ENCYCLOPEDIA OF THE SCIENTIFIC REVOLUTION FROM COPERNICUS TO NEWTON

GARLAND REFERENCE LIBRARY OF THE HUMANITIES (VOL. 1800)

Encyclopedia of the Scientific Revolution From Copernicus to Newton

Editor
Wilbur Applebaum

Garland Publishing, Inc.
A member of the Taylor & Francis Group
New York & London
2000

Published in 2000 by
Garland Publishing, Inc.
A member of the Taylor & Francis Group
29 West 35th Street
New York, NY 10001

Library of Congress Cataloging-in-Publication Data

Encyclopedia of the scientific revolution : from Copernicus to Newton / editor Wilbur Applebaum.
    p.   cm. — (Garland reference library of the humanities ; vol. 1800)
    Includes bibliographical references and index.
    ISBN 0-8153-1503-1
    1. Science—Europe—History—16th century—Encyclopedias. 2. Science—Europe—History—17th century—Encyclopedias. I. Applebaum, Wilbur. II. Series

Q125.E53 2000
509.4'03—dc21   00-025149

To the memory
of
Stella Prizand Applebaum

CONTENTS

PREFACE

When Garland Publishing invited me several years ago to edit an encyclopedia of the Scientific Revolution, I welcomed the opportunity. Here was a means of providing a wider audience with the fruits of the most recent scholarly research on a fascinating complex of events that helped shape the modern world. The study of the origins of modern science in the sixteenth and seventeenth centuries has been a widely expanding field that, in recent years, has undergone significant changes in emphasis and outlook—as have studies in the history of science as a whole. Interest in the subject has grown enormously since World War II. In the mid-twentieth century, only a handful of universities offered courses in the history of science; at the century's end, hundreds of universities did, and many of them offered doctoral programs in the field. There are now dozens of journals devoted to the history of science, and thousands of books and articles are published each year.

As the history of science has developed as an area of study, its course has exhibited patterns similar to those seen in the natural sciences. Both have undergone processes of fission and fusion, with research areas branching out into subfields, and two or more uniting to create new fields of research. The history of science, initially practiced by historians, philosophers, and retired scientists, now attracts social historians, sociologists, anthropologists, historians of religion and of technology, and literary historians. It has come to embrace biographies of scientists; the histories of scientific disciplines and their branches; scientific institutions; the analysis and development of broad concepts such as matter, motion, and life; the support of scientific activities; the philosophical foundations and implications of science; the relation of science to fields such as medicine and technology; and the social contexts within which scientific ideas and practices emerged.

The expertise required for the creation of an encyclopedia as complex as one on the Scientific Revolution led to the recruitment of more than 160 contributors from fourteen countries. The 441 articles, however, were designed to appeal to a wide readership. A user's guide has been provided as an aid for the reader in finding his or her way in the subject matter of the encyclopedia as a whole, and a number of entries on various historiographical approaches to the history of science are included.

The creation of the *Encyclopedia of the Scientific Revolution* has been a lengthy and complex task. Its difficulties were eased by the suggestions and assistance, particularly in the design of the encyclopedia, of the members of the advisory board: Ernan McMullin, Paolo Rossi, John A. Schuster, Richard S. Westfall, and Robert S. Westman. Of particular value was the counsel of the late "Sam" Westfall, who also wrote more words for this volume than any other contributor. Many of his former students are also contributors, a testimonial to his excellence as a scholar and teacher. Special thanks are due also to a number of contributors who provided criticism, advice, and suggestions. They include William Eamon, Robert A. Hatch, John Henry, David Kubrin, John Lankford, Margaret Osler, and Albert Van Helden. Naomi Bernards Polonsky provided helpful advice and encouragement on my own authorial efforts. There were others as well, too numerous to list, who graciously responded to my queries or calls for assistance. I am grateful to them all and hereby relieve them of responsibility for whatever flaws may be found in this volume. Special thanks for contributing illustrations or their help making photographs or photocopies are owed to Vincent Golden of the Galvin Library of Illinois Institute of Technology, Marilyn Ogilvie of the University of Oklahoma's History of Science Collections, Renzo Baldasso of the University of Oklahoma, R. Russell Maylone and the staff of Special Collections at Northwestern University Library, Liba Taub and Catriona West of the Whipple Museum of the History of Science at Cambridge University, and to those individuals who contributed pictures from their own collections.

Coping with computer disks using an astonishing variety of software submitted by the encyclopedia's contributors as well as with a number of computer problems would have been more difficult without the helpful assistance of Emad Al Shawakfa and the staff of the Academic Computing Center at Illinois Institute of Technology. For important and necessary editorial and technical assistance, I am grateful to several former and present members of the editorial staff of Garland Publishing. The help provided by Earl Roy and Marianne Lown of Garland Publishing was indispensable; they were also quite patient with a novice at this sort of enterprise, as were Joanne Daniels and Tim Roberts. Kenny Lyman deserves credit, if that is the right word, for persuading me to undertake what has taken a substantial chunk out of my working life and proven more difficult than I had imagined. Now that the work has issued from the press, however, I want to express my thanks to her.

Wilbur Applebaum

INTRODUCTION AND USER'S GUIDE

For several centuries, the study of the natural world has been perceived as having undergone unusually significant changes in sixteenth- and seventeenth-century Europe, changes that broke decisively with earlier conceptions and practices and paved the way for the emergence of modern science. Only since the mid-twentieth century, however, has the term "Scientific Revolution" been applied to those changes and those two centuries. "Revolution" was thought to be apt in light of the emergence in that era of novel concepts concerning the structure of the universe, as well as of the nature of matter and motion and the means of acquiring knowledge of them. It was a period rich in radical transformations of ideas about the natural world that were inherited from the ancients and modified in the Middle Ages by Muslim scholars and western Scholastics.

At the beginning of the sixteenth century, the universe was thought to be spherical, finite, geocentric, and completely filled with matter. By the end of the seventeenth century, the universe had come to be thought of as infinite, heliocentric, and possessed of vacuous spaces large and small. In the course of those two centuries, the belief that the heavens obeyed different laws from those on earth was abandoned. Analogies to mechanical action largely replaced explanations of natural events in terms of purpose, values, inherent qualities, and occult powers. Although the universe increasingly came to be seen as operating on principles similar to those determining the workings of a clock, the seventeenth century also gave birth to the immensely fruitful, yet decidedly non-mechanistic concept of universal gravitation; it also provided room for the operation of other nonmechanical principles.

In the study of living things, as well, long-held traditional ideas were replaced by new ones. Blood circulated rather than flowed and ebbed through arteries and veins. Reproduction, it was learned, began with the union of egg and sperm. Sexual reproduction was noted in plants, and new taxonomical arrangements were proposed as a great many new plant and animal species were discovered. Related patterns in anatomical organization and embryological development were discerned in comparative studies of a variety of species. Living things were divested of souls as governors of their activities; life functions were understood as analogs of physical and chemical processes.

The increasing employment of experiment, mathematics, and novel instruments was decisive in the creation of many of these changing ideas. Experiments were designed to gain new facts, test hypotheses, yield quantifiable results where possible, and be capable of replication. Close and detailed observation and increasingly precise measurement became important desiderata, as did the ability to observe the very small and the very distant.

Some historians of science have questioned the use of the term "Scientific Revolution" to characterize these changes, stating that it has misleading and anachronistic implications. Scientific ideas would seem to be disembodied from their cultural contexts. "Revolution," it is objected, implies an ahistorical, "triumphalist" account, in which a few scientific geniuses, responding to "crises" in their disciplines, rapidly overturned certain concepts and methods and led us from ignorance, superstition, and error to the truths and successes embodied in modern science.

Further, the characterization of early modern science as revolutionary tends to ignore the sometimes piecemeal processes by which new ideas emerged in its various branches and the often lengthy periods during which, for sound reasons, opposed theories were simultaneously held. Nor was due credit given to the roles played by the gradual recovery and translation of influential classical Greek texts and the questioning of traditional principles in the late Middle Ages. These medieval efforts led to important developments upon which the recasting of fundamental concepts in the sixteenth and seventeenth centuries was based. Moreover, some of the scientific disciplines pursued during the period do not exhibit the very marked changes that were true of astronomy and some of the physical sciences; instead, these disciplines underwent slow changes without radical alterations in their underlying principles. Although the transformation of scientific ideas and practice in the sixteenth and seventeenth centuries was a significant turning point in the creation of modern science, it is objected that an even greater role in that process was played by events in the nineteenth and twentieth centuries. One could say, therefore, that there were two or more scientific revolutions.

A good case, however, can be made for retention of the term Scientific Revolution as unique to the sixteenth and seventeenth centuries. Whether or not events during this period represent the beginnings of what we call modern science, they certainly constituted a decisive break with the past. Prime axioms of ancient and medieval sciences, their modes of investigation and scientific explanation, however modified over the centuries, were overturned. The sometimes slow processes by which old scientific theories were challenged and new ones emerged and debated do not invalidate the concept of the Scientific Revolution, which was not an event, but a complex of events.

In the course of two centuries the tempo of change in the replacement of old scientific ideas and methods with new ones was much more rapid and radical than had been the case in the preceding two millennia. Although the scientists of the period did not characterize their efforts as revolutionary, they were nevertheless aware that they were creating a wholly new enterprise. The authors of some of the truly revolutionary scientific ideas of the nineteenth and twentieth centuries had no such sense that they were transforming the scientific enterprise as a whole. More to the point, one may as well take issue with such historical categories as the Industrial Revolution and the Renaissance. They, along with the term Scientific Revolution, encompass periods and complexes of events broad enough to provide an identifiable framework for investigation, analysis, and understanding. Just as the Renaissance has come to embrace a field far beyond a "rebirth" of classical languages, learning, and style, so has the Scientific Revolution come to stand for much more than the creation of new scientific concepts and practices.

Developments in the world of science, or natural philosophy as it was then called, took place amid significant social and economic changes in European society, in its institutions and in intellectual life. The Renaissance and early modern period was the era of exploration, geographical discovery, encounters with hitherto unknown peoples, and the creation of colonial empires. These early stages in the creation of a world economy coincided with the efforts of monarchs and princes to consolidate and enlarge their powers. To enhance their prestige, and in the hope of practical benefits, rulers became patrons of mathematicians and natural philosophers. Interest in natural philosophy became fashionable among the social elites, and themes from the new science appeared in the works of poets. Improvements in the technologies employed in mining, hydraulics, horology, cartography, navigation, and warfare resulted in new respect for artisans and their crafts. The idea inherited from the ancient Greeks—that thinking was superior to doing—came under challenge. In the course of the sixteenth century, an interventionist style emerged in the pursuit of natural philosophy, emphasizing practice united to reflection. Anti-Aristotelian sentiments grew in the universities, as well as impatience with Scholastic logic-chopping. Magic and alchemy grew in importance and complexity, reflecting an increase in the desire to know by doing, by the manipulation of nature. Professors of anatomy, such as Andreas Vesalius (1514–1564), began to perform dissections to see what could be learned, rather than having their assistants dissect to demonstrate traditional views.

New institutions for the conduct of scientific activities and their promotion were created. The printing press and the establishment of postal services permitted the exchange of ideas and collaborative efforts to a degree impossible before the Scientific Revolution. Scientific societies were founded in the seventeenth century, and scientific knowledge began to become available to those who had not been schooled in Latin or attended universities. Scientific works were beginning to be written in and translated into the vernaculars. Works written for the nonscientist attracted an audience, and institutions offering lectures to the public were established.

In the realm of religion, traditional beliefs were challenged both by the Protestant Reformation and by scientific developments. Boundaries to human knowledge once thought to derive from theological certitudes were called into question by practitioners of the new natural philosophy. They argued that man, despite his limitations, was made in the image of an omniscient God, who had given humans the ability to gain greater knowledge of the Creator's works. The new science was charged with denying divine Providence and the Creation as well as promoting atheism. In response, its defenders argued that the pursuit of natural philosophy was justified on theological grounds as revealing in new ways the infinite wisdom and power of the Creator. The argument from design—that the observed ordered complexity of the natural world is evidence of divine purpose—received fresh impetus with every new discovery. When scientific positions were challenged on the grounds of scriptural authority, natural philosophers felt compelled to insist that science and religion were distinct areas of human knowledge and authorities in each should not insist on making claims in the other field. Implications of scientific developments for religion, of little concern in the sixteenth century, became significant in the early years of the seventeenth century. Nicolaus Copernicus's (1473–1543) work on sun-centered astronomy, published in 1543, received little attention on religious grounds until Galileo Galilei (1564–1642) began to promote it about seven decades later.

Not only the Catholic Church found the idea of a moving earth objectionable; the concept violated the most fundamental principles of the science of motion as then known. In the first half of the seventeenth century, the study of motions of various kinds proved highly significant. Motion was slowed and broken down into small increments in order to yield new principles at odds with those of the ancients. Johannes Kepler (1571–1630) figuratively slowed down the motions of planets by breaking their orbits into one-degree arc-segments to determine the relationship between the speed of a planet and its distance from the Sun. The result was the overthrow of the ancient axiom that all celestial motions must be circular and uniform. William Harvey (1578–1657), in his experiments slowing down the beating hearts of dying mammals and cold-blooded animals to study the motion

of the blood, showed how blood circulates, thus refuting the traditional doctrine that the blood ebbs and flows in its channels. Galileo, slowing the motion of falling balls by rolling them down inclined planes, determined that the rate at which bodies fall is independent of their weights—contrary to what had long been thought—and that falling bodies accelerate uniformly during equal time periods.

The decisive events determining the nature of the Scientific Revolution were focused in the first half of the seventeenth century. Aristotle's theory of matter, its elements and qualities, was discarded in favor of new particulate theories of matter. It was in these few decades that experiment, precise observation, and mathematics were employed to challenge ancient, long-held scientific principles and to create new ones. It is no mere coincidence that, in this relatively short period, logarithms, the slide rule, calculating machines, the pendulum clock, the microscope, the telescope, the air pump, and heat-measuring devices were invented. During the Renaissance, the pursuit and attainment of scientific knowledge had been justified by arguments stated in terms of the restoration of long-lost truths. By the early seventeenth century, emphasis was on the renovation of the sciences, on novelty, on the discovery of things the ancients had never known. Francis Bacon (1561–1626) put forward the rapidly adopted idea that science is a progressive and collective enterprise. The pursuit of natural philosophy was newly justified on the grounds of its practical benefits. René Descartes (1596–1650) explained that the natural world and all in it, other than parts of the human soul, operates on mechanical principles.

This uniquely creative segment of the Scientific Revolution was followed by one in which its achievements were absorbed and developed further. New discoveries were made and new theories proposed in astronomy, mechanics, pneumatics, optics, chemistry, and physiology, aided by the increased use of experimentation, the telescope, and the microscope. The earlier development of algebra and analytic geometry culminated with the invention of calculus by Gottfried Wilhelm Leibniz (1646–1716) and Isaac Newton (1642–1727). Newton's unparalleled achievements in the creation of the calculus, a new systematic mechanics embracing both celestial and terrestrial phenomena, and his light and color discoveries in the latter part of the seventeenth century mark a useful culminating boundary for the Scientific Revolution.

User's Guide

The topics chosen for the *Encyclopedia of the Scientific Revolution* reflect the recent expansion of history of science studies to include issues of social and cultural context. Here one can find not only scientific ideas and individuals, but also categories and topics that would never have found their way into such a work several decades ago. Among them are aspects of the occult (sometimes called the pseudo-sciences), technology, medicine, scientific institutions, religion, language and literature, and social conditions that have some bearing on the development of science or that were affected by the development of science. Interpretations of the Scientific Revolution, its scope and meaning, are many and include challenges to the concept itself. Various entries will reflect those differing interpretations and are chiefly encountered in several essays dealing with historiographical issues.

A word of caution concerning certain expressions used in this encyclopedia: the history of science is replete with examples of the changing meanings and connotations of certain terms. We have seen this in the case of the concept of the Scientific Revolution itself. An atom was understood quite differently in ancient Greece, the seventeenth century, and the twentieth, as was the word "soul." Our use of the word "science" has a more restricted meaning than it had during the Scientific Revolution; the closest to it in meaning at that time is the term "natural philosophy." For much of the period, astrology and alchemy were considered valid sciences. Words such as "scientist," "biology," or "psychology" did not exist. To be intelligible to the modern reader, however, such words are occasionally used with the understanding that their meanings embody concepts similar to but not identical with those used during the Scientific Revolution.

As far as possible, entries reflect a sense of the development of the topic over time, whether a decade, a lifetime, or the approximately two centuries covered by this encyclopedia. Dates given in the various articles are in the Christian era unless designated as B.C.E. Authors of entries on the various disciplines and broad subject areas, such as Mathematics, Astronomy, Medicine, and Botany, aim at elucidating, within the limits of space, such aspects of the subject as its scope, branches, theoretical basis, methodologies, relation to other fields, means of preparation of its practitioners, and how all of these may have changed over time. The longer entries on individuals emphasize the development of their ideas, methods, and practices. Entries ending in "ism," or associated with major figures and including an adjectival form of the person's name, such as Copernicanism, Cartesianism, and so on, deal with the reception of the ideas of that individual.

The taxonomical listing that follows is intended to give the reader some idea of the organizational structure of the work and the criteria for choice of topics. Topics on persons have been omitted here on the grounds that many individuals did not restrict their activities to a single discipline. General categories followed by an asterisk are also entries, as are the topics listed under them.

TOPICAL OUTLINE

Bibliography

Each entry has a brief bibliography appended, as well as appropriate *See also* entries. A number of general works are listed below to provide greater detail on a number of issues raised in the entries and narrative accounts of the Scientific Revolution as a whole.

Dear, Peter. *Discipline and Experience: The Mathematical Way in the Scientific Revolution.* Chicago: University of Chicago Press, 1995.

Gillispie, Charles C., ed. *Dictionary of Scientific Biography.* 16 vols. New York: Scribners, 1970–1980.

Goodman, David, and Colin A. Russell, ed. *The Rise of Scientific Europe 1500–1800.* Sevenoaks, Kent, England: Hodder and Stoughton, 1991.

Hall, A. R. *The Revolution in Science, 1500–1750.* 3rd ed. New York and London: Longman, 1983.

Henry, John. *The Scientific Revolution and the Origins of Modern Science.* New York: St. Martin's, 1997.

Lindberg, David C., and Robert S. Westman, eds. *Reappraisals of the Scientific Revolution.* Cambridge: Cambridge University Press, 1990.

Olby, R. C. et al. *Companion to the History of Modern Science.* London and New York: Routledge, 1990.

Olson, Richard. *Science Deified and Science Defied: The Historical Significance of Science in Western Culture.* 2 vols. Berkeley and Los Angeles: University of California Press, 1982.

Porter, Roy, and Mikulás Teich, ed. *The Scientific Revolution in National Context.* Cambridge: Cambridge University Press, 1990.

Shapin, Steven. *The Scientific Revolution.* Chicago: University of Chicago Press, 1996.

Westfall, Richard S. *The Construction of Modern Science: Mechanisms and Mechanics.* New York: Wiley, 1971.

CHRONOLOGY

1462 Publication of the widely read *Epitome of Ptolemy's Almagest* by Georg Peurbach (1423–1461) and Johannes Regiomontanus (1436–1476)

1469 Initial Latin translation of the *Corpus Hermeticum,* an influential series of tracts on theology and the occult, believed to have been written by Hermes Trismegistus, an ancient Egyptian sage

1472 Georg Peurbach's *New Theory of the Planets,* written in 1454, attempts to reconcile geometric models for predicting planetary positions with Aristotle's homocentric celestial spheres

1486 Publication of *The Hammer of Witches,* on the nature of witchcraft and the necessity of its punishment

1494 Giovanni Pico della Mirandola (1463–1494) attacks the practice of astrology as interfering with belief in Providence and human free will

The introduction to Europe of Arabic numerals for arithmetic computation, including their use in fractions and the extraction of square roots, is published by Luca Pacioli (ca. 1445–1517)

1503 Founding of the influential Casa de la Contratación in Seville by the Spanish monarchy for the teaching and improvement of navigation and cartography

1514 A draft of the heliocentric theory of Nicolaus Copernicus (1473–1543), the *Commentariolus* (Little Commentary) circulates among astronomers

1518 Granting of a royal charter to the London College of Physicians, functioning as a guild, but also as a learned society

1522 Completion of the first circumnavigation of the globe by the expedition initially led by Ferdinand Magellan

1530 A description of and speculation on the causes of a disease new to Europe is published in *Syphilis, or the French Disease* by Girolamo Fracastoro (1478–1553)

Establishment of the Collège Royal in Paris for the advancement of learning by providing free lectures to the public on, among other subjects, philosophy, mathematics, and medicine

1530–1536 Publication of Otto Brunfels's (ca. 1489–1534) *Portraits of Living Plants,* the first publication by a botanist to incorporate illustrations from nature rather than from copies and narratives in traditional accounts

1531 The first emblem book, the enormously popular *Emblemata* by Andrea Alciati (1492–1550), providing a visual language through the use of symbolic images associated with brief mottoes frequently taken from classical and religious sources, influenced representations of plants and animals in books of natural history

Juan Luis Vives (1492–1540) urges the reform of education and the importance of empirical knowledge by learning from craftsmen in his *On the Disciplines*

1532 Peter Apian (1495–1552) and Girolamo Fracastoro note that the tail of the comet seen in that year—later known as Halley's Comet—points away from the Sun

1533 Publication of Heinrich Cornelius Agrippa's (1486–1535) *On Occult Philosophy,* an influential compendium of the occult sciences

1538 An effort to eliminate apparent contradictions between Ptolemaic astronomy and Aristotelian cosmology is made in *Homocentrics, or On the Stars* by Girolamo Fracastoro

1539 Establishment of clinical teaching and the use of patients' medical histories at the University of Padua

1540 Vannoccio Biringuccio (1480–ca. 1540) publishes the first comprehensive text on metallurgy

A description of Nicolaus Copernicus's heliocentric astronomy is provided by Georg Joachim Rheticus (1514–1574) in his *Narratio prima* (First Account)

1541 Giovan Battista Canano's (1550–1579) work on anatomy, based on some of his own observations, showing in a novel way, through etchings, the relations of the muscles to their functions

1542 A novel, widely influential, and masterfully illustrated herbal by Leonhart Fuchs (1501–1566), *On the History of Plants,* depicts plant forms with their essential generalized features

1543 Andreas Vesalius's (1514–1564) *On the Fabric of the Human Body,* the most influential text on anatomy in its time, based on his own dissections and beautifully illustrated, notes a number of errors in the classical anatomy of Galen

Nicolaus Copernicus's heliocentric theory is published in his *De revolutionibus orbium coelestium* (On the Revolutions of the Celestial Spheres)

1545 Girolamo Cardano's (1501–1576) *The Great Art* brings together many earlier algebraic innovations and introduces his novel methods for dealing with equations of the third degree

Establishment of the first medicinal plant gardens at the universities of Padua and Pisa

Ambroise Paré (ca. 1510–1590) publishes the first of his innovative methods in surgery—the use of mild dressings instead of cautery in the treatment of wounds and incisions

1546 The spread of plague is explained by Girolamo Fracastoro in his *On Contagion,* by the spread of disease "seeds" through personal contact, the common use of "seed"-carrying objects, or through the air

1547 Preparation of the first standardized pharmacopoeia in Nürnberg

1551 Publication of Erasmus Reinhold's (1511–1553) *Prutenic Tables,* based on Copernicus's planetary models, perceived as the most accurate of their time

Founding of the Collegio Romano as a Jesuit university, many of whose teachers and students were active scientists during the Scientific Revolution

1553 Michael Servetus (1511–1553) puts forward his description of the pulmonary circulation of the blood in a heretical theological work, for which he was burned at the stake by John Calvin, in Geneva

1554 Giovanni Battista Benedetti (1530–1590) challenges Aristotle's theory that falling bodies move with speeds proportional to their weights

1555 Pierre Belon's (1517–1564) *History of the Nature of Birds* features illustrations that had all been made from his own observations rather than from traditional and sometimes imaginary accounts and presents an anatomical comparison between a human and an avian skeleton

1556 Georgius Agricola's (1494–1555) comprehensive and highly influential text on mining and metallurgy, *De re metallica,* is illustrated with detailed woodcuts

Juan Valverde's (ca. 1525–ca. 1588) anatomical text, *Account of the Structure of the Human Body,* the most widely read in Renaissance Europe, included thirty novel anatomical discoveries and the first anatomical engravings in copperplate, some by a student of Michelangelo

1558 Giambattista della Porta's (1535–1615) *Natural Magic* is intended to demonstrate that this collection of marvelous phenomena was natural and not demonic

Gioseffo Zarlino (1517–1590) challenges the traditional theory of consonance and intonation with adaptations suitable for the music of his time

1559 Realdo Colombo's (1510–1559) *On Anatomy* describes his independently discovered pulmonary circulation of the blood—an important step in the later discovery of its circulation through the entire body—and asserts, contra Galen, that systole, the contraction of the heart, is its active phase

1561 Discovery of the fallopian tubes, described in the *Anatomical Observations* of Gabriele Falloppio (1523–1562)

1564 Bartolomeo Eustachio (ca. 1510–1574) discovers the aural passage that came to bear his name and makes improvements on Vesalian anatomy

1566 Publication of the works of Pedro Nuñes (1502–1578) on navigation, explaining the use of new instruments and how to sail on a great circle course

1569 The cartographic projection system of Gerardus Mercator (1512–1594) enables navigators to choose constant courses in any part of the world

Paracelsus's (1493–1541) works, most unpublished in his lifetime and written approximately four decades earlier, begin to be published, explaining his views on the nature of matter, physiology, diseases, and the use of chemical medicines

1570 The use and importance of mathematics in many fields is strongly urged by John Dee (1527–1608) in a much-noted Preface to an English translation of Euclid's geometry by Henry Billingsley

Abraham Ortelius (1527–1598) publishes the first atlas

1572 Observations of a striking supernova appeared to indicate that it was beyond the sphere of the Moon, challenging the traditional idea of the unchanging nature of the heavens

1576 An early sympathetic and brief account of Copernicus's heliocentric theory and a description of the stars as infinite in extent is given by Thomas Digges (ca. 1546–1595)

Construction begins on Tycho Brahe's (1541–1601) observatory, Uraniborg, on the Danish island of Hven, site of the most precise and detailed collection of astronomical data of its time

1577 Francisco Hernández (1515–1587) leaves Mexico after six years, having compiled a great mass of data and illustrations on the environmental conditions of many plant and animal species unknown in Europe and on the inhabitants of Mexico

Observations of a comet indicated that its path was beyond the sphere of the Moon, challenging the Aristotelian conception of the solidity of the

celestial spheres and that comets were sublunar phenomena

Guidobaldo del Monte's (1545–1607) *Book of Machines* applies Archimedean statics to the study of machines

1582 Reform of the Julian calendar completed, with publication of a papal bull by Pope Gregory XIII

Giovanni Antonio Magini (1555–1617), although rejecting heliocentrism, begins to publish ephemerides making use of Copernican data and methods

1583 Andrea Cesalpino's (1519–1603) influential *On Plants* proposes a classification system based on reproduction, emphasizing seed, flower, and fruit

1584 Joost Bürgi (1552–1632), the most ingenious watch and clockmaker of his time, devises an escapement making clocks more accurate than any in use

1585 The first systematic presentation of decimal numeration, published by Simon Stevin (1548–1620)

1587 Completion of the publication of Conrad Gessner's (1516–1565) monumental multivolume *Histories of Animals,* for which numerous zoologists had supplied data from their own observations of animal morphology and behavior

1588 The first account of the inhabitants and resources of North America, by Thomas Harriot (ca. 1560–1621), in *A Briefe and True Report of the New Found Land of Virginia*

The influential translation by Federico Commandino (1509–1579) of the main Greek texts of Archimedes into Latin

Publication of Tycho Brahe's geoheliocentric system, in which the planets revolve around the Sun, with the Sun revolving about the stationary earth

The most comprehensive illustrated work on machines and their design, published by the military engineer Agostino Ramelli (1531–1590)

1591 Publication of François Viète's (1540–1603) *Introduction to the Analytical Art,* a pioneering work in the creation of analytic geometry

Francesco Patrizi (1529–1597) cites correlations between the tides and lunar positions

1596 Gresham College, founded by bequest of the prosperous London merchant Sir Thomas Gresham to provide public lectures on, among other subjects, astronomy, geometry, and medicine; it later becomes the locus of a group that founded the Royal Society of London

The *Cosmographic Mystery,* by Johannes Kepler (1571–1630), improves upon Copernican astronomy, putting forward Kepler's goal of uniting mathematical astronomy, physics, and religion in the creation of a new astronomy

1600 Giordano Bruno (1548–1600), an early Copernican and a believer in the infinity of the universe and a plurality of worlds, is burned at the stake for heretical religious opinions

1600 The first detailed and observation- and experiment-based study of magnetism as a cosmological principle, in *On the Magnet,* by William Gilbert (1540–1603)

For his astronomical work, Tycho Brahe gains the patronage of the Holy Roman Emperor in Prague

1601 The sine law of refraction obtained by Thomas Harriot (ca. 1560–1521), but never published by him

The Holy Roman Emperor, Rudolph II, becomes the patron of Johannes Kepler

1603 The Accademia dei Lincei (Academy of Lynxes) founded in Rome as a scientific society

The discovery of the valves in the veins, by Girolamo Fabrici (ca. 1533–1619), significant for the later determination that the blood circulates

Thomas Harriot succeeds in obtaining the area of a spherical triangle

1604 Johannes Kepler holds that light rays are rectilinear, that they diminish in intensity by the inverse square of their distance as they travel from the light source, and that it is on the retina that an inverted image is formed and transmitted to the nerves

1607 Galileo Galilei (1564–1642) demonstrates that a projectile follows a parabolic path

1608 The telescope, utilizing a convex objective and a concave eyepiece, invented in the Netherlands

1609 Johannes Kepler's (1571–1630) *New Astronomy* shows that Mars moves nonuniformly in an elliptical orbit and proposes a quasi-magnetic force as the cause of planetary motion

Installation at the University of Marburg of the first professorship of medical chemistry, with the introduction of laboratory teaching

Galileo reinvents the telescope and uses it to observe the heavens

Thomas Harriot independently obtains or builds a telescope and begins to observe the heavens

Approximate date of the invention of the microscope

1610 Galileo presents the results of his earliest telescopic observations, including innumerable stars invisible to the naked eye, mountains on the Moon, and four of Jupiter's satellites, in his *Sidereal Messenger.* Later that year he discovers the phases of Venus and the peculiar appearance of Saturn

1611 Johannes Kepler's *Dioptrics* analyzes optical refraction and proposes an improvement in the Galilean telescope, making it more effective for astronomical observation

1612 Santorio Santorio (1561–1636) publishes the first account of a thermometer using air as the expanding and contracting fluid

1613 Galileo's *Letters on Sunspots* debates the nature of sunspots with Christoph Scheiner (1573–1650) and comes out in favor of the Copernican system

1614 John Napier (1550–1617) puts forward foundational rules for the concept of logarithms

The influence of the *Corpus Hermeticum* begins to wane when it is shown to have been written well after the classical Greek and early Christian eras

Publication of the first of two tracts announcing the goal of the Rosicrucian movement to reform knowledge through the application of numerology, alchemy, and Paracelsian medical chemistry

1616 Galileo is admonished by Cardinal Bellarmine, a member of the Inquisition, to abandon the teaching of the Copernican system, and Copernicus's *On the Revolutions* is placed on the Index of Prohibited Books until it should be corrected

1617 Robert Fludd's (1574–1637) *History of the Two Cosmoses,* in a series of allegorical plates, represents the unity of God, His creation, and human knowledge through the concept of the microcosm reflecting the macrocosm

Foundation of the Worshipful Society of Apothecaries in London

1618 Publication in London of the *Pharmacopoeia Londinensis,* the first national pharmacopoeia possessing legal standing

1619 Johannes Kepler's *Harmonics of the Universe* presents his Third Law, relating the periods of the planets to their distances from the Sun

1620 Francis Bacon's (1561–1626) *Novum organum* analyzes the barriers to effective thinking and proposes observation and experiment as necessary foundations for the acquisition of new knowledge

Johann Valentin Andreae (1586–1654) proposes a model scientific society with scientific work as a collective enterprise

Approximate date of Willibrord Snel's (1591–1626) discovery of the sine law of refraction

1621 Girolamo Fabricius's posthumous *On the Formation of the Egg and the Chick* postulates that in viviparous generation, an embryo is created by the union of semen and blood supplied by the parents

1622 Publication of Tommaso Campanella's (1568–1639) *Apologia pro Galilaeo* in support of Galileo's Copernicanism and his views on the separation of science from religion

Christian Severin (Longomontanus) (1563–1647), who had been Tycho Brahe's chief assistant, shows the geometrical equivalence of the Ptolemaic, Tychonic, and Copernican systems, but opts for a central rotating earth

William Oughtred (1575–1660) invents the slide rule

1623 Galileo's *The Assayer* presents his arguments opposing Scholastic methods in the study of nature and advocates the use of mathematical and experimental methods

1624 Pierre Gassendi (1592–1655) redefines the goal of empirical science as determining probable, rather than certain, results

1625 Wilhelm Schickard (1592–1635) designs the first arithmetic calculating machine

1626 Francis Bacon's *New Atlantis* describes a fictionalized institution for collaborative scientific research, later seen as a model for subsequently founded scientific societies

1627 Johannes Kepler's *Rudolphine Tables,* based on his laws of planetary motion, provides the most accurate astronomical tables up to that time

Lorenzo Bellini (1643–1704), by close examination of the anatomy of the kidney, challenges the traditional Galenic account by noting that the kidney operates like a sieve, separating urine from blood

Approximate date of René Descartes's (1596–1650) independent discovery of the sine law of refraction

1628 William Harvey (1578–1657) publishes his *Anatomical Exercises on the Movement of the Heart and Blood,* demonstrating how the blood circulates

In his *On the Measure of Running Waters,* Benedetto Castelli (1577–1643) establishes the basis for the science of hydraulics

1630 Founding of the Bureau d'Adresse, a clearinghouse for information, goods, and services in Paris that offered weekly conferences to the public on scientific issues

Christoph Scheiner presents his detailed observations on sunspots, challenging Aristotelian concepts on the nature of the heavens

1631 Thomas Harriot's posthumous work advances algebra by relating roots to binomial factors of polynomials and creates new forms of algebraic notation

1632 Galileo's *Dialogue Concerning the Two Chief World Systems, Ptolemaic and Copernican* argues forcefully for the Copernican system by employing his discoveries with the telescope and his novel ideas on the nature of motion

1633 Galileo's trial before the Inquisition for his advocacy of Copernicanism results in his conviction on vehement suspicion of heresy and his abjuration. He is placed under house arrest for the remainder of his life, and his *Dialogue on the Two Chief World Systems* is put on the Index of Prohibited Books

1634 Johannes Kepler's posthumous *The Dream,* an imaginative account of a trip to the Moon and of the life of its inhabitants, provides the elements of Copernican astronomy in popular form

1635 Bonaventura Cavalieri (1598–1647) publishes a means of calculating the areas and volumes of various planes and solids by the use of indivisibles

Declination of a compass needle is noted as varying over time and not constant for a given latitude

1637 Publication of René Descartes's *Discourse on Method* and his *Geometry,* a foundation work on analytic geometry. The appearance of colors when light is refracted is explained in mechanistic terms in Descartes's *Dioptrics*, attributed to particles of light acquiring different rotational speeds

1638 Galileo's *Discourses on Two New Sciences* presents his ideas on the nature of motion and strength of materials

John Wilkins's (1614–1672) *Discovery of a World in the Moone* brings some of the discoveries of Kepler and Galileo to the general reader

1639 The first observation of a transit of Venus across the Sun, a rare phenomenon used in the eighteenth and nineteenth centuries for determining the distance of the earth from the Sun, is made by Jeremiah Horrocks (1618–1641)

1641 René Descartes's *Meditations* presents the dualistic metaphysical foundations—material and spiritual—of his mechanistic natural philosophy

1644 Evangelista Torricelli (1608–1647) fills a tube sealed at one end with mercury, and with the open end immersed in mercury, notes its fall in the tube to a certain level, leaving a void above it

René Descartes's *Principles of Philosophy* puts forward his ideas on matter, mechanics, and the universe as a plenous mechanical system

1645 Ismael Boulliau's (1605–1694) *Philolaic Astronomy* becomes widely influential in promoting Johannes Kepler's theory of elliptical planetary orbits but rejects his idea of a physical cause for planetary motions

Publication by Michael Florent van Langren (1598–1675) of the first engraved lunar map showing the features of the Moon and their names

1647 A much more detailed description with illustrations of the surface features of the Moon is given by Johannes Hevelius (1611–1687) in his *Selenographia*

Construction of the first air pump by Otto von Guericke (1602–1686)

Blaise Pascal's (1623–1662) *New Experiments Concerning the Void* describes a series of experiments demonstrating that the presence of matter above the mercury in a Torricelli tube cannot be detected

1648 The theory that the height of the mercury in a tube that is sealed at the top and has its open end immersed in a dish of mercury will vary with altitude is successfully tested by Pascal

Johannes Baptista van Helmont (1579–1644) strongly supports the development of medical chemistry and the role of chemistry in physiological function

Initial meetings of the experiment-oriented Oxford Philosophical Society, many of whose members would later help found the Royal Society of London

Publication of John Wilkins's (1614–1672) popular *Mathematical Magick,* a primer on mechanics designed for the general public

1650 A classic clinical description of rickets published by Francis Glisson (1597–1677) and others

1651 Thomas Hobbes's (1588–1679) classic work of political theory, *Leviathan,* utilizes a concept of human nature influenced by his familiarity with contemporary mechanistic ideas on physiology and sensation

Giovanni Battista Riccioli (1598–1671) presents the astronomical work of Copernicus and Kepler in a detailed effort to demonstrate that the earth does not move

1653 First meetings of the Montmor Academy, an early French scientific society, at the home of H. L. Habert de Montmor (ca. 1600–1679)

Christiaan Huygens applies the sine law of refraction to spherical lenses

1654 The first presentation and promotion of Epicurean atomism in English in Walter Charleton's (1620–1707) *Physiologia Epicuro-Gassendo-Charletoniana,* a translation of Pierre Gassendi's work on the subject

Establishment in Tuscany of a network of meteorological stations to collect data on weather conditions

James Ussher (1581–1656), Archbishop of Armagh, through close analysis of biblical passages, determines the date of Creation as October 23, 4004 B.C.E.

1656 Christiaan Huygens's pendulum clock allows for significantly greater precision in time measurement

1657 Founding of the Accademia del Cimento (Academy of Experiment) in Florence

A theory of epigenesis, the development of organisms through successive stages of organ development from unformed fertilized ova, is presented by William Harvey (1578–1657) in his *Exercises Concerning the Generation of Animals*

Otto von Guericke (1602–1686) demonstrates the pressure of the air by showing that two teams of horses are unable to pull apart two joined metal hemispheres from which the air had been evacuated

1658 Christiaan Huygens provides a description of an improved pendulum clock yielding a substantial increase in accuracy

Publication of a detailed exposition of Epicurean philosophy by Pierre Gassendi incorporates Christian elements and aspects of contemporaneous natural philosophy, influential in the development of atomic theories of matter and of the existence of vacua

Contagion is held by Athanasius Kircher (1602–1689) to occur through the spread of animate and sticky particles

1659 Christiaan Huygens explains the changing appearance of Saturn as due to its being surrounded by a flat ring of matter

1661 Marcello Malpighi (1628–1694), using the microscope, observes the capillaries joining arteries and veins, demonstrating conclusively the ability of the blood to circulate

Robert Boyle's *Sceptical Chymist* argues against Aristotelian and Paracelsian chemical theories in favor of the use of more practical and experimental means of enlarging chemical knowledge

Joseph Glanvill's (1636–1680) *Vanity of Dogmatizing* puts forth a skeptical attack on Aristotelian methods in the practice of natural philosophy and strongly supports the use of experimentation

1662 René Descartes's posthumous *Treatise on Man* presents human physiology as operating on mechanical principles

Establishment, by royal charter, of the Royal Society of London for the Improvement of Natural Knowledge, the oldest of today's scientific societies, and the appointment of Robert Hooke (1635–1702) as Curator of Experiments, charged with conducting experiments at the Society's weekly meetings

The second edition of Robert Boyle's (1627–1691) *New Experiments Physico-Mechanicall, Touching the Spring of the Air and its Effects* details his experiments with the vacuum pump and states the inverse relation between the pressure and volume of a gas

Lorenzo Bellini (1643–1704), by detailed anatomical investigation of the kidney, challenges the traditional Galenic idea of its function by showing that it operates like a sieve, separating urine from blood

John Graunt (1620–1674) publishes the first statistical tables in his *Observations upon the Bills of Mortality,* with data on London's population and its characteristics

1663 Girolamo Gardano's *Book of Games of Chance,* although written a century earlier, is published in response to increased interest by mathematicians in probability theory

1664 René Descartes's posthumous *The World* puts forth a theory of the transmission of light as pressure in a medium consisting of a "subtle matter"

Thomas Willis (1621–1675) significantly advances neuroanatomy through his investigations of the brain and nervous system

1665 Robert Hooke's (1635–1702) *Micrographia* provides detailed etchings of his microscopic observations, including the cells in cork, and popularizes the compound microscope

Publication in Paris of the *Journal des Sçavans,* the first journal to feature scientific news

Initial publication of the *Philosophical Transactions of the Royal Society*

Francesco Maria Grimaldi (1618–1663) describes the diffraction of light and proposes a theory that light is "split apart" when flowing past the edges of bodies

1666 The Académie Royale des Sciences is established in Paris, under the patronage of King Louis XIV, to advance science and mathematics

Giovanni Alfonso Borelli's (1608–1679) *Theories of the Medicean Planets* proposes that the orbits of celestial bodies are governed by an attraction to their centers and a quasi-inertial tendency to remain in motion

Explanation of chemical processes by "corpuscularianism," a particulate theory of matter, is put forward by Robert Boyle (1627–1691) in his *Origine of Formes and Qualities*

1667 Establishment of the Paris Observatory under royal patronage

On religious principles and Baconian grounds, Thomas Sprat's *History of the Royal Society* defends the institution against attacks, describing it as capable of providing for the improvement of life through its effective utilization of inductive methods in the study of nature

1668 In *Experiments on the Generation of Insects,* Francesco Redi (1626–1679) demonstrates that insects and other lower forms of life are not generated spontaneously, but instead come from eggs

John Wilkins publishes *An Essay Towards a Real Character and Philosophical Language,* an effort to create a scientific, universal, unambiguous language with a vocabulary capturing the essences of its referents

1669 Isaac Newton (1642–1727) builds the first reflecting telescope

Isaac Barrow (1630–1677), first holder of the Lucasian Chair of Mathematics at Cambridge University, resigns it in favor of Isaac Newton

Description of the heart's function as a muscle and details of his experiments with blood transfusion are published in *Treatise on the Heart* by Richard Lower (1631–1691)

Nicolaus Steno (1638–1686) explains the sequential deposition of sedimentary strata and proposes a theory of the calcification of the remains of once-living animals

Jan Swammerdam's (1637–1680) microscopical work on the development of insects leads him to reject the notion of their spontaneous generation and to speculate whether organisms are fully formed before fetal development

1670 Newton makes the first reflecting telescope and begins his decades-long involvement with the theory and practice of alchemy

1671 Jacques Rohault's (1618–1672) *Traité de Physique* (Treatise on Physics) published as an important text on Cartesian natural philosophy

Jean Picard's (1620–1682) *Measure of the Earth,* a description of his precise measurement of a meridional arc, influential in geodesy, cartography, and celestial mechanics

One of the earliest attempts, by Jan de Witt (1625–1672), to apply statistical methods for economic goals by using life expectancy to calculate premiums for annuities

1672 Creation of the first electrical machine—a sulfur globe rubbed and electrified by a dry hand—described by Otto von Guericke (1602–1686) in his *Experimenta nova*

In an article in the *Philosophical Transactions of the Royal Society,* Isaac Newton establishes, by experiment with a prism, that white light is composed of a spectrum of colors and that light of each color is refracted at a different angle

A detailed study of the anatomy and physiology of the female reproductive system by Regnier de Graaf (1641–1673) leads to the discovery of the follicles bearing his name and his support of the theory of ovistic preformation

Detailed microscopic observation by Marcello Malpighi (1628–1694) of the first hours of embryonic development of the chick, with descriptions of the initial formation of various organs

1672–1673 Jean Richer's (1630–1696) expedition to Cayenne in French Guyana results in an adjustment of 90 arc-minutes in the obliquity of the ecliptic and a revision in the horizontal solar parallax, enabling a more precise measure of the distance of the earth from the Sun

1673 *An Essay to Revive the Ancient Education of Gentlewomen* by Bethsua Makin (ca. 1612–ca. 1674), is one among a number of works published in the seventeenth century urging equality of education and the ability of women to study natural philosophy

Publication of Christiaan Huygens's book on the pendulum clock contains a more refined and accurate version of the timepiece

Initial publication in the *Philosophical Transactions of the Royal Society* of the microscopical discoveries of Antoni van Leeuwenhoek (1632–1723)

1674 John Mayow (1641–1679) proposes that certain particles in the air are necessary for combustion and are transmitted by the lungs to the blood, where they serve to maintain body heat and other functions

1675 Ole Römer's precise astronomical observations lead him to conclude that the speed of light is finite

Gian Domenico Cassini (1625–1712) discovers the gap in Saturn's ring system

Establishment of the Royal Observatory at Greenwich, England, and the appointment of John Flamsteed (1646–1719) as its director

Nicolas Lemery's (1645–1715) *Cours de chemie* presents the most influential corpuscular account of chemical reactions

Robert Boyle proposes in his *Experiments and Notes about the Mechanical Origin and Production of Electricity* that electrical effects can be explained by the emission and refraction of electrical effluvia

Thomas Shadwell's *The Virtuoso* satirizes the work of the Royal Society of London as silly and impractical

1677 Discovery of spermatozoa by use of the microscope, reported by Antoni van Leeuwenhoek

Francis Glisson (1597–1677), in a study of muscle fibers, proposes the influential theory that the basic property of living matter is irritability, the ability to be stimulated and to respond by contracting

1678 Ralph Cudworth (1617–1688), in his *True Intellectual System of the Universe,* strongly challenges, on theological grounds, the idea that the universe is composed of inert matter

Edmond Halley (ca. 1646–1743) presents a catalogue of the stars in the Southern Hemisphere

"Hooke's Law," based on several years' study with watch springs, states that the "power" of any spring is proportional to its tension

1679 A work by Johannes Hevelius describes his instruments and gives over 20,000 measurements of positions of celestial objects, useful for later astronomers as the most extensive database for the period

Edmé Mariotte (ca. 1620–1684), in an analogy with the circulation of the blood, describes the sap in plants as circulating

Robert Hooke solicits Isaac Newton's opinion on the possibility of explaining the motions of the planets by the assumption of inertia and an attractive force from the Sun, initiating a train of events leading to Newton's monumental achievement in his *Mathematical Principles of Natural Philosophy* of 1687

Publication of the first nautical almanac in Paris

John Mayow (1640–1679) shows that air is necessary for combustion as well as respiration

1681 The application of mechanical principles to analysis of the movements of animals undertaken by Giovanni Alfonso Borelli (1608–1689) is published in his posthumous *On the Motions of Animals*

Publication of the first two volumes of Thomas Burnet's (ca. 1635–1715) *Sacred Theory of the Earth,* which, following the biblical account, stimulated discussion of the changing nature of the earth's surface over time

1683 Opening of the Ashmolean Museum at Oxford University, the first English public museum, established with the donation by Elias Ashmole (1617–1692) of his library and artifacts

1684 Publication of Gottfried Wilhelm Leibniz's (1646–1716) first paper outlining his symbolism for and approach to the calculus, utilizing infinitesimals

Discovery of the third and fourth of Saturn's satellites by Gian Domenico Cassini (1625–1712), after having discovered two others in 1671 and 1672

Francesco Redi (1626–1698) publishes an encyclopedic account of hundreds of parasites

1686 Publication of the first edition of *Conversations on the Plurality of Worlds* by Bernard le Bovier de Fontenelle (1657–1757), a classic popularization of the Cartesian version of Copernicanism

Correction of René Descartes's measure of force as *mv* by Gottfried Wilhelm Leibniz (1646–1716) to *mv²*, which he termed "living force"

1687 Isaac Newton's *Mathematical Principles of Natural Philosophy* establishes fundamental principles of classical mechanics—his concepts of force, mass, space, and time and his laws of motion and universal gravitation

1690 John Locke's (1632–1704) *Essay Concerning Human Understanding* proposes that knowledge about the nature of matter can be probable at best, rather than of demonstrable certainty

Christiaan Huygens's *Treatise on Light* advances a wave theory of the propagation of light

Posthumous publication of Johannes Hevelius's catalog of the positions of over 1,500 stars, a standard reference source for his successors

William Petty's (1623–1687) pioneering *Political Arithmetic* develops mathematical methods as a foundation for political economy

John Ray (1620–1705), in his book on British plants, uses multiple criteria to distinguish species

1693 Edmond Halley provides a mathematical equation for finding the focal lengths of lenses of all shapes

1694 First detailed explanation of plant sexuality by Rudolph Jacob Camerarius (1665–1721), in his *A Letter on Plant Sexuality*

Emphasis on the genus as the primary category of plant taxonomy, based mostly on general characteristics of flower and fruit, is given in *Elements of Botany* by Joseph Pitton de Tournefort (1656–1708)

1696 Publication of the first textbook on the calculus by the Marquis de L'Hôpital (1661–1704)

1697 Samuel Clarke (1618–1672) translates Jacques Rohault's Cartesian *Traité de physique* (1671) as *System of Natural Philosophy* with Newtonian footnotes, for use as a university textbook of physics

1700 Founding of the Berlin Academy of Science by Gottfried Wilhelm Leibniz

1701 Edmond Halley prepares the first map showing magnetic variation

1702 Publication of one of the earliest mathematically informed popular works on Newtonian astronomy, David Gregory's (1659–1708) *Elements of Physical and Geometrical Astronomy,* with an anonymous preface by Newton claiming ancient authority for the concept of gravity

1703 Herman Boerhaave (1668–1738), the most influential medical teacher of his time and for some time after, lays down the principles of an effective medical curriculum, emphasizing a sound scientific foundation

1704 The first edition of Isaac Newton's (1642–1727) *Opticks,* based on his experiments and including his "Queries" on important and unresolved issues on various aspects of nature

1705 The comet that now bears Edmond Halley's name, and that he had observed in 1682, is determined by him to have an elongated elliptical orbit

Maria Merian (1647–1717) publishes her work on the metamorphoses of insects, based on her field work in Surinam, contributing to the rejection of the idea of spontaneous generation

1706 Isaac Newton postulates as a fundamental principle of physics forces of attraction and repulsion between particles of matter

1713 Posthumous publication of *The Art of Conjecturing* by Jakob Bernoulli (1654–1705), intended as a guide to sound thinking by utilizing probabilistic analysis, presents a proof for the law of large numbers

William Derham's (1657–1735) *Physico-theology* and the second edition of Isaac Newton's *Mathematical Principles of Natural Philosophy* establish a trend to promote the discoveries of science as evidence for the greatness, wisdom, and goodness of God

1715 Gottfried Wilhelm Leibniz sends his list of objections to Isaac Newton's philosophy to the Princess of Wales, initiating a debate with Newton's defender, Samuel Clarke, on the relation of God to a universe conceived as mechanical in nature

Contributors

Ferdinando Abbri
Dipartimento di Studi Storico-Sociale Filosofici
Università degli Studi di Siena
Arezzo, Italy

Amir R. Alexander
Humanities Consortium
University of California at Los Angeles

Wilbur Applebaum
Department of Humanities
Illinois Institute of Technology

Roger Ariew
Virginia Polytechnic Institute

Renzo Baldasso
Department of History of Science
University of Oklahoma

Martha Baldwin
Program in History and Philosophy of Science
Stonehill College

Peter Barker
Department of History of Science
University of Oklahoma

Barbara G. Beddall†
Independent Scholar

Klaas van Berkel
Department of History
University of Groningen, The Netherlands

Domenico Bertoloni Meli
Department of History and Philosophy of Science
Indiana University

Amalia Bettini
Milan, Italy

Richard Blackwell, Jr.
Department of Philosophy
Saint Louis University

Ann Blair
Department of History
Harvard University

Michel Blay
Gif sur Yvette, France

Harold Brown
Department of Philosophy
Northern Illinois University

David J. Bryden
Edinburgh, Scotland

David Buisseret
Department of History
University of Texas at Arlington

William Burns
Department of History and Sociology of Science
University of Pennsylvania

Jerome J. Bylebyl
Department of History of Science, Medicine
and Technology
The Johns Hopkins University

Andrea Carlino
Institut Louis Jeantet d'Histoire et la Médecine
Université de Genève, Switzerland

Juan Casanovas
Specolo Vaticana
Castelgandolfo, Italy

Desmond M. Clarke
Philosophy Department
University College
Cork, Ireland

Antonio Clericuzio
Department of History and Philology
University of Cassino
Cassino, Italy

Nicholas Clulee
Department of History
Frostburg State University

Lisa Forman Cody
Department of History
Claremont McKenna College

H. Floris Cohen
Department of History
University of Twente
Enschede, The Netherlands

I. Bernard Cohen
History of Science Department
Harvard University

Alix Cooper
History of Science Department
Harvard University

Lesley Cormack
Department of History and Classics
University of Alberta

Allison P. Coudert
University Honors College
Arizona State University

Maurice Crosland
Rutherford College
University of Kent at Canterbury
United Kingdom

Edward B. Davis
Department of Natural Sciences
Messiah College

Peter Dear
Department of History
Cornell University

Allen G. Debus
The Morris Fishbein Center
University of Chicago

Elly Dekker
Linschooten, The Netherlands

David De Vidi
Department of Philosophy
University of Waterloo

Steven J. Dick
U.S. Naval Observatory
Washington D.C. 20392-5420

Fokko J. Dijksterhuis
Department of History
University of Twente
Enschede, The Netherlands

Peter Dilg
Philipps-Universität Marburg
Marburg-Lahn, Germany

William H. Donahue
Santa Fe, New Mexico

William Eamon
Department of History
New Mexico State University

Berna K. Eden
Bogazici University
Istanbul, Turkey

J. Worth Estes
Department of Pharmacology
Boston University School of Medicine

Bernardino Fantini
Institut Louis Jeantet d'Histoire de la Médecine
Université de Genève, Switzerland

Annibale Fantoli
Victoria, British Columbia

Sister Maureen Farrell
St. Peter's House
Manchester, United Kingdom

Paula Findlen
Department of History
Stanford University

Saul Fisher
Mellon Foundation

Sophie Forgan
Institute of Design
University of Teesside
Cleveland, United Kingdom

Marian Fournier
Museum Boerhaave
Leiden, The Netherlands

Roger K. French
Wellcome Unit for the History of Medicine
University of Cambridge
Cambridge, England

Don Garrett
Department of Philosophy
University of Utah

John Gascoigne
School of History
University of New South Wales
Sydney, Australia

Owen Gingerich
Harvard-Smithsonian Center for Astrophysics
Harvard University

Chiara Giuntini
Dipartimento di Scienze Filosofiche e Storico-Sociali
Università degli Studi di Udine
Udine, Italy

André Goddu
History of Science Department
Stonehill College

Elsa L. Gonzalez
Chicago, Illinois

Edward A. Gosselin
Department of History
California State University

Pamela Gossin
The University of Texas at Dallas

Penelope M. Gouk
Wellcome Unit for the History of Medicine
University of Manchester
Manchester, England

Paolo Gozza
Dipartimento di Musica e Spettacolo
Università degli Studi di Bologna
Bologna, Italy

Mark Greengrass
Hartlib Papers Project
University of Sheffield
Sheffield, England

Mario Grilli
Dipartimento di Fisica
Università degli Studi di Roma "La Sapienza"
Rome, Italy

Emily R. Grosholz
Department of Philosophy
Pennsylvania State University

Richard W. Hadden
Department of Sociology
St. Mary's University
Halifax, Nova Scotia Canada

Marie B. Hall
Oxford, United Kingdom

Robert A. Hatch
Department of History
University of Florida

Helen Hattab
Department of Philosophy
Southern Illinois University

David Haycock
London, United Kingdom

Anne van Helden
Museum Boerhaave
Leiden, The Netherlands

Marcus Hellyer
Department of History
Brandeis University

John Henry
Science Studies Unit
University of Edinburgh
Edinburgh, Scotland

Reinhard Hildebrand
Institut für Anatomie
Münster, Germany

Katherine Hill
Science Studies Unit
University of Edinburgh
Edinburgh, Scotland

William L. Hine
Science Studies
Atkinson College
York University

Kenneth J. Howell
Newman Foundation
University of Illinois

William H. Huffman
Independent Scholar

Keith Hutchison
Department of History and Philosophy of Science
University of Melbourne, Australia

Robert Iliffe
Imperial College of Science, Technology
and Medicine
London, United Kingdom

Bruce Janacek
Department of History
University of California at Davis

Nicholas Jardine
Department of History
and Philosophy of Science
University of Cambridge, United Kingdom

Richard A. Jarrell
Department of Natural Science
Atkinson College
York University

Jane E. Jenkins
St. Thomas University
New Brunswick

Douglas Jesseph
Department of History
North Carolina State University

Adrian Johns
University of Chicago

Alex G. Keller
Department of History
University of Leicester
Leicester, United Kingdom

Peggy A. Kidwell
National Museum of American History
Smithsonian Institution

Ursula Klein
Max-Planck-Institut
für Naturwissenschaftsgeschichte
Berlin, Germany

Lewis A. Knafla
Department of History
University of Calgary

Fritz Krafft
Institut für Geschichte der Pharmazie
Philipps-Universität Marburg
Marburg/Lahn, Germany

Helge Kragh
History of Science Department
Aarhus University
Aarhus, Denmark

Peter van der Krogt
Map Historian, Explokart Research Program
Faculty of Geographical Sciences
University of Utrecht, The Netherlands

David Kubrin
San Francisco, California

W. Roy Laird
Department of History
Carleton University

James Lattis
Space Astronomy Laboratory
University of Wisconsin
Madison WI 53706

Michel-Pierre Lerner
Observatoire de Paris
Paris, France

Pamela O. Long
Washington, D.C.

José Maria López-Piñero
Facultad de Medicina
Universitat de Valencia, Spain

Peter Loptson
Department of Philosophy
University of Saskatchewan

Antonie M. Luyendijk-Elshout
Museum Boerhaave
Leiden, The Netherlands

Yasukatsu Maeyama
Institut für Geschichte der Naturwissenschaften
Universität Frankfurt
Frankfurt, Germany

Cesare S. Maffioli
Luxembourg

Antoni Malet
Universitat Pompeu Fabra
Departament d'Humanitats
Barcelona, Spain

Paolo Mancosu
Department of Philosophy
University of California at Berkeley

Otto Mayr
Leesburg, Virginia

Gary McIntyre
Institute for History of Science
and Technology
University of Toronto

Stephen McKnight
Department of History
University of Florida

Emerson T. McMullen
Department of History
Georgia Southern University

Ernan McMullin
Program in History and Philosophy
of Science
University of Notre Dame

Frederick G. Meyer
Takoma Park, Maryland

Guy Meynell
Dover, United Kingdom

Mara Miniati
Istituto e Museo di Storia
della Scienza
Florence, Italy

Bruce T. Moran
Department of History
University of Nevada

John Morgan
Department of History
Ryerson Polytechnic University

Jean D. Moss
Catholic University

Ioanna Mountriza
Formation doctorale d'épistémologie et histoire
des sciences
Université Paris, France

Madeline M. Muntersbjorn
Department of Philosophy
University of Toledo

Steven M. Nadler
Department of Philosophy
University of Wisconsin

Charles G. Nauert
Department of History
University of Missouri

Malcolm Nicolson
Wellcome Unit for the History
of Medicine
Glasgow, United Kingdom

Cornelius O'Boyle
University of Notre Dame

Kathleen Ochs
International Institute
Colorado School of Mines

David R. Oldroyd
School of Science and Technology Studies
University of New South Wales, Australia

Richard G. Olson
Department of Humanities and
Social Science
Harvey Mudd College

Ynez V. O'Neill
Medical History Division
University of California at Los Angeles

Margaret J. Osler
Department of History
University of Calgary

Lodewijk C. Palm
Institute for the History of Science
Utrecht, The Netherlands

John Parker
Keswick Cumbria, United Kingdom

Jeanne Peiffer
Centre Alexandre Koyre
France

Jon V. Pepper
Department of Mathematics
University College London, United Kingdom

Marcello Pera
Lucca, Italy

Edward Peters
Department of History
University of Pennsylvania

Guy Picolet
Laboratoire d'Histoire des Sciences
et des Techniques (UPR 21)
Centre National de la Recherche
Scientifique
Paris, France

Joseph C. Pitt
Department of Philosophy
Virginia Polytechnic and State University

Claus Priesner
Neue Deutsche Biographie
Munich, Germany

Lawrence M. Principe
Department of Chemistry
The Johns Hopkins University

Stephen Pumfrey
Department of History
Furness College
University of Lancaster, United Kingdom

Cynthia Pyle
New York University

Sheila Rabin
Department of History
St. Peter's College

Rhoda Rappaport
Department of History
Vassar College

Karen Reeds
Independent Scholar

Graham Rees
University of London
London, United Kingdom

David Reid
Department of History of Science
University of Wisconsin–Madison

Louise E. Robbins
Department of the History of Science
University of Wisconsin–Madison

Paolo Rossi
Dipartimento di Filosofia
Università degli Studi di Firenze, Italy

James A. Ruffner
Independent Scholar

Alison Sandman
Department of the History of Science
University of Wisconsin–Madison

Lisa Sarasohn
Department of History
Oregon State University

John Schuster
School of Science and Technology Studies
University of New South Wales, Australia

Michael Segre
Govone, Italy

Thomas B. Settle
Polytechnic University

Jole R. Shackelford
University of Minnesota

Timothy Shanahan
Department of Philosophy
Loyola Marymount University

Michael H. Shank
Department of History of Science
University of Wisconsin–Madison

Barbara Shapiro
University of California at Berkeley

William Sherman
Department of English
University of Maryland

M. M. Slaughter
Kent Law School
University of Kent at Canterbury

Pamela H. Smith
History Department
Pomona College

Peter G. Sobol
Department of History of Science
University of Wisconsin–Madison

Beverley C. Southgate
University of Hertfordshire, United Kingdom

Steven Straker
Department of History
University of British Columbia

Alice Stroup
Department of History
Bard College

Noel Swerdlow
Department of Astronomy and Astrophysics
University of Chicago

Sascha Talmor
Kibbutz Nachshonim
Mercaz, Israel

Victor Tammone
Department of History and
Philosophy of Science
University of Indiana

Kevin Tapp
Independent Scholar

Liba Taub
Whipple Museum of the History of Science
Cambridge, United Kingdom

Timothy Taylor
Program in History and Philosophy of Science
University of Notre Dame

E. H. Thompson
Department of Economics
University of Dundee, Scotland

Gerard L'E. Turner
Oxford, United Kingdom

Eric Urbanc
Independent Scholar

Albert Van Helden
Department of History
Rice University

Denys Vaughan
Horsham, Sussex
United Kingdom

Rienk Vermij
Utrecht, The Netherlands

R. P. W. Visser
Instutute for the History of Science
Utrecht University, The Netherlands

James Voelkel
Department of History of Science, Medicine
and Technology
The Johns Hopkins University

William Wallace
Department of Philosophy
University of Maryland

Michael T. Walton
Salt Lake City, Utah

Andrew Wear
Wellcome Institute for the History of Medicine
London, United Kingdom

Kathleen Wellman
Department of History
Southern Methodist University

Richard S. Westfall[†]
Indiana University

Robert S. Westman
Department of History
University of California at San Diego

Kathleen Whalen
Birkbeck College
University of London
London, United Kingdom

Frances H. Willmoth
Cambridge, United Kingdom

Catherine Wilson
Department of Philosophy
University of British Columbia

Mary G. Winkler
Institute for the Medical Humanities
University of Texas Medical Branch
Galveston, Texas

Joella G. Yoder
Independent Scholar

[†] indicates that the author is deceased

A

Académie Royale des Sciences

Founded in Paris in 1666 under Louis XIV. Its mission was to advance natural philosophy and mathematics and to apply the laws of nature to practical reforms. The academy quickly became a preeminent arbiter of scientific thought, a role it sustained until 1793, when it was dissolved, to be reincarnated in 1795 as part of the Institut de France. From the start, this company of savants was a monument to royal patronage and to the ideals of the Scientific Revolution. Moreover, its work addressed the theoretical controversies that dominated natural philosophy after René Descartes (1596–1650).

Royal patronage guaranteed the academy prestige and generous funding, but at the price of close supervision by its ministerial protectors. Aside from a fashionable enthusiasm for exotic fauna and flora, Louis XIV had little interest in matters mathematical or scientific, except insofar as they might advance matters of state. He is on record as visiting the academy only twice, once in December 1681 at its rooms in the Royal Library and again in May 1682 at its observatory. Otherwise, the academy came to Court, whether to survey for the water supply or fountains of Versailles, to instruct the dauphin or dissect an elephant, to conduct observations of an eclipse or to assist in specific diplomatic occasions.

It fell, therefore, to the ministers in charge of the Academy to oversee its functioning. They were the chief minister, Colbert; the minister of state and war, Louvois; and the finance minister, Pontchartrain. In the name of the king and in consultation with academicians, these three successively appointed members and fixed their annual pay, proposed and approved research, admonished or praised academicians, arranged publication of books at the royal press, and authorized expenditure on research and travel.

In fact, the academy benefited from the most generous scientific patronage of the seventeenth century. From 1666 through 1699, more than two million livres were disbursed on its infrastructure, research, and the pensions of the members, with ministerial protectors using these funds to shape the program and image of the academy.

It was, above all, by naming academicians that the three ministers shaped the company. The early absence of administrative protocol reflects Colbert's close ties to the academicians he appointed and with whose cooperation he guided the company's affairs. Apart from designating Jean-Baptiste Du Hamel (1623–1706) as secretary, he informally tested other categories of membership—student, external, corresponding, honorary—in response to circumstances. To supplant Colbert's posthumous authority, Louvois appointed as his spokesmen in the academy new members who did not always represent the interests of the other academicians. Pontchartrain, in turn, instituted the positions of president in 1691 and treasurer in 1696; he also guaranteed the succession to the secretaryship in 1697 and ratified a formal institutional hierarchy in 1699. In the process, he consolidated under the control of his nephew, the Abbé Jean-Paul Bignon (1662–1743), not only the royal academies but also the Royal Library and publishing houses, giving him sway over a considerable portion of French intellectual life.

The undisputed celebrities of the early academy were two foreign savants with powerful families or patrons, international reputations, and technical expertise: the Dutch mathematician Christiaan Huygens (1629–1695), who was entitled to 6,000 livres a year from

An imagined visit of King Louis XIV to the Académie. The observatory under construction is visible through the window. From Claude Perrault, Mémoires pour servir à l'histoire naturelle des animaux *(1671).*

The ambitious research agendas of Huygens, Cassini, Duclos, and Perrault shaped the academy's intellectual program in astronomy, chemistry, and natural history for several decades. New members were expected to enlist in collective research projects and to review the relevant notebooks and minutes. Thus, the institution instilled in its members a corporate esprit and respect for its own role in the advancement of the sciences. That process is reflected from the 1690s in the minutes, in which memoirs rehearse a history of the problem to be solved and recount the accomplishments of earlier academicians. It was realized more systematically by the annual history and memoirs edited after 1699 by Bernard le Bovier de Fontenelle (1657–1757), made Permanent Secretary in 1697.

Surprisingly, given its influence and longevity, the early academy was small and intimate, numbering between 20 and 34 members in any given year before 1699. Drawn together by the apartments and research facilities available to them at the Royal Library and the observatory, academicians not only met formally on Wednesdays and Saturdays, but also rubbed shoulders daily at the dissection table and laboratory furnaces, over the latest inventions and ingenious experiments, or at games of cards. But by the late 1680s, academicians worked increasingly out of facilities at the Royal Botanical Gardens and other Parisian establishments, and during the 1690s they found the academy's own meetings less congenial than the learned salons.

Although the academy's mission—to advance knowledge and serve the king—necessitated publication, discretion governed its formative years. In the 1660s, members referred simply to "the Company that meets in the Royal Library" and pledged not to divulge its activities to outsiders, except with the permission of the company; they issued early anatomical and astronomical findings anonymously, in pamphlets and in articles to the *Journal des sçavans*. But in 1671 Perrault and Jean Picard (1620–1682) inaugurated a series whose large format and lavish illustrations were the envy of the learned world. That series encompassed a comparative anatomy of exotic animals from the Versailles menagerie, mathematical treatises, and natural history of rare plants, as well as a report on the measurement of the earth. Besides collective works identified as the product of the entire academy, academicians published under their own names treatises based on research conducted at, or presented to, the academy.

1666 and Jean-Dominique Cassini (1625–1712), the Bolognese astronomer who entered the company in 1669 with an annual pension of 9,000 livres. By attracting foreigners to Paris, Colbert intended to rob other countries of their best talent to the benefit of France. Colbert also appointed four gifted and well-connected French savants—the Huguenot alchemist Samuel Cottereau Duclos (d. 1685), the anatomist and architect Claude Perrault (1613–1688), the physician and philosopher Marin Cureau de La Chambre (1596–1669), and the mathematician Pierre de Carcavi (ca. 1603–1684)—with pensions of 2,000 livres. Savants were appointed to the academy because of their associations in learned and official circles; they, in turn, put their new affiliation to the advancement both of their families and of knowledge. Once established, the academy gained new members more cheaply, and after 1699 academicians tended to come from higher social ranks, in part because the liberal professions were gaining in prestige.

In their research and publications, members espoused the credo of the Scientific Revolution. They preferred experiment over discourse, vaunted communal investigation as the path to scientific progress, and affirmed that learning transcended geopolitical boundaries. They claimed that their discoveries would not only advance understanding of nature, but also serve industry, commerce, medicine, and public health. Although academicians were disinclined to theorize collectively, the rectification of Cartesian natural philosophy formed an important, if implicit, agenda in much of their work.

The academy may be understood as being composed of three learned companies. To that of mathematicians and geometers, established at the Royal Library by the spring or summer of 1666, was added another company of chemists, anatomists, botanists, and natural philosophers in December 1666. In 1699 three members of a company of arts and crafts that had, since 1691, operated out of Jean-Paul Bignon's house joined the academy; that merger formalized the institution's responsibility to reform technology and industry as well as mathematics and the sciences. While an academician was expected to work primarily within one of these companies, a defining characteristic of the early academy is that its members were polymaths whose research spanned several disciplines.

From the start, Colbert and his academicians underscored astronomy and its practical applications. Besides improving the instruments and techniques of positional astronomy, Adrien Auzout (1622–1691), Jacques Buot (d. ca. 1678), Picard, Cassini, and Huygens took the measure of the heavens and of the earth. The voyage of Jean Richer (1630–1696) to Cayenne in 1672, designed to test Huygens's clocks, called into question whether the earth was perfectly spherical. Systematic observations of the satellites of Jupiter prompted the announcement in 1676 by Ole Römer (1644–1710) of the finite propagation of light, which, in turn, confirmed Huygens's views about the nature and finite speed of light (1678, 1690). Building on Huygens's previous studies of Saturn, Cassini identified four additional satellites (1671, 1672, 1684) and perceived that the planet was circled by two rings, thereby confirming its variable aspect (1675). During the 1670s he mapped the Moon, and from 1694 his nephew Giacomo Filippo Maraldi (1665–1729) mapped the fixed stars. Taken together, the academy's astronomical work bolstered heliocentricity while calling into question certain Cartesian assumptions

about light, magnetism, and the shape of the earth. But academicians disagreed in their interpretations, with Cassini and Huygens at the head of opposing camps.

These astronomical researches served the practical interests of the state, particularly in the domains of longitude, cartography, and hydrography. By attracting Huygens and Cassini to the academy, Colbert had effectively monopolized for France the best practitioners of the two most promising methods—time-telling by the pendulum clock or the satellites of Jupiter—then known for determining longitude at sea; their expertise also put the academy in a position to unmask false solutions. On Colbert's instructions, academicians also began in 1668 a comprehensive survey of France, starting with the tax district around Paris and extending the meridian from the observatory north and south of Paris. By 1681 they could challenge traditional maps of the kingdom, and in 1693 their coastal surveys appeared in an atlas called *Le Neptune François* (The French Neptune). Eclipse observations at the observatory and around the world established longitudes of provincial and foreign cities for a world map recorded on the observatory floor, with the academy supplying telescope lenses to its provincial collaborators. In carrying out these practical projects, the academy trained young mathematicians who later served the Crown as engineers or geographers.

Colbert quickly established the practice of demanding technical counsel from the academy. Besides his concern for longitude and cartography, he asked academicians to study theoretical and applied mechanics; the models of machines collected in that investigation were displayed to the public at the observatory from the 1680s, serving, in part, as a historical museum of military technology. Under both Colbert and Louvois, academicians applied their surveying skills to planning the aqueducts and fountains for Versailles. In addition, Duclos advised on methods of assaying for gold and silver in American mines, and several academicians tested inventions destined for use by the king's armies. Such chauvinist inquiries corresponded to the competitive spirit of the academy's foundation by Colbert, who was determined that his French company should outshine those of London and Florence. Academicians shared these chauvinistic sentiments despite their pride in belonging to the international republic of letters.

Academicians turned their studies of comparative anatomy to understanding physiological processes. Perrault related the structure of feathers to the mechanics of

flight and debunked time-honored myths about sala-
manders, pelicans, and chameleons, but he emphasized
the organs of the sensory, digestive, respiratory, and circulatory systems (1671, 1676). The organs of sense drew
the attention of Edmé Mariotte (ca. 1620–1684), Jean
Pecquet (1622–1674), and Joseph-Guichard Duverney
(1648–1730). Academicians experimented controver-
sially with blood transfusion in 1667, and during the
1680s and 1690s Duverney and Jean Méry (1645–1722)
debated the movement of the blood in the fetus. But academicians did not investigate animalcules, even though
Huygens communicated a letter from Antoni van Leeuwenhoek (1632–1723) in 1678 and displayed animalcules
to his astonished colleagues with a bead-glass microscope designed by Nicolas Hartsoeker (1656–1725), who
in 1687 went on to explain the implications of animalcules for theories of generation. As a rule, academicians
were inspired by an experimental model based on the
work of William Harvey (1578–1657), while drawing on
chemical processes and Cartesian mechanism for their
explanatory hypotheses.

To study plants, academicians employed both traditional and innovative approaches. The natural-history
group appropriated the artists of the Jardin Royal (Royal
Botanical Gardens) and the late duke of Orléans, yet set
new standards for botanical illustration. Stimulated by
theories about the circulation of the blood, academicians
investigated the rise and descent of sap: in studies that
bear little resemblance to English and Italian models,
Mariotte and Perrault developed experimental evidence
for the existence of two saps (1668), combining mechanistic with chemical explanations to account for the rise
of sap above 32 feet, while Philippe de La Hire (1640–
1718) searched experimentally and microscopically for
valves in vegetable vessels (1690). La Hire and Picard
used Hartsoeker's microscope to compare plant pollens
(1678). At the same time, academicians continued to
seek the medical implications of their plant studies.
Denis Dodart (1634–1707), for example, established
that ergot was the cause of the hallucinatory and gan-
grenous malady known as Saint Anthony's Fire, and he
published his findings in the *Journal des sçavans* (1676)
with recommendations for safeguarding public health.

Chemistry was at once an ancillary and a natural-
philosophical study for academicians. Duclos evoked
Helmontian and Neoplatonist traditions that embarrassed colleagues who nonetheless admired his analyses
of French mineral waters (1675). The laboratory Duclos

established for the academy at the Royal Library was in
use 24 hours a day from 1669; in it, Claude Bourdelin
(1621–1699) examined the chemical constituents of organic matter. Although Bourdelin's work did not advance
the academy's natural history of plants as intended, it
served Dodart's studies of nutrition, digestion, and tran-
spiration. Guillaume Homberg (1652–1715), remembered
for studying acids and alkalis, drew on Bourdelin's analyses to explain the food chain. In general, academicians
combined chemical and corpuscularian philosophies to
explain physiological processes or matter itself.

The company's conspicuous experimentalism has
concealed the theoretical preoccupations that shaped its
program. Surviving minutes, laboratory records, dissection notes, and drafts of books have a positivist tone that
camouflages the controversial implications of the academy's work. But from the 1660s the academy constituted
a forum within which Cartesian physics could be dis-
creetly tested and modified. When academicians discussed cohesion, the causes of the weight of the air, and
the implications of the air pump during the 1660s, or
when they debated motion, light, magnetism, and the
impact of bodies in the 1670s, they rarely referred to
Descartes by name. Nonetheless, his theories were at
issue. At the forefront of the academy's efforts to correct
Cartesian natural philosophy was Huygens, whose influence continued to be felt well after his death. In
the opposite camp were Cassini, Mariotte, and Gilles
Personne de Roberval (1602–1675).

Thanks, in part, to its prestige and publications,
the academy shaped scientific inquiry even by non-
academicians from its earliest years. Aspirants to membership submitted their findings and inventions to the
academy's scrutiny; visitors observed or contributed to
meetings, learned from watching dissections, and consulted individual academicians. Cassini instructed provincial astronomers by correspondence, and naturalists
reported from the Americas, Europe, and the Mediterranean. Significantly, academicians were among the first
to champion the Leibnizian calculus, thanks to the Marquis de L'Hospital (1661–1704) and Pierre Varignon
(1654–1722).

In its structure and work, the academy celebrated
the collective, experimental, and utilitarian ideals of the
time. The results impressed contemporaries and influenced subsequent scientific thought. Even those discoveries rightfully recalled as the accomplishment of specific
members are indebted to the institution itself. With its

extensive quarters and excellent equipment, the academy functioned as a laboratory for the research, individual or collective, of members. Moreover, because the twice weekly meetings were an obligatory forum for examining evidence or debating arguments, academicians not only refereed each other's work, but also followed a broad spectrum of scientific inquiry. Academicians learned from one another, formally and informally. It was thanks to Huygens that Perrault embraced Cartesian mechanism, Mariotte read Galileo Galilei (1564–1642), and Gottfried Wilhelm Leibniz (1646–1716) discovered Blaise Pascal (1623–1662). Indeed, Mariotte's treatise on the impact of bodies (1673) reflected both his own and the experiments and reasoning of his colleagues, as Huygens was to recall bitterly in 1690.

In sum, the academy quickly became an arbiter of scientific data and theories. It also forged lasting links between science and the state. Academicians repaid generous patronage in the currency of discovery and invention, practical accomplishments, and methodological advice. While brandishing experimental method and contributions to positive science, academicians also explored competing theories about the nature of the world, testing in particular the claims and limits of Cartesian mechanism.

BIBLIOGRAPHY

Académie des Sciences. *Histoire et mémoire de l'Académie des sciences: Guide de recherches.* Ed. Éric Brian and Christiane Demeulenaere-Douyère. Paris, London, and New York: Technique et Documentation, 1996.

Hahn, Roger. *The Anatomy of a Scientific Institution: The Paris Academy of Sciences, 1666–1803.* Berkeley, Los Angeles, and London: University of California Press, 1971.

———. "Louis XIV and Science Policy." In *Sun King: The Ascendancy of French Culture During the Reign of Louis XIV,* ed. David Lee Rubin. Washington D.C.: Folger Shakespeare Library; Cranbury, NJ, and London: Associated University Presses, 1992, pp. 195–206.

Stroup, Alice. *A Company of Scientists: Botany, Patronage, and Community at the Seventeenth-Century Parisian Royal Academy of Sciences.* Berkeley, Los Angeles, and Oxford: University of California Press, 1990.

———. "Louis XIV as Patron of the Parisian Academy of Sciences." In *Sun King: The Ascendancy of French Culture During the Reign of Louis XIV,* ed. David Lee Rubin. Washington D.C.: Folger Shakespeare Library; Cranbury, NJ, and London: Associated University Presses, 1992, pp. 221–240.

———. *Royal Funding of the Parisian Académie Royale des Sciences During the 1690s. Transactions of the American Philosophical Society,* vol. 77, part 4. Philadelphia, 1987.

Sturdy, David. *Science and Social Status: The Members of the Académie des Sciences, 1666–1750.* Woodbridge and Rochester: Boydell, 1995.

ALICE STROUP

See also Descartes, René; Fontenelle; *Journal des sçavans;* Montmor Academy; Observatoire de Paris

Academies

The birth of scientific academies in seventeenth-century Europe was part of the process of transition toward a new culture. Aristotelian science and the old methodology that assumed the existence of universal truths by which the processes of nature could be explained had come under persistent questioning. The truth, no longer a given, was coming to be thought of as capable of being continually transformed, revised, and corrected. Descriptions and explanations of natural phenomena emerged from novel researches and were communicated and popularized in order to be discussed and verified. This new and different mode in the investigation of nature constituted a revision in the practice of natural philosophy. The result was that, during the seventeenth century, a growing exchange of information created extraordinary networks, thanks to which there was a continual discourse between natural philosophers and interested amateurs, enthusiasts and politicians, and laymen and clerics throughout Europe.

While a number of societies for the discussion of literary, philosophical, or theological issues had been organized during the Renaissance, it was primarily in the seventeenth century that formal organizations devoted to the study and promotion of natural philosophy came into being. Some were inspired by the urgings of those like Francis Bacon (1561–1626) and Johann Valentin Andreae (1586–1654) that natural philosophy and the arts could best be promoted by organized collaborative efforts. Others were founded in emulation of existing societies or for reasons of national or local prestige.

Discussions of issues in natural philosophy or the related arts took place not only during personal meetings, but also, and above all, through a whole series of letters, reports and diaries of scientific travels, notes on lessons, and comments on cultural and social events. While international communication was most frequently in Latin, there was a marked and growing tendency for the publications of the societies to be in the vernaculars and in a simple, easily understandable prose. This diffusion of knowledge had significant effects on subsequent cultural, political, and social institutions. In this lively intellectual movement, the academies provided a means of uniting men with common interests in the comparison of hypotheses, the verification of phenomena, and the close examination of printed works.

The development of the academies was an international phenomenon. Between the seventeenth and nineteenth centuries, their diffusion was so great that almost every country claimed at least one academy, "royal" or otherwise, and some had several in different provincial towns. At the same time, every institution was unique, as the nature of the academies varied according to their predominant scientific interests. Groups emerged that privileged one discipline or another and gave their attention to instruments for scientific research. The differences among the academies depended also upon the degree of their submission to the Court or the patron who made their work possible and who sometimes determined their choices. Some were self-financed; others managed without financial resources at all. They differed, too, in the ties each of them had with its civil community. Every institution emphasized its uniqueness, with investigative themes of particular interest to its members. The participants in the discussions and work became more and more "professional," more and more "specialized" in the subjects and techniques examined. Those involved in the meetings and work groups of the academies prepared experiments and tested various hypotheses, thus participating in the development and transformation of the various scientific disciplines. New instruments for research were invented, and the research itself often led either to the creation of still more apparatus or to the perfecting of existing instruments.

The "experimenters," as many of the members of the societies termed themselves, became innovators within innovative research and activity programs, and they, often very young, received an important contribution to their vocational training from the academies. They matured within the discussions on the disciplines and in their diffusion and definition. The academies also had a larger public function. They shared their experiences, compared their results, and debated scientific problems that were being discussed by intellectuals and were the focus of many a conversation in salons throughout Europe. Some of the academies published the results of individual research; thus, the scientific patrimony of a few specialists became common wealth accessible to everyone.

The situation and development of the academies differed from country to country. The origin of the academies in Italy has been explained as an intellectual movement outside the university and as an answer to the progressive loss of reference points due to the political, social, and cultural transformation of the country. In Italy, the academies were numerous, but none were organizationally or intellectually as strong as the French or the English, and most of them were decidedly short-lived. Among the most important Italian scientific academies were the Accademia dei Lincei and the Accademia del Cimento. The Lincei was founded in Rome in 1603 by Federico Cesi (1585–1630), a wealthy nobleman. A number of scientists took part in its activities, notably Galileo Galilei (1564–1642), and it was there that Galileo presented his *occhiale* and his *occhialino,* which the academicians would rename, respectively, the telescope and the microscope. The Accademia dei Lincei was active for few years but could not survive the death of Cesi in 1630 and the condemnation of Galileo in 1633. The Accademia del Cimento was founded in Florence in 1657. It had neither statutes nor official members; rather, it was under the rule and protection of the grand duke Ferdinand II de' Medici, and his brother, Prince, later Cardinal, Leopold. Its seat was the Pitti Palace. During the ten years of its activity (1657–1667), its members performed experiments on heat, on the density and non-compressibility of fluids, and on atmospheric pressure. Many of these experiments were published as *Saggi di naturali esperienze* (Trials of Natural Experiments, 1667). The introduction, written by the secretary Lorenzo Magalotti (1637–1712), was revised with great care by the grand duke himself.

In England, the Royal Society for the Promotion of Natural Knowledge, chartered by the Crown in 1662, was born out of the common interest held by a number of scientists in experimental science. Among its founding members were some who earlier had been associated with the Oxford Philosophical Society and a few who had met informally each week after lectures at Gresham College in London, the site of the meetings of the society for a few decades after its founding. It had a charter, providing for a president, a council, and officers, with a single paid position, curator of experiments, held by Robert Hooke (1635–1702). The society was financed by the dues of its members. Its membership, larger than that of any other academy, was self-selected and included not only a number of the leading natural philosophers of the Scientific Revolution, including Isaac Newton (1642–1727), but also not a few individuals chosen for reasons of prestige or for their social or political connections. The secretary of the society, Henry Oldenburg (ca. 1618–1677), undertook the publication of a journal, the *Philosophical Transactions,* reflecting the society's interests and activities, as a private venture, but it was taken over by the society itself upon Oldenburg's death.

In France, several informal associations to discuss literary, political, and scientific matters were organized under the patronage of various individuals. Under the leadership of Marin Mersenne (1588–1648), a Minim friar, however, a group meeting periodically at the house of his order devoted itself expressly to natural philosophy and mathematics. Upon his death, the center of weekly discussions of topics in natural philosophy as well as medicine and the liberal arts became the home of Habert de Montmor (ca. 1600–1679), presided over by Pierre Gassendi (1592–1655). It established a formal constitution as the Montmor Academy in 1657 and, after the founding of the Royal Society, kept in close touch with its activities.

Some of the academy's members were instrumental in persuading Louis XIV's chief minister, Colbert, to establish the Académie Royale des Sciences, which began its regular meetings in Paris in December 1666. Many scientists and scholars from different fields of study took part in the academy's work sessions, and they regularly wrote reports on their meetings and on the discussions and experiments. The Académie had neither statutes nor rules until 1699. In fact, it worked under the direct authority of the royal ministers, first of all Colbert. These ministers played a very important role in the election of the academicians, in providing financial resources, and also in the scientific choices. From 1699 on, however, the Académie was guided by precise regulations that would remain in place until the French Revolution (1789). Several classes of members were created, with different salary levels. The work of its members and others was initially published in the *Journal des sçavans.* The role of the Parisian academy was important, in particular in the eighteenth century for the diffusion of Newtonianism throughout Europe and for the renewal of the monarchy and of the state.

The academies of the German states were less important than those of England, France, or Italy in the seventeenth century, and most were short-lived. In 1651, however, the Collegium Naturae Curiosum, a society of physicians, was founded in Schweinfurt to hear papers on innovative work in medicine. A few years later, the society began to publish its *Miscellanea curiosa,* which, along with articles on medicine, also included some on related fields, such as botany, anatomy, and chemistry. It obtained imperial patronage after 1677. The Collegium Curiosum sive Experimentale was founded in 1672 in Altdorf by Johann Christoph Sturm (1635–1703), a talented experimenter and professor at the University of Altdorf, who was influenced by the example of the Accademia del Cimento. The society published two volumes describing its experiments. In 1700, the example set by the Académie Royale des Sciences led Gottfried Wilhelm Leibniz (1646–1716) to undertake the establishment of an academy in Berlin. A number of academies with royal or princely patronage were similarly founded in the eighteenth century.

BIBLIOGRAPHY

Boehm, Laetitia, and Ezio Raimondi, eds. *Università, accademie e società scientifiche in Italia e in Germania dal cinquecento al settecento.* Bologna: Società editrice il Mulino, 1981.

Brown, Harcourt. *Scientific Organizations in Seventeenth-Century France.* Baltimore: Johns Hopkins University Press, 1934.

Hunter, Michael. *The Royal Society and Its Fellows, 1660–1700: The Morphology of an Early Scientific Institution.* Chalfont St. Giles: British Society for the History of Science, 1982.

Maylender, Michele. *Storia delle accademie d'Italia.* 5 vols. Bologna: Arnaldo Forni Editore, 1976.

Ornstein, Martha. *The Role of Scientific Societies in the Seventeenth Century.* Chicago: University of Chicago Press, 1938.

Sturdy, David. *Science and Social Status: The Members of the Académie des Sciences, 1666–1750.* Woodbridge and Rochester: Boydell, 1995.

MARA MINIATI

See also Bureau d'adresse; Correspondence Networks; Mersenne, Marin; Montmor Academy; Oxford Philosophical Society

Accademia dei Lincei

The Academy of Lynxes was founded in Rome by Federico Cesi (1585–1630), later Prince Cesi, who hailed from a rich and noble family. Cesi was deeply involved in scientific debate and was extremely interested in exploring and uncovering the mechanisms regulating the natural world. He was, however, also firmly convinced that such a task could not be realized alone but, rather, necessitated a close collaboration among scholars through the creation of an authentic scientific community.

He joined forces with three young scholars not much older than himself and in 1603 formed a society that had as its symbol the lynx, which is no longer found in Italy but at that time was common. The symbolic animal was accompanied by the motto *Sagacius ista,* referring to its perceived attribute of extremely acute eyesight; the eyesight to which Cesi alluded was not only corporeal but intellectual, capable of penetrating phenomena to their core and of discovering their causes and effects. Cesi's three companions were the poet and scholar Francesco Stelluti (1577–1652), the Dutch doctor Joannes van Heeck (1577–post-1618), and Anastasio de Filiis (1577–1608). The aim of the academy was announced in the *Lynceographum,* probably begun around 1605, which constituted the programmatic statutes of the academy. The text established the regulations for the admission of new members and, above all, sanctioned the commitment of the academy's members to cultivate the scientific disciplines, to lead a life devoted to study, to work always in collaboration with others, and to make known the results of research.

The academy's first years of activity would prove difficult. At first the studies were carried out in great secrecy, provoking a reaction by Cesi's father, who launched a fierce persecution, above all of Heeck, who was suspected of heresy and was compelled to emigrate. Stelluti and de Filiis also returned to their native places. Federico Cesi was sent to Naples, and he used the occasion to get to know the philosophers and naturalists of that city. He met, among others, Giambattista della Porta (1535–1615) and Ferrante Imperato (1550–1625), who had his own museum, rich with natural-history specimens, scientific instruments, and books. Cesi laid the foundations for relationships of friendship and collaboration that would allow for the enlistment of some illustrious new Neapolitan members.

After 1609, activities were resumed thanks to the acquisition of family property, which permitted Cesi to finance the academy. New members joined its founders: in 1610, Giambattista della Porta; in 1611, Galileo Galilei (1564–1642) and then Johann Schmidt (Joannes Faber, 1574–1629), a doctor at the Hospital of Santo Spirito in Rome, who would become the secretary of the academy; Fabio Colonna, a botanist from Naples; Cassiano dal Pozzo, a Piedmontese collector; and Johann Schreck (1576–1630), later known as Giovanni Terrentius, who would become a famous missionary in China, where he would play a prominent role in science. The participation of Galileo in the academy is particularly important. The scientist had already constructed his *occhiale,* which the Linceans would then baptize *telescopio.* Galileo would also, in 1624, offer Cesi his *occhialino,* which he had constructed in 1612. Upon the suggestion of Faber, the instrument, which enlarged minute bodies, would be renamed *microscopio.*

These two instruments, fundamental to research, were perfected in the milieu of the society, other models were made, and, above all, these instruments were applied to the study of both the cosmos and the microcosmos. New branches and sources of knowledge in astronomy and the biological and medical sciences were born. In 1625 Stelluti published the first microscopic observations of bees, with engravings by Mathäus Greuter.

The attention that Cesi hoped to draw to scientific research and the importance he gave it found full confirmation in the Galilean instruments and the kind of research Galileo conducted; he refused to acknowledge the authority of Aristotle (384–322 B.C.E.) and proudly affirmed the autonomy of thought and of free research. This is the importance of the academy itself, as a place independent even of the university, where respect for the "masters" reigned and where the ultimate aim was not so much the studies themselves as the attainment of practical benefits. The Accademia dei Lincei represented an association dedicated to freedom of research; in this spirit it sustained Galileo in his defense of the Copernican theory.

After the condemnation of Copernicanism in 1616, the death of Cesi in 1630, and the definitive condemnation of Galileo in 1633, the academy ceased its activities, and the library and documents were dispersed, though some books were acquired by Cassiano del Pozzo, a Lincean scholar from 1622 on, who also secured the findings of the museum collected by Cesi, consisting of minerals, scientific instruments, artistic objects, and much else.

It was not until later in the seventeenth and eighteenth centuries that there were attempts to resurrect the academy. These attempts would finally prove fruitful in

1874, after the unification of Italy, when it was reconstituted under the name of Reale Accademia dei Lincei, later modified in 1944 to the present-day Accademia Nazionale dei Lincei.

BIBLIOGRAPHY

Biagioli, Mario. "Scientific Revolution and Aristocratic Ethos: Federico Cesi and the Accademia dei Lincei." In *Alexandre Koyré: L'avventura intellettuale,* ed. Carlo Vinti. Naples: Edizioni Scientifiche Italiane, 1994, pp. 279–295.

Clericuzio, Antonio, and Silvia De Renzi. "Medicine, Alchemy, and Natural Philosophy in the Early Accademia dei Lincei." In *Italian Academies of the 16th Century,* ed. D. S. Chambers and F. Quiviger. London: Warburg Institute, 1995, pp. 175–194.

Gardair, Jean-Michel. "I Lincei: i soggetti, i luoghi, le attività." *Quaderni storici* 16 (1981), 763–787.

Maylender, Michele. *Storie delle accademie d'Italia.* 5 vols. Bologna: Arnaldo Forni Editore, 1976, vol. 3, pp. 430–503.

MARA MINIATI

See also Academies; Accademia del Cimento; Public Knowledge

Accademia del Cimento

The Academy of Experiment drew its name from *cimentare,* (assay), a term characteristic of the art of working metals, and was active in Florence from 1657 to 1667. It was a sort of scientific society with neither members nor statutes, protected by Grand Duke Ferdinand II de'Medici and by his brother, Prince, subsequently Cardinal, Leopold.

Numerous scientists and simple enthusiasts, some of whom had been followers or students of Galileo Galilei (1564–1642), took part in the academy's activities. Among them was the Neapolitan Giovanni Alfonso Borelli (1608–1679), who had been a pupil of Benedetto Castelli (1578–1643) in Rome. Borelli carried out numerous scientific missions for the grand duke and was one of the academy's most attentive observers and experimenters. He left Tuscany for Messina in 1665 and finally went to Rome, where he would die. Other academics included Carlo Rinaldini (1615–1679), professor of philosophy at the University of Pisa; and Antonio Oliva (1624–1691).

The Florentine Vincenzo Viviani (1622–1703) became so skilled at mathematics that the grand duke presented him with a monthly subsidy and recommended him to Galileo. Taken in by the renowned scholar in

1639, Viviani would remain with Galileo until his death in 1642. After the death of Evangelista Torricelli (1608–1647), Viviani would succeed him as the grand duke's mathematician and was often called upon to assume the role of engineer and consultant for various projects. He was admitted to the Accademia del Cimento at Leopold's request. King Louis XIV of France gave him a substantial pension and named him one of the eight foreign members of the Académie Royale des Sciences at Paris. Viviani wrote on geometry in numerous celebrated and widely read works. He would have liked to publish a complete edition of Galileo's works, which would have included the banned *Dialogue Concerning the Two Chief World Systems* (1632) but was, unfortunately, unable to do so.

Lorenzo Magalotti (1637–1712) was the academy's secretary and edited the *Saggi di naturali esperienze* (Trials of Natural Experiments, 1667). He had a good knowledge of the science of his day, was a courtier, widely traveled, and a high-ranking diplomat. The academy's seat was in the Pitti Palace and made use of a *fornace da bicchieri* (glass furnace) situated in the adjacent Boboli Gardens. Its motto was "Try and try again," by which was meant successive testing and attempts to verify experimental results. Its seal bore the image of a furnace for assaying metals, an appropriate image, as the experiments conducted were concerned primarily with heat.

The Torricellian "barometric" experiment was repeated. It involved placing an unsealed tube containing mercury inside a container. The difference in the height of the liquid due to atmospheric pressure and the vacuum it created within the tube led to experiments on the effects of the liquid's level within a sealed tube, in which the height of the liquid would depend exclusively on temperature and no longer on pressure. These experiments were the basis for the Florentine thermometer, an instrument made of a ball of glass and a tube sealed *alla fiamma* (with a flame). The gradations were marked on the tube with small black dots of enamel for each degree, a white mark for every ten, and a blue one for every hundred degrees. Some experiments were done before the work at the academy itself began; Prince Leopold dedicated himself to thermometry, designing the so-called *termometri infingardi* (lazy thermometers), tubes filled with alcohol and containing floating glass balls of diverse densities. Varying the heat, the alcohol varied in volume, causing different balls to begin to descend slowly at different temperatures. He also attempted experiments in incubation in the Boboli Gardens, trying to hatch eggs at different temperatures without the use of chickens.

The academy's members oversaw the construction of equipment to be used for the experiments—glass instruments designed by them and made by glassblowers (*gonfia*) commissioned by the grand dukes for the creation of china, glasses, and goblets. Among the instruments produced were long-stemmed and spiral thermometers and densimeters called *palle d'oncia* (ounce balls).

The scientists followed the movements of the Court and the will of the prince, so that the academy's ten-year life span did not amount to ten years of work. There were long pauses and moves to other cities. For example, in January 1658 experiments on the *agghiacciamenti,* or freezing of water with varying levels of salt content, were done on the coast of Livorno, where the scholars had been led by the Court. The year 1667 brought the publication of *Saggi di naturali esperienze,* which constituted the official presentation of the research that had been undertaken. The experiments were rigorously selected,

and only the most spectacular ones were presented with the instruments that had been used. There was no trace of the astronomical research present in the diaries and manuscripts of the academy, nor of those experiments considered less significant. The secretary's draft underwent numerous revisions and a veritable censure by the prince to guarantee the absence of words considered "dangerous" or not consistent with the political or religious requirements of the period. Copies of the *Saggi* were sent everywhere, often accompanied by the very precise "Florentine" thermometer, the new pride of the grand duke.

The academy's activities came to an end in 1667; Leopold had become a cardinal, there was bad blood among the scientists, and in reality the Florentine academy never reached the levels of other European scientific societies, nor their autonomy or achievements in scientific research. It never had statutes or members: it continued its irregular activities as a palace society. The results of the method of research it adopted, although influenced by Galilean experimentation, underwent censorship imposed by the difficult situation created by the condemnation of the heliocentric theory and the trial of Galileo.

The scientists who in some way played a role in the academy's activities had researches of their own, which did not fall expressly within the life of the academy itself. We must, therefore, seek to trace the life of the academy not through its official documents but within the dense correspondence that the scientists maintained among themselves and with colleagues in other countries. There one can find the scientific exchanges worthy of a great and active community of scholars. But they were, after all, private exchanges that went beyond the princely control and the censorship imposed both on that kind of experience and on the scientific conclusions that could be drawn from it.

Title page of the first edition of the Accademia's Saggi.

BIBLIOGRAPHY

Galluzzi, Paolo. "L'Accademia del Cimento: 'Gusti' de principe, filosofia e ideologia dell'esperimento." *Quaderni storici* 16 (1981), 788–844.

Maylender, Michele. *Storie delle accademie d'Italia.* 5 vols. Bologna: Arnaldo Forni Editore, 1976, vol. 2, 7–16.

Middleton, W. E. Knowles. *The Experimenters: A Study of the Accademia del Cimento.* Baltimore: Johns Hopkins University Press, 1971.

Segre, Michael. "Die Accademia del Cimento: Wissenschaft zwischen Kirche und Politik." *Historisches Jahrbuch: Im Auftrag des Görres-Gesellschaft* 111 (1991), 148–154.

Tribby, Jay. "Club Medici: Natural Experiment and the Imagineering of 'Tuscany.'" *Configurations* 2 (1994), 215–235.

MARA MINIATI

See also Academies; Barometer; Patronage; Thermoscope/Thermometer

Acosta, José de (ca. 1540–1600)

A Spanish Jesuit (possibly a Jewish convert), he served as a missionary in Peru (1572–1586). He attempted to "explain the causes and reasons" of "the works of nature." The presence in the New World of men and animals unknown to the ancients was a source of wonder, contradicting, as it did, biblical teachings about Adam and the Ark. He concluded that men had reached the New World on foot, walking from the Old World to the New by way of a northern connection between the two. European animals, some of them dangerous, also could have walked, but animals known only from the New World presented a puzzle that he never resolved. To say that European and New World animals were the same, was, he said, to call "an egg a chestnut." New World plants posed no such difficulty because plants were not included in the Ark. According to Aristotle (384–322 B.C.E.), the leading ancient authority, only part of the earth was habitable, tropical regions being too hot and dry, as they were burnt by the Sun, and northern regions too cold. Acosta was surprised to find that the tropical climate was both temperate and humid. He explained such inconsistencies by saying that things sometimes worked one way and sometimes another, depending on the circumstances, thus saving many Aristotelian principles. He also discussed winds and tides; the magnetic compass; the mining of gold, silver, and mercury; the rivers; the skies; and the comet of 1577.

BIBLIOGRAPHY

Acosta, José de. *The Natural and Moral History of the Indies.* Trans. Edward Grimston[e], London, 1604. Repr. Clements R. Markham. London: Hakluyt Society, 1880.

Beddall, Barbara G. Introducción, apéndice y antología (Spanish and English). In José de Acosta. *Historia natural y moral de las Indias.* Seville: Juan de Léon, 1590. Facs. ed. Valencia: Albatros, 1977, pp. 12–129.

Jarcho, Saul. "Origin of the American Indian as Suggested by Fray Joseph de Acosta (1589)." *Isis* 50 (1959), 430–438.

BARBARA G. BEDDALL

See also Anthropology and Race

Acoustics

A

First became clearly identified as a distinct branch of physics in the seventeenth century. Francis Bacon (1561–1626) proposed that the "Acoustique Art" should embrace both the investigation of the nature and causes of sound (speculative natural philosophy) and the practical harnessing of its effects (operative natural magic). The broad program of experimental inquiry he sketched out in the *New Atlantis* (1627) and *Sylva sylvarum* (1627) proved a compelling model for later natural philosophers. In England the first documented use of the term "acoustics" was by Narcissus Marsh in 1684, while in France Joseph Sauveur (1653–1716) first proposed a new science of *acoustique* in 1701.

Sound as the object of hearing had always constituted a part of Aristotelian physics. Within the Scholastic system, however, music was generally classified as a mathematical discipline addressing the arithmetic of pitch relationships. What revolutionized traditional understandings and contributed to the mathematization of physics was the discovery that the numerical ratios that had characterized musical intervals since Pythagoras (fl. sixth century B.C.E.) corresponded to frequencies of vibration. This insight was first clearly articulated in Galileo Galilei's (1564–1642) *Two New Sciences* (1638).

The earliest significant contribution to the development of acoustics was made by Marin Mersenne (1588–1648) in his *Harmonie universelle* (1636). By rigorous experimental observation, he established the relationship between the physical variables determining the frequency of a vibrating string and expressed them as mathematical laws. This success led natural philosophers to look for similar laws in optics and other areas of mechanics. Mersenne investigated many other properties of sound, and his work was fundamental to all later developments in acoustics.

Throughout the Scientific Revolution, a twofold approach to acoustics is discernable. The first was a mathematical, analytical approach exemplified by Isaac Newton's (1642–1727) determination of the speed of sound in the *Principia* (1687), Robert Hooke (1635–1702) and Christiaan Huygens (1629–1695) on absolute frequency, and John Wallis (1616–1703) and Francis Robartes (1650–1718) on overtones.

The second was a more "Baconian" approach concerned with collecting data on unusual aural phenomena in nature or those produced by instruments. This is exemplified by the acoustical interests of the Accademia del Cimento in Florence, the Royal Society of London, and the Académie Royale des Sciences in Paris. International collaboration from both of these perspectives underpinned Joseph Sauveur's (1653–1716) work on modes of vibration, which, in turn, set the stage for Leonhard Euler's (1707–1783) achievements in the eighteenth century.

BIBLIOGRAPHY

Dostrovsky, Sigalia. "Early Vibration Theory: Physics and Music in the Seventeenth Century." *Archive for History of Exact Sciences* 14 (1974–1975), 169–218.

Gouk, Penelope Mary. "Acoustics in the Early Royal Society, 1660–1680." *Notes and Records of the Royal Society* 36 (1982), 155–175.

Hunt, Frederick Vinton. *Origins in Acoustics: The Science of Sound from Antiquity to the Age of Newton.* New Haven, CT, and London: Yale University Press, 1978.

PENELOPE GOUK

See also Music/Harmonics

Acta eruditorum

Literally *Records of the Learned,* the *Acta* was a journal published in Latin in the German city of Leipzig from 1682 until 1782. Consciously modeled on the *Journal des sçavans* and the *Philosophical Transactions* of the Royal Society, it sought to make international works available to a German audience and to spread the reputation of German learning abroad by publishing reviews of important books from all of Europe. Such reviews were meant to enable the man of universal learning (the *polyhistor*) to keep up with the exponential increase in published works. The first editor, Leipzig Professor of Ethics and Politics Otto Mencke (1644–1707), used a wide network of contacts throughout Europe to acquire important books, which were reviewed primarily by northern German scholars, the *Collectores.* Although he and the *Collectores* were all Protestants, Mencke strenuously sought to present the works of authors of all denominations fairly and to avoid acrimonious debate. Although the *Acta* published primarily reviews (89 percent of the total content, according to a survey of 1682–1706 volumes, of which only 30 percent were on scientific subjects), Mencke consciously tried to raise the prestige of the journal by publishing articles on mathematics and natural philosophy (7 percent of the total content, of which 85 percent were on science in the broadest sense). This

ACTA
ERUDITORUM
ANNO M DCLXXXIII
publicata,
ac
SERENISSIMO FRATRUM PARI,
DN. JOHANNI
GEORGIO IV,
Electoratus Saxonici Hæredi,
&
DN. FRIDERICO
AUGUSTO,
Ducibus Saxoniæ &c.&c.&c.
PRINCIPIBUS JUVENTUTIS
dicata.
Cum S.Cæfareæ Majeftatis & Potentisfimi Electoris Saxoniæ Privilegiis.

LIPSIÆ,
Proftant apud J. GROSSIUM & J. P. GLETITSCHIUM.
Typis CHRISTOPHORI GüNTHERI.
Anno M DCLXXXIII.

Although publication of the journal began in 1682, the first several numbers were published collectively the following year.

heavy emphasis on science was also apparent in articles translated from foreign journals and reprinted in the journal (3.7 percent of the total, 96 percent on science).

Foremost among the journal's contributors was Gottfried Wilhelm Leibniz (1646–1716), who contributed a piece almost every year until his death. In an essay of October 1684, he presented for the first time the fundamentals of his differential calculus, although it remained for a time misunderstood. Leibniz continued to develop infinitesimal calculus in further issues of the *Acta.* This close connection with Leibniz discouraged Isaac Newton (1642–1727)and his English colleagues from publishing in the *Acta,* although the journal published an accurate and influential early review of Newton's *Principia* (1687) that appreciated the achievement of Newton's work. Other contributors included the elder Johann (1667–1748) and Jakob (1654–1705) Bernoulli, Niklaus and Daniel Bernoulli, François de l'Hôpital, Walter von Tschirnhaus, Christiaan Huygens (1629–1695), and Christian Wolff.

After Mencke's death, the editorship was assumed by his son Johann Burckhard, then, in turn, by Burckhard's son Friedrich Otto, and finally by Andreas Bel. The standard and prestige of the journal declined over time, and the *Acta* folded with the publication of the 1776 issue considerably behind schedule in 1782. By then its role had been supplanted by the specialized scientific and academic periodical.

BIBLIOGRAPHY

Cohen, I. Bernard. "The Review of the First Edition of Newton's *Principia* in the *Acta eruditorum,* with Notes on the Other Reviews." In *The Investigation of Difficult Things: Essays on Newton and the History of the Exact Sciences in Honour of D. T. Whiteside,* ed. P. M. Harman and Alan E. Shapiro. Cambridge: Cambridge University Press, 1992, pp. 323–353.

Laeven, Hubertus. *The* Acta eruditorum *Under the Editorship of Otto Mencke (1644–1707): The History of an International Learned Journal Between 1682 and 1707.* Amsterdam: APA-Holland University Press, 1990.

MARCUS HELLYER

See also Journal des sçavans; Leibniz, Gottfried Wilhelm; Philosophical Transactions

Active Principles

From ancient times through the Scientific Revolution, there was a debate among natural philosophers about the nature of matter. Formalists, such as Plato (428–348 B.C.E.) and Aristotle (384–322 B.C.E.), conceived of matter as passive; therefore, it required an actualizing principle or form, either internal or external, to shape it. Materialists, such as Democritos (ca. 460–370 B.C.E.), Epicuros of Samos (341–270 B.C.E.), and Lucretius (ca. 95–55 B.C.E.), taught that the motion of atoms was sufficient to produce natural phenomena.

Alchemical thought tended to follow formalism and involved active principles as shapers of chaotic matter. In alchemy, these principles were often described in terms of male and female. When brought into perfect balance, the male and female principles produced the Philosopher's Stone, which could both transmute base metals and heal sickness. Theophrastus Bombastus von Hohenheim (Paracelsus) (ca. 1493–1541) built an elaborate chemical theory using active agents he called *semina* (seeds) and *archei* (artificers) that informed chaotic matter. Paracelsus's noted follower and systematizer Petrus Severinus (1542–1602) explained that *semina* were the fundamental immaterial principles from which bodies arise and to which they return. Robert Fludd (1574–

1637), an English chemical physician, spoke of the Kabbalistic *ruach Elohim* (spirit of God) as the primary active principle, which worked through rarefaction and condensation. The Dutch chemical philosopher Johannes Baptista van Helmont (1579–1644) developed the *semina* doctrine and worked out experimental proofs for the existence of such active principles. He attributed the creation of the world to *semina* working on the primordial waters of Genesis. This creative action continued in biological activities, such as the growth of plants, in which water is transformed into plant matter by *semina*.

The reemphasis on atomism and the development of Cartesianism in the sixteenth and seventeenth centuries gave rise to the mechanical philosophy, which posited that the motion of matter alone accounted for natural phenomena. René Descartes (1596–1650) taught that the motion imparted to matter by God was sufficient to explain all phenomena. The antipodal approaches to matter represented by the chemical philosophy and mechanism provided a framework for more syncretistic views of matter and active principles. Robert Boyle (1627–1691) was an atomist, or corpuscularian, with mechanistic leanings, yet he also invoked Helmontian *semina* as the active principles that transformed the waters of Genesis into the physical world through the action of the *ruach Elohim*. He reported hydroponic experiments that showed *semina* at work in plant growth. *Semina* were essential to his corpuscularianism.

Isaac Newton (1642–1727) was a quasi-Cartesian mechanist. He accepted that matter in motion largely accounted for physical reality. He agreed, however, with the Neoplatonist Henry More (1614–1687) that motion alone was an insufficient explanation of nature. Gravity, for example, was the active force on which all "great motions depended." Newton also shared Boyle's Helmontian corpuscularianism. Newton's limited, but crucial, use of active principles was deeply disturbing to Gottfried Wilhelm Leibniz (1646–1716). Leibniz believed that passive matter was merely a manifestation of what was ultimately active force. His monads were active principles, each of which reflected the entire universe from its perspective. He thought that Newton was irrational and misplaced in his halfway position. Leibniz's mathematical active principles, which were the basis of matter, differed considerably from the *semina* of the chemists, which worked on passive matter. Whatever the theoretical context, the disagreement about the sufficiency of matter in motion or the necessity of active principles to account for nature was a major issue in early-modern science.

BIBLIOGRAPHY

Debus, Allen G. *The Chemical Philosophy of the Renaissance.* New York: Science History Publications, 1977.

McGuire, J. E. "Force, Active Principles, and Newton's Invisible Realm." *Ambix* 25 (1968), 154–208.

Shackelford, Jole. "Seeds with a Mechanical Purpose: Severinus' *Semina* and Seventeenth-Century Matter Theory." In *Reading the Book of Nature: The Other Side of the Scientific Revolution,* ed. Allen G. Debus and Michael T. Walton. Kirksville, MO: Sixteenth Century Journal Publishers, 1998, pp. 15–44.

Walton, Michael T. "Boyle and Newton on the Transmutation of Water and Air, from the Root of Helmont's Tree." *Ambix* 27 (1980), 11–18.

MICHAEL T. WALTON

See also Cambridge Platonists; Chemical Philosophy; Paracelsus

Aerostatics. *See* Pneumatics

Agricola, Georgius (1494–1555)

Nicknamed the Saxon Pliny, he was primarily a humanist scholar concerned with reviving and extending ancient learning through direct observations of life, places, and things without reference to hidden meanings. A flourishing school teaching career in Zwickau was cut short in 1522 after his reform-minded Catholicism clashed with the views of radical Protestants. He switched briefly to theology and then medicine, soon joining the team in Venice preparing Latin translations of the works of Galen (second century) and Hippocrates. His interest in minerals and their medical applications whetted, he visited mining districts in the Austrian Alps before settling in ore-rich areas of Bohemia and Saxony as town physician at Joachimsthal and later Chemnitz. Agricola's plan to annotate the works of Dioscorides and Galen expanded to elucidate everything about minerals, German mines, and metalworking in the light of the body of knowledge also found in other authorities, such as Pliny and Theophrastus. In particular, their scientific terminology needed to be clarified and standardized, and Agricola's major works featured glossaries listing Latin and Greek terms with German equivalents.

Agricola's first scientific work, *Bermannus,* published in 1530, is a dialogue between a mining expert, named

An illustration from Agricola's De re metallica (1556) *showing three stages in the digging of shafts to create a mining tunnel.*

after Lorenz Berman (d.1532), one of his mentors, and two physicians, one knowledgeable about Greek and Roman sources and one familiar with Arabic sources. Mines and remote places were frightening or in disrepute, but Agricola saw them as essential in the support and spread of civilization. Despite wealth from mining investments and duties as mayor of Chemnitz and ambassadorships, Agricola continued observations at mines and smelteries. He also maintained contact with Valerius Cordus (1515–1544), Conrad Gessner (1516–1565), and others who provided mineral samples and information from different places. These new sources extended his vision and allowed him to rethink some conclusions. He rarely relied on Neoplatonic or occult explanations. A folio volume containing *De ortu et causis subterraneorum* (On the Origin and Cause of Subterranean Things) and *De natura fossilium* (On the Nature of Excavations), among other works, was published in 1546. His landmark *De re metallica* (On Metals) appeared posthumously in 1556 and was quickly translated into German to serve practitioners. And still, Agricola's Catholicism followed him in death with burial denied in the parish church alongside other mayors. Despite the early success of his scientific writings, little was done to extend his lead for nearly another century. Even today, he is better known than understood.

BIBLIOGRAPHY

Agricola, Georgius. *De re metallica*. Trans. Herbert C. Hoover and Lou H. Hoover. New York: Dover, 1950.

Craddock, P. T. "Agricola, *De re metallica:* A Landmark in the History of Metallurgy." *Endeavour* n.s. 18 (1994), 67–73.

Hannaway, Owen. "Georgius Agricola as Humanist." *Journal of the History of Ideas* 53 (1992), 553–560.

JAMES A. RUFFNER

See also Mining and Metallurgy

Agriculture

Early-modern Europe saw gradual but significant changes in agricultural practice that encouraged, much more than benefited from, contemporary scientific activity. Natural philosophers were unable to offer improved understanding of plant generation, growth, nutrition, and breeding. Rather, particularly in western Europe, economic, social, and political events such as increasing urbanization, mercantilism, and exploration and colonization of newly encountered lands encouraged the replacement of a self-sufficient economy with one that emphasized farming for profit.

The Low Countries exhibited Europe's most advanced agriculture, characterized by field rotations that included a fodder crop instead of a fallow period to replenish soil. Entrepreneurial landlords, notably in England, Switzerland, and the environs of Paris, adopted these profitable rotations. Market farming, however, necessitated changes in land management. Landowners enclosed and farmed community common and waste lands and consolidated tenant's scattered fields. They eliminated many tenants and established control over crops and methods. Agricultural workers resisted, and enclosure and consolidation were not uniformly in place in some areas until well into the nineteenth century.

This period is characterized by an avid interest in agricultural innovation; many believed that widespread agricultural improvements, while benefiting landowners, would also ease serious social problems such as unemployment, intermittent famines, and rising food prices. Social reformer Samuel Hartlib (ca. 1600–1662) collected and published literature in which landlords discussed agricultural experiments and recommended new methods. This literature influenced natural philosophers in England and on the Continent, many themselves landowners. The new science emphasized manipulation of nature, and natural philosophers turned its methods on plants and agriculture. Francis Bacon (1561–1626) attempted to immunize seeds against diseases; Johannes Baptista van Helmont (1579–1644) experimented on methods of plant generation and, like Bernard Palissy (ca. 1510–ca. 1590) and Robert Boyle (1627–1691), investigated soil composition and manuring requirements. Francesco Redi (1626–1697) explored plant propagation; John Evelyn (1620–1706) performed grafting experiments; and Nehemiah Grew (1641–1712), Kenelm Digby (1603–1655), and Marcello Malpighi (1628–1694) worked on plant anatomy and physiology.

Scientific institutions also explored agricultural matters. The Royal Society of London, the Académie Royale des Sciences, the Accademia Secretorum Naturae, and the Accademia del Cimento all gathered information on agricultural practice and experimented on plant growth and nutrition.

Whether and how plants reproduced sexually was also a topic of much interest, and the study of floral anatomy led Grew and John Ray (1620–1705) to propose that stamens and pollen functioned in plants as did male organs and semen in animals. Rudolph Camerarius (1665–1721), director of a botanical garden in Tübingen, in 1694 experimentally confirmed sexual reproduction in plants and the fertilizing role of pollen.

Though progress was made in many of these areas, little emerged that was applicable to agriculture. Agricultural chemistry, an eighteenth- and nineteenth-century development, would mark the interjection of scientifically derived knowledge into agricultural practice in Europe.

BIBLIOGRAPHY

Ambrosoli, Mauro. *Scienziati, contadini e proprietari: Botanica e agricoltura nell'Europa occidentale, 1350–1850.* Turin: Einaudi, 1992.

Fussell, G. E. *Farms, Farmers and Society: Systems of Food Production and Population Numbers.* Lawrence, KS: Coronado, 1976.

———. "History and Agricultural Science." *Agricultural History* 19 (1945), 126–127.

Grigg, David. *The Agricultural Systems of the World: An Evolutionary Approach*. Cambridge: Cambridge University Press.

KATHLEEN WHALEN

See also Botany; Taxonomy

Agrippa von Nettesheim, Heinrich Cornelius (1486–1535)

A polymath, claiming academic degrees in the liberal arts, medicine, and law and profound knowledge, though not a degree, in theology. A native of Cologne, he received an arts degree from the local university in 1502 and seems to have studied or lectured at the Universities of Dôle, Paris, and Pavia. His exact relation to these three universities and the extent to which he spent his years in Italy (1512–1518) engaged in formal study remain unclear, but he claimed doctorates in law and medicine, and contemporaries accepted these claims. Especially after returning to northern Europe in 1518, he became involved in humanistic criticism of ecclesiastical abuses and in agitation for reform, but he was never a committed follower of Martin Luther (1483–1546).

Far more persistent than reformist activities was his commitment to the study of the occult sciences (especially astrology, alchemy, and Kabbalah), which were related to the profession of medicine. He practiced medicine at Geneva, Fribourg im Uchtland, and the Netherlands and served for at least two years as a physician to the queen-mother of France, Louise of Savoy. His major publication in occult science was *De occulta philosophia*. He dedicated an early draft to Abbot Trithemius of Sponheim in 1510 but added new material down to the time of publication (Book I, Antwerp, 1531; complete text, Cologne, 1533). Agrippa shared the belief of Renaissance Neoplatonists in an ancient tradition of divine wisdom going back to the origins of human society, passed down through Zoroastrian and Egyptian as well as Jewish priests and scholars, and expressed in the Hebrew scriptures, the Orphic hymns, the Hermetic books, and Jewish Kabbalah, as well as by Plato (428–348 B.C.E.), the ancient Neoplatonists, recent Florentine Neoplatonists like Marsilio Ficino (1433–1499) and Giovanni Pico della Mirandola (1463–1494), and modern Kabbalists like Paolo Ricci, Pietro Galatino, Francesco Zorzi, and Johann Reuchlin. He would have named his book *De magia* except for the undeserved evil reputation

of magic. In fact, Agrippa's avowed goal was to restore the pure, genuine, holy magic of ancient times through study of ancient texts and to cleanse magical science from the gross popular superstitions that had contaminated it in recent times.

The shaky philosophical superstructure of his magical treatise is the hierarchical worldview of the Neoplatonists. His book incorporates much material from the Florentine Neoplatonists, the Hermetic treatises (first translated into Latin by Ficino), and the Christian Kabbalists. Although Agrippa accepts the traditional belief that material substances are compounded from the four elements of classical science and that most properties of things can be explained on that basis, some properties cannot be derived through reason but are occult, knowable only from long experience, which he conceives in terms of the wisdom discovered in ancient books rather than personal experiment. Knowledge of occult properties can be used for operations of natural magic. He also defines a second realm of astral magic and a third realm of spiritual or demonic magic, a tripartite division derived from the Neoplatonists. Although he did warn against the dangers of spiritual magic if evil spirits were invoked, his open endorsement of invoking spiritual agents, controlled through use of symbols such as numbers, geometrical figures, music, and divine and angelic names, explains why ecclesiastical censors sought to block publication of *De occulta philosophia*.

Although the latter work became an influential encyclopedia of magic, the author's own ambivalence is expressed in other works that emphasize human dependence on divine grace and attack trust in the power of human reason. The chief of these works is *De incertitudine et vanitate scientiarum et artium* (On the Uncertainty and Vanity of the Sciences and Arts), written about 1526 in France and first published at Antwerp in 1531. This book explicitly recants his magical books. Rather oddly, this recantation was reprinted as an appendix to the full edition of *De occulta philosophia* in 1533. Much of *De incertitudine et vanitate* consists of social satire directed against abuses by the clergy, rulers, aristocrats, and various occupational groups, but it also calls in question the ability of human reason to attain certainty and shows unmistakable influence from ancient Academic and Pyrrhonist skepticism. Recent scholarship has struggled with the problem of reconciling the magical with the skeptical elements in Agrippa's two chief publications, both of which were frequently reprinted and translated into vernacular languages. His own solution, clearly expressed in the closing chapters of *De incertitudine et vanitate,* is a simple, undogmatic faith in the power and grace of God.

BIBLIOGRAPHY

Agrippa, Cornelius. *De occulta philosophia libri tres.* Ed. Vittoria Perrone Compagni. Leiden: Brill, 1992.

Keefer, Michael H. "Agrippa's Dilemma: Hermetic 'Rebirth' and the Ambivalence of *De vanitate* and *De occulta philosophia.*" *Renaissance Quarterly* 41 (1988), 614–653.

Nauert, Charles G., Jr. *Agrippa and the Crisis of Renaissance Thought.* Urbana: University of Illinois Press, 1965.

CHARLES G. NAUERT JR.

See also Hermetism; Magic; Neoplatonism; Skepticism

Air Pump

Around 1647 the Magdeburg diplomat Otto von Guericke (1602–1686) had the first vacuum pump constructed. He used it to prove the possibility of a macroscopic void. More, and more important, experiments were done with it from 1659 onward by Robert Boyle (1627–1691) and Robert Hooke (1635–1702). They used the instrument to investigate the properties of air, the vacuum, and everything else they could put into it. Their experiments became the prototype example of the experimental method in science, but it did not immediately result in widespread use. The air pump was too much of a high-tech instrument to allow cheap production. This situation changed toward the end of the seventeenth century, just in time for the pump to become one of the standard tools for itinerant lecturers.

The idea of pumping air was not a new one; compressors of some sort had been known since antiquity. But Guericke was the first to use a pump to create a vacuum, and in doing so he entered into an old debate on the possibility of a macroscopic void. With considerable effort, he managed to get his pump operational, but his experimental reasoning did not convince the Aristotelian scholars who argued on logical grounds against the possibility of a vacuum. What is more, he was not even the first to create a (near) void of macroscopic size. One might, in fact, say that Guericke's most important contribution was that he inspired Robert Boyle.

Boyle was not as much interested in the old vacuum debate as he was in the instrumental possibilities of the air pump. He recognized it as the prototypical Baconian instrument. Together with his assistant Robert Hooke, who did the actual work, he conducted an extensive series of experiments to discover the properties of air and the vacuum. Owing to Boyle, the air pump changed from merely a means to create a void to an established research tool and eventually to the emblem of Baconian science. Boyle also introduced Christiaan Huygens (1629–1695) to the merits of pumping, and it was Huygens who constructed the first air pumps in Holland and France.

Guericke had designed his first air pump on the basis of a fire syringe: a piston moving back and forth in a brass cylinder. During the outward motion, it took in air from a spherical recipient. The pump was emptied during the inward stroke, while a leather valve prevented the air from flowing back to the recipient. The outlet was supplied with a valve as well, to prevent the atmospheric air from being taken in during the suction stroke. Hooke and Huygens improved on this design, but the overall idea remained the same.

Leakage was the largest problem with the earliest vacuum pumps. To reduce it, the pump cylinder had to be perfectly straight with a smooth inner surface. Requirements like this made the construction of a vacuum pump extremely expensive and difficult. No more than fifteen scholars and institutions succeeded in obtaining a vacuum pump before 1670, and most of these depended on Guericke, Hooke, or Huygens for the construction and maintenance of their instruments.

Instrument makers contributed little to the earliest air pumps. Scientists designed and assembled the instruments themselves. Often enough, they had trouble finding craftsmen capable of making the constituent parts to their specifications, but gradually the pattern changed. In the 1670s, Parisian craftsmen began to produce air pumps, soon to be followed by the Musschenbroek workshop in Leiden. Typical customers of these instrument makers were societies, rich individuals, and, somewhat later, universities. Most of these used their air pumps to duplicate or demonstrate the experiments of Boyle and Guericke. Notable exceptions were Francis Hauksbee (1666–1713) and Huygens, but the number of scientists doing new research with the air pump was never very large.

Progress in air-pump design initially meant less leakage and larger recipients. But around 1680 the emphasis shifted to convenience and pumping speed. An important representative of this trend was Denis Papin

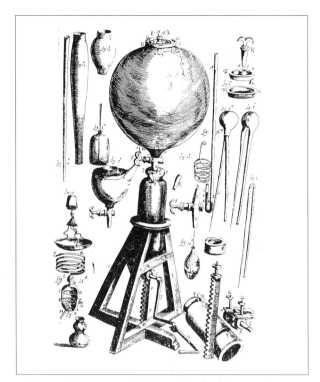

Robert Boyle's air pump, displaying details of the parts that compose it. Robert Boyle, New Experiments Physico-Mechanical, *2nd ed. (1662).*

(1647–ca. 1712), who invented the double-barrel air pump. Compared with single-barrel pumps, this instrument required less force and pumped twice as fast. Another useful innovation was introduced by the Leiden physics professor Wolferd Senguerd (1646–1724) in 1679. His pump could both evacuate and compress. The instrument was no longer merely a tool to produce a vacuum. It was designed to allow for as many experiments and demonstrations as possible.

BIBLIOGRAPHY

Helden, Anne C. van. "The Age of the Air-Pump." *Tractrix: Yearbook for the History of Science, Medicine, Technology, & Mathematics* 3 (1991), 149–172.

Shapin, Steven, and Simon Schaffer. *Leviathan and the Air-Pump: Hobbes, Boyle, and the Experimental Life.* Princeton, NJ: Princeton University Press, 1985.

ANNE C. VAN HELDEN

See also Barometer; Pneumatics; Void

Alchemy

The claims associated with the practice of alchemy in the sixteenth and seventeenth centuries were many and extended beyond the traditional understanding that it was concerned primarily with the transmutation of lead into gold. Alchemists claimed that the material they sought, sometimes called an "Elixir," or more commonly the "Philosopher's Stone," could heal illnesses, extend one's life span, and even purify and redeem an individual's spirit. An anonymous sixteenth-century manuscript published by Elias Ashmole (1617–1692) in 1658 entitled *The Way to Bliss* noted that a ring made from material from the Philosopher's Stone could heal the political divisions of a kingdom.

Arabic Alchemy

To understand the vast claims associated with alchemy is to understand the indiscrete associations made by individuals of the early-modern period. Alchemy is a particularly helpful instrument with which to view early-modern intellectual, religious, and scientific history precisely because the practice had such broad associations. The practice of alchemy was not unique to the West. There was a Chinese, an Indian, a Jewish, and an Arabic tradition of alchemy. While Western alchemy would eventurally incorporate many elements of Jewish alchemy, particularly its tradition of Kabbalah, Arabic alchemy was most likely the tradition responsible for its transmission to Europe. Following the Crusades, Arabic alchemical and other texts were translated into Latin in the twelfth century, making Arabic alchemical theory and tradition available to medieval intellectuals in Europe. This last point is important because, although there were certainly unlearned charlatans who claimed, often at great risk, to know how to change lead into gold, alchemy was seen from its twelfth-century inception in the West to the early eighteenth century, when Sir Isaac Newton (1642–1727) was copying and writing alchemical texts, as an intellectual pursuit. Further, even though medieval alchemy was distinct in its own right, early-modern alchemical theory was its progeny, and one cannot understand the latter without understanding the former.

The Arabic texts that twelfth-century scholars encountered and translated composed a vast and heterogeneous body of literature that was largely, if spuriously, associated with the work of the eighth-century Persian alchemist Jabir ibn Hayyan, who eventually became more commonly known as Geber. The Jabirian school assumed that all material substances contained their hidden opposites, and that, therefore, every substance held a "manifest" and an "occult" quality, or an "internal" and an "external" quality. For example, gold manifested hot and wet qualities externally, but its cold and dry qualities were hidden internally, while silver had precisely the opposite qualities. Jabir argued that because transmutation occurred through the interchange of elementary qualities, silver ought to be able to transmute into gold by inverting its qualities.

Well grounded in Aristotelian physics, Jabirian alchemy by the thirteenth century had acquired a corpuscular theory of matter, but, more significant, it began to acquire a distinct Western interpretation by shedding some aspects of the Arabic tradition and developing others. When a collection of texts known as the *Seventy Books,* the major Jabirian work, was translated and circulated, it became so widely regarded on the Continent that it was not long before its many imitators appeared. These alchemical texts of the late thirteenth and fourteenth centuries, the most famous of which was the *Summa perfectionis,* claimed to be the writings of the Latinized figure "Geber." Although this authorship was as spurious as the texts attributed to Jabir, the authors succeeded in making the alchemical theories contained therein conformable to accepted Scholastic physics.

At the same time, a dearth of precious metals in Europe was frustrating the expansionist political ambitions of many territorial rulers. The practical skills of alchemists allowed princes to stretch their resources by alloying the gold and silver that they possessed with other metals, producing more coins than they would have been able without alchemical assistance. Edward III of England (1312–1377) demanded that two notable alchemists of the day, John le Rous and William of Dalby, be brought to him whether they consented or not because, as he said, "they will be able to do much good for us and for our kingdom."

Church Opposition

Because the Church, however, did not suffer from the financial exigencies that confounded so many secular rulers, it viewed alchemy and alchemists with hostility. In 1317, Pope John XXII condemned alchemists both for practicing deceit and for counterfeiting coins, thereby making the issue both a moral and a legal one. Pope John's condemnation did little, however, to stave off the interest in alchemy within the religious orders of the Church itself. Religious orders poured enormous amounts of money and effort into obtaining the Philoso-

pher's Stone. Johannes Trithemius (1462–1516) believed that the practice was impoverishing the Catholic Church, and he urged others not accept the claims of alchemists. Even though Trithemius was an intellectual colleague of such notable occultists as Marsilio Ficino (1433–1499) (whose translations of the texts attributed to Hermes Trismegistus further fueled the interest in alchemy), Giovanni Pico della Mirandola (1463–1494), Johannes Reuchlin, Heinrich Cornelius Agrippa von Nettesheim (1486–1535), and Paracelsus (ca. 1491–1541), he was, above all, a faithful servant of the Church, and he excoriated alchemists, calling them fools and disciples of apes who were enemies of nature and despisers of heaven. He saw the pursuit of alchemy as a cancer that was destroying the monasteries and religous orders and, therefore, attacked it because of the damage he thought it was doing to the Church.

Yet, despite the Catholic Church's persistent concerns, perhaps one of the most distinguishing aspects of early-modern alchemical theory was its spirituality. One of the earliest appearences of a spiritual association with alchemy occurred in the *Summa perfectionis,* in which the author associated alchemy with the *donum dei* (gift from God). During the fourteenth and fifteenth centuries, the search for the Philosopher's Stone became associated for the first time with a search for the salvation of an individual's soul. In the early fifteenth century, a German alchemical text appeared known as *Das Buch der heiligen Dreifaltigkeit* (The Book of the Sacred Trinity), the author of which appears to have been a Franciscan monk named Ulmannus. This alchemical text constructs a close parallel between the suffering, death, and resurrection of Christ and the alchemical process. Alchemy would retain its spiritual associations throughout the early-modern period, but it would also retain its political associations as well, and alchemical texts were routinely commissioned and dedicated to the rulers and emperors of medieval and early-modern Europe.

Gold was, according to the Paracelsian physician and occultist Robert Fludd (1574–1637), the least of its appeal. He wrote in one of his many defenses of alchemy, *Truth's Golden Harrow* (ca. 1623) that "thos which zealously seeke after it and with a true intent, and by Gods blessing doth attayne unto it, shall easily perceave that gold is the meanest possession and the least to be esteemed of ten thousand other mysteryes which it bringeth with it."

A

Alchemists spoke often of the process of "multiplication" or "extension" of the Philospher's Stone, and an important and often central concern were the efforts of alchemists (or their patrons) to multiply and extend their wealth. However, multiplication held important religious significance as well. It was believed by some alchemists that God's command to Adam and Eve to be fruitful and multiply extended beyond humanity to include the entire natural world, and the Philosopher's Stone held that secret. Such knowledge was far more valuable to a Christian natural philosopher than mere riches.

The biblical basis for the Philosopher's Stone was as clear to Fludd as it was for so many other Christian occultists, and to call upon both the Old and the New Testaments was one of the most common defense strategies of alchemists. Many alchemists—both in England and on the Continent—claimed that they were heirs to Old Testament prophets, many of whom allegedly possessed the secret knowledge of the Philosopher's Stone. Alchemists of the early-modern period scoured the biblical texts searching for any and all references to gold or riches. For example, some alchemists believed that the brief line in the Hebrew Scriptures referring to Abraham's wealth, "Now Abram was very rich in cattle, in silver, and in gold" (Genesis 13:3), confirmed Abraham's practice of alchemy. Abraham, Jacob, Job, David, Solomon, Elijah, Isaiah, Moses, even Adam himself were all thought to have known the alchemical secrets.

Paracelsus and "Vegetation"

Nowhere were spirituality and natural philosophy more closely entwined than in the natural philosophy of Paracelsus. Paracelsus was a deeply religious individual but was not affiliated with either the Catholic Church or any of the Protestant denominations. The system he developed was never intended to be rational but was instead, first and foremost, intensely spiritual and mystical, requiring both a strong will and a powerful imagination. In addition to this strong mystical element, Paracelsus's system incorporated his belief that salt, sulfur, and mercury were even more fundamental to matter than the four Aristotelian elements of earth, air, fire, and water. Alchemy, for Paracelsus, was a part of a larger natural philosophy in which mystical spirituality was integrated with physical principles. One of the most notable aspects of Paracelsianism was its proposition that the Creation was an alchemical process; alchemists, there-

fore, examined the Book of Genesis through Paracelsian lenses to discern and, they hoped, re-create God's Creation. Many early-modern alchemists claimed that acquiring the Philosopher's Stone not only would transmute base metals into precious ones, but also could transform and redeem the fallen natural world itself. Paracelsian efforts to imitate the creative process through alchemy coincided with the larger early-modern effort to recapture and re-create an Edenic world. To Paracelsian alchemists, to understand alchemy was to understand God's creative process itself.

Alchemy was also never very far from the early-modern interest in the ancient world and other occult pursuits such as astrology or numerology. By the seventeenth century, when interest in alchemy burgeoned more than at any previous time, principles borrowed from the ancients were integrated with the new mechanical philosophy to create yet another stratum in the history of alchemical theory. Many seventeenth-century alchemists assumed, like the ancients, that metals could be "fermented" and allowed to "grow" like dough or vegetation. The processes that were labeled "fermentation" and "vegetation" were thought to be critical to the alchemical process. Robert Boyle (1627–1691) and Isaac Newton (1642–1727) both practiced alchemy, and both recorded in their notes their observations of metals sprouting tendrils and changing colors. Their observations were presumably of some unstable intermetallic compounds that experienced fairly rapid shifts in color and form by the energy caused by the fire of their furnaces. However, because neither gentleman, despite their formidable contributions to what we recognize as science, had discarded ancient presuppostions about matter, they could not help but make their observations with them in mind and, therefore, believed they were witnessing the "vegetation" of metals. In addition, neither rejected the spiritual elements of alchemy, and both men, until the end of their lives, believed that alchemy held crucial theological significance.

Although the Enlightenment and the increasingly secular pursuit of science began to address the reasons that the legitimacy of alchemy diminished by the end of the seventeenth century and became virtually discredited by the middle of the eighteenth, the specific reasons that alchemy could no longer engage the greatest minds of natural philosophy as it had for so many centuries remain unresolved. Contemporary scholarship on alchemy has recognized the complexity of the issue and has, therefore, been devoted to specific individuals and case studies rather than to the syntheses that characterized the study of alchemy in the nineteenth and early twentieth centuries.

BIBLIOGRAPHY

Debus, Allen G. *The Chemical Philosophy: Paracelsian Science and Medicine in the Sixteenth and Seventeenth Centuries.* 2 vols. New York: Science History Publications, 1977.

Dobbs, B. J. T. *The Foundations of Newton's Alchemy, or "The Hunting of the Greene Lyon."* Cambridge: Cambridge University Press, 1975.

———. *The Janus Face of Genius: The Role of Alchemy in Newton's Thought.* Cambridge: Cambridge University Press, 1991.

Moran, Bruce T. *The Alchemical World of the German Court: Occult Philosophy and Chemical Medicine in the Circle of Moritz of Hessen, 1572–1632.* Stuttgart: Franz Steiner, 1991.

Newman, William R. *Gehennical Fire: The Lives of George Starkey, an American Alchemist in the Scientific Revolution.* Cambridge, MA: Harvard University Press, 1991.

Smith, Pamela. *The Business of Alchemy: Science and Culture in the Holy Roman Empire.* Princeton, NJ: Princeton University Press, 1994.

BRUCE JANACEK

See also Chemical Philosophy; Chemistry; Hermetism; Paracelsus

One of the hundreds of finely engraved plates of birds from the second printing of Aldrovandi's Ornithologiae hoc est, de avibus historiae libri xii *(1610–1640).*

Aldrovandi, Ulisse (1522-1605)

One of the great Renaissance naturalists, Aldrovandi spent the majority of his life in north-central Italy, where he taught natural history at the University of Bologna. The son of a Bolognese notary, Aldrovandi traveled throughout Europe as a youth, studying philosophy and mathematics at the University of Padua (1548–1549) and receiving a medical degree at Bologna (1553). He developed his interest in natural history and collecting, in part, through an encounter with the French naturalist Guillaume Rondelet (1507–1566) and through subsequent study with the Bolognese naturalist Luca Ghini (ca. 1490–1556), one of the first professors of medicine to take students on botanical field trips. Aldrovandi succeeded Ghini as professor of natural history at Bologna in 1556.

Aldrovandi expanded the teaching of natural history within the medical faculty at Bologna and founded its first botanical garden (1568). His reputation as "the Bolognese Aristotle" rested on his collection of natural objects, one of the earliest natural-history museums. Aldrovandi used it to demonstrate anatomies, to improve the state of pharmacy by checking medicinal ingredients, and to interest patrons in assisting in the publication of his *Natural History.* He engaged in extensive correspondence with scholars and collectors throughout Europe. In 1603, two years prior to his death, he donated his collection to the Senate of Bologna so that his museum would continue to be a center for scientific activity.

Few of Aldrovandi's publications appeared in his lifetime. While he wrote hundreds of treatises, he published only three volumes of his work on natural history—the *Ornithologia* (1599–1603); another ten volumes—on bloodless animals, quadrupeds, fish, metals, monsters, and trees—appeared between 1606 and 1668. Aldrovandi made some specific contributions to our understanding of nature—dividing animals according to the shape of their hooves, for example, and continuing Aristotle's (384–322 B.C.E.) embryological work on chicks. But the primary importance of his work lay in his desire to institutionalize natural history as a legitimate field of study and to make careful empirical observation a precondition for understanding nature.

BIBLIOGRAPHY

Findlen, Paula. *Possessing Nature: Museums, Collecting, and Scientific Culture in Early Modern Italy.* Berkeley and Los Angeles: University of California Press, 1994.

Lind, L. R., ed. and trans. *Aldrovandi on Chickens: The Ornithology of Ulisse Aldrovandi (1600) Volume II, Book XIV.* Norman: University of Oklahoma Press, 1963.

Olmi, Giuseppe. *Ulisse Aldrovandi. Scienza e natura nel secondo Cinquecento.* Trent: Libera Università degli Studi di Trento, 1976.

PAULA FINDLEN

See also Botany; Museums and Collections; Natural History; Zoology

Algebra

Although doubts have been cast on both its origin and its etymology, the word "algebra" is usually said to derive from the title of an early-ninth-century work by al-Khwarizmi in Baghdad; it refers to the process of completing or restoring terms in an equation, such terms being expressed in words rather than by any special symbols. Algebra now signifies to mathematicians the study of specific structures, such as rings, fields, and vector spaces, but school algebra still deals with equations and formal manipulations of symbolic arithmetic. The first meaning is barely a hundred years old, even if prefigured by earlier mathematicians.

Because of its general structural features, mathematicians often claim to see algebra in some of the purely geometric or arithmetic work of antiquity. The matter is controversial, but such hindsight may obscure, conflate, or alter the ideas originally involved. In the second or third century Diophantus of Alexandria, in his *Arithmetic,* often regarded as the founding work of algebra, used a variety of abbreviations for exponents of a single unknown and for subtraction, but he may not have been the first to do so.

Omar Khayyam (ca. 1050–1123) added to earlier work when he solved cubic equations geometrically, using intersecting curves and giving conditions for solubility; this was an extension of Archimedes's notable solution of a specific cubic in his *Sphere and Cylinder.* The twelfth-century revival of learning in the West, asso-

ciated with the new universities founded as independent corporations, led to many translations of Arabic works into Latin, including in the mid-twelfth-century work of al-Khwarizmi by Robert of Chester, who worked at Toledo and also translated the Koran. Following this, Leonardo of Pisa's famously misnamed *Liber abaci* (Book of the Abacus, 1202) dealt with equations and Hindu-Arabic numerals. At the same time, the beginnings of symbolism can be seen in Jordanus de Nemore's (fl. ca. 1220) *De numeris datis* (On a Given Number). Later, Nicole Oresme (mid-fourteenth century) gave rules for exponents and attempted notations for indices. He and others were able to sum certain infinite series, using graphical ideas, and even to prove the divergence of the harmonic series.

The main advanced application of mathematics, and the source of employment for skilled practitioners, was still, as it had almost always been, in surveying, engineering, astronomy and related calendar studies, and astrology. For this, trigonometry was of more use than algebra, as is seen in the mid-fifteenth-century work of Georg Peurbach (1423–1461) and Johannes Regiomontanus (1436–1476). The latter wished to see Latin translations produced of Diophantus, but this was not taken up until 1550 by Rafael Bombelli (1526–1572). Simon Stevin (1548–1620) translated Diophantus's *Arithmetic* into French in 1585. Later, Pierre de Fermat (1601–1665) used Claude-Gaspar Bachet's version of 1621; the original text may derive from Hypatia's early-fifth-century commentary.

Before this, the last decades of the fifteenth century saw Nicholas Chuquet (fl. ca. 1480) develop ideas about exponents and even freestanding negative numbers, but he did not publish. Luca Pacioli (ca. 1445–1517), who did (1494), was less innovative in his notations.

Shortly after 1500, the otherwise little-known Bologna professor Scipione del Ferro (1465–1526) found a remarkable algorithmic solution in square and cube roots for certain cubic equations. Perhaps this arose as an extension of Euclid's surds in the recently printed *Elements.* The solution, extended to other cases by Niccolo of Brescia (ca. 1500–1557), known as Tartaglia, was eventually published, together with Ludovico Ferrari's (1522–1565) method for biquadratic equations, by Girolamo Cardano (1501–1576) in the *Ars magna* (The Great Art) of 1545, the most famous purely mathematical work of the century. The presentation, like Khayyam's, is geometrical, but the methods are more intrinsic to the specific equations.

This High Renaissance work was paralleled by the so-called "cossic" studies in Italy, France, and Germany, leading to extended notations for exponents. The "cos" was the Italian *cosa,* or thing, French *chose,* itself the unknown, as we say. In Germany, algebra became known as *die Cos* and was associated with Christoff Rudolff, Michael Stifel and Peter Apian. In 1572, Bombelli published his *Algebra.* In addition to solving simple geometrical problems using a sort of symbolism—modern machine codes make us more sympathetic to such schemes—he analyzed complex numbers and recognized their conjugates; some of his content was based on original studies of a Diophantine manuscript.

The key figure at this time was François Viète (1540–1603), who disliked the term "algebra." In addition to solving many interesting and important specific problems, including the numerical solution of equations, he took big steps toward the formalization of a symbolic arithmetic in nearly the form of modern elementary algebra. This work was virtually completed by Thomas Harriot (ca. 1560–1621)—published posthumously in 1631—who also introduced the important inequality signs, associated roots of equations with binomial factors, and applied algebra to problems of geometry, cartography, interpolation, impacts, projectiles, and optics.

A little later, Albert Girard (1595–1632) gave initial results on symmetric functions of roots, and René Descartes's (1596–1650) geometrical appendix (1637) showed the power of algebra in many areas. His solution of Pappus of Alexandria's three- and four-line problem and its extensions not only went beyond the older results of Alhazen (early eleventh century), but also showed a general geometrical method, which he also applied to optics. Descartes gave general rules for the transformation of equations and the detection of roots—the latter leading, via Isaac Newton (1642–1727), to the results of Jean Baptiste Joseph Fourier, Jacques Sturm, and James Joseph Sylvester in the nineteenth century. Descartes was less innovative in solving equations by the intersection of curves; Khayyam had done the same 500 years previously, albeit geometrically rather than algebraically.

At the same time, Fermat was developing algebra in geometry in a more abstract way and improving Descartes's method for tangents. The peak of algebra in the seventeenth century was seen in the development of the calculus. John Wallis's (1616–1703) *Arithmetica infinitorum* (1656) was influential in the differing calculuses of Newton and Gottfried Wilhelm Leibniz (1646–1716), but for Newton the key influence was Frans van Schooten's (ca. 1615–1660) second Latin edition (1659–1661) of Descartes's geometry, with the extensive appendices of later work. Newton extended the algebra to general infinite series, the basis of much of his calculus. Leibniz sought a more general logical formalism, but this is also a form of algebra, as developed later by George Boole (1854) and Friedrich Wilhelm Karl Ernst Schröder (1890). Newton's analysis of cubic curves, completed in the 1690s, is an algebraic tour de force; this and his *Arithmetica universalis* of the 1670s both belie his remark that "algebra is the analysis of bunglers." One important result went unproved until Sylvester (1865); another dealt with sequences of sums of powers of roots and limits of roots. Newton's reconstruction of a solution of Diophantus prefigures the Weil-Mordell theorem of the 1920s, itself related to the 1995 proof of Fermat's "last theorem."

By 1700, formal algebra and some structural algebra was in place, even if the fuller mysteries of complex numbers awaited clarification by Carl Friedrick Gauss and William Rowan Hamilton in the nineteenth century. One general point remains to be made. We see not only the development of algebraic symbolism and the solution of specific problems, but the increasing algebraicization of mathematics as a whole. Often placed as late as the eighteenth century, this really goes back to Viète's publications of the 1590s. Geometric formulations were slow to fade, but such late formulations by Isaac Barrow (1630–1677) and Christiaan Huygens (1629–1695) were less indicative and, hence, less influential.

BIBLIOGRAPHY

Cardano, Girolamo. *The Great Art.* Trans. T. Richard Witmer. Cambridge, MA: MIT Press, 1958.

Descartes, René. *The Geometry.* Trans. D. E. Smith and M. C. Latham. New York: Dover, 1954.

Rashed, Roshdi. "Algebra." In *Encyclopedia of the History of Arabic Science,* ed. Roshdi Rashed. 3 vols. London: Routledge, 1996, vol. 2, pp. 349–375.

Rose, Paul L. *The Italian Renaissance of Mathematics.* Geneva: Droz, 1975.

Viète, François. *The Analytic Art.* Trans. T. Richard Witmer. Kent, OH: Kent State University Press, 1983.

JON V. PEPPER

See also Analytic Geometry; Cardano, Girolamo; Viète, François; Mathematics

Almanacs

Movable type made these publications easy and inexpensive to produce, and the Crusades against the Turks brought a request to Johannes Gutenberg to publish the first almanac in 1448. At first, they were a means of introducing astrology to a wide audience; later, they became a means of disseminating the new astronomy.

Almanacs were written in the vernacular. They generally consisted of three parts. The almanac proper showed major astronomical events of the coming year, such as eclipses and conjunctions, which were believed to have astrological significance, and movable feasts, like Easter, that depended on astronomical data. The second part was a calendar, which listed the days of the weeks, the months, and the fixed church festivals. The third part consisted of prognostications—astrological predictions of upcoming events, including the weather, favorable hours for such matters as medicinal bleedings and planting or even taking a bath, and anticipated political occurrences. Almanacs sold as broadsheets were the ancestor of the modern calendar. There were also pocket almanacs. Like the modern pocket diary, they often contained useful information: a list of markets and fairs, a guide to highways and distances by road, a brief chronology of historical events since the Creation, medical preparations, legal formulas, suggestions for gardening.

During the Middle Ages, astrology had been the preserve of the educated and the powerful. Publications about the subject were in Latin, and wealthy patrons sought the advice of astrologers. The vernacular almanacs gave the less-educated members of society access to such information, sometimes with interesting results. For example, in 1499 the influential astrologer Johann Stöffler (1452–1531) published *Ephemerides,* in which he predicted that multiple planetary conjunctions in the sign of Pisces during 1524 would produce a second great flood on 25 February. This prediction was reproduced in almanacs for the next quarter-century. Although the almanacs themselves were not read by the illiterate majority and were often mocked by them in carnivals, the prediction was spread among the lowest classes by preachers who saw the upcoming flood as divine punishment. People moved their places of residence in anticipation, and in Rome there was general panic. Of course, the flood never materialized, which reinforced common mockery of almanacs and astro-

logers, but the incident shows how these almanacs had an influence beyond their readership.

The most important information the almanacs contained concerned astrological predictions of the weather for farming and gardening and for traveling and predictions of the best times for medical procedures. Astrology was the most successful means of forecasting the weather in the early-modern period. Since both agriculture and commerce depend on the weather, almanacs became very important to the economy. Farmers used them to make decisions about planting; merchants were anxious to know of any impending storms before sending their ships out. Physicians generally believed that the heavenly bodies influenced the health of both individuals and society. Not only did they check birth charts to study the physical and emotional constitution of the patient, but they also used the astrological information in almanacs to vary treatment according to the celestial configurations (for example, bleeding was believed to be affected by the phases of the Moon), to take note of critical days in the course of the disease, and to predict or explain epidemics.

Since medical practice in the late-medieval–early-modern period usually involved astrology, many of the early almanacs were written by physicians and surgeons. One of the most popular publications was by the Laet family. The works of these Flemish astrologer-physicians appeared annually from 1469 to 1550 and were translated into French and English. The popularity of these almanacs spurred publishers of books in these languages to enter into the lucrative business. In England, the university presses of Oxford and Cambridge were anxious to break the Stationers Company's monopoly on the publication of almanacs. Generally, however, the writers of these almanacs did not profit so well from the endeavor. For them, the almanac produced pecuniary advantages as an advertisement of their astrology practice, and authors often devoted a page to listing the services they provided.

These authors were anxious to show that their predictions were based on the most accurate astronomical assumptions. Therefore, they would discuss astronomical discoveries of their day. They debated the relative merits of the various cosmic systems. Already in 1576, Leonard Digges (ca. 1520–ca. 1559) introduced his almanac with a lengthy defense of the Copernican system. Almanacs were the major source in the vernacular for the ideas not only of Nicolaus Copernicus (1473–

1543), but of Johannes Kepler (1571–1630) Galileo Galilei (1564–1642), and Isaac Newton (1642–1727) as well. Thus, they became an important means of popularizing the new astronomy.

BIBLIOGRAPHY

Capp, Bernard. *English Almanacs, 1500-1800: Astrology and the Popular Press*. Ithaca, NY: Cornell University Press, 1979.

Thomas, Keith. *Religion and the Decline of Magic: Studies in Popular Beliefs in Sixteenth- and Seventeenth-Century England*. Harmondsworth and New York: Penguin, 1973.

Thorndike, Lynn. *A History of Magic and Experimental Science*. 8 vols., vols. 5–8. New York: Columbia University Press, 1923–1958.

SHEILA J. RABIN

Analytic Geometry

If one defines algebra as a set of problems that include establishing basic algebraic identities and formulating and solving quadratic and cubic equations, then its beginnings go back four thousand years, and ancient mathematics is rife with the geometrical treatment of algebraic problems. But the modern origins of analytic geometry, which combines algebra and geometry by formulating certain correspondences between curves and equations, are generally assigned to the work of François Viète (1540–1603), René Descartes (1596–1650), and Pierre de Fermat (1601–1665). In general, geometry, rather than an abstract symbolic structure, was the universal language of antiquity, and the domains of geometry and number were segregated. Viète, Descartes, and Fermat introduced an essentially modern form of mathematics, in which the domains of geometry and number could be deeply and fruitfully integrated under the aegis of an abstract symbolic structure.

Viète's greatest contribution was to raise algebra to a general form of reasoning by freeing it from its reference to number; in the Greek and Arab world, algebra was mostly preoccupied with the treatment of special cases, finding the numerical unknown in equations with numerical coefficients. In his *In artem analyticem isagoge* (Introduction to the Analytical Art, 1591), Viète announced a program for solving all mathematical problems by means of a *logistica speciosa,* an abstract algebra (in almost the modern sense of the term: a system endowed with a variety of interpretations and implicitly defined by a set of rules and axioms) with a homogeneity

law. This system included rules for addition, subtraction, multiplication, division, scalar multiplication, and extraction of roots; the notation was expressed partly in symbols (addition and subtraction), partly in words and abbreviations (multiplication, division, equality, powers). Differing symbols were used for the first time to register the important distinction between parameters and unknowns.

Viète left both the magnitudes and the operations of his system undefined. He stipulated only that magnitude always has a well-defined dimension (any natural number) and that operations must respect dimensionality: only magnitudes of the same dimension can be added or subtracted; two magnitudes of dimensions m and n, when multiplied, give rise to a magnitude of dimension (m + n); and so forth. Viète has often been reproached for his allegiance to the condition of homogeneity; Dirk Struik (1948) says baldly that it vitiated his system. But respect for the condition of homogeneity was a commonplace in the seventeenth century; moreover, it saved Viète an extra assumption—that is, the stipulation of a unit.

When Viète applied his *logistica speciosa* to geometry, he was able to show that all geometrical problems that can be recast as algebraic equations of the fourth degree or lower can be either constructed by ruler and compass or reduced to the trisection of an angle or the determination of two mean proportionals between two given line segments. Viète also began to enunciate certain important relations among the roots and coefficients of an equation, approaching the theory of symmetric functions of roots in the theory of equations. In both of these results, Viète's gift for generalization is evident.

Descartes shared Viète's wish to discover more general algebraic methods for attacking problems in mathematics. But whereas Viète begins with an abstract algebra, Descartes begins with an algebra interpreted as operations on magnitudes that are finite line segments. Descartes's algebra is a closed algebra: operations on line segments produce line segments. Multiplication, for example, is interpreted as the construction of a line that stands in the same ratio to one of the factors as the other factor stands to the unit. Homogeneity is dropped as a condition, but then a unit must be stipulated.

Like Viète, Descartes is interested in recasting traditional problems from the canon of classical geometry in algebraic form. By choosing "Pappus's Problem," a family of locus problems, as the centerpiece of his *Géométrie*

(Geometry, 1637), he broadens the scope of his project beyond that of Viète in two significant ways. In his attempt to give a general solution to Pappus's Problem, Descartes offers two classifications, one of determinate construction problems and the other of curves. His classifications project a hierarchy of problems (or curves) and, thus, opens up the investigation of algebraic equations of any finite degree in one (or two) unknowns. In principle, the second classification also opens up the investigation of higher algebraic curves, though the *Géométrie* makes that innovation far from clear. Descartes is not so much interested in curves per se but, rather, as constructional tools—generalizations of ruler and compass—for the construction of determinate problems represented by equations of finite degree in one unknown.

The power of Descartes's method in the *Géométrie* is not simply that he shows how to translate a geometrical problem into an algebraic equation, solve the equation, and then translate back to the geometrical problem. Rather, at its best (as in the case of the so-called Cartesian parabola, a cubic curve), it allows the mathematician to think geometrically and algebraically at the same time. The Cartesian parabola, for example, is understood as a curve traced by certain instruments, as a point-wise construction, and as an equation, and the problems in which it figures in the *Géométrie* are addressed by making use of both results from geometry and results from the newly expanded theory of equations, as it were simultaneously.

The mathematician who most clearly enunciated the central insight of analytic geometry, that curves may be correlated with equations in two unknowns, was Pierre de Fermat. He wrote his *Ad locos planos et solidos isagoge* (Introduction to the Loci of Planes and Solids) and its *Appendix* in 1636; thereafter it circulated in manuscript, but it was not published until 1679. Applying the *logistica speciosa* of Viète to the study of loci in Apollonius, Fermat concentrated on the sketching of curves correlated with equations in two unknowns, rather than the construction of roots of equations in one unknown as Descartes had. He showed first that linear equations correspond to the line, and then that quadratic equations reducible to various canonical forms correspond to the hyperbola, parabola, circle, and ellipse. (For example, an equation reducible by a translation of axes to the form $xy = k$ corresponds to a hyperbola.) Though his work makes no mention of algebraic curves more complex than the conics, it goes beyond that of Descartes, in that

Fermat showed how to reduce a certain kind of problem to two equations in two unknowns and then construct it by the intersection of the loci corresponding to the equations.

On balance, the work of Descartes was more influential in the seventeenth century than that of Viète or Fermat, though the approach of Viète was more abstract and rigorous, and that of Fermat more didactic and clearer. Descartes's analytic geometry was promulgated and regularized through the labors of a school of Dutch mathematicians, of which the *Geometria a Renato Des Cartes* (1659–1661, 1683, and 1695), edited with commentary by Frans van Schooten (ca. 1615–1660), was the most important. In these works, for example, the coordinate axes were stipulated to be orthogonal, and canonical forms for equations were established.

BIBLIOGRAPHY

Bos, H. J. M. "On the Representation of Curves in Descartes' *Géométrie.*" *Archive for History of Exact Sciences* 24 (1981), 295–338.

Boyer, Carl B. *A History of Mathematics*. Princeton, NJ: Princeton University Press, 1968, chs. 16–18.

Grosholz, Emily. *Cartesian Method and the Problem of Reduction*. Oxford: Clarendon, 1991, chs. 1–2.

Mahoney, Michael. *The Mathematical Career of Pierre de Fermat, 1601–1665*. Princeton, NJ: Princeton University Press, 1973, 1994.

Struik, Dirk J. *A Concise History of Mathematics*. New York: Dover, 1948, vol. 2.

Zeuthen, H. G. *Geschichte der Mathematik im 16. und 17. Jahrhundert*. Stuttgart: B. G. Teubner, 1966, sec. 2.

                                        EMILY GROSHOLZ

See also Algebra; Descartes, René; Fermat, Pierre de; Mathematics; Schooten, Frans van; Viète, François

Anatomy

When the French physician Jean Fernel (1497–1558) reflected on the necessity and excellence of anatomy in the epilogue of the first book of his physiological treatise *De naturali parte medicinae* (1542), he concluded by drawing a particularly important comparison: just as geography is pertinent to the veracity of history, medical practice requires a knowledge of how the human body is described. In his analogy, both the geographer and the anatomist state characteristics of places in which something is going on. In the instance of anatomy, such descriptions not only result in medical practice on the living body, but, in a figurative sense, they also indicate action within, and of, the body itself. Because of this intimate connection between the body—seen as a place—and its functions, anatomy, according to the Renaissance notion of it, has to be understood as a discipline that deals with the *fabrica* (structure) of the human body. Precisely hence stems the title of Andreas Vesalius's (1514–1564) monumental *De humani corporis fabrica* (1543), which was to become the most influential of all anatomical texts ever published. As a result of what could be compared to a foreshortened view of the long-term process of the Scientific Revolution—a process that was anything but undirectional—the beginnings of modern anatomy, of medicine, and even of modern science in general have been seen in connection with this book. In the context of Fernel's comparison between the sciences of anatomy and geography, Vesalius may be, and has been, regarded as the Columbus of the human body, as a man who literally discovered a new world. The full impact of the *Fabrica* on anatomy and science, however, has to be evaluated on the basis of the achievements of his predecessors and with regard to Renaissance medicine as a whole, with all that this implies for our understanding of the conditions that gave rise to modern science.

When medicine, in line with Renaissance humanism, turned back to the newly emended texts of the ancients during the fifteenth century and increasingly during the sixteenth, the canon of anatomical literature had been reduced to Galen's (second century) writings. However, any understanding of antiquity could become fecund only where it tied in with the period's own achievements. This implied that, in accord with the ancients, nature itself had to be studied through the reborn art of dissection of the human body. Such a mode of proceeding did not lead back to the canonical writings of Galen (who had never dissected a human body), but to what Vesalius considered to be the true Galen—that is, back to the anatomists of Alexandria, who had trained in, and practiced, human dissection in antiquity. This development did not go unopposed by dogmatic Galenists like Jacques Dubois (1478–1555), himself an astute observer, who in an anti-Vesalian reaction had overstated his case by taking the view that it was more likely for the human body to have changed since Galen's time than for the venerated master to have erred.

Even so, Vesalius was not alone in trusting observation more than books and in employing his own eyes and hands with the help of suitable tools; indeed, such priorities were common among early-sixteenth-century anatomists. In spite of their more or less scrupulous attitude toward Galen, authors like Giacomo Berengario da Carpi (1460–1530), Charles Estienne (ca. 1505–1564), and Giovanni Battista Canano (1515–1579) had become convinced of the correctness of their own observations and judgments. Along with others who had written anatomical treatises in the years between 1490 and 1543, these anatomists, commonly labeled as pre-Vesalians, have not been given their fair share of prominence by medical historians, who, until the mid-twentieth century, favored Vesalius in what was an unbalanced representation of Renaissance medicine. It has since been shown how pre-Vesalian anatomists strove to develop their own concepts and to attain their somewhat differing goals.

For example, to convince his readers and fellow scholars of what he believed anatomy should be and do, in 1521 Berengario published an anatomical treatise based on dissection in the form of a commentary on Mondino de Luzzi's (ca. 1275–1326) *Anatomia,* completed in 1316. Mondino is reputed to have reintroduced human dissection into medieval medical education after a period of relative stagnation during which medicine followed late antique—Byzantine and Arabic—traditions and was determined by respect for the Church. Although Mondino's book had already been criticized by the Galenist naturalist Leonhart Fuchs (1501–1566) for what he saw as an addiction to Arabism and speculations, it had temporarily gained canonic character and was, in Berengario's opinion, the best available text; the one most suitable, that is, for serving as a practical handbook covering anatomy as conducted by manual operations in the course of dissection.

Berengario's endeavors to work like a craftsman on structures visible to the eye, and to prove his observations through repeated inquiry, thus form an early attempt to acquire anatomical knowledge, not least with a view to the long-neglected practice of surgeons. Such a line of investigation lay exactly within the scope of Vesalius's interest in the employment of the hands in anatomy, and in medical treatment by means of the hands in surgery, which at that time was not regarded as forming part of medicine proper.

Canano, in his treatise on the muscles of the upper limb published in 1541, pursued a course similar to that of Berengario. Illustrating an approach that already was directed at function rather than merely at form, the engravings in his work show the skeleton in positions that correspond to the primary action of the respective muscle; in other words, each muscle is individually depicted in action. Nothing comparable can be found in Vesalius's *Fabrica,* in which, in plates representing muscle-men, the musculature is fully and fluently portrayed with differing degrees of anatomization and by variations of pose.

Vesalius, following the cues of his predecessors, not least where anatomical illustration was concerned, completed the work that Berengario had initiated. Though still in the tradition of Galen, his extensive textbook more perspicuously emphasizes the revival of anatomy in the process of the Scientific Revolution. The composition of Vesalius's *Fabrica* no longer follows Mondino's medieval principles of dissection, according to which the description of the body proceeds from the inside toward

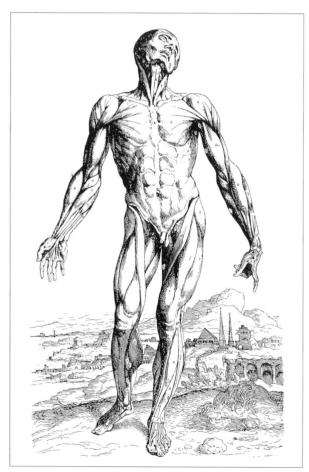

The first of the "muscle-men" plates in Andreas Vesalius's De humani corporis fabrica *(1543). Successive plates showed the outer muscles peeled back to illustrate interior muscles.*

the outside, starting with the viscera in the abdominal and thoracic cavities before moving on to the head and finally to the limbs. Instead, Vesalius returned to Galen's system and, in what might be termed a "structuralist" approach, took the bones as his starting point, developing his description of the *fabrica* of the body in relation to its basis, the skeleton. Each part of the body that he describes in his anatomical work is analyzed with the aim of reconstructing the entity of the living body, into whose function and design the anatomist gains insight through its structure—a structure that, according to Vesalius, is fashioned by God's wisdom for an ultimate purpose. Whereas in pre-Vesalian anatomy the structure of the body had been deduced from that final cause, a result of which it was seen to be, with Vesalius structure becomes the key to deciphering that very purpose. Thus, favoring an interpretation that is no longer ontological but epistemological, he exchanges a deductive for an inductive method. From the way in which the parts of the body are seen to be structured and equipped, he concludes what the purpose of its construction must be and how this purpose points to the body's Creator. Thus, in the *fabrica* of the body, its *faber* (maker) becomes visible.

In the late seventeenth century and during the eighteenth, these notions gained importance in demonstrations of God's providential design, promoting a mechanistic and teleological view of the body. With the methodological change thus initiated, beliefs in a relationship between macrocosm and microcosm and in genuine correspondences between man and the universe broke up. Man as microcosm assumed a new quality, turning into an anthropological concept. In anatomy, he now met himself as an object of his own observation and thought, acquiring valuable philosophical material from the knowledge of the human body. The analogy between macrocosm and microcosm, though still an object of philosophy up to the seventeenth century, fails to explain the complex organ functions recognized by the developing modern physiology of that time through generalized correspondences with a universe that had become equally multifold.

In the plates showing muscle-men and skeletons in Vesalius's *Fabrica,* the gigantic human figures in front of landscapes receding into the distance give direct expression to his new concept of man through uniting anatomy with art. When the background landscapes of Vesalius's plates are assembled so as to form an uninterrupted panorama, the individual figures in the foreground are linked up in a dance of death in which all become equal.

Interest in anatomical research, however, was not centered on man alone or, indeed, tied to the Vesalian tradition only. Renaissance humanism is commonly credited with the discovery of man, but, in addition to this, it also redefined his place in nature. Forming only part of a broader scientific enterprise, investigations of the human body uncovered its relation to that of animals; on the basis of the perceptible matter of nature, such investigations generated a new idea of the order of the world. One of the most captivating subtleties of nature was detected by Pierre Belon (1517–1564), who, in a classic and endlessly reproduced illustration to his comparative anatomical work, *L'histoire de la nature des oyseaux* (1555), drew attention to the structural conformity of the skeletons of man and bird. Regrettably, the "inquisitive" gaze of the age eventually faded into a generalizing overview that, by the end of the seventeenth century, resulted in the prosy analytical empiricism betrayed by so much natural-history writing of the period.

Although structural aspects undoubtedly fueled comparative studies, function also attracted particular interest, as is evident from the work of authors like Girolamo Fabrici (ca. 1533–1619) and his pupil Giulio Casseri (1552–1616), both of whom focused some of their efforts on the vocal and auditory organs. However, Fabrici's Aristotelian reflections on animal and human anatomy and generation (the formation of the fetus) were not confined to structure and function alone. As his most famous pupil, William Harvey (1578–1657), indicated, in his comprehensive account of a universal approach to anatomy Fabrici deals with underlying common causes from the point of view of natural philosophy quite apart from medical application. With Fabrici, anatomy became a science that was not only independent of, but regarded as in some ways superior to, medicine.

Vesalius's descriptions made the whole of the human body known to man. Although the principles he established were not fundamentally questioned by his successors, this knowledge cleared the way for corrections and new discoveries—for example, those made by Vesalius's pupil Gabriele Falloppio (1523–1562) or his vehement critic Bartolomeo Eustachio (ca. 1510–1574). With the knowledge of the body's shapes established, around 1600 anatomical interest turned to its cavities, including the organs and their interior structures, which were diligently inspected. Eustachio's early research into the vascular system, as well as Fabrici's account of the venous valves (1604), complete with its mechanical implications, made Harvey's discovery of circulation possible; this, in turn, marked the step from anatomy to physiology.

Harvey's doctrine certainly had a great influence on attempts to study the vascular bed of organs and developing organisms. In equal measure, it affected efforts to apply injection techniques to vessels and ductular systems—which Frederik Ruysch (1638–1731) mastered brilliantly—and to visualize their ramifications and distribution as a part of interior organic formation. The detection, with the aid of the microscope, of the lung's capillaries by Marcello Malpighi (1628–1694) in 1661, and their rediscovery and correct interpretation by Antoni van Leeuwenhoek (1632–1723) in 1683, provided the missing link between the arteries and the veins and made Harvey's theory complete. Already in 1622, when he observed that the chylous vessels of the intestinal tract were filled with milky lymph by a "natural injection," Gaspare Aselli (1581–1626) had succeeded in discovering another vascular system that was distinct from the veins.

Ever since the microscope extended the range of human perception, Francis Bacon's (1561–1626) program of an inquisitorial interrogation of nature has been put into relentless practice. Nature no longer "speaks for itself," as it had in the Renaissance, even though its "words" have always had to be interpreted. Rigorous observation and reason became the only legitimate sources of knowledge. Physical experimentation, mathematical discourse, and René Descartes's (1596–1650) constitutive image of men and animals as machines promoted Niels Stensen's (1638–1686) seminal studies of muscular mechanics and Giovanni Alfonso Borelli's (1608–1679) investigations of the movements of the joints and working points of muscular power. The development of anatomy at the end of the seventeenth century is well reflected in the still life–like presentation of the human body and its parts—particularly the glands—down to microscopical structures and in the comparative analyses of muscles based on a mechanical model, which all make Govard Bidloo's (1649–1713) *Anatomia humani corporis* (1685) the anatomical book most characteristic of its time.

BIBLIOGRAPHY

Cunningham, Andrew. *The Anatomical Renaissance: The Res-urrection of the Anatomical Projects of the Ancients.* Aldershot: Scolar, 1997.

Magner, Lois N. *A History of the Life Sciences.* New York: Marcel Dekker, 1979.

Putscher, Marielene. *Geschichte der medizinischen Abbildung: Von 1600 bis zur Gegenwart.* Munich: Heinz Moos, 1967.

Roberts, K. B., and J. D. W. Tomlinson. *The Fabric of the Body: European Traditions of Anatomical Illustration.* Oxford: Oxford University Press, 1992.

Sawday, Jonathan. *The Body Emblazoned: Dissection and the Human Body in Renaissance Culture.* London: Routledge, 1995.

Wear, Andrew, R. K. French, and Iain M. Lonie, eds. *The Medical Renaissance of the Sixteenth Century.* Cambridge: Cambridge University Press, 1985.

REINHARD HILDEBRAND

See also Berengario da Carpi, Giacomo; Dissection; Fabrici Girolamo (Fabricius ab Acquapendente); Falloppio, Gabriele; Galenism; Physiology; Vesalius, Andreas

Andreae, Johann Valentin (1586–1654)

Educated at Tübingen university, he combined an interest in science with his career in the Lutheran ministry. His *Collectaneorum mathematicorum* (1614) uses 110 of his own etchings to illustrate a wide range of mathematical topics, including "cossic numbers" (algebra), astronomy, horology, mechanics, fortification, perspective, and human proportions. His *Christianopolis* (1619) describes a utopian community of scholar-craftsmen who treat work as applied science and who engage in research using the most up-to-date equipment—an observatory equipped like Tycho Brahe's (1546–1601) Uraniborg, including the newly invented telescope, an anatomy theater with occasional human dissections, pharmacology and chemistry laboratories. No one may hold office in Christianopolis who is not expert in mathematics, but the book is also a critique of contemporary society and religion, and the ultimate goal of science is, through understanding Creation, to approach the Creator and reject the world.

Christianae societatis imago (1620) is a model of a scientific society in which teams of specialists would work collectively to advance knowledge. This proposal was subsequently circulated in England by Samuel Hartlib (ca. 1600–1662) and may have helped pave the way for the Royal Society of London. Elsewhere, as in *Christianopolis* and *Theophilus* (1649), Andreae proposed a program of educational reform aimed at boys and girls alike, emphasizing hands-on experience and the development of observation and recording skills.

The extent of Andreae's involvement in Rosicrucianism remains controversial. His *Chemical Wedding of Christian Rosenkreuz* (1616), an allegorical work with an alchemical theme, is often claimed to be a Rosicrucian text, but from 1617 on he distanced himself from the movement.

BIBLIOGRAPHY

Dickson, Donald R. *The Tessera of Antilia: Utopian Brotherhoods in the 17th Century.* Leiden: Brill, 1997.

Held, F. E. *Christianopolis: An Ideal State of the 17th Century.* New York: Oxford University Press, 1916.

Montgomery, J. W. *Cross and Crucible: Johann Valentin Andreae.* The Hague: Archives Internationales d'Histoire des Idées, 1973.

EDWARD H. THOMPSON

See also Educational Reform; Rosicrucianism; Utopias

Anthropology and Race

Anthropology was not an independent discipline during the Scientific Revolution. The term referred to the science of man in general, and subjects that we would now call anthropological were discussed by theologians, geographers, philosophers, physicians, experts in Roman law, travelers, and others.

The influx of new information about the peoples of the world during the great age of European expansion posed questions concerning differences of peoples and cultures in a particularly urgent form. The accounts of travelers and missionaries (particularly the Jesuits), varied widely in accuracy, but they were the most important sources of information on other societies and were sometimes compiled into massive ethnographies. All of this new information had to be fitted into a body of knowledge derived from the Bible and the Greek and Roman classics. Writers traced the descent of foreign peoples from Noah or argued that the natives of America were descendants of the ten lost tribes of Israel. Lack of evidence meant decreasing credibility for the traditional monstrous races, thought since classical times to inhabit areas remote from Europe—the one-legged and headless races, among others—although some continued to believe in their existence throughout the period.

A

Regulorum aut Principum in Virginia typus. III

One of the first drawings from life of North American Indians by Theodore de Bry. From De Bry's Admiranda narratio fida tamen, de commodis et incolarum ritibus Virginiae *(1590), a Latin translation, with the original plates, of Thomas Harriot's* A Briefe and True Report of the New Found Land of Virginia *(1590).*

Although significant, the category of race did not have the centrality for European scientific thought at this time that it attained later. Religion remained the most important way of categorizing peoples to most early moderns. A roughly fourfold division of the world into Christians, Jews, Muslims, and "idolaters" was common, although the Jews were increasingly seen as a race. African slavery was often explained and legitimated by the non-Christian beliefs of Africans or by the biblical curse on the descendants of Ham. Another common way of categorizing differences was the climatic theory that the character of different societies was determined by their natural environments. Thus, the darker pigments of Africans and Americans was due to their exposure to the heat of the Sun. Some, such as the French essayist Michel de Montaigne (1533–1592), used the experience of other cultures to argue against assumptions of European or Christian superiority. Much more common, however, was the belief in the superiority of European to other cultures.

The most important intellectual debate on the subject of race was provoked by the Spanish conquests in America. The question of whether native Americans had souls and were, therefore, human (a position supported by the Catholic missionary orders) was settled in the affirmative by a papal bull in 1537. Vigorous debate on whether Indians were barbarians in the Aristotelian sense and, therefore, naturally slaves was carried on in Scholastic terms during the sixteenth century in the Spanish universities, where the Spanish conquests remained highly controversial. Both sides produced voluminous treatises, one side stigmatizing native American societies, the other arguing that, since the Aztecs and Incas had lived in urbanized and political societies, they were not barbarous, merely idolaters in need of the Christian revelation. Although the opponents of natural slavery won the debate, their influence on actual Spanish practice in the New World was slight.

BIBLIOGRAPHY

Hannaford, Ivan. *Race: The History of an Idea in the West.* Washington, D.C.: Woodrow Wilson Center Press, 1996.

Hodgen, Margaret. *Early Anthropology in the Sixteenth and Seventeenth Centuries.* Philadelphia: University of Pennsylvania Press, 1964.

Pagden, Anthony. *European Encounters with the New World: From Renaissance to Romanticism.* New Haven, CT: Yale University Press, 1993.

Spence, Jonathan. *The Memory Palace of Matteo Ricci.* New York: Viking Penguin, 1984.

WILLIAM E. BURNS

See also Exploration and Discovery

Apian, Peter (1495–1552)

Inspired by his teacher, Viennese mathematician Georg Tanstetter, he became a leading German editor and publisher of various works on geography and astronomy, including the *Sphere of Sacrobosco* (ca. 1220), Georg Peurbach's (1423–1461) *New Theories of the Planets* (1454), and one of the first world maps to include "America" as the name of the newly discovered continent.

Apian also proved to be a capable and popular author. From his first geographical textbook—his *Isagoge* (Introduction, 1520) to his major works, the *Cosmography* of 1524 and the *Astronomicum Caesareum* of 1540—his books treated their subjects clearly and simply and included cardboard instruments and diagrams with revolving pieces. His textbooks proved extremely popular—particularly the later editions of the *Cosmography* edited by Reiner Gemma Frisius (1508–1555)—and became the standard in European universities for the rest of the century. They established Apian's reputation and afforded him the patronage of Emperor Charles V and a lifelong post as professor of mathematics at the University of Ingolstadt.

In addition to training the next generation of mathematicians, Apian contributed greatly to the observation of comets and the development of improved instruments and mathematical tools for cosmographical calculations. On the occasion of the great comet of 1531 (later known as Halley's), he was the first to report that a comet's tail pointed away from the Sun and became one of the first to

Peter Apian, from Paul Freher, Theatrum virorum eruditione clarorum *(1688).*

suggest the use of parallax theory to determine its distance from the earth. He also designed an improved cross-staff for surveying and a new version of the quadrant for determining the time of day and created the first comprehensive table of sines in spherical trigonometry (according to each minute) designed to be used in calculating angular distances.

BIBLIOGRAPHY

Günther, Siegmund. *Peter und Philipp Apian: Zwei deutshe Mathematiker und Kartographen.* Amsterdam: Meridian, 1968.

Van Ostoy, Fernand Gratien. *Bibliographie de l'oeuvre de Pierre Apian.* Amsterdam: Meridian, 1963.

Wattenberg, Dietrich. *Peter Apianus and His Astronomicum Caesareum.* Trans. G. Archenhold. Leipzig: Edition Leipzig, 1967.

GARY MCINTYRE

See also Comets; Cross-Staff; Parallax; Trigonometry

Apothecaries. See Pharmacy

Archaeology and Antiquities

Archaeology (understood as the study of the human past through the scientific analysis of material remains) had its origins in antiquarianism, but it was not until the mid-eighteenth century that it really began to acquire its modern meaning. Although an awareness of, and a historical interest in, the debris of previous cultures had existed in most civilizations of the ancient and medieval worlds, it was the Renaissance that produced the first sophisticated studies and collections of "antique" materials.

Antiquarianism as a subject, therefore, developed out of the collection from the Renaissance onward of varied and disparate objects, which were displayed by gentlemen in their "cabinets of curiosities." In Rome, the papal rebuilding of the city led to exciting discoveries of classical antiquities and their collection and recording by humanist scholars throughout Europe. But these collections would often include natural-historical objects such as fossils, and "anthropological" objects such as those gathered from the natives of the New World, as well as antiquities such as coins and medals. As these collections grew, attempts were made at sorting and ordering and at systematization and classification. Important early collections, or "museums," included those of the Dane Ole Worm (1588–1654), variously a professor of Latin, Greek, physic, and medicine, and of Elias Ashmole (1617–1692), who founded the Ashmolean Museum in Oxford. Antiquarianism tended to form one of only a number of interests for gentlemen and scholars. An atypical example was the German Jesuit scholar, collector, and polymath Athanasius Kircher (1602–1680), who devoted himself to researching and publishing on various studies, including optics, astronomy, philology, geology, theology, acoustics, and mathematics, as well as antiquities. This eclecticism tends to characterize antiquarian studies in the period of the Scientific Revolution.

Kircher's interests included ancient Egypt, and he wrote a three-volume work, *Oedipus Aegyptiacus* (1652–1654). As Egypt and the Near East was generally considered to have been the source of all science, including mathematics, geometry, and astronomy, and civilization itself, great interest was taken in Egyptian antiquities and hieroglyphs in the Renaissance and early-modern period. Through the Florentine humanist Marsilio Ficino's (1433–1499) translation of Plotinus's *Enneads,* Egyptian hieroglyphs were interpreted as a divinely inspired form of symbolic writing. It was believed that an understand-

ing of their meaning might provide understanding of ancient religious, philosophic, and scientific knowledge. But scholars largely relied on Egyptian antiquities brought to Italy by the ancient Romans or corrupt copies made by them. An early "scientist" to actually visit Egypt itself was John Greaves (1602–1652), professor of astronomy and mathematics at Oxford University, who in 1646 published *Pyramidographia: Or a Description of the Pyramids in AEgypt,* the first treatise by an Englishman solely concerned with Egyptian antiquities.

Antiquarian studies also became tied to the attempt to unravel the origins both of nations and of the populating of the world. The European voyages of discovery developed awareness of the human race's presence throughout the world and led to attempts to explain all human history, and the history of the earth, in terms acceptable to the biblical account of Genesis. Several seventeenth-century European scholars made use of synchronistic and euhemeristic theories. They looked to the past in their attempts to explain the dissemination and subsequent corruption of true religion throughout the world and suggested possible theories for the populating of the Americas and the Pacific. Their work, in turn, influenced the work and ideas of other antiquarians with more local or provincial interests.

Following the Reformation, there was also a growing concern with national origins and identity, especially in Protestant countries attempting to distance themselves from the authority of the Roman Church. In seventeenth-century England, some scholars tried to form a clearer understanding of the origins of the nation and to trace the verifiable course of English history through Saxon times. The first Antiquarian Society, which met in the 1580s and 1590s, showed a persistent concern with the beginnings of British institutions and customs and, for this reason, met the opposition of James I, who feared that it might undermine royal authority and the prerogatives of the king.

In the later seventeenth century, a number of Fellows of the Royal Society of London took an interest in antiquarian subjects, submitting papers to its *Philosophical Transactions*. A principal figure of the Scientific Revolution to pursue an interest in history and antiquities of nations was Isaac Newton (1642–1727), who devoted a substantial amount of time to studying the history of religion and idolatry, and biblical chronology. He believed that the ancients had known of the heliocentric universe and of universal gravitation, as well as that all matter consisted of atoms. Newton thought that these ideas had been expressed in their temples, which were built in the shape of the universe, and in their myths and legends. Many of these ideas were taken up by Newton's acquaintance, the antiquarian William Stukeley (1687–1765), who developed them in his own researches into the "Celtic" temples of Avebury and Stonehenge in Wiltshire, England. Stukeley is one of the earliest examples of a scholar combining the physical activity of fieldwork, excavation, and recording with the study of written historical sources, marking the move toward modern archaeological techniques.

BIBLIOGRAPHY

Gaukroger, Stephen, ed. *The Uses of Antiquity: The Scientific Revolution and the Classical Tradition.* Dordrecht: Kluwer Academic, 1991.

Malina, Jaroslav, and Zdenek Vasicek. *Archaeology Yesterday and Today: The Development of Archaeology in the Sciences and Humanities.* Cambridge: Cambridge University Press, 1990.

Rossi, Paolo. *The Dark Abyss of Time: The History of the Earth and the History of Nations from Hooke to Vico.* Chicago: University of Chicago Press, 1984.

Schnapp, Alain. *The Discovery of the Past.* London: British Museum Press, 1996.

                                        DAVID A. B. HAYCOCK

See also Ashmole, Elias; Museums and Collections

Architecture

Before the seventeenth century, the discipline encompassed a wider sphere than it does today; it included civil and military engineering, as well as building design and construction. Vitruvius's *De architectura,* the only architectural treatise to survive intact from antiquity, treats clocks, hydraulics, and machines in addition to building. Vitruvius (fl. 20s B.C.E.) suggests that his most significant contribution to architecture is his treatise, in which he has collected the principles of the discipline. The Roman architect advocates the open, written dissemination of knowledge and insists upon the importance of bestowing credit upon past writers. He enumerates the disciplines in which the architect should be trained and suggests that he should be experienced in both reasoning (*ratiocinatio*) and construction (*fabrica*).

An extensive manuscript tradition of the *De architectura* points to medieval interest in Vitruvius, but that era did not produce its own tradition of architectural

writings. The crowning achievement of medieval architecture was the Gothic cathedral. The teams of masons who constructed these great monuments created plans by manipulating geometric figures such as triangles and squares and put them into construction by using measuring rods and instruments such as the level, square, triangle, compass, and straightedge. Structural soundness was achieved through the mason's practical knowledge of construction with a variety of materials and under diverse conditions. Such practitioners paid careful attention to signs of stress such as cracking in walls.

In late-medieval–early-modern Europe, princes, oligarchs, and city-states frequently undertook large construction projects involving the redesign of urban space and the building of great palaces, cathedrals, and other edifices, thereby helping legitimize their political power. Such construction occasionally involved spectacular engineering achievements, such as Filippo Brunelleschi's (1377–1446) massive double-shelled dome for the cathedral of Florence. More often, it entailed a new classicizing style of architecture in which proportionate modules were duplicated throughout the building in precise mathematical ratio to one another. From the mid-fifteenth century, the properly designed building came to be seen as a microcosm reflecting the mathematical proportions of the universe itself. The discipline of architecture thereby joined the material and the mathematical in a new relationship that informed both construction and the cosmos.

This development was accompanied by the flowering of architectural authorship in the fifteenth and sixteenth centuries. The new writings included independent treatises, first and most important, *De re aedificatoria* (ca. 1450) by Leon Battista Alberti (1404–1472), as well as commentaries on Vitruvius's *De architectura.* Authorship facilitated the written elaboration of architectural principles as it also raised the status of the discipline from a mechanical to a liberal art. Although architectural authors embraced Neoplatonic mathematics, they did not move away from the physical world but tended, rather, to bring the material and the mathematical realms closer together.

Practitioners, such as Antonio Averlino, known as Filarete (ca. 1400–1462), Francesco di Giorgio (1439–1501), and Andrea Palladio (1508–1580), and university-trained men, such as Alberti and Daniele Barbaro (1513–1570), undertook architectural authorship. This textual tradition in both Latin and the vernacular languages promoted architecture as a discipline that combined reason, mathematics, and construction, theory and practice. The new literature treated machines and mechanical apparatuses as well as design and construction of buildings.

In the sixteenth century, architecture and engineering split into separate disciplines accompanied by the increased professionalization of the architect and military engineer. No longer considered artisans, successful architect-engineers such as Francesco di Giorgio acquired the patronage of princes and gained status and employment through authorship as well as through concrete projects of construction and design.

Particularly through treatises and commentaries, architecture as a discipline contributed to the construction of knowledge. It is perhaps no accident that one of the canonical texts of the scientific revolution, Galileo Galilei's (1564–1642) *Two New Sciences* (1638), is set in the Venetian arsenal (an impressive site for the constructive and military arts) and involves a lengthy mathematical analysis of the strength of beams. Whereas Galileo's solutions were often original, his application of Euclidean geometry to material problems had many antecedents within the architectural traditions that preceded him.

BIBLIOGRAPHY

Long, Pamela O. "The Contribution of Architectural Writers to a 'Scientific' Outlook in the Fifteenth and Sixteenth Centuries." *Journal of Medieval and Renaissance Studies* 15 (1985), 265–298.

Mark, Robert, ed. *Architectural Technology up to the Scientific Revolution: The Art and Structure of Large-Scale Buildings.* Cambridge, MA: MIT Press, 1993.

Pérez-Gómez, Alberto. *Architecture and the Crisis of Modern Science.* Cambridge, MA: MIT Press, 1982.

Wittkower, Rudolf. *Architectural Principles in the Age of Humanism.* London: Alec Tiranti, 1952. 4th ed. New York: Norton, 1971.

PAMELA O. LONG

See also Fortification; Wren, Christopher

Aristotelianism

The general approach to philosophy and the sciences taken by the followers of the ancient philosopher Aristotle (384–322 B.C.E.). In the history of the Scientific Revolution, Aristotelianism usually stands as the ancien régime. From the preeminent place in science and philosophy he had held in the West since antiquity, after 1550 Aristotle generally fell sharply in influence and reputation. Once known as the "master of those who know," Aristotle was first attacked, then dismissed, and finally neglected, while his followers were often characterized by contemporary humanists and scientists alike as slavish, dull, and pedantic. Yet, this judgment, too often taken up uncritically by historians of the Scientific Revolution, conceals the real historical place of the study and interpretation of Aristotle in the early-modern period and obscures the relation Aristotelianism bears to modern science. Aristotelianism in general was not so much what opposed the new science (though many Aristotelian positions were overturned by it) as the major intellectual circumstance of its emergence.

Despite the singular name, Aristotelianism was never a monolithic philosophy, and individuals characterized as Aristotelians, when looked at closely, are often found to have had little in common beyond a knowledge of his works. In fact, Aristotle had so pervaded Western intellectual life since antiquity that most thinking persons before 1600—and many afterward—could, with much justification, be called Aristotelians.

The Middle Ages

Aristotle's works constitute a comprehensive body of knowledge of astonishing scope and unprecedented depth, treating almost all of the then-existing branches of knowledge except medicine and mathematics. As the founder of one of the more influential schools of thought in Greek antiquity, Aristotle exercised considerable influence in the centuries following his death, especially in logic, where he was considered preeminent. Aristotelian geocentric cosmology was incorporated to some extent into Greek mathematical astronomy, culminating in the astronomy of Claudius Ptolemy (ca. 100–ca. 170), and Aristotelian elemental theory was incorporated into Greek medicine in the works of Galen (second century). In late antiquity, philosophers from Plotinus (205–270) to Proclus (410–485) combined Aristotelian logic and philosophical concepts with a Platonic-inspired metaphysics to produce a syncretic philosophy now called Neoplatonism, which was the main channel for the transmission of Platonic thought into the Middle Ages and a major influence on the interpretation of Aristotle. Neoplatonic philosophy passed into Arabic following the expansion of Islam beginning in the seventh century, and later Arabic physicians and philosophers, such as Avicenna in the eleventh century and Averroes in the twelfth, became important commentators on Aristotle in the Latin West.

In western Europe in the Middle Ages, when the full range of Aristotle's works were made available in Latin translation together with the Arabic commentaries, they introduced whole new subject areas, gave content to subjects previously known only by name, and displaced many earlier texts in existing subjects. By 1255, despite initial opposition by some theologians, the works of Aristotle had become largely synonymous with the undergraduate curriculum of the medieval university and fundamental to the study of medicine, law, and theology in the higher faculties. While hardly any issue enjoyed universal agreement among the Scholastic Aristotelians, there was, nevertheless, a body of assumptions and conclusions generally understood as having been held by Aristotle, if not as necessarily true.

The Means to Knowledge

Aristotelian philosophy depends on logic. It was a logic of terms, in which one term (the predicate) is said or predicated of another term (the subject) to form a proposition. Propositions are, in turn, combined into inferences, or syllogisms, of the general form, if A is B, and B is C, then A is C. Aristotle identified and classified all of the valid forms of syllogism, and he discussed the requirements for scientific demonstration—that is, for the syllogistic proof of an effect through its proper cause, which was the aim and culmination of Aristotelian logic.

Logic, the formal laws of thought, mirror reality. Reality, for Aristotle, consists of individual substances that possess attributes. Certain attributes make a substance the sort of substance it is and are called properties; others may or may not be present in some particular substance and are called accidents. Substances may be immaterial—for example, the prime mover (about which more later) and the human intellect—or material, such as rocks, trees, and human beings. Whatever makes a substance that kind of substance and no other is its nature or essence; this nature or essence is expressed in the definition of the substance as its genus and specific difference. So, for example, the definition of human being is "rational animal," animal being the genus and "rational" being the property that distinguishes this animal from all others. The Aristotelian method in philosophy, then, consists in finding general and specific differences, distinguishing them from accidents, and using the resulting definitions in syllogisms to arrive at new conclusions.

Although knowledge can be had only of universals and not of particular things (which are only perceived by the senses), universals can be known only through the sensible apprehension of particular things.

Natural Philosophy

The branch of philosophy concerned with material substances and their natures, properties, and accidents is called natural philosophy, or physics. The other branches are philosophy, or metaphysics, concerned with Being in general; mathematics, concerned with the quantitative accidents of material substances; and practical philosophy—ethics, economics, and politics.

Aristotle's concern with hierarchy and classification led him to develop a long-lived and influential taxonomy of animate beings. There were three general categories, encompassing many genera and species, whose life functions were governed by "souls" with differing properties: vegetative (such as in trees, shrubs, or plants), sensitive and vegetative (as in animals possessing perception and mobility), and rational, along with the other two, possessed only by humans.

All natural or physical substances are composites of matter (the subject) and form (its attributes), though all have a third principle called potency, which is what the substance could be but is not. Motion or change, possible only for natural, material, and spatially extended substances, is the gradual passing of a substance from potentially having some attribute to actually having it, or from actually having some attribute to lacking it. (Substantial change—the generation or the annihilation of a substance or the change of one sort of substance into another—happens not gradually, step by step, but suddenly and all at once and so is not motion but mutation.) All motion and change, then, is between contraries, and the fundamental contraries are act (having the attribute) and potency (not having it but able to). There are three kinds of motion or change, depending on the sort of attribute acquired or lost: change of quality, change of quantity or size, and change of place. Natural motions are motions that arise out of the nature of the material body: rocks fall, plants grow, fire rises. Unnatural motions are imposed from the outside and in opposition to the nature of the body and so are called violent or forced motions: the motion of a stone thrown upward is violent motion, and it is opposed and eventually overcome by the stone's natural tendency to fall downward. This inherent tendency is precisely the nature of the thing, the internal principle or source of its motion and rest. The object of natural philosophy, then, is to grasp the natures, principles, and causes of natural substances and of the changes that they undergo by nature.

For natural things, Aristotle distinguished four kinds of cause: the material cause (out of which something is), the formal cause (what it is), the efficient cause (what made or effected it), and the final cause (what its purpose or goal is). Each nature acts toward a specific goal or end: rocks fall toward the center of the cosmos (which coincides with the center of the earth); acorns grow into oak trees (not into pine trees or carrots); and men are meant to enjoy happiness. Natures, for Aristotle, are goal directed or teleological, so that the final cause or goal is the most important cause and often determines the others.

A number of Aristotle's conclusions drawn from these principles were to prove especially contentious among his ancient, medieval, and early-modern interpreters. For instance, he argued that a void or vacuum is physically impossible because the speed of any motion depends on the resistance to it: where the resistance is zero, as it would be in a void, the speed would be infinite, which is impossible. Further, since size or extension is a property of bodies, there is no such thing as empty space—just as there can be no weight or any other property or accident without a body. Similarly, time, for Aristotle, is not an independent physical reality but merely a measure of motion, and it is especially identified with the motion of the *primum mobile* (see below).

Every motion, according to Aristotle, requires a cause distinct from the body moved. The cause of forced motions is readily seen to be outside of the body undergoing the motion. Bodies that move themselves, such as animals, move themselves part by part. In an inanimate natural body, such as a rock, its motion is neither from the outside nor does it move itself part by part. Still less is its nature (e.g., heaviness) the cause of its motion; heaviness is merely the principle (the source or origin) of its motion, and the cause of that motion is whatever made it a heavy body in the first place. Aristotle was also often taken to have suggested that, since the tendency of heavy bodies to fall depends on their weight, so will their speeds, so that the heavier body will fall proportionally more swiftly than the lighter.

Aristotle argued that, since all motions must have a cause, there must be a first motion—not first in time, because the cosmos, for Aristotle, always was and always will be—but first in priority. And since all motions can never cease all at the same time (for if they did they could never get started again), there must be at least one motion that never ceases and that is perfectly uniform, regular, continuous, and circular motion. This is the first motion, and the body that is so moved is called the first moved body, or *primum mobile*. Aristotle placed this body—a perfect sphere—on the outermost circumference of the spherical cosmos, just outside the sphere of the fixed stars. The *primum mobile* must itself be moved by something, but it is neither self-moved nor is it moved like a projectile. For a projectile, according to Aristotle, is kept in motion by the various parts of the medium (the air or the water) through which it passes and that are set in motion by the body before it leaves the hand or sling that throws it. This sort of motion quickly decays because it is caused by different parts of the medium and so is not absolutely one and continuous. But whatever moves the *primum mobile* cannot itself be moved, for if it were it would then also need a mover, and so on without end. Since all bodies are at least potentially mobile, this mover, therefore, cannot be a body and so must be an immaterial substance or intelligence. This, the unmoved mover, is called the prime mover, or *primum movens,* and it moves the *primum mobile* not by any mechanical or material connection but as final cause—that is, as its goal or purpose. In its uniform, continuous, and eternal revolving, the *primum mobile* seeks to emulate the eternal, immaterial being of the prime mover. With the prime mover, an immaterial substance, Aristotle has passed beyond the bounds of natural philosophy and provided later Christian thinkers evidence that his philosophy was consistent with belief in God.

Cosmology

The Aristotelian cosmos, then, is a huge sphere, with the earth, a tiny sphere, fixed at the center. Surrounding the earth are the proper spheres of the other three elements: water, air, and fire. Each of the four elements has its natural place, though, in fact, none is ever found pure and each is always mixed with the others, in constant turmoil and motion—moving up and down, increasing and decreasing, and altering in numerous ways. Since all change, for Aristotle, occurs between two contraries, each of the four elements has one from each of two pairs of fundamental contrary qualities: fire is hot and dry; air, hot and moist; water, cold and moist; and earth, cold and dry. Their combinations and mixtures give rise to all of the chemical and physical changes of the elemental world.

Concentric with the elemental spheres and containing them is the sphere of the Moon, the first of the nine celestial spheres (the others are those of Mercury, Venus, the Sun, Mars, Jupiter, Saturn, the fixed stars, and the *primum mobile*). Each of the planetary bodies is fixed in its own sphere, which revolves from west to east at its own speed around the earth, but each is assisted by a few additional spheres with different axes of rotation to account for the *apparent* nonuniform and periodic retrograde motions of the planets. The fixed stars, so-called because they never change their relationships to one another, as do the planets, are all fixed on one sphere, which is the highest of the visible spheres and the most regular in motion. It alone revolves from east to west, carried by the perfectly regular motion of the *primum mobile* and carrying with it, in turn, all of the lower spheres. This system of concentric spheres is called the homocentric cosmos, since all of the spheres have the same center.

The celestial spheres and the luminous celestial bodies they carry cannot be made of any of the four elements, since the elements possess contraries (hot and cold, wet and dry) and move naturally with contrary motions (e.g., up and down). But the heavens move only with circular motion, which has no contrary. Thus, they must be composed of some fifth element or essence that is without contrary and to which circular motion is natural. This fifth essence is called the quintessence, or ether. In a similar way, Aristotle reasoned that the heavens are unique, all-encompassing, ungenerated, incorruptible, and incapable of any motion or change, alteration, increase, or decrease other than their regular, circular motion. Beyond the cosmos there is nothing—no body, no space, no emptiness, just nothing.

Scholastic Aristotelianism

From the thirteenth century on, there was an alliance of sorts between Aristotelian philosophy and Christian faith, but it was never without controversy. Most of the conclusions of Aristotle seen as contrary to Christian doctrine (such as the mortality of the human soul and the eternity of the world) were resolved, and Aristotelian principles, in turn, were used to great effect in explaining mysteries of the faith such as the Trinity and the Eucharist. These tendencies reached their zenith in the synthesis of Thomas Aquinas (d. 1274), in which the natural knowledge of Aristotle and the revelations of Christian faith were reconciled as two complementary ways of knowing the world and its Creator. Most medieval philosophers and theologians did not go so far, however, and though few rejected Aristotle outright as useless or even dangerous for Christians, none accepted his teachings uncritically.

The Scholastic method of the medieval university was, above all, a method of critical and exhaustive questioning and examination. The characteristic forms this took were the commentary and the question, in which many of Aristotle's positions were extended, qualified, or rejected, as often on the grounds of reason and experience as of faith. Scholastics in the late thirteenth and early fourteenth centuries questioned Aristotle's accounts of the cause of projectile motion and discussed the possibility of an actual void and the behavior of moving bodies in it, the possibility of an infinite cosmos, multiple worlds, and the motion of the earth, all of which were directly contrary to Aristotle's positions. For all of this speculation, Aristotle nevertheless served as the common foundation, although the superstructures built on it were often very un-Aristotelian.

The Renaissance

In the early fourteenth century, at the same time that Scholastic philosophers and theologians were submitting Aristotle to this vigorous and critical examination, another kind of scholar was beginning to give new attention to ancient Greek and Latin literature, history, ethics, politics, and rhetoric. The humanists, as they are called, sought to recover the wisdom of the ancients by recovering their ancient texts from the distortions of commentators and translators and by studying them in historical context. Their goal was less the search for theoretical truth than the cultivation of practical wisdom. The humanist program thus complemented the curriculum of the university by taking up literary and historical texts that held little interest in the advanced Scholastic curriculum but opposed the Scholastic method, with its highly technical terminology and its emphasis on logical distinctions, disputations, and objective truth.

The opposition of the humanists to Scholasticism, however, entailed an opposition neither to Aristotle nor to Christian faith. Rather, humanists launched virulent attacks on Latin Scholastics for their quibbles and logic-chopping, as well as on the followers of the infidel Averroes, who introduced both irreligion and barbarous

Latin into philosophy. But Aristotle, the saying went, also wrote in Greek, and he received more attention from humanist editors and printers than perhaps any other Greek author. This, together with his still-dominant place in the university curriculum and among almost everyone with any claim to learning, made Aristotle one of the most frequently printed ancient authors in the Renaissance. Between 1450 and 1600, three thousand to four thousand editions of Aristotle were printed, while the same period saw fewer than five hundred editions of Plato (428–348 B.C.E.).

In their search for all things Greek, humanist scholars also recovered and translated the ancient Greek commentaries on Aristotle, and these works, often highly critical of Aristotle's doctrines, were avidly taken up by many university Aristotelians to be used alongside the commentaries of Averroes and the Latin Scholastics. Thus, while the works of Aristotle remained at the core of undergraduate teaching at the sixteenth-century university, the method and the content of the teaching were changing. The scope and the variety of Aristotelianism in the sixteenth century defy summary, though two strands deserve special attention: Paduan Aristotelianism and the Aristotelianism of the Jesuits.

Very soon after its formation in the thirteenth century, the university at Padua emerged as a prominent center for the study of medicine. The arts curriculum, in which the works of Aristotle were predominant, was studied there primarily in preparation for medicine rather than for theology as at Oxford and Paris. This, together with the fact that the masters of arts at Padua, Bologna, and other northern Italian universities were more often seculars than clerics or regular friars (Franciscans or Dominicans), meant that the study of Aristotle was largely independent of theological concerns. Averroes was especially favored by Paduan masters from the thirteenth century, while later masters in the early sixteenth century were among the first to use the newly recovered Greek commentators. In general, the treatment of Aristotle at Padua and other Italian universities among the secular masters was more naturalistic, empirical, and secular and less theological than elsewhere, and the general goal was a better understanding of nature and the world through the exercise of reason and the correct reading of Aristotle independent of Christian doctrine.

This led some Aristotelians to assert controversial conclusions: in the early sixteenth century, for example, Pietro Pomponazzi argued that Aristotle had held the human soul to be mortal and that its immortality could not be proved in philosophy despite its truth in faith. Cesare Cremonini (1550–1631), professor of natural philosophy at Padua, defended himself before the Venetian Inquisition against charges of religious heterodoxy by asserting that he was paid to teach what he understood Aristotle to have meant. Cremonini used a similar argument to explain why he did not need to look through Galileo Galilei's (1564–1642) telescope: he preferred to rely on Aristotle's account of the heavens. In contrast was Jacopo Zabarella (1533–1589), Cremonini's predecessor, who, citing Aristotle as his example, claimed always to have appealed to reason and experience over any authority, even that of Aristotle himself.

Paduan Aristotelians are credited with developing Aristotle's logic of demonstration into a scientific method of discovery and proof, in which one first reasons from effects back to their causes (resolution), and then from those causes back to the effects (composition). John Herman Randall (1961), in particular, has argued that this twofold method of resolution and composition, called *regressus* (or the demonstrative regress), was the forerunner of Galileo's scientific method.

In contrast to the secular bent of the Paduan Aristotelians, the Order of the Society of Jesus, established in 1540, enlisted Aristotle into the service of the Catholic Church to combat heresy and the Protestant Reformation. Its members instituted a rigorous and intellectually disciplined curriculum for the numerous colleges they founded throughout Europe in the sixteenth century, among which the Collegio Romano in Rome and the Collège Royal in Paris are the most notable. This curriculum was founded on Aristotle in logic and philosophy and Thomas Aquinas in theology. Jesuit lecturers published works on logic, natural philosophy, and metaphysics that were widely influential, and a set of commentaries on all of the logical and natural works of Aristotle was assembled and published by Jesuits in an ambitious attempt to provide a complete and exhaustive aid to the study of Aristotle. These commentaries were reprinted well into the seventeenth century and were widely read outside Jesuit colleges. William A. Wallace (1992) has argued that Galileo owed his knowledge of *regressus* and his mature scientific method not to the School of Padua but to Jesuit lectures on Aristotelian scientific demonstration.

One pseudo-Aristotelian text merits special attention: the *Mechanical Problems,* or *Questions on Mechanics.*

Recovered in the late fifteenth century, this brief treatise was edited and translated by humanists and printed in all of the major editions of Aristotle's works. It was the only mechanical text taught at a sixteenth-century university; Galileo was one of several professors who lectured on it at Padua. The *Mechanical Problems* was by far the most influential work on mechanics until it was displaced in the late sixteenth century by Archimedes and the works he inspired, though commentaries were written on it well into the seventeenth century. Its attribution to Aristotle, though always doubtful, lent the *Mechanical Problems* authority and helped establish mechanics as a theoretical and mathematical science.

The Decline of Aristotle

The reasons for the decline of Aristotelianism are numerous and complex. Most obvious were new scientific discoveries and conclusions that called Aristotle's science into doubt, such as the discovery in the 1570s that comets and novae were in the allegedly unchanging supralunar realm, and Johannes Kepler's (1571–1630) demonstration in the early seventeenth century that the planetary orbits were not homocentric and their motions were neither uniform nor circular. Galileo's telescopic observations of mountains on the Moon, the moons of Jupiter, and sunspots also broke down Aristotle's distinction between the terrestrial and the celestial realms and opened the way for a new physics that applied everywhere. Galileo refuted many of Aristotle's conclusions (or reputed conclusions) about the fall of heavy bodies and projectile motion, and the principle of inertia directly challenged Aristotle's proposition that everything that moved must have a mover. Experiments with the barometer and the air pump cast doubt on Aristotle's denial of the possibility of a vacuum. The mechanical philosophy emerging in the seventeenth century proposed alternative concepts of matter and tended toward rejection of Aristotle's fourfold concept of causality, retaining only the efficient cause.

In university education, the teaching of Aristotle's books by commentary and question gave way to new humanist methods of teaching and new or expanded subject areas, especially mathematics, classical literary and historical studies, and the study of other ancient philosophers, especially Plato, Epicurus (341–271 B.C.E.), and the Stoics. Non-Aristotelian and even anti-Aristotelian natural philosophies were proposed by Girolamo Cardano (1501–1576), Bernardino Telesio (1509–1588), and Francesco Patrizi (1529–1597), to name only a few. Humanist theologians, such as Erasmus, turned away from Aristotle-based scholastic theology to a simpler, practical Christian wisdom based directly on the Gospels and the Fathers of the Church, and many Churchmen, both Catholic and Protestant, looked with suspicion on the claims of secular philosophers in general and of Aristotle and his followers in particular.

Even in logic Aristotle did not remain unchallenged: newly recovered Stoic texts offered a propositional logic to vie with Aristotle's syllogistic, while Petrus Ramus (1515–1572) developed what he claimed was a new logic to replace Aristotle's. Mathematicians such as Christopher Clavius (1538–1612), Francesco Maurolico (1494–1575), Federico Commandino (1509–1575), and Galileo began to recognize that Aristotle's syllogistic method did not extend to the axiomatic-deductive method of Euclid and Archimedes. Francis Bacon (1561–1626) even proposed what he thought was a new method for the sciences explicitly to replace Aristotle's. Aristotle was not the only authority to fall in the general challenging of established powers and authorities: when the Royal Society of London adopted as its motto the phrase *nullius in verba* ("on the word of no man") from Horace (65–8 B.C.E.) its members were merely repeating what had by then become a commonplace posture: I carry a brief for no master. In an age of political absolutism and religious dogmatism, the critical spirit of inquiry cultivated by Aristotle and the best of his followers eventually turned against him, and Aristotelianism as a system of philosophy and as a way of understanding the world began to crumble under the assault.

BIBLIOGRAPHY

Gilbert, Neal Ward. *Renaissance Concepts of Method*. New York: Columbia University Press, 1960.

Kristeller, Paul Oskar. *Renaissance Thought: The Classic, Scholastic and Humanist Strains*. New York: Harper and Row, 1961.

Lloyd, G. E. R. *Aristotle: The Growth and Structure of His Thought*. Cambridge: Cambridge University Press, 1968.

Lohr, Charles H. *Latin Aristotle Commentaries II: Renaissance Authors*. Florence: Leo S. Olschki, 1988.

Randall, John Herman., Jr. *The School of Padua and the Emergence of Modern Science*. (Saggi e Testi 1). Padua: Antenore, 1961.

Rose, Paul Lawrence, and Stillman Drake. "The Pseudo-Aristotelian Questions in Mechanics in Renaissance Culture." *Studies in the Renaissance* 18 (1971), 65–104.

Schmitt, Charles B. *Aristotle in the Renaissance*. Cambridge, MA: Harvard University Press, 1983.

Van Steenberghen, Fernand. *Aristotle in the West: The Origins of Latin Aristotelianism.* Trans. Leonard Johnston. Louvain: Nauwelaerts, 1970.

Wallace, William A. *Aristotle's Logic of Discovery and Proof.* Dordrecht: Kluwer, 1992.

W. R. LAIRD

See also Demonstration; Dialectic; Matter; Mixed Sciences; Motion; Resolution and Composition; Teleology

Arnauld, Antoine (1612–1694)

A French theologian and philosopher, Arnauld was the most important and well-known intellectual associated with the Jansenist community at Port-Royal, as well as a staunch and orthodox champion of Cartesian philosophy. In his theological writings, Arnauld defended the Augustinian doctrine of efficacious grace, according to which a person's salvation is not earned by his or her own acts but granted by the irresistible grace of God. In addition to his role in the theological controversies surrounding Jansenism, Arnauld was also constantly engaged in philosophical disputation and was regarded as one of the sharpest and most philosophically acute thinkers of his time.

His influence on several major philosophers of the period resulted mainly from his penetrating criticism of their systems. In 1641, Arnauld was asked to comment on René Descartes's (1596–1650) *Meditations*. The objections he sent—regarding, among other topics, the representational nature of ideas, the circularity of Descartes's proofs for the existence of God, and the apparent irreconcilability of Descartes's conception of material substance with the Catholic doctrine of Eucharistic transubstantiation—were considered by Descartes to be the most intelligent and serious of all. Arnauld offered his objections in a constructive spirit and soon became an enthusiastic defender of Descartes's philosophy, regarding it as beneficial both to the advancement of human learning and to Christian piety. He supported the mechanistic program in natural philosophy but was concerned to ensure that it be consistent with the proper understanding of God's freedom, omnipotence, and providence.

In 1662, Arnauld composed (with Pierre Nicole) *La logique, ou l'art de penser* (Logic; or, The Art of Thinking), also known as the "Port-Royal Logic," an influential treatise on language and reasoning. After several decades of theological polemic, during which he fled France in exile to the Netherlands, Arnauld resumed his philosophical activities with a number of works attacking Nicolas Malebranche's (1638–1715) theology and its philosophical foundations, as well as a fruitful philosophical correspondence with Gottfried Wilhelm Leibniz over metaphysics and the concept of substance.

BIBLIOGRAPHY

Kremer, Elmar, ed. *The Great Arnauld.* Toronto: University of Toronto Press, 1994.

———, ed. *Interpreting Arnauld.* Toronto: University of Toronto Press, 1996.

Nadler, Steven. *Arnauld and the Cartesian Philosophy of Ideas.* Princeton, NJ: Princeton University Press, 1989.

STEVEN NADLER

See also Cartesianism; Descartes, René; Leibniz, Gottfried Wilhelm; Logic; Malebranche, Nicolas

Art

The visual arts in particular played a crucial role in developing the early-modern understanding of the natural world. By their nature, the visual arts concern themselves with sensory phenomenon (light, color, form). It is in the art of the Renaissance, however, that one discerns an interest in the operations and the details of nature unlike that of preceding centuries. Characteristic of Renaissance interest is a stress on empirical observation allied with a desire to harmonize those observations with underlying principles. Giorgio Vasari (1511–1574), the artist and biographer of artists, singled out these characteristics in his *Lives of the Artists* (1550) when he praised the "accomplished artists" that preceded him for "setting themselves to the intelligent investigation and zealous imitation of the true properties of the natural world." Verisimilitude achieved through observation of "the true properties" and conformity to nature's laws were the goal of the artists.

From the thirteenth century, artists had shown an increasing interest in capturing the details of the natural world in a sometimes serious, sometimes playful fashion (as manuscript illustrations testify), but increasingly the trend was toward naturalistic illusionism, particularly in painting. Although this trend was marked both in Italy (where Giotto [1266/1267–1337] is accepted as the pioneer) and north of the Alps, the emphases were different.

North of the Alps, the emphasis fell on the accumulation of almost microscopically observed, accurately depicted detail and on the use of light to achieve concreteness and spatial unity. Rendering of both detail and light was facilitated by the development of painting that allows a depth of color and a lucidity not to be achieved in tempera. The works of fifteenth-century Flemish painters, notably those of Jan Van Eyck (1390–1441) and Rogier Van der Weyden (1399/1400–1461), possess a kind of documentary quality derived from intense focus on the material details of bourgeois life and personality coexisting with a mysterious solemnity conveyed through the use of clear but gentle light—they treated domestic detail as both real and sublime. Artists used empirical observation to convey not only information about the visible world, but also invisible significance. The metaphysical use of light corresponds to late-medieval scientific understanding of light as the medium of grace.

Italian artists of the same period turned their interests in another direction. In Italy, artists concentrated on harmonizing optics and geometry with naturalistic representation. The artistic method for achieving verisimilitude in accordance with mathematical principles is linear perspective, the pictorial invention by which Renaissance art is chiefly known. Filippo Brunelleschi (1377–1446), a Florentine goldsmith, engineer, and architect, is acknowledged as the inventor of linear perspective. Brunelleschi made his first perspective demonstration in 1425 in two small paintings of Florentine landmarks. His demonstration was followed quickly by the experiments of other artists, one of the earliest and most significant being Masaccio's *Trinity* (1426) in the Church of Santa Maria Novella. Subsequently, several influential treatises describing the perspective method and formulating its theoretical principles appeared. Probably the most well-known early theoretical discussion appears in Leon Battista Alberti's (1404–1472) *On Painting* (1455). Lorenzo Ghiberti (1381–1455) and Piero della Francesco (ca. 1420–1492) also wrote treatises on perspective construction and theory.

The importance of linear perspective to early-modern science has long been acknowledged, as has the significance of the visual model for exploring and understanding the natural world. The significance for artists and scientists was that perspective seemed to derive from and obey the principles of Euclidean geometry and optics. Renaissance painters and theoreticians were convinced that linear perspective corresponds with mathe-

matical truths and is consonant with visual perception: a picture in linear perspective is a true approximation of reality.

The invention or development of a mode of representation that allows a "true" image of the visible world has important ramifications for the development of observational science. Perspective creates the illusion of three-dimensionality on a two-dimensional surface, making objects appear to be drawn or painted in the round. Moreover, by rationalizing pictorial space, perspective provides a mode for depicting objects in correct relationship to each other as they appear to the viewer. The concept of relationship between the viewer and the objects viewed is important for understanding the influence of the perspective mode. The perspective picture is represented as a view through a window into which the static viewer gazes. The convincing quality of perspective depends on a relationship between the fixed vantage point of the viewer and the scene being viewed: the eye of the artist/viewer determines the relationship among objects as they advance or recede in space. Perspective sets up an objective view, with the observer standing outside and looking into the scene under scrutiny. Linear perspective is an excellent method for the demonstration of the details of the natural world.

The convergence of art and science in the fifteenth and sixteenth centuries is attributable to several interrelated factors. An intense interest in natural phenomena and the search for pattern and underlying principles have been discussed. Another factor was the blurring of boundaries between practice and theory, craft and art. An interchangeability of interests and a renunciation of disciplinary or academic definitions characterizes the work of the most well-known artist-scientists and theorists. Men trained in craft traditions and those pursuing humanist studies were deeply interested in the application of knowledge to practical problems. Brunelleschi was trained as a goldsmith and became an architect; Alberti had studied law but was devoted to the pursuit of his interests in art theory and architecture. Many artists undertook the study of anatomy to make their art more rational and realistic. Leonardo da Vinci (1452–1519) and Michelangelo (1475–1564) are only the most well-known artists-anatomists. Da Vinci also experimented in, and theorized about, hydraulics, engineering, geology, and optics and developed techniques for atmospheric perspective. Albrecht Dürer (1471–1528), who merged the traditions of German art with the classicizing focus of Italian art (learned during two visits to Venice), undertook detailed nature studies, wrote treatises on measurement, perspective, and human proportion, and made important contributions to perspectival printing and engraving.

Renaissance artists and theorists approached their studies of nature via the authoritative texts of classical antiquity and by means of empirical observation. Their aim was to be factual, detailed, and exact in their discovery of natural laws and in their translation of the observations according to mathematical principles.

It is not insignificant to art and science that perspective and printing developed at the same time. Perspective would become a very important tool for scientific illustration, and the printing of perspective woodcuts and engravings resulted in an unprecedented dissemination of observations and theoretical drawings.

In the first decades, printed pictures lacked the subtlety and depth to make them real descriptions of the visible world, but, after about 1520, artists, form cutters, and engravers had invented means for making true pictorial illustrations of the verbal text. These illustrators translated the techniques of perspective and chiaroscuro from drawing and painting, thereby allowing the possibility of conveying accurate and detailed visual information. By the middle of the sixteenth century, there were any number of technical and scientific books on the market, each containing large numbers of sophisticated printed illustrations. Subject matter ranged from geometry, engineering, and ballistics to botany, zoology, and, of course, anatomy.

Dürer's treatises on measurement and proportion, *Treatise on Measurement* (1525) and *Four Books on Human Proportion* (1528), were followed by other essays demonstrating how the human body conforms to geometrical natural laws.

The life sciences were represented by the work of Pierre Belon (1517–1564) in *La nature et diversité des poissons* (1551) and *Portraits* (1557), Guillaume Rondelet (1507–1566), and Conrad Gessner (1516–1565). Gessner's work was multifaceted and grew from his humanist and medical education. In 1551 he published his encyclopedic *Historiae animalium,* an illustrated zoological compendium based on both ancient and contemporary sources. At his death in 1565 he was preparing his *Historia plantarum,* for which he had drawn and col-

ored more than fifteen hundred plants to be made into woodcuts.

Botany, a part of medical education, entered a new theoretical phase as illustrated books spread knowledge of plants from Europe and the Americas. Sixteenth-century scholars worked closely with artists and form cutters to visualize their syntheses of ancient texts and empirical observation. In 1539 the artist Hans Weiditz (fl. 1500–1536) collaborated with the physician Otto Brunfels (ca. 1489–1534) to produce the three-volume *Herbarum vivae eicones* (1530, 1532, 1536) and its German translation, *Contrafayt Kreuterbuch,* with more than 230 illustrations.

Perhaps the most well-known connection between art and science resulted from the anatomical studies of both artists and medical humanists. The detailed depiction of a skeleton at the base of Masaccio's *Trinity* suggests that the artist had made some kind of study of anatomical structure. Vasari attributed the accuracy of Antonio Pollaiuolo's (1431–1498) rendering of the human body to his participation in dissections. Although the source of Pollaiuolo's anatomical knowledge is contested, engravings such as *Battle of the Ten Naked Men,* printed in the 1470s, were a source of knowledge for other artists. Both Leonardo da Vinci and Michelangelo made empirical anatomical studies based on dissection.

The most famous of Renaissance anatomical texts, Andreas Vesalius's (1514–1564) *De humani corporis fabrica,* was published in 1543, two years after Michelangelo completed his *Last Judgment* in the Sistine Chapel. The more than two hundred woodcuts, designed by Jan Stefan van Calcar (1499–ca. 1546), are the result of a collaborative effort whereby new anatomical knowledge and the artistic developments of the previous century were united in a work that combined aesthetic and pedagogical value.

Although the artistic innovators of the fifteenth and sixteenth centuries may have begun with a desire to "restore" art to its ancient status as a mirror of nature, they, in effect, developed a new way of imagining space. The ability to imagine and picture "Cartesian space" (i.e., a three-dimensional infinite space) from the viewpoint of an observer situated outside the milieu of the observed had philosophical, phenomenological, and political ramifications: the eye of the observer became "objective."

The political nature of the objective gaze continues to be the subject of discussion and debate. It remains in question to what extent the transformation of natural phenomena into objects for scrutiny and metaphorical (or actual) dissection may be an innocent mode of perception. Nevertheless, the relationship between the work of those artists whose interests escape the boundaries of their craft traditions to range over the mathematical and life sciences, and the development of modern scientific understanding, is clear and uncontested.

BIBLIOGRAPHY

Alpers, Svetlana. *The Art of Describing: Dutch Art in the Seventeenth Century.* Chicago: University of Chicago Press, 1983.

Baigrie, Brian S., ed. *Picturing Knowledge: Historical and Philosophical Problems Concerning the Use of Art in Science.* Toronto: University of Toronto Press, 1966.

Dunning, William V. *Changing Images of Pictorial Space: A History of Spatial Illusion in Painting.* New York: Syracuse University Press, 1991.

Edgerton, Samuel, Jr. *The Heritage of Giotto's Geometry: Art and Science on the Eve of the Scientific Revolution.* Ithaca, NY: Cornell University Press, 1991.

Kemp, Martin. *The Science of Art: Optical Themes in Western Art from Brunelleschi to Seurat.* New Haven, CT: Yale University Press, 1990.

Schultz, Bernard. *Art and Anatomy in Renaissance Italy.* Ann Arbor, MI: UMI Research Press, 1985.

MARY G. WINKLER

See also Dürer, Albrecht; Emblematics; Illustration; Leonardo da Vinci; Perspective; Printing

Ashmole, Elias (1617–1692)

Antiquarian, astrologer, and alchemist. After legal training in London, he settled at Oxford, where he studied mathematics, astronomy, and astrology. During the Civil War, Ashmole, who was a Royalist, was associated both with the Royalist astrologer and mathematician George Wharton (1617–1681) and the Parliamentarian astrologer William Lilly (1602–1681), who became his lifelong friends.

His marriage to Lady Manwaring provided him with a steady income, which made it possible for Ashmole to pursue his antiquarian interests and to collect books and scientific instruments. Ashmole studied alchemy under William Backhouse (1593–1662), and in 1650 he published the *Fasciculus chemicus,* a translation of works of

From Elias Ashmole, The Way to Bliss *(1658).*

Arthur Dee (1579–1651). In 1652 he published *Theatrum chemicum Britannicum,* a collection of verse alchemical works, to which he added *Prolegomena* and notes. In the *Prolegomena,* he conceived alchemy as part of the ancient wisdom, which the Druids had shared. For Ashmole, astrology, magic, and alchemy were the key to unlock the secrets of nature.

Ashmole's commitment to astrology and alchemy did not prevent him from cultivating experimental knowledge. He developed a keen interest in botany, especially in the medical uses of plants, and, under the influence of Thomas Wharton (1614–1673), he studied anatomy. Ashmole was a very early member of the Royal Society, but his scientific contributions were negligible.

Ashmole was a man of encyclopedic knowledge, and his collections of books, manuscripts, and scientific rarities were offered to the University of Oxford, where they became the first English public museum, which opened in 1683. The Ashmolean Museum, which was equipped with a laboratory, played a prominent part in Oxford science.

BIBLIOGRAPHY

Debus, Allen G. "Introduction." In E. Ashmole. *Theatrum chemicum Britannicum*. Repr. New York: Johnson Reprint, 1967, pp. ix–xlix.

Josten, C. H., ed. *Elias Ashmole (1617–1692): His Autobiographical and Historical Notes, His Correspondence . . . with a Biographical Introduction*. 5 vols. Oxford: Clarendon, 1966.

ANTONIO CLERICUZIO

See also Alchemy; Museums and Collections

Astrolabe

The planispheric astrolabe is the archetypal scientific instrument because of its antiquity and remarkable sophistication. It is a flat, circular brass instrument, which embodies a stereographic projection of the earth and of the hemisphere of the heavens. The point of the projection is nearly always the South Pole, and the plane of the projection the equator. The user can take an altitude measurement of the Sun or a star with the sighting device (*alidade*) on the back, and set the position of the Sun on the front or the pointer for the selected star on the celestial part (*rete*), over the appropriate altitude circle on the stereographic plate, representing the earth. The combination gives the configuration of the heavens at the time the sighting is made at a particular location on the earth.

Basically used for telling the time either by the stars or by the Sun, the astrolabe has an additional function as an analogue computer, important for solving mathematical problems. It had a great variety of applications in astronomy and astrology, in which it was used to determine the positions of the heavenly bodies at a chosen time and date, and in the professions of surveying and navigation.

The astrolabe was introduced to Europe through Spain at the time of the Islamic invasions in the tenth century. With the Christian reconquest of Spain, knowledge of the astrolabe penetrated medieval Europe during the eleventh century, and craft centers were established by the thirteenth in France, Germany, the Low Countries, and England. The *Treatise on the Astrolabe* written in 1391 by Geoffrey Chaucer, the English literary figure, is an excellent introduction to the use of the instrument.

The European university arose from the cathedral schools during the twelfth century, and by 1350 thirty

A sixteenth-century astrolabe of gilded copper plate. Courtesy Whipple Museum of the History of Science, Cambridge, England.

existed. Science was taught in the arts faculties as part of the "quadrivium": arithmetic, geometry, astronomy, and music. The astrolabe had, at that time, an obvious role in such teaching, which encompassed astrology, since, in the medieval cosmological view, the planets ruled the life of mankind. By 1500 the number of universities had increased to seventy, which explains the fifteenth-century increase in astronomical texts and in the making and use of astrolabes and associated instruments. Examples have survived of fairly simple and small astrolabes that were made at that period in Germany for aspiring scholars.

The Renaissance craftsmen of the sixteenth century made large astrolabes, 1–2 feet in diameter, for greater accuracy in measuring angles. To avoid cutting projections for a sequence of latitudes on several plates, the "universal" projection was invented. Thus, a single projection on the north-south plane of the globe could be marked with the positions of thirty or more stars, making the astrolabe lighter, quicker to produce, and less expensive.

The finest astrolabes were produced between 1540 and 1590 at Louvain in the Low Countries, where the most skilled craftsmen were Thomas Gemini (fl. 1524–1562), who moved to London; Gerard Mercator (1512–1594), the map and globe engraver; and Walter Arsenius. Other craft centers were in Nuremberg, Florence, and Prague. After 1600 the astrolabe was made obsolete by new observatory instruments, calculators, and accurate clocks.

BIBLIOGRAPHY

Gibbs, Sharon, with George Saliba. *Planispheric Astrolabes from the National Museum of American History*. Washington, D.C.: Smithsonian Institution Press, 1984.

National Maritime Museum. *The Planispheric Astrolabe*. London: National Maritime Museum, Greenwich, 1976.

North, J. D. "The Astrolabe." *Scientific American* 230 (1) (January 1974), 96–106.

Turner, Gerard L'E. "The Three Astrolabes of Gerard Mercator." *Annals of Science* 51 (1994), 329–353.

G. L'E. TURNER

Astrology

According to Ptolemy (ca. 100–ca. 170), the science of the stars had two parts: the theoretical and the practical. In the seventh century, Isadore of Seville gave these parts the different names of *astronomy* and *astrology*. At this time in western Europe, however, neither astronomy nor astrology was very much studied. Moreover, throughout the Middle Ages and into the early-modern period, the two terms were often used interchangeably. Only in the twelfth century, with the revival of classical learning and the translations of Greek and Arabic philosophical texts, did the science of the stars become once again of major interest to western scholars. At this point, Aristotelian philosophy began to dominate the schools, and Aristotle's view of the cosmos underlay the study of the heavens. In particular, Aristotle's (384–322 B.C.E.) concept that all existence depended on immutability and eternity, which are in the empyrean, suggested to the medieval reader that knowledge of the heavens could give the student special insight into occurrences on Earth, including foreknowledge of future events.

There are three basic parts of traditional astrology. The first is what we would call astronomy proper, the mathematical computation of the positions of the various heavenly bodies. In the geocentric system, there were seven planets. Measured by the lengths of their pre-

sumed orbits around the earth, they were the Moon, Mercury, Venus, the Sun, Mars, Jupiter, and Saturn. The Sun seemed to make an annual orbit along the ecliptic through the fixed stars that became the constellations of the zodiac: Aries, Taurus, Gemini, Cancer, Leo, Virgo, Libra, Scorpio, Sagittarius, Capricorn, Aquarius, and Pisces. Until Tycho Brahe (1546–1601) proved otherwise, comets were thought to be sublunar phenomena, and their appearance had to be noted. Even after astrologers began to accept the heliocentric system, astrology was earth centered because it focused on how the heavens affected the earth; it did not matter whether the Sun went around the earth or the earth went around the Sun. Thus, they could still use the apparent movement of the Sun. As new planets and asteroids were discovered in later centuries, astrologers readily added them to their calculations.

Next, the apparatus had to be calculated from the movements of the heavenly bodies. The zodiacal signs, which are each 30°, are divided into three decans of 10°, and three signs forming an equilateral triangle constitute trigons or triplicities. The angles formed by the light of two planets are called aspects. The major aspects—conjunction (0°), opposition (180°), trine (120°), square (90°), sextile (60°)—were established by Ptolemy; the earliest minor aspects—sesquiquadrate (135°), quintile (72°), biquintile (144°)—were derived from Johannes Kepler's (1571–1630) writings, the only part of his attempt to reform astrology that was accepted generally by astrologers. Other aspects, the quincunx (150°) and semisextile (30°), were added later. Astrologers also divide the sky into twelve sections apart from the zodiacal signs, which they call houses; no universally accepted method of making this division has ever been established.

Finally, astrology involves interpretation. The houses, for example, traditionally represented the self, possessions, siblings, parents, children, health, marriage, legacies, duty, career, benefits, and difficulties. The signs of the zodiac and each of the "planets" had special characteristics attached to them. Aspects could be good or bad, or, in the case of conjunction, they depended on the nature of the "planets" involved. Each sign was said to be ruled by a planet, but, in the second and third decans (groups of ten zodiacal degrees), the sign was ruled by the ruler of its partners in the triplicity. Triplicities were associated with one of the elements—earth, water, air, or fire. Comets were portents of evil. Predictions were also made through progressions, a system whereby each day following the natal chart represented a year in the subject's life.

Traditional astrology was divided into natural astrology and judicial astrology. Natural astrology dealt with the weather and medicine. Astrology was the most successful means of forecasting the weather in the late-medieval–early-modern period. Farmers used these forecasts to make decisions about planting, and merchants were anxious to know of any impending storms before sending their ships out, so astrology was considered useful to the economy. Of course, these forecasts had mixed results. In 1499 the influential astrologer Johann Stöffler (1452–1531) published *Ephemerides,* in which he predicted that multiple planetary conjunctions in the sign of Pisces during 1524 would produce a second great flood on February 25. This prediction produced widespread consternation, but there was not even a minor storm on that date. On the other hand, Kepler, who kept careful records of his weather predictions and was proud of their relative accuracy, predicted a terrible hailstorm for March 1, 1609, from a conjunction of Jupiter and Mars in the sextile of the Sun and Mercury, which, he observed, came to pass as predicted.

Physicians generally believed that the heavenly bodies influenced both individual and public health. They checked birth charts to study the physical and emotional constitution of the patient, much as the modern physician uses a case history. They studied the heavens so that they would know when to administer certain treatments because, for example, they believed that bleeding was affected by the phases of the Moon. They would use astrology to predict the course of a disease, especially to watch for "critical days," times at which the disease would undergo a significant change. In fact, physicians like Robert Fludd (1574–1637) considered it more important to watch the stars than to watch the patient. Astrology was also used to predict and explain the occurrence of epidemics. The Medical Faculty of the University of Paris explained the Black Death of 1348 by the fact that on March 20, 1345, at 1 p.m., there was a conjunction of Saturn, Jupiter, and Mars in the sign of Aquarius; a conjunction of Saturn and Jupiter is believed to cause disaster, and a conjunction of Mars and Jupiter to cause pestilence, while Aquarius is considered a carrier associated with the element of air.

Judicial or divinatory astrology involved readings of personal characteristics and predictions of human events. In the late-medieval–early-modern period, there were four categories of judicial astrology. General predictions were based on future movements of the heavenly bodies and dealt with society as a whole. Nativities, more commonly known as horoscopes, were maps of the sky at the moment of birth. These would give information about the person's innate character and predispositions. In his 1608 horoscope of Count Albrecht von Wallenstein, the notorious general who switched sides in the middle of the Thirty Years War, Kepler wrote that Saturn on the ascendant in his birth chart showed that he was untrusting and untrustworthy and scorned human laws and religion, while the low Moon made him prejudiced and contemptuous and without sympathy toward others. Astrologers became advisers particularly because of the category of elections, or deciding the right moment to undertake a certain action. Queen Elizabeth I consulted with John Dee (1527–1608) about the most propitious time for her coronation, and she did, indeed, have a successful reign. Pope Julius II not only fixed the day of his coronation but also the day for his return from Bologna in consultation with his astrologers. The most controversial category of judicial astrology were the horary questions. This category did not come from the "classical" astrology of Ptolemy but was developed by Arab astrologers. In this category, it was assumed that the astrologer could answer any question by considering the heavens at the exact moment the question was asked, under the assumption that that moment represented the birth of the question and worked the same way as the nativity.

Early astrology flourished in Hellenistic culture, when it was nurtured by the fusion of Mesopotamian, Egyptian, and Greek thought, but the Romans regarded it with ambivalence. In the early Christian centuries, it was identified with pagan worship and was opposed by the Church. Saint Augustine's (354–430) condemnation of astrology made all study of the heavens suspect. Such study reentered western Europe primarily through translations from the Arabic and became part of the accepted Aristotelian outlook of the schools. Opposition to astrology became identified with opposition to the study of the book of nature—the other side of divine revelation. Saint Thomas Aquinas (d. 1274) considered the heavenly bodies divine instruments for ruling the sublunar world, and he believed that human passions were controlled by the heavenly bodies, so that it was possible to study human character and predict events through astrology. Dante

(1265–1321) put the diviners in hell, but in heaven he apostrophized Gemini, his birth sign, as the source of his poetic creativity. In fact, even those who opposed astrology accepted its basic premises. Nicole Oresme (ca. 1323–1382) was one of the few Scholastic natural philosophers who wrote polemics against astrology. He accepted the idea of the stars as divine instruments and of heavenly motion as a cause of motion on Earth, but he did not think it possible to make calculations accurate enough to predict from astrology. He also considered astrology more useful for medicine than for predicting the weather. Most opponents of astrology, however, were primarily motivated by religious reasons: astrology interfered with belief in divine providence and human free will, and it provided a secular explanation for phenomena. There was no need for recourse to divine retribution for human sinfulness if the state of the heavens could explain the Black Death. John Calvin (1509–1564) opposed any attempt to penetrate the mysteries of human destiny, and his followers objected to the way astrologers substituted astral fate for predestination.

Most opponents of astrology would have approved of Giovanni Pico della Mirandola's (1463–1494) belief in an absolute contradiction between human free will and astrological prediction. Pico's *Disputations Against Judicial Astrology*, written in 1494, was the most widely cited work against astrology in the early-modern period. He had assimilated all of the available literature on astrology and brought to bear as many different arguments against astrology—natural as well as judicial—as he could find. But the underlying theme was the necessary opposition he perceived between astrology and religion. The fact that he had had no experience either observing the heavens or calculating their courses gave supporters of astrology ammunition against his work.

In fact, astrology was part of the mathematics curriculum of every Western university from their founding in the twelfth century to the seventeenth century, and *mathematicus* was a synonym for astrologer. Students of the heavens took astrology for granted as one facet of their discipline. The study of astronomy was often motivated by its necessity in the practice of astrology. Nicolaus Copernicus (1473–1543), Tycho Brahe, Kepler, and Galileo Galilei (1564–1642) had all studied astrology. Copernicus mostly ignored it in his writings and probably opposed it, but Tycho and Kepler were both practicing astrologers, although Kepler often expressed doubts about it and tried to reform it so that it could conform to

his view of the universe. Galileo was more skeptical than Kepler, but he cast horoscopes from which he made predictions, and he taught astrology to medical students at the University of Padua. The astronomical work of Tycho, Kepler, and Galileo, however, destroyed the foundations on which the belief in astrology rested at that time, for they challenged the doctrine that the motion of an immutable, immaterial heaven affects the sublunar world. By the time Isaac Newton (1642–1727) was composing his great synthesis of the universe at the end of the century, there was no need to mention astrology. Among astronomers, it was dead.

BIBLIOGRAPHY

Garin, Eugenio. *Astrology in the Renaissance: The Zodiac of Life*. Trans. Eugenio Garin and Clare Robertson. London: Routledge and Kegan Paul, 1983.

Hone, Margaret E. *The Modern Text Book of Astrology*. Rev. ed. Romford: Fowler, 1978.

Shumaker, Wayne. *The Occult Sciences in the Renaissance*. Berkeley and Los Angeles: University of California Press, 1972.

Tester, Jim. *A History of Western Astrology*. Woodbridge and Wolfeboro: Boydell, 1987.

Thomas, Keith. *Religion and the Decline of Magic: Studies in Popular Beliefs in Sixteenth- and Seventeenth-Century England*. Harmondsworth and New York: Penguin Books, 1973.

Thorndike, Lynn. *A History of Magic and Experimental Science*. 8 vols. New York: Columbia University Press, 1923–1958, vols. 5–8.

SHEILA J. RABIN

See also Pico della Mirandola, Giovanni

Astronomical tables and Ephemerides

Astronomical tables provide the means for computing the celestial positions of the Sun, Moon, and planets at any time, based on a self-consistent theory; and ephemerides provide a continuous reference system of observations to meet practical requirements by giving daily geocentric positions of the Sun, Moon, and planets, generally deduced from particular astronomical tables. They are two indispensable mediators between astronomical observation and theory (consisting of a hypothesis on planetary motion and fundamental orbital parameters), the four components thus forming a synthesis. The confrontation with one another within this synthesis has, throughout the history of astronomy, been the ultimate source for the development of this observational science. An example is Johannes Kepler's (1571–1630) search for a theory in his *Astronomia nova* (1609), using Erasmus Reinhold's (1511–1553) Prutenic Tables of 1551, based on the Copernican theory, several late-sixteenth-century ephemerides, and Tycho Brahe's (1546–1601) observations.

In the long search for a fundamental law in the reference system of time and position of the celestial bodies, every epoch shows its unique characteristics in the attention it pays to the relationship between observation and theory through those two mediators; every achievement appears almost proportional to the attention so paid. The relationship became particularly intense in the sixteenth and seventeenth centuries, but the process was complex and long lasting, as may be seen by the increasingly close attention with which the observed planetary positions were compared with those given by many different tables and ephemerides. Among the tables were the Alfonsine, based on Ptolemy (ca. 100–ca. 170); the Prutenic, based on Nicolaus Copernicus (1473–1543); the Danish, based on Tycho Brahe by Longomontanus (1562–1647); the Rudolphine, by Kepler; as well as a number of variations on these four. Although all planetary theories show systematic deviations from one another, and one was mathematically able to reduce any systematic deviation to a minimum, no theory at that time accurately reproduced the observations available, a phenomenon that can only be ascribed to the problem of observation.

The immediate observations are, by nature, normally distributed about the true value, and their average value tends to yield it accurately. Other values, deduced from the immediate observations such as the so-called observed planetary positions in the orbit, contain various error sources and, therefore, tend to show systematic errors. Hence, two sorts of observations, immediate and deduced, are to be distinguished. Tycho's tropical year, the interval between two vernal equinoxes, for example, is accurate to three seconds (immmediate observation), but his length of the half-year is erroneous by six hours (deduced observation). For every planetary theory, the mean periods of the planets are fundamental. Their accurate values and deductive method (immediate observation of the synodic periods—the interval between two successive conjunctions of a planet with the Sun—in terms of the sidereal solar years—the time for a complete revolution of Earth about the Sun relative to the

fixed stars) survived from ancient Babylonian astronomy, so that the mean periods and the corresponding mean longitudes at a particular epoch could later, easily and frequently, be improved, as they were in Ptolemy's *Almagest* (ca. 140), Copernicus's *De revolutionibus* (On the Revolutions, 1543) and Kepler's *Astronomia nova* (New Astronomy, 1609). The mean periods of, for example, Mars from Babylonian times to the eighteenth century are all accurate to within about ten minutes of time. Its sidereal period of 686 days, 23 hours, 32 minutes, as given in the Prutenic Tables differs from its modern value by about one minute, compared to the Babylonian error of about ten minutes. The former was used by Kepler for deducing his laws and his frequent corrections of the mean longitude in his *Astronomia nova*.

The further accuracy within the periodic returns of the planets (mean periods and mean longitudes) is given by the hypothesis and orbital elements (dependent parameters such as eccentricity) of the theory, the latter derived from the observed positions as deduced from the immediate observations, corrected for independent and dependent parameters (geographic latitude, parallax, refraction, obliquity of the ecliptic, etc.) by means of a method based on a definite hypothesis, such as those of Ptolemy and François Viète (1540–1603)—a circular orbit with an equant, a point not in the center of the orbit about which a radius to the planet generates equal angles in equal times—or of Pierre Hérigone (d. ca. 1643) and Jean-Dominique Cassini (1625–1712)—an elliptical orbit with an equant. In this procedure, the solar parallax, or angle at the Sun determined by the earth's radius, as a fundamental independent parameter affects practically all parameters; thus, for example, the eccentricity, the main indicator of accuracy, showed systematic errors depending on the value adopted for the solar parallax. As the value decreased from about 3' (ca. 140–ca. 1630, i.e., from Ptolemy to Kepler) to approximately 10" (ca. 1670 in Cassini and Flamsteed), the eccentricity of the Sun's orbit decreased from about 0.018 in Tycho and Kepler to approximately 0.0169 in Cassini, John Flamsteed (1646–1719), Isaac Newton (1642–1727), and Edmond Halley (ca. 1656–1743), and that of Mars increased from 0.09265 for Kepler to about 0.093 for Jeremiah Horrocks (1618–1641), Nicolaus Mercator (ca. 1619–1687), and Halley, all according to the configuration of the planetary orbits. As the values adopted for the solar parallax converged to the modern value (8.8"), all theories—first solar and then, necessarily, planetary theories—had also to converge to the modern theories.

Due to the erroneous parameters involved in the whole confrontation of observation and theory, each theory can strictly reproduce only those three or four underlying observations from which the theory was deduced. As soon as any new value of the solar parallax obtained as an independent parameter—17" by Remus Quietanus (fl. 1615–1631), 14" by Gottfried Wendelin (1580–1667) and Jeremiah Horrocks—is applied to those underlying immediate observations, the theory consisting of a planetary hypothesis and the erroneous dependent parameters turns out to be inconsistent with the heavens, the phenomena valid for all theories of that time. The Rudolphine Tables—based on Kepler's laws and the erroneous dependent parameters deduced by means of his erroneous value of the solar parallax as 3'—had also to show a systematic deviation from even Tycho's observations, once corrected for all of those new accurate values of the solar parallax. Kepler's tables soon underwent a series of revisions. For the further development from 1660 onward, the correct recognition of the above astronomical reference system, the distinction between independent and dependent parameters, and between these and the hypothesis within a theory was essential.

Surprisingly, the profoundly important evolution of astronomy from 1609 to about 1670 had occurred virtually behind the scenes, notably through the work from 1637 to 1640 of Horrocks, whose determination of the solar parallax as 14", examination of Kepler's Rudolphine Tables, correction of his orbital parameters, and recognition of the agreement between observation and theory led to his acceptance of Kepler's hypotheses and laws as correct.

The role of the astronomical tables and ephemerides at that time in the confrontation between observation and theory is perhaps best exemplified by man's first observations of the conjunctions of the inner planets with the Sun as transits over the Sun's disc in 1631 and 1639, corresponding to the oppositions of the outer planets as observed in past millennia, both dealing with the planetary positions as directly subject to the heliocentric laws—immediately followed by the substantial improvements of the orbital elements predicted in Kepler's tables of 1627 and reflected in subsequent ephemerides.

BIBLIOGRAPHY

Gingerich, Owen. "Early Copernican Ephemerides." *Studia Copernicana* 16 (1978), 403–417.

Kennedy, E. S. "A Survey of Islamic Astronomical Tables." *Transactions of the American Philosophical Society* 46 (1956), 123–175.

Maeyama, Y. "The Historical Development of Solar Theories in the Late Sixteenth and Seventeenth Centuries." *Vistas in Astronomy* 16 (1974), 35–60.

———. "Kepler's *hypothesis vicaria*." *Archive for History of Exact Sciences* 41 (1990), 53–92.

Russell, J. L. "Kepler's Laws of Planetary Motion: 1609–1666." *British Journal for the History of Science* 2 (1964), 1–24.

Y. MAEYAMA

See also Astronomy; Keplerianism; Parallax; Ptolemaic Astronomy

Astronomy

Astronomy in many ways provides the model for the development of a science during the Scientific Revolution. Changes in its theoretical basis, its place within the divisions of knowledge, its observational content, and its institutional structures are all characteristic of the changes that took place during the Scientific Revolution and, in many instances, precede and provide the model for the other sciences.

Astronomy led the other sciences largely because it inherited from antiquity a large body of technically sophisticated theory wedded to a consistent natural philosophy. The technical theory came from Ptolemy (ca. 100–ca. 170) and his Islamic commentators. The Ptolemaic planetary models included many of the classical geometric constructions of planetary theory. The so-called first anomaly of planetary motion was modeled by a large sphere (called the deferent) that was slightly eccentric from the center of the planetary system, namely the earth. The eccentricity would cause a point on the uniformly rotating deferent to appear to move faster or slower when it was nearer or farther from the earth, which mimicked observed variations in the speed of the motions of the planets among the stars. In addition, the model included a smaller sphere, the epicycle, whose center was carried around on the deferent. The planet was attached to a point on this smaller sphere, which rotated in the same sense as the deferent. The epicycle had the effect, when the planet was in the lowest part of the epicycle, of overcoming the continuing forward motion of the deferent and causing the planet to appear periodically to come to a halt among the stars, briefly reverse course, and then continue its normal course. Thus the epicycle modeled observed episodes of retrograde motion, the second anomaly of planetary motion. Ptolemy's own innovation was the equant. By shifting the point of uniform angular motion of a planet on its deferent to a position equally distant and on the opposite side from its center as the eccentric earth, the equant was able to accentuate the nonuniformity of motion caused by the eccentric placement of the observer on the earth, but without exaggerating the component of motion of the epicycle. Since the orbits of the planets are nearly circles, and the equant very nearly reproduces Johannes Kepler's (1571–1630) second law, Ptolemy's planetary theories were remarkably accurate and robust. Coupled with his comprehensive treatise on constructing planetary models, his work became the foundation for astronomy for nearly fifteen hundred years.

Ptolemy's planetary theory, along with the works of some of his Islamic commentators, had been recovered and assimilated in the late-medieval period and were used for planetary tables and ephemerides. The full sophistication of Ptolemy's achievement and the cogent criticisms of his Islamic commentators became apparent only near the beginning of the sixteenth century. The fall of Constantinople in 1453 brought original Greek manuscripts of Ptolemy's *Almagest* and refugees fluent in Greek to the West. The advent of printing in the same year made the wide dissemination of original sources possible. These events became particularly influential in the sixteenth century with the first publication of the *Almagest* in 1515, an event that occurred in the midst of Nicolaus Copernicus's (1473–1543) development of his planetary theory and that contributed greatly to the technical sophistication of his *De revolutionibus* (On the Revolutions, 1543).

Increasingly sophisticated reading of Ptolemy brought home to sixteenth-century astronomers a lingering inconsistency between Ptolemaic astronomy and Scholastic philosophy. Aristotle (384–322 B.C.E.) had provided a remarkably consistent and wide-ranging natural philosophy that became the foundation of medieval science and also the natural philosophical backbone of Ptolemaic astronomy. In the realm of astronomy, Aristotle had put forward the doctrine that the heavens are entirely unworldly—that is, they consist of a fifth element, ether, which has no earthly qualities and whose natural motion is uniformly circular around the center of the world, namely the earth. Aristotelian natural philosophy was well compatible with Eudoxus's contemporary doctrine of homocentric planetary spheres, but Ptolemy's later innovations constituted an unresolved challenge.

This incompatiblity between Ptolemaic theory and Aristotelian natural philosophy was, to a certain extent, embodied in a division in astronomy between *spherica* and *theorica* that had been established during the medieval period. The former, deriving from Johannes de Sacrobosco's (d. ca. 1256) *De spera* (On the Sphere) and Aristotle's *De caelo* (On the Heavens), dealt largely with spherical astronomy—the daily and yearly motion of the Sun and stars. It was elementary and cosmological and was considered part of natural philosophy. *Theorica* derived from Ptolemy, contained technical planetary theory, and was deemed part of mathematics. Because of the well-known fact that alternative arrangements of planetary spheres could represent identical appearances, there was considerable skepticism as to whether mathematical astronomy had any claim to demonstrative certainty.

Attempts to reconcile Ptolemaic theory and Aristotelian philosophy had advanced far with Islamic commentators and, in the sixteenth century particularly, began to percolate into the West. An arrangement of space-filling spheres proposed in Ptolemy's *Planetary Hypotheses* passed through Islamic sources and became the basis for the system described in Georg Peurbach's (1423–1461) *Theorica novae planetarum* (New Theory of the Planets) of 1472. This system reconciled Ptolemy's eccentrics and epicycles with Aristotlean homocentric spheres by carefully embodying the Ptolemaic mechanisms as systems of ether spheres whose peripheries were homocentric with the Sun. The Ptolemaic equant, however, was particularly troublesome. Although, on the one hand, angular motion around the equant was uniform and thus perfectly acceptable, on the other hand, the physical motion of the epicycle center around the deferent could not be, which cast doubt either on the uniformity of motion or on the rigidity of the planetary spheres. By the late-medieval period, Islamic astronomers had succeeded in eliminating this problem by recasting the Ptolemaic equant into ingenious, more complex compounds of uniform circular motion that largely mimicked the Ptolemaic equant.

Against this backdrop, the achievement of Copernicus should be seen as a continuation of a tradition of astronomical humanism begun by Peurbach and Johannes Regiomontanus (1436–1476) and devoted to reforming astronomy within the constraints of classical thought. As it was seen in the sixteenth century, the significance of Copernicus's *De revolutionibus orbium coelestium* (On the Revolutions of the Celestial Spheres, 1543) lay in its elimination of the nonuniformity of motion inherent in the Ptolemaic equant, which Copernicus seems to have accomplished on the basis of the models of the Islamic astronomers, though the means of their transmission remains unknown. Modern analysis has shown that Copernican planetary models, which achieved their widest influence through Erasmus Reinhold's (1511–1553) *Tabulae Prutenicae* (Prutenic Tables, 1551), were not unambiguously more accurate than Ptolemaic tables, although in the sixteenth century they were widely perceived to be so. The fact that Copernicus's planetary theories were framed in a heliocentric system—which itself had at least some classical precedent—was treated with widespread ambivalence. The "Wittenberg Interpretation" of Copernicus, as Robert Westman has named it, in which the planetary theories were avidly studied while the cosmological claims were treated with indifference, was widely followed by astronomers regardless of their faith. Manifest physical experience of the earth's immobility and the testimony of Scripture stood in the way of heliocentrism's acceptance.

A number of factors accumulated in the late sixteenth century that did not so much lend support to Copernicus as undermine the Aristotelo-Ptolemaic orthodoxy. There was a Renaissance curiosity about competing scientific systems of antiquity and, thus, a renewed interest in Neoplatonism and Stoicism. Exegetical trends issuing from the Reformation also strained the Aristotelian scheme of the heavens, which influenced an unsophisticated reading of Aristotle that allowed the ether spheres to solidify. Contrary to the original doctrine, by the late sixteenth century ether was understood to possess the earthly qualities of materiality, rigidity, and impenetrability; they had become "crystalline spheres." Skepticism from proponents of alternative views of nature and the, unfortunately, unsophisticated philosophical position of Aristotelians with regard to the ether paved the way for a cosmological crisis.

Some singular observational phenomena hastened the attacks on Aristotelian cosmology. The novae of 1572 and 1604, which showed no measurable parallax and were, thus, demonstrably supralunar and most probably belonged to the sphere of the fixed stars, showed that the heavens were not immutable. And the spectacular comet of 1577, which was observed by some—most notably Tycho Brahe (1546–1601) and Michael Maestlin (1550–1631)—also to be supralunar and, thus, to travel among the planetary spheres, cast doubt both on the Aristotelean notion that comets were atmospheric phenomena and on the solidity or reality of the celestial spheres. The meaning of these phenomena was not manifestly clear, but they did provide the impetus to reconsider the reigning paradigm and to entertain closer examination of the elegance provided by the Copernican scheme.

Analysis of observations of the comet of 1577 eventually provided the evidence of the immateriality of the celestial spheres that Tycho needed to put forward his hybrid cosmological system, first published in 1588, in which the Sun revolved around the earth while the planets revolved around the Sun. The attractiveness of this compromise is evident in the number of people who quickly started teaching it as their own. Tycho reacted bitterly to the infringement, as he saw it, of Paul Wittich (ca. 1546–1586), Nicolaus Reimers Ursus (1551–1600), Helisaeus Röslin (1544–1616), and Duncan Liddel (1561–1613). The Tychonic system, by incorporating some of the simplicity of heliocentrism while avoiding physical and theological objections to the earth's mobility, provided an attractive compromise in the cosmological debate of the early seventeenth century.

Apart from the novae and comets, observational evidence played a reasonably small role in the cosmological debate around the turn of the seventeenth century. Only with Tycho Brahe did astronomical instruments achieve great sophistication. Prior to Tycho's time, accurate, utilitarian astronomical instruments were virtually nonexistent in the West, Bernard Walther's (1430–1504) instruments and the observatory of Wilhelm IV, Landgrave of Hesse (1532–1592), being the only real precedents. Tycho's accomplishment rested on his fundamental belief that the state of astronomical theory required a reformation and that such a reformation could be accomplished only on the basis of an accurate series of observations. With lavish support from the Danish Crown, he embarked upon a twenty-year program of observation and instrumental development. Tychonic instruments converged on a type that was large and entirely of metal, with finely divided arcs and accu-

A

rate sights. With repeated use, the best instruments were capable of measuring the location of a star to the limit of resolution of the naked eye. His final triumph was that he disseminated knowledge of his innovative instruments in his *Astronomiae instauratae mechanica* (Instruments for the Restoration of Astronomy, 1598). In addition to being perhaps the greatest naked-eye observer of all time, Tycho was also one of the last. The invention of the telescope about ten years after Tycho's death made possible another series of instrumental improvements, but it was some time before his accuracy was matched and exceeded.

Johannes Kepler (1571–1630) was the first to argue vigorously for the physical reality of heliocentrism, for the inclusion of physical reasoning in astronomy, and for the dissolution of the barrier between *sphaerica* and *theorica*. He aimed to let astronomy take its rightful place as a part of natural philosophy. That he was armed for this effort with Tycho Brahe's unprecedentedly accurate observations must be counted as the most fortuitous turn of events during the Scientific Revolution. Using the observations with great originality and creativity, Kepler was able to derive a physical theory of the motions of the planets, which entailed his first and second "laws" of planetary motion and abandoned circles and uniform circular motion. He published his theory of Mars first in the *Astronomia nova* (New Astronomy, 1609) and followed with the remaining planets in the *Tabulae Rudolphinae* (Rudolphine Tables, 1627). Kepler published his third "law" relating the periods of the planets and distances in his *Harmonice mundi* (Harmonics of the Universe, 1619). It had great cosmological significance for him, but its relation to the rest of his work was forced, and he never exploited its utility in determining the parameters of planetary theory. It was not so used until the publication of Thomas Streete's (1622–1689) tables in 1661.

Kepler's theories were undeniably accurate. His most spectacular predictions were of the transits of Mercury and Venus in 1631—phenomena that had never been witnessed before. But his program of physical astronomy was not widely accepted by astronomers. The notion of a quasi-magnetic solar effluvium he used to explain the motions of the planets was regarded by many as bizarre. Moreover, with the ellipse and the area law, he had introduced into astronomy "Kepler's problem," which made it impossible to calculate a planet's position directly as a function of time. Thus, most of the history of technical planetary theory between Kepler and Newton

Frontispiece of Johannes Kepler's Tabulae Rudolphinae *(1627), illustrating various aspects of the science of astronomy. The physical and mathematical foundations of astronomy are represented at the top of the structure, along with some astronomical instruments. The pillars and the figures next to them represent the great astronomers from antiquity to Kepler's time; the strongest pillars are those associated with Copernicus and Tycho Brahe. Attached to the columns are various instruments, including an astrolabe, a sextant, a quadrant, a cross staff, and a celestial globe.*

is devoted to recasting Kepler's elliptical orbits and the area law into some more manageable mathematical model. In the 1630s Bonaventura Cavalieri (1598–1647) and Jeremiah Horrocks (1618–1641) developed identical approximate solutions to Kepler's problem. And similar kinds of "empty focus" theories, in which the empty focus of the ellipse acts as a Ptolemaic equant, were introduced by Ismaël Boulliau (1605–1694), Seth Ward (1617–1689), and Blaise François de Pagan (1604–1665) in the 1640s and 1650s. Finally, it should be noted that accepting Kepler's theories did not entail being a Copernican; both Noël Durret (ca. 1590–ca. 1650) and Jean-Baptiste Morin (1583–1656) published Keplerian tables and were simultaneously anti-Copernican.

Kepler had pushed toward physics from mathematical astronomy. But the greatest strides in unifying the two came from physics and natural philosophy toward astronomy. Galileo Galilei (1564–1642) played a decisive role in two respects. First, his telescopic discoveries of 1609–1610 fundamentally changed the nature of astronomy. Until that time, the subject matter of astronomy largely involved predicting the motion of the Sun, Moon, and planets against the backdrop of the stars. The nature of those dots of light was largely unknowable and speculative and was the province of natural philosophers. The observations of the heavens that Galileo described in the *Sidereus nuncius* (The Sidereal Messenger, 1610) created more of a sensation than any other work of the Scientific Revolution. In addition to creating a new subject matter for astronomy, the discoveries in the *Sidereus nuncius* and those made during the flurry of activity within the first year or two of telescopic observation after its publication played an important role in clarifying the cosmological debate. The rough features on the lunar surface—which lent support to those who believed it was essentially earthlike—and sunspots dealt a serious blow to the Aristotelian notion of celestial perfection. The gibbous phases of Venus effectively ruled out the Ptolemaic system. And the moons of Jupiter, in showing that another planet could retain its satellites, provided some analogical support for heliocentrism. Astronomers settled into Tychonic and Copernican camps. Because of the observational equivalence of the two systems, the decision between them could be made only on physical or religious grounds.

This state of affairs made Galileo's omission of the Tychonic system in his *Dialogo sopra i due massimi sistemi del mondo, Tolemaico e Copernicano* (Dialogue Concerning the Two Chief World Systems, Ptolemaic and Copernican, 1632) a false dichotomy. However, it was in Galileo's study of motion that he made his other great contribution toward the physicalization of astronomy. Galileo recast the age-old problem of a body's motion from being a process that required a mover to maintain it to being a simple state of existence that would persist as long as the body was not acted upon. In so doing, he was able to address the greatest physical objection to the motion of the earth: that it might move and we would not perceive it. In addition, by his analysis of falling bodies, he provided a quantification of the acceleration of gravity that would be an important element in the formulation of the law of gravity. Although

his overzealous and masterfully rhetorical advocacy of Copernicanism in the *Dialogue* ended badly for him and gave others, like René Descartes (1596–1650) pause, it had the greatest effect in crippling Aristotelianism and clearing the way for the acceptance of heliocentrism.

The advent of the telescope also breathed new life into another, longer-term observational investigation of heliocentrism having to do with the scale of the solar system. In the Ptolemaic system, the size of the universe had been determined by nesting the planetary theories one on top of another and calculating the total space they took up. The distance to the sphere of stars, located just beyond Saturn, was reckoned to be ca. 20,000 earth-radii (e.r.). In the heliocentric system, however, the annual motion of Earth around the Sun should have induced a measurable shift in the observed position of the stars at different times of the year (stellar parallax). The absence of observable stellar parallax led Copernicus to conclude simply that the stars are very far away. Careful investigation by Tycho Brahe placed a lower limit on their distance of ca. 8 million e.r. Spurious naked-eye estimates of the angular size of stars implied that, at such a distance, the stars would be enormous bodies comparable in size to the earth's entire orbit. Such absurd sizes and distances bolstered Tycho's rejection of the heliocentric system. Galileo discovered, however, that the telescope stripped stars of the adventitious rays that made them appear to have any angular size whatsoever. The problem of their size was resolved, but their distance remained elusive. Stellar parallax eluded detection throughout the Scientific Revolution, even after the heliocentric system had achieved widespread acceptance. One of the most concerted such efforts was that of Robert Hooke (1635–1702), who claimed (mistakenly) to have measured stellar parallax in 1669 using a special telescope built into his house. Stellar parallax would not be measured successfully until the nineteenth century.

The acceptance of heliocentrism progressed without decisive observational proof. Rather, the cogent explanatory power of the heliocentric system when coupled with sophisticated physics made the doctrine increasingly persuasive. Studies of mechanics, which revolutionized physics and, at the same time, addressed the physics of planetary motion, were essential for melding physics and astronomy. Along with Galileo's example in mechanics, Descartes's contribution was certainly foundational. In reaction to contemporary philosophies of nature, he purged physical thought of the excesses of Renaissance naturalism, as well as Aristotelean qualities, and produced an austere ontology that admitted only matter and motion. Since motion is conserved, given correct laws of impact (where he fell short), there is the inherent expectation in his philosophy that physical processes are quantifiable and intelligible. Although the vortex theory of the planetary motion put forth by Descartes in its mature form in the *Principia philosophiae* (Principles of Philosophy, 1644) was qualitative and could contribute little of substance to planetary theory, his work contained some essential elements of mechanics, such as rectilinear inertia, and inspired mechanical philosophers. In correcting Descartes's badly flawed laws of impact, Christiaan Huygens (1629–1695) elucidated notions of momentum and kinetic energy. Moreover, he was able to quantify the relation for centrifugal force and provide an essential element in the dynamics of circular motion that could be applied to the case of planetary motion. Characteristically, Isaac Newton (1642–1727) came to these same thoughts independently.

The Newtonian synthesis was certainly the culmination of the Scientific Revolution, and many of its elements either came from astronomy or were influenced by the cosmological debate. From Kepler came the laws of planetary motion; from Galileo, the law of falling bodies; and from Descartes, rectilinear inertia and the foundations of the mechanical philosophy. In addition, Newton received one essential idea from Robert Hooke: that the motion of a planet should be seen as a compound of motion along the tangent and an attraction toward a center. Spurred by correspondence with John Flamsteed (1646–1719) regarding the comet of 1680–1681 and by an inquiry from Edmond Halley (ca. 1656–1743) about the shape of an orbit caused by an inverse-square force toward the center, Newton erected a foundation for celestial mechanics that has scarcely been superseded to this time. The laws of motion and universal gravitation he put forth in his *Principia mathematica philosophiae naturalis* (Mathematical Principles of Natural Philosophy, 1687) not only provided a new basis for Kepler's laws and Galileo's observation of falling bodies, but also were extended to the cause of tides, the figure of the earth, the precession of the equinoxes, and the perturbations of the planets on one another. Mathematical tools needed to be developed to handle the more difficult cases, and Cartesian resistance continued into the eighteenth century, but no other single work has comparable significance in the history of astronomy.

Along with the theoretical synthesis that put astronomy in the forefront of sciences, there was a corresponding development of instrumentation, which was a hallmark of the Scientific Revolution. This development could proceed beyond the level achieved by Tycho Brahe only with the further development of the telescope. The phenomena discovered with the telescope in the second decade of the seventeenth century lay just beyond visual perception. Most of these were either made by Galileo or he claimed priority for them. Thereafter, a long lull ensued while telescopes were improved. The first step, taken by a number of observers by around 1640, involved abandoning Galileo's convex-concave system of lenses for the convex-convex system described by Kepler in his *Dioptrice* (Dioptrics, 1611), which inverted the image but had a larger, clearer field of view. To achieve greater magnification, it was then necessary to grind lenses of longer and longer focal length. The quest for longer focal length culminated in Christiaan Huygens's so-called aerial telescope, in which the objective lens was raised on a high pole while the observer stood on the ground with the eyepiece. Huygens's efforts paid off with the discovery of Saturn's moon Titan in 1655. His observations also helped elucidate the cause of Saturn's odd tripartite appearance, which, as he explained in his *Systema saturnium* (The Saturnian System, 1659), was due to a flat ring surrounding but not touching the planet. The further telescopic discoveries of the late seventeenth century were all made by Jean-Dominique Cassini (1625–1712), who discovered four additional satellites of Saturn between 1671 and 1684. Such discoveries were certainly hard-won but—like the various lunar maps published during the seventeenth century—of questionable significance.

The telescope was far more significant for the effect it had on the prosaic matter of accurately measuring positions. Tycho's method of open-sight observing—equaled only by the Danzig astronomer Johannes Hevelius (1611–1687)—was limited ultimately by the resolving power of the human eye. Properly constructed telescopic sights, however, could overcome this limit after the technique of fitting crosshairs in the focal plane of the telescope was introduced by Jean Picard (1620–1682) in 1667. A similar technique developed by Adrien Auzout (1622–1691) in the same year involved placing a fixed wire and one mounted to a micrometer. Such a filar micrometer could be used to measure very small angles accurately. The pendulum clock, perfected by Huygens

A

in 1656, used in conjunction with a meridian transit first developed by Ole Römer (1644–1710), made the collection of accurate positions routine and completed the arsenals of state observatories that were founded toward the end of the century. High-precision measurements of angles and time were essential for subtle but important astronomical discoveries in the second half of the seventeenth century. In 1675 Römer was able to conclude from anomalous times for eclipses of Jupiter's moons that the speed of light was finite. And observations of Mars's opposition in 1672 by Cassini and Flamsteed provided the first realistic measurements of the distance to the Sun.

The development of patronage and institutional support made astronomy the best-supported science during the sixteenth and seventeenth centuries and was also characteristic of its status as the queen of the sciences during the Scientific Revolution. Although in the early sixteenth century astronomers supported themselves largely by occupying low-status chairs in mathematics at universities and by publishing calendars and ephemerides, around the turn of the seventeenth century a fortunate few obtained positions at Court that provided the resources for important research projects. Tycho Brahe set the standard in this regard. His research institute—which supported alchemical research in addition to astronomically related fields such as meteorology—was lavishly funded by the Danish Crown, and, when that support collapsed, he was able to arrange a similar position with the Holy Roman Emperor Rudolph II. Kepler inherited this position upon Tycho's death, although at a significantly lower salary. Galileo, too, was able to fashion a lavish position for himself as court philosopher and mathematician to the grand duke of Tuscany, Cosimo II de'Medici, a title that reflected astronomy's changing content and importance. It must not be overlooked that all of these positions existed, at least partly, because of the importance of astrological advice to men in positions of power. Later in the seventeenth century, when belief in astrology was waning and the utility of astronomy as an aid to navigation became apparent, the English and the French governments established permanent state observatories. Cassini, in particular, as director of the Observatoire de Paris, was able to make good use of the resources of the state, such as the sending of an astronomical expedition to Cayenne. In addition, the foundation of both the Observatoire de Paris (1667) and the Greenwich Observatory (1675) in England are bound up with the newly formed scientific societies in those countries. The changes in its institutional status and its close affiliation with scientific societies represent a final indication of the centrality of astronomy in the Scientific Revolution.

BIBLIOGRAPHY

Grant, Edward. *Planets, Stars, and Orbs: The Medieval Cosmos, 1200–1687.* Cambridge: Cambridge University Press, 1994.

Koyré, Alexandre. *The Astronomical Revolution: Copernicus-Kepler-Borelli.* Trans. R. E. W. Maddison. London: Methuen, 1980.

North, J. D. *The Norton History of Astronomy and Cosmology.* New York: Norton, 1995.

Pannekoek, A. *A History of Astronomy.* London: Allen and Unwin, 1961.

Swerdlow, N. M. "Astronomy in the Renaissance." In *Astronomy Before the Telescope,* ed. Christopher Walker. London: British Museum Press, 1996, pp. 187–230.

Taton, René, and Curtis Wilson, eds. *Planetary Astronomy from the Renaissance to the Rise of Astrophysics;* Part A: *Tycho Brahe to Newton.* (The General History of Astronomy, vol. 2). Cambridge: Cambridge University Press, 1989.

Van Helden, Albert. *Measuring the Universe: Cosmic Dimensions from Aristarchus to Halley.* Chicago: University of Chicago Press, 1985.

JAMES R. VOELKEL

See also Astronomical Tables and Ephemerides; Celestial Spheres; Cosmic Dimensions; Geoheliocentrism; Ptolemaic Astronomy; Telescopic Astronomy

Atomism

The seventeenth century saw the robust reemergence of the ancient view that we best account for the nature of matter and manifest qualities of familiar material objects by postulating invisible elemental particles from which all such objects are constituted. Atomist views and related corpuscularian doctrines were principally designed by their authors as fundamental ontologies for physical theories, and, in the early-modern era, these theories were generally associated with one or another mechanical outlook. Yet, for several epistemological and physical reasons, atomism failed adequately to furnish a universe conceived as mechanical, and it proved dispensible to the classical mechanics developed in the wake of Isaac Newton's (1642–1727) *Principia mathematica philosophiae naturalis* (Mathematical Principles of Natural Philosophy, 1687). Nonetheless, early-modern atomism paved the way for particulate-matter theories of greater sophistication by suggesting how grasping macrophenomena might depend on first understanding the structure and behavior of ultimate building blocks on the microlevel.

Broadly, the diverse early-modern atomist theories all suggest that matter is composed of extraordinarily small, indivisible particles, which, according to the various theories, may be uniform or vary with respect to size, shape, weight, or motion. Another central claim of atomism is the explanatory principle that the combinations of such invisible particles yield not only the aggregate structure of familiar objects, but also their specific qualities, such as density, fluidity, temperature, elasticity, taste, and color. Competing corpuscularian theories of matter suggested either that the basic particles are infinitely divisible or that, while such ultimate particles may provide a structural basis for bodies of greater scale, we best account for their qualities by appealing to Aristotelian forms arising from the mixtures of fundamental elements. Thus, atomism is a species of corpuscularianism, distinguished at least by the rejection of both this Scholastic view regarding mixtures and the thesis that matter is infinitely divisible. As a consequence of rejecting that last thesis, the atomists were also committed to the existence of the void. If there is a definable smallest particle that cannot be divided, then between any two such particles that do not fit together seamlessly there will be gaps, and matter cannot be continuous; thus, there must be matter-free spaces, or voids, that separate each solid particle.

From its initial, ancient formulations onward, atomism was not simply an ontological or explanatory view pertinent to physics but a systematic metaphysical theory with wide-ranging scientific and cultural consequences. Theologically dutiful physical theorists ignored or condemned the materialist implications of strict atomism through the earliest years of the Scientific Revolution, at which point an effort was made by Pierre Gassendi (1592–1655), Walter Charleton (1620–1707), and others to "sanitize" atomism so as to have it better conform to Christian doctrine. As in the ancient world, this more palatable atomism shaped the natural and human sciences of the seventeenth century, from particulate assumptions in theories of sound propagation to materialist underpinnings of social and political philosophy in Thomas Hobbes (1588–1679) and, to a degree, Gassendi.

At the beginning of the seventeenth century, a generation of investigators, inspired by advances in experimental technique, wove together elements of atomism and medieval natural-minima matter theory (broadly, the view that each type of matter has its characteristic smallest particle). In the eclectic theories of Daniel Sennert (1572–1637), David Van Goorle (fl. 1590), and Sebastian Basso (fl. 1560–1623), elementary particles were understood, respectively, to have chemical properties; to account for rarefaction and condensation; and to form secondary aggregates, which, in turn, form tertiary aggregates—higher-order compounds having generally greater stability than lower-order ones.

Galileo Galilei (1564–1642) also played a key role in the transition from Aristotelian and medieval matter theories. In *The Assayer* (1623), he hints at atomism by proposing to explain the perceived qualities of bodies in terms of those qualities of their minute constituent parts, to which we lack perceptual access. Though he never spells out a detailed particulate structure of matter, this distinction between primary and secondary qualities was frequently cited by other corpuscularians as a phenomenon for which their matter theory offered a suitable corresponding ontology.

Like Galileo, René Descartes (1596–1650) was not an atomist, yet contributed to the conceptual development of those common points with his own corpuscularian views, which include counting extension among the necessary properties of matter and taking matter's particulate structure as requisite for mechanical explanation. Descartes, however, openly opposed atomism, primarily on the ground that space, as extended, must be a material plenum with no room for void—which rules out the possibility of discrete, indivisible bodies separated by extended, unoccupied space. Nevertheless, his popular physics influenced many to adopt a corpuscularian ontology.

One great achievement of seventeenth-century atomism was the development of those explanatory schema that, if only in sketch or fable, suggested the parameters of a successful particulate ontology and that range of phenomena for which, armed with such an ontology, we might hope for our physics to account. In just this vein, Isaac Beeckman (1588–1637) developed a somewhat novel view, which, unfortunately, was unknown to his contemporaries save through the filters of his student René Descartes and his acquaintance Pierre Gassendi. From Beeckman's diaries, though, we learn of

A

his view that atoms are organized into molecular structures that are the actual basic structures underlying macrosize objects. Like the little-known Sebastian Basso and the widely read Joachim Jungius (1587–1657), Beeckman associated the four Aristotelian elements— air, fire, water, and earth—with varying molecular structures and proposed that such an interpretation could yield sophisticated analyses of chemical phenomena. His interests in physics were quite diverse, and we find atomist (or, rather, molecularist) suggestions throughout his optics, hydrostatics, and other mechanical studies.

Gassendi's atomism is frequently seen as a spiritual "cleansing" of Epicureanism, but it also represented an attempt to draw out the significance of this ancient philosophy for experimental physics and other sciences. Gassendi suggested that the barometric experiments of Blaise Pascal (1623–1662) gave empirical evidence for the existence of the void—and thereby atoms—and he tried, if without success, to integrate an account of atomic motion with a dynamics of wider grain. Though many of his atomist explanations in the special sciences, from geology to the study of generation to psychology, are fanciful or ridiculous, his very attempts to employ his theory of matter across these different disciplines likely spurred the search in these fields for microlevel answers to macrolevel questions. To his credit, even Gassendi suggested that these answers awaited further developments in microscopy.

The atomism of the early-modern era reached an apotheosis at the turn of the eighteenth century in Robert Boyle's (1627–1691) chemistry, Isaac Newton's (1642–1727) physics, and John Locke's (1632–1704) philosophy. Boyle amassed a battery of rhetorical and empirical arguments against the Scholastics and for a particulate-matter theory, though he was agnostic regarding the Cartesian and Gassendist versions. As a great experimenter, he employed the methods of resolution and composition in researching the structure of matter and interpreted the resulting evidence in favor of those "real" qualities he attriibuted to corpuscles. Yet, as a careful scientist, he proposed that corpuscularianism is merely sufficient for explaining macrolevel phenomena. That there is nothing necessary about this or any other matter theory suggested to him that it may be overturned by future experiences.

In the 1706 edition of his *Optics,* Newton proposes that matter is created by God in the form of impenetrable, solid, "massy" particles, the motion of which is ensured by divine maintenance. Newton does not think his mathematical physics is directly predicated on an atomist ontology, and so he does not weave atoms directly into his phenomenal accounts. He agrees with earlier atomists, however, that no other matter theory provides adequate causal explanations of macrosize phenomena, and in this sense he holds that it is indispensable. As for Locke, the corpuscularian hypothesis and its varieties generally suits, and likely inspired, his discussion of primary and secondary qualities, distinction between real and nominal essences, and doubts concerning our ability to know with certainty about the ultimate constitution of matter.

Atomism's significance in the Scientific Revolution is best grasped by exploring the larger conceptual framework in which that ontology was generally developed—the mechanical philosophy. The mechanical philosophers held, broadly, that material objects behave in the ways of artificial machines such as clocks: in principle, their behavior is regular, measurable, repeatable, and predictable, and it is the product of the behavior of their component parts. Mechanists generally held that their accounts should explain all manifest physical phenomena by reference to the "real" and quantifiable qualities of matter, and the atomists conceived of their proposed ontology as providing the locus of such real qualities. Accordingly, such explanations of macrolevel physical phenomena should consist in giving precise descriptions of the sets and relations of basic properties of atoms, and showing how these descriptions can be derived from, or are at least consistent with, our primary physical (and metaphysical) commitments—whether derived from experience, reason, or both.

Many historians have suggested that the mechanical philosophers faced an inherent conflict in attempting to link atomism with their dynamics or kinematics because of the impossibility of giving quantified accounts of the fixed characteristics of atoms, let alone their motion. Yet, for some writers like Descartes or Christiaan Huygens (1629–1695), a corpuscular ontology is a key thesis of a mechanical philosophy from which dynamical considerations are inseparable. Such principles as govern the motion of matter fulfill the promise of the machine metaphor—that mechanistic accounts of matter with a particulate structure have predictive power and the phenomena are repeatable (at least in principle), given that the physical behavior is law- or principle abiding. This suggests that, at least from the vantage point of that era, those two elements might well be thought of as parts of an integral natural philosophy.

Yet, other aspects of the Scientific Revolution engendered problems for the atomists. One methodological difficulty concerns their claim that there is better empirical evidence for their matter theory than for any other: it is not even clear what such evidence would look like, given the supposition that atomic bodies and their behavior are below the threshold of perception. By default, the arguments of the atomists tend to rely on a priori reasoning; further, historical analysis and tribute significantly shape the content of their claims. However, some of these historically based arguments and other, more original arguments depend on what at least a number of the atomists following Gassendi (who, in turn, follows Epicurus) would construe as empirical evidence. Gassendi suggests that our inferences based on the signs of unobserved phenomena constitute empirical reasoning, such that the beliefs we thereby acquire or develop are the stuff of empirical knowledge.

Another difficulty is that the atomists no better account for phenomena on the microlevel than on the macrolevel. This is the charge that the mysterious, if familiar, qualities of the experienced world are explained by reference to equally, if not more mysterious, qualities of the atomic world. To explain familiar, experienced properties, atomists routinely appealed to the distinctive character of particular sorts of atoms, or (as per Basso, Jungius, Beeckman, and Gassendi) the special molecules they form, or (as per Sennert) the Aristotelian elements of which they are minimal parts. The challenge to such accounts is to say how or why those atoms, aggregates, or elements have their particular qualities. Two responses available to the early moderns include an appeal to theology or inference to the best explanation. This first response is to suggest that this is just the way God made such-and-so atoms. The second response is to suggest that the assumption that such-and-so atoms have such-and-so properties better explains macrolevel properties and phenomena than any competing candidate-explanation does. Whether or not there is good motivation for accepting either response, the problem remains that neither tells us how those properties came to be characteristic of the atoms that bear them, nor why they should be the basic ones as opposed to any others. If only in this respect the atomists earn Boyle's criticisms of those Aristotelian and Paracelsan theories that bestow us with one set of mysteries in lieu of another.

Another, physics-related set of difficulties emerges when we consider the contribution atoms are supposed to make to aggregate properties of bodies they compose—against the background of what some atomists intend in this context by *vis,* or "force." One question, no longer posed after Newton's treatment, is: how can "force" be understood as a feature of atoms? Clearly, any sense of "force" that is applied differently to atoms and to bodies composed of them is inconsistent with the idea of universal laws of dynamics. It is, instead, closer to the intuitive sense of "capacity to create motion" or, as it was frequently referred to, "motive force." As to the origin of such a capacity, Gassendi, Newton, and Boyle held that the ultimate particles of matter are endowed with this internal impetuslike force by divine investiture. For these atomists, the difficulty is to square such an ineradicable, inherent force with the very much eradicable force typically attributed to bodies by the developing dynamics of the time.

Still other problems arose from the prevalent view that there are infinitely hard, thus inelastic, atoms and that no impact between such bodies could entail their compression. This view suggests that change in, or cessation of, atomic motion upon impact takes zero time, yet Newton's second law of motion accordingly requires an infinite force to account for such change in motion. Hence, those holding the prevalent view were committed to the existence of such forces as are physically and theologically impossible. Two confusions prevented atomists from recognizing this problem: first, their failure adequately to define "force" and, second, their grasp of, and significance accorded to, elasticity. For his part, Newton proposed that we retain atoms as hard, inelastic bodies, hold on to the (atomist) delusion that our physics requires only macrolevel elasticity, and rely on God's external maintenance of matter in motion. Subsequent attempts to accommodate rebounding bodies acknowledged the elasticity of matter, a move made easier by the demise of neoclassical atomism.

The flourishing of atomism in the seventeenth century might be regarded as simply another example of post-Renaissance interest in antiquity, except that, in this case, scientists and philosophers attempted not only to revive a classical matter theory, but also to integrate it into contemporary physics. This effort was doomed to failure, for even a renewed, improved version of ancient atomism could not meet the methodological requirements of the new science. Yet, aspects of atomism suited seventeenth-century physics and contributed to the development of a mature chemistry.

The atomist revival provided what seemed at first glance as a mechanically plausible way to account for all physical phenomena in strictly materialist and non-scholastic terms. As the shape of Newtonian mechanics became clear, it turned out that atomism had no intrinsic part in it, but such a matter theory marked the incipient steps toward molecular and chemical element models of change in substances. Atomism, therefore, may be counted as a conceptual advance requisite for the far better empirically grounded atomism of the nineteenth century. And, while atomists could produce direct empirical corroboration of the specifics of their rough, hopeful hypotheses, few among them expected as much, and it is to their credit if they could produce any slight, indirect experimental evidence. More pertinent, we should judge their efforts as imaginative steps in the direction of an ontology worthy of contemporary trends toward quantification and normativity in the natural sciences.

BIBLIOGRAPHY

Garber, Daniel, John Henry, Lynn Joy, and Alan Gabbey. "New Doctrines of Body and Its Powers, Place, and Space." In *The Cambridge History of 17th Century Philosophy,* ed. Daniel Garber and Michael Ayers. 4 vols. Cambridge: Cambridge University Press, 1998, vol. 1, pp. 553–623.

Lasswitz, Kurd. *Geschichte der Atomistik vom Mittelalterbis Newton.* 2 vols. Hamburg and Leipzig: L. Voss, 1890.

Pyle, Andrew. *Atomism and Its Critics.* Bristol: Thoemmes, 1995.

Scott, Wilson. *The Conflict Between Atomism and Conservation Theory, 1644–1860.* New York: Elsevier, 1970.

Tamny, Martin. "Atomism and the Mechanical Philosophy." In *Companion to the History of Modern Science,* ed. R. C. Olby, G. N. Cantor, J. R. R. Christie, and M. V. S. Hodge. London: Routledge, 1990, pp. 597–609.

Van Melsen, Andreas G. M. *From Atomos to Atom: The History of the Concept* Atom. Trans. Henry J. Koren. Pittsburgh: Duquesne University Press, 1952.

SAUL FISHER

See also Active Principles; Charleton, Walter; Epicureanism; Gassendi, Pierre; Matter; Void

Attraction

The force of attraction, whereby one body could draw another toward it, was widely acknowledged in ancient and medieval natural philosophy. The Hellenistic philosopher Galen (second century), primarily known as a medical authority, distinguished three kinds of attraction in nature. First was attraction due to an elemental quality. The prime examples of this were attractions due to heat (we would say due to the current of air toward a burning body) or to moisture or wetness (an idea that seems to have arisen from observations of cohesion brought about by moisture or, in some cases, by the surface tension of water). Second were attractions brought about to avoid the formation of a vacuum. And finally, there were attractions brought about by the "whole substance" of a body, which is to say, attractions that were brought about by some natural property of the body as a whole and that could not be explained in terms of the manifest qualities (hotness, coldness, wetness, and dryness) of any of the four elements that were held to constitute the body. The prime examples of bodies that attracted according to their whole substance were magnets and "electrics" like amber and jet, but there were also a number of other supposedly attracting substances that were frequently used in the medical tradition, notably purgatives or medicines supposed to draw out venom from snakebites or wounds caused by poisoned arrows, which were believed to act by attracting like substances toward them. This last idea seems to relate closely to notions of sympathy and sympathetic attraction, which were one of the mainstays of the magical tradition. The theory of magic was based on the assumption that God had created the world on a hierarchical pattern, the Great Chain of Being, in which all creatures were linked to those immediately above and below them. There were, however, resonating or corresponding planes within the Chain of Being, so that the noblest metal, gold, corresponds to the noblest beast, the lion, the noblest planet, the Sun, and to kings, the noblest of men. Sympathetic attractions were held to operate across these corresponding planes.

Although known to the ancient Greeks and to the medieval magical tradition, the magnet achieved an important place in natural philosophy only during the Renaissance, when its use in the directional compass led to increased familiarity with, and awareness of, its remarkable properties, as well as a recognition of its importance to trade and other maritime pursuits. The first, and in many ways the most impressive study of magnets and magnetism, *De magnete* (On the Magnet) was published by William Gilbert (1544–1603), a leading English physician, in 1600. Among other things,

Gilbert took pains to distinguish magnetic from electrical phenomena. Having developed an elaborate and idiosyncratic philosophy in which the magnet's spontaneous ability to rotate was used as a model of the earth's ability, recently claimed by Nicolaus Copernicus (1473–1543), to rotate on its axis every twenty-four hours, Gilbert insisted that the substance of the lodestone was essentially elemental earth and that the earth itself was a giant lodestone. Accordingly, he needed to emphasize the differences between electrical and magnetic phenomena. One of the most significant of Gilbert's distinctions was his insistence that electrical attractions were brought about by material effluvia sent out by the electrical body and returning to it. There was no equivalent material cause of magnetic attraction, according to Gilbert. In fact, he regarded magnets as animated bodies that come together by mutual action or that attract iron, a debased form of elemental earth, by exciting or inciting its own dormant soul, so that it, too, can join to the magnet by mutual action. Part of the reason for Gilbert's emphasis on the mutual involvement of lodestone and iron in what he preferred to call magnetic "coition," rather than attraction, was his reluctance to deviate from the Aristotelian principle that action at a distance was impossible. Some, at least, of Gilbert's later followers had no such scruples and reinterpreted Gilbert's views in a more openly magical way, accepting that magnets are capable of acting at a distance.

One of the more spectacular examples of this kind of interpretation of Gilbert's ideas is to be seen in the work of Johannes Kepler (1571–1630), who drew upon Gilbert's magnetic philosophy to provide him with a model for the physical explanation he needed to account for the fact that the orbits of the planets are elliptical, not circular as previously assumed. Being unable to give a satisfactory mathematical reason why planets might move in ellipses rather than circles, Kepler felt obliged to defend his discovery by providing a plausible physical explanation. He did so by supposing that the Sun might operate like a unique form of magnetic monopole that first attracted and then repelled a planet, according to which pole of the planet was turned closest to it, so resulting in an elliptical orbit.

With the advent of the mechanical philosophy in the seventeenth century, notions of attraction were usually rejected. The atomistic, or corpuscularian, matter theories of the various versions of the mechanical philosophy spelled the end of theories of attraction due to elemental properties. Although attraction due to avoidance of vacuum was forcefully invoked by no less a thinker than Galileo Galilei (1564–1642) to explain the cohesion of countless atomic particles to form a body, this idea, which involved the assumption that every body was made up of an infinite number of indivisible particles held together by an infinite number of indivisibly small vacua, never won any adherents. A more traditional use of the antivacuist theory of attraction was invoked by Francis Linus (1595–1675) in his dispute with Robert Boyle (1627–1691) about the cause of the elevation of water or mercury in a barometer, but the mechanistic view that the elevation of the fluid was due to the pressure of the surrounding atmosphere fairly easily prevailed.

The traditional notion of attraction due to the whole substance, as manifested most clearly in magnets and electrics, had a more complicated history. In strict versions of the mechanical philosophy, such as that developed by René Descartes (1596–1650), all occult notions were eschewed, and magnetic, electrical, and gravitational attractions were explained in terms of the behavior of invisible streams of particles, flowing out and returning to the "attracting" body. In principle, if not always in practice, the incessant movements of these streams of particles were explained mechanistically. In less strict versions of the mechanical philosophy, however, something close to sympathetic attractions often seemed to creep in. The English Roman Catholic thinker Kenelm Digby (1603–1665), for example, gave what he saw as a mechanistic explanation of the so-called weapon salve, an ointment that supposedly cured wounds by being applied to the weapon that caused the wound. The efficacy of the ointment, according to Digby, lay in the fact that invisibly small particles of the ointment were carried from the weapon to the wound by invisibly small particles of blood left on the weapon returning to the wound (the idea being that the smallness of the particles guaranteed that they were more penetrating into the recesses of the wound, without clogging up the wound or the natural movements of the blood and other bodily fluids). The particles of blood on the weapon were held to return to the wound because of what sounds, in Digby's description, exactly like a sympathetic attraction to the blood in the open wound.

Other English thinkers, like John Wilkins (1614–1672) and William Petty (1623–1687), promoted a deanimated version of Gilbert's magnetic philosophy, in which magnets were said to have an energy or a vigor extending outward in a sphere of activity by which they could attract other magnetic bodies. Petty even went so far as to make magnetic atoms the basis of his matter theory. While Descartes explained magnetic phenomena in terms of the movements of invisible corpuscles, Petty suggested that the invisible particles that constituted all bodies may be tiny magnets whose interactions with one another could account for cohesion, contraction, and expansion (depending upon the orientation of the particles to bring about mutual attractions or repulsions) and other phenomena.

This English group of mechanical philosophers was also sympathetic to Kepler's attempt to explain planetary motions by drawing upon Gilbert's magnetic philosophy. In his *Attempt to Prove the Motion of the Earth* (1674), Robert Hooke (1635–1703) suggested that it might be possible to explain the elliptical orbits of the planets on the assumption of a tangential motion in a straight line, bent around by an attractive force operating between the planet and the Sun and varying in an inverse proportion to the distance between them. Hooke wrote to ask Isaac Newton (1642–1727) his opinion of this theory in 1679 and so should be given some credit for the development of the universal principle of gravitation even though he, unlike Newton, was incapable of providing a precise mathematical analysis and confirmation of the theory.

Prior to this correspondence with Hooke, Newton had been thinking of planetary movements in terms of a balance between inward and outward pressures caused by particles moving toward and away from the Sun; only now did he think in terms of a single attractive force operating across vast distances of empty space. As is well known, however, Newton went on to develop a theory of gravitational attraction between all bodies that was judged by Continental mechanical philosophers, if not by English thinkers, to be too occult to be acceptable. Furthermore, Newton expressed a hope in the Preface to his first great work, his *Principia mathematica philosophiae naturalis* (Mathematical Principles of Natural Philosophy, 1687), that we might one day be able to explain all phenomena in terms of attractive and repulsive forces between particles. Newton indicated how such a philosophy might work in a series of speculative "Queries," which he appended to his second major work, *Opticks* (1704, 1706, 1717). These speculations proved immensely influential upon eighteenth-century natural philosophy, particularly in the field of chemistry, in which notions of differential attractiveness between substances gave rise to the important notion of chemical affinity.

Influential as Newtonian attraction was, it is important to note that Newton himself was somewhat ambivalent about the notion of attraction. Although in a number of places he writes freely of attractive (and repulsive) forces operating between bodies, there is evidence to suggest that he believed that magnetic and electrical attractions could be explained in mechanistic terms by the circulation of invisible particles emitted from the magnetic or electric body. Accordingly, at one point in the *Opticks* he cautioned that "What I call Attraction may be perform'd by impulse." Even so, in the second edition of the *Principia* (1713) Newton added a third Rule of Reasoning about universal qualities in which he insisted that gravitational attraction had more right to be considered a universal property of body than impenetrability, since we have no manner of observing the impenetrability of celestial bodies, but astronomical observations enable us to confirm their mutual gravitation.

BIBLIOGRAPHY

Bennett, J. A. "Magnetical Philosophy and Astronomy from Wilkins to Hooke." In *Planetary Astronomy from the Renaissance to the Rise of Astrophysics,* Part A: *Tycho Brahe to Newton,* ed. René Taton and Curtis Wilson. (The General History of Astronomy, vol. 2). Cambridge: Cambridge University Press, 1989, pp. 222–230.

Heilbron, John L. *Electricity in the 17th and 18th Centuries: A Study of Early Modern Physics.* Berkeley and Los Angeles: University of California Press, 1979.

Hesse, Mary B., *Forces and Fields: The Concept of Action at a Distance in the History of Physics.* London: Thomas Nelson, 1961.

Home, R. W. "'Newtonianism' and the Theory of the Magnet." *History of Science* 15 (1977), 252–266.

McGuire, J. E. "Force, Active Principles, and Newton's Invisible Realm." *Ambix* 15 (1968), 154–208.

Pumfrey, Stephen. "Magnetical Philosophy and Astronomy, 1600–1650." In *Planetary Astronomy from the Renaissance to the Rise of Astrophysics,* Part A: *Tycho Brahe to Newton,* ed. René Taton and Curtis Wilson. (The General History of Astronomy, vol. 2). Cambridge: Cambridge University Press, 1989, pp. 45–53.

JOHN HENRY

See also Electricity; Gilbert, William; Magnetism; Mechanical Philosophy

Automata

Traditionally, automata were understood to be self-moving mechanical devices that contained not only a source of power, but also their own plan of action. "Automata are Mechanical or Mathematical Instruments or Engines, that going by a Spring, Weight, etc. seem to move of them selves, as a Watch, Clock, etc." (John Harris, *Lexicon technicum,* 1736). Mechanical clocks were subsumed under this category; other automata were capable of imitating humans and animals, of performing music, of replicating the motions of celestial bodies, and so on.

Inventions of automata have been reported in ancient, Hellenistic, and Byzantine Greece, in ancient China, and in the classical Islamic world. Some of these reports are inherently improbable; others, usually involving water clocks or related hydraulic devices (examples are the books of Hero of Alexandria in the first century and al-Jazari in Mesopotamia, ca. 1200), convince by providing realistic technical details and illustrations.

With the invention of the mechanical clock in western Europe in the late thirteenth century, weight-driven and regulated by a verge-and-foliot escapement, automata became part of daily life. Clocks, installed in public buildings, spread quickly over Europe, indicating the time on large dials visible from outside and by striking the hours on bells, but often also giving astronomical indications, playing music, or displaying animated figures. Well-known early examples are the astronomical clock of Richard of Wallingford, abbot of Saint Albans in Hertfordshire (ca. 1330); the monumental clock of Strasbourg cathedral (1352) with its celebrated crowing cock; and Giovanni de' Dondi's planetarium clock (Padua, 1348–1364).

The adoption of spring power to clockwork in the mid-fifteenth century made clocks small, portable, and mass-producible. Clocks with the basic time indications, but often also capable of serving as an alarm clock and of performing, in any combination, the full range of automata functions, were produced by the thousands. Increasingly, automata, dispensing with timekeeping, were dedicated to a single function, such as impersonating animals or humans. Centers of this technology, to the middle of the seventeenth century, were the south German cities of Augsburg and Nuremberg. In the eighteenth century, the skill of automata building was brought to pinnacles of perfection by Jacques de Vaucanson, whose much admired automatic duck

(Paris, 1739) appeared to eat and digest, and by Pierre Jacquet-Droz, whose *androids,* lifelike automata in human form, could, for example, write with pen on paper (Neuchâtel, ca. 1772). By the end of the nineteenth century, the technology of automata had declined to the level of mass-produced sheet-metal toys. When the concept of the automaton recovered new currency in twentieth-century cybernetics and computer science, it benefited more from the intellectual glamor of the ancient automata tradition than from any of its technological ideas.

The intellectual history of the automaton was fueled by one idea: man's quest for replicating God's act of Creation by building machines that showed the characteristics of living beings or of the universe. Three phases are notable in this history. From antiquity to the end of the Renaissance, there was a continuous tradition of automata legends: accounts of inventors of superhuman, if not supernatural, power creating mechanical life. Often these legends were attached to famous names: Daedalus, Archytas of Tarentum, Vergil, Albertus Magnus, Leonardo da Vinci, René Descartes; they were consistently uncritical, celebrating miraculous feats without discussing what was behind them; they presented events from antiquity, from the Middle Ages, and the Renaissance as linked in unbroken continuity; they were repeated so often that they must have been familiar to any literate person.

In the Scientific Revolution, the automaton concept was alive mainly through two ideas: the image of the *clockwork universe,* comparing the movements of celestial bodies with that of clockwork; and the image of *animal automatism,* comparing the functioning of animal bodies with that of automata. Implied in these comparisons was a belief in a similarity of origins (the act of Creation was compared with the work of an inventor-craftsman) and in a program-controlled (i.e., deterministic) manner of operation. Prominent advocates of the clockwork-universe analogy were G. W. Leibniz (1646–1716) and his follower Christian Wolff (1679–1754)); champions of animal automatism were René Descartes (1596–1650), who based a comprehensive theory of physiology upon it, and J. O. de La Mettrie (1709–1751), whose book *L'Homme machine* (Man Is a Machine, 1747) presented it in the most radical form.

In the nineteenth century, the notion of artificial man was kept alive in Romantic novels. The impact of the stories of E. T. A. Hoffmann carried over even into opera (*The Tales of Hoffmann*) and ballet (*Coppelia, Nutcracker*). Karel Čapek's robot is a late representative of this tradition.

BIBLIOGRAPHY

Beyer, Annette. *Faszinierende Welt der Automaten: Uhren, Puppen, Spielereien*. Munich: Callwey Verlag, 1983.

Chapuis, Alfred, and Edmond Droz. *Automata: A Historical and Technological Study*. Trans. Alec Reid. Neuchâtel, Switzerland: Editions du Griffon, 1958.

Maurice, Klaus, and Otto Mayr, eds. *The Clockwork Universe: German Clocks and Automata, 1550–1650*. New York: Neale Watson Academic Publications, 1980.

Mayr, Otto. *Authority, Liberty, and Automatic Machinery in Early Modern Europe*. Baltimore and London: Johns Hopkins University Press, 1986.

OTTO MAYR

See also Clockwork Universe; Horology

Auzout, Adrien (1622–1691)

An early member of the Paris Academy of Sciences, Auzout was highly regarded for his skill in astronomy, mathematics, and physics and is best remembered for his work with the telescopic micrometer. A member of several scientific societies, he first joined the Mersenne Circle and the Cabinet Dupuy and later became an habitué of the Montmor group. In 1664, following an audience with Louis XIV, Auzout dedicated his *Ephemerides du comete* (1664) to the king with an open letter calling for a royal academy and construction of an observatory.

Auzout's most creative work was in concert with Christiaan Huygens (1629–1695) and Jean Picard (1620–1682) developing the crosshair (filar) micrometer eyepiece. Although he was not a systematic observer, Auzout encouraged optical over open-sight observation and was an early champion of telescopes with long focal lengths. When Isaac Newton (1642–1727) announced his new reflecting telescope, Auzout wrote expressing reservations about its durability.

Auzout was easily drawn into controversy, notably with Giuseppe Campani (1635–1715) on telescopes, Johannes Hevelius (1611–1687) on comets (1665), and Claude Perrault (1613–1688), the architect, concerning plans for the Paris Observatory. This last dispute, foreshadowed by a scathing critique of Perrault's translation of Vitruvius, somehow angered Colbert, Louis XIV's chief minister. For whatever reason, Auzout soon ceased to be an *academicien*. According to Ismaël Boulliau (1605–1694), his longtime friend had been branded *"un contradicteur et paresseux"* ("a lazy gainsayer"). Auzout left for Italy in 1668. Although he later returned to France (1676) and toured England (1683), he spent his last years in Rome (1685), where he died. Auzout published pamphlets, not books; many appear in the *Mémoires* of the Académie Royale des Sciences in Paris (Paris, 1729). Most of his letters are lost; his unpublished journals for research projects can be found in the unpublished minutes in the academy's archives.

BIBLIOGRAPHY

McKeon, Robert. "Etablissement de l'astronomie de precision et Oeuvre d'Adrien Auzout." Ph.D. diss. University of Paris, 1965.

Hetherington, Norriss S. "The Hevelius-Auzout Controversy." *Notes and Records of the Royal Society of London* 27 (1972), 103–106.

Sturdy, David J. *Science and Social Status: The Members of the Academie des Sciences, 1666–1750*. Woodbridge: Boydell, 1995.

ROBERT A. HATCH

See also Académie Royale des Sciences; Montmor Academy; Observatoire de Paris; Picard, Jean; Telescope

B

Bacon, Francis (1561–1626)

British philosopher, historian, essayist, jurist, and states-man. Born to Sir Nicholas and Lady Anne Bacon, promi-nent and learned members of the new Tudor political class, Francis was educated at Trinity College, Cam-bridge (1573–1575), and afterward at Gray's Inn (1576), where he pursued the legal studies that provided him with an income and raison d'être until he obtained the preferment that eventually carried him to the lord chan-cellorship, an office from which, charged with taking bribes, he fell in 1621. He spent his last days pursuing the philosophical and literary projects that he had been developing for more than thirty years.

The grand design unifying Bacon's writings, career in government, and efforts to reform the natural sciences was the vision of Great Britain as an efficient, central-ized, and expansionist monarchy. This design was, above all, knowledge-based. Knowledge, in Bacon's famous dictum, was power. Knowledge was for *use*, and, if unfit for use, it must be rebuilt to enable humankind to recover the losses of the Fall. In pursuit of this vision, he wrote in the early 1600s a number of short studies, the most important of which were *Temporis partus masculus* (The Masculine Birth of Time, ca. 1602) and *Valerius Terminus of the Interpretation of Nature* (ca. 1603), *Cogi-tata et visa* (Thoughts and Conclusions, ca. 1607), and *Redargutio philosophiarum* (The Refutation of Philoso-phies, ca. 1608). These and other texts were rehearsals for the large-scale texts of the *Instauratio magna* (The Great Instauration).

The *Instauratio* (1620–1626)—a colossal, unfinished (and unfinishable) six-part sequence of works—was the crowning achievement of Bacon's philosophical career.

According to the plan of the *Instauratio,* Part I was to be a survey of knowledge that would identify its deficiencies and give directions and advice for their correction. The requirements for Part I were met by the *De augmentis sci-entiarum* (On the Growth of Knowledge, 1623). The restrained language of this huge work expresses a bold and original conception of knowledge: Bacon did not construct an erudite, encyclopædic summation of exist-ing knowledge (the project of many Renaissance schol-ars) but shaped an *anti*-encyclopædia dedicated to the notion that knowledge should grow. This notion helps explain the originality of the classification of knowledge in the *De augmentis.* The classification gives unprece-dented weight to history in general and to natural history and the history of the mechanical arts in particular. The classification enshrines a revaluation of the empirical, the experimental, and the technological. True science must rest upon empirical and experimental data and data derived from mechanical arts (i.e., from technology). Technological data would help guarantee that natural philosophy would embody the idea of progress. Technol-ogy, Bacon believed, was the engine of history. History was not propelled by social struggle, economics, stellar influences, or the rise and fall of empires and religions but by technological change. Chance discoveries like the printing press, gunpowder, and the mariner's compass had changed everything, and, if chance could do that, how much greater would be the changes if technological advance could be procured *deliberately* and by rational methods. What if rational science and technology could be brought into a new relationship and so simultaneously deflect Pyrrhonist attacks on the possibility of knowl-edge and displace the sterile systems of everyone from Aristotle to Copernicus?

Courtesy Whipple Museum of the History of Science, Cambridge, England.

Bacon's proposals for realizing these ambitions appear in Part II of the *Instauratio,* which contains the celebrated two-book *Novum organum* (1620). Book I is a brilliant critique of extant philosophical systems and ways of acquiring knowledge. Its centerpiece is the Doctrine of Idols (illusions), a doctrine aimed at countervailing inherent and acquired intellectual vices. There are four kinds of idol: Idols of the Tribe, illusions generated by the innate weaknesses of the senses and understanding; Idols of the Cave, which arise from the particular circumstances of one's unique upbringing, education, and enthusiasms; Idols of the Marketplace, imposed on the mind by words; and, lastly, Idols of Theater, which spring from the dogmas of the philosophers.

Book II is an account of the new method designed to counteract the idols and generate the new sciences—though Bacon never used the word "method" (*methodus*) in this context; he preferred to speak of his new "way" (*via*) or "means" (*modus*), which proceeds by applying inductive routines to the data of natural history to yield progressively more powerful "axioms." Natural philosophy rises from physics to metaphysics, and these two

sciences are differentiated by the causes they seek. Physics deals with material and efficient causes; metaphysics, with formal and final. Here Bacon was engaged in a typical maneuver—the appropriation of Aristotelian terminology for non-Aristotelian ends. For instance, Baconian matter was not passive, abstract, pure potentiality (a view he attacked vigorously) but has its own sources of activity. Likewise, with metaphysics Bacon was really concerned with formal causes alone. Like René Descartes (1596–1650), he was no teleologist who consecrated final causes (explanations in terms of purpose or end) to God, and banished them from natural philosophy altogether. Bacon believed that physics would yield an applied knowledge called mechanics, while metaphysics, the highest grade of human knowledge, would yield magic. For Bacon, as for many Renaissance thinkers, magic signified not black magic but the ultimate legitimate power over nature.

The early part of Book II culminates in the famous trial investigation of the form of heat. The rest is devoted to a lengthy discussion of "prerogative instances" and is implicitly a reservoir of materials relating to Bacon's *speculative* philosophy (see below) and explicitly an analysis of privileged classes of data. This analysis comprises the most sophisticated treatment of the theory of experiment and, in particular, of crucial experiments written up until that time. However, the analysis is but one of the nine topics planned for Book II. If Bacon had tackled the other eight, the unfinished *Novum organum* could well have been four times longer than it is. As so often with Bacon's writings, we are left with a partial realization of a colossal program.

Part III of the *Instauratio* was reserved for natural history, but not natural history in the Renaissance tradition. Turning against the philological, antiquarian, and authority-ridden styles characteristic of earlier activity in the field, Bacon defined natural history in *functional* terms (i.e., as the foundation upon which the new sciences were to be raised). Bacon believed that the standards the new natural history would have to meet were so high that the new sciences would come into being only after generations of cooperative work conducted within a state-funded institutional framework. The instauration of philosophy could not be accomplished by any single individual. Nevertheless, fearing that his idea of natural history might be misunderstood, Bacon planned to produce six prototype natural histories, six imperfect representations of the ideal subsequent generations might achieve.

The plan was another that Bacon left unfinished. The first of the histories, the *Historia ventorum* (History of the Winds), was published in 1622; the second, the *Historia vitæ et mortis* (History of Life and Death), in 1623; and the third, *Historia densi et rari* (History of Dense and Rare), which he left incomplete, was published posthumously by his secretary, William Rawley, in 1658. The other three histories never progressed beyond their prefaces. But for all that, the natural histories are important documents. In the *Historia ventorum,* Bacon accomplished the considerable feat of making the weather boring. Here is a history without marvels or prodigies that insists on the importance of a systematic and thoroughly empirical approach to meteorology. As for the *Historia vitæ et mortis,* it was concerned with an objective—the prolongation of life—that he regarded as one of the highest his new, operative science could achieve. The work is an elaborate collection of data on factors governing durability in things animate and inanimate and mortality in living ones. And, like the *Historia densi et rari,* the *Historia vitæ* exhibits great faith in the efficacy of quantitative data in natural philosophy, a faith with which he has seldom been credited with by his critics.

Besides those mentioned above, Bacon wrote another natural history, the *Sylva sylvarum.* Published in 1626, it is quite unlike the others. Despite its Latin title (translated freely: A Storehouse of Building Materials), the work is in English and so may not have been destined for Part III of the Latin *Instauratio* at all. Moreover, unlike the Latin ones, it was not a single-subject history but a miscellany of one thousand "experiments" (Bacon here uses the word in its most multivocal Renaissance senses) arranged, often arbitrarily, into ten "centuries." A mélange of Bacon's own experiments and materials from the writings of authors ancient and modern, the *Sylva* was unquestionably his most popular scientific work up to the end of the seventeenth century. Its success can no doubt be attributed, in part, to the fact that it was published with the *New Atlantis,* Bacon's celebrated excursion into utopian fiction. This extraordinary prefiguration of a society based on *institutionalized* scientific research was perhaps the only such fiction ever to have been partly realized, as it was, almost thirty-five years after Bacon's death, with the foundation of the Royal Society of London.

With the last three parts of the *Instauratio,* the *necessary* incompleteness of Bacon's program is particularly apparent. In Part IV Bacon had intended to present worked examples of his methodological precepts in action. Part IV would enable the reader to see what investigations conducted in terms of the doctrines embodied in Parts II and III would actually look like. But apart from a few preliminary sketches written toward the end of his life, he wrote only the introduction to Part IV, the *Abecedarium novum naturae* (New ABC of Nature, ca. 1623) which tells us quite bluntly why Part IV was beyond his powers: he simply did not have data of sufficient quantity and quality to make its fulfillment a realistic possibility. Parts V and VI of the *Instauratio* met a similar fate. Part VI was reserved for the new natural philosophy itself, but it remained empty: the nature of Bacon's program was such that he knew he would not live to see its fruition. He nevertheless hoped that, once his program was implemented, materials in Part V might one day be promoted into Part VI. What then was the function of Part V?

Although Bacon wrote nothing specifically for it, Part V was for provisional theories reached not by his new method but by ordinary reasoning. These theories constituted an entire *speculative* system, organized aspects of which appear in the *De fluxu et refluxu maris* (Ebb and Flow of the Sea, ca. 1611) and *Thema coeli* (Theory of the Heavens, ca. 1612). Eclectic to a fault, Bacon raided disparate traditions to fashion a hybrid that embodied peculiar alliances of ideas developed in response to philosophies ancient and modern. The system was, in effect, an emulative meditation on atomism, Aristotelianism, Copernicanism, Galileo Galilei's (1564–1642) discoveries, the writings of Paracelsus (ca. 1491–1541), William Gilbert (1544–1603), Bernardino Telesio (1509–1588), Francesco Patrizi (1529–1597), and many others besides.

This system represented the universe as a finite, geocentric plenum. The earth consisted of passive, *tangible* matter; the rest of the universe contained active *pneumatic,* or spirit, matter. The earth's pure tangible insides were surrounded by a crust that belonged to the frontier zone between the interior and the pure pneumatic heavens. This zone reached some miles into the crust and some into air. Only here did pneumatic matter mix with tangible, and from this mixture many terrestrial phenomena originated.

Pneumatics mixed with tangible matter were "attached spirits" and distinct from the "free spirits" outside tangible bodies. There are four kinds of free spirit. Two, air and terrestrial fire, were sublunary; the

TABLE 1. The Two Quaternions

	SULFUR QUATERNION	MERCURY QUATERNION
TANGIBLE SUBSTANCES (WITH ATTACHED SPIRITS)	Sulfur (subterranean)	Mercury (subterranean)
	Oil and oily inflammable substances (terrestrial)	Water and "crude" noninflammable substances (terrestrial)
PNEUMATIC SUBSTANCES	Terrestrial fire (sublunary)	Air (sublunary)
	Sidereal fire (planets)	Ether (medium of the planets)

other two, ether and sidereal fire, were celestial. Ether, the medium in which the planets (globular aggregations of sidereal fire) moved around the central earth, was a tenuous kind of air; both air and ether belonged to a family—the *mercury quaternion*—that also included watery bodies and mercury (see Table 1).

Terrestrial fire was a feeble version of sidereal fire, and both of these join with oily substances and sulfur in the *sulfur quaternion*. The quaternions expressed antithetical qualities, so air and ether warred upon their opposite numbers, fire and sidereal fire. The issue of the struggle depended on distance from the Earth: air and ether became progressively weaker as terrestrial and sidereal fire grew stronger.

Bacon used the quaternion theory (which owed much to Renaissance pneumatology and Paracelsian thought) to develop a view of planetary motion that estranged him from the major systems of his day: the diurnal motion, driven by sympathy, carried the heavens westward about the earth. Where sidereal fire was powerful the motion was swift, so the stars completed a revolution in exactly twenty-four hours. But sidereal fire became weaker nearer to the earth, so that a lower planet moved more slowly and erratically than a higher. This consensual motion was not confined to the heavens. Aiming at a unified physics, Bacon extended the explanatory powers of the quaternions to wind, tide, and verticity; this brought him into conflict with William Gilbert's philosophy and Galileo's theory of the tides. The conflict was inevitable; Gilbert and Galileo thought the earth moved, Bacon did not.

Bacon's system had two interlocking departments: one comprised the cosmological phenomena summarized above; the other embraced terrestrial things. The second was logically dependent on the first, for explanations applied to the terrestrial domain were integrated with, but subordinated to, those deployed in the cosmological. The latter were dominated by the quaternion theory; the former, by explanations framed in terms of *intermediates*. These combined the qualities of members of one quaternion with those of their counterparts in the other (see Table 2).

Each quaternion had four members, so there were four types of intermediate. From a theoretical point of view, the principal intermediates were the fire-air intermediates, the "attached" animate and inanimate spirits. Inanimate spirits were incarcerated in all tangible bodies, including living ones; animate spirits were found in living bodies alone. Bacon's matter theory thus comprised twelve major categories: the eight substances of the quaternions and the four classes of intermediate. These categories constituted a framework for interpreting all natural phenomena, including terrestrial phenomena as diverse as spontaneous generation, projectile motion, plant growth, and the workings of the nervous system.

This provisional system is important not least because it reminds us that, for all of his apparent modernity, the architect of the great instauration thought in ways remote from our own.

BIBLIOGRAPHY

Bacon, Francis. *Letters and Life of Francis Bacon.* Ed. James Spedding. 7 vols. London: Longman, 1861–1874.

B

TABLE 2. Bacon's Theory of Matter

	SULFUR QUATERNION	INTERMEDIATES	MERCURY QUATERNION
TANGIBLE SUBSTANCES (WITH ATTACHED SPIRITS)	Sulfur (subterranean)	Salts (subterranean and inorganic beings)	Mercury (subterranean)
	Oil and oily inflammable substances (terrestrial)	Juices of animals and plants	Water and "crude" noninflammable substances (terrestrial)
PNEUMATIC SUBSTANCES	Terrestrial fire (sublunary)	Attached animate and inanimate spirits (in tangible bodies)	Air (sublunary)
	Sidereal fire (planets)	Heaven of the fixed stars	Ether (medium of the planets)

———. *Philosophical Studies, c.1611–c.1619.* Ed. Graham Rees, Oxford: Clarendon, 1996.

Jardine, Lisa. *Francis Bacon: Discovery and the Art of Discourse.* London and New York: Cambridge University Press, 1974.

Martin, Julian. *Francis Bacon, the State, and the Reform of Natural Philosophy.* Cambridge and New York: Cambridge University Press, 1992.

Peltonen, Markku, ed. *The Cambridge Companion to Francis Bacon.* London and New York: Cambridge University Press, 1996.

Pérez-Ramos, Antonio. *Francis Bacon's Idea of Science and the Maker's Knowledge Tradition.* Oxford: Clarendon, 1988.

Quinton, Antony. *Francis Bacon.* Oxford: Oxford University Press, 1980.

Sessions, William A. "Recent Studies in Francis Bacon." *English Literary Renaissance* 17 (1987), 351–371.

GRAHAM REES

See also Baconianism; Empiricism; Histories of Trades

Baconianism

There is no such thing. The term is a reification denoting the alleged "influence" of Francis Bacon (1561–1626) on the turbulent intellectual cultures of seventeenth-century Europe. It is seldom a good idea to speak of "influences" and never a good idea to speak of Baconianism in the singular. Rather, there were *Baconianisms,* though probably never quite as many as there were people who took the lord chancellor's name in vain. During the seventeenth century, Bacon's words were on everyone's lips, though not always fixed in their understandings. His writings were invoked by all sorts and conditions of individuals: virtuosi on the make, provincial projectors, improving colonialists, millenarian visionaries, Royalists and radicals, Anglicans and Puritans, Calvinists and Latitudinarians, educational and social reformers, promoters of the New Science and defenders of the Old Erudition. The celebrities of the Royal Society were seemingly as keen to associate themselves with Bacon's program as was the host of lesser figures who, as self-interest or philanthropy prompted, flocked to the noble but amorphous banner of the Experimental Philosophy.

That may, at any rate, have been the case in Great Britain from the early 1640s onward. But it is possible (though not certain) that, before then, Bacon's reputation stood higher on the European continent than in his native land and that various brands of Baconianism were subsequently reimported to mix with, reinforce, and shape emergent homegrown Baconianisms that came to the fore during the protracted crises of the Interregnum. In France, and the Low Countries, for instance, Bacon's name was well known from the early 1620s. In France, Pierre Gassendi (1592–1655) and Marin Mersenne (1588–1648) were among Bacon's earliest admirers and critics. The Dupuy brothers, Pierre (1582–1651) and Jacques (1586–1656), librarians to the king of France, were instrumental in preserving manuscripts stolen from Bacon by Philippe Fortin de la Hoguette (1585–ca. 1668). Hoguette's copy of Bacon's 1623 *De augmentis scientiarum* (On the Growth of Knowledge), hot off the press, was broken up by N-C. Fabri de Peiresc (1580–1637) to provide copy for the 1624 Paris edition of the work. Peiresc and members of his circle had evidently been longing for this publication: it would at last give them access to Bacon's compelling survey of the intellectual globe, a survey now rescued from the provincial obscurity of the English language (i.e., *The Advancement of Learning,* 1605) and released into the big, wide world of Latin erudition. In the Netherlands, Constantijn Huygens (1596–1687) and Isaac Beeckman (1588–1637) were among Bacon's earliest and most prominent readers. Huygens had actually met Bacon; he disliked the man but admired his philosophy. As early as 1621, he solicited Daniel Heinsius's opinion of the *Instauratio magna* (The Great Instauration); by the end of the decade, he was being pestered by Jan Brosterhuysen (1596–1650) for a copy of the *Sylva sylvarum* (1626). Between 1623 and 1628, Beeckman wrote copious notes on Bacon's philosophy and, in particular, on the experiments of the *Sylva*. In this, Beeckman was one of the first commentators on what was to become by far Bacon's most popular work in the seventeenth century, a work later translated into Latin (1648) by another Dutchman, Jacob Gruter (1614–1652), whose brother Isaac (1610–1680) not long afterward published a number of important Bacon manuscripts that he had inherited from the British diplomat Sir William Boswell (ca. 1580–ca. 1650).

But among the propagators of Bacon's fame in England, the most important came not from western but from central Europe. Notable here are Jan Amos Comenius (1592–1670), pansophist and educational theorist; John Dury (1596–1680), preacher of ecclesiastical reconciliation; and, above all, Samuel Hartlib (ca. 1600–1662), whose indefatigable activity has come to occupy the center ground of our understanding of his age. Hartlib, with all of his shallow originality and insatiable curiosity, stood at the focus of Protestant and, particularly, Calvinist thinking about education, science, philosophy, colonialism, and economic affairs during the Interregnum. He was a promoter of the mercantilist-imperialist Baconianism also canvassed by his friend Benjamin Worsley (1618–1677) and practiced with mixed results by the Irish Protestants and their apologists. He tirelessly promoted schemes for institutionalizing the production and exchange of scientific and technological information, schemes with Baconian roots, schemes that aligned Hartlib with individuals who were to become founder

members of Royal Society. He espoused an eclectic approach to epistemological questions, an approach that was broadly Baconian in some of its essentials and had much in common with the natural-historical Baconianism developed by Ralph Austen (d. 1676), John Evelyn (1620–1706), William Petty (1623–1687), and John Graunt (1620–1674) and (later) by Robert Hooke (1635–1702), Robert Plot (1640–1696), and others too numerous to mention.

Hartlib promoted the various manifestations of his eclectic brand of Baconianism during the unprecedented intellectual ferment that marked the Interregnum and, with it, the collapse of official censorship. In that period, Bacon's writings were more than ripe for selective appropriation, for they offered an ideology of remarkable consistency and force, yet one that (like all good ideologies) could be adopted flexibly and piecemeal. From Robert Boyle (1627–1691) and Thomas Vaughan (1622–1666) to John Beale (ca. 1613–1682) and John Wilkins (1614–1672), an alphabet of notabilities pressed Bacon's name into the service of many causes, not all of which were in mutual harmony. People from quite different political and religious positions felt that Bacon belonged to them. For instance, John Webster (1610–1682), the chemist and metallurgist, enlisted Bacon in the struggle for university reform, while Webster's opponent, Seth Ward (1617–1689), tried to capture the Great Instaurator for the status quo. The Webster-Ward controversy is but one sign of the remarkable plurality of Commonwealth Baconianisms, a plurality that stands in contrast to the would-be "official" Restoration Baconianisms to be seen in the writings of Thomas Sprat (1635–1713), Boyle, Hooke, and later still in the work of Isaac Newton's (1642–1727) popularizers.

The sheer range of seventeenth-century Baconianisms makes them difficult to generalize about—especially so for historians who believe that it is risky to talk about Bacon's *influence* (talk that implies an unnatural passivity on the part of the influenced) but proper to talk of *responses* to Bacon (talk that implies difference, debate, and differential absorption on the part of the responders). What Bacon meant to seventeenth-century writers was almost as various as the writers themselves. However, one can say that, with differences of emphasis and application, Bacon's appropriators claimed to be in favor of some or all of the following: *negotium* (employment, activity) rather than *otium* (leisure); an experimental, natural-historical, and broadly inductive approach to the natural sciences; the institutionalization of science and of the means of gathering, collating, and communicating knowledge; planned, cooperative research; rational "utilitaria" and technological solutions to social problems (not least if there was money in it). Likewise, they claimed to be opposed to some or all of these: useless erudition, premature system building, metaphysical speculation, superstition, theological controversy, undue reliance on unaided reason, Aristotelianism, and anything that smacked of Scholasticism.

One of the principal elements of Bacon's philosophy appropriated by seventeenth-century authors was the natural-historical program. Once again, responses to this program were protean. There was, for instance, a widespread "demotic" appeal to Bacon's name. His writings were used to legitimize the "democratization" of seventeenth-century English natural philosophy (i.e., the growing belief that anyone with a barometer and a passion for mere data could get in on the act as far as the New Philosophy was concerned and that anyone, however unlettered, might make what could be represented as a serious contribution to the sciences). The natural-historical program also proved to be a rich source of arguments and examples to individuals who moved in more exalted circles. This may be seen in (1) the "statistical" Baconianism of Graunt and Petty (inspired by Bacon's *Historia vitæ et mortis* [History of Life and Death, 1623]); (2) the economic and topographical Baconianism of Arnold (ca. 1600–ca. 1653) and Gerard Boate (1604–1650), Joshua Childrey (1623–1670), Petty, and Plot; (3) the highly developed, critical experimentalism and methodological thought of Boyle and Hooke; and (4) the collective and "official" labors of the Royal Society in its early years.

Prominent among these last were Sprat's *History of the Royal Society* (1667) and the History of the Trades project. The former, often and perhaps wrongly taken for a statement of the official ideology of the Royal Society, echoed Bacon at every turn. In fact, it may be that Sprat, in his search for a comprehensive justification of the New Philosophy, failed properly to address the complexities of the contemporary situation and so, in his selection of examples of the society's work, presented an uncontentious picture that played down the role of hypothesis and exaggerated Baconian accumulation of natural-historical data. As for the History of the Trades, it was a quintessentially Baconian project, embodying the conviction that technology was crucial to natural his-

tory and the key to social progress. Yet, the project's achievements were destined to fall short of its aspirations. It turned out to be very difficult to accumulate technological data, to derive genuine improvements from the energy invested, and so to capture the enthusiasm of members in the last two decades of the century. Among scientific intellectuals, this aspect of Bacon's program had to wait for its apotheosis until the eighteenth century and the revolution represented by the French Encyclopaedia. But that is another story.

BIBLIOGRAPHY

Greengrass, Mark, Michael Leslie, and Timothy Raylor, eds. *Samuel Hartlib & Universal Reformation: Studies in Intellectual Communication*. Cambridge: Cambridge University Press, 1994.

Hunter, Michael. *Science and Society in Restoration England*. Cambridge: Cambridge University Press, 1981.

Kroll, R., R. Ashcraft, and Perez Zagorin, eds. *Philosophy, Science, and Religion in England, 1640–1700*. Cambridge: Cambridge University Press, 1992.

Le Doeuff, Michèle. M. "Bacon chez les grands au siècle de Louis XIII." In *Francis Bacon: terminologia e fortuna nel XVII secolo,* ed. Marta Fattori. Rome: Edizioni dell'Ateneo, 1984, pp. 155–178.

Webster, Charles. *The Great Instauration: Science, Medicine, and Reform, 1626–1660*. London: Duckworth, 1975.

GRAHAM REES

See also Bacon, Francis; Empiricism; Experience and Experiment; Gassendi, Pierre; Histories of Trades; Mersennen, Marin; Royal Society of London

Baliani, Giovanni Battista (1582–1666)

Trained as a lawyer, he did important work in physics, though he spent most of his life in public service. While in charge of the fortress at Savona in 1611, he noted that cannon balls of varying weights fall at the same speed. Informed of Galileo Galilei's (1564–1642) interest in this subject, in 1614 he opened a correspondence with him that lasted many years. His publications include a treatise on the natural motion of heavy bodies, published in 1638, in which he discussed free fall, the pendulum, and motion on inclined planes. He expanded this work in 1646 to discuss the cause of acceleration in falling bodies, which he attributed to a building up of impetus during the fall, and to include the motion of liquids. There is evidence that Baliani actually performed the "ship's mast" experiment, in which a weight dropped from the top of the mast of a moving ship lands at the foot of the mast rather than toward the rear of the vessel.

Baliani also had correspondence with Marin Mersenne (1588–1648) over the barometer and was the first to explain the operation of the siphon in terms of the "ocean of air" (*il pelago d'aria*), or atmospheric pressure. He favored the Tychonian system of the world over that of Nicolaus Copernicus (1473–1543) and though that the earth's motion might be the cause of the tides. In 1647 he composed a work on the plague and the way it was propagated; in this, he anticipated ideas later expounded by Thomas Malthus (1766–1834). Baliani's previously unpublished writings were printed in the year of his death and then reissued in 1792, along with a brief biography by an unnamed author. His correspondence with Galileo, which was intermittent, is found in the National Edition of Galileo's works, volumes 12–18; that with Mersenne (to 1640), in *Correspondance de P. Marin Mersenne* (1945–1965).

BIBLIOGRAPHY

Arrioto, Piero E. "From the Top to the Foot of the Mast of a Moving Ship." *Annals of Science* 28 (1972), 191–203.

Moscovici, Serge. "Les développements historique de la théorie galiléenne des marées." *Revue d'histoire des sciences et de leurs applications* 18 (1965), 193–220.

Natucci, Apinolo. "Giovan Battista Baliani letterato e scienzato del secolo XVII." *Archives internationales d'histoire des sciences* 12 (1959), 267–283.

Nonnoi, Giancarlo. *Il pelago d'aria: Galileo, Baliani, Beeckman.* Rome: Bulzoni, 1988.

WILLIAM A. WALLACE

See also Galilei, Galileo; Geoheliocentrism; Motion; Pneumatics; Tides

Ballistics and Gunnery

The theoretical study of motion, relevant to exterior ballistics, predated the introduction of gunpowder in the West in the fourteenth century and was linked to arrows and other projectiles. Aristotle's (384–322 B.C.E.) views on dynamics reappeared in Europe during the revival of learning in the twelfth century and, although increasingly criticized, were still held in the sixteenth century and for much of the seventeenth. The idea of impetus, however, associated with Jean Buridan had an enduring effect, as did kinematical views from Gerard of Brussels (early thirteenth century) to the fourteenth-century Merton school at Oxford, which clarified the notions of uniform velocity and accelerations, allowing the use of numerical results.

This background was made widely available in the early sixteenth century by Alvaro Tomas (fl. 1509). Leonardo da Vinci (1452–1519) showed a knowledge of the medieval background and attempted to unite theory and practice, but the mathematicians were far from successful in this. Niccolò Tartaglia's (ca. 1499–1557) result in 1537 that maximum range on level ground is obtained by a firing elevation of 45° was questionable in practice, whatever its application in the vacuum, against which many earlier writers had advanced strong arguments. However, the sighting and surveying instruments he suggested became increasingly important. This tradition was continued by several persons in the sixteenth and early seventeenth centuries but with sometimes exaggerated accuracy of detail.

The construction, charge, and shot of both large and small pieces was essentially a practical trade, with numerous practitioners vying for suppport and markets. Cannons appear just after 1300, mainly for use against city and castle walls; thereafter, progress in firearms and powder mills was rapid, with numerous developments, including the matchlock ca. 1450 and rifling near the end of the next century. Accounts of individual battles and sieges show the varied tactics used aginst footsoldiers and cavalry. By 1500, castles were no longer safe (even

The gunners are using a sighting device and a quadrant to gauge the proper elevation for the cannon. From Johannes Stöffler, Der . . . mathematischen und mechanischen Künst (1541).

Constantinople had fallen in 1453), and soon cannon were used in the open field. The arquebus challenged the supremacy of the pike, and musketeers could hold defensive positions by 1522. Actions at sea involved cannon shot aimed at timber, men, or sails, either directly or indirectly off the water and sometimes at point blank range.

The first century of printing led to great developments in mathematics, and these bore fruit in ballistics early in the seventeenth century. Developing François Viète's (1540–1603) algebraic methods, Thomas Harriot (ca. 1560–1621) compounded constant velocities and accelerations to demonstrate the parabolic orbit in a vacuum, and, allowing the motion (either horizontally or obliquely) to vary as certain arithmetic sequences, he obtained the tilted ballistic parabolas and their ranges. This has been described by Johannes Lohne (1979) as the emergence of ballistics as a science, had Harriot published; it was rediscovered by James Gregory (1638–1675) in 1672. The basic parabolic orbit, however, was first published by Bonaventura Cavalieri (1598–1647) in 1632. Galileo Galilei's (1564–1642) results on such trajectories did not appear until 1638, together with tables of height attained and ranges. Air resistance, particularly at higher velocities, vitiated such work from the practical point of view. A little later, in 1644, Evangelista Torricelli (1608–1647) discovered the enveloping paraboloid of safety, outside which no shot of given initial speed may penetrate, whatever its inclination. Internal points can be attined by either a high-angle shot (howitzer was the later name given it in 1695), or a low-angle shot. Torricelli, too, gave tables relating inclination and range and, like Galileo, wrote (in part, at least) in Italian rather than Latin for the practical user.

Harriot's arithmetic sequences summed to squares, but it was Christiaan Huygens (1629–1695) who, having suggested in 1668 and earlier that air resistance varied directly with velocity, next asserted in 1669 that the square of the velocity gave a better account. This work was published in 1690. Just before this, Isaac Newton (1642–1727) transformed the subject by adopting the linear inertia of René Descartes (1596–1650) and allying it openly with the recent infinitesimal methods and less openly with his own fluxions. His second law is stated not in terms of acceleration, but of changes in motion (the old impetus, in a sense), as is made clear in his *Principia mathematica philosophiae naturalis* (Mathematical Principles of Natural Philosophy, 1687).

Newton dealt with linear motion as a limiting case of motion in a conic section and solved many problems of resisting motion depending on the velocity, including that of a particle in a descending spiral (reentrant satellite, as we may think). He argued for the squared resistance and the importance of such resistance and elasticity of the air. These became increasingly recognized after further contributions by Gottfried Wilhelm Leibniz (1646–1716) and Johann Bernoulli (1667–1748).

BIBLIOGRAPHY

Cipolla, Carlo M. *European Culture and Overseas Expansion.* London: Penguin, 1970, pp. 29–109.

Hall, A. Rupert. "Gunnery, Science, and the Royal Society." In *The Uses of Science in the Age of Newton,* ed. John Burke. Berkeley and Los Angeles: University of California Press, 1983, pp. 111–141.

———. "Military Technology." In *A History of Technology.* Ed. Charles Singer. 5 vols. Oxford: Oxford University Press, 1957, vol. 3, pp. 347–376.

Lohne, Johannes A. "Harriot Studies II: Ballistic Parabolae." *Archive for History of Exact Sciences* 20 (1979), 230–264.

JON V. PEPPER

See also Fortification; Torricelli, Evangelista

Barometer

In two letters of June 11 and 28, 1644, Evangelista Torricelli (1608–1647) reported to Michelangelo Ricci on certain experiments he had performed "not simply to produce a vacuum, but to make an instrument which would show the changes in the air, which is at times heavier and thicker and at times lighter and more rarefied." One experiment consisted of filling with quicksilver several glass tubes of different diameter but with the same height of two cubits, inverting them into a basin also containing quicksilver, and letting the quicksilver fall down into the basin. The tubes "remained always filled to the height of a cubit and a quarter and an inch besides." Another experiment consisted of filling the basin with water and slowly raising the vessel. "One could see the quicksilver fall from the neck, whereupon with a violent impetus the vessel was filled with water completely."

As a result, Torricelli maintained that the vacuum "can be produced without effort and without resistance on he part of Nature"; that "we live submerged at the bottom of an ocean of the element air, which by unquestioned experiments is known to have weight"; and that "the cause for the resistance which is felt when one needs to produce a vacuum . . . is the weight of the air."

Although Torricelli's instrument is a barometer—as it was later called by Robert Boyle (1627–1691)—the question of whether it was first invented by Torricelli raises historical and philosophical puzzles. If the barometer is to *measure* the weight of the air, then Torricelli's tube was no such instrument because it had no scale. If the barometer is to *confirm* the theory of the atmospheric pressure and the vacuum, then Torricelli was anticipated by Isaac Beeckman (1588–1637), Giovanni Battista Baliani (1582–1666), and (although this is still disputed) Gasparo Berti (ca. 1600–1643). And if the barometer is to measure the change of the atmospheric pressure, then Torricelli's tube was a failure because he admits that his "principal intention . . . has not been fulfilled." In the end, what Torricelli can be credited with is assembling the relevant hydrostatic concepts, performing simple experiments, making a manageable instrument, and providing a heuristics for further research.

This research was pursued in France and England, not in Italy, where, afraid of another possible case (vacuum was associated with atomism and atheism), the young followers of Galileo Galilei (1564–1642) kept Torricelli's experiments almost secret until 1663. When further experimental results were obtained by others, they confirmed Torricelli's insight. In his second letter to Ricci, he had anticipated that, "if the air were infinitely rarefied—that is, a vacuum—then the metal would descend entirely." At the end of the seventeenth century, these bold predictions had become ordinary facts.

BIBLIOGRAPHY

Cioffari, V., trans. "Torricelli's Letters to M. Ricci." In *The Physical Treatises of Pascal*. Trans. I. H. B. Spiers and A. G. H. Spiers, with Introduction and Notes by F. Barry. New York: Columbia University Press, 1937.

De Waard, Cornelis. *L'expérience barométrique: Ses antécedents et ses explications*. Thouars: J. Gamon, 1936.

Middleton, W. E. Knowles. *The History of the Barometer*. Baltimore: Johns Hopkins University Press, 1971.

Webster, Charles. "The Discovery of Boyle's Law, and the Concept of the Elasticity of the Air in the Seventeenth Century." *Archive for History of Exact Sciences* 2 (1965), 441–502.

MARCELLO PERA

See also Boyle, Robert; Pascal, Blaise; Pneumatics; Torricelli, Evangelista; Viviani, Vincenzo

Barrow, Isaac (1630–1677)

Wrote on optics (1669) and published editions of Euclid, Apollonius, Archimedes, and Theodosius. His forceful sermons and tracts occupy nine volumes in an edition published in 1859. A leading scholar and Royalist, Barrow graduated B.A. (1648) and M.A. (1652) from Trinity College, Cambridge. Elected Fellow in 1649, by 1655, during the Commonwealth, he was persuaded to leave Cambridge to go on his travels, which took him through Europe to Turkey. Returning in 1659, at the Restoration of the Monarchy (1660), he obtained the chair in Greek, which he had earlier been denied. In 1662 he added the Gresham Chair of Geometry (London) and Fellowship of the new Royal Society. In 1663 he became the first holder of the new Lucasian Chair of Mathematics at Cambridge, but he resigned it in 1669 in favor of Isaac Newton (who, although not his pupil, was often his protégé) to become royal chaplain in London. The king mandated his D.D. (1670) and appointed him Master of Trinity College in 1673. Himself the nephew of a bishop, Barrow probably expected similar elevation, but he died suddenly, seemingly of a medicinal overdose.

Isaac Barrow. Courtesy Whipple Museum of the History of Science, Cambridge, England.

While Barrow's *Lectiones geometricae* (1670) and *Lectiones mathematicae* (1683) are the works of an able mathematician, who had absorbed much of the precalculus writings on tangents, quadrature, and rectification from René Descartes (1596–1650) to Christiaan Huygens (1629–1695) and especially James Gregory (1638–1675), modern claims for their originality and importance are exaggerated; they are more the culmination of earlier geometrical investigations.

Barrow opposed the trend to algebraic formulations, which he thought more suitable to logic than mathematics. His backward-looking geometrical approach brought out neither the algorithmic nature of the calculus nor the potential importance of his many interesting but disconnected results, which had little effect on the calculus of Isaac Newton (1642–1727) or Gottfried Wilhelm Leibniz (1646–1716).

BIBLIOGRAPHY

Baron, Margaret E. *The Origins of the Infinitesimal Calculus.* Oxford and New York: Pergamon, 1969.

Feingold, Mordechai, ed. *Before Newton: The Life and Times of Isaac Barrow.* Cambridge: Cambridge University Press, 1990.

———. "Newton, Leibniz, and Barrow, Too: An Attempt at a Reinterpretation." *Isis* 84 (1993), 310–338.

JON V. PEPPER

See also Analytic Geometry; Gregory, James

Bartholin, Erasmus (1625–1698)

Best known for his study of the refraction of light in Iceland spar, which he published in *Experimenta crystalli Islandici* (1669), he was professor of mathematics and medicine at the University of Copenhagen. He had matriculated in Leiden in 1646 and traveled in France, Italy, and England before he returned to Copenhagen in 1656. He was well versed in mathematics and collaborated in publishing editions of works of René Descartes (1596–1650), Frans van Schooten (ca. 1615–1660), and Florimond de Beaune (1601–1652). In Copenhagen he published for many years a *Dissertatio de problematibus geometricis,* containing mathematical problems to be studied by his students.

Bartholin presented Iceland spar as an interesting curiosity, the strange refractional properties of which he tried to integrate into contemporary optics. The "diop-

tric rarity" of the crystal is twofold. In the first place, objects seen through the crystal appear double. In the second place, the secondary image moves about when the crystal is rotated, which means that light rays are not refracted according to the sine law of refraction. To account for this extraordinary refraction, Bartholin retained the geometrical structure of the sine law. According to the sine law, there is a constant ratio between the sines of the angle of incidence and the angle of refraction. The angles are measured with respect to the perpendicular to the surface. Bartholin stated that, for extraordinary refraction, the sine law holds if the angles are measured with respect to the line parallel to the edge of the crystal. He had investigated this experimentally. In his sketchy explanation of both the duplicate refraction and the extraordinary character of the secondary refraction, Bartholin drew upon the Cartesian theory of light. He supposed that the crystal has "pores" running parallel to the faces of the crystal, in addition to the pores also found in glass and water. *Experimenta crystalli Islandici* received much attention from scholars. Jean Picard (1620–1682) brought the book, along with some specimens of the crystal, to Paris soon after its publication. There Christiaan Huygens (1629–1695) studied it and refuted Bartholin's account of extraordinary refraction. Huygens's own explanation of it would be the foundation of his theory of light in *Traité de la lumière* (1695).

BIBLIOGRAPHY

Buchwald, Jed Z., and Kurt Møller Pedersen. "Bartholin, His Discovery, and Its Significance." In Erasmus Bartholin, *Experiments on Birefringent Icelandic Crystal.* Trans. Th. Archibald. Copenhagen: Danish National Library of Science and Medicine, 1991.

Lohne, J. A. "Nova experimenta crystalli Islandici disdiaclastici." *Centaurus* 21 (1977), 106–148.

FOKKO J. DIJKSTERHUIS

See also Optics; Refraction; Schooten, Frans van; Snel (Snellius or Snel van Royen), Willebrord

Bartholin, Thomas (1616–1680)

A famous Danish physician and skilled anatomist, Bartholin is best known as the physician most responsible for circulating throughout the European medical community the numerous anatomical discoveries and experiments of the sixteenth and seventeenth centuries. The

B

vehicles by which Bartholin accomplished this were his professional correspondence with an astonishing array of Continental, English, and Scandinavian physicians and his textbook, *Bartholinus' Anatomy* (1641, with numerous subsequent editions). Ten years' study at the best medical schools in Italy and the Low Countries and extensive travel in his formative years made Bartholin well qualified to do this. Upon his return to his native country in 1646, Bartholin kept in close contact with the many physicians whom he had met during his earlier years. His textbook, while officially a reedition of a work of his father, Caspar Bartholin (1585–1629), went through numerous editions and was popular throughout Europe. By inserting in parentheses medical novelties and experiments that had surfaced since his father's death, Thomas Bartholin was able continually to revise and update his father's and his own work. By citing the works of others, he carefully avoided refuting his father, although his sympathies clearly lay with the moderns. Not vituperative or combative, he often sought a compromise reading of medical disputes. Hence, for example, he endorsed William Harvey's (1578–1657) circulation of the blood but noted the reservations of certain others, including René Descartes (1596–1650) and Johannes Walaeus (1604–1649).

Appointed dean of the medical faculty at the University of Copenhagen in 1656 and physician in charge of supervising apothecaries and midwives in the kingdom of Denmark in 1658, Bartholin was also directly involved with medicine in his homeland. Tightly allied to the monarchy, he helped defend the state policy of promoting native medicaments over exotic medicinal ingredients. As a prolific author on a host of medical subjects, Bartholin represents well the state of learned medicine in seventeenth-century Europe. As a spokesman for the New Anatomy, he also made significant discoveries related to the human lymphatic system, which earned him the enmity of committed Galenists.

BIBLIOGRAPHY

French, Roger. *William Harvey's Natural Philosophy*. Cambridge: Cambridge University Press, 1995, pp. 152–168.
Schioldann-Nielsen, Johan, and Kurt Sørensen, eds. "Introduction." In Thomas Bartholin, *On Diseases in the Bible: A Medical Miscellany 1672*. Trans. James Willis (Acta Historica Scientiarum Naturalium et Medicinalium 41) Copenhagen: Danish National Library of Medicine, 1994, pp. 8–23.

MARTHA BALDWIN

See also Anatomy; Galenism; Medicine; Pharmacy

Basso, Sebastian (fl. 1560–1625)

A French physician and natural philosopher, noted for his opposition to Aristotle, although educated by Jesuits, Basso was born in Lorraine and spent time in Rome and Lausanne. After converting to Protestantism, he taught at the Huguenot academy at Die-en-Dauphiné (1611–1625), composed at least one tragedy (*De virginia*—now lost), and served as tutor to the Protestant nobleman Charles Tonard (1601–1670). In 1621 his *Philosophiae naturalis adversus Aristotelem, libri XII* (Twelve Books of Natural Philosophy Against Aristotle) appeared at Geneva.

Basso's critique of Aristotle (384–322 B.C.E.) combines Epicurean and Stoic ideas. The smallest particles of the conventional elements fire, air, earth, and water are atoms. A definite number of atoms appeared at the Creation of the world. They are permanent existents and cannot be further divided. But, unlike the classical atomists, Basso rejects vacua. The space between atoms is filled by a universal fluid identified with the Stoic pneuma and responsible for all physical change. God, in turn, directs the pneuma. Although he continues to regard the earth as the center of the cosmos, Basso rejects Aristotle's distinction between the heavens and the earth. He abandons the spheres that support the planets in Aristotle's account for a fluid heaven filled with the element fire. Unlike the Stoics, he does not regard the planets as capable of moving themselves but offers a mechanical account of planetary motion. Each planet is supplied with "innumerable windows" leading from the surface into a hollow interior. As different shutters open and close, the celestial fire rushes into the planet, propelling it in different directions. His critique of Aristotle is frequently cited by later writers, including Isaac Beeckman (1588–1637), René Descartes (1596–1650), and Marin Mersenne (1588–1648).

BIBLIOGRAPHY

Ariew, Roger. "Descartes, Basso, and Toletus: Three Kinds of Corpuscularions." In *Descartes and the Last Scholastics*. Ithica, NY: Cornell University Press, 1999, ch. 6, 123–139.
Lüthy, C. H. "Thoughts and Circumstances of Sébastien Basson: Analysis, Micro-History, Questions." *Early Science and Medicine* 2 (1997), 1–73.
Nielsen, Lauge Olaf. "A Seventeenth Century Physician on God and Atoms: Sebastian Basso." In *Meaning and Inference in Medieval Philosophy*, ed. Norman Kretzmann. Boston: Kluwer, 1988, pp. 297–369.

PETER BARKER

See also Atomism; Epicureanism; Pneuma; Stoicism

Bauhin, Gaspard (1560–1624) and Jean (1541–1613)

The Bauhin brothers—the sons of a French physician and his French wife who had fled religious persecution in the Lowlands to settle in Basel ca. 1540—represent two generations of the Scientific Revolution. In their careers and contributions to botany in particular, Jean and Gaspard Bauhin epitomize the effect of humanist educational reforms, the impact of printing on science and medicine, and the international character of scientific communication in early-modern Europe.

Jean Bauhin studied classical languages and medicine with his father and other Basel humanists before making the grand tour of European medical schools. In the 1560s, he studied, corresponded, and exchanged plants with, among others, Guillaume Rondelet (1507–1566) in Montpellier, Leonhart Fuchs (1501–1566) in Tübingen, Conrad Gessner (1516–1565) in Zurich, and Ulisse Aldrovandi (1522–1605) in Italy. In Count Frederick of Württemburg, Jean Bauhin found a patron who encouraged his investigations of botany, horticulture, balneology, and entomology.

Like others in his generation, Jean Bauhin directed his efforts to purging dangerous errors from the classical botanical texts and producing large illustrated herbals. He was one of the anonymous coauthors (with Jacques Daléchamps [1513–1588] of Lyon) of the huge, error-filled (but afterward corrected by Gaspard Bauhin) herbal known as *Historia generalis plantarum* (1586–1587). His little book *De plantis a divis sanctisve nomen habentibus* (1591) reflects both his Protestant and his humanist beliefs in its attack on the use of the names of saints for plants. Bauhin's *Historia plantarum universalis* (1650–1651), which described more than four thousand plants, including many new species, was not published until long after his death.

Gaspard Bauhin's interests in botany and anatomy were stirred by his family's example and the rich heritage of Basel medical and scientific publishing. His own tour of Italy and France (1577–1581) established lasting ties with botanists throughout Europe, who sent him plants they had received from the New World and Asia. At the University of Basel, Bauhin was appointed the first professor of anatomy and botany; under Bauhin and Felix Platter, the Basel medical school attracted students from all parts of Europe.

At the age of nineteen, during a private dissection, Gaspard Bauhin deduced and then demonstrated the existence of the ileo-caecal valve (*Valvula Bauhini*). Andreas Vesalius (1514–1564) served as the model for his teaching and textbooks. Bauhin shows respect for Galen (second century C.E.) but notes that Galen never dissected a human body. The authority of Bauhin's *Theatrum anatomicum* (1605) is suggested by William Harvey's (1578–1657) many citations.

Gaspard Bauhin's seven botanical books include revisions of three widely used sixteenth-century herbals and four original works. He also projected an illustrated encyclopedia of plants, but only one volume was ever published. In *Prodomos theatri botanici* (1620), he set a model for clear, comprehensive descriptions of previously undescribed plants. In *Pinax theatri botanici* (1623), he sorted out the enormous array of synonyms of plant names that had grown up over the centuries—and gave Carl Linnaeus (or von Linné, 1707–1778) a firm basis for nomenclatural reform in 1753. (*Pinax* remains the most reliable guide to establishing the identities of plants named in Renaissance herbals.) In their striking omission of the medical uses of plants, *Prodomos* and *Pinax* represent the culmination of the sixteenth century's steadily increasing interest in the scientific study of plants for their own sake.

BIBLIOGRAPHY

Hasler, F., and M-L. Portmann. "Joannes Bauhin d. (1541–1613)." *Gesnerus* 20 (1963), 1–21.

Hess, Johann Wahrmund. *Kaspar Bauhins, des ersten Professors der Anatomie und Botanik an der Universität Basel, Leben und Charakter.* Separatdruck, *Beiträge für Vaterländische Geschichte* VII (Basel: Schweighauser, 1860).

Reeds, Karen Meier. *Botany in Medieval and Renaissance Universities.* New York: Garland, 1991.

KAREN MEIER REEDS

See also Botany; Galenism; Harvey, William; Vesalius, Andreas

Becher, Johann Joachim (1635–1682)

In common with a number of German writers after the Thirty Years War, Becher believed that the pursuit of natural knowledge, particularly through the work of alchemy and chemistry, was a key part of the religious and material reform of the world. Son of a Lutheran pastor, Becher received very little formal education, leaving

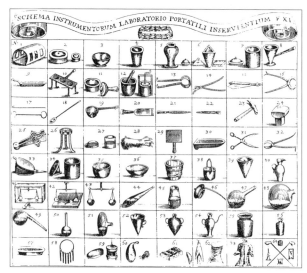

Becher's illustrations of the vessels and tools required for a well-equipped portable laboratory, from his Tripus hermeticus *(1689).*

his native Speyer after his father's death to wander the Continent. He somehow acquired mechanical and chemical expertise and attracted the attention of the elector of Mainz in 1660 with his proposal for a perpetual-motion machine. He became Court physician and mathematician in Mainz and, after minimal training, received a doctorate of medicine from the university, giving an inaugural lecture on the reality of the Philosopher's Stone. In 1664 the elector of Bavaria called him to Munich, and in 1670 Becher moved on to Vienna, where he remained as commercial adviser until 1676, when, falling from favor at Court, he attempted to find patrons in Holland and England, where he spent his last years.

His numerous books ranged from works on universal language to moral philosophy, but those with chemical and economic themes predominated. His theoretical writings in chemistry posited three earths, one of which, the *terra pinguis,* was taken up in the eighteenth century by Georg Ernst Stahl (1660–1734) as the basis for the phlogiston theory and formed a framework for chemical thinking before Antoine-Laurent Lavoisier's (1743–1794) discovery of oxygen (1770s).

More important during his lifetime, however, was Becher's promotion of practice and experience as the basis of natural knowledge. It was through the practical orientation of numerous individuals like Becher that the New Epistemology of experiment and experience came to be accepted as the method by which all natural knowledge should be pursued. Significant among Becher's practical activities were his commercial projects (some involving chemical processes such as dyemaking and saltpeter production) designed to bring in revenue to the impoverished German princely territories. Both his natural philosophy and his commercial schemes were part of the same effort to reform knowledge, informed by the humanist emphasis on *praxis* and the work of Paracelsus (ca. 1491–1544). Paracelsus's idea that knowledge was not to be gained by the study of books, but instead through the active experience and observation of the "Book of Nature," formed a model for figures like Becher, who claimed authority in the natural realm through mechanical and practical capabilities rather than through their university training. The New Philosophy thus constituted an opportunity for Becher, who previously would have remained marginal to established intellectual networks.

Paracelsus's view that alchemy represented in microcosm the redemption of the world and humankind was taken up by Becher and others, although in a transmuted form that emphasized the material rather than religious potential of the new science. This was a message attractive to the potentates of Europe in need of new sources of revenue and established an early relationship between science and the central state. In numerous books and practical proposals made to the electors of Mainz and Bavaria and to Emperor Leopold I, Becher linked the productive possibilities of natural knowledge (especially alchemy and its multiplication of wealth) to the workings of commerce to make his commercial projects more palatable to his noble patrons.

BIBLIOGRAPHY

Frühsorge, G., and G. F. Strasser, eds. *Johann Joachim Becher (1635–1682).* Wiesbaden: Otto Harrassowitz, 1993.

Hassinger, H. *Johann Joachim Becher, 1635–1682: Ein Beitrag zur Geschichte des Merkantilismus.* Vienna: Adolf Holzhausen, 1951.

Smith, P. H. *The Business of Alchemy: Science and Culture in the Holy Roman Empire.* Princeton, NJ: Princeton University Press, 1994.

Steinhüser, F. A. *Johann Joachim Becher und die Einzelwirtschaft.* Nuremberg: Verlag der Hochschulbuchhandlung Krische, 1931.

PAMELA H. SMITH

See also Alchemy; Chemical Philosophy; Paracelsus; Stahl, Georg Ernst

Beeckman, Isaac (1588–1637)

A natural philosopher who developed one of the first mechanical philosophies of the seventeenth century. With his new approach to nature he exercised considerable influence on some of his contemporaries, especially René Descartes (1596–1650). But, whereas Descartes made every effort to be known as the philosopher whose ideas would replace the Aristotelian system, Beeckman's natural shyness and irresolution prevented him from publishing his ideas. If it had not been for Cornelis de Waard, who in 1905 discovered Beeckman's supposedly lost scientific diary and subsequently published it, Beeckman would have remained a shadowy figure in the background of the Scientific Revolution.

Beeckman studied theology and mathematics in Leiden, where the Ramist philosopher Rudolf Snellius was his main tutor. Unable to find a living as a minister because of the ultraorthodox views of his father, Beeckman settled as a candlemaker (his father's trade) in Zierikzee. In 1616, however, he handed over his shop to his assistant and started to study medicine, meanwhile helping his father in the construction of water conduits for breweries. Beeckman became doctor of medicine at the University of Caen in 1618. After his return to the Netherlands, Beeckman met Descartes, then a young French officer in the Dutch army. In November and December 1618, they discussed several topics in mathematics and mechanics. The next year, Beeckman became a teacher in the grammar school in Utrecht, but in 1620 he moved to Rotterdam. There he became assistant to his brother Jacob, who was the principal of the local grammar school. Although he liked the practical atmosphere of Rotterdam, problems within the Dutch Reformed Church forced him in 1627 to move to nearby Dordrecht, where he became principal of the grammar school. In Dordrecht Beeckman became a well-respected intellectual, who also established several international contacts, among them Marin Mersenne (1588–1648) and Pierre Gassendi (1592–1655). The relationship with Descartes, however, cooled in 1631 after Descartes had gotten the unfounded impression that Beeckman was boasting of being Descartes's teacher. In his last years, Beeckman spent much time learning the art of lens grinding.

From his days as a schoolboy, Beeckman kept a diary, his *Journaal*. This miscellaneous collection of notes contains remarks pertaining to his personal life, the weather, and the milieu in which he lived, but also to medicine, logic, music, physics, and mathematics. From this *Journaal*, it is clear that, already in Zierikzee, Beeckman had developed a mechanistic philosophy of nature, in which atomism, a modern principle of inertia, and a drive for a mathematical formulation of natural philosophy are the main ingredients.

Although Beeckman called his philosophy *"philosophia physico-mathematica,"* the mathematical part of his thought is not strongly developed. It was his physical intuition that proved to be his main asset. He started from the assumption that no explanation in physics was acceptable that did not allow for a picturable model; therefore, in mechanics he rejected the concept of impetus and opted for the idea that motion that is not interrupted or deflected will always continue in the state it is in, which is an important step toward the modern concept of inertia. He also rejected the Aristotelian matter theory and opted for atomism, though he was aware of the problems involved in the concept of perfectly hard atoms that nevertheless are able to bounce back after collision.

Starting from these ideas, Beeckman was able to give a mechanistic explanation of many physical problems. The tides, the propagation of sound, the problem of the consonance and the movements of the planets were all reduced to the behavior of matter in motion. Problems in hydrostatics Beeckman explained with the concept of air pressure, a force exercised by particles of air, themselves struck by particles of ether streaming in from the heavens. Magnetism was explained by recourse to a model of particles streaming through and around the magnet. Differences in the properties of substances with the same chemical composition were explained by different arrangements of the individual particles (a precursor of the concept of isomerism). The law of free fall was formulated by the combined effort of Descartes and Beeckman, the latter providing the physical explanation—a falling body retains its motion but acquires new motion each time it is hit by an ether particle, resulting in the phenomenon of acceleration—while Descartes brought his mathematical skills to the solution of the problem.

Although very little of Beeckman's natural philosophy was published during his lifetime, many of his ideas were discussed with Mersenne, Gassendi, and Descartes, and, through their work, at least some of them found their way to the larger scientific community.

BIBLIOGRAPHY

Beeckman, Isaac. *Journal tenu par Isaac Beeckman de 1604 à 1634.* Ed. C. de Waard. 4 vols. The Hague: Nijhoff, 1939–1953.

Cohen, H. F. *Quantifying Music: The Science of Music at the First Stage of the Scientific Revolution, 1580–1650.* Dordrecht: Reidel, 1984.

Van Berkel, K. *Isaac Beeckman (1588–1637) en de mechanisering van het wereldbeeld.* Amsterdam: Rodopi, 1983. (An English translation is due to appear in 1998.)

KLAAS VAN BERKEL

See also Descartes, René; Gassendi, Pierre; Mechanical Philosophy; Mersenne, Marin

Beguin, Jean (ca. 1550–ca. 1620)

French chemist and author of *Tyrocinium chymicum* (1610), one of the most popular chemical textbooks of the seventeenth century. Born in Lorraine, Beguin traveled in central Europe, where he visited the mines of Hungary and Slovenia. With the support of Jean Ribit (ca. 1571–1605) and of Theodore Turquet de Mayerne (1573–1655), he set up a laboratory in Paris and gave public lectures, teaching the preparation of new chemical remedies. His *Tyrocinium,* which depended on Andreas Libavius's (1540–1616) *Alchemia* (1597), was practical in nature and was intended to explain the processes carried out in the laboratory. For Beguin, chemistry was the art of separating and recombining mixed bodies and of producing medicines. He adopted the Paracelsian theory of the three chemical principles—salt, sulfur, and mercury. He defined mercury as an acid, volatile, and penetrating liquor, bearing a principle of life; sulfur as a viscous and oily substance and as the cause of odors in natural bodies; salt as a dry substance having the power to prevent the corruption of bodies. For Beguin, all natural bodies contained a quintessence, namely a celestial substance, or universal spirit.

Besides the preparation of numerous substances, Beguin described various chemical operations, like calcination, precipitation, fermentation, extraction, coagulation, and distillation. A moderate Paracelsian, Beguin advocated the use of metals and minerals in the preparation of medicines, but he did not rule out traditional Galenic medicines.

The *Tyrocinium* went through forty-one editions between 1610 and 1690 and was translated into many European languages. It became the pattern of subsequent French chemical textbooks in the second half of the seventeenth century.

BIBLIOGRAPHY

Patterson, T. S. "Jean Beguin and His 'Tyrocinium chymicum.'" *Annals of Science* 2 (1937), 243–298.

Kent, A., and O. Hannaway. "Some New Considerations on Beguin and Libavius." *Annals of Science* 16 (1960), 241–250.

ANTONIO CLERICUZIO

See also Chemistry; Iatrochemistry; Libavius, Andreas; Paracelsus

Bellini, Lorenzo (1643–1704)

A physiologist with a successful career in Tuscany as a professor of medicine and anatomy and personal physician to the duke, he saw the key to physiology in the laws of mechanics. Under the patronage of the duke, he studied at the University of Pisa, where he was greatly influenced by Giovanni Alfonso Borelli (1608–1679). At the age of nineteen, he published his first work—on the anatomy and function of the kidneys; the following year, was appointed professor of medicine at Pisa. Five years later, he was awarded the chair of anatomy.

He challenged the Galenic account of kidney function as dependent on the operation of a special "faculty" separating urine from blood in an organ composed of undifferentiated tissue, by his discovery that the kidney was a complex structure of fibers, spaces, and tubules, acting as a sieve, separating urine from blood and returning the latter to the bloodstream. Influenced by the attempts of Borelli and Thomas Willis (1621–1675) to explain physiological processes in mechanical terms, Bellini developed his iatromechanical ideas in detail in works published in 1683 and 1695. In what has been called a hydraulic iatromechanism, he held that health consists in proper circulation of the blood, and illness in interference with it. His ideas were widely influential throughout Europe until the mid-eighteenth century.

BIBLIOGRAPHY

Grondona, Felice. "L'esercitazione anatomica di Lorenzo Bellini sulla struttura e funzione dei reni." *Physis* 5 (1963), 423–463.

Klass, G. M. "Bellini's Concept of Catarrh: An Examination of a Seventeenth Century Iatromedical Viewpoint." *Clio medica* 9 (1974), 317–323.

Partington, J. R. *A History of Chemistry.* 4 vols. London: Macmillan, 1962, vol. 2, ch. 16.

ELSA L. GONZALEZ

See also Borelli, Giovanni Alfonso; Iatromechanics; Physiology; Willis, Thomas

Belon, Pierre (1517–1564)

A French naturalist who traveled widely and published his observations in several books devoted to the natural history of birds and marine animals, as well as his impressions of the Levant. Trained as an apothecary, Belon broadened his knowledge under the auspices of powerful patrons who sent him to Wittenberg to study with the botanist Valerius Cordus (1515–1544) and to the Levant as official botanist of a royal embassy to the Ottoman Empire. His research into Levantine flora and fauna focused on the sources of valuable drugs, and after returning to France he unsuccessfully solicited royal financing for a botanical garden in which to cultivate exotic plants with pharmaceutical and other useful properties.

Belon's major publications appeared between 1551 and 1555, beginning with a treatise on dolphins entitled *L'histoire naturelle des estranges poissons* (The Natural History of Strange Fish, 1551). His natural histories combined contemporary descriptions and illustrations of their subjects with an eclectic array of ancient and modern knowledge, with special attention paid to the various names by which they had been previously identified. He emphasized the importance of firsthand observation yet borrowed many illustrations from colleagues and drew liberally upon contemporary publications in composing his own works. Although fantastical creatures appear in some of his other books, Belon boasted in his masterpiece, *L'histoire de la nature des oyseaux* (History of the Nature of Birds, 1555): "there is in this work no description nor portrait of any bird which is not found in nature nor which has not been before the eyes of the artist." Among these illustrations is a famous juxtaposition of human and avian skeletons, intended to demonstrate their "affinity." His third major work, *Observations of Several Singularities and Memorable Things Found in . . . Foreign Countries* (1553), which was based on his tour of the Levant, served as a reference for generations of Orientalists.

BIBLIOGRAPHY

Delaunay, Paul. "L'aventureuse existence de Pierre Belon du Mans." *Revue du seizième siècle* 9 (1922), 251–268; 10 (1923), 1–34, 125–147; 11 (1924), 30–48, 222–232; 12 (1925), 78–97, 256–282.

———. *Pierre Belon naturaliste.* Le Mans: Monnoyer, 1926.

Glardon, Philippe. "Introduction." In *L'histoire de la nature des oyseaux: Fac-similé de l'édition de 1555.* Geneva: Librairie Droz, 1997, pp. vii–lxxi.

ERIC A. URBANC

See also Natural History; Zoology

The skeletons of a man and bird compared. From Pierre Belon, Portraits d'oyseaux, animaux, serpens, herbes, hommes et femmes d'Arabie & Egypte *(1557).*

Benedetti, Giovanni Battista (1530–1590)

A mathematician and physicist who was among the first to criticize Aristotle's laws of falling bodies and prepare the way for Galileo Galilei (1564–1642). He studied briefly under Niccolò Tartaglia (1500–1557) and served as mathematician to the duke of Parma from 1558 and then as mathematician to the Court of Savoy from 1567. His most important works are his *Resolutio* of 1553, concerned with problems in Euclid's *Elements;* his *Demonstratio* of 1554, concerned with ratios of motions; and his *Speculationes* of 1585, collected essays on mathematics and mechanics. Benedetti's *Demonstratio* was plagiarized by Jean Taisnier and published in 1562 under a different title, which had a much larger circulation than the original. Through it, for example, Benedetti's ideas were transmitted to the Jesuits of the Collegio Romano.

Benedetti is best known for his buoyancy theory of fall in which he invoked Archimedes to show that the absolute weight of a body is not what determines its speed of fall but rather the weight of the body in the medium. On this account, bodies of the same material but of different sizes will fall through a given medium at the same speed, not at speeds proportional to their weights, as Aristotle (384–322 B.C.E.) held. Benedetti also proposed a thought experiment in which one considers, first, a body joined by a line to another body of equal size and falling in a vacuum, then a single body of double the size doing the same. Intuitively, he argued, one should be able to see that the smaller bodies will fall at the same speed as the larger body whether they are connected or not. He subscribed to a theory of impetus, attributing the increase of speed of a falling body to increments of impetus built up in the body during its fall. And he correctly saw that a body subjected to rapid circular motion would, when released, have an impetus that directs it tangentially and in a straight line.

Galileo nowhere mentions Benedetti in his writings, but the many similarities in their thought suggest that Galileo was acquainted with his work, most probably through Jacopo Mazzoni, with whom Galileo studied in 1590.

BIBLIOGRAPHY

Koyré, Alexandre. *Galileo Studies*. Trans. John Mepham. Atlantic Highlands, NJ: Humanities Press, 1978.

Wallace, William A. "Science and Philosophy at the Collegio Romano in the Time of Benedetti." In W. A. Wallace. *Galileo, the Jesuits, and the Medieval Aristotle*. Hampshire, UK: Variorum, 1991.

WILLIAM A. WALLACE

See also Galilei, Galileo; Impetus

Berengario da Carpi, Giacomo (1460–1530)

The son of a surgeon, Berengario da Carpi was a teacher of practical medicine in early-sixteenth-century Bologna. He believed himself to be in a tradition of Bolognese anatomy that had begun two hundred years before with Mondino de'Luzzi (1275–1326), who had been the first to systematically dissect the human body for teaching purposes. Berengario's main work was a commentary on Mondino's short text.

There are three principal features of Berengario's commentary. It is large: Berengario drew on almost the whole of extant anatomical literature, including ancient texts not known to Mondino, especially Galen's (second century C.E.) *On the Use of the Parts of the Body*. Second, his commentary had the elaborate structure that was perfected by university teachers before the Black Death of 1348. In Berengario's time, this structure was beginning to be be called "scholastic" in a pejorative way by Hellenists who wanted anatomy to be a business of presenting good translations of ancient Greek texts, but Berengario and his colleagues in the schools were proud of being Scholastic, claiming that only full academic rigor and dialectical presentation could deal with the complexities of the structure of the body.

Third, Berengario clearly delimited the roles of sense and reason in anatomy. He accepted that anatomical knowledge of a part was knowledge of its action as well as of its structure but did not allow inferring structure from action (as in the case of very small parts). He also held that words could not adequately describe some complex shapes (like the vertebrae), and the illustrations he included to demonstrate such shapes make this the first pictorial anatomy text. He stressed the sensory nature of such anatomical knowledge by calling it *anatomia sensibilis*.

The amount of technical information presented by anatomists like Berengario was large (whether correct or not in our view) and much greater than could be used in the medicine and limited surgery of the time. Anatomy and the public dissections also had the social role of identifying the group of university physicians who practiced them and of persuading educated people that a medicine based on an anatomical rationality was best.

BIBLIOGRAPHY

Berengario da Carpi, Giacomo. *Isagoge brevis: A Short Introduction to Anatomy*. Trans. with an Introduction and Historical Notes by L. R. Lind; Anatomical Notes by Paul G. Roofe. Chicago: University of Chicago Press, 1959.

Busacchi, V. "Berengario da Carpi e l'anatomia." *Proceedings of the Nineteenth International Congress of the History of Medicine*. Basel: Karger, 1966, pp. 267–271.

French, R. K. "Berengario da Carpi and the Use of Commentary in Anatomical Teaching." In A. Wear, R. K. French, and I. Lonie. *The Medical Renaissance of the Sixteenth Century*. Cambridge: Cambridge University Press, 1985, pp. 42–74.

ROGER FRENCH

See also Anatomy; Dissection

Bernoulli, Jakob I (1654–1705)

Professor of mathematics at the University of Basel from 1687 until his death, he made important contributions to the areas of mathematics (algebra, infinitesimal analysis, probability theory) and mechanics. He studied the Leibnizian calculus soon after the groundbreaking publications by Gottfried Wilhelm Leibniz (1684, 1686) and extended its applications to a wide range of problems. The term *integral* was adopted by Leibniz (1646–1716) after a suggestion by Bernoulli.

Of particular importance are his general method for the determinations of evolutes (1692) and his work on the brachistochrone. The brachistochrone problem is that of determining the curve described by a body moving under the influence of gravity (ignoring friction and air resistance) that starts from rest at point A and reaches a point B (lower than A and not directly under it) in the least time. The problem was proposed by his brother Johann in 1696. Several solutions were presented, by, among others, Leibniz and Jacob Bernoulli himself in 1697, which showed the brachistochrone to be a cycloid. The importance of Bernoulli's solution consists in being one of the first results in the area of analysis known as calculus of variations.

To the same branch of mathematics belongs a problem proposed and solved by Bernoulli known as the isoperimetric problem. For example, given a segment with endpoints A and B and a class of curves of given length d passing through A and B, the problem consists of singling out from this class the curve for which the area contained between the segment AB and the curve is largest. It is in this context that Jakob and Johann fiercely opposed each other in one of the most vitriolic scientific debates of the century.

Other results by Bernoulli in the area of infinitesimal analysis include his work on the catenary (a curve made by a hanging chain suspended from its endpoints), the isochrone (a class of curves in which a moving point generates equal segments in equal times), the lemniscate (a curve resembling the figure eight), and the tractrix (the characteristic of a curve tangent to a straight line). He also determined in 1694 the differential equation for the radius of curvature of a curve. In a series of five *mémoires* published between 1682 and 1705, Bernoulli also investigated the theory of infinite series. Although many of the results could be found previously in the literature, the *mémoires* provide a comprehensive account of results in

this area. One of Bernoulli's most important works is *Ars conjectandi* (The Art of Conjecturing, 1713), which was published after his death. It can be considered the first book in probability theory. It is divided into five parts. The first part contains a commentary to a previous introduction to the subject by Christiaan Huygens (1629–1695). The second part offers a survey of the theory of permutations and combinations. The rest of the book is devoted to applications in probability theory. The fourth part is of great philosophical and mathematical interest. Bernoulli offers the first explicit "subjective" conception of probability, defining it as "degree of certainty." Moreover, he proves the celebrated "weak law of large numbers." Let p be the (unknown) probability of an event, and m/n is the proportion of (observed) positive outcomes in n trials. Then for any e > 0, the probability of $|p\text{-}m/n| < e$ increases to 1 as n grows to infinity—or, the larger the number of trials (as in throws of dice, for example), the greater the probability that all faces will come up an equal number of times. This is the first limit theorem ever proved in probability theory.

BIBLIOGRAPHY

Bernoulli, Jakob. *Die Werke von Jakob Bernoulli.* (Herausgegeben von der Naturforschenden Gesellschaft in Basel). Basel and Boston: Birkhäuser, 1969–1993.

Hacking, Ian. *The Emergence of Probability.* Cambridge: Cambridge University Press, 1975.

Hess, Hans-Jürgen, and Fritz Nagel, eds. *Der Ausbau des Calculus durch Leibniz und die Brüder Bernoulli.* (Studia Leibniziana, Special Issue 17). Stuttgart: Franz Steiner Verlag, 1989.

Sylla, Edith. "Political, Moral, and Economic Decisions and the Origins of the Mathematical Theory of Probability: The Case of Jakob Bernoulli's *The Art of Conjecturing.*" In *Acting Under Uncertainty: Multidisciplinary Conceptions,* ed. George M. von Furstenburg. Dordrecht: Kluwer Academic, 1990, pp. 19–44.

PAOLO MANCOSU

See also Bernoulli, Johann I; Huygens, Christiaan; Leibniz, Gottfried Wilhelm; Probability

Bernoulli, Johann I (1667–1748)

Professor of mathematics at the University of Groningen from 1695, and then at the University of Basel from 1705 as a successor to his brother Jakob (1654–1705). His main contributions are in the areas of infinitesimal calculus and mechanics. After the publication of Gottfried

Wilhelm Leibniz's (1646–1716) *mémoires* on the calculus, Bernoulli familiarized himself with the new infinitesimal techniques under the guidance of his older brother Jakob. His first outstanding contribution to the calculus was the determination in 1691 of the solution to the problem of the catenary, the shape of the curve formed by a chain hanging between two points. Bernoulli was able to show that the curve "depended on the quadrature of the hyperbola." Other contributions to the calculus include the determination of the radius of curvature of a curve (also discovered by Jakob), the study of the integration of differential equations, and the development of the exponential calculus, which extends Leibniz's differential calculus to curves of the form $z = yx$.

In 1696 he challenged the mathematical community by asking for the shape of the brachistochrone (from the Greek "quickest time"), the path described by a freely falling body to a point not directly under the position from which it commenced its fall. Several solutions were proposed, including one by Johann himself, who showed that the curve must be a cycloid by appealing to the law of refraction in optics. The solution by his brother Jakob is at the origin of the calculus of variations. As a counter-challenge, Jakob proposed the isoperimetric problem: to find the curve of a given length passing between two endpoints AB, which encloses the largest area between it and the segment AB, for example. This was solved by Johann in a defective manner and set the stage for a discord between the two brothers that grew worse with the passing of time. Johann, however, played an extremely important role in the spread of the infinitesimal calculus on the Continent. Bernoulli's teachings enabled a group of French mathematicians centered around Nicolas Malebranche (1638–1715), including Pierre Varignon (1654–1722) and the marquis de L'Hôpital (1661–1704), to master the new infinitesimalist techniques. During his stay in Paris in the winter of 1691–1692, Bernoulli gave lectures to L'Hôpital on the differential and integral calculus. These lectures were instrumental in enabling L'Hôpital to write the first textbook in the calculus, *Analyse des infiniment petits pour l'intelligence des lignes courbes* (1696). Bernoulli's extensive correspondence with Leibniz and Varignon is an essential source for the history of the calculus during this period. He also played a role in the priority debate between Leibniz and Isaac Newton (1642–1727) concerning the discovery of the calculus. In 1713 Bernoulli sided with Leibniz and

attacked Newton's understanding of higher-order differentials, which he deemed erroneous.

His work in the field of mechanics is notable, among other things, for the first analytical expression of the principle of virtual velocities and for the analytical solution to the inverse two-body problem for central forces. In physics, he was a staunch defender of the Cartesian vortex theory. He also contributed to experimental physics and hydraulics. In 1714 he published a book on navigational theory entitled *Théorie de la manoeuvre des vaisseaux*.

BIBLIOGRAPHY

Bernoulli, Johann. *Der Briefwechsel von Johann I Bernoulli*, vol. 1. Ed. Otto Spiess. Basel and Boston: Birkhäuser, 1955.

Bernoulli, Jakob, and Johann Bernoulli. *Die Streitschriften von Jacob und Johann Bernoulli: Variationsrechnung.* Ed. with Commentary by Herman Goldstine; Historical Notes by Patricia Rodelet-de Grave. Basel: Birkhäuser, 1991.

Hess, Hans-Jürgen, and Fritz Nagel, eds. *Der Ausbau des Calculus durch Leibniz und die Brüder Bernoulli.* (Studia Leibniziana, Special Issue 17). Stuttgart: Franz Steiner Verlag, 1989.

Van Maanen, J. A. *Een complexe grootheid: Leven en werk van Johann Bernoulli, 1667–1748.* Utrecht: Epsilon, 1995.

PAOLO MANCOSU

See also Bernoulli, Jakob I; Calculus; Infinitesimals; Leibniz, Gottfried Wilhelm; Newton, Isaac; Varignon, Pierre

Biblical Chronology

The dating of the precise years in which biblical events occurred was of central importance to intellectuals in the early-modern period, not least because there was a pressing need to reform the Church year, which was becoming out of phase with the Julian calendar. Although the Old Testament was the most ancient and authentic source for ancient history, historians had to reconcile this with pagan histories that often told of the same events, while new astronomical techniques promised to aid them in pinpointing specific historical dates more precisely.

The most important chronology of the sixteenth century was Joseph Scaliger's *Opus novum de emendatione temporum* (A New Work on the Reform of Chronology, 1583), published a year after Pope Gregory VIII had initiated the new Gregorian calendar. Scaliger (1540–1609) made use of both philological evidence and the latest astronomical data, such as that from Nicolaus Copernicus's (1473–1543) heliocentric *De revolutionibus orbium coelestium* (On the Revolutions of the Celestial Spheres, 1543) in order to date on the calendar eclipses mentioned in ancient pagan treatises. Although these techniques had been used before, Scaliger's work systematized the different strands of evidence in an unprecedented manner. In composing a work that he hoped would aid calendrical reform, he emphasized and reintroduced the so-called Julian period of 7,980 years (the product found by multiplying the number of years in a Metonic cycle—19; the lowest number of solar years equal to a multiple of lunar months, namely 235—by those in a solar cycle (28); the periodicity of recurrence of a particular day of the month coinciding with a particular day of the week (this product gives 532, probably the most influential period in early modern chronology); and also by the number of years in the Roman Indiction cycle—15; a period that was used to denote a particular year in the Julian ecclesiastical calendar and that originally derived from the announcement of obligatory donation of food to the Roman government—which was to be influential for chronologers in the following century.

The most authoritative chronologist in the seventeenth century was the archbishop of Armagh, James Ussher (1581–1656). He began a lifelong study in the history of the reigns of Old Testament figures. In his two-part *Annals of the Old Testament,* published in 1650 and 1654, Ussher adopted Scaliger's notion of the Julian period and redated Creation to Sunday, October 23, 4004 B.C.E., fifty-four years earlier than Scaliger had placed it. In fact, he was even more precise and claimed that the creation of the chaotic matter from which God effected the Creation proper had taken place at ca. 6 P.M. on the previous evening. He was able to connect Old Testament to nonscriptural sources, the most significant of these being the accession of the reign of Nabonassar in Babylon to February 26, 747 B.C.E., which was linked to the reigns of the biblical figure Nebuchadnezzar and the Persian ruler Cyrus the Great. From here, one could work backward to the Creation, using the numbers for the length of reigns of kings found in the Hebrew text of the Old Testament. This gave a shorter period for the length of the reigns of the patriarchs than did the Greek Septuagint, which he considered a forgery.

Ussher's figure for the Creation had the advantage of being sufficiently close to periodizations, such as that in the Talmud, that attached great importance to events that happened in dates with significant round numbers.

He put the completion of Solomon's Temple at three thousand years after the Creation and the appearance of the Messiah a thousand years after that, but since scholars accepted—from independent evidence—that Herod had died in 4 B.C.E., and he was known to have been alive when Christ was born, Christ's birthdate had to be put back to just before that period. Adding this to the convenient figure of 4,000 gave the date of Creation. Ussher's dates became authoritative and were inserted into the King James Bible from the beginning of the eighteenth century.

Perhaps the most stunning use of astronomical techniques for the reordering and dating of Old Testament events was to be found in the research of Isaac Newton (1642–1727), whose *Chronology of Ancient Kingdoms Amended* was published posthumously in 1728. By adopting the euhemerist technique of supposing that pagan myths referred to real people, and then showing how many characters in these various mythical traditions were actually the same person, Newton cut down the length of various pagan histories such as that of the Greeks. By also assuming the radical notion that the average length of reign of kings in history was between eighteen and twenty years, he redated the Argonautic expedition to 936 B.C.E., thereby lopping at least four hundred years off the standard histories. All of this reinforced the notion that the Old Testament contained the oldest and most authentic historical records extant, and Newton ended up with a relatively orthodox date for Creation of 3988 B.C.E. (some five years later than that published by Johannes Kepler [1571–1630] in his *Rudolphine Tables* of 1627). Newton was less precise in his dating than was one of his favorite authors, the Jesuit Denis Petau (1583–1652), who in his *De doctrina temporum* (On the Principles of Chronology, 1627), set the time of Creation at nine hours, five minutes, and forty-two seconds into October 27, 3983 B.C.E. The fierce debates that followed the publication of his work continued into the nineteenth century, although they were superseded by new evidence coming from the sciences of geology and natural history that gave a much greater age for the earth.

BIBLIOGRAPHY

Grafton, Anthony. "From *De die natali* to *De emendatione temporum:* The Origins and Setting of Scaliger's Chronology." *Journal of the Warburg and Courtauld Institutes* 48 (1985), 100–143.

———. *Joseph Scaliger: A Study in the History of Classical Scholarship.* Oxford: Oxford University Press, 1983.

B

Manuel, Frank. *Isaac Newton, Historian*. Cambridge: Cambridge University Press, 1963.

Trevor-Roper, Hugh. "James Ussher, Archbishop of Armagh." In *Catholics, Anglicans, and Puritans: Seventeenth Century Essays*. London: Secker and Warburg, 1987, 120–165.

ROB ILIFFE

See also Calendar Reform; Cosmogony; Theories of the Earth; Whiston, William

Biblical Interpretation

During the sixteenth and seventeenth centuries, the Bible was almost universally believed to be the word of God, a major source of truth not only about theology but about virtually any subject. Because the Scientific Revolution coincided with the Protestant and Catholic Reformations, the number of books on theology and interpretation grew to staggering proportions during this period, although most of these volumes had little to do with natural philosophy. That subset that bore on the knowledge of nature employed a wide range of hermeneutic strategies based on different models of the relation of the book of Scripture to the book of nature. Three major approaches revolving around different problems in natural philosophy are: the Copernican problem, the chemical philosophy, and the hexaemeral (six days of Creation) tradition.

The Copernican theory of the solar system immediately raised interpretative questions among learned men in Europe because the Bible clearly stated that the earth cannot move (Psalm 93:1) and that the Sun, instead, is in motion (Ecclesiastes [Qoheleth] 1:4–5). One of the most widely debated texts was the story of Joshua commanding the Sun to stand still so the Israelites could engage in battle against their enemies (Joshua 10:12–13). To the opponents of Nicolaus Copernicus (1473–1543), this text implied the immobility of the earth and the motion of the Sun. The Copernicans contended that all of these biblical texts employed phenomenal (or accommodated) language so that the Bible spoke according to what everyday experience indicates rather than according to the actual truth of nature. It is important to understand what all of these disputants had in common. None of them simply dismissed the Bible as irrelevant because they all believed it to be authoritative in some sense. They also faced the problem of how to interpret Copernicus's heliocentric claim. An ancient tradition held that the task of the astronomer was simply to predict the positions and movements of the planets, employing whatever mathematical devices fit the phenomena. On this account, there was no requirement that astronomy seek the truth about celestial motions. Predictive success was enough. On the other hand, natural philosophy aimed at the truth about the heavens by postulating causal mechanisms that carried the planets. Mathematical astronomy and physical philosophy (cosmology) were separate disciplines and issues. One of Copernicus's major innovations was to claim that his mathematical system represented, in fact, the true system of the universe, but this did not keep his readers from interpreting his work as an attempt only to predict the celestial motions.

So long as Copernicus's readers understood his work simply as prediction (instrumentalism), no conflict with the Bible resulted, since the moving earth in his system was not understood physically but only as a necessary postulate to save the phenomena. Those who read his work as representing truth about the universe (realism) found themselves embroiled in controversy over how to reconcile this new theory with the biblical texts mentioned above. The differences in interpretative strategies surfaced as soon as Georg Joachim Rheticus (1514–1574) returned from his sojourn with Copernicus. The leading educational figure at Wittenberg, Philip Melanchthon (1497–1560), opposed the motion of the earth by appealing to traditional physics and biblical texts. At that time (1540s), no adequate substitute for Aristotle's (384–322 B.C.E.) earth-centered physical theory was available, a situation that was remedied only in the seventeenth century by Galileo's work. For that reason, Melanchthon did not believe he had any reason to depart from the physical meaning of these texts. Rheticus defended the new theory against theological objections by appealing to Saint Augustine's (354–430) authority in distinguishing questions of natural philosophy from theology. In a treatise that was rediscovered only in the 1970s, Rheticus explained how the Holy Spirit did not intend to teach a theory of the heavens and, therefore, employed the language of sight rather than a theoretical vocabulary such as astronomy used. The most famous Protestant Copernican, Johannes Kepler (1571–1630), used the same type of approach in the introduction to his groundbreaking *Astronomia nova* (New Astronomy, 1609), in which he argued that nature and the Bible are distinct but complementary sources of knowledge. Among Catholic Copernicans—including Galileo Galilei (1564–1642), Tommaso Campanella (1568–1639), and Paolo Foscarini (ca. 1565–1616)—one finds a similar distinction between scientific and theological questions based on different views of the Bible and the Church Fathers. Both Protestants and Catholics acknowledged the inviolable truth of Scripture, but Catholics stressed the Church as the supreme interpreter of the Scriptures. Since the Council of Trent (1545–1563) had required that the unanimous consent of the Church Fathers was binding in determining a doctrinal matter, Catholic Copernicans were also obliged to argue that no consensus could be found in the Fathers on the matter of terrestrial motion. Therefore, they did not consider the Copernican issue a matter of faith (*de fide*).

The chemical philosophy represented another distinct use of the Bible in connection with nature. For the followers of Paracelsus (ca. 1491–1541), the truth expressed in the Bible can be found in nature in the chemical processes of Creation; nature was but another expression of the divine word. Alchemy in the hands of the Paracelsians became a basis of medical practice and a natural philosophy that they hoped would supplant the philosophies of the ancients and those of moderns based on mathematics. Although the hermetic and alchemical traditions did not survive their era with the success of the Copernican theory, they were important for their attempt to found a new science based on the interpretation of Genesis. The alchemists believed that the Creation narratives of Genesis gave divine sanction to their work because Creation itself was a result of chemical separation, the secrets of which the alchemical art would reveal. Thus, these Paracelsians found the three principles (Salt, Sulfur, Mercury) of alchemy in the Bible, and, conversely, they found specific Christian doctrines (e.g., the Trinity) in nature. Nature and the Bible were thought to be mirrors of each another through correspondences. Similarly, they also expected to discover the causes of disease in humans by unlocking the secrets of the universe as a whole because of the correspondences between the macrocosm and the microcosm. These correspondences were predicated on the notion of the Judeo-Christian tradition that human beings represented the crown of Creation and were the goal of all the universe. The chemical philosophy also cut across denominational lines, but it did so only by a transformation of the doctrinal content of the original groups. The Catholic Paracelsus, the Lutheran Valentin Weigel (1533–1588), and the Calvinist Oswald Croll (1560–

1609) were united by their common natural philosophy to such an extent that their original theological differences paled into insignificance. It is doubtful that orthodox Catholics, Lutherans, and Calvinists would have found much sympathy with the biblical interpretations of the chemical philosophers.

Unlike the first two approaches, the hexaemeral tradition of commentary on Genesis was rooted in ancient Christianity and flourished in the Renaissance apart from specific movements in natural philosophy. However, since Chapters 1–2 of Genesis touch on natural phenomena in an obvious way, this hermeneutical tradition often interacted with contemporaneous philosophy in multifaceted ways. The considerable diversity among interpreters on the relation between Genesis and natural philosophy cannot hide a common belief that the Bible contains the seeds of natural-philosophical truth. For almost all exegetes, Genesis was the fountain from which a right knowledge of nature flowed, but how that belief worked itself out in the actual interpretation of the text appeared in very different ways. The degree to which Genesis was taken as an authority on natural philosophy by the commentators varied widely. The Catholics Marin Mersenne (1588–1648) and Benito Pereyra (1535–1610), as well as the Protestant convert Jerome Zanchius (1516–1590), gave considerable treatment to questions of natural philosophy that were suggested by the text. Many of these commentators based their views on Aristotelian science, probably because they possessed a high degree of natural knowledge. Mersenne is a striking exception to this pattern of Aristotelian interpretation. Most of these interpretations attempted to expound the literal sense (*sensus literalis*), understood as giving a historical description of the events of the six days of Creation. They also drew on the medieval notion of the scale of being, which they found correlated well with the creative acts of the six days. They all affirmed the centrality of humans in the universe and seemed constrained to relate the rest of Creation to them. The recognition of the presence of accommodating language in the Bible, so frequently appealed to in the Copernican debates, is found abundantly in the hexaemeral commentaries. When Genesis 1:16 spoke of the two great lights in the heavens (Sun, Moon), the commentators asked how the Moon could be called a great light when it is known that Saturn is bigger than the Moon. Their answer usually appealed to the appearance of the Moon being greater because of its proximity to the earth. They clearly distinguished

B

between the appearances spoken of in the Bible and the celestial reality itself. This aspect of the hexaemeral tradition, reaching back into ancient and medieval commentaries, also provided the Copernicans with a ready-made argument for their claim that the Bible did not intend to teach astronomical truth.

BIBLIOGRAPHY

Blackwell, Richard. *Galileo, Bellarmine, and the Bible.* Notre Dame, IN: University of Notre Dame Press, 1991.

Debus, Alan G. *The Chemical Philosophy.* 2 vols. New York: Science History Publications, 1977.

Hooykaas, Reijer. *G. J. Rheticus' Treatise on Holy Scripture and the Motion of the Earth.* With translation, annotations, commentary, and additional chapters on Ramus-Rheticus and the development of the problem before 1650. Amsterdam: North-Holland, 1984.

Howell, Kenneth J. "Copernicanism and the Bible in Early Modern Science." In *Facets of Faith and Science,* ed. Jitse van der Meer. Lanham, MD: University Press of America, 1996.

Moss, Jean Dietz. *Novelties in the Heavens: Rhetoric and Science in the Copernican Controversy.* Chicago: University of Chicago Press, 1993.

Williams, Arnold. *The Common Expositor.* Chapel Hill: University of North Carolina Press, 1948.

KENNETH J. HOWELL

See also Book of Nature; Chemical Philosophy; Copernicanism; Galileo and the Church; Reformation, Protestant; Religion and Natural Philosophy; Warfare of Science and Theology

Biringuccio, Vannoccio (1480–ca. 1540)

The son of an architect in Siena, he traveled extensively in Italy and Germany during his early years, observing mining and metallurgical operations and thus laying the foundations of his work, *Pirotechnia.* After returning to Siena, he was appointed to run an iron mine and forge at Boccheggiano, and in 1513 he was appointed to a post with the Sienese armory. When a popular uprising forced his patrons, the Petrucci family, from Siena, Biringuccio was exiled on a charge of having debased the coinage. He returned to Siena with the Petruccis in 1523 and was granted a monopoly on saltpeter production but was again exiled when the Petruccis were expelled forever in 1526. After serving Alfonso I d'Este, duke of Ferrara, in 1531, he returned to Siena and worked for the Republic as an architect and director of building construction of

the Duomo, the cathedral of Florence. He later moved to Rome (where he lived the rest of his life) and became head of the papal foundry and director of munitions.

Biringuccio's only work, the *Pirotechnia,* was published posthumously in 1540. The first comprehensive treatise on the "fire arts" to be printed, the *Pirotechnia* covers virtually the entire field of metallurgy as it was then known. The work includes chapters on the various metallic ores, assaying, smelting, parting gold from silver, metallic alloys, casting, building furnaces, wiredrawing, silversmithing, and the making of saltpeter and gunpowder. Biringuccio was extremely skeptical of alchemy, deriding the art as "childish folly." His work evidences a remarkably experimental character, although he did not use experiment to test theory. In typical Renaissance fashion, he insisted that the vagaries of fortune could be conquered by careful, methodical attention to details. In bringing the crafts to the attention of natural philosophers, Biringuccio's classic work played an instrumental role in framing the background to the Scientific Revolution.

BIBLIOGRAPHY

Biringuccio, Vannoccio. *Pirotechnia.* Trans. Cyril Stanley Smith and Martha Teach Gnudi. Cambridge, MA: MIT Press, 1966.

Rossi, Paolo. *Philosophy, Technology, and the Arts in the Early Modern Era.* Trans. S. Attanasio. New York: Harper and Row, 1970.

Zilsel, Edgar. "The Sociological Roots of Science." *American Journal of Sociology* 47 (1941–1942), 544–562.

WILLIAM EAMON

See also Books of Secrets; Mining and Metallurgy.

Blaeu, Willem Janszoon (1571–1638)

Born into a prosperous Amsterdam Anabaptist family, Blaeu was trained to be a herring merchant, but he was more interested in scientific matters, particularly astronomy. In 1595 he left for Denmark to study the stars with Tycho Brahe (1546–1601) and stayed for a whole winter. After his return in May or June of 1596, he published, in cooperation with Adriaan Anthoniszoon, a celestial globe, on which Tycho Brahe's observations are included. In 1598 or 1599, he started a shop in Amsterdam for the manufacturing of globes and navigational instruments, later also publishing maps, charts, and navigational books. His first printed map sheet (*Map of the Nether-*

A copy, ca. 1645, of a terrestrial globe made by Blaeu in 1617. Courtesy Amsterdams Historisch Museum, The Netherlands.

BIBLIOGRAPHY

Krogt, Peter van der. *Globi Neerlandici: The Production of Globes in the Low Countries.* Utrecht: HES, 1993.
——. *Koeman's atlantes Neerlandici,* vol. 2: *The Folio Atlases by the Blaeus.* 't Goy-Houten: HES, 2000.

Schilder, Günter. *Single-sheet Maps and Topographical Prints Published by Willem Jansz Blaeu.* (Monumenta cartographica Neerlandica 3). Alphen aan den Rijn: Uitgeverij Canaletto, 1993.
——. *Two Wall-Maps of the World by Blaeu: 1619 and 1645/46.* (Monumenta cartographica Neerlandica 3). Alphen aan den Rijn: Uitgeverij Canaletto, 1990.

PETER VAN DER KROGT

See also Cartography; Geography

Boerhaave, Hermann (1668–1738)

This *Communis Europae Praeceptor* (Teacher of all Europe) at the University of Leiden is known as the most famous physician of the eighteenth century. He was a gifted teacher, whose lectures were copied by his students and, indeed, all over Europe. Boerhaave tried to eliminate all irrational elements from medical theories and to present a system that was based upon rational mechanical principles as postulated in the physics of Isaac Newton (1642–1727). Medicine was to become a logical discipline without reliance on allegories and mysticism. It could serve as the starting point for the development of modern physiology and pathology. Moreover, Boerhaave drew the attention of his students to Hippocrates (460–370 B.C.E.). He praised the Greek father of medicine for drawing his attention to the individual patient and his direct environment. Boerhaave emphasized the importance of this attitude in the first of his academic lectures when he was nominated as a reader in medicine at the University of Leiden in 1701.

Boerhaave was born in a small village behind the dunes of Holland, where his father was a minister. He was sent to the grammar school in Leiden when he was fourteen years old, and in 1684 he was enrolled in the university as a student of theology and philosophy. In 1690 he graduated in philosophy, but his study of theology was interrupted by his growing interest in medicine. In 1693 he graduated in medicine at the University of Harderwijk. His intention to follow a career as the healer of both spirit and body was struck down when he was accused by ecclesiastical authorities of being a follower of the condemned doctrines of the Jewish philosopher Benedict de Spinoza (1632–1677).

lands) dates from 1604. Analysis of Blaeu's earliest works shows that he began his activities as a scholar, producing a number of globes himself. After he found himself in the world of navigational and cartographic publishers, he continued in this field.

He specialized in maritime cartography and published the first edition of the pilot guide *Het licht der zeevaert* (The Light of Navigation) in 1608; he was appointed hydrographer of the United [Dutch] East India Company in 1633. After thirty years of publishing books, wall maps, globes, charts, and pilot guides, he brought out his first atlas, *Atlantis appendix* (1630). This was the beginning of the great tradition of atlas making by the Blaeus, which reached its apex under his son and successor Joan Blaeu (1596–1673) with the publication of the *Atlas maior* in 1662.

The family name Blaeu was not used until 1621. About 1621 Willem Janszoon decided to put an end to the confusion of his name with that of his competitor and neighbor, Jan Janszoon, and assumed his grandfather's sobriquet, "blauwe Willem" (blue Willem), as the family name, calling himself Willem Janszoon Blaeu.

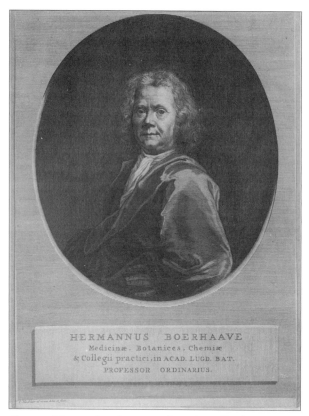

HERMANNUS BOERHAAVE
Medicinæ, Botanices, Chemiæ
& Collegii practici, in ACAD. LUGD. BAT.
PROFESSOR ORDINARIUS.

Courtesy Museum Boerhaave, Leiden, The Netherlands.

Boerhaave thereupon established himself in Leiden as a physician. His practice was modest, and, as he needed extra income, he gave private lessons in mathematics to students. He also studied chemistry and spent much time in the library near his home. As a student, he had assisted the librarian in cataloging the collection of Isaac Vossius (1618–1689), the English scientist, which was bought by the university in 1690. Boerhaave became well versed in modern scientific literature, since the collection held the works of Francis Bacon (1561–1626) and the first edition of Newton's *Principia mathematica philosophiae naturalis* (Mathematical Principles of Natural Philosophy, 1687), among other works in natural philosophy.

In 1701 he was invited to become a lector, a reader in medicine. His oration recommending the study of Hippocrates was well received. In 1703 Boerhaave was offered a chair in the medical faculty. This time his address was on the usefulness of the mechanical method in medicine. In 1709 Boerhaave was appointed to the chair of botany and in 1718 to the chair of chemistry. With the exception of anatomy, all medical subjects were taught by Boerhaave until 1729, when he resigned his

professorships in botany and chemistry. In 1730 he laid down his office as rector of the University with an address: "On the Honor of the Physician in Serving." In his early years, Boerhaave chose for his motto *Simplex veri sigillum* (Simplicity is the hallmark of truth). But in his last years he could no longer take for his theme the mechanical principles as the most simple explanation of the working of the human body. The experienced clinician, so highly admired by his students for his bedside manner and his individual treatment of the patient, had humbly returned to medicine as a servant of nature.

In the thirty-seven years Boerhaave taught, he helped educate a great number of young men as physicians. The main part of foreign students came from German-speaking countries, followed by English-speaking countries and other countries from Europe. His lectures and notebooks were translated into German, English, and French. The *Institutiones medicae* (1708), in which Boerhaave gave the basic principles of medicine, were even translated into Turkish and Japanese. His *Aphorisms* (1709) and *Elementa chemiae* (1732) also found their way to many countries.

Boerhaave's pattern of medical education, which he unfolded in his address of 1703, became the prototype, even of present-day teaching programs and the medical curriculum. It was transplanted from Leiden to other countries, such as Austria, Russia, Germany, Scotland, and, via Edinburgh, to Philadelphia on the other side of the Atlantic. His most famous pupils were Gerard van Swieten (1700–1772), who founded the medical school in Vienna; Albrecht von Haller (1708–1777), the Swiss scientist; and John Monro, (1670–1740), who helped found a medical school at Edinburgh on the Leiden model.

Boerhaave had a great knowledge of literature. Besides his well-known textbooks, he paid much attention to editing and republishing outstanding medical works, such as the *Opuscula anatomica* (1707), originally published in 1564, by the Italian anatomist Bartholomeo Eustachio (ca. 1510–1574). He convinced the young anatomist B. S. Albinus (1697–1770) to assist him in the republication in 1725 of the anatomical atlas *De humani corporis fabrica* of Andreas Vesalius (1514–1564). In 1732 he also edited some ancient Greek texts on the signs and symptoms of acute and chronic diseases by the Cappadocian physician Aretaeus, the successor of Hippocrates. He would refer to these works in his lectures.

Boerhaave's lectures, such as the *Praelectiones publice habitae de morbis nervorum* (Lectures on Nervous Diseases), constitute the first text embodying everything on which present-day medicine, in this case neuropsychiatry, is based. While he made no important discoveries himself, he made an eclectic compilation of all conceptions prior to his time. He praised the English physician Thomas Sydenham (1624–1689) in his lectures, and he was on good terms with the Italian anatomist and pathologist G. B. Morgagni (1682–1771), with whom he corresponded on several subjects.

Boerhaave's concept of chemistry and his lectures on this subject were directed toward the expulsion of alchemistic elements. In his *Elementa chemiae,* he used *motion* and *attraction* as the basic principles of chemical processes. For twenty years, Boerhaave taught botany to the students in the garden during the summer semester and published an *Index alter,* a catalog of plants. He also took an active part in the *commercium,* the botanical correspondence and exchange of plants.

Indeed, Boerhaave was the "teacher of all Europe," but the power of his spirit and the influence of his work reached much farther in time and space.

BIBLIOGRAPHY

Gibbs, F. W. "Boerhaave's Chemical Writings." *Ambix* 6 (1958), 117–137.

Kegel-Brinkgreve, E., and A. M. Luyendijk-Elshout, eds. *Boerhaave's Orations.* Leiden: Brill, 1983.

Lindeboom, G. A. *Hermann Boerhaave: The Man and His Work.* London: Methuen, 1968.

———, ed. *Boerhaave and His Time. Papers Read at the International Symposium in Commemoration of the Tercentenary of Boerhaave's Birth, Leiden 15–16 November 1968.* (Analecta Boerhaaviana 6). Leiden: Brill, 1970.

Underwood, E. Ashworth. *Boerhaave's Men at Leyden and After.* Edinburgh: Edinburgh University Press, 1983.

ANTONIE M. LUYENDIJK-ELSHOUT

See also Iatromechanics; Medicine

Book of Nature

A metaphor commonly employed by leading figures of the Scientific Revolution that expressed an analogy with the Bible. The Book of Nature (sometimes called the Book of Creatures) was created by God to be read, just as the Book of Scripture was also read, because both were considered means of revelation of God's will for the universe and humankind. The roots of the concept lie much earlier in Christian thought than the sixteenth and seventeenth centuries. Nature in the Judeo-Christian heritage of the West was never thought to be simply brute fact but, rather, had a semiotic function of pointing to the creator and providential sustainer of the world. Scholars who created the extensive hexaemeral (six-day) tradition of commentary on the Creation narratives of Genesis (Chapters 1–2) often invoked this metaphor to justify investigation into nature as a divinely imposed obligation.

While this concept appears pervasively in the writings of natural philosophers during the Scientific Revolution, it was subject to a variety of interpretations and uses, all of which required nature's readers to know the language in which it was written. The most prominent of these interpretations held that nature was written in the language of mathematics. Galileo Galilei (1564–1642), for example, argued in *The Assayer* (1623) that the lines, areas, and polygons of geometry constituted the only language through which one might have access to a true knowledge of nature. Earlier, Johannes Kepler (1571–1630), in both his *Mysterium cosmographicum* (1596) and *Astronomia nova* (New Astronomy, 1609), claimed that truth of the heavens required an intimate acquaintance with Euclidean geometry. These and others believed that the precision of mathematics conferred on nature a clarity that would lead to indubitable knowledge of the universe. Both Kepler and Galileo, as well as figures like Philip van Lansberge (1561–1632) and John Wilkins (1614–1672), contended that the two great books of Nature and Scripture stood in a complementary relation with each other. The Book of Nature yielded a knowledge of God but was not designed to teach the human family about salvation, while the Book of Scripture had the intention of teaching the way of salvation and only incidentally commented on nature. For the most part, these thinkers did not consider the Bible and nature to be in any real conflict since each book had its own intention. What united the two books was that these different intentions had the same Author. This tradition found its roots in the writings of Saint Augustine (354–430), particularly his lengthy commentary on the first chapters of Genesis. Augustine contended that the purpose of Scripture was not to theorize about nature in a manner similar to natural philosophers, so the words of the Bible should not be misjudged by trying to make them say something they never intended to teach. True, bona fide natural knowledge could be depended on to clarify what the

B

Scriptures did and did not teach, although Augustine often invoked the Bible to counter views of nature that were false on other grounds.

A lesser-known tradition, associated with the chemical philosophy, viewed nature and Scripture as mirror images of each other, so that what was found in the one might be expected in the other. Rather than a complementary relation, nature and Scripture taught essentially the same truths. For a number of complex reasons, this tradition did not survive beyond the Scientific Revolution.

A third tradition, which numbered among its advocates many of those in the first two already mentioned, involved astrology and saw celestial events as pointing to earthly events by way of prediction. Both Tycho Brahe (1546–1601) and Johannes Kepler engaged in astrological predictions in behalf of their patrons, Frederick II and Rudolph II, respectively. Tycho Brahe particularly defended astrology against objections from the Lutheran theologian Niels Hemmingsen by appealing to the significatory function of celestial events implied in the Book of Scripture. These different interpretations of the relation of the Book of Nature to that of Scripture are developments of ambiguities resident in earlier Christian tradition that were occasioned by the new challenges of the emerging sciences and philosophies of the early-modern era.

BIBLIOGRAPHY

Galilei, Galileo. *Discoveries and Opinions of Galileo.* Trans. with Introduction and Notes by Stillman Drake. Garden City, NY: Doubleday, 1957.

Kepler, Johannes. "Introduction" to the *New Astronomy.* Trans. William H. Donahue. New York: Cambridge University Press, 1992.

KENNETH J. HOWELL

See also Biblical Interpretation; Chemical Philosophy; Religion and Natural Philosophy

Books of Secrets

In the mid-sixteenth century, European presses published large numbers of collections of recipes known as books of secrets. These popular books contained medical recipes; household hints; technical recipes on metallurgy, alchemy, dyeing, and making perfume, oil and incense; and cosmetic recipes, such as how to dye one's hair or apply makeup to the face. The books of secrets supplied a great deal of practical information to an emerging middle-class of readers. At the same time, they brought new experimental attitudes to the lay public. Underlying the books of secrets was the premise that nature was a repository of hidden forces that might be discovered and manipulated by using the right techniques. The utilitarian character of the books of secrets gave substance to this implicit claim. Unlike treatises on magic and the occult arts, the books of secrets were grounded upon a concrete, experimental outlook.

One of the most famous books of secrets was a work attributed to Alessio Piemontese, *I secreti del reverendo donno Alessio Piemontese* (The Secrets of Alessio, 1555). Alessio's *Secreti* went through more than a hundred editions and was still being reprinted in the 1790s. The humanist Girolamo Ruscelli (1500–1566), the real author of the *Secreti,* reported that the work contained the experimental results of an Academy of Secrets that he and a group of humanists and noblemen founded in Naples in the 1540s. Ruscelli's Academy of Secrets is the first recorded example of an experimental scientific society. The academy was later imitated by Giambattista della Porta (1535–1615), who founded an Accademia dei Secreti in Naples in the 1560s.

Alessio Piemontese was the prototypical "professor of secrets." The description of Alessio's hunt for secrets in the Preface to the *Secreti* gave rise to a legend of the wandering empiric in search of technological and scientific secrets. Its enormous popularity made the work play a key role contributing to the emergence of the conception of science as a hunt for the secrets of nature. The concept of science as a hunt pervaded experimental science during the Scientific Revolution.

In the books of secrets, experimental science shaded into natural magic. Giambattista della Porta's *Magia naturalis* (Natural Magic, 1558) deployed practical recipes in an effort to demonstrate the principles of natural magic. Other books of secrets, such as Isabella Cortese's *Secreti* (1564), a compilation of alchemical recipes, disseminated experimental techniques and practical information to a wide readership. Numerous encyclopedic compilations such as Johann Jacob Wecker's *De secretis* (1582) were also published. The books of secrets were intermediaries between the private and esoteric "secrets" of medieval alchemists and magi and the public Baconian "experiments" that characterized the research programs of the seventeenth-century experimental academies.

Books of secrets continued to be published until well into the nineteenth century, but by then they had lost any credible claim to revealing the secrets of nature. No longer considered scientific or experimental books, the modern descendants of the books of secrets are found in bookstores under "self-help."

BIBLIOGRAPHY

Eamon, William. *Science and the Secrets of Nature: Books of Secrets in Medieval and Early Modern Culture*. Princeton, NJ: Princeton University Press, 1994.

———. "Science as a Hunt." *Physis* 31 (1994), 393–432.

Eamon, William, and Françoise Paheau. "The Accademia Segreta of Girolamo Ruscelli. A Sixteenth-Century Scientific Society." *Isis* 75 (1984), 327–342.

Ferguson, John K. *Bibliographical Notes on Histories of Inventions and Books of Secrets*. 2 vols. London: Holland, 1959.

WILLIAM EAMON

See also Porta, Giambattista della; Secrets of Nature

Borelli, Giovanni Alfonso (1608–1679)

From Fielding H. Garrison, An Introduction to the History of Medicine, *3rd ed. (Philadelphia and London: Saunders, 1921).*

One of the protagonists of Italian intellectual life in the seventeenth century and the most active member at the Accademia del Cimento in Florence. He was the son of a Spanish soldier, Miguel Alonso, and Laura Borrello. He changed his name from Giovanni Alonso to Giovanni Alonso Borrelli, and lastly to Giovanni Alfonso Borelli. His first mentor was Tommaso Campanella (1568–1639), then imprisoned in the Neapolitan castles, who called him a son of virtue. Probably ca. 1626, together with Campanella, Giovanni Alfonso moved to Rome, where he studied under Benedetto Castelli (1578–1643). His intellectual apprenticeship places Borelli at the crossroads between the southern Italian philosophical tradition and the Galilean school, as well as the medical and mathematical disciplines. Campanella, in a manuscript copy of his book on medicine, acknowledged his use of Borelli's work.

From ca. 1635 to 1656, Borelli lived at Messina, where in 1639 he obtained the chair of mathematics against competition from the Jesuits. His first publications concerned mathematics and medicine. In *Discorso del Signor Gio. Alfonso Borrelli* (1646), he defended the mathematical competence of the Galilean school. In another work, published in 1649, he attacked astrology and defended iatrochemistry and William Harvey

(1578–1657). Although his name does not appear in print, Borelli was involved in the edition of *Emendatio, et restitutio Conicorum Apollonii Pergaei* (1654) by Francesco Maurolico (1494–1575). During his two decades in Sicily, Borelli established lifelong intellectual and political links with the Sicilian aristocracy. He was probably involved in the 1649 plot seeking to overturn Spanish rule and establish an autonomous kingdom under a Sicilian king.

Between 1656 and 1667, Borelli taught mathematics at Pisa University and participated in Leopold de'Medici's (1617–1675) Accademia del Cimento. In the Cimento, Borelli advocated a radical position in defense of atomism and the void. He was dissatisfied with the published version of the experiments performed at the academy, the *Saggi di naturali esperienze* (1667), both because of the neutral philosophical stance imposed by Leopold and because the names of the academicians were not mentioned, thus penalizing the most active members.

The Tuscan years are the best-documented period of Borelli's life, thanks to the surviving correspondence, diaries of the Cimento, and his publications. All of his publications of this period deal with the mathematical disciplines, and many of them have their roots in problems left unsolved by Galileo Galilei (1564–1642). In *Euclides restitutus* (1658), Borelli reformulated Euclid's *Elements* and especially the problematic theory of proportions, an area that Galileo, Evangelista Torricelli (1608–1647), and others had already tried to systematize. The edition of Apollonius's *Conics* (1661) resulted from a collaboration with Abramo Ecchellense (d. 1664) and was based on an Arabic Codex in the Laurentian Library containing the previously unknown Books 5–7. *Theoricae Mediceorum planetarum* (Theories of the Medicean Planets, 1666) is a study of the motions of the satellites of Jupiter, with transparent analogies to the solar system. Borelli's work and his subtle analysis of orbital motion were praised by Isaac Newton (1642–1727) in the mid-1680s. *De vi percussionis* (On the Force of Percussion, 1667), too, like the previous work, was related to Galileo, who had planned and drafted an additional part to his *Discourses on Two New Sciences* (1638) on the force of percussion. Lastly, the short tract *Del movimento della cometa* (1665), though published under the name of Pier Maria Mutoli, is attributed to Borelli. During his Tuscan years, Borelli's house was the site of important anatomical investigations carried out with Claudius Auberius (d. 1658), Marcello Malpighi (1628–1694), Lorenzo Bellini (1643–1704), and Carlo Fracassati (d. 1672). Their publications bear the mark of Borelli's influence and at times contain entire passages from his pen.

Between 1667 and 1672, Borelli lived at Messina with his patron Iacopo Ruffo. He became involved in a controversy with Stefano degli Angeli (1623–1697) and Giambattista Riccioli (1598–1671) on the problem of falling bodies and its relations to Copernicanism, and one with Honoré Fabri (1607–1688) on the force of percussion. His major publications over this period were *Historia, et meteorologia incendii Aetnae* (1670) on the Aetna eruption and *De motionibus naturalibus a gravitate pedentibus* (1670), dealing with a range of physico-mathematical themes, such as motion of heavy bodies in a fluid medium and the nature of air. The latter work was dedicated to Andrea Concublet (d. 1675), patron of the Neapolitan Investiganti Academy, to which Borelli had been elected in 1667. In this work, Borelli accomplished a double appropriation of many of the Cimento experiments on topics such as levity and capillarity by claiming authorship and presenting them in his own philosophical framework. Borelli was involved in anti-Spanish activi-

ties, and in 1672 a ban was issued against him and others, offering a large sum for his capture. He lived in hiding and had to abandon the nearly completed edition of Archimedes—*Ex traditione Francisci Maurolyci*—later published in 1685 with no mention of his name. Borelli reached Rome in the late spring of 1673.

There he was associated with the academy of Queen Christina of Sweden (1626–1689), to whom he dedicated his posthumous masterpiece *De motu animalium* (1680–1681), in which he applied mechanical reasoning to anatomy and claimed to have raised it to the level of a physico-mathematical discipline. Book I deals with the so-called external motions, such as walking, flying, and swimming, whereas Book II deals with the so-called internal motions, namely muscular contraction, breathing, and the functions of all of the main organs. In 1674 Messina rebelled against Spain and received French support for about four years. Borelli supported the revolt and acted as the chief Messina representative with the French ambassador. His hopes of overturning Spanish rule and creating an autonomous kingdom under a resident king were dashed in 1678, when Messina was abandoned by the French and severely punished by Spain. From 1677 Borelli taught mathematics to the Piarists at S. Pantaleo, near Piazza Navona, were he died on the last day of 1679.

Thanks to his contacts with the Medici and the Messina ruling class, Borelli was able to exert considerable influence on Italian intellectual life and procure university positions for his followers, such as Alessandro Marchetti (1633–1714), Donato Rossetti (1633–1686), Diego Zerilli (d. 1706), Bellini, Malpighi, and Fracassati. While establishing a major iatromechanical school, Borelli failed to leave a mathematical tradition at a time when Italian mathematics was being overtaken by developments in northern Europe.

BIBLIOGRAPHY

Baldini, U. "Gli studi su Giovanni Alfonso Borelli." In G. Arrighi et al. *La scuola galileiana: Prospettive di ricerca.* Firenze: La Nuova Italia, 1979.

Bertoloni Meli, D. "The Neoterics and Political Power in Spanish Italy: Giovanni Alfonso Borelli and His Circle." *History of Science* 34 (1996), 57–89.

Koyré, A. *La révolution astronomique.* Paris: Hermann, 1961, Part III.

Middleton, W. E. K. *The Experimenters: A Study of the Accademia del Cimento.* Baltimore: Johns Hopkins University Press, 1971.

DOMENICO BERTOLONI MELI

See also Accademia del Cimento; Campanella, Tommaso; Iatromechanics

Botanical Gardens

Typically defined as a collection of living plants, assembled for the purposes of scientific study, the term *botanical garden* is generally used to refer to systematic gardens in the tradition of the university medical gardens that originated in Renaissance and early-modern Europe. In fact, the cultivation of plants has long contributed to knowledge, as seen, for example, in the gardens of ancient China and the Near East and the herbals they generated. The ancient Greek botanist Theophrastus of Eresos reputedly pursued his studies in a garden attached to Aristotle's Lyceum, in a grove near Athens. During the European Middle Ages, monastic gardens were used to grow not only fruits and vegetables for the use of monks, but medicinal herbs as well, preserving much botanical knowledge along the way. Nor was Europe the only site of botanical activity as the Middle Ages drew to a close; a network of Islamic gardens benefited scholars, while Hernán Cortés, stumbling through the undergrowth of Mexico in 1519, was awed by the sight of the splendid royal Aztec gardens of Iztapaplan, two full decades before the foundation of the earliest European university gardens.

It was in Renaissance Italy, however, that the characteristic form of the European botanical garden came to be shaped. The age saw a proliferation of gardens of all kinds, as new attitudes favoring nature appreciation and openness toward the world led princes and merchants alike to construct gardens for their private pleasure. With its flourishing urban life and extensive trade contacts, Italy was at the center of these developments, though the enthusiasm for gardening touched many other areas of sixteenth-century Europe as well; the Swiss polymath Conrad Gessner (1516–1565), for example, devoted an entire book—*De hortis Germaniae* (On the Gardens of Germany, 1561)—to an admiring enumeration of gardens in the German territories. But it was in Italy that the botanical garden first entered the university, assuming in the process its classic ambitions and design. In the years 1543–1544, medical professor Luca Ghini (ca. 1490–1556), recently called to Pisa, constructed there a systematic garden for the use of his pupils. Within a few years, similar gardens had sprung up throughout Italy, most notably in Padua, Florence, Bologna, and Rome. The next century showed a wave of foundations of public botanical gardens across Europe, as northern universities sought to emulate their southern counterparts and as princes likewise aspired to adorn their capitals. The process of chartering and equipping gardens was often a lengthy one, so much debate still exists about their dates of origin; to provide merely a partial list, botanical gardens were established in Zurich (1560), Leiden (1577), Leipzig (1579), Heidelberg (1593), Paris (1597 and 1626), Montpellier (1598), Giessen (1605), Strasbourg (1620), Oxford (1621), Altdorf (1626), Jena (1629), Uppsala (1657–1665), Chelsea (1673), Berlin (1679), Edinburgh (1680), Amsterdam (1682), Halle (1698), and St. Petersburg (1713). By 1653, Simon Paulli's (1603–1680) *Viridaria varia regia et academia publica* (Various Royal Gardens and Public Academies) offered readers an intellectual tour through seven of the most prominent royal and university gardens, documenting the extent to which the culture of the botanic garden had by this time become truly international.

The typical *hortus medicus,* or physic garden (the term *hortus botanicus* is also to be found, but less frequently), displayed certain characteristic features. Geometrically laid out in rows of tiny beds, in which plants were grouped according to various systems, it enabled the easy demonstration of "simples" (medicinal herbs) by medical professors, who could literally lead their students through the vegetable kingdom. Recent scholarship has stressed another aspect of this highly formalized garden design: the way in which early-modern botanical gardens evoked images of the Garden of Eden. Enclosed by square or circular walls and often divided into quarters planted to represent the four corners of the world, botanical gardens symbolically assembled species from around the globe, seeming to reunite them in a new earthly Paradise. In fact, the earliest botanical gardens were largely composed of European plants, like the medieval monastic gardens that preceded them; but garden directors increasingly sought out rare and exotic specimens for their own installations. Successive editions of garden catalogs show a steady rise in the number of species cultivated, with a late-sixteenth-century influx of Oriental bulbs from the eastern Mediterranean, followed by seventeenth-century waves of plants from the more distant shores of America, Africa, and Asia. To house these newcomers, gardens would often add a *hibernaculum* (greenhouse), with increasingly elaborate

B

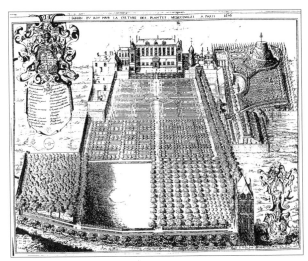

The Royal Garden was established in Paris in 1630. It contained plants from all parts of the world and served as a botanical research center. From Frédéric Scalberge, Le jardin du roy *(1636).*

heating systems designed to keep tropical plants alive during cold winter months. Such structures and extensions became highly visible features of the botanical garden as it expanded.

This shift in focus paralleled an equally important development. Whereas medicinal plants had provided the primary inspiration for the earliest botanical gardens, later gardens increasingly opened their horizons to the systematic study of *all* plants, regardless of medicinal properties. In the process, they contributed greatly to the development of botany as a discipline no longer merely ancillary to medicine. Often integrated with such other institutions of the New Science as anatomy theaters, chemical laboratories, and collections of curiosities, botanical gardens came to serve as key centers for the practice of natural history and philosophy during the Scientific Revolution. Much research remains to be done on the role of botanical gardens as sites for such important activities as the compiling of *herbaria* (collections of dried plants), the organization of botanical excursions or field trips to study the local flora, and the shaping of early-modern attitudes toward diversity and change in the natural world.

BIBLIOGRAPHY

Adams, William Howard. *Nature Perfected: Gardens Through History.* New York: Abbeville, 1991.
Cunningham, Andrew. "The Culture of Gardens." In *Cultures of Natural History,* ed. N. Jardine, J. A. Secord, and E. C. Spary. Cambridge: Cambridge University Press, pp. 38–56.

Prest, John. *The Garden of Eden: The Botanic Garden and the Re-Creation of Paradise.* New Haven, CT: Yale University Press, 1981.
Reeds, Karen Meier. *Botany in Medieval and Renaissance Universities.* New York: Garland, 1991.
Stafleu, Frans A. "Botanical Gardens Before 1818." *Boissiera* 14 (1969), 31–46.

ALIX COOPER

See also Aldrovandi, Ulisel; Botany; Gessner, Conrad; Natural History

Botany

The words *botanique* and *botany* were, respectively, sixteenth-century French and seventeenth-century English neologisms. The Greek root of these modern words refers to the description and gathering of plants useful in medicine and industry. But, for moderns, the term came to encompass the hunt for new species, the study of the cultivation and properties of plants, the art of naming and classifying plants, and investigation into the chemical components, internal structure, and functions of the parts of plants.

In the sixteenth and seventeenth centuries, botany was transformed. In editions published by Renaissance humanists, the treatises of Theophrastus (ca. 372–ca. 287 B.C.E.), Pliny (23–79 C.E.), Dioscorides (first century), and Galen (second century) inspired direct observation of plants, whether in the field or in specially created gardens and herbaria. Herborizations in Europe and abroad disclosed thousands of species unknown to the ancients. Some yielded new medicaments (quinine) or foods (pineapple, potato), while others (the sensitive plants) challenged the Aristotelian distinction between vegetative and animal kingdoms.

At the same time, university medical faculties developed new ways of teaching botany. At Montpellier, for example, humanist professors replaced Avicenna (980–1037) with Dioscorides and took their students into the countryside to cull "simples" (medicinal plants). Chairs in medical botany were established at several universities, including Padua in 1533, Basel in 1588, Montpellier in 1593, Paris in 1647, and Aix in 1658. University botanical gardens were established at Padua and Pisa in the 1540s, at Bologna in 1568, at Leiden and Leipzig in the 1570s, and at Heidelberg and Montpellier in the 1590s.

These trends ignited a taste, inside and outside medical circles, for collecting botanical exotica. Private

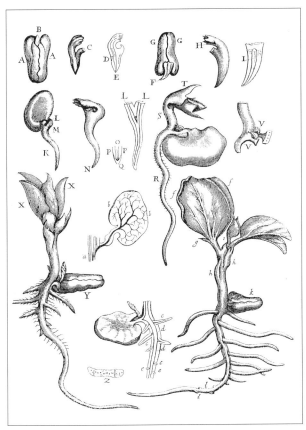

Germination of the lima bean. From Marcello Malpighi,
Anatome plantarum *(1675–1679).*

gardens expanded from kitchen or pharmaceutical plots to ambitious evocations of the Garden of Eden. Their owners supplemented the offerings of urban flower markets by exchanging seeds and cuttings along with advice about cultivating difficult varieties; those overcome by "tulip fever" paid ruinous prices for rare bulbs. Artists who could render "all but the scent" of plants were much in demand, and cognoscenti valued their work as much for its accuracy as for its metaphysical evocations. Books on plants addressed an increasingly diverse audience, and public lectures at the Paris Jardin Royal founded by Louis XIII (1601–1643) drew an international audience of savants, collectors, and medical students.

With woodblock and copperplate permitting detailed, delicate, and replicable representations, authors and readers came to demand naturalistic illustrations in botanical treatises. The resulting plates might be collected independently of the books. Several styles of illustration evolved. Blossoms on their stems served the decorative purposes of Nicolas Robert (1614–1685) in his "garlands," but the Académie Royale des Sciences

(Paris) required its artists (Robert, Abraham Bosse, 1602–1676, and Louis de Chastillon, 1639–1734) to render in scale the entire plant, including roots, and to represent the stages of growth from seed or bulb to mature plant. Charles Plumier (1646–1704) suggested the Caribbean habitat of his flora, while Maria Sybilla Merian (1647–1717) linked plants and insects to evoke ecological and allegorical associations.

In the late seventeenth century, newly invented instruments stimulated savants to examine vegetable parts and processes. In his *Micrographia,* Robert Hooke (1635–1702) described mushroom spores, mosses, and the cell membranes in cork. Using the glass-bead microscope developed by Nicolas Hartsoeker (1656–1725), Christiaan Huygens (1629–1695) and Jean Picard (d. 1682) compared the shapes of pollens in 1678; Huygens also speculated on the connection between pollen and beeswax. With a simple convex lens, Edmé Mariotte (ca. 1620–1684) studied bulbs in 1677 and 1678 to argue against preformation; in the 1690s, Joseph Pitton de Tournefort (1656–1708) identified seeds in plants previously thought to have been generated spontaneously. With the air pump, Robert Boyle (1627–1691), Huygens, and Guillaume Homberg (1652–1715) tested whether air was necessary to plants.

Innovative experiments and theories about plants were modeled after the latest developments in animal anatomy and physiology. The controversial studies of plant sexuality published in 1694 by Rudolph Camerarius (1665–1721) were taken up by Sébastien Vaillant (1669–1722) and Carl Linnaeus (1707–1778) in the eighteenth century. William Harvey's (1578–1657) theory of the circulation of blood inspired speculation and research on the circulation of the sap by Hooke, Johann Daniel Major (1634–1693), Marcello Malpighi (1628–1694), Mariotte, Claude Perrault (1613–1688), and Nehemiah Grew (1641–1712) after 1660. Such studies, in turn, inspired illustrations (showing roots and stems cut transversally and longitudinally) of internal vegetable structures.

The influx of new species prompted descriptive encyclopedias, with new classificatory systems prompting debate in the late seventeenth century. Robert Morison (1620–1683) favored the form and structure of the fruit and John Ray (1620–1705) used both flowers and fruits, while Augustus Quirinus Bachmann (1652–1723) and Tournefort relied on flowers or corollas in their physiognomic systems.

Finally, for savants who explained the invisible workings of the world in terms of chemical elements and processes, plants offered an important test case. Chemists and doctors at the Académie Royale des Sciences distilled fruits and vegetables, whole and in their parts, trying to correlate known nutritive and medical properties with the chemical components found in plants or soils.

By 1650, botany was no mere ancillary to medical study. Newly discovered species shattered old categories of thought while attracting a broader public. Theories and experiments adapted from the animal world affirmed the interest in plants not only as living things in themselves, but also as problematic test cases in debates about the nature of life and matter.

BIBLIOGRAPHY

Delaporte, François. *Nature's Second Kingdom*. Trans. Arthur Goldhammer. Cambridge, MA: MIT Press, 1979, 1982.

Greene, Edward Lee. *Landmarks of Botanical History*. Ed. Frank N. Egerton. 2 vols. Stanford: Stanford University Press for the Hunt Institute for Botanical Documentation, 1983.

Reeds, Karen Meier. *Botany in Medieval and Renaissance Universities*. New York and London: Garland, 1991.

Stroup, Alice. *A Company of Scientists: Botany, Patronage, and Community at the Seventeenth-Century Parisian Royal Academy of Sciences*. Berkeley, Los Angeles, and Oxford: University of California Press, 1990.

ALICE STROUP

See also Aldrovandi, Ulisse; Botanical Gardens; Brunfels, Otto; Camerarius, Rudolph Jakob; Freda, Leonhart; Greiv, Nehemiah; Natural History; Ray, John; Taxonomy

Boulliau, Ismaël (1605–1694)

An early Copernican, Keplerian, and defender of Galileo Galilei (1564–1642), Boulliau was the most noted astronomer of his generation. Although his career reflects many of the movements associated with the Scientific Revolution, Boulliau was widely known in the Republic of Letters as a historian, classical scholar, and philologist. Arguably, his correspondence network (which rivals the combined efforts of Marin Mersenne and Henry Oldenburg) marks the transition from humanism to science, from scholarly correspondence to the first scientific journals.

Born to Calvinist parents in Loudun, Boulliau converted to Catholicism and moved to Paris in the early 1630s. During the next thirty years, he enjoyed the patronage of the family De Thou and assisted the brothers Dupuy at the Bibliothèque du Roi (Royal Library), home of their famous Cabinet (one of the principal informal societies of Paris). Here Boulliau extended the humanist ideal of intelligencer to matters of science.

Boulliau's first book, *De natura lucis* (On the Nature of Light, 1638), grew out of an ongoing conversation on the nature of light with his friend Pierre Gassendi (1592–1655). Against Gassendi's atomist claims, Boulliau defended Johannes Kepler's punctiform analysis, but he argued against Kepler (1571–1630) that light behaved three-dimensionally and could be understood as a mean proportional "between corporeal and incorporeal substance." Later in the volume, Boulliau provided one of the first statements of the law of illumination: the intensity of light diminishes inversely as the square of the distance.

In the following year, Boulliau published his *Philolaus* (1639), which had circulated in manuscript in the years following Galileo's condemnation by the Roman Catholic Church (1633). Thoroughly Copernican, there was perhaps little remarkable about the book except, as René Descartes (1596–1650) noted, that it was published at all. Boulliau's purpose was to provide new geometrical and optical arguments for the motion of the earth. Although he was attacked by J-B. Morin (1583–1656) and several Italian astronomers, Boulliau continued to embrace Kepler's central claim, that nature "loves simplicity, she loves unity . . . she uses one cause for many effects," to explain the motions of the planets.

Struck by the elegance of Galileo's "Platonic cosmogony" and Kepler's Platonic solids, Boulliau sought a single solution to two longstanding problems: accelerated circular free fall (Galileo's problem) and the cause of planetary motion and the true orbital paths of the planets (Kepler's problem). The solution, Boulliau argued, would be found in the "secret that lay hidden in uniform acceleration" and in the rule that governed the attenuation of light. Alas, a solution proved no mean feat, and Boulliau was not equal to the task. But his *Philolaus* received wide notice; it underscored his belief that a deeper unity—simple and elegant—would unite heaven and Earth.

The clearest expression of these commitments came in his *Astronomia Philolaica* (1645), arguably the most important book in astronomy between Kepler and Isaac Newton (1642–1727). Without doubt, this work extended awareness of Kepler's planetary ellipses. But where Kepler sought a physical cause for planetary motion—and called on astronomers and mathematicians for assistance—Boulliau provided an entirely new cosmology, the "Conical Hypothesis."

Arguing that planets orbit the Sun in an elliptical path, Boulliau again sought a single solution to two problems. For astronomers, the problem was to locate the planet at a given time; for cosmologists, the problem was to explain orbital motion. Because circles and ellipses are conic sections, Boulliau imagined each planet moving on the surface of a cone in an elliptical orbit, with the Sun at the lower focus. By construction, the axis of the cone lay in the center of the base, which simultaneously defined the empty focus of the ellipse and the centers of circular motion. The position of a planet on the ellipse at a given time (Kepler's problem) was thus defined by the intersecting circles (parallel to the base of the cone) where the planet's motion, at any instant, was uniform and circular around its center (Plato's dictum). But where Kepler invoked analogies of the lever and magnetic attractions and repulsions, Boulliau explained acceleration and deceleration along the ellipse as the natural motion of the planet from smaller or larger circles. The result was elegant and practical. Kepler's "area rule" was suspect on physical and geometrical grounds, and it was also difficult to apply. By contrast, Boulliau provided a model of simplicity: planetary motion was not caused by external forces but by reason of geometry; tedious trial-and-error calculation was now simple and direct. Arguably—in context—Kepler's construction was ingenious but useless.

The foundations of Boulliau's cosmology, however, were soon called into question. In 1653 Seth Ward (1617–1689) attacked his hypothesis, claiming to provide a more simple and accurate model. In his published response (1657), Boulliau acknowledged a difficulty (noted in his *Philolaica*) but showed that Ward's alternative (the "simple elliptical" model) was not equivalent to the Conical Hypothesis. If they were observationally equivalent, the latter would show a maximum error of 8' in heliocentric longitude, not Boulliau's 2.5'. Ward failed to note the difference. Boulliau nevertheless supplied a new "modified elliptical" model; compared to Kepler's calculations (using the same Tychonic data), the new model was slightly more accurate for several of the planets. Although the Boulliau-Ward debate ended abruptly—and Boulliau's tables were widely copied in England and Italy—the "problem of the planets" was far from resolved.

Boulliau published a number of works that blurred the distinction between "science" and "humanism," among them editions of several classical works on philosophy, astronomy, and mathematics. In his *Ad astronomos monita duo* (1667), Boulliau employed historical and scientific analysis to establish the period of Mira Ceti, a long-period variable star.

BIBLIOGRAPHY

Hatch, Robert. "Coherence, Correspondence, and Choice: Gassendi and Boulliau on Light and Vision." *Quadricentenaire de la naissance de Pierre Gassendi (1592–1992)*. 2 vols. Digne-les-Bains: Société Scientific et Littéraire, 1994, vol. 2, 365–385.

———. *The Collection Boulliau (FF. 13019–13059): An Inventory*. Philadelphia: American Philosophical Society, 1982.

Koyré, Alexandre. "A Documentary History of the Problem of Fall from Kepler to Newton." *Transactions of the American Philosophical Society* n.s. 45 (4) (1955), 329–395.

Wilson, Curtis. "From Kepler's Laws, So-Called, to Universal Gravitation: Empirical Factors." *Archive for History of Exact Sciences* 6 (1970), 89–170.

ROBERT A. HATCH

See also Correspondence Networks; Keplerianism; Ward, Seth

Boyle, Robert (1627–1691)

A superb experimentalist and an influential polemicist, Boyle wrote extensively about practical and theoretical chemistry and medicine, physical properties of matter (especially air), natural history, alchemy, philosophy of science, morality, theology, and the relationship between scientific and religious knowledge.

The fourteenth child and seventh son of Richard Boyle (1566–1643), the first earl of Cork, Boyle was born into the wealthiest, most influential family in Ireland and one of the most powerful families in the whole realm, at Lismore Castle in Munster on January 25, 1627. Robert and his brother Francis studied for three years at Eton College prior to embarking on a Grand Tour of the Continent under the supervision of Isaac Marcombes (d. ca. 1654), a French Protestant in whose Genevan home they stayed for nearly two years. During this time, Boyle later recalled, he underwent a conversion experience when he prayed for divine deliverance in the midst of a terrifying thunderstorm, vowing to live piously if he should survive—a vow he kept with remarkable

Courtesy Oklahoma University Library.

consistency for the rest of his life. He also perfected his French while learning the traditional subjects of rhetoric, logic, mathematics, natural philosophy, ethics, history, and the art of fortification. When in 1642 the Irish Rebellion and other circumstances rendered their father unable to forward funds for their support, Francis returned to Ireland to fight while Robert continued his studies with Marcombes in Geneva on credit. Around the middle of 1644, he returned to England and took up lodging with his sister Katherine, Lady Ranelagh (1615–1691) in London.

A year or so later, Boyle moved to Stalbridge Manor in Dorset, which he had inherited upon his father's death in 1643. He lived there until the mid-1650s, though he often visited London and spent almost two years in Ireland, where William Petty (1623–1687) taught him dissection and vivisection. His earliest writings, some of which were published many years later, date from the first part of this period: an ethical treatise, the autobiographical "Account of Philaretus During his Minority," and essays, reflections, and romances on moral and reli-

gious subjects (including *The Martyrdom of Theodora and Didymus, A Free Discourse Against Customary Swearing,* and early versions of *Seraphick Love* and *Occasional Reflections*). These writings have an emotional tone and an evangelical fervor to renew the spirituality of his countrymen that are not found to a similar degree in Boyle's mature works; indeed, though Boyle later reworked some of these treatises, he did not start any new ones on similar subjects after the early 1650s. The profound sense of divine sovereignty manifest throughout these works, however, remains undiminished in his later works and undoubtedly underlies his deep commitment to a voluntarist theology of Creation, which, in turn, underlies his advocacy of an empirical science based on the direct study of phenomena rather than a rationalistic science derived from metaphysical or mathematical axioms.

In the years 1649–1650, Boyle initiated a program of experimentation that apparently triggered an excitement for practical science that he never lost. Although he had been in contact with members of the Hartlib circle and other scientifically informed men in London since the mid-1640s, prior to this he had shown no more than a casual, "gentleman's interest" in natural philosophy. He also met the American alchemist George Starkey (1628–1665), who shared alchemical secrets with Boyle and spurred him on to additional experimentation. Like Francis Bacon (1561–1626), Boyle believed that the New Science held the key to improving the human condition; like the iatrochemists and the Hartlibians, he had particularly strong hopes for what might come through the application of chemical knowledge to medicine. These beliefs are the central themes of his longest book, *Some Considerations Touching the Usefulnesse of Experimental Naturall Philosophy* (1663 and 1671), parts of which were begun at this time and constitute Boyle's earliest scientific writings.

Yet, his religious interests were not being neglected. Influenced by his father's friend James Ussher (1581–1656), archbishop of Armagh, Boyle began to study biblical languages, acquiring linguistic skills that served him well later in his many theological treatises. About this time (late 1650s) he wrote an unpublished "Essay of the Holy Scripture," a work about reason and revelation written partly in response to Socinianism, brief passages from which were later incorporated into *Some Considerations Touching the Style of the Holy Scriptures* (1661) and *Some Considerations About the Reconcileableness of*

Reason and Religion and the tract that accompanied it, *Some Physico-Theological Considerations About the Possibility of the Resurrection* (1675).

In the winter of 1655–1656, Boyle moved to Oxford to join a group of natural philosophers that met in the rooms of John Wilkins (1614–1672), the warden of Wadham College. After Wilkins moved to Cambridge in 1659, Boyle hosted the meetings himself. Clearly, regular contact with accomplished natural philosophers was a great stimulus, for the next twelve years were perhaps the most productive of his life. His most famous project was a series of brilliantly conceived experiments on air, inspired by several demonstrations carried out at Regensburg by Otto von Guericke (1602–1686). Crucial to Boyle's success was the assistance of Robert Hooke (1635–1702), a gifted mechanician who helped Boyle perfect his air pump and prove that the properly equipped natural philosopher could, indeed, produce a vacuum—a fact that flew in the face of the Aristotelian principle that "nature abhors a vacuum." Boyle published his results in *New Experiments Physico-Mechanicall, Touching the Spring of the Air and its Effects* (1660) and in a much expanded second edition (1662), in which he answered the objections of Thomas Hobbes (1588–1679) and Francis Line (1595–1675). The latter also contained a statement of the inverse relation between the pressure and volume of a gas that has come to be called Boyle's Law, even though Boyle himself credited others with the original discovery.

Simultaneously with his work on pneumatics, Boyle wrote two other major scientific treatises: *Certain Physiological Essays* (1661), which includes a splendid account of the practical and philosophical problems posed by experiments, and *The Sceptical Chymist* (1661), a rambling dialogue in which he weighed the Aristotelian and Paracelsian traditions and called for practical chemists to show greater philosophical sophistication. He also helped found the Royal Society of London in 1660. A few years later, he published two large collections of experiments on cold and colors, drawing heavily on reports from travelers to various parts of the world.

In the early and mid-1660s, Boyle wrote his two most subtle and analytical works of natural philosophy, *The Origine of Formes and Qualities* (1666) and *A Free Enquiry into the Vulgarly Receiv'd Notion of Nature*, published after much revision in 1686. In these works, taken together, Boyle stated his reservations about the Scholastic mode of explaining natural phenomena and

argued for the superiority of what he called "the mechanical philosophy." Boyle saw mechanical explanations as more coherent and intelligible than the "vulgar" Aristotelian philosophy and, thus, more likely to lead to technological progress. In addition, Boyle argued for the theological merits of the mechanical philosophy: by focusing on the properties and powers given to brute matter at the Creation rather than on purposive principles within nature that functioned as intermediaries between God and the Creation, it represented an effective foil to various forms of Renaissance naturalism that tended to personify nature and circumscribe the sovereignty of God. Indeed, the support that Christianity and the New Science provided each other is the most obvious unifying theme of Boyle's voluminous writings, of which his last major work, *The Christian Virtuoso* (1690), is simply the culmination.

Beyond this general appreciation for mechanical explanation, Boyle typically did not venture too deeply. Although he recognized differences between competing versions of the mechanical philosophy—such as that of Pierre Gassendi (1592–1655), which postulated forces between atoms moving through empty space, and that of René Descartes (1596–1650), which denied the existence of all three—Boyle tended to gloss over these in favor of an eclectic, practical corpuscularianism that was well suited to his active, experimental life. Boyle's approach to the philosophy of science was equally moderate, drawing on both empiricist and rationalist elements and influenced by contemporary legal theory, a wide knowledge of natural phenomena gleaned from physicians and natural philosophers, and his own extensive laboratory experience. His scientific works were admired not so much for the theoretical views they espoused as for the observations and experiments they contained—most of the former attributed to specific authorities thought to be reliable, and most of the latter described in sufficient detail to enable curious readers to repeat them. Thereby Boyle carried out one of his primary intentions: to compile a Baconian history of nature.

In October 1668 Boyle moved to London, where he lived at Lady Ranelagh's house in Pall Mall for the rest of his life. Foreign dignitaries and distinguished natural philosophers routinely stopped by to visit—his work was well known on the Continent, owing to the availability of numerous authorized and pirated Latin editions—leading Boyle eventually to limit visitors to certain hours of the day. In his rooms and in a laboratory he established on the premises, Boyle continued his investigations in practical chemistry and pneumatics; wrote several treatises on aspects of medicine, natural philosophy, and theology; defended himself amicably against various critics; and pursued with some circumspection his alchemical interests, the extent of which is only now being fully realized. He also became involved in various scientific and religious projects—joining the Hudson's Bay Company to get more information about the effects of extreme cold; helping his nephew, Robert Fitzgerald (b. ca. 1637), in an effort to produce fresh water from the ocean; supporting both a Gaelic translation of the Bible for use in Ireland and Scotland and John Eliot's (1604–1690) translation of the Bible for the Indians in Massachusetts; serving as governor of the revitalized Society or Company for the Propagation of the Gospel in New England; underwriting Gilbert Burnet's (1643–1715) *History of the Reformation of the Church of England* (1680); and, in his will, endowing a perpetual lectureship in defense of Christianity. When the Royal Society elected him president in 1680, Boyle declined the honor on the ground that he did not wish to take the oaths required; he had earlier refused ordination, claiming that, if he remained a virtuoso rather than a cleric, his arguments using science to support Christianity would carry more weight.

Boyle died on December 31, 1691, partly from grief over the death eight days before of his beloved sister Katherine. The enormous set of papers he had accumulated at his death, along with some additional items associated with his eighteenth-century editor Henry Miles (1698–1763), is now housed at the Royal Society. The recent cataloging of this previously chaotic archive has made possible for the first time a systematic study of its contents. The more this has progressed and the more seriously his entire output of published writings is taken, the more our image of Boyle changes, from that of the systematic "rationalizer" of chemistry with a regrettable tendency to waste his time trying in vain to reconcile the New Science with theology, to that of a highly eclectic, somewhat ambivalent thinker, committed equally to moral and scientific reform, with an uncommon openness to new ideas coupled with a sincere desire to be fair to his opponents, driven even in his scientific investigations by an intense piety and a powerful vision of the unity of truth.

BIBLIOGRAPHY

Boyle, Robert. *The Works of Robert Boyle.* Ed. Michael Hunter and Edward B. Davis. 14 vols. London: Pickering and Chatto, 1999.

Hunter, Michael, ed. *Robert Boyle Reconsidered.* Cambridge: Cambridge University Press, 1994.

Maddison, R. E. W. *The Life of the Honourable Robert Boyle, F.R.S.* London: Taylor and Francis, 1969.

Principe, Lawrence M. *The Aspiring Adept: Robert Boyle and Alchemical Quest.* Princeton, NJ: Princeton University Press, 1998.

Sargent, Rose-Mary. *The Diffident Naturalist: Robert Boyle and the Philosophy of Experiment.* Chicago: University of Chicago Press, 1995.

Shapin, Steven, and Simon Schaffer. *Leviathan and the Air Pump: Hobbes, Boyle, and the Experimental Life.* Princeton, NJ: Princeton University Press, 1985.

Wojcik, Jan W. *Robert Boyle and the Limits of Reason.* Cambridge: Cambridge University Press, 1997.

EDWARD B. DAVIS

See also Air Pump; Alchemy; Atomism; Chemistry; Pneumatics

Brahe, Tycho (1546–1601)

The greatest observational astronomer prior to the invention of the telescope in the early seventeenth century, he formulated of one of the most influential models of the universe during the Scientific Revolution. Born in Skaane, Denmark, Brahe's early career in astronomy and his contacts with other scholars in Europe explain how he developed his geoheliocentric system and why he took the cosmological positions he espoused. Tycho stated that his interest in astronomy was greatly spurred by observations he made when he was but seventeen years of age. At the time, he was traveling through German university towns, where he met with many leading intellectuals. Of particular importance was his meeting in Augsburg with Peter Ramus (1515–1572), who advocated a reconstruction of astronomy based on observations and denied the value of using hypotheses. The term *hypothesis* traditionally had a different meaning from its modern sense. At that time, hypotheses were understood as fictional constructs used to predict celestial motions but were not thought to be true reflections of the actual state of nature. Although Tycho agreed that more accurate observations were essential, he did not see how astronomy could be improved by abandoning the traditional use of hypotheses.

From Tychonis Brahe epistolarum astronomicarum *(1596),*
showing Brahe surrounded by the names and coats of arms of
the Danish nobility.

During this time, Brahe also began assembling what was, for his day, an impressive panoply of instruments, beginning with his purchase of an astronomical radius, or cross-staff. While still a student, Brahe constructed his own celestial compass, which he employed in correcting the accepted astronomical tables of his day. The most important instrument was his Great Quadrant (*Quadrans maximus*), built at Augsburg in March 1570 before he returned to Denmark. These instruments, described by Tycho in a book many years later, emboldened him to believe that he could achieve a greater observational accuracy than anyone who preceded him. When Tycho returned to Denmark in 1570 because of his father's failing health, he had already concluded that his life would be devoted to the restoration of astronomy. Late in the year 1572, Brahe began to observe systematically a new star in the constellation Cassiopeia that had never before

been seen. He published an account of his observations in *De nova stella* (1573), in which he argued, contrary to the teachings of Aristotle (384–322 B.C.E.), that the star was supralunar. By this time, Brahe had studied Nicolaus Copernicus's *De revolutionibus* (On the Revolutions, 1543) carefully enough to conclude that this revived Aristarchan system was mathematically superior to Ptolemy's Earth-centered model. As a result of his work, Brahe gave a lecture (*Oratio*) at the University of Copenhagen in which he announced his intention to transform Copernican parameters into a geocentric model of the universe that would surpass the adequacy of both Ptolemy (ca. 100–ca. 170) and Copernicus (1473–1543). Brahe's intention might have never been fulfilled had it not been for the gift of the island of Hveen from his patron, Frederick II, king of Denmark. Here Brahe built the first modern observatory in Europe (called Uraniborg) and conducted an extensive program of studying the heavens by night.

Over the course of ca. twenty years, Brahe's nocturnal observations yielded many significant results for astronomy, with particular advances in the theory of lunar motion. Copernicus had reduced the distance of the Moon's orbit from the earth to half that of Ptolemy's theory. Drawing on Copernicus's work, Brahe made systematic observations of the Moon for several years and proved to his own satisfaction that there were still gross inaccuracies in previous theories. Most significant was his discovery of variation in the Moon's velocity, a discovery that ran contrary to the traditional notion of uniform celestial motions. Johannes Kepler (1571–1630) later developed this idea of the variable speeds of the planets in his laws of planetary motion. Another important observation was of the comet of 1577, which was investigated by almost all the learned astronomers of Europe. From his own observations, Brahe concluded that the comet displayed no perceptible parallax and, therefore, must be above the sphere of the Moon, another challenge to Aristotle's view of comets as sublunar phenomena.

Brahe eventually published his new system in 1588 in the eighth chapter of his *De mundi aetheris recentioribus phenomenis*. His system solved all of the major problems facing planetary theory in his own mind, even though today it is thought of as a trivial inversion of the Copernican system. Brahe was convinced of the geometric superiority of Copernicus's work, but he could not

B

conceive of how the earth could be physically moving. Furthermore, as he often repeated, the very idea was "contrary to Sacred Scripture." His solution placed the earth at the center of the universe with its moon and the Sun circumnavigating the earth. The Sun, then, was the center of the remaining five planetary orbits known at that time: Mercury, Venus, Mars, Jupiter, and Saturn. This system was mathematically equivalent to Copernicus's, yet it did not violate Aristotelian physical theory in most respects or the common interpretation of Scripture.

How did Brahe come to this system? Taking his own words in *De mundi* as its cue, the standard historical account claims that the comets of 1577 and 1585 made him give up his belief in the solid spheres on which, according to much of medieval cosmology, the planets travel. Further, his construction is not surprising because many astronomers in the late sixteenth century were, in fact, attempting to transform Copernican parameters into a geostatic model. While the comets no doubt played an important role in his deliberations, they do not explain the features of his system in detail. In a long letter to Caspar Peucer (1525–1602) in 1588, Brahe outlined how he arrived at his model, yet other statements in his letters suggest that this account does not tell the whole story. Brahe refers obliquely to the year 1583 or 1584 as the year in which he formulated his system in his mind, but the process began in the 1570s. As he became aware of the inadequacies of the Ptolemaic system, he searched for a necessary cause and a natural ordering of the planets that would answer to his sense of systemic elegance. He particuarly noticed that the orbits of the superior planets (Mars, Jupiter, and Saturn) and the inferior planets (Mercury and Venus) were related to the apparent motion of the Sun, a regularity that made no sense in a geocentric system. These problems made him look carefully at Copernicus's modern alternative but, as noted above, he thought the attribution of triple motion to the earth both physically absurd and theologically unacceptable. He found himself in an untenable position. On the one hand, he had to have Copernican parameters in his model, but, unlike Copernicus, he could not have a system with a moving earth. Brahe considered himself first of all a celestial observer and many times insisted that the restoration of astronomy had to be founded on indisputable observations.

He must have been happy, then, to have the opportunity to construct an observational experiment that would decide between Ptolemy and Copernicus. His opportunity came in 1582, when Mars was in opposition to the Sun. On Ptolemy's model, Mars is always farther from the earth than the Sun, but, on Copernicus's model, Mars should be closer to the earth at opposition. We know today that Brahe and his assistants could not have viewed what he said he did without a telescope because the phenomenon was well below the threshold of naked-eye observation. Yet, in 1584, in a letter to Henry Brucaeus, he wrote that the parallax of Mars was far less than the solar value, a conclusion that would confirm the Ptolemaic system. In a letter to Caspar Peucer in 1588, however, he argued that the parallax of Mars was greater than the Sun's and thus confirmed the Copernican system. Many scholars have attempted to explain Brahe's reversal, but none have been completely convincing. What does seem clear is that Brahe's system needed to have the Copernican prediction since his system predicts the same outcome.

While many astronomers of that era attempted to fit Copernican parameters to a geocentric model, only Brahe's system contains the innovative intersection of the orbits of Mars and the Sun. This feature violated the traditional notion of solid spheres and would have been impossible prior to the establishment of the supralunar location of comets. Brahe relates that the solid spheres prevented him from embracing a model with intersecting orbits for some time. When he realized, however, that there were no solid spheres, he knew he could allow such an intersection. His knowledge that the orbits of Mars and the Sun must intersect led him to recognize that another astronomer, Nicolaus Raimarus Bär (Ursus) (1551–1600), had stolen Brahe's ideas when the German astronomer had visited Uraniborg in the early 1580s. When Brahe sent copies of his system to leading astronomers of Europe in 1588, they informed him that they had already seen such a system published by Ursus. But Ursus's system did not contain the intersecting orbits, and Brahe knew that Ursus had absconded with an earlier and inaccurate version of the planetary system. He pursued Ursus until the end of his life in the hope of vindicating his claim to originality.

Most accounts of the Tychonic system fail to explain why Brahe opposed the motion of the earth other than cite his general denial of its physical impossibility and theological acceptability. We may infer from his comments to his correspondents that Brahe operated on an implicit disciplinary hierarchy. For him, discovering the true world system required the agreement of all three relevant disciplines: astronomy, physics, and theology. Terrestrial motion was not a question that astronomy could answer; it was a physical question. Astronomy could only construct tests to refute the motion of the earth but it could not prove it. If the question of Earth's motion were left open by astronomy (i.e., not refuted), then one must turn directly to physics. In that sphere, Brahe knew of no reason to abandon the traditional immobility of the earth, and there was, in fact, none at the time. If there had been physical reasons to believe in the earth's motion, he would have had to turn to theology to search for an answer and interpret those controversial biblical texts. Since there was no physical question in his mind, a detailed examination of biblical texts was unnecessary. This explains what appears to be his hasty dismissal of terrestrial motion by an appeal to physics and the Bible.

Brahe's planetary system does not cover other cosmological issues he thought important, the most prominent of which was the traditional question of celestial matter. Christopher Rothmann (fl. 1555–1597), the Court astronomer of Wilhelm IV, the landgrave of Hesse, insisted that the heavens below and above the Moon were homogeneous, consisting only of air. In contrast, Brahe held that the heavens above the Moon consisted of a quintessence, a fifth substance that differed from the traditional four posited for the sublunar world by Aristotle. Because this substance allowed for the free movement of heavenly bodies, Brahe insisted, it must be some type of liquid that was "very pure, fine and penetrable," but he was unwilling to deliver on what the specific nature of that substance might be. In this matter astronomy could be no help, so Brahe sought answers in the current natural philosophies of his day and the exegesis of biblical texts.

Brahe's geoheliocentric system was eventually rejected in favor of the Copernican system by the end of the seventeenth century, but it enjoyed immense popularity among astronomers in the earlier part of that century. The eventual demise of the Tychonic system, however, did not obscure his invaluable contributions to astronomy, the most important of which was his catalog of observations that became an essential part of the Copernican revolution.

BIBLIOGRAPHY

Brahe, Tycho. *Tychonis Brahe Dani opera omnia*. Ed. J. L. E. Dreyer. 15 vols. Copenhagen: Hauniae, 1913–1929.

Gingerich, Owen, and Robert S. Westman. "The Wittich Connection: Conflict and Priority in Late Sixteenth-Century Cosmology." *Transactions of the American Philosophical Society* 78 (1988), part 7, pp. 1–148.

Shackelford, Jole. "Tycho Brahe, Laboratory Design, and the Aim of Science." *Isis* 84 (1993), 211–230.

Schofield, Christine. *Tychonic and Semi-Tychonic Systems*. New York: Arno, 1981.

Thoren, Victor. *The Lord of Uraniborg: A Biography of Tycho Brahe*. Cambridge: Cambridge University Press, 1990.

Westman, Robert S. "The Astronomer's Role in the Sixteenth Century: A Preliminary Study." *History of Science* 23 (1980), 105–147.

KENNETH J. HOWELL

See also Comets; Copernicanism; Copernicus, Nicolaus; Geoheliocentrism; Kepler, Johannes; Novae; Parallax; Ramus, Peter; Rothmann, Christopher; Uraniborg; Ursus (Bär), Nicolaus Raimarus

Briggs, Henry (1561–1631)

Briggs was educated at Cambridge (B.A. 1581, M.A. 1585). A Fellow of his college from 1588, he became reader in physic (medicine) in 1592. In 1596 he was made the first professor of geometry at Gresham College, London; in 1619 he moved to Oxford as Savilian Professor of Geometry. His monuments are his logarithmic and trigonometrical tables.

Most of his life was spent as a blameless if busy university or college teacher, with contacts among the mathematical practitioners of the day, and he might now be little known but for John Napier's (1550–1617) publication of logarithms in 1614. Briggs saw how these could be improved to the more practically useful form with, as would later be recognized, a base of 10, and he published a short table (1617) of such logarithms from 1 to 1000, to fourteen places. This was followed by his extensive tables from 1 to 20,000 and 90,001 to 100,000 (101,000 in some copies), also to fourteen places, in his *Arithmetica logarithmica* (1624). In the extensive Preface, he explains his construction (although few, if any, seem to have read it in his own century), involving a case of the binomial theorem and interpolation formulae. The tables were completed by Adrian Vlacq (1628), but only to ten places; a London printing is dated 1631. After this,

Briggs turned to the production of trigonometrical and logtrigonometrical tables, completed by his Gresham College colleague Henry Gellibrand (1597–1636) and published in the *Trigonometria Britannica* (1633).

Briggs made other lesser but useful contributions to science and navigation. For example, he contributed tables to Thomas Blundeville's *Theoriques of the Seven Planets* (1602) and to Edward Wright's *Certaine Errors in Navigation* (2nd ed., 1610). Other tables by Briggs appear in Wright's translation of Napier's tables (1616, 1618). He also wrote on the Northwest Passage, was a friend of the Archbishop of Armagh James Ussher (the chronologist), and a member of a company trading to Virginia.

Although Briggs's standing is now less than it was during the "logarithmic centuries" (ca. 1614–ca. 1964), when virtually all calculations, large and small, relied on the existence of the extensive tables developed by him and his successors, he was a mathematician of some stature, whose methods, of wider-ranging interest, were extended by Carl Friedrich Gauss and others in the nineteenth century.

BIBLIOGRAPHY

Henderson, James. *Bibliotheca tabularum mathematicarum* (in English), part I. London: Cambridge University Press, 1926.

Thompson, A. J. *Logarithmica Britannica*. 2 vols. Cambridge: Cambridge University Press, 1952.

                                        JON V. PEPPER

See also Logarithms; Napier, John

Brouncker, William (1620–1684)

Born in Ireland to an aristocratic family, Brouncker succeeded to the title of viscount in 1645. He was educated at Oxford, where he took the degree Doctor of Physick in 1647. Brouncker held a number of government and administrative offices and was an active participant in British scientific life: he was president of Gresham College (1664–1667), a member of the Royal Society from 1660 to his death, and served as President of the Royal Society (on the king's nomination) from 1662 to 1677, actively promoting the society's experimental work. His principal area of scientific interest, however, was mathematics, and he is best known for his use of continued fractions. His most famous results include the expression

$$\frac{4}{\pi} = 1 + \cfrac{1^2}{2+\cfrac{3^2}{2+\cfrac{5^2}{2+\cfrac{7^2}{2+\ldots}}}}$$

as well as numerous other continued fractions for other geometric quantities.

In correspondence with Pierre de Fermat (1601–1665) and John Wallis (1616–1703), Brouncker supplied a solution to the Diophantine equation $ax^2 + 1 = y^2$ equivalent to $x = 2r/r^2 - a; y = r^2 + a/r^2 - a,$ for r any integer.

Brouncker published no mathematical works; his forte was solving problems set by others. Most of his results were made public by Wallis, who published several letters from Brouncker in his own books.

BIBLIOGRAPHY

Hartley, Harold, and J. F. Scott. "William Viscount Brouncker, P. R. S." *Notes and Records of the Royal Society* 15 (1960–1961), 147–156.

Whiteside, D. T. "Brouncker's Mathematical Papers." *Notes and Records of the Royal Society* 15 (1960–1961), 157.

                                 DOUGLAS M. JESSEPH

See also Fermat, Pierre de; Series; Wallis, John

Brunfels, Otto (ca. 1489–1534)

Initiated a new era in herbals with his aptly named *Herbarum vivae eicones* (Living Portraits of Plants, 1530–1536). Brunfels, often called (with Jerome Bock, Leonhart Fuchs, and Valerius Cordus) a German father of botany and referred to by Carl Linnaeus (1707–1778) as the father of botany, was the first to feature illustrations drawn from nature in his text. He also wrote and edited many theologial, medical, and pharmacological works, including the influential *Reformation der Apotecken,* which was used as the city ordinance for apothecaries in Bern.

Brunfels's knowledge of botany derived primarily from Italian herbalists who focused on identifying plants in their areas with those described in Dioscorides's (fl. 50–70) *Materia medica*. Brunfels, too, attempted to correlate plants he discussed with those mentioned by Dioscorides, but his *Herbarum* was the first herbal to

Creating medical preparations. From Otto Brunfels, Onomastikon medicinae *(1534), a dictionary for physicians and apothecaries that included information on botany, dosages, alchemy, and magic.*

incorporate descriptions and illustrations of plants native to Germany. He explained therapeutic usage in terms of Galenic "temperaments" and relied heavily on ancient and contemporary commentators on Dioscorides. Brunfels also published the *Contrafayt Kreuterbuoch,* a German adaptation of the *Herbarum,* which included still more German plants and illustrations.

Early-sixteenth-century graphic artists began including exact imitations of nature in book illustrations and by 1550 had developed techniques allowing naturalistic renderings to be transferred to woodblocks. Previous herbal illustrations were simple line drawings copied imperfectly from ancient texts, but lifelike illustrations such as those of Leonardo da Vinci (1452–1519) and Albrecht Dürer (1471–1528) led herbalists to demand similar verisimilitude. Hans Weiditz, Brunfels's illustrator, drew from nature, even depicting plants with broken stems and insect damage. His illustrations were original, realistic, and much superior to Brunfels's descriptions,

which uncritically copied predecessors. The importance of the *Herbarum* to contemporaries and successors alike was due largely to Weiditz's illustrations, which prompted others to attempt increasingly naturalistic illustrations in herbals.

B

BIBLIOGRAPHY

Baader, Gerhard. "Mittelalter und Neuzeit in Werk von Otto Brunfels." *Medizinhistorischer Journal* 13 (1978), 186–203.

Dilg, Peter. "Die Reformation der Apotecken (1536) des Berner Stadtarztes Otto Brunfels." *Gesnerus* 36 (1979), 181–205.

Weigelt, Sylvia. *Otto Brunfels: Seine Wirksamkeit in der frühbürgerlichen Revolution unter besonderer Berucksichtigung seiner Flugschrift "Vom Pfaffenzehnten."* Stuttgart: H-D. Heinz, 1986.

KATHLEEN WHALEN

See also Botany; Dürer, Albrecht; Leonardo da Vinci; Natural History; Taxonomy

Bruno, Giordano (1548–1600)

Philosopher, born Filippo Bruno in Nola, Italy, he became renowned as a defender of Copernicanism, the infinity of the universe, and the plurality of worlds and practitioner of the art of memory. He entered the Dominican Order in 1563 but fled his monastery in 1572. His religious transformation resulted from having read works of Desiderius Erasmus (ca. 1469–1536), which led him to question orthodox ideas, particularly those on the Trinity.

Bruno spent two years traveling throughout Italy, earning a meager income teaching the thirteenth-century astronomical treatise *De sphaera* by Johannes de (John of Holywood) Sacrobosco. He retained the tonsure, indicating that he kept certain elements of his Catholic belief. In fact, after 1578, for safety's sake, he donned homemade Dominican garb.

In 1578, Bruno taught part-time at the University of Toulouse. However, because of Protestant and Catholic acrimony there, Bruno moved to Lyons, where he encountered the ideas of Ramon Lull (ca. 1235–1316) on artificial memory, which became the foundation for his own work, including *De umbris idearum* (On the Shadows of Ideas, 1582). Still dressed as a Dominican, he entered Calvinist Geneva in 1580. Italian refugees urged him "to dress like a layman" and to wear a cap, presumably to cover his tonsure. He quickly insulted the

Courtesy Burndy Library, Dibner Institute for the History of Science and Technology, Cambridge, MA.

authorities and was incarcerated. He was strictly questioned on his ideas concerning the Lord's Supper and was finally released. Bruno left Geneva and went to Paris.

He became an acquaintance of Court intellectuals such as Pontus de Tyard and perhaps even of King Henry III. It was probably in Paris that Bruno first learned about Copernican heliocentricity. Certainly his later discussion of the Copernican model, in *La cena de le ceneri* (The Ash Wednesday Supper, 1584), contains errors also found in Pontus de Tyard's *Deux discours de la nature du monde et de ses parties* (Two Discourses on the Nature of the World and its Parts, 1578). Bruno went to England in 1583 on a mission from the king of France, he later said, to unite liberal English Protestants with liberal Catholics in the French Court). He wrote his Italian dialogues in London, including *La cena de le ceneri, De l'infinito universo e mondi* (On the Infinite Universe and Worlds, 1584) and *Lo spaccio della bestia trionfante* (The Appearance of the Triumphant Beast, 1584). These works dealt with Bruno's religious interpretation of Copernicanism, his discussion of the infinity of the centerless universe, his belief in the plurality of worlds, and his interpretation of the ancient Egyptian (i.e., Hermetic) religion.

Bruno returned to France in 1585. However, he no longer enjoyed Court favor, and he fled Paris in 1586. He went to Lutheran Wittenberg, where he enrolled briefly in the university, to Frankfurt, and then to Prague, where he hoped to attach himself to the Court of the occultist Emperor Rudolph II. In 1590, he returned to Frankfurt, where he wrote and published his last works, *De magia* (On Magic) and *De imaginum compositione* (On the Composition of Images).

In 1591, the Venetian nobleman Zuan Mocenigo invited Bruno to Venice to teach him the art of memory. But Mocenigo turned him over to the Venetian Inquisition in 1592. A year later, Bruno was transferred to the Inquisition in Rome, where he remained the last seven years of his life. He was sentenced to death as a heretic on February 7, 1600, and was burned at the stake in Rome on February 17.

The charges on which Bruno was found guilty are not precisely known. A wide panoply of questions were put to him. Interestingly enough, the Inquisitors were less concerned with his Copernicanism and praise of Nicolaus Copernicus (1473–1543) in *La cena de le ceneri* and other works than they were with his praise of Queen Elizabeth and other heretical princes. They were alarmed at his apostasy, his consequent neglect of fasting regulations, and his views on Christ and the Trinity.

While Bruno has been characterized as a "wild man" in terms of religion (Yates 1964) and as one of the "philosophers of nature" along with Bernardino Telesio and Francesco Patrizi (Kristeller 1964), it seems that the "sins" that led to his death were the sins of a religious dissident rather than those of a scientist. It is clear, nonetheless, that he played an important role in the Scientific Revolution (positing the idea of the infinity of the universe and the plurality of worlds). His contributions to Galileo's troubles with the Inquisition (1632–1633) were due more to supposed similarities in their relationships with Protestant leaders and causes than to their ideas about nature.

Bruno was influenced by the Neoplatonists and the Hermetic texts, Lucretius, Ramon Lull, Nicholas of Cusa, and various contemporary writers. Although few directly cited him after his condemnation and execution, he seems to have influenced Galileo Galilei (1564–1642) in certain formalistic manners of writing. His concept of the monad influenced Benedict de Spinoza (1632–1677) and, in the early eighteenth century, when John Toland published Bruno's *Lo spaccio della bestia trionfante,* he became associated with Toland's pantheistic doctrines. In the late nineteenth century, he became a hero of the Italian nationalists.

BIBLIOGRAPHY

Gosselin, Edward A. "Fran Giordano Bruno's Catholic Passion." In *Supplementum Festivum: Essays in Honor of Paul Oskar Kristeller,* eds. James Hankins, John Monfasani, and Frederick Purnell Jr. Binghamton, NY: Medieval and Renaissance Texts and Studies, 1989, 537–561.

Gosselin, Edward A., and Lawrence S. Lerner. "Galileo and the Long Specter of Giordano Bruno." *Scientific American* 255 (1986), 126–133.

Kristeller, Paul O. "Giordano Bruno." In *Eight Philosophers of the Italian Renaissance.* Stanford: Stanford University Press, 1964.

Yates, Frances A. *Giordano Bruno and the Hermetic Tradition.* Chicago: University of Chicago Press, 1964.

EDWARD A. GOSSELIN

See also Copernicanism; Hermetism; Infinity of the World

Buonamici, Francesco (ca. 1535–1603)

Physician and professor of natural philosophy at the University of Pisa, teacher of Galileo Galilei, and author of *De motu* (On Motion, 1591), which exposed Aristotle's teachings in ten books and focused on the four causes of motion, the types of motion, and the relation of motion to the heavenly bodies. In effect, an entire course in natural philosophy, this was published at Florence in 1591. At one time it was thought that Buonamici was the source of Galileo's early notebook containing the physical questions, but this has been disproved. Buonamici's influence is detectable in other of Galileo's writings, however, mainly in the notebook containing his early treatises on motion. In his later works, Galileo (1564–1642) was expressly critical of his former teacher.

Buonamici presents himself as a classical, if somewhat eclectic, Aristotelian, making use of Greek commentators on the texts of Aristotle (384–322 B.C.E.) and the works of his contemporaries at Italian universities, mainly Padua and Bologna, but showing little acquaintance with fourteenth-century authors. In mechanics, Buonamici held a theory of self-expending impetus, thought that projectiles increase velocity after leaving the projector, and rejected the medieval conception of a build-up of accidental gravity in falling bodies to explain their acceleration. Similarly, he preferred Aristotle's rules

for calculating the ratios of motions, velocities, and distances of travel over those proposed by Albert of Saxony and other Scholastic authors.

Despite their differences, Mario Helbing (1989) has advanced the thesis that Buonamici exerted a substantial influence on the young Galileo, whose own writings reflect a prolonged polemic dialogue with his onetime teacher. These influences are manifest in three areas. The first is the autonomy they both grant to the natural sciences; the second is their common commitment to a *methodus* of resolution and composition in their search for causes; and the third is the status each accords to mathematics as a science in its own right and as an aid in investigating the secrets of nature. These set Galileo on a course that would bring him ultimately to Christoph Clavius (1538–1612) and the professors of the Collegio Romano.

BIBLIOGRAPHY

Helbing, Mario. *La filosofia di Francesco Buonamici, professore di Galileo a Pisa.* Pisa: Nistri-Lischi Editore, 1989.

Koyré, Alexandre. *Galileo Studies.* Trans. John Mepham. Atlantic Highlands, NJ: Humanities Press, 1978, Part I, ch. 2.

WILLIAM A. WALLACE

See also Collegio Romano; Impetus; Motion; Resolution and Composition

Bureau d'adresse

A clearinghouse for information, goods, and services founded in Paris by Theophraste Renaudot (1586–1653) in 1630. It provided listings of real-estate offerings, experimental medical treatments, job opportunities, and the professional services of physicians, surgeons, apothecaries, and tradesmen. It tracked down elusive information about missing persons and documents. Renaudot intended to facilitate the efficiency of society, particularly through increased commerce and employment, by bringing people into contact with each other. The bureau also served the poor through low-interest loans, pawn shops, and free medical treatment. (Poor relief was one of Renaudot's vital interests and was reflected in his appointment by Cardinal Richelieu, Louis XIII's chief minister, as commissioner to the poor.)

Several activities of the bureau are particularly relevant to the Scientific Revolution. The bureau challenged the authority and hegemony of the Faculty of Medicine in Paris over medical education and practice. Renaudot and other Montpellier-trained physicians provided medical consultations and prescribed chemical remedies at the bureau. Bureau physicians produced a medical questionnaire to facilitate diagnosis at a distance for patients without access to medical practitioners, particularly the rural poor. Perhaps most significant for the dissemination of the new science, the bureau was the site of a weekly series of conferences for nine years (1633–1642). These conferences treated scientific issues extensively and demonstrated a wide-ranging, eclectic understanding of science. Because they took place in a public setting and were disseminated through published proceedings, they illuminate both the character of seventeenth-century scientific discussion as an interplay of many competing scientific paradigms and the increasingly important role of science in French public culture.

BIBLIOGRAPHY

Solomon, Howard. *Public Welfare, Science, and Propaganda in Seventeenth-Century France*. Princeton, NJ: Princeton University Press, 1972.

Brown, Harcourt. *Scientific Organizations in Seventeenth-Century France (1620–1680)*. Baltimore: Johns Hopkins University Press, 1934.

Sutton, Geoffrey. *Science for a Polite Society*. Boulder, CO: Westview, 1995.

KATHLEEN WELLMAN

See also Academies

Bürgi, Joost (1552–1632)

Born in Lichtensteig (St. Gall canton), Switzerland, Bürgi had no formal academic education but apprenticed as a watchmaker. Wilhelm IV, landgrave of Hesse (1532–1592), hired him in 1579 as a Court clockmaker at Kassel but soon also employed him as an instrument maker, observer, and calculator. Due to Bürgi's mechanical skill, the Kassel observatory had instruments second only to Tycho Brahe's (1546–1601) Uraniborg, and Wilhelm commended him to the latter as a "second Archimedes." He designed a proportional compass—described in 1607—about the same time as Galileo Galilei (1564–1642).

Bürgi was the most ingenious clock and watchmaker of the period. In his watches, the mainspring repeatedly rewound a second spring, which, in turn, drove the escapement. He also employed a remontoir, superior to the fusee. His cross-beat escapement (1584) ensured clocks vastly superior to any in use. Wilhelm claimed they had an accuracy of one minute per day. Bürgi is said to have built the first clock with a second hand.

Although untutored, he had significant mathematical talent. Paul Wittich (ca. 1546–1586), visiting Kassel ca. 1583, showed him Johannes Werner's formula for *prosthapaeresis,* a method of converting the product of sines into an addition—namely, $2 \sin \alpha \sin \beta = \cos (\alpha - \beta) - \cos (\alpha + \beta)$. Bürgi provided a demonstration and suggested a formula for the product of two cosines. He also produced a table of sines and was one of the first to employ the decimal point.

In 1603 he entered the employ of Rudolf II in Prague as Court watchmaker and also worked with Johannes Kepler (1571–1630) as a computer on reductions of Tycho's observations. Bürgi independently developed a system of natural logarithms, probably before John Napier (1550–1617), but did not publish tables based upon his method until 1620. He remained in Prague after the Imperial Court left in 1620 but returned to Kassel, perhaps in 1631, and died there the following year.

BIBLIOGRAPHY

Von Mackensen, Ludolf. *Die erste Sternwarte Europas mit ihren Instrumenten und Uhren: 400 Jahre Jost Bürgi in Kassel.* Munich: Callwey, 1979.

RICHARD A. JARRELL

See also Horology; Logarithms; Triponometry

Burnet, Thomas (ca. 1635–1715)

A disciple of Ralph Cudworth (1617–1688) at Christ's College, Cambridge, he was master of the Charterhouse of London, corresponded with Isaac Newton (1642–1727), and, above all, was widely known as the author of *Telluris theoria sacra,* a narration of the history of the earth. Already in 1681 (the year of publication of its first two volumes) it had become an epicenter of the cosmological dispute involving English and European scholars and helped promote the idea that the face of the earth had undergone change. The cyclic structure of his cosmology follows closely the cosmology of the Bible—chaos, flood, conflagration, and the end of the world, which are characterized by traumas and catastrophes, each of which mark off a cycle. The stages of the catastrophes are: the origin of the earth, its development into its present form, the conflagration, and the millennium. Burnet's several concerns are evinced by the composition of his work. The first two books, which constitute the scientific section, deal, respectively, with the Deluge and the formation of the present form of the earth. The third book announces the imminent conflagration of the terraqueus globe, and the fourth describes the restoration of Paradise.

Burnet's attempts to support his *Theory* may be seen in his *Archeologia philosophica* (1692), in which he argues that his hypothesis is proved both by an ancient philosophical tradition and by its compatibility with the Mosaic tale of Genesis, if correctly read and rightly interpreted. In several works, some of them posthumously published, Burnet replied to criticisms of his theories and developed his theological points. In them, the author engages in a rational inquiry into theological foundations and acknowledges salvation as the main theme of Christian faith. His emphasis on man, man's history, and man's future is also evident in remarks on John Locke's *Essay Concerning Human Understanding* that Burnet issued between 1697 and 1699. Against Locke (1632–1704), he argues for the natural morality of men, their original purity, and their possibility of recapturing such a state of intellectual and spiritual perfection after the millennium.

BIBLIOGRAPHY

Bettini, A. *Cosmo e apocalisse: teorie del millennio e storia della terra nell'Inghilterra del seicento.* Firenze: Olschki, 1997.

Gould, S. J. *Time's Arrow, Time's Cycle: Myth and Metaphor in the Discovery of Geological Time.* Cambridge, MA: Harvard University Press, 1987.

Jacob, M. C. *The Newtonians and the English Revolution, 1689–1720.* Ithaca, NY: Cornell University Press, 1976.

Pasini, M. *Thomas Burnet: Una storia del mondo tra ragione, mito e rivelazione.* Firenze: La Nuove Italia, 1981.

AMALIA BETTINI

See also Geology/Mineralogy; Theories of the Earth

B

C

Cabala. See Kabbalah

Calculating Machine

Seventeenth-century natural philosophers devoted considerable attention to improved techniques of computation. Early in the century, John Napier (1550–1617) not only proposed a tool, known as Napier's rods, for assisting in multiplication, but also discovered logarithms, providing the mathematical basis of the slide rule. In Italy, Galileo Galilei (1564–1642) invented a military compass, or sector, for use in artillery computations. Later in the century, Claude Perrault (1613–1688) of the Parisian Academy of Sciences proposed an arrangement of sliding bars that could be used to keep track of the digits in addition and subtraction problems. Numerous nineteenth-century adders operated on Perrault's principle.

Calculating machines, instruments that perform arithmetic operations automatically, were proposed in the seventeenth century by the Tübingen professor and minister Wilhelm Schickard (1592–1635), the French mathematician and philosopher Blaise Pascal (1623–1662), and the German mathematician and philosopher Gottfried Wilhelm Leibniz (1646–1716). Schickard's machine is known only from letters he wrote to Johannes Kepler (1571–1630) in 1624, which were discovered in the twentieth century. It was designed to assist in multiplying a large number by a single digit. Multiples of each digit of the large number were entered by hand—the machine had rotating multiplication tables, similar to Napier rods, to assist in finding these multiples and a limited mechanical carry to accumulate totals.

Pascal was the son of a tax collector, which may have impressed him with the need for precise calculations. In 1642 he invented a stylus-operated machine that would add and subtract. The work of carrying numbers was done by falling weights linked to pegs in the machine. In the course of his life, Pascal made ca. fifty machines of this sort, several of which survive. Pascal's demonstration that machines could calculate, and his specific use of stylus-operated machines with rotating wheels, inspired later inventors of sturdier machines, such as Jean Lepine.

In 1671 Leibniz, then a diplomat in the service of the elector of Mainz, envisioned a machine that carried out all four arithmetic operations. Leibniz spent the next five years in Paris, where he and the watchmaker Olivier (fl. 1673) built calculating machines. In early 1673, Leibniz demonstrated a rough wooden model of this machine at a meeting of the Royal Society of London. By the summer of the next year, Olivier had completed a proper working instrument. In Leibniz's calculating machine, digits were represented by the position of a gear along a cylinder with teeth of varying length. The larger the digit, the greater the number of teeth engaged. Operations were carried out by rotating the drums with a crank. The direction of motion determined whether numbers were added or subtracted. Multiplication took place through repeated addition, division through repeated subtraction.

Unable to find permanent work, Leibniz left Paris in 1676 to become the librarian to the duke of Hanover. In Hanover, he continued to work on improvements to his calculating machine, although he never completed a commercial product, and only one machine associated with him survives. Stepped drums would be used in the eighteenth-century calculating machine of Philipp

Matthäus Hahn and in numerous nineteenth- and twentieth-century commercial calculating machines.

BIBLIOGRAPHY

Graef, Martin, ed. *350 Jahre Rechenmaschinen.* Munich: Carl Hanser Verlag, 1973.

Hofmann, Joseph E. *Leibniz in Paris, 1672–1676.* Cambridge: Cambridge University Press, 1974.

Kidwell, Peggy A. "Adders Made and Used in the United States." *Rittenhouse* 8 (1994), 78–96.

Williams, Michael R. *A History of Computing Technology.* Englewood Cliffs, NJ: Prentice-Hall, 1985. 2nd ed. 1997.

PEGGY ALDRICH KIDWELL

See also Proportional Dividers; Slide Rule

Calculus

The development of the calculus has, for three hundred years, been regarded as one of the main achievements of seventeenth-century science. The importance of this algebraically expressed general method for dealing with areas, tangents, and their extensions and applications, chiefly associated in its beginnings with Isaac Newton (1642–1727) and Gottfried Wilhelm Leibniz (1646–1716), has not been diminished by subsequent discoveries in other fields.

Many results now obtainable by elementary calculus were rigorously demonstrated in the ancient world by Euclid (fl. 300 B.C.E.) and Archimedes (ca. 287–212 B.C.E.) using the so-called exhaustion method of Eudoxus (fifth century B.C.E.). One result, the volume of a specific pyramidal frustum, had been given much earlier in the anonymous *Moscow Papyrus* (ca. 1900 B.C.E.). Such work, however, does not give the great mathematicians involved a true claim to the calculus; their methods, though ingenious, are not of sufficient generality. The same applies to Apollonius and Pappus, who solved various extremal problems.

Even after the revival of learning in the Latin West, the quantitative consideration of change by such as Thomas Bradwardine (ca. 1290–1349) was hampered, as it had always been, by the lack of an adequate symbolism, but his ideas were spread in the sixteenth century. Another important impulse was the printing of editions of Euclid (1482) and Archimedes (1544). However, Greek methods were mainly applicable to rather restricted problems, and their lengthy and rigorous methods of proof did not show how results could be found.

By 1600 the belief that the ancients had all knowledge that study and luck might recover was becoming less tenable, although the mechanical method of Archimedes, recovered as late as 1906, showed that long-lost discovery methods had existed.

The century before Newton and Leibniz saw many contributions to what may be called "precalculus." Sometimes these were special cases, but degrees of generality were also obtained. Simon Stevin (1548–1620) and Thomas Harriot (ca. 1560–1621) experimented with infinitesimals (i.e., small nonzero elements). By 1600 Harriot had produced the first known rectifications, by double limits, summations, and geometrical dissection. John Napier's (1550–1617) logarithms and Harriot's meridional parts (both completed in 1614) became classic examples to which infinitesimals and series methods were later applied. Mathematical tables from Ptolemy (ca. 100–ca. 170) onward had given ideas of functionality and stationary values. Johannes Kepler (1571–1630), himself a notable calculator, used infinitesimals to estimate various volumes of revolution (1615), without the sterile Archimedean demonstrations.

Later, in 1635, Bonaventura Cavalieri (1598–1647) used indivisibles (i.e., lines or planes of zero content) to obtain new results via the transformations now that became possible. The equivalent of the integration of integral powers was found. In 1637 René Descartes (1596–1650) made algebraic ideas and notation more available. He included an algebraic method of finding normals (hence, tangents), easily verified for well-known simple cases but harder beyond that. This was based on equality of roots, but Pierre de Fermat (1601–1665) in the 1630s (but not published until 1679), studying François Viète (1540–1603), used Diophantus's idea of adequality, a sort of "almost equals," to solve similar problems and those related to maxima and minima by an incremental method not unlike those of Newton and Leibniz later on. He also obtained notable quadratures of conics and spirals by infinitesimal methods involving variable intervals.

Descartes had denied that rectification was possible, even conceptually, but in the early 1640s Evangelista Torricelli (1608–1647) repeated Harriot's spiral results, and in the late 1650s both William Neil (1637–1670) and Hendrik van Heuraet (1633–ca. 1660) gave rectifications of the semicubical parabola. The latter's method converted infinitesimal tangent lengths into areas, which were then summed. It used one of the rules given by Jan

Hudde (1629–1704), that for finding equal roots to determine stationary values. Other contributors at this time were Gregory of St. Vincent and Paul Guldin. At the same time, both Blaise Pascal (1623–1662) and Gilles Personne de Roberval (1702–1675) in France were working on the cycloid. Pascal provided a transmutation method that converted problems into the determination of a simpler area or volume. Leibniz subsequently acknowledged his influence on him. Roberval, using Cavalierian indivisibles, gave a neat quadrature of the cycloid, and Christopher Wren (1632–1723) rectified the curve (1659).

Further contributors were Pietro Mengoli, Michelangelo Ricci, and Stefano Degli Angeli, Gregory's teacher at Padua. In 1638 Descartes had only partly solved an inverse-tangent problem of F. de Beaune (1601–1652); the fuller solution was left to Leibniz (1676). Christiaan Huygens (1629–1695) produced results similar to those already mentioned, including a method for points of inflection, but his chief contribution here was the encouragement of the young Leibniz in Paris in the early 1670s. Isaac Barrow (1630–1677), in a work (1670) seen through the press by Newton, constructed tangents rather like Fermat and even gave, in geometric form, a result equivalent to the fundamental theorem of the calculus, relating tangents to areas, but he did not seem to see its fuller importance.

James Gregory (1638–1675) was another notable contributor, giving the quadrature of conic sectors by an extension of Archimedean methods, series expansions of trigonometric and logarithmic functions, and the fundamental theorem. In 1668 Nicolaus Mercator (ca. 1619–1687) gave the famous series for log $(1 + x)$, obtained by quadrature of the series expansion of $1/(1 + x)$. The identity of the logarithm with hyperbolic areas was noticed by Alfonso Antonio de Sarasa on reading St. Vincent's work of 1647 and became widely known by the 1660s.

It will be clear that the years before Newton had produced many ingenious methods and results, some more general than others. But Newton's work in the mid-1660s went beyond this and produced an algebraic and algorithmic unification of approach. Heavily influenced by Frans van Schooten's (ca. 1615–1660) much extended editions of Descartes, Newton, in a series of papers not published until after 1700 (some only very recently), produced his kinematical model of fluxions, the rate of change of flowing quantities or fluents (although time

was not essential to them), and involving motion during infinitely short intervals. His *Principia mathematica philosophiae naturalis* (Mathematical Principles of Natural Philosophy, 1687) contains both overt infinitesimals and covert calculus, and it was published in the form in which it was first written, contrary to the myth that it had been reworked as geometry.

Newton showed the inverse problem to be that of quadrature and gave numerous examples. He also used his method of infinite series, including the binomial theorem, particularly in rectification, as an extension of Descartes's finite algebra. Newton explained to Leibniz in 1676 that this result arose from extending to an algebraic, rather than an arithmetic, conclusion John Wallis's (1616–1703) rather different interpolation method of 1656, which had led to the infinite product for π. Newton's papers include all of the usual elementary systematic rules and give numerous examples of the now standard series, as well as tables of integrals obtained by substitutions and the solution of many problems. In the 1680s and early 1690s, he produced further treatises, only in the latter decade introducing the dot notation since associated with him.

Newton did not publish his calculus until Leibniz's calculus, developed in the 1670s and published after short delays, had been developed further by the Bernoulli brothers Jakob (1654–1705) and Johann (1667–1748) and partly published in textbook form by Guillaume-François-Antoine de l'Hôpital (1696). Leibniz's approach was different from Newton's. He started with summation as the inverse of difference methods, and his work made greater use of symbols. His writing was somewhat careless and obscure, but it is his notations that have stood the test of time, despite being based on unclear ideas (e.g., his use of "dx" in calculating the derivation of a function). His first relevant paper was published in 1684, but in the early to mid-1670s, he had already given the basic rules and a powerful transmutation that led to the series for $\pi/4$ (known also to James Gregory) and to integration by parts. Later papers, giving the integral sign and the fundamental theorem, appeared in 1686 and 1693. Whether the nonstandard analysis of the 1960s shows that Leibniz's differentials, which long embarrassed mathematicians, have a proper logical foundation remains controversial.

In their different ways, the algorithmic calculuses of Newton and Leibniz both relied on, and extended, algebraic symbolisms developed since Viète. Whereas

Newton's ideas were essentially kinematic, Leibniz's involved sequences of infinitesimally close values; the fluxion was a velocity, or at least a rate of change, whereas the differential was a difference. Newton had defined his integration as an inverse and had no special notation for it, but for Leibniz it arose as a summation, and the fundamental theorem became more prominent. Leibniz's notation lent itself more easily to functions of more than one variable and relied less on geometric representation, as befitted his search for a universal symbolic language. To Leibniz and his followers, Newton's method of infinite series was a last resort and not part of the calculus, but few problems have exact (finite) solutions, and, in the end, Newton's judgment has proved the sounder. Newton's creation of the calculus has always loomed large in the English-speaking world, but its influence elsewhere was slight; the best eighteenth- and nineteenth-century work was in Continental Europe and followed the Leibnizian tradition.

The first printed account by Isaac Newton of his work on the calculus and the binomial theorem. The vignette on the title page has a portrait of Newton emitting the light of understanding.

The notorious Newton-Leibniz priority dispute, in which neither protagonist was entirely straightforward, is a minor subject in its own right. The Bernoulli brothers developed the Leibnizian calculus very quickly in the 1690s, Johann working hard to put the *Principia* into analytical form, something largely completed by Joseph Louis Lagrange (1788). The modern form of elementary calculus is due mainly to a series of textbooks by Leonhard Euler from the 1740s onward. Although, as some recognized at the time, the new calculus was not rigorous, it set the basis and agenda for two centuries of mathematical development, eventually including the introduction of sounder foundational studies.

BIBLIOGRAPHY

Baron, Margaret E. *The Origins of the Infinitesimal Calculus.* Oxford and New York: Pergamon, 1969.

Boyer, Carl B. *The History of the Calculus and Its Conceptual Development.* New York: Dover, 1959.

Edwards, Charles E. *The Historical Development of the Calculus.* New York and Berlin: Springer, 1979. Corrected ed. 1982.

Fauvel, John, and Jeremy Gray. *The History of Mathematics: A Reader.* London: Macmillan, 1987, chs. 11–13.

Hall, A. Rupert. *Philosophers at War.* Cambridge: Cambridge University Press, 1980.

JON V. PEPPER

See also Infinitesimals; Mathematics

Calendar Reform

The reform of the Julian calendar was accomplished in 1582 with the publication of Pope Gregory XIII's bull *Inter gravissimas.* Most Catholic countries adopted the new calendar immediately; other countries, at later dates and not without long controversies. England and its colonies did not adopt it until 1752. It replaced the calendar introduced by Julius Caesar in 46 B.C.E.

The Julian calendar was designed to have the seasons begin approximately on the same days every year. To this end, its length in days needed to coincide with length of the "tropical" year, the time it takes for the Sun to come back to the same point on the ecliptic (e.g., the vernal equinox). As the year does not contain an exact number of days, any calendar has to provide unambiguous rules for the intercalation of a number of days, when needed. It was known that the tropical year had a duration of a little less than 365.25 days. The Julian calendar, therefore, provided that, after three succesive years of

365 days, the fourth year should have 366. To avoid confusion, the longer year (or leap year) would be each year whose number is divisible by four.

At the time of the Nicaean Council in 325, the vernal equinox was ca. March 21. But the actual value of the tropical year was a little shorter than the calendar year. This secular effect meant that, by the sixteenth century, the true equinox occurred ten days earlier. The calendars of those times would indicate the day of the astronomical and of the official equinox. Any generation could get used to it, but it interfered with the computation of Easter Sunday.

The Gregorian reform followed the project proposed by Luigi Liglio (ca. 1510–1578) before his death. It dealt first with the solar, or civil, calendar and then with the religious part, or the rules for the determination of Easter. Taking the value of the tropical year from the Alfonsine Tables (1252), Liglio used a suggestion of P. Petati (1560). Both supposed that the drift of the equinox was ca. one day in 134 years. This comes to ca. three days in four hundred years. Liglio thought it would be impractical to intercalate one day any time within a century; instead he proposed, as a fundamental rule, that any change would have to be on the centurial years (ending with two zeros): no centurial year would be a leap year except when divisible by four hundred. In practice, it means that the "adopted" year has 365.2425 days.

The reformers estimated an error of one day in ca. twenty thousand years. They were aware that the year value used was not exact, but they desisted from further corrections. The adopted year, compared to the modern value (still not well known in its secular variations), has an error of one day in twenty-five hundred years. Even so, the Gregorian calendar is a still a very good approximation for centuries to come.

Christianity agreed to celebrate Easter on the first Sunday that follows the first full Moon after March 21. But, instead of actual observations of the Moon's phases, the traditional practice was the use of tables for their computation. The Metonic cycle of nineteen years proved sufficient for this. This cycle is based on the fact that 235 mean lunations equals almost nineteen years. A set of tables allowed one to find the Moon's approximate phase. The Gregorian reformers accepted this cycle, but with the new value of the tropical year and also with a slightly different value of the lunation. Liglio was the auther of the new scheme approved with a set of rules for the intercalation or omission of days, when needed, to keep the computed moon's phases as close as possible to the true Moon. As before, such intercalation or omission was allowed only on centurial years. The reformers did not accept the suggestion of using astronomical tables because they were not reliable at the time. It would be all right today, but back then it would have been a source of dissent and lack of unity.

The Gregorian reform was an attempt to return the calendar to the way it was at the time of the Nicaean Council. The vernal equinox was fixed again on March 21 with the suppression of ten days in October 1582, the year of the reform. The distribution of days in the months was left intact, and the seven-day-week cycle never had an interruption.

BIBLIOGRAPHY

Clavius, C. *Explicatio Romani calendarii a Gregorio XIII P. M. restituti.* Rome: Zannettum, 1603.

Coyne, G. V., M. A. Hoskin, and O. Pedersen, eds. *Gregorian Reform of the Calendar.* Vatican City: Specolo Vaticana, 1983.

Ginzel, F. K. *Handbuch der mathematischen und technischen chronologie.* 3 vols. Leipzig: Hinrichs, 1906–1914.

Nautical Almanac Offices of the United Kingdom and of the United States of America. *Explanatory Supplement to the Astronomical Ephemeris. . . .* London: HMSO, 1961, pp. 410–430.

Seidelmann, K. *A Revision of the Explanatory Supplement. . . .* Mill Valley, CA: University Science Books, 1992, pp. 575–608.

JUAN CASANOVAS

See also Clavius, Christoph

Cambridge Platonists

The Cambridge Platonists were a group of seventeenth-century divines, emanating chiefly from Emmanuel College, Cambridge, who can be seen to have shared some moral, religious, and theological principles. Although there were undoubted similarities among them, they were by no means entirely uniform in their thinking. The term *Cambridge Platonists* has to be used, therefore, with some caution; particularly so as there is no consensus among historians about who is to count as a Cambridge Platonist and who is not. Those who are more or less guaranteed a place in the ranks are Benjamin Whichcote (1609–1683), John Smith (1616–1652), Ralph Cudworth (1617–1688), and Henry More (1614–1687).

In general, it seems true to say that the Cambridge Platonists shared a common favorable attitude to the use of reason in religion; opposed the Calvinist doctrine of predestination, seeing it as a threat to sound moral principles; and subscribed, to a greater or lesser extent, to a Latitudinarian theology in which things that were deemed to be indifferent to the faith were excluded from dispute. They have also been seen as taking a favorable view of the so-called New Philosophy, particularly the mechanical philosophy of René Descartes (1596–1650).

For the Cambridge Platonists, reason was a "partial likeness of the Eternal Reason," a faculty bestowed upon man by God to enable him to see the truth. They were committed, therefore, to the belief that reason and revelation could not be at odds with each other. This led them to an admiration for Plato (428–348 B.C.E.) and later Neoplatonist philosophers like Proclus (410–485) and, especially, Plotinus (205–270). They were not Platonists to the extent that they adhered to specific Platonic or Neoplatonic principles but simply insofar as they admired the rationalist and idealist approach to knowledge. The similarities between Platonism and Neoplatonism, on the one hand, and Christian doctrines, on the other, which we now know to derive simply from Platonic influences upon the early Church Fathers, served the Cambridge theologians as ample testimony to the ability of reason to lead even pagans to Christian truths.

If Platonism seemed to them to be compatible with both reason and faith, however, Calvinism did not. The notion of predestination and the associated doctrine of absolute reprobation seemed particularly indefensible on moral grounds. Henry More recounted in later life how, when still a pupil at Eton, he refused to believe that, even if he were not one of the Elect, if he continued to live a godly afterlife in Hell God should not save him. Their rationalism and anti-Calvinism led many to accuse them of Socinianism and Arminianism, and there were certain similarities between them and the latter. They were also close to another movement in the English Church, however—Latitudinarianism. Originally coined as a pejorative charge of religious indifference and laxity, Latitudinarianism was, in fact, a would-be irenic movement intended to remove dissent from within the Church. Latitudinarians developed a religion of doctrinal minimalism, declaring most theological and religious niceties to be indifferent to one's salvation. The truth of such contentious matters would one day be revealed, but, meanwhile, the important thing was to establish and subscribe to the undeniable and uncontentious doctrines

of the true faith. It is important to note, however, that, just as the Cambridge Platonists were not the only rationalists in seventeenth-century religion, so they were not the only Latitudinarians. Indeed, while Whichcote's proud declaration, "I am not a Christian of any denomination," marks him as truly Latitudinarian, there must be some doubts about Henry More, for example, who was rather too insistent in his writings upon the supposedly undeniable truth of such nonfundamental doctrines as the preexistence of souls and the incorporeality of animal souls.

Of the four leading members of the Cambridge school, all but Whichcote were clearly impressed and influenced by the usefulness of the Cartesian mechanical philosophy for religion. Smith, More, and Cudworth embraced Cartesian dualism and used it to insist upon the truth of the existence and immortality of the soul.

The influence of the Cambridge Platonists is hard to assess. Their rationalism and Latitudinarianism certainly became characteristic of the Anglican Church in the eighteenth century, but the Cambridge theologians themselves were only participants in these more widespread movements in contemporary theology. Their rationalism and their use of the new philosophies of nature to establish the fundamental truths of religion proved influential in the subsequent development of natural theology. These features of their work may also have contributed to the rise of deism, if not atheism, but here again they were not the only influence in this direction. The moral philosophy of More and Cudworth, with its emphasis on rationally evident, absolute, and immutable principles of morality, by which even God had to abide, was also highly influential in the eighteenth-century English Church.

BIBLIOGRAPHY

Cassirer, Ernst. *The Platonic Renaissance in England*. Trans. James P. Pettegrove. Edinburgh: Nelson, 1953.

Colie, Rosalie L. *Light and Enlightenment: A Study of the Cambridge Platonists and the Dutch Arminians*. Cambridge: Cambridge University Press, 1957.

Powicke, Frederick J. *The Cambridge Platonists: A Study*. London and Toronto: Dent, 1926.

Tulloch, J. *Rational Theology and Christian Philosophy in England in the Seventeenth Century,* vol. 2: *The Cambridge Platonists*. Edinburgh and London: Blackwood, 1874.

JOHN HENRY

See also Cartesianism; Cudworth, Ralph; More, Henry; Natural Theology; Neoplatonism

Camera Obscura

Camera clausa, camera ottica, and other variants refer to a "darkened chamber" into which an image or a picture of a scene outside is cast on a wall or screen through a small opening, or aperture. The phenomenon seems to have been known in several ancient cultures, particularly for casting images of the Sun, especially during eclipses.

The pseudo-Aristotelian *Problemata* reported round (or crescent-shaped) solar images beneath the openings of overlapping leaves of trees, through the angular holes in wickerwork and even crossed fingers and saw the phenomenon as possibly incompatible with a rectilinear path of light.

It became an instrument of optical demonstration, teaching the art of perspective, revealing the marvels of "natural magic," and offering a model of the role of the eye in vision. By artificially isolating a beam of light, the camera allowed experimental investigations of the propagation of light.

The puzzle concerning rectilinearity continued to be addressed in the Middle Ages. The problem of "pinhole images" was definitively solved early in the Scientific Revolution by Johannes Kepler (1571–1630), whose insight had been anticipated, subsequent scholarship has revealed, by Ibn al-Haytham (Alhazen) (965–ca. 1040), Levi ben Gerson (1288–1344), Francesco Maurolico (1494–1575), and possibly others.

With Kepler's general demonstration of how geometrical rays of light produce images of bodies of any shape behind apertures of any shape, investigators were now able to isolate beams of presumptively rectilinear light for further study, as, for example, in experiments concerning prismatic colors by Isaac Newton (1642–1727) and the investigations of diffraction begun by Francesco Maria Grimaldi (1618–1663).

BIBLIOGRAPHY

Hammond, John H. *The Camera Obscura: A Chronicle.* Bristol: Adam Hilger, 1981.

Kemp, Martin. *The Science of Art: Optical Themes in Western Art from Brunelleschi to Seurat.* New Haven, CT: Yale University Press, 1990.

Straker, Stephen M. "Kepler, Tycho, and 'The Optical Part of Astronomy': The Genesis of Kepler's Theory of Pinhole Images." *Archive for History of Exact Sciences* 24 (1981), 267–293.

STEPHEN STRAKER

See also Light Transmission; Optics; Vision

Camerarius (Camerer), Rudolph Jacob (1665–1721)

A German botanist who was the first to discover and to prove experimentally that all plants reproduce sexually (i.e., by means of distinct male and female reproductive organs). This had been known since ancient times about a few plants but without specific details as to how it happens, as some plants like date palms are dioecious (i.e., some individual plants have only male flowers and others only female flowers). The question of whether bisexuality, so obviously found in animals, also applies generally or universally to plants was debated during the century before Camerarius but remained unanswered.

Camerarius was able to extend this notion to all plants by means of a series of experiments in which he carefully removed various components from the flowers to see the effect this had on reproduction. He thereby succeeded in identifying the sexual anatomy of monoecious plants (those having male and female flowers on the same individual plant) as consisting of the female pistil (ovary, style, and stigma) and the male stamen (filament and anther with its pollen).

However, the exact role of the pollen in fertilization was not determined until the middle of the nineteenth century. Camerarius's understandable conclusion that plants having both male and female organs in the same flower reproduce hermaphroditically was later proven to be incorrect. Although he recognized the role of the wind in pollination, it had not yet been discovered that flying insects are the main agents.

Camerarius's important findings were published in 1694 in his *De sexu plantarum epistola.* However, it was only a century-and-a-half later that his findings came to be accepted as conclusive. His work opened the door to experimental plant hybridization and to an understanding of genetically transmitted traits in plants.

BIBLIOGRAPHY

Camerarius, Rudolph Jacob. *De sexu plantarum epistola.* Tübingen, 1694.

Wickert, Konrad. *Das Camerarius-Florilegium.* Erlangen-Nürnberg: Universitätsbibliothek, 1993.

RICHARD J. BLACKWELL

See also Botany; Taxonomy

Campanella, Tommaso (1568–1639)

An Italian natural philosopher and Dominican priest whose lifelong intellectual project was the creation of a new synthesis of all knowledge. This universal philosophy, or metaphysics as he called it, was conceived as a bridge uniting the realms of religion (God as revealed in the Scriptures) and the physical world (God as revealed in his Creation). Theology and science were understood to be distinct modes of knowing but completely consistent and conducive to a unification that should be the goal of a Christian culture.

One result was that, throughout his career, Campanella was very opposed to the philosophy of Aristotle (384–322 B.C.E.), which was not only pre-Christian, but also contradicted religion in its denial of Creation, divine providence, and the immortality of the human soul. But since Aristotle's philosophy was generally dominant in the schools of his day, it was inevitable that Campanella would run into conflict with the religious authorities.

His universal philosophy was a tapestry woven of several different threads. He was influenced by the writings of Bernardino Telesio (1509–1588), who advocated the direct empirical study of nature (in place of the then common practice of appealing to established authors) and who maintained that the operations of the natural world consisted of the interactions between the active forces of hot and cold and the passive sensible matter of the world. Telesio also argued for an earth-centered model of the universe, a view that Campanella maintained throughout his life, even though in his heroic *A Defense of Galileo* (1622), he vigorously defended the thesis that Galileo Galilei (1564–1642) should, for the good even of the Church itself, be free to carry on his own scientific work and arguments in favor of the Copernican sun-centered model.

Campanella's synthesis also included elements of magic, astrology, and the occult, based on his view that spirits of various types inhabited all bodies. As a result, the theme of animism, if not pantheism, that flows through his writings makes him appear antirational and antiscientific. These themes brought him into further conflict with the religious authorities.

His final metaphysical synthesis was built on the claim that the whole of reality, including both God and nature, is everywhere composed of three "primalities" or principles: power, knowlege, and love. He applied this to

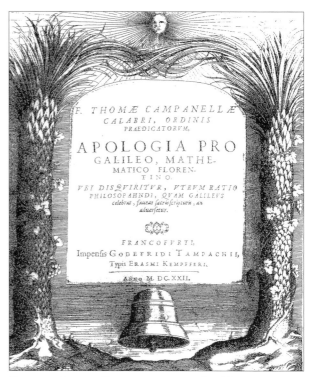

Tommaso Campanella's tract in support of Galileo's Copernicanism.

the Divine Trinity, to the body, spirit, and soul in humans, and to all material things in various ways.

On the political side, he argued vigorously for the reform of the Church, the religious orders, and civil government, envisioning instead a universal Church-State governed by reason. His best-known writing is *The City of the Sun* (ca. 1602), a utopian discussion of this ideal state. These political views led him to become an active opponent of the Spanish rule then exercised in southern Italy.

In 1599 he was charged with conspiracy against the state and heresy against the faith, and, after a complex trial that included torture on several occasions, he spent the next thirty years in the prisons of the Inquistion. Nevertheless, in such harsh conditions, and with only a few books available to him, he managed to write voluminously during his long imprisonment, which was made possible in large part by his possession of a truly prodigious verbatim memory of most of what he had read.

BIBLIOGRAPHY

Blanchet, Léon. *Campanella*. New York: Burt Franklin, 1964.

Bonansea, Bernardino. *Tonmaso Campanella: Renaissance Pioneer of Modern Thought*. Washington, D.C.: Catholic University of America Press, 1969.

Campanella, Thomas. *A Defense of Galileo.* Trans. R. J. Black-well. Notre Dame, IN: University of Notre Dame Press, 1994.

RICHARD J. BLACKWELL

See also Copernicanism; Telesio, Bernardino; Utopias

Cardano, Girolamo (1501–1576)

During the course of his life, he wrote more than two hundred books on medicine, mathematics, mechanics, astrology, natural philosophy, music, and the immortality of the soul. Cardano began his university studies in 1520 at Pavia and obtained a doctorate in medicine at Padua in 1526. His first publication, *De malo recentiorum medicorum usu libellus* (On the Bad Practice of Medicine in Common Use), appeared in 1536. He had a successful career in medicine, including holding the chair of medicine at Pavia, until his imprisonment by the Inquisition in 1570, after which he was forced to recant and to abandon teaching.

Famous for revealing, after being sworn to secrecy, Niccolò Tartaglia's procedure for solving third-degree equations, his *Ars magna* (The Great Art, 1545) presented systematically many of the new techniques in algebra. One of the most important of these, now called Cardano's Rule, is a method for solving reduced third-degree equations (equations that lack the second-degree term); he also included the linear transformations that eliminate the second-degree term in a complete cubic equation. His *Liber de ludo aleae* (Book on the Game of Dice), a work on games of chance, published posthumously in his collected works (1663), is considered a precursor of probability theory. Although he enunciated the law of large numbers, the principle that there is an approximate fit between observed frequencies and "true" probabilities that improves as the numbers of observations increase, and tested the extent to which a priori probabilities were borne out by a posteriori observations on the dice, he also believed that luck could play an important part in the final outcome. Additionally, he was a well-known advocate of astrology who proposed that events, even Christ's life, are influenced by the stars. He attempted a complete systematization of astrology that strove for rigor both in mathematics and in accounts of celestial change, but he was hostile to Copernicanism.

Cardano's interest in medicine led to his attempts to account for fevers and other medical phenomena

Frontispiece of Cardano's Cl. Ptolemaei Peluensis *(1554).*

through a radical reformation of Aristotle's (384–322 B.C.E.) four qualities (hot, cold, wet, and dry); he reduced the four qualities to two (hot and wet), considering coldness and dryness to be merely the privation of heat and wetness, respectively. Moreover, he also reduced the elements from four to three (air, earth, and water), considering fire to be merely a mode of existence of matter.

Cardano published two encyclopaedias of natural philosophy, *De subtilitate* (On Subtlety, 1550) and *De rerum varietate* (On the Variety of Things, 1557). Showing a wide-ranging display of erudition, they contain a diverse range of topics: from cosmology to the construction of machines; from the evil influences of demons to cryptology; they also discss the current status of various sciences, alchemy, and several branches of the occult. Additionally, they explicitly reject Aristotelianism and argue that, in the end, experience is the only convincing and trustworthy guide. These works also display an interest in the forms in which knowledge was expressed, formulating a contrast between "human knowledge" and "natural knowledge." In other words, they develop the beginnings of a distinction between a rhetorical-moral type of knowledge used for dominating and deceiving others and a knowledge supposedly derived from nature, constructed from facts and capable of expansion over time. These distinctions were developed partly through Cardano's interest in improving the conditions of human life by exploiting nature. Additionally, he suggested that the limitations on our knowledge imply that the deciphering of nature could not be the work of a single individual but would eventually be achieved through the collaboration of all researchers, all heedful of the practical aspects of knowledge. His work exemplifies the growing significance of concreteness and specific explanation.

BIBLIOGRAPHY

Eckman, James. *Jerome Cardano.* (Supplements to the Bulletin of the History of Medicine no. 7). Baltimore: Johns Hopkins University Press, 1946.

Maclean, Ian. "The Interpretation of Natural Signs: Cardano's *De subtilitate* versus Scaliger's *Exercitationes.* In *Occult and Scientific Mentalities in the Renaissance,* ed. Brian Vickers. Cambridge: Cambridge University Press, 1984, pp. 231–252.

Morley, Henry. *The Life of Jerome Cardan of Milan, Physician.* 2 vols. London: Chapman and Hall, 1854.

Ore, Oystein. *Cardano the Gambling Scholar.* Princeton, NJ: Princeton University Press, 1953.

Siraisi, Nancy. "Girolamo Cardano and the Art of Medical Narrative." *Journal of the History of Ideas* 52 (1991), 581–602.

KATHERINE HILL

See also Algebra; Probability

Cartesianism

A distinctive approach to scientific knowledge based on the work of René Descartes (1596–1650), which included the establishment of a new metaphysical foundation for science, the adoption of a hypothetical method in search of mechanical explanations of natural phenomena, and a recognition of the probabilistic character of scientific hypotheses.

Cartesianism developed especially in France during the century after Descartes's death, until it was challenged in the eighteenth century by Newtonian theory as the dominant framework for scientific theorizing. It included among its followers in France Jacques Rohault (1620–1675), Pierre-Sylvain Régis (1631–1707), Louis de la Forge (1632–1666), Nicolas Malebranche (1638–1715), Geraud de Cordemoy (1626–1684), Nicolas Poisson (1639–1710), Bernard Lamy (1640–1715) and, in Geneva, Jean-Robert Chouet (1642–1731). It also attracted attention in England from the Cambridge Platonists and from Samuel Clarke (1675–1729), who translated Jacques Rohault's *Traité de physique* (1671) as *System of Natural Philosophy* in 1697, adding Newtonian footnotes for use as a university textbook of physics.

Colleges and universities in Europe in the seventeenth and early eighteenth centuries were slow to adapt to new scientific theories. In France, the association of Cartesians with dissident theological movements, especially Jansenism, and with democratically inspired critiques of the monarchy meant that they were challenging simultaneously the received teaching of the schools, the Churches, and the political system. Consequently, Cartesianism flourished in independent academies and informal meeting houses, outside the established centers of higher education, with the exception of some Oratorian colleges operated by the religious order to which Malebranche and other Cartesians belonged. It also attracted women among its early supporters because, as Poulain de la Barre argued in *The Equality of the Sexes* (1673), men had no natural advantage over women in studying science but labored under the disadvantage of having their minds clouded by traditional learning. By the beginning of the eighteenth century, the spirit of Cartesianism was established as a progressive force in the sciences; universities gradually adopted elements of Cartesian science, and those officially recognized as proponents of the new sciences, the members of the Académie Royale des Sciences, acknowledged their intellectual debt to this "sect" in natural philosophy: Bernard le Bovier de Fontenelle (1657–1757), Christiaan Huygens (1629–1695), Gottfried Wilhelm Leibniz (1646–1716), Edmé Mariotte (ca. 1620–1684), and Claude Perrault (1613–1688) all contributed to science in conversation with the Cartesian legacy.

The metaphysical foundation of Cartesianism included a clear distinction between matter and spirit and a foundationalist theory of knowledge that claimed to answer the skeptical objections of the age. The sharp metaphysical distinction between matter and spirit was reflected in a similar division in disciplines. While religious faith and philosophy were concerned with the human soul and God, the scope of scientific knowledge was limited to the properties of extended matter. Adopting a distinction between primary and secondary qualities that was commonly accepted by scientific contemporaries, including Galileo Galilei (1564–1642) and Robert Boyle (1627–1691), Cartesians argued that we have no reason to believe that our perceptions are qualitatively similar to the objects that trigger them and that even reliable sensations are, at best, a basis for constructing hypotheses about the most likely objects to which they correspond. Thus, the legendary reluctance of the Cartesian tradition about sensations as a basis for knowledge was not an objection to using our senses to make observations or perform experiments, but to the naive epistemology of the schools that assumed that natural phenomena correspond exactly to our perceptions of them. A Cartesian scientist, like any other scientist of the Scientific Revolution, had to make observations and perform experiments; the results provided the basis for reasoning toward a hypothetical explanation or theory of the phenomenon in question. In this sense, Cartesians favored reason (i.e., theory) over experience (i.e., uninterpreted perception).

They also favored mechanical explanations rather than Scholastic explanations, which relied on substantial forms. They characterized the latter as "occult powers" because, they argued, they were unintelligible and were nonexplanatory to the extent that they merely renamed, in apparently technical terms, the phenomena to be explained. In the famous example used by Molière (1622–1673), it is not an explanation to say that sleeping powder induces sleep because it has a dormitive power. Cartesians also rejected teleological principles in nature as the mistake of applying to material realities properties that apply properly only to intentional realities such as the human mind. Thus, in embryology and, generally, in biology, Cartesians assumed that it was possible in principle to construct explanations as if the realities to be explained were machines; the only relevant factors were the size, shape, position, and movement of parts of matter, which, in many cases, were unobservable. This raised a question that was central to the developing science of dynamics, whether it was possible to use the concept of force in explaining the movements of pieces of matter, on which the explanation of all other natural phenomena depended. Most Cartesians argued against the use of forces in physics, claiming that they were as dubious as Scholastic forms. Others, such as Antoine Arnauld (1612–1694) in his *True and False Ideas* (1683), adopted a more tolerant attitude, similar to that of Isaac Newton

(1642–1727) in the *Opticks* (1604), according to which there was both a legitimate and an illegitimate use of forces, and the former was compatible with mechanism.

The ontological status of forces was linked with two other features of Cartesianism: occasionalism and the concept of matter that was widely adopted within this tradition. Occasionalism emerged early, in Louis de La Forge's *Traité de l'esprit* (Treatise on the Soul, 1683), as a theoretical attempt to protect God's providence from compromise by apparently independent secondary causes. In this version of the theory, moving bodies were genuine causes of the motion that they communicated to other bodies on impact, but their causality depended on the general causality of God in creating material things, in establishing the laws of their interaction, and in contributing his constant concurrence to the maintenance of that created structure. The development of this theory of causality coincided, in Malebranche, with a more general critique of forces that provided the arguments and examples for David Hume's (1711–1776) critique of causality in La Forge's *Treatise*.

In contrast to its contribution to methodology, the Cartesian concept of matter was less fruitful for subsequent scientific developments. Descartes emphasized the mathematical features of matter and seemed almost to have defined matter in terms of its geometrical properties. Matter was indefinitely divisible; hence, there could be no atoms. Matter was also identical with space; therefore, it was impossible, by definition, to have a genuine vacuum. The conceptual parsimony of this approach was understandable in response to the corresponding prodigality of the Scholastics, but it provided too few parameters with which to construct a plausible account of many natural phenomena. Many phenomena, such as the elasticity of some bodies and the magnetism of others, required a richer ontology of basic properties. Cartesians soon lapsed from the rigor of this ontology. Geraud de Cordemoy adopted a form of atomism as early as 1666, in *Le discernement du corps et de l'ame* (Distinction Between the Body and the Soul), and others struggled with the conceptual limitations of their concept of matter in the face of refractory phenomena. The strain involved in trying to construct viable hypotheses within the metaphysical and methodological constraints of a particular tradition was not confined to Cartesianism; it is equally evident in Newton, although he was clearly not a Cartesian, and in Christiaan Huygens's (1629–1695) treatise on the cause of gravity (1690).

Despite the language of certainty and demonstration that characterized the methodological works of Descartes, the Cartesian tradition in science is most notable for the exact opposite, namely, an almost cavalier attitude toward the adoption of untested hypotheses. This is partly explained in terms of the emancipation from traditional theories that was central to the Cartesian enterprise; it also resulted from a recognition that the particles of matter that ultimately explain natural phenomena are too small to be observable, even with the aid of powerful microscopes, and that the most one can hope to do in science is to construct viable hypotheses that tally with the available facts. Even here, one might have expected a greater respect for the experimental results that were widely reported from meetings of scientific societies, such as the Royal Society in London or the Académie Royale des Sciences in Paris. But Cartesians also argued that the number of variables involved in any given experimental situation was likely to be vastly greater than their current theory could cope with. Consequently, Cartesianism was less a coherent group of scientific theories than a philosophical attitude to the development of new theories.

This is reflected in its subsequent history. Descartes made significant contributions to optics and mathematics and supported a vortex theory of planetary motion that survived, in various forms, into the nineteenth century in parallel with the mathematically more demanding theory of Newton. Cartesianism added few major scientific discoveries to rival these accomplishments. La Forge discussed possible neural mechanisms for conditioned responses the anticipated the work of Ivan Petrovich Pavlov (1849–1936), and the theory of biological machines supported the first unsuccessful attempts at blood transfusions, by Jean-Baptiste Denis (d. 1704). The development of Cartesianism represented a paradigm shift in traditional learning. It provided the philosophical framework that successfully challenged traditional learning and contributed significantly to the transition from Scholastic natural philosophy to scientific explanation.

BIBLIOGRAPHY

Aiton, E. J. *The Vortex Theory of Planetry Motions*. London: Macdonald, 1972.

Clarke, Desmond M. *Descartes' Philosophy of Science*. Manchester: Manchester University Press, 1982.

———. *Occult Powers and Hypotheses: Cartesian Natural Philosophy Under Louis XIV*. Oxford: Clarendon, 1989.

Laudan, Larry. "The Clock Metaphor and Probabilism: The Impact of Descartes on English Methodological Thought, 1650–65." *Annals of Science* 22 (1966), 73–104.

Mouy, Paul. *Le développement de la physique cartésienne, 1646–1712*. Paris: Vrin, 1934.

DESMOND M. CLARKE

See also Descartes, René; Fontenelle, Bernard le Bovier de; Matter; Mechanical Philosophy; Motion; Rohault, Jacques

Cartography

The relationship between Western cartography and the Scientific Revolution is a puzzling one. In one sense, the great proliferation of maps between 1400 and 1600 seems an outcome of the same mental developments; what, after all, could be more Cartesian than attempting to plot geographical reality in a network of mathematical coordinates? However, viewed more closely, it does not seem that mapmaking bore any simple relationship to the Scientific Revolution.

Several of the elements leading to what we can call the cartographic revolution of the sixteenth century go far back into the Middle Ages. It would seem, for instance, that the basically new way of "seeing" the world, found in the imagery and maps of the early fifteenth century, was eventually rooted in new theological attitudes toward the faculty of sight, which came to be regarded as, in some sense, specially divine. Hence, it would seem, the alliance between cartography and art that can be traced down from the Van Eyck brothers (fl. 1425) to artists like Pieter Bruegel the Elder (ca. 1525–1569).

Some of the techniques of the New Cartography were rooted further back in the Middle Ages. Such was the case with the portolan chart, using which the Europeans began charting the world outside Europe. Once the utility of maps became apparent to the ruling elites, a phenomenon that varied from country to country but may generally be detected in the early sixteenth century, all kinds of new map forms emerged: topographical maps for governors to envisage territories, estate maps for landowners to exploit their holdings more effectively, military maps to control and maneuver the newly large and complex armies, and so forth. For many of these map types, it is not clear that any influence could have been felt from the early Scientific Revolution.

In one respect, though, there was a close connection. The rediscovery in the early fifteenth century of

C

the cartographic knowledge of Claudius Ptolemy (ca. 100–ca. 170) introduced the Europeans to a type of mapmaking that relied essentially upon mathematical coordinates, even if the resultant maps often needed much correction in the light of later investigation. Such scientific precursors as Leon Battista Alberti (1404–1472) and Leonardo da Vinci (1452–1519) adapted the Ptolemaic method to the mapping of smaller areas of the countryside and to the delineation of city plans.

The portolan chart, showing compass headings between pairs of ports and innocent of mathematical coordinates, offered no solutions to the problem of providing a projection useful throughout the world in all latitudes. The cartographers of the House of Navigation (Cosa de la Contratación) in Seville attempted to resolve this problem by establishing variable scales for different parts of the world, but this was clearly not a satisfactory solution, and it was not until 1569 that the projection sys-

tem of Gerard Mercator (1512–1594) provided navigators with a chart that enabled them to choose constant courses in any part of the world. Of course, the Mercatorian system relied upon the Ptolemaic system of coordinates, even when, in other respects, the cartographic information supplied by the great Alexandrian was being radically corrected.

The cartography of early-modern Europe relied not only on the theoretical structure of Ptolemy, but also on the mathematical principles first developed in antiquity and then taken up with renewed vigor at the time of the Scientific Revolution. Thus, the idea of locating a place by triangulation, explained more or less fully from the fifteenth century onward, eventually led to huge national programs designed to extend triangulation points over whole countries in order to create maps of hitherto unimagined accuracy. In something of the same way, the coming of scaled drawings, probably used first in the

The western hemisphere, from the first modern atlas, Abraham Ortelius's Theatrum orbis terrarum *(1570).*

delineation of fortifications, led, in the end, to maps that could reliably be used for a great variety of scientific purposes.

In these developments, cartography was not so much the outcome of the Scientific Revolution as the beneficiary of many of the same ideas and developments as those that inspired the later movement. Peter Apian (1495–1552), Willem Janszoon Blaeu (1571–1638), Gian Domenico Cassini (1625–1712), Regnier Gemma Frisius (1508–1555), and Gerard Mercator used some of the techniques developed at the time of the Scientific Revolution in constructing their maps. But they also drew upon techniques and concepts that long antedated the Scientific Revolution, having roots deep in the Middle Ages.

BIBLIOGRAPHY

Bagrow, Leo. *History of Cartography*. Chicago: Precedent, 1985.

Brown, Lloyd A. *The Story of Maps*. New York: Dover, 1977.

Karrow, Robert W. *Mapmakers of the Sixteenth Century and Their Maps*. Chicago: Newberry Library and Speculum Orbis, 1993.

Thrower, Norman J. W. *Maps and Civilization: Cartography in Culture and Society*. Chicago: University of Chicago Press, 1996.

DAVID BUISSERET

See also Blaeu, Willem Janszoon; Casa de la Contratación; Geography; Navigation; Ortelius, Abraham

Casa de la Contratación

The Casa was founded in 1503 in Seville as the monarch's agency for regulating the movement of men and merchandise to and from America. In addition to administrative tasks, the Casa also dealt with matters related to technical navigation problems and, in doing so, became a prominent center of applied science. Its first technical position was that of senior pilot (1508), who was responsible for teaching and examining pilots and supervising the maps and nautical instruments used on voyages to America. In 1523 the position of senior cosmographer was created, with responsibility for maps and instruments and directing the work of the other cosmographers in the Casa authorized to prepare the devices needed by the pilots. Teaching was reorganized in 1552 when a chair of navigation and cosmography was established. Theoretical studies, comprising the astronomical fundamentals of the "art of sailing" were followed by training in the use of astrolabes, quadrants, and cross-staffs, particularly to establish latitudes; compasses—with emphasis on magnetic declination; navigational charts, and the like. At a later date, the position of shipbuilding supervisor was created and also the chair of artillery and fortifications. During the sixteenth century, the Casa's golden period, these positions were held by such prominent Spanish and Portuguese cosmographers as Alonso de Chaves (d. 1587), Diogo Ribeiro (d. 1533), Alonso de Santa Cruz (1505–1567), and Pedro Medina (1493–1567) and by Italians such as Amerigo Vespucci (1451–1512) and Sebastiano Caboto (ca. 1476–1557).

One of the Casa's outstanding works was the organization of shipping cartography. The *padrón real* (royal cartographical pattern) created in 1512 was housed in the Casa and was constantly enlarged and updated to take into account the innovations contributed by pilots, which were discussed and evaluated beforehand at a weekly meeting of cosmographers. The Casa was also the source of many inventions and improvements in nautical instruments and in the fitting out of ships. However, the Casa's major achievement was, as highlighted by U. Lamb (1992), the transformation of the art of sailing into a systematic discipline based on a series of treatises and handbooks that were translated into a variety of languages and diffused throughout the rest of Europe, often with numerous reprintings.

BIBLIOGRAPHY

Lamb, U. *A Navigator's Universe: The "Libro" of Cosmographie of 1538 by Pedro de Medina*. Chicago: University of Chicago Press, 1992.

López-Piñero, J. M. *El arte de navegar en la España del Renacimiento*. 2nd ed. Barcelona: Labor, 1986.

———. *Ciencia y técnica en la sociedad española de los siglos XVI y XVII*. Barcelona: Labor, 1979.

Pulido Rubio, J. *El Piloto Mayor de la Casa de la Contratación de Sevilla: Pilotos mayores, catedráticos de cosmografía y cosmógrafos*. Seville: Consejo Superior de Investigaciones Científicas, 1950.

JOSÉ M. LÓPEZ-PIÑERO

See also Cartography; Navigation

Cassini, Gian Domenico (Jean-Dominique) (1625–1712)

Born in Perinaldo in Liguria, he was educated at the Jesuit college in Genoa. Through patronage connections, he was appointed professor of astronomy at the

University of Bologna in 1651. In Bologna, Cassini constructed a gnomon, or meridian line, in the church of San Petronio for measurements of solar declinations. His measurements allowed him to make important adjustments to the corrections for solar parallax and atmospheric refraction, and these led to a marked improvement in the accuracy of solar theory. He published new solar tables in 1662.

During this period, Cassini served the commune of Bologna and the papacy as a consultant on fortification and hydrology. During his stays in Rome, he became friendly with Giuseppe Campani (1635–1715), then emerging as Europe's most able telescope maker, and, with Campani telescopes, he determined the rotation periods of Mars and Jupiter and observed the satellites of Jupiter. One of his most remarkable observations was that of the shadow of Jupiter's satellites on the body of the planet. In 1668 he published new tables of Jupiter's satellites, *Ephemerides Bononienses Mediceorum Syderum,* the first reasonably accurate tables of these bodies. Cassini's tables allowed Ole Römer (1644–1710) to demonstrate the finite speed of light in 1675, and, from this time onward, observations of the eclipses of Jupiter's satellites became the standard method of determining longitudes.

In 1669 Cassini became a member of the Académie Royale des Sciences and moved to Paris, where he spent the rest of his life. He was able to make architectural changes to the observatory then under construction and assumed its leadership when it was finished. Under his guidance, the Observatoire de Paris became the leading astronomical institution in Europe. Cassini was able to organize a number of astronomical expeditions. In 1671 he sent Jean Picard (1620–1682) to Denmark to determine the position of Tycho Brahe's (1546–1601) observatory; in the years 1672–1673, Jean Richer (1630–1696) led an expedition to Cayenne (French Guyana) to observe solar declinations and to try to determine the parallax of Mars. This expedition led to an adjustment of 90 arc-minutes to the obliquity of the ecliptic and confirmed Cassini's combination of parallax- and refraction-corrections that he had formulated during his tenure in Bologna. The result was a new value for horizontal solar parallax of 9.5 arc-seconds.

With Campani telescopes, Cassini discovered four satellites of Saturn: by their modern names, Iapetus (1671), Rhea (1672), Tethys (1684), and Dione (1684). In 1675 he observed for the first time the gap in Saturn's

Cassini, with the Paris observatory and a telescope in the background. Courtesy Oklahoma University Library.

ring system known today as Cassini's division. In 1679 he published a new moon map, and in 1683 he observed the zodiacal light. Cassini was the most able telescopic observer of his day.

Under Cassini's direction, a survey of France was begun in the 1670s. Observations of latitude and longitude (using Jupiter's satellites) were made all over France. This project eventually led to the first accurate map of France. In the question about the shape of the earth, Cassini measured a meridian from Paris to Perpignan and concluded that the earth was a prolate spheroid, a conclusion defended by his heirs and successors until the middle of the eighteenth century. Cassini's son, Jacques (1677–1756), his grandson César-François (1714–1784), and his great-grandson Jean Dominique (1748–1845) succeeded him as directors of the observatory.

BIBLIOGRAPHY

Cassini, Anna. *Gio. Domenico Cassini: Uno scienziato del seicento.* Perinaldo, Italy: Comune di Perinaldo, 1995.

Cohen, I. Bernard. "G. D. Cassini and the Number of the Planets: An Example of Seventeenth-Century Astro-Numerological Patronage." In *Nature, Experiment, and the Sciences: Essays on Galileo and the History of Sciene in Honour of Stilllman Drake,* ed. Trevor H. Levere and William R. Shea. Dordrecht: Kluwer Academic, 1990, pp. 199–205.

Swerdlow, N. M. "Astronomical Chronology and Prophecy: Jean-Dominique Cassini's Discovery of Josephus's Great Lunisolar Period of the Patriarchs." *Journal of the Warburg and Courtauld Institutes* 53 (1990), 1–13.

Taton, René, and Curtis A. Wilson, eds. *Planetary Astronomy from the Renaissance to the Rise of Astrophysics,* vol. 2A: *The General History of Astronomy,* ed. Michael Hoskin. Cambridge: Cambridge University Press, 1989–, passim.

ALBERT VAN HELDEN

See also Académie Royale des Sciences; Observatoire de Paris; Picard, Jean; Ricker, Jean

Causality

A concept that has its origins in Greek philosophy and that played a significant role in the Scientific Revolution, particularly in the thought of Galileo Galilei (1564–1642), William Harvey (1578–1657), and Sir Isaac Newton (1642–1727). Generally it designates anything that has the character of a cause; more specifically it describes the relationship between cause and effect. Cause in the traditional sense is that from which something proceeds with a dependence in being. Effect, the correlative of cause, is then what proceeds. Essential to the classical notion of causality is the idea of dependence in being, that is, an ontological link or necessary connection between cause and effect, sometimes referred to as causal efficacy.

This notion is lacking in the related concept of causation, proposed by David Hume (1711–1776) and subsequently adopted by empiricist philosophers. As Hume defines the causal relationship, it is a relationship between events rather than things and involves two objective factors and an additional subjective factor. The objective factors are temporal antecedence, whereby the cause occurs before the effect; and concomitance, whereby the effect invariably accompanies the cause. The subjective factor is human expectation, whereby previous experience of causes and effects leads one, on the appearance of a cause, to expect the usually attendant effect. In Hume's philosophy, this third factor replaces the notion of necessary connection in the traditional concept.

This essay treats causality, not causation, since the former was the common understanding throughout the Scientific Revolution, although the path to the Humean concept was prepared for by developments within its period. On this account, the Humean notion is sometimes anticipated in analyses of that revolution by empiricist philosophers.

The Aristotelian Concept

As originally proposed by Aristotle (384–322 B.C.E.), a cause is a positive principle that exerts an influence on something that is coming to be and, in this way, involves an influx into being. The way it exerts this influence varies in four important ways and, thus, gives rise to its fourfold division into formal, material, efficient, and final causes. The first two are said to be intrinsic causes because they are within the thing to which causing is attributed; the last two, extrinsic causes because they are in some way outside it. The four types can best be understood in terms of the meanings given to form, matter, agent, and end within the Aristotelian tradition as this developed in medieval and Renaissance thought.

Formal causality is the type exerted by a definable form, which can be of various kinds, such as a substantial or accidental form, a nature or essence, a definition or pattern, an idea or whole. Material causality, its correlate, refers to the matter that is being formed, such as the substrate acted upon by the form, that out of which a thing is made, a constituent or element or part entering into its composition. Efficient causality designates agency of some kind or other, any primary source of change or stability, whatever initiates a process or its cessation. And final causality is that of the end, what it is that causes an agent to act, anything that terminates a process and brings it to rest, the goal or purpose for which a thing is done, a good or perfection it aims to achieve. These meanings are very general and apply in analogous ways wherever there is change—thus, in all areas of natural and human activity.

In Aristotle's view, the priority of cause over effect is not one of time, as it is for Hume, but of nature, in the sense that the effect flows from the cause but not conversely. Strictly speaking a cause is only a cause when it is actually causing, that is, when it is producing an effect, and on this basis the two must be simultaneous. The temporal antecedence of cause comes about when the cause begins a process whose terminus is seen as the effect. There is also a kind of reciprocity between the four types of cause: form actualizes or determines matter, and matter is potential to the reception of form; the end explains why the agent causes, and the agent, in turn, makes the end come to be. In Hume's analysis, interactions of these causal types drop out of consideration: causality itself comes to be equated simply with the operation of efficient causes in mechanistic fashion.

Causality and Scientific Explanation

The importance of causality in the history of science derives from the fact that science itself has traditionally been defined as causal knowledge. For Aristotle, to have scientific knowledge is to know perfectly, to know that something is so because it cannot be otherwise, and this, in turn, because of the causes that make it be what it is. The most satisfactory explanation of a phenomenon, the best answer to the question "why?" is, for him, one of identifying the cause that accounts for it. Similarly, the ideal definition is one given in terms of all four causes. Each of these, or all together, can function as the middle term in a demonstration, and this itself is productive of *episteme* or *scientia,* classical terms for scientific knowing.

The clearest and most certain demonstrations are those given in the science of mathematics. These employ formal or material causes, the first usually in terms of definitions and the second in terms of the parts or components of the entities to which they apply. Proofs in natural science, by contrast, additionally employ efficient and final causes. The need for the last arises from the contingency of nature, which makes it necessary to demonstrate in a special way, that is, "from the supposition of the end." If a particular end is to be achieved, one can reason to the agent that would be required to produce the form from the matter at hand. The necessity in such a case is not absolute, as it is in mathematics, but suppositional. For example, planting an olive seed does not necessarily produce an olive tree. But, supposing that an olive tree is to be produced, one can reason back to the causes that must be had to produce it—the olive seed as matter and the additional agencies of soil, water, and sunlight. In this way, one can arrive at a science of olive trees and, along similar lines, sciences of rainbows, and eclipses, and other contingent phenomena.

A special type of science that combines elements of natural and mathematical science was known to Aristotle and highly developed by Archimedes (ca. 287–212 B.C.E.) and Ptolemy (ca. 100–ca. 170). Known as mixed science (*scientia mixta*) or middle science (*scientia media*), this is best exemplified in the sciences of statics, mechanics, optics, and astronomy. Through the use of appropriate suppositions, such sciences apply mathematics to the study of nature and, in some instances, achieve a higher degree of certitude in their conclusions than would be attainable through the use of natural principles alone. The development of these sciences in the High Middle Ages and the Renaissance led proximately to the Scientific Revolution. How the transition occurred may be illustrated in the ways causal analysis was variously employed by Galileo, Harvey, and Newton.

Galileo Galilei

Galileo was thoroughly trained in causal methodology from his studies under Francesco Buonamici (ca. 1540–1603) at the University of Pisa and then from notes he appropriated from Jesuit sources when he returned to teach mathematics at that university in 1589. The best source is a series of questions he extracted at that time from the logic course taught at the Collegio Romano by Paolo Della Valle, S. J. (1561–1622), in 1588. Not only does it explain the various types of cause, but it also goes into detail on the causal regress, a process of discovery and proof developed earlier at the University of Padua. There is evidence that Galileo used the regress in scientific work throughout his life. Some authors, unaware of this teaching (most notably Stillman Drake), have argued that it was Galileo's rejection of causal reasoning that enabled him to found his "new sciences." In this they are clearly mistaken.

The causal regress involves a twofold process of reasoning, one a *progressus,* going from effect to cause, and the second a reversal of this and, thus, a *regressus,* going back from cause to effect. Between the two, there is an intermediate stage during which one certifies that the cause arrived at in the first process is the proper cause of the effect, convertible with it, and so serves to explain it. Galileo's particular innovation was his employment of mathematical reasoning and experimentation in this intermediate stage of the regress.

Galileo first employed the regress, but without complete success, in his earlier treatises on motion written at Pisa ca. 1590. In these, he sought to use Archimedean principles in a way already pioneered by Giovanni Battista Benedetti (1530–1590) to find the "true cause" of falling motion. He had more success with the method later at the University of Padua in his *Trattato della sfera,*

C

his *Le meccaniche,* and his investigation of uniformly accelerated motion with "table-top" experiments between 1602 and 1609. His most spectacular results, however, came in 1609–1610, when he used the regress to explain his observations with the telescope, thus certifying his discovery of mountains on the Moon, satellites of Jupiter, and the phases of Venus. Here he favored the formal causality of projective geometry to assure the convertibility of his results. His later uses of efficient causality in the regress, when studying buoyancy phenomena and the causes of tides on Earth, failed mainly because of inadequate empirical data. Still, Galileo used the causal regress to overthrow many of Aristotle's teachings in physics and astronomy. His claim was that, were Aristotle alive, he would agree with his results rather than those of the Peripatetics of his day.

William Harvey

Whereas Galileo came to see Aristotle as an adversary, Harvey subscribed to his teachings wholeheartedly. He learned Aristotelian methodology while studying with Fabricius of Aquapendente (ca. 1533–1619) at the University of Padua and used it against Galen (second century) when investigating the motion of the heart and the blood in animals. With the aid of precise experiments and measurements, Harvey determined that a finite quantity of blood, too great to be supplied by the daily ingestion of food, was passing continuously through animal arteries and, thus, had to be moved in a circle. Here he employed a material cause, the actual blood moved and its quantity, to show the necessity of the circulation. This much established, Harvey saw that the heart functions as a pump to move the blood. This led to his classical definition of the heart in terms of the four causes: formal, its precise anatomical structure and function; material, its muscular and other tissue sustaining its structure and operation; final, its circulating the blood; and efficient, its contraction and expansion whereby it fulfills that function. His conclusion: "It would be difficult to explain in any other way for what cause all is constructed and arranged as we have seen it to be."

A similar spirit informs Harvey's *Exercationes de generatione animalium* (Anatomical Exercises on the Generation of Animals, 1651), which begins with an essay on method that is solidly Aristotelian, stressing the importance of personal experience to establish the facts rather than depending on what others have said about them. He stresses that "inquiry must begin from the causes, especially the material and efficient ones," and lays out a program for causal analysis based on careful observation and experimentation.

Isaac Newton

When Newton began his studies at Trinity College, Cambridge, in 1661, the curriculum was still largely based on Aristotle, as can be seen from the Latin portions of Newton's *Trinity Notebook* (1661–1665). His use of causal terminology suggests a competent knowledge of the tradition of the schools, although there are evidences in the English portions of the notebook of an incipient interest in Galileo and René Descartes (1596–1650). Significant examples of causal reasoning are found in his first published paper in the *Philosophical Transactions of the Royal Society* of 1671–1672, on a new theory of light and colors, and in his *Principia mathematica philosophiae naturalis* (Mathematical Principles of Natural Philosophy, 1687), in which he formulates his "Rules of Reasoning in Philosophy" at the beginning of the third book.

Newton's early work on light and color laid the foundations for his *Opticks* (1704). A central feature of his investigations was what he called his *experimentum crucis* (crucial experiment), in which he proposed to ascertain the "true cause" of the elongation of the image produced by a light ray when passing through a prism. This experiment, which involves two prisms, purports to show that light is composed of rays that are "differently refrangible," that is, composed of many rays, each disposed to exhibit a different color, and each with a distinctive angle of refraction. What is interesting is that Newton is seeking to explain the quantitative form of a multicolored image, its elongation (such that its length is five times its width), and concludes that its cause lies in the parts of which light is composed, clearly a material cause. Newton's critics, thinking in terms of Descartes's theory of light being composed of particles, quickly challenged the experiment on the ground that it failed to reveal the nature of light. At the time, Newton probably thought that his colored rays were made up of pulses, as opposed to Descartes's luminiferous particles, but he refused to commit himself on that subject. Unable to puzzle out how the rays might be present in the light before its refraction, Newton maintained simply that he had discovered a true property of light rays and so preferred to remain agnostic about light's nature. (A Peripatetic, not seeking a mechanical explanation, might have answered that the rays were present virtually or potentially in the light, but by then such an account would not have appealed to Newton.)

The first two books of the *Principia* are concerned mainly with mathematical definitions and demonstrations relating to the local motion of bodies first in empty space (Book I) and then in resistive media (Book II). Being mathematical in the classical sense, these invoke causes of the formal and material types. The application to natural philosophy comes in Book III, in which Newton proposes to explain the system of the world in terms of the force of gravity. His rules of reasoning are drawn up so that he can use causal argument, particularly effect-to-cause reasoning, to establish the existence of gravity throughout the known universe. This is expressed in the law of universal gravitation, which sees gravity as an agent or efficient cause that explains the fall of bodies on Earth, the motions of planets around the Sun, the motions of satellites around planets, and the tides on the earth's surface. The empirical evidence Newton cites is that all of these phenomena exhibit a uniformly accelerated type of motion. If this type of motion actually occurs in the heavens, he argues, the inference inescapably follows, by a posteriori demonstration, that celestial matter is no different from terrestrial matter in the respect that both matters undergo a "falling" motion. Gravity is, thus, for him, the universal cause, the *vera causa* of naturally accelerated motion.

Newton ran into problems, however, when his critics raised the question: how, specifically, does gravity cause this motion, or, better, what is the cause of gravity? To invoke a quasi-mechanical explanation, Newton proposed the concept of *attraction,* but taken in a mathematical way and not as a physical cause. As to what the physical cause might be, he preferred to remain agnostic on the ground that he did not "feign hypotheses" (his famous "*hypotheses non fingo*"). His situation here is remarkably similar to that he encountered in optics: he knew the *vera causa* of the elongation of the spectrum, but he did not know light's nature and so could not really explain how the elongation was caused; he knew that gravity exists in the universe, but he did not know the cause of gravity and so could not really explain why bodies fell. All he could do was invoke "attraction," an "occult quality," as it was characterized by critics, to explain it.

From Agnosticism to Skepticism

Newton's selective agnosticism in these matters had strong repercussions on the classical concept of causality. All of the founders of modern science, Francis Bacon (1561–1626), Johannes Kepler (1571–1630), Gottfried Wilhelm Leibniz (1646–1716), Christian Huygens (1629–1695), and those we have already mentioned, were committed to causality in the strong sense, that of causal efficacy. Many, such as Bacon and Leibniz, still subscribed to the four types of cause, though they interpreted them in ways different from Aristotle's. Those who did not do so had become mechanists, and, for these, efficient causality as instantiated in force or energy was real and efficacious beyond any doubt.

The move to causation came about when philosophers, especially John Locke (1632–1704) and David Hume, began to consider another of Newton's proposals—extending the force concept to the minute but insensible particles of which all matter was then believed to be composed. Locke proposed that there are powers in such particles that produce sensations in us, but that, because of their minuteness, they do so in ways forever unknowable to us. Hume went Locke a step further. He argued that, even were we to know these powers, our method of acquiring knowledge through the senses prohibits our detecting any necessary connection between such powers as causes and the effects they produce. It was in this context that he elaborated his philosophy of empiricism. Where Newton had been agnostic about a particular type of causality, Hume became a skeptic about causality in general. His skepticism has appealed to many philosophers since, but it was not a part of the mentality of the scientists who brought about the Scientific Revolution.

BIBLIOGRAPHY

Drake, Stillman. *Galileo*. New York: Hill and Wang, 1980.
Galilei, Galileo. *Galileo's Logical Treatises*. Trans. with Notes and Commentary by W. A. Wallace. Boston and London: Kluwer Academic, 1992.
Koyré, Alexandre. *Newtonian Studies*. Cambridge, MA: Harvard University Press, 1965.
Wallace, William A. *Causality and Scientific Explanation*. 2 vols. Ann Arbor: University of Michigan Press, 1972–1974.
———. *Galileo's Logic of Discovery and Proof*. Dordrecht: Kluwer, 1992.

WILLIAM A. WALLACE

See also Aristotelianism; Demonstration; Empiricism; Mixed Sciences

Cavalieri, Bonaventura (1598–1647)

Italian mathematician and author of the controversial *method of indivisibles*. Cavalieri was born in Milan and, at the age of fifteen, joined the monastic order of the Jesuits of St. Jerome. From 1616 to 1620 he resided in Pisa and Florence, where he became acquainted with Benedetto Castelli and Galileo Galilei (1564–1642). In 1629 he was appointed to the chair of mathematics at the University of Bologna, where he remained until his death.

During his years in Bologna, Cavalieri published numerous works on astrology, trigonometry, and logarithms. His reputation, however, rests squarely on his method of indivisibles, elaborated in his 1635 book *Geometria indivisibilibus continuorum nova quadam ratione promota* (Geometry, Put Forth in a New Account by the Indivisibles of the Continuum) and defended in his last work, the *Exercitationes geometricae sex* (Six Exercises in Geometry, 1647). The method was designed to calculate the areas and volumes of various geometrical figures and solids. Rather than treat the objects as a whole, Cavalieri suggested "that plane figures should be conceived by us in the same manner as cloths are made up of parallel threads. And solids are in fact like books, which are composed of parallel pages." Planes, in other words, are construed as composed of indivisible parallel lines, and solids as made up of indivisible parallel planes. In order to determine, for example, the area of a given figure, it must be compared to a figure of known dimensions. If each of its "indivisible lines" is in a given ratio to an "indivisible line" of the known figure, then, according to Cavalieri, "all the lines" of the given figure stand in the same ratio to "all the lines" of the other figure. From this he concluded that their areas are also in that ratio.

Cavalieri's method of indivisibles was extremely effective in producing new results as well as in simplifying traditional proofs. Its fundamental assumption, however, was extremely problematic. The notion that continuous magnitudes could be viewed as composed of an infinite number of indivisible discrete parts seemed to contradict the ancient paradoxes of Zeno (ca. 490–ca. 425 B.C.E.) and ignore the problem of incommensurability. Cavalieri was well aware of these problems, and in the *Geometria* and the *Exercitationes* he attempted to bring the method in compliance with the classical theory of magnitudes. Not everyone, however, was satisfied with

his efforts. In 1641 the Jesuit mathematician Paul Guldin (1577–1643) published a scathing attack on Cavalieri's method. "All the lines" of a magnitude, Guldin charged, constituted an infinite sum and could not, therefore, be compared with one another. Cavalieri, he argued, had violated an ancient mathematical maxim, and his method was unfounded and unreliable.

Recent scholarship indicates that Guldin's attack represented not only his own personal views, but those of the Society of Jesus as a whole. As early as 1632 and again in 1641, the Collegio Romano, the leading Jesuit academy, condemned the notion that the continuum is composed of indivisibles and banned it from being taught in Jesuit schools. It is hardly surprising, then, that almost all Jesuit mathematicians were highly critical of Cavalieri's methods. Despite their hostility, however, the "indivisiblist" approach proved extremely popular and became one of the mainstays of seventeenth-century mathematics. Various versions of the method were developed by Evangelista Torricelli (1608–1647), Gilles Personne de Roberval (1602–1675), John Wallis (1616–1703), and others. Even Isaac Newton's (1642–1727) and Gottfried Wilhelm Leibniz's (1646–1716) calculus may well be viewed as an elaboration and systematization of Cavalieri's rudimentary method.

BIBLIOGRAPHY

Andersen, Kirsti. "Cavalieri's Method of Indivisibles." *Archive for History of Exact Sciences* 31 (1985), 291–367.

Festa, Egidio. "Quelques aspects de la controversie sur les indivisibles." In *Geometria e atomismo nella scuola Galileiana,* ed. Massimo Bucciantini and Maurizio Torrini. Florence: Olschki, 1992, pp. 193–207.

Gandt, François de. "Cavalieri's Indivisibles and Euclid's Canons." In *Revolution and Continuity,* ed. Peter Barker and Roger Ariew. Washington, D.C.: The Catholic University of America Press, 1991, pp. 157–182.

Giusti, Enrico. *Bonaventura Cavalieri and the Theory of Indivisibles.* Bologna: Cremonese, 1980.

                                        AMIR ALEXANDER

See also Calculus; Infinity, Mathematical

Cavendish, Margaret, Duchess of Newcastle (née Lucas) (1623–1673)

Philosophical writer, biographer, dramatist, essayist; possibly the first woman to publish books of metaphysics or natural philosophy. Daughter of a Royalist squire, she was, as she herself later acknowledged, not well educated; she seems to have known only English. She married William Cavendish, first marquess of Newcastle (1592–1676), an extremely wealthy Royalist landowner with extensive interest in the "New Philosophy" and a correspondent of René Descartes (1596–1650). In impoverished European exile during the Protectorate, the Newcastles met Descartes and other European thinkers. They returned to England at the Restoration, whereupon Cavendish was created duke of Newcastle. He supported and financed a series of Margaret's publications between 1653 and 1671. Several of them were concerned in whole or in part with issues of natural philosophy, most notably *Philosophical Opinions* (1663) and *Philosophical Letters* (1664). Margaret was viewed by contemporaries as eccentric—Samuel Pepys's description of her as "a mad, conceited, ridiculous woman" is well known.

Her visit to the Royal Society in 1667—the only participation by a woman in Royal Society meetings before 1945—was much talked of. She had secured an invitation to a meeting (her brother was a member and there were numerous other connections) and arrived with a large train of followers. Robert Boyle (1627–1691) and others performed experiments for her, which much impressed her. Henry More (1614–1687) was also present.

Newcastle's natural philosophy included analyses of various material processes and attempts a series of reductions of all phenomena (including space and time) to individual material particulars. The latter idea is more impressively comprehensive than Newcastle's execution of it, but she is an original thinker and important as an early advocate of women's rational capacities and female education and as someone engaged on a popular level in natural philosophy. Margaret Cavendish may be seen as having a real, if marginal, place in the Scientific Revolution. Would-be patroness of, and contributor to, natural philosophy, she makes a claim for a female presence in the New Science and its public and institutional processes as well as its theoretical work.

BIBLIOGRAPHY

Grant, Douglas. *Margaret the First.* London: Rupert Hart-Davis, 1957.

Newcastle, Margaret Cavendish, Duchess of. "Selections from *Philosphical Letters*." In *Women Philosophers of the Early Modern Period,* ed. Margaret Atherton. Indianapolis: Hackett, 1944.

Sarasohn, Lisa T. "A Science Turned Upside Down: Feminism and the Natural Philosophy of Margaret Cavendish." *Huntington Library Quarterly* 47 (1984), 289–307.

PETER LOPTSON

See also Women and Natural Philosophy

Celestial Spheres

The theory of celestial spheres draws its origin from two chief sources in antiquity: Aristotle and Ptolemy. In *On the Heavens,* Aristotle (384–322 B.C.E.) argued that the heavens are filled with a peculiar substance: it had none of the properties (hot, cold, wet, dry, hard, soft, and so on) of ordinary matter and was, accordingly, not subject to any kind of change other than its innate tendency to move in a circle around the center of the universe. In the *Metaphysics,* he described a nest of spheres, leaving it to the astronomers (he mentioned Eudoxus and Callippus) to decide how many spheres would be necessary.

Ptolemy (ca. 100–ca. 170) approached the spheres from a different perspective: his main concern was to construct a mathematical theory that would accurately predict planetary positions. His circles were not concentric, and it was not clear from his presentation of them whether he considered them to be physically real. He did not even consider Aristotle's question of whether the spheres must be concentric with the center of the universe. Nevertheless, he did arrange their sizes in such a way that the apparatus of orbs belonging to each planet as a whole fit exactly between the apparatus of the adjacent planets. The Moon was lowest, followed by Mercury, Venus, the Sun (which was a planet in his earth-centered system), and so on.

There was, thus, an inherent tension in the idea of celestial spheres as it was inherited by medieval scholastics. They argued a wide variety of views, from complete acceptance of the physical reality of all the astronomers' spheres to denial of all as mere mathematical fictions. However, the most commonly accepted view was a compromise that asserted the reality of the major orbs, both concentric and eccentric, while leaving the reality of the smaller orbs and circles an open question. It should be remarked that none of the planetary orbs was ever described as "crystalline." The *coelum crystallinum,* or crystalline heaven, was sometimes included as a sphere beyond the fixed stars. It was called "crystalline" to harmonize with the bibical account of waters above the heavens (Genesis 1.7).

In the sixteenth century, debate over the nature of the celestial substance and of the orbs was vigorous, and there was no clear consensus. Nevertheless, several important trends are evident. First, there was the Reformation and the Catholic reaction to it, both of which tended to emphasize the biblical cosmology rather than Aristotle's. Second, other non-Aristotelian views, such as those of the Stoics and of the alchemists, were attracting followers. Both of these trends tended to make the idea of the heavens as somewhat like the earth more acceptable. Third, a number of technically competent astronomers, such as Nicolaus Copernicus (1473–1543), Tycho Brahe (1546–1601), and William, landgrave of Hesse-Kassel (1532–1592), found ways of supporting their work outside of the universities and so were less constrained by the official curriculum. And fourth, there was a tendency even among traditional astronomical and philosophical writers to give mathematical astronomy more weight in determining physical reality.

The result was a tendency to allow the heavens to be somewhat like the earth (though still usually more pure and unchangeable), and to consider the question, seldom raised before, whether the heavens are solid (i.e., hard) or fluid. Once the question was framed in this way, it became possible to answer it by appealing to observations. The Danish astronomer Tycho Brahe, philosophically an alchemist, made careful observations of the comet of 1577 and determined that it had been passing through the celestial regions, thereby arguing against the spheres. He published his results along with letters from other astronomers whose observations supported his conclusion. Proponents of real spheres had no effective response, and those who attempted to impugn Brahe's technical arguments only managed to display their ignorance. Observations of other comets in the ensuing decades supported Brahe's conclusions, and, by the mid-1620s, even mainstream Aristotelians were comfortable with the idea of fluid-filled heavens through which the planets moved "like birds in the air, or fish in the water," as Cicero had put it.

The sphere of the fixed stars, though it lasted somewhat longer, had likewise lost its function. For the Copernicans, the stars were at rest and so did not need to be attached to anything to keep in formation. But the geocentrists also had no compelling reason to keep the stellar sphere. For, if the planets could move with perfect regularity without spheres, why could the stars not do the same?

The final, limiting sphere proved more durable. The chief difficulty in abandoning it was the question of the place of God's heaven. The medieval universe, perhaps best exemplified by Dante's *Divine Comedy,* was hierarchically ordered, with angels and saints, and even God himself, primarily present in an invisible region (the empyrean heaven) beyond the stars. As the hierarchical structure weakened in the early seventeenth century and the spherical organization came into question, the empyrean heaven came to receive an unusual amount of attention, chiefly from Spanish Jesuits, but also from several Italian and French writers. The empyrean proposed by these authors differed from the traditional empyrean of earlier times in that it played an active role in governing and moving the otherwise inert physical universe below it.

This last defense of finitude was very effectively countered by the dualistic approaches of René Descartes (1596–1650) and Galileo Galilei (1564–1642). By placing God and spirits decisively in a different ontological category, so that they did not exist in space, Descartes rendered the surrounding empyrean superfluous. Moreover, all physical actions, whether celestial or terrestrial, took place in accord with natural principles, without the interference of God or angels. Galileo's dualism was more pragmatic and methodological. He argued that God and the heaven of theology are beyond the reach of physics and, therefore, should not be included in such theories. He expressed ignorance as to whether the universe did or did not have a boundary, though he believed it impious to set prior limits on God's power to create a universe whose size exceeds our comprehension.

Although defenders of the spherical universe, and even of the planetary spheres, were not entirely lacking in the latter part of the seventeenth century, theirs was increasingly a minority opinion. Once the hierarchy of the medieval cosmos with its nest of increasingly exalted spheres fell apart, the spherical cosmos was hard to justify. Even those who professed belief in a central and motionless Earth, such as the Jesuit Athanasius Kircher (1602–1680), were able to allow the starry region to extend indefinitely outward, its velocity increasing jubilantly with its altitude.

BIBLIOGRAPHY
Donahue, William H. *The Dissolution of the Celestial Spheres.* New York: Arno, 1981.

Grant, Edward. "Medieval Cosmology." In *Cosmology: Historical, Literary, Philosophical, Religious, and Scientific Perspectives,* ed. Norris Hetherington. New York and London: Garland, 1993, pp. 181–199.

———. *Planets, Stars, and Orbs: The Medieval Cosmos, 1200–1687.* Cambridge: Cambridge University Press, 1994.

WILLIAM H. DONAHUE

See also Brahe, Tycho; Comets; Infinity of the World

Cesalpino, Andrea (1519–1603)

An Italian physician, physiologist, and botanist who also wrote on anatomy, mineralogy, and metallurgy. He studied medicine and philosophy at Pisa under Realdo Colombo (ca. 1510–1559) and Luca Ghini (ca. 1490–1556), receiving his doctorate in 1551. Cesalpino succeeded Ghini as professor of medicine and director of the Pisan botanical gardens in 1555 and was one of the first generation of educators to include *materia medica* (the use and preparation of medicinal drugs) in the medical curriculum. In 1592 he was appointed to the post of papal physician in Rome; during this period, he also taught medicine at the Sapienza.

Cesalpino's approach was Aristotelian, and, in his *Quaestionum peripateticarum* (1571), he articulated a comprehensive theory of nature consistent with Aristotle's theories and methodology. Here and elsewhere (*Quaestionum medicarum,* 1593) Cesalpino argued, against Galen (second century C.E.) that the heart, not the liver, was the organ of sanguification. He described the cardiac valves and pulmonary vessels and insisted that both the veins and the nerves had their origin in the heart. One of his students later taught William Harvey (1578–1657), leading some to argue that Cesalpino, not Harvey, should be credited with the discovery of the circulation of the blood.

Cesalpino is best remembered, however, for *De plantis* (1583), the first work to elaborate a system of plant classification derived from, and consistent with, philosophical principles. In Book I, Cesalpino outlined his theory of botany, which is teleological in character. Cesalpino looked for *differentia*—the essential characteristics of plants—and declared medical usage, traditionally central to understanding of plants, merely an *accidentia,* or unessential feature. As a plant's purpose was reproduction, the seed, fruit, and flowers must be its essential parts. These, then, served as the basis for his

Andrea Cesalpino's attempt to classify flora based on their forms.

classification system. The remaining books of *De plantis* organize about fifteen hundred plants into four genera, *Arbores* (Trees), *Frutices* (Shrubs), *Herbae* (Herbs), and *Suffrutices* (Shrubby Herbs), which Cesalpino then subdivided according to the kind of fruit each produces. He also discussed seedless plants, which he thought arose from putrefaction.

Though Georges Cuvier (1769–1832) called him the creator of the doctrines of mineralogy, Cesalpino's chief contribution to science was his insistence on the importance of the reproductive organs of plants. His work had little effect on his peers, but the focus on reproductive organs, and the internal consistency and comprehensiveness of his classification system, influenced successors, such as Joachim Jung (1587–1657), Joseph Pitton de Tournefort (1656–1708), John Ray (1620–1705), and Carl Linnaeus (1707–1778).

BIBLIOGRAPHY

Bremerkamp, C. E. B. "A Re-Examination of Cesalpino's Classification." *Acta botanica Neerlandica* 1 (1953), 580–593.

Capecci, Angelo. "Meccanicismo e finalismo nella biologia di A. Cesalpino." In *Medicina e biologia nella rivoluzione scientifica,* ed. Lino Conti. Assisi: Edizioni Porziuncola, 1990, pp. 34–64.

Silvano, C., ed. *Antologia storica relativa a scoperta della circolazione del sangue fatta da Andrea Cesalpino.* 2 vols. Pisa: Ciardini, 1970.

Viviani, U. *Vita e opera de Andrea Cesalpino.* Arezzo: p.p., 1922.

KATHLEEN WHALEN

See also Botany; Taxonomy

Cesi. See Accademia dei Lincei

Charleton, Walter (1620–1707)

Appointed Court physician to Charles I in 1643, Charleton was elected to the Royal Society of London in 1663. He served as president of the Royal College of Physicians from 1689 to 1691 and wrote nearly thirty books on topics ranging from medicine (*Exercitationes pathologicae,* 1661) to the origins of Stonehenge (*Chorea gigantum,* 1663). Through correspondence with well-known natural philosophers in England and on the Continent, Charleton participated in discussions of the search for a philosophy of nature to replace Aristotelianism and added his voice to calls for university reform.

Charleton's most important contribution was his translations of the works of other natural philosophers. Most notable of these is his English translation of Pierre Gassendi's *Philosophiae Epicuri syntagma* (1658), a revised and Christianized version of ancient Epicurean atomism. This work, *Physiologia Epicuro-Gassendo-Charltoniana* (1654), was the first complete English presentation of Epicureanism and confirmed Charleton as an active promoter of atomism and the new mechanical philosophy of nature in England. Explicit in his atomism was the acceptance of interparticulate void, a controversial notion the other English natural philosophers, such as Robert Boyle (1627–1691), avoided. Charleton did, however, share with Boyle the conviction that promoting the mechanical philosophy would enhance rather than destroy Christian piety.

Earlier translations by Charleton included works by the Hermeist Johannes Baptista van Helmont (1579–1644), such as *The Magnetic Cure of Wounds* (included in *A Ternary of Paradoxes,* 1650). Scholars disagree on whether Charleton accepted the Hermetism of Van Helmont, which emphasized spiritual illumination, and subsequently abandoned it for the rationalism of the mechanical philosophy. While some say he converted from mysticism to mechanism, others argue that his development was less dramatic, never wholly supporting either philosophy but embodying the complex eclecticism of seventeenth-century natural philosophy.

BIBLIOGRAPHY

Charleton, Walter. *Physiologia Epicuro-Gassendo-Charltoniana.* Introduction by Robert Kargon. New York: Johnson Reprint, 1966.

Fleitmann, Sabrina. *Walter Charleton (1620–1707), "Virtuoso": Leben und Werk.* Frankfurt am Main: Lang, 1986.

Osler, Margaret J. "Descartes and Charleton on Nature and God." *Journal of the History of Ideas* 40 (1979), 445–456.

JANE JENKINS

See also Atomism; Epicureanism; Gassendi, Pierre; Van Helmont, Johannes Baptista

Chemical Philosophy

A philosophy of nature and man founded on chemistry was proposed by the followers of Paracelsus (ca. 1491–1541) in the last half of the sixteenth century and into the seventeenth. Few of the works of Paracelsus had appeared before his death, and it was a decade before physicians began to look for his manuscripts and to publish them, often with commentaries. By 1570 many of his works were in print.

In these works, there is a strong challenge to the educational establishment. The Paracelsians rejected the traditional reliance on the ancient authorities with their emphasis on logic. They demanded educational reform that would permit teaching of their doctrines. However, with little evidence of change, some of these Paracelsians took pride in the fact that they had had little formal education, thus avoiding the useless knowledge they would have been taught.

They turned instead to the two-book theory, relying first on Holy Scripture and then on personal observations and experience—the "Book of Nature." Here they found chemistry particularly valuable since it required laboratory operations. Beyond this, chemistry became a basis for explaining both macrocosmic and microcosmic phenomena. Even the Creator was pictured as a divine alchemist in commentaries on the first chapter of Genesis.

The Paracelsians differed sharply from the ancients in their discussion of mathematics. In his summary of Paracelsian medicine, Peter Severinus (1542–1602) argued that Aristotle's work was flawed by its overemphasis on mathematical logic (1571). Galen (second century) had sought to emulate Aristotle (384–322 B.C.E.) in his medical work. For Severinus, such an approach was hopeless. The use of weights and measures was acceptable for the physician as was the mystical use of numbers such as one might find in the Hermetic texts, but not the logical-geometrical use of mathematics. Far more acceptable was the analogy of the great world and man that might be used as a guide to truth. Paracelsus had written that "everything which astronomical theory had searched deeply and gravely by aspects, astronomical tables, and so forth—this self-same knowledge should be a lesson and teaching to you concerning the bodily firmament."

Another subject of attack was the ancient system of elements: earth, air, water, and fire with their attendant qualities and humors. This was a complex system, but a potentially fragile one, since a rejection of even one might result in a collapse of the whole. But they argued that nowhere in Holy Scripture is there reference to the creation of fire, and, therefore, it cannot be considered an element. Paracelsus introduced the three principles, Salt, Sulfur, and Mercury as primary substances. Still, the four elements were not categorically denied by all—even by Paracelsus—and, in the course of the seventeenth century, a five-element-principle system evolved in the works of the chemists and the chemical physicians.

Element theory was only one aspect of macrocosmic interest. If the Creation was to be understood primarily as an alchemical separation from an initial chaos, then it seemed appropriate to use this analogy in geocosmic explanations. Distillation was the model employed for rain, volcanic eruptions, and the origin of mountain streams. Indeed, the earth itself was viewed as a large distillation flask with a fiery center that heated underground reservoirs of water and lava, both of which might erupt at this surface.

But if the Paracelsians rejected much of the ancient legacy, they remained wedded to the ancient vitalistic worldview. Metals originated in the earth from a union of an astral seed and a proper matrix. The resultant ore matured in the earth much as a fetus in the mother. They also believed that there is a life spirit essential for both the organic and the inorganic worlds. By the final decade of the sixteenth century, this spirit was identified as an aerial niter or saltpeter in a tract ascribed to Paracelsus. Paracelsus and his followers clearly sought a new world system based upon the macrocosm/microcosm analogy. Chemistry was to be the key to this new philosophy, and this placed an emphasis on new observations and the use of the laboratory. Yet, these reformers had a special interest in medicine. This was unavoidable since a knowledge of the macrocosm led directly to hitherto unknown secrets of man.

Practical medicine played an important part in the acceptance of Paracelsian medicine. The *Grosse Wundartzney* (1536), one of the most influential works of Paracelsus, was a book dealing with specific medical problems, as well as the preparations of balms and plasters that were widely accepted even among those who rejected his cosmological views. The chapters on the cure of wounds caused by gunshot clearly spoke to a growing problem in sixteenth-century medicine. But Paracelsus was aware of other current problems as well. In his *Von der Bergsucht oder Bergkranckheiten* (1533–1534), he prepared the first book on diseases of miners. And in his treatment of venereal diseases, *Vom Holtz Guaico gründlicher Heylung* (1529) and *Von der Französischen Kranckheit* (1530), he criticized current methods of treatment, including the popular use of guaiac wood.

However, works on specific medical problems were less inflammatory than concepts that seemed to directly challenge Galenic authority. Here Paracelsus's repeated use of chemistry and chemical analogies was particularly objectionable to the medical establishment. As an example, one may cite his conviction that each bodily organ acted as an alchemist, separating pure from impure. Thus, the stomach separated the nutritional part of foodstuffs from the dross, which was eliminated through the intestines. Similarly, other organs had their function in maintaining the health of the body. Illness occurred when the directive force in an organ failed and poisons accumulated. Examples were the tartaric diseases in which stony precipitates developed in the kidneys, or the bladder, or—as in the case of tuberculosis—in the lungs.

The Paracelsian rejection of humoral medicine was clearly a fundamental break with tradition. No less so was their method of cure. The Galenists argued that contraries cure: a disease of a certain quality and magnitude would be cured by a medicine of opposed quality and

C

magnitude. The Paracelsians turned, rather, to folk tradition, arguing that like cures like: a poison in the body would be cured by a similar poison. And if the Galenists charged that the Paracelsians were a legion of homicide physicians, the Paracelsians replied that their medicines were safe because they had been altered chemically and practitioners paid careful attention to dosage.

The Paracelsian chemical philosophers not only proposed a new approach to cure, they also emphasized a new class of *materia medica* (medicinal drugs). To be sure, some metallic and mineral substances had been employed by the ancients, but the great bulk of traditional remedies were derived from plant substances. This balance was to shift with the chemists who argued that the new and violent diseases of their age required stronger medicines. Neither the medieval herbals nor the works of the ancients described substances that could combat syphilis and other new diseases successfully. The internal use of metals and their compounds seemed essential for that purpose. Used as purges and vomitives, their action was truly more violent than the old herbal mixtures. In some cases, the new medicines proved too strong, and the Galenists accused their opponents of murder. When we examine the chemical and pharmaceutical books of the late sixteenth and the seventeenth centuries, we see directions for the preparation of numerous compounds of mercury, lead, arsenic, and antimony, almost all of which would be avoided today.

The growing interest in the works of Paracelsus in the third quarter of the sixteenth century led to an increasing number of publications, translations, and commentaries on his works. At stake was the question of educational reform, the relative value of ancient authority to fresh observational evidence, and even the relation of religion to science and medicine. The chemical philosophers played a role in all of these.

It would be wrong to picture the growing confrontation in terms of stark contrasts. To be sure, Peter Severinus sought to establish the superiority of Paracelsism to Galenism in his important *Idea medicinae philosophicae* (1571), while Thomas Erastus (1524–1583) upheld the authority of Aristotle and Galen and damned the innovations of Paracelsus in his *Disputationes de medicina nova Paracelsi* (1572–1574). But there were others who sought a middle course, such as the venerable Joannes Guinter of Andernach (ca. 1505–1574), who had taught both Andreas Vesalius (1514–1564) and Michael Servetus (1511–1553) at Paris in the 1530s. A renowned medical

humanist, he began to read the Paracelsian texts late in life. The result was his massive *De medicina veteri et noua . . .* (1571), in which he held to much of traditional medical theory but lauded the new chemically prepared medicines.

Nevertheless, there was debate on many levels. In his defense of the macrocosm/microcosm world, Robert Fludd (1574–1637) was opposed by Johannes Kepler (1571–1630), Marin Mersenne (1588–1648), and Pierre Gassendi (1592–1655). Significant points raised related to the roles of mathematics, observational evidence, and religion in the understanding of nature. But perhaps the most acrid confrontation concerned the use of chemically prepared medicines. In France, this problem centered on the internal use of antimony and its compounds, which were forbidden by the medical faculty of Paris as early as 1566. It was not until 1666 that this decree was rescinded. In the meantime, the Parisian debate had resulted in an extensive polemical literature. One of the most prominent casualties of this exchange, Theodore Turquet de Mayerne (1573–1655), was ostracized by his colleagues for his defense of medical chemistry. He left France for England, where he became first physician to King James I and was instrumental in introducing chemicals into the *Pharmacopoeia Londinensis* (1618), the first national pharmacopoeia.

As chemical medicines became more acceptable, the medical faculties of European universities gradually saw the need to establish chairs in chemistry. The first of these was in 1609 at Marburg, where Johannes Hartmann was appointed to teach the preparation of pharmaceuticals. By mid-century, chemistry was well established in European universities; by the end of the century, it had become almost universal in major medical schools.

In the second half of the seventeenth century, chemical philosophers found themselves competing with mechanists for the attention of scientists. Johannes Baptista van Helmont (1579–1644) presented a less mystical approach to chemistry and medicine than his predecessors and emphasized observational evidence. His work influenced the young Robert Boyle (1627–1691) as well as the prominent Oxford physiologist Thomas Willis (1621–1675), who maintained an interest in chemical explanations in his *De fermentatione* (1659). However, unlike earlier chemists, Willis insisted on the importance of anatomical studies, and in this he was seconded by the Leiden chemical physician Franz de la Boë Sylvius (1614–1672).

The *Principia mathematica philosophiae naturalis* (Mathematical Principles of Natural Philosophy, 1687) of Isaac Newton (1642–1727) encouraged many physicians to think that medicine should be reformed through mathematical and mechanical means rather than through chemistry. A number of confrontations at the close of the century and in the early decades of the new one pitted the iatrochemists against iatrophysicists. But, although the hopes of the sixteenth-century chemical physicians had succeeded primarily in practical areas, they had established a close connection between chemistry and medicine that still exists. The influence of eighteenth-century mechanists was to result in a chemistry independent of medical faculties (other than in pharmacy), and this formed the background for the chemical revolution of Antoine Lavoisier (1743–1794) and his colleagues.

BIBLIOGRAPHY

Debus, Allen G. *The Chemical Philosophy: Paracelsian Science and Medicine in the Sixteenth and Seventeenth Centuries.* 2 vols. New York: Science History Publications, 1977.

———. *The English Paracelsians.* London: Oldbourne, 1965.

———. *The French Paracelsians: The Chemical Challenge to Medical and Scientific Tradition in Early Modern France.* Cambridge: Cambridge University Press, 1991.

Hannaway, Owen. *The Chemists and the Word: The Didactic Origins of Chemistry.* Baltimore and London: Johns Hopkins University Press, 1975.

Moran, Bruce T. *The Alchemical World of the German Court: Occult Philosophy and Chemical Medicine in the Circle of Moritz of Hessen (1572–1632).* (Sudhoffs Archiv. Beiheft 29). Stuttgart: Steiner Verlag, 1991.

Pagel, Walter. *Paracelsus: An Introduction to Philosophical Medicine in the Era of the Renaissance.* Basel: Karger, 1958. 2nd ed. 1982.

———. *The Smiling Spleen: Paracelsianism in Storm and Stress.* Basel: Karger, 1984.

ALLEN G. DEBUS

See also Alchemy; Chemistry; Iatrochemistry; Macrocosm/ Microcosm; Paracelsus; Pharmacology

Chemistry

In the early-modern period, the term *chemistry* encompassed a wide spectrum of pursuits. Chemical practitioners could be involved in diverse studies involving the knowledge, use, manipulation, or production of chemical substances. The most important branches of chemistry were the search for metallic transmutation (now retrospectively labeled *alchemy*); chemical manufacture and technology; matter theory; chemical medicine, or pharmacy; and the employment of chemical phenomena for the elaboration of natural philosophy. Many "chemists" were actively involved in several branches simultaneously.

The search after the secret of metallic transmutation (properly termed *chrysopoeia,* from the Greek words for "the making of gold," and *argyropoeya,* "the making of silver") continued throughout the period of the Scientific Revolution. While the pursuit of the agent of metallic transmutation—called the Philosophers Stone or the Elixir—dates to the late-classical period, the climax of its activity dates to the seventeenth century. These chemical practitioners sought to prepare the Stone from a variety of substances, including vitriol (copper or iron sulfate), niter (potassium nitrate), mercury, the metals, dew, dung, urine, and many other substances. Differences in approach to the process led to the creation of "schools" of practice, thus providing considerable internal diversity to this subset of chemistry. The lure of the production of precious metals naturally attracted a number of charlatans, whose cheating practices tended to give a bad name to the whole of chemistry. Rulers across Europe maintained aspiring transmutors of metals at their Courts, paying them a stipend to labor on the problem of making gold.

An important development in chemistry was the beginning of chemical medicine, known as either *iatrochemistry* or *chemiatria* (both from the Greek *iatros,* physician). The earliest employment of chemistry for medicine in Europe appears in the writings of the fourteenth-century radical Franciscan John of Rupescissa, but a more renowned advocate of chemical medicine was the Swiss physician and iconoclast Theophrastus von Hohenheim, known as Paracelsus (ca. 1491–1541). Paracelsus downplayed the importance of traditional transmutational chemistry and emphasized the confection of pharmaceuticals from metallic and mineral bodies. He believed that such preparations were of greater power than the predominantly herbal remedies canonical to the medical establishment based on Galen (second century) and Ibn Sina (Avicenna, 930–1037). Additionally, Paracelsus constructed a cosmology with chemistry at its core. For example, he saw the world as a great distillation vessel, and its changes as parallel to the operations of chemistry. For Paracelsus and his followers, the human body itself (the "microcosm") bore resemblances not only to the universe (the "macrocosm") but also to chemical processes. This "chemical worldview" attracted a very large following, particularly after the late-sixteenth-century elaboration of Paracelsus's rather incoherent writings into more systematic forms by Petrus Severinus, Joseph DuChesne (Quercetanus), and others. For many, it provided an alternative to both the Aristotelian world system and the Galenic medical system.

Paracelsianism spread widely across Europe. In France, violent debates ensued between the Paracelsian (and Protestant) medical faculty at Montpellier, and the orthodox Galenic (and Catholic) college of physicians at Paris. Their debate crystallized in the so-called antimony wars of the late sixteenth century, wherein the former asserted that preparations (largely emetics and cathartics) based on antimony were powerful but safe, while the latter claimed (with considerable accuracy) that they were poisonous. Paracelsianism also gained great popularity in England, particularly during the Interregnum. The works of Paracelsians were then joined by those of the Flemish iatrochemist Johannes Baptista van Helmont (1579–1644). While Van Helmont disagreed with Paracelsus on a number of medical issues, he continued to champion chemically prepared medicines and to view many of the functions of the human body as chemical or analogous to chemical processes. Helmontianism was extremely influential in English scientific and medical thought. In 1665, the year of the Great Plague, an (ultimately unsuccessful) attempt was made to organize a College of Chymical Physicians as a rival to the Royal College of Physicians. In German lands as well, chemical medicine spread widely. In 1609 Johannes Hartmann (1568–1631) was installed at the University of Marburg as what is often termed the "first professor of chemistry," but his studies and lectures are more accurately defined as *chemiatria.*

Numerous "textbooks" of chemistry appeared throughout the seventeenth century and had the effect of widely propagating a working knowledge of basic chemical operations and preparations, although with little theory. Some, like Oswald Crollius's (ca. 1560–1609) *Basilica chymica* of 1609 and the very popular *Tyrocinium chymicum* of Jean Beguin (ca. 1550–ca. 1620), were of strongly Paracelsian character and contained mostly medicinal receipts; others, like Andreas Libavius's (1540–1616) *Alchemia* of 1597, were less Paracelsian and emphasized both chemical operations and pharmaceutical preparations. The emphasis on chemical medicine drew much attention away from more traditional trans-

mutational pursuits, and several authors tried to reduce the scope of chemistry to mere *chemiatria.* For example, Werner Rolfinck (1599–1673), in his 1661 textbook *Chimia in formatis redacta* (Chemistry Reduced to the Form of an Art), claimed that chemistry was "a part of medicine" (i.e., pharmacy alone). It is in such attempted reductions of the scope of chemistry that the origin of the British usage of "chemist" to mean "pharmacist" lies.

Chemistry was key to many manufacturing applications, and the chemical industry draws its origins from the increasing importance and output of workshops in the sixteenth and seventeenth centuries. Dyes, pigments, prepared salts, metals and alloys, glass, gunpowder, and a host of other materials were produced in increasing quantities. Distillation was crucial for a large number of industrial productions, including the preparation of the mineral acids (sulfuric, nitric, and hydrochloric), essential oils, perfumes, and liquors. The importance of this operation led to the term *distillatory art* as a synonym for chemistry and to the publication of distillation manuals, including Hieronymus Brunschwygk's *Little Book of Distillation* (1500), John French's *Art of Distillation,* and the more broadly technical *Furni novi philosophici* (New Philosophical Furnaces, 1648–1650) of Johann Rudolf Glauber (1604–1670). Distilled mineral acids were necessary, for example, for assaying and separating precious metals, and related chemical techniques were important to mining for the testing and refining of ores. Such chemical-minerological technology was showcased in the 1556 *De re metallica* (Of Metallic Things) by the humanist Georgius Agricola (Georg Bauer) and (1494–1555) *De la pirotechnia* (On the Craft of the Fire, 1540) by Vannoccio Biringuccio (1480–ca. 1540). A tradition of mining handbooks (*Bergbüchlein*), describing mining techniques and the treatment of ores, flourished in Germany.

Conceptions about the nature of matter developed throughout the period. An important feature of chemical thought was that its practitioners frequently conceived of matter as composed of tiny particles, in contrast to most orthodox Aristotelian physics, which rejected atomistic models. The major source of Latin medieval chemical thought, the thirteenth-century *Summa perfectionis* (Sum of Perfection) of the pseudo-Geber (actually the Franciscan Paul of Taranto), employs the language of "minimal parts"—imperceptibly small particles of matter—to explain chemical phenomena using the varying sizes and "compositions" of these particles. This particulate system was propagated through several branches of chemistry, appearing, for example, in the transmutational theories of Gasto DuClo (ca. 1530–ca. 1595) and those of the highly esteemed Eirenaeus Philalethes, alias George Starkey (1628–1665), as well as in the iatrochemical writings of Daniel Sennert (1572–1637). While atomistic theories were revived from classical sources by Pierre Gassendi (1592–1655) and René Descartes (1596–1650) in the seventeenth century, similar notions had already become traditional in chemical thought.

In conjunction with particulate theories, there generally existed a theory of "principles"—substances either fundamental or of very simple or resilient composition. In the oldest literature and among those writers adhering most closely to Aristotle (384–322 B.C.E.), the elements were four—fire, air, earth, and water—and the combinations and reshuffling of these four elements provided all material substances, their properties, and interactions. Most chemical workers however, preferred a more complex scheme. Following the formulations of Arabic authors, the Latin medieval tradition recognized two principles, called Mercury and Sulfur, as the constituents of minerals and metals. These principles corresponded only by analogy to the common substances with the same names. They represented, instead, the condensed forms of the moist and smoky exhalations that, according to Aristotle's *Meteors,* arose from the center of the earth to produce stones and minerals. In this system, the different metals were composed of Mercury and Sulfur of differing qualities mixed in differing proportions. Gold, as the pinnacle of metallic perfection, was composed of pure Mercury mixed perfectly and in the perfect proportion with pure Sulfur. Consequently, since all metals shared the same ingredients, transmutation was possible by adjusting the mixtures.

Under Paracelsus and his followers, these two principles were joined by a third, Salt, thus composing the Three Principles (*tria prima*). Additionally, whereas Mercury and Sulfur had earlier been postulated as the constituents of metals and minerals only, the Paracelsians extended their triad to include *all* substances. In cosmological schemes, this material trinity was drawn into analogy with the triune nature of man (body-soul-spirit) and the Holy Trinity. The classic experiment for exhibiting the Principles was a burning twig—the flame shows the presence of an inflammable Sulfur, the smoke a the volatile Mercury, and the ashes, when extracted with water and evaporated, a Salt. Seventeenth-century chemists, noting the existence of an "Earth" and an insipid water, or "Phlegm," added these to the roster of constitutive substances, producing a pentad.

While chemistry as broadly defined here has a long history, the subject as we would define it today began seriously to take shape as a branch of science independent of production (whether of gold and silver, pharmaceuticals, or manufactured substances) and medicine in the latter half of the seventeenth century. That period witnessed the elaboration of the medieval particulate-matter theories into broader corpuscularian schemes that eventually became the fundamental theoretical basis of modern chemistry. Many thinkers played a role in this development, but perhaps chief among them was the English natural philosopher Robert Boyle (1627–1691). Boyle insisted upon the great value of chemical knowledge and practice for solving larger problems in natural philosophy. He drew upon both the accumulated wealth of practical and experimental chemical knowledge—in *chrysopoeia, chemiatria,* and chemical trades—and the long tradition of particulate-matter theories he found among "the Chymists" to argue on behalf of the new mechanical philosophy. Boyle's corpuscularian system was better able to explain real chemical effects than were the more jejune and abstracted formulations of Gassendi and Descartes. With Boyle (and some of his contemporaries), the corpuscles took on specific shapes that explained their reactivity. Some had hooks to connect them together; some had pores that could receive the pointed parts of others; some were smooth and spherical; others rough; others shaped like snakes or eels. This mechanical view received its most sustained expression in 1675 in the *Cours de chemie* (Course of Chemistry) of Nicolas Lemery (1645–1715).

It has often been said that chemistry was "left out" of the Scientific Revolution and that it had to await the late-eighteenth-century works of Antoine Lavoisier (1743–1794) to undergo a "delayed chemical revolution." But this conception arises out of an ill-conceived positivist notion that the progress of any branch of science must mimic that of physics. While there may not have been a change in chemistry analogous to that experienced by physics at the hands of Galileo Galilei (1564–1742) and Isaac Newton (1642–1727), it cannot be denied there was intense activity, interest, and development in chemistry throughout the sixteenth and seventeenth centuries. This development occurred along many lines and in many different subsets of the discipline. By the start of the eighteenth century, chemistry had

C

become a recognized branch of natural philosophy pursued by such important scientific organizations as the Académie Royale des Sciences in Paris and the Royal Society of London and taught in various forms at many universities. Outside of natural-philosophical circles, its importance to trade and manufacture continued to burgeon, and its contibutions to medicine for both confecting new pharmaceuticals and understanding bodily process had become widely accepted.

BIBLIOGRAPHY

Brock, William H. *The Norton History of Chemistry.* New York: Norton, 1992.

Clericuzio, Antonio. "A Redefinition of Boyle's Chemistry and Corpuscular Philosophy." *Annals of Science* 47 (1990), 561–589.

Debus, Allen G. *The Chemical Philosophy: Paracelsian Science and Medicine in the Sixteenth and Seventeenth Centuries.* 2 vols. New York: Science History Publications, 1977.

Moran, Bruce T. *Chemical Pharmacy Enters the University.* Madison WI: American Institute of the History of Pharmacy, 1991.

Newman, William R. *Gehennical Fire: The Lives of George Starkey, an American Alchemist in the Scientific Revolution.* Cambridge, MA: Harvard University Press, 1994.

Principe, Lawrence M. *The Aspiring Adept: Robert Boyle and His Alchemcial Quest.* Princeton, NJ: Princeton University Press, 1997.

LAWRENCE M. PRINCIPE

See also Alchemy; Chemical Philosophy; Matter; Paracelsus; Pharmacy

Cimento. See Accademia del Cimento

Class. See Social Class and Science

Classification of the Sciences

A useful myth about the history of classifying the sciences suggests that, before the Scientific Revolution, Scholastics categorized the sciences by simply reflecting on their relations to an ultimate Aristotelian metaphysics, whereas during the Scientific Revolution the modern view arose that, by the lights of experience, physics is the queen of the sciences, mathematics its handmaiden, and all the special sciences follow suit. Yet, even late into the seventeenth century, scientists and philosophers continued to shape their conceptions of

what counts as a science, and what kinds of science there are, based on what was logically and metaphysically viable. The primary shift in the early-modern era was the emergence of the notion that such concerns about the nature of science stand apart from the empirical inquiries of natural science.

Like many other historical myths, though, this one is useful because it relates an important element of the historical truth. The Aristotelians indeed viewed what we today think of as physics and the special sciences as all subordinate to a more general "science of being," the object of which is to uncover the conceptually and physically necessary elements of existence, and the range of which is anything that we could even conceive of as existing. Only by grasping highly abstract descriptions of things, such as that any identifiable bit of substance would have to feature both matter and form together, could we hope to successfully pursue more specialized studies. Indeed, all other sciences were seen as "specialized"; for example, physics looks at the properties, changes, and interactions of identifiable bits of matter, whereas biology looks at the specific class of living bits of matter. While, in modern times, we may be inclined to consider biology as subordinate to, or at least as borrowing many foundational elements from, physics and chemistry, the Aristotelians saw all sciences below the "science of being" as on an equal level of distinctness and specialization. Quite to the contrary of viewing physics as the model for other sciences, Aristotelians held that biology offers important insights into goal-directed behavior of matter, and many sought to identify such behavior in inanimate matter as well. It was widely held, for example, that the free fall of bodies results from a natural, form-constrained tendency of bodies to fall toward the center of the earth. Such elements of metaphysics commonly guided the pursuit of empirical inquiry by the Aristotelians and so, as well, their picture of all sciences as equally specialized studies playing a secondary role to metaphysics.

Aristotle (384–322 B.C.E.) himself does not simply crown metaphysics as First Philosophy but further classifies the sciences according to their aims and corresponding cognitive virtues. Thus, in the *Metaphysics* he distinguishes among theoretical, productive, and practical knowledge, and in the *Nicomachean Ethics* he distinguishes art, scientific knowledge, rational intuition, practical intelligence, and wisdom. Most significantly for the Scholastics, however, the divisions of Aristotle's treatises (really fashioned by his latter-day editors) best illuminated what they believed to be the proper boundaries of physics, the study of the heavens, the natural histories of terrestrial beings, ethics, and other areas of learning.

Yet, the classificatory schemes that truly shaped the curricula of the Scholastic world were the *trivium* of grammar, rhetoric, and dialectic or logic and the *quadrivium* of arithmetic, geometry, astronomy, and music; the roots of these schemes may be traced to Plato's (428–348 B.C.E.) educational proposals in *The Republic*. And during the Renaissance, there is a rising recognition of the importance of law, medicine, and literary studies, as a reflection of still other ancient priorities. But for all this classicist demarcation of areas of knowledge, the prevailing view before the Scientific Revolution was that Aristotle was particularly correct about two matters: that the key to carving up the special sciences is their subject matter and associated method and that metaphysics provides the general principles governing all of the sciences. Hence, the mythic tale goes, big changes emerge in the way the sciences are classified when René Descartes (1596–1650) proposes to reject the first point, and Francis Bacon (1561–1626) proposes to reject the second.

Thus, Descartes, in his *Rules for the Direction of the Mind* (written 1619–1628, but published posthumously), rejects the view that we distinguish among the sciences by their subject matter and corresponding method, on the ground that scientific method is actually universal and so unites all science into a web of interrelated truths: "Whoever would seriously seek after the truth of things cannot . . . choose [to find this in] a particular science, because they are all united between them by a connection of reciprocal dependence." The method is the same across the sciences, Descartes contends, because we employ the same cognitive tools toward a goal common to all science—certain knowledge. Insofar as he accepts, in this early work, that the sciences share a universal method, some part of the myth holds true. But in later works, such as the *Principles of Philosophy* (1644), Descartes proposes that we base our explanations and understanding of data from special sciences like mechanics, astronomy, and optics on those general and indubitable foundational principles we use to characterize the natural world. This mature view suggests, contrary to the myth, that, even if scientific method is universal, the subject matter of the sciences is still what distinguishes among them.

Bacon similarly promises but fails to take us far beyond the pre-Revolutionary picture. In the *Plan of the Great Instauration* (1620–1626), he appears to reject the Aristotelian program of founding scientific thought on general principles—metaphysical or otherwise—in favor of the project of building science on specific reports of natural and experimental histories. So it is fitting that, in *The Advancement of Learning* (1605), Bacon proposes to classify the sciences by dividing the broad areas of history, poetry, and philosophy by criteria reflecting our experience: their objects of study, their "narrative" versus "inductive" use, or the kinds of causes studied. Quite apart from this approach to classification, however, he suggests that there is a First Philosophy, or unifying basis of the sciences, that consists of those axioms found across the sciences but special to none. He takes some of these principles as belonging to logic, such as "if equals be added to unequals the wholes will be unequal," and others rather as the stuff of metaphysics, "as they have efficacy in nature and not logically." It appears, then, that while Bacon places a great premium on building the individual sciences on the basis of gathering particulars, he believes, with the Aristotelians, that we can tie the sciences together by their common foundational metaphysics.

If these two cases are representative, then the myth is wrong to suggest that those who classify the sciences after the Scientific Revolution follow empirical criteria alone and throw out the Aristotelian view of metaphysics as a source of general principles to which all other kinds of knowledge must conform. For Descartes, at least, we continue to divide the sciences in the same way we carve up the world, on the basis of reflection before experience and in accordance with metaphysical constraints. And for Bacon, at the highest level of science we seek logical and metaphysical principles with which our physics and other empirical studies must agree. Each of these thinkers retains the principal ancient and Scholastic criterion for classification: we divide the sciences along the lines of nature's actual structure, and we grasp this structure when, through metaphysical inquiry, we identify the underlying general features of the world and their relations. But, while this myth is not wholly accurate, it is useful nevertheless. It conveys the notion that, when areas of knowledge are reclassified during the Scientific Revolution, physics provides the foundations of a group of natural sciences clearly characterized as empirical inquiry, among which we will not find metaphysics. By distinguishing "summary philosophy," as Bacon calls metaphysics, from experimental and observational natural philosophy, these thinkers demarcate the modern boundary between philosophy and science. This constitutes a real change, not perhaps in the character of criteria for classifying the sciences but in their actual hierarchy or ordering.

Aside from the philosophically inspired changes related by this myth, the Scientific Revolution also brought reclassifications of the areas of knowledge through new ways of viewing practical concerns and the increasingly formal character of science. Studies of medicine, artillery, navigation, and actuarial data (and many other diverse fields of practical knowledge) came to be considered not only as optimally shaped by rigorous, theoretical science, but also as possibly shaping the nature of such scientific inquiry. One factor that previously contributed to keeping such theoretical and practical pursuits apart was a common perception that theoretical science is uniquely abstract and, correspondingly, that what makes practical studies nontheoretical is their inherent concreteness. During the Scientific Revolution, this distinction is partly eliminated with the mathematicization of science—when scientists like Galileo Galilei (1564–1642) advocate idealization and precision through quantified descriptions of physical phenomena—which makes it clear that studies of physical phenomena previously thought of in practical terms alone (such as cannonball trajectories or ocean depths) are subsumable under a common physics. This newly robust, mathematicized physics heralds a worthy applied science, in which technological development follows quickly on the heels of pure scientific research. Just as significant, it became commonplace for pure research to advance with the practical knowledge of scientist and nonscientist alike; refined techniques in lens grinding, for example, led directly to an explosion in microscopy and telescopy. By integrating applied areas of knowledge with the theoretical sciences, the notion of what could be considered a science—pneumatics or statistics, for example—was greatly broadened.

BIBLIOGRAPHY

Fisher, Nicholas. "The Classification of the Sciences." In *Companion to the History of Modern Science,* ed. R. C. Olby, G. N. Cantor, J. R. R. Christie, and M. J. S. Hodge. London: Routledge, 1990, pp. 853–868.

Freedman, Joseph S. "Classifications of Philosophy, the Sciences, and the Arts in Sixteenth- and Seventeenth-Century Europe." *Modern Schoolman* 72 (1994), 37–65.

McRae, Robert. "The Unity of the Sciences: Bacon, Descartes, Leibniz." In *Roots of Scientific Thought: A Cultural Perspective,* ed. Philip P. Weiner and Aaron Noland. New York: Basic Books, 1957, pp. 390–411.

Schmidt-Biggemann, Wilhelm. *Topica universalis: eine Modellgeschichte humanistischen und barocker Wissenschaft.* Hamburg: Meiner, 1983.

Speziali, Pierre. "Classification of the Sciences." In *Dictionary of the History of Ideas,* vol. 1, ed. Philip P. Weiner. New York: Scribner, 1973, pp. 462–467.

SAUL FISHER

See also Aristotelianism; Bacon, Francis; Mixed Sciences

Clavius, Christoph (1538–1612)

Promoted the mathematical sciences, including astronomy, and established their place in the curriculum of the far-flung and influential Jesuit college network. He designed and put into practice a mathematics curriculum that shaped generations of Jesuit-educated scholars. While Clavius also helped start the Jesuit colleges at Messina and Naples, he spent most of his life teaching in Rome at the Jesuit Collegio Romano. He also wrote many books, including a very early printed edition and commentary on Euclid's *Elements.* He produced a long series of revised editions of his *Commentary on Sacrobosco's Sphere,* which served as an introductory astronomy textbook for much of sixteenth-century Europe and which is an important source for the history of cosmology in that period. Clavius was one of the technical advisers on the papal committee that formulated the Gregorian-calendar reform and became Pope Gregory's principal expositor and defender of the reform. He also wrote treatises on geometry, arithmetic, gnomonics, the astrolabe, and the like.

Clavius's position at the Collegio Romano gave his opinions great weight, and he was very interested in the astronomical and cosmological controversies of his era. He gathered observations, first published in his *Sphere* commentary of 1585, that confirmed the celestial nature of the nova of 1572 (i.e., that it was located above the sphere of the Moon) and used that conclusion to call into question the Aristotelian doctrine of celestial incorruptibility. Clavius was also influential in the acceptance of the Copernican heliocentric theory. In the successive editions of his *Sphere* commentary, Clavius critically reviewed the competing cosmological alternatives that he saw in competition with the Ptolemaic cosmology, which he defended. He praised aspects of Nicolaus Copernicus's (1473–1543) work and steadily accepted several Copernican innovations, culminating in Clavius's rejection in 1593 of the traditional Alfonsine theory of trepidation (an oscillation of the equinoxes) in favor of a geocentric theory, adapted from Copernicus, of the motion of the fixed stars. Clavius, however, never accepted Copernican heliocentrism but criticized it strongly in his *Sphere* commentary's survey of cosmological alternatives, in which he also rejected other cosmological rivals to the Ptolemaic. Clavius rejected Copernican cosmology on several grounds. Not only did it conflict with Scripture, common sense, and Aristotelian physics, but, Clavius believed, its methodology was flawed so the Copernican theory would never contribute any reliable knowledge to astronomy.

Clavius's influence was important in Galileo Galilei's (1564–1642) advocacy of heliocentrism. When Galileo, who had known Clavius for some time, made public his early telescopic discoveries, Cardinal Robert Bellarmine, who had been one of Clavius's colleagues at the Collegio Romano, requested an opinion from the astronomer. The response from Clavius and three of his students was an early and influential endorsement of the validity of Galileo's claims, though Clavius was careful to deny, correctly, that Galileo's observations were proof of the Copernican theory. In the final *Sphere* commentary, published shortly before his death, Clavius described Galileo's discoveries and remarked on their enormous significance for the development of astronomy.

BIBLIOGRAPHY

Baldini, Ugo. "Christoph Clavius and the Scientific Scene in Rome." In *Gregorian Reform of the Calendar: Proceedings of the Vatican Conference to Commemorate Its 400th Anniversary, 1582–1982,* ed. George V. Coyne, M. A. Hoskin, and A. Pedersen. Vatican City: Pontificia Academia Scientiarum, Specola Vaticana, 1983.
———. *Legem impone subactis: Studi su filosofia e scienza dei Gesuiti in Italia, 1540–1632.* Rome: Bulzoni Editore, 1992.
Lattis, James M. *Between Copernicus and Galileo: Christoph Clavius and the Collapse of Ptolemaic Cosmology.* Chicago: University of Chicago Press, 1994.

JAMES M. LATTIS

See also Calendar Reform; Collegio Romano; Copernicanism

Clocks. See Horology

Clockwork Universe

The metaphor of the clockwork universe played a central role in the discussions of the Scientific Revolution at its height. Leading champions were René Descartes, Robert Boyle, and Gottfried Wilhelm Leibniz; the chief adversary was Isaac Newton. After Newton, the use of the metaphor declined, rapidly in England, more gradually on the Continent.

The mechanical clock, even in its simplest form an automaton simulating the rotations of the earth in real time, soon after its invention (late thirteenth century) acquired astronomical capabilities to indicate, for example, the length of the day; the age, phases, and aspects of the Moon; the position of the Sun in the zodiac; and even the position of some, or all, planets. The claim of an essential affinity between this machine and the universe was, thus, strongly stated. This affinity was soon recognized in literature.

Early clock metaphors are found in the fourteenth century in Dante's *Divine Comedy* and works by Jean

Cristoph Clavius. From Paul Freher, Theatrum virorum eruditione clarorum *(1688).*

Froissart, Christine de Pisan, and Nicole Oresme; after the fifteenth century, their use increased. The points of comparison ranged widely, but uniformly the clock was invoked to convey approval and praise. The clockwork-universe analogy, anticipated in the ancient *machina mundi* (world machine) concept, was introduced by Nicole Oresme ca. 1350 and soon became popular among poets, theologians, and natural philosophers. Implied in it was the idea of the Clockmaker-God, which was expandable into a formal proof of the existence of God, the *argument from design,* which had the form of the syllogism: A clock is made by a maker (and not by chance); the universe is a large clock; therefore, it, too, must have been made by a maker: God.

From the mid-seventeenth to the mid-eighteenth century, the clockwork-universe metaphor was used in the discussions of natural philosophy with great variety and frequency. Early champions of the new scientific outlook had employed the clock metaphor sparingly; not only had any belief in the physical reality of a clockwork universe become untenable long before, but it was also one of the chief priorities of the movement to create a new literary style of scientific discourse, characterized as a "close, naked, natural way of speaking," rejecting the use of metaphor and other rhetorical devices.

Clockwork imagery became popular in scientific discourse with the writings of René Descartes (1596–1650), who adopted a program of describing "the visible world in general as if it were only a machine in which there is nothing to consider but the shapes and movements of its parts." He realized this program most fully by applying the clock/automaton image not to astronomy but to living things. His elaborate human physiology, published posthumously as *Traité de l'homme* (1662), is rigorously based upon the automaton analogy. Animals are identified with automata; humans, distinguished from animals only by their free will, are given a special status with the help of an ingenious theory of the soul.

Most of the philosophers of the generation following Descartes—including Blaise Pascal (1623–1662), Christiaan Huygens (1629–1695), Benedict de Spinoza (1632–1677), Nicolas Malebranche (1638–1715), François Fénelon (1651–1715), Bernard le Bovier de Fontenelle (1657–1757) on the Continent; Kenelm Digby (1603–1665), Henry More (1614–1687), Joseph Glanvill (1636–1680), Roger Cotes (1682–1716), John Locke (1632–1704), and Robert Hooke (1635–1702) in Bri-

tain—used clock metaphors occasionally in many contexts of the mechanical philosophy. Robert Boyle (1627–1691) and Gottfried Wilhelm Leibniz (1646–1716), clearly partial to the metaphor, drew upon it extensively.

Boyle compared the method of the modern natural philosopher with that of the clockmaker taking apart a defective clock, and he demanded the same logical stringency of a scientific deduction as that seen in the cause-and-effect relationship among the parts of a watch. But he rejected, as did most of his compatriots, the theory of animal automatism. Boyle's references to the argument from design, which recur in his writings throughout his career, undergo a gradual shift in emphasis. This argument, it was recognized, not only demonstrated the existence of God, it also defined his essential characteristics. Initially, Boyle had repeated the conventional argument, that the Creation did not require subsequent divine intervention because it was perfect: an omniscient Creator could not make an imperfect work. This argument, however, implied that there was no further need for the Creator: God would become a passive bystander, of limited power, *omniscient* but not *omnipotent.* An omnipotent God, conversely, could not be omniscient, because a creation that required continued maintainance by its maker had to be faulty. God could not be both, all-wise and all-powerful. A theological debate arose whether supreme wisdom or supreme power was God's chief characteristic, with the opposing camps known as *intellectualists* and *voluntarists,* a debate equivalent to that over *determinism* versus *free will.* While Continental philosophers gravitated to the intellectualist position, in Britain a voluntarist consensus soon emerged to which Boyle adjusted his position, eventually leaving the clock image out of his formulation of the argument from design.

Leibniz, whose philosophy was deeply rooted in determinism, employed metaphors of clock and automaton frequently. His strong commitment to the argument from design in its intellectualist form brought him into conflict with Newton, a passionate voluntarist. Newton had frequently referred to the design argument but never mentioned the image of the clock. In 1715 Leibniz sent to his friend the princess of Wales a list of his objections to Newton's philosophy. The letter reached Samuel Clarke (1675–1729), who replied on behalf of Newton, his friend and mentor. The ensuing correspondence has become famous as the *Leibniz-Clarke debate.* In his first letter, Leibniz attacked Newton's voluntarism by outlining his own intellectualist position in terms of the classical formulation of the design argument. Clarke bluntly rejected the analogy. Speaking of clockmakers, he stated: "with regard to God, the case is quite different," and he concluded that "the notion of the world's being a great machine, going on without the interposition of God, . . . is the notion of materialism and fate." Leibniz let this stand without objection in his subsequent letters; his death terminated the debate. In Britain, this certified the death of the clockwork-universe analogy. On the Continent, the idea survived in the philosophy of Leibniz's disciple Christian Wolff but quickly lost all significance in the following decades.

BIBLIOGRAPHY

Alexander, H. G., ed. *The Leibniz-Clarke Correspondence.* Manchester: Manchester University Press, 1956.

Kubrin, David. "Newton and the Cyclical Cosmos: Providence and the Mechanical Philosophy." *Journal of the History of Ideas* 28 (1967), 235–296.

Mayr, Otto. *Authority, Liberty, and Automatic Machinery in Early Modern Europe.* Baltimore and London: Johns Hopkins University Press,1986.

Maurice, Klaus, and Otto Mayr, eds. *The Clockwork Universe: German Clocks and Automata, 1550–1650.* New York: Neale Watson, 1980.

OTTO MAYR

See also Automata; Mechanical Philosophy; Physico-theology; Providence

Coiter, Volcher (1534–1576)

Dutch anatomist, a key figure in the later stages of Renaissance anatomy. Coiter was a typical Peripatetic scholar-anatomist, learned in classical medicine but willing to test it by using eyesight observation, the hallmark of sixteenth-century anatomy. In 1555 the city council of his native Groningen awarded Coiter a scholarship to travel and study abroad. Gabriele Falloppio (1523–1562) at Padua and Bartolomeo Eustachio (ca. 1520–1574) in Rome were among his teachers in anatomy.

Coiter's work in anatomy forms part of a decisive development in Renaissance anatomy. Coiter moved away from human anatomy as exemplified by the work of Andreas Vesalius (1514–1564) and into comparative anatomy. The motivation for this came from a comment by the naturalist Ulisse Aldrovandi (1522–1605) to Coiter at Bologna that the natural philosophers were ignorant and often in error in anatomy. As Coiter noted,

anatomical knowledge of the human body alone was considered sufficient for physicians, but philosophers needed to dissect all animals, as they studied all of nature. Much of Coiter's work and that of his contemporaries was concerned with integrating the methods and approaches of Aristotle (384–322 B.C.E.), the great authority on comparative anatomy, into late-Renaissance anatomy, as well as checking the accuracy of his observations. In embryology, Coiter repeated and expanded upon Aristotle's systematic observations on the development of the chick embryo, and, like Aristotle, he described the anatomical structure of many different vertebrate skeletons. He dissected the heart, in Aristotle's opinion, the principal organ of the body, in serpents, fishes, frogs, and cats. He also made a study of the anatomy of birds. Coiter's work represents a broadening of the vision of the anatomists and looks forward to the Aristotelian-inspired anatomy of Girolamo Fabrici (ca. 1533–1619) and William Harvey (1578–1657).

BIBLIOGRAPHY

Bäumer, Änne. "Der Nürnberger Artz Volcher Coiter: Anatom und Zoologe." *Medizinhistorische Journal* 23 (1988), 224–234.

Herrlinger, Robert. *Volcher Coiter, 1534–1576.* Nuremberg: Edelmann, 1952.

Nuyens, B., and A. Schierbeck, ed. *Opuscula selecta Neerlandicorum de arte medica.* Vol. 18, *Volcher Coiter.* Amsterdam, 1955.

ANDREW WEAR

See also Anatomy; Dissection; Embryology

Collège Royal

A humanist and royal foundation, the Institution des Lecteurs Royaux was established at Paris in 1530 by Francis I. Called the Collège Royal from 1610 and renamed the Collège de France in the nineteenth century, the institution has shaped intellectual life in France and abroad from the sixteenth century to the present day.

Several institutional idiosyncrasies allowed the Collège Royal a distinctive intellectual role. These include a fiercely guarded administrative independence from the University of Paris; the early establishment of chairs in mathematics, medicine, and Greek and Latin philosophy as well as in ancient languages; the recruitment of foreign lecturers; the relative latitude enjoyed by the professors in determining their courses; and the practice of offering lectures (and competitions for chairs) free of charge to the interested public. In addition, the Crown paid (albeit irregularly) annual stipends to lecturers and provided permanent quarters in the seventeenth and eighteenth centuries.

Royal patronage is traditionally credited with protecting the Collège Royal against the university and the parlement. Nonetheless, the three Paris institutions were closely linked. In the century after 1568, the chairs in medicine were largely monopolized by the same few Parisian medical dynasties that served the royal family. After 1671, the Collège Royal fell increasingly under the influence of the Académie Royale des Sciences.

Lectures at the college exhibited no overarching intellectual consensus. Aristotle (384–322 B.C.E.) had his defenders in the sixteenth century, but a strong Platonist tradition also survived into the seventeenth century. Pierre Gassendi (1592–1655), the atomist and heliocentrist, and Jean-Baptiste Morin (1583–1656), the anti-Copernican astrologer, held chairs in mathematics contemporaneously. Despite the bans on teaching Cartesianism, the college accommodated both opponents and supporters of René Descartes (1596–1650) under Louis XIV. Finally, confessional discord intruded on the institution, notably in the sixteenth-century religious wars.

The mission of the institution was, from the start, to reform education and learning. Dubbed the "tri-lingual academy" because its first chairs were in Latin, Greek, and Hebrew, the college soon added posts in mathematics, Oriental languages, philosophy, and medicine. Professors of Greek and Latin philosophy sought to reconcile competing natural philosophies with one another and with religion.

In medicine, respect for the ancients was tempered by fresh anatomical research. In mathematics, lectures encompassed ancient theory, modern invention, and practical applications. Sixteenth-century professors commented in humanistic fashion on texts of Euclid, Archimedes, and Theodosius and taught algebra. In the final years of Louis XIV, Pierre Varignon (1564–1722) introduced the infinitesimal calculus to Parisians, and Philippe de La Hire (1640–1718) lectured on navigation, astronomy, optics, mechanics, and hydrostatics. If its originality and influence waned in the seventeenth century, the Collège Royal continued to reflect the tension between ancients and moderns that dominated learning in early-modern Europe.

BIBLIOGRAPHY
Lefranc, Abel. *Histoire du Collège de France depuis ses origines jusqu'à la fin du premier empire.* Paris: Hachette, 1893.
Raulet, Lucien. "Billets mortuaires et autre documents concernant des professeurs du Collège royale de France (1622–1660)." *Société de l'histoire de Paris et de l'Ile-de-France* 34 (1907), 127–147.
Torlais, Jean. "Le Collège royal." In *Enseignement et diffusion des sciences en France au six-huitième siècle,* ed. René Taton. Paris: Hermann, 1986, pp. 261–286.
                                          ALICE STROUP

See also Académie Royale des Sciences; Educational Reform; Gresham College

Colleges of Physicians

Established in the towns of northern Italy in the late Middle Ages to examine prospective practitioners, regulate medical practice, and advise the civic authorities on public-health matters. The charter granted to the London College of Physicians in 1518 by Henry VIII alluded to the role played by such institutions in the efficient governance of the Italian cities. Several of the founders of the London College had studied in Padua and had developed an admiration for the Italian revival of humanistic scholarship. They sought to use the college to inculcate the values and ethos of Renaissance learning within English physic. But the London College also had some of the functions of a city guild, operating as a local licensing body to maintain a monopoly of trade for its members against surgeons, apothecaries, and irregular practitioners. The London College was thus simultaneously a learned society, an agent of royal administration, and a trade organization. Similar institutions were established in Glasgow in 1599, Dublin in 1654, and Edinburgh in 1681. However, of all of the European colleges, the London one was the most involved in scientific endeavor in the seventeenth century.

In the intellectual and political turbulence of the seventeenth century, an elite and monopolist body, associated closely with the established social order, could not escape criticism. The troubles of the London College were exacerbated by the problems it experienced in balancing its various functions. The Fellowship of the College was reserved to physicians with the degree M.D. from Oxford or Cambridge. Such men had been trained in classical philosophy and tended to be practitioners of a more or less orthodox Galenic physic. However much it had been purified and renewed by humanist scholarship, Galenism was inevitably regarded by many as Scholastic and conservative in the radical intellectual context of the Scientific Revolution. Proponents of the new chemical remedies, associated with Paracelsus (ca. 1491–1541) and Johannes Baptista van Helmont (1579–1644), particularly criticized the collegian physicians for their continued adherence to a traditional pharmacopoeia. The necessity to defend the honor and authority of orthodox physic against medical chemistry could be combined only with difficulty with the college's desire to present itself as being at the forefront of the intellectual developments of the time. Throughout the seventeenth century, the collegian physicians engaged in an uneasy balancing act between the defense of their privileged social position and their orthodox practice, on the one hand, and the encouragement and assimilation of new learning, on the other.

In the early decades of the seventeenth century, the collegian physicians were determined in their defense of Galenic therapeutics. However, chemical drugs were so popular among the surgeons, apothecaries, and patients of London that the college could not afford to ignore them completely. The 1618 *College Pharmacopoeia* acknowledged the value of 122 chemical remedies, and the revised edition, published in 1650, listed 130. After 1648 the college installed a chemical laboratory on its own premises and appointed a chemist, William Johnson (1610–1665), to manufacture and test new drugs. This innovation stopped well short, however, of an official endorsement of the chemical philosophy, in any of its varieties.

In emulation of the Italian example, the London College of Physicians organized surgical and anatomical demonstrations for the edification of its Fellows. William Harvey (1578–1657) was Lumleian Lecturer to the College from 1615 to 1656. The work that led up to his discovery of the circulation of the blood was first publicly presented in the course of these lectures. His college audiences undoubtedly provided Harvey with an important sounding board upon which to try out his ideas. Nevertheless, Harvey was virtually unique among the collegian physicians of the 1620s and 1630s in his enthusiasm for the experimental philosophy. His colleagues were largely indifferent to his discoveries, which they saw as irrelevant to medical practice.

As the seventeenth century progressed, however, opinion within the college shifted as to the value and pertinence of the experimental method as applied to medical and biological subjects. Harvey gradually built up a coterie of supporters among the younger college Fellows. Roger Drake (1608–1669) in 1639 and George Ent (1604–1689) in 1641 publicly defended the theory of the circulation of the blood. With increasing frequency throughout the 1640s and 1650s, the college's anatomy lecturers acknowledged the force of Harvey's arguments and praised the magnitude of his scientific achievement. By this time, with the publications of Francis Glisson (1597–1677), Thomas Wharton (1614–1673), and Thomas Willis (1621–1675), a strong indigenous school of anatomists was developing in England. All of these authors were Fellows of the London College and disciples of Harvey.

Harvey's work was important to the collegian anatomists for the vivid practical exemplars it provided for the undertaking of experimental investigations in physiology. But Harvey was also of great symbolic importance to the college in the context of the attacks being made upon it by Helmontians and other radical critics. The key point is that Harvey's reconceptualization of the action of the heart and the role of the blood did not alter his consulting or therapeutic practice. Harvey's example thus seemed to show that the collegian physician was by no means indifferent to the exciting scientific discoveries of the age. The college, indeed, could play a leading role in the support of investigation and the dissemination of its results. Harvey's career also indicated that anatomical discovery did not threaten, could indeed even endorse, the authority of traditional therapeutics. The great physiologist had managed to combine a brilliant program of original experimentation with an unshakable commitment to orthodox physic. In 1657 Walter Charleton (1620–1707), a leading apologist for the college, even claimed that all of Hippocrates's (460–ca. 370 B.C.E.) aphorisms could be deduced from the hypothesis of the circulation of the blood. The revolution in anatomy had improved medicine, but it had not shaken its foundations nor discredited the college in its role as the conservative guardian of proper practice.

By the mid-1650s, the London College had developed a fine range of facilities for the scientific endeavors of its Fellows. Its library was not narrowly medical in scope and had been greatly enhanced by Harvey's gift of his books. The resources of the museum included a wide range of anatomical specimens and surgical instruments. As well as its laboratory, the college also supported a botanical garden. Its premises provided a meeting place for groups of enthusiasts. Important new books, notably on anatomy and iatromechanics, were published under its imprimatur. Overall, the college made a substantial contribution to the continued development of observational and experimental science in Britain. The Colleges of Physicians in Dublin and Edinburgh played similar, if somewhat lesser, roles in the encouragement of anatomy and experimentation.

Some collegian physicians, however, saw dangers for the social and professional status of the graduate physician if medicine should become wholly dominated by the experimental philosophy. First, there was the danger that experimental scrutiny might reveal that the remedies of their arch rivals, the apothecaries and empirics, were, indeed, of greater therapeutic value than the prescriptions of the physicians. Second, and more important, the graduate physician did not seek merely to intervene therapeutically when his patients became ill. A distinguishing aspect of his professional practice, as against that of other practitioners, was that the physician provided his healthy patients with advice for the maintenance of their well-being. The physicians maintained that their lengthy educations uniquely equipped them with the wisdom and intellectual acumen to undertake this task successfully. But the emphasis of the chemical and experimental philosophers was overwhelmingly upon the narrowly therapeutic aspects of medicine, upon finding specific drug remedies. It seemed to many collegial physicians that, if medicine was to be reduced to a drug-based therapeutics, then something distinctive and centrally important, to them at least, would be lost.

In the later decades of the seventeenth century, the status of the London College was somewhat reduced in several respects. The Royal Society, founded in 1660, rose to become indubitably the preeminent learned society in England, displacing the college from that position. Erosion of the absolute power of the monarchy eventually led to the loss of the college's monopolistic control over the practice of medicine. Ultimately, the defense of orthodox Galenic physic in the face of scientific innovation and social change was to prove an impossible task—in London and elsewhere.

BIBLIOGRAPHY

Clark, George. *A History of the Royal College of Physicians of London*. Oxford: Clarendon, 1964.

Craig, William S. *History of the Royal College of Physicians of Edinburgh*. Oxford: Blackwell, 1976.

Whitteridge, Gweneth. "Some Italian Precursors of the Royal College of Physicians." *Journal of the Royal College of Physicians* 12 (1977), 57–80.

Webster, Charles. "The College of Physicians: Solomon's House in Commonwealth England." *Bulletin for the History of Medicine* 41 (1967), 393–412.

MALCOLM NICOLSON

See also Galenism; Harvey, William; Medicine; Pharmacy

Collegio Romano

A Jesuit university in Rome founded in 1551 by Ignatius of Loyola (1491–1556), who had studied at the Universities of Alcalá, Salamanca, and Paris and chose the latter as his model. Later it became known as the Gregorian University because of benefactions for a new building received from Pope Gregory XIII in 1567, at which time more than a thousand students attended its classes from all parts of Europe. To its original faculties in the humanities and science, faculties of philosophy and theology were added in 1553. The university became a model for Jesuit universities and set standards to be met by other universities, secular as well as Catholic, during the Scientific Revolution.

Two features are of particular importance for historians of science. The first is that many of the Jesuits who achieved distinction in science studied or taught at the Collegio Romano. Among these should be included Christoph Clavius (1538–1612), Christoph Grienberger (1561–1636), Odo van Maelcote (1572–1615), Orazio Grassi (1590–1654), Niccolò Zucchi (1586–1670), and Athanasius Kircher (1602–1680).

The second point is the relationship of Galileo Galilei (1564–1642) with the professors of the Collegio Romano, which took place in three different periods: 1587–1590, 1610–1611, and 1618–1623. The extent of the first contact had not been discovered until recently. Three of Galileo's manuscripts from his early period, written in his own hand and in Latin, are still extant: the first contains questions on logic; the second, questions on the universe, the heavens, and the elements; the third, various treatises on motion. The editor of the National Edition of Galileo's works, Antonio Favaro, excluded the first from the edition on the ground that it was a Scholastic composition copied by Galileo before entering the University of Pisa. The second and third he published, dating the second in 1584, while Galileo was studying there, and the third ca. 1590, while Galileo was at Pisa again, teaching mathematics. It is known that in 1587 Galileo visited Clavius at the Collegio Romano and left with him some theorems on the center of gravity of solids. Correspondence between the two in 1588 shows that Clavius was concerned about a *petitio principii* (assuming the premise of an argument the argument is intended to prove) in Galileo's reasoning. Since this expression occurs in the first manuscript, it became a clue for its renewed study; similarly, Galileo's citation of the *Doctores Parisienses* in the second manuscript re-awakened interest in it. Serious study since the 1980s has yielded the following surprising results. The first manuscript contains notes appropriated by Galileo from the portion of a logic course covering Aristotle's *Posterior Analytics* taught at the Collegio Romano and ending in August 1588 and so probably dates from early 1589. The second similarly contains notes from a course covering Aristotle's *De caelo* and *De generatione* taught at the Collegio Romano in 1589. The third contains Galileo's own original compositions, now referred to as his *De motu antiquiora,* but in its later portions employs Aristotelian concepts contained in the same course and so was written ca. 1590. These results require extensive revision of previously held views on Galileo's Pisan period and his relationships with the Jesuits.

Galileo's second contact with the Collegio Romano occurred after his discoveries with the telescope. Astronomers at the Collegio had difficulty building a good telescope to verify his results. They had done so by March 1611, however, and confirmed Galileo's findings in the *Sidereus nuncius* (Sidereal Messenger) of 1610, as well as his discovery that Venus has phases. Later that year, the mathematicians of the Collegio feted Galileo, and Odo van Maelcote gave an address in which he praised the *Sidereus nuncius* and expressed his agreement with Galileo's results.

The third contact, that of 1618–1623, was less fortunate, for it relates to Galileo's acrimonious interchanges with Orazio Grassi over the nature of comets. By that time, Clavius had died and Galileo had had a similar interchange with a German Jesuit teaching at Ingolstadt, Christoph Scheiner (1573–1650), over the nature of sunspots. Galileo's relationships with the Jesuits continued to deteriorate until his trial by the Roman Inquisition on 1633. Some have argued that the Jesuits actually brought about the trial, but this is contested in recent scholarship.

It may finally be noted that the first discovery of stellar parallax was made by an astronomer at the Collegio Romano, Giuseppe Calandrelli (1749–1827), who reported it in a work published in 1806 and dedicated to Pope Pius VII. The star was Alpha in the constellation Lyra, and the measurement was a factor in the Church's finally removing its prohibition against Copernican teaching in 1820.

BIBLIOGRAPHY

Villoslada, Riccardo G. *Storia del Collegio Romano dal suo inizio (1551) alla soppressione della Compagnia di Gesù (1773).* Rome: Gregorian University, 1954.

Wallace, William A. *Galileo and His Sources: The Heritage of the Collegio Romano in Galileo's Science.* Princeton, NJ: Princeton University Press, 1984.

WILLIAM A. WALLACE

See also Causality; Clavius Christoph; Society of Jesus

Colombo, Realdo (ca. 1510–1559)

Italian anatomist who provided some of the essential preliminary discoveries for William Harvey's work on the circulation of the blood. In his lifetime, Colombo strengthened in the anatomical tradition belief in the primacy of direct observation, criticism of previous observational errors, and the need to establish priority in the making of new observations as a means of gaining a professional reputation. Colombo's only published work was his *De re anatomica* (1559). In it, he was highly critical of his former friend Andreas Vesalius (1514–1564), and he also showed himself to be an original anatomist and vivisectionist. Colombo's dispute with Vesalius began when he had temporarily replaced him at Padua and had publicly criticized him for errors in anatomy and for passing off descriptions of animal anatomy as human (precisely the fault that Vesalius criticized in Galen). Vesalius responded with bitter hostility in his *Epistola . . . radicis chynae* (Letter . . . [on] China Root, 1546).

In 1548 Colombo tried to get Michelangelo (1475–1564) to collaborate with him in producing an illustrated anatomy text to surpass Vesalius's *De humani corporis fabrica* (On the Structure of the Human Body, 1543), but the age of the painter and perhaps also his reported stomach-churning disgust when present at dissections prevented this, and *De re anatomica* was published without illustrations. It gave a succinct and complete account

Realdo Colombo's De re anatomica *(1559) shows Colombo, as professor, dissecting a cadaver by himself, a practice that had only recently become common at the University of Padua.*

of human anatomy, and, appended at the end, were two chapters of observations drawn from animal-vivisection experiments and pathological anatomy. The pulmonary transit of the blood and the elucidation of the heartbeat provided important cornerstones for Harvey's (1578–1657) discovery of the circulation of the blood. By vivisecting dogs, Colombo showed that blood went from the right side of the heart through the flesh of the lungs to the left side and that the pulmonary vein always contained blood, not air as was previously thought. Colombo observed that the blood in the pulmonary vein was arterial blood, and he concluded that it was in the lungs, rather than in the heart, that dark venous blood was altered into "shining thin and beautiful" blood. Previous anatomists had denied the Galenic doctrine that there were pores through the intraventricular septum by which blood flowed from the right to the left side of the heart, but they had produced no alternative pathway— the work of Ibu al-Nafis (thirteenth century) and

Michael Servetus (1511–1553) was unknown to anatomists at this time. Colombo also described the movement of the heart, and from vivisection he concluded that its active phase was when it was raised up, swollen, and constricted, not when it dilated; this contradicted the Galenic view that the active phase of the heart was in diastole, when it drew blood in to itself. Despite confusion in Colombo's text where he used the word *diastole* when he meant *systole,* Harvey grasped his meaning and confirmed Colombo's findings with his own experiments.

BIBLIOGRAPHY

Colombo, Realdo. *De re anatomica*. Venice: 1559.

Pagel, Walter. *William Harvey's Biological Ideas*. Basel: Karger, 1964, pp. 154–156, 166–169, 215–218.

Whitteridge, Gweneth. *William Harvey and the Circulation of the Blood*. London: Macdonald; New York: American Elsevier, 1971, pp. 41–77.

ANDREW WEAR

See also Anatomy; Harvey, William; Servetus, Michael; Vesalius, Andreas

Color

Until the early seventeenth century, Aristotle's ideas dominated natural-philosophical thinking on colors. Before that time, new views on colors, as had been developed by artists since 1400, did not have any impact on scholarly thinking. In Renaissance painting, color mixing had become commonly accepted. Painters had begun to reject Aristotle's opinion that black and white are the fundamental colors from which all others are composed. Leon Battista Alberti (1404–1472), in *De pictura* (1435), strictly separated black and white from the chromatic primaries from which others colors can be derived. François de Aguilón (1567–1617) was one of the first scholars who adopted the painter's primaries. In *Opticorum libri sex* (1611), Aguilón proposed a scheme of color mixing in which black and white are dismissed as generators of colors, although not unequivocally as being colors. In the course of the seventeenth century, the scheme of colors based on black and white as primaries was generally abandoned.

According to Aristotle (384–322 B.C.E.), the rainbow is caused by reflection of sunlight in a black cloud, whereby colors are produced by weakening of the light. During the sixteenth and seventeenth centuries, the explanation of Theodoric of Freiburg (d. ca. 1311), based on internal reflection in raindrops, was only slowly rediscovered. Francesco Maurolico (1494–1575) tried to account for the size of the rainbow by considering the behavior of rays in raindrops, including internal reflection. Through purely mathematical reasoning, he arrived at a broadly right value. Marco Antonio de Dominis (1564–1624) gave, in 1611 in *De radiis visus et lucis,* an almost modern account of the path of rays through a spherical raindrop. René Descartes (1596–1650) was the first to acquire a full understanding of the reflections and refractions in raindrops. By mathematically tracing the paths of rays through a drop, Descartes was able to determine the extreme limits of the radii of the primary and secondary bows. His cumbersome calculations of *Les meteores* (1637) were simplified and generalized by several mathematicians, most notably Edmond Halley (ca. 1656–1743) and Jakob Hermann (1678–1733) ca. 1700.

Explaining the colors of the rainbow was a different matter, for it entailed a conception of the nature of colors. According to Aristotle, colors are inherent qualities of an object that light enables to be transmitted to the observer. In the Middle Ages, the problem was raised whether radiant colors, like those of the rainbow, are real colors. The answer had been that those colors are apparent and are the result of a modification of pure light. According to mechanistic philosophy, all colors, including those of bodies, are apparent and caused by the interaction of light and objects. Colors produced by prisms and, later on, in thin films became central in seventeenth-century accounts of the nature of colors. Descartes gave a mechanistic account of the nature of color in the eighth discourse of *Les meteores, based on his pressure theory of light. When light is refracted,* the particles that transmit light acquire a rotational motion that can cause the sensation of color.

According to Robert Hooke (1635–1702), this theory could not explain how colors are produced in the spherical raindrops of the rainbow, for the second refraction would neutralize the effect of the first refraction. In *Micrographia* (1665), he put forward an alternative explanation of colors produced by refraction, based on his pulse conception of light. According to him, in white light, pulses are perpendicular to the sides of the rays, the direction of propagation of the waves. After refraction of light, however, the pulse makes an angle with the ray. The obtuse and acute angles at each side of the pulse cause the perception of colors. To explain the colors in thin films, Hooke formulated a second theory of colors. In this case, the reflections at the upper and lower surface of the film produce two waves to propagate at a small distance at each other. Depending on the order of the waves reflected at each surface and their distance, the various colors are produced. Hooke's was the most elaborated attempt to explain colors by means of a wave theory of light, for Christiaan Huygens (1629–1695) did not treat colors at all.

Isaac Newton (1642–1727), in his turn, developed the most elaborate account of colors based on an emission conception of light. Throughout his life, he considered two possible explanations: colors are dependent on the mass of particles or on their velocity. In the end, the correlation of color with mass seems to have had his preference. In the several editions of *Opticks* since 1704, he

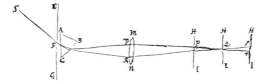

(3086)

about three foot radius (suppose a broad Object-glass of a three foot Telescope,) at the distance of about four or five foot from thence, through which all those colours may at once be transmitted, and made by its Refraction to convene at a further distance of about ten or twelve feet. If at that distance you intercept this light with a sheet of white paper, you will see the colours converted into whiteness again by being mingled. But it is requisite, that the *Prisme* and *Lens* be placed steddy, and that the paper, on which the colours are cast, be moved to and fro ; for, by such motion, you will not only find, at what distance the whiteness is most perfect, but also see, how the colours gradually convene, and vanish into whiteness, and afterwards having crossed one another in that place where they compound Whiteness, are again dissipated and severed, and in an inverted order retain the same colours, which they had before they entered the composition. You may also see, that, if any of the Colours at the *Lens* be intercepted, the Whiteness will be changed into the other colours. And therefore, that the composition of whiteness be perfect, care must be taken, that none of the colours fall besides the *Lens*.

In the annexed design of this Experiment, A B C expresseth the Prism set endwise to sight, close by the hole F of the window

E G. Its vertical Angle A C B may conveniently be about 60 degrees: *M N* designeth the *Lens.* Its breadth 2½ or 3 inches. S F one of the streight lines, in which difform Rays may be conceived to flow successively from the Sun. F P, and F R two of those Rays unequally refracted, which the *Lens* makes to converge towards Q, and after decussation to diverge again. And H I the paper, at divers distances, on which the colours are projected : which in Q constitute *Whiteness,* but are *Red* and *Yellow* in R, r, and *t,* and *Blew* and *Purple* in P, p, and π.

.If

A page from Isaac Newton's "New Theory about Light and Colors," published in the Philosophical Transactions of the Royal Society *of February 19, 1672, illustrating how white light is made up of light rays of various colors.*

separated these explanations, however, strictly from his experimentally proven theory of colors. The core of this revolutionary theory was that colored light instead of white light is pure and homogeneous. According to Newton, colored light is not generated by some modification of white light but by separation of one or more colors from white light. He first published his "New Theory About Light and Colours" in the *Philosophical Transactions* of January 1672. According to Newton, his theory was proved by the experiments he described. His critics, however, thought it depended on an emission conception of light they ascribed to him and focused on this. Because of his frustration over these disputes, he withheld his complete theory of colors from publication.

Newton's 1672 paper did not make clear that his theory was the result not only of extensive experiments with prisms, but also of his mathematical approach. Positioning a prism in such a way that an incident beam of light is maximally refracted, an elongated spectrum is produced, whereas a circular would have been expected. According to Newton, this dispersion of colors is the result of the different refrangibility of colored rays. To prove that light of a specific color is refracted at a specific angle, Newton performed the famous *experimentum crucis* (crucial experiment). He projected part of the spectrum through a second prism and showed that no further dispersion was caused and that the angle of refraction for each color remained the same. Newton never succeeded in developing a complete mathematical science of colors based on his discovery of different refrangibilities. He searched in vain for a dispersion law, a mathematical relationship between the refrangibilities of each of the colors. In *Opticks,* he included his theory of colors in thin films, but it was primarily an experimental theory of light and colors.

BIBLIOGRAPHY

Boyer, Carl B. *The Rainbow, from Myth to Mathematics.* New York: Sagamore, 1959. Princeton, NJ: Princeton University Press, 1987.

Sabra, A. I. *Theories of Light from Descartes to Newton.* London: Oldbourne, 1967.

Shapiro, Alan E. "Artists' Colors and Newton's Colors." *Isis* 85 (1994), 600–630.

———. "Introduction." In *The Optical Papers of Isaac Newton,* vol. 1: *The Optical Lectures, 1670–1672,* ed. Alan E. Shapiro. Cambridge: Cambridge University Press, 1985, pp. 1–25.

FOKKO J. DIJKSTERHUIS

See also Grimaldi, Francesco Maria; Light Transmission; Optics; Refraction

Comets

At the beginning of the Scientific Revolution, the dominant account of comets was that of Aristotle, who believed them to be fires located nearer than the Moon, and thus meteorological not astronomical. Later writers attributed astrological meaning to comets, linking them with heavenly phenomena. During the sixteenth century, many important astronomers adopted a new account that treated comets as spherical lenses, with tails created by focusing the rays of the Sun. At the same time, the first attempts to track the distance of comets from the earth established that they were beyond the Moon and raised serious questions about Aristotle's doctrine that the planets were supported by spheres of ether. In the first half of the seventeenth century, many accounts of the origin, composition, and motion of comets competed. Isaac Newton's classification of comets as returning or nonreturning laid the foundation for modern theories, although he continued to ascribe an important providential role to comets.

Aristotle's universe is divided into two regions: the heavens and the earth. Their boundary is the earth-centered sphere in which Aristotle (384–322 B.C.E.) imagined the Moon to be embedded. As the heavens are composed of a single substance, nothing that changed could exist there. Comets were a problem for Aristotle: they appeared to move like a heavenly body, but they came to be and passed away, which could not happen in the heavens. They also varied greatly in appearance, sometimes from night to night. Aristotle concluded, in his *Meteorology,* that comets must be some kind of fire in the upper regions of the terrestrial world and, hence, closer than the Moon. Later Greek and Roman writers almost universally accepted this account.

Later writers also began to treat comets as warning signs of political catastrophes, plagues, dry weather, and droughts (the last three, at least, resulting from the comet's heat). During the Middle Ages, medically trained astrologers began to observe comets with new and more precise instruments designed originally for use in astronomy. Thus, although regarded as atmospheric phenomena, comets came to linked with the study of the heavens because, like the stars and planets, they had astrological meaning, and the same instruments could be used to examine them.

The first attempt to measure the distance of a comet from the earth was probably made by Levi ben

Gerson (1288–1344), who devised a new instrument later known as the *radius astronomicus* or Jacob's staff. The results of his measurement have not survived. Johannes Regiomontanus (1436–1476) adopted Levi's instrument, probably using it in 1472 to measure the altitude of a comet, which he found to be well inside the sphere of the Moon. He suggested that the tail was smoke rising from the comet's flames, which in Aristotle's physics would be expected to move radially away from the earth.

Based on the bright comet of 1532, Peter Apian (1495–1552) in Germany and Girolamo Fracastoro (ca. 1478–1553) in Italy both concluded that the real orientation of comets' tails was away from the Sun, on a great circle from the Sun through the head of the comet. This new observation led Girolamo Cardano (1501–1576) and Ioannes Pena (1528–1558) to suggest, during the 1550s, that comets were not fires but spherical lenses condensed from celestial material, with tails created as the rays of the Sun were focused by passing through the comet's head. Pena also allowed that at least some comets were beyond the Moon and noted, against Aristotle, that fires lacked the power to focus light rays. Later figures who endorsed this view include Christoph Rothmann (fl. 1555–1597), Michael Maestlin (1550–1631), Tycho Brahe (1546–1601), and the young Johannes Kepler (1571–1630). Brahe was unable to line up the tail of the comet of 1577 with the Sun and concluded that it was created by light from the bright planet Venus. Equally important, Maestlin and Brahe determined the distance from the earth to this comet over a number of months. These showed that, if plotted in an earth-centered universe, the comet's path would pass through a series of Aristotle's spheres of ether. Both concluded that Aristotle's account of the heavens was mistaken and that the motion of the comet was centered on the Sun.

Although Kepler initially accepted the optical account of comets, he soon became its critic, pointing out that light rays focused by the head of a comet would be not be visible unless there was something behind the comet for the rays to shine on. He preferred the view that comets are temporary condensations of celestial matter and that the tail is a stream of fine particles left behind as the comet moves through the heavens (essentially the modern view). In place of the heliocentric paths of Brahe and Maestlin, he insisted that comets move in straight lines. Among major figures of the Scientific Revolution,

only Galileo Galilei (1564–1642) refused to accept that comets were celestial objects, although he rejected Aristotle's account of the heavens on other grounds. In universities, Aristotle's doctrines about comets remained prominent.

René Descartes (1596–1650) freed comets from the Sun. He regarded them as stars that had become so encrusted with denser matter that they had become detached from their native vortex. The dead star was then free to travel through surrounding vortexes until captured by one of them. Newton (1642–1727) set Descartes's conjecture on a mathematical footing by distinguishing returning and nonreturning comets. Newtonian orbits around the Sun are either closed (ellipses, with circles as a special case) or open (parabolas and hyperbolas). Plotting the path of a comet established once and for all that the pairs of comets seen a short interval apart were the same object approaching and leaving the Sun. If the comet's path was open, it would never return. If its path was closed, a precise date for its reappearance could be calculated. Newton and Edmond Halley (ca. 1656–1743) established that the 1682 comet, which now bears the latter's name, had an elongated elliptical orbit and successfully predicted its return. Newton also continued to give an important role to comets in God's providential plan for the universe. Like the Stoics, he assumed that the Sun required new supplies of fuel on a regular basis and believed that this was supplied by comets falling into the Sun as their orbits decayed. A particularly large comet would cause the Sun to swell and brighten, sterilizing the earth and preparing the way for a new cycle of creation. The bright comet of 1680 was expected to fulfill this function after five or six more revolutions.

BIBLIOGRAPHY

Barker, P. "The Optical Theory of Comets from Apian to Kepler." *Physis* 30 (1993), 1–25.

Barker, Peter, and Bernard R. Goldstein. "The Role of Comets in the Copernican Revolution." *Studies in History and Philosophy of Science* 19 (1988), 299–319.

Hellman, C. Doris. *The Comet of 1577: Its Place in the History of Astronomy*. New York: Columbia University Press, 1944.

Jervis, Jane L. *Cometary Theory in Fifteenth-Century Europe*. (Studia Copernicana 26). Warsaw: Polish Academy of Sciences Press, 1985.

PETER BARKER

See also Astrology; Brahe, Tycho; Celestial Spheres; Ether; Parallax

C

Commandino, Federico (1509–1579)

Physician, mathematician, and translator, a native of Urbino, he studied Latin and Greek in his youth, then pursued courses in philosophy and medicine at the University of Padua for ten years, and finally took his medical degree from the University of Ferrara in 1546. Withdrawing soon after from the practice of medicine "because of its uncertainty," he settled into editing, translating, and commenting on the classics of ancient Greek mathematics, a career he pursued to the end of his life. His only original publications were a brief treatise *On the Calibrating of Sundials* (1562) and a work on the center of gravity of solids (1565). From 1569 onward, he lived at Urbino, where he was the teacher of Guidobaldo del Monte (1545–1607) and Bernadino Baldi (1553–1617).

Commandino's importance derives from his extensive work on Archimedes (ca. 287–212 B.C.E.), translating his main Greek texts into Latin and providing a commentary, published in a single volume in 1588. Seeking the source of some propositions in *Floating Bodies,* he further investigated and translated portions of Apollonius's *Conics* and Pappus's *Collection,* as well as writings of Eutocius and Serenus. He also translated into Latin Euclid's *Elements,* providing an extensive commentary; a work of Aristarchus, with Pappus's explanations; Ptolemy's *Planisphere;* and Hero's *Pneumatics.* Finally, to aid his students, he supervised a translation of Euclid's *Elements* into Italian. One could argue that it was Commandino's translating activity that made possible the rapid recovery of Western mathematics in the sixteenth century.

BIBLIOGRAPHY

Commandino, Federico. *La prospettiva.* Ed. Rocco Sinisgalli. (Domus Perspectivae: Documenti e studi di prospettiva 3). Florence: Cadmo, 1993.

———. *La rappresentazione degli orologi di Federico Commandino.* Ed. Rocco Sinisgalli and Salvatore Vastola. (Domus Perspectivae: Documenti e studi di prospettiva 4). Florence: Cadmo, 1994.

Losito, Maria. "La gnomonica, il IX libro dei Commentari Vitruviani di Daniele Barbaro e gli studi analemmatici di Federico Commandino." *Studi Veneziani* 18 (1989), 177–237.

WILLIAM A. WALLACE

See also Translations

Compass, Magnetic

It played three walk-on parts in the Scientific Revolution. First, it was a major symbol of the "battle of the ancients and the moderns," a battle conclusively won for the moderns by late-seventeenth-century science. Second, it was the main piece of apparatus used in navigation, a vital field of study that fruitfully united the "hand knowledge" of navigators with the "head knowledge" of philosophers into recognizably experimental science. Third, throughout the Scientific Revolution, the compass was believed to offer a solution to the problem of finding longitude at sea, the scientific-cum-technical problem that arguably received more state encouragement than any other in the seventeenth century.

A precondition of the Scientific Revolution was belief in a concept of progress. As late-Renaissance humanists sought proofs of the superiority, or at least equality, of their age with classical antiquity, they always cited the magnetic compass. Although ancient Greeks knew of the magnet's attractive power, they did not discover its directional property, unlike the Chinese, who developed the first north-seeking devices. As knowledge of them penetrated late-medieval Europe, development of the nautical compass made possible transoceanic voyages such as Columbus's to America in 1492. Jean Bodin could write in 1560 of the compass (as well as of printing and gunpowder—also Chinese inventions) as proof of progress in technology. "What, for example, is there more marvellous."

Francis Bacon (1561–1626) famously extended the argument for progress in technology to science in Aphorism 129 of his *New Organon:* "printing, gunpowder and the compass . . . have changed the appearance and state of the whole world." For Bacon, the sciences should progress like the arts and for the same reason: that the philosopher, like the navigator, should pay attention to useful things, not Scholastic words. Indeed, Bacon elevated the navigational revolution occasioned by the compass into a general symbol of intellectual progress. Just as navigators had sailed beyond the Pillars of Hercules (the fabulous western Mediterranean limits of navigability) to discover the New World, so should philosophers move beyond the philosophical limits of adherence to Plato (428–348 B.C.E.) and Aristotle (384–322 B.C.E.) into a new intellectual world. Bacon also interpreted a prophecy in the Book of Daniel, that "many shall go to and fro, and knowledge shall be increased," to mean that the end of the world was being marked both by oceanic navigation and his yet-to-be-accomplished reformation of science.

Bacon's confidence in an imminent scientific revolution was partially fueled by contemporary progress in the science of the compass itself, notably that made by William Gilbert (1544–1603) in his *De magnete* of 1600. Although Bacon was characteristically critical of Gilbert's magnetic philosophy, he praised his novel experimentalism in this useful area. Gilbert's science of the magnet demonstrated to the seventeenth century the reality of new, experimental sciences that improved on classical natural philosophy. Magnetic philosophy depended upon the compass in two ways. First, miniature compasses, which Gilbert called *versoria* and used as detectors of magnetic fields, were crucial apparatus in his demonstration of the earth's magnetic field. Second, Gilbert's book attracted attention because it explained the hitherto "marvellous" behavior of the nautical compass. As Edgar Zilsel argued in 1940, the experimentalism that Bacon advocated and that *De magnete* exemplified was born out of the compass's mediating function as an object of interest to both practical investigators (of navigation) and philosophical analysts (of the "occult virtue" of magnetism).

Navigators and instrument makers had advanced the subject, notably through the discovery of magnetic dip in 1581 by the unlearned compass maker Robert Norman. As well as adapting his apparatus from the compass, Gilbert's empirical proof relied upon his replication in the laboratory of the patterns of compass variation measured at sea. Furthermore, there is evidence that Gilbert's philosophical interests were tempered and given empirical rigor by the navigation lecturer Edward Wright (1558–1615). Seventeenth-century magnetic science continued to combine technical and scientific expertise. Gilbert's science was studied intensively for several reasons, which included Gilbert's suggestion that the earth rotated magnetically, but primarily for its navigational applications. Gilbert's theory of why compasses varied from true north was that the earth itself was not a homogeneous magnetic sphere. A corollary was that local geology would produce local patterns of compass variation that could be used to determine one's position at sea. This and other magnetic schemes seemed the most likely solution to the pressing problem of longitude.

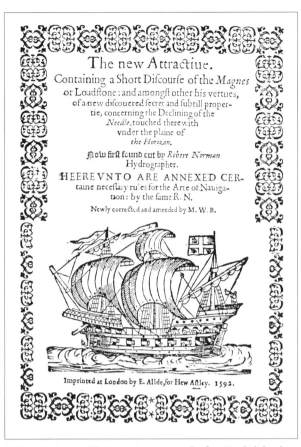

Robert Norman's The New Attractive, *the first English book on the compass, described the variation of the compass and magnetic dip, based on his own experiments and experience as a navigator.*

Emerging nation-states such as Philip II's Spain, Louis XIII's France, and Charles II's England offered huge prizes for a successful longitude scheme. Research into the magnetic philosophy of the compass thus represents some of the earliest state support for the new science. The Baconian and Puritan circle of Samuel Hartlib (ca. 1600–1662) gave it a high priority. In the 1660s and 1670s in England, the newly formed Royal Society and the Admiralty both investigated a method propounded by the navigation teacher Henry Bond, which allowed for the new discovery of the secular variation of the compass. It and other attempts failed, and by 1700 the compass, like magnetic philosophy itself, no longer represented the vanguard of scientific progress.

BIBLIOGRAPHY

Keller, Alex. "Mathematical Progress in the Technologies and the Growth of the Idea of Progress in the Sixteenth Century." In *Science, Medicine, and Society in the Renaissance,* ed. Allen G. Debus. 2 vols. New York: Science History Publications, 1972, vol. 1, pp. 11–27.

Pumfrey, Stephen. "'O tempora, O magnes!' A Sociological Analysis of the Discovery of Secular Variation in 1634." *British Journal for the History of Science* 22 (1989), 181–214.

———. "'These 2 Hundred Years not the Like Published as Gellibrand Has Done de Magnete': The Hartlib Circle and Magnetic Philosophy." In *Samuel Hartlib and Universal Reformation: Studies in Intellectual Communication,* ed. Mark Greengrass, Michael Leslie, and Timothy Railor. Cambridge: Cambridge University Press, 1994, ch. 13.

Waters, D. W. *The Art of Navigation in Elizabethan and Early Stuart Times.* New Haven, CT: Yale University Press, 1958.

STEPHEN PUMFREY

See also Gilbert, William; Magnetism; Navigation; Wright, Edward

Contagion. See Etiology

Conway, Anne, Viscountess Conway (née Finch) (1631–1679)

A Neoplatonist metaphysician, the invalid wife of Viscount Conway, she spent most of her adult life as a recluse at Ragley Hall, Warwickshire. Deeply interested in theology, metaphysics, and mathematics from childhood, she entered into correspondence with the Cambridge Platonist Henry More (1614–1687). This led to a lifelong friendship and mutual influence. Another close associate was F. M. van Helmont (ca. 1614–1699), through whose influence she became acquainted with Quakerism, to which she converted in 1674. All three (More, van Helmont, Conway) were very involved in study of the Kabbalah.

Conway left a posthumously published treatise, *Principles of the Most Ancient and Modern Philosophy,* setting out her system of interconvertible created substances and of Christ as the medium through which God makes them. Conway is important as the advocate of an original *essentialist* theory. Perhaps inspired in part by Ovid's *Metamorphoses,* Conway viewed all created substances as possessing some degree of corporeality and some degree of thought, the differing degrees of each corresponding to substance types. These views bear similarity to Robert Boyle's (1627–1691) theory of corporeal substance (his so-called corpuscularian hypothesis), but Conway extends them to all of animate, as well as inanimate, nature.

Gottfried Wilhelm Leibniz (1646–1716) was told of Conway's life and work by van Helmont and refers to her views with praise more than once. Her system is, indeed, a sort of proto-monadology. (The term *monad* appears in her treatise, and she views the world as a scene of progressive moral amelioration through its transformation.)

Situating Conway with respect to the Scientific Revolution is not straightforward. Formally, her Neoplatonist system is backward looking or premodern. Like More, she attempted accommodation to the new currents with doubtful success. On the otther hand, Conway's system is genuinely monistic, as More's is not. Her affinities to Leibniz are striking, whatever the degree of actual influence may have been.

BIBLIOGRAPHY

Conway, Anne. *The Principles of the Most Ancient and Modern Philosophy*. Ed. with Introduction by Peter Loptson. The Hague: Nijhoff, 1982.

Duran, Jane. "Anne Viscountess Conway: A Seventeenth-Century Rationalist." *Hypatia* 4 (1989), 64–79.

Merchant, Carolyn. "The Vitalism of Anne Conway: Its Impact on Leibniz's Concept of the Monad." *Journal of the History of Philosophy* 17 (1979), 255–269.

PETER LOPTSON

See also Kabbalah; Leibniz, Gottfried Wilhelm; Neoplatonism; Women and Natural Philosophy

Copernicanism

Copernican astronomy is the general name for a heliocentric theory of the solar system, wherein Earth turns around the Sun and around its own axis, thus causing the apparent movements of the heavenly bodies. It does not cover just Nicolaus Copernicus's own work, which first challenged the long-accepted Ptolemaic astronomy, but also all subsequent modifications of it—for instance, those by Johannes Kepler (1571–1630).

Copernicus's work is often regarded as a kind of watershed, having inaugurated a new era in astronomy. This dichotomous conception certainly had a lengthy history. Still, one should keep in mind that initially, matters were less clear-cut. Copernicus's ideas, after publication of his *De revolutionibus* (On the Revolutions) in 1543, gained acceptance only very slowly. In the course of this process, many compromises between Copernican and Ptolemaic astronomy were sought. It was possible to accept just those elements of Copernicus's theories that were compatible with a geocentric worldview: the theory of the Moon, the theory of precession, or the construction of planetary movements from uniform circular movements. The last element especially appears to have appealed to Copernicus's fellow-astronomers. Copernicus (1473–1543) had done away with Ptolemy's (ca. 100–ca. 170) *punctum equans* (a point not at the center of an orbit with respect to which the planet maintains a constant angular velocity, resulting in a nonuniform movement in its orbit), thereby fulfilling the ancient demand to "save the phenomena" by reducing the celestial movements to constant circular movements. This accomplishment was, in fact, independent of his heliocentric theory. Mathematicians could use Copernicus's calculations without bothering about the reality of the underlying cosmological model. This strategy, for which good medieval precedents existed, was already advocated in Andreas Osiander's Preface to Copernicus's book and was put to practice in the *Prutenic Tables* (1551) of Erasmus Reinhold (1511–1553). In modern historiography, it is sometimes called the "Wittenberg interpretation," after the German university where Reinhold taught and where it was particularly advocated.

Copernicus's cosmological system could be rejected or accepted, partly or entirely. Some authors accepted the daily rotation of the earth but rejected its annual movement around the Sun. Of all such compromises, the Tychonic system remains the best known. It is important to note that the appeal of Copernicus's theories was not in their practical use or their correspondence with observations. As such, Copernican theory initially hardly superseded Ptolemy's. Only Kepler's *Rudolphine Tables* (1627) offered substantial progress in terms of accuracy.

Moreover, the question of the movement (or rest) of the earth was only one aspect of a much larger cosmological debate. Other topics included celestial (in)corruptibility, the existence of celestial spheres, and the plurality of worlds, which were largely independent of the planetary system proposed. Still, one should acknowledge that the whole debate was largely inaugurated by Copernicus's innovation and that his ideas remained at the heart of it. Copernicus's innovation is, therefore, generally regarded as a key element in the Scientific Revolution.

In an age that venerated humanist scholarship, Copernicus's ambitious attempt to emulate Ptolemy's classical astronomical work, carried out in a thorough and technically highly competent way, could not fail to impress his contemporaries. People quickly gave the heliocentric theory a respectable classical pedigree.

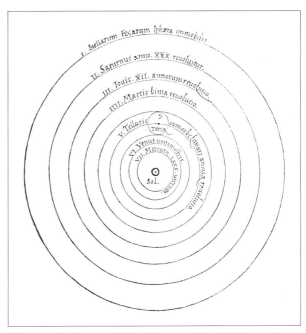

Copernicus's diagram of the solar system, from his De revolutionibus *(1543).*

Copernicus, partly on his own claim, was said to have revived the ancient Pythagorean theory. Placing it on the intellectual map, however, did not entail agreeing with its content. The world-system proposed by Copernicus was too much at odds with accepted ideas on the universe to be easily accepted. Various arguments were advanced against Copernicus's ideas. For simplicity's sake, one could reduce them to three main ones:

1. The yearly movement of the earth should result in a corresponding annual apparent change in the position of the fixed stars (parallax). Since, with the instruments then available, no such parallax was observable, the stars in the Copernican universe had to be at a distance incredibly larger than anything accepted before. Most people regarded such a universe as absurd. The Copernicans, for their part, could counterargue that the immense velocity of the fixed stars in the system of Ptolemy was just as absurd. Both problems could be solved, of course, by having recourse to God's omnipotence.

2. If the earth were moving, objects in the air around it, if not the air itself, would lag behind. The swift movement of the earth should be clearly discernible on its surface. Copernicans generally countered this argument by assuming that the

movement of the earth was also in the surrounding air, which communicated it to loose objects.

3. According to accepted theory, the earth, being heavy, had its proper place in the center of the universe, hence could not be moving around the Sun. This argument seems to have been somewhat less important, as alternative theories of heaviness were being put forward at the time. Copernicans assumed that heavy objects were naturally attracted to one another or that different kinds of objects were drawn to different places.

In spite of these objections, Copernicus's system was cogent enough to be felt as a serious challenge to established theory. In France, it was used as an argument for an all-encompassing skepticism: how could one arrive at sure knowledge if even such an ancient and venerated theory as Ptolemy's could seriously be doubted? In any case, a realist interpretation of Copernicus's theories, accepting the motion of the earth as physically true, gained ground only very slowly and hesitatingly. The following four factors can be said to have allowed in course of time the acceptance of heliocentrism:

The Growing Importance of Mathematics. The main asset of the Copernican model lay in its simplicity and coherence. This argument appealed to mathematicians rather than to philosophers: in medieval scholarship, mathematical elegance did not carry much weight. From the sixteenth century onward, however, mathematics became an increasingly important field of study, in engineering, instrument making, navigation, and warfare. Mathematicians established themselves in society, and, increasingly, they arrived at asserting their intellectual independence against traditional scholarship. In some cases, they regarded mathematical explanations of the world as superior to traditional philosophy. Simon Stevin (1548–1620) and Galileo Galilei (1564–1642) could be seen as examples of such self-assertive new men, who did not hesitate to defend Copernicanism against received scholarly knowledge.

The Decline of Aristotelian Philosophy. Copernican astronomy was in flagrant contradiction to Aristotelian philosophy, whereas Ptolemaic astronomy was based in it. As long as there was no real alternative to Aristotelianism, Copernicanism could never become the dominant theory. Although it cannot be denied that Aristotelian-

ism dominated university education well into the seventeenth (and at many places the eighteenth) century, it is equally clear that, outside the universities, European intellectuals began to feel some unease with it already in the sixteenth century. This led to no new philosophy for the time being, but alternative ideas, whether ancient or modern, were studied eagerly. Quite popular for some time was the spectrum of ideas associated with Neoplatonism and Hermeticism. Their importance for the reception of Copernicanism has been the subject of some dispute, but by now most people agree that their influence in this respect was fairly limited. There are a few examples of people defending heliocentrism in the framework of a general Neoplatonic worldview (Giordano Bruno, Philip van Lansberge), but most Neoplatonists remained traditional in their cosmology.

Of somewhat more importance was the so-called magnetical philosophy, deriving from the work of William Gilbert (1544–1603), according to which the universe was governed by magnetic forces. Gilbert defended the daily rotation of the earth as deriving from magnetism. Copernicans like Kepler and Stevin used magnetic forces to argue for the physical plausibility of the heliocentric cosmos. One should add, however, that the link between heliocentrism and magnetical philosophy was rather loose. At most, such ideas could make Copernicanism philosophically acceptable to people who already were committed to it for other reasons. The Jesuit Niccolo Cabeo, on the other hand, defended the earth's immobility as founded on cosmic magnetic forces.

New Astronomical Observations A factor that contributed heavily to the downfall of traditional Aristotelian cosmology was the discovery of new phenomena in the heavens: the new stars of 1572 and 1604, the supralunar position of the comet of 1577, and, above all, the telescopic observations published by Galileo in 1610. These made the nature of the heavens a pressing problem. Again, none of these observations forced one to adopt heliocentrism. The discovery of the phases of Venus by Galileo in 1610 was in direct contradiction to Ptolemaic astronomy, but it was still possible to defend a geoheliocentric system. The new phenomena, however, did affect the credibility of traditional philosophy, in particular with regard to the division of the universe into supralunar and sublunar regions. People began to believe that the universe was basically uniform, and the earth just another planet.

The 1640s, finally, saw the rise of a real rival to Aristotelianism: the new mechanical philosophy. It sought not to adapt Aristotelian philosophy on certain points, but to supplant it in its entirety. In particular, the ideas of René Descartes (1596–1650) gained a foothold in a number of universities. Descartes's mechanical cosmos of matter in motion, unlimited and without a definite center, shattered ancient ideas on order and hierarchy. Where the mechanical philosophy gained the upper hand, Ptolemaic astronomy lost all credit, and heliocentrism won the day. Whereas, in Aristotelianism, the movement of the earth could never be more than a strange anomaly, it fitted perfectly into the Cartesian worldview. Not that Cartesian physics really answered the traditional objections against the motion of the earth regarding the movement of falling objects; these were only finally solved by Isaac Newton (1642–1727). But they were no longer seen as a problem. For scholars like Christiaan Huygens (1629–1695), Gian Domenico Cassini (1625–1712), Gottfried Wilhelm Leibniz (1646–1716), and others, the movement of the earth was settled beyond dispute. In university education as well, Copernicanism usually was accepted only within the wider framework of Cartesian philosophy. Newton's explanation of the solar system by means of universal gravitation and the laws of motion has been of great scientific importance, but it could add little to the acceptance of Copernican astronomy.

Religious Controversy. There could be other arguments, however, that kept many from adhering to Copernicanism. It had been realized quite early that the movement of the earth and the immobility of the Sun accorded ill with the common interpretation of several biblical passages. As long as Copernicanism was just a daring hypothesis, few people bothered about its theological implications, but when Copernicanism began to prove a viable theory, objections were loudly made.

The Roman Catholic Church was moved into action mainly by Galileo's polemical defense of Copernicanism. In 1616 Copernicanism was formally banned by the Congregation of the Index, and in 1633 Galileo himself was sentenced to house arrest. From then on, the Catholic Church was committed to an anti-Copernican stance. This affected particularly the many Catholic scientists in religious orders, who were bound to obedience to papal decrees. As the Ptolemaic system proved scientifically untenable, most of them choose to uphold some

kind of Tychonic cosmology. In most astronomical calculations, however, Copernicus's theories could still be used in an instrumental way, with a disclaimer. Indeed, instrumentalism became particularly important in this way, as it could justify the use of up-to-date Copernican theories that one was forbidden to defend as constituting reality. As for Catholic laymen, the situation varied, depending upon how rigorously the local authorities enforced the papal decree. In Italy censorship was alert, whereas in France the government refused to authorize the decree altogether.

Copernicanism became a matter of theological dispute in Protestant countries also. Here, however, the matter was never settled by an authoritative decree. Copernicanism was opposed—and, one should never forget, supported—by individual theologians. The dispute on Copernicanism arose with the advent of Cartesianism and, in fact, appears closely linked to it. For several reasons, Descartes's ideas were highly controverted by many theologians. As Copernicanism was regarded as a central element of Cartesianism, which moreover could be made quite understandable to the common man (quite unlike discussions on Cartesian metaphysics), Copernicanism came to take a prominent place in this debate. Where the controversy over Cartesianism ran high, as in the Dutch Republic, Copernicanism met violent opposition; where Cartesianism failed to impose itself as a self-conscious movement, as in England, Copernicanism met with less resistance. The opposing theologians generally took little account of scientific developments, nor did they think this necessary. In consequence, the theological debate was inconclusive. Pro- and anti-Cartesian/Copernican theologians simply kept the positions wherein, by the middle of the seventeenth century, they had entrenched themselves, in many cases well into the eighteenth century. When Cartesianism finally disappeared from the scene, to be replaced by less offensive systems of natural philosophy, the debate lost much of its acerbity. This happened at most places in the course of the eighteenth century. By then, Copernicanism was accepted by the major part of the formerly hostile theologians as well.

BIBLIOGRAPHY

Brockliss, L. W. B. "Copernicus in the University: The French Experience." In *New Perspectives on Renaissance Thought: Essays . . . in Memory of Charles B. Schmitt,* ed. J. Henry and S. Hutton. London: Duckworth, 1990, pp. 190–213.

Dobrzycki, J., ed. *The Reception of Copernicus' Heliocentric Theory. Proceedings from a Symposium Organised by the Nicolas Copernicus Committee of the International Union of the History and Philosophy of Science.* Torún: Ossolineum, 1973. Dordrecht and Boston: Reidel, 1972. Also published as *Colloquia Copernicana,* I. Wroctaw: Ossolineum, 1972.

Kuhn, T. S. *The Copernican Revolution: Planetary Astronomy in the Development of Western Thought.* Cambridge, MA: Harvard University Press, 1957, chs. 6–7.

Russell, J. L. "Catholic Astronomers and the Copernican System after the Condemnation of Galileo." *Annals of Science* 46 (1989), 365–386.

Taton, R., and C. Wilson, eds. *Planetary Astronomy from the Renaissance to the Rise of Astrophysics: Tycho Brahe to Newton.* (The General History of Astronomy, ed. M. Hoskin, vol. 2A). Cambridge: Cambridge University Press, 1989.

Westman, R. S. "Two Cultures or One? A Second Look at Kuhn's *The Copernican Revolution.*" *Isis* 85 (1994), 79–115.

———. "The Wittenberg Interpretation of the Copernican Theory" and "Discussion: The Reception of Heliocentrism in the Sixteenth Century." In *The Nature of Scientific Discovery,* ed. Owen Gingerich. Washington, D.C.: Smithsonian Institution Press, 1975, pp. 393–457.

RIENK VERMIJ

See also Aristotelianism; Copernicus, Nicolaus; Digges, Thomas; Galileo and the Church; Geoheliocentrism; Keplerianism

A copy, by an unknown artist, of an earlier painting of Copernicus, thought to have been made in his lifetime. Courtesy Burndy Library, Dibner Institute for the History of Science and Technology, Cambridge, MA.

Copernicus, Nicolaus (1473–1543)

Copernicus is known today for a single contribution to astronomy, but it is an important one, the heliocentric theory. He was born to a prosperous merchant family in Torun in Royal Prussia, now a part of Poland. His parents died when he was young, and he was raised in the household of his mother's brother, Lucas Watzenrode, who became bishop of Warmia in 1489 and intended an ecclesiastical career for his nephew. In 1491 Copernicus entered the University of Cracow, where courses were given in mathematics, astronomy, and astrology, but he left without a degree in 1495, following which his uncle obtained for him a canonry of the Cathedral Chapter of Warmia. From 1496 to 1501, he studied canon and civil law at the University of Bologna; from 1501 to 1503, medicine at the University of Padua; finally, in 1503, he received a degree in canon law from the University of Ferrara. While at Bologna, he worked as assistant to the professor of astronomy, Domenico Maria Novara (1454–1504), and made his earliest-known observations; in 1500 he delivered a lecture in Rome on mathematics, which could mean astronomy. After he returned to Warmia, he lived with his uncle, serving as his physician, but in 1510 he moved to Frauenburg, the headquarters of the Cathedral Chapter, where he spent most of the rest of his life working at various administrative duties.

It is possible that his new theory came to him at about the time he left his uncle's service; perhaps he gave up further ecclesiastical advancement to devote more time to astronomy. He wrote a description of his discoveries, which circulated in manuscript before 1514 and later came into the hands of Tycho Brahe (1546–1601), who had copies made under the title *Memoir (Commentariolus) by Nicolaus Copernicus on the Hypotheses of the Motions of the Heavens that He Invented.* The theory of the *Commentariolus* is similar to that of *De revolutionibus* (On the Revolutions, 1543) but has deficiencies that Copernicus himself must have recognized, in that little evidence is given for the heliocentric theory, and the parameters of the "hypotheses" (mathematical models) are merely extracted from the Alfonsine Tables. He had promised a longer treatment in the *Commentariolus* but

C

must soon have decided that something far more substantial was required—a new *Almagest*, in fact—that would require many years of work. From ca. 1512 to 1529, he made the necessary observations, following which came years of labor over the derivation of parameters, the computation of tables, and finally the writing of his treatise, *On the Revolutions of the Heavenly Spheres*, which was nearly complete when he was visited in 1539 by Georg Joachim Rheticus (1514–1574), a young professor of mathematics from Wittenberg.

Although Copernicus seems to have been reluctant to finish and publish his work, he allowed Rheticus to read his manuscript and write a description of it, published in 1540 as the *Narratio prima* (First Account) in the form of a letter to Johannes Schöner, a noted writer on astronomy, astrology, and geography, whom Rheticus had just visited in Nuremberg. This may have provided some encouragement to Copernicus to finish; by May 1542, Rheticus was supervising the printing of the book by Johann Petreius in Nuremberg. When Rheticus left in October to take up an appointment at Leipzig, the supervision was turned over to Andreas Osiander, a Lutheran minister, who added an unsigned Preface stating that Copernicus's new theories, like all astronomical hypotheses, were intended only for computation and were not to be considered true or even probable. This was not Copernicus's view at all, nor was it Rheticus's, but it is possible that Copernicus never knew what Osiander had done since he suffered a stroke in December 1542 that left him comatose until his death on May 24, 1543. Tradition has it that he was given a copy of his book before he died.

Copernicus's astronomy is built upon Ptolemy's (ca. 100–ca. 170), of which it is a transformation and exten-sion. Copernicus's principal and only original innovation in the theory of the planets is his accounting for the second inequality—the apparent periodic reversals of the superior planets, Mars, Jupiter, and Saturn with respect to the fixed stars—and the first inequality—the non-uniform motion—of the inferior planets, Mercury and Venus, by the annual motion of Earth about the Sun. He arrived at his theory by way of transformations of Ptolemy's, as explained by Johannes Regiomontanus (1436–1476) in the *Epitome of the Almagest,* a work Copernicus used even in preference to Ptolemy's *Almagest* as his guide to the latter's astronomy. The relation of Ptolemy's and Copernicus's models for the superior planets is shown in Figure 1, in which we assume only circular motions. In Ptolemy's model, the earth O is at rest, about it is described a circle of radius R', on which moves an epicycle with center C and radius r'. The planet P moves on the epicycle through the mean anomaly $\bar{\alpha}$ measured from the apogee of the epicycle $\bar{\alpha}$ such that the radius CP is parallel to the direction $O\bar{S}'$ from the earth to the "mean sun," the Sun with only its uniform motion. The distance $O\bar{S}'$ is arbitrary in Ptolemy's model, but if a parallelogram $OCP\bar{S}$ is constructed and it is assumed that the mean sun is at $\bar{S}$, then both Earth O and the planet P may be taken to move about $\bar{S}$ in circles of radii r and R, where $r/R = r'/R'$, and the direction OP from the earth to the planet, the diagonal of the parallelogram, is identical in both models. The relation of the models for the inferior planets is shown in Figure 2, again assuming only circular motions. As before in Ptolemy's model, about

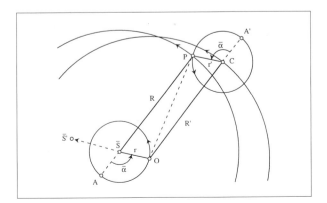

Figure 1

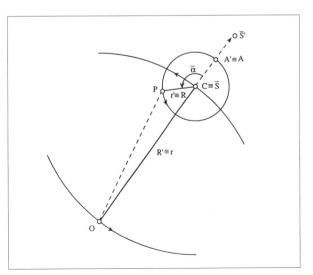

Figure 2

the earth O at rest is described a circle of radius R', on which is an epicycle with center C and radius r'. But now OC lies in the direction $O\bar{S}'$ from the earth to the mean sun, where the distance $O\bar{S}'$ is arbitrary, and the planet P again moves on the epicycle through the mean anomaly $\bar{\alpha}$ measured from the apogee of the epicycle A'. If it is assumed that the mean sun $\bar{S}$ coincides with C, is identical to ($\equiv$) C, then, again, both Earth O and the planet P may be taken to move about $\bar{S}$ in circles of radii r and R, where $r/R = r'/R'$, and the direction OP from the earth to the planet is identical in both models.

The essential advantage of the Copernican theory lies in the order and distances of the planets, the unification of the planetary models into a single system in which everything is determined and nothing is arbitrary. In Ptolemy's models, the radii r' and R' are arbitrary for each planet, and only the ratio r'/R' is determined by observation; thus, there is no common measure of distances within the planetary system, and even the order of the planets is arbitrary without further assumptions. However, in Copernicus's models, the radii R of the orbits of all of the planets are measured in terms of the unit r, the radius of Earth's orbit, which is common to the model for every planet, so neither the distances nor the order of the planets are arbitrary, for they are fixed by the ratio r/R, which, as in Ptolemy's models, is determined by observation. There are also certain arbitrary rules governing Ptolemy's models that are explained when it is seen that geocentric planetary models are actually transformations of underlying heliocentric models. The most obvious in the Figures are why the radii of the epicycles of the superior planets are parallel to the direction from the earth to the mean sun, and why the centers of the epicycles of the inferior planets lie in the direction of the mean sun, but there are many more properties of geocentric models, even as basic as why the superior planets move in the same directions on their epicycles, that are only explained as transformations of heliocentric models. The most well-known consequence of the heliocentric theory is the explanation of retrogradation, which takes place in Ptolemy's models near the perigee of the epicycle when the apparent backward motion of the planet on the epicycle exceeds the forward motion of the center of the epicycle, which happens to be near opposition for a superior planet and near inferior conjunction for an inferior. In Copernicus's models, retrogradation occurs when Earth passes a slower superior planet near opposition or is passed by a faster infe-

rior planet near inferior conjunction, so the location of the retrogradation is also explained.

It is precisely the fixing of the order and distances of the planets into a unified system and the explanations of retrogradation and of the rules of geocentric models that convinced Copernicus that his system was correct. But this came at a price, for the heliocentric theory creates problems of its own, namely, the effect of the motion of Earth on the sphere of the fixed stars and on the earth itself. If the distance of the stars is ca. 20,000 earth-radii and the distance of the earth from the Sun ca. 1,200 earth-radii, both canonical in Copernicus's time, then the motion of Earth about the Sun ought to produce unequal divisions of the sphere of the fixed stars by the horizon and an annual displacement in the positions of stars of ca. 7°, but nothing of the kind was seen. If then, as Copernicus supposed, the fixed stars were located at so great a distance that such effects would be undetectable, say, 1' of arc, there is another problem, raised by Brahe: if the apparent diameters of bright stars are 1' or 2', as was also supposed, then the true diameters of such stars must be as large as, or even larger than, the diameter of Earth's orbit around the Sun, 1,200 earth-diameters, which appeared absurd since the diameter of the Sun, the largest body in the planetary system, was ca. 5.5 earth-diameters. This serious objection to the Copernican theory was not answered until Galileo found with his telescope that the apparent diameters of stars were far smaller than they appeared to the unaided eye, so they could be removed to great distances without being any larger than the Sun.

Then, if Earth moves about the Sun, it is hard to understand why heavy bodies fall in straight lines toward the center of the earth, particularly if the earth also possess a daily rotation about its axis, a necessary consequence of the annual motion about the Sun, since the entire universe could hardly rotate each day about an earth that continuously shifts its position and thus cannot remain in the center of the universe. For these physical problems raised by the motions of the earth, which should also affect the motion of birds, clouds, and projectiles, Copernicus made what he considered to be a minimal alteration of Aristotelian natural motion of the elements, such that the natural motion of a spherical body, whatever its substance, is to rotate in place by virtue of its form alone. The daily rotation of the spherical earth together with the surrounding water and air is, therefore, entirely natural; projectiles, birds, and clouds are simply carried along with the rotating earth; and heaviness (*gravitas*), the descent of heavy bodies to their natural place, the surface of the earth, in straight lines, is due to a "natural inclination placed in the parts" to come together to form a globe. In proposing this explanation, Copernicus did not intend to overthrow or displace Aristotelian physics but to adapt it to the motion of the earth, unlike Galileo Galilei (1564–1642), who later used much the same principles as Copernicus for a devastating attack on Aristotle. In fact, the objections to the motion of the earth were not completely answered until Isaac Newton (1642–1727).

Nor should it be thought that, as is commonly said, Copernicus eliminated the distinction between the heavens and the earth, between celestial and terrestrial physics, by making the earth a planet. In so far as he had anything to say about it, terrestrial physics is still Aristotelian, with natural downward motion of Earth and water and natural upward motion of air and fire, along with the additional principle that the natural motion of a spherical body is rotation, which is, of course, the Aristotelian principle of the motion of the spheres of the heavens. This brings us to the second important aspect of Copernicus's work: his strict adherence to the principle of uniform, circular motion and its consequences for his model for the first inequality of the planets. It was, in fact, this concern with uniform, circular motion and its violation by Ptolemy's planetary models that initiated Copernicus's investigations of planetary theory in the first place, as he explains in the *Commentariolus*. The reason for this concern was entirely physical. The motions of the bodies in the heavens are produced by the rotation of spheres, and the motion natural to a sphere, the only motion possible to a sphere, which is taken to be a rigid body, is a uniform rotation in place about an axis passing through its center. It cannot rotate uniformly about an axis passing through any other point, for then it would also be displaced, nor can it rotate nonuniformly, for this would require some cause other than the natural rotation of a spherical body.

Some two hundred years before Copernicus, the same physical concern led a number of Arabic astronomers, originally associated with the observatory of Maragha in northwestern Persia, to develop alternatives to Ptolemy's models for the motions of the planets compatible with the uniform rotation of spheres. The models of one in particular, Ibn ash-Shāṭir of Damascus (1304–1376), are identical to the models used by Copernicus in the *Commentariolus* except that they are geocentric; in *De revolutionibus,* Copernicus alters these models into forms that were also anticipated by the astronomers of the Maragha school, as they have come to be called. How Copernicus learned of the models of his predecessors is not known—a transmission through Italy is the most likely path—but the relation between the models is so close that independent invention by Copernicus is all but impossible.

Before taking up Copernicus's model for the first inequality, we consider the parts of *De revolutionibus* preceding the planetary theory, in which Copernicus treats every subject covered in the *Almagest,* although not necessarily in the same detail. Spherical astronomy, the geometry and motion of the circles on the celestial sphere, is identical in both works since it makes no difference whether the daily rotation by which bodies rise and set belongs to the earth or the heavens. The catalog of stars is Ptolemy's catalog converted to sidereal longitude by subtracting from all longitudes 6° 40', Ptolemy's tropical longitude of the first star in Aries, which is for Copernicus the zero point of sidereal longitude, and mean motions of the Sun and planets are likewise tabulated for sidereal longitude. The reason is that, following theories of the motion of the sphere of the fixed stars in medieval Arabic and European treatises and tables, Copernicus believed the motion of the equinoxes with respect to the fixed stars, the precession of the equinoxes, to be nonuniform; hence, mean motions could be uniform only if measured with respect to the fixed stars. Since motion can no longer belong to the fixed stars, both a uniform and a nonuniform component of the precession are produced by motions of the axis of the earth, and a related motion of the axis varies the obliquity of the ecliptic. The solar theory is the same as Ptolemy's, a simple eccentric, but, again following medieval sources, Copernicus found a smaller solar eccentricity than did Ptolemy. Consequently, just as for the inequality of the precession, he developed a model to produce a variation in the eccentricity, along with an inequality in the motion of the solar apsidal line, such that the eccentricity is near maximum at Ptolemy's time and near minimum at his own—the same variation he found in the obliquity of the ecliptic and, with the same period, twice that of the inequality of the precession. All of these inequalities are thus related, and all are really illusory, due to errors of observation by Ptolemy and Copernicus.

Following the Maragha astronomers, Copernicus objected to Ptolemy's lunar model on the grounds that it violates uniform, circular motion, since the center of the epicycle does not move uniformly about the center of the eccentric on which it is carried, and that it produces a large variation in lunar distance contradicted by the small variation in the apparent size and parallax of the Moon. His model, identical to that of Ibn ash-Shāṭir, is shown in Figure 3, in which the earth is at O, and the apogee, which moves about 7' per day or 40° per year, is A, from which the center C_1 of the larger epicycle of radius r_1 moves through the mean anomaly $\bar{\alpha}$ and through the mean elongation $\bar{\eta}$ with respect to the mean sun $\bar{S}$. The radius r_1 moves in the opposite direction through $\bar{\alpha}$, thus remaining parallel to OA, and the radius r_2 of the smaller epicycle, with center C_2, carries the Moon M in the same direction as C_1 through $2\bar{\eta}$, twice the elongation from the mean sun. The effect of r_2 is to introduce a correction c_1 to the mean anomaly, and to vary the equation of the anomaly c_2 from a minimum at conjunction and opposition when $2\bar{\eta} = 0°$ to a maximum at quadrature when $2\bar{\eta} = 180°$. Both effects are also found in Ptolemy's model, but at the cost of a large variation in lunar distance, which is greatly reduced in the model of Ibn ash-Shāṭir and Copernicus. This advantage was immediately appreciated by Copernicus's contemporaries, who adopted his lunar model even if they accepted no other part of his astronomy. Copernicus found the lunar distance to vary from ca. 65 to 55 earth-radii at syzygy (in opposition or conjunction with the Sun) and ca. 68 to 52 at quadrature (90° from opposition or conjunction) far smaller than the variation in

Ptolemy's model of 64 at syzygy to 33 at quadrature. Nevertheless, the variation of distance is still more than twice as great as it should be and was reduced to about its correct value by Brahe, whose lunar model is a great improvement over all previous lunar theory. For the distance of the Sun, using Ptolemy's method, Copernicus found a greatest distance of 1,179 earth-radii, compared with a mean distance of 1,210 found by Ptolemy, both too small by a factor of twenty, but in both cases the diurnal parallax is ca. 3', small enough to be neglected.

Copernicus's model for the first inequality of the superior planets is shown superimposed on Ptolemy's model in a heliocentric form in Figure 4. The center of the earth's sphere, the mean sun, is $\bar{S}$, the center of the eccentric in Ptolemy's model is M, the center of the equant is E, and the two eccentricities e are equal; the planet P moves in a circle of radius R about M such that its angular motion, the mean eccentric anomaly $\bar{\kappa}$, is uniform about E. In Copernicus's model, the center C_1 of a larger epicycle of radius r_1 moves through $\bar{\kappa}$ in a circle of radius R about $\bar{S}$, and the center C_2 of a smaller epicycle of radius r_2 moves in the opposite direction through $\bar{\kappa}$ so that r_1 is always parallel to the apsidal line $\bar{S}A$. The planet P' moves in the same direction as C_1 through $2\bar{\kappa}$ such that r_2 coincides with r_1 when C_1 is in the apsidal line. Provided that $r_1 = \frac{3}{2}e$ and $r_2 = \frac{1}{2}e$, P' will lie on the line EP, thus moving uniformly about E, and the apparent directions $\bar{S}P$ and $\bar{S}P'$ will nearly coincide, the greatest difference, for Mars, amounting to ca. 3'. It follows that Copernicus's model (1) preserves uniform motion about

![Figure 3 diagram]

Figure 3

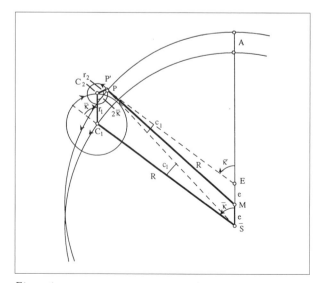

Figure 4

the equant and (2) is observationally indistinguishable from Ptolemy's. The common belief that Copernicus did away with the equant, or wished to do away with the equant, is simply false, for it was as fundamental to his planetary theory as to Ptolemy's, and even in the time of Brahe and Kepler, there was no observational distinction between the models of Ptolemy and Copernicus. The motivation for Copernicus's model was entirely physical: to preserve the uniform rotation of spheres.

The model is altered in *De revolutionibus* to the form of Figure 5, which shows both inequalities. The larger epicycle is replaced by an equal eccentricity $e_1 = r_1 = \frac{3}{2}e$, which has the same effect since r_1 is always parallel to e_1; r_2 is unchanged although its motion, because measured from C_1C_2, is now $\bar{\kappa}$, and thus P still moves uniformly about E. The second inequality is accounted for by the motion of the earth O in a circle of radius s about the mean sun $\bar{S}$ through the mean anomaly $\bar{\alpha}$, uniformly with respect to a line *FH*, which is drawn parallel to *EP*; the true anomaly, from line $G\bar{S}$, is $\bar{\alpha} \pm c_1$. The true position of the planet as seen from the earth is found through two corrections: c_1, the equation of center, the difference in direction between the uniform motion of the planet about the equant and the nonuniform motion about the mean sun; and c_2, the equation of the anomaly, found from the true anomaly, which reduces the heliocentric direction of the planet $\bar{S}P$ to the geocentric direction *OP*.

Given the longitude of the apogee λ_A, the longitude of the planet is $\lambda_A + \bar{\kappa} \pm c_1 \pm c_2$. The corrections are nearly identical to those used by Ptolemy, and Copernicus's tabulations of the corrections are also nearly identical to Ptolemy's. Likewise, Copernicus finds the parameters of the model for each planet by observation through exactly the same methods used by Ptolemy, and, except for the directions of the apsidal lines, his results are the same or quite close.

What we have seen here is Copernicus's model for the superior planets. The inferior planets are somewhat different in that the equation of center, c_1 in the Figure, depends not upon the distance of the planet from its own apogee, but, remarkably, upon the distance of the earth from the planet's apogee, due to a direct adaptation of Ptolemy's model; and there are yet further complications for Mercury, which are identical to those of Ibn ash-Shāṭir's model. The models for the latitudes of the planets are also direct adaptations of Ptolemy's, which require oscillations of orbital planes that Kepler found implausible and prompted his famous remark: "Copernicus, ignorant of his own riches, took it upon himself for the most part to represent Ptolemy, not nature, to which he had nevertheless come the closest of all." Kepler, as usual, could not be more correct. Copernicus's astronomy was built upon Ptolemy's descriptions of the apparent motions of the heavens, upon Ptolemy's observations, upon transformations of Ptolemy's models, and upon Ptolemy's methods of deriving parameters from observation. Thus, he did, as Kepler said, represent Ptolemy rather than nature.

BIBLIOGRAPHY

Armitage, A. *Copernicus: The Founder of Modern Astronomy.* New York: Thomas Yoseloff, 1957.

Copernicus, N. *Complete Works II: On the Revolutions of the Heavenly Spheres. Complete Works III: Minor Works.* Trans. E. Rosen. Warsaw: Polish Scientific Publishers, 1985.

———. *On the Revolutions of the Heavenly Spheres.* Trans. A. M. Duncan. Newton Abbot: David and Charles; New York: Barnes and Noble, 1976.

Crowe, M. J. *Theories of the World from Antiquity to the Copernican Revolution.* New York: Dover, 1990.

Kuhn, T. S. *The Copernican Revolution: Planetary Astronomy in the Development of Western Thought.* Cambridge, MA: Harvard University Press, 1957.

Rosen, E. *Three Copernican Treatises.* 3rd ed. New York: Octagon Books, 1971.

Swerdlow, N. M. "The Derivation and First Draft of Copernicus's Planetary Theory: A Translation of the Commentariolus with Commentary." *Proceedings of the American Philosophical Society* 117 (1973), 423–512.

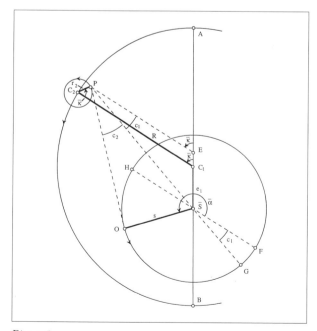

Figure 5

Swerdlow, N. M., and O. Neugebauer. *Mathematical Astronomy in Copernicus's De Revolutionibus.* 2 vols. New York: Springer, 1984.

N. M. SWERDLOW

See also Astronomy; Brahe, Tycho; Celestial Spheres; Copernicanism; Kepler, Johannes; Ptolemaic Astronomy; Regiomontanus, Johannes

Corpuscularianism. See Atomism

Correspondence Networks

Letters were the most common form of writing in the seventeenth century. Because they were "swift, certain, and cheap," letters were easily adapted to the needs of the new science and quickly earned an enduring niche in the exchange of information. Throughout the Scientific Revolution, the size and number of correspondence networks continued to expand, and, in the course of the century, *intelligencers* adapted the Renaissance ideal of a Republic of Letters to the realities of the new science—a learned world divided by distance, time, and censorship.

Although historians have long acknowledged the importance of scientific correspondence, no synthetic study of intelligencers or detailed analysis of correspondence networks has been undertaken. Scholars generally agree, however, that, as traditional boundaries of learning were redrawn (between universities, Court culture, private patronage, and informal societies), new lines of communication emerged with the expansion of the postal system and increased use of print. Some scholars have focused on the mid-1660s. In these accounts, if the first half of the century was marked by the proliferation of private societies and correspondence networks, the second half was dominated by state-sponsored academies and printed journals. Although explicit theories about these changes have yet to appear, several scholars, among them Elizabeth Eisenstein (1979), have suggested that intelligencers were replaced by the periodical press. What remains unclear is the nature and the pace of these changes.

However humble and ordinary, handwritten letters were a powerful form of communication and a fact of daily life. By existing standards, letters were not only convenient and inexpensive, they were the fastest and most unrestricted form of science writing. From the first decades of the century, letters could be sent and received within weeks anywhere in Europe; before the century was over, the "ordinary" post combined with diplomatic couriers to establish wider, faster, and more reliable service.

The letter was particularly suited to a small, diverse, and isolated community. Although bookstalls and salons were popular meeting places, most members of the Republic of Letters never met face to face. The letter was perfectly suited to these conditions, as it easily cut across traditional boundaries of space, time, language, religion, class, and confessional domain. The speed of the letter made it particularly useful for organizing simultaneous observation of events (for example, in astronomy) and for disseminating and comparing time-sensitive information from widely dispersed sites.

Characteristically, scientific letters were relatively free from censorship. In an age of vested interests, regimentation, and systematic persecution, the great correspondence networks were unrivaled throughout the century as a vehicle for free expression. Letters could be dangerous; but with proper precautions, controversial issues circulated freely "under the cloak" or under the "seal of friendship." Here questionable opinions were often expressed in "half-words" or with full-blown irony (i.e., with a meaning clear to the recipient but not, should the letter be intercepted, to a potential censor). Less-rhetorical precautions were also employed: sometimes letters were written in a second language or, if particularly suspect, in personal code, cipher, or anagram. When anonymity was required, authors often replaced their signature with a pseudonym or acronym or simply sent the letter unsigned. Ironically, while these "masks" veiled authorship and collusion from public view, within the community they tended to dramatize identity and group cooperation. Freethinkers had to be thick as thieves.

Freedom of expression took various forms, from idle gossip to critical debate. Against the claim of several historians, no issue was beyond discussion; indeed, ridiculing Richelieu or commenting on the undergarments of Queen Christina of Sweden was fair game. Many topics flirted with heresy or reprisal. Even in the 1630s, scholars openly discussed the Galileo affair, Copernicanism, the immortality of the soul, and the mysteries of transubstantiation. Unthinkable in print, private opinions shared in these letters would not be publicly debated until the next century. In this context, the significance of Galileo's trial might easily be misconstrued if judged solely on the printed word—whether from the 1630s or the mid-1660s. Here public opinion and public reason were dubious ideals in the face of certain realities—excommunication, incarceration, or execution.

To all appearances, the Republic of Letters reflected civil society more generally, its patterns of patronage and polite conversation, its flourishes of form. But scientific correspondence dealt with more substantial matters. Arguably, letters supplied what daily relations lacked; they socially intervened and personally persisted as no printed text could. Although epistolary conventions continued to reflect stability and order, the daily circulation of scientific letters tended to erase social boundaries, while the new science shifted grounds of knowledge and belief. If the new science undermined the old order—and there is evidence it did—scientific correspondence challenged traditional hierarchies by substituting natural ability for social status, acquired skill for inherited wealth.

More than any other form of science writing, correspondence opens a historical window on these changes. Spontaneous and fresh, letters show science in the making. At the most practical level, letters help historians pinpoint the date of an observation or experiment, or, more generally, they explain problem selection, changes in approach, or the fate of a failed hypothesis. Letters sometimes provide frank appraisals of the work of others and often supply the only written record of private activities, friendships, and rivalries, not to mention the collaborations, controversies, and inner workings of informal groups. Unlike the printed book, letters repeatedly fail to separate public and private. At their best, they tell the story behind the book—the first inklings, second guesses, second thoughts.

A great deal of scientific correspondence has been published. While the best-known editions are associated with the major figures of the Scientific Revolution—Nicolaus Copernicus (1473–1543), Tycho Brahe (1546–1601), Johannes Kepler (1571–1630), Galileo Galilei (1564–1642), René Descartes (1596–1650), Blaise Pascal (1623–1662), John Flamsteed (1646–1719), Christiaan Huygens (1629–1695), and Isaac Newton (1642–1727)—the major "intelligencers" are also well represented. Serving as "unofficial secretaries" in the "Commonwealth of Learning," these self-styled "conduit pipes" sent and received letters that were often copied, forwarded, circulated in groups, and read aloud at informal meetings. Though often described as "invisible," their

correspondence networks were real, and their "geography" can be mapped. Surveyed in sequence, they offer a glimpse of the Republic of Letters in transition.

Known as the "prince of erudition," N-C. Fabri de Peiresc (1580–1637) once sent forty-two letters in a single day, and commonly sent two or three to the same person. At his death, he left between ten thousand and fourteen thousand letters, about half of which are extant; of these, thirty-two hundred letters from 1598 to 1637 to or from Peiresc have been published. Boasting nearly five hundred correspondents throughout Europe, Peiresc's network focused on the major centers of learning, particularly Paris and Rome. Although Peiresc took an active interest in astronomy and optics—and conducted numerous experiments and dissections—his chief influence was through mediating intellectual commerce across space, time, and theme, traditionally representing the translation of learning from Italy to France, Provence to Paris, humanism to science.

One of Peiresc's chief contacts in Paris came to be known as the "mailbox of Europe." Representing the second generation of intelligencers, Marin Mersenne (1588–1648) was a prominent publicist for Galileo and a principal correspondent of Descartes. His interests in mathematics, mechanics, music, theology, and languages are immediately evident in his published letters (*Correspondance du P. Marin Mersenne,* 16 vols., 1932–1986). While his network is often cited as one of the major ones of the century, the actual number of letters (eleven hundred) to or from Mersenne from 1617 to 1648 is surprisingly small, the early years actually containing more entries for Peiresc. Although it focused heavily on relations between Paris and the provinces, Mersenne's network dominated the second quarter of the seventeenth century; its importance was in cutting across national and religious boundaries that traditionally divided France, Belgium, England, Germany, Holland, and Italy.

Samuel Hartlib (ca. 1600–1662) was known to contemporaries as the "great intelligencer of Europe." Committed to universal learning, Hartlib was a tireless promoter, and his correspondence supplies an important context for understanding reform movements (educational, religious, utopian) and the useful arts (agriculture, commerce, medicine). The vast majority of Hartlib's letters (letters sent) are presumed lost, though some two thousand letters sent to Hartlib for the years 1640–1661 have been published in electronic form (CD-ROM). Although Hartlib was not a practicing scientist, the

C

significance of his network is its portrayal of learning during the middle third of the century and the clear outline it provides of an emerging "Invisible College."

A friend of Peiresc and Mersenne, Ismaël Boulliau (1605–1694) represents the middle generation of intelligencers. Although his letters have not been published, Boulliau's network was one of the most extensive of the century, representing five thousand letters for the years 1632–1693. An early Copernican and admirer of Kepler and Galileo, Boulliau used his network to coordinate and compare astronomical observations, and he was a major correspondent of Pierre Gassendi (1592–1655), Johannes Hevelius (1611–1687), Prince Leopold of Tuscany, and Huygens. Although his letters reflect strong interests in classical studies, philology, politics, and diplomacy, the significance of Boulliau's network is its sharper scientific focus and broader geographical scope, which now stretched beyond France, Holland, Italy, and England to Poland, Scandinavia, and the Levant.

Henry Oldenburg (ca. 1619–1677)—first secretary of the Royal Society of London and editor of its *Philosophical Transactions* (1665)—has been called the English "clearinghouse" of science. As his letters make clear (*Correspondence of Henry Oldenburg,* 13 vols., 1975–1986), Oldenburg sought to realize Hartlib's hopes for a universal "office of address." Oldenburg's published correspondence includes thirty-one hundred letters for the years 1641–1677. As editor and intelligencer, Oldenburg extended his network beyond Europe and the Levant to the American Colonies, and the frequency of his letters as secretary is unrivaled by any previous scientific correspondent.

From the earliest decades of the Scientific Revolution, letters foreshadowed and underwrote subsequent forms of scientific exchange. As is clear from Oldenburg's career, handwritten letters were daily facts of life that entered his work from start to finish—as part of the editorial process and as "prototype" for the final published product. The difficulty embodied in Oldenburg's career as intelligencer and editor is not in distinguishing two roles, two functions, or two technologies but in imagining how "scribal and print culture" could be kept apart. The mistaken impression that printed journals overshadowed or suddenly replaced intelligencers overlooks the order and pace of events, assumes competing technologies, and separates facts of life that actually belong together.

BIBLIOGRAPHY

Dewald, Jonathan. *Aristocratic Experience and the Origins of Modern Culture, France, 1570–1715.* Berkeley and Los Angeles: University of California Press, 1993.

Eisenstein, Elizabeth L. *The Printing Press as an Agent of Change: Communications and Cultural Transformations in Early-Modern Europe.* 2 vols. Cambridge: Cambridge University Press, 1979.

Goldar, Anne. *Impolite Learning: Conduct and Community in the Republic of Letters, 1680–1750.* New Haven, CT: Yale University Press, 1995.

Hatch, Robert A. "Between Erudition and Science: The Archive and Correspondence Network of Ismaël Boulliau." *Archives of the Scientific Revolution: The Formation and Exchange of Ideas in Seventeenth-Century Europe,* ed. Michael Hunter. Woodbridge, England: Boydell and Brewer, 1998, ch. 4.

———. "Peiresc as Correspondent: The Republic of Letters and the Geography of Ideas." *Science Unbound: Geography, Space, Discipline,* ed. Brian P. Dolan. Umeå, Umeå University, Sweden, 1998, ch. 1.

Ultee, Maarten. "The Republic of Letters: Learned Correspondence, 1680–1720." *Seventeenth Century 2* (1987), 95–112.

ROBERT A. HATCH

See also Mersenne, Marin; Oldenburg, Henry; Peiresc, Nicolas-Claude Fabri de; Printing

Correspondences

By the doctrine of *correspondences,* often referred to in the language of the macrocosm/microcosm contrast, is meant a simple belief, widely held in premodern Europe: the idea that the different components of the universe possessed deeply analogous structures. In its most general form, such a belief remains routine today—it is surely the backbone of biology and mathematical physics—so one must descend to details, the precise items that get compared, to adequately characterize the earlier version of the doctrine. Before the Scientific Revolution, it was a standard belief that the human body (the microcosm par excellence) was similar to the whole universe (the macrocosm), for instance, with planets corresponding to the organs, the head to the stellar sphere, and so forth. Both, furthermore, were similar to the ideal government; or to the ranks of saints and angels in heaven; and to the ranks of metals in the earth—though the precise details varied from case to case. On these basic facts historians are in wide agreement; they differ only in the uses they make of their understandings.

The belief in question here can be readily traced back to the very beginnings of Western philosophy among the presocratics, and presumably much further, though overt defenses and expositions of it are surprisingly rare; familiarity is simply presumed. Correspondences are evident in Aristotle (384–322 B.C.E.) and ever-present in Plato (428–348 B.C.E.). The doctrine fits particularly well with Platonic metaphysics, for a version of it is effectively built into the doctrine of forms: if material objects are created in imitation of immaterial patterns, then objects that share the same pattern will, of necessity, have analogous structures.

Instances of this belief from the era of the Scientific Revolution are easy to find. William Shakespeare's *Coriolanus* is full of it, and a nice example is provided by the long exposition of basic numerology in Agrippa von Nettesheim's *Occult Philosophy* (1531–1533): "the Pythagorians call [four] the perpetuall fountain of nature: for there are four degrees in the Scale of nature, viz. to be, to live, to be sensible, to understand. . . .There are four Elements under Heaven, viz. Fire, Aire, Water and Earth. . . . There are four first qualities under the Heaven, viz. Cold, Heat, Driness, and Moystness, from these are the four Humours, Blood, Flegm, Choller, Melancholy. Also the year is divided into four parts." Such a view remains quite bland, however, until two extra standard ingredients are added to it: one, causal efficacy; the other epistemic.

For a variant of the doctrine, one associating *causes* with correspondences, was particularly common in the Renaissance. It built upon the popular idea that all things in the cosmos were linked together and proposed that objects deemed similar to each other (or particularly dissimilar) also exerted influences on each other, often known as *sympathies* or *antipathies*. Because sheep are wary of wolves, for instance, a guitar strung with gut from each of these animals will never play in tune. Or since gold among the metals is analogous to the Sun among the planets, or the heart within the body, wearing gold on the body near the heart, perhaps while uttering golden words, will attract beneficial solar influences to the body and enhance their efficacy. This is the sort of thinking that rationalized medical astrology, and the use of talismans, but, as the processes involved are not particularly obvious, there was much room for disagreement about the details. Some questioned the causality altogether: wearing gold near the heart may, indeed, benefit the health, but the cause may not be solar rays at all, but

some demon summoned by the gold or by the prayer uttered at the time of its application. So the practice was sometimes condemned as idolatrous and might well seem to others to depend on knowledge that God had not intended humans to possess. This is just one case of the dubious status of magic in medieval and Renaissance Europe, but it is widely accepted that the revival of explicit interest in Platonism that is part of the early stages of the Scientific Revolution, and the attached interest in Hermetism, greatly enhanced the plausibility of this causal thinking. It became one of the issues of seventeenth-century philosophical debate, and the weapons-salve debate, a dispute about how whether to treat wounds by applying remedies to the wounded body or to the remote weapon, is a famous instance.

The doctrine was also applied epistemically and provided a metaphysical support for the very common premodern tendency to interpret the universe symbolically. If one object has the same structure as another, one can find out about the first by studying the second, and each becomes symbolic of the other. So the visible motions of the planets can teach us about less visible matters to do with health, or politics, and so on. Furthermore, if all were created by God, each can be interpreted as an instance of divine rhetoric, as God's means of telling us what he wants us to know, and the similarities that one observes are likely to be a reliable guide to unobserved reality.

Such a view easily extends to the doctrine of *signatures,* the belief that some of the hidden powers and properties of objects can be discerned in the superficialities of their external appearances, so that the latter indicate commonalities more profound than might initially be supposed. So, the claim that a herb was able to make a mother produce milk could be defended on the ground that the herb itself had a milky sap—yet, many of those making such claims did continue to cite ancient authority as well, and other occult properties, such as the ability of garlic to neutralize magnetism, were not thought to be so easy to ascertain. Although God had generally restricted the human capacity to acquire knowledge—to that which is obtainable via the senses— he did provide us, sometimes, with keys that enable us to go a little further.

The fate of these modes of thought in the course of the Scientific Revolution have not been well studied, and it is remarkably unclear how quickly, and to what extent, and for what reasons, they declined. The question

C

is difficult, for the use of analogies does survive into the Enlightenment and beyond, yet often they function as mere figures of speech. But in individual cases, it is hard to be sure that that is all they are.

BIBLIOGRAPHY

Ashworth, William. "Natural History and the Emblematic World View." In *Reappraisals of the Scientific Revolution*, ed. David Lindberg and Robert Westman. Cambridge: Cambridge University Press, 1990, pp. 303–332.

Eamon, William. *Science and the Secrets of Nature: Books of Secrets in Medieval and Early Modern Culture*. Princeton, NJ: Princeton University Press, 1994.

Gombrich, Ernst. "Icones Symbolicae." In *Symbolic Images: Studies in the Art of the Renaissance*. London: Phaidon, 1972, pp. 123–195.

Praz, Mario. *Studies in Seventeenth Century Imagery*. 2nd rev. ed. Rome: Edizioni di Storia e Letteratura, 1964. Addendum published as Part 2 in 1974. 1st ed. London: Warburg Institute, 1939–1947.

Shumaker, Wayne *The Occult Sciences in the Renaissance: A Study in Intellectual Patterns*. Berkeley and Los Angeles: University of California Press, 1972.

Tillyard, Eustace. *The Elizabethan World Picture*. London: Chatto and Windus, 1943. Numerous reprints.

KEITH HUTCHINSON

See also Macrocosm/Microcosm

Cosmic Dimensions

A coherent scheme of sizes and distances first put forward by Ptolemy (ca. 100–170), and consistent with geocentric cosmology, was replaced in the seventeenth century by a new scheme, consistent with heliocentric cosmology. The change was partly the result of telescopic observations but depended as well on theoretical considerations.

In his *Planetary Hypotheses,* Ptolemy put forward a system of planetary distances based on two premises. First, there were no empty spaces in the cosmos, and, therefore, the spherical shell containing one planet was enclosed without spaces in the shell of the next planet. The sphere of Saturn was tightly enclosed in the sphere of the fixed stars. Second, the relative thickness of a spherical shell was determined by the ratio of a planet's greatest-to-least distance derived from the geometrical model of that planet in the *Almagest*. With these premises, Ptolemy needed to determine only one absolute distance: by parallax measurements, he found the distance to the Moon in terms of earth-radii. The

Moon's apogee (greatest distance) had to be equal to Mercury's perigee (least distance), and so on. Through this procedure, all of the absolute distances of all heavenly bodies could be calculated. Ptolemy put the distance of the sphere of the fixed stars (i.e., the radius of the cosmos) at 20,000 earth-radii, ca. four million miles. Accepting the estimates of the angular diameters of heavenly bodies made by Hipparchus, Ptolemy could calculate the sizes of all heavenly bodies. Thus, the Sun was ca. 1200 earth-radii away and was 5.5 times as large as the earth.

This complete scheme of the sizes and distances of heavenly bodies was accepted by Ptolemy's successors and found its way into the West through the works of Moslem astronomers. In the Latin West, the scheme was enshrined in the mathematical curriculum of universities and can be found in nonscientific works such as Dante's *Divine Comedy*.

Although until the coming of the telescope estimates of the angular diameters of heavenly bodies did not change significantly, the Copernican system necessitated changes in the system of distances. The order of the planets was no longer a convention, as it had been in geocentric astronomy. The relative distances (expressed in the new astronomical unit, the radius of Earth's orbit around the Sun), and therefore the order, of the planets now followed directly from Nicolaus Copernicus's (1473–1543) geometrical constructions of the motions of the planets. The eccentricity of the planet (the distance of the center of its orbit from the Sun) gave the thickness of its sphere. In this new system of distances, there were large empty spaces between the spheres of successive planets, and, since Copernicus's solar distance was no different from Ptolemy's, the sphere of Saturn and everything in it (the solar system) had shrunk by almost half. The fixed stars, on the other hand, were now no longer positioned immediately beyond Saturn but at an inconceivably farther distance.

Changes in the solar distances and the angular diameters of the planets began with Johannes Kepler (1571–1630) and Galileo Galilei (1564–1642). During his lifetime, Kepler successively enlarged the radius of Earth's orbit to 3,500 earth-radii, corresponding to a horizontal solar parallax of 1 arc-minute (down from Ptolemy's 3 arc-minutes). In this process, he was guided by measurements and harmonic speculations. Through observations with his telescope, Galileo was able to show that estimates of angular diameters had been too large by an order of magnitude. Their successors continued their efforts to improve on these numbers because they were important for the accuracy of observations, as well as for predictive models.

Following in Kepler's footsteps, Gian Domenico Cassini (1625–1712) studied the combination of the opposing corrections for atmospheric refraction and solar parallax and concluded by 1660 that solar parallax was perhaps 12 arc-seconds, which corresponded to a solar distance of ca. 20,000 earth-radii. In 1673 his conclusion was confirmed by Jean Richer's (1630–1696) measurements of solar declinations in Cayenne and by John Flamsteed's (1646–1719) attempts to measure the parallax of Mars by means of a micrometer. By the end of the seventeenth century, the consensus was that the solar distance was more than 20,000 earth-radii, or eighty million miles, and that the radius of the solar system was ten times as great. Measurements of the angular diameters became systematized with the telescopic micrometer after the middle of the seventeenth century. By the end of the century, these measurements stabilized around values much lower than the traditional ones. A new system of sizes and distances was thus established. If the consensus solar parallax of 10 arc-seconds represented little more than an upper limit on this measure, the measurements made during the transits of Venus of 1761 and 1769 constrained the value to within perhaps 2 arc-seconds.

BIBLIOGRAPHY

Goldstein, Bernard R. "The Arabic Version of Ptolemy's Planetary Hypotheses II." *Transactions of the American Philosophical Society* 57 (1967), Part 4, pp. 3–55.

Van Helden, Albert. *Measuring the Universe: Cosmic Dimensions from Aristarchus to Halley.* Chicago: University of Chicago Press, 1985.

ALBERT VAN HELDEN

See also Celestial Spheres; Horrocks, Jeremiah; Parallax; Telescopic Astronomy

Cosmogony

Refers to myth or doctrine concerning the origins of the world, and is of two types: first, those that celebrate a supreme being that creates directly, gives birth to a mechanical-evolutionary process, or is the author of all things and men; and, second, those that are tied into the idea of a cosmic egg and that often explain the origin of things as the result of forces produced by conflicting principles.

Every civilization has produced its own cosmogony. Most influential in the West were the creation myths of the Hebrews and the Greeks. In Genesis, the God of the Hebrews created the universe from nothing, and water was the prime element from which even the earth was created. In the *Timaeus,* Plato (428–348 B.C.E.) shifts attention from the problem of creation to that of the succession of worlds. Plato, by rationally explaining the myth of Phaethon, the son of the Sun who steals his father's chariot and, unable to control it, destroys the earth, gives a vision of the world characterized by cycles that alternate between the destruction and rebirth of the planet where the catastrophic events are determined by fire or water. Although he never developed his own cosmogony, Aristotle (384–322 B.C.E.), in the first book of *Metaphysics,* summarizes the principal works of the ancients with regard to the first causes of the world and places their research in a sort of limbo caught between myth and philosophy. According to Aristotle, the first philosophers of physics—Thales, Anaximenes, and Heraclitus—celebrating the natural elements— earth, water, air, and fire—demonstrated a desire for the inquiry characteristic of *logos* but were, in reality, tied to *mythos*. Aristotle held to the eternity of the world, and this concept constitutes one of the principal problems of Patristic and Scholastic philosophy because of its contradiction of the idea of creation ex nihilo (from nothing). The solution proposed by Saint Thomas Aquinas (d. 1274) interprets the Aristotelian first cause not as a material cause but as a starting point for a logical succession.

In the modern era, Johannes Kepler (1571–1630) united Copernican astronomy with Neoplatonic and Neopythagorean doctrines. He held that mathematical thought is capable of understanding the laws of divine will with regard to the creation of the world. He compared the number of planets and the sizes of their orbs with the relationships among the five regular solids. René Descartes (1596–1650) considers that God created a plenous universe, of indefinite extent, whose matter was subject to determinate laws of motion.

In the sixteenth and seventeenth centuries, interest in cosmogony continued, probably directly linked to the concept of a succession of worlds in the *Timaeus*. The main characteristic of these new cosmogonies is that they supported traditional explanations of the origin of the world with a history of its evolutionary stages in which myth is not associated exclusively with the origin of the world but finds new space and function in each cycle. Francesco Patrizi (1529–1597), in the first dialogue his *Della retorica* (1562), renews the idea of catastrophic changes of the world. He puts forward a history of the earth in which Jupiter and Pluto punish arrogant and overly proud mortals by making the earth's surface collapse into the surrounding abyss, the world's original form. In consequence, the earth undergoes a change in size and a transformation of its surface from smooth and uniform to deformed and rough.

The topography of the current earth as set forth by Patrizi is found in *Telluris theoria sacra* (1681) by Thomas Burnet (ca. 1635–1715), who was, for this reason, accused of plagiarism. The intent of Burnet's ambiguous and complex work is to marry an archaic and mythological awareness of the world with Cartesian philosophical principles. Burnet reconstructs the principal stages of the history of the earth: chaos, the creation of the original Earth, the universal flood, the current world, the imminent destruction of the terraqueous globe, and, at the end, the restoration of paradise. He also superimposes the history and destiny of humankind and the earth in both the fall and the rebirth of the world: humankind's moral condition corresponds directly to the earth's physical condition: paradise is the natural element for the original purity of Adam, just as our Earth is the consequence of sin, and the future earth, purified by the conflagration, will be the seat of a kingdom lasting a thousand years.

The *Theoria* is, in this way, "sacred" inasmuch as it goes beyond the limits of a scientific narration of events and takes the point of view that divine providence is the primary cause of the world and the omniscient spectator of the misadventures of humankind and the earth. In response to Burnet's opus, a number of works were published in the last ten years of the seventeenth century that, although intended as alternatives to the *Theoria*, followed the same evolutionary cycle and differed only in the historical-scientific narration. *Discourses Concerning the Dissolution and Changes of the World* (1692) by John Ray (1620–1705) reproposes the fundamental moments of Burnet's narration but gives more attention to the universal conflagration because, according to Ray, a great desire and curiosity to know future events in advance is rooted in the nature of humankind.

Burnet's conviction that traumatic events were necessary to explain the current configuration of the planet

is shared by William Whiston (1667–1752) who published *A New Theory of the Earth* in 1696. His is a history of the earth built around the laws of motion, but it remains tied to the idea of a periodic divine intervention and identifies in comets the cyclical instruments of divine providence. In the midst of this debate, John Woodward's (1665–1728) *An Essay Towards a Natural History of the Earth* (1695) appears to be a renewal of premodern cosmogonies because, despite presenting itself as a history that excludes the unobservable events of creation and destruction, myth reemerges prepotently in the guise of post-Deluge chaos. Myth in seventeenth-century cosmogonies is not relegated to the origins of the world but includes its end as well, distancing itself in the process from classical tradition and absorbing the influences of the Judeo-Christian religions.

BIBLIOGRAPHY

Cohn, N. *Cosmos, Chaos, and the World to Come: The Ancient Roots of Apocalyptic Faith.* New Haven, CT: Yale University Press, 1993.

Collier, K. B. *Cosmogonies of Our Fathers: Some Theories of the Seventeenth and Eighteenth Centuries.* New York: Octagon Books, 1968.

Fehling, D. *Materie und Weltbau in der Zeit der frühen Vorsokratiker: Wirklichkeit und Tradition.* Innsbruck: Verlag des Instituts für Sprachwissenschaft der Universität Innsbruck, 1994.

AMALIA BETTINI

See also Burnet, Thomas; Theories of the Earth; Whiston, William

Court Cultures. See Patronage

Craftsman-and-Scholar Thesis

In the early 1940s, Edgar Zilsel (1899–1944) published in the United States a series of essays in which he underlined the decisive role the Renaissance craftsmen and engineers had in creating the modern image of science. The first formulation of a new concept of science and scientific progress can be found, according to Zilsel, in many texts written by the master craftsmen and engineers of the sixteenth century. With a felicitous image, Zilsel contrasted the workshop, arsenal, and *bottega*, which were places where men worked together, to a monk's cell and a humanist's study. The ends and goals of knowledge for these men were very different and certainly more impersonal than those of individual sanctification or of literary immortality.

The appeal to *nature* and *experience,* the rejection of authority, do not of themselves imply the acceptance of an ideal view of science, which has a public, democratic, and collaborative character and is composed of individual contributions organized in the form of scientific discourse and offered with the view of achieving a success that becomes the patrimony of mankind. This conception of science played a crucial role in the formation of the idea of progress. According to this image, knowledge increases and grows, actuated through a process to which generations of scholars successively contributes; this process, or any of its stages, is never complete, being ever needful of successive additions, revisions, or integrations. In the classical period, Zilsel concluded, similar ideas were not taken over by scholars; in early-modern capitalism, they were. The absence of slavery, the existence of machinery, and the capitalistic spirit of enterprise seem to be prerequisites without which the idea of scientific progress cannot unfold.

Zilsel's works, since he was very close to the logical-positivist program and contributed to making it known among American historians of science, reflect ideas present in Max Weber's work (published in Germany between 1904 and 1924) on the connections between the birth of modern science and the capitalistic spirit and in Max Scheler's essay *Wissensformen und die Gesellschaft* (1926). However, the subject of technique and the importance of craftsmen and engineers at the orgins of the Scientific Revolution had been strongly revalued in English-speaking culture during the Second International Congress on the History of Science and Technology in London, 1931. A delegation of Soviet scientists and historians of science directed by N. I. Bukharin presented, on that occasion, a series of essays published as *Science at the Crossroads* (1931). To J. D. Bernal, J. S. Haldane, L. Hogben, J. Needham, V. G. Childe, B. Farrington, S. Lilley, and C. Hill, the book appeared as the starting point for a new interpretation of the history of science. As Joseph Needham wrote in the Preface to the English edition of the book, it offered a model of the Marxist form of externalism in the history of science. Many of the delegates at the London congress later became victims of Joseph Stalin's (1879–1953) ferocious dictatorship, but, because of one of the not infrequent ironies of history, the enormous esteem that in Russia followed J. D. Bernal's work helped keep in circulation in the Stalinist Soviet Union many of the ideas that Bernal had directly taken from the "renegade" and "traitor" Nikolai Bukharin (1888–1938). The book explicity stated that every single research had to be subordinated to the dialectical Marxist method, but, in spite of this, it contained interesting analyses in a new and unusual fashion.

R. K. Merton's book (1910–) *Science, Technology, and Society in Seventeenth Century England* (1938) provided substantial help in delineating problems concerning the relations among science, the structures of society, and technological growth at the beginning of the modern age. In his book, Merton not only asked himself which were the ways in which science and the other expressions of culture could interact, but he also pointed out the issue of the interaction between technique and science at the beginning of modernity. Merton also looked with great interest at the many pages, written by English historians of science linked to Marxist perspectives, but he also noticed, in those studies, the complete absence of empirical or systematic research of a quantitative or qualitative nature. A large part of the discussion that took place during the 1950s between the supporters of an internal history and the supporters of an external history of science seems to be connected to discussions and perspectives that have to do more with the relationship between craftsmen and scientists in the sixteenth and seventeenth centuries, or, more generally, with the relation between technology and science, but that also make reference to the perspectives of Marxism. This helps explain, at least to a minor extent, the strength of some of the opposed positions and the rigidity, which today seems extreme, of the contrasting approaches.

Alexandre Koyré (1892–1964) was an ardent believer in a panmathematical image of science that came in part from Edmund Husserl (1859–1938) and in part from Ernst Cassirer (1874–1945). According to this view, science is always and only *theory.* Against Needham's approximate Marxism, Koyré claimed that science is not in any way necessary to the life of society. The development of scientific knowledge needs specific social conditions: it needs the presence of men who find satisfaction in the comprehension of reality or in theory; it needs that theorizing, in which scientific activity consists, may appear of a some value to society. Science, Koyré said, is the road that we must walk to truth: *itinerarium mentis in veritatem.* For this reason, Koyré defended a type of history of science as history that is immanent or internal.

Arguing against Marxism, Koyré claimed that there was a clear distinction and separation between theory and practice. It was not true for him either that theories led to practice or that practice led to theories. It was not Egyptians, while measuring the fields in the Nile Valley, who created geometry, but Greeks, who didn't have to measure anything that mattered. It was not Babylonians, because of their belief in astrology and need to foresee the positions of planets, who elaborated a system of celestial motions, but once again Greeks, who didn't even believe in astrology. The Egyptians and Babylonians contented themselves with ingenious methods of calculation. The appearance of cannons did not lead to the new dynamics, and it was not the needs of navigation, or the necessary calculations for the calendar, or of astrology that encouraged Nicolaus Copernicus (1473–1543) to reorganize completely the order of planets and to put the Sun at the center of the universe.

The controversy concerning the function of technicians and superior craftsmen during the Scientific Revolution was to tie itself closely to the one between internal and external history. This controversy gains even more significance, and not only to a simple erudite debate, if one keeps in mind an even wider discussion closely concerned with the relation between theory and practice, theory and technique, science and society. A. R. Hall (b. 1920) offered strong arguments against this new image of the modern scientist as some kind of hybrid between a philosopher of nature and a craftsman, and argued against the kind of historiography that interprets the birth of modern science as a marriage between the figure of the philosopher of nature, who thinks a lot and operates poorly, and that of the craftsman, who handily operates, but without ideas. Neither Copernicus, nor Andreas Vesalius (1514–1564), nor René Descartes (1596–1650) was more craftsmanlike than Ptolemy (ca. 100–170), Galen (second century C.E.), or Aristotle (384–322 B.C.E.). Hall's position was less univocal than Koyré's: the roles of the scholar and the craftsman in the Scientific Revolution are complementary, and, if the former holds the prime place in its story, the plot would lack many rich overtones had the latter also not played his part. The decisive changes, also for Hall, happen only on a theoretical level. Hall also believes that theories aren't generated by anything that is outside of science. The different solutions brought to this problem drive our attention back to our understanding of science. Is it an intellectual adventure whose ultimate goal is to derive and express our understanding of the universe in rational terms? Or do we have to understand and observe the scientific venture as a sort of manual that teaches us a series of expedients by which human beings can finally achieve their domination over nature and other humans?

The problem concerning the relationship between craftsmen and scientists, between technique and theories, between science seen as knowledge and science seen as the possibility of intervening on the world has presented itself in ways different from those we have been stating, when, during the extensive discussion following Thomas Kuhn's (1922–1996) work *The Structure of Scientific Revolutions* (1962), the relation between internal and external history of science began to assume a different configuration. As a matter of fact, many considered (after the second half of the 1960s) that the validity of a distinction between external history and internal history should be discussed. Many realized that, accepting that dichotomy, we are brought, on the one side, toward a dissolution of the history of science into a sort of epistemology and, on the other, toward a dissolution of the history of science into a sociology of scientific institutions that considers unimportant or not too relevant the analysis of theories; on one side, rational reconstructions that end up in "footnotes" of the real history; on the other, descriptions (instinct with literary zest) of culture atmospheres that come to rest as though in front of an unknown world, in front of hard-core problems and demonstrations. The crisis of the distinction between internal and external history has been enormously helped and encouraged by the discussion of one of the central issues of neopositivist epistemology: the distinction between the context of discovery and the context of justification.

Nowadays the discussion of the relation between scientists and superior craftsmen is only of historical interest. As it was formulated in the past, it lost its fashion and up-to-dateness. It has helped demonstrate how science has never been, and never will be, only a pure ensemble of theory but is, rather, a grand social and cultural phenomenon subject to influences that have to do not only with the development of thought, with implications of logic, with the internal dialectic between theories, but also with magic and literature, with religious sects and politics, with philosophy and industry, with ways of thinking and living, with institutions, metaphysics, economy: all things, these, on which science in its turn has a not negligible influence. Nowadays historians of science seem exclusively interested in finding ways in which we can achieve *consent* concerning hypotheses and theories; they are (almost *exclusively*) interested in the making and procedure of *negotiation*. As Kuhn said in 1991, power and interests seem to be the only things worthy of consideration for historians of science. Nature, whatever we might think of it, seems not to have had any influence on the growth of the beliefs that we have about her. Science appears only as an ensemble of the beliefs of winners. Even the more avid defenders of the importance of the craftsman and the mechanics of the Scientific Revolution would never have accepted a thesis such as this.

BIBLIOGRAPHY

Bukharin, Nikolai, ed. *Science at the Crossroads*. London: Kniga, 1931.

Hall, A. R. "The Scholar and the Craftsman in the Scientific Revolution." In *Critical Problems in the History of Science,* ed. M. Clagett. Madison: University of Wisconsin Press, 1962, pp. 3–24.

Koyré, A. *Études d'histoire de la pensée scientifique*. Paris: Presses Universitaires de France, 1966.

Kuhn, T. S. *The Trouble with the Historical Philosophy of Science* (Robert and Maurine Rothschild Distinguished Lecture, November 19, 1991). Cambridge, MA: Department of the History of Science, Harvard University, 1992.

Rossi, P. *Philosophy, Technology, and the Arts in the Early Modern Era*. Trans. Salvatore Attanasio. New York: Harper and Row, 1970.

Werskey, P. G., ed. *Science at the Crossroads*. London: Frank Cass, 1971.

Zilsel, E. "The Genesis of the Concept of Scientific Progress." In *Roots of Scientific Thought,* ed. P. Wiener and A. Noland. New York: Basic Books, 1957, pp. 250–275.

PAOLO ROSSI

See also Experience and Experiment; Internalist/Externalist Historiography; Marxist Historiography; Puritanism and Science

Crollius, Oswald (ca. 1560–1609)

An iatrochemist and member of a circle of Paracelsian critics of Aristotelianism, he studied medicine in Geneva, Strasbourg, and Heidelberg and received a doctorate in medicine ca. 1582. After finishing his studies, Crollius became a tutor for the children of the French family D'Esnes and the Counts of Pappenheim-Stühlingen. From ca. 1593 he traveled through Poland, Hungary, Silesia, and Bohemia as a physician and from 1597 he practiced in Prague. A sensational healing of Prince Christian I of Anhalt-Bernburg made him well known,

and Emperor Rudolph II consulted him repeatedly. Crollius was granted a coat of arms by Elector Friedrich IV of the Palatinate in 1591.

His most important work is the *Basilica chymica* (1609), which shows Crollius to be an ardent supporter of Paracelsian medicine, although he attacks Paracelsus's theory of the *Tartarus* as a general cause of illness and also disagrees with the concept of the *Archeus* as a kind of inner demon that separates the pure from the impure parts of ingested food. The whole first part of the *Basilica* is written in a somewhat dark and scarcely comprehensible manner and was influenced by Petrus Severinus (1542–1602), who had tried to solve some of the contradictions in the writings of Paracelsus (ca. 1491–1541).

The second part of the book, however, is particularly important, as it deals with practical iatrochemistry (the preparation of synthetic medicines rather than the traditional compounding of drugs from plants). Crollius gives clear prescriptions for the preparation of his medicines, often relying on his own laboratory experience,

The title-page of Oswald Crollius's very popular work illustrates his interest in hermetism, alchemy, and Kabbalah. Among the portraits are those representing Roger Bacon, the medieval alchemist Jabir ibn Hayyan, as well as Paracelsus, and the mythical Hermes Trismegistus.

and describes their effects and usage. His treatise *De signaturis internis rerum* of 1609 also had a lasting effect because it laid the foundations for the theory of signatures. The idea was based on the assumption that the outer appearance of plants, animals, or minerals indicates a sympathetic relationship between them and similar-appearing parts of the human body. The theory of signatures offered a genuine alternative to the humoral pathology of Galen.

BIBLIOGRAPHY

Crollius, Oswald. *Basilica Chymica et Praxis Chemiatricae, or Royal and Practical Chymistry in Three Treatises etc. Translated, Augmented, and Inlarged by John Hartmann etc. Englished by a Lover of Chemistry.* London, 1670.

Klutz, Monika. *Die Rezepte in Oswald Crolls* Basilica Chymica *(1609) und ihre Beziehungen zu Paracelsus.* Braunschweig: Technische Universität, Pharmaziegeschichtliches Seminar, 1974.

Kühlmann, Wilhelm. "Oswald Crollius und seine Signaturenlehre: Zum Profil hermetischer Naturphilosophie in der Ära Rudolphs II." In *Die occulten Wissenschaften in der Renaissance,* ed. August Buck. Wiesbaden: Harrassowitz, 1992, pp. 103–123.

Partington, J. R. *A History of Chemistry.* 4 vols. London: Macmillan, 1961–1964, vol. 2, 174–177.

CLAUS PRIESNER

See also Correspondences; Iatrochemistry; Paracelsus

Cross-Staff

An instrument for measuring angular distances, used by astronomers, mariners, and others. An early astronomical staff was described by Levi ben Gerson (1288–1344), who may have been the inventor. Some historians have suggested that the cross-staff was inspired by the *kamal,* used to measure altitude at sea by the Arabs.

The cross-staff consists of a wooden crosspiece sliding on a longer wooden rod, which is held close to the eye while the crosspiece is moved until its ends subtend the object(s) being measured. Depending on the manner in which the scale on the staff was divided, the distance could be either read off directly or determined indirectly by consulting a table of calculations. (A staff for direct measurement was more difficult to produce, requiring nonlinear divisions.) While a cross-staff might have several crosspieces, for measuring a range of angles, only one would be used at a time; illustrations depicting several crosses are incorrect.

The cross-staff was a standard astronomical instrument during the fifteenth and sixteenth centuries, used by Johannes Regiomontanus (1436–1476), Peter Apian (1495–1552), and Tycho Brahe (1546–1601). Larger versions were mounted on stands. Like many other astronomical instruments, the cross-staff was adapted for use by mariners and surveyors. A navigational aid for determining latitude, the cross-staff was relatively inexpensive and easy to make as well as use, although there were certain inherent difficulties. Holding the end close to the eye on the deck of a rolling ship was probably not unproblematic. While the cross-staff proved useful until the end of the eighteenth century, few examples survive because they were somewhat easily broken; most surviving examples are Dutch. The cross-staff was also adapted for surveying; many contemporary illustrations depict its use on land and at sea.

BIBLIOGRAPHY

Mörzer Bruyns, W. F. J. *The Cross-Staff: History and Development of a Navigational Instrument.* [Amsterdam]: Vereeniging Nederlandsch Historisch Scheepvaart Museum, Rijksmuseum Nederlands Scheepvaartmuseum Amsterdam, Walburg Instituut, 1994.

Stimson, Alan Neale, and Christopher St. John Hume Daniel. *The Cross Staff: Historic Development and Modern Use.* London: Harriet Wynter, 1977.

LIBA TAUB

See also Quadrant

Cudworth, Ralph (1617–1688)

Known as one of the leading members of the so-called Cambridge Platonists, and for his contributions to moral philosophy, he also made an important contribution to late-seventeenth-century debates about the relationship between natural philosophy and religion.

His monumental *True Intellectual System of the Universe* (1678) was intended to be merely the first part of a much larger examination and refutation of three kinds of fatalism: atheistic, pantheistic, and Calvinistic. It is a major study of intellectual, or philosophical, irreligion. Cudworth sought to refute several kinds of atheism, all of which assumed some principle of activity within matter, by insisting that it was a logical requirement for matter to be totally passive and inert. Although it followed from this that these forms of atheism were contradictory, it left mechanical atheism, with its assumption of inert matter, unharmed. But Cudworth went on to argue that a mechanical philosophy based upon the behavior of particles of matter that are supposedly devoid of all capacity to act is equally untenable. While rejecting the atheistic atomism of the mechanical philosophy, Cudworth insisted that there was a pre-Democritean form of atomism, deriving from a shadowy Phoenician philosopher called Moschus whom Cudworth, following a minor exegetical tradition, tentatively identified with Moses. This form of atomism, needless to say, was regarded as the true natural philosophy. Far from being atheistic, this atomism, when correctly understood, pointed to the need for an active (and, for Cudworth, necessarily spiritual) principle at work in the world to account for the interactions, motions, and other activities of inert matter. Cudworth referred to this spiritual principle as the *plastic nature* and saw it as a real entity, a universal secondary cause responsible for blindly carrying out the laws of nature ordained by God. There are a number of very close similarities between Cudworth's philosophy and that of his friend Henry More (1614–1687); both advocated a strict dualist distinction between active spirit and passive matter, and Cudworth's plastic nature serves the same philosophical and theological function as More's Spirit of Nature.

BIBLIOGRAPHY

Gysi, Lydia. *Platonism and Cartesianism in the Philosophy of Ralph Cudworth*. Bern: Herbert Lang, 1962.

Passmore, J. A. *Ralph Cudworth: An Interpretation*. Cambridge: Cambridge University Press, 1951.

Sailor, Danton B. "Moses and Atomism." *Journal of the History of Ideas* 25 (1964), 3–16.

JOHN HENRY

See also Active Principles; Cambridge Platonists; More, Henry

D

Decimals

Although the theoretical principle underlying decimal fractions was explicitly articulated by some medieval mathematicians, decimal fractions were not widely used before the seventeenth century. Up to 1500, only common fractions were used in all sorts of applied mathematics (surveying, gauging, mercantile transactions, and so on), with the exception of astronomical computations. Here angles as well as chord- or sine-lengths were handled in sexagesimal fractions. The German astronomer Johannes Regiomontanus (1436–1476) was influential in moving astronomical computations to the decimal camp. His tables, well known and used in the sixteenth century, gave sines and tangents as an integer number of parts of a radius measuring 6.10^n or 10^n ($n = 4, 5, 6, 7$) units.

After 1500, but mostly after 1550, we find proper decimal fractions occasionally used in books and tables, although explicit recognition of their algorismic power and a systematic account of their computational techniques are nowhere to be found before 1585, when the Flemish engineer Simon Stevin (1548–1620) published *De thiende* (The Tenth, or Dime). This small booklet begins by introducing the notion of decimal numbers and their notation. Integers are represented by ⓪, tenths are called *primes* and represented by ①, hundredths (②) are *seconds,* and so on. Thus, 0.27 would in Stevin's notation look like 0⓪ 2① 7②. Succinctly and by example, *The Tenth* also explains how to add, subtract, multiply, and divide with such numbers. The notation is clumsy, but the techniques are modern. They are demonstrated by rewriting decimal numbers as common fractions with a denominator of the form 10^n (say, 27/100 instead of 0.27) and then grounding the operations with decimal numbers on the operations with common fractions. Finally, in an appendix, Stevin emphasizes the advantages to be gained from using decimal systems of weights and measures and currency. In this, Stevin was not heeded for two hundred years, but his booklet was otherwise instrumental in spreading the use of decimal numbers. Originally written in Flemish, in 1685 it was also printed in French. It was often reprinted and was twice translated into English (in 1608 and 1619) through the first decades of the seventeenth century.

At about the same time, other works were published teaching the new fractional calculations. The invention of logarithms (the first tables were published in the 1610s) and the task of computing more extensive and accurate tables were no doubt powerful stimuli for using decimal numbers—indeed, they were taken for granted in seventeenth-century trigonometric and logarithmic tables. By 1700, their place was secure among the basic arithmetic tools. What was not achieved before 1700 was a standard notation. John Napier (1550–1617) recommended the use of a mere period or coma as decimal separatrix, but this simple notation did not come into universal use until the eighteenth century. Many contemporary books on decimals numbers, including Stevin's, emphasized that they provided "a kind of arithmetic" allowing the performing of all computations "by whole numbers, without fractions"—suggesting that involved computations could now be performed by wider audiences. The suggestion is reinforced by the exclusive use of vernacular languages and by the redundant notations employed. That decimals gained a wide currency in the seventeenth century may thus be related to the increasing social importance of mathematical literacy in early-modern Europe.

BIBLIOGRAPHY

Cajori, F. *A History of Mathematical Notations,* vol. 1: *Notations in Elementary Mathematics.* Chicago: Open Court, 1928, pp. 314–335.

Sarton, G. "The First Explanation of Decimal Fractions and Measures (1585): Together with a History of the Decimal Idea and a Facsimile of Stevin's Disme." *Isis* 23 (1935), 153–244.

Smith, D. E. *History of Mathematics.* 2 vols. New York: Dover, 1925. 2nd ed. 1958, vol. 2, pp. 235–247.

Stevin, S. *The Tenth.* Trans. R. Norton. In *The Principal Works of Simon Stevin,* vol. 2: *Mathematics,* ed. D. J. Struik. Amsterdam: Swets and Zeitlinger, 1958, pp. 371–455.

ANTONI MALET

See also Logarithms; Stevin, Simon

Dee, John (1527–1608)

John Dee From David Lysons, The Environs of London *(1793–1796).*

This Elizabethan polymath built one of the largest personal libraries of the time. It was rich in mathematics, sciences of all sorts, and philosophy, not only in the ancient texts prized in the Renaissance, but also in unusually large numbers of medieval texts. Dee mined this material in a number of ways. He translated it into usable knowledge for contemporaries by promoting mathematics in his *Preface* (1570) to the English Euclid, providing mathematical instruction and treatises for patrons, teaching navigational techniques to English navigators, and consulting at Court on calendar reform and supporting British imperial claims. Like others in the Renaissance, he sought new insights into the natural world as a reflection of divinity and to achieve personal spiritual insight. His inspiration was primarily Roger Bacon (ca. 1214/1220–ca. 1292), enhanced by ancient, medieval, and Renaissance magical texts. In the *Propaedeumata* (1558), he developed a mathematical theory of astrological causation founded on Bacon's concept of the multiplication of species. His *Monas hieroglyphica* (1564) presents an unusual blend of alchemy, astrology, and magic that is as much an allegory of spiritual ascent as a study of nature. Later, he became increasingly absorbed in "spiritual exercises" in a quest for direct spiritual insight from angels contacted through a crystal gazer.

The extensive occult interests that coexist with elements of what seem "real" science in Dee's work have made his contribution to science ambiguous. Early in the twentieth century, scholars highlighted just what they thought were his positive contributions at the expense of the whole person. In the 1960s Frances Yates's (1969) contention that Hermetic occultism directly contributed to science supported a positive contribution for all of Dee's activities. More recently, scholarly attention to context and the social construction of knowledge has reduced the concern to find a place for Dee in the Scientific Revolution.

BIBLIOGRAPHY

Clulee, Nicholas H. *John Dee's Natural Philosophy: Between Science and Religion.* London: Routledge, 1988.

French, Peter J. *John Dee: The World of an Elizabethan Magus.* London: Routledge, 1972.

Sherman, William H. *John Dee: The Politics of Reading and Writing in the English Renaissance.* Amherst: University of Massachusetts Press, 1995.

Yates, Frances A. *The Occult Philosophy in the Elizabethan Age.* London: Routledge, 1969.

NICHOLAS H. CLULEE

See also Alchemy; Hermetism; Magic

Della Porta. See Porta, Giambattista della

Demonstration

A logical and methodological term (Gr. *apodeixis,* Lat. *demonstratio*), first used by Aristotle (384–322 B.C.E.) to designate an argument or proof that is necessarily true and certain. The concept was developed with the revival of Aristotelianism in the High Middle Ages and the Renaissance and was frequently employed throughout the Scientific Revolution, in which its meaning was modified in various ways. This essay explains the classical concept at the onset of the revolution and representative views that later served to characterize it.

The Classical Notion

Within the Aristotelian tradition, a demonstration is a syllogism that is productive of scientific knowledge (i.e., knowledge that is true and certain because it is based on a causal connection that makes the conclusion be as it is). It is most intelligible when placed in the form of a syllogism such as "M is P; S is M; therefore S is P," in which S is the subject of the demonstration, P an attribute predicated of it, and M the middle term joining the two together. It is concerned with matter that is said to be necessary because the terms of the argument cannot be related otherwise than they are. When they can be related otherwise, the matter is said to be contingent, and the argument is probable or dialectical, as opposed to demonstrative.

Effectively, a demonstration is had whenever a statement is made together with the reason, or cause, or explanation for its truth or whenever the question "why?" is answered. Because there are different senses of "why," there are different kinds of demonstration. These are indicated by the character of the middle term. If the middle gives the proper cause of the attribute's inherence in the subject, the demonstration is *propter quid,* or "of the reasoned fact"; if the middle gives a remote or common cause, or an effect through which the cause is known, the demonstration is *quia,* or "of the fact" only. In the most perfect type of *propter quid,* all of the terms are convertible, or commensurately universal, and then it is called "most powerful" (*potissima*); at the least, the middle term and the attribute must be convertible. If the middle term is a cause of the attribute, the demonstration is *a priori;* if it is an effect, the demonstration is *a posteriori.* Should it happen that the cause reached through *a posteriori* demonstration is of commensurate universality with the effect, the demonstration may without circularity be recast as a *propter quid* demonstration in a process known as the *demonstrative regress.* In this, the first step is that of resolution, resolving the effect to its cause, and the second that of compo-

sition, combining the cause with the effect to give its proper explanation.

Special conditions attach to the premises of a demonstration (i.e., to "M is P" and "S is M"). They must be known to be "true" either as self-evident or from prior demonstration, in which case all prior demonstrations must ultimately be reducible to premises that are "immediate" and do not themselves require a middle term. This occurs when a connection can be made directly from the meanings of their terms, as when the thing defined is joined with an essential or causal definition involving any of the four causes, once this has been grasped by induction (*epagoge*) from sense experience. Again, the premises must be "prior to and better known than" the conclusion, since they are known on their own terms whereas the conclusion is not, being made known through the premises. Finally, the premises are "causes" of the conclusion, and this in two ways: epistemologically, in that they are causes of one's knowledge of the conclusion; and ontologically, in that they explain the attribute's actual inherence in the subject or "why" it is there.

Role in the Scientific Revolution

These conditions are extraordinarily difficult to fulfill. Prior to the Scientific Revolution, they were usually explained with the aid of simple examples from Euclidean geometry or from mixed sciences in which the "M is P" premise is taken from mathematics, as the demonstration that the Moon is a sphere from its having phases. In the revolution, the stress on mathematical premises continued, but the arguments gain strength from the extension of "sense experience" to include observation with instruments, measurements, and experimentation. This brought problems, too, for many lacked access to these new tools and could not verify the results attributed to them, thus having to rely on the authority of the scientist and his community for their acceptance.

William Harvey (1578–1657) was the most adept at incorporating these techniques within an Aristotelian framework in proving the blood's circulation through "ocular demonstration." Thomas Hobbes (1588–1679) employed the traditional terminology and placed emphasis on resolution and composition but tended to reduce all causes to the cause of motion (efficient causality) and generally read Aristotle as a nominalist. Robert Boyle (1627–1691) was wary of demonstrative claims such as Hobbes's but had difficulty himself establishing the authority of his air pump as a scientific instrument. Galileo Galilei (1564–1642) encountered a similar problem with his telescope, and so did Isaac Newton (1642–1727) with the prisms he used in the *experimentum crucis* (crucial experiment) to display the composition of white light.

René Descartes (1596–1650) subscribed to the method of resolution and composition, which he termed analysis and synthesis, but, rather than establish the truth of his premises from sense experience, he sought to do so by invoking "clear and distinct" ideas, thus elevating all science to the level of mathematical reasoning. Galileo rejected much of the Aristotelian corpus but in logic claimed to have been a Peripatetic all his life; most of his scientific contributions can be seen as resulting from the successful employment of the demonstrative regress. Newton proclaimed the method of resolution and composition as his own for both the *Principia mathematica philosophiae naturalis* (Mathematical Principles of Natural Philosophy, 1687) and the *Opticks* (1704) but, somewhat like Descartes, was content to defend his science on a mathematical plane, leaving it ambiguous at the level of physics. One could argue that it was the resulting failure to validate a mathematical physics in realist terms that led to the weakening of knowledge claims in all of philosophy and to the rise of skepticism and positivism in later centuries.

BIBLIOGRAPHY

Aristotle. *Posterior Analytics.* Book I, chs. 1–2, 10, 13; Book II, ch. 11.

Glutz, M. A. "Demonstration." *New Catholic Encyclopedia.* New York: McGraw-Hill, 1967, vol. 4, pp. 757–760.

Wallace, W. A. "Circularity and the Demonstrative *Regressus:* From Pietro D'Abano to Galileo Galilei." *Vivarium* 33 (1995), 76–97.

WILLIAM A. WALLACE

See also Causality; Logic; Resolution and Composition

Descartes, René (1596–1650)

Born in La Haye (now known as Descartes) near Tours, he was educated at the Jesuit College of La Flèche (1606–1614) before studying civil and canon law at Poitiers (1614–1615). He then set out to the Low Countries to begin a lifetime of private study, voluminous correspondence, and, after the age of forty, extensive publication. Descartes is sometimes termed the father of

modern philosophy. This reflects the interest of modern philosophers in epistemological issues stemming originally from Descartes's famous doctrine of the ontological distinction between matter, taken as pure spatial extension, and soul, taken as an immaterial, immortal, unextended thinking substance. Considered in the context of his time, however, Descartes was a pioneer of the mechanistic philosophy of nature and a master practitioner of mathematics and a number of the sciences.

Descartes lived during a period of intense competition amongst natural philosophers, as the still-dominant Scholastic Aristotelianism was challenged by varieties of Platonism, some imbued with magical aims or tied to programs of religious and political reform. The mechanical philosophy of nature was constructed by Descartes and a handful of others, who hoped to resolve the conflict of natural philosophies in a way that promised scientific progress and increasing command of nature, without the need for social reform or political or religious upheaval. Descartes's version of the program of the mechanists was developed in two treatises, *The World; or, A Treatise on Light* (1629–1633) unpublished in his lifetime, and *The Principles of Philosophy* (Latin edition 1644, French edition 1647).

Unlike most other mechanical philosophers, Descartes was no atomist. He thought that the notion of a void space was unclear and that a conceptual analysis of our ideas showed that every extended space is filled with matter—indeed, is matter. The impossibility of any void spaces meant that, if a particle is to move, the space it is about to vacate must be simultaneously filled by another particle of equivalent volume. This further implied that any motion at all entrains an instantaneous circuit of displacement, leading to the filling of the about-to-be-voided space.

Descartes applied these notions to a speculative cosmogony. He starts with an "indefinitely" large chunk of divinely created matter-extension. The term *indefinite* is supposed to camouflage the move to an infinite universe. When God injects motion into this matter-extension, it is shattered to microparticles, and myriads of "circular" displacements ensue. These lead to a steady state in which an infinite array of gigantic whirlpools, or vortices, is formed. Each vortex carries a family of planets around a central star. Vortex formation is accompanied by the emergence of three species of microscopic particle, or elements. The so-called third element forms all solid and liquid bodies on earth and other planets throughout the

explanatory strategy in *The World* and the *Principles of Philosophy,* in which it is legitimated by appeal to God's declaration of these laws and his constant governance of natural processes according to them.

Descartes's vortex theory signals his commitment to the truth of Copernicanism as an account not just of our solar system but of star and planet systems throughout an infinite universe. Descartes's vortex theory, employing his characteristic dynamical concepts, was a considerable achievement at the time and persisted well into the eighteenth century. More was involved than the vague idea of planets being swept along in a vortex of the second element. For example, as a vortex whirls about on its axis, each planet tends to recede from the center, its orbital radius being established by the dynamic balance between the centrifugal tendency of the planet and the counterforce arising from the centrifugal tendency of the second element composing the vortex in the vicinity of the planet. Descartes's model also deals with the behavior of comets and the celestial mechanical function of the central stars. In broad terms, he was trying to translate into a mechanistic framework the revolutionary celestial mechanical approach of the arch Neoplatonist Johannes Kepler (1571–1630).

To this end, Descartes's vortex theory also embodied cosmological mechanical theories of light and magnetism. Light had traditionally seemed to be the phenomenon least obviously grounded in base matter. Now it, too, was explained by the centrifugal tendency of the particles of the second element constituting each vortex. For Descartes, light consists in the instantaneous passage through the vortex of lines of tendency to centrifugal motion. As in the case of planetary motion, the mainly first-element seething star in the center of each vortex also plays a role, adding further centrifugal agitation to the vortex. Descartes deals with magnetism at length in the *Principles of Philosophy,* having omitted it in the earlier *The World.* In *On the Magnet* (1600), William Gilbert (1544–1603) had constructed a Neoplatonic natural philosophy centered upon magnetism as an immaterial, spiritual force. He had argued that not only Earth, but also the other planets are large, living magnets possessing high-level magnetic minds or intelligences. Buttressed with a wide range of experiments, this dazzling cosmological philosophy of the magnet could not be ignored by mechanists. According to Descartes, magnetism is caused by certain particles of the first element shaped into right- and left-hand screws by being

Courtesy Oklahoma University Library.

cosmos and constitutes the main portion of the air. Interspersed in the pores of such planetary bodies are the spherical particles of the second element. In addition, the second element fills what we would call space between the Sun and the planets in each solar system. The second element being spherical, there are spaces left between its particles, which were filled by the so-called first element, which also constitutes the body of the stars, including our Sun.

The behavior of Descartes's microparticles was governed by a carefully articulated theory of dynamics. Descartes held that bodies in motion or even merely tending to motion can be characterized from moment to moment by the possession of two sorts of dynamical quantity: (1) the absolute quantity of the *force of motion;* and (2) the directional modes of that quantity of force, which Descartes termed *determinations.* As corpuscles undergo instantaneous collisions with each other, their quantities of force of motion and determinations are adjusted according to certain universal laws of nature, rules of collision. This style of explanation is present in Descartes's earliest physico-mathematical researches undertaken with Isaac Beeckman (1588–1637) in 1618–1619, and it subsists as the basis of his natural-philosophical

squeezed through arrays of the spheres of the second element as they travel into a stellar vortex from above or below along the axis of rotation of the central star. If a star eventually cools down, dies, and becomes a planet like earth, the screwlike particles can continue to enter from its north and south poles. Thus, Descartes glossed Gilbert's experimental work in mechanistic terms and co-opted Gilbert's discovery of the "cosmic" significance of magnetism.

Descartes was a skilled practitioner of several of the specialized sciences inherited from antiquity and rapidly developing in his time. He excelled at mathematics, optics, mechanics, and physiology. His achievements in the latter three areas both shaped and were shaped by his system of mechanical philosophy. Descartes's most important optical discovery was his specification of the law of refraction of light, which probably occurred ca. 1627. This discovery was based on the analysis of empirical data on angles of incidence and refraction, taken in conjunction with a traditional geometrical assumption concerning the location of the refracted images of point sources. With his collaborator, the geometer Claude Mydorge, Descartes deployed the law of refraction in a theory of lenses, presented later in refined form in his *Dioptrics* of 1637, along with, in the accompanying *Meteorology* (1637), a solution to the ancient problem of the formation of the rainbow.

Although Descartes had dabbled with a qualitative mechanical theory of light since 1619, it contained assumptions that hindered the search for the law. After his discovery of the law of refraction by purely geometrical optical means, he looked for better mechanical conceptions of light by which to explain the law. These he found by literally transcribing into dynamical terms some of the geometrical parameters embodied in his initial diagrammatic representation of the law. The resulting principles concerning the mechanical nature of light foreshadow the two central tenets of his mature dynamics mentioned above. Later, in the *Dioptrics,* he tried to model these underlying dynamical principles through a kinematic model involving tennis balls, but this presentation created more difficulties than it clarified.

Descartes's approach to physiology, medicine, and anatomy was dominated by his mechanistic approach and underlying ontological dualism. Human beings he considered unique among all of God's creations. They are constituted by the "substantial union" of a mechanistic, machine body to an immortal, immaterial reasoning soul. Other animals are soulless machines, lacking subjective awareness, sensory perception, emotions, and feelings. In this spirit, Descartes appropriated and attempted to mechanize William Harvey's (1578–1657) neo-Aristotelian account of the circulation of the blood, in the process considerably altering Harvey's theory and complicating debate about it. Descartes's two other most significant developments of mechanistic physiology were his rewriting into mechanical terms of Kepler's new (1604) theory of vision and his groundbreaking explanation of the nature of certain involuntary muscular reflexes. These he held to be mediated entirely through mechanical feedback pathways, with no conscious intervention by the willing "soul." Descartes's mechanistic physiology was inspired by the contemporary vogue for automata and moving statues. What humans could do with gross pieces of matter and the flow of water or air, surely God could accomplish even better with finely designed microscopic structures and the smallest, most mobile corpuscles. Such, then, was "life" as conceived in Descartes's strictly mechanist approach.

Descartes's mathematical achievements were cataloged in his *Geometry,* published along with the *Dioptrics* and *Meteors* with the *Discourse on Method* in 1637. The *Geometry* was the climax of a late Renaissance tradition in analytical mathematics that had looked to contemporary algebra for the key to the presumed hidden analytical method by which the ancient mathematicians had produced their astounding results before presenting them in a synthetic, deductive style. Hence, *Geometry* has in some degree a misleading title, for Descartes's focus was on the algebraic theory of equations used for analysis of geometrical and algebraic problems. He begins by showing that all of the basic operations of algebra have interpretations in terms of line segments. This is done less in the service of representing algebraic equations through geometrical curves than to show that geometrical problems (as well as algebraic ones) are amenable to an increasingly powerful theory of equations. He then applies his techniques to obtain a limited, but promising, solution to some cases of the so-called problem of Pappus's complex locus which the ancients had stated but had not been able to solve. Finally, in Book Three of the *Geometry,* Descartes presents an improved version of algebraic notation and a theory of equations, before offering his method of construction by means of a circle and parabola the solutions to all cubic and quartic equations. He then indicates how one might move up to ever higher levels of curves, represented and manipulated through ever higher orders of equations. This accords with his hope that progress in the algebraic theory of equations would dictate a systematic and cumulative program of analysis. With the appearance of Descartes's *Geometry,* along with the mature work of Pierre de Fermat (1601–1665), the ancient geometers were definitively surpassed and new vistas of work emerged that led to the invention of the calculus later in the century.

Such, then, were Descartes's basic contributions to mechanistic natural philosophy, mathematics, and the technical sciences. Comprehension of them, however, is often obstructed by two pitfalls that have long troubled scholars. The first pitfall consists in the widespread belief that Descartes's work in mechanistic natural philosophy, mathematics, and the sciences was guided by his method as taught in his *Discourse on Method* and the earlier *Rules for the Direction of the Mind* (1619–1628). According to the method, all rationally obtainable truths subsist in a unitary network of deductive linkages, which humans may explore by intuiting individual truths and deducing valid links between them. Method essentially consists in a set of practical hints or heuristic rules to aid the intuiting and deducing mind in traversing this network. The key point here is that many modern scholars now hold that grand, set-piece doctrines of scientific method, such as Descartes's, cannot and do not control and guide living practice in any given field of research, let alone across the entire gamut of disciplines. Descartes's technical achievements in mathematics and the sciences, discussed above, cannot, therefore, be explained as applications of his method, and more plausible reconstructions are being found by modern scholars.

Of course, Descartes may have believed in the efficacy of his method, at least until it met severe difficulties in the late 1620s. Descartes had constructed the core of the method in late 1619 and early 1620. It was the third and final of a sequence of youthful, overblown, and ineffective programs he dreamt up between 1618 and 1620. It was preceded by a "physico-mathematics" promoted by Descartes and his mentor Isaac Beeckman as a properly mathematical approach to corpuscular-mechanical natural philosophy, and by "universal mathematics," a supposedly general analytical discipline spanning mathematics and "physico-mathematics." So enthused was Descartes for his third project, the method commanding all rational disciplines, that on St. Martin's Eve 1619 he

dreamt that the project had been consecrated by God himself. Descartes's methodological honeymoon lasted less than a decade. By the late 1620s, he returned to the text of the *Rules* to explicate the method in detail. There he met severe internal difficulties, involving the application of the method to problems of higher mathematics, as well as to cases of mechanistic explanation involving the invisible realm of microparticles. Recognizing these problems, Descartes abandoned the text of the *Rules* in late 1628 and retreated to the United Provinces, there to work out the dualist metaphysics and systematic corpuscular mechanism that could supply the answers to his difficulties. Until the collapse of the renewed method project in 1628, Descartes probably believed in his method. After 1628, his use of it, for example in the *Discourse* and three *Essays* of 1637, probably betrays a calculated rhetorical strategy of presentation and persuasion.

The second pitfall besetting the comprehension of Descartes's work involves the belief that he claimed to deduce his entire system of natural philosophy from absolutely certain metaphysical principles. This folklore arose from the strictly deductivist tone of Descartes's abortive method and from some of his more offhand public and private statements about the issue. It is clear that in his mature work, after 1628, Descartes increasingly came to see that neither the details of particular explanatory models nor the facts to be explained could be deduced from metaphysics. In the *Principles of Philosophy,* his position became very clear: We may know with certainty from metaphysical deduction that the essence of matter is extension, but we cannot deduce from this truth more detailed explanatory models for such phenomena as gravity, light, magnetism, planetary motion, sensory perception, and animal locomotion. The best one can say is that such models should not contradict metaphysically derived certainties and that relevant facts must also be considered in shaping explanatory models. Hence, such lower-level models are necessarily hypothetical and can achieve, at best, only "moral certainty." Clearing these pitfalls is necessary for anyone hoping to analyze Descartes's struggle, after 1629, to legitimate and communicate his system of mechanistic natural philosophy. After the collapse of the *Rules,* Descartes began to elaborate his dualist metaphysics. At the same time, he was drawn into writing what became *The World.* However, the latter treatise makes no explicit appeal to metaphysical grounding and certainty. Descartes was relying on the persuasive effect of his mechanization of Copernicanism and its extension to an infinite number of solar systems. Hence his alarm in 1633 when the Catholic Church condemned Galileo Galilei (1564–1642) for openly teaching that Copernicanism is true. Descartes withdrew plans to publish *The World*. Different tactics would be needed, including the explicit attachment of the mechanical natural philosophy to metaphysical arguments for ontological dualism. In 1637, Descartes finally produced his first publication, the *Discourse on Method* and three supporting *Essays*—the *Geometry, Dioptrics,* and *Meteorology*. The *Discourse* introduced his method as well as an initial version of the metaphysical construction of ontological dualism. Descartes hoped that these abbreviated versions of his doctrines would lead the savants of Europe to his door, raising the public's appetite for the full system. The *Discourse* and *Essays* triggered much correspondence and debate, along with some recruitment to the Cartesian program in the United Provinces, scene of the first spread of Cartesianism into university teaching. But the overall reception was disappointing, and Descartes could not move directly to the intended triumphal unfolding of his full system. In 1641, he took a strategic detour, publishing his *Meditations,* the fullest elaboration of the metaphysical arguments for dualism. Since the *Meditations* contain virtually no natural-philosophical detail, it is often studied anachronistically, in isolation, as Descartes's inauguration of modern philosophical debate. However, it should be seen in context as Descartes's attempt to set in place the metaphysical foundations of a mechanistic natural philosophy, without having to offer up debatable details. Finally, in the *Principles of Philosophy* (1644, 1647), Descartes presented, in the form of a textbook, his full system of mechanical natural philosophy and its explicit metaphysical legitimation. None of this activity, however, achieved what Descartes so much desired—the winning over of the learned world to his system of mechanism, his form of metaphysical legitimation, and his particular achievements and techniques in optics, mechanics, and physiology. Descartes's later career was engulfed in controversy, debate, and a constant struggle to defend and explicate his system. One can illustrate his later struggles by considering the shifting history of his aims in medicine.

Through the mid-1630s, Descartes had thought that medical theory and therapy could follow directly from his mechanistic physiology. But, unsurprisingly, his medical program stumbled on the very complexity of the human condition as conceived in Cartesian ontological dualism. In humans, the intimate and "substantial" union of a reasoning, immortal, and immaterial mind with a machine body entailed the existence of a subjective realm of emotions and internal sensations. From the late 1630s onward, Descartes increasingly recognized these difficulties, and, by the 1640s, his medical theory had become focused on psychosomatic aspects of ethical and therapeutic issues. Accordingly, his last work, the *Passions of the Soul* (1649), explores the passions, emotions, and internal sensations arising from, and characteristic of, the human mind-body union. Descartes's mechanistic medicine was, in short, derailed by the dualism that he otherwise had to supply to shore up his overall natural philosophy. In his resulting engagement with ethics, the passions, and the human condition, he tried to exploit the implications of that dualism for humans, while engaging the criticisms that his astringent dualism had elicited. In the end, Descartes bequeathed to the next generation of the Scientific Revolution a powerful but particular version of the mechanistic philosophy, as well as startling, if often hotly debated, achievements in the traditional sciences and mathematics. He did not succeed in imposing upon his successors his personal program of mechanism, method, and dualist metaphysics. Bits of his personal vision were variously altered, revised, adopted, and rejected by the next generation of mechanists, who, unlike Descartes, had the luxury of being relaxed heirs to, rather than tortured inventors of, the mechanistic world vision and its program for the scientific domination of nature.

BIBLIOGRAPHY

Buchdahl, Gerd. *Metaphysics and the Philosophy of Science.* Oxford: Blackwell, 1969, pp. 79–180.

Garber, Daniel. *Descartes' Metaphysical Physics.* Chicago: University of Chicago Press, 1992.

Gaukroger, Stephen. *Descartes: An Intellectual Biography.* Oxford: Oxford University Press, 1995.

———. *Descartes: Philosophy, Mathematics, and Physics.* Brighton, England: Harvester, 1980.

Milhaud, Gaston. *Descartes savant.* Paris: Felix Alcan, 1921.

Shea, William. *The Magic of Numbers and Motion: The Scientific Career of René Descartes.* Canton, MA: Science History Publications, 1991.

JOHN A. SCHUSTER

See also Beeckman, Isaac; Cartesianism; Copernicanism; Laws of Nature; Mechanical Philosophy

Dialectic

During the sixteenth and seventeenth centuries, the terms *dialectic* and *logic* were frequently used interchangeably. When speaking more strictly, however, philosophers often distinguished between the two on the Aristotelian ground that the former dealt with deductive inference from first principles that were accepted only as being probable, whereas the latter dealt with deductive inference from first principles that were accepted as certain. In both cases, the conclusions arrived at by such inference were themselves as solidly established as the premises from which they were derived.

During the sixteenth century, the traditional Scholastic approach to the teaching of logic was increasingly challenged by newer approaches associated with the educational-reform program of the humanists. Humanist approaches to what they usually preferred to call *dialectic* took its province to be argumentation in general rather than following the strict Scholastic Aristotelian sense of rigorous demonstration from certain principles. As a result, humanist dialectic had much in common with another Aristotelian category, that of *rhetoric* (drawing especially on Aristotle's *Topics*). The five parts of rhetoric in the Latin Aristotelian tradition were *inventio, dispositio, elocutio, memoria,* and *pronunciatio*: invention, disposition, style of presentation, memory (to control the material deployed), and delivery. In keeping with the tendencies that had become established in the new humanist dialectic, the French pedagogue Peter Ramus (Pierre de la Ramée, 1515–1572), in the second half of the sixteenth century, introduced a formal separation of the five parts of rhetoric by removing *inventio* and *dispositio* from rhetoric altogether and placing them under dialectic. Ramus treated dialectic as a discipline that encompassed formal deductive logic, whether or not rooted in premises warranted as certain, and rhetorical persuasion, leaving to the category "rhetoric" itself little more than its performative aspects. Any discourse structured with the aim of persuasion counted, for Ramus, as dialectic. His (by no means universally accepted) innovation represented an extreme version of the humanist conception of dialectic.

One common feature of humanist dialectic in contrast to Scholastic logic concerns its epistemological stance. The widespread adoption of the humanist approach in the sixteenth century, with its incorporation of merely probable as well as certain arguments, simultaneously encouraged a focus on the realm of the uncertain. A virtue of the humanist approach was that it could deal with many more kinds of argument, concerning many more topics, because it did not restrict itself to matters admitting of demonstrative certainty. Thus, its proponents often emphasized the vast array of topics and questions that could be determined only with probability and yet were accessible to their kind of dialectic.

The contemporary senses of the terms *probable* and *probability* should be specified in this connection. To label an opinion probable meant, as its etymology suggests, that it was fit to be approved and accepted. The grounds on which such probability rested were various; an opinion might be rendered approvable (probable) by virtue of particular pieces of sensory evidence, as when a fire is inferred from smoke, or by virtue of common experience, as with the view that the Sun rises every day; but it might also be done by virtue of the pronouncement of someone accepted as an authority, such as Aristotle, or one of the Church Fathers. These sources of probability were traditional resources of rhetoricians, but the extension of dialectic beyond the demonstratively certain made them part of its purview, too.

During the seventeenth century, the teaching of dialectic (logic) continued to bear the stamp of the humanist program. The syllogism had been the fundamental tool of Scholastic logic in the Middle Ages; it retained an important place alongside probable arguments. In a syllogistic demonstration, the conclusion was rigorously deduced from starting premises, according to the following basic model:

(Major premise): All men are mortal.
(Minor premise): Socrates is a man.
(Conclusion): Socrates is mortal.

Textbooks continued throughout the period to explain and codify the various forms of syllogism, separating valid from invalid forms. At the same time, they emphasized the new role of probable arguments; the syllogism was now only one part of the subject rather than dominant aspect.

Even apparently novel departures owed much to the reforms of the sixteenth century. The 1662 Port-Royal *Logique,* closely associated with Jansenism, is famous for its expression of Cartesian and Pascalian ideas about right reasoning. Yet, it, too, follows in the well-trodden footsteps of countless earlier textbooks, even down to its topical division into four parts. The meanings and connotations of the word *dialectic* throughout the period of the Scientific Revolution, therefore, became loosened, no longer invoking the image of iron logic and its syllogistic demonstrations, but signaling a rhetoricized art of argument and persuasion that was prepared to discuss opinions and probabilities. Whether this change promoted an increased emphasis on the uncertainty of natural knowledge, or whether views of that uncertainty themselves encouraged the new dialectic, is less clear.

BIBLIOGRAPHY

Hacking, Ian. *The Emergence of Probability*. Cambridge: Cambridge University Press, 1976.

Howell, W. S. *Logic and Rhetoric in England, 1500–1700*. Princeton, NJ: Princeton University Press, 1956.

Jardine, Lisa. *Francis Bacon: Discovery and the Art of Discourse*. Cambridge: Cambridge University Press, 1974.

———. "Lorenzo Valla and the Intellectual Origins of Humanist Dialectic." *Journal of the History of Philosophy* 15 (1977), 143–164. Revised as "Lorenzo Valla: Academic Skepticism and the New Humanist Dialectic." In *The Skeptical Tradition,* ed. Myles Burnyeat. Berkeley and Los Angeles: University of California Press, 1983, pp. 253–286.

PETER R. DEAR

See also Humanism, Logic; Ramus, Peter; Rhetoric

Diffraction

First identified by Francesco Maria Grimaldi (1618–1663), diffraction refers to nonrectilinear deviations of light passing by, around, or through openings in opaque objects that cannot be ascribed to reflection or refraction. The phenomenon was initially observed as a small widening of the shadow and penumbra of a narrow object, accompanied by bands or fringes of light and color both outside and (more weakly) inside the edges of the shadow. Grimaldi called this *diffractio* in accord with the view—set forth and supported by these and other experiments in his *Physico-mathesis de lumine* (1665)—that light is a rapidly moving undulating fluid that is "split apart" and its undulations altered when flowing past the edges of corporeal objects.

The decades preceding Grimaldi's surprising observations had seen the demonstration of rectilinear propagation, not only in common and ancient experience, but also by careful studies of: eclipses and occultations; the artistic portrayal of light, shadow and penumbra (called *sfumato*); pinhole images in the camera obscura; and general solar projections, as, for example, by Girard Desargues (1591–1661) for sundials.

Grimaldi describes a series of observations for which "especially strong sunlight is required" and that demonstrate "a fourth mode" of the diffusion of light. Next to the outside edges of the shadow are as many as three bands of light, decreasing in size and intensity, each one bordered by colored lights, bluish toward, and reddish on the side away from, the shadow. They follow cornered edges and on inside corners concur and are "augmented intensely or mixed." Also noted was a pair of bands inside the shadow parallel to the edges, and at the inside corner Grimaldi's diagram shows a set of five dark-bordered feather-shaped lights crossing these bands, apparently emanating from the corner. A second aperture casts a bright cone whose edges are colored "partly red and most especially blue." No detailed measurements are reported.

In the 1670s, various incomplete accounts of Grimaldi's hypotheses and observations circulated. Citing "the affinity" of Grimaldi's views to his own pulse theory, Robert Hooke (1635–1702) added observations in which "rays deflect into the shadow" (Steuwer 1970, 192). Relying solely on such reports, Isaac Newton (1642–1727) described rows of colors both outside and inside the shadow. Convinced that light is not a pulse or pression, else, as with sound, there would be no shadows, Newton explained these bands as an "inflection" of light corpuscles through the same ether gradient that causes refractions. Diffraction had joined the phenomena to be observed and explained; thus, for example, Newton asked for reports of sudden changes in the apparent colors of Jupiter's moons as they were occulted by the planet.

Some time before completing the *Principia* (1687), Newton observed diffraction for himself (Book I, Props. 94–96) and now explained it (and refraction) by the action of attractive and repulsive forces. By 1704 (in the *Opticks*), Newton had carried out his own detailed measurements with which he inconclusively ended the text (Book III), his "Design" having been "interrupted"; there the "Queries" begin in which, in 1717, he reintroduced an ether gradient. Returning to a force dynamics (*Principia,* 1726), Newton saw that the causes of inflection must be different from those causing refraction.

Investigation and speculation along both wave and corpuscular lines continued inconclusively for nearly a century but was secured by the wave-theorist Augustin Fresnel's (1788–1827) successful account in 1819.

BIBLIOGRAPHY

Buchwald, Jed Z. *The Rise of the Wave Theory of Light: Optical Theory and Experiment in the Early Nineteenth Century.* Chicago: University of Chicago Press, 1989.

Cantor, G. N. *Optics After Newton: Theories of Light in Britain and Ireland, 1704–1840.* Manchester: Manchester University Press, 1983.

Grimaldi, Francesco Maria. *Physico-mathesis de lvmine, coloribvs, et iride, ...* Bologna, 1665. Repr. Bologna: Forni, 1963. London: Dawsons of Pall Mall, 1966.

Hakfoort, Casper. *Optics in the Age of Euler: Conceptions on the Nature of Light, 1700–1795.* Cambridge: Cambridge University Press, 1995.

Hall, A. Rupert. *All Was Light: An Introduction to Newton's Opticks.* Oxford: Clarendon, 1993.

Stuewer, Roger H. "A Critical Analysis of Newton's Work on Diffraction." *Isis* 61 (1970), 188–205.

STEPHEN STRAKER

See also Camera Obscura; Grimaldi, Francesco Maria; Light Transmission; Optics

Digby, Kenelm (1603–1665)

A diplomat, soldier, and natural philosopher, Digby studied mathematics and astronomy in Oxford at Gloucester Hall from 1618 to 1620 but did not obtain a degree. Born and raised a Catholic, he converted to Anglicanism briefly in 1630 but returned to the Catholic Church shortly after the sudden death of his wife, Venetia, in 1633 and became a vocal apologist for Catholicism for the remainder of his life. Beginning in the late 1630s, Digby devoted himself to the study of religion, natural philosophy, and occultism.

An Aristotelian, Digby is best known in natural philosophy for his study *Two Treatises, in One . . . the Nature of Bodies; in the Other, the Nature of Mans Soule* (1644). Deeply influenced by Cartesian philosophy and logic, Digby begins the first treatise with basic definitions of physical properties and proceeds to discuss particles in matter—often called *atoms*—arguing that light is material and in motion.

Digby was a consummate virtuoso of the seventeenth century, and his qualitative discussion of mechanical philosophy is often seen as indicative of his superficial knowledge of it. However, Digby said his main goal in the treatises was to prove that souls were immaterial and immortal, indicating that his contribution may have been intended to be more spiritual than scientific. He also wrote a treatise in 1658 on the efficacy of the "weapon salve," which healed by being placed on the weapon that had caused the injury. Digby also studied alchemy, obtaining many alchemical "recipes," and wrote commentaries on alchemy as well.

BIBLIOGRAPHY

Dobbs, Betty Jo T. "Studies in the Natural Philosophy of Sir Kenelm Digby," Parts I–III. *Ambix* 18 (1971), 1–25; 20 (1973), 143–163; 21 (1974), 1–28.

Petersson, R. T. *Sir Keneim Digby: The Ornament of England, 1603–1665.* London: Jonathan Cape, 1956.

BRUCE JANACEK

See also Religion and Natural Philosophy

Digges, Thomas (ca. 1546–1595)

An English mathematician and politician known for his Copernicanism. Educated by his father, Leonard, and by John Dee (1527–1608), he edited and expanded his father's mathematical works after the elder Digges's death in 1559. These included a work concerning the geometry of surveying—his *Pantometria* of 1571 and his *Stratioticos* of 1579, a guide to mathematics and military affairs of use to the common soldier. In subsequent editions, he appended fresh discussions of ballistics to them, derived partly from his own experiments and partly from his father's research.

The younger Digges was also keenly interested in astronomy. His short tract on the new star of 1572—*Alae sue scalae mathematicae* (1573)—contained a very accurate observational record that is considered to be second in accuracy only to the work of Tycho Brahe (1546–1601). Brahe himself devoted some thirty pages in his own work on the new star to Digges's results.

However, it is an appendix to his father's work that has received the most attention from modern scholars. At the end of the 1576 edition of his father's *Prognostication Everlastinge,* Thomas Digges added *A Perfit Description of the Caelestiall Orbes.* Essentially a summary and endorsement of the first book of Nicolaus Copernicus's (1473–1543) *De revolutionibus* (1543), it placed special emphasis on the physical arguments in favor of a moving earth. It is distinguished by Digges's conception of an infinite universe, or at least a sphere of fixed stars that has no visible limit. In his universe, the stars were distributed throughout this limitless space. Stars situated at greater distances from the earth faded until they could not be seen. For some modern historians, this description has lent additional circumstantial evidence to the claim that Thomas Digges or his father had experimented with a sort of telescopic instrument.

BIBLIOGRAPHY

Johnson, Francis R., and S. V. Larkey. "Thomas Digges, the Copernican System, and the Idea of Infinity of the Universe in 1576." *Huntington Library Bulletin* 5 (1934), 69–117.

Ronan, Colin A. "Leonard and Thomas Digges." *Endeavour: Review of the Progress of Science* 16 (1992), 91–94.

GARY MCINTYRE

See also Brahe, Tycho; Copernicanism; Infinity of the World

Discourse, Styles of

The term *discourse* refers generally to substantial oral or written communication addressed to an audience, as opposed to an expressive utterance, brief comment, or conversation. In this essay, style refers to both the genre or kind of work and the manner of expression. In the Renaissance, rhetorical discussions of style treated many figures of speech involving word patterns (schemes), comparisons, turns of meaning (tropes), and strategies of thought. Authors during the Scientific Revolution expanded and altered the genres of scientific discourse commonly employed in the Middle Ages, and they adopted a wider range of stylistic expression.

During the High Middle Ages, natural philosophers generally chose genres of discourse in which demonstrative and dialectical argument predominated: tracts, treatises, commentaries, and questionaries. As A. C. Crombie (1994) has pointed out, in this period the participants in scientific discussion were primarily philosophers who were concerned with theoretical knowledge and with explicating for their students newly recovered texts of the Greeks and commentaries on these works.

Since the conventional genres of scientific discourse of the Middle Ages and variations on these continued to be found in the late sixteenth century and in the seventeenth, a brief description of these styles follows. Exposition and description served to communicate a range of purposes, from demonstrations to speculations, from observations to axiomatic and discursive proofs. In the treatises and commentaries on recovered texts, the style

of presentation could range from the conversational prose of Albert the Great, Peter Peregrinus, or Nicole Oresme to the terse, spare approach of Thomas Bradwardine, William of Heytesbury, or Thomas Aquinas. Introductions to such treatises sometimes contained more expansive and figured prose, particularly if the author desired to situate his work in relation to the hierarchy of academic disciplines or to relate it to knowledge in general. Figures of speech, such as metaphor and analogy, appeared often in the texts themselves, where they were employed to illuminate difficult material. But eloquence, for the sheer love of eloquent expression, was not characteristic.

Demonstration was the preferred method of attaining or guaranteeing scientific knowledge. It required both logical and material rigor for its perfection, knowledge of causes or principles that could be presented in a sound syllogism. Its mode of presentation varied from the axiomatic to the discursive. When demonstrations were not possible, matter being contingent or causes unknown, dialectical argument came into play. Dialectical argument as practiced in the Middle Ages was generally concise and precise in style. The disputation genre, or its related form the "questionary," proved to be particularly economical and effective in treating problems arising from texts or from nature itself. Differences of opinion could be carefully aired, and a resolution of these problems reached based on the most acceptable or the most probable opinion. Scholars focused the inquiry by framing a central question. The author then proceeded to examine all of the opinions deemed relevant or worthy of consideration. Refutations of less probable opinions in the form of doubts or objections followed. When an opinion appeared to offer the best solution to the question, the scholar brought the disputation to a close, adding whatever qualifications seemed appropriate. This genre proved to be an excellent tool for instruction, for it provided a focused, exhaustive consideration and an economical and efficient method of arriving at the most probable answer to a scientific question.

Questionaries were employed during the sixteenth and seventeenth centuries, and the disputation continued to furnish the format for theoretical inquiry, as well as for academic examinations. Changes in discourse styles occurred as applications of theory to nature claimed more and more attention. At the same time, scientific inquiry extended beyond the universities and was often addressed to less expert audiences. The directions of these stylistic changes was influenced by the new tastes associated with the Renaissance.

Italian humanism ushered in an appreciation for Ciceronian style, gathered from the orations and letters of the Roman senator. His rhetorical arguments were interwoven with appeals to the emotions and from the character of the speaker. Ciceronian prose was replete with imaginative comparisons, vivid description, figures of speech, humor, and digressions, all characteristic of rhetoric.

At the beginning of the Scientific Revolution, the new taste in expression not only affected the style of scientific writing, it also evoked an expansion of the conventional genres. The letter became less formal and formulaic than medieval letters had been as authors chose to communicate scientific matters in the Ciceronian informal, friendly manner. While addressed ostensibly to one person, these letters—often quite lengthy—were meant to be published. Printing offered the possibility of large, international audiences. Latin was preferred for reaching these larger audiences. Galileo Galilei (1564–1642), however, broke with tradition, preferring to write his scientific letters in the vernacular. He was engaged in published correspondence on matters of great significance to science with such scholars as Christoph Scheiner (1573–1650), (through Mark Welser) on sunspots, with Orazio Grassi (1583–1654) on comets, and with Johannes Kepler (1571–1630) on Galileo's discoveries with the telescope.

Letters were also to become a medium for exchange of information in the new scientific societies. In the Royal Society, these began as simple letters addressed to the secretary of the society, Henry Oldenburg (ca. 1619–1677) when the *Transactions* were first published in 1665. Under the influence of Francis Bacon (1561–1626), Thomas Sprat (1635–1713), and John Wilkins (1614–1672), these letters eschewed ornate language or figures of speech. As Charles Bazerman (1988) has shown, the letter became less laconic and descriptions of procedures more detailed as scientists began to defend their experiments from the criticisms of readers. Isaac Newton's (1642–1727) exchanges with Ignace Pardies (1636–1673) in the *Transactions* of 1672 illustrate these changes. The scientific article began to take form.

The disputation at the start of the Scientific Revolution continued to be a fruitful vehicle for the investigation of a theoretical question or a scientific problem. But the question-answer format no longer satisfied the

humanist-natural philosophers who used it. For example, when Orazio Grassi argued for the presence of comets beyond the sphere of the Moon, he wrote his *Disputation* in continuous prose, framed it with a prologue and a postscript, and included metaphors and humor. Delivered initially as a dialogue at the Collegio Romano in 1618, Grassi presents arguments for his thesis and refutes possible objections to these consecutively rather than in the pro and contra sections of Scholastic dialectics. He creates thereby a hybrid genre that more nearly resembles an oration than a disputation. The dialectical concern with airing both sides of an argument continues to be important to natural philosophers, but rhetorical touches and continuous prose became more common.

The questionary form of the disputation also underwent a transformation in Galileo's hand. In his treatise *On Motion* (1590), Galileo considers questions of dialectical nature in an essay form. He poses questions that have been treated in questionaries, but he approaches them in a more fluent fashion, offering "demonstrations" of his contentions in successive sections. Objections are considered along the way and refuted in the course of his discussion. His style here is dialectical in character, spare and neutral.

The dialectical impulse also found expression in another humanistic genre, dialogue. The recovery of Plato's dialogues and Cicero's dialogue *De oratore* inspired scholars to take up scientific subjects in that genre. Galileo wrote his most famous and fateful work, *Dialogue on the Two Chief World Systems* (1632), as a humanistic text composed in the vernacular. Closely related to the disputation, the dialogue genre enabled authors to consider both sides of a question but to do so in a real-life context, with real or fictive interlocutors. Such treatment permitted the introduction of rhetorical elements, persuasive techniques that went beyond barebones deductive or inferential arguments. The rhetorical aspects were not always helpful in advancing the scientific argument, however, as the case of Galileo's trial demonstrates. Giordano Bruno (1548–1600) also received severe criticism after the publication of his extravagantly rhetorical dialogue in defense of Copernicanism, *The Ash Wednesday Supper* (1586).

Even Galileo seems to have decided not to rely on the Platonic style of dialogue alone by the time he wrote *Discourses Concerning the Two New Sciences* (1638). Although he cast this work as a dialogue in Italian with the same interlocutors as his earlier *Dialogue,* he included also a lengthy discussion of a Latin work by "the Academician" (Galileo) that absorbs two days of the four days of dialogue Galileo was to complete. The title "Discourses" (*Discoursi*) indicates a shift in stylistic treatment. Galileo couches the interlocutors discussion in Italian when a looser discussion of observations and experiments is desired. But as William A. Wallace has pointed out, Galileo's intent to reach an international audience of scholars is manifest in his choice of Latin for the development of his most important arguments. This dual treatment permitted more flexibility, allowing Galileo to reserve dialectical and demonstrative science for the systematic Latin treatise and allot to the Italian exchanges a more entertaining rhetorical consideration.

Overt rhetorical appeals and flourishes were to fade from the texts of scientific works as the Scientific Revolution advanced. The low opinion of rhetoric voiced by René Descartes (1596–1650) and John Locke (1632–1704) and the views of Thomas Sprat expressed in his *History of the Royal Society* (1667) made scientists wary of the free use of rhetoric such as had been enjoyed by Galileo. Treatises and articles gradually replaced the hybrid disputation, the letter, and the dialogue as serious scientific texts.

BIBLIOGRAPHY

Bazerman, Charles. *Shaping Written Knowledge: The Genre and Activity of the Experimental Article in Science.* Madison: University of Wisconsin Press, 1988.

Crombie. A. C. *Styles of Scientific Thinking in the European Tradition: The History of Argument and Explanation Especially in the Mathematical and Biomedical Sciences and Arts.* 3 vols. London: Duckworth, 1994.

Moss, Jean Dietz. *Novelties in the Heavens: Rhetoric and Science in the Copernican Controversy.* Chicago: University of Chicago Press, 1993.

Wisan, Winifred. "Galileo and the Emergence of a New Scientific Style." In *Pisa Conference Proceedings,* ed. J. Hintikka, D. Gruender, and E. Agazzi. Dordrecht: Reidel, 1980, vol. 1, 311–339.

JEAN DIETZ MOSS

See also Correspondence Networks; Demonstration; Dialectic; Logic; Rhetoric; Universal Languages

Dissection

In teaching situations during medieval times, surgeons dissected, while physicians, who had higher societal status, read the commentary of Galen of Pergamum (sec-

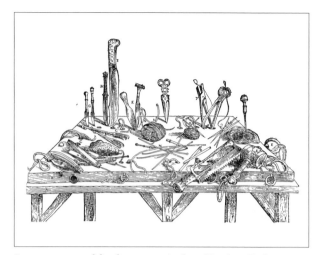

Instruments used for dissection. Andreas Vesalius, De humani corporis fabrica *(1543).*

ond century). The Black Death, entering Europe in 1348, changed some of these attitudes. Galen had written nothing about plague, and medical theory, the province of the university-educated physicians, was as ineffective against it as the doctors were. As a result, the physicians lost some of their status while the practical, empirically minded surgeons gained. The plague may have been the reason cities pushed for more dissections and made the bodies of executed criminals more readily available. For instance, in 1368 the Great Council of Venice decreed that the College of Surgeons would conduct at least one human dissection annually. In 1370 the council ordered the city's doctors to contribute to the costs of these dissections because their attendance would improve medical knowledge. By this time, anatomies had become regular features of medical schools.

Another change was that doctors started to do portions of anatomies themselves. This became the full-time practice of the most famous anatomist of all, Andreas Vesalius (1514–1564). One of his teachers was Joannes Guinter (ca. 1505–1574), who actually did some dissecting himself and even let his students participate. Guinter's dissection manual, published in 1536, did advocate that anatomy, formally considered mostly for study by surgeons, be fundamental to the education of the physician. Vesalius criticized Guinter's technique but followed his advice. While doing human dissections himself, Vesalius discovered many Galenic anatomical errors. The mores of Galen's day allowed him to dissect only animals. Thus, he sometimes made incorrect extrapolations to human anatomy. The authority of observation came to the forefront as Vesalius and others began a program of making new anatomical discoveries and correcting the mistakes of the old authorities.

William Harvey (1578–1657) and his famous teacher, Girolamo Fabrici (ca. 1533–1619), realized that the revolution occurring in anatomy should be extended into physiology. Harvey was more successful in doing this. His very careful and extensive dissections laid the groundwork for him to both observe and reason that Galen's explanation for the motion of the heart and blood was wrong. They also helped Harvey to arrive at the correct explanation.

The last great change concerning dissection during the Scientific Revolution came with the discovery of the microscope. It extended the vision of the anatomist into new realms, and naturally new discoveries continued to be made. One example of these microanatomists is Marcello Malpighi (1628–1694). While microscopically examining the lungs and learning their correct structure, he discovered the capillaries. This confirmed Harvey's theory that the blood circulated and assured its general acceptance. Examples of other discoveries are the pancreatic duct (by Wirsung in 1642), the testicular duct (by Highmore in 1651), the submandibular duct (by Wharton in 1656), and the parotid duct (by Steno in 1660).

The changes involving dissection that occurred during the Scientific Revolution paved the way toward modern medical approaches and methods. They also directed researchers into new paths, such as the search for the life-supporting component of the air.

BIBLIOGRAPHY

Wear, Andrew. "William Harvey and the 'Way of the Anatomists.'" *History of Science* 21 (1983), 223–249.

French, Roger, and Andrew Wear, eds. *The Medical Revolution of the Seventeenth Century.* Cambridge: Cambridge University Press, 1989.

EMERSON T. MCMULLEN

See also Anatomy; Harvey, William; Malpijhi, Marcello; Vesalius, Andreas

Dodoens, Rembert (1516–1585)

Born in Mechelen, Belgium, he read medicine at the University of Louvain, from which he graduated in 1535. After traveling about France, Italy, and Germany for a decade, he returned to his native city, where he lived until 1574, the year he was appointed physician to Emperor Rudolph II. He was in Vienna at the same time as Charles de l'Écluse (Clusius, 1526–1609), already a friend of his because they both belonged to the group of scientists and intellectuals that held its meetings at the home of the famous typographer of Antwerp Cristophe Plantin (d. 1589). Later he lived in Cologne and Antwerp, and in 1582 he moved to the University of Leiden, where he taught general therapeutics and pathology.

Although Dodoens penned books on cosmography and medicine, his historical importance is owed to the work on botany he carried out in close conjunction with his friends Clusius and Matias L'Obel (Lobelius, 1538–1616). Following several essays on botany, he published a comprehensive herbarium in Flemish entitled *Cruydeboeck* (1554). This work was illustrated using the engravings from the smaller edition of *De historia stirpium* of Leonhart Fuchs (1501–1566), the text of which was also used, although *Cruydeboeck* is more than just a translation of Fuchs's treatise. The French edition, translated by Clusius and revised by Dodoens himself, came out in 1557. It was published by Plantin, who also printed Dodoens's main work on botany, *Stirpium historiae pemptades* (1583), an early attempt at classifying plants within a general framework, which introduced numerous innovations based mainly on the materials and engravings he shared with Clusius and L'Obel.

BIBLIOGRAPHY

Dodoens, R. *Histoire des plantes.* Trans. C. de l'Écluse (1557). *Facsimilé avec introduction, commentaires et la concordance avec la terminologie scientifique moderne par* J. E. Opsomer. Bruxelles: Centre National d'Histoire des Sciences, 1978.

Hunger, F. W. T. "Dodonée comme botaniste." *Janus* 22 (1917), 151–162.

JOSÉ M. LÓPEZ-PIÑERO

See also Botany; Fuchs, Leonhart

Dürer, Albrecht (1471–1528)

Printmaker, painter, art theorist, he received his early training in Nuremberg, a city exemplary for its artistic production and patronage. He learned the goldsmith's craft in his father's workshop and then was taught painting and printmaking as an apprentice to Michael Wolgemut. He later traveled in southern Germany, northern Italy, and the Netherlands. Although his childhood and adolescence were passed in the milieu of late-medieval craft traditions, he very early evinced an interest in the

Dürer's self-portrait. From Albrecht Dürers Randzeichnungen aus dem Gebetbuche des Kaisers Maximilian I *(1845).*

artistic concepts of the Italian Renaissance. His mature art was a synthesis of Italian mathematical precepts and northern focus on particularity. He was justly praised during his lifetime for his skill as a printmaker and an engraver, and his paintings of sacred scenes and portraits gained him prosperity and social standing. From his circle of humanist friends (Willibald Pirckheimer, Konrad Celtis), he gained access to ideas then current: ideas about a new role for the artist and a new position for the visual arts. He became acquainted with the theories of Leon Battista Alberti (1404–1472) and the teaching of Marsilio Ficino (1433–1499), who argued that the artist and the scholar share similar functions. Where the scholar explores the secrets of nature, the artist uses his creative power to make visible the power of the Creator.

Dürer accepted this almost religious calling as his own and set about to reform German art. Arguing that boys were trained in their craft with no knowledge of underlying mathematical principles (like wild plants), he spent his last years writing a series of treatises for the education of young artists. His aim was to raise the practice of art to a science. His theoretical interests were

broad. He studied architectural proportions, animal anatomy, plants, and human proportions. Onto the more abstract ideas of the Italian theorists, he grafted the practical concerns of the mercantile culture of Nuremberg. In 1515 he published his work *The Painter's Manual: A Manual of Measurement of Lines, Areas, and Solids by Means of Compass and Ruler,* which he dedicated to his friend Willibald Pirckheimer. His *Treatise on Proportions,* a work based on the studies on proportion of Vitruvius, was published only after his sudden death in 1528.

Although Dürer wanted to establish his fame as the founder of rational and mathematical principles in German art, he is now most widely known for his exquisite engraving skills and for the particularistic intensity of his animal and plant studies.

BIBLIOGRAPHY

Dürer, Albrecht. *The Painter's Manual: A Manual of Measurement of Lines, Areas, and Solids by Means of Compass and Ruler.* Trans. and Commentary by Walter L. Strauss. New York: Abaris Books, 1977.

Hutchison, Jane. *Albrecht Dürer: A Biography.* Princeton, NJ: Princeton University Press, 1992.

Koren, Fritz. *Albrecht Dürer und die Tier-und Pflanzenstudien der Renaissance.* Munich: Prestel Verlag, 1985.

Smith, Jeffrey Chipps. *Nuremberg: A Renaissance City, 1500–1618.* Austin: University of Texas Press, 1983.

MARY G. WINKLER

See also Art; Perspective

Dynamics

Dynamica is a term coined by Gottfried Wilhelm Leibniz (1646–1716) in 1689 during his Italian journey, referring to his doctrine of forces. In that year, he composed an extensive work called *Dynamica,* which remained unpublished at the time. His major publication on the subject is "Specimen Dynamicum," which appeared in the *Acta eruditorum* for 1695, in which he tried to reconcile a variety of metaphysical and mechanical traditions relevant to the notion of force on the basis of a grid of the following four notions: (1) active primitive force is a purely metaphysical entity expressing the activity of substances and is also called *entelechy;* (2) active derivative force is somehow the phenomenal manifestation of an aggregate of metaphysical substances and is measured by living force, or *vis viva;* (3) passive primitive force is purely metaphysical and expresses the imperfection of substances; (4) is passive derivative force, which is also called *inertia,* is its phenomenal manifestation. The connection between metaphysical and phenomenal levels was and still is especially problematic in this account. Leibniz further introduced the distinction between *vis viva,* which pertains to actual motion and is proportional to the square of velocity, and *vis mortua,* or dead force, which pertains to the very beginning of motion and is proportional to infinitesimal velocity. Examples of the latter are Christiaan Huygens's (1629–1695) centrifugal, and Isaac Newton's (1642–1727) centripetal, forces. Leibniz developed his views in several works and tried to establish many laws of nature, such as the law of conservation of force, or *vis viva,* on the metaphysical foundations provided in his system. Although Leibniz's metaphysical preoccupations are extreme even by seventeenth-century standards, at the time notions like motion and force had much larger philosophical dimensions than the modern reader may suspect.

Ca. 1700 the notion of dynamics had a distinctive Leibnizian flavor that Newton found particularly irritating and distasteful. In a manuscript, he complained that "Galileo began to consider the effect of Gravity upon Projectiles. Mr Newton in his *Principia Philosophiae* improved that consideration into a large science. Mr Leibniz christened the child by a new name as if it had been his own, calling it *Dynamica*. . . . But his mark must be set upon all new inventions. And if one may judge by the multitude of new names and characters invented by him, he would go for a great inventor." Although Leibniz's dynamics was primarily a science of living forces, in the quotation above Newton portrayed it as dealing with his own force, a notion more similar to Leibniz's dead force.

Almost exactly a century after Leibniz had coined the term, Joseph-Louis Lagrange (1736–1813), in his classic *Mécanique analytique* (1788), defined dynamics as the science of accelerative forces and of the motions they produce. In his historical outline, he portrayed Galileo Galilei (1564–1642) as the founder of dynamics, a science later perfected by Huygens. Lagrange went on to argue with involuntary irony that mechanics and, therefore, dynamics were then revolutionized by Newton. Thus, by that time it had become customary to call dynamics a doctrine of forces based, unlike Leibniz's, on accelerations, such as Newton's. Newton himself had given the greatest possible emphasis to his doctrine of forces by stating in his *Principia mathematica philosophiae naturalis* (1687) that the whole burden of philosophy consists in investigating the forces from the phenomena of motion and then from the forces to demonstrate the phenomena.

The term *dynamics* is also used by some historians in the sense of science of motion, rather than strictly of forces, and is contrasted to *statics,* or the science of equilibrium of bodies. Ernst Mach (1838–1916), for example, devoted the first two parts of his influential *Die Mechanik in ihrer Entwickelung* (1883; ninth edition, 1933) to the development of the principles of statics and of dynamics, which in his view had been founded by Galileo and by which he meant a science of motion.

These preliminary reflections leave the scholar of the Scientific Revolution with the problem of whether it is legitimate or helpful to talk of a history of dynamics in the seventeenth century, including such actors as Galileo and Huygens, and extending back to the medieval *scientia de motu* (science of motion) and *scientia de ponderibus* (science of weight) and even to the *Quaestiones mechanicae* attributed to Aristotle (384–322 B.C.E.) or to one of his immediate disciples. The answer to this question depends on several factors, such as whether dynamics is taken to mean a science of accelerative forces, a science of motion, or a science of the causes of motion. Further, it depends on the aims and purposes of one's historical research. Historians, however, ought to be aware of the categories of their actors, even if for a variety of reasons they decide not to follow them, and make a conscious and deliberate decision, as opposed to taking for granted that dynamics always existed and that its history can, therefore, be written unproblematically.

BIBLIOGRAPHY

Barbour, J. B. *Absolute or Relative Motion? A Study from a Machian Point of View of the Discovery and Structure of Dynamical Theories.* Cambridge: Cambridge University Press, 1989.

Brackenridge, J. B. *The Key to Newton's Dynamics: The Kepler Problem and the "Principia."* Berkeley and Los Angeles: University of California Press, 1995.

Cohen, I. B. *The Newtonian Revolution: With Illustrations of the Transformation of Scientific Ideas.* Cambridge: Cambridge University Press, 1980.

Gabbey, A. "Force and Inertia in Seventeenth-century Dynamics." *Studies in History and Philosophy of Science* 2 (1971), 1–67.

Westfall, R. S. *Force in Newton's Physics: The Science of Dynamics in the Seventeenth Century.* London: Macdonald; New York: American Elsevier, 1971.

DOMENICO BERTOLONI MELI

See also Kinematics; Leibniz; Gottfried Wilhelm; Mechanics; Motion

E

Educational Reform

In the sixteenth and seventeenth centuries, self-proclaimed educational reformers suggested broad changes in both school curricula and teaching methods. Reformers like Peter Ramus (1515–1572) and Samuel Hartlib (ca. 1600–1662) generally couched their proposals within the context of a general reformation of society, but their vision of a top-down restructuring of the schools experienced only limited success, for they lacked the political power and social organization to implement their plans. Nonetheless, numerous educators of the period found elements of the programs of the reformers attractive and incorporated them alongside more traditional subject matter and methods.

Perhaps the most important change during this period arose as a response to the pressures of humanism. By the late fifteenth century, Italian humanists had successfully promoted a neoclassical pedagogy that sought to train cultured and morally upright citizens who could speak and write in an elegant Ciceronian Latin. While appealing to the European aristocracy as a means for training effective political leaders, humanism experienced staunch resistance in the universities, where Aristotelian natural philosophy and syllogistic disputation continued to be the norm until the late seventeenth century.

Despite this resistance, humanism's primary influence on schooling came in the field of rhetoric. By 1539 Rudolph Agricola's *Dialectical Invention* (*De inventione dialectica;* written ca. 1480 but first published in 1515) had become the standard text in humanist schools throughout northern Europe, replacing the Scholastic *Compendium of Logic* (*Summulae logicales*) of Peter of Spain (fl. ca. 1250). In his text, Agricola (1444–1485) provided the teacher and the student with a methodical introduction to the variety of compositional styles, which students were to master and emulate. Building on Agricola's reforms, the French humanist Peter Ramus sharply derided Scholasticism for its emphasis on abstruse and complex strings of logical arguments. Instead, Ramus and his followers promoted a much simplified logic that stressed diagrammatic methods for analyzing dialectical arguments. Purportedly, Ramus's simplified system of argumentation would allow the student to apply logic to the practicalities of everyday life. This may explain why Ramist reforms were so popular among artisan classes, especially in England where Puritan reformers joined Ramist logic to biblical exegesis.

Practical concerns were even more prominent among the circle of reformers surrounding Samuel Hartlib, who was active in England, between 1628 and 1662. In anticipation of the biblical end times, the Hartlib Circle made educational reform a central part of its sweeping plan for the social and religious reformation of society. Based on Baconian empiricism, their educational system emphasized natural philosophy and mathematics in order to prepare the student for commercial life. Furthermore, since it was believed that knowledge of the natural world would also lead to a greater understanding of God's divine powers, a belief central to natural theology, the study of empirical science also helped advance notions of Puritan piety. Although the political realities of England's Interregnum government prevented the circle's proposals from becoming social reality, the association of its members with members of the future Royal Society helped guarantee that aspects of these reforms, such as the interest in chemical and agricultural knowledge, found a permanent home.

Because of its comprehensiveness and logical coherence, as well as the general conservatism of university faculties, Aristotelian natural philosophy continued to function as the core of the university curriculum throughout the sixteenth and seventeenth centuries. Nevertheless, Scholastic pedagogy proved remarkably open to innovative ideas. Thus, for instance, the heliocentric astronomy of Nicolaus Copernicus (1473–1543) and the geoheliocentric system of Tycho Brahe (1546–1601) were often studied alongside the geocentric astronomies of Aristotle (384–322 B.C.E.) and Ptolemy (ca. 100–ca. 170) without actually replacing them. In Reformation Germany, in particular, the group of mathematicians and astronomers associated with the Lutheran Phillip Melanchthon (1497–1560) was fairly open to Copernican astronomy. A humanist devoted to astronomy and astrology, Melanchthon was responsible for the reformation of the German universities and created numerous new chairs in mathematics and astronomy, thus helping to spread the study of heliocentrism.

During the latter half of the seventeenth century, René Descartes (1596–1650) formulated the first comprehensive new philosophical system to challenge that of Aristotle's and thus attracted considerable support and strong criticism. In short, Descartes provided a method of philosophizing based on deductive arguments arising from first principles and a mechanical philosophy of nature that accepted and accounted for a heliocentric astronomy. Although defenders of Aristotle sharply criticized Cartesian philosophy on cosmological and epistemological grounds, the new philosophy had effectively replaced Aristotle's at the University of Paris by the start of the eighteenth century due, in part, to the growing inability of Aristotelian cosmology to account adequately for new experimental discoveries. In England, the Cambridge Platonists helped introduce Cartesian philosophy to university students, but Cartesianism did not replace the Aristotelian worldview in the English universities as Newtonian natural philosophy was to do in the eighteenth century.

Thus, by the end of the seventeenth century, education in Europe combined traditional and revised methods of Scholastic pedagogy with the philosophical and, eventually, experimental approaches to nature developed during the Scientific Revolution. But the process of educational reform had been both gradual and controversial, involving the efforts of educators throughout Europe and at all levels of education.

BIBLIOGRAPHY

Brockliss, L. W. B. *French Higher Education in the Seventeenth and Eighteenth Centuries: A Cultural History.* Oxford: Clarendon, 1987.

Gascoigne, John. *Cambridge in the Age of the Enlightenment: Science, Religion, and Politics from the Restoration to the French Revolution.* Cambridge: Cambridge University Press, 1989.

———. "A Reappraisal of the Role of the Universities in the Scientific Revolution." In *Reappraisals of the Scientific Revolution,* ed. David C. Lindberg and Robert S. Westman. Cambridge: Cambridge University Press, 1990, pp. 207–260.

Grafton, Anthony, and Lisa Jardine. *From Humanism to the Humanities: Education and the Liberal Arts in Fifteenth- and Sixteenth-Century Europe.* Cambridge, MA: Harvard University Press, 1986.

Grendler, Paul F. *Schooling in Renaissance Italy: Literacy and Learning, 1300–1600.* Baltimore: Johns Hopkins University Press, 1989.

Lawn, Brian. *The Rise and Decline of the Scholastic "Quaestio Disputa": With Special Emphasis on Its Use in the Teaching of Medicine and Science.* Leiden: Brill, 1993.

Webster, Charles. *The Great Instauration: Science, Medicine, and Reform, 1626–1660.* London: Duckworth, 1975.

DAVID A. REID

See also Aristotelianism; Gresham College; Hartlib, Samuel; Humanism; Medical Education; Ramus, Peter

Electricity

This concept emerged during the first quarter of the seventeenth century, closely associated with magnetism. It soon became important within the development of matter theory and the treatment of occult qualities.

William Gilbert (1544–1603) is often credited as the founder of the science of electricity. He was the first to use the term *electricity,* which he derived from the Greek word for the attractive properties of amber. Gilbert's key contribution consists of the experimental discovery of many "electric" substances—beyond the already known amber—that caused the attraction and repulsion of a variety of substances when rubbed. Rejecting medieval and Renaissance "sympathies" and seeking instead a material mode of interaction, he explained the electric phenomena by combining concepts taken from alchemy and Aristotelian viscosity and cohesion. Without providing many details, he claimed that emanations of electical vapor, or effluvia, were the vehicle of the attraction.

Niccolò Cabeo (1585–1650), a leading Jesuit mathematician and natural philosopher, challenged Gilbert's presentation of both magnetism and electricity. Implementing the Jesuit program aimed at achieving intellectual supremacy, Cabeo first established himself as an authority in electricity through the finding of many new phenomena and electric substances and then replaced Gilbert's effluvia, explaining electrical attraction through emitted streams that displace the surrounding air, forming a wind that can either attract or repel bodies.

In the second quarter of the century, mechanical philosophers offered another explanation for electrical phenomena. Noting that not all of the electric substances emit effluvia, René Descartes (1596–1650) proposed invisible elastic particles. Also trying to rationally explain directly unintelligible powers, Pierre Gassendi (1592–1655) compared the action of these particles to the movement of the chameleon's tongue.

In England, electrical experiments became popular in the Royal Society; Robert Boyle (1627–1691) intervened in the debate in 1675 with a book entitled *Experiments and Notes About the Mechanical Origin and Production of Electricity,* in which he countered Cabeo's and the Cartesian theories and proposed an explanation based upon emission and refraction of effluvia. Within the Royal Society are found the major subsequent developments in both electric theory and experimentation. On the Continent, Otto von Guericke (1602–1686) carried out important experimental work.

BIBLIOGRAPHY

Freudenthal, Gad. "Clandestine Stoic Concepts in Mechanical Philosophy: The Problem of Electrical Attraction." In *Renaissance and Revolution,* ed. J. V. Field and Frank A. J. L. James. Cambridge: Cambridge University Press, 1993, pp. 161–172.

Heilbron, J. L. *Electricity in the Seventeenth and Eighteenth Centuries.* Los Angeles: University of California Press, 1979.

RENZO BALDASSO

See also Gilbert, William

Elements

One can distinguish among methodological, ontological or philosophical and chemical concepts of element in early-modern and modern times. Methodologically, *elements* meant fundamental principles or axioms of a science. There were different philosophical concepts of elements from the sixteenth until the late eighteenth century. The Scholastic tradition, which goes back to

Aristotle (384–322 B.C.E.), and the Paracelsian philosophy of the sixteenth and seventeenth centuries conceived of elements not as observable natural bodies but as their *constituents.* All natural bodies were seen as *mixta* generated from different elemental constituents. *Constituent* here means not a corporeal part but a generator of natural bodies and a carrier of irreducible qualitites. In accordance with this, a natural body was called a *mixtum* because it was generated from different entities and because its properties were derived from the irreducible qualities of these entities. But it was seen as being completely homogeneous in all of its corporeal parts. This homogeneity was brought about through the development of a relationship of dominance between the qualities of the constituents. These *philosophical* concepts of elements have causal explanatory functions for (1) the generation of natural bodies; (2) their multiplicity and their observable properties; and (3) their alterations.

The Scholastic tradition understood all natural bodies as *mixta* generated from, and consisting of, four elements: fire, water, air, and earth. Each element was a carrier of two opposite qualities. Fire was hot and dry, water cold and wet, air warm and wet, earth dry and cold. The elements could be transformed into one another by transferring a quality. Within the dichotomy of the Aristotelian concepts of matter and form, elements were *formed matter* when compared with the unformed primary matter, but *matter* when compared with the form of the natural *mixta.*

The Paracelsian philosophy amalgamated the Scholastic tradition of the concept of elements with similar concepts from different Renaissance philosophies, mainly Neoplatonism and the alchemical philosophy. The Paracelsians distinguished between elements and principles. Like the Aristotelians, they assumed four elements. The two elements fire and air belonged exclusively to the two spheres next to the earth and were constituents of planets and stars. The elements earth and water belonged to the sphere of the earth. They were *matter* or *matrixes* of all natural bodies. Principles were form-endowing *semina.* The Paracelsians assumed three principles— Mercury, Sulfur, and Salt—each bearing its characteristic irreducible qualities. These form-endowing *semina* were thought of as noncorporeal or spiritual carriers of qualities that would invest the natural *mixta* with corporeality and all perceptible properties. In the generation of the natural bodies of the earth, all three principles should unite with an elemental matrix, either earth or water, thus creating observable natural bodies. The cause of the multiplicity of natural bodies was seen in the difference in the dominance of one or the other principle. This relationship of dominance could be altered in natural alterations or in chemical operations. The great majority of chemists in the sixteenth century and the first half of the seventeenth were adherents of this Paracelsian theory of elements and principles. They interpreted the flame that develops during a combustion as the indicator of the principle Sulfur, the fume as that of Mercury, and the remaining ashes as that of Salt.

During the seventeenth century, chemists altered the Paracelsian concept of elements and principles, mainly by referring to dry distillation as a source of experimental knowledge about elements and principles. The five tangible substances into which some natural bodies, mainly vegetable materials, could be decomposed by distillation—water, acid or alcoholic spirits, combustible oil, salt, and earth—were first seen as representatives of the five principles of all natural bodies. During the last three decades of the seventeenth century, chemists attempted to identify the distilled substances with the principles. This went hand in hand with the establishment of the concepts of chemical combination, affinity, and chemical compound. From this, a multiplicity of empirical and theoretical problems emerged, thus initiating a slow process of fundamental alteration of the traditional philosophical concept of elements.

In the seventeenth century, the two main opponents of both the Scholastic and the Paracelsian concepts of the elements were atomistic philosophies, which attempted to integrate the philosophical concept of elements, and mechanical-corpuscular philosophies. Representatives of the first are Daniel Sennert (1572–1637) and Joachim Jungius (1587–1657) in Germany, Claude Gillermet de Bérigard (1578–1653/64) and Johann Chrysostomos Magnenus (1590–1679) in Italy, and Sebastian Basso (fl. 1560–1623) and Etienne de Clave (fl. 1646) in France. The atomistic theory of elements differed in many aspects from the modern chemical concept of elements: (1) the atoms of elements were seen as the ultimate and irreducible entities of matter, and they, in turn, cause the multiplicity of natural bodies; (2) in accordance with this, there were only a few (five) kinds of elemental atoms; (3) elements were not themselves natural bodies but exclusively constituents of natural bodies; and (4) all natural bodies were *mixta* that consist of all five elements. De Clave wrote in his *Cours de chimie*

(1646) that the five elements that chemists admit are simple bodies that actually preexist as bodily parts in all natural *mixta* and can be obtained through their analysis. Joachim Jungius's concept of hypostatical principles has much in common with both De Clave's and Daniel Sennert's atomistic theory of elements. *Hypostatical* is the opposite of *synhypostatical* and refers to parts of a body that can exist outside that body after their decomposition. Refuting the Aristotelian concept of the synhypostatical parts of natural *mixta* that cannot be separated from each other (i.e., matter and form), Jungius claimed that natural mixta consist of different hypostatical elementary atoms. They were conceived of as undecomposable, intransmutable, and irreducible causes of the multiplicity of natural bodies and their alterations. The consequence of this explanatory status is that only a few kind of different atoms or a few elements were admitted. Jungius did not specify the physical and chemical nature of these elements.

Seventeenth-century mechanical-corpuscular philosophy was either hostile or skeptical toward the concept of elements. As in ancient atomism, the ultimate constituents of matter were seen as differently sized, shaped, and moved particles of a qualitatively indifferent universal matter. The mechanical-corpuscular philosopher who dealt most deeply with the concept of elements was Robert Boyle (1627–1691). In *The Sceptical Chymist* (1661), he tried to answer the question of whether hypostatical elements in the sense of the seventeenth-century atomistic theory of elements exist or not. He investigated it both theoretically and empirically, referring to natural alterations of the bodies and, mainly, to chemical procedures. In his theoretical investigation, Boyle questioned and criticized all fundamental meanings of the atomistic concept of elements. However, this critique did not end in a positive definition of elements. From a theoretical point of view, Boyle considered the existence of elements to be possible but not necessary. The empirical investigation led to a similar result. Boyle interpreted many natural alterations of bodies and artificial chemical transformations as transmutations, thus challenging the atomistic concept of unchangeable atoms of elements. Other procedures were understood as chemical analysis or as combinations of basic substances that conserve their integrity during the chemical process. These stable substances were possible candidates for elements. The result of both his theoretical and his empirical investigation was skepticism regarding the existence of elements.

The concept of the *chemical element* developed slowly during the eighteenth century alongside, and independently of, the philosophical concept of the element, culminating in Antoine Lavoisier's concept of the chemical element. Lavoisier (1743–1794) defined chemical elements as substances into which bodies can be reduced by decomposition. In contrast to the philosophical concept of elements, chemical elements are not absolutely irreducible constituents of natural bodies but substances that are (1) irreducible by a *chemical* operation (i.e., by chemical analysis); (2) not exclusively constituents of natural bodies but natural bodies themselves; and (3) not all found in every natural or artificial chemical compound but in specific parts of specific compounds. Furthermore, a great number of elements is assumed. Besides elements in the sense of the ultimate and irreducible entities of matter, a second concept emerged within the framework of eighteenth-century theory of acids, alkalis, and salts and the phlogiston theory, both of which were closely tied to experimental practice. A set of substances was seen as chemically undecomposable (i.e., acids, alkalis, metal calces, and phlogiston), later enlarged by the different "kinds of air." In his new theories of combustion and of acids, alkalis, and salts, Lavoisier reorganized the reference of *analysis* and *combination,* or synthesis. Metal calces, for example, were now conceived of as chemical compounds, whereas metals were seen as chemically undecomposable substances. Lavoisier thus reversed the reference of the concept of undecomposable substances and defined them as chemical elements, thereby separating them definitively from the philosophical concept of elements.

BIBLIOGRAPHY

Debus, Allen G. "Fire Analysis and the Elements in the Sixteenth and the Seventeenth Centuries." *Annals of Science* 23 (1967), 127–147.

Guerlac, Henry. *Lavoisier—The Crucial Year: The Background and Origin of His First Experiments on Combustion in 1772.* Ithaca, NY: Cornell University Press, 1961. Repr. New York: Gordon and Breach, 1990, pp. 93–101 and passim.

Hall, Marie Boas. "The History of the Concept of Element." In *John Dalton and the Progress of Science,* ed. D. S. L. Cardwell. Manchester: Manchester University Press, 1968, pp. 21–39.

Klein, Ursula. *Verbindung und Affinität.* Basel: Birkhäuser, 1994, pp. 36–87 and passim.

Meinel, Christoph. "Der Begriff des chemischen Elementes bei Joachim Jungius." *Sudhoffs Archiv* 66 (1982), 313–338.

Pagel, Walter. *Paracelsus: An Introduction to Philosophical Medicine in the Era of the Renaissance.* Basel: Karger, 1958. 2nd ed. 1982, pp. 82–104 and passim.

Perrin, C. E. "Lavoisier's Table of the Elements: A Reappraisal." *Ambix* 20 (1973), 95–105.

Siegfried, Robert. "Lavoisier's Table of Simple Substances: Its Origin and Interpretation." *Ambix* 29 (1982), 29–48.

URSULA KLEIN

See also Chemical Philosophy; Chemistry; Paracelsus

Emblematics

In the sixteenth and seventeenth centuries, a new genre of literature known as the emblem book became popular. A rich, visual language of symbolic images was created that soon spread far beyond the pages of the emblem book and had an impact on many aspects of society, including the practice of science.

Andrea Alciati (1492–1550), an Italian lawyer and humanist, published the first emblem book in 1531, entitled *Emblemata*. This work is a collection of emblems, each consisting of an engraved image and text. Taken together, the image and the text form a puzzle that was meant to entertain and also often to impart a moral lesson. Alciati's *Emblemata* went through more than two hundred editions, and by the early seventeenth century hundreds of other authors had produced emblem books.

A typical emblem consisted of a picture, a brief motto—often taken from a classical source—and a longer epigram that explained the lesson in more detail. One emblem, for example, has a picture of a hunter aiming his bow at a bird flying overhead, while a snake curls around his leg. The motto declares: "Those who contemplate the heights come to grief." The epigram relates a story, taken from one of Aesop's fables, of a man who was so intent on his high-flying prey that he failed to notice a snake attacking him. Emblem-book writers drew on many earlier traditions for their ideas, including Egyptian hieroglyphics, Aesopic fables, ancient books of proverbs, and even the images on antique coins.

The scientific discipline most directly affected by the emblem tradition was natural history. Although Alciati had included some emblems of animals and plants, later writers, such as Joachim Camerarius (1534–1598), produced emblem books that focused exclusively on animal and plant emblems. Camerarius was a highly respected botanist and physician, and he saw his collection of emblems as a contribution to natural history as well as to the

ILLVSTR. XX.   Book.3

Looke here, and marke (her fickly birds to feed)
How freely this kinde *Pelican* doth bleed.
See, how (when other *Salves* could not be found)
To cure their forrowes, fhe, her felfe doth wound ;
And, when this holy *Emblem,* thou fhalt fee,
Lift up thy foule to him, who dy'd for thee.
    For, this our *Hieroglyphick* would expreffe
That *Pelican,* which in the *Wilderneffe*
Of this vaft *World,* was left (as all alone)
Our miferable *Nature* to bemone ;
And, in whofe eyes, the teares of pitty ftood,
When he beheld his owne unthankfull *Brood*
His *Favours,* and his *Mercies,* then, contemne,
When with his wings he would have brooded them :
And, fought their endleffe peace to have confirm'd,
Though, to procure his ruine, they were arm'd.
    To be their *Food,* himfelfe he freely gave ;
His *Heart* was pierc'd, that he their *Soules* might fave.
Becaufe, they difobey'd the *Sacred will,*
He, did the *Law of Righteoufneffe* fulfill ;
And, to that end (though guiltleffe he had bin)
Was offred, for our *Vniverfall finne.*
    Let mee Oh *God !* forever, fixe mine eyes
Vpon the Merit of that *Sacrifize :*
Let me retaine a due commemoration
Of thofe deare *Mercies, and* that bloudy *Paffion,*
Which here is meant ; and, by true *Faith,* ftill, feed
Vpon the drops, this *Pelican* did bleed ;
    Yea, let me firme unto thy *Law* abide,
    And, ever love that *Flocke,* for which he dy'd.
                                        Bee

emblem literature. Other naturalists agreed, and Ulisse Aldrovandi (1522–1605) included many of Camerarius's emblems in his authoritative encyclopedias of natural history. Naturalists in the sixteenth and seventeenth centuries were concerned not merely with empirical observations, but also with exploring all of the symbolic meanings attached to a creature. The emblem books, therefore, provided these naturalists with important insights. One example of an animal emblem that was included in all of the important natural-history

books is seen in Fig. 1. There are different versions of this emblem, but the pelican is always shown pecking open its breast to allow the young to feed on its own blood. The text explains that the pelican represents Christ's mercy, and this religious imagery is strengthened by the crucifix in the background of the emblem shown here.

This symbolic language of the emblem was not limited to emblem books and natural history. Emblematics played an important role in Court culture. The Courts in which many of the most important figures of the Scientific Revolution worked each had their own emblems. These emblems allowed the rulers to legitimate their power by weaving themselves into a rich mythological tradition and also gave them a kind of visual stamp, which would remind people of their power wherever it was spotted. These royal emblems appeared in public ceremonies, festivals, paintings, operas, and also on the title pages of scientific books. To gain the patronage of a powerful ruler, a scientist had to be skilled at framing his work in the context of the emblematic language of that particular Court. For example, when Galileo Galilei (1564–1642) presented his discovery of the moons of Jupiter to Cosimo II de' Medici (1590–1621) in 1610, he tied this discovery into the imagery of the Medici Court. The Medici family had created for itself an elaborate myth, in which each member of the family was associated with one of the gods. Cosimo I (1519–1574), the dynasty's founder, was associated with Jupiter. Galileo named the moons of Jupiter the Medicean Stars and explained in the dedication of *Sidereus nuncius* (1610) how these stars actually played an astrological role in transmitting certain qualities from Cosimo I to his successors. The Medicean Stars then became a standard part of the symbolic language of the Medici Court, and they were featured in paintings, theatrical presentations, and even sonnets. A new emblem had been created, and the image of Jupiter sitting on a cloud surrounded by the four Medicean Stars became an emblematic representation of Cosimo II.

Emblem books became less and less popular in the late seventeenth and early eighteenth centuries, but the visual language they had created lived on in children's books and also in the imagery found on the title pages of scientific books. Even in the works of Carl Linnaeus (1707–1778), one still finds elaborate, emblematic title pages that carry on the rich symbolic tradition of the emblem book.

BIBLIOGRAPHY

Ashworth, William B., Jr. "Natural History and the Emblematic World View." In *Reappraisals of the Scientific Revolution,* ed. David C. Lindberg and Robert S. Westman. Cambridge: Cambridge University Press, 1990, pp. 303–332.

Bath, Michael. *Speaking Pictures: English Emblem Books and Renaissance Culture.* London: Longman, 1994.

Biagioli, Mario. "Galileo the Emblem Maker." *Isis* 81 (1990), 230–258.

Daly, Peter M., and Mary V. Silcox. *The English Emblem: Bibliography of Secondary Literature.* Munich and New York: K. G. Saur, 1990.

KEVIN TAPP

See also Aldrovandi, Ulisse; Illustration

Embryology

Aristotelian doctrines on embryonic development remained in force, with certain variations, until the seventeenth century. Aristotle (384–322 B.C.E.) had created an embryonic research technique using chick embryos that were henceforth required subject matter in papers on this subject. He upheld epigenesis from a theoretical viewpoint, identifying embryo development with a configuration process. This doctrine gave configurational force priority over form, the complete opposite of seventeenth- and eighteenth-century preformationism, according to which form was more important and embryonic development was merely enlargement. Unlike embryologists in the first centuries of modern times, Aristotle had no problem dealing with the concept of configurational force because in ancient Greece *physis,* or nature, was deemed to be the metaphysical principle that generated and configured all change. Epigenesis was, furthermore, in keeping with the Aristotelian theory of spontaneous generation, according to which the configurational force of nature could generate grubs, larvae, and other inferior living creatures in mud or any other organic substance in a state of decomposition.

The same three variations that Aristotelian epigenesis had had in the late Middle Ages continued to be expounded in the Renaissance. The main difference concerned the first visible organ in the embryo, which the strict Aristotelian line held to be the heart, the Galenic variation held to be brain, and Arab physicians believed to be the three vesicles corresponding to the three organ cavities and their main organs (brain, heart, and liver).

However, together with these Scholastic questions, Renaissance anatomists, particularly the Italians, began to collect observations on the embryonic process. At the University of Bologna, Ulisse Aldrovandi (1522–1605) and his Dutch disciple Volcher Coiter (1534–1576) worked methodically to describe the successive appearance of the organs in incubated hen eggs. At Padua University, Girolamo Fabrici (ca. 1533–1619), in addition to comparing the embryos of different species of mammals and other animals, studied the development of chick embryos and provided a description that was clearly influenced by Andreas Vesalius's (1514–1564) architectural approach to anatomy: first the sustaining parts (skeleton) would appear, followed by the muscles, and finally the viscera.

William Harvey (1578–1657), Fabrici's great English disciple, carried on with his master's embryological works, studying in minute detail how the chick inside the egg and the embryo of other animals developed. His works went beyond mere description and led him to expound in *Exercitationes de generatione animalium* (1657) a renewed version of epigenesis. He believed embryonic development to be a progressive configuration starting from a shapeless substance, which he called *ovum* in a very general sense. He stated that all animals, from the inferior creatures to man, develop from ova, but he distinguished two basic types of generation. He thought that inferior creatures were generated by metamorphosis, in which the shapeless germinal substance is configured by distribution like a mass of clay in the sculptor's hands. Higher animals, however, were generated, according to Harvey, by epigenesis, in which the parts successively appear and grow in a set order of importance determined by *vis,* or the configurational force of each specific species. The only set species would be those of higher animals with epigenetic embryonic development.

In the two decades following the publication of Harvey's work, three converging factors led to epigenesis being superseded and replaced by preformationism, which was to remain in force for more than a century. The first of said factors was the introduction of the microscope in embryological research. Marcello Malpighi (1628–1694), the most prominent of the classic microscopists, expounded in *De formatione pulli in ovo* (1672) and *De ovo incubato* (1675) the first hours in the development of the embryo, providing a precise description of the formation of the blastula, the appearance of

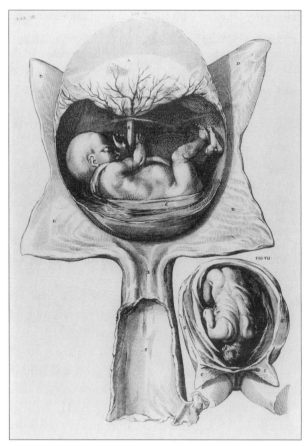

A fetus in utero. From Fabrici ab Acquapendente, De formato foetu *(1600).*

the nervous system, eyeballs, blood vessels, and so on. These contributions were later elaborated upon by other microscopists. Regnier de Graaf (1641–1673) investigated the macro- and microscopic structure of the genitals of mammals and discovered the seminal ducts and ovarian follicle, now known as *De Graaf's follicle.* He thought the follicles were the ova of mammals, and this idea was upheld until the discovery of the ovule in 1827 by Karl Ernst von Baer (1796–1876). De Graaf stated, moreover, that the function of the ovary was to produce ova, superseding the traditional doctrine according to which they were some sort of testicle secreting "female semen." Shortly afterward, in 1677, Antoni van Leeuwenhoek (1632–1723) informed the Royal Society of the discovery of spermatozoa by the student Jan Ham (1650–1723), having personally confirmed and enlarged upon the discovery.

The second factor was the experimental demonstration by Francesco Redi (1626–1697) that macroscopic inferior creatures are not produced by spontaneous generation. Redi rigorously proved that, when the rotting organic substance is in tightly sealed jars, no larvae are generated because the corresponding species are unable to lay their eggs there. From this he deduced the famous formula *omne vivum ex vivo* (all life [comes] from an egg).

The third factor was the existence of an anti-Aristotelian mentality, predominantly mechanist, that conditioned new facts to be interpreted giving priority to form. Unlike the authors of ancient Greece and those who had retained their metaphysical conception of the *physis,* or nature of, organisms for fifteen hundred years, the configurational force had turned into a serious problem. In the mid-seventeenth century, Thomas Browne (1605–1682) had attempted to clarify the causes of the embryo-configuration process of hens, frogs, and other species by heating them and treating them with substances such as oil, salts, and vinegar. During the final third of that century, however, and at the turn of the eighteenth, the predominant approach was to discard this problem and consider embryonic development to be simply the growth of a structure already preformed in the ovum or spermatozoon. Preformationism had two lines of thought: the ovistic trend situated this preformed structure of living creatures in the ovum, and the animalculist trend held that it was in the spermatozoon. The ovistic theory was specifically stated by Malpighi and other authors, but its first systematic formulation was largely the work of Antonio Vallisneri (1661–1730), who held that the specific "primary form" of different species was already constituted in the ova of each, albeit on an infinitely small scale.

Hence, preformationism absorbed the infinitism mentality, which also appeared in mathematics and other scientific areas. At the hands of the greatest researchers during the Enlightenment, the ovistic branch of preformism became the embryological theory in force throughout the academic world. The only note of criticism was found in the works of Caspar Friedrich Wolff (1734–1794), which were the starting point of modern epigenesis and the theory of germinal layers at the turn of the nineteenth century by Karl Ernst von Baer and other embryologists.

Animalculism followed a different path. Leeuwenhoek himself was the first to affirm that spermatozoon were seminal animalcules, or, in the case of man, "homunculi," in the shape of the corresponding species. Nicolas Andry (1658–1731) and Nicolas Hartsoeker

(1656–1725), later to be the most outspoken defenders of animaculist preformationism, indulged in excessive speculation, in both their illustrations of spermatozoa and their theorizings. Speculation became increasingly excessive during the eighteenth century and caused animalculism to be discredited and left on the scientific sidelines.

Preformationism moved from biology to philosophy and even to theology, turning into intricate theoretical structures. During the seventeenth and eighteenth centuries, it was commonly known as the theory of evolution because it implied the *evolutio,* or development, of predetermined models of form since Creation. Today's meaning of evolution and evolutionism, however, come from the nineteenth century.

BIBLIOGRAPHY

Adelmann, H. B. *The Embryological Treatises of Hieronymus Fabricius ab Aquapendente.* 2 vols. Ithaca, NY: Cornell University Press, 1942.

———. *Marcello Malpighi and the Evolution of Embryology.* 5 vols. Ithaca, NY: Cornell University Press, 1966.

Castellani, C. *La storia della generazione: Idee e teorie dal diciassettesimo al diciottetsiemo secolo.* Milan: Longanesi, 1965.

Guyénot, E. *Les sciences de la vie aux XVIIᵉ et XVIIIᵉ siècles.* Paris: Albin Michel, 1941.

Needham, J. *A History of Embryology.* 2nd ed. Cambridge, Cambridge University Press, 1959.

JOSÉ M. LÓPEZ-PIÑERO

See also Epigenesis; Fabrici, Girolamo; Generation; Graaf, Regnier de; Harvey, William; Leewenholk, Antoni van; Malpighi, Marcello; Preformation; Spontaneous Generation

Empiricism

The central thesis of empiricism is that all knowledge of the natural world derives from experience. This view was held by Aristotelians, who were under attack in the Scientific Revolution. However, new developments in science and philosophy led to the recognition that the dominant features of the world are not necessarily those that appear to our unaided senses. As a result, the acquisition of empirical knowledge was seen to be more complex and indirect—and the results less certain—than had previously been assumed.

Rethinking the nature of empirical knowledge began with Francis Bacon (1561–1626), who sought to establish a proper marriage between reason and experience. Four linked themes are central to this marriage.

First, the key to empirical knowledge is *induction,* but, Bacon insisted, things are not always as they appear on the surface because sense perception is prone to error, although less so than the unaided intellect. Thus, induction requires more than observing correlations: we must actively seek out *counterinstances* to apparent correlations. The need to seek negative instances is enhanced by our natural tendency to look for instances that confirm beliefs we already hold. Second, Bacon insisted on a central role for *experiments* rather than passive observation. Experiments enhance our means of discovering new facts and weeding out false beliefs by creating situations that do not naturally occur, thereby increasing the range of our observations of nature. Bacon's third theme was his doctrine of the *idols.* These are features of human cognition that interfere with our attempts to learn about nature. Idols of the Tribe are limitations inherent in human nature, such as the limits of our senses; these are the hardest to overcome. Idols of the Cave, Market Place, and Theater are false beliefs deriving, respectively, from the individual, human society and language, and philosophical systems. The attempt to get at the truth about the world requires that we work to overcome biases generated by the idols. Experiments and the active search for negative instances are central to this project. Fourth, Bacon's doctrine of *forms* further underlined the need for science to go beyond passive observing. Forms (or "laws") are the underlying features of nature that really determine the properties of entities. Forms are not apparent in our experience, even though experience provides our only means for studying the forms. We thus require indirect means to their discovery. Bacon held that the aim of knowledge is to gain control over nature, and our ability to control nature ultimately depends on understanding the forms.

Scientific developments supported this more complex view of the role of experience in studying nature. Galileo Galilei's (1564–1642) telescopic discoveries did more than just reveal unknown items. Examples such as the phases of Venus and the resolution of the Milky Way into stars provided observations that directly contradicted what appeared to our unaided senses. Thus, Galileo argued, our unaided senses cannot always be trusted; they have inherent defects that become dominant when we observe small, bright points of light. The telescope corrects these defects and provides a superior source of astronomical information than we can acquire with the naked eye.

Many of Galileo's telescopic discoveries supported Copernican astronomy, which also challenged naive sensory experience. Galileo replied to many traditional arguments against the motion of the earth—such as that a stone dropped from a tower falls at the foot of the tower—by arguing that these observations follow from both the geostatic and the Copernican views. Other, carefully selected, experiments are required to make the choice. Experience remains the final court of appeal in the study of nature, but we must use experience intelligently. Galileo also argued that properties that appear to us in perception need not all characterize physical objects. We experience sensations when external objects act on our senses, but some of these sensations, such as itches and tickles, do not exist in physical objects. Galileo argued that the same holds for other sensations such as color, odor, taste, and heat. Only those properties that are encompassed in geometry—shape, number, and motion—actually exist in physical objects. Again, sensory appearances are not to be taken at face value in our exploration of nature.

The distinction between those qualities that appear to our senses and those that actually characterize physical objects was developed in greater detail by Robert Boyle (1627–1691). An avid experimenter, Boyle argued that physical objects are composed of minute corpuscles that have size, shape, and motion as their only properties. Larger bodies are systems of corpuscles, and the properties of composite objects are determined by the properties of the corpuscles and the way they are connected together to form a particular texture. Size, shape, motion, and texture are the only intrinsic (primary) qualities of physical objects; these are the only properties that an object would have if it were alone in the universe. But physical objects also have an unlimited number of relational (secondary) qualities, such as the ability of a hot coal to melt a piece of wax or cause us to feel pain. Secondary qualities, and all behavior of physical objects, reduce to, and are explained by, the primary qualities. Since the underlying corpuscles are too small for us to perceive, the grounds for accepting the corpuscular hypothesis must derive from its ability to provide detailed explanations of physical and chemical phenomena that we can perceive, and do to so better than competing hypotheses.

An additional theme derives from René Descartes (1596–1650), who, although not an empiricist, introduced a framework that was largely adopted by later empiricist philosophers. Reflecting on both the causal process that generates our sensations and the occurrence of perceptual illusions, Descartes concluded that the objects we directly perceive are *ideas:* entities that exist only in our minds, although they are caused by the action of physical objects on our senses. This raises the question of how we determine which of our precepts actually characterize physical objects in a more radical form. Descartes continued Galileo's quest for a physical science that would be captured in a mathematical description of the physical world, although Descartes maintained that the ultimate evidence for this physics rests on the ability of the mind to grasp the indubitable truth of mathematical propositions.

Isaac Newton (1642–1727), who succeeded in constructing a mathematical physics, returns us to the empiricist theme that only experience can justify scientific claims. Newton distinguished between laws of nature, such as the law of gravitation, that he thought could be inferred directly from experienced phenomena, and the underlying causes of these phenomena. He argued that the discovery of laws was the main task of natural philosophy, and he was generally hesitant to propose deeper causes—although he did accept the corpuscular view of nature.

The image of a world made up of corpuscles that are characterized by only a small subset of the properties they appear to have, and the view that we directly perceive ideas caused by the action of physical objects on our senses, came together in John Locke (1632–1704). Following Boyle, Locke distinguished primary from secondary qualities of physical objects. In addition, Locke stressed that awareness of physical objects is indirect and that we are directly aware only of our own ideas. Some of these ideas may copy properties of physical objects—these are "ideas of primary qualities"; the rest are "ideas of secondary qualities." Ideas of secondary qualities are not illusions; they are caused by the object being perceived and thus provide information about that object that must be taken into account in attempting to determine an object's primary qualities. Determining the primary qualities of a physical object is a scientific task, not a subject for philosophical reflection. Philosophy, however, does have much to say about the nature and limits of the knowledge we can acquire. Since ideas are our only source of information about physical objects, we must proceed by hypothesizing qualities of physical objects and showing that these qualities can account for the full range of ideas we experience when we perceive those objects—including the full range of changes we perceive the object in question to cause in other physical objects.

On this account, science provides only sufficient conditions for what we experience, not necessary conditions. This makes our account of the physical world, in principle, tentative and subject to revision as science develops. In this regard, Locke departs significantly from such predecessors as Bacon, Galileo, and Newton, who maintained that science can establish conclusions about nature that are necessarily true. The most we can achieve, according to Locke, is probable knowledge of the nature of physical objects. Even here, Locke doubted our ability to proceed very far in understanding the physical world because of our inability to grasp why some qualities regularly coexist in physical objects (e.g., malleability and resistance to rust in gold), how specific primary qualities cause specific secondary qualities, and how physical interactions cause ideas. An extreme form of this skepticism became a dominant theme among eighteenth-century empiricists.

BIBLIOGRAPHY

Brown, Harold I. "Galileo on the Telescope and the Eye." *Journal of the History of Ideas* 46 (1985), 487–501.

Galilei, Galileo. *Dialogue Concerning the Two Chief World Systems.* Trans. Stillman Drake. Berkeley and Los Angeles: University of California Press, 1967.

Locke, John. *An Essay Concerning Human Understanding.* Ed. P. Nidditch. Oxford: Oxford University Press, 1984.

Mandelbaum, Maurice. *Philosophy, Science, and Sense Perception.* Baltimore: Johns Hopkins University Press, 1964.

McMullin, Ernan. "Conceptions of Science in the Scientific Revolution." In *Reappraisals of the Scientific Revolution,* ed. David C. Lindberg and Robert S. Westman. Cambridge: Cambridge University Press, 1990, pp. 27–92.

HAROLD I. BROWN

See also Bacon, Francis; Causality; Descartes, René; Experience and Experiment; Galilei, Galileo; Hypothesis; Laws of Nature; Locke, John; Qualities

Encyclopedias

Attempts to provide a comprehensive coverage of knowledge predate the first use of the term *encyclopedia* in the sixteenth century. Pliny the Elder's (23/24–79) *Natural Histories* (77) and, among the many medieval encyclopedias, Vincent of Beauvais's *Speculum maius*

(The Great Mirror, composed 1245–1260, printed six times down to 1624) remained influential as sources and models for early-modern works that sought to cope with ever-increasing amounts of knowledge.

During the Renaissance, much new knowledge was generated by the humanist recovery of ancient texts, the discovery of new worlds and the new interest in the natural phenomena of old ones, and the accelerated production and diffusion of texts through printing. In addition, the Reformation challenged the unity of the Christian faith, and the new awareness of the great variety of ancient philosophers and commentators undermined confidence in the singular authority of Aristotle (384–322 B.C.E.); at the same time, the growing number of students during the sixteenth century increased the demand for compact summaries of philosophy. These crises of information and authority impelled new syntheses of knowledge and new tools of scholarship and instruction.

On the one hand, many humanists were enthusiastic about the notion of the *encyclopedia,* a term coined ca. 1500 from a misreading of a passage in Quintilian in the first century. Held to mean the "circle of learning," it promised an underlying unity to the increasing complexity of knowledge and fueled many schemes for the classification and treatment of the disciplines—such as the method of Peter Ramus (1515–1572) using embranching tables—though such schemes were often devoid of detailed content. On the other hand, more practically oriented authors developed diverse types of bulky reference works, which were rarely entitled "encyclopedia" ("theatrum," "thesaurus," "systema" or "silva" are some of the colorful metaphors used instead). These included well-established genres like the dictionary, arranged alphabetically but containing more than strictly linguistic explanations (e.g., Ambrogio Calepino's, 1435–1511, *Dictionarium,* first published 1502), and the encyclopedic commentary, modeled on Aulus Gellius (ca. 130–170), which contained much information in a self-consciously rambling order, made usable by an alphabetical topical index (e.g., Caelius Rhodiginus, 1453–1425, *Lectiones antiquae* (Ancient Selections), first published 1542). New genres included bibliographies like Conrad Gessner's (1516–1565) *Bibliotheca universalis* (1545) designed as a guide to all known books and, in principle, as the first step toward a complete index of the contents of the books (the goal of Gessner's unfinished *Pandectae,* 1548–1549). Commonplace books like Theodor Zwinger's (1533–1588) *Theatrum humanae vitae,* first published 1565, sorted information under systematically arranged topical headings but were also accessible through multiple alphabetical indices. Subject encyclopedias focused on specific fields were especially numerous in natural history, with authors like Ulisse Aldrovandi (1522–1605) and Jan Jonston (1603–1675) generating many volumes on birds, fish, quadrupeds, and insects.

Johann Heinrich Alsted's (1588–1638) *Encyclopaedia* (1630) was one of the few works to combine the title with a philosophical organizational scheme and a detailed treatment of each discipline. In the next major work of that title, the *Encyclopédie* of Denis Diderot and Jean le Rond d'Alembert (1750), alphabetical order structured the whole work rather than a simple index at the back, and the philosophical scheme instead was relegated to a "Preliminary Discourse": the encyclopedia had become the reference work that it is today, while the classification of the disciplines became the purview of speculative philosophy.

Encyclopedic works are a rich and largely untapped source for the history of science, in which one can trace the wide range of interactions between old and new scientific knowledge (simple juxtapositions, attempts at reconciliation, or forthright rejections of old for new) and gauge the rhythms of the diffusion of these ideas to nonspecialist audiences of more or less learned and more and less wealthy readers.

BIBLIOGRAPHY

Collison, Robert. *Encyclopedias: Their History Throughout the Ages.* New York: Hafner, 1964. 2nd ed. 1966.

Kafker, Frank, ed. *Notable Encyclopedias of the Seventeenth and Eighteenth Centuries: Nine Predecessors of the Encyclopédie.* Oxford: Voltaire Foundation, 1981.

Loemker, Leroy. *Struggle for Synthesis: The Seventeenth-Century Background of Leibniz's Synthesis of Order and Freedom.* Cambridge, MA: Harvard University Press, 1972.

ANN BLAIR

See also Classification of the Sciences; Humanism

Ephemerides. See Astronomical Tables and Ephemerides

Epicureanism

A philosophy consisting of a hedonistic ethics, an atomic philosophy of nature, and an empiricist theory of knowledge. During the period of the Scientific Revolution, Epicureanism influenced the development of the mechanical philosophy, empiricist philosophies of science, and the political philosophies of Thomas Hobbes (1588–1679) and John Locke (1632–1704).

Epicureanism arose in the late fourth century B.C.E. Drawing on the theories of the fifth-century B.C.E. atomists Leucippus of Miletus and Democritus of Abdera, Epicurus (341–271 B.C.E.) developed his philosophy in response to prevailing Platonism and Aristotelianism. Epicurus's aim was ethical: how to lead the good life. He believed that a good life leads to a state of mental tranquility called *ataraxia,* which can be attained by maximizing pleasure and minimizing pain, both physical and mental. Epicurus believed that the chief causes of mental pain are fear of the gods and fear of punishment in life after death. To dispel these fears, he espoused a materialistic philosophy of nature in which all phenomena can be explained in terms of the chance collisions of atoms moving in infinite, void space. Epicurus considered the present world to be one in an unending series formed by the collisions of atoms swirling through empty space. The atoms collide because their eternal downward motion is occasionally interrupted by random swerves. This swerve (*clinamen*) also provided Epicurus with an explanation for human free will. Everything in the universe is composed of atoms. The qualities of physical objects can be explained in terms of the motions and configurations of their constituent atoms, which impinge on our sense organs. Epicurus relegated the gods to a beatified existence, in which they are unconcerned with human affairs; and he claimed that the human soul is material and mortal. Composed of atoms, the soul leaves the body at the time of death, and its constituent atoms are dispersed through the universe.

Epicurean ideas were popularized in Latin in *De rerum natura* (On the Nature of Things), an epic poem by Titus Lucretius Carus (99–55 B.C.E.), as well as in several writings by Marcus Tullius Cicero (106–43 B.C.E.). Because Epicurus was commonly misunderstood to advocate atheism and unrestrained sensuality, his philosophy had little following in the Christian Middle Ages.

Epicurean ideas did not receive serious attention until the fifteenth century, when Italian humanists recovered the manuscript of Lucretius's poem. First edited by Poggio Bracciolini in 1417, *De rerum natura* finally became a permanent part of European intellectual resources when it was printed in 1473. Early interest in the recovered poem focused on Lucretius's literary style and, later, on Epicurean ethics. Further interest in Epicureanism was sparked by the recovery of Diogenes Laertius's third-century *Lives of Eminent Philosophers,* which was published by Ambrogio Traversari (1386–1439) in 1431. This work, containing three letters and two collections of maxims by Epicurus himself, was a major source for knowledge of Epicureanism and other ancient philosophies. Epicureanism received serious consideration in Lorenzo Valla's (1407–1457) *De voluptate,* a discussion of Christian morality and Epicurean sensuality first published in 1431.

There were a few discussions of atomism in the sixteenth and early seventeenth centuries. Daniel Sennert (1572–1637) attempted to combine the atomism of Democritus with the Aristotelian theory of substantial forms, which he thought were innate to the atoms. Isaac Beeckman (1588–1637) promoted an atomic theory of matter, influencing the thinking of both Pierre Gassendi (1592–1655) and René Descartes (1596–1650), who both adopted mechanical philosophies of nature after meeting with him.

The first serious consideration of Epicurean natural philosophy was undertaken by Gassendi, a French Catholic priest, who embarked on a lifelong project to produce a Christianized version of Epicureanism. Rejecting Aristotelianism, which had provided philosophical foundations for natural philosophy during the Middle Ages and much of the Renaissance, Gassendi undertook the articulation of a complete philosophy based on Epicurean principles, publishing three major works as the fruit of his Epicurean project: *De vita et moribus Epicuri libri octo* (1647), in which he attempted to rehabilitate Epicurus's philosophy and reputation; *Animadversiones in decimum librum Diogenis Laertii, qui est de vita, moribus, placitisque Epicuri* (1649), which is a commentary on the tenth book of Diogenes Laertius containing the extant letters and maxims of Epicurus; and the posthumous *Syntagma philosophicum* (1658), which is a complete exposition of his Christianized Epicureanism, containing sections on the three traditional fields of philosophy: logic, physics, and ethics. The *Syntagma philosophicum,* though still written in a humanist style, incorporates material from contemporary natural philosophy into a full account of Epicureanism.

Gassendi modified the ancient philosophy in order to ensure the orthodoxy of his Christianized Epicureanism. He rejected polytheism, a corporeal conception of the gods, the denial of creation ex nihilo, the infinitude of atoms, the swerve (*clinamen*), the eternity of the universe, a materialistic cosmogony, the denial of finality, and the corporeality and mortality of the human soul. In the place of these objectionable doctrines, he asserted the existence of an omnipotent God who created the world and rules it providentially, the existence of a single world consisting of a large but finite number of atoms created by God, the evidence of wise design in the Creation, a role for final causes in natural philosophy, and the immortality of an immaterial human soul.

Gassendi believed that the world is composed of atoms moving in void space. He argued for the existence of the void by appealing to the ancient Epicurean arguments as well as evidence drawn from the barometric experiments of his contemporaries Evangelista Torricelli (1608–1647) and Blaise Pascal (1623–1662). He claimed that atoms possess only the primary qualities of magnitude, solidity, and heaviness. All other qualities—the secondary qualities such as color, taste, and smell as well as the so-called occult qualities—can be explained in terms of the motions and configurations of the atoms and their impact on our senses. Accepting the canonic of Epicurus, Gassendi accepted an empiricist theory of knowledge that maintained that all of the ideas in our minds come from experience. He believed that a science built from such empirical foundations can at best attain probability.

In the *Syntagma philosophicum,* Gassendi undertook the explanation of all of the phenomena in the universe, including the heavens, the inorganic world, plants, and animals, in terms of atoms and the void. Although he favored Copernican astronomy and published an account of Galileo Galilei's (1564–1642) new science of motion, he proposed the system of Tycho Brahe (1546–1601) as a compromise acceptable to the Church. He rejected astrology because he regarded its principles as unproven and its practitioners as deceptive. He believed that the design evident in the structure of animals is important evidence of divine providence and made extensive use of the argument from design in affirming God's role as creator and ruler of the world. His argument for the immortality of the human soul was the crowning touch of his natural philosophy. Adapting the distinction between the sentient, material soul (*anima*) and the incorporeal, rational soul (*animus*) from Lucretius, he demonstrated that the rational soul, unique to humans, is immortal. He explicitly argued against the

E

Epicurean arguments for the mortality of the soul. Gassendi's insistence on the immortality of the human, rational soul marked the boundary of his mechanization of the world as well as an important departure from traditional Epicureanism.

To complete his baptism of Epicureanism, Gassendi reinterpreted Epicurean ethics on Christian lines. He thought that God endowed humans with free will and with an innate desire for pleasure. Thus, when people use the calculus of pleasure and pain and exercise their capacity to make free choices, they participate in God's providential plan for the Creation. Since the greatest possible pleasure is the beatific vision of God after death, the idea of Christian salvation fits perfectly, in Gassendi's view, with Epicurean hedonism. Gassendi advocated a theory of social contract on the ground that people can achieve greater happiness for themselves by forming societies than they can find in the state of nature. Civil society is, thus, a natural consequence of human nature. He favored monarchy but believed that the monarch remains accountable to the consent of the governed. Gassendi developed his political philosophy in close association with Thomas Hobbes, and these ideas, in turn, influenced the thinking of John Locke, who is usually regarded as the founder of the liberal tradition in political philosophy.

Epicurean ideas came to England primarily in the works of Walter Charleton (1620–1707), a member of the circle of Royalists surrounding William Cavendish. In *The Darknes of Atheism Dispelled by the Light of Nature* (1652), Charleton announced his adherence to Gassendi's Christianized Epicureanism and dealt with some of the theological implications of the New Philosophy. Arguing that knowledge of God and his relationship to the Creation is a necessary preliminary to a philosophy of nature, he followed Gassendi closely in demonstrating the existence of God who created the world ex nihilo, designed nature so that it reflects his creation, and rules it providentially. Charleton's *Physiologia Epicuro-Gassendo-Charltoniana* (1654) is a translation and expansion of the physical part of Gassendi's *Animadversiones in decimum librum Diogenis Laertii*. In *The Immortality of the Human Soul Demonstrated by the Light of Nature* (1657), Charleton rehearsed Gassendi's arguments for the immortality of the soul. Taken together, the three works introduced many of Gassendi's key ideas to the English reader. Another important source of Epicurean ideas in England was Thomas Stan-

ley's (1625–1678) *History of Philosophy* (1655). This work contains a lengthy section on the philosophy of Epicurus that is a translation of Gassendi's uncharacteristically brief *Philosophiae Epicuri syntagma,* originally published as an appendix to the *Animadversiones in decimum librum Diogenis Laertii.* Epicurean ideas were popularized in France by François Bernier's (1620–1688) *Abregé de la philosophie de Gassendi,* published in many editions from 1674 on.

Together with Cartesianism, Epicurean atomism exerted a major influence on the formation of the mechanical philosophy, which was adopted by such important natural philosophers as Robert Boyle (1627–1691) and Isaac Newton (1642–1727). Despite the fact that these natural philosophers adopted many aspects of Epicurean atomism, as modified by Gassendi, they remained nervous about the dangers of atheism and materialism that were always associated with the name of the ancient atomist.

Boyle advocated a mechanical philosophy that he called *corpuscularianism* to indicate that he sought to explain natural phenomena in terms of matter and motion without committing himself on the metaphysical questions of whether or not matter is composed of indivisible atoms and whether or not vacuum exists. His most systematic exposition of this theory of matter is his *Origine of Formes and Qualities* (1666). Combining Gassendi's Christianized version of Epicurean atomism and Descartes's version of the mechanical philosophy, which denied the existence of void space and claimed that matter is infinitely divisible, Boyle devoted himself to demonstrating that chemical phenomena could be explained in terms of small particles of matter. He claimed that matter is composed of *minima naturalia,* which are never divided except possibly by divine omnipotence. These smallest of particles form clusters, which, in turn, form observable bodies. Boyle endorsed mechanical explanations of various phenomena. For example, he used his air pump to prove that the pressure of the atmosphere is what supports the column of mercury in the barometer in place of the Aristotelian *horror vacui.* Nonetheless, he was unwilling to say that the empty space above the column of mercury is actually void. Although there is unpublished evidence that Boyle actually favored atomism over the Cartesian theory of matter, his reluctance to do so in print was the consequence of the atheistic and materialistic associations that continued to adhere to Epicureanism. He expressed his differences from Epicurus explicitly in *The Usefulness of Experimental Philosophy* (1663). Gassendi's effort to baptize the ancient philosophy had not been entirely successful.

Newton was deeply influenced by Epicurean atomism, but he introduced profound modifications into the ancient theory. He favored an atomic theory of matter, from the time he opened his early student notebook on natural philosophy in the 1660s all the way through the "Queries" appended to the *Opticks* in the first quarter of the eighteenth century. Despite the fact that he believed "that God in the Beginning form'd Matter in solid, massy, hard, impenetrable, moveable Particles" (*Opticks,* Query 31), Newton felt the need to modify Epicureanism for theological, philosophical, and scientific reasons. Newton insisted that God had created the atoms, had given them their motions, and continuously guided their motions, thus ensuring divine providence in the Creation. Because the theory of discrete atoms made it difficult to explain either the cohesion of bodies or the phenomenon of gravitation, Newton modified Epicurean atomism even further, adding forces or active principles to atomism, ideas he drew from alchemical and Stoic sources. These modifications of atomism marked a serious departure from Epicureanism as well as from the orthodox mechanical philosophy.

Both atomism and ethical hedonism continued to influence scientific and philosophical thinking long after explicit debates about the acceptance of Epicureanism subsided. The philosophy of John Locke presupposed an atomic theory of matter, which lay at the foundation of his theory of primary and secondary qualities and his epistemology more generally. His political philosophy had roots in Gassendi's ethics and the Epicurean calculus of pleasure and pain lay at the heart of later utilitarian social philosophies. An atomic theory of matter has continued to influence chemistry and physics, although modern scientific theories bear little direct resemblance to ancient Epicurean atomism.

BIBLIOGRAPHY

Jones, Howard. *The Epicurean Tradition*. London and New York: Routledge, 1989.

Kargon, Robert. *Atomism in England from Hariot to Newton*. Oxford: Oxford University Press, 1966.

Kroll, Richard W. F. *The Material Word: Literate Culture in the Restoration and Early Eighteenth Century*. Baltimore and London: Johns Hopkins University Press, 1991.

Long, A. A., and D. N. Sedley. *The Hellenistic Philosophers*. 2 vols. Cambridge: Cambridge University Press, 1987.

Osler, Margaret J., ed. *Atoms, Pneuma, and Tranquillity: Epicurean and Stoic Themes in European Thought*. Cambridge: Cambridge University Press, 1991.

———. *Divine Will and the Mechanical Philosophy: Gassendi and Descartes on Contingency and Necessity in the Created World*. Cambridge: Cambridge University Press, 1994.

Sarasohn, Lisa T. *Freedom in a Deterministic Universe: Gassendi's Ethical Philosophy*. Ithaca, NY: Cornell University Press, 1996.

MARGARET J. OSLER

See also Atomism; Charleton, Walter; Gassendi, Pierre; Matter; Mechanical Philosophy

Epigenesis

The theory that the embryo develops successively in stages, progressively forming structures not originally present in the egg. Aristotle originally discussed this idea but did not use the name *epigenesis*. In the Scientific Revolution, William Harvey (1578–1657) wrote about it in 1651 and used the name, mainly in exercise 45 of *Exercitationes de generatione animalium* (Exercises Concerning the Generation of Animals).

Harvey contrasted epigenesis, differentiation from an amorphous beginning, to the idea of metamorphosis, enlargement only from the embryo. An example of metamorphosis that Harvey used is the development of an insect. An example of epigenesis that Harvey gave is the growth of an acorn into an oak tree:

> in the same way, for instance, as the bud bursting from the top of the acorn, in the course of its growth, has its parts separately taking the form of root, wood, pith, bark, boughs, branches, leaves, flowers, and fruit, until at length out comes a perfect tree; just so is it with the creation of the chick in the egg.

All this happens from the original material. An analogy Harvey drew to illustrate this is God's commands in creating the world from the first chapter of the Book of Genesis:

> Just as if the whole chick was created by a command to this effect, of the Divine Architect: "Let there be a similar colourless mass, and let it be divided into parts and made to increase, and in the meantime, while it is growing, let there be

a separation and delineation of parts; and let this part be harder, and denser, and more glistening, that be softer and more coloured," and it was so. Now it is in this very manner that the structure of the chick in the egg goes on day by day; all its parts are formed, nourished, and augmented out of the same material.

Harvey also pointed out that his position is different from that of his old professor at Padua, Hieronymous Fabricius (Girolamo Fabrici, 1533–1619), whose position on chick development Harvey says is akin to metamorphosis.

Harvey's promotion of epigenesis did not greatly influence the majority of researchers on embryology in the Scientific Revolution. They were more interested in the various forms of the theory of preformation, which stated that the organism exists preformed in the egg. In other words, the adult existed in miniature, which they called the *homunculus,* in the material forming the embryo. It was not until the late eighteenth century that Caspar Friedrich Wolff (1734–1794) successfully urged the return to epigenesis. In the next century, Karl Ernst von Baer (1792–1876) found empirical evidence against preformation and laid the foundations of modern embryology along the lines than Harvey had discussed, albeit in a much simpler fashion than Von Baer.

BIBLIOGRAPHY
Needham, Joseph. *A History of Embryology.* New York: Arno, 1975.
Oppenheimer, Jane. *Essays in the History of Embryology and Biology.* Cambridge, MA: MIT Press, 1967.

EMERSON T. MCMULLEN

See also Embryology; Fabrici, Girolamo (Fabricius ab Acquapendente); Generation; Harvey, William; Preformation

Ercker, Lazarus (ca. 1530–1594)

This skilled metallurgist and overseer of mining and mint operations in the German territories also wrote books on mining and metallurgy. He published his masterpiece, a treatise on ores and assaying, *Beschreibung der allervornehmsten mineralischen Erze und Bergwerksarten,* in 1574. Born in central Europe in an era of prolific metal production, as a young man Ercker obtained a position as assayer of Dresden. He received his appointment from the Elector Augustus, one of a number of German

princes who earned substantial income from mines in their territories and who enthusiastically promoted mine, metallurgical, and alchemical operations. Ercker dedicated a pamphlet on assaying to the elector and was thereby promoted.

In his subsequent career, Ercker acquired similar positions in Germany and Bohemia and, at the same time, wrote technical books that he inscribed to his patrons. As assay warden at the mint of Goslar, he dedicated a book on minting to Julius, duke of Braunschweig-Wolfenbüttel (1528–1589). While working as control assayer in Kutnà Hora (Kuttenberg) in Bohemia, he wrote his masterpiece on ores and mining, dedicating it to the Emperor Maximilian II (1564–1576). Promotions came from Maximilian and subsequently from his successor, Rudolf II (1576–1612), who also knighted him.

Inspired by the success of *De re metallica* (1555) by Georgius Agricola (1494–1555), Ercker wrote his own treatise on metallurgy. It is an original and systematic

Washing of ores, from Ercker's Aula subterranea domina dominatium subdita subditorum *(1703), the seventh ediction of a work first published in 1574.*

treatment of ores and of assaying metals, including silver, gold, copper, tin, lead, bismuth, and mercury. It also treats salts, acids, and other compounds, including salt-peter, and instructs as well on cupellation and on equipment such as furnaces. Ercker's lifelong experience as an assayer and metallurgist is evident on every page and contributed to the originality and comprehnsive nature of his masterpiece. Hostile to alchemy and a proponent of the clear explication of technical material, he wrote one of the most important early treatises on practical metallurgical chemistry. It was translated into English in the seventeenth century and published (1683) under the auspices of the Royal Society of London.

BIBLIOGRAPHY

Beierlein, Paul R. *Lazarus Ercker: Bergmann, Hüttenmann, und Münzmeister im 16. Jahrhundert.* Berlin: Akademie Verlag Berlin, 1955.

Long, Pamela O. "The Openness of Knowledge: An Ideal and Its Context in Sixteenth-Century Writings on Mining and Metallurgy." *Technology and Culture* 32 (1991), 318–355.

Sisco, Anneliese Grünhaldt, and Cyril Stanley Smith, trans. and eds. *Lazarus Ercker's Treatise on Ores and Assaying.* Chicago: University of Chicago Press, 1951.

PAMELA O. LONG

See also Agricola, Georgius; Mining and Metallurgy

Ether

Aristotle (384–322 B.C.E.) taught that the ether was a fifth element that carried the stars and planets embedded in it. Plato (428–348 B.C.E.) and the Stoics regarded it as a fluid and the source of life. During the sixteenth century, Aristotle's account was attacked, first by substituting the Stoic view and later by introducing new kinds of ether. Both René Descartes (1596–1650) and Isaac Newton (1642–1727) employed ethers as central features of their cosmologies. Seventeenth- and eighteenth-century scientists adopted ethers as working fluids in physics and chemistry.

In antiquity, the substance of the heavens was known as ether, although there was no general agreement on its nature or extent. When Aristotle adopted Eudoxus of Cnidus's construction to explain planetary motion, he began a tradition that treated the substance of the heavens as a series of shells surrounding a central earth. He regarded the substance of these shells as a fifth element, distinct from the four terrestrial elements and possessing a natural tendency to move at uniform speed in a circle. The stars and the planets (including the Sun and the Moon) did not move freely. They were merely denser parts of one particular shell, and their motions were the result of the rotation of that shell and the rotation of other shells to which it was attached at its axes.

For Aristotle, the ether began above the sphere of the outermost terrestrial element—the sphere of fire—extending from the sphere of the Moon to the sphere of fixed stars that formed the boundary of the whole cosmos. Claudius Ptolemy (ca. 100–ca. 170) accepted this topology, although he replaced Eudoxus's concentric shells with a system of deferents and epicycles for purposes of calculation. In the *Planetary Hypotheses,* composed shortly after the better-known *Almagest,* Ptolemy introduced an alternative set of shell models. When placed in uniform motion, these shells, centered on the earth, would oblige a planet to perform the motions required by the deferent and the epicycle. The ether spheres of both Aristotle and Ptolemy were in immediate contact and excluded vacua. Ptolemy's shell construction was transmitted to the Latin West by Arabic intermediaries, but Ptolemy was not identified as its author. The thirteenth-century Arab astronomer al-Tusi solved Ptolemy's outstanding problem—that the equant (a point not at the center of a deferent) motion could not be modeled by uniformly rotating spheres—but his solution did not reach the West, and the equant problem became a main motivation of the reform of astronomy by Nicolaus Copernicus (1473–1543).

In contrast to Aristotle's inanimate but naturally rotating ether, Plato had taught that the heavens were filled with life-giving fire. The Stoics adopted and modified this view, making the *pneuma* the fundamental substance of their entire cosmology. Their *pneuma* was a mixture of air and fire. Its key property was its ability to animate objects it penetrated. Rather than being sharply separated from the substance of the heavens, the terrestrial elements diffused into the ether to form the lower air, and this blended imperceptibly into the pure celestial ether that stretched to the sphere of fixed stars. Epicureans also accepted that a fluid ether filled the heavens, although, in keeping with their general ontology, it consisted of atoms separated by void.

During the sixteenth century, Ioannes Pena (1528–1558) revived the Stoic account of the substance of the heavens. Following him, Tycho Brahe (1546–1601) and Michael Maestlin (1550–1631) showed that the comet of 1577 had a path that was incompatible with the existence of Aristotle's or Ptolemy's earth-centered spheres, and Johannes Kepler (1571–1630) described the ether as a life-giving air that penetrated into the very center of bodies.

Descartes introduced the most important seventeenth-century incarnation of the ether. Like the Stoic pneuma, his ether was a fluid that operated by contact, but, like the Epicurean ether, it was composed of finely divided matter, both the spherical second element and the even finer particles of the first. These elements existed in such intimate contact that vacua were excluded, and were able to move only when linked circles or vortices of particles moved in unison. Etherial matter filled the heavens and propelled the planets; stars were aggregates of the first element that collected at vortex centers. Although this finely divided matter appeared in the "animal spirits" that activated living organisms, Descartes treated animals, and human bodies, as hydraulic machines. Only humans were endowed with a reasoning soul, and this was entirely nonmechanical in nature. Descartes thus separated the life-giving and the intellectual functions of earlier ethers.

Descartes's position was criticized by the Cambridge Platonists, who wished to retain an active role for spiritual substances. Against this background, Isaac Newton began a research program to recover the spiritual and physical truths known to the ancients, pursuing research in fields as diverse as kinematics and alchemy. He rejected Descartes's ether vortices when he found that they could not generate Kepler's elliptical planetary orbits, although he continued to seek an ether as the cause of gravitation and to endow nonliving systems with life. His views on the ether evolved throughout his life. Ultimately, he seems to have accepted (but never published) at least two ethers. Impressed by electrical demonstrations at the Royal Society, Newton introduced an electrical ether that was the source of animation in living things. Believing that any ether that excluded vacua would resist planetary motion to an unacceptable extent, he postulated a related but extremely tenuous ether of rapidly moving, widely spaced particles as the cause of gravity. These ethers were agents of God in the providential direction of the cosmos and closer to the Stoics and the Neoplatonists than to Descartes.

After Newton, ethers and etherial effluvia became a stock in trade of working scientists. Important examples from the next century include the explanation of electrical attraction by etherial atmospheres surrounding elec-

trified bodies, the caloric theory of heat, and the three states of matter; chemical theories like those of Hermann Boerhaave (1668–1738), who endowed the element fire with many of the properties of earlier ethers; and the phlogiston theory of chemical change, with its similar fundamental substance.

BIBLIOGRAPHY

Cantor, G. N., and M. J. S. Hodge. *Conceptions of Ether: Studies in the History of Ether Theories, 1740–1900.* Cambridge: Cambridge University Press, 1981.

Dobbs, B. J. T. *The Janus Faces of Genius: The Role of Alchemy in Newton's Thought.* Cambridge: Cambridge University Press, 1991.

PETER BARKER

See also Celestial Spheres; Comets; Descartes, René; Matter; Newton, Isaac; Pneuma; Stoicism

Etiology

Infection, contagion, miasma, and *epidemic* are very old words and concepts. Until the second half of the nineteenth century, they were closely associated with "corruption," putrefaction, and fermentation. There is an extraordinary continuity of ideas concerning the causes and the nature of plague between the Black Death of the fourteenth century and the mid-eighteenth century. The main idea was a correspondence between the corruption of the air and the corruption of the body. The origin of infectious diseases was to be found in a change in the "temperament" of the air, an *intempery,* in favorable atmospheric conditions. Air-borne putrefaction was universally considered as the ultimate cause of a pestilential disease.

Precise distinctions between miasma, infection, and contagion are anachronistic. Renaissance authors, both medical and lay, could easily pass from one term to the other. The word *contagion* was far from incompatible with a theory of noxious air, or miasma. A hypothesis of the nature, specificity, and importance of contagion, as distinguished from traditional miasmas, was first proposed by Girolamo Fracastoro (ca. 1478–1553) in 1546. The predominant idea about plague was that it originated from venomous atoms, or "seeds." Whether generated by rotting matter or emanating from infected persons, animals, or objects, the venomous atoms would infect salubrious air and make it "miasmatic"—that is, poisonous. In addition, the atoms were also exceptionally "sticky," and they would stick to inanimate objects and living beings in the same way that perfumes and disgusting odors permeate fabrics and other materials. By contact or by inhalation of the "corrupted air," the "contagion" would pass from one person or object to another. The logical conclusion was that the only way to avoid the spreading of the disease was to stop all intercourse with people, animals, and objects coming from areas afflicted by the plague.

During the Renaissance, people, including physicians, recognized that plague prevailed in the summer, and that observation, which from our modern point of view is linked with the life cycles of rats and fleas, fitted perfectly well with the accepted theory: during the hottest months of the year, people smelled the worst odors from the dirty streets and the defective sewers. That was considered "proof" that the venomous particles grew out of rotting material in the hot and humid climate of the summer. The most important thing to do in this situation was to clean up the environment.

Thomas Sydenham's (1624–1689) conception of contagion held that "particles of the atmosphere . . . first insinuate themselves up with the blood; and finally, taint the whole frame with the contagion of the disease." Epidemics are the result of "pestilential virus" or "murderous miasma," in addition to the atmospheric "constitution," but Sydenham would not allow that the "virus" alone could transmit the disease for, if this were the case, "deaths would succeed deaths in one continuous and indefinite series."

In Johannes Baptista van Helmont's (1579–1644) opinion, the agent of the plague is a poisonous "gas," a spirit of a specific nature. The disease is not simply an abnormal bodily condition but a process of struggle between the patient's inner *archaeus* (a sort of control center of the organism) and an internal or external "irritant"—for example, the saliva of the rabid dog, a plague "virus," or the venom of the tarantula: "A disease is from an efficient seminal cause, positive, actual and real, with a seed, manner, species and order."

Robert Boyle (1627–1691) wrote two essays related to the question of the causes of diseases. His central idea is that diseases are caused by material particles of extreme smallness that mechanically disrupt organs and bodily processes, a sort of widespread chemical poisoning, caused by exhalations from the earth. The unaltered persistence of these morbific particles (*fomites*) and their easy distribution explain the wide and rapid diffusion of epidemic diseases. Boyle called attention to the diseases of miners, which were recognized as due to emissions of effluvia, and he noted that arsenic poisoning produces inflammations, pustules, and fevers, exactly like contagious diseases. Boyle considered that the multiplicative faculty of the disease implied some kind of analogy to the aggressive processes of fermentation and putrefaction.

The theory of contagion played a minor role in the medical systems of the seventeenth century. However, the doctrine of *contagium animatum* (contagion by living entities) acquired a larger empirical basis with the discovery of the "microscopical world" in the seventeenth century. The discovery of microparasites and the almost inconceivable number of animalcula that could be observed in fluids made plausible a special role of animalcula in the different functions of the living world, including generation, fermentation, and contagion.

A different understanding emerged in the thirty years between 1650 and 1680 when the increasing use of the microscope led to a renewal of the doctrine of contagion by "microscopic insects." Athanasius Kircher (1602–1680) published his animalculist theory in the tract *Scrutinium physico-medicum* (1658): all rotting substances are full of "worms" that propagate infection. Plague, as well as leprosy and venereal diseases, are caused by *effluvia animata*: all substances in nature "exhale certain effluvia composed of extremely minute invisible corpuscles." Corpuscles of this kind are commonly without life, but, if the air is already tainted by pollution, they are transformed into countless invisible worms, "so that the effluvia may now be called, not lifeless but animate."

The link between putrefaction, fermentation, and contagion gave new energy to the idea of spontaneous generation. Microscopical worms were thought of as arising from the corruption of humors in the body, chemical reactions within it caused by bad food, poisonous plants, or the breath of malignant animals, such as serpents, toads, and rabid dogs. According to Kircher, putrefaction is not the cause but the product of the life processes of microscopical organisms. Contagion is explained in the same way: its cause is the diffusion of "living corpuscles," endowed with viscosity and stickiness. As such, they can penetrate the fibers of clothing and porous materials, such as wood and cork, bringing forth new seeds of contagion.

Antonio Vallisneri (1661–1730) reintroduced the idea of *contagium vivum* through minute worms (*vermicelli*), able to enter the circulatory system and penetrate deeply into the body. This theory survived into the eighteenth century but faced strong opposition and was practically abandoned at its end. From the very beginning, many writers underlined the limits of the compound microscope and what has been called an illusory micrography. The great clinicians continued to adhere to the classical chemical or mechanical explanations. Philosophers, physicians and natural historians were rather hostile to the idea of a *contagium vivum* and preferred to account for the replicative aspects of disease not by appeal to the replication of a form or a living entity but simply by reference to the distribution of a toxic substance.

The contagion theory, however, played a minor role in Sydenham's main system and in the medical systems of the eighteenth century, which were based on the analysis and classification of the phenomenal or "nominal" essence of the disease, the cluster of symptoms that characterize it and distinguish it from other diseases.

BIBLIOGRAPHY

Belloni, Luigi. Le "contagium vivum" avant Pasteur. Paris: Palais de la Découverte, 1961.

Cipolla, Carlo M. *Fighting the Plague in Seventeenth-Century Italy*. Madison: University of Wisconsin Press. 1981.

————. *Miasma and Disease: Public Health and Environment in the Pre-Industrial Age*. New Haven, CT: Yale University Press, 1992.

Henderson, John. "Epidemics in Renaissance Florence: Medical Theory and Government Response." In *Maladie et société (XIIᵉ–XVIIIᵉ siècles), Colloque de Bielefeld*. Paris: Éditions du CNRS, 1989, pp. 165–186.

Nutton, Vivian. "The Reception of Fracastoro's Theory of Contagion: The Seed That Fell Among Thorns?" *Osiris* 6 (1990), 196–234.

————. "The Seeds of Disease: An Explanation of Contagion and Infection from the Greeks to the Renaissance." *Medical History* 27 (1983), 1–34.

BERNARDINO FANTINI

See also Fermentation; Fracastoro, Girolamo; Helmont, Johannes Baptista van; Humors; Vallisneri, Antonio

Eustachio, Bartolomeo (ca. 1510–1574)

Eustachio was born in San Severino, the son of a doctor. In addition to paternal encouragement to study the original texts of the medical tradition, he could rely upon a solid humanistic education and on his familiarity with Latin, Greek, and Arabic. He moved to Rome as a member of the staff of Cardinal Giulio della Rovere. He quickly advanced through the medical hierarchy, attaining the highest position in the medical guild (the Collegium Medicorum), and later teaching practical medicine at the Archiginnasio della Sapienza from 1555 to 1568.

Apart from writing some texts qualified by his philological education (for instance, he applied it to the analysis of the Hippocratic terminology), Eustachio dedicated most of his efforts to the study of anatomy. In Rome, in order to better conduct his investigations—and quite unusual for the time—the authorities granted him permission to dissect cadavers of deceased patients in the Santo Spirito and Consolazione hospitals. Combining erudition with his human anatomical studies, Eustachio published several treatises focused on specific body parts; there, he presented an anatomy distinctly different from that of Andreas Vesalius (1514–1564). Among these publications, the most important is the treatise dedicated to hearing, in which Eustachio described aural physiology in a new way, including the role of the passage bearing his name. These texts, which were published in Venice in 1564, are collected in his *Opuscola anatomica*.

In one of the *Opuscula*, entitled *Tabulae et figurae anatomicae*, Eustachio explained how to make illustrations of the human body and its sections in several media (paper, wood, and metal). In the *Libellus de renibus*, published in 1563, Eustachio announced the imminent publication of forty-six engravings on copper plates illustrating the complete human anatomy. In fact, these plates were published only many decades later, in 1714, by Giovanni Maria Lancisi; they constitute the first example in an anatomical atlas of the possibility of exactly identifying the described body parts through a system of coordinates—a technique borrowed from geometry.

BIBLIOGRAPHY

Belloni, Luigi. "Bartolomeo Eustachio anatomico del cinquecento, al lume di recenti richerche." *Archives internationales d'histoire des sciences* 29 (1979), 5–50.

————. "Il manoscritto senese de dissensionibus et controversiis anatomicis de Bartolomeo Eustachi (ed altri manoscritti del medesimo Eustachio)." *Physis* 14 (1972), 194–200.

Eustachio, Bartolomeo. "An Epistle on the Organs of Hearing." Trans. and annotated by Charles D. O'Malley. *Clio medica* 8 (1971), 49–62.

Pazzini, Alfredo. "Introduzione e commento storico alle Tavole Anatomiche di Bartolomeo Eustachio." In *Le tavole anatomiche di Bartolomeo Eustachio.* Rome: Bottega dell'antiquario, 1944, pp. 13–79.

ANDREA CARLINO
TRANSLATED BY RENZO BALDASSO

See also Anatomy; Vesalius, Andreas

Experience and Experiment

Experience and experiment lay at the heart of the conceptions of natural knowledge that dominated European learning at both the beginning and the end of the Scientific Revolution. Nonetheless, many of the proponents during the seventeenth century of what came to be called by some (rather obscurely) the New Science criticized the earlier orthodoxy of Aristotelian natural philosophy on the ground that it took insufficiently seriously the lessons of experience. For example, Francis Bacon (1561–1626) wrote in the *New Organon* (1620) that Aristotle (384–322 B.C.E.) "did not consult experience, as he should have done . . . but having first determined the question according to his will, he then resorts to experience, and bending her into conformity with his placets, leads her about like a captive in a procession." Aristotelian philosophy was commonly represented as being obsessed with logic and wordplay rather than attempting to come to grips with things themselves.

Bacon's remark suggests that the Aristotelian approach put experience in a subordinate position to abstract reasoning, using experience only as a means of confirming preconceptions. This was, indeed, a common criticism in the seventeenth century. Nonetheless, Scholastic philosophers who took their lead from Aristotle's texts stressed, following the master himself, that all knowledge took its origin from the senses: "nothing in the mind which was not first in the senses," ran a Scholastic maxim. This emphasis on the sensory origin of knowledge looks like a radical empiricism that makes experience paramount. Indeed, Aristotle himself had regarded even mathematics, apparently the most intellectual field of knowledge and the farthest removed from the messiness of experience, as being rooted in the senses: we gain our ideas of number from seeing collections of things in the world and our ideas of geometrical figures from spatial experience. Clearly, Bacon's criticisms involved a perception of Aristotelian procedures that discounted such considerations.

The explanation for this disjunction lies in the ways in which experience was *used* in the making of knowledge during the Scientific Revolution. The Aristotelian account of a science of the physical world, widely accepted throughout educated Europe during the sixteenth century and much of the seventeenth, regarded it as a logical deductive structure derived from uncontestable basic statements or premises. The model was the structure of classical Greek geometry as exemplified in Euclid's (fl. 300 B.C.E.) *Elements,* in which the truth of unexpected conclusions can be demonstrated by deduction from a delimited set of prior, and supposedly obvious, accepted axioms (such as that "when equals are subtracted from equals, the remainders are equal"). In the case of sciences that concerned the natural world, however, such axioms could obviously not be known by simple introspection. In those cases, the axioms had to be rooted in familiar and commonly accepted experience. Thus, "the sun rises in the east" was unshakeably and universally known through experience, as was the apparently slightly more recondite principle that, in a homogeneous medium, vision (and hence perhaps light rays, depending on one's theory) occurs in straight lines—because everyone knows that it is impossible to see around corners—or that acorns grow into oak trees. On the basis of such experiences, firm deductive sciences of astronomy, of optics, and of plants could be erected. To do this in practice was, of course, much more difficult than to lay it out as an ideal, but as an ideal it dominated Scholastic Aristotelianism into the seventeenth century.

The kind of experience that was involved, therefore, was of a universal, rather than a particular, kind: the Sun *always* rises in the east; acorns *always* (barring accidents) grow into oak trees. Singular experiences were more problematic because they could only subsequently be known by historical report, as something that had happened on a particular occasion. They were thus unfit to act as scientific axioms because they could not receive immediate free assent. A science needed to be *certain,* whereas histories were matters of fallible record and testimony. Of course, the difficulty was unavoidable; most, if not all, of an individual's knowledge of the world relies very heavily on things believed from the testimony of others. Those subscribing to an Aristotelian ideal of science in this sense, therefore, developed a variety of techniques to "universalize" their own specialist empirical work.

E

The areas in which this proved most essential were the so-called mathematical sciences. These were branches of natural knowledge that concerned only the quantitative, measurable properties of things rather than questions to do with what *kinds* of things they were. These latter questions fell under the general disciplinary heading of "natural philosophy," as distinct from "mathematics." Thus, such sciences as astronomy (studying the arrangement and movements of celestial objects) and geometrical optics (studying the quantitative behavior of geometrically construed light rays) were branches of "mathematics"; they were also the sciences that made greatest use of specialized instruments, sometimes including custom-made experimental apparatus, to generate precise empirical results. This meant that they provided to their practitioners recondite knowledge that was, for that reason, hard to fit into the mold of a demonstrative science because it was not rooted in generally accepted experiential data.

By way of compensation, therefore, astronomers and others relied on their individual and corporate reputations (in the case of university practitioners) as reliable truth-tellers, so as to lend weight to their empirical claims. They did not need to rely exclusively on such a weak foundation, however, because astronomers were not in the habit of publishing raw astronomical data. The proof of the astronomical pudding was in the testing. Rather than present observational results certified on their say-so, they used their data as a means of generating, via geometrical models of celestial motions, predictive tables of planetary, solar, or lunar positions; there was no formal separation between the observational and the calculatory parts of the enterprise. Nicolaus Copernicus's (1473–1543) reputation as an astronomer lay in the sixteenth century with his mathematical abilities not with his presumed competence as an observer. In the later sixteenth century, Tycho Brahe (1546–1601), although famous as an indefatigable observer, did not publish his vast accumulation of observational results but instead published calculations of cometary parallax and his new earth-centered astronomical system, while hiring Johannes Kepler (1571–1630) to compute a new, more accurate model for the motion of Mars from his raw data.

The Aristotelian kind of scientific experience continued to hold sway even among figures later regarded as being in the vanguard of the Scientific Revolution. Galileo Galilei (1564–1642) adduced the results of experiments in such a way as to avoid as much as pos-

sible calling on his own authority to render his claimed results credible. In his famous account of fall along inclined planes, published in his *Two New Sciences* (1638), rather than describe a specific experiment or set of experiments carried out at a particular time, together with a detailed quantitative record of the outcomes, Galileo just says that, with apparatus of a certain sort, he had found that the results agreed exactly with his theoretical assumptions—and he says that he repeated the trials "a full hundred times." The phrase (found frequently, in various forms, in Scholastic writings) means something like "more than enough times." Galileo, that is, tries to establish the authenticity of the experience that falling bodies do behave as he says they do by basing it on the memory of many individual instances.

Galileo is not here presenting a report of an *experiment,* in the sense of a reported, singular historical event; instead, he tells the reader what *happens.* The reader is assured, in effect, that it is entirely to be expected that the world would behave in this particular way; that the empirical assertions are perfectly consonant with ordinary events. Thus, for Galileo, the proper construal of experience was unproblematically Aristotelian, to the extent that it was not even recognized as being Aristotelian: in Galileo's world, this was simply what experience was.

Galileo's approach is mirrored in many contemporary Scholastic texts (such as those by Jesuits like Giovanni Battista Riccioli) in the mathematical sciences of the natural world: detailed accounts of experimental or observational apparatus—a precedent for which might be found in Ptolemy's (ca. 100–ca. 170) account of astronomical-sighting instruments in his classic *Almagest* from the second century—were commonly followed by assertions of the results of their use. By ignoring the issue of trust altogether, such writers evidently hoped to win assent for their less-than-obvious empirical principles; distrust was not presented as a relevant option.

Beyond the confines of academic practice, "experience" had other connotations as well. In the sixteenth century, opponents of university learning, most prominently Paracelsus (ca. 1491–1541) in the 1530s and 1540s, held up experience as an alternative to the elaborate epistemology of the Aristotelians. Paracelsus advocated a closer acquaintance with things themselves as the way to acquire knowledge of a practical, operational kind—in contrast to the Aristotelian focus on philosophical *understanding.* His particular concern was with medicine, an unavoidably practical specialty. By stressing knowledge of the properties of things and how to make use of them, Paracelsus turned attention squarely to the practical experience of the artisan, taken to have an intimate, almost mystical rapport with things themselves.

Others subsequently in the century, particularly but by no means exclusively in England, advocated a similar upgrading of artisanal knowledge, their most accomplished representative being Francis Bacon. In the closing decade of the sixteenth century and the first quarter-century or so thereafter, Bacon promoted a reformed "natural philosophy" directed toward different ends from that of the schools, again emphasizing the practical benefits to be derived from knowledge of nature and praising the craft knowledge of artisans. Bacon held up "experience" as the route to such knowledge, by which he meant the scrupulous examination of, and the collection of facts regarding, the properties and behaviors of physical phenomena. These facts remained, however, generic: they concerned "how things behave" and took for granted the establishment of such general facts from singular instances, much like the Aristotelian conception. The main exception was Bacon's concern with "monsters"—that is, individual cases in which nature does *not* behave in its normal, regular way.

In a major way, specific set-piece experiments seem first to have entered into knowledge-making practices regarding the inanimate world in the domain of the mathematical sciences. It is in these that we first find regular use of historical reports of particular events to justify universal statements about how some aspect of nature behaves. Hints of this departure are found in Galileo's work as discussed above; but where Galileo tried to avoid placing the justification for his claims on historical reports, other writers on similar quantitatively focused "mathematical" sciences began on occasion to describe particular, contrived events. Thus, Jesuit mathematical scientists, including Riccioli, reported experiments that involved dropping weights from the tops of church towers to determine their rates of acceleration and gave places, dates, and witnesses to underwrite their stories. One of the most famous such instances in the seventeenth century, organized by Blaise Pascal (1623–1662), took place in 1648. Pascal had asked his brother-in-law, Florin Périer, off in the provinces, to take a mercury barometer up a nearby mountain so as to determine whether the mercury's height in the glass tube decreased with increasing altitude. Pascal expected that it would

and believed that such an eventuality would confirm his conviction that the mercury column in its tube was sustained by the weight of the air—there being less atmospheric air to weigh down and thus counterweight the mercury at higher elevations.

Périer's report, quickly published by Pascal, gives a detailed circumstantial account of his trip up the mountain and back, in named company, one day in September, and the measurements that were made along the way. Pascal turned the narrative to account by using its results to predict the expected drop in height of mercury to be expected in ascents of church towers in Paris, promptly asserting that actual trials bore out those predictions. While not an unequivocal use of a recorded event as justifying evidence for a claim about nature, Pascal's promotion of the trial indicates the role that contrived, set-piece experiments, historically reported, were beginning to play. It is with the Royal Society of London, founded in the early 1660s, and especially with the exemplary work of Robert Boyle (1627–1691), that concern with such reports becomes solidly established as the foundation of a new natural philosophy.

The sources of the Royal Society's predilection for historical reports as the core of its communal enterprise are difficult to pin down. The Fellows of the early Society credited Francis Bacon with having inspired their enterprise, and their professed concern with useful knowledge, and with empirical investigation as the means to its acquisition, has many resonances with Bacon's work. But concern with particularities could also be found in the well-established traditions of medical practice.

The case history goes back to the Hippocratic writings (ca. 450–ca. 350 B.C.E.) of Greek antiquity. Case histories recorded in detail the progression of a disease in a particular patient, from onset to resolution (either death or a return to health). Their meaning was contested in antiquity itself, with different medical sects interpreting them as either particular instances of independently existing disease entities (a case of measles, for example) or as wholly specific to the individual patient. Through most of the sixteenth and seventeenth centuries, the usual academic approach to medicine (the one so violently opposed by Paracelsus and his later followers) derived from the writings of the ancient Greco-Roman physician Galen (second century C.E.), and, following his general theoretical approach, physicians usually treated case histories as means to determine the generic nature of the ailment (typically in terms of an imbalance of the

E

four humors). The teaching of human anatomy formed an integral part of an early-modern medical education in the universities, and it, too, had its established ways of doing things. In the sixteenth century, again with frequent bows to the example set by Galen, anatomists conceived of their enterprise as being, above all, one of disciplined *seeing,* and what they saw in the corpses that they dissected was generally taken to be representative of all human beings. William Harvey (1578–1657), writing in the 1620s, regarded his work on the circulation of the blood as fundamentally a matter of looking in the right way, rather than as active experimentation—which would have posed methodological problems to an Aristotelian such as Harvey.

Indeed, this is why experimentation seems to have grown up most vigorously, during the seventeenth century, in the mathematical sciences of nature. Aristotle's natural philosophy was especially concerned with "final causes," the purposes or ends toward which processes tended or that explained the conformation and capacities of something. Living creatures were model instances of this: all of the parts of an animal's body seem to be fitted to their particular functions, and, by studying their behaviors passively, one could find out what they were doing—that is, what they were *for.* Interference, by setting up artificial conditions, would risk subverting the natural course of things, hence yielding misleading results; experimentation would be just such interference. Experiments in the inanimate world ran into the same problem: to the extent that Aristotle's natural philosophy sought the final causes of things, thereby to determine their natures, experimental science was disallowed. But the mathematical sciences dealt only with quantitative characteristics—those properties of things that could be approached through arithmetic or geometry. Careless of final causes and essential natures, the kind of knowledge that they sought was uncompromised by experimental contrivance.

A combination of mathematical unconcern with teleology and the favoring of historical particulars in the empirical establishment of (potentially useful) natural knowledge may be seen in the work of the early Royal Society and, to some degree, of the early Royal Academy of Sciences in Paris (founded 1666), among a variety of locations. Isaac Newton (1642–1727) represents the fullest expression of this development; as a result of his work, the "experimental philosophy" touted by Robert Boyle became wedded to the traditional quasi-experimental

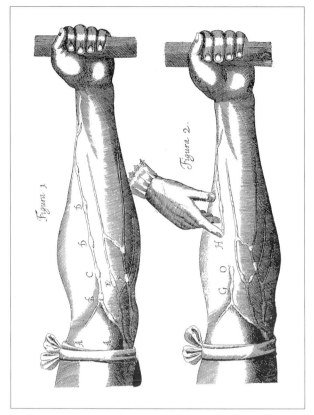

William Harvey invited readers of his De motu cordis *(1628) to experiment with their arms. By pushing their blood certain ways in the distended veins, they could see for themselves that the valves in the veins allowed the blood to flow only toward the heart, thereby challenging accepted Galenic beliefs on the motion of the blood.*

practices of the mathematical sciences to yield a new synthesis that became established in the eighteenth century as Newtonianism. The methodological hallmark of Newtonianism was a characteristically agnostic stance toward fundamental causal claims regarding the inner natures, or essences, of the things being investigated. Thus, Newton put forward his ideas on light and colors as being solidly rooted in experience, not venturing beyond the high degree of certainty that the mathematical science of optics traditionally afforded. He claimed only to show by experiment that white light was a mixture of the colors. When undergoing refraction to yield a spectrum, white light separated into its components, rather than the refractive colors being newly created from the white light. Newton denied that his claims relied in any way on a particular notion of the true *nature* of light—whether it be made up of particles or of waves, for example. Similarly, in speaking of inverse-square-law universal gravitation, Newton wished to be understood as demonstrating (again, through experiment and observation) the existence of such a universally distributed force acting between particles of matter, but *not* to be asserting any theoretical *cause* of that force. Whatever caused gravitational attraction, the quantitative *properties* of gravity remained as he had demonstrated them to be.

Newton's use of historically reported experiments and the character of his mathematical-scientific work thereby represented to the eighteenth century a newly consolidated, alternative conception of scientific experience. Where for Aristotelians scientific "experience" was a matter of what one learned about the ways of the world (and then needed to explain) by virtue of living and moving around in it every day, for a natural philosopher of the eighteenth century it had become a technique for interrogating nature (if necessary, "torturing" it, in Bacon's word). No longer a matter of "what everyone knows," the experimental approach to knowledge aimed at accumulating records of natural behavior that would be accepted by others on the secure word of witnesses or institutional authority. It was a kind of science that aimed at operational effects and took increasingly less interest in extraneous matters of underlying natures or causes.

BIBLIOGRAPHY

Baroncini, Gabriele. *Forme di esperienza e rivoluzione scientifica.* (Bibliotheca di Nuncius, Studi e testi IX). Florence: Leo S. Olschki, 1992.

Daston, Lorraine J. "Baconian Facts, Academic Civility, and the Prehistory of Objectivity." *Annals of Scholarship* 8 (1991), 337–363.

Dear, Peter. *Discipline and Experience: The Mathematical Way in the Scientific Revolution.* Chicago: University of Chicago Press, 1995.

Garber, Daniel. "Descartes and Experiment in the *Discourse* and the *Essays.*" In *Essays on the Philosophy and Science of René Descartes,* ed. Stephen Voss. Oxford: Oxford University Press, 1993, pp. 288–310.

Koyré, Alexandre. "An Experiment in Measurement." In Koyré, Alexandre. *Metaphysics and Measurement.* London: Chapman and Hall, 1968, pp. 89–117.

Licoppe, Christian. *La formation de la pratique scientifique: Le discours de l'expérience en France et en Angleterre (1630–1820).* Paris: Éditions la Découverte, 1996.

Schmitt, Charles B. "Experience and Experiment: A Comparison of Zabarella's View with Galileo's in *De motu.*" *Studies in the Renaissance* 16 (1969), 80–138.

Shapin, Steven. "Pump and Circumstance: Robert Boyle's Literary Technology." *Social Studies of Science* 14 (1984), 481–520.

Wear, Andrew. "William Harvey and the 'Way of the Anatomists.'" *History of Science* 21 (1983), 223–249.

PETER R. DEAR

See also Aristotelianism; Demonstration; Empiricism; Laws of Nature; Logic; Teleology; Theory

Exploration and Discovery

Between the fifteenth and the seventeenth centuries, Europeans greatly increased their knowledge of the globe and of the people, animals, and plants found in it. While exploration was never unique to Europeans, the voyages of the fifteenth century, culminating in the Portuguese discovery of a sea route to India and the Spanish discovery of the Americas, set the stage for centuries of expansion to both east and west. The resulting encounters eventually caused Europeans to rethink their ideas about the world.

Much exploration was driven by attempts to find new routes to India and China, in order to trade directly for spices and silks. Spices were in high demand, to both preserve and flavor food, and thus offered the lure of huge profits. The medieval silk road went overland across central Asia, and in the fifteenth century it was becoming increasingly dangerous and expensive with the expansion of the Ottoman Empire. Since travel by land was slower and more arduous than water transport, and the European end of the silk road was largely monopolized by the Venetian Republic, a sea route would give other countries the opportunity to bypass intermediaries and join in this lucrative trade.

The motivations for exploration were never simply economic. In Africa, the Portuguese searched not only for a way to India, but also for a legendary Christian king, Prester John, who as a rich and powerful Christian was seen as a natural ally against Islamic rulers. Missionaries attempting to convert the local inhabitants often pressed into new areas and sent back detailed reports of their findings. Many explorers also sought for legendary islands such as Hy-Brasil or followed local reports of fabulous wealth, as in the search for El Dorado.

The Portuguese were the first to search actively for a route to the East. Lured by evidence of gold in Africa and potential rich trade with the East, Prince Henry the Navigator (1398–1460) sent many expeditions south along the coast of Africa. Vasco da Gama (ca. 1460–1524) reached India in 1498. Subsequent Portuguese voyagers established bases and local trade networks, as they fought for control of the Indian Ocean and founded fortresses in Goa and Malacca. The knowledge gained of the local weather systems, while long familiar to Chinese and Arab traders, proved invaluable for later European trade and exploration in the Indian Ocean. Portuguese trade envoys, then followed by missionaries, also reached Japan, Persia, and China, where in 1557 they received permission to found a trading base at Macao.

By the end of the century, Portuguese influence was declining and was replaced by that of the Dutch and the English. The English tried to reach the East both via the New World and by sailing to the northeast, but, though the latter search opened trade with Russia, both routes proved too arduous to be commercially viable. Though the English next tried the sea route around Africa, the Dutch had better luck in their early voyages and formed the Dutch East India Company in 1602. Subsequent Dutch voyages concentrated almost exclusively on Java and the Spice Islands, leading to great economic success and supplanting the Portuguese in the spice trade.

The Dutch traders favored a southerly route through the Indian Ocean, initially avoiding India and the fortified Portuguese bases. Beginning in 1605, a series of ships dropped anchor in various parts of what is now known as Australia. Abel Janszoon Tasman (1603–1659) explored the northern coast of Australia and made a wide circle around the rest in the 1640s, discovering Tasmania and New Zealand. However, the coast looked inhospitable, and little organized exploration was done until the eighteenth century.

The other major focus of exploration was to the west. As the Portuguese were exploring the coast of Africa, Christopher Columbus (ca. 1451–1506) persuaded the Spanish monarchs to fund his expedition west across the Atlantic. Encouraged by a mistaken calculation of the size of the earth, he hoped to sail around the world and reach the Indies from the other side. His three ships left in 1492 and made landfall in the Caribbean, which he thought was near Japan.

After Columbus's return, the Spanish focused most of their energy in the new lands to the west. In 1503 Seville's newly founded House of Trade began to regulate all voyages to the Indies. Hernán Cortes (1485–1547) conquered the Aztec Empire, and Francisco Pizarro (1476–1541) that of the Incas. Their successes and rich booty encouraged others merchants, missionaries, and colonists to follow them. Much of the overland

Thomas Harriot's report of the discovery, resources, and people of Virginia, published in 1590.

exploration was driven by the search for gold, as groups of Conquistadors followed what they interpreted as reports of riches across the continent.

While some worked to exploit the new lands, others saw them as an obstacle in the path of trade with the East and explored the coasts in search of a passage through the continent. A 1519–1522 expedition led by Ferdinand Magellan (ca. 1480–1521) found a strait far to the south. Though Magellan died along the way, the sole returning ship completed the first circumnavigation of the globe and opened a Spanish claim to a share of the Eastern trade.

The inevitably disappointed search for a northwest passage attracted England and France to explore the New World. Sailing for the English, John Cabot (ca. 1450–ca. 1499) had reached what is now Newfoundland in 1497, finding valuable fishing grounds. Subsequent English and French voyages greatly increased knowledge of the coast and river systems of North America, harvested large quantities of fish and furs, and planted colonies. The English privateer Sir Francis Drake (ca. 1540–1596) searched parts of the Pacific coast, while also attacking Spanish colonies and treasure ships and eventually circumnavigating the globe. But no convenient passage was forthcoming.

Exploration led to new discoveries, fostering new needs and encouraging different ways of thinking about the world. Most obviously, it increased geographical knowledge and gave new impetus to progress in navigation. As reliable ocean travel became economically and strategically important, various nations began to regulate navigation and fund research into cartography, navigational instruments, and ways of finding longitude at sea, using astronomical observation or compass declination.

Explorations also emphasized the political importance of geography and cartography. The Treaty of Tordesillas (1494) used longitude to divide the world into Spanish and Portuguese spheres of influence. During the sixteenth century, both governments summoned geographers to give their opinions on the locations of disputed lands, making geographic and cartographic expertise a weapon in the hands of the diplomats.

As interest in exploration increased, so did books about voyages and associated discoveries. Richard Hakluyt (1552–1616), who was perhaps exploration's most influential propagandist, published accounts of voyages to promote English investment. Others, such as the Spaniards José de Acosta (ca. 1540–1600) and Bernardino de Sahugun (1499–1590), focused less on explorations per se than on the New World itself and the customs of the newly encountered peoples. New peoples, animals, and plants spurred an interest in collections, ethnology, and natural history as the Europeans struggled to fit this New World into their system of knowledge. Plants such as tobacco were interesting both for possible economic and medicinal value and for their novelty. The existence in the New World of flora and fauna unknown in classical texts, and the errors in these texts revealed by these and other discoveries, eventually transformed attitudes about the relative importance of authorities and empirical evidence.

BIBLIOGRAPHY

Boxer, C. R. *The Portuguese Seaborne Empire, 1415–1825.* New York: Knopf, 1969.

Fernandez-Armesto, Felipe, ed. *The Times Atlas of World Exploration: Three Thousand Years of Exploring, Explorers, and Map Making.* New York: HarperCollins, 1991.

Grafton, Anthony, with April Shelford and Nancy Siraisi. *New Worlds, Ancient Texts: The Power of Tradition and the Shock of Discovery.* Cambridge, MA: Belknap Press of Harvard University Press, 1992.

Morison, Samuel Eliot. *The European Discovery of America.* 2 vols. New York: Oxford University Press, 1971–1974.

Parry, J. H. *The Age of Reconnaissance: Discovery, Exploration, and Settlement, 1450–1650.* London: Weidenfeld and Nicolson, 1963.

ALISON SANDMAN

See also Anthropology and Race; Cartography; Casa de la Contratación; Geography; Navigation

F

Fabri, Honoré (1607–1688)

A French Jesuit who taught philosophy in the Jesuit college at Lyon (1640–1646). He then had a career in the Church hierarchy in Rome as theologian and confessor but continued to pursue his interests in natural philosophy, publishing numerous works. He was made corresponding member of the Accademia del Cimento in Florence and engaged in correspondence with many prominent contemporaries on numerous topical physical and mathematical issues in geometry, optics, astronomy, and dynamics.

Fabri can best be regarded as an adherent of Aristotelian natural philosophy who sought to maintain the core of the traditional philosophy while integrating into it what he regarded as the best elements of the new natural philosophy. He was an enthusiastic proponent of mathematics and experiment but not of the metaphysical basis of the New Physics. He believed, for example, that materialist physics, such as René Descartes's (1596–1650), was dangerous to the Catholic faith (although he was himself accused of being a Cartesian). He admired Galileo Galilei's (1564–1642) studies of motion but thought that such mathematical dynamics were merely descriptive and not truly scientific according to the standards of Aristotle's (384–322 B.C.E.) *Posterior Analytics* and that it was also necessary to give a causal account of motion. He sought to provide this, ultimately unsuccessfully, by using the late-medieval concept of impetus.

He admitted the fluidity of the heavens, and, after first questioning Christiaan Huygens's (1629–1695) ring theory of Saturn, he acknowledged its correctness. Fabri never accepted heliocentrism, however, stating that there was not enough physical evidence in favor of it to overcome the scriptural passages against it, and he wrote a dialogue attempting to prove physically the immobility of the earth. Fabri made several contributions in mathematics, in particular in the geometry of curves and solids. Gottfried Wilhelm Leibniz (1646–1716) studied Fabri's geometry, acknowledged its influence on his own work, and unintentionally provoked the irascible Isaac Newton (1642–1727) by identifying similarities in Newton's mathematics and Fabri's geometry.

BIBLIOGRAPHY
Boehm, A. "L'aristotélisme d'Honoré Fabri." *Revue des sciences religieuses* 39 (1965), 305–360.
Dear, Peter. *Discipline and Experience: The Mathematical Way in the Scientific Revolution.* Chicago: University of Chicago Press, 1995.
Fellmann, E. A. "Die mathematischen Werke von Honoratus Fabry (1607–1688)." *Physis* 1 (1959), 6–25, 73–102.

MARCUS HELLYER

See also Aristotelianism; Calculus; Impetus

Fabrici, Girolamo (Fabricius ab Acquapendente) (ca. 1533–1619)

Born at Acquapendente, a small village north of Rome, he moved to Padua, where he studied with the great anatomist Gabriele Falloppio (1523–1562), succeeding him at his death in 1562 as teacher of anatomy. In 1565 Fabrici was named professor of anatomy and surgery at the Padua medical school, a post he held until he retired in 1613. In 1594 Fabrici convinced the faculty to build a permanent anatomical theater, which is still preserved. Among his students were Caspar Bartholin, Ole Worm, Gaspard Bauhin, Peter Paaw, and William Harvey.

Fabrici's importance for the history of medicine and the Scientific Revolution rests on his anatomical and embryological works and in his role as teacher of William Harvey (1578–1657), who referred often to his theories and observations. Almost all of Fabrici's treatises were published at the end of his life, a first group ca. 1600, another in his late years. Many of his treatises were meant as part of an unfinished *Totius animalis fabricae anatomicae* (The Complete Anatomical Structures of Living Things). A total of 167 anatomical plates are preserved in St. Mark's Library in Venice, part of the three hundred color plates that Fabrici produced in 1600.

As a surgeon and physician, Fabrici enjoyed a high professional reputation. His surgical works were published in 1592 and republished in 1619 with an addendum. This was the most complete surgical treatise at the time and contains many plates illustrating surgical instruments. In surgery, however, Fabrici's diagnostic and therapeutics methods conform to the Hippocratic and Galenic tradition.

The treatise *De venarum ostiolis* (On the Valves in the Veins, 1603) reports the observations made by Fabrici in 1574, in particular the valves at the opening of collateral branches of the veins. He proposed a teleological and Galenic explanation, interpreting the function of the valves to be the slowing down of the centrifugal flux of blood in order to obtain an even distribution to the various parts of the body. In addition, the valves have a static function, reinforcing the walls of the veins and preventing the stretching of the blood vessels. He carried out an experiment, ligating the veins and observing the valves in action, applying pressure with a finger. This treatise was used by William Harvey as the starting point of his study of the circulation of blood.

Fabrici's anatomical observations are centered on three aspects of each organ: its structure (i.e., anatomy), its action, and its utility. He devoted several treatises to the anatomy of different sensory organs and their function. His primary research field was the study of fetal anatomy in order to find the purpose of the different organs on teleological grounds, aiming at reconciling his observations with the traditional Galenic concepts. He gave much attention to the link between structure and function of the organs of the body, and in this context he wrote that he was unwillingly obliged by his daily observations to affirm his disagreement with Aristotle (384–322 B.C.E.) and Galen (second century).

Fabrici's embryological studies include *De formatione ovi et pulli* (On the Formation of the Egg and Chick), published posthumously in 1621, and his last treatise on the subject, *De formato foetu* (On the Formed Fetus, 1603), both containing many plates. In the first treatise, Fabrici discusses the causes and conditions of generation, the role of the egg and the sperm, and the order in which the various parts of the embryo are formed during development. For the last question, he refutes both the Aristotelian theory that gave priority to the heart and the Galenic one that considered that the liver was formed first, giving priority instead to the blood. *On the Formed Fetus* concentrates on the organs needed to provide for the necessities of the fetus during intrauterine life and includes comparative studies of, among other things, the placenta, the umbilical vessels, and the fetal membranes in different animals. For this reason, Fabrici is considered a comparative anatomist, even if he did not analyze the affinities and homology of

Girolamo Fabrici. From Hieronymus Fabricius ab Acquapendente, Opera omnia *(1738).*

function and structure. His study of the placenta and its significance is the most original part of this treatise, limiting the use of the term, first introduced by Realdo Colombo (ca. 1510–1559), to the type found in humans and other animals. In the last years of his life, Fabrici published several physiological treatises, which were probably influenced by his contacts with the new generation of scientists, in particular Galileo Galilei (1564–1642), who had left Padua in 1610. The new scientific style aimed at general laws based on empirical evidence. In this style, Fabrici, taking up the challenge, wished to study movement "in general," trying to explain animal movement by simple physical laws. He seems to have been the first to apply physical laws to the study of movement, establishing in particular the muscular progression needed to overcome resistance, anticipating the analogous researches by Galileo and Giovanni Alfonso Borelli, published respectively in 1638 and 1680. Because of this new approach, Fabrizi's last treatises have been considered the weakest part of his scientific work, but they are also an effort to overcome the limits of purely anatomical description and to establish a close relationship between the study of form and the explanation of function.

BIBLIOGRAPHY

Fabrizi d'Acquapendente, Girolamo. *Opera omnia anatomica et physiologica*. Leipzig, 1687.

Fabricius ab Acquapendente. *The Embryological Treatises of Hieronymus Fabricius of Acquapendente*. Ed. and trans. with Introduction and Commentary by Howard Bernhardt Adelmann. 2 vols. Ithaca, NY: Cornell University Press, 1942, 1967.

Fossati, Pier Maria, ed. *Girolamo Fabrizi da Acquapendente, Medico e anatomista: La vita e le opere*. Acquapendente, 1988.

Scipio, Rosario, ed. *Girolamo Fabrici, l'Acquapendente*. Viterbo: Agnesotti, 1978.

BERNARDINO FANTINI

See also Anatomy; Embryology; Generation; Harvey, William; Surgery

Falloppio, Gabriele (1523–1562)

Falloppio was born in Modena and remained there until 1544. During his adolescence, he obtained a humanistic education as a prelude to an ecclesiastical career. During those years, Falloppio developed interests in both medicine and botany. Because the University of Modena did not offer the medical degree, Falloppio completed his partly self-taught education studying, possibly first, in Padua and later in Ferrara.

Falloppio taught in Ferrara (1547–1548), in Pisa (1548–1551), and in Padua (1551–1562). In these universities, he taught courses in anatomy, surgery, and *semplici* (pharmaceutical botany). At the same time, he continued to be a practicing doctor, counting among his patients many from the ranks of political and intellectual elites.

The name Falloppio is usually associated with his studies in anatomy. He enjoyed high esteem among his contemporaries because of his ability in dissecting human and animal bodies. The studies and results of his anatomical research are presented in *Observationes anatomicae* (1561). This book demonstrates Falloppio's subscription to the theories of the New Anatomy proposed by Andreas Vesalius (1514–1564); furthermore, it presents some important anatomical discoveries, such as the seminal ducts. In addition to anatomical studies, Falloppio distinguished himself for the wide breadth of his knowledge and for the many research projects—in a variety of areas—he undertook during his career. These

Gabriele Falloppio. From Fielding H. Garrison, An Introduction to the History of Medicine, *3rd ed. (Philadelphia and London: W. B. Saunders, 1921).*

accomplishments are confirmed by the numerous books published posthumously by his students, based on the manuscripts of lecture notes taken from the courses he taught at the university.

Throughout his scientific career, botany and the art of drugmaking always remained very important; in fact, through accurate textual analysis, Falloppio dedicated himself to identifying the plants described in Greek, Latin, and Arabic herbals. His interests in the natural world, especially in the study of plants and minerals, were associated with therapeutic experiments on human subjects with remedies based on organic and inorganic substances.

Falloppio's researches in pharmacology and anatomy were guided by an approach that relied on experiment, direct observation, and empirical verification of the canonical texts in the medico-naturalistic tradition.

BIBLIOGRAPHY

Favaro, Giuseppe. *Gabrielle Falloppia, Modenese (MDXXIII–MDLXII): Studio biografico.* Modena: Immacolata Consezione, 1928.

Franceschini, Pietro. "Luci e ombre nella stori delle tube di Falloppia." *Physis* 7 (1965), 215–250.

O'Malley, Charles D. "Gabrielle Falloppia's Account of the Orbital Muscles." In *Medicine, Science, and Culture: Historical Essays in Honor of Owsei Temkin,* ed. Lloyd G. Stevenson and Robert P. Multhauf. Baltimore: Johns Hopkins University Press, 1968, pp. 77–85.

Zanier, Giancarlo. "Gabriele Falloppia e la filosofia dei minerali." In Zanier, G. *Medicina e filosofia tra '500 e '600.* Milan: Franco Angeli Editore, 1983, pp. 5–19.

ANDREA CARLINO
TRANSLATED BY RENZO BALDASSO

See also Anatomy; Botany; Pharmacology; Vesalius, Andreas

Fermat, Pierre de (1601–1665)

A lawyer by profession but a mathematician by preference, he was a mathematical amateur only in the sense that he sought no payment for the considerable results he generated at his leisure. Following François Viète (1540–1603), Fermat fashioned algebraic tools that he employed in the solution of previously unsolved geometric problems involving properties of curved lines and figures, such as the determination of maxima and minima, tangents, and quadratures. Literally, "quadrature" comes from the Latin verb *quadrare,* meaning "to square." Mathematically, determining the quadrature of a curve

involves finding rectilinear areas comparable to curvilinear areas under the curve. Historically, quadrature is the precursor of integration. Many of the problems Fermat investigated had been studied in a piecemeal fashion by Archimedes (ca. 287–212 B.C.E.), and Fermat's respect for the Greek geometry of antiquity is evident in his writings. Yet, Fermat shares the credit with René Descartes (1596–1650) for the invention of analytic geometry because of his novel use of algebra in his treatment of classical problems. The unprecedented generality and uniformity of Fermat's solutions contributed to the invention of the infinitesimal calculus.

Fermat's contributions have not always been evident to his successors, as he was loath to publish his results. Reading his correspondence, one gets the impression that the painstaking work of preparing material for publication would take all the fun out of his otherwise relaxing hobby. Fermat's reluctance to publish annoyed his contemporaries, who recognized the value of his work and contributed to the relative historical neglect of Fermat. Recent scholarship rescues Fermat from undeserved obscurity as evidence emerges that both Isaac Newton (1642–1727) (via John Wallis) and Gottfried Wilhelm Leibniz (1646–1716) (via Christiaan Huygens) were exposed to Fermat's inventive problem-solving techniques. To see Fermat's most enduring contribution to mathematics, however, one must not view the invention of analytic geometry as separate from those methods that anticipated the nascent infinitesimal calculus. Fermat not only developed notational tools characteristic of modern mathematics, he demonstrated their effectiveness by employing them successfully in the solution of a broad spectrum of mathematical problems. Particular results, like his quadrature technique, were eclipsed by the infinitesimal calculus, but the algebraic representational strategy that Fermat employed endures as a defining characteristic of modern mathematics.

Ironically, Fermat is most famous for something he did not do. In addition to studying Viète and Archimedes, Fermat studied the *Arithmetica* of Diophantus of Alexendria in an edition published by Bachet in 1621. In the margin of his copy of this book, Fermat wrote that he could demonstrate a theorem, which may be expressed in modern language as: there are no positive integers $x, y,$ and z such that,

$$x^n + y^n = z^n$$

when $n > 2$. However, he did not jot down the demonstration itself, claiming that the margin of the book was too small. Fermat's demonstration of the particular claim that there are no positive integers x, y, and z that satisfy the equation when $n = 3$ survives. If he had a truly general proof of what became known as "Fermat's last theorem" the proof is now lost. A proof of this conjecture was recently found by Andrew Wiles and is accepted by the mathematical community. Fermat's efforts to excite interest in the problem among his seventeenth-century contemporaries was to no avail. Nevertheless, Fermat's largely solitary investigations of the properties of numbers represent the origins of modern number theory.

In correspondence with Blaise Pascal (1623–1662) on various games of chance, Fermat brought his abilities to bear on the study of probability. Together, they contributed to the edifice that became the foundation of modern probability theory. Like many of his contemporaries, Fermat's interests went beyond pure mathematics to include geostatics and optics.

BIBLIOGRAPHY

Breger, Herbert. "The Mysteries of Adaequare: A Vindication of Fermat." *Archive for History of the Exact Sciences* 46 (1994), 193–219.

Cifoletti, Giovanna Cleonice. *La méthode de Fermat: Sa statut et sa diffusion: Algèbre et comparaison de figures dans l'histoire de la méthode de Fermat.* Paris: Société Française d'Histoire des Sciences et des Techniques, 1990.

Fermat, Pierre de. *Oeuvres.* Ed. Paul Tannery and Charles Henry. 4 vols. and supp. Paris: Gauthier-Villars et fils, 1891–1922.

Mahoney, Michael S. *The Mathematical Career of Pierre de Fermat, 1601–1665.* Princeton, NJ: Princeton University Press, 1973. 2nd ed. 1994.

MADELINE M. MUNTERSBJORN

See also Algebra; Analytic Geometry; Probability

Fermentation

The concept of fermentation was quite literally the general factotum or do-all of early-modern science. It was used to explain an extraordinary number of phenomena, both organic and inorganic. These included digestion; sanguification; body heat; glandular secretion; fever; contagious disease; the motion of the heart; muscular contraction; the conversion of blood into flesh; the generation and growth of animals, plants, and minerals; the rusting of iron; subterranean fires; hot springs; and even tempests and hurricanes.

Just as remarkable as the number of phenomena explained in terms of fermentation was the number of natural philosophers putting forth those explanations. In addition to scores of lesser-known figures, this included such important personages in the history of science as Giovanni Alfonso Borelli (1608–1679), Robert Boyle (1627–1691), Walter Charleton (1620–1707), René Descartes (1596–1650), Pierre Gassendi (1592–1655), William Harvey (1578–1657), Johannes Baptista van Helmont (1579–1644), Marcello Malpighi (1628–1694), John Mayow (1641–1679), Isaac Newton (1642–1727), Franciscus Sylvius (1614–1672), and Thomas Willis (1621–1675). In short, the doctrine of fermentation proved to be so appealing that it was adopted (to varying degrees) by virtually everyone in the European scientific community during the latter decades of the seventeenth century. Even after that point, it continued to attract adherents well into the nineteenth century.

The doctrine of fermentation first took shape in the writings of Joseph Duchesne (1544–1609) and Pietro Castelli (ca. 1575–1661). Both of these physicians utilized fermentation in their attempts to develop new explanations for gastric digestion. For centuries, the process of digestion had been regarded as the archetype of natural change in general and physiological change in particular. Scholastic medicine—which was based largely on the writings of Aristotle (384–322 B.C.E.) and Galen (second century)—taught that much of physiology should be seen as a series of digestions: the first of these takes place in the stomach and involves the transmutation of food into chyle; the second takes place in the liver and involves the conversion of chyle into blood; the third takes place in the tissues and involves the conversion of blood into flesh.

Because digestion was so significant in premodern physiological thought, any change in the explanation of this seemingly simple process was bound to shake the very foundations of medical science as a whole. According to the Scholastics, all digestions are caused by (what Galen called) the "alterative faculty" of the soul and its primary instrument, "innate heat." Though it was never quite clear what "innate heat" and the "alterative faculty" were, this explanation of digestion went unchallenged for more than a millennium.

In the 1620s, however, Castelli argued that the Scholastic theory of digestion was untenable. He pointed out that, if heat were the cause of digestion, then one should be able to duplicate this process in a cooking pot.

He also noted that fish are perfectly capable of digestion, despite being totally devoid of body heat.

Castelli was well versed in alchemy, which taught that all physical transmutations (including the transmutation of lead into gold) are produced by fermentations. With this in mind, Castelli argued in the first place that gastric digestion must be caused by fermentation. He also insisted that animal generation is a fermentative process. In the ensuing decades, others went much further. Johannes Baptista van Helmont, for example, contended that all "digestions" formerly attributed by the Scholastics to heat are actually caused by fermentations.

Though its intellectual roots could be traced to alchemy (which was thoroughly vitalistic), by the mid-seventeenth century the doctrine of fermentation was also adopted by the advocates of the mechanical philosophy. Conceived in corpuscular terms, fermentation was generally defined as "an intestine motion of particles." The mechanical philosophers saw fermentation as a mechanism by which one form of corpuscular matter could put another into motion. Once matter is in motion, they reasoned, almost anything can happen.

The widespread adoption of the doctrine of fermentation was a significant step in the history of science. In physiology, in particular, the concept of fermentation served as a plausible substitute for innate heat and Galenic alterative faculties. By his own admission, when Galen said that various physiological processes are caused by alterative faculties, he was conceding that he did not know the cause of those processes.

But it was not until the early seventeenth century that natural philosophers began to voice their dissatisfaction with this lack of understanding. Thus, not only was the adoption of the doctrine of fermentation closely associated with the rejection of Scholasticism and the rise of the mechanical philosophy, even more fundamentally it represented the end of a centuries-long complacency with ignorance and, thus, the beginning of a new era in the history of science.

BIBLIOGRAPHY

Davis, Audrey B. *Circulation Physiology and Medical Chemistry in England, 1650–1680.* Lawrence, KS: Coronado, 1973.

Debus, Allen G. *The Chemical Philosophy: Paracelsian Science and Medicine in the Sixteenth and Seventeenth Centuries.* New York: Science History Publications, 1977.

Frank, Robert G., Jr. *Harvey and the Oxford Physiologists: A Study of Scientific Ideas.* Berkeley and Los Angeles: University of California Press, 1980.

Pagel, Walter. *Joan Baptista Van Helmont: Reformer of Science and Medicine.* Cambridge and New York: Cambridge University Press, 1982.

WILLIAM TAMMONE

See also Galenism; Mechanical Philosophy; Physiology

Fernel, Jean François (1497–1558)

A renowned French physician and medical author, noted for his identification and use of the terms *physiology, pathology,* and *therapeutics.* He helped establish a new approach to medicine by campaigning against the use of astrological prediction, magical cures, and sorcery in the diagnosis and treatment of disease. He maintained that the whole art of healing was subject to an inviolable code of laws observable in nature.

The son of a wealthy innkeeper from Montdidier, Fernel received his M.A. at the University of Paris in 1519. For the next six years, he read widely in philosophy and published in the fields of astronomy and mathematics. Choosing medicine as his vocation, he graduated M.D. in 1530 and settled down to a successful career as a teacher and practitioner of medicine in Paris, eventually becoming personal physician to Henry II of France.

Fernel's chief work, *Medicina* (1554), comprises three sections. The first, entitled "Physiology," reproduces his earlier treatise on the topic (*De naturali parte medicinae,* 1542). This was the first systematic exposition of contemporary theory concerning the natural processes of the healthy human body. Presented as an introduction to the theory of medicine, this section first discusses anatomy and then examines the causes of the actions of the body in terms of the elements, temperaments, -spirits, innate heat, faculties, humors, and procreation. In the course of this traditional humoral theory of medicine, Fernel emphasizes that observation of sickness and health is the only way to understand the functioning of the human body.

The second section of the work, entitled "Pathology," provides a new method for discussing the facts of morbidity by organizing diseases according to each organ of the body. Localized diseases are classified as simple when they are confined to a single organ and as complex when they affect a set of organs. The third section, on "Therapeutics," contains a reissue of Fernel's earlier treatise on venesection (*De vacuandi ratione,* 1545). This three-part work became the standard textbook in medical theory for more than a century, with more than thirty editions, printings, and translations.

BIBLIOGRAPHY

Capitaine, Pierre Albéric. *Un grand médecin au XVIe siècle, Jean Fernel*. Paris: Librairie Le François, 1925.

Figard, Léon. *Un médecin philosophe au XVIe siècle: Étude sur la psychologie de Jean Fernel*. Paris: F. Alcan, 1903.

Herpin, Alexandre. *Jean Fernel, médecin et philosophe*. Paris: J-B. Baillière, 1949.

Sherrington, Charles S. *The Endeavour of Jean Fernel, with a List of the Editions of His Writings*. Cambridge: Cambridge University Press, 1946.

CORNELIUS O'BOYLE

See also Etiology; Humors; Medicine; Physiology

Flamsteed, John (1646–1719)

The leading English practical astronomer of his day. Flamsteed was appointed on March 4, 1675, as Charles II's astronomical observator and director of the new observatory to be built shortly by the Ordnance Office in Greenwich Park. In effect he was the first Astronomer Royal, though this title was not yet formally used; he occasionally termed himself Astronomicus Regius but preferred to be Mathematicus Regius in imitation of Tycho Brahe (1564–1601) and Johannes Kepler (1571–1630). Despite perennial complaints about his slowness to publish results, and despite bitter public quarrels with Isaac Newton (1642–1727) and Edmond Halley (ca. 1656–1742) in his later years, he kept the post under five subsequent monarchs until his death. The publication of his star catalog and observations was initially assisted by sponsorship obtained from Prince George of Denmark (1653–1708), but this resulted only in the appearance of a volume edited by Edmond Halley as *Historia coelestis* (1712). In 1715 Flamsteed obtained the unsold copies of this work and burnt the parts he had not approved. His own three-volume *Historia coelestis Britannica* (1725) and *Atlas coelestis* (1729) were posthumous publications, produced by his wife, Margaret (née Cooke, ca. 1670–1730), with the aid of some of his former assistants.

Flamsteed's distinctive view of the nature of astronomy derived from his own early experience of the subject. As the eldest child and only son of a businessman from the provincial town of Derby, he received a grammar-school education, was taught arithmetic by his father, and was encouraged to further study by local

John Flamsteed. From E. F. Mac Pike, Hevelius, Flamsteed and Halley *(London: Taylor and Francis, 1937).*

friends interested in practical mathematics, astronomy, and astrology. In November 1669, he addressed a long letter to the Royal Society enclosing astronomical predictions; this led to publication of his predictions in the *Philosophical Transactions* and to correspondence with Henry Oldenburg (ca. 1619–1677) and John Collins (1625–1683). In 1670 he visited London, and Collins introduced him to Jonas Moore (1617–1679), who presented him with a Towneley/Gascoigne micrometer; soon afterward a business trip to Lancashire enabled him to meet Richard Towneley (1629–1707), with whom he was to maintain a regular correspondence for many years. In June 1674, he was awarded the degree M.A. in the University of Cambridge by royal mandate, as a nominal member of Jesus College. He then went on to London, as the guest of Moore (now Sir Jonas); when Moore's plan to establish an observatory came to fruition in the following March, Flamsteed appears to have been the only candidate considered for the post of director.

According to the royal warrant of appointment, he was "to apply himselfe . . . to the rectifieing the Tables of the motions of the Heavens, and the places of the fixed stars, so as to find out the . . . Longitude of places for perfecteing the Art of Navigation." Moore was initially influential in deciding how this was to be achieved and exerting pressure for speedy results; after his death in August 1679, Flamsteed secured sufficient backing from other patrons to continue in a more independent manner. He retained a commitment to improving positional astronomy but interpreted this in a broad fashion; his particular interests and approach to the subject are conveyed in the lectures he delivered at Gresham College in the early 1680s. He was also drawn into international astronomical concerns through corresponding with Johannes Hevelius (1611–1687), Jean-Dominique Cassini (1625–1712), and others; this led him, for instance, to imitate Cassini's work on Jupiter's satellites. From 1689, on completion of a large mural arc, he worked intensively on the fixed stars. He also continued to make lunar and planetary observations, many of which he supplied to Isaac Newton.

Flamsteed's reputation has only recently begun to recover from the controversy stirred up in the nineteenth century over his dealings with Newton regarding the latter's unauthorized publication of Flamsteed's observations. He is now of interest to historians of science as the custodian and interpreter of highly sophisticated instruments and as the conscious constructor of a public role for astronomy. His star catalog was soon superseded, with the discovery of aberration (which Flamsteed had detected but misinterpreted as stellar parallax); his observations are nevertheless the earliest accurate enough to be of use to modern astronomers.

BIBLIOGRAPHY

Baily, Francis. *An Account of the Reverend John Flamsteed, the First Astronomer-Royal.* London: Lords Commissioners of the Admiralty, 1835. Repr. London: Dawsons of Pall Mall, 1966.

Forbes, Eric G. *Greenwich Observatory,* vol. 1: *Origins and Early History, 1675–1875.* London: Taylor and Francis, 1975.

Forbes, Eric G., Lesley Murdin, and Frances Willmoth, eds. *The Correspondence of John Flamsteed, the First Astronomer Royal,* vols. 1–2. Bristol and Philadelphia: Institute of Physics Publishing, 1995, 1997. Vol. 3 forthcoming.

Willmoth, Frances, ed. *"Flamsteed's Stars": New Perspectives on the Life and Work of the First Astronomer Royal.* Woodbridge, UK: Boydell and Brewer in association with the National Maritime Museum, 1997.

FRANCES WILLMOTH

See also Astronomy; Royal Observatory at Greenwich

Fludd, Robert (1574–1637)

An English physician and philosopher, Fludd produced encyclopedic publications that were a summation of ancient, medieval, and Renaissance Platonist thought and contained many notable copperplate illustrations. Fludd's publications were dedicated to King James I, Fludd's patron after a personal audience (Charles I also gave him an estate in Suffolk); the archbishop of Canterbury; the bishops of Lincoln and Worcester; Sir William Paddy; and Sir Robert Bruce Cotton. Some disagreed with Fludd in print, most notably Marin Mersenne (1588–1648), Pierre Gassendi (1592–1655), and Johannes Kepler (1571–1630), who advanced his own Neoplatonist mathematical cosmos against Fludd's mystical harmonies.

Following Plato (428–348 B.C.E.), the Neoplatonists, and Christian theology and utilizing some elements from Aristotle (384–322 B.C.E.), Fludd constructed a hierarchy of being that descended from the Trinity, the most spiritual and ethereal, to the most dense and material. Contained within God were two opposite principles:

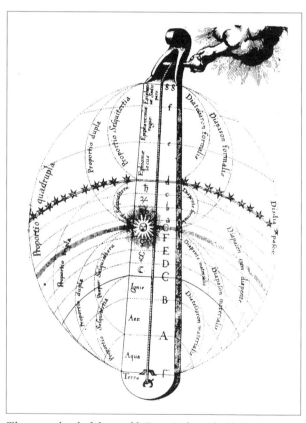

The monochord of the world. From Robert Fludd, Utriusque cosmi . . . historia *(1617–1621).*

life-giving and sustaining light, and a darkness of privation and stillness. An outpouring of light at Creation transformed the void into a mass containing five elements: earth, water, air, fire, and quintessence. Subsequently, three realms were created: the highest contains the angelic hierarchy; the middle contains the Sun in the center, the planets, and the Moon; and the lower contains the earth and physical elements. The central Sun is the physical manifestation of life-giving divine spirit, the quintessence, and is analogous to the heart in man. Each part of the hierarchy is related as the major musical harmonies of a monochord. Man, the microcosm, replicates the heavenly macrocosm. This scheme is coordinated with the Kabbalah. Divine spirit pervades all of Creation. Heat or cold (physical light/darkness) interacts with the primeval water, giving the hot-cold-moist-dry basis for the earthly elements and four humors in man. The outpouring or indrawing of divine light causes concord or discord in the heavenly and corporeal worlds. Disease is cured by restoring balance by administering missing elements with medical equivalents. Fludd set up a chemical laboratory in London ca. 1606 and conducted experiments with wheat, which he thought proved his cosmological beliefs. He also produced a superior-quality steel, for which he was granted a patent by the Privy Council in 1620.

BIBLIOGRAPHY

Debus, Allen G. *Robert Fludd and His Philosophical Key*. New York: Science History Publications, 1979.

Godwin, Joscelyn. *Robert Fludd: Hermetic Philospher and Surveyor of Two Worlds*. Boulder: Shambala; London: Thames and Hudson, 1979.

Huffman, William H. *Robert Fludd and the End of the Renaissance*. London: Routledge, 1988.

WILLIAM H. HUFFMAN

See also Kabbalah; Macrocosm/Microcosm; Neoplatonism

Fontenelle, Bernard le Bovier de (1657–1757)

A talented, lucid interpreter of scientific research for the literate nonspecialist, Fontenelle long held (1697–1740) the position of permanent secretary of the Royal Academy of Sciences in Paris. He began his career as a poet and playwright but had more success with his philosophical essays. His *New Dialogues of the Dead* (1683) may be described as an exercise in skepticism, displaying also

From Fontenelle's Entretiens sur la pluralité des mondes *(1821).*

some traces of the newer Spinozism. The *History of Oracles* (1686), based on a scholarly work by A. van Dale (1638–1708), characterized ancient pagan oracles as priestly frauds and popular delusions; by implication, the text attacked all forms of superstition and prophecy. His essay on myths, written early but not published until 1724, offered an explanation of the origin of religions that anticipates the more detailed analysis later produced by David Hume (1711–1776). In his *Plurality of Worlds* (1686, enlarged in 1687), he presented Cartesian cosmology and an expanded universe in so informative, elegant, and enjoyable a fashion that it became an instant classic of high-level popular science, reprinted and translated for decades after its Cartesian features had been superseded by Newtonianism.

As an academician, Fontenelle prefaced each annual volume of the academy's *Mémoires* with a lengthy *Histoire,* summarizing in largely nontechnical terms the research of his colleagues and placing their work in suitable contexts. How accurately he summed up papers in so many fields of science remains to be investigated; what can be said with certainty is that he sometimes developed further the interpretations advanced in the memoirs, differed on some points from the original papers, and added reflections of his own. The annual *Histoire* also carried eulogies of deceased academicians, and here, too, Fontenelle presented his own views. Famous in his eulogy of Isaac Newton (1642–1727) was his dislike of gravitational attraction, which he considered a regrettable departure from the mechanical philosophy. More significant, these eulogies, individually and collectively, presented scientists as disinterested seekers of truth, the inquirers taking on the dispassionate qualities of nature itself.

Fontenelle's success as a spokesman for science may be gauged in part by the many editions of the eulogies, the first collection of which appeared as early as 1708. Book-review journals, reporting on the academy's annual volumes, usually relied more on Fontenelle's *Histoire* than on the technical *Mémoires;* one detects even among academicians a tendency to quote Fontenelle rather than the original papers. In 1734, D-F. Camusat assessed Fontenelle's work as being above criticism: he had presented abstruse papers with a clarity that the authors themselves could not achieve, and he had accustomed readers "to believe and to think as he does."

BIBLIOGRAPHY

Camusat, D-F. *Histoire critique des journaux.* 2 vols. Amsterdam: J-F. Bernard, 1734.

Fontenelle, Bernard le Bovier de. *Oeuvres.* Ed. J-B-J. Champagnac. 5 vols. Paris: Salmon, 1825.

Marsak, Leonard M. "Bernard de Fontenelle: The Idea of Science in the French Enlightenment." *Transactions of the American Philosophical Society* n.s. 49 (1959), no. 7.

Niderst, Alain, ed. *Fontenelle: Actes du colloque tenu à Rouen du 6 au 10 Octobre 1987.* Paris: Presses Universitaires de France, 1989.

RHODA RAPPAPORT

See also Académie Royale des Sciences; Cartesianism; Popularization

Force

The problem of force in the seventeenth century had three distinct dimensions. The first and easiest was nomenclature. From the tradition of natural philosophy, mechanics inherited a plethora of terms expressing activity. In a passage in Galileo Galilei's *Discourses on Two New Sciences* (1638), the author referred to "the impetus, the ability, the energy, or we might say the momentum" of a moving body. To these four he added at other places "virtue," "propensity to motion," and "force." Other words were also available, such as "endeavor" and "power." Most of the terms, employed more or less interchangeably, continued in use through the century. In the 1650s, Evangelista Torricelli (1608–1647) constructed a promising dynamics on the concept of "moment," and later Christiaan Huygens (1629–1695) sketched out one based on "incitation." In his second law of motion, near the beginning of the *Principia mathematica philosophiae naturalis* (1687), Isaac Newton (1642–1727) chose "force" (or *vis* in Latin, universally translated into English in this context as "force"), and, with the precision the *Principia* bestowed, that word has since prevailed.

Far more important than the word was the measure of the concept it denoted. From the tradition of statics, the Scientific Revolution had received a universally accepted quantitative rule, the law of the lever. The lever and the other simple machines were ambiguous. The law of the lever, which established the ratio between the force applied and the load moved in a given arrangement, analyzed the conditions of equilibrium, but the simple machines existed not to hold loads in place but to move them. It is not surprising that students of mechanics kept trying to extract a quantitative system of dynamics from the statics of simple machines.

Here they confronted a second ambiguity. One possible measure of dynamic action was the product of force times its velocity. This was Galileo's (1564–1642) usual analysis. A small force applied to the longer end of a lever is able to move a larger load because it moves faster, in the exact ratio of the two lever arms, which is identical to the ratio of the load to the force. To put this in terms we readily recognize, let us use for the load, instead of its weight, its mass, although a clear concept of mass did not come into mechanics until Newton's *Principia*. Then we might say that the force (which we use here, as seventeenth century scientists frequently did, in a slightly different sense) to move a load of mass m must be equal to *mv*, where *v* is the velocity. There was another possible analysis of the lever, however. What counts is not the velocity of movement but the height through which the load is lifted. A smaller force can lift a larger load because the force moves a greater distance, again in the exact ratio of the two lever arms or of the load to the force. In his analysis of the simple machines, René Descartes (1596–1650) insisted on this measure. Using the anachronistic concept of mass again, we could say in this case that the force to move a load of mass *m* must be equal to *ms,* where *s* is the vertical displacement. These two quantities, *mv* and *ms,* continued to appear in the literature of attempted dynamics through the century. Because both measures apply successfully to the lever, the majority of writers did not see any disparity between them; the two measures of force sometimes appear within a single paragraph as though they were synonymous.

Most of the attempts to construct a dynamics during the seventeenth century drew upon the model of impact, and most of them called upon the idea of the force of a body's motion as the measure of its capacity to act. They usually expressed the force of a body's motion by the quantity *mv* (*m* still being anachronistic). The model of impact was as filled with ambiguities as the law of the lever from which the quantity *mv* came, and it invariably led efforts to build a science of dynamics on it into confusion.

The concept of the force of a body's motion, in turn, led to a third possible measure of force. Late in the century, Gottfried Wilhelm Leibniz (1646–1716) reasoned that the same amount of force must be expended to lift a body of four pounds one foot and a body of one pound four feet. Everyone agreed that a body falling from a given height gains force sufficient to lift it back to that height. But if the body of four pounds gains a velocity *v* in falling from a height of one foot, then, by Galileo's kinematics, the body of one pound gains a velocity only of 2*v* in falling from four feet. Clearly, *mv* cannot be the measure of force, but rather *mv*^{2}, a quantity that Leibniz called *vis viva* (living force). The argument as to whether *mv* or *mv*^{2} measures force continued well into the eighteenth century and was not finally settled until it was agreed that momentum and kinetic energy are different concepts, both essential to the science of motion.

The model of impact was not the only possible model. There was also free fall. Free fall stood behind Torricelli's dynamics based on the concept of moment and Huygens's based on incitation. It was the model that

Newton drew upon for his dynamics. Free fall suggested a different point of view for the measurement of force: not the force in a body that moves but the force that generates the velocity with which a body moves. Ambiguities about its measure still remained. The second law of motion in Newton's *Principia* states that the change of motion is proportional to the force impressed. That is, *f* = Δ *mv,* not *f* = *ma*. In this case, however, the confusion was minimal. In propositions in the *Principia* that use Δ *mv,* successive impacts are separated by uniform, brief intervals of time. In the limit, Δ *mv* merges into *ma,* a formulation that Newton also employed in some propositions, and the small conceptual lack of clarity did not lead to faulty demonstrations.

Newton's dynamics established another point important for the concept of force. Behind the model of free fall stood the principle of inertia and the perception that any change in a body's state of rest or of uniform motion requires a cause external to the body—that is, in the language of the second law, the action of an impressed force. Uniformly accelerated motion results when a constant force moves a body along the straight line in which the force acts. But the principle of inertia implies as well that any deviation from a straight line is as much a change as acceleration in a straight line and also requires the action of a force. No theory of force within a body, be it medieval impetus or Cartesian force of a body's motion, succeeded in accommodating curvilinear motion. The triumph of Newtonian dynamics stemmed from its capacity to treat, with equal quantitative precision, all alterations in a body's inertial state. In effect, Newton's second law defined force in terms of a strict proportionality between it and the change of motion it generates. This conception of force has endured in the science of mechanics. The other three quantities have all been perceived to measure concepts also essential to mechanics but different from force—momentum and kinetic energy as already mentioned, and *fs* (not quite identical to *ms*) as work.

The third dimension of the problem of force was its ontological status. Philosophies prevalent in Europe during the sixteenth century had filled nature with a range of mysterious agents or powers. The primary goal of the seventeenth century's mechanical philosophy had been to banish these agents, which were referred to pejoratively as "occult qualities." Nature consists solely of particles of inert matter in motion; all of nature's phenomena are produced by particles of matter in motion; the moving particle is the sole agent of causation. After

F

the middle of the century, there was hardly anyone who was not at least influenced by the mechanical philosophy, and it is no wonder that the model of impact seemed like the key to dynamics. An appeal to forces that act on bodies appeared like a retreat to a rejected natural philosophy.

In the *Principia,* Newton insisted repeatedly that he was proposing an abstract concept that made a mathematical dynamics possible and that he was not asserting anything about the status or cause of given forces. Dynamics since his time has worked with the concept in precisely this abstract meaning; wherever there is an acceleration, a force proportional to it must act, and where a force acts, it must produce a proportional acceleration. Nevertheless, Newton's second law appeared in a book that asserted the existence of a universal force of attraction among all of the bodies in the universe. The attraction was mathematically defined, and Newton claimed that he was merely deriving mathematically the consequences of such a force and making no assertion about its status or cause. It might result, for example, from the mechanical action of an ether spread throughout the universe. Mechanical philosophers were not appeased. For a generation, there was a heated dispute between mechanical philosophers of strict persuasion and Newtonians, whom they accused of reintroducing occult qualities into science.

In the end, the mathematical power of the *Principia* and its science of dynamics based on the Newtonian concept of force prevailed. After a generation, an attraction that explained so many phenomena in exact quantitative terms became familiar and ceased to sound mysterious. Gravity, and a range of other forces, all defined mathematically and subject then to precise quantitative treatment according to Newton's laws of motion, came to be admitted into the ontology of nature, and this model, embodying at once Newtonian dynamics and the reality of forces, became the continuing framework of Western science.

BIBLIOGRAPHY

De Gandt, François. *Force and Geometry in Newton's Principia.* Trans. Curtis Wilson. Princeton, NJ: Princeton University Press, 1995.

Gabbey, Alan. "Force and Inertia in Seventeenth Century Dynamics." *Studies in the History and Philosophy of Science* 2 (1971), 1–67.

Grosholz, Emily R. "Geometry, Time, and Force in the Diagrams of Descartes, Galileo, Torricelli, and Newton." *PSA:*

Proceedings of the Biennial Meeting of the Philosophy of Science Association 2 (1988), 237–248.

Needham, Tristan. "Newton and the Transmutation of Force." *American Mathematical Monthly* 100 (1993), 119–137.

Westfall, Richard S. *Force in Newton's Physics: The Science of Dynamics in the Seventeenth Century.* London: Macdonald, 1971.

RICHARD S. WESTFALL

See also Dynamics; Huygens, Christiaan; Impetus; Mass; Mechanical Philosophy; Newton, Isaac; Torricelli, Evangelista

Fortification

The appearance of artillery in the fourteenth century changed the face of warfare. At first, guns were too cumbersome and unreliable to do more than strike terror into an enemy. However, the development of cast-metal cannon in bronze and later in iron and of cast-iron shot made them more effective, while mounting guns on carriages made them more mobile. By the early sixteenth century, the traditional style of castle had become obsolete, for their towers were now too vulnerable. Italian architects experimented with new types of tower, usually rounded, so as not to offer corners to hostile fire, and relatively low. The result was the bastion, the characteristic feature of the new style of fortification. In essence, a bastion was a gun platform, with maximum field of fire but exposing minimum target area to an opponent. Bastions had to project to sweep the curtain walls, which linked them to form a complete circuit, or *enceinte*. From ca. the 1530s, rounded bastions were replaced by pentagons; the ideal fortification was a polygon with pentagonal bastions at its corners. Often the base corners were rounded off while the two that projected were short and recessed, presenting an appearance like the spades in a pack of cards. From the middle years of the century, wars of religion racked Germany and France, while in the Netherlands religious conflict became a national war of independence. Such wars involved much of the population so that cities became the military objectives of a campaign, as well as the linchpins of a state's defenses. Armies tended to concentrate on besieging hostile towns and to avoid pitched battles, which were in this period less common and often less decisive than in the Middle Ages. Whereas battles lasted a few days at most, a siege could last for weeks, or months, or even years in some famous cases in which the besieged could be supplied by sea. Taking such a place by storm became very difficult;

starving the besieged might be the only means of success; at the least it would force the other side to try to raise the siege. Thus, two rings of temporary works might be thrown up—one to pen in the besieged, the other to keep out a relieving force and impose on it the dangers of a frontal assault.

The new style of fortification is sometimes described as scientific; *rationalized* might be a better term. Certainly, the layout of fortification and siegeworks alike required a grounding in geometry to establish the best line for the *enceinte* and the best position for the bastions. Since the bastions themselves now became the points of attack, defenders protected the line with a ditch, and beyond that a low wall with a parapet from which they could fire on any advance, while they themselves were protected by covering fire from the bastions. In front of this might be outworks—ravelins (angled salients), demi-lunes, hornworks—differing only in shape, from which retreat could be made without too much risk. Sometimes, *cavaliers* (elevated positions) were constructed behind the outer line and higher up so as to provide further cover.

Places to be fortified might be on high ground, to command a valley or a pass, or as citadels within a town, or on rivers or bays, so geometrically ideal plans were often modified. Some new towns were laid out as key fortresses, such as Palma Nova in the Venetian republic, Naarden in the Netherlands, and Neuf-Brisach in France. In order that this new type of structure might be explained properly, a technical literature grew up, numbering dozens of texts by 1600, while more continued to appear regularly thereafter. Most of the earlier books were written by Italians, but French and German authors such as Jean Errard (1554–1610) and Daniel Speckle (1536–1589) published important contributions. In this literature, mathematical skill was treated as the key factor in design; some authors did, however, debate whether the experience of the practiced soldier might not count for more than the learning of the mathematical scholar. In any case, military architects, now usually known as "engineers," came to be regularly attached to the armed forces of most states as a recognized and respectable profession.

Besiegers would have to measure heights and distances accurately across a field of fire, which allowed the engineer an occupation in peacetime, although, in practice, periods of peace were as often spent in expanding and reconstructing fortifications for the next war. Even

army officers who did not intend to specialize in engineering still had to learn enough geometry to appreciate the work of the professionals—René Descartes (1596–1650) would be a good example. So, by the seventeenth century, the new art of fortification had become an organized body of knowledge.

BIBLIOGRAPHY

Duffy, Christopher. *Siege Warfare: The Fortress in the Early Modern World, 1494–1660*. London: Routledge and Kegan Paul, 1979.

Hughes, Quentin. *Military Architecture*. London: Hugh Evelyn, 1974.

Pepper, Simon, and Nicholas Adams. *Firearms and Fortifications: Military Architecture and Siege Warfare in Sixteenth Century Siena*. Chicago: University of Chicago Press, 1986.

ALEX KELLER

See also Ballistics and Gunnery; Vauban, Sébastien Le Prestre

Fracastoro, Girolamo (ca. 1478–1553)

A Renaissance man, he studied mathematics, medicine, botany, geology, astronomy, and philosophy in Padua and acquired an extensive knowledge of Latin and Latin literature. In 1501 he was named lecturer on logic at the University of Padua. A doctor and a poet, Fracastoro enjoyed a notable reputation as an astronomer, mathematician, and geographer. He participated actively in the construction of the new geography and cartography in the wake of the voyages of exploration. He was interested in cosmography throughout his life, and in his astronomical treatise *Homocentrica sive de stellis* (Homocentrics; or, On the Stars, 1538) he elaborated a cosmological system in an effort to eliminate the complex eccentrics, epicycles, and equants of Ptolemaic astronomy. The work also discusses refraction and includes some of his own astronomical observations and hypotheses, notably about comets. He also studied mechanics, experimented with magnets and the compass, and traveled throughout his region seeking medicinal plants and studying geological formations. Fracastoro had a great interest in philosophical issues and wrote dialogues on aesthetics, epistemology, and psychology.

Fracastoro's significance in the Scientific Revolution rests on two major works, both devoted to epidemic diseases: the beautiful poem in Latin hexameters *Syphilis sive morbus Gallicus* (1530) and the treatise *De contagione*

Girolamo Fracastoro From Fielding H. Garrison, An Introduction to the History of Medicine, *3rd ed. (Philadelphia and London: Saunders, 1921).*

et contagiosis morbis et eorum curatione (1546). The poem tells how Syphilus, a shepherd in Haiti, was the first victim of a new disease. The final version (1547) was in three books. In Book I, Fracastoro discusses the causes and diffusion of the disease, rejecting both the "American theory" for its origins, because it seemed to have broken out in several countries simultaneously, as well as its attribution to a peculiar conjuncture of planets. The agent of the disease is the air, and it transmits contagion through *semina* (seeds). Book II is devoted to remedies and suggests mercury as the best remedy; Book III is devoted to guaiac, derived from a sacred wood and imported to Europe from Haiti, where it was used by natives for curing a disease of the skin. The poem shows a detailed knowledge of the clinical manifestations of the disease and of the different therapeutic tools used at the time. The central theme of the poem is the possibility of new diseases emerging in nature, independently of divine intervention.

At the time, contagion was defined as the passage from one body to another of a similar corruption. The *semina* of contagion were of different types and could be produced by "infection" within the body, in the air itself, or by the effect of astral conjunction. They have an antipathy for the animal organism, provoking an alteration of the humors and thus the disease. The role of astral influences was discussed in 1538 in a treatise by Fracastoro on the cause of critical days in illness. Stating that knowledge must be based on experience, on observation, Fracastoro criticizes the traditional idea that the real existence of critical days in a disease depends on astral influences or on the mysticism of number. The cause must be found in the nature of the disease itself, the crisis being the result of the reaction of the body to the qualitative and quantitative modification of the humors.

Fracastoro's book on contagion was published together with a treatise *On the Sympathy and Antipathy of Things.* Both were aimed against the explanations of natural phenomena in terms of occult qualities. Magnetism can be explained logically by the principle of sympathy and antipathy, and the same principle can explain why a sponge absorbs water and why some bodies are more receptive than others to particular diseases. Fracastoro described different infectious diseases, in particular typhus and tuberculosis, distinguished them from nonspecific "fevers," and discussed their affinities with particular organs of the body. He tried to explain how contagion takes place, its different types, and why only some diseases are contagious, and he emphasized receptivity as a possible explanation of the fact that, even in the most terrible epidemic, some escape. Rather than the first statement of the modern theory that infectious diseases are transmitted by a living agent, Fracastoro's theory is, on the contrary, the most advanced classical theory, the most relevant contribution to the learned debate on contagious diseases that had started with the Black Death of the fourteenth century. Most of the plague treatises discuss plague in term of "contact," "contagion," or "seeds of disease."

Fracastoro's theory conforms well to the standard Galenic medical culture of his time. He defines contagion as "an infection that passes from one thing to another," comparing contagion to the emanations of an onion. He noticed the close relationship between fermentation and putrefaction and argued that putrefying bodies emit invisible corpuscles. This may explain how they are communicable, how one rotten apple infects the whole barrel. All infections may be reduced ultimately to putrefactions; Fracastoro makes, however, a subtle distinction between contagion and putrefaction: the *seminaria* cause putrefaction, but they do not need to be putrid themselves.

Fracastoro's originality lies in the mechanisms he implies for the diffusion of the diseases. He distinguishes three types of contagion: (1) by direct contact with a sick person; (2) by indirect contact through fomites; and (3) at a distance through the air originating with a sick person. The term *fomites* designated at the time a generic cause of epidemic diseases. Fracastoro appears to be the first to use the word *fomites* as a technical term for substances deposited on or in clothing and wood and to describe the transferred infectious agent as "seedlets of contagion," gelatinous or "dispersed" systems, that adhere to people, wood, or cloth, similar to the traditional idea of "sticky venomous atoms." Fracastoro suggested that *seminaria* were able to propagate and engender themselves. They have specific affinities for plants, animals, and organs or fluids in the body.

He underlines the importance of contagion in the diffusion of a plague, rather than simply blaming "bad air," as in the classical miasmatic theories. Fracastoro believed in humors, but he considers that infectious diseases are independent of a particular humoral equilibrium within the body. The *De contagione* is a philosophical contribution to the debate on disease causation, in particular on action at a distance. Contagion is only one case of a series of phenomena pertaining to the realm of antipathy and sympathy (magnets, poisons, and the like), part of a new view of the cosmos based on Lucretian atomism.

BIBLIOGRAPHY

Fracastoro, Girolamo. *Syphilis.* Trans. with Notes by Geoffrey Eatough. Liverpool: F. Cairns, 1984.

Howard-Jones, N. "Fracastoro and Henle: A Reappraisal of Their Contribution to the Concept of Communicable Disease." *Medical History* 21 (1977), 61–68.

Pellegrini, F. *Fracastoro.* Trieste: Zigiotti, 1948.

Pellegrini, F. ed. *Studie memorie nel IV° centenario. A cura della Revista "Il Fracastoro" Ginolamo Francastono.* Verona Instituto degli Øspitalieri, 1954.

Singer, Charles, and Dorothea Singer. "The Scientific Position of Girolamo Fracastoro (1478?–1553)." *Annals of Medical History* 1 (1917) 1–34.

BERNARDINO FANTINI

See also Etiology

Fuchs, Leonhart (1501–1566)

F

Leonhart Fuchs is best known for his *De historia stirpium commentarii insignes* (Notable Commentaries on the History of Plants, 1542), a masterpiece of Renaissance scientific illustration. Fuchs's woodcuts of approximately 511 plants set a precedent in their deliberate use of naturalistic representation of the perfect plant forms, as opposed to the naturalistic depiction of individual specimens found in the 1530 work, *Herbarum vivae eicones* (Living Images of Plants), of Otto Brunfels (ca. 1489–1534).

For each plant (arranged alphabetically by its Greek name), Fuchs gave synonyms in ancient and modern languages, quoted pertinent classical and medieval accounts, and added his own observations of the plant's uses and appearance. He also provided the first glossary of technical botanical terms. Fuchs, who never traveled

Frontispiece of Fuchs's De historia stirpium *(1542).*

outside Germany, showed little awareness that the plants found growing in Germany (including maize, squash, and other New World introductions illustrated for the first time) did not always correspond to the Mediterranean flora described by his classical authorities.

Fuchs's herbal appeared in a wide variety of formats, sizes, translations, pirated editions, hand-colorings, and popularizations. He hoped to publish a much enlarged herbal—for which nine volumes of draft manuscript, paintings of more than fifteen hundred plants, and twenty-three woodcut proofs survive—but never found a printer willing to take on the mammoth project.

For most of his life, Fuchs lived with his wife and ten children in Tübingen, where he practiced medicine, served as Court physician to the local duke, and taught at the university. He took an active part in the Lutheran reforms of medical education there in 1539. He declined prestigious invitations to teach in Denmark and Italy, generated by his fame as the prolific author of medical textbooks (which had incorporated Vesalian anatomy by 1550) and as a participant in medical/botanical controversies. His scientific correspondents and friends included Andreas Vesalius (1514–1564), Conrad Gessner (1516–1565), Luca Ghini (ca. 1490–1556), Joachim Camerarius the Elder (1500–1578), and Guillaume Rondelet (1507–1566).

BIBLIOGRAPHY

Meyer, Frederick G., Emily Emmart Trueblood, and John L. Heller. *The Great Herbal of Leonhart Fuchs: De historia stirpium commentarii insignes*. 2 vols. Stanford: Stanford University Press, 1998.

Stübler, Eberhard. *Leonhart Fuchs: Leben und Werk*. Munich: Verlag der Münchener Drucke, 1928.

KAREN MEIER REEDS
FREDERICK G. MEYER

See also Botany; Brunfels, Otto; Gessner, Conrad; Rondelet, Guillaume

G

Galenism

A medical system based on the work by Galen of Perga-mon (second century). This system was successively elab-orated upon in detail in Byzantium, the Islamic world, and Europe during the Middle Ages, cumulating in the rather heteogenous Galenism practiced in sixteenth- and seventeenth-century Europe. The dialectic between tra-dition and renovation in this period brought about the fragmentation of Galenism into several trends, the understanding of the development of which is crucial if the process of the Scientific Revolution is to be correctly situated within the field of medical science. Broadly speaking, four major trends can be identified, which can best be characterized on the basis of their relations with ideological and cultural tendencies.

The first of these trends was simply a continuation of the Galenism of the later Middle Ages in Europe. The works of Galen and those of the main Greek physicians of ancient times were translated into Arabic from the eighth century onward, and Avicenna (980–1037), in his *Canon,* systematized all medical knowledge in accor-dance with Galenism. From the eleventh to the thir-teenth century, the texts by classic Greek authors were translated from Arabic to Latin, together with those of Avicenna and other Islamic physicians, particularly in the cities of Salerno, Italy, and Toledo, Spain. These transla-tions full of Arabic words were fundamental to the assimilation of Galenism in late-medieval Europe, where they were rewritten in keeping with the tendencies of Scholastic thought at that time. The fundamental system-atic text was the Latin version of the *Canon* by Avicenna; hence, this trend was generally known as Arabized Scholastic Galenism or Avicennist Galenism. It remained in force until the first half of the sixteenth century despite clashes with the new approach to Galenism adopted by the physicians who followed Renaissance humanism.

Renaissance humanism was a multifaceted move-ment involved in all spheres of culture. In the field of science, it attempted inter alia to fully recover the knowl-edge of classical times by establishing direct links with the original scientific texts by using editions with an accurate terminology and direct translations, free of the mistakes found in the versions from the late Middle Ages. In the sphere of medicine, the humanists meticu-lously corrected and published the texts of Galen, Hip-pocrates (ca. 460–ca. 370 B.C.E.), and the other ancient authors in Greek and also the Latin translations of each. They scathed those who remained true to Avicennist Galenism, referring to them as "barbarians," because the classical medical doctrines they used were gleaned from medieval translations and "distorted" interpretations by Arabs. They disregarded Avicenna's *Canon* and concen-trated on the works of Galen himself, some of which were unknown in the Middle Ages, and wrote a consid-erable number of new commentaries on them. Like the other branches of this movement, humanist Galenism began in Italy and was led by notable authors such as Niccolò Leoniceno (1428–1524) and Ermolao Barbaro (1454–1493). It spread later to other countries as a result of the activities of certain physicians, the majority of whom had been educated in, or maintained links with, Italy, in particular the Englishman Thomas Linacre (1461–1524), the German Johannes Guinter of Ander-nach (ca. 1505–1574), the Spaniard Andrés Laguna (1494–1560), and the Frenchman Jacques Houllier (1498–1562).

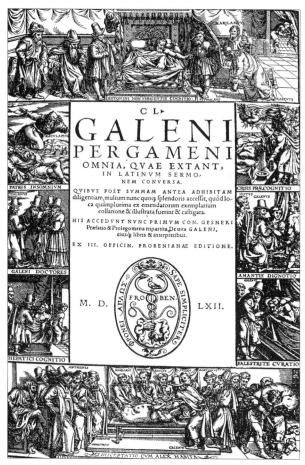

Title page of one of the many editions of Galen's Opera omnia
that were published in the fifteenth and sixteenth centuries.
The illustrations depict Galen in various capacities as a prac-
ticing physician.

Their contribution was not merely to recover the ancient medical texts but to expound the need to genuinely understand them. This task was facilitated by the printing press, which enabled said texts to be distributed on a far greater scale than had been possible during the classical period. After overcoming the "barbarisms" in medieval interpretations and translations, the comparison of texts by ancient authors was undertaken, shedding light on the contradictions they contained. In keeping with the original intention of exemplifying the classic doctrines, the contents were linked to the phenomena observed in healthy and sick human bodies. The outcome, however, had far-reaching implications because the lacunae and errors discovered were one of the reasons leading to the crisis concerning the criteria of ancient authority as the basis of medical knowledge.

From the mid-sixteenth century onward, some adherents of humanist Galenism vested observation with increasing importance. The most immediate result of this trend was the new descriptive anatomy of the human body, led by Andreas Vesalius (1514–1564), which based morphological knowledge on observations obtained from dissecting human corpses and clashed openly with Galenist doctrines. Epidemiological and clinical observations began in a more gradual fashion. The medical histories referred to as *consilia* (counsels) because their purpose was to exemplify Galenist doctrines came to be known as "observations." A series of "new illnesses" was described, including syphilis, exanthematic typhus, and suffocating diphtheria, so-called because classical physicians were believed to have had no knowledge of them and, hence, had no authority in the matter. The precision and scope of the information gathered on epidemic and endemic illnesses in relation to ambient conditions continually increased. The Hippocratic clinical observations and environmentalist conceptions became models for all of these activities, and, although the Galenist system remained in force on the whole, pride of place was occupied by the Hippocratic treatises. Furthermore, the majority of the followers of what may be called Hippocratic Galenism adopted the New Anatomy and began applying it not only to theories on the localization of illness, but also to the clarification of specific clinical cases by necroscopy. The most prominent figures of this trend who penned highly influential works over a period of almost two centuries were Jean François Fernel (1497–1558) and Francisco Valles (1524–1592).

During the last third of the sixteenth century, European academic medicine reached a dead end. Disappointment reigned among the most clearsighted individuals and groups when the expectations aroused by the rebirth of medical science as a result of the humanist program were thwarted. This crisis led to two opposite viewpoints, one for and the other against the scientific renewal, both conditioned by conflicting ideological, sociocultural, and political factors.

The pro-renewal standpoint did not merely incorporate the breakthroughs made in New Anatomy, the necroscopic, clinical, and epidemiological observations, and a variety of detailed rectifications of Galenist doctrines that had been taking place, including some as outstanding as the discovery of pulmonary circulation. It also gradually assimilated elements of Paracelsianism, the only system in the sixteenth century that had broken away from Galenism completely, and was based mainly on alchemical concepts and techniques. The very few of

Paracelsus's (ca. 1491–1541) own works published during his lifetime had had little impact at that time. From the 1560s onward, however, coinciding with the crisis in the humanist program, the so-called Paracelsian Revival occurred. All of his numerous manuscript texts were published in the original German and in Latin translations, which were distributed outside Germany. Until that time, very few Galenists had accepted Paracelsian principles. This movement was spearheaded by Conrad Gessner (1516–1565), who had defended Paracelsian chemical medicines in a book published in 1552 under a pseudonym. Following the Paracelsian Revival, the majority of the pro-innovation Galenists also came to accept the use of chemical medicines, although almost always merely as a partial modification of the traditional system. There were, however, others who not only accepted such medicines, but also tried to reconcile Galenism with chemical interpretations of physiological and pathological phenomena. The main figure of this "eclectic Galenism" in the first half of the seventeenth century was Daniel Sennert (1572–1637), whose synthesis of Galenism, Paracelsianism, and atomism influenced the whole of Europe to an extraordinary degree, helping pave the way for the iatrochemical system of the second half of the seventeenth century.

Although it is not possible to establish a simplistic relationship, there is no doubt that the sociocultural conditions and ideology of the Protestant Reformation facilitated the development of eclecticism. It is not just by chance that Gessner was a professor in Zurich, and Sennert in Wittenberg, both prominent cities in the Protestant world. At the other extreme, the Catholic Counter-Reformation was, by all accounts, a fitting backdrop to the anti-innovation Galenism. The main aim of this Galenism was to return to traditional doctrines, outlaw any contradictory innovations, and systematically rewrite Galenism in accordance with Counter-Reformation neo-scholasticism. Its most noteworthy adherent at the end of the sixteenth century was Luis Mercado (1520–1606), a professor at the Spanish University of Valladolid. He was well informed on innovations and an excellent clinical observer, but he carried out a comprehensive systematization of Galenism that was published several times and widely distributed throughout Europe. In it, he attempted to refute all criticism of Galenism, including the new Vesalian anatomy ands the pulmonary circulation. During the seventeenth century, this anti-innovation Galenism was led by the dean of the Faculty of Medicine, Paris, Guy Patin (1601–1672), who succeeded in having Paracelsianism condemned and the use of chemical medicines banned. Until the formulation of the iatrochemical system by Thomas Willis (1621–1675) and Franz de le Boë (Franciscus Sylvius, 1614–1672), the clash between the "ancients and moderns" in the field of medicine took place largely in the shape of bitter conflicts between the unyielding partisans of Galenism and the adherents of eclecticism.

BIBLIOGRAPHY

Baader, G. "Medizinisches Reformdenken und Arabismus in Deutschland des 16 Jahrhunderts." *Sudhoffs Archiv* 63 (1979), 261–296.

López-Piñero, J. M., and F. Calero. *Los temas polémicos de la medicina renacentista: Las "Controversias" (1556), de Francisco Valles.* Madrid: CSIC, 1988.

Müller, I. W. *Humoralmedizin: Physiologische, pathologische, und therapeutische Grundlagen der galenistischen Heilkunst.* Heidelberg: K. F. Haug, 1993.

Siraisi, N. *Medieval and Early Renaissance Medicine: An Introduction to Knowledge and Practice.* Chicago: University of Chicago Press, 1990.

Temkin, O. *Galenism: Rise and Decline of a Medical Philosophy.* Ithaca, NY, and London: Cornell University Press, 1973.

Wear, A., K. French, and M. Lonie, eds. *The Medical Renaissance of the Sixteenth Century.* Cambridge: Cambridge University Press, 1985.

JOSÉ M. LÓPEZ-PIÑERO

See also Anatomy; Humors; Paracelsus; Physiology; Vesalius, Andreas

Galilei, Galileo (1564–1642)

A major contributor to the Scientific Revolution. His lifelong studies of natural motions yielded the law of free fall, the laws of the isochronism of the simple pendulum, the parabolic trajectory of projectiles and, not least, a rejection of much of the ancient and Renaissance Aristotelian teachings on free and forced motions. His researches exhibited from the beginning his basic assumptions of the primacy of the material world as the object of knowledge and the reasonableness of expecting near-mathematical precision in the representation of that world. As a consequence, his work contributed importantly to the emergence in the seventeenth century of experimental natural philosophy in place of the discursive natural philosophy of the schools and to the replacement of the traditional, organic-biological view of the

Courtesy Whipple Museum of the History of Science, Cambridge, England.

world with what would become known as the mechanical philosophy.

When he turned his improved telescopes on the heavens in 1609, Galileo found convincing evidence that the Greek and Scholastic division of the cosmos into two distinct regions, the terrestrial and the celestial, could no longer be upheld and that the Ptolemaic system required serious revision at the very least. He took the occasion to begin defending the Copernican system publicly, constructing his support for it on a thorough critique of accepted views, his own telescopic discoveries, and his analysis of the nature of the tides, the latter a product of his studies of natural oscillating motion. This brought him into conflict with the Roman Catholic Church, and he argued for the right of the mathematician-natural philosopher to work and publish, free from any restraint by authority or tradition, civil or ecclesiastical. In the end, his trial in 1633 and subsequent confinement to house arrest made him a semimartyr to the cause of the new learning; however, he did arrange to publish, in 1638, his final scientific work, *Discourses on Two New Sciences,* thus bringing together results from his investigations into a whole range of topics over the fifty-odd years of his active career.

It is important to understand the social and intellectual milieu from which Galileo came. By the turn of the sixteenth century, northern Italy had created a class, generally, though not exclusively, nonuniversity and non-Latinate, whose members were highly trained in the more recent and demanding technical fields and who were already accustomed to a combined empirical-mathematical handling of nature. It included skilled and innovative instrument makers, engineers, mathematicians, and translators of classical Greek mathematical works. Cosimo I de' Medici (1519–1574), grand duke of Tuscany, encouraged the new professions, creating a cadre of architect-engineers. In the later sixteenth century, an informal engineering academy met in a Medici palazzo. Galileo attended and profited from its teachings in the arts of fortification and military architecture; he used copies of its circulated manuscripts in his own private tutoring of those subjects after he moved to Padua.

Galileo likely began his education in music under his father, Vincenzo (1520–1591), a noted musical theorist, and became an accomplished lutanist with an excellent sense of musical tone and tempo. After his early study of classical learning and languages, Galileo entered the University of Pisa in the fall of 1580 in the Faculty of Arts. It is quite likely that he attended the lectures of the philosopher Girolamo Borro (1512–1592), a generally conservative, yet heterodox, Aristotelian. He published two works of which Galileo owned copies: one on the tides and one on motion. Rather than by Borro's proposed explanation of the cause of the tides, he may have been inspired by the comment in a treatise by Andrea Cesalpino (1519–1603), professor of medicine at the university: "the ebb and flow of the waters are not provoked by the motion of the moon but by that of the earth." One aspect of the second of Borro's works stands out: his empirical testing of the notion that a heavy object ought to fall more quickly than a light one; Galileo made specific reference to these passages in his early manuscript tract *De motu (antiquiora),* ca. 1590.

If he had been introduced to problems that would concern him afterward, he also had developed a strong antipathy to the normal modes of natural philosophy in the universities. But it was in these same student years that he took the initial steps of his own career. Tradition and some corroborative evidence indicate that it was at Pisa that he discovered the isochronous properties of the simple pendulum. A swinging lamp in the cathedral may have attracted his attention; one of his early biographers wrote that Galileo checked the constancy of the period of the swings against his own practiced sense of musical timing. How he later satisfied himself that the properties were fundamental natural phenomena is suggested in passages in his *Two New Sciences*—that is, a systematic comparison of several pendula checked against each other in varying configurations. These passages also connect pendular isochronism with speculations on the nature of harmony in musical acoustics. The properties of naturally oscillating systems would be one of the prime foci of his researches from this time forward.

Galileo left Pisa in 1585 without taking a degree but continued laying important foundations for future research. Dissatisfied with the traditional story of how Archimedes (ca. 287–212 B.C.E.) discovered the laws of floating bodies, he devised an instrument appropriate for the task, a hydrostatic balance, elegant both in theory and in the precision with which he could obtain experimental results. His account, *La bilancetta* (1586), was his first original work, and he circulated copies in manuscript. He also used the classical Archimedean techniques of exhaustion to develop a set of theorems on the centers of gravity of certain solids of revolution, which he also circulated in manuscript.

His father had undertaken experimental investigations of the variables pertaining to tones in various types of musical instruments; Galileo very likely participated in the work. Part of the effort would have involved finding the way in which the tone of a plucked string depends on an applied tension. Initially the tone is loud, but, as both the amplitude of the sound and the visual amplitude of the excursions of the string diminish, the tone itself remains constant. But a weight hanging by a thin lute string (the likely experimental arrangement) is also a pendulum, and at some point Galileo must have been struck by the fact that, when a pendulum bob is drawn aside and released, the amplitude of its excursions diminishes even as the frequency of its swing remains the same. Could it be that the stable tone of a plucked string was a result of a constant frequency of vibration of that string? By 1587–1588, Galileo had probably already satisfied himself of the intrinsic and not just approximate nature of pendular isochronism. He continued to search for further experimental evidence as well as demonstrative proof connecting frequency with tone. He had discovered, not least, a new "natural motion" to add to that of free fall and had confirmed his sense of a need for a physical-experimental basis for a science.

Thus prepared, with a growing reputation and with influential support, Galileo returned to the University of Pisa in 1589 in the chair of mathematics. It is possible that, in his three years there, he introduced a comparison of the Ptolemaic and Copernican systems. Comments in the manuscript *De motu,* in composition in these years, do hint that he was beginning to wrestle with the notion of a movable earth. His *De motu* shows that he made a major attempt systematically to reformulate the standard late-Aristotelian accounts of natural motion. First, he attacked the supposition that there were two natural motions on the earth: one upward, a result of a natural "levity," and one downward, a result of a natural "gravity." On Archimedean grounds, he reduced the first to the second, arguing that those bodies that appear to rise naturally in a medium are really being pushed up by a buoyant force in that medium. Next, already aware that the Aristotelian teaching about the free fall of heavy bodies—that they fall with a speed proportional to their absolute weights—was wrong empirically, he began to erect an alternative account. He still assumed that bodies should fall with a uniform speed, not a uniform acceleration, but supposed that the speed should depend on its specific, not absolute, gravity. Unfortunately, when he tested the idea by dropping objects of widely differing specific gravities from high places, he found that they hit the ground almost simultaneously.

To account for it, he made a third assumption, importing a version of the medieval *impetus,* a quality that could be added from a source outside a body and that would slowly diminish when the source was removed. A ball not on the surface of the earth had, therefore, received an upward impetus, and, when released, its impetus drained away slowly. It was in this context that Galileo used a heavy weight, set swinging on the end of a cord, to find how long it took for its impetus to drain away and come to rest. Since it took much longer than the interval required for a body to reach the ground from any free vertical height available to him, he realized that he would not find uniform motion in vertical fall. Undiscouraged, he began to observe balls rolling down inclined planes, hoping to find an experimental example of his assumed uniform motion. In this he was also disappointed. He could produce an approximation to a uniform motion on a very shallow inclination, but he realized that this was probably a result of friction and imperfections in the wood of the plane itself, not because the equivalent impetus had vanished.

G

To this point, Galileo, looking for his postulated natural uniform motion, had always found what he initially called an "accidental" acceleration; while the acceleration was an empirical fact, it could not be reduced to mathematical or rational rule. He then imagined a model of acceleration in which a body could continuously increase in speed, never exceeding a given value but asymptotically approaching it. In this way, Galileo could preserve his initial assumption of an essential uniform speed of fall, the asymptotic upper limit, while accommodating and rationalizing the acceleration he was observing.

Meanwhile, he began to consider evidence that would lead him to abandon impetus. A ball, pushed to start rolling on a horizontal surface, continued to roll on that surface until its acquired impetus vanished and it, too, came to a natural stop. From his use of inclined planes, however, Galileo realized that a ball moved spontaneously only when allowed to roll down the plane, toward the center of the earth. When, given an impulse to move it up the plane, it would spontaneously decelerate. He reasoned that a ball placed on a horizontal surface should be indifferent to rest or motion and that, if started in motion on that surface, it would have no reason to either accelerate or decelerate. Moreover, if that surface were a frictionless sphere concentric with the center of the earth, the ball ought to continue at the same speed indefinitely. Impetus was, therefore, superfluous. He would eventually conclude that acceleration, not uniform motion, was the natural mode of falling bodies.

But was the acceleration to be limited, as in his initial, asymptotic speculation, or open and unbounded? How could it be characterized mathematically? The answer came from precise measurements of motions on inclined planes. Galileo had no way of measuring speed directly, so he had to measure distance and time intervals for balls rolling down those planes. Distance was no problem; needing, however, to measure continuous time intervals, he used an elevated water container with a small tube through its bottom. He could simultaneously release a ball at the top of the plane and open the tube to the flow of water, closing the tube when he heard the impact of the ball against a block set at a determined length along the plane. The water flowing through the tube was collected in a container and weighed, the weights of the water collected indicating the time intervals. Needing to express the results only in terms of ratios, he did not have to convert those weights into time

units. He found from experience that the distances covered in equal intervals of time were as the odd numbers from one, or, in terms of total times, the distances were as the squares of the times: the relationships we have come to know as Galileo's law of free fall. Galileo's systematic pursuit of the initial assumptions of his *De motu* project, in many respects a coherent and substantial revision of what he had been taught as a student, had eventually voided them and produced a cornerstone for a yet newer science of natural motion, in all probability by ca. 1595.

In 1592 Galileo moved to the University of Padua, where he augmented his salary by teaching private students and selling a device he invented. Combining elements of instruments already in existence, he designed a rather precise calculating and measuring device for engineers. He hired an artisan to produce copies, and he provided instruction in their use to interested students. The design underwent changes over several years; eventually (1606) Galileo published *Le operazioni del compasso geometrico militare,* describing the instrument and its use; it was his first printed work.

In the meantime, his research continued apace. By ca. 1595, or at the latest 1597, he had become engaged in another and larger project. He had convinced himself of the plausibility of the Copernican system and conceived a possible observational proof of it. Possibly recalling Cesalpino's suggestion, he sought a mechanical explanation of the tides. He found a rationale in his understanding of natural oscillation and experimented with containers of water. In the Copernican system, the earth spun on its axis as it moved around the Sun; a sea basin on the surface of the earth must move more swiftly in space when it was away from the Sun (at midnight), its total speed being the sum of the earth's speed in orbit and the speed of the surface of the spinning earth. Conversely, when the basin was closest to the Sun (midday), its speed in space was less, being the speed of the earth in orbit minus the speed of the earth's surface. The sea basins, periodically speeding up and slowing down, were, therefore, periodically pushing the water and causing the sloshing we observe as tides. In short, tides, as the product of naturally oscillating systems, constituted solid empirical evidence for the double motion of the earth. By 1615, he had drafted a version of his theory, *De flusso e reflusso del mare,* which he circulated in manuscript.

Galileo's related and other researches while at Padua were of at least equal long-term importance. Though he had moved from uniform motion to uniform acceleration as the basis for a science of motion, he still had problems to solve. One was to find a natural definition or axiom from which he could deduce as a theorem what he had already found experimentally, the law of free fall. He found it by 1607 or 1608—for a body in free fall, its velocity increases in direct proportion to the time—and he had constructed a demonstrative bridge from the definition to the law.

Galileo had satisfied himself empirically that a body falling from a given height would acquire the same speed whatever path it followed. He had no way of analyzing the difference between a ball rolling down an inclined plane and one falling (not spinning) vertically. He had more success, however, with trajectories. In the early 1590s, he had realized that projectile trajectories were continuously curved, and he had become convinced that an initial rising curve was symmetrical with its descending counterpart. By 1607 he had demonstrated the curve to be parabolic.

In Padua, Galileo also wanted to create a general, unified science of mechanics. He began developing a concept he called *momentum,* here a product of a weight times a speed, hoping initially to use it as a tool for understanding the effects of percussion, but had no success. He did use the concept, however, in his *Discourse on Floating Bodies,* essentially tying this Archimedean science to his mechanics. He also began working out a new branch of mechanics, the science of the resistance of beams to failure. He understood that he had to distinguish problems requiring independent treatment: the resistance of bodies to being pulled apart and how the properties of a body depend on its geometrical form; he viewed the latter as an extension of mechanics. His was the first, and largely successful, attempt to reduce a body of know-how, much of which had accumulated in the various building trades, to demonstration and to provide the starting tools for further investigations.

In the course of all of this and other work, Galileo heard about the invention in the Low Countries of a device that could make distant objects appear nearer. By the end of August 1609, he had constructed a nine-power instrument and presented it to the government of the Republic of Venice. Realizing its obvious practical value to a maritime nation, Republic officials gave him a lifetime appointment at Padua, with a substantial raise in salary.

By mid-November, with a twenty-power instrument, he began a systematic study of the Moon. He quickly sat-isfied himself that the Moon's surface was not the smooth one of a perfect sphere, as required in Aristotelean cosmology, but rough and mountainous like the surface of the earth. He could even calculate the heights of some of its mountains. He also found many more stars and constellations than anyone had ever seen or imagined previously. By January 13, 1610, he had seen all four of Jupiter's major moons. Two weeks later, he was in Venice arranging to print the *Sidereus nuncius* (Sidereal Messenger). The book was an immediate sensation, engendering widespread praise and strong opposition. Galileo's final comments left no doubt about its Copernican implications, but the initial opposition seemed more based on a combination of traditional Aristotelian views of the cosmos and doubts about the spyglass as a reliable vehicle for valid information.

His overture to the Tuscan Court of Cosimo II de' Medici (1590–1621) through the dedication of the book and naming the moons of Jupiter the Medice an Stars resulted in an offer to become senior mathematical lecturer at the University of Pisa (without obligations to teach or reside there) and philosopher and mathematician to the grand duke. In October, now in Florence, Galileo began to observe Venus closely and learned of its phases and changes in apparent size. Venus (and, by implication, Mercury) did not shine by its own light and apparently revolved about the Sun, in the space between the earth and the Sun. In March 1611, the Jesuits at the Collegio Romano, as well as a number of others previously, confirmed the moons of Jupiter and accepted the rest, including the phases of Venus, tacitly endorsing the spyglass as a legitimate means for investigating the heavens. On a visit to Rome, Galileo also showed a few people another recent discovery, the sunspots. The Sun itself, for millennia a symbol of heavenly purity and perfection, proved maculate, and it turned on its axis much as the earth was thought to do by Copernicus. Capping this trip was a banquet at the Accademia dei Lincei, during which Galileo was inducted as a member and his optic tube received the name it has been known by since, the telescope.

In 1612 Galileo entered into a debate on the nature of sunspots with Christoph Scheiner (1573–1650), a Jesuit, through correspondence with an intermediary, in the course of which he came out fairly unambiguously in favor of the Copernican system. The Lincei published the correspondence, *Letters on the Sunspots,* in 1613 to general acclaim, but Galileo had probably sown some seeds of animosity within the Jesuit Order. The grounds for the opposition to Galileo and Copernicanism were beginning to shift to the theological.

In February 1615, Galileo was denounced to the Holy Office. To express his views and defend his loyalty to the Church, Galileo wrote out his opinions on the relation between science and theology by that summer. It became the *Letter to the Grand Duchess Christina,* which was circulated but not published at the time. Meanwhile, a Carmelite friar and theologian, Paolo Antonio Foscarini, published a work, *Letter of the Reverend Father Paolo Antonio Foscarini, on the Pythagorean and Copernican Opinion of the Earth's Motion and the Sun's Rest and on the New Pythagorean World System* (1615), spelling out the implications of Galileo's discoveries and showing how the Copernican system was not inconsistent with the Bible. He sent a copy to Robert Cardinal Bellarmine (1542–1621), a Jesuit and, as member of the Congregation of the Holy Office, a Cardinal Inquisitor, requesting his opinion. Bellarmine replied, extolling the virtue of speaking only hypothetically about the Copernican system and warning against contradicting both the Scriptures and theologians. Though he admitted that, if there were real proof of the Sun's centrality and the motions of the earth, interpretations would have to be reconsidered, he had not seen such proofs and he believed that none existed. Galileo saw a copy of this letter, and it was probably then that he completed a draft and began to circulate his tract *Discourse on the Ebb and Flow of the Sea.* Meanwhile, the theologians of the Holy Office decided that a heliocentric system was absurd in philosophy and formally heretical, while a noncentral, moving earth was merely erroneous theologically. Bellarmine was directed by the pope to summon Galileo and admonish him to abandon the Copernican opinions, to which, by March 3, Galileo acquiesced. On the same day, the Congregation of the Index issued a decree condemning the Copernican teachings and suspending Copernicus's exposition of his system, *De revolutionibus,* until corrected. Foscarini's book was absolutely condemned. By mid-1616, Galileo's immediate campaign for the Copernican system was over, but there was no shadow on him personally.

In the fall of 1616, the appearance of three comets led to a debate between Galileo and Orazio Grassi (1592–1654), a Jesuit, who tried to explain them in the context of the Tychonian system, maintaining a stationary earth. Galileo's response was published as *Il saggia-* tore (The Assayer) in 1623 with the sponsorship of the Lincei and dedicated to the recently elected pope, Galileo's friend Maffeo Cardinal Barberini (1568–1644), who had taken the name Urban VIII.

It was a brilliant combination of polemic against the logical and disputative modes of the universities and manifesto for the new experimental-mathematical mode of investigating and understanding nature. It gave clear expression to a distinction between what we have come to call the primary and the secondary qualities. The first are the mathematical ones, the sizes, shapes, weights, and relative motions of bodies; the second, such as color, taste, and smell, reside only in the consciousness of the individuals sensing them. *Il saggiatore* was well received, and Galileo journeyed to Rome in the spring of 1624, hoping that the Church under Urban VIII might be persuaded to soften its stance on Copernicus. He had six cordial audiences with the pope, who praised the book highly and gave Galileo the impression that he might cautiously revive the heliocentric debate, though he insisted that Galileo would be safe only if he stayed within the bounds of the 1616 decree. Encouraged, Galileo finished the draft in 1630 of the project he had begun even before his telescopic discoveries, initially entitled *Dialogue on the Ebb and Flow of the Sea.* Authorization to print arrived in July 1631. It specified, among other things, that the title had to be changed. Galileo accepted all of the changes, choosing the new title: *Dialogue Concerning the Two Chief World Systems, Ptolemaic and Copernican,* and the work was published in February 1632.

Galileo structured the *Dialogue* in the form of an extended conversation among three acquaintances over a period of four "days." The discussion in the first three days covers many topics central to the theme, including questions about the traditional distinction between celestial and terrestrial substances; the telescopic discoveries and their implications; Galileo's new science of local motions and what it can tell us about whether the earth is actually moving or not; and the problems and ways of making astronomical observations.

To this point, Galileo by and large presented the Copernican issues reasonably evenhandedly, strongly, but arguably not going beyond the hypothetical. In the Fourth Day, however, the tone and effect change drastically. Salviati, presenting the views of Galileo, offers a tight, technical presentation of tidal phenomena and their causes in the two motions of the earth (with an obviously related digression on the properties of pendular motions). Then, in the final paragraphs, Simplicio, who had represented Aristotelian positions, comes alive and gives voice to what we might call the Barberini reservation—that God, in his infinite wisdom, could have arranged things differently to produce the effects that we see. For Barberini-Urban, of course, this was sound theology, and Galileo may well have thought that, by ending the *Dialogue* in this way, he was only following the rules he had been given. In a human and rhetorical sense, however, he could well have been seen as thumbing his nose at the pope.

Through the licensing process and even the publication of the book, Urban had continued to encourage Galileo; he had probably even seen parts of the draft. Then something happened to enrage him, and he ordered proceedings against Galileo for violating the 1616 decree. After a trial of several weeks without resolution, the Commissary of the Holy Office (the Inquisition) received permission to treat Galileo extrajudiciously, hoping to persuade him to confess that he had, in fact, overrepresented the strength of his arguments out of "vainglorious ambition and of pure ignorance and inadvertence." Galileo eventually agreed but, after review, was nevertheless found guilty of vehement suspicion of heresy, condemned to abjure his Copernican beliefs, and sentenced to imprisonment at the pleasure of the Holy Office; the *Dialogue* was prohibited.

After several months, he was allowed to return to his small villa in Arcetri, near Florence. Galileo now continued his earlier reworking of his old notes and redrafting portions of what would become his final work, the *Discourses on Two New Sciences,* issued in 1638. As with the *Dialogue,* the *Discourses* is divided into four days of discussions among three friends. Here, however, Galileo had different expository aims. Instead of trying to make controversial cosmological notions acceptable to bureaucrats, intellectuals, and theologians, he wanted to discuss the technically complex scientific issues that had engaged him for half a century and to present some of his solutions, the new sciences.

The second, third, and fourth days contain the two "sciences," those subjects for which Galileo had been able, at least in part, to provide a demonstrative, mathematical backbone, uniting sets of observational or experimentally refined phenomena. In the second day, Galileo presented that aspect of the resistance of beams to fracture depending only on their geometrical forms. In the third and fourth days, he dealt with local motions: uniform motion as on a horizontal surface; uniformly accelerated motion as in free fall; nonuniformly accelerated motion as in the natural oscillation of a pendulum; and combined motion as in the parabolic trajectory of a projectile.

The first day is entirely different. Here were presented the research projects that he had not brought to satisfactory resolution; those that had some bearing on the topics of the later days but that were distinct from them, both introducing the later topics and clarifying and distinguishing the issues. He speculated that matter might be composed of "minimal" or infinitesimal atoms, which in solids might have minimal vacua interspersed, thus accounting for their tensile properties. Then he introduced and discussed several of the paradoxes of the infinite, adducing properties of the infinitely large and small while recognizing the difficulties of comparing the infinite to the finite. Finally, he returned to what, for him, were the related topics of the nature of musical tones and harmonics and the isochronism of pendulums.

Though growing progressively blind and often confined to bed with infirmities, he continued his attempts to solve many outstanding problems and kept up an active personal and scientific correspondence. Vincenzo Viviani (1622–1703), who had moved in to assist him, stimulated Galileo to find a demonstration for a theorem to the effect that bodies falling through a given height would acquire the same speed independent of the path of fall, a demonstration that had eluded him for many years and would be added to subsequent editions of the *Discourses.* He had already used a pendulum device to help him time the periods of the revolutions of Jupiter's moons; it was manually activated, unconnected to any driving mechanism. He now designed a pendulum-regulated clock. Clocks were later constructed from his plans and worked quite well.

In October 1641, Galileo's health began to deteriorate markedly, and he died the following January.

BIBLIOGRAPHY

Drake, Stillman. *Galileo at Work: His Scientific Biography*. Chicago: University of Chicago Press, 1978.

Finocchiaro, Maurice A., ed. and trans. *The Galileo Affair: A Documentary History*. Berkeley and Los Angeles: University of California Press, 1989.

Galilei, Galileo. *Dialogue Concerning the Two Chief World Systems, Ptolemaic and Copernican.* Trans. Stillman Drake. Berkeley and Los Angeles: University of California Press, 1962.

G

———. *Discoveries and Opinions of Galileo*. Ed. and trans. with an Introduction by Stillman Drake. Garden City, NY: Doubleday, 1957.

———. *Galileo's Early Notebooks: The Physical Questions*. Ed. and trans. William A. Wallace. Notre Dame, IN: University of Notre Dame Press, 1977.

———. *On Motion* and *On Mechanics*. Trans. with Introductions by I. E. Drabkin and Stillman Drake. Madison: University of Wisconsin Press, 1960.

———. *Le Opere di Galilei Galilei*. Ed. Antonio Favaro. Edizione Nazionale, 20 vols. Florence: Barbèra, 1890–1909. Repr. with additions, 1929–1939, 1964–1966.

———. *Sidereus Nuncius, or the Sidereal Messenger*. Ed. and trans. Albert van Helden. Chicago: University of Chicago Press, 1989.

———. *Two New Sciences Including Centers of Gravity and Force of Percussion*. Trans. with an Introduction by Stillman Drake. Madison: University of Wisconsin Press, 1974.

McMullin, Ernan, ed. *Galileo: Man of Science*. New York: Basic Books, 1967.

THOMAS B. SETTLE

See also Copernicanism; Galileo and the Church; Mechanics; Motion; Telescope; Telescopic Astronomy; Tides

Galileo and the Church

Apart from his scientific achievements, Galileo Galilei (1564–1642) is also and perhaps even more known for his conflict with the Catholic Church on the issue of Copernicanism and its dramatic conclusion with his condemnation and abjuration. This essay aims to clarify the cultural factors (both philosophical and theological) as well as the historical facts that played a decisive role in the so-called Galileo affair.

At the time Galileo first announced his astronomical discoveries with his book *Sidereus nuncius* (Sidereal Messenger, 1610), the almost universally accepted vision of the world, both in Catholic and in Protestant Europe, was that of geocentrism. It was preferred by the Greeks both in its philosophical form, expressed by Aristotle (384–322 B.C.E.), and in the mathematical one, expressed by Ptolemy (second century), to various forms of geokinetism. Geocentrism had been adopted in the Middle Ages in place of the primitive world picture of the Bible. The great intellectual open-mindedness thus shown by the medieval Christian thinkers was unfortunately progressively lost in the following centuries.

On the one hand, the Aristotelian philosophy, seen as the best intellectual preparation (*praeamblum*) to the Christian faith, ended up appearing inseparable from it.

On the other hand, the harsh polemics between Catholics and Protestants on the biblical foundations of the Church structure contributed to a much more rigid emphasis from both sides on the literal interpretation of Holy Scripture. At the same time, the necessity of preserving Catholic "orthodoxy" against the dangers of Protestant "heresy" brought ever-increasing control of thought in the Catholic world. This control was entrusted to the Congregation of the Roman and Universal Inquisition (or Holy Office, 1542) and later also to the Congregation of the Index of the Forbidden Books (1571).

Notwithstanding such an increasingly rigid intellectual climate, the publication of Nicolaus Copernicus's (1473–1543) major work *De revolutionibus* (1543) failed to provoke the virulent opposition that Copernicus himself had feared. As a matter of fact, Copernicus's geokinetism did not offer, in general, predictions of celestial phenomena more accurate than those of geocentric astronomy and, thus, did not compel most astronomers to abandon geocentrism. To philosophers, it appeared false and even absurd, being so much in contrast with the fundamental assertions of Aristotelian cosmology, considered by them as the only true one. Thus, Copernicanism failed to appear as a real alternative to geocentrism. This is perhaps the chief reason why the criticism of the Copernican theory, as opposed to the literal interpretation of the Bible, though present in both Protestant and Catholic Europe, did not materialize into authoritative condemnations.

An important exception to this apparent lack of concern of the Catholic Church authorities toward Copernicanism is, however, noticeable in the case of Giordano Bruno (1548–1600). Though not the chief cause of his condemnation, Bruno's Copernican convictions and especially his bold extension of the Copernican vision to that of an infinite universe with an infinite number of solar systems inhabited by living beings similar to man were considered by his judges as incompatible with the Christian faith.

The publication of Galileo's *Sidereus nuncius* marks a turning point in the acceptance of Copernicanism by the cultural European elite. Galileo's discovery of the Moon's mountains and of the Jupiter satellites contradicted two fundamental tenets of Aristotelian cosmology: the essential difference between celestial and terrestrial matter and the earth as the only center of all celestial motions. To be sure, Copernicanism was not proved by these discoveries (nor by the soon to follow observation of the phases of Venus), which were still compatible with new forms of geocentrism like that of Tycho Brahe (1546–1601). But it ceased by now to be a mere mathematical hypothesis and became a real possibility, if not a probability.

Endorsed by the authority of Johannes Kepler (1571–1630) and of the Jesuit mathematicians of the Collegio Romano, Galileo's discoveries soon became an unquestionable fact, gaining for Copernicanism an ever-growing number of supporters, or at least sympathizers. Galileo's trip to Rome in 1611, with the celebration held in his honor at the Collegio Romano and his admission into the newly founded Accademia dei Lincei, represented the climax of his success, though his open profession of Copernicanism did not fail to arouse concern in the Holy Office.

After Galileo's return to Florence, a fateful development took place in the Copernican debate. Unable by now to put in doubt Galileo's discoveries, his opponents started to stress the incompatibility of Copernicanism with the literal interpretation of many biblical passages. That was, in fact, the thesis presented by the Aristotelian philosopher Cosimo Boscaglia at a lunch offered by the Tuscan Grand Duke Cosimo II de' Medici (1590–1621). Informed by his Benedictine disciple Benedetto Castelli (1578–1643), also present at the lunch, Galileo felt all of the danger of this turning of a scientific question into a theological one and hastened to compose a written answer, the *Letter to Castelli, to be circulated among their friends*. In it, he stressed that Holy Scripture, while giving the ultimate answers in questions pertaining to Christian faith and morals, did not pretend to teach astronomy or natural philosophy. The debate on Copernicanism ought, therefore, not to be solved on the basis of a literal interpretation of biblical passages seemingly opposed to it, which expressed only the common way of thinking of ancient people.

This letter was deemed by the Dominicans of the convent of St. Mark in Florence to be a dangerous example of the kind of private interpretation (moreover by a simple layman!) of Holy Scripture that the Catholic Church had condemned at the Council of Trent (1546). Sent in February 1615 by the Dominican Niccolò Lorini to Rome, the *Letter* was examined by a consultor of the Holy Office, who, however, did not have serious objections to its theological content. An even more dangerous accusation against Galileo and his followers was person-

ally brought to Rome by another Dominican, Tommaso Caccini, who had previously attacked them from the pulpit of a Florentine Church. Even though, in this case as well, the accusation could not be substantiated, the preoccupation of the Church authorities was on the rise.

An even deeper preoccupation was caused by the appearance of a letter written by the Neapolitan Carmelite Paolo Antonio Foscarini in defense of the compatibility of Copernicanism with Holy Scripture. He sent a copy of it to the most authoritative Catholic theologian of the time, the Jesuit Robert Cardinal Bellarmine (1542–1621). In his answer to Foscarini, the cardinal admitted that, in the case (for him extremely improbable) of strict scientific proofs in favor of Copernicanism, one should reconsider the traditional interpretation of the biblical passages opposed to it. But he recommended to Foscarini, and indirectly to Galileo, that, in the meantime, they were to treat Copernicanism as a mere hypothetical theory.

Galileo became aware of this answer, as well as the action pushed ahead against him by the Dominicans. Deeply concerned about the possibility of a hasty condemnation of Copernicanism by Church authorities, he decided to go to Rome, hoping to ward off the danger through contacts and discussions with influential Roman clergymen. This decision proved to be ill advised. Galileo's heated discussions with the opponents of Copernicanism, together with the stir caused by the intervention of a theologian, Foscarini, in favor of heliocentrism, convinced Church authorities that a decision on the matter had to be taken without further delay. On February 19, 1616, two propositions summing up the principal tenets of the Copernican system held by Galileo were submitted for examination to the theological experts of the Holy Office. In their answer, they judged the immobility of the Sun to be "foolish and absurd in philosophy and formally heretical" since it explicitly contradicted in many places "the sense of Holy Scripture, according to the literal meaning of the words and the common interpretation and understanding of the Church Fathers and the doctors of theology." As for the mobility of the earth, the experts said that this affirmation of Copernicanism, too, was foolish and absurd in philosophy, while in regard to theological truth it was "at least erroneous in faith."

Approved in the plenary session of the Holy Office on February 24, 1616, this answer was made known to Pope Paul V, who decided that Galileo should be summoned by Cardinal Bellarmine and warned by him to abandon his opinions. In the case he should refuse to obey, the Commissary of the Holy Office, Michelangelo Segizzi, in the presence of notary and witnesses, would order him to abstain completely from teaching or defending this doctrine or even from discussing it. In case of failure to acquiesce, Galileo was to be imprisoned. From the documents of the Holy Office, as well as from a declaration released later by Bellarmine himself to Galileo, it appears that the notification was made by Bellarmine to Galileo on Friday, February 26, in the presence of the Commissary Segizzi. Perhaps dissatisfied with the kind way in which Bellarmine had carried out his task, Segizzi intervened without delay, imposing on Galileo the much harsher precept of abstaining from dealing with Copernicanism in any way. Galileo acquiesced. Though lacking the signature of Bellarmine (who may have been displeased with the premature intervention of Segizzi) and of the witnesses, the written document on the matter was put in the files of the Holy Office and came to play an important role in the process against Galileo in 1633.

As to Copernicanism, a doctrinaire decree was published by the Congregation of the Index on March 5, 1616. Copernicus's theory was declared "false and altogether opposed to Holy Scripture," and Copernicus's book *De revolutionibus* was suspended until corrected, while Foscarini's book was prohibited and condemned. The decree thus stopped short of declaring Copernicanism heretical. This was most probably due to the opposition of some cardinals of the congregation, among whom was Galileo's old admirer Maffeo Cardinal Barberini (1568–1644). As for the correction of Copernicus's work, it was aimed at making his theory appear as a mere mathematical one, not as a real explanation of the system of the world. Thus ended the so-called first process of Galileo. He had been spared a formal process, no doubt because of his status as first philosopher and mathematician of the grand duke of Tuscany, as well as his renown throughout Europe. But the way had been found (at least in the opinion of Church authorities) to silence him forever and, with him, the whole Copernican debate.

Galileo, having returned to Florence, remained silent on the Copernican issue until a fateful event occurred in August 1623—the election of his friend Barberini as the new Pope Urban VIII. With great hopes, Galileo went to Rome in April 1624 and was received in audience by the pope several times. Urban VIII did not

Title page of Galileo's Dialogue on the Two Great World Systems *(1632), the publication of which led him to be brought before the Inquisition. The characters represent an Aristotelian, an open-minded participant, and a Copernican.*

show any intention of abolishing the decree of the Index against Copernicanism. But he seemingly gave to Galileo permission to write a work in which the Aristotelian-Ptolemaic and the Copernican systems of the world might to be expounded in an impartial way, without taking a position in favor of either of them. Completed after six years, the work was submitted in Rome to the Master of the Sacred Palace, Niccolò Riccardi, for permission to publish. Concerned about the content of the book, which in spite of the author's protestations appeared heavily biased in favor of Copernicanism, Riccardi delayed the ecclesiastical permission. Riccardi's apprehensions were well grounded. When the book, finally printed in Florence with the title of *Dialogue Concerning the Two Chief World Systems,* reached Rome in the spring of 1632, there was an increasing uproar against such a patently pro-Copernican work. Feeling betrayed by his friend, Urban VIII ordered the book to be examined by a commission of theologians, who confirmed the *Dialogue*'s pro-Copernican stand. The concomitant discovery in the Holy Office's archives of the document on Segizzi's injunction to Galileo was a further and even heavier blow against him. Galileo was thus found guilty on two accounts: of having written a defense of Copernicanism against the decree of the Index of 1616, and of having fraudulently omitted to mention, at the time of the request for permission to publish, the existence of an inquisitorial precept that prevented him altogether from dealing with the Copernican issue. Galileo had thus become "vehemently suspect of heresy" (in the wider Inquisitorial sense of the term "heresy").

Summoned to Rome, he was subjected to a formal process by the Holy Office, which started on April 12, 1633. Galileo consistently denied having taken a position in favor of Copernicanism in the *Dialogue,* even asserting that, on the contrary, he had intended to prove it false. As to his silence about Segizzi's injunction, he affirmed not to have any memory of it, but only of Bellarmine's notification, which did not forbid him from dealing with Copernicanism but only from defending it. As a proof of his position, he submitted the attestation given to him by the cardinal. To his judges, however, Galileo's answers appeared insincere, the more so since a new commission of theologians confirmed that, in defending Copernicanism, he had violated the decree of the Index and, thus, even the more general notification of Bellarmine, not to speak of Segizzi's injunction. A condemnation of Galileo for "vehement suspicion of heresy" was thus unavoidable, with the abjuration of Copernicanism by Galileo aimed at removing that suspicion. On June 22, 1633, at the Dominican convent of S. Maria sopra Minerva, kneeling down before the cardinals and other officials of the Holy Office, Galileo heard the sentence of condemnation and then read the formula of abjuration. The *Dialogue* was put on the Index of Forbidden Books, and Galileo was condemned to house arrest in his residence near Florence, until his death on January 8, 1642.

As a whole, Galileo's process was carried out in an objective way and with unusual consideration paid to Galileo (who was spared the prison at the Holy Office and torture). As to its outcome, it was the only one possible under the Inquisitorial jurisprudence of the epoch, given Galileo's infringement of the decree of 1616 and of Segizzi's injunction. The real abuse of authority, both doctrinal and disciplinary, goes back to the fateful decisions taken by the Catholic Church in 1616. Surely enough, Galileo was then (as later, at the time of the composition of the *Dialogue*) unable to give unques-

tionable proofs in favor of Copernicanism. But the new observational data were already sufficient to show the Aristotelian-Ptolemaic system to be untenable, while Copernicanism increasingly appeared to be a real possibility. The grave mistake of the Church decisions in 1616 consisted, thus, in having pretended to definitively close a question that should have been left open, as Galileo had recommended.

The first to suffer for such an unwise authoritarianism was the Church itself, confronted in the following centuries with the fact of the scientific proof of Copernicanism and, thus, with the unpleasant task of admitting its mistakes. It took more than two hundred years to see the works of Copernicus and of Galileo removed from the Index of Forbidden Books (1835). It took another three hundred fifty years for the frank recognition of the Church's responsibilities for its unjust treatment of Galileo made by Pope John Paul II in 1979 and later, in a conclusive way, in 1992.

BIBLIOGRAPHY

Drake, Stillman. *Galileo at Work: His Scientific Biography.* Chicago: University of Chicago Press, 1978.

Fantoli, Annibale. *Galileo: For Copernicanism and for the Church.* Trans. George Coyne. (Vatican Observatory Publications). Notre Dame, IN: University of Notre Dame Press, 1994. 2nd ed. 1996.

Feldhay, Rivka. *Galileo and the Church: Political Inquisition or Political Dialogue?* Cambridge: Cambridge University Press, 1995.

Finocchiaro, Maurice, ed. and trans. *The Galileo Affair: A Documentary History.* Berkeley and Los Angeles: University of California Press, 1989.

Langford, Jerome J. *Galileo, Science, and the Church.* Ann Arbor: University of Michigan Press, 1966.

Redondi, Pietro. *Galileo Heretic.* Trans. Raymond Rosenthal. Princeton, NJ: Princeton University Press, 1987.

Santillana, Giorgio de. *The Crime of Galileo.* Chicago: University of Chicago Press, 1955.

ANNIBALE FANTOLI

See also Biblical Interpretations; Copernicanism; Galilei, Galileo; Religion and Natural Philosophy

Gascoigne, William (ca. 1612–ca. 1644)

An astronomer and the inventor of the micrometer, which enabled effective telescopic sights to be applied to angle-measuring astronomical instruments for the first time. After being educated in London and Oxford (and, reputedly, in Rome), he lived at Middleton, near Leeds, in Yorkshire; during the English Civil War he served as a "providore" to the Royalist army and died in battle in 1644 or 1645. From 1638 to 1642, he corresponded with the Manchester astronomer William Crabtree (ca. 1610–1644), who passed on news of Gascoigne's invention to Jeremiah Horrocks (1618–1641); this has led to Gascoigne being identified by Edward Sherburne (1618–1702) and later historians as a member of a supposed "Towneley Circle." It was, however, through Gascoigne's description of the micrometer in a letter to the mathematician William Oughtred (1575–1660) that it became known to other contemporary astronomers. It was more widely publicized only in 1667, when a rival claim by the French led to the publication of accounts by Richard Towneley (1629–1707) and Robert Hooke (1635–1702) in the *Philosophical Transactions* over several years beginning in 1667. Soon afterward, a Towneley-Gascoigne micrometer was presented to the young John Flamsteed (1646–1719) by Jonas Moore (1617–1679); this and modified copies were utilized in instruments at the Royal Observatory at Greenwich, founded in 1675, and were essential to the institution's claims to achieve unprecedented accuracy. Flamsteed directly imitated some of Gascoigne's micrometric observations and claimed to have learned much from his writings on optics; he also preserved extracts from the Gascoigne-Crabtree correspondence and published observations from this source in Volume 1 of his *Historia coelestis Britannica* (1725).

BIBLIOGRAPHY

Chapman, Allan. *Three North Country Astronomers.* Swinton, England: N. Richardson, 1982.

Rigaud, S. J. *Correspondence of Scientific Men of the Seventeenth Century.* Oxford: Oxford University Press, 1891. Repr. Hildesheim: G. Olms, 1965.

FRANCES WILLMOTH

See also Philosophical Transactions; Picard, Jean; Royal Observatory at Greenwich; Telescope; Towneley, Richard

Gassendi, Pierre (1592–1655)

A French Catholic priest who introduced the philosophy of the ancient atomist Epicurus into the mainstream of European thought. Like many of his contemporaries in the first half of the seventeenth century, Gassendi sought to articulate a new philosophy of nature to replace the Aristotelianism that had traditionally provided the foundation for natural philosophy. Before European intellectuals could accept the philosophy of Epicurus (341–270 B.C.E.), it had to be purged of various heterodox notions. Accordingly, Gassendi modified the philosophy of his ancient model to make it conform to the demands of Christian theology. He was an enthusiastic supporter of new developments in natural philosophy and in 1642 published an exposition of Galileo Galilei's (1564–1642) new science of motion that contains the first correct statement of the principle of inertia in print.

Gassendi was born in Provence and obtained a clerical education in preparation for the priesthood. He studied Aristotelian philosophy and Catholic theology at the college of Aix-en-Provence and received the doctorate in theology at Avignon in 1614. Assuming the chair of philosophy at Aix-en-Provence, he taught Aristotelian philosophy there from 1616 until 1622, when the university was taken over by the Jesuits and the faculty was forced to leave. He had been a member canon of the Cathedral of Digne since his student days, and in 1634 he became provost of the cathedral, a position he retained for the rest of his life. He was appointed professor of mathematics at the Collège Royal in 1645.

Gassendi's first published work, *Exercitationes paradoxicae adversus Aristoteleos* (Paradoxical Exercises Against the Aristotelians, 1624) was a skeptical critique of Aristotelianism. Gassendi adopted "mitigated skepticism," which claimed that a science of appearances can attain, at best, probable knowledge of things. Denying the possibility of knowing essences, he allied himself with the nominalists. Empiricism and nominalism were central themes in his philosophical writings. In a series of works, starting in the 1630s, Gassendi addressed the problem of restoring Epicureanism, beginning with philological studies of the main Epicurean texts. The culmination of his project was the posthumous *Syntagma philosophicum* (1658), which incorporated material from contemporary natural philosophy into a thoroughly Christianized exposition of Epicureanism.

Gassendi rejected the the parts of Epicureanism that were inconsistent with Christian theology, namely polytheism, a corporeal conception of the divine nature, the negation of all providence, the denial of creation ex nihilo, the infinitude and eternity of atoms and the universe, the plurality of worlds, the attribution of the cause of the world to chance, a materialistic cosmogony, the denial of all finality in biology, and the corporeality and mortality of the human soul. He asserted that a wise and

Pierre Gassendi. From Johannes Hevelius, The Illustrated Account Given by Hevelius in his *"Machina celestis" (1882).*

In the first part of the *Syntagma philosophicum,* entitled "Logic," Gassendi attempted to substitute the canonic of Epicurus for Aristotelian dialectic, which he deemed useless as a tool for finding out about the world. Gassendi developed a theory of knowledge and a primitive psychology to explain how we acquire ideas. He endorsed an empirical approach to knowledge, which, he thought, could, at best, attain probability.

The "Physics" is the longest part of Gassendi's *Syntagma philosophicum.* Here Gassendi stated that atoms and the void are the ultimate components of the physical world. Using concepts borrowed from the Renaissance Platonist Francesco Patrizi (1529–1597), Gassendi considered space to be neither substance nor accident but, rather, a kind of incorporeal extension. He appealed to arguments taken from the ancient atomists, as well as evidence from the barometric experiments of his contemporaries Evangelista Toricelli (1608-1647) and Blaise Pascal (1623–1662), to support the existence of void. He rejected the Aristotelian explanation that appealed to the *horror vacui,* appealing instead to the pressure of the atmosphere as the explanation of various barometric phenomena.

Atoms possess only a few primary qualities: magnitude and figure, resistance or solidity, and heaviness. Gassendi cited observations with the microscope, as well as traditional observations such as the dispersion of pigment in water and the large quantity of smoke emanating from a smoldering log, as evidence for their small size. He used Zeno's (ca. 490–ca. 425 B.C.E.) paradoxes to argue for the indivisibility of atoms, interpreting the paradoxes as demonstrating the absurdity of the idea of the infinite divisibility of matter. Gassendi tried to explain all of the qualities of bodies in terms of the motions and configurations of their constituent atoms. He gave mechanical explanations of all of the observable qualities of bodies, including the so-called occult qualities, which, he argued, can be explained in mechanical terms rather than by any kind of action at a distance.

Having considered the universal principles of physics, Gassendi turned to all of the phenomena of the world. Two topics regarding the heavens are particularly noteworthy: his attitude to Copernicanism and his rejection of astrology. Although the Roman Catholic Church's condemnation of Galileo in 1633 dampened his enthusiasm for Copernicanism, at least in print, where he expressed skeptical doubts about being able to prove any of the three main world systems—Ptolemaic, Copernican,

omnipotent God had created the world and its constituent atoms, that God rules the world providentially, that the number of atoms in the world is finite, that there is evidence of design throughout the Creation, that final causes play an important role in natural philosophy, and that the human soul is immaterial and immortal.

Gassendi's theology was voluntarist, emphasizing God's omnipotence and freedom. The laws of nature are simply descriptions of the regularities we observe in the operations of nature. Like everything else God created, the laws of nature are contingent on divine will. God could have created an entirely different natural order, a possibility limited only by the principle of noncontradiction. Noting that God is the first cause of the world, including the atoms, Gassendi reduced second causes, the natural causes operating in the physical world, to collisions among atoms moving in void space. He rejected the random swerve of atoms (*clinamen*) introduced by Epicurus to account for the collisions of atoms that would otherwise only fall downward in parallel paths. For Gassendi, God created the motions of atoms at the time of the Creation. Evidence of design throughout the world establishes God's continuing providential relationship to his creation.

or Tychonic—conclusively, Gassendi proposed the system of Tycho Brahe (1546–1601) as a compromise approved by the Church, but not before having stated that the Copernican theory was "more probable and evident." As for the effects of the stars, Gassendi rejected astrology as "inane and futile." He thought that, although sidereal and planetary configurations may be signs of some events on earth, such as the seasons or the weather, they are not the causes of terrestrial phenomena and cannot be used to prognosticate the future. God alone has foreknowledge of future events. Gassendi found horoscopes based on the moment of nativity absurd. Why, he asked, should the heavenly bodies have more influence at the moment of birth than at any other moment in a person's life? He thought that the principles of astrology were based on insufficient evidence and that astrologers often resort to deception.

Turning to terrestrial phenomena, Gassendi considered the properties of the earth, the distribution of water and land, the tides, subterranean heat, the saltiness of the sea, and meteorological phenomena. Shifting his attention to smaller things, he wrote about stones and metals, paying particular attention to recent observations of the magnet and to the question of the transmutation of gold, which he considered possible. He included plants among inanimate things because, he believed, they lack souls. Gassendi discussed the varieties of plants and their parts, considering their various physiological processes, including grafting, nutrition, germination, growth, and death.

The final section of the "Physics" was devoted to terrestrial living things, or animals, including the varieties of animals, the parts of animals, their uses, and various physiological topics, including generation, nutrition, respiration, and motion. Gassendi devoted about half of this lengthy section to the topics of sensation, perception, and the immortality of the human soul, topics of particular philosophical interest. Gassendi's argument for the immortality of the soul was central to his Christianization of Epicureanism. Against Epicurus, who had claimed that the soul is material and mortal, Gassendi argued that the sentient soul is material and present throughout the body but that the rational soul is incorporeal and, therefore, immortal. The sentient soul is composed of very fine and intensely active atoms. It is the principle of organization and activity for the organism and the source of the animal's vital heat. It is also responsible for perception, forming the imagination, or "phantasy," a physical organ that forms images derived from perception. The sentient soul is transmitted from one generation to the next at the moment of conception.

The rational soul is an incorporeal substance, created by God and infused in the body, and functions like an informing form. It is distinct from the corporeal imagination, or phantasy, because it is possible to understand some things of which we cannot form images, such as that the Sun is 160 times larger than the earth. In contrast to corporeal things, the rational soul is capable of reflecting on itself and the nature of universality per se, abilities that distinguish humans from animals. Gassendi's claim that the rational soul, in contrast with the animal soul, is incorporeal established one of the boundaries of his mechanization of the world.

BIBLIOGRAPHY

Brundell, B. *Pierre Gassendi: From Aristotelianism to a New Natural Philosophy*. Dordrecht: Reidel, 1987.

Gassendi, P. *The Selected Works of Pierre Gassendi*. Trans. Craig Brush. New York: Johnson Reprint, 1972.

Jones, H. *Pierre Gassendi, 1592–1655: An Intellectual Biography*. Nieuwkoop: B. de Graaf, 1981.

Joy, L. S. *Gassendi the Atomist: Advocate of History in an Age of Science*. Cambridge: Cambridge University Press, 1987.

Osler, M. J. *Divine Will and the Mechanical Philosophy: Gassendi and Descartes on Contingency and Necessity in the Created World*. Cambridge: Cambridge University Press, 1994.

Sarasohn, L. T. *Gassendi's Ethics: Freedom in a Mechanistic Universe*. Ithaca, NY: Cornell University Press, 1996.

MARGARET J. OSLER

See also Atomism; Charleton, Walter; Epicureanism; Mechanical Philosophy; Religion and Natural Philosophy; Skepticism; Soul

Gemma Frisius, Reiner (1508–1555)

Born to humble parents in the Dutch province of Friesland, he trained and was employed at the Faculty of Medicine at the University at Louvain. By all accounts, he was a successful physician and devoted some of the proceeds from his practice to his work in astronomy and geography.

At the age of twenty-two, he published his first book, a revised edition of Peter Apian's (1495–1552) *Cosmographicus liber,* which enjoyed thirty editions to 1609. His first original work, *Gemma Phrysius de principiis astronomiae et cosmographiae* (1530), and a popular introduction to mathematics, *Arithmeticae practicae methodus facilis* (1540), were also extremely successful and were subsequently published throughout Europe. He also taught geography to such men as Gerard Mercator (1512–1594) and John Dee (1527–1608), was renowned for the quality of his globes, and improved the astronomical cross-staff and the astrolabe of his day.

Today he is best known for his original contributions to navigation and surveying. In the first edition of his *De principiis astronomiae,* he became the first to propose the use of a portable mechanical clock to determine longitude at sea, a suggestion that would await the invention of more reliable clocks. In addition, he became one of the first to recommend—in a chapter first included in the 1533 edition of the *Cosmographicus liber*—the use of triangulation to improve the practices of surveyors and cartographers.

BIBLIOGRAPHY

Frisius, Gemma. *De principiis astronomiae et cosmographiae.* A facsimile reproduction, with an Introduction by C. A. Davids. Demar, NY: Scholars' Facsimiles and Reprints, 1992.

Haasbroek, N. D. *Gemma Frisius, Tycho Brahe, and Snellius and Their Triangulations.* Delft: Netherlands Geodetic Commission, 1968.

Kish, George. *Medicina, Mensura, Mathematica: The Life and Works of Gemma Frisius, 1508–1555.* (James Ford Bell Lectures 4). Minneapolis: Associates of the James Ford Bell Collection, 1967.

GARY MCINTYRE

See also Apian, Peter; Mercator, Gerard; Navigation; Surveying

Generation

The origins of individual plants and animals and of entire species, the regeneration of lost limbs and organs, and the "equivocal" generation of one kind of substance from another were questions that received renewed attention in the second quarter of the seventeenth century. Although advances in descriptive and theoretical embryology were not steady, Aristotelian and Renaissance concepts of generation were subject to powerful criticism, and rival models proliferated. By 1690, several philosophers envisioned common and exclusive mechanisms of plant and animal generation and repudiated the generation and corruption of metals and minerals as envisioned by Aristotle (384–322 B.C.E.) and many later theorists.

Thanks to their ubiquity and constant seasonal reappearances, it had long been thought self-evident that "imperfect" (nonsanguineous) animals such as insects, as well as vermin such as mice, and some plants, notably mushrooms, originated in dew, stagnant water, earth, debris, or putrefying matter, or, in the case of parasites, in the bodies of animals and galls on plants, from and within the tissues of the organism itself. The introduction of the microscope was crucial in challenging this plausible view by revealing sexual organs and eggs in all manner of insects. Controlled experiments by Nicolas Malebranche (1638–1715) and Louis Joblot (1645–1723) involving covered and uncovered vessels revealed that larval worms did not appear in a nutritive material unless flies had access to it. Francesco Redi (1626–1697) continued to allow that plants might produce insects spontaneously; he denied only that lower forms (putrefying matter) could bring forth higher forms (animal life). A more decisive position was taken by Antoni van Leeuwenhoek (1632–1723), who argued that all animals, including insects, were generated from similar parents; however, it was difficult to extend this conclusion to microscopical *animalcula,* which did appear after a time in apparently pure water kept in closed vessels. Equivocal generation (e.g., that of bees from the carcasses of bulls) was abandoned, but spontaneous generation continued to vie with creationism as an explanation for the ultimate origins of life. Debates conducted in theological and scientific terms continued through the nineteenth century.

Theories of *reproduction*—a term introduced by Abraham Trembley (1710–1784) in 1740—may be broadly classified as epigenetical or preformationist. But epigenetic theories themselves could be predominantly mechanistic or vitalistic. William Harvey (1578–1657), who continued a traditional mode of experimentation, opening eggs on successive days of generation and describing what he saw, was assisted by a lens in his early researches. He was able to pronounce against Aristotle's claim that the parts of the organism appeared simultaneously and the claims of his Renaissance predecessors that the skeleton developed first, and then the flesh and vital organs. The heart and vascular system and the blood, the seat of the soul for Harvey, were the first elements to appear: they were the architects of the body, creating its matter as well as its form. At the same time, Harvey rejected Aristotle's view that the modes of reproduction of viviparous and oviparous animals were fundamentally different, arguing that, in both cases, the male semen exercised a fructifying effect on a female "egg" before vanishing without trace. The egg, he thought, was not visible in mammals until the process of development was well underway. Though Harvey is sometimes regarded as a mechanist on the basis of his quantitative research methods and his conception of the heart as a pump, his account of generation was spiritistic. He rejected Aristotle's suggestions that the sperm physically "curdled" the female's menstrual blood and that the sequence of development set in motion was in any way automatic. Rather, fertilization transmitted a vital principle from parent to offspring, by means of which the fetus created its own form and its own matter and transmitted its generative power to the next generation.

An epigenetic account that differed from Harvey's in rejecting the action of any spiritual principle in favor of assembly from individual particles of matter was defended by René Descartes (1596–1650) and by Kenelm Digby (1603–1665). These mechanistic accounts were criticized as fantastic and ceded the preformation theories preferred by post-Cartesian Christian mechanical philosophers like Malebranche and Gottfried Wilhelm Leibniz (1646–1716). Jan Swammerdam opposed Harvey's theory of insect metamorphosis (1637–1680) with his own theory that the mature, winged, form of the insect preexists in the wormlike larva, which he demonstrated by unwrapping the pupa of the mutating insect and showing the rudiments of the adult structures. Swammerdam defended a theory of emboîtement, which implied the preexistence of an endless nested set of organisms for the larger animals against Harveian epigenesis; there is no generation but only growth, and the ground plan of every organism, by contrast with its mature appearance and habits, is identical.

The mammalian ovaries had long been regarded as analogous to male testicles and were thought by many physicians to produce a female semen, a view Harvey opposed vehemently. That their extirpation in the living female prevented generation was discovered shortly after Harvey's death, and egg follicles, incorrectly but usefully identified as the egg itself, were discovered and rediscovered in mammalian and fish ovaries within a period of a few years by Regnier de Graaf (1641–1673) and other Dutch microscopists. Shortly thereafter, the fertilized egg itself was observed in the fallopian tubes by Leeuwenhoek. The analogy between the plant "ovum" and the female egg and plant pollen and the male sperm was

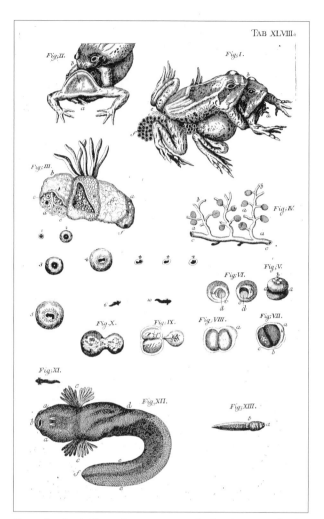

Reproduction in frogs, from mating to the development of tadpoles. John Swammerdam, *The Book of Nature, trans. Thomas Flloyd, ed. John Hill (1758). The development of microscopy made possible a more detailed knowledge of development from egg to mature animal.*

evident to Marcello Malpighi (1628–1694), who took it as the basis of his comparative approach to anatomy.

Living spermatozoa were discovered in fresh semen by a young Dutchman, Johan Ham, in 1677, and rediscovered by Leeuwenhoek, though Nicolaas Hartsoeker (1656–1725) claimed priority. The discovery was confusing, as the Malpighian revision to Harvey had left the priority of the egg intact and seemed a workable system. Yet, spermatozoa of unnervingly similar appearance could be demonstrated in a variety of male animals and were evidently indispensable for generation. Leeuwenhoek maintained that the spermatozoon was the future animal itself and accepted the consequence that millions upon millions of undeveloped humans were sacrificed to no purpose on a daily basis. (The number of eggs in a female, though recognized as very large, was not so large.) Ovists, who regarded the egg as the basis for the future animal and the sperm as the chemical trigger that set off the course of development by a kind of "fermentation," remained in the majority well into the eighteenth century, some going so far as to claim that the spermatozoa were useless parasites.

The relations between generation and regeneration were studied by experimentation with the polyp and the starfish, both of which possessed the plantlike ability to regrow missing limbs. This ability was difficult to reconcile with either preformation or mechanistic epigenesis and suggested the presence of a vital force that was intentional and possessed an "image" of the complete organism. In the eighteenth century, theorists sought to incorporate and, at the same time, to demystify vital forces in generation, assisted by the introduction of Newtonian attractive forces into physics and chemistry.

BIBLIOGRAPHY

Cole, Francis J. *Early Theories of Sexual Generation*. Oxford: Oxford University Press, 1930.

Gasking, Elizabeth. *Investigations into Generation, 1651–1828*. Baltimore: Johns Hopkins University Press, 1967.

Lindeboom, Gerrit A. "Leeuwenhoek and the Problem of Sexual Reproduction." In *Antoni van Leeuwenhoek, 1632–1723: Studies on His Life and Work*, ed. L. C. Palm and H. A. M. Snelders. Amsterdam: Rodopi, 1982, pp. 129–152.

Needham, Joseph T. *A History of Embryology*. 2nd ed. Cambridge: Cambridge University Press, 1959.

CATHERINE WILSON

See also Embryology; Epigenesis; Leeuwenhoek, Antoni van; Microscopy; Preformation; Spontaneous Generation

Geography

A complex and wide-ranging discipline; changing from cosmography to geography in the period; divided into three subdisciplines of mathematical geography, descriptive geography, and chorography or local history; combined theory and practice; aided in the ideology of the "new science."

Geography was a complex and wide-ranging discipline in early-modern Europe, providing a focus for both exploration and nationbuilding. It was a lively study, involving the work of many men and closely followed by scores of students and readers. Geography had both a theoretical underpinning and a practical purpose. Be-

cause of this, it corresponds neither to a model of disinterested natural philosophy nor to one of craft-oriented technology. Rather, geography was an intermediate discipline that combined aspects of theory and practice, adopting its own ideology and methodology. That new ideology had three components: an immense value placed on mathematics; an emphasis on the importance of gathering information in an incremental and inductive way; and a desire to make the knowledge so obtained into a public and useful science. Geography thus provides an example of the type of investigation that encouraged its seventeenth-century practitioners to develop a new, engaged approach to natural inquiry. Such an approach is emblematic of the "new science."

During the Scientific Revolution, geography was developing into a discipline distinct from the older study of cosmography. Although both terms continued to be used, sometimes interchangeably, a distinction was increasingly made. Cosmography, as John Dee (1527–1608) proclaimed, "matcheth Heaven, and the Earth, in one frame," requiring "*Astronomie, Geographie, Hydrographie,* and *Musike*" to be complete. Geography, on the other hand, "teacheth wayes, by which, in sundry formes, (as *Sphaerike, Plaine,* or other), the Situation of Cities, Townes, Villages, Fortes, Castells, Mountaines, Woods, Havens, Rivers, Crekes, and such other things, upon the outface of the earthly Globe . . . may be described and designed" (*Mathematicall Praeface,* 1570). In other words, while the subject of cosmography was the globe and its relationship with the heavens as a whole, picturing the earth as an integral part of the cosmos, geography had a narrower focus, concentrating specifically on the earth itself. Geographers abstracted the globe from its surrounding cosmos and began to classify its parts by separation, rather than by union.

Geography developed into three related branches: mathematical, descriptive, and chorographical geography, each with distinct practitioners and different topics of investigation. Mathematical geography had its roots in Ptolemy's (ca. 100–ca. 170) *Geographia*. It was most closely akin to the modern study of geodesy, that branch of applied mathematics that determines the exact positions of points and the figures and areas of large portions of the earth's surface, the shape and size of the earth, and the variations of terrestrial gravity and magnetism. Cartography, the study of maps and mapmaking, was related to mathematical geography, although cartography depended more on guild methods of transfer of knowledge and so remained separate from the more academic discipline of geography.

The second branch, descriptive geography, developed as a subdiscipline quite separate from mathematical geography. Using Strabo (ca. 63 B.C.E.–25) as its classical model, descriptive geography portrayed the physical and political structures of other lands, usually in an inductive and relatively unsophisticated manner. Because of this relative lack of rigorous analysis, and because its primary goal was utility of knowledge, descriptive geography was the most easily accessible of the three geographical subdisciplines. It encompassed everything from practical descriptions of European road conditions to outlandish yarns of exotic locales, providing intriguing reading and practical information alike. This form of geography helped people from different countries establish their own identity against that of other European and non-European nations.

The final type of geography, chorography, combined a medieval-chronicle tradition with the Italian Renaissance study of local description. Chorography was the most wideranging of the geographical subdisciplines, since it included an interest in genealogy, chronology, and antiquities, as well as local history and topography. Chorography thus united an anecdotal interest in local families and wonders with the mathematically arduous task of genealogical and chronological research.

All three subdisciplines of geography attracted practitioners from within and outside the halls of academe. Most men interested in geography pursued careers that called for a combination of practical and theoretical experience, placing the study of geography within the context of the new scientific methods and ideologies developing in the seventeenth century. As well, many of the men interested in geography pursued active careers that required the support of patrons, either noble or royal. Much of the imperial rhetoric used by these geographers was designed to impress and flatter patrons. Thus, imperial images, expansionist or occasionally isolationist, as portrayed by geographers were intimately linked with the political state.

Geography was most closely allied with mathematics at one instance and history at another. Mathematicians such as Henry Briggs (1561–1631), for example, were interested in the use of mathematics in navigation and surveying. J. J. Scaliger's (1540–1609) work with chronology allied this branch of geography with biblical studies and history. The similarities between geography and these other disciplines included a desire for utility of knowledge and a belief in the ability of such geographical understanding to aid in the creation of the common weal.

Geography provided an impetus to the new mathematized vision of the world, part of the transformation of "science" in this period. The changes that are often characterized as the Scientific Revolution included a new attitude to methodology based on the behavior of a recently empowered gentry; a strong value placed on mathematics; a new, more "objective" way of seeing the world; and an attitude that claimed the possibility of controlling that world. All of these characteristics were present in the study of geography. Geography, as the science of seeing and developing narratives to explain the world, provided a new key for natural philosophers and mechanics alike. Implicit in geographical narratives was the belief that the world was, ultimately, a knowable, describable place, a place that could be predicted, mastered, and governed. This belief was to be central to the impact and evolution of scientific thought in the seventeenth century.

Historians of science have often consigned geography, the study of the earth and its inhabitants, to a peripheral position in the Scientific Revolution. This interpretation has begun to change, as this interactive science is seen as important for the changing knowledge, methodology, and culture of investigation of the natural world in the period known at the Scientific Revolution. Likewise, historians of cartography have recently begun to examine the contextually rich nature of maps and atlases in this period. Since the mid-1980s, historians have begun to deconstruct maps for their ideological messages, most successfully seeing their importance for state and government control.

Early-modern geography remains understudied. Almost nothing has been examined of geography in countries other than England, France, and Spain. From this preliminary work, it is clear that geography was necessary to people about to discover and exploit large sections of the globe. It was important to the changing political structure of Europe itself. As well, geography helped create a new ideology that was to influence both the social and the political sphere and the formation of a new organization, methodology, and value for scientific knowledge.

BIBLIOGRAPHY

Buisseret, David, ed. *Monarchs, Ministers, and Maps: The Emergence of Cartography as a Tool of Government in Early*

Modern Europe. Chicago: University of Chicago Press, 1992.

Cormack, Lesley B. *Charting an Empire: Geography at the English Universities, 1580–1620.* Chicago: University of Chicago Press, 1997.

Lestringant, Frank. *Mapping the Renaissance World.* Trans. David Fausett. Cambridge: Polity, 1994.

Livingstone, David. *The Geographical Tradition.* Oxford: Blackwells, 1992.

Withers, Charles. "Geography, Science, and National Identity in Early Modern Britain: The Case of Scotland and the Role of Sir Robert Sibbald (1641–1722)." *Annals of Science* 53 (1996), 29–73.

LESLEY B. CORMACK

See also Cartography; Exploration and Discovery; Globes, Astronomical and Terrestrial; Navigation; Surveying

Geoheliocentrism

Compromise world models, utilizing features of both Copernican and Ptolemaic theories, allowing for some or all planetary orbits to be referred to the Sun, while retaining a fixed earth as the center of the universe.

It is now well known that Nicolaus Copernicus's (1475–1543) theory of a moving earth convinced almost no one during the sixteenth century. While astronomers admired and used his technical solutions to various kinematical problems, few were willing to accept his theory as reality. Tycho Brahe (1546–1601), the most formidable observational and theoretical astronomer of the century's second half, himself uncomfortable with the physical implications of Copernicanism, authored a third alternative. Although Erasmus Reinhold (1511–1553) and Reiner Gemma Frisius (1508–1555) realized that one could utilize Copernican planetary theory in a geostatic framework, it was Brahe who first described it in detail. He developed his view in three stages. First, by 1578, he accepted an idea of the ancient writer Martianus Capella (cited by Copernicus in *De revolutionibus*) suggesting that Mercury and Venus might circle the Sun, which, in turn, moved about the earth. This would explain why Mercury and Venus are never far from the Sun in the course of a year, while the remaining planets are at times 180° from the Sun. Six years later, he entertained the idea that Mars, Jupiter, and Saturn might also orbit the Sun. He may have been stimulated by Paul Wittich (ca. 1546–1586) of Wrocław, who visited Brahe on the island of Hven, off the Danish coast, in 1580. Wittich seems to have developed a Capellan-type model in 1578.

The next step, accomplished by 1584, was to incorporate the superior planets. If, however, one accepts Copernicus's scale in the translation, which Tycho did, then the orbit of the Sun intersects the orbit of Mars. He, like nearly all of his contemporaries, assumed that planetary orbs were solid and could not physically intersect.

The solution to this conundrum was at hand. In reviewing the many tracts on the great comet of 1577, Tycho believed from his own comet observations, along with those of Michael Maestlin (1550–1631), Gemma Frisius, Landgrave Wilhelm of Hesse (1532–1592), and Helisaeus Röslin (1548–1616), that the comet was supralunary. Tycho's data suggested that the comet moved through the spheres of both Venus and Mercury. Probably by early 1587, he realized that solid spheres could not exist. The way was open for a full-blown geoheliocentric model, which he published in his *De mundi* in 1588.

The mature Tychonic model assumed a fixed earth at the center, with all planets circling the Sun, which, in turn, circled the earth. He retained the sphere of the fixed stars, not far removed from Saturn's orbit, so that the entire universe revolved daily. Such a system had several advantages. The Copernican scale and nearly the same order, along with the explanation for the retrogradation of the superior planets, could be preserved. The geometric equality of two systems allowed one to adopt Copernican techniques without embracing his physical ideas. The solution was thus both radical and conservative, retaining much, but not all, of Aristotelian physics.

Tycho Brahe was not alone in the field, though he acknowledged no debts in this matter. A number of astronomers were in contact with Wittich, who had also visited Wilhelm of Hesse in Kassel in the early 1580s. In 1588, Nicolaus Reimarus Bär (Ursus) (1551–1600) published a similar theory. It had two important differences from Tycho's: the earth rotated daily and Mars's orbit did *not* intersect the Sun's, suggesting that Ursus did not quite understand the Copernican scale or had appropriated an earlier version of Tycho's scheme. Röslin, in 1597, offered another variant, more like Brahe's but retaining solid spheres. Both claimed originality, and Brahe charged both with plagiarism. Neither can be proven. Ursus was certainly in Hven in 1584 but was also a visitor to Kassel. Röslin could have read both Tycho and Ursus.

The Tychonic system was attractive because it sidestepped the vexing issue of annual parallax, which the Copernican model required but which no astronomer

G

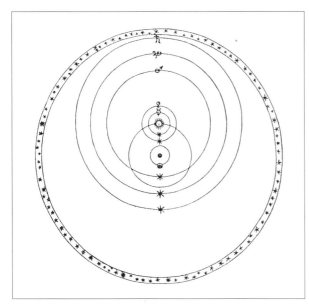

Tycho Brahe's system of the world, with the Sun circling a motionless Earth and the planets orbiting the Sun. From Brahe's De mundi aetherei reconforibus phaenomensis *(1588).*

could discover. For those who were repelled by the necessity of the rapid diurnal motion of the fixed stars, the Semi-Tychonic model of Ursus, which allowed for the earth's rotation, was more appealing. David Origanus published another such model in 1609, followed by Brahe's principal disciple, Christian Severin (Longomontanus) (1562–1647), in his *Astronomia danica* of 1622 and later editions. The telescopic discoveries of Galileo Galilei (1564–1642) and others after 1610 added fuel to the controversy. Probably the most inventive seventeenth-century variant was described by Giambattista Riccioli (1598–1671) in his *Almagestum novum* of 1651, in which he argued that Mercury, Venus, and Mars orbited the Sun, while the Sun, the Moon, Jupiter, and Saturn circled a fixed earth.

After the decree of 1633 banning Copernicanism among Catholics, Italian Jesuit writers in particular found Tychonic models a safe halfway house between religious orthodoxy and modern planetary theory. In Italy, such ideas were still current to ca. 1690. The English, though introduced early to Tycho, were not enthusiastic, nor were the Germans, the Dutch, or the French. The rise of Cartesianism and, later, of Newtonian mechanics spelled the end to Tychonic-style compromises.

BIBLIOGRAPHY

Gingerich, Owen, and Robert S. Westman. "The Wittich Connection: Conflict and Priority in Late Sixteenth-Century Cosmology." *Transactions of the American Philosophical Society* 78 (1988), Part 7.

Schofield, Christine Jones. *Tychonic and Semi-Tychonic World Systems.* New York: Arno, 1981.

Thoren, Victor E. *The Lord of Uraniborg: A Biography of Tycho Brahe.* Cambridge: Cambridge University Press, 1990.

RICHARD A. JARRELL

See also Brahe, Tycho; Copernicanism; Parallax; Wittich, Paul

Geology/Mineralogy

A science of geology did not emerge as such in the period of the Scientific Revolution. Rather, it emerged toward the end of the eighteenth century when studies of the earth assumed a marked historical character and the word *geology,* as understood today, came into use.

However, a number of seventeenth-century writers interested themselves in the earth. Some, such as René Descartes (1596–1650) and Gottfried Wilhelm Leibniz (1646–1716), developed grand "theories of the earth." Others, working at a finer grain, interested themselves in details of minerals, crystals, and (what are today called) fossils and made substantial collections of such objects. They were figured accurately and attractively, and attempts were made to classify them. A good example of such work is provided by the English virtuoso John Woodward (1665–1728), who endowed the Woodwardian Chair at Cambridge University and bequeathed a notable collection of fossils that formed the basis of its subsequent collections.

Woodward was also a collector of antiquities. His Oxford contemporary Edward Lhwyd (1660–1709), who likewise made a substantial fossil collection, was a philologist. Martin Lister of York (ca. 1639–1712), another assiduous fossil collector, studied Roman inscriptions. There was, thus, a continuity of interest between studies of human remains and of other objects deposited in the earth, the investigators being "archaeologists" as much as "geologists" or "mineralists." Significantly, the Bible was taken as a reliable source of information about the past for both the earth and the human race, with the result that earth history was compressed into a time-scale of ca. six thousand years.

Regarding rocks, minerals, and fossils, there was no agreed classification system, and numerous incompatible proposals were made as to how materials might be sorted. There were also doubts about whether certain objects were or were not the remains of former living organisms. For those who believed in an organic origin, it was sometimes suggested that fossils had been emplaced by the agency of Noah's Flood.

With respect to minerals, some older ideas about organic origins were still extant in the seventeenth century, showing indications of the continuing influence of Neoplatonic and Stoic ideas. There were also ideas based on chemical doctrines such as those of the phlogiston theory. However, a growing preference for mechanical ideas about mineral growth (involving the notion of the accretion of invisible, hypothetical corpuscles) made possible the eighteenth-century development of studies in crystallography.

Among seventeenth-century investigators, the most important were Robert Hooke (1635–1702) and Niels Stensen (1638–1686). Hooke's theory of the wandering of the earth's poles rejected the Noachian Flood as an agent of geological change; and he had the idea of "raising a chronologie" of the earth on the basis of fossils (even if he did not himself carry through such a project). Stensen also saw fossils as the remains of former living organisms; with his geological sections for part of Tuscany, his ideas on the growth of crystals, and his understanding that sediments are laid down by the deposition of suspended matter from moving water—with the older sediments being deposited below those laid down subsequently—he established fundamental principles for the study of earth history. These were utilized when geology became an independent historical science, distinct from archaeology, theology, crystallography, chemistry, and cosmogony.

BIBLIOGRAPHY

Herries-Davies, Gordon L. "A Science Receives Its Character." In *Two Centuries of Earth Science, 1650–1850,* ed. G. L. Herries-Davies and A. R. Orme. Los Angeles: University of California Press, 1989, pp. 1–28.

Laudan, Rachel, *From Mineralogy to Geology: The Foundations of a Science, 1650–1830.* Chicago and London: University of Chicago Press, 1987.

Oldroyd, David R. *Thinking About the Earth: A History of Ideas in Geology.* London: Athlone; and Boston: Harvard University Press, 1996.

Rossi, Paolo. *The Dark Abyss of Time: The History of the Earth and the History of Nations from Hooke to Vico.* Trans. Lydia G. Cochrane. Chicago and London: University of Chicago Press, 1984.

DAVID OLDROYD

See also Cosmogony; Steno, Nicolaus (Niels Stensen); Theories of the Earth

Geometry. See Analytic Geometry

Gessner, Conrad (1516–1565)

(The name has a number of variants: Cuonrat, Cunrat; Conradus Gesnerus; the erroneous spelling "Gesner" derives from the Latin.) Encyclopedist, bibliographer, illustrator, professor of philosophy, and practicing town physician of Zürich, he was educated at Zürich, Bourges, Paris, Lausanne, and Basel in the classical languages, theology, and medicine. Gessner's first published works were philological, historical, and bibliographical (*Lexicon Graecolatinum,* 1537; *Bibliotheca universalis,* 1545; editions of Stobaeus, Martial, et al.) He is the acknowledged father of modern bibliographical methods and of modern scientific botany and could also be termed the father of modern scientific zoology.

Although he was not alone in collecting and publishing natural specimens (he corresponded and exchanged specimens with many other collectors and writers of his

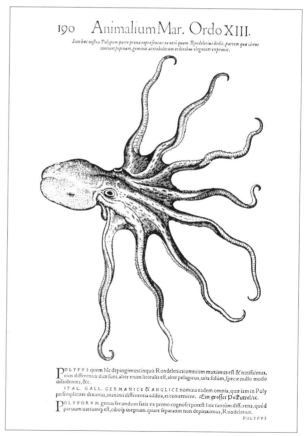

An octopus, depicted in Gessner's Historia animalium *(1551–1587).*

day), his attempts at systematization of the materials outstripped even contemporaries like Ulisse Aldrovandi (1522–1605), whose publications postdate his. His enormous intellectual capacity enabled him to see the whole picture while simultaneously delving in great detail into the physical characteristics and developmental stages of each specimen. His grounding in the science of philology gave him the background needed for a critical assessment of facts at his disposal on their own terms. In bibliography, this resulted in a reclassification of the entries of his *Bibliotheca* by subject in the *Pandectarum libri* (1548). In zoology, his five-volume *Historiae animalium* (1551–1587) became a standard, and, in the epitomes (*Icones animalium, Icones avium, Nomenclator aquatilium animantium,* 1553–1560), he began attempting to classify entries according to their morphology. Similarly, in his unpublished botanical work (now in facsimile), he was concerned with classification on the basis of morphology, including flower, fruit, and seed types. He wrote also on pharmacopeia and medicine, on fossils and metallurgy, and edited the works of Aelian, of Galen (second century) and of Valerius Cordus (on Dioscorides), as well as a number of theological texts. Sixty-three of his works (authored or edited) were published during his lifetime in various editions, followed by thirteen works published posthumously by his friends and disciples.

BIBLIOGRAPHY

Fischer, Hans, et al. *Conrad Gessner, 1516–1565: Universalgelehrter, Naturforscher, Arzt.* Zürich: Orell Füssli Verlag, 1967.

Gessner, Conrad. *Historia plantarum: Faksimile-ausgabe. Aquarelle aus dem botanischen Nachlass von Conrad Gessner (1516–1565) in der Universitätsbibliothek Erlangen.* Ed. Heinrich Zoller, Martin Steinmann, and Karl Schmid. 10 vols. Zürich: Urs Graf Verlag Dietikon, 1972–1991.

Gmelig-Nijboer, C. A. *Conrad Gessner's "Historia animalium": An Inventory of Renaissance Zoology.* (Communicationes Biohistoricae Ultrajectinae 72). Meppel: Krips Repro B.V., 1977.

Wellisch, Hans H. *Conrad Gessner: A Bio-Bibliography.* Zug, Switzerland: Inter Documentation, 1984.

CYNTHIA M. PYLE

See also Aldrovandi, Ulisse; Botany; Fuchs, Leonhart; Taxonomy; Zoology.

Gilbert, William (1544–1603)

Acquired a prominent place in the Scientific Revolution through his experimental demonstration of terrestrial magnetism. His influence derives from the one work published in his lifetime, *A New Natural Philosophy of the Magnet, Magnetic Bodies, and the Great Terrestrial Magnet* (1600), or *De magnete.* He published it when his medical career culminated in his appointment as a physician to Elizabeth I. His previous obscurity, early death from plague, and the absence of manuscripts and correspondence leave enigmatic the origin and development of his novel work. Some undated manuscripts were assembled into a posthumous *New Philosophy of the Sublunary World, in Opposition to Aristotle* (*De mundo*), which was published in 1651 and only adds to the puzzle.

From the nineteenth century, when classical electromagnetism and positivist views of experimental method were being forged, until the 1960s, historians explored Gilbert as a forerunner of experimentalism. What impressed them was his vehement rejection of the received scholarship of Aristotelian natural philosophers and his twenty-odd years of magnetic researches, which he conducted through experiments of unprecedented thoroughness. They agreed with Gilbert's contemporaries that he had established the principles and facts of a genuinely new science, which, significantly, Gilbert called *philosophia magnetica.* Recent historians have modified the empiricist image of Gilbert and asked why an Elizabethan, in the critical words of his Court contemporary Francis Bacon (1561–1626), made "a philosophy out of the lodestone." And why *De magnete* adopted the unusually modern, experimental mode of exposition.

The first question has made central Gilbert's cosmological beliefs, which previous historians dismissed as premodern speculation. Gilbert rejected the Aristotelian conception of the earth as a corrupt, inert globe around which moved the perfect heavens. The climactic sixth book of *De magnete* argues, in a Neoplatonic vein, that a magnetic virtue was the earth's ennobling and "as it were, animate" force, which literally empowered it to rotate. His outline of a magnetic dynamics for Copernican astronomy was what most interested pre-Newtonian natural philosophers.

The core of Gilbert's elegant, groundbreaking experimental method is his use of laboratory models and argument by analogy from them to the earth. The analogy was the central principle of magnetic philosophy. For the earth, he substituted lathe-turned spherical lodestones, which he called *terrellae* (little earths). He acknowledged the thirteenth-century philosopher Petrus Peregrinus's influence in the idea. Over the *terrella*'s sur-

William Gilbert. From Gilbert's On the Loadstone and Magnetic Bodies and on the Great Magnet the Earth, *trans. P. Fleury Mottelay (New York, 1893).*

face, Gilbert moved *versoria* (rotation detectors), which were effectively miniature compass needles. In other experiments, he floated *terrellae* on cork rafts to permit their free movement. His apparatus thus privileged torque effects, of rotation into alignment with a magnetic field. Gilbert denied that repulsion existed and replaced it and attraction, Aristotelian terms for violent motion, with the more natural *coition*.

Gilbert also deplored the common treatment of lodestone as one of many substances, especially amber, that exhibited occult qualities of attraction. He was anxious to show that magnetism was a unique, cosmic, spatially extended, immaterial virtue, while electricity was a ubiquitous, local, and material phenomenon. He designed experiments to discriminate between them, in which he considerably extended the range of substances exhibiting *electricitas*—another Gilbertian term. He was not, however, concerned to establish a parallel science of electricity.

In successive books of *De magnete,* Gilbert took one of five magnetic motions and presented experiments to establish the central principle. Book III, covering vertic-

ity, or north and south pole–seeking motions, and Book IV, investigating magnetic variation from the true north pole, best exemplify his method. Using *terrellae* modeled with continent- and oceanlike irregularities, he produced alignments in *versoria* that, he claimed, imitated the best tables of variation data that navigators could give him. The hypothesis that terrestrial variation was caused by the earth's geological irregularities had great navigational significance as a method for position finding at sea. It was also necessary to save his principle that the earth's astronomical poles and axis were real, magnetic phenomena and not the mathematical projections of traditional geography.

Gilbert closed *De magnete* with a confident extension of his analogy to the earth's daily rotation. He could not make a *terrella* replicate it, and his argument was based on possibility and probability. Because rotation was a natural motion for magnets, and because the earth possessed a real, stabilizing magnetic axis, its daily rotation was possible. Gilbert then added magnetic reasons to those of Nicolaus Copernicus (1573–1543) (sometimes reproduced verbatim) for the greater economy and harmony of a moving earth.

Whether Gilbert was one of the first full Copernicans or a semi-Tychonian has exercised historians. He was more explicit about an annual orbit, though still guarded, in *De mundo*. There he argued that all planets had a motive virtue (earth's and the Moon's being magnetic) and were incited into harmonious orbits by the Sun's luminous virtue. He considered that the complex interactions between the forces were beyond calculation. Thus, unusually for a Copernican, Gilbert maintained the traditional demarcation between natural philosophy and mathematical astronomy, which only "saved the appearances." That did not stop readers like Johannes Kepler (1571–1630) and Simon Stevin (1548–1620) from building a physical astronomy upon his magnetic principles.

The cosmological discussion in *De mundo,* together with combative sections on standard Aristotelian topics such as the four elements and qualities, show that Gilbert was in many ways a typical late-sixteenth-century system builder like Bernardino Telesio (1509–1588) or, Francesco Patrizi (1529–1597). More surprisingly, its equally typical discursive, philosophical style of exposition shows that Gilbert was no thorough-going experimentalist. There is no interesting new experiment in *De mundo*.

De magnete's experimentalism may have developed out of Gilbert's collaboration with navigators and practical mathematicians. They explained Copernican astronomy to him and provided knowledge of the compass and its behavior at sea. Edward Wright (1558–1615), England's leading expert, supplied practical information and wrote *De magnete*'s "Address," which stressed practical applications of magnetic philosophy. But he also contributed to Book V, on magnetic inclination, in which a correlation between inclination and latitude was announced. Wright wrote Chapter XII, designed the instrument for measuring inclination, and was rumored to have discovered the correlation himself and so may have had a general editorial role.

We might have to modify Edgar Zilsel's (1941) suggestion that the groundbreaking experimentalism of *De magnete* stemmed from the union of head- and hand-knowledge, to incorporate Wright's moderation of Gilbert's preference for philosophy. Nevertheless, Gilbert turned his idiosyncratic distrust of all prior natural-philosophical authorities, especially ancient ones, into a philosophy matched only by Francis Bacon. He preempted Bacon in his belief that natural philosophy had to make a new start from new observations and principles and in his general ideology that knowledge had progressed, not declined, since ancient times. These convictions, surprisingly iconoclastic and "modern" in 1600, provide the context for his development of a new, magnetic philosophy.

BIBLIOGRAPHY

Freudenthal, Gad. "Theory of Matter and Cosmology in William Gilbert's 'De magnete.'" *Isis* 74 (1983), 22–37.

Gilbert, William. *De magnete.* Trans. P. Fleury Mottelay. New York: Dover, 1958. Repr. of 1893 ed.

Hesse, M. B. "Gilbert and the Historians." *British Journal for the History of Science* 11 (1960), 1–10, 130–142.

Kelly, Suzanne. *The De mundo of William Gilbert.* Amsterdam: Elsevier, 1965.

Pumfrey, Stephen. "Magnetical Philosophy and Astronomy, 1600–1650." In *The General History of Astronomy,* ed. R. Taton and C. Wilson. Cambridge: Cambridge University Press, 1989, vol. 2A, pp. 45–53.

Zilsel, Edgar. "The Origins of William Gilbert's Scientific Method." *Journal of the History of Ideas* 2 (1941), 1–32.

STEPHEN PUMFREY

See also Compass; Magnetism; Wright, Edward

Glanvill, Joseph (1636–1680)

British philosopher and author of *The Vanity of Dogmatizing* (1661) (source of Matthew Arnold's poem "The Scholar Gypsy," 1853) and other works on philosophical, theological, and scientific subjects, Glanvill is generally regarded as an upholder of the "modern" against the "ancient," a fervent propagandist of the "new science" and experimental method, and even as a precursor of David Hume (1711–1776), especially on the problem of causality. He is also presented as an Anglican apologist intent on proving the agreement of reason and faith. But since he was a believer in the preexistence of souls in *Lux orientalis* (1662) and witches and witchcraft in his posthumous *Saducismus triumphatus* (1681), historians of ideas find it difficult to reconcile this with his modern philosophical outlook.

A Fellow of the newly founded Royal Society (1662) and an advocate of its scientific methods, like most of its members he regarded the testimonies of respectable witnesses as scientifically valid. He rejected Aristotle's formal, material, and final causes and accepted only the efficient cause. This very fact made him a member of the coalition of daring thinkers ready to fight against the sterile Aristotelian concept of science.

For Glanvill, skepticism was a form of revolt against Aristotle (384–322 B.C.E.), the "Dictator of Philosophy," and the Scholastics, who only studied the writings of other philosophers. But he and the Free Philosophers used the new experimental method "to seek Truth in the Great Book of Nature."

Glanvill the "skeptic" was part of the new religious establishment that sided with the party of the Scientific Revolution. This establishment included thinkers like Glanvill, Henry More (1614–1687), and other Cambridge Platonists, who, while defending Cartesian physics and mathematics, saw the world as inhabited by spiritual and supernatural powers. Thus, Glanvill belongs to the transition period between the Renaissance and the Scientific Revolution. So Glanvill, Fellow of the Royal Society, felt at home both in the animated world of witches and in the inert, mechanical universe of the New Science.

BIBLIOGRAPHY

Cope, Jackson I. *Joseph Glanvill: Anglican Apologist.* St. Louis: Washington University Press, 1956.

Glanvill, Joseph. *The Vanity of Dogmatizing: The Three Versions.* With a critical Introduction by Stephen Medcalf. Sussex: Harvester, 1970.

Popkin, Richard H. "The Development of the Philosophical Reputation of Joseph Glanvill." *Journal of the History of Ideas* 15 (1954), 305–311.

Talmor, Sascha. *Glanvill: The Uses, and Abuses of Scepticism.* Oxford: Pergamon, 1981.

SASCHA TALMOR

See also Aristolelianism; Cambridge Platonists; More, Henry; Royal Society of London

Glauber, Johann Rudolf (1604–1670)

Chemical entrepreneur and project maker who manufactured chemical medicines and a variety of other products, such as chemical instruments, artificial jewels, mirrors, mineral fertilizer, and food extracts. He improved metallurgical operations, as well as the production of linen, wine, and vinegar. Glauber never attended a university. He traveled in several countries and worked in the laboratories of apothecaries and alchemists. In Amsterdam, where he settled at the end of the Thirty Years War, and in the last period of his life, he had a famous laboratory of his own and a garden for his agricultural experiments. Much of his reputation depended on his books, which demonstrate his technological know-how and advertise his manufactures. They have Latin titles but were written in German. Most of them are compiled in the seven volumes of his *Opera omnia* (1661), an English translation of which appeared in 1689 in London.

Glauber's most famous chemical book is his *Furni novi philosophici* (1646–1649), a compilation of contemporary chemical-technological knowledge and a description of his own projects. The organization of the book follows the technology of operations. Each description of a new distilling furnace is followed by that of its use in manufacturing medicines. Besides the famous Glauber's salt (sodium sulfate), Glauber introduced hydrochloric acid as a medicine and explored systematically the salts that could be produced out of it. He also described metallurgical operations, alchemical experiments, and chemical instruments. There is no comprehensive theoretical part in the book, but Glauber's view on chemical transformations is apparent in many descriptions of chemical operations.

On the one hand, Glauber lived in an alchemical and Paracelsian world. He understood most of the operations he performed as transmutation, enhancement of qualities, or extraction of an "essence." On the other hand, he lived in the world of manufacturing laboratories. As a practitioner, he interpreted chemical operations with the knowledge of a craftsman. Thus, he explained some chemical transformations on the model of a building-block principle that integrated the idea of mutual love between the substances.

BIBLIOGRAPHY

Gugel, Kurt F. *Johann Rudolph Glauber, 1604–1670: Leben und Werk.* Würzburg: Freunde mainfränk. Kunst und Geschichte, 1955.

Walden, Paul. "Glauber." In *Great Chemists,* ed. Eduard Farber. New York: Interscience, 1961, pp. 115–134.

URSULA KLEIN

See also Alchemy; Paracelsus; Pharmacology; Pharmacy

Glisson, Francis (1597–1677)

Made significant contributions to anatomy, physiology, and pathology. He was educated at the University of Cambridge and graduated in medicine in 1634. The following year, he was named Fellow of the Royal College of Physicians of London, where he practiced as a physician and continued his scientific activities until his death. He was also a member of the "Invisible College," meeting regularly to discuss scientific matters and, consequently, was one of the first members of the Royal Society. He was commissioned by the Royal College of Physicians and, together with several contributors, published a book entitled *De rachitide* (1650), now considered a classic title of the the clinical and pathological description of rickets. In this book, Glisson interpreted disease as an alteration of an indwelling principle, a subject to which he returned in later works. His *Anatomia hepatis,* the outcome of his research into the structure of the liver over more than a decade, appeared in 1654. One of the contributions it includes is the description of a fibrous capsule that encases the ramifications of the portal vein and biliary ducts, now known as *Glisson's capsule.* The book begins with several prolegomena that attempt to reconcile the Galenist doctrine of elements with Paracelsian doctrine from an eclectic viewpoint widespread among the most prominent physicians of the period. In his last work, *Tractatus de ventriculo et intestinis* (Treatise on the Stomach and Intestines, 1677), Glisson expounded his most influential theoretical conception. While dealing with innervation and the contraction of muscles, he affirmed that the basic property of living matter, consisting of strings of atoms in the form of fibers, is *irritability,* which he defined as the ability to be stimulated and respond by contracting. During the eighteenth century, irritability became the fundamental concept of vitalism, particularly when Albrecht von Haller (1708–1777) differentiated between sensitivity and irritability, strictly speaking.

BIBLIOGRAPHY

Clarke, E. "Whistler and Glisson on Rickets." *Bulletin of the History of Medicine* 36 (1962) 45–61.

López Piñero, J. M. "Eighteenth-Century Medical Vitalism: The Paracelsan Connection." In *Revolutions in Science,* ed. W. R. Shea. Canton: Science History Publications, 1988, pp. 117–132.

Temkin, O. "The Classical Roots of Glisson's Doctrine of Irritation." *Bulletin of the History of Medicine* 38 (1964), 297–323.

Walker, R. M. "Francis Glisson and His Capsule." *Annals of the Royal College of Surgeons of England* 38 (1966), 71–91.

JOSÉ M. LÓPEZ-PIÑERO

See also Anatomy; Etiology; Physiology

Globes, Astronomical and Terrestrial

Next to showing the lands and seas on earth and the stars with their constellations in the sky, the main use of globes throughout the ages has been to demonstrate the natural phenomena as these are observed from a geocentric perspective. With a terrestrial globe, one can find when the Sun is rising and setting; with a celestial globe, the rising and setting of the stars can be worked out. For these purposes, both the earth and the celestial sphere were made mobile around the axis of the world. In western Europe, the production of such globes started in the fifteenth century. Following the voyages of exploration, the pair of globes became the most popular model for the universe in the sixteenth century. The use of the printing press ca. 1500 for globe making made new and cheaper ways of production possible.

Globes were not affected by the change from the geocentric Ptolemaic to the heliocentric Copernican world system. A conceptual change took place only when, in the nineteenth century, the need for the demonstration of the natural phenomena diminished. For centuries, the globe had been fitted in a meridian ring for

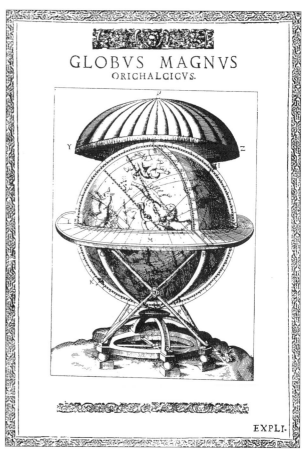

Tycho Brahe's brass celestial globe was about five feet in diameter. From Brahe's Astronomiae instauratae mechanica *(1598).*

varying the latitude and mounted in a stand with a horizon ring for finding the times of rising and setting. These parts disappeared altogether. Nowadays globes are mounted under a fixed angle of 23.5' with the horizontal plane, reflecting the position of the earth in its orbital plane around the Sun. Such modern globes should be turned from west to east to represent the rotation of the earth on its own axis, in contrast to the traditional globe, which should be turned from east to west to represent the observed phenomena. The celestial globe has almost given way to the flat planisphere, by which the configurations of the stars visible at a given time can be worked out. Instead, globes of the Moon and Mars have become fashionable, a development that was closely connected with the extraterrestrial-life debate triggered by the Copernican hypothesis.

BIBLIOGRAPHY

Dekker, Elly, and Peter van der Krogt. *Globes from the Western World.* London: Zwemmer, 1993.

Krogt, Peter van der. *Globi Neerlandici: The Production of Globes in the Low Countries.* Utrecht: HES Publishers, 1993.

Muris, O., and G. Saarmann. *Der Globus im Wandel der Zeiten: Eine Geschichte der Globen.* Berlin: Columbus Verlag Paul Oestergaard, 1961.

Stevenson, Edward Luther. *Terrestrial and Celestial Globes: Their History and Construction Including a Consideration of Their Value as Aids in the Study of Geography and Astronomy.* 2 vols. New Haven: Yale University Press, 1921.

ELLY DEKKER

See also Blaeu, Willem Jansgoon; Cartography; Mercator, Gerard

Government and Science

Extrauniversity scientific activities continued to be supported largely through personal patronage within Europeann Courts and wealthy households throughout most of the period of the Scientific Revolution. Thus, for example, the Court of Rudolph II at Prague supported the work of Tycho Brahe (1546–1601) and Johnnnes Kepler (1571–1630) as well as that of numerous alchemists and mechanics, and the Florentine Grand Dukes Ferdinand II and Leopold provided the Accademia del Cimento with the elaborate and expensive barometers, thermometers, clocks, and the like that enabled its members, including Giovanni Alfonso Borelli (1608–1679) and Evangelista Torricelli (1608–1647), to do some of the most outstanding experimental natural philosophy of their time. Though it was not uncommon for scholars seeking Court patronage to claim that their knowledge would lead to military or economic advantage to the potential patron, it is also clear that the glory that came to a patron from conspicuous cultural display was a primary consideration. This is why so much Renaissance mechanical knowledge was devoted to stage machinery and the production of hydraulic devices for gardens and why the performance of public alchemical "transformations" was such a popular public entertainment.

During the mid-seventeenth century, the personal patronage of princes began to be transformed into an impersonal state support of science by governments, usually in response to the persistent claims by scientists that their work would produce economic benefit to the state. Such utilitarian claims were advanced by many, but because Francis Bacon (1561–1626) was among the most effective promoters of the notion that scientific knowledge must confer power to better the human condition, they are often associated with his name. The notion that science was a cultural activity that might reflect glory on the nation that supported it was not totally abandoned, but Baconian motives increased dramatically in importance, at least in public pronouncements regarding state support of scientific activity.

The Royal Society of London for the Promotion of Natural Knowledge, chartered by Charles I in 1661, is often identified as the first institution to be self-consciously grounded in Baconian principles and to reflect the new relationships between science and government, but in its early years, except for its charter, the Royal Society received virtually no support from the state, nor did it directly serve the state in any systematic way. It was a private association supported erratically by dues from its members so that it was able to purchase instruments and hire two paid servants—Robert Hooke (1635–1703), who built and maintained instruments and planned experiments to be performed before the group, and Henry Oldenburg (1615–1677), who acted as corresponding secretary and editor of the society's immensely important *Philosophical Transactions,* which was initiated in 1665. The society did receive a gift of real property from the king, which was converted into a small endowment in 1682. The society was given a vague charge to oversee the Royal Observatory, which was founded in 1675 with one paid staff member, John Flamsteed (1649–1719), but the relations between the royal astronomer and the Royal Society were strained and there was little constructive interaction. If the society provided any significant service to the state, it was an informal one in which government officials, who were often members by virtue of their casual amateur interest in natural philosophy, came into contact with serious scientists, whom they consulted as private advisers on technical matters or pressed into government service as individuals. Not until the early nineteenth century, under the impetus of Utilitarianism, did the British government begin to regularize the use of technical expertise; and not until the late nineteenth century did it begin to subsidize the pursuit of science on a large scale.

A quite different pattern of government/science relations—one that served as the primary model followed by other European states—was initiated on December 22, l666, when the Paris Academy of Sciences held its first meeting in Louis XIV's private library. This academy was created by Chief Minister Jean-Baptiste Colbert, partly as a part of Colbert's general policy of centralizing French cultural activities and partly in response to a scientist-initiated proposal for a Compagnie des Sciences et des Arts that would engage in commercially and militarily relevant research and provide an advisory council of technical experts for the Crown in return for funding to build laboratories, purchase equipment, and pay salaries. Under Colbert, an observatory was built with meeting rooms for the academy, two classes of paid academicians—one in the mathematical sciences and one in experimental natural philosophy and natural history—were established, a number of scientific expeditions were funded, the Jardin du Roi was subsidized to become a research center for natural history, and the *Journal des sçavans* was established to communicate the results of the studies of the academicians. They were asked to evaluate new inventions, do cartographic work, and undertake some militarily relevant research; but most of the problems investigated were initiated by the academicians themselves, with relatively little government interference. Under Colbert's successor, Louvois, there was much greater insistence on dealing with practical problems; but under the next chief minister, Pontchartrain, scientist-initiated studies were once again emphasized. This pattern of combined support for "pure" and "applied" science—with continuously negotiated changes in the balance between the two—became a long-term feature of government/science interations vitually everywhere on the Continent, as academies emulating the Parisian Academy were established in Prussia, Russia, Sweden, and elsewhere.

In the former Holy Roman Empire and in Scandinavia, the French Academy system was transposed into a situation in which governmental officials expected scientific knowledge to be directly translatable into economic benefits. There, a class of alchemically oriented scientific projectors typified by Johann Joachim Becher (1635–1682) were able to convince numerous princes that their economic well-being depended on commercial expansion, which, in turn, depended on expanded scientific knowledge. As a result, in central and eastern Europe, government support for science became both more extensive and more tightly linked to commercial and agricultural concerns during the seventeenth and eighteenth centuries than it was in western Europe. Furthermore, broad-based state-supported technical education became more common. This situation undoubtedly set the stage for rapid industrial growth grounded in scientific and technical innovation during the nineteenth century.

BIBLIOGRAPHY

Hahn, Roger. *The Anatomy of a Scientific Institution: The Paris Academy of Sciences, 1666–1803.* Berkeley, Los Angeles, and London: University of Califomia Press, 1971.

Hunter, Michael. *Science and Society in Restoration England.* Cambridge: Cambridge University Press, 1981.

McClellan, James E., III. *Science Reorganized: Scientific Societies in the Eighteenth Century.* New York: Columbia University Press, 1985.

Smith, Pamela. *The Business of Alchemy: Science and Culture in the Holy Roman Empire.* Princeton, NJ: Princeton University Press, 1994.

RICHARD OLSEN

See also Académie Royale des Sciences; *Journal des sçavans;* Patronage; Royal Society of London

Graaf, Regnier de (1641–1673)

Born in Schoonhoven, the Netherlands, he read medicine in Utrecht, then in Leiden, and finally received his doctorate in Angers, France, in 1665. He settled in Delft, where he practiced medicine until his death. While still a student in Leiden, he carried out research on pancreatic juice (1664) under the guidance of Franciscus Sylvius (Franz de le Boë) (1614–1672), using for the first time the Wirsung duct artificial fistula technique, by means of which direct collection of pancreatic juice in a bottle is feasible. He concluded that pancreatic juice was acid, enabling Sylvius—whose iatrochemical doctrine was based on acid-alkali polarity—to affirm that its contact with alkaline bile in the duodenum triggered a fermentation process that separated feces from chyle. When Johann Bohn (1640–1718) demonstrated later that pancreatic juice was not acid, he dealt severe blow to iatrochemistry.

De Graaf pursued his research in Delft, concentrating mainly on reproduction. He studied the macro- and microscopic structure of the genitals of mammals and discovered the seminal ducts and the ovarian follicle, now known as *De Graaf's follicle.* He thought that follicles were the ova of mammals, and this idea was upheld until the discovery of the ovule in 1827. De Graaf stated, morever, that the function of the ovary was to produce ova, superseding the traditional doctrine according to which they were some sort of testicle secreting "female

From De Graaf's De mulierum organis generationi inservientibus *(1672).*

semen." He practiced staggered autopsies on female rabbits from thirty minutes to twelve days after mating in order to observe the growth of ova and their journey to the uterus. His main treatise, *De mulierum organis generationi inservientibus* (The Organs of Women Related to Generation, 1672), upheld ovistic preformationism (i.e., embryonic development being simply the growth of a structure preformed in the ovum). A bitter priority dispute with Jan Swammerdam (1637–1680), a former fellow student in Leiden, over the technique of injecting colored fluids in bodily vessels, soured his final years.

BIBLIOGRAPHY

Castellani, C. *La storia della generazione: Idee e teorie dal diciassetesimo al diciottesimo secolo.* Milan: Longanesi, 1965.

Houtzager, H. L., ed. *Reinier de Graaf, 1641–1673: In sijn leven Naukering Ontleder en gelukkig Geneesheer tot Delft.* Rotterdam: Erasmus, 1991.

Needham, J. A. *History of Embryology.* 2nd. ed. With A. Hughes. Cambridge: Cambridge University Press, 1959.

JOSÉ M. LÓPEZ-PIÑERO

See also Generation; Iatrochemistry; Preformation; Sylvius, Franciscus (Franz de la Boë); Swammerdam, Jan

Gravitation. See Attraction

Greenwich Observatory. See Royal Observatory at Greenwich

Gregory, David (1659–1708)

The nephew of James Gregory (1638–1675), whose mathematical and philosophical papers, containing substantial unpublished contributions, he inherited. David Gregory's 1684 *Exercitatio geometrica de dimensione figurarum* competently summarizes methods for calculating series expansions and their applications—a new field in which both J. Gregory and Isaac Newton (1642–1727) had done pioneering work, although little had appeared in print. Both in the *Exercitatio* and in his 1695 *Catoptricae et dioptricae sphaericae elementa,* a textbook in geometrical optics, David set forth without proper acknowledgment some of James's contributions.

Appointed Savilian Professor of Astronomy at Oxford on Newton's recommendation, Gregory became an influential figure among Newton's early followers. His manuscript remains contain interesting mathematical and philosophical comments by Newton. Gregory is best remembered for his 1702 *Astronomiae physicae et geometricae elementa* (second edition, 1726; English edition, 1726), an able introduction to Newtonian astronomy.

Among the many popularizations of Newton's ideas, Gregory's is one of the earliest and most mathematically informed. Perhaps its most notorious feature is its prefatory remarks on the ancientness of Newton's physical astronomy. They introduce the law of gravity as a law already known by "the Ancients" (Thales, Pythagoras, and so on), as regards both the universal attractive effect and its mathematical law. This rather defensive stance is perhaps a consequence of the criticism most Continental philosophers and mathematicians leveled against Newton's universal gravitation and its role in his *Principia mathematica philosophiae naturalis* (1687). Since the Preface was discovered to have been written by Newton himself, it has been interpreted as a reflection of Newton's interest in the *prisca philosophia,* or wisdom of the ancients.

BIBLIOGRAPHY

Eagles, C. M. "David Gregory and Newtonian Science." *British Journal for the History of Science* 10 (1977), 216–225.

Guerrini, A. "The Tory Newtonians: Gregory, Pitcairne, and Their Circle." *Journal of British Studies* 25 (1986), 288–311.

Lawrence, P. D., and A. G. Molland. "David Gregory's Inaugural Lecture at Oxford." *Notes and Records of the Royal Society of London* 25 (1970), 143–178.

Steward, A. M. *The Academic Gregories.* Edinburgh: Oliphant Anderson and Ferrier, 1901, pp. 52–76.

ANTONI MALET

See also Gregory, James; Series, Mathematical

Gregory, James (1638–1675)

The son of a Scottish clergyman, Gregory contributed to astronomy and the development of the calculus. After graduating from Aberdeen University, he traveled to London, Paris, and Padua, where he studied with Stefano degli Angeli (1623–1697), a pupil of Evangelista Torricelli (1608–1647). There he published the important *Vera quadratura* (1667) and *Geometria pars universalis* (1668); returning to London, he was elected to the Royal Society and published his *Exercitationes geometricae* (1668). Gaining appointment to the new chair of mathematics at St. Andrews University, he taught elementary courses and continued his researches, maintaining contact with the wider world of learning through the London mathematical correspondent John Collins (1625–1683). A plan for him to move to the Académie Royale des Sciences in Paris fell through, and, Gregory's own plans for building a public observatory at St. Andrews having been thwarted, he moved to a more congenial new professorship at Edinburgh but died suddenly a year later, with little of his post-Italian work in print.

Although he died before producing results that would impress the wider public, Gregory was a worthy contemporary of Isaac Newton (1642–1727), who admired his work. In optics, Gregory proposed a practical reflecting telescope, and showed both the promise and the limitations of his isolated education, not having seen, for example, René Descartes's (1596–1650) *Dioptrics* (1637); his astronomy was ingenious but defective. He developed considerably during his Italian years. In the *Vera quadratura,* he extended Archimedes's (ca. 287–212 B.C.E.) methods for the circle to the hyperbola, obtaining bounding convergent sequences of geometric and harmonic means, and he tried to use the algorithmic structure to show that neither π nor e is rational or even algebraic. In the *Geometria pars universalis,* following Blaise Pascal 1623–1662) and others, he sought transmutation rules to turn one problem into another— Got-

tfried Wilhelm Leibniz's (1646–1716) later integration-by-parts arose in this way. Gregory knew the inverse nature of tangents and quadrature but made little of the result, now called the fundamental theorem of calculus.

The *Vera quadratura* was harshly criticized by Christiaan Huygens (1629–1695); answering this, Gregory gave series expansions of elementary functions, including the logarithmic tangent solution of Nicolaus Mercator's (ca. 1619–1687) problem. Gregory's unpublished work also broke new ground in algebra and number theory, in interpolation and the binomial theorem, and in the general expansion of a function. A short published essay (1672) dealt with the pendulum and resisted projectile motion. Some of Gregory's results had been known to others; he himself sometimes anticipated Newton, Edmond Halley (ca. 1656–1743), Brook Taylor (1685–1731), and the Continentals.

BIBLIOGRAPHY

Malet, Antoni. "James Gregorie on Tangents and the 'Taylor' Rule for Series Expansions." *Archive for History of Exact Sciences* 46 (1993), 97–137.

Simpson, A. D. "James Gregory and the Reflecting Telescope." *Journal for the History of Astronomy* 23 (1992), 77–92.

Turnbull, Herbert W., ed. *James Gregory: Tercentenary Memorial Volume.* London: Bell, 1939.

JON V. PEPPER

See also Gregory, David; Series, Mathematical

Gresham College

Founded in 1596 under the terms of the will of the prosperous London merchant Sir Thomas Gresham (ca. 1519–1579), founder of the Royal Exchange. The significance of Gresham College in the context of the Scientific Revolution rests on two issues: first, the extent to which it represents an institution that rejected the traditional Scholastic learning of the universities and, second, its role in the foundation of the Royal Society.

The claims of Gresham College as an institution that was more open to new scientific currents than the universities—largely because it was more responsive to the practical technological needs of the citizens of London— have been advanced most vigorously by Christopher Hill (1965). In his interpretation, Gresham College represents an instance of the way in which the traditional order, as embodied by Oxford and Cambridge, was being supplanted by an intellectually more adventurous

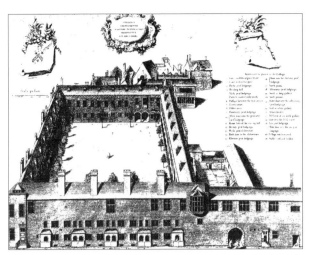

Gresham College. From John Ward, Lives of the Professors of Gresham College *(1740).*

capital that benefited from the stimulation provided by craftsmen and technically innovative seamen. Gresham College was, in turn, to leave its mark on the universities through the forced appointments made following the parliamentary visitation of Oxford in 1648–1649.

Later historians, such as I. R. Adamson (1980) and Mordechai Feingold (1984), are more inclined to emphasize the traditional character of Gresham College. Sir Thomas Gresham, the college's founder, envisaged a fairly conventional curriculum since, along with the chairs of astronomy, geometry, and physic, he also specified those of divinity, music, law, and rhetoric. True, he did make provision for lectures in English as well as in Latin, thereby making them accessible to a much wider range of the citizens of London, but, in practice, many of the lectures continued to be delivered in the ancient academic language. This reflects the fact that most of the professors came from Oxford and Cambridge universities and continued to follow its practices. Along with academics who regarded Gresham College as a stepping-stone toward an appointment back at Oxford and Cambridge, another major category of professors was Court favorites who regarded their posts as sinecures.

Overall, then, as a teaching institution Gresham College proved to be something of a disappointment. However, its location in central London helped make it a natural meeting place for those interested in science. This tradition owed much to Henry Briggs (1561–1631), the first professor of mathematics—a post he held from 1596 until 1620, when he followed the familiar route of

moving on to a chair at Oxford. The mathematician John Wallis (1616–1703) records that, ca. 1645, some of the key individuals in the prehistory of the Royal Society used to gather at Gresham to pursue their scientific interests. When the Royal Society was founded after the Restoration of the monarchy in 1660, Gresham College became its home until, in 1705, the trustees insisted that the society should find its own accommodation. This eventual divorce between the society and Gresham College underlines the fact the society was fundamentally extraneous to the original purposes of the college and that it was a guest (which ultimately outstayed its welcome) rather than an integral part of the college. Nonetheless, the term *Greshamites* was frequently used, particularly during the Restoration period, as a synonym for members of the Royal Society.

With the departure of the Royal Society in 1710, Gresham College faded into increasing obscurity—its role as a teaching institution being undermined by the inability of the trustees to discipline or control the professors. Ultimately, in 1768, the college was demolished, although some lectures continued to be delivered in the Royal Exchange. The erection of new buildings in 1842 and 1912 did little to revive the college's fortunes.

BIBLIOGRAPHY

Adamson, I. R. "The Administration of Gresham College and Its Fluctuating Fortunes as a Scientific Institution in the Seventeenth Century." *History of Education* 9 (1980), 13–25.

Feingold, Mordechai. *The Mathematicians' Apprenticeship: Science, Universities, and Society in England, 1560–1640.* Cambridge: Cambridge University Press, 1984.

Hill, Christopher. *Intellectual Origins of the English Revolution.* Oxford: Oxford University Press, 1965.

Johnson, F. R. "Gresham College: Precursor of the Royal Society." *Journal of the History of Ideas* 1 (1940), 414–421.

JOHN GASCOIGNE

See also Briggs, Henry; Collège Royal; Oxford Philosophical Society; Royal Society of London

Grew, Nehemiah (1641–1712)

He realized his scientific work within the ambience of the Royal Society, having been appointed a member of that body in November 1671 and, after some months, becoming curator for the anatomy of plants. During the 1670s Grew accomplished a program of research on plants, which covered a wide range of problems, including growth, nutrition, the form and dimensions of all

From R. T. Gunther, Early Science in Cambridge *(Oxford: p.p., 1937).*

plant parts, development, and propagation. His ultimate goal was the elucidation of the "nature of vegetation."

Grew proposed the use of five general methods of investigation, or *means* as he called them: a survey of the external parts; the disposition of the original parts; analysis of the contents (e.g., saps); analysis of what he called the *principles* (i.e., the chemical constituents, such as salt or water) of the organic parts; and, lastly, an examination of the raw materials from which the plant grows. Grew concluded his researches on plants by the end of 1677 and published in 1682 his earlier published books and lectures read to the members of the Royal Society in his *Anatomy of Plants.*

The most important part of Grew's investigations, for which he is famous, are his microscopic observations. Through the microscope he observed that all of the parts of the plant are formed from two basic elements: what he termed the *bladders* (the plant cells) and the vessels, but in an infinitely varied way as to number, size, and configuration. Both the bladders and the vessels he perceived to be constructed from an intricate network of fibers.

Another, lesser known part of Grew's research are his chemical analyses. He expanded his findings con-

cerning the fabric of plants with a detailed investigation of their chemical composition. In his opinion, the chemical composition of the parts determined their form. As like attracts like, a particle of a certain substance would preferably adhere to another particle of the same kind. Thus, Grew explained the longitudinal form of the vessels by their high proportion of alkaline salts, which of themselves shoot out lengthwise.

BIBLIOGRAPHY

Fournier, Marian. *The Fabric of Life: Microscopy in the Seventeenth Century.* Baltimore: Johns Hopkins University Press, 1996, pp. 72–79, 121–128.

Hunter, Michael. "Early Problems in Professionalizing Scientific Research: Nehemiah Grew (1641–1712) and the Royal Society, with an Unpublished Letter to Henry Oldenburg." *Notes and Records of the Royal Society of London* 36 (1982), 189–209.

LeFanu, William. *Nehemiah Grew, M.D, F.R.S.: A Study and Bibliography of His Writings.* Winchester, England: St. Paul's Biographies; Detroit: Omnigraphics, 1990.

MARIAN FOURNIER

See also Botany

Grimaldi, Francesco Maria (1618–1663)

An exemplary disciple of the new scientific humanism, a merger of traditional Scholasticism with the recently enriched practices of rigorous measurement, experiment, and mathematics, which had been established by the Society of Jesus under the leadership of Christoph Clavius (1538–1612) at the Order's College Rio Romano.

Grimaldi entered the Society in his fourteenth year and began to teach in Bologna (Santa Lucia) six years later (1638). Continuing his studies to a doctorate in 1647, he subsequently reduced his collegiate responsibilities due to poor health and took the vows of the priesthood in 1651.

During his twenty-five years at the college in Bologna, Grimaldi was actively engaged in scientific work, much of it in collaboration with (and surely under the supervision of) Giovanni Battista Riccioli (1598–1671), director of studies and Grimaldi's senior by twenty years.

In an affectionate *Elogium* appended to Grimaldi's posthumous *Physico-mathesis* (1665), Riccioli praised his colleague's exceptional experimental and observational abilities. Together they had perfected a pendulum clock to measure the acceleration of falling bodies. Grimaldi's

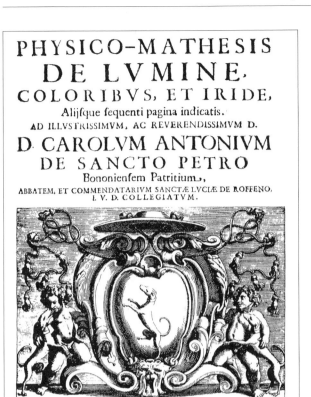

PHYSICO-MATHESIS
DE LVMINE,
COLORIBVS, ET IRIDE,
Alijfque fequenti pagina indicatis.
AD ILLVSTRISSIMVM, AC REVERENDISSIMVM D.
D. CAROLVM ANTONIVM
DE SANCTO PETRO
Bononienfem Patritium,
ABBATEM, ET COMMENDATARIVM SANCTÆ LVCIÆ DE ROFFENO,
I. V. D. COLLEGIATVM.

BONONIÆ, M. DC. LXV.

Ex Typographia Hæredis Victorij Benatij.　Superiorum permiffu,

Title page of Grimaldi's work on light, color, and the rainbow.

skill was indispensable for the completion of "our *Almagestum novum* (1651) and no less the *Geographiae et hydrographiae reformatae* (1661) or our volumes on astronomy," which work included astronomical measurements, especially to produce a catalog of fixed stars (in Riccioli, *Astronomia reformatae,* 1665); mapping the surface of the Moon, measuring the heights of lunar mountains and initiating the practice of naming lunar features after eminent astronomers; terrestrial mapping and measuring the heights of clouds; and establishing the meridian line for Bologna, in collaboration with Gian Domenico Cassini (1625–1712).

But in empirical and theoretical optics—a well-developed Jesuit topic—Grimaldi pursued his own project and devoted the last years of his life to the experimental and theoretical disputations of the monumental *Physico-mathesis de lumine, coloribus, et iride* (1665). In the sixty "Propositions" of Book I (90 percent of the text), Grimaldi advanced the hypothesis that light is an extremely subtle, rapidly propagated, undulating, and vibrating fluid substance, the colors of which arise from variations in the vibrations of this fluid caused by

its interaction with corporeal matter. In addition to the colors of bodies, the prism, and the rainbow, especially significant are those colors due to "a fourth mode" of diffusion that Grimaldi discovered and named *diffraction*: light flowing past the edges of bodies is "split apart," the geometrical shadow is widened, and bands of light and color appear both inside and outside its edges. On the title page of Book II, the reader is told that the strongly supported "opinions" of Book I "are refuted and the peripatetic teaching of the accidentality of light"—that light is a property of something that is not itself light— "is upheld as probable," while most especially "the arguments of the atomists" are attacked.

With the extension and defense of the hypothesis of the "substantiality of light," Grimaldi had set out a viable materialist alternative to the traditional peripatetic theory, and, with his discovery of diffraction, he left a new and puzzling optical phenomenon to succeeding generations of natural scientists.

BIBLIOGRAPHY

Dear, Peter. "Jesuit Mathematical Science and the Reconstitution of Experience in the Early Seventeenth Century." *Studies in History and Philosophy of Science* 18 (1987), 133–175.

Grimaldi, Francesco Maria. *Physico-mathesis de lumine, coloribus, et iride . . .* Bologna, 1665. Repr. Bologna: Forni, 1963; London: Dawsons of Pall Mall, 1966.

Marek, Jiri. "The Diffraction of Light and the Ideas of Kepler." *Physis* 12 (1970), 237–248.

STEPHEN STRAKER

See also Diffraction; Optics; Riccioli, Giovanni Battista

Guericke, Otto von (1602–1686)

German statesman, engineer, and physicist. Educated at the Universities of Leipzig, Helmstedt, Jena, and Leiden in law and mathematics/fortification, he was elected councilor of his hometown, Magdeburg, in 1626 and its chief architect in 1630. After the destruction of the city in 1631, he worked as an engineer for the occupying forces before he was elected a member of the council once again in 1642; he was also elected one of the four mayors in 1646, which post he held until 1676.

In 1644 there were discussions about the existence of a vacuum outside the earth in the context of a heliocentric universe. René Descartes (1596–1650) denied the possibility of a vacuum and insisted that—because of the identity of space and matter—the walls of a vessel emptied of matter would adjoin. Guericke began to think about the subject, and in 1647 he converted a fire syringe into a suction pump by adding two flap valves. He used it initially to pump water and later air out of a well-caulked beer barrel. He thereafter exchanged that pump for a spherical container forged out of copper and provided with a spigot to achieve better results. He thus invented the air pump, found that air can be be pumped, and thereby discovered its elasticity. He was convinced that he had artificially produced a vacuum on earth, such as naturally exists between planets and stars. He differentiated between the "weight of air" and atmospheric "air pressure," resulting from the weight of the air and causing the effects formerly ascribed to the *horror vacui.*

Guericke discovered not only the variation in air pressure, which he took as evidence of an extraatmospheric vacuum and as an indicator of weather (he constructed also a special barometer for forecasting storms),

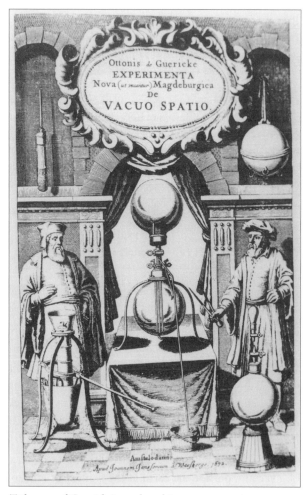

Title page of Guericke's work on his vacuum experiments.

but also its ability to perform work, and he demonstrated its power again and again by means of new experiments, especially with the so-called Magdeburg hemispheres. These, after evacuation, could be separated only by hanging a very heavy weight on the lower of the two hemispheres. This demonstration was also performed with a team of horses that were unable to pull the hemispheres apart, first in Magdeburg in 1657, then repeated at the Berlin Court in 1663. Guericke also tested the behavior and reaction of various things placed in an evacuated glass flask, such as a shriveled apple, a burning candle, a bird, beer, and a bell struck by means of a magnet.

Guericke demonstrated all of these experiments (except the horse experiment) on several occasions at the 1653–1654 Imperial Diet in Regensburg, where Johann Philipp von Schönborn, the elector and archbishop of Mainz, bought the equipment from him, brought it to his residence at Würzburg, and called upon the Professor of Mathematics Caspar Schott (1608–1666) to repeat the experiments there. Through letters from Guericke, Schott obtained more information about them and published them, together with a description of the instruments and experiments, as an Appendix in his *Mechanica hydraulica-pneumatica* (1657)—supplemented with additional information about new experiments and improvements of the air pump in his *Technica curiosa* (1664). It was mainly Schott's first book that stimulated Christiaan Huygens (1629–1695) and Robert Boyle (1627–1691) to construct another air pump and repeat Guericke's experiments, to which Boyle added several new ones.

Guericke's own description of the instruments and experiments in his book *Experimenta nova* was published only in 1672. It shows that his interests were much broader, as these experiments became the foundation of his attempt to create a new physics of the moving earth in an immensely expanded universe. His book assumes the infinity of an empty, absolute space independent of the creation within it, as well as immaterial and mutually acting forces among stellar, planetary, and terrestrial bodies. Guericke claimed to demonstrate these various forces by means of the first electrical machine—a sulfur globe rubbed and electrified by his dry hand—that showed repulsive, attractive, sparking, and other effects of frictional electricity.

BIBLIOGRAPHY

Guericke, Otto von. *Neue (sogenannte) Magdeburger Versuche über den leeren Raum. Nebst Briefen, Urkunden, und anderen*

Zeugnissen seiner Lebens-und Schaffensgeschichte. Trans. and ed. Hans Schimank. Düsseldorf: VDI-Verlag, 1968.

———. *The New (So-Called) Magdeburg Experiments of Otto von Guericke.* Trans. Margaret G. F. Ames. Dordrecht/Boston: Kluwer Academic, 1994.

Krafft, Fritz. *Otto von Guericke.* Darmstadt: Wissenschaftliche Buchgesellschaft, 1978.

FRITZ KRAFFT

See also Air Pump; Boyle, Robert; Electricity; Huygens, Christiaan; Pneumatics; Void

Guinter of Andernach, Joannes (ca. 1505–1574)

Medical humanist, anatomist, and chemist. After taking his M.D. at Paris (1532), Guinter was appointed there as one of two professors of medicine (1534). A Lutheran, he later moved from Paris to Metz (1538) and finally to Strasbourg. One of his students at Paris was Andreas Vesalius (1514–1564), who aided him in the preparation of the *Institutiones anatomicae* (1536). In later years, Vesalius strongly criticized Guinter's ability as an anatomist; nevertheless, the *Institutiones* remaines a pioneering manual, being preceded only by the works of Mondino da Luzzi (1316) and Berengario da Carpi (1522). Although Guinter published on practical medicine (the plague and the medicinal properties of spas), he was especially noted for his many translations of ancient medical texts.

No less important is Guinter's reaction to the Paracelsian literature that was beginning to appear in quantity by the 1560s, which had attacked the bases of traditional medicine (the four elements, the four humors, Galenic disease theory). It also called for the use of chemically prepared medicines to counter the stronger diseases of the time. The Paracelsian world system was based on the interaction of the macrocosm and the microcosm through sympathetic action.

Among the first to react to this new medical literature was Guinter in his *De medicina veteri et nova* (1571). Here he acted as a conciliator between the two systems. He rejected the arrogance of the Paracelsians, but he found much of value in their medicines. He sought similarities between the elements of the Aristotelians and the principles (Salt, Sulfur and Mercury) of the Paracelsians and even argued that the chemical processes employed by them in the preparation of their medicines altered their action so that their belief that "like cures like" might agree with the Galenic dictum that contraries cure. For Guinter, there was only one valid conclusion: both Galenic and Paracelsian medicines were needed. "The Ancients on account of time-honored authority ought to be given first place," but there was much in the work of the more recent chemists of great value. Physicians must choose the best from each. This was enough for late-sixteenth- and early-seventeenth-century Paracelsians and chemists to look on Guinter as one of their most valued authorities.

BIBLIOGRAPHY

Debus, Allen G. "Guintherius-Libavius-Sennert: The Chemical Compromise in Early Modern Medicine." In Debus, Allen G. *Science, Medicine, and Society in the Renaissance: Essays to Honor Walter Pagel.* 2 vols. New York: Science History Publications, 1972, vol. 1, pp. 151–165.

O'Malley, C. D. *Andreas Vesalius of Brussels 1514–1564.* Berkeley and Los Angeles: University of California Press, 1964, pp. 56–61 and passim.

ALLEN G. DEBUS

See also Anatomy; Galenism; Iatrochemistry; Paracelsus; Vesalins, Andreas

Gunnery. See Ballistics and Gunnery

G

H

Halley, Edmond (ca. 1656–1743)

Through his theoretical analyses of many critical problems of early-modern science, Edmond Halley set the course for much of eighteenth- and nineteenth-century astronomy and physics. We see this, for example, in his suggestions about using the transit of Venus for determining the distance of the earth from the Sun and in his researches on lunar motion during its eighteen-year cycle, on magnetic variation, on the aurora borealis, on the nature of nebulae and the distribution of stars in space, and on cometary orbits. Halley's observational work was less acute; despite this lack of precision, his observations were, nonetheless, frequently fruitful, such as his discovery of the proper motion of stars (1718) and his determination of the Moon's acceleration (1695).

It is his theory of comets for which Halley is best known. That work, including his successful and dramatic prediction of the return of the comet in 1756 that has since borne his name, resulted from his collaboration with Isaac Newton (1642–1727), beginning when Halley coaxed out of a coy and petulant Newton the first propositions of what, under Halley's sure hand, became the pinnacle of seventeenth-century science, the *Principia mathematica philosophiae naturalis* (1687). In the nearly suppressed Book III, Newton showed that comets followed the same laws of motion as the planets, which both Newton and Halley saw as the crowning achievement of the *Principia*.

Halley had demonstrated his prodigious appetite for learning early in life. He was born in London, the son of a prosperous soapmaker and landowner. When he entered Queens College, Oxford, in 1673, the year after the death of his mother, he already possessed a respectable collection of astronomical instruments. That year he assisted John Flamsteed (1646–1719), with whom he later had a falling out, in observations and conferred with Johannes Hevelius (1611–1687) in Danzig regarding the use of telescopic sights for observation. In 1682 Halley married Mary Tooke, with whom he had two daughters and a son. Newton, as warden of the mint, named Halley deputy controller of the mint in Chester in 1696.

Thinking it important to have accurate positions for the stars visible from the Southern Hemisphere, like the ones Hevelius and Flamsteed were finding for the Northern, Halley left Oxford without his degree, obtained a letter from Charles II to the East India Company to facilitate his work, and sailed to St. Helena at 16° south latitude in November 1676. Weather there limited his observations, but Halley was able to study the longer period of a pendulum in the lower latitudes, observations that were later used by Newton in his mechanics. Halley's *Catalogus stellarum australum* was presented to the Royal Society in November 1678, and he was elected a Fellow of the society shortly after.

Newton's threat to suppress his extended discussion of comets in Book III of the *Principia* was due to Robert Hooke's (1835–1702) claim that some of the key ideas of Newton's treatise came from a letter he wrote Newton in 1679. Not only was Halley able to convince Newton to include Book III, Halley also systematically did battle against the alternative system of nature that Hooke, Newton's rival on many subjects for decades, pointed to as the basis for his claim. Beginning in February 1687, Halley delivered a series of papers proposing, in opposition to the grand scheme being put to the Royal Society at the same time by Hooke (in what was later published as his *Lectures on Earthquakes,* 1705), that the impact or

Edmond Halley. From A. Wolf, A History of Science, Technology, and Philosophy in the Sixteenth and Seventeenth Centuries *(London: Allen and Unwin, 1935).*

close passage to the earth of comets was the agent of change for the wide range of phenomena mentioned in Hooke's discourses, including the magnetic variation; a hypothetical change in the earth's axis of rotation, with simultaneous continent-shattering terrestrial devastation, as is recounted in many archaic legends; the ancient "figured stones" found in rocks that resembled no living creatures; a change in the length of the year and the day; and the cause of mountains (therefore, in another paper of Halley's, the cause of the water cycle). Hooke had proposed processes internal to the earth for all of these. The sweeping transformative role of comets was a common Newtonian alternative explanation, but it was Halley who first spoke publicly about it.

As Halley's views on these and related matters became known, however, Halley acquired a reputation as a skeptic and a materialist. He was passed over for the chair of Savilian Professor of Astronomy in 1691 because of rumors that he believed in the eternity of the world, the same fear later leading to Halley's famous ode to Newton in the first edition of the *Principia* being significantly rewritten by both Richard Bentley (1662–1742) and Henry Pemberton (1694–1771), the editors of the second (1713) and third (1726) editions. Halley turned

to studying just how one could find the age of the earth, looking for cycles in nature that might be measured. Based on what he thought would be a progressive and linear salinization of the seas, he proposed making measurements over many decades as a means of establishing the age of the oceans. Several of his researches set out to find cycles in the "immutable" heavens, which is how Halley found the secular acceleration of the Moon and later the first proper motion of three nearby stars. In one of his discourses for the Royal Society, Halley hypothesized a progressive retardation of the motions of the planets, so that, as he now frequently remarked in his papers, "the eternity of the world was hence to be demonstrated impossible."

Halley had mathematical interests as well. Named Savilian Professor of Geometry in 1704, he undertook translations of Apollonius's *Conics* with David Gregory (1659–1708) and the *Sphaerica* of Menelaus of Alexandria. He published papers on finding the roots of equations, on calculating gunnery trajectories, on finding the focal length of thick lenses, on computational methods, and on constructing actuarial statistics.

In addition to his scientific work, Halley served as a diplomat, surveyed harbors and fortifications for Queen Anne, wrote on archaeology, and was a sea captain, in which capacity he led a crew between 1698 and 1701 in surveys of the southern and northern Atlantic, from which, in 1701, he prepared the first map showing magnetic variation. He designed a diving bell and diving helmet and established a company to use them for salvaging wrecks. Besides acting as secretary of the Royal Society for fourteen years and editor of its *Philosophical Transactions* for eight, Halley was named astronomer royal in 1721, for which he moved to Greenwich, where he tried without success to work out his theory of the Moon.

BIBLIOGRAPHY

Armitage, Angus. *Edmond Halley*. London: Nelson, 1965.

Cohen, I. Bernard. *Introduction to Newton's Principia*. Cambridge, MA: Harvard University Press, 1978.

Halley, Edmond. *Correspondence and Papers of Edmond Halley*. Ed. Eugene Fairfield MacPike. London: Taylor and Francis, 1937.

Ronan, Colin A. *Edmond Halley: Genius in Eclipse*. Garden City, NY: Doubleday, 1969. 2nd ed. 1970.

Thrower, Norman J. W., ed. *Standing on the Shoulders of Giants: A Longer View of Newton and Halley*. Berkeley and Los Angeles: University of California Press, 1990.

DAVID KUBRIN

See also Comets; Theories of the Earth

Harmonics. See Music/Harmonics

Harriot, Thomas (ca. 1560–1621)

The leading mathematician of his time and a notable scientist, he graduated B.A. from Oxford in 1580. By 1584 he was established in London in the service of Sir Walter Ralegh (1554–1618) as a scientific adviser, working on navigational matters for voyages to the Americas.

Harriot was a senior member of the Roanoke Settlement of 1585–1586 and wrote the first English account of North America, *A Briefe and True Report of the New Found Land of Virginia,* first published in London in 1588 and reissued in four languages in Frankfurt in 1590 and many times subsequently. It gave a fair, if hopeful, account of the resources and a sympathetic description of the native inhabitants. Harriot was also involved in Ralegh's ventures in Ireland and prepared navigational material and instruments for the latter's Guiana voyage of 1595. In the 1590s, he was implicated with Ralegh and others in accusations of impiety and atheism; he may, in fact, have held Arminian views, then or later. In 1597 he became a pensioned member of the household of Henry Percy, ninth earl of Northumberland, a noted amateur of science, and in 1608 he occupied a house built for him by the earl at his Sion House seat near London. He continued to act for both Ralegh and Percy in various business matters during their long years as state prisoners, and in 1605–1606 he was himself briefly a prisoner following the Gunpowder Plot.

In the years 1606–1609, in a correspondence initiated by Johannes Kepler (1571–1630) in Prague, Harriot and Kepler considered matters of optics and specific gravities. Harriot was a careful and sympathetic student of Kepler's theory of planetary motion and one of its earliest converts. During the period 1609–1612, Harriot, like Galileo Galilei (1564–1642), was active in mapping telescopic observations of the Moon, sunspots (leading him to conclude that the Sun rotated), and Jupiter's satellites. He also observed the comets of 1607 and 1618 and estimated their paths.

Even now it is hard to give a full summary of Harriot's numerous and wide-ranging contributions to science and mathematics. Although none of his work after 1588 was published in his lifetime, knowledge of it was widespread in northwest Europe by 1600. The *Artis analyticae praxis* (1631) was a posthumous work selected

ARTIS ANALYTICAE
PRAXIS,

Ad æquationes Algebraïcas nouâ, expeditâ, & generali methodo, refoluendas:

TRACTATVS

E pofthumis THOMÆ HARRIOTI Philofophi ac Mathematici celeberrimi fchediafmatis fummâ fide & diligentiâ defcriptus:

ET

ILLVSTRISSIMO DOMINO
DOM. HENRICO PERCIO,
NORTHVMBRIÆ COMITI,

Qui bæc primò, fub Patronatus & Munificentiæ fuæ aufpicijs ad proprios vfus elucubrata, in communem Mathematicorum vtilitatem, denuò reuifenda, defcribenda, & publicanda mandauit, meritiffimi Honoris ergò Nuncupatus.

LONDINI
Apud ROBERTVM BARKER, Typographum Regium: Et Hæred. Io. BILLII.
Anno 1631.

Title page of Harriot's posthumous work on algebra.

from his algebraic papers and is important for its extensions of François Viète's (1540–1603) work on algebraic notation, including the inequality signs; for relating roots to binomial factors of polynomials; and for numerical methods of solution.

In his navigational work, in addition to problems of amplitudes and latitudes, he solved the problem of constructing a conformal mapping of the globe proposed by Gerard Mercator (1512–1594) in 1569, first by the addition of secants and later by a method structurally equivalent to the modern logarithmic formula, and constructed the necessary tables of meridional parts. Using the geometry of the sphere, he proved (stating probably for the first time) the conformality of stereographic projection and achieved the rectification of both the plane equiangular spiral and the spherical loxodrome, the first known rectifications and a notable achievement before the calculus.

He also gave the binomial expansion for fractional indices and applied this both to interpolation by finite differences and to obtaining the limiting exponential series. This work applied algebra to geometry, with extensions to loci in optics and projectile theory. He wrote on ship design (1608), introduced binary arithmetic, constructed a good if imperfect theory of elastic impacts (perhaps related to optics), and wrote on geodesy. In 1603 he obtained the area of a spherical triangle, a result recognized at the time as unknown to antiquity. Arising from his work in America, he constructed a soundly based phonetic alphabet.

His work on optics in the late 1590s led to the sine rule of refraction—now named for Willebrord Snel (1580–1626)—dated in his manuscript to 10:30 a.m. on July 22, 1601. He verified it experimentally and applied it to the calculation of the height of the primary rainbow and dispersion. He solved Alhazen's (Ibn al-Haytham [965–ca. 1040]) problem in optics of determining the points of reflection in a spherical mirror, given two points on the ray, accepted Copernicanism (but not always the accuracy of the resultant tables), and was sympathetic to atomism, which he related to ideas of infinities and perhaps to finding centers of mass via infinitesimals.

After Viète's death in 1603, there was no European mathematician to match Harriot, but the nature of his employments contributed to his neglect of wider publication, so that his subsequent influence was reduced. Without this neglect, his name might now be nearly as well known as that of Kepler or Galileo. Many of his methods and results were rediscovered later by such as Gottfried Wilhelm Leibniz (1646–1716), Isaac Newton (1642–1727), Isaac Barrow (1630–1677), Willebrord Snel (1580–1626), René Descartes (1596–1650), James Gregory (1638–1675), and Edmond Halley (ca. 1656–1743). George Chapman's translations of Homer come with a fine poem of dedication to Harriot (1598) and praise of him as one "whose judgement and knowledge in all kinds, I know to be incomparable." Harriot was a man of many parts. Perhaps his failure to gain the fullest recognition in history was because he had too many ideas in his head at any one time.

BIBLIOGRAPHY

Harriot, Thomas. *A Briefe and True Report of the New Found Land of Virginia.* New York: Dover, 1972. Repr. of 1590 Frankfurt ed.

Lohne, Johannes. "Thomas Harriot (1560–1621), the Tycho Brahe of Optics." *Centaurus* 6 (1959), 113–121.

Shirley, John W. *Thomas Harriot: A Biography.* Oxford: Clarendon, 1983.

———, ed. *A Source-Book for the Study of Thomas Harriot.* New York: Garland, 1981.

JON V. PEPPER

See also Algebra; Cartography; Keplerianism; Optics; Telescopic Astronomy

Hartlib, Samuel (ca. 1600–1662)

One of the most respected and thoughtful intelligencers (disseminators of news) of the seventeenth century, Hartlib was born into a family of merchant notables from Elbing, Prussia. After an education at the Calvinist academy of Brieg in Silesia and the newly Calvinist University of Koenigsberg, he continued his studies in Cambridge. His mother was English, and it was to London that he returned in the later 1620s to escape the ravages of the Thirty Years War. There he cultivated a vast network of correspondents (based, in part, on his refugee contacts in northern Europe, England, and North America). His correspondents gave him news, scientific ideas and methods, and information about innovations. A welcoming host to various indigent "strangers" to London, he also gained a reputation as an imparter of scientific ideas and information. From 1647 onward, he devoted himself to establishing an "Office of Address" with elements borrowed from Théophraste Renaudot's (1586–1653) French model. Although he never succeeded in having the office funded by the English Parliament, he employed scriveners and translators on his own account to copy portions of letters and treatises for others. Although he became well known as the publisher of numerous pamphlets written mainly by others, he was even more influential scientifically as a scribal publisher and communicator. He also acted as an agent for those seeking patents for new inventions; more than half of the known patents issued by the English government during the Commonwealth and Protectorate (1649–1660) engaged Hartlib's attentions. His closeness to that regime ensured that he was marginalized after the Restoration, and he died in penury, after progressively greater ill health.

Hartlib readily adopted the dominant ideas and language of others. He promoted the "pansophy" (universal of encyclopedic knowledge) of the Czech educationalist and philosopher John Amos Comenius (1592–1670) in England. Comenius eventually accepted his invitation to stay with him in London, arriving there just as the political crisis that led to the English Civil War (1642–1646) reached its climax. He regularly supported the laudable but unrealistic efforts of his friend John Dury to be the peacemaker among Europe's divergent Protestant traditions. Francis Bacon's (1561–1626) blueprint for a reformed natural philosophy became Hartlib's, and he was keen to find surviving Baconian manuscripts and to advance Bacon's practical ideas for change. But Hartlib's adoption of other people's ideas also involved thought and adaptation. When he was advancing practical ideas for change, as in his writings on husbandry (his most successful being *Samuel Hartlib His Legacie,* 1651), Hartlib went beyond any individual influence in his shrewd advocacy of sharing information for the common good about the possibilities for agricultural change. It was Hartlib's perception that only through the dissemination of knowledge would the coming of the millennium (in which he profoundly believed) be achieved. His commitment to that dissemination gave him a distinctive voice, even though it was a goal that would be achieved in very different ways by the Royal Society.

BIBLIOGRAPHY

Greengrass, Mark, Michael Leslie, and Timothy Raylor, eds. *Samuel Hartlib and Universal Reformation.* Cambridge: Cambridge University Press, 1994.

Webster, Charles. *The Great Instauration.* London: Duckworth, 1975.

MARK GREENGRASS

See also Bureau d'adresse; Correspondence Networks

Harvey, William (1578–1657)

Harvey is best known for the discovery of the circulation of the blood, which he published in his *Anatomical Exercise on the Movement of the Heart and Blood in Animals* (1628). This work is commonly cited as *De motu cordis* (On the Movement of the Heart), although it is the parallel phrase "movement of the blood" that alludes to the circulation proper. This theory became widely accepted among European physicians and scientists within a few decades. Shortly after its publication, René Descartes (1596–1650) co-opted the circulation into his influential new system of philosophy. In 1636 a colleague wrote to Galileo Galilei (1564–1642): "This is the circulation which the blood traverses within us. It has been ob-

served in our time, and will suffice to revolutionize all of medicine, just as the invention of the telescope has done for astronomy, the compass has done for commerce, and artillery has done for the whole military art."

Older medical thinking presupposed that the bodily humors or fluids (especially the blood) can collect in various organs to cause harm, and medical practices were often aimed at overcoming these imbalances to restore health. By establishing that all the blood is in constant, rapid motion throughout the body, Harvey ushered in a fundamental reform of medical theory, as well as a significant reevaluation of medical practices. Beyond medicine, the circulation provided an impressive example of the value of experiment in the investigation of nature, so that well before his death in 1657 Harvey had become one of the major figures of the Scientific Revolution.

Harvey attended the King's School, Canterbury, and then Gonville and Caius College, Cambridge, where he took his B.A. in 1599. In 1600 he went to study medicine and natural philosophy at Padua, Italy, the leading European school for those subjects. Padua was also a major center of anatomical teaching and research. In Harvey's time, the professor of anatomy was Hieronymus Fabricius (Girolamo Fabrici, ca. 1533–1619), who particularly emphasized the broadening of human anatomy by the study of all other kinds of animals, as well as by attention to the functions of the organs. Fabricius and his former student Giulio Casseri (1552–1616) served as faculty sponsors for Harvey's Paduan doctorate in 1602. Harvey would later see his own research as fitting within the Fabrician methodological tradition, though he often disagreed with Fabricius in matters of substance.

Harvey's other two sponsors at Padua were professors of medical practice and of Aristotelian natural philosophy, respectively. Subsequently, his main professional identity was that of a physician, a medical practitioner who depended upon knowledge of the human body gained through philosophical speculation and anatomical research. After settling in London in 1602, Harvey became first a licentiate and then a Fellow of the London College of Physicians and subsequently held a variety of offices within the college. He was also named physician to St. Bartholomew's Hospital and a physician to the English Royal Court. Eventually, he would serve as the chief physician to King Charles I and, as a result, would be profoundly affected by the English Civil War (1642–1646). Under the Commonwealth, Harvey

William Harvey. From Fielding H. Garrison, An Introduction to the History of Medicine, *3rd ed. (Philadelphia and London: Saunders, 1921).*

emerged as the much-honored hero of the London College of Physicians. In turn, he provided the college with a new library, to which he donated his own books and manuscripts. This library was, however, destroyed in the Great Fire of London of 1666.

In addition to these other duties, in 1616 Harvey became lecturer on anatomy at the London College. This required him to give, periodically, a short survey of all of human anatomy accompanied by the dissection of a human cadaver. The manuscript notes that he prepared for this course show him to have been especially interested in the functions of the various organs, concerning which he frequently advanced his own positions rather than those of the authorities. Reflecting his training with Fabricius are the many digressions on the comparative anatomy of the organs. To satisfy his specifically medical interests, he also enumerated the variety of pathological changes that he had observed at autopsy.

Harvey clearly had no idea of the circulation when he wrote his notes in 1616, but he did have definite ideas about the blood and the heart. He vigorously advanced the notion of the primacy of the blood, according to which the blood is the most living part of the animal, the first part to be formed in embryonic development, and the vital principle throughout subsequent life. Since the time of Aristotle (384–322 B.C.E.), philosophers and physicians had considered life to reside within the solid parts of the body, especially the heart; the blood was essentially the body's nutriment, intermediate between the nonliving food and the living organs that would ultimately assimilate the blood. Harvey reversed this relationship: liquid blood is itself fully alive, and other parts continually renew their vital powers through the consumption of blood.

But Harvey's early views about the formation of blood were fairly conventional. Freshly ingested food is converted to a whitish *chyle* in the stomach and intestines and from there is conveyed by the mesenteric and portal veins to the liver, where the conversion to blood is completed. From the liver, the blood passes into the vena cava and its branches, from which it is gradually eaten up by all the parts of the body. But whereas many contemporaries (including Fabricius) regarded the heart and arteries chiefly as the body's heating and ventilating system, Harvey accepted a newer view that owed much to Aristotelians of the late sixteenth and early seventeenth centuries. For Harvey, the veins provided the basic nutriment that is required by the bodies of all animals, but, as one ascends the scale of perfection among animals, their bodies have increasing need of a more perfect kind of nutriment that is supplied by the heart and arteries, until, in the most perfect animals (including humans), this second kind of blood is the one that is needed most. Thus, in such animals, the greater part of the blood from the vena cava is taken up by the right ventricle of the heart and transmitted to the lungs, where the conversion of venous into arterial blood takes place. From the lungs, the arterial blood then passes on to the left ventricle of the heart, which distributes it through the arteries to nourish and vivify the entire body.

Along with this general conception of the blood flow, Harvey had, by 1616, devoted great attention to determining exactly how the heart, by its movement, transmits blood from the veins, through the lungs, to the arteries. In this one respect, his early ideas owed much to animal vivisection in addition to comparative anatomy. The heartbeat itself was universally familiar, but among Harvey's predecessors and contemporaries there was wide disagreement as to what the heart does at what time, in relation to the beat that it makes against the chest wall and to the pulse of the arteries. The more generally held view was that the heart actively dilates, thereby sucking in air from the lungs into the left ventricle to ventilate the heart, and blood from the vena cava into the right ventricle. At this time, the heart also strikes the chest wall. During its less vigorous contraction, the heart expels materials—blood, air, smoky vapors—from its ventricles. Furthermore, the arteries dilate and contract actively and at the same time as the heart, thereby extending the ventilating process to the whole body.

In his lectures of 1616, Harvey concluded that the heart undergoes only one active movement, namely contraction, during which it vigorously expels blood from both of its ventricles and also strikes the chest. The pulse of the arteries is nothing but the mechanical consequence of the heart's forceful impulsion of blood, so that the dilation of the arteries follows immediately upon the contraction of the heart. After contraction, the heart relaxes, during which time the right and the left ventricles are passively refilled with blood from the vena cava and pulmonary veins, respectively. Thus, the heartbeat and the arterial pulse can be understood entirely with reference to the heart's transmission of blood, from the vena cava, through the lungs, to the arteries, and so to the whole body. Harvey's discussion was mostly in Latin, but he switched to English when summing up: "Action [of the heart]: thus relaxed, receives blood, contracted scups it over; in the entire body the arteries respond as my breath in a glove." Harvey also argued that the contraction of the heart is the underlying cause of arterial hemorrhage and of the swelling that occurs when a band is applied to the arm, as in bloodletting. Furthermore, he proposed that the purpose of the valves in the veins is to prevent the heart from propelling the venous blood away from itself.

All of these issues would later figure prominently in Harvey's argument for the circulation, but, as of 1616, he probably regarded the investigation of the movement of the heart as a finished piece of work. Indeed, there is some evidence that he wrote significant portions of *De motu cordis* before the discovery of the circulation, as a separate monograph on the heartbeat alone. In 1627 he also wrote the first draft of a treatise on animal locomotion, in which he discussed muscles as the underlying organs in all bodily movements. He concluded that muscles have an inherent ability to contract but that the maintenance of this power depended upon a constant supply of arterial blood from the heart. He seems still to have had in mind a one-time distribution of blood, but in this context he also took account of the effects of the emotions on bodily activity: in fear, all of the blood rushes to the center of the body, leaving the muscles weak and unresponsive, while, in anger, there is an enhanced outward flow of blood, which invigorates the muscles and readies them for action. Harvey was thus concerned with rapid inward and outward movements of the blood, but he saw them as the result of special circumstances.

Soon afterward, Harvey concluded that these movements of the blood to and from the center of the body must be constant, natural processes, in which the same blood repeatedly traverses this pathway. This crucial breakthrough resulted from his shifting attention from the *individual* beat of the heart to the cumulative effect of *many beats in succession*: there is simply not enough blood in the body for the heart to ceaselessly transmit blood on a one-time basis. His thinking may have been stimulated by the consideration of certain kinds of mechanical pumps having a limited reservoir of water: such pumps frequently run out of water, whereas the heart seems never to run out of blood. In what may be his earliest surviving account of the circulation, Harvey stated: "The panting [beating] of the heart is but the pumping about of the blood, in the expansion receiving, and in the contraction sending it out; and it receives so much at every expansion that considering the great proportion and the many beatings of the heart in half an hour, the blood must of necessity come round about." Or, as he put it in a somewhat more mature formulation: "It has been demonstrated that a perpetual movement of the blood in a circle is caused by the beat of the heart." In Harvey's view, the arteries and the veins were important as the pathways through which the circulation occurs, but his primary emphasis was on two kinds of movement: the vigorous contraction of the heart and the resulting circulation of the blood.

In *De motu cordis*, Harvey refined his calculations to show that the blood must circulate repeatedly within half an hour. He also proposed a number of more directly empirical proofs of the circulation: arterial hemorrhage shows that the heart can easily evacuate all of the blood from the whole body within half an hour; ligatures applied to the human arm can be manipulated to show that blood ordinarily flows forcefully into the arm through the arteries and then out again through the veins; and experiments involving the valves in the veins show that the venous blood moves exclusively inward through the veins.

Harvey's *De motu cordis* was printed at Frankfurt in mid-1628 and was on sale by the autumn of that year. Within less than a year, the theory of circulation was being favorably discussed in leading medical centers of Continental Europe. The philosopher Thomas Hobbes (1588–1679) later wrote that his friend Harvey was "the only man that I know of who, overcoming envy, established a new doctrine within his own lifetime." But there were also not a few critics who feared that acceptance of the circulation would undermine much of traditional medical practice. In 1649 Harvey published *Anatomical Exercises on the Circulation of the Blood* in response to some of these opponents, especially Jean Riolan, Jr. (1580–1657), the professor of anatomy at Paris.

Harvey had long planned monographs on various other topics, but the only one that came to fruition was *Exercises on the Generation of Animals* (1651). Fabricius, in *On the Formation of the Egg and the Chick* (published posthumously in 1621), had treated the fertilized egg as a distinct organ whose function is the generation of the chick embryo. But Fabricius maintained that, in viviparous generation, which he regarded as the more fundamental kind, semen and blood supplied by the parents are the direct progenitors of the embryo. Harvey maintained, on the contrary, that an egg is the agent of generation in all kinds of animals. Citing his detailed investigations of generation in both oviparous and viviparous animals, he maintained that there is no evidence that parental blood or semen (in the sense of visible masses of material) enters directly into the makeup of the embryo. He therefore held that the formation of a fetus from a fertilized egg is the only demonstrable kind of generation in animals, and, by appealing to a principle of uniformity in nature, he extended this model to viviparous species. The frontispiece of *On Generation* epitomizes his major conclusion: Zeus is shown opening up an egg, from which emerge insects, birds, reptiles, and mammals, including a human infant; on the egg is inscribed *Ex ovo omnia* (All things come from an egg).

BIBLIOGRAPHY

Bylebyl, Jerome, ed. *William Harvey and His Age: The Professional and Social Context of the Discovery of the Circulation.* (The Henry E. Sigerist Supplements to the *Bulletin of the History of Medicine* n.s., no. 2). Baltimore: Johns Hopkins University Press, 1979.

———. *William Harvey: From Heartbeat to Circulation* (forthcoming).

Frank, Robert G. *Harvey and the Oxford Physiologists: A Study of Scientific Ideas and Social Interaction.* Berkeley and Los Angeles: University of California Press, 1980.

French, R. K. *William Harvey's Natural Philosophy.* Cambridge and New York: Cambridge University Press, 1994.

Keynes, G. *The Life of William Harvey.* Oxford: Clarendon, 1966.

Pagel, Walter. *William Harvey's Biological Ideas: Selected Aspects and Historical Background.* Basel: Karger; New York: Hafner, 1967.

Whitteridge, Gweneth. *William Harvey and the Circulation of the Blood.* London: MacDonald's; New York: American Elsevier, 1971.

JEROME J. BYLEBYL

See also Colombo, Realdo; Fabrici, Girolamo (Fabricius ab Acquapendente); Galenism; Lower, Richard; Physiology

Heat

The physics of heat, during the Scientific Revolution, was less advanced, in terms of principles, than mechanics, probably on account of the intrinsic complexity of thermal processes. At that time, a deeper empirical knowledge of these processes was achieved, resulting from researches on artificially generated processes and no longer only from the observation of natural phenomena. This semiquantitative experimentation was made possible thanks to some basic technical developments and was connected to the birth of famous scientific institutions: the Accademia del Cimento in Florence, the Académie Royale des Sciences in Paris, and the Royal Society of London.

The subjects explored were, schematically, the construction and calibration of thermometers, the properties of bodies and temperature, change of state, and the production and transmission of heat or cold. The first subject—a good level was reached only at the beginning of the eighteenth century—was one of the basic problems investigated during the seventeenth century in order "to devise a universal and determinate measure of cold and heat," according to Christiaan Huygens (1629–1695). The evaluation of the thermic level of a body required an understanding of the conceptual difference between temperature and heat quantity. This basic point, definitively explained only in the eighteenth century, was discussed in the late Middle Ages, following the Aristotelian classification of the quantity of heat or cold and the temperature of the qualities of a body. Before the seventeenth century, cold and heat were both regarded as a positive and opposite quality of a body, delimited within a maximum degree.

In the seventeenth century, the physical nature of cold was clarified as absence of heat, particularly thanks to Galileo Galilei (1564–1642) and Robert Boyle (1627–1691), who linked quantity of heat to motion of the particles comprising matter. Overcoming the heat/cold dualism was an outstanding result of the developing physics of heat. The concept was associated with different conceptions of heat, which can roughly be traced back to two theories of heat: the material theory and the kinetic theory. According to the first theory, heat is a sui generis (unique) substance. In the seventeenth century, this conception prevailed among chemists, who examined thermal processes like dissolution, incalescence, calcination, and fermentation. They regarded heat (or fire) "a peculiar fluid provided with specific properties that differentiate it from other fluids," in the words of Nicolas Lemery (1645–1715).

Some chemists, like N. Lemery, Louis Lemery (1677–1743), and Nicolaas Hartsoeker (1656–1725), also considered it essential that, for the production of heat, the parts of this special fluid be in a state of rapid motion. Boyle, a firm champion of the kinetic nature of heat, invoked such a conception in an attempt to explain the gain in weight shown by metals in calcination. According to the kinetic theory, the distinctive feature of heat is motion. Francis Bacon (1561–1626) specifically alluded to "motion which is the form of heat." During the seventeenth century, the leading natural philosophers espoused, more or less completely, this last theory. According to Galileo and Pierre Gassendi (1592–1655), the "calorific motion" of the constituents of a body was due to the injection of swarms of igneous corpuscles (*ignicoli* for Galilei, "heat atoms" for Gassendi). These corpuscles are present "inside those substances that give us a sensation of warmth" (Galileo, 1626) and are provided by very fast motion. Closer to the modern kinetic theory of heat were the ideas of Bacon, René Descartes (1596–1650), Boyle, Edmé Mariotte (ca. 1620–1684) and Isaac Newton (1642–1727), who thought that the calorific motion inside a body could be "mechanically producible" by percussion, collision, or friction without the intervention of igneous corpuscles. The motion of

the particles of a hot body must be, according to Boyle, "vehement" and "very various," "some particles moving towards the right, some on the left hand, some directly upwards, some downwards, and some obliquely." Note that none of the mentioned conceptions on the nature of heat reached, during the seventeenth century, a quantitative stage; quantification of heat phenomena and theory would begin only in the eighteenth century and come to full maturity in the nineteenth.

BIBLIOGRAPHY

Grilli, Mario, and Fabio Sebastiani. "Le origini della fisica del calore: le teorie sulla natura del calore da Galileo a Newton." *Physis* 24 (1982), 301–356.

Roller, Duane. "The Early Development of the Concepts of Temperature and Heat." In *Harvard Case Histories in Experimental Science,* ed. J. B. Conant and L. K. Nash. Cambridge: Cambridge University Press, 1957, pp. 119–214.

Sebastiani, Fabio. "Quantification of Heat." In *Scritti di storia della scienza,* ed. A. Ballio and L. Paoloni. Rome: Accademia Nazionale delle Scienze (detta dei XL), 1990, pp. 53–68.

MARIO GRILLI

See also Accademia del Cimento; Thermoscope/Thermometer

Helmont, Johannes Baptista van (1579-1644)

Van Helmont was born into the Flemish landed gentry in Brussels; his father died a year after his birth, a loss that deeply marked his development and personality. He studied at the University of Louvain, but his belief that he had learned nothing from philosophy, astronomy, and mathematics led him to refuse his M.A. He studied geography at the Jesuit college opened shortly before in Louvain and attended classes by the Jesuit Martín del Río (1551–1609), whose great treatise (*Disquisitionum magitarum,* 1599) aimed at refuting magic from the orthodox Catholic viewpoint and also served as an erudite encyclopedia for advocates of the occult. In his disappointment, van Helmont turned to reading the Stoics and many works on botany, medicine, and law intensively, only to be disappointed yet again. For a while, he considered entering a monastery but finally chose to study medicine, a decision inspired, according to his autobiography, by the Archangel Raphael. He graduated as a doctor in 1599, but his dissatisfaction as a practitioner led him to abandon the profession.

He set out on a long journey across Switzerland, Italy, France, and England and became familiar with Paracelsianism, which became one of the mainstays of his work. He deemed chemical medicines to be more effective than the natural remedies of academic Galenism and began practicing as a physician again in 1605. His marriage four years later to the rich heiress of a landowner family consolidated his position in the upper class. A practicing physician and writer until his death, he was also a devout Catholic with a mystic tendency, who deemed Galen (second century) and Seneca (ca. 4 B.C.E.–65), for example, to be not only mistaken but pagan and, hence, unacceptable. He was, however, a stubborn opponent of the Jesuits for political reasons and over differences in scientific outlook. He was condemned by the University of Louvain in 1623 and by the Inquisition in 1625 for his treatise *De magnetica vulnerum . . . curatione* (On the Magnetic Healing of Wounds, 1621), in which he defended the remote curing of wounds by applying a Paracelsian prescription, which included mold from the skull of a hanged person, to the sword that had inflicted the wound.

Johannes Baptista van Helmont. From Fielding H. Garrison, An Introduction to the History of Medicine, *3rd ed. (Philadelphia and London: Saunders, 1921).*

His work was, in fact, an intricate synthesis of science and faith. He categorically rejected Scholastic logic as a means of knowledge, confronting it with two different types of experience: the "sympathetic" experience of reality, based on feelings of affinity, and the quantitative experience based on weight and measurement—the first stemming from Paracelsianism and the second basically from Nicholas of Cusa (1401–1464). Like Paracelsus (ca. 1491–1541), van Helmont conceived of the universe as an organism in which matter was configured by a series of forces. He modified certain Paracelsian ideas, differentiating between *fermentum*—the causal force in material processes such as digestion, the formation of minerals, and the transformation of water into animal or vegetable substances; *semen* (seed)—the working principle responsible for the production of particular forms of plants, animals, and diseases; and *archeus*—the vital principle that directs specific organisms. The influence of Nicholas of Cusa led him to consider water to be a universal element.

Van Helmont's ontological concept of disease was in line with these ideas, deeming diseases to be individual beings (*entia*) produced by a specific seed (*semen*) generated like the embryo by the interaction of the sick person's archeus and that of a harmful agent. Unlike the Galenist concept of catarrh, in which humors supposedly flow from the brain to different parts of the body, he held that seeds entered the body and produced local reactions in the part of the body where they took root. He also rejected Galenist therapy, especially purging and bloodletting. In his opinion, medicines did not act by specifically destroying the seeds of disease, as propounded by Paracelsus, but cured people by modifying their archeus. He demonstrated that acid is the digestive agent in the stomach, as well the role of bile in the gut, and provided good descriptions of several diseases, especially tuberculosis, asthma, epilepsy, and the association of hydrops with the kidneys.

As a physician, van Helmont made noteworthy contributions to other scientific fields. He introduced the expression and concept of "gas," differentiating air and water vapor from the "specific smokes" produced by the combustion or fermentation of different substances. He emphasized that said gases were the same substances in the volatile state and used chemical analysis systematically to describe several. The concept of water as a universal element provided the theory behind one of his most famous experiments: a willow tree was planted in a certain amount of soil and watered every day with the same amount of water. The balance showed that the weight of the soil remained constant while the tree grew heavier in proportion to the weight of the water used. Using the same quantitative approach, he obtained the specific weight of urine from healthy and sick persons and proposed this as a means of diagnosis, replacing the traditional and chemical uroscopy. He used the pendulum to measure time and another device to measure pressure and temperature and also invented methods for the preparation of *spiritus salis marini* (hydrochloric acid) and other acids.

The influence of van Helmont was felt in two different historical lines. First, his influence was an important factor in iatrochemistry, the medical system led during the seventeenth century by Franciscus Sylvius (1614–1672) and Thomas Willis (1621–1675) that aimed to integrate all of the anatomical, physiological, and pathological innovations in conflict with Galenism since the Renaissance with Paracelsian concepts and techniques, while substituting Paracelsian panvitalism with a more or less marked mechanism. Second, van Helmont bridged the gap between Paracelsianism and eighteenth-century medical vitalism, mainly due to the influence his work had on Francis Glisson's (1597–1677) notion of "irritability" as the basic property of living matter, on the "anima" concept formulated by Willis in his *De anima brutorum* (1672) as the dynamic principle of animal life, and, above all, on the animistic system of Georg Ernest Stahl (1660–1734).

BIBLIOGRAPHY

Debus, A. G. *The Chemical Philosophy: Paracelsian Science and Medicine in the Sixteenth and Seventeenth Centuries.* 2 vols. New York: Science History Publications, 1977.

———. *Chemistry, Alchemy, and the New Philosophy, 1550–1700.* London: Variorum, 1987.

López Piñero, J. M. "Eighteenth-Century Medical Vitalism: The Paracelsan Connection." In *Revolutions in Science,* ed. W. R. Shea. Canton: Science History Publications, 1988, pp. 117–132.

Pagel, W. *Joan Baptista van Helmont: Reformer of Science and Medicine.* Cambridge: Cambridge University Press, 1982.

———. *The Religious and Philosophical Aspects of Van Helmont's Science and Medicine.* (Supplement to *Bulletin of the History of Medicine,* no. 2). Baltimore: Johns Hopkins University Press, 1944.

JOSÉ M. LÓPEZ-PIÑERO

See also Chemistry; Etiology; Fermentation; Iatrochemistry; Paracelsus; Vitalism

Herbals. See Botany

Hermetism

As commonly happens with ism-words, *hermetism* has been greatly debased. Like its cognate *hermeticism,* it is often used in an extremely vague sense to refer to magic or occultism generally, but in such a way as avoids the necessity to decide what any of these terms really mean; it sometimes refers to alchemy alone; and it is often used as if it referred to a clearly defined and coherent tradition of esoteric thought, though experts are in wide agreement that this is not true. Accordingly, it is much better to use the adjective *hermetic,* for this has a reference that is quite clear: it denotes a body of literature, much (but not all) of it derived from antiquity, that claims Hermes (or some closely related demigod) as its author or perhaps as the source of its inspiration. This literature is very diffuse and presents no obvious coherent doctrine beyond the general notion that it deals with issues seemingly beyond the range of unaided human reason, hence derived from some superior source. Yet, as we eventually see below, it is important to the student of the Scientific Revolution because of the role it appears to have played in diminishing the authority of medieval Scholasticism.

The experts on Hermetic literature agree in dividing it into two groups, variously categorized: the "philosophical," "theological," or "theoretical" texts, on the one hand, and the "popular," "practical," or "technical" ones, on the other. There remains, however, severe doubt about whether this categorization reflects anything more than the accidents of a millenium of editing, but the distinction remains vital to understanding early-modern thought. For it is the "practical" texts that provide a warrant for the common identification of Hermetism with occultism, since these often deal with astrology, alchemy, and magic. The brief *Tabula smaragdina* (The Emerald Tablet of Hermes), or the long *Picatrix* (= Goal of the Wise, eleventh century) are well-known examples of this literature. The latter is preoccupied with astrological theories of talismatic operations and tends to attribute divinity to the planets, while the former is an enigmatic "poem" about how to use a special "one thing" (presumably, the Philosopher's Stone) to "accomplish . . . miracles" and "works of wonder"—the very essence of magic. "This thing is the strong fortitude of all strenth, for it overcometh every subtle thing and doth penetrate every cold substance. Thus was the world created. Hence will there be marvelous adaptions achieved, of which the matter is this. For this reason I am called Hermes Trismegistus, because I hold three parts of the wisdom of the world" (from *The Emerald Tablet*).

Because of the abundance of texts in this "technical" category, Hermetic literature had become closely associated with magic by the time of the Renaissance and thus shared the latter's reputation as intellectually dubious and theologically unorthodox.

The "theoretical" texts, by contrast, contain very little that we would categorize as magic. They deal instead with theosophy, "philosophy" in the popular sense of the word: "the nature of things as a whole" (*Hermetica*). So it asks how knowledge of God can be found in the order of the universe about us; it observes the superiority of the soul to the body, and the moral necessity of escaping corporeal sensuality; and it discusses salvation and immortality, among other things. As these themes should suggest, many of the questions handled are extremely reminiscent of Plato (428–348 B.C.E.), and so are the answers provided. But the latter are presented as dogmatic pronouncements and clearly presuppose that spiritual assistance is required if we are to succeed in grasping such divine mysteries of the cosmos. So the texts still share many of the presumptions of the European traditions of occultism, and one was overtly condemned by Saint Augustine (354–430) for its endorsement of what it calls "the art of making gods," some seemingly magical and demonic processes for bringing statues alive. The same text generally presents an astrological view of the operation of the cosmos, while the activity of demons is an ongoing presumption of the other texts, too.

Yet, this "theological" literature also contains numerous passages (and much specific language) extremely reminiscent of the Hebrew Bible. A spirit, for instance, moves upon the waters at Creation, and man is later made in his "father's image." Furthermore, various Christian doctrines, like the last judgment (*Hermetica*), are mirrored in them.

The most prominent of these "philosophical" texts are seventeen possibly independent Greek tracts (numbered 1–14 and 16–18 since the Renaissance and known since the Middle Ages as the *Corpus Hermeticum,* or sometimes by the name of the first tract, *Poimandres*) and the *Asclepius* (surviving in Latin and named after the Greek god of healing). But there are a number of other

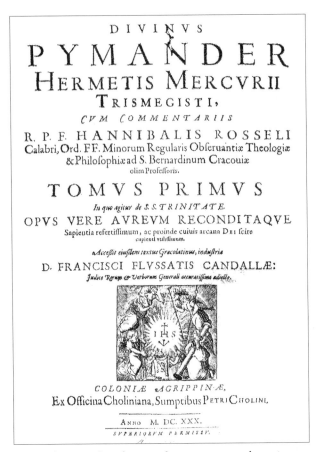

A six-volume work with text and commentary on the major work attributed to Hermes Trismegistus.

texts as well, some in Coptic. All of these pieces date from antiquity, particularly (but less certainly) from the syncretism of Hellenistic and Roman Egypt, in which the author they commonly claim, the traditional Egyptian god Thoth/Tat, became identified with the Greek god Hermes (also identified with the Roman god Mercury), but who, as well, split into several individuals with the same name, to one of whom the epithet "Thrice-Great" (Trismegistus in Latin) was eventually applied.

For the student of early-modern science, the details of the genesis of these texts, and the debates (noted by Brian Copenhaver in the Introduction to his 1992 translation) about the extent to which their contents are Greek or Egyptian, are presumably irrelevant. What matters here is the immense popularity of Hermetic literature in sixteenth- and seventeenth-century Europe, a popularity closely associated with that new enthusiasm for Platonism widely regarded as integral to the Scientific Revolution. Indeed, in the mid-fifteenth century, Cosimo de' Medici urged Marsilio Ficino

(1433–1499) to interrupt his translating of Plato to prepare a Latin version of the *Corpus Hermeticum,* the first fourteen tracts of which appeared a decade later in 1471. The *Asclepius* was printed in 1469, and a Greek edition of the *Corpus* was published in 1554. Many other translations and editions appeared in the sixteenth century, but there was a big gap after the mid-seventeenth century.

It is vital to an understanding of the historical role played by the hermetic texts to note that, at the time of the Renaissance, their words were widely believed to have been written in the extremely dim past—before the birth of Christ and before the time of Plato and Aristotle (384–322 B.C.E.), and their author was sometimes thought to have been a contemporary of Moses, the accepted author of the biblical Book of Genesis. In itself, this gave the *Hermetica* great authority because of the standard belief that the world was in a state of decay, so that knowledge was more apt to be lost than got. Texts of great antiquity were thus closer to that ample knowledge of the material world given to Adam by God.

Furthermore, the patent coincidences with "later" Greek thought, especially with Platonism, were routinely interpreted as revealing Hermes to have been one of the teachers of the Greeks, while the Christian resonances similarly indicated that Plato's philosophy was not genuinely pagan. Aristotle, by contrast, was widely seen as non-Christian in the Renaissance, and it was routinely accepted, even by his medieval supporters, that the doctrines of his natural philosophy needed supplementation by divine revelation; unlike Hermes and Plato, Aristotle did not even allow the universe to have been created, for example.

Plato's philosophy, furthermore, became widely associated with occultism because of the importance it accorded to unseen realities. When coupled with the obvious piety of the theological *Corpus,* this suggested that the occultism and magic found in the *Hermetica* as a whole, and hence occultism and magic in general, were not as unorthodox as had been traditionally believed, and it reduced suspicion that the knowledge hidden in their oracular pronouncements was illicit. So the texts greatly supported—and, indeed, became an integral part of—that enhanced enthusiasm for magic embedded in Renaissance naturalism—"naturalism" because belief in magic as a whole tends to presume that nature is full of invisible powers, not known to the ignorant masses. The medieval worldview, by contrast, tended to see apparently magical actions as really caused preternaturally, by demons.

The precise significance of these facts for the Scientific Revolution is, however, not at all clear and is the subject of dispute. It has been famously proposed, especially by Frances Yates, that the hermetic texts were particulary important here and spearheaded the revolt against medieval Aristotelianism, and that, despite the great contrast between their essential spirit and that of the new science of the seventeenth century, some of their specific doctrines promoted the new knowledge. Yates notes (1964, 1967), for example, the "sun-worship" of the *Hermetica* and also its obvious rejection of the characteristic medieval presumption that humanity is profoundly incompetent. So she sees hermetism as generating both the new vision of the universe and the new "engaged" approach to human knowledge. But Yates did not argue her case particularly well, and many have queried the details of her claims, suggesting that the influences she saw were not really an impact of the *Corpus* at all but a much broader impact of occultism and Neoplatonism as a whole. Copenhaver notes (1988), for example, that Ficino's *Heavenly Life* (*De vita coelitus comparanda,* a key magical text of 1489) makes few references to Hermes but does depend heavily on Proclus (410–485).

The issue remains unresolved and is certainly muddied by the confusions noted in the opening paragraph of this essay. The specific claims about Hermetism need to be distinguished from the broader claims, and Yates must be recognized as pursuing two separate goals. Many of the attacks on her do not diminish the strength of the more profound claim.

All agree, however, that the specific influence of hermetism eventually waned in the seventeenth century—even if the influence of occultism did not. The key event here was a redating of the texts, by the Protestant philologist Isaac Casaubon, in 1614. Using linguistic evidence, Casaubon enlarged upon some earlier suspicions to argue that the texts could not be Greek translations from the Egyptian and that they certainly postdated both Plato and Christianity. Given this, their authority must collapse. By the time of the Enlightenment, it had.

BIBLIOGRAPHY

Copenhaver, Brian. "Hermes Trismegistus, Proclus, and the Question of a Philosophy of Magic in the Renaissance." In *Hermeticism and the Renaissance,* ed. Ingrid Merkel and Allen G. Debus. Washington: Folger Library, 1988, pp. 79–110.

———. "Natural Magic, Hermetism, and Occultism in Early Modern Science." In *Reappraisals of the Scientific Revolution,* ed. David Lindberg and Robert Westman. Cambridge: Cambridge University Press, 1990, pp. 261–301.

Hermes Trismegistus [nominal author]. *Hermetica: The Greek Corpus Hermeticum and the Latin Asclepius in a New English Translation, with Notes and Introduction.* Trans. and annotated by Brian Copenhaver. Cambridge: Cambridge University Press, 1992.

Westman, Robert, and J. E. McGuire. *Hermeticism and the Scientific Revolution.* Los Angeles: Clark Memorial Library, 1977.

Yates, Frances. *Giordano Bruno and the Hermetic Tradition.* London: Routledge and Kegan Paul, 1964.

———. "The Hermetic Tradition in Renaissance Science." In *Art, Science, and History in the Renaissance,* ed. Charles Singleton. Baltimore: Johns Hopkins University Press, 1967, pp. 255–274.

———. *The Rosicrucian Enlightenment.* London: Routledge and Kegan Paul, 1972.

KEITH HUTCHISON

See also Magic; Magic and the Scientific Revolution; Neoplatonism

Hernández, Francisco (1515–1587)

Born in 1515 in the town of Puebla de Montalbán, near Toledo, Spain, he studied medicine at the University of Alcalá de Henares at a time when it was the most outstanding Spanish center of Renaissance learning. After practicing medicine in several cities and studying plants and animals in different places on the Iberian Peninsula, in 1569 Hernández was appointed by Philip II of Spain to direct an expedition to investigate the natural history of America. This expedition—the first scientific expedition of modern times—covered the territory of Mexico between 1571 and 1577 and collected a vast amount of material. In his *Historia naturalis Novae Hispaniae,* Hernández applied methodical guidelines and noted all of the environmental conditions and zones. He described some three thousand plants, almost five hundred animals, and some minerals and illustrated this work with more than two thousand paintings. Most of the species were unknown in Europe. He therefore used Amerindian terms, particularly those of the Nahuatl people, which he relied on when establishing taxonomic groups. The work was not published during the lifetime of the author. During the first half of the seventeenth century, however, most of its contents were distributed in several

Hernández's work describing the flora and fauna of Mexico.

editions, the most important of which was published in Rome by the Accademia dei Lincei in the first half of the seventeenth century; it included the ample selection of the *Historia naturalis Novae Hispaniae.* This work had considerable influence on the subsequent development of botany and zoology up to the time of Linnaeus and Buffon in the eighteenth century. For example, in his *Historia plantarum* (1686–1704), John Ray (1620–1705) included many chapters and a complete summary of the Roman edition, stating that Hernández's work provided the major fundamentals of his treatise.

BIBLIOGRAPHY

López-Piñero, J. M. and J. Tomás Pardo. *La influencia de Francisco Hernández en la constitución de la botánica y la materia médica modernas.* Valencia: Instituto de Estudios Documentales e Históricos sobre la Ciencia, 1996.

———. *Nuevos materiales y noticias sobre la 'Historia de las Plantas de Nueva España' de Francisco Hernández.* Valencia: Instituto de Estudios Documentales e Históricos sobre la Ciencia, 1994.

Varey, S., ed. *The World of Francisco Hernández.* 2 vols. Stanford: Stanford University Press, 1997.

JOSÉ M. LÓPEZ-PIÑERO

See also Botany; Ray, John; Zoology

Hevelius, Johannes (1611–1687)

The son of a prosperous brewer in Gdansk, he was educated at the local gymnasium and then studied in the Netherlands and France, after which he joined his father's business. For the rest of his life he resided in Gdansk, running the brewery and serving in the city government in various capacities. On the urging of his former teacher Peter Crüger, under whom he had studied astronomy, he took up serious observing, beginning with the solar eclipse of 1639. Over the next two decades, he built a sumptuous observatory, supervising the building of instruments, grinding his own lenses, making observations, doing his own engraving, and supervising the publication of his works. He kept up an active correspondence with astronomers in other countries.

Hevelius's first major research project was mapping the Moon. He set out to observe and draw every phase of the Moon, a task that took him years because of the variable weather in Gdansk. In 1647 he published *Selenographia, sive lunae descriptio.* In this ambitious work, he reviewed all of telescopic astronomy, but the centerpiece was the section containing engravings of all of the phases of the Moon, both waxing and waning, and three large plates of the full Moon that showed the parts of the Moon revealed by libration, a slow oscillation as seen from the earth. *Selenographia* established Hevelius's reputation as one of the foremost astronomers of Europe. In 1668 Hevelius published *Cometographia,* containing a complete "history" of comets (in the Baconian sense), which, although it contained no startling insights, became the standard source for information on comets up to that point.

His next great work was *Machina coelestis,* published in two volumes in 1673 and 1679. In the first volume, he described his instruments, including the longest telescope with a tube ever mounted—140 feet. All of the instruments were made by Hevelius and his workmen. But although he was a leader in telescope building, for positional astronomy he was committed to naked-eye sights. By the early 1670s, astronomers at Paris and Greenwich had made the shift to telescopic

Johannes Hevelius. From his Selenographia *(1647).*

sights on their measuring arcs, because such instruments promised an increase in accuracy of an order of magnitude. Hevelius was roundly criticized by Robert Hooke (1635–1702) and John Flamsteed (1646–1719) for clinging to open sights, but he did not change his practice. In the second volume of *Machina coelestis,* he reported more than twenty thousand position measurements made over more than three decades. These observations were the primary database for that period used by later astronomers.

In 1679 Hevelius's observatory and houses burned to the ground, and all of his instruments were destroyed. Most of his manuscripts were saved, however. After his death, Catherina Elizabeth Koopman, his second wife, who had assisted him in his observations, published two of his greatest works in 1690: *Prodromus astronomica,* a star catalog containing the positions of more than fifteen hundred stars—more than Ptolemy's (ca. 100–ca. 170) and Tycho Brahe's (1546–1601)—and *Firmamentum sobiescianum, sive uranographia,* a collection of fifty-six plates of constellations. Both became standard reference sources.

BIBLIOGRAPHY

Béziat, L. C. "La vie et les travaux de Jean Hévélius." *Bullettino di bibliografia et di storia matematiche e fisiche* 8 (1875), 497–558, 589–669.

Glebocki, Robert, and Andrezej Zbierske, eds. *On the Three Hundredth Anniversary of the Death of Johanne Hevelius.* Wrocław: Ossolineum, the Polish Academy of Sciences, 1992.

MacPike, E. F. *Hevelius, Flamsteed, and Halley.* London: Taylor and Francis, 1937.

Winkler, Mary G., and Albert van Helden. "Johannes Hevelius and the Visual Language of Astronomy." In *Renaissance and Revolution: Humanists, Scholars, Craftsmen, and Natural Philosophers in Early Modern Europe,* ed. J. V. Field and Frank A. J. L. James. Cambridge: Cambridge University Press, 1993, pp. 97–116.

ALBERT VAN HELDEN

See also Comets; Telescope; Telescopic Astronomy

Histories of Trades

The idea for the history of trades project originated with Francis Bacon (1561–1626) in the early seventeenth century. Bacon suggested that complete descriptions of all of the relevant facts about the crafts, "histories," would provide information about nature and additionally enable students of nature to improve craft production. In the mid-seventeenth century, during the Commonwealth, the Continental reformer and educator Samuel Hartlib (ca. 1600–1662) continued the project; he attracted several men to carry out the program. Hartlib's program stressed social improvements as well as scientific aspects. In 1660, when the Royal Society of London formed, several founding members continued, under the society's auspices, the work that they had begun with Hartlib. History of Trades activists argued that since the project would improve English economic life, government should support the Royal Society. By the time of the "Glorious Revolution" of 1688, when the Protestant King William III and Queen Mary II were brought to the English throne, the program was in decline, partly because its social aspects had became a liability. The Royal Society ceased to collect, record, and publish the histories. The program was already in decline well before the Glorious Revolution for a variety of reasons: the inadequacies of seventeenth-century science and the limitations in Bacon's program, the preference of members of the society to remain in London, their inability to do cooperative work, the differing interests of new members, the reluctance of artisans to reveal trade secrets, and class distinctions between the artisans and society members. The program produced some histories and gathered much empirical data useful to scientists. The goal of improving manufactures took more time; it was not until the nineteenth century that college-educated engineers used science-based methods to provide consumer goods.

Several authors of histories and activists in the program had been directly or indirectly associated with Hartlib, including John Beale (1603–1683), Robert Boyle (1627–1691), John Evelyn (1620–1706), Robert Hooke (1653–1702), Christopher Merrett (1614–1695), Henry Oldenburg (ca. 1619–1677), and William Petty (1623–1687). Only Robert Moray (1608–1673) was not so connected. The men, and their allies outside London, covered many topics during the forty years they were active: wool and silk textile production, textile dyeing, leather processing, building and shipbuilding, mining and ferrous-metals production, the substitution of coal for charcoal, glassmaking, printing and papermaking, mechanical devices, a wide variety of industrial chemicals, salt production, soap making, and agriculture and food production, including brewing. At least 12 percent of the entries in the official record, the *Philosophical Transactions of the Royal Society of London,* were related to trades topics during the society's first twenty-three years (excluding agriculture, navigation, and other topics not related to industrial crafts, although they were part of the original project's design).

The society initiated the program by asking Christopher Merrett to create a catalog of all possible histories. Even before the official catalog was developed, members investigated topics that interested them. They also conducted systematic experiments, privately and collectively. Questions were given to travelers. The partial or complete histories were recorded in the *Record Books,* the *Letter Books,* and the *Philosophical Transactions.*

The program resulted in two published histories, many shorter histories included as parts of books, and manuscripts in the society's collections. The socially oriented project to increase cider production was not successfully implemented. The program did collect facts helpful for the development of science; Roy Porter (1997) argues, for example, that geology benefited from the program. Finally, Hooke's observations of program-related experiments may have helped him develop the law named after him—Hooke's Law, which states that the ratio of stress to strain is always the same for any one material.

The program's class implications are clear. One society propagandist, Thomas Sprat (1635–1713), following Boyle, argued that artisans should cooperate because study would improve their craft's technology. However, artisans apparently remained unwilling to part with trade secrets. Sprat continued that, if artisans did not reveal their secrets to researchers, scientists would discover them unaided and put the artisans out of business.

An interesting, and as yet uninvestigated, aspect of the program is its gender implications. Several scholars have studied the impact that the Scientific Revolution had on women both as subjects of knowledge and as scientists. For example, as gynecological knowledge became "scientific," women ceased to be midwives, while men became obstetricians. How the History of Trades program—as part of the history of the transfer of knowledge from artisans to engineers—affected women's roles in industrial production is as yet unclear.

BIBLIOGRAPHY

Houghton, Walter E., Jr. "The History of Trades: Its Relation to Seventeenth Century Thought." *Journal of the History of Ideas* 2 (1941), 3–60.

Ochs, Kathleen. The Failed Revolution in Applied Science: Studies of Industry by Members of the Royal Society of London, 1660–1688." Ph.D. diss. University of Toronto, 1981.

———. "The Royal Society of London's History of Trades Programme: An Early Episode in Applied Science." *Notes and Records of the Royal Society of London* 39 (1985), 129–158.

Porter, Roy. *The Making of Geology.* Cambridge: Cambridge University Press, 1977.

KATHLEEN H. OCHS

See also Baconianism; Hartlib, Samuel

Hobbes, Thomas (1588–1679)

English philosopher, best known for his political theory, but also closely involved with developments in the Scientific Revolution. Hobbes was sent to Oxford's Magdalen Hall at the age of fourteen and took the degree of B.A. in 1608. He then entered into the service of William Cavendish (1555–1526), who would become the first earl of Devonshire in 1618. Hobbes was little impressed with the state of learning at Oxford—he later described the university as entirely under the sway of the Aristotelian philosophy, and he had little interest in or contact with the "new philosophy" when he took his degree.

As tutor and companion to William Cavendish's son (also named William), in 1614–1615 Hobbes toured the Continent, where he apparently came to understand how widely the "school philosophy" was held in contempt by progressive thinkers on the Continent. He joined the service of Sir Gervase Clifton (1587–1666), whose son he accompanied to the Continent (1629–1630). In the course of his journey, Hobbes reportedly came across a copy of Euclid's (fl. 300 B.C.E.) *Elements* and was so fascinated by the deductive structure of geometry that he acquired a passion for mathematics and a desire to develop a philosophical system *more geometrico.*

Hobbes returned to the service of the Cavendish family in 1631 as a tutor to the third earl of Devonshire (1617–1684). During the 1630s, he pursued his scientific interests, particularly in optics. The leading idea in Hobbes's optical theory is that light is motion propagated through a uniformly dense ethereal medium by the

Thomas Hobbes. From A. Wolf, A History of Science, Technology, and Philosophy in the Sixteenth and Seventeenth Centuries *(London: Allen and Unwin, 1935).*

dilation and contraction of the luminous body. Hobbes denied the possibility of a vacuum, and his "mediumistic" optics seeks to explain light as a specific kind of motion, without supposing a "corpuscularian" theory that assumes atoms and a void.

Hobbes's contacts with the scientific community were greatly fostered by his connection with the Cavendish family. It is through this connection that Hobbes and Francis Bacon (1561–1626) became acquainted. This acquaintance eventually led to Hobbes's brief service as a kind of secretary to Bacon, which involved taking dictation and helping with the Latin translation of Bacon's *Essays*.

In 1634 Hobbes made his third Continental tour. This sojourn lasted more than two years and included two prolonged stays in Paris, where he became familiar with the network of scientists grouped around Marin Mersenne (1588–1648) that included René Descartes (1596–1650), Gilles Personne de Roberval (1602–1675), Kenelm Digby (1603–1665), and Pierre Gassendi (1592–1655). Legend even has it that Hobbes met Galileo Galilei (1564–1642) during this third trip to the Continent and was inspired to pursue the goal of presenting moral and political philosophy in the form of a rigorously geometric method.

By the time he returned to England in 1636, Hobbes was committed to a philosophical vision that entailed the rejection of Scholasticism and its replacement by a thoroughgoing materialism that regarded all phenomena of nature as produced by motion. He also came to deny (after 1648) the possibility of a vacuum and advocated a "plenist" physics, which held that apparently empty space is really filled with a subtle ether. In the late 1630s, Hobbes wrote a treatise on optics that contained an extensive critique of Descartes's optical theory, notwithstanding the fact that they both held broadly similar theories of light. Although this particular Hobbesian treatise remained in manuscript, the ideas in it were aired in an acrimonious correspondence with Descartes (1640–1641). Mersenne would later publish a version of Hobbes's optics in his 1644 *Cogita physico-mathematica*.

Hobbes's research into natural philosophy was interrupted by political events in England, specifically the conflict between Charles I and Parliament over the extent of royal authority. Hobbes composed his brief treatise *The Elements of Law* (1650), which purported to derive the necessity of absolute sovereign power from first principles. These principles were psychological tenets concerning human motivation, from which Hobbes argued that conflict can be avoided only by the imposition of unchallengeable sovereign authority. He combined this political theory with a purely mechanistic account of human physiology rooted in his materialistic metaphysics.

Fearing Parliamentary censure for his adamantly pro-Royalist stance in *The Elements of Law*, in late 1640 Hobbes returned to France, where he would remain for nearly eleven years. He immediately resumed his contacts with the Mersenne circle and returned to the task of working out a comprehensive treatment of his philosophical system. He had by this time acquired a considerable reputation as a natural philosopher and metaphysician and was asked by Mersenne to contribute a set of "Objections" to Descartes's *Meditations* (1641). These, together with five other sets of objections and Descartes's replies, were published in 1641.

As the English Civil War (1642–1646) raged on and the Court of Charles I assumed exile in Paris, Hobbes worked steadily on a projected tripartite system of philosophy that would include treatises on the nature of body (*De corpore*), man (*De homine*), and the citizen (*De cive*). The treatise *De cive*, although the third in the projected order, appeared in 1642 as a remodeled version of the argument from *The Elements of Law*. His passion for mathematics remained unabated, and he was appointed tutor in mathematics to the Prince of Wales (the future Charles II) in 1646.

With the defeat of the Royalist cause and the execution of Charles I, Hobbes's thoughts again turned to politics. He composed his masterpiece, *Leviathan*, in 1650, recasting his earlier arguments for the necessity of absolute sovereign power and including both a statement of his materialism and a number of inflammatory anticlerical passages. *Leviathan* was published in 1651, and it made life difficult for Hobbes in Paris. It angered the exiled Court of Charles II (by implying that submission to a victorious faction in a civil conflict is both lawful and rational), and his harsh denunciation of the Catholic Church angered the French clergy. He therefore returned to England at the end of 1651.

By this time, Hobbes possessed a substantial reputation as natural philosopher, but it was based on little published work. His *Leviathan* had, however, made him notorious as a materialist, a presumed atheist, and an enemy of the Church. He intended to secure his scientific credentials with the publication of *De corpore*, which included an exposition of the foundations of his physics and attempts to prove many long-sought mathematical results, including the squaring of the circle. When *De corpore* appeared in 1655, John Wallis (1616–1703) immediately published a book refuting its mathematical claims, while Seth Ward (1617–1689) denounced Hobbesian physics and metaphysics in a publication of his own. Hobbes thus became involved in a long-running dispute with Wallis and Ward, which lasted until his death in 1679. In the course of this controversy, and another with Robert Boyle (1627–1691) concerning pneumatics, Hobbes's scientific reputation was demolished, and he became a bitter adversary of the Royal Society.

BIBLIOGRAPHY

Brandt, Frithiof. *Thomas Hobbes' Mechanical Conception of Nature.* Copenhagen: Levin and Munksgaard, 1928.

Shapin, Steven, and Simon Schaffer. *Leviathan and the Air-Pump: Hobbes, Boyle, and the Experimental Life.* Princeton, NJ: Princeton University Press, 1985.

Sorell, Tom. "Arguments of the Philosophers." In *Hobbes,* ed. Tom Sorell. London and New York: Routledge and Kegan Paul, 1986.

———, ed. *The Cambridge Companion to Hobbes.* Cambridge: Cambridge University Press, 1996.

Spragens, Thomas A. *The Politics of Motion: The World of Thomas Hobbes.* Lexington, KY: University Press of Kentucky, 1973.

DOUGLAS M. JESSEPH

See also Light Transmission; Mersenne, Marin; Void

Hooke, Robert (1635–1703)

A leading member of the scientific movement in seventeenth-century England. As a youth he displayed great mechanical ingenuity and soon became one of the leading experimentalists of his age. His first employment was as assistant to Robert Boyle (1627–1691), with whom he made celebrated investigations on the "spring of air" with the air pump. The discovery of Boyle's Law owed much to Hooke, who actually devised the pump.

In 1662 Hooke was appointed curator of experiments to the Royal Society, charged with conducting experiments for the edification of Fellows at their weekly meetings. Following the death of Henry Oldenburg (ca. 1619–1677), with whom Hooke had difficult personal relations, Hooke was appointed secretary of the society in 1677. From 1664 he had served as Gresham Professor of Geometry and Cutlerian Lecturer in Mechanics.

Besides being an exceptional experimentalist, Hooke made significant theoretical and practical contributions to many fields of science, including astronomy, mechanics, chemistry, physiology, geology, optics, psychology, music theory, microscopy, and horology. He also did much architectural work, assisting in the rebuilding of London after the Great Fire of 1666.

Hooke was of "gentle birth," but not wealthy. He was willing to associate with tradesmen, and, in keeping with his Baconianism, he thought that scholars could learn much from artisans; under his urging, the early Royal Society sought to collect and compile information from such sources. While Hooke was a collector of information, his experimentalism was always prominent, and he was a strong advocate of the use of instruments as aids to observation and research.

Early in his career, Hooke toyed with the idea of there being a kind of algorithmic method for prosecuting

H

Lectiones Cutlerianæ,

OR A

COLLECTION

OF

LECTURES:

PHYSICAL,
MECHANICAL,
GEOGRAPHICAL,
&
ASTRONOMICAL.

Made before the *Royal Society* on several Occasions at GRESHAM Colledge.

To which are added divers

MISCELLANEOUS DISCOURSES.

By *ROBERT HOOKE,* S.R.S.

LONDON:

Printed for *John Martyn* Printer to the *Royal Society,* at the Bell in S. *Pauls* Church-yard. 1679.

Publication of some of Hooke's presentations to the Royal Society.

scientific inquiries. But as time went on, he gave up the notion of there being a universally successful general procedure. What he had proposed, however, was essentially a kind of hypothetico-deductivism.

In traditional historiography of science, one of the features of the Scientific Revolution was that it saw the end of magic, occult forces, incorporeal substances, notions of sympathy and antipathy, and the like as explanatory concepts. As a mechanical philosopher, Hooke might well be thought to exemplify this trend. He believed that the most intelligible forms of scientific explanation were mechanical: the world was to be understood in terms of the mechanical interactions of minute hypothetical corpuscles. The two grand explanatory principles for science were matter and motion.

But recent work by, for example, John Henry (1989), has challenged this view. Henry contends that Hooke made use of notions such as active principles and ethers of various kinds and that his scientific/experimental method was directed toward investigating hidden or occult powers by means of their effects. There was, Henry suggests, a continuation of the tradition of "natural magic" in Hooke's work.

However, such interpretations of Hooke have been contested by Mark Ehrlich (1995), who has reasserted the traditional historiography. For Henry, when Hooke used such terms as *congruity* and *incongruity,* these had meaning similar to the older terms *sympathy* and *antipathy.* But, Ehrlich argues, the question of whether or not materials mingled (were "*congruent*") with one another was taken by Hooke to depend on fundamentally mechanical properties, such as the shapes and motions of the constituent particles. The revisionism of writers such as Henry has not, then, been universally accepted.

As a theoretician and an experimentalist in mechanics, Hooke is particularly known for his generalization concerning the behavior of springs (applicable also to stretched strings), namely Hooke's Law, which he expressed in 1678 as: "*Ut tensio sic vis,*" or "The 'power' of [any spring] is in the same proportion as its tension." This generalization emerged from Hooke's investigations of springs in relation to watches, which went back to 1660. Other of Hooke's important mechanical inventions included the universal joint, the clock-driven telescope, the iris diaphragm for telescopes, and (probably) the anchor escapement.

Through much of his career Hooke wrestled with problems concerning gravity and the elliptical orbits of planets. It was Hooke who gave Isaac Newton (1642–1727) the idea regarding the motion of a planet as being compounded of two motions: (1) inertial, in a straight line, and (2) directed toward the Sun. Hooke speculated on the force for the centrally directed motion being inversely proportional to the square of the distance between the planet and the Sun. But he did not have the mathematical ability to show that the laws of planetary motion (Kepler's Laws) were congruent with an inverse-square law of gravity. When Newton later published a proof of this, Hooke, unfortunately, claimed that Newton's demonstration was dependent on ideas derived from Hooke. This led to regrettable conflict between Hooke and Newton.

There were several other disputes during Hooke's career. There was, for example, a fight with Henry Oldenburg about the work on watch springs (Hooke was plagiarized by the secretary of the Royal Society). There was an earlier dispute with Newton about work on optics. And there were claims that Hooke's geological ideas were partly purloined by the Dane Niels Stensen (1638–1686). There was also an acrimonious squabble with the Polish astronomer Johannes Hevelius (1611–1687) about the relative merits of instrument-aided and naked-eye observations in astronomy. Hooke was evidently willing to engage in controversy. But he was ill treated by several of his peers, and it might be said that he was only standing up for his rights, as he saw them.

Hooke's claims regarding refraction were based on ideas expressed in his remarkable *Micrographia* (1665), which gave an illustrated account of his investigations with the microscope, along with thoughts about scientific method. According to Hooke's theory of refraction, red and blue are primary colors while the others are "dilutions" of these. As light entered a new medium, its "orbicular pulse" in the ether supposedly became oblique to the direction of propagation, instead of perpendicular, and the color supposedly arose from the differences in motion between such pulses and that of the adjacent matter. This was a speculative, essentially qualitative, hypothesis, of a kind often proposed in the early years of the Scientific Revolution.

Also in the *Micrographia,* Hooke developed a prescient theory of combustion, according to which air was "the universal dissolvent" for "sulphureous" (inflammable) bodies. Further, the "dissolution" was brought about by a substance "inherent, and mixt with the Air" similar to "that which is fixt in *Salt-peter.*" The process of "dissolution" was again thought to be mechanical, in keeping with Hooke's general philosophy.

Also in line with his mechanistic views, Hooke envisaged a speculative theory of mind and memory, according to which the very material of the brain was shaped mechanically, receiving "impressions" as a result of stimulation of the sense organs. These impressions were supposedly stored in the head and could be looked over by the soul as memories are recovered. Since the impressions might slowly lose their form, information could be forgotten.

Hooke proposed one of his most creative ideas in geology. He correctly supposed that the earth's rotating envelope of water was spheroidal. So, he thought, waters would be deeper nearer the equator. But in addition to the earth's daily, annual, and precessional motions, Hooke postulated a motion of the poles, such that parts of the earth's surface near the equator might move poleward, and vice versa. Thus, there would be cyclic changes, with land successively moving out of the oceans and undergoing erosion, while other parts sank beneath the oceans, receiving thereby deposits of sediment. Then, thinking that animal forms might change over time (a protoevolutionary idea), Hooke thought there might be a recognizable record of such changes in the earth's strata.

The theory accounted for the presence of fossils far from the sea. It might account for volcanoes and earthquakes—as parts of the earth's crust underwent changing stresses according to the shifts in latitude. And the theory might be tested by looking for slow changes in the directions of meridians, ascertainable by careful astronomical observation. Hooke used this example to exemplify his ideas on scientific method.

In the event, Hooke never carried out the necessary astronomical observations over an extended time period, and the idea was for long forgotten. Moreover, his ideas were thought unacceptable by his contemporaries, since biblical history did not seem to support the kinds of secular changes that Hooke envisaged. In response, he spent much time looking through the mythological writings of the ancients for evidence in support of his theory. His efforts did not convince his contemporaries.

Such was the tragedy of Hooke's career. He tried to do too much, and with insufficient "carry-through," to become a scientist of first rank. Much of his thinking was speculative, and the linkage between mathematics and observation/experiment that Newton achieved lay

beyond Hooke. But, as a man epitomizing the Scientific Revolution, he was almost without equal. His philosophy of matter, his work for scientific institutions, his experimentalism and inventive capacity, his recognition of the great importance of the practical application of knowledge, his fondness for the informal exchange of ideas (typically in coffeehouses), and his piety were found to different degrees in many of his contemporaries. But hardly anyone combined them all in one frenetic life.

BIBLIOGRAPHY

Drake, Ellen T. *Restless Genius: Robert Hooke and His Earthly Thoughts.* New York and Oxford: Oxford University Press, 1996.

Ehrlich, Mark E. "Mechanism and Activity in the Scientific Revolution: The Case of Robert Hooke." *Annals of Science* 52 (1995), 127–151.

'Espinasse, Margaret. *Robert Hooke.* Berkeley and Los Angeles: University of California Press; London: William Heinemann, 1956.

Henry, John. "Robert Hooke, the Incongruous Mechanist." In *Robert Hooke: New Studies,* ed. Michael Hunter and Simon Schaffer. Woodbridge: Boydell, 1989, pp. 149–180.

Oldroyd, David R. "Robert Hooke's Methodology of Science as Exemplified in His Discourse of Earthquakes." *British Journal for the History of Science* 6 (1972), 109–130.

Westfall, Richard S. "Hooke and the Law of Universal Gravitation." *British Journal for the History of Science* 3 (1967) 245–261.

DAVID OLDROYD

See also Air Pump; Attraction; Color; Geology/Mineralogy; Horology; Mechanical Philosophy; Royal Society of London; Theories of the Earth

Horology

The science that deals with the construction of instruments to measure time. During the period of the Scientific Revolution, these consisted of nonmechanical timekeepers: clepsydra, sandglasses, sundials and nocturnals (astronomical instruments for determining the hour at night), and mechanical clocks and watches. Clepsydra and sandglasses were generally used to measure short time intervals, and portable sundials provided a cheaper alternative to watches. Fixed sundials and nocturnals served the same purpose as clocks but were also necessary to correct the cumulative error of mechanical timepieces, which was of the order of fifteen minutes per day up to the middle of the seventeenth century. The demand for precision timekeepers by astronomers, cartographers, and navigators (who needed them to locate stellar and terrestrial objects) provided the incentive for the introduction of the pendulum clock and the balance spring watch during the third quarter of the seventeenth century. The resulting dramatic improvement in accuracy made the pendulum clock a viable tool for the astronomer, but portable timekeepers required further development during the eighteenth century before they were able to meet the needs of cartographers and navigators.

Despite the improvements in mechanical timekeepers, nonmechanical timekeepers continued to be important; sandglasses, for example, were essential for use at sea to determine the distance that had been covered on a particular course (*dead reckoning*). At the end of each four-hour watch, the distance was computed from an estimate of the speed of the vessel during the watch. Sandglasses of half-hour duration were used to time the watch, and smaller sandglasses of half-minute duration were used with a "log" to determine the speed. The log consisted of a piece of shaped wood attached to a line that was knotted at fixed intervals. A seaman cast the log over the stern of the vessel and measured the speed by the number of knots that slipped through his fingers while the sandglass was running. Clepsydra, although similar in principle to sandglasses, were very little used for time measurement in the West, although Tycho Brahe (1546–1601) claimed to have measured the time interval between star transits with a mercury clepsydra. By the sixteenth century, almost all of the standard types of sundial had been established, but, after the introduction of the pendulum clock, a change of design was necessary to improve the precision with which they displayed the time. The improved accuracy of the pendulum clock also revealed the difference between sun time and clock time, the former being less regular. Both Christiaan Huygens (1629–1695) and John Flamsteed (1646–1719) prepared tables that gave the difference between apparent solar time and mean solar time throughout the year (*equation of time*). Meridian dials, which only indicated noon, offered a more accurate way of setting clocks, and later the shape of the noon line was drawn so that local mean time could be read directly without recourse to tables. Time at night could be determined from the position of the stars, using a nocturnal, and this had the advantage that the equation of time was not involved. Astronomers would, of course, be able to set their clocks to sidereal time far more accurately by observing star transits.

Prior to the introduction of the pendulum clock, the timekeeping element in clocks and watches had remained virtually unchanged since the first mechanical clocks appeared in the thirteenth century. It consisted of either a bar with adjustable weights at its end (*foliot*) or a wheel (*balance*), which was made to oscillate by a force provided by a weight or a spring. This force, which alternated in direction, was applied to the foliot or the balance by means of a mechanism known as a *verge escapement*. The escapement also allowed the clockwork train to advance by a discrete amount with each swing of the oscillating element, effectively measuring time by counting the number of oscillations. Unfortunately, this arrangement had no natural frequency of oscillation, the period of oscillation being dependent on the driving force. Although the force produced by the weight was constant, variations occurred as it was transmitted through the train of gears to the foliot or balance. The first attempts to improve timekeeping tried to alleviate this effect rather than adopt the more radical approach of using an oscillator with a natural frequency. This culminated in the clocks that Joost Bürgi (1552–1632) made for use in the observatory of Landgrave William IV (1532–1592) of Hesse, which indicated seconds and, according to contemporary evidence, had an accuracy of about a minute per day. The friction in the train of gears was reduced by improving the shape of the teeth; this was done empirically, but in the seventeenth century the correct epicyclic form was derived mathematically. Bürgi's great innovation was the *remontoire*, which bypassed the train of gears and applied the force directly to the oscillating element. These clocks also had a novel cross-beat escapement with two coupled foliots moving in opposition, but this probably had only a small effect on the timekeeping, which owed more to Bürgi's superb craftsmanship. Although these clocks were used by the landgrave to compile his star atlas, very few similar clocks were made, and the long-term solution lay in the use of an oscillator with a natural period of oscillation.

Such an oscillator existed in a free-swinging pendulum, which Galileo Galilei (1564–1642) had already used to time astronomical events, such as the eclipses of the satellites of Jupiter, first observed in 1610. However, this was an exceedingly tedious process as the oscillations had to be maintained and counted manually, and it

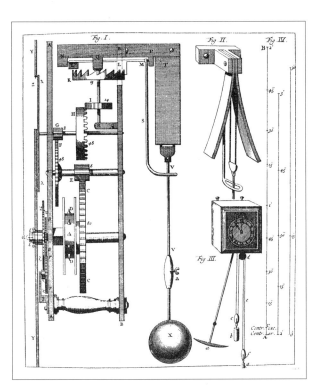

Christiaan Huygens's diagram of his pendulum clock with its cycloidal cheeks, from his Horologium oscillatorium *(1658).*

was not immediately obvious how the process could be automated by using the pendulum to control a clock. Toward the end of his life, Galileo described such a mechanism to his son Vincenzio, but the model had not been completed when the son died in 1649. Galileo's model used a novel form of escapement, but a much simpler approach was used by Huygens, who was unaware of Galileo's work. On Christmas Day 1656, he modified an existing spring-driven table clock so that the verge escapement was impulsed and controlled by a pendulum. This produced a dramatic improvement in timekeeping, reducing the error from minutes to seconds a day. The time lost while the clock was being wound now became important, and, in his *Horologium* of 1658, Huygens illustrates an ingenious mechanism (maintaining power) that ensured that the weight still drove the clock even when it was being rewound. Galileo and Huygens were aware that the pendulum was not truly isochronous because it took slightly longer to swing through a large arc than a small one: the so-called *circular error*. Galileo thought that this was due to the friction of the air, but Huygens had deduced that it was because the pendulum bob moved in a circular arc. In his *Horologium,* Huygens

proposed to minimize this effect by inserting a reduction gear between the escapement and the pendulum so that the arc of the pendulum was reduced. However, because of increased friction, this was not a practical solution, and, having deduced that the path of the pendulum should be cycloidal if it was to be truly isochronous, Huygens achieved this in a very elegant manner by fitting cycloidal cheeks to the pendulum suspension. These cheeks proved to be less than satisfactory in practice as they could introduce greater errors if the clock was not mounted absolutely vertically. The solution lay in reducing the arc through which the pendulum swung, as Huygens had suggested earlier, but this was achieved by using a new escapement rather than the method he had proposed. This was the *anchor,* or *recoil, escapement,* which was introduced in England ca. 1670, although it is not clear who was the inventor. A near-contemporary account gives the honor to William Clement, and, although this was contested by Robert Hooke (1635–1703), there is little evidence to support his claim. The earliest surviving example of the escapement is in a turret clock made in 1670 by Joseph Knibb (1640–1711) for Wadham College, Oxford.

A weight-driven clock with an anchor escapement and a seconds pendulum then became the standard timepiece for use in both the home and the observatory. It had an accuracy of about ten seconds a day, but two serious sources of error remained. The first arose from the anchor escapement, which interfered with the free motion of the pendulum and was, therefore, detrimental to good timekeeping. In fact, at the end of its swing, the pendulum momentarily drove the clock in reverse as implied by its alternative title of the recoil escapement. Thomas Tompion (1639–1713) attempted to overcome this defect in the clocks he made for the Royal Observatory at Greenwich in 1676. Although these clocks enabled Flamsteed to prove that the earth rotated at a constant speed (an application of the pendulum clock that Huygens had suggested in his *Horologium*), they were not entirely successful, and the problem was solved only in the eighteenth century with the introduction of George Graham's (ca. 1674–1751) dead-beat escapement. The other major source of error was the change in the length of the pendulum rod that occurred when the temperature changed. This was barely acknowledged in the seventeenth century; even Huygens refuted Gottfried Wendelin's (1580–1667) assertion that the oscillations of a pendulum were faster in winter than in summer, and he never accepted that the length of the pendulum was temperature dependent. The temperature compensation of pendulums, therefore, had to wait until early in the next century.

Ever since Reiner Gemma Frisius (1508–1555), in his *De principiis astronomiae cosmographicae* of 1530, had suggested that a clock might be used to determine longitude, it had been a powerful stimulus to horological development, and the potential financial rewards increased as trade with the New World and the Indies expanded. Huygens hoped that his pendulum clock would offer a solution to this problem, and he devoted much time to devising ingenious ways of ensuring that the motion of the ship did not affect the motion of the pendulum, without success. From his earlier work on the pendulum, he was aware of the conditions necessary for an oscillating system to be isochronous; in 1675 this enabled him to make the balance of a watch approximately isochronous, by controlling its oscillations with a spiral spring. When he attempted to obtain a patent for his invention in England, Robert Hooke immediately claimed priority. Hooke had experimented with the application of springs to a balance during the 1660s, and a watch with such a device had been constructed. However, when he failed to secure the promise of what he regarded as an adequate financial reward, Hooke made only a partial revelation of his invention. There is, therefore, some doubt about the shape of the spring and whether it produced an isochronous balance, and his watch does not appear to have been successful. Although the application of the balance spring resulted in a great improvement in the timekeeping of watches, it was still insufficient to fulfill the very stringent requirement of a longitude timekeeper. Huygens lost interest in it as a solution to the longitude problem when it became apparent that its timekeeping was very susceptible to temperature changes, which could not be corrected at that time. It did, however, lay the basis for the development of the marine chronometer and the successful solution to the longitude problem in the next century.

BIBLIOGRAPHY

Baillie, G. H. *Clocks and Watches: An Historical Bibliography.* London: NAG, 1951.

Hall, A. Rupert. "Horology and Criticism: Robert Hooke." In *Science and History: Studies in Honor of Edward Rosen,* ed. Erna Hilfstein, Pawel Czartoryski, and Frank D. Grande.

(Studia Copernicana 16). Wrocław: Ossolineum, 1978, pp. 261–281.

Huygens, Christiaan. *Horologium* (1658). Trans. E. L. Edwardes. In *The Story of the Pendulum Clock.* Altrincham, England: Sherratt, 1977.

Huygens, Christiaan. *Horologium oscillatorium* (1673). Trans. Richard J. Blackwell. Ames: Iowa State University Press, 1986.

Landes, David S. *Revolution in Time: Clocks and the Making of the Modern World.* Cambridge, MA: Harvard University Press, 1983.

Leopold, J. H. "L'invention par Christiaan Huygens du ressort spiral réglant pour les montres." In *Huygens et la France.* Paris: Vrin, 1981, pp. 154–157.

DENYS VAUGHAN

See also Automata; Clockwork Universe; Hooke, Robert; Huygens, Christiaan; Time

Horrocks, Jeremiah (1618–1641)

An astronomer who championed Keplerian astronomy before it was accepted by most astronomers, he made notable contributions of his own during his short life. He corrected the parameters for Johannes Kepler's tables—the best extant—improving them considerably and enabling him to be the first to predict and observe a transit of Venus. His lunar theory yielded the most accurate predictions up to that time and provided the basis for Isaac Newton's (1642–1727).

Horrocks was born in Toxteth Park, a village three miles from Liverpool. He attended Cambridge University, where, self-taught, he quickly mastered the fundamentals of the discipline and acquainted himself with the works of the most important astronomers, notably Ptolemy (ca. 100–170), Nicolaus Copernicus (1473–1543), and Tycho Brahe (1546–1601). Upon his return to Toxteth Park, he actively pursued an intensive program of observation with angle-measuring instruments of his own construction and two telescopes he purchased. He soon befriended William Crabtree, residing near Manchester, who introduced him to the works of Kepler (1571–1630). In the summer of 1639, Horrocks gained employment (its nature unknown) with the most prominent family in Hoole, a village twenty miles north of Liverpool, where he resided for a year. He then returned to Toxteth Park and continued his observations and revisions of the drafts of treatises he intended to publish on his discoveries and in support of Keplerian astronomy.

Horrocks was a keen observer, always concerned to test and improve his methods. He continually revised his earlier data and corrected subsequent observations as he became aware of distorting effects caused by his instruments, the weather, atmospheric refraction, and other sources. He adopted a practice, becoming increasingly common in the first half of the seventeenth century, of comparing several tables based on different systems—Ptolemaic, Copernican, Tychonic, and Keplerian—with his own observations of celestial phenomena. It was this, among other factors, that led him to conclude that Keplerian astronomy represented the true system of the universe.

He accepted Kepler's fundamental ideas on planetary motion: that the Sun lies in the planes of all of the elliptical planetary orbits and is the cause of the motions of the planets, that the planets move more rapidly in proximity to the Sun and more slowly the more distant from it, and that the squares of the planetary periods are proportional to the cubes of their mean distances from the Sun (Kepler's third law). He disagreed, however, with Kepler's quasi-magnetic solar forces and speculated instead on other means involving mechanical analogies on the causes of planetary motion.

Among the important results of his careful observations were his verification of Kepler's third law and—together with a dash of speculation involving harmonics—a radical change in the figure for solar parallax (the angle at the Sun subtending the radius of the earth), thereby yielding more accurate data for predicting planetary positions and extending considerably the distance of the solar system from the stars. His observation of the transit of Venus—the passage of Venus across the face of the Sun, which occurs alternately every 121.5 and eight years—in the fall of 1639 led to further revisions in his figures for solar parallax and a number of planetary parameters.

Horrocks's lunar theory, as did Kepler's, had the Moon moving in an elliptical orbit, but Horrocks surpassed Kepler in accounting for the complex inequalities in the Moon's motion. He achieved this by providing a varying distance between the earth and the center of the Moon's orbit and an oscillation of the line passing through the earth from the Moon's minimum and maximum distances, while the mean position of that line slowly rotated. He hinted that a physical relationship among Sun, Moon, and Earth might explain the numerous lunar inequalities.

JEREMIÆ HORROCCII, LIVERPOLIENSIS ANGLI, ex Palatinatu LANCASTRIÆ, OPERA POSTHUMA; viz. Astronomia *Kepleriana*, defensa & promota. Excerpta ex Epistolis ad *Crabtræum* suum. Observationum Cœlestium Catalogus. Lunæ Theoria nova.

Accedunt
GUILIELMI CRABTRÆI, *Mancestriensis*, Observationes Cœlestes.

In calce adjiciuntur
JOHANNIS FLAMSTEDII, *Derbiensis*, De Temporis Æquatione Diatriba. Numeri ad Lunæ Theoriam *Horroccianam*.

LONDINI,
Typis GULIELMI GODBID, Impensis J. MARTYN Regalis Societatis Typographi, ad insigne Campanæ in Cœmeterio D. *Pauli*, Anno Domini M.DC.LXXIII.

Title page of Horrocks's posthumously published manuscripts.

Horrocks's manuscript of his transit observation was published in 1662 by Johannes Hevelius (1611–1687) and much of the rest a decade later by the Royal Society of London.

BIBLIOGRAPHY

Applebaum, Wilbur. "Between Kepler and Newton: The Celestial Dynamics of Jeremiah Horrocks." *Proceedings of the Thirteenth International Congress of the History of Science, Moscow, August 18–24, 1972.* 7 vols. Moscow: 1974, vol. 4, pp. 292–299.

Gaythorpe, Sydney B. "Horrocks's Observation of the Transit of Venus 1639 November 24 (O.S.)." *Journal of the British Astronomical Association* 47 (1936), 60–68; 64 (1954), 309–315.

Wilson, Curtis. "Horrocks, Harmonies, and the Exactitude of Kepler's Third Law." In *Studia Copernicana XVI: Science and History: Studies in Honor of Edward Rosen,* ed. Erna Hilfstein, Pawel Czartoryski, and Frank D. Grande. Wrocław: Ossolineum, 1978, pp. 235–259.

———. "On the Origin of Horrocks's Lunar Theory." *Journal for the History of Astronomy* 18 (1987), 77–94.

WILBUR APPLEBAUM

See also Astronomical Tables and Ephemerides; Cosmic Dimensions; Kepler, Johannes; Keplerianism

Humanism

This educational and cultural movement developed in the urban centers of Italy and northern Europe from the fourteenth to the seventeenth centuries. Humanists often served as secretaries, notaries, and diplomats for princes and republics. They devoted themselves to what they called the *studia humanitatis,* comprising history, grammar, rhetoric, poetry, and moral philosophy. They greatly admired the ancients and realized with a newly developed sense of history that antiquity was an era profoundly different from their own. They attempted to reinstate ancient, usually Ciceronian, Latin in place of what they considered the barbarisms of medieval Latin. From the early fifteenth century, they also began to learn Greek. Avidly searching for the writings of the ancients, they found many manuscript copies of known works, as well as works that had been unknown to medieval scholars. They edited, translated, and retranslated many of these ancient texts.

The humanists advocated an active life in opposition to the medieval ideal of contemplation. They favored particular forms of writing, especially the dialogue and the letter. Criticizing the Scholasticism of the universities, they claimed that the schoolmen used texts that had been corrupted by the errors of medieval copyists. They also disparaged the Scholastic emphasis on Aristotelian logic and philosophy. Instead, they stressed rhetoric and grammar—necessary tools to persuade humans to the good life and (especially in the early fifteenth century) to the good civic life.

Historians have assessed the influence of the humanists upon early-modern science in terms that have ranged from highly negative judgments to (more recently) an appreciation for humanist influence accompanied by detailed specific investigations. In the early twentieth century, Pierre Duhem (1861–1916) developed a thesis of continuity between the fourteenth-century Parisian nominalists and the mechanics of Galileo Galilei (1564–1642). Yet, Duhem disregarded the humanist culture that was intrinsic to Galileo's milieu. Early historians of medieval science, such as Anneliese Maier (1905–1971) and Charles Homer Haskins (1870–1937), ignored the humanists as not relevant to their medieval focus. Other scholars investigating the connections between medieval and seventeenth-century thought, such as Lynn Thorndike (1882–1965) and John H. Randall, Jr. (1899–1980), derided the humanists as shallow, ignorant men

whose work was irrelevant to the development of science. More recently, the positive contributions of the humanists have been recognized and investigated in detail.

The most important figure associated with the founding of humanism is Francesco Petrarch (1304–1374). Petrarch's substantial, complex literary output includes numerous letters and epistolary tracts (including an invective against Scholasticism), Latin and vernacular poetry, and essays. Petrarch admired Cicero (106–43 B.C.E.) and cultivated Ciceronian Latin. He condemned the Scholastics for their excessive reliance on the authority of Aristotle (384–322 B.C.E.). Articulating the conflict between a contemplative life and an active one, Petrarch longed for a peaceful, unified Italy and placed his hopes successively in the popular tyrant of Rome Cola di Rienzo (1313–1354), the Holy Roman Emperor Charles IV (1316–1378), and various rulers of the Italian territorial states. Petrarch's interest in governance is evident in his essay on good government addressed to Francesco Carrara of Padua (1325–1393). Among much other advice, Petrarch urges Carrara to drain the swamps near the city, to build walls, and to stop herds of pigs from running through the streets. Such admonitions exemplify the fundamental interest of the humanists in political praxis that included practical and technical issues of urban administration.

The humanist movement has often been described exclusively in terms of its literary and educational achievements. Yet, the humanists concerned themselves with political and ethical matters, and they served patrons who ruled city-states and territories. These merchant oligarchs and princes also patronized the visual and constructive arts, thereby contributing to their political legitimacy and status by transforming public and private space. They accomplished this by the construction of palaces, loggias, and other major buildings, by ornamentation with painting and sculpture, and by the consumption of luxury items. The patronage system promoted stylistic changes in sculpture, painting, and architecture that were inspired by classical motifs and by Pythagorean proportional systems. The humanists were by no means passive bystanders in this development. Visual and architectural transformations occurred in civic and courtly arenas in which artisan-practitioners, engineers, and learned humanists worked in close proximity, shared common patronage, and influenced one another.

Humanists played an important role in bringing the mechanical arts into closer proximity to the learned disciplines, including natural philosophy and mathematics. For example, the early-fifteenth-century development of artist's perspective involved the bringing together of the learned discipline of optics with the "mechanical" art of painting. Linear perspective creates the illusion of a three-dimensional space on a flat surface by means of geometric techniques. Although the circumstances of its invention are not entirely known, an important contributor was the architect-engineer Filippo Brunelleschi (1377–1446), who may have been influenced by the learned Paolo Toscanelli (1397–1482). Artist's perspective also may have been influenced by the study of projective techniques discussed by Claudius Ptolemy (ca. 100–ca. 170) in the *Geographia,* a second-century text carried to Florence in 1400 by the teacher of Greek Manuel Chrysolaras (ca. 1350–1414). In the 1430s, Leon Battista Alberti (1404–1472), one of the most important humanists of the fifteenth century, wrote treatises on painting and sculpture. Alberti knew the major artists working in Florence and explicated his own version of linear perspective. He elevated the status of the "mechanical art" of painting by making it mathematical and by treating its principles in writing.

Ca. 1450, the work of three men—Alberti, Nicholas of Cusa (1401–1464), and Roberto Valturio (1405–1475)—exemplifies the convergence of learning, political praxis, and technology within humanist culture. Alberti and the humanist Pope Nicholas V (1397–1455) worked together to redesign the city of Rome. During the same period, Alberti wrote his treatise on architecture, *De re aedificatoria,* a masterpiece indebted to the *De architectura* of the Roman architect Vitruvius (fl. 20s B.C.E.) but also highly original. Alberti based architecture on principles of proportionate design, grounded it in material construction, and placed it emphatically within the ethical world of civic society. About the same time, the humanist Cardinal Nicholas of Cusa wrote *Idiota: De sapientia, De mente, De staticis experimentis,* in which he suggests that wisdom can be found in the streets and marketplace, where ordinary weighing and measuring occur. Cusa presents an untutored maker of spoons and pots, the *idiota,* as an exemplary figure for a learned orator and a philosopher seeking wisdom. In a third example, Roberto Valturio, at the bequest of his patron Sigismund Malatesta of Rimini (1417–1468), wrote a learned military treatise, *Elenchus et index rerum mili-*

tarum, based on the extensive compilation of ancient writings. Yet, unlike most ancient military authors, Valturio combined a discussion of strategy and military leadership with an extensive treatment of military technology, both ancient and contemporary.

The university education of the humanists diverged sharply from the workshop training of artisans. Yet, in the fifteenth century for the first time, artisan-practitioners wrote a significant number of treatises on the arts that they practiced. Often dedicating their books to patrons that they shared with the humanists, practitioners, including Antonio Averlino called Filarete (ca. 1400–1469), Leonardo da Vinci (1452–1519), and Francesco di Giorgio (1439–1502), wrote books on sculpture, architecture, painting, machines and mechanics, fortification, gunpowder, artillery, and other aspects of the military arts. Practitioner authorship was inspired by humanist writings such as those of Alberti and could not have developed as it did without humanist models.

Printing greatly increased the production of all kinds of books, including those on technical subjects. Printed books on architecture, navigation, the visual arts, mining and metallurgy, pottery, and the military arts proliferated. Taking into account the writing, illustration, book production, and readership, such authorship often involved collaboration among humanists, patrons, and practitioners.

Humanists frequently associated themselves with the new presses, including that of the humanist scholar-printer Aldus Manutius (ca. 1450–1515). For example, Georgius Agricola (1494–1555), author of a famous treatise on mining and ore processing (*De re metallica,* 1556), spent several years at the Aldine press before returning to Germany to work as a physician and prolific author. In *De re metallica,* Agricola advocated openness and clarity of expression. He developed a Latin technical vocabulary for mining and metallurgy and included a defense of mining based on the Roman author Columella's (fl. first century) defense of agriculture.

The significance of humanist technical authorship extends beyond the particular topics treated because it brought together categories that previously had been separated. Aristotle had distinguished *techne* (technical production), *praxis* (political and military action), and *episteme* (knowledge of unchanging things) and had insisted that categories should be analyzed on their own terms. For Aristotle and many of his successors in the early-modern period, to analyze aspects of *physics* was to inquire into the causes of phenomena in the natural world. To apply mathematical analysis to local motion (an aspect of physics) would involve a category mistake. Moreover, Greek mathematics was conceived as an abstract, not an applied, topic. In general, as Aristotelianism was incorporated into the curricula of medieval universities, natural philosophy tended to maintain its separation from the mechanical arts and from mathematics as well. Before Galileo could apply extended mathematical analysis to physical phenomena, as he did in his foundational work in mechanics, the *Two New Sciences* (1638), it was necessary that the separation between mathematics and physics be eliminated and that the distance between the mechanical arts and learned discourse be narrowed. Although there are also important medieval precedents, humanist and practitioner-authored technical literature played an important role in bringing together previously separated categories.

Humanist influence on the study of mechanics is particularly evident in the sixteenth century. As W. R. Laird has shown, one aspect of this work was the study of the Pseudo-Aristotelian *Mechanical Problems,* an ancient text rediscovered by humanists. The first translators were humanist philosophers such as Alessandro Piccolomini (1508–1579). Subsequent humanist-trained scholars who worked on the text included Guidobaldo del Monte (1545–1607), who published his *Liber mechanicorum* in 1577, and Giuseppe Moletti (1531–1588), who lectured on the *Mechanical Problems* at the University of Padua. Sixteenth-century interest in mechanics also developed from practical problems, such as the aiming of cannon (including the study of the projectile motion of cannonballs) and the strength of materials. Galileo, who participated in this discourse about mechanics, finally succeeded in incorporating Archimedean statics into a mechanics of moving weights. Humanist investigations and textual work brought particular mechanical problems under sustained study and helped change mechanics from a manual art to a mathematical and philosophical discipline.

Humanist study of ancient texts is better described as critical and creative appropriation than slavish imitation. This can be seen in what Paul Lawrence Rose (1975) describes as the Renaissance recovery of Greek mathematics. The humanists discovered and/or edited the texts of Euclid (fl. ca. 300 B.C.E.), Apollonius (fl. second half of the third century B.C.E.), Archimedes (ca. 287–212 B.C.E.), and Pappus (fl. 320), among others.

They found unknown texts and created new editions and translations. For example, the Latin translations of Federigo Commandino (1509–1575) included the works of Euclid, Apollonius, Archimedes, and Aristarchus (fl. first half of the third century B.C.E.). Commandino's fluency in Greek and his mathematical skill allowed him to elucidate passages that for centuries had been garbled by copyists. Humanist textual work provided mathematicians with techniques beyond those of the Middle Ages and created the basis for the rapid development of mathematics in the seventeenth century.

Mathematics was relevant to disciplines such as astronomy and was studied by humanists who had wide literary and scholarly interests. For example, Georg Peurbach (1423–1461), an important early humanist and mathematician from Vienna, wrote and lectured on the Latin poets and on rhetoric and oratory, in addition to his mathematical and astronomical pursuits. Peurbach was persuaded by Cardinal Johannes Bessarion (ca. 1403–1472) to write an epitome of Ptolemy's *Almagest* for university classroom use. Bessarion, whose native language was Greek, zealously worked to increase the transmission of Greek learning to the West. At his urging, Peuerbach began an intensive study and summary of the *Almagest,* a text with which he was thoroughly familiar despite his lack of Greek.

After Peurbach's premature death at the age of thirty-six, his student Johannes Regiomontanus (1436–1476) continued this work. Regiomontanus, who had studied both astronomy and mathematics and had mastered Greek, was able to study the Greek original of the *Almagest* and to compare Greek manuscripts. He pointed out discrepancies between observations (such as the size of the Moon at the perigee of the epicycle) and Ptolemy's account. The *Epitome Almagesti Ptolemaei,* a product of humanist collaboration, remained the most important work on Ptolemaic astronomy until the time of Johannes Kepler (1571–1630) and Galileo.

At the University of Padua, a student of Regiomontanus, Domenico Maria de Novara (1454–1504), became the astronomy teacher of Nicolaus Copernicus (1473–1543). Copernicus owned a copy of the *Epitome* and was intrigued by the discrepancies there noted between Ptolemy's statements and observational data. Robert S. Westman (1990) has emphasized that Copernicus was profoundly influenced by humanism—that he learned Greek, translated Greek poetry, and participated in an appreciation for the visual arts, perhaps painting his own portrait. Copernicus's elaboration of a heliocentric cosmological system was influenced by the humanist mathematical astronomers who preceded him, as well as by the humanist revitalization of Platonism.

A key figure in the revival of Platonism is Marsilio Ficino (1433–1499), who was appointed by Cosimo de' Medici (1389–1464) to be the head of the new Florentine Platonic Academy. Ficino's translations included the dialogues of Plato (ca. 428–348 B.C.E.) and a group of third-century writings known as the *Hermetic Corpus* that were believed to have been written by an Egyptian, Hermes Trismegistus, who lived before Moses. Ficino's widespread influence and the resulting enthusiasm for Platonism encouraged the view that the cosmos was essentially mathematical. Hermetic writings pointed to sun worship and a Sun-centered universe. The significance of Renaissance Platonism can be seen in the work of Johannes Kepler, who was not only the best mathematical astronomer of his generation but was also a Platonist who believed that his discovery of the five regular solids situated between the planets was as important as his explication of the laws of planetary motion.

The significance of humanist textual work is evident in many different areas. For example, the humanist discovery of *On the Nature of Things* by the Roman Epicurean Lucretius (99–55 B.C.E.) influenced the development of seventeenth-century corpuscularianism. A second example involves the *Naturalis historia* by Pliny the Elder (23–79). Humanists began the study of Pliny's *Natural History* with attempts to establish accurate readings for the complicated, corrupt text. They ended, however, by criticizing his confused terminology concerning medicinal and botanical information—confusions that had negative implications for actual medical practice. This progression of scholarship—from attempts to establish an accurate text to critiques of that text on the basis of fresh observation and study—was characteristic of humanist work on other ancient texts of natural philosophy as well.

Independent treatises on subjects such as botany and anatomy suggest a similar development from intensive study of ancient texts to critical assessments that include considerations derived from direct observation. In both anatomy and botany, moreover, the interaction of visual artists and humanists is of crucial importance. Karen Reeds (1991) has shown that humanist-illustrated herbals such as that of Otto Brunfels (ca. 1489–1534) displayed a new interest in the observation of plants and

their accurate description. In related disciplines, the humanist study of both the Hippocratic corpus (a group of ancient medical writings) and the writings of the physician Galen (second century) furthered the development of early-modern anatomy and medicine. In anatomy, Leonardo da Vinci's extensive anatomical drawings began with an interest in observational accuracy. But Leonardo also studied Galen with the help of a humanist professor of anatomy at Pavia, Marc Antonio della Torre (ca. 1480–1511). Della Torre wanted to replace traditional university medical texts with those of Galen. For his part, Leonardo attempted to correlate his observations of actual bodies and body parts with some of the precepts of Galen. In the mid-sixteenth century, Andreas Vesalius (1514–1564), who was also a careful student of Galen, published his famous illustrated *De humani corporis fabrica*. Vesalius's own observations caused him to reject some, but by no means all, of Galen's views.

The humanists made important contributions to specific disciplines such as botany and astronomy by means of their philological work of comparing manuscripts and establishing texts and through their translations and commentaries. However, they also contributed to methodological shifts that produced an emphasis on observation, experiment, and mathematics. Peter Dear has explored the seventeenth-century conflict between the use of experience in Aristotelian natural philosophy (common experience upon which everyone agrees without question) and the use of experiment (constructed experience using specialized apparatus and requiring expert evaluation). The experimentalism that allowed generalizations from very particular constructed experiences was preceded by two centuries of humanist culture in which individual particular experience was given central importance and used to exemplify and validate broader general truths. Lisa Jardine (1988) has emphasized the development of a humanist logic or dialectic in which compelling argumentation for probable conclusions (a process indebted to rhetoric) took precedence over the formal logical procedures endorsed by the Scholastics. Humanist dialectic also influenced scientific argumentation in the seventeenth century. Ann Blair (1992) has studied the growth of humanist encyclopedism and its interest in collecting multifarious interesting "facts." Natural philosophy in the seventeenth century was not a unified conceptual entity. It was characterized by numerous methodological debates and conflicts, to which humanism made significant contributions.

Humanism affected specific disciplines and methodologies in complex and various ways, the more so given its growing authority within the universities during the sixteenth century. Humanism should not be seen as starkly in contrast to a petrified Scholasticism but, rather, as a cultural movement in a state of creative interaction with a Scholasticism that was also changing and developing during the same time period. The humanists' appropriation of texts from the past, and their creative use of that material to develop new points of view, might also be said to characterize the work of the canonical figures of the Scientific Revolution as well, most of whom were beneficiaries of humanist culture.

BIBLIOGRAPHY

Blair, Ann, and Anthony Grafton, eds. "Reassessing Humanism and Science." *Journal of the History of Ideas* 53 (1992), 535–584.

Field, J. V., and Frank A. J. L. James, eds. *Renaissance and Revolution: Humanists, Scholars, Craftsmen, and Natural Philosophers in Early Modern Europe.* Cambridge: Cambridge University Press. 1993.

Jardine, Lisa. "Humanistic Logic." In *The Cambridge History of Renaissance Philosophy,* ed. Charles B. Schmitt and Quentin Skinner. Cambridge: Cambridge University Press, 1988, pp. 173–198.

Kraye, Jill, ed. *The Cambridge Companion to Renaissance Humanism.* Cambridge: Cambridge University Press, 1996.

Kristeller, Paul O. *Renaissance Thought,* vol. 1: *The Classic, Scholastic, and Humanist Strains,* vol. 2: *Papers on Humanism and the Arts.* New York: Harper and Row, 1961–1965.

Long, Pamela O. "Humanism and Science." In *Renaissance Humanism: Foundations, Forms, and Legacy,* vol. 3: *Humanism and the Disciplines,* ed. Albert Rabil, Jr. Philadelphia: University of Pennsylvania Press, 1988, pp. 486–512.

Nauert, Charles G., Jr. "Humanists, Scientists, and Pliny: Changing Approaches to a Classical Author." *American Historical Review* 84 (1979), 72–85.

Reeds, Karen Meier. *Botany in Medieval and Renaissance Universities.* New York: Garland, 1991.

Rose, Paul Lawrence. *The Italian Renaissance of Mathematics: Studies on Humanists and Mathematicians from Petrarch to Galileo.* Geneva: Librairie Droz, 1975.

Westman, Robert S. "Proof, Poetics, and Patronage: Copernicus's Preface to *De revolutionibus.*" In *Reappraisals of the Scientific Revolution,* ed. David C. Lindberg and Robert S. Westman. Cambridge: Cambridge University Press, 1990.

PAMELA O. LONG

See also Art; Craftsman-and-Scholar Thesis; Encyclopedias; Neoplatonism; Printing; Translations

Humors

The notion of the four humors and its conflation into a formal theory often termed *humoral pathology* began in the speculations of the pre-Socratic philosophers. Empedocles (ca. 492–ca. 432 B.C.E.) maintained that human beings, as well as the physical universe, were composed exclusively of four principle elements: earth, air, fire, and water. Health resulted from the harmony of the elements, and disease from their disturbance. One of Empedocles's disciples added the idea that each of the four elements possessed a distinctive quality: fire with heat; earth, cold; water, moisture; and air, dryness.

The theory of the four humors was likely first advanced by the author of the Hippocratic treatise *Of the Nature of Man,* composed no later than 400 B.C.E. According to his theory, four humors—blood, yellow bile, black bile, and phlegm—were always present in the human body and determined its relative health or illness. Moreover, this author also hypothesized links between the humors, the qualities, the elements, and even the seasons into a doctrine of humoralism that was maintained for more than two thousand years.

In the second century, Galen (second century) molded these concepts into a comprehensive theory of medicine. Galen believed that food and drink consisted of the basic elements, which, through the process of digestion, were transformed into the four humors, or, as he termed them, the "daughters of the elements." Each humor corresponded to an element as well as to two qualities. Blood was considered hot and wet and corresponded to air; yellow bile was hot and dry and corresponded to fire; black bile was cold and dry, a symbol of earth; and phlegm, cold and wet, related to water. Generally, illness was thought to result from an imbalance of the humors. Such an imbalance was caused when one humor dominated, or was lacking, in comparison to the other three. As treatment of one such an imbalance, foods or drinks opposing in form but equal in strength to the dominant humor were prescribed. Other treatments that aimed at correcting humoral imbalance included bleeding and the use of emetics. Thus, the humors played a major role in the early development of the diagnosis and treatment of illness.

External factors such as occupation, heredity, climate, season of the year, age, and position of astronomical bodies affected the dominance of humors in the body.

Furthermore, an individual's habits could also influence his or her natural complexion or disposition, which might be described as sanguine, phlegmatic, choleric, or melancholic.

Having studied and absorbed the work of the sixteenth-century anatomists and philosophers, Paracelsus (ca. 1491–1541) launched an attack on humoral pathology that would ultimately destroy it. He rejected the traditional four elements and denied the ancillary system of the humors. He described physiological functions in chemical terms, thus rejecting the idea of health as a balance of the humors. Illness was no longer held to result from an imbalance of bodily fluids but was localized and believed to be basically chemical in origin. Thoughout the later sixteenth century, important thinkers strove to integrate Paracelsian ideas into conventional medicine. Despite these efforts, however, humoralism remained deeply rooted in the thought and practice of many.

A definitive break from the humoral theory occurred, however, when Johannes Baptista van Helmont (1579–1644) denied Galen's humoral theory entirely. Believing strictly in a chemical approach to medicine, he made every effort to prove that the body's general health was not the result of humoral balance. He did not advocate integration of the old and the new ideas but strove to completely eliminate the teaching of the humors. His endeavors eventually led to the repudiation of humoral theory.

Though eclipsed by the chemical theory introduced by Paracelsus, the theory of the humors was integral to the ensuing revolution in medical and scientific thought. Humoralism served as the ancient and increasingly fragmented foundation from which several ideas regarding the cause of illness and treatment of disease germinated. The controversy that arose as a result of the attack on this essential theory, which is generally thought to have been initiated by Paracelsus, was eventually to produce a genuine revolution that led to the acceptance of a universe essentially chemical in nature and operation.

BIBLIOGRAPHY

Debus, Allen. *The Chemical Philosophy.* New York: Science History Publications, 1977.

Dols, Michael W. "Introduction." *Medieval Islamic Medicine: Ibn Ridwan's Treatise On the Prevention of Bodily Ills in Egypt.* Berkeley and Los Angeles: University of California Press, 1984.

Klibansky, Raymond, Erwin Panofsky, and Fritz Saxl. *Saturn and Melancholy: Studies in the History of Natural Philosophy, Religion, and Art.* New York: Basic Books, 1964.

YNEZ V. O'NEILL

See also Etiology; Galenism; Helmont, Johannes Baptista van; Paracelsus

Huygens, Christiaan (1629–1695)

In the 1660s, the fame of this Dutchman was so great that he was hired by Louis XIV to lead the newly formed Académie Royale des Sciences in Paris. At the same time, he was elected the first foreign member of the Royal Society of London. Little recognized today, Huygens was a transitional figure whose primary achievements were subsumed by later developments; thus, his contributions tend to be underreported or even assigned to other, more famous names. Yet, Huygens was one of the founders of modern science, particularly mathematical physics.

In his early treatises, Huygens absorbed and responded to the mathematics of Archimedes (ca. 287–212 B.C.E.). *De iis quae liquido supernatant* (1650), which he never published, extends Archimedes's treatment of floating geometrical bodies to other shapes. *Theoremata de quadratura hyperboles* (1651) emulates Archimedean techniques for relating areas under curves to their centers of gravity; its appendix is a critique of James Gregory's (1638–1675) proof that the circle cannot be squared (that is, in modern terminology, pi is not rational). *De circuli magnitudine inventa* (1654) is a more advanced method for approximating pi using inscribed and circumscribed circles; its appendix contains solutions to famous classical problems. By imitating the ancient master, Huygens himself became a master of Greek mathematical methods.

René Descartes (1596–1650) was another major figure who influenced the young Huygens. Descartes had been a personal friend of his father, who took a keen, though amateur, interest in scientific matters. While at the University of Leiden, Huygens studied with Frans van Schooten (ca. 1615–1660), the major promoter of Cartesian mathematics, in which geometrical problems were solved using algebraic symbols (analytic geometry) and of which Huygens also became a master. Like many young thinkers at the time, Huygens was attracted to Cartesian physics, especially its paring down of the

Christiaan Huygens. From volume VII of Oeuvres complètes de Christiaan Huygens *(1888–1950).*

universe to a few causal principles involving matter in motion. Throughout his life, he accepted this framework as an adequate basis for explanations of the natural world, although he certainly differed with particulars of Cartesianism.

Another of his father's friendships, with Marin Mersenne (1588–1648) in Paris, brought Huygens his first international contacts and encouraged his study of the third great influence on his work, Galileo Galilei (1564–1642). When he was seventeen, he was already so confident of his abilities that he sent Mersenne his refutation of Galileo's claim that the catenary is a parabola. Their correspondence ended with Mersenne's death two years later, but the French scientific community remained interested in his work and welcomed him when he came visiting in 1655. One fashionable subject in Paris at the time was the mathematics of predicting outcomes of games of chance, which led to the creation of the theory of probability by Blaise Pascal (1623–1662) and Pierre de Fermat (1601–1665). Characteristically, Huygens returned home and developed his own independent theory, centered on the concept of expectation (*Van rekeningh in spelen van geluck,* 1657).

By his late twenties, Huygens had focused on the topics that would dominate his mature research: the

mathematics of light, the laws of motion, and the development of instruments. These areas of interest were not independent in his work but intersected in creative ways.

In 1653 he began a study of the refraction of light in lenses that he continually supplemented (e.g., by including aberration) but never published, although he provided for a posthumous edition of his *Dioptrica* in his will. Concomitantly, he and his brother built their own machines for grinding telescopic lenses and eventually cowrote instructions on how to build an accurate machine, also published posthumously. With one of their early telescopes, Huygens discovered Saturn's largest moon, Titan, and observed Saturn's changing profile, from which he correctly theorized that it was surrounded by a ring (*Systema Saturnium,* 1659). During his residency in Paris, he turned his attention to the phenomenon of double refraction, which he explained by a wave theory of light (*Traité de la lumière,* 1690). In what is now called Huygens's Principle, each point on a wave front is the center of a weak secondary wave, and the resulting new wave front is the curve (envelope) that is tangent to all of those secondary waves. Huygens also maintained that the speed of light is finite. In his treatise on light, Huygens justifies the probable certainty of his results by appealing to a hypothetico-deductive method.

His studies on motion began in the 1650s with an analysis and refutation of Descartes's rules of impact. Huygens developed his own rules regarding the collision of bodies (*De motu corporum ex percussione*), which he eventually published in abbreviated notices to London and Paris in 1669. Fundamental to all of his work on motion was his belief in its relativity, that there is no privileged, absolute frame of reference. In 1659 an unsatisfactory attempt to measure the constant of gravitational acceleration experimentally prompted Huygens to try a mathematical analysis instead. *Horologium oscillatorium* (1673), his greatest work and one of the few published in his lifetime, presents the results, which include a proof of the isochronism of the cycloid, a theory of companion curves called *evolutes,* the description of a pendulum clock that embodies these mathematical discoveries, an analysis of the compound pendulum, as well as an accurate value for the constant. In the final chapter, Huygens lists propositions concerning related mathematical work on circular motion; the proofs appeared posthumously under the title *De vi centrifuga.* During his tenure at the Académie Royale des Sciences, Huygens tried to provide a mechanical explanation of gravity using a modified vortex theory, which he later revised and published as an appendix to his treatise on light (*Discours de la cause de la pesanteur*, 1690).

Huygens had a talent for improving upon a technological invention by substantially revising its design, which often led to priority disputes with other designers. In 1656 he created the first accurate clock driven by a pendulum; in 1658 he published a description of its design; and by 1659 his personal pendulum clocks (both free swinging and cycloidal) were accurate to within seconds. Thus, he could be said to have given science its most important tool, precise timekeeping. He also attempted, with variable success, to replicate at sea the accuracy of his clocks in order to solve the pressing problem of determining the longitude of ships. Although he created an improved spiral spring watch and used springs in some of his seagoing clocks, he usually relied on exotic variations of the isochronous pendulum to guarantee precision. A visit to London in 1661 introduced him to the air pump newly created by Robert Boyle (1627–1691) and Robert Hooke 1635–1703). A few months after his return home, he was reporting back on discoveries made with his own improved model. Likewise, he and his father took an early interest in Antoni van Leeuwenhoek's (1632–1723) microscopes, and he was soon making observations of his own.

In the last decade of his life, Huygens was overtaken by the new generation. Because his own techniques had always yielded solutions to the challenge problems out of which the calculus grew, he was slow to recognize the power of the new mathematics, even though Gottfried Wilhelm Leibniz (1646–1716) pressed for his approval. On the other hand, he readily accepted that Isaac Newton (1642–1727) had decimated much of the Cartesian system in his *Principia mathematica philosophiae naturalis* (1687) and tried to salvage what he considered essential.

Unlike Descartes or Leibniz, Huygens did not attempt to structure his discoveries into an integrated system. Nor did a search for God in nature inspire him as it did Robert Boyle (1627–1691) and Newton. Instead, he focused on limited problems with definable parameters and achievable solutions. Of all of his contemporaries, Huygens was the most startlingly modern in attitude.

BIBLIOGRAPHY

Bell, A. E. *Christian Huygens and the Development of Science in the Seventeenth Century*. London: Arnold, 1947.

Bos, H. J. M., et al. *Studies on Christiaan Huygens: Invited Papers from the Symposium on the Life and Work of Christiaan Huygens, Amsterdam, 22-25 August 1979*. Lisse: Swets and Zeitlinger, 1980.

Huygens, Christiaan. *Oeuvres complètes de Christiaan Huygens, publiées par la Société Hollandaise des Sciences*. Ed. by a Committee of Dutch Scholars. 22 vols. The Hague: Nijhoff, 1888–1950.

Shapiro, Alan E. "Kinematic Optics: A Study of the Wave Theory of Light in the Seventeenth Century." *Archive for History of Exact Sciences* 11 (1973), 134–266.

Taton, René. "Introduction." *Huygens et la France: Table ronde du Centre National de la Recherche Scientifique, Paris, 27-29 mars 1979*. Paris: Vrin, 1982.

Yoder, Joella G. *Unrolling Time: Christiaan Huygens and the Mathematization of Nature*. Cambridge: Cambridge University Press, 1988.

JOELLA G. YODER

See also Air Pump; Mathematics; Motion; Optics; Pneumatics; Telescopic Astronomy

Hydraulics and Hydrostatics

The gap between Renaissance hydraulic engineering and the mathematical science of fluids that developed two centuries later is so deep that historians, while acknowledging the main developments in hydrostatics, have usually displaced the science of hydraulics to the periphery of the Scientific Revolution. This attitude is scarcely justified. Fifty-six (8.9 percent) of the 631 scientists of the sixteenth and seventeenth centuries that are included in the *Dictionary of Scientific Biography* (1970–1980) were engaged in hydraulic engineering. This percentage rises to almost 50 percent if we consider only the mathematicians born in some geographic areas like the Po Valley in northern Italy.

In this area, the process of reclaiming land for cultivation reached a peak in the second half of the sixteenth century, stimulated by population growth and the rise in grain prices. While land reclamation was carried out by drainage with windmills in Holland, in Italy it was pursued either by canalization or by landfill (thanks to the silt deposited by river water artificially conveyed into marshes and swamps). Both techniques needed suitable river management. For this and other public needs, each town of the Po Valley was provided with a water-management administration. Although the technical expertise involved in these projects required a certain knowledge of practical mathematics, the technical staff received little or no mathematical education. Even though experts in water management like Rafael Bombelli (1526–ca. 1572) were to win their renown as mathematicians, their commitment to land-reclamation schemes and their mathematical research remained largely unrelated. The two fields slowly converged, however. In the late Renaissance, mathematics became fashionable at Court, attracted princes and courtiers, and found its way into the engineering profession. For example, Giambattista Aleotti (1546–1636), besides reclaiming marshes and defending the territory of Ferrara from floods, translated Hero's *Pneumatica* into Italian and wrote for the benefit of his profession the *Hidrologia*. This work, if published, would have been the first modern treatise on hydraulics.

The links between the engineering and the mathematical professions in the field of water management were strongly favored by the Archimedean revival in hydrostatics. In 1543 Niccolò Tartaglia (ca. 1499–1557) published a Latin translation of Book I of Archimedes's (ca. 287–212 B.C.E.) *On Floating Bodies*. It was followed in 1551 by Tartaglia's Italian translation of it and in 1565 by Federico Commandino's (1509–1579) Latin version of Books I and II. In 1586 the first real improvement on Archimedes's hydrostatics was achieved by Simon Stevin (1548–1620). In *De beghinselen des waterwichts,* the Flemish mathematician was able to explain the hydrostatic paradox by evaluating the force exerted by superincumbent water on a plane surface of whatever orientation.

Tartaglia's and Stevin's works emphasize the manifold facets of the Renaissance engineering profession. While Tartaglia was granted a privilege for his *Travagliata inventione* (1551), a new salvage technique based on Archimedean principles, Stevin acted as a military engineer and applied his hydrostatic skills in the service of the Dutch army. A nice example is his discussion *Vande vlietende topswaerheyt* (1605), in which he dealt with the problem of the stable equilibrium of assault boats equipped with ladders employed by soldiers for storming ramparts.

In spite of the emergence of the professional mathematician specialized in hydraulics, early in the seventeenth century the science of moving water was not yet born. Even if the contents of Leonardo da Vinci's (1452–1519) notebooks, filled as they were with accurate observations and extraordinarily keen intuition on the behavior of water, had been spread throughout the engineering

profession, this would not have been enough to build a new science. The Benedictine monk Benedetto Castelli (ca. 1577–1643), a close friend of Galileo Galilei (1564–1642) and a university lecturer in mathematics at Pisa and Rome, must be credited with opening this new field to the mathematical sciences by applying Galileo's geometry of motion to the case of running water. In Castelli's book *Della misura dell'acque correnti* (On the Mensuration of Running Waters), for the first time, the law of continuity was established in a geometric form as the basic principle of the kinematics of fluids. Its publication in 1628 in Rome was also a move in favor of the town of Bologna in a controversy about the river Reno, which caused strife between the papal towns of Ferrara and Bologna. It is, thus, not coincidental that the first serious criticism of Castelli's formulation of the law of continuity came from the Ferrara Jesuit Niccolò Cabeo (1586–1650), who proposed a physical approach to fluvial hydraulics based on the measurement of the velocity of rivers.

Meanwhile, Evangelista Torricelli (1608–1647) developed the mathematical approach by showing that a jet of water follows the Galilean law of falling bodies. The law of efflux was independently investigated in France and Holland by Marin Mersenne (1588–1648) and René Descartes (1596–1650) and, subsequently, at the Paris Academy of Sciences by Christiaan Huygens (1629–1695) and others. In spite of this, at least until the second edition of Isaac Newton's (1642–1727) *Principia mathematica philosophiae naturalis* (1713), it was far from settled whether or not the actual velocities of the issuing jet and of a falling body were the same. Torricelli and other Galileans had few doubts on this matter. According to their views, the drops issuing from the orifice in a tank actually fall from the free surface of water. By extrapolating this reasoning to the case of rivers, it followed that the current is swifter at the bottom and that the profile of velocities in a given perpendicular of a river has a parabolic shape. Scientists like Edmé Mariotte (ca. 1620–1684) were more cautious. They sought an explanation of the law of efflux by referring to the pressure exerted on the issuing jet and preferred to investigate experimentally the velocities of rivers.

The Torricellian analogy shows a basic incomprehension of the concept of fluid pressure in fluids in motion. Even in hydrostatics, however, the Galileans were not well equipped to grasp this concept. Galileo tried to reduce hydrostatics to statics by means of the

H

Poleni's apparatus to study the efflux of water from conical mouthpieces that modeled the entrance mouth of a flood relief channel. From G. Poleni, De castellis *(1718).*

vanni Poleni (1683–1761), built their academic careers on water management and studied lagoon hydraulics by means of accurate experiments and a consistent use of algebra and differential calculus. The science of hydraulics was changing, and new avenues of research were to develop modeled on Newton's mathematical physics.

BIBLIOGRAPHY

Blay, Michel. "Recherches sur les forces exercées par les fluides en mouvement à l'Académie royale des sciences, 1668–1669." In *Mariotte savant et philosophe.* Paris: Vrin, 1986, pp. 91–124.

Cazzola, Franco. "Le bonifiche nella Valle Padana: Un profilo." *Rivista di storia dell'agricoltura* 27 (1987), 37–66.

Clagett, Marshall. *Archimedes in the Middle Ages.* 3 vols., vol. 3: *The Fate of the Medieval Archimedes, 1300–1565.* Philadelphia: American Philosophical Society, 1978.

Maffioli, Cesare S. *Out of Galileo: The Science of Waters, 1628–1718.* Rotterdam: Erasmus, 1994.

Westfall, Richard S. "Science and Technology During the Scientific Revolution: An Empirical Approach." In *Renaissance and Revolution,* ed. J. V. Field and Frank A. J. L. James. Cambridge: Cambridge University Press, 1993, pp. 63–72.

C. S. MAFFIOLI

See also Pascal, Blaise; Stevin, Simon

Hydrostatics. See Hydraulics and Hydrostatics

Hypothesis

One of the most troubling problems that faced the innovative thinkers whom we identify collectively today as the instigators of the Scientific Revolution was how to deal with hypothetical reasoning. According to a tradition stretching back to Aristotle (384–322 B.C.E.), the ideal to be aimed at in our knowledge of nature is demonstration, a definitive form of causal understanding yielding knowledge that is, in Aristotle's words, "eternal and necessary." The new sciences of the seventeenth century seemed to fall short, in most cases far short, of that. Ought one, then, settle for a lesser standard? Or ought one still try to conform to the demands of the older tradition?

The term *hypothesis* derives from a Greek root meaning "to place under" (hence, the Latin equivalent *su(b)ppositio*), "to put forward," "to postulate." Aristotle distinguishes between different senses of the term, the two most important being an assertion put forward

principle of virtual velocities, and this led him and his disciples astray from the fundamental concept of hydrostatic pressure acting at every point within a liquid independent of direction. However, it was Torricelli who, through his barometric experiment, stimulated Blaise Pascal (1623–1662) to follow a line of research that led to his *Traités de l'équilibre des liqueurs et de la pesanteur de la masse de l'air* (1663), in which the idea of pressure played the central role.

In the 1690s, thanks to Domenico Guglielmini (1655–1710), the science of waters began to be acknowledged as an autonomous university subject. Guglielmini was the superintendent of the waters of Bologna and the first incumbent of the chair of hydrometry of the Bologna Studium. In 1697 he published his *Della natura de' fiumi,* a landmark in river hydraulics, in which he studied the dynamics of forces that modify the shape and the longitudinal profile of riverbeds. Meanwhile, water management became an academic business even in Venice. Lecturers of the Padua Studium, such as Gio-

simply or "absolutely" and one proposed conditionally. The latter he usually signifies by the expression *ex hupothéseos* (in later Latin translation, *ex suppositione*). A strict demonstration requires unconditional premises since it must yield unqualified truth. He distinguishes between two types of demonstration: one that produces "knowledge of the fact" (*hoti, quia*), the other, "knowledge of the reasoned fact" (*dioti, propter quid*). Only the latter yields the sort of causal understanding that is required for science (*episteme*) proper.

It is straightforward to argue deductively from cause to effect. But to argue from effect to cause can be deductive only if all potential causes save one can be eliminated. And this will rarely be possible. In modern parlance, effects ordinarily underdetermine their causes.

One further feature of Aristotle's system also influenced the status given hypothetical reasoning. He explained the motions of the planets by postulating a complex of concentric carrier spheres moving uniformly about the earth. The main merit of this proposal was that it allowed one to understand *how* the planets moved. When Ptolemy (ca. 100–ca. 170) later proposed a scheme that would more accurately "save the phenomena" (i.e., account for the positions of the planets, which were observed to move with nonuniform motion and at varying distances from the earth), he abandoned the concentric spheres for a much more complicated geometrical combination of epicycles and equants. The two systems were obviously not physically compatible with each other. Each appealed to a different virtue: causal explanation in one case, and saving the phenomena in the other. Generations of natural philosophers struggled with this issue. A favored response was that a *causal* ("physical") account ought to be given priority if *truth* were in question, whereas a "mathematical" model could be preferred if one's aim were the practical one of accurate prediction. And the term *hypothesis* was customarily used for this latter sort of construction. It conveyed the notion of a postulate that was useful for practical purposes but that made no claim on truth or even on likelihood, since it did not appeal to the physical natures of the entities involved.

It was in this sense that Andreas Osiander, in his celebrated Introduction to Nicolaus Copernicus's (1473–1543) *De revolutionibus* (1543), asserted that the "hypotheses" of the heliocentric model are not to be taken as true or even probable; they are calculational devices, no more than that. The true causes of the planetary motions lie outside the reach of the mathematical astronomer. This was the reading of Copernicus's book that Johannes Kepler (1571–1630) set out to oppose. In his unpublished *Apologia pro Tychone contra Ursum* (1600), he responded to the charge that an astronomy that was mathematical in form could do no more than save the appearances. Saving the appearances, he allowed, is not enough to establish the reality of the postulated planetary motions. But if the hypothesis can also *explain* what the rival account can only postulate in an ad hoc way (the exact one-year periodicity of one of the components of each planetary motion, for example), and if, furthermore, the hypothesis continues to incorporate the observed phenomena successfully, one can eventually and appropriately come to assert its truth. False hypotheses, he suggests, must ultimately betray themselves. In his *Astronomia nova* (1609), he refines this argument further. To convert a mere saving of the appearances into a true account of planetary motions requires a physical explanation of those motions in terms of their causes. The discovery of the elliptical shape of the orbit of Mars, announced in this work, allows him to formulate at least the beginnings of such an explanation.

When Cardinal Robert Bellarmine (1542–1621) advised Paolo Antonio Foscarini and Galileo Galilei (1564–1642) in 1615 that it was legitimate for them to propose the Copernican system *ex suppositione* but not "absolutely," he made it clear that he meant that it might save the appearances better than did the eccentrics and epicycles of Ptolemy but that this was not to be taken to give it any standing as a possibly true assertion. It was, in fact, he argued, definitively false, for a series of reasons he proceeds to spell out. In the context of astronomy, at least, the notion of a hypothesis as an instrument of prediction, no more, still lingered. Galileo did not deny, any more than Kepler had done, that saving the phenomena of the apparent planetary motions was not enough for demonstration. But he was convinced that the Copernican system could give "reasons" for the planetary appearances that its rival could not do. And this was one of the things he set out to do in his *Dialogue on the Two Chief World Systems* (1632). But he was never quite sure how to regard knowledge claims that fell short of the status of demonstration. Many readers of his book would have been convinced that the Copernican construction could never be more than a hypothesis in the instrumental sense. Others would have conceded to it the status of hypothesis in the stronger sense of a postulate for which evidence of its truth can be given and which has, in consequence, some degree of likelihood short of certainty. But they would have insisted that anything short of demonstration was not sufficient to secure the Copernican theses against theological objection. Throughout this fateful debate, the ambiguous claim of hypothesis to the status of knowledge was a critical factor.

René Descartes (1596–1650) paid more explicit attention to questions of method than Galileo had done. He was convinced that he could claim certainty for the principles of his mechanics. But in his *Discourse on Method* (1637), he conceded that these principles are so general that they leave open a multiplicity of different possible underlying causes when one is inferring backward from effect to (hidden) cause. The only way, then, to decide on the true cause is to test the different alternatives by drawing inferences from them and checking these against experience. Though this was to legitimate hypothesis and its assessment by the consequences drawn from it, Descartes still retained the older goal of demonstration. In his *Principles of Philosophy* (1644), he keeps stressing that his principles account for all that there is in the world and that it is, thus, impossible that they should be false. Yet, he has to admit that the sizes, shapes, and motions of the imperceptibly small corpuscles on which the properties of the bodies of our everyday experience depend cannot be deduced from the principles. God could have regulated these in an infinity of ways; only experience can tell us, he says, which of these ways he chose. But how? He is vague about this and concludes eventually on a strikingly pragmatic note: even if the postulated configurations are false, as long as they get the effects right, "we shall do as well as if these were the true causes."

Galileo and Descartes were willing to employ hypothesis in their work but evidently retained the hope that science could still aim at something like demonstration. A hypothesis, even if well supported, did not qualify as science proper. Their focus was on mechanics, in which a plausible claim might still be made for the intuitive self-evidence of their axioms. But, with Robert Boyle (1627–1691), a significant shift began. His concerns were not with mechanics but with the underlying structures responsible for such phenomena as chemical change and the behavior of confined gases. He had no illusions about the hypothetical character of the causal claims he was making about such newly postulated entities as the atmosphere. He realized that something other

than the traditional canons of deduction and induction would be needed for the task of assessing hypothesis. In a short, unpublished paper, "The Requisites of a Good Hypothesis," he enumerated six criteria for a "good" hypothesis and four for an "excellent" one. Hypothesis was coming at last to be recognized as a legitimate part of scientific knowledge; the fact that it could not claim certainty would not exclude its possessing epistemic value.

How was that value to be characterized? More a philosopher than a scientist, two professions just beginning to separate, John Locke (1632–1704) took this issue very seriously. In his *Essay Concerning Human Understanding* (1690), he returned to Descartes's puzzle about the quality of our knowledge of the hidden configurations of corpuscles on which the properties of the visible world depend. He was much more pessimistic than Descartes had been, arguing that a "science of bodies" in the traditional sense of science as demonstration was forever out of reach. This is because we cannot come to know the sizes and motions of the corpuscles in an assured way, and, even more serious, we cannot know what the conceptual connections are between these and the properties they are to explain. But another alternative may be open: the acceptance of *probability* as a sufficient goal, though it be "twilight" instead of the broad daylight once hoped for. Hypotheses based on analogy and tested carefully against experiment can yield probable knowledge, the best to which a science of bodies can aspire.

In the same year, Christiaan Huygens (1629–1695) published his *Traité de la lumière* (1690), in which he makes exactly the same point, relating it directly to the optical inquiries in which he had been engaged. In such a science, the assertions made are to be verified indirectly by the consequences drawn from them; this is the only way open, and it admits of "a degree of probability often scarcely less than complete proof." And he notes, as Boyle had done, that the evaluation of hypotheses requires an oblique approach. One has to determine first whether the hypothesis corresponds perfectly to the known phenomena, then whether it applies to a wide variety of phenomena, and, above all, whether it predicts novel phenomena. Taken together, these permit "strong confirmation."

The story so far has been of a gradual, if reluctant, acceptance of the legitimacy of hypothetical reasoning in natural science. With Isaac Newton (1642–1727), however, the story takes a very different turn. From the beginning of his career, he attacked the "conjectures and probabilities" he saw his contemporaries indulging in and sought to construct a science without hypothesis. To do this, both in optics and mechanics, he distinguished between the "mathematical" approach to which he limited himself and a "physical" approach that would, in addition, inquire into underlying causal mechanisms. In this way, he could claim to be deducing directly from the phenomena, needing only to generalize his conclusions by means of a straightforward induction.

His hostility to admitting hypothesis into science proper, expressed in his famous *hypotheses non fingo* ("I feign no hypotheses"), had many sources. One was undoubtedly a matter of temperament: Newton was constitutionally averse to the sort of challenge to which hypothesis is always open. He was impatient with the sort of speculative causal hypotheses that the Cartesians delighted in, which, though perhaps in a broad sense explanatory, were incapable of test. But what may have encouraged him most to believe that he could do without hypothesis in his "finished" science was the peculiarity of optics and mechanics that one could abstract a mathematical formalism directly from the observed behavior of light or the observed motions of planets and bracket further causal questioning. The convenient ambiguity of terms like *attraction* allowed his treatment of planetary motion to *appear* explanatory, yet without any commitment to a specific underlying mechanism.

Yet, of course, he could not cut off further causal questioning. And, in the *Opticks* (1604), he speculated freely about ether-pulses, about corpuscles that attract and repel, about active principles. But he labels all of this as no more than "queries," leaving it to be understood that, at some later time, these "queries" could yield a science of a suitably deductive kind with no taint of hypothesis to mar it. His legacy to later generations was in this regard a deeply divided one: an ideal of science that was as close to the traditional ideal of demonstration as he could make it, yet admitting at the margins a profusion of explanatory mechanisms of the most imaginative kind. It was only with such theorists of science as John Herschel and William Whewell in the nineteenth century that hypothesis finally became domesticated within the structure of natural science proper.

BIBLIOGRAPHY

Farr, James. "The Way of Hypotheses: Locke on Method." *Journal of the History of Ideas* 48 (1987), 51–72.

Kepler, Johannes. *A Defence of Tycho Against Ursus.* In *The Birth of History and Philosophy of Science.* Trans. Nicholas Jardine. Cambridge: Cambridge University Press, 1984, pp. 83–207.

Laudan, Larry. *Science and Hypothesis.* Dordrecht: Reidel, 1981.

McMullin, Ernan. "Conceptions of Science in the Scientific Revolution." In *Reappraisals of the Scientific Revolution,* ed. David C. Lindberg and Robert S. Westman. Cambridge: Cambridge University Press, 1990, pp. 27–92.

Shapiro, Alan. "Hypothesis and the Quest for Certainty." In Shapiro, Alan. *Fits, Passions, and Paroxysms.* Cambridge: Cambridge University Press, 1993, pp. 12–40.

Westfall, R. S. "Unpublished Boyle Papers Relating to Scientific Method." *Annals of Science* 12 (1956), 63–73, 103–117.

ERNAN MCMULLIN

See also Descartes, René; Galileo and the Church; Realism; Resolution and Composition; Theory

I

Iatrochemistry

This "medical chemistry" was developed in the sixteenth century as a new medicine rooted in chemistry. Iatrochemistry viewed biological processes and medical remedies in chemical terms and initially rejected traditional humoral medicine. A synthesis of traditional and chemical medicine occurred in the late sixteenth and early seventeenth centuries as the value of chemical remedies was recognized. By the eighteenth century, iatrochemistry was subsumed by medicine as chemical medical theories developed more accepted medical applications.

Iatrochemistry's genesis in the thought and work of Theophrastus Bombastus of Hohenheim, known as Paracelsus (ca. 1491–1541), determined much of its early history. Paracelsus rejected classical humoral causality in favor of a chemical causality and called a physician using chemistry an *iatrochemist*. He viewed man as a microcosm of the greater world, both functioning on chemical principles. The organs of the body were chemical factories (*archei*), and external forces and materials caused disease when they interfered with the function of the *archei*. Paracelsus believed that alchemy was to be used to make medicaments, not gold, and that chemically prepared medicines contained arcana, active principles, that could restore the *archei* to their proper role of separating poison from nourishment.

The medical-chemical tradition was, in fact, much older than Paracelsus. Alchemical remedies had passed from late antiquity to both the Arab and the Latin worlds. Medieval treatises on alchemy, such as the one attributed to Albertus Magnus (1193–1280), presented methods of chemical preparation. Adepts like Roger Bacon (ca. 1214–ca. 1294) and Arnold de Villanova (ca.

1235–ca. 1313) suggest chemical remedies. Paracelsus's teacher Johannes Trithemius (1462–1516) was an alchemist, magician, and student of medicine. It is likely that seeds of Paracelsus's radical chemical model for medicine came from the tradition taught him by Trithemius.

The New Medicine was presented in the nine authentic books of Paracelsus's *Archidoxis,* written ca. 1526 but not published until 1569. Like the extravagant and egotistical personality of Paracelsus, his theories engendered conflict among medical theorists and practitioners. The debate over the validity of iatrochemistry was fueled in no small measure by Paracelsus's lack of systematic exposition, his use of strange terms to describe physiological and disease processes, and his vituperative attack on classical medicine and its practitioners. However, because he used the well-accepted macrocosm/microcosm analogy and alchemical information, his ideas found a receptive audience.

Although Paracelsus left no disciples, his theories did not lack advocates. Adam von Bodenstein (1528–1577) taught iatrochemistry at the University of Basel. Leonhart Thurneisser zum Thurn (1531–1596) taught Paracelsian chemistry in England, France, Spain, Germany, and Italy, as well as in his native Basel. Paracelsianism was promulgated by several learned and well-published chemists, including Gerard Dorn (fl. 1560–1585), Oswald Crollius (ca. 1560–1609), and Robert Fludd (1574–1637). The expositions of Peter Severinus (1542–1602) and Joseph DuChesne (1544–1609) greatly influenced the acceptance of iatrochemistry. Severinus, physician at the Danish Court, wrote the first systematic iatrochemical text, *Idea medicina* (1571). Presenting the progress of medicine from the ancients to the modern age, he pictured Paracelsus's chemical breakthrough as the culmination of medical knowledge. Before Paracelsus, medicine had been founded on pagan principles; the New Medicine was rooted in Mosaical philosophy and observation of God's great Book of Nature.

DuChesne, a physician in the French Court of Henri IV, battled the Galenists at the University of Paris. His use of chemistry to explain phenomena like respiration (he analogized it to distillation) and his successful use of chemical remedies helped convince some traditionalists, such as Andreas Vesalius's (1514–1564) teacher Johannes Guinter (ca. 1505–1574), to integrate chemical remedies into conventional medicine. DuChesne's associate Theodore Turquet de Mayerne (1573–1655), a Huguenot refugee, popularized chemical medicine in English Court circles. Other chemical physicians advertised and sold chemical medicaments. In Germany, Georg am Wald (1554–1616) lived well by selling his secret concoctions, *Terra sigillata amwaldina* and *Panacea amwaldina*.

Soon after the publication of Paracelsus's work, the theologian-physician Thomas Erastus (Lieber) (1524–1583) challenged iatrochemistry. In his *Disputationum de medicina nova Philippi Paracelsi* (1572–1573), he criticized Paracelsus's character, his confused chemical ideas, and his nonconformist religiosity. Erastus's attack on Paracelsus, however, did not stem the growing popularity of iatrochemistry. Paracelsus's personality, no matter how distasteful, could not indefinitely obscure the value of understanding the chemical nature of physiology and the possible efficacy of chemical remedies. Andreas Libavius (1540–1616), chemist and professor of rhetoric at Jena, bitterly attacked the "bombast" of the "herd" of Paracelsians but defended chemistry and chemical remedies against a proposed ban by the faculty of Paris. By the early seventeenth century, Johannes Baptista van Helmont (1579–1644) had made significant strides in rethinking the theoretical and experimental basis of chemical medicine. His *Ortus medicinae* (1648) reached beyond the medical community, influencing both Robert Boyle (1627–1691) and Isaac Newton (1642–1727).

The work of the major chemical writers of the seventeenth century contributed to the idea that chemistry explains biological functions and that chemical remedies can cure. Daniel Sennert (1572–1637), Franciscus Sylvius (Franz de Le Boë, 1614–1672), Otto Tachenius (fl. 1699), Michael Ettmuller (ca. 1644–1683), Thomas Willis (1621–1675), Johann Rudolf Glauber (1604–1670), John Mayow (1641–1679), and Robert Boyle all drew medical-biological conclusions from their chemical studies. The success of iatrochemistry was further demonstrated by the editing by chemical physicians of official pharmacopoeias. The iatrochemist Raymond Minder (ca. 1570–1621) prepared the 1613 edition of *Pharmacopoeia Augustana,* which specifically authorized *spagyric,* or chemical remedies. The 1618 London *Pharmacopoaeia* was assembled in part by Turquet de Mayerne and gives many chemical formulas.

Chemistry and chemical medicaments were a routine part of medicine by the time the New Philosophy of mechanism, which grew up in the eddy currents of Newton's theories, gave birth to iatromechanism. Iatromechanism accepted the fusion of medicine and chemistry, suggesting mechanical models for chemical processes. The success of chemical medicine, integrated into traditional medicine, two centuries after Paracelsus challenged "pagan" medicine, is evinced by the well-established program of chemical study at Leiden brought to great heights and rigor by Hermann Boerhaave (1668–1738).

BIBLIOGRAPHY

Debus, A. G. *The Chemical Philosophy*. 2 vols. New York: Science History Publications, 1977.

Pagel, Walter. *Paracelsus: An Introduction to Philosophical Medicine in the Era of the Renaissance*. Basel and New York: Karger, 1958.

Partington, J. R. *A History of Chemistry*. 4 vols. London: Macmillan, 1961–1970.

MICHAEL T. WALTON

See also Alchemy; Chemical Philosophy; Galenism; Paracelsus; Pharmacology

Iatromechanics

Iatromechanics is the application of mechanics to medicine. Interest in biomechanical approaches grew during the Scientific Revolution as the older theories of medicine began to be questioned. An early influence for iatromechanics was the work of Santorio Sanctorius (1561–1636). He devised a scale that enabled him to study quantitatively the fluctuations of his body weight as it related to the ingestion of food and the elimination of wastes (i.e., his basal metabolism).

Sanctorius's approach and experiments had a strong effect on the movement toward biomechanism. In France, Denis Dodart (1634–1707) repeated the scale experiments on himself. In Italy, Georgius Baglivi

(1668–1707), also influenced by William Harvey's (1578–1657) mechanical explanation of the blood's circulation, sought to develop a theory concerning fluid circulating in the nerves.

A key member of the Italian iatromechanical school was Giovanni Alfonso Borelli (1608–1679), who applied mechanics to the movement of animals. Under the influence of Borelli, Lorenzo Bellini (1643–1704) rejected Galenic theory as absurd and joined the prevailing mechanical philosophy with physiology. In reaction to Thomas Willis (1621–1675), who had applied Robert Boyle's (1627–1691) corpuscular hypothesis to medical theory, Bellini produced a hydraulic iatromechanism. This initially had a few supporters, such as Johannes Bohn (1640–1718) and Baglivi. Bellini's ideas languished until, stimulated by the interest of Archibald Pitcairn (1652–1713), he organized and systemized them, thereby gaining an international reputation. Pitcairn's "mathematical physick" was influenced heavily by Bellini and somewhat by Isaac Newton (1642–1727). It generated interest in Scotland, especially with James Keill (1673–1719); in England with Stephen Hales (1677–1761); and on the Continent with Hermann Boerhaave (1668–1738). Boerhaave effectively joined the wide variety of iatromechanical theories into a systematic synthesis.

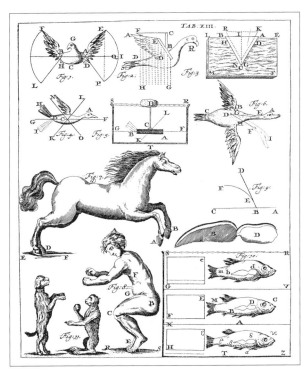

Examples of the centers of gravity in moving animals. From Giovanni Alfonso Borelli, De motu animalium *(1680–1681).*

Boerhaave was the last great iatromechanical theorist. The mechanization of life was attacked by later physiologists, such as Paul-Joseph Barthez (1734–1806), and was displaced by the competing ideas of vitalism and irritability.

BIBLIOGRAPHY

Coulter, Harris L. *Divided Legacy: A History of the Schism in Medical Thought,* vol. 1: *The Patterns Emerge: Hippocrates to Paracelsus.* 2 vols. Berkeley, CA: North Atlantic Books, 1973.

Debus, Allen G. "The English Paracelsians: A Study of Iatrochemistry in England to 1640." Ph.D. diss. Harvard University. 1961.

———. *The French Paracelsians: The Chemical Challenge to Medical and Scientific Tradition in Early Modern France.* Cambridge: Cambridge University Press, 1992.

EMERSON T. MCMULLEN

See also Bellini, Lorenzo; Boerhaave, Hermann; Borelli, Giovanni Alfonso; Vitalism

Ideology, Science as

Ideology is a very difficult concept. Whereas it initially meant the systematic study of ideas in terms of their origin or context, it has come to refer to sets of ideas themselves. This kind of reference is often employed pejoratively, indicating a more limited validity for a set of ideas than their holders would like. This limitation, furthermore, often entails the ascription or imputation of a rationale or motivation for holding a set of beliefs or giving expression to a particular constellation of ideas. While those expressing ideas would prefer to see the ideas expressed as having a rather universal validity or correspondence to reality, those claiming the ideological status of those ideas are thereby imputing a self-serving motive or interested position to those claiming universality on behalf of their beliefs.

The concept of ideology begins its life in eighteenth-century France. The ideologues of that century set themselves the task of uncovering the origin of sensory experience in material conditions and, in turn, of the bases of thought in sensory experience. They hoped thereby to wrest knowledge from a ruling class and to make it the property of a scientific elite. What they wanted to accomplish was a remaking of the social environment to change ideas: a scientific reconstruction of France. It is, thus, ideology in the sense of an account of the interested, social sources of human error and truth, and *an* ideology in the sense of a spirited promotion of the status of a particular group. The claim to repair knowledge after a period of corruption and the recommendation that purer knowledge resided in a particular group were advanced by a number of thinkers of the Scientific Revolution.

According to Thomas Sprat (1635–1713), official historian of the Royal Society, it is to the philosophy of the East (Assyrians, Chaldeans, and Egyptians) that we owe both the origin and the corruption of true and useful knowledge. "It was the custom of their Wise men, to wrap up their Observations on Nature, and the Manners of Men, in the dark shadows of *Hieroglyphicks;* and to conceal them, as sacred *Mysteries,* from the apprehensions of the vulgar. This was a sure way to beget a Reverence in the Peoples Hearts towards *themselves;* but not to advance the true Philosophy of *Nature.*"

Sprat's own promotion of the experimental philosophy of the Royal Society excluded the participation of both the "vulgar" and the "faithless." After presenting his view of the deficiencies of other philosophies and of the nations and faiths that have housed them, he proceeded to outline the virtues of the Royal Society and of the philosophy and status of its members. Under the subtitle "They admit men of all Religions," Sprat goes on to claim that the reason promoted by the Church of England is closest to the "general Reason of Mankind." Even though the society admits men "Of all Professions," it "consists chiefly of Gentlemen," and Sprat claims that this latter condition may prevent the corruption of learning. He recommends the practice of experimental philosophy to gentry and nobility but emphasizes its importance in improving commerce and ensuring obedience to civil government.

Sprat was neither the first nor the last in the early-modern period to employ the device of claiming the universality *and* particular advantage for the promotion of particular interests and natural-philosophical viewpoints. The sixteenth-century French mathematician François Viète (1540–1603) claimed that the art (algebra) that he was advancing, although invented by the ancients, was "so spoiled and defiled by the barbarians" that he had to clear up its formulation "lest is should retain its filth and continue to stink in the old way." Similarly, according to René Descartes (1596–1650), the ancient world, principally in the figures of Pappus and Diophantus, had traces of the science of algebra but they suppressed it by a "low cunning deplorable indeed."

The work of Francis Bacon (1561–1626) is ideological in the complete sense noted above. The path to knowledge that he recommended was designed to restore the human condition to its pre-Fall status. This recommendation included a treatment of what he terms "the idols of the mind," which are responsible for error and corruption. Although the idols are not completely eliminable, this method is supposed to reduce their effects as much as possible. The idols are those of the Tribe, the Cave, the Market Place, and the Theater, and these refer to the clouding influence of the nature of the human understanding (fallible senses), of the idiosyncrasies of individual biography, of imprecise language, and of received false philosophies, respectively. Because of this formulation of the means of removing sources of error, many modern commentators regard Bacon as the first sociologist of knowledge.

In Bacon's view, religion and science can be mutually repairing. The innocence and dominion over nature that humans lost in the Fall from grace can be restored through work and the study of works, both human and natural. In this scheme, divine providence grants a "legal plea" to the sciences to interrogate nature; this was part of Bacon's plea to government for financial support for the "spies of nature." The plan originates in the legal practices of interrogating Spanish prisoners, and the "schedule of interrogatories" drawn up for that purpose finds its way into Bacon's natural philosophy. Amidst all of this are many gendered references to the practices of conquest and vexation of nature.

The theme of religious motivation and justification of natural philosophy also resonates in the work of Robert Boyle (1627–1691). The sort of moral philosophy customary for someone of Boyle's station would have been to suggest that fortune allows one the wealth and leisure necessary to cultivate virtue. In Boyle's case, however, the civil wars in England and Ireland caused a reduction in his family's estates. Lacking the wealth necessary to pursue the customary aristocratic path to virtue, he argued that defying fortune by a rather puritan devotion to work, especially the study of God's works evident in nature, will lead to virtue, which providence will then reward. This rational pursuit of self-interest, according to Boyle, is in harmony with religious peace and the public good. With changes in regime, however, Boyle changed affiliations but retained the same form of moral philosophy. The proper study of nature, he argued, will reveal the true religion, politics, and morals.

ILLUSTRATION   323

The ideological character of his experimental philosophy is best illustrated through his dispute with Thomas Hobbes (1588–1679). Whereas Hobbes preferred to establish first principles on a parallel with geometry and develop ratiocination as the way of producing valid claims about nature, Boyle preferred to establish knowledge on the basis of matters of fact, experimentally produced and witnessed by credible persons. Dispute about interpretations would be allowed but would be limited to the group of experimental philosophers. Boyle claimed that he kept experimental philosophy separate from politics, but also that it represented the best form of politics and the best way of informing public life.

Whereas Hobbes vehemently maintained a value position and argued for its preferability, Boyle claimed both that his experimental philosophy was politically and metaphysically neutral and, at the same time, that it represented the best form of politics. Just as Boyle's moral philosophy could recommend itself to any regime, so could Boyle separate matters of fact from metaphysical interpretation and, thus, "market" his natural philosophy to various interests in Restoration England.

Each of the positions above represents a claim to purify knowledge from an earlier, corrupted state and an argument that the purified form is universally valid, although it is also recommended that a particular group should have preference in purveying such knowledge.

BIBLIOGRAPHY

Jacob, J. R. "The Ideological Origins of Robert Boyle's Natural Philosophy." *Journal of European Studies* 2 (1972), 1–21.

Martin, Julian. *Francis Bacon, the State, and the Reform of Natural Philosophy.* Cambridge: Cambridge University Press, 1992.

Shapin, Steven, and Simon Schaffer. *Leviathan and the Air Pump: Hobbes, Boyle, and the Experimental Life.* Princeton, NJ: Princeton University Press, 1985.

Sprat, Thomas. *History of the Royal Society.* Ed. with Critical Apparatus by Jackson I. Cope and Harold Whitmore Jones. St. Louis: Washington University Press; London: Routledge and Kegan Paul, 1959; 1667 1st ed.

RICHARD W. HADDEN

See also Bacon, Francis; Marxist Historiography; Social Class and Science

Illustration

During the sixteenth and seventeenth centuries, the techniques and conventions used by scientific illustrators underwent profound changes. These changes transformed scientific illustration from a largely decorative, symbolic art into a highly refined, universally understood visual language that became an essential part of transmission, teaching, and research in the sciences. Two types of changes played a role in this evolution: changes in the technological tools available to artists and changes in the psychological and social tools at their disposal. To understand the significance of these changes, it is first necessary to examine the state of scientific illustration before the advent of printing.

Prior to the introduction of the printing press, pictures that accompanied the text of a scientific book were prone to one overwhelming problem: they could not be reproduced accurately. Although the skill of painting lifelike illustrations of birds and plants was highly developed among certain painters, these skills could, at best, be used to decorate the margins of one special copy of a book to be given to a wealthy patron. If scribes attempted to copy the images, the illustrations would inevitably degenerate over time and lose any scientific value they once had. The ability of text and image to work together also degenerated as books were copied and recopied; diagrams and illustrations became separated from the books that once referred to them, and labels drifted away from diagrams.

The introduction of the printing press in the late fifteenth century did not immediately change the role that images played in science. The first printed images were simply copies of earlier hand-painted images and tended to be merely decorative and symbolic rather than functional. For the first time, however, it was technically possible to create images that could be exactly reproduced.

The woodcut was the first type of medium for creating reproducible illustrations. To create a woodcut, a picture first had to be drawn on a block of wood. A woodcutter would then carve away all of the wood except the drawn lines, leaving them standing out in relief. These woodblocks could then be passed through the printing press along with text. These relief lines, however, could only be so thin, and it was, therefore, difficult to represent small details and shading effects. In the early days of printing, woodcutters were not, in general, respected artists but were, rather, part of lower-class carpenter guilds. Woodcutting was a craft that enjoyed no tradition, history, or specialized guilds, and so early woodcuts were often low-quality imitations of existing images. All of these factors limited the amount of functional information that illustrations could carry.

During the first several decades of the sixteenth century, the craft of woodcutting improved dramatically. Artists like Albrecht Dürer (1471–1528) took the art of woodcutting to a new level. Dürer showed how woodcuts could approach, in detail and beauty, the images created in other preprint media. He also showed how artists could gain a wider audience by producing images that would be reproduced in printed books. As woodcutters became more skilled, they also became more respected, and specialization within the printshops led to higher- and higher-quality woodcuts.

Even the best illustrations during this time period, however, continued to follow certain earlier conventions that kept them from reaching their full didactic potential. For example, the *Herbarum vivae eicones* (1530) of Otto Brunfels (ca. 1489–1534) contains beautiful, high-quality woodcuts of plants, but Brunfels still attempted to represent individual specimens, with each torn leaf or bent stem. The idea of using an illustration to highlight what is scientifically significant about a class of organisms, rather than record a unique encounter between artist and organism, was one that was foreign to artists. A major shift in thinking was required for such a convention to develop, and this shift was the result of scientists and artists working in close collaboration. It is this type of collaboration that made possible works such as *De historia stirpium* (1542), written by Leonhart Fuchs (1501–1566). Fuchs hired three artists: one to make color drawings, one to redraw them on woodblocks, and a trained cutter to make the blocks that would be sent through the press. Fuchs states in his Preface that the goal was to limit the artistic expression of each individual artist and instead create images that would communicate the maximum amount of scientific information. Fuchs, for example, uses illustrations to show the important stages of the life cycle of a plant.

Scientists who studied the nonliving world also developed conventions that made images more powerful. Figure 1 shows an illustration by Georgius Agricola (1494–1555) of a pump being used in a mine shaft. Several important conventions are apparent in this illustration. The cutaway view allows the viewer to see the pump in operation, as if looking in through a hole torn in the earth. This cutaway view, also used in anatomical drawings to show internal organs, is taken for granted by modern readers, but its introduction greatly enhanced the ability of an image to communicate technical information. The alphabetical labels in this diagram are keyed

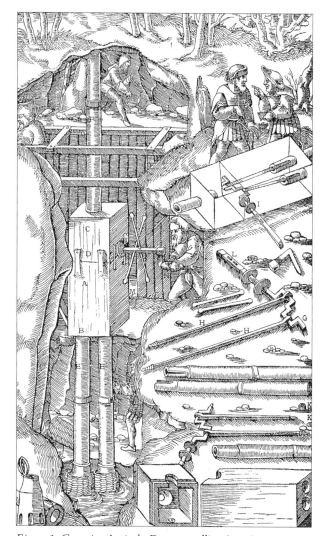

Figure 1. Georgius Agricola, De re metallica *(1556).*

to descriptions in the text. This type of label was problematic in preprint media because, as the diagrams and text were copied, scribes would often mix up the letters, making the labels useless.

The box labeled ABC is shown again using another important psychological tool, the transparent view. The outer casing is drawn only in outline, as if transparent, allowing the viewer to see the internal parts (H and I) and how they fit together. Then, in the lower right quarter of the diagram, all of the parts are shown again, completely disassembled and spread out on the ground. This last method allows the depiction of details not visible any other way, such as the holes that the pistons fit into.

The illustrations used by scientists like Fuchs and Agricola were so effective that they were often copied by later scientists. The same woodcuts were used again and again, and the art of woodcutting remained at a plateau.

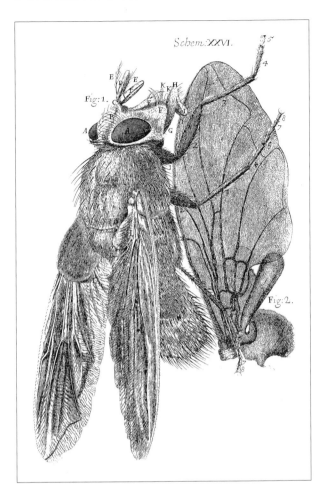

Figure 2. Robert Hooke, Micrographia *(1665).*

The next important development was a technical one, as the art of metal engraving was perfected and became the preferred method for creating detailed illustrations. Metal engraving could create images with finer detail and more subtle shading effects than woodcuts. Whereas woodcuts were made by leaving the image standing up in relief, engravings were produced by incising the image into the metal. The carved image was then filled with ink. When this metal plate was run through the press, pressure forced the paper into the inked lines, resulting in a line slightly raised above the surface of the paper.

Although woodcuts did not completely disappear, by the early seventeenth century the majority of scientific books were illustrated using metal engravings. The technique of metal engraving provided seventeenth-century scientists and artists with the precision and flexibility needed to represent the new world visible through the microscope. In engravings such as the one shown in Figure 2, from *Micrographia* (1665) by Robert Hooke (1635–1703), the technological and psychological develop-

ments discussed above reached their climax to produce images that are both spectacular and scientifically meaningful. Although further refinements were made in the technology of engraving during the seventeenth and eighteenth centuries, these refinements were minor in comparison with the groundbreaking changes outlined in this essay. By the time Hooke's *Micrographia* was published, illustrations had become a vital part of the transmission of scientific information, and many of the conventions and techniques developed during the sixteenth and seventeenth centuries can still be seen in scientific illustrations today.

BIBLIOGRAPHY

Baigrie, Brian S., ed. *Picturing Knowledge: Historical and Philosophical Problems Concerning the Use of Art in Science.* Toronto: Toronto University Press, 1996.

Bridson, Gavin D. R. "From Xylography to Holography: Five Centuries of Natural History Illustration." *Archives of Natural History* 16 (1989), 121–141.

Ford, Brian J. *Images of Science: A History of Scientific Illustration.* New York: Oxford University Press, 1993.

Edgerton, Samuel Y., Jr. *The Heritage of Giotto's Geometry: Art and Science on the Eve of the Scientific Revolution.* Ithaca, NY: Cornell University Press, 1991.

Ivins, William M., Jr. *Prints and Visual Communication.* London: Routledge and Kegan Paul, 1953.

KEVIN TAPP

See also Art; Dürer, Albrecht; Emblematics; Printing

Impetus

A concept to characterize a quality that is transferred from one thing to another, originating in antiquity. Hipparchus (second century B.C.E.) rejected the Aristotelian requirement of immediate contact between the mover and the moved in the account of projectile motion and argued instead that a projectile receives a motive principle from its mover. John Philoponus (sixth century) adopted impetus in his critique of Aristotle's (384–322 B.C.E.) accounts of both projectile motion and the acceleration of falling bodies. Several Arabic authors also used the theory in critiques of Aristotle's account of motion. Medieval Latin authors learned of impetus indirectly by way of reports that were critical of the theory; nevertheless, several fourteenth-century authors adopted the theory to account for some theological doctrines as well as the motions of bodies. By the middle of the fourteenth century, Latin authors restricted use of the concept to account for projectile motions, acceleration of falling bodies, and the uniform motions of celestial bodies. These authors developed two versions: a self-expending impetus (Franciscus of Marchia, d. ca. 1344, and Nicole Oresme, ca. 1320–1382) and a permanent impetus (John Buridan, ca. 1295–ca. 1358, and Albert of Saxony, ca. 1316–1390). The majority of authors up to the seventeenth century held that impetus is self-expending. The adherents of the theory understood impetus as a quality that functions both as a cause of motion and as an effect (dependent on quantity of matter and speed). Some of these authors (e.g., Buridan) suggested that God imparted an impetus to celestial bodies, which accounts for their uniform motions. Although such discussions were not based on rigorous empirical investigation, the theory seems to represent a transitional stage between Aristotelian dynamics and modern classical dynamics. Though ontologically different, impetus is analogous to Galileo Galilei's early use of *impeto* and Isaac Newton's "quantity of motion."

By the sixteenth century, the majority of authors, especially Italian followers of Averroës (the Latin form of the name of the twelfth-century Arabic commentator on Aristotle, Ibn Rushd, 1126–1198), portrayed the theory as Aristotelian or as compatible with Aristotle's account; nevertheless, some discussions clarified a number of confusions present in the earlier accounts. Luiz Coronel (d. 1531), a Spanish master at Paris, published a treatise in 1511 in which he considered impetus as an effect produced in falling bodies. In a treatise on mechanics from 1585, Giovanni Battista Benedetti (1530–1590) asserted that a body moved when a power has been impressed on it by some external mover has a tendency to move on a rectilinear, not a curved, path. If the mover acts continuously, the velocity increases continually, although Benedetti concluded that impetus decreases gradually and continuously.

In his early work on motion, Galileo (1564–1642) accepted a version of impetus as held by Buridan, and even in *Two Chief World Systems* (1632) he spoke of impetus as an impressed motive power. In *Two New Sciences* (1638), however, Galileo removed some of the ambiguity present in earlier versions. First, Galileo eliminated the notion of impetus as a cause and unambiguously characterized it as an effect and measure of motion. Second, in his treatment of ideal cases, he transferred the idea of a permanent uniform motion from celestial to terrestrial mechanics. Third, in his version of inertial motion, he treated impetus as a function of weight and speed.

By way of Galileo, then, impetus approaches the modern conceptions of kinetic energy and momentum. Among Galileo's successors, Giovanni Baliani (1582–1666) recognized the ambiguity between cause and effect and observed that a motion continues of its own accord even though we commonly speak of an impetus impelling a body forward. René Descartes (1596–1650) clearly formulated quantity of motion or momentum as the product of quantity of matter and speed, and he maintained that the total momentum in the universe conserved by God remains constant.

Much as one would like to say that Newton (1642–1727) corrected all previous misconceptions and defined the concepts of force, mass, momentum, inertia, and so forth unambiguously, the fact is that late-medieval notions and considerations remain in his language. For example, Newton used the concept of an impressed force as an external force that changes the momentum of the body on which it operates. Still, Newton's *Principia mathematica philosophiae naturalis* (1687) puts these discussions decisively on a path that leads from the medieval conception of impetus to the understanding of kinetic energy as the energy of an inertial mass in motion, and of momentum as the product of inertial mass and velocity.

BIBLIOGRAPHY

Clagett, Marshall. *The Science of Mechanics in the Middle Ages.* Madison: University of Wisconsin Press, 1959.

Drake, Stillman, and I. E. Drabkin. *Mechanics in Sixteenth-Century Italy.* Madison: University of Wisconsin Press, 1969.

Franklin, Allan. *The Principle of Inertia in the Middle Ages.* Boulder: Colorado Associated University Press, 1976.

Wolff, Michael. *Geschichte der Impetustheorie.* Frankfurt am Main: Suhrkamp Verlag, 1978.

ANDRÉ GODDU

See also Baliani, Giovanni Battista; Benedetti, Giovanni Battista; Dynamics; Galilei, Galileo; Mechanics; Newton, Isaac

Inertia

In the course of the seventeenth century, the notion of inertia underwent important changes and has to be treated with considerable care. Several historians adopted a univocal definition without considering that the term *inertia* was understood in different ways by different actors. Seventeenth-century philosophers and mathematicians charged each other with having improperly used it, though the criteria according to which usage was proper or improper were themselves a matter of contention. This essay contrasts four interpretations to show that the notion of inertia cannot be isolated from a broad disciplinary matrix involving such issues as the philosophy of matter, properties of motion, the nature of space, and cosmological beliefs.

Johannes Kepler (1571–1630) was generally credited in the seventeenth century, and still is today, with having introduced the term *inertia*. Kepler still adhered to some aspects of Aristotelian physics; for him, a body tends to resist being set in motion, and a moving body tends to come to rest, because matter tends naturally toward rest. Inertia meant the natural tendency of a moving body to come to rest. In the 1621 edition of his *Mysterium cosmographicum,* for example, he wrote of inertia in the context of planetary motion, arguing that planets need to be continually impelled by the Sun to prevent their coming to a halt. Moreover, Kepler believed that, if a body moves in a small circle, it tends to escape along the tangent, as he stated in his 1619 *Epitome astronomiae Copernicanae.* If the circle is very large, however, namely comparable to the size of planetary orbits, circular motion would not produce an outward tendency. Thus, Keplerian inertia is radically different from what has become known as the principle of inertia, whereby a body continues in its state of rest or rectilinear uniform motion unless that state is altered by an external action.

Toward the middle of the seventeenth century, several authors, notably René Descartes (1596–1650) and Pierre Gassendi (1592–1655), published their views on motion, arguing that motion is a state in the same way as rest is and that a body set in motion and left to its own devices would move in a straight line with a uniform speed. This view was closely associated with the belief in an infinite and homogeneous space. In his correspondence of the late 1630s, published posthumously by Claude Clerselier (1614–1684), Descartes denied any inherent tendency of bodies toward rest, though he admitted that they have inertia, namely a reluctance to change their state dependent on the law of conservation of quantity of motion, by which he meant the product of matter and speed. In other words, he reinterpreted the notion of inertia in the context of impact, arguing that, if two unequal bodies are impelled at successive times by the same body moving with the same speed, thus having the same amount of quantity of motion, the speeds they acquire will be inversely proportional to their matter or natural inertia. Therefore, Cartesian inertia is embedded in his views on space and laws of impact and differs profoundly from Keplerian inertia.

Gottfried Wilhelm Leibniz (1646–1716) was aware of both Kepler's and Descartes's usage of the term *inertia*. Although he recognized the differences between Keplerian physics and late-seventeenth-century views on motion, he tried to retrieve Kepler's terminology largely on metaphysical grounds, arguing that inertia is the phenomenal manifestation of the imperfection of creatures. For Leibniz, too, phenomena of impact occupy center stage, though for him the true impact laws concern conservation of living force, or mass times the square of velocity, rather than quantity of motion as believed by Descartes. In his 1710 *Essais de théodicée,* Leibniz discussed his position in relation to Kepler and to the physical example of boats differently laden in a river. Comparing the flowing water to the impact of a body, Leibniz argued that the boats most heavily laden will go more slowly than the others because the same living force of the river has to move a larger mass. Although both his reference to Kepler and his example were subject to ambiguities, many commentators correctly interpreted Leibnizian inertia as resistance to impressed motion. Despite important differences of metaphysical beliefs and conservation laws, both Leibniz and Descartes consciously reinterpreted Keplerian inertia within their views on motion and impact physics.

In Definition 3 of his *Principia mathematica philosophiae naturalis,* Isaac Newton (1642–1727) stated that *vis insita* (innate force) or *vis inertiae* is a body's power to resist change to its state of rest or motion, which differ only relatively. *Vis insita* or the force of inertia can be conceived both passively, as a body's resistance to the force of another body to change its state, and actively, because the body's resistance is a tendency to alter the state of the other body. In this sense, Newton's force of inertia seems to be linked to his third law of motion, stating that action and reaction are equal and opposite. Whereas for Descartes and Leibniz the change to the state of a body could be produced only through impact, Newton believed that both impacts and a continuous force, such as centripetal force, could change the direction and magnitude of a body's speed. Typical examples were planetary and cometary paths round the Sun. On a small piece of paper in his own copy of the second edition of his *Principia* (1713), Newton felt the need to clarify that, by *vis inertiae,* he did not mean Keplerian inertia, whereby bodies incline to rest. This clarification was not inserted in the third edition of 1726 either because Leibniz, the likely addressee of the remark, was dead or because Newton thought that by that time the issue was sufficiently clear.

The notion of inertia is closely intertwined with the so-called *principle of inertia,* which is generally considered as one of the cornerstones of the new science of motion. In the work of Alexandre Koyré (1892–1964), this principle has taken the broader role of a key historiographic tool for interpreting the Scientific Revolution and for assessing the contributions of seventeenth-century philosophers and mathematicians to the historical process. The possession of a clear and correct understanding of the principle of inertia was almost considered to be a mark of modernity. Take, for example, Galileo Galilei (1564–1642). Historians often mention his principle of circular inertia, referring to several passages in which Galileo argued that, if a moving body is left to its own devices, it will not come to rest but, under ideal conditions, such as a sphere rolling on a perfectly smooth, frictionless plane, will continue to move with a uniform motion. From other passages, it appears that this motion, however, was not rectilinear but circular, the circle being of a size comparable to the circumference of the earth or planetary orbits. While moving away from the belief that, in the absence of friction, motion needs to be maintained by an external action, Galileo still attributed a special status to circular motion. Thus, he is depicted as occupying a crucial position in the transition from Aristotelian physics and the medieval *impetus* theory to the novel horizon of Gassendi and Descartes. Within this historiography emphasizing ideas and their development, the principle of inertia has at times been discussed without paying much attention to the terminology employed by historical actors, including the very word *inertia,* and to the relevant disciplinary contexts and specific problems. One of the problems related to the principle of inertia concerns the very definition of motion, including rectilinear uniform motion, with respect to space. According to Leibniz, for example, space is a relation among material bodies, and motion can be defined only with respect to those bodies. Newton, by contrast, believed in absolute space and argued that only relative motion can be measured with respect to material bodies but that real motion occurs in absolute

space and can be measured, at least in the case of rotations, from the outward tendencies of truly rotating bodies. Descartes, too, held interesting and complex views on how the motion of a body can be defined and whether it is absolute or relative to other bodies.

This survey is of necessity incomplete for the limited number of actors investigated and for the brief analyses of their views. The scholar of the Scientific Revolution, however, may see it as a tool for the identification of some problems and authors and for studying their works in a more pluralistic way, without imposing a Newtonian framework.

BIBLIOGRAPHY

Barbour, J. B. *Absolute or Relative Motion? A Study from a Machian Point of View of the Discovery and Structure of Dynamical Theories.* Cambridge: Cambridge University Press, 1989.

Cohen, I. B. *The Newtonian Revolution: With Illustrations of the Transformation of Scientific Ideas.* Cambridge: Cambridge University Press, 1980.

Gabbey, A. "Force and Inertia in Seventeenth-Century Dynamics." *Studies in History and Philosophy of Science* 2 (1971), 1–67.

Garber, D. *Descartes' Metaphysical Physics.* Chicago: University of Chicago Press, 1992.

Koyré, A. *Metaphysics and Measurement: Essays in Scientific Revolution.* London: Chapman and Hall; Cambridge, MA: Harvard University Press, 1968.

Westfall, R. S. *Force in Newton's Physics: The Science of Dynamics in the Seventeenth Century.* London: Macdonald; New York: American Elsevier, 1971.

DOMENICO BERTOLONI MELI

See also Descartes, René; Dynamics; Force; Galilei, Galileo; Impetus; Mechanics

Infinitesimals

The Greek mathematical tradition rarely brought into play considerations about infinity for dealing with measurements of areas or determinations of tangents. Although the heuristic underpinnings of the classical Greek proofs might have relied on considerations of infinity, such considerations simply do not appear in their formal developments. By the end of the seventeenth century, the use of infinitistic methods had become widespread. In particular, indivisibles and infinitesimals played a central role in the development of one of the main mathematical achievements of the seventeenth century, the infinitesimal calculus.

To visualize the difference between indivisibles and infinitesimals, consider a square with bases AB and CD. Bonaventura Cavalieri (1598–1647), the founder of the indivisibilist method, considers the square as being characterized by the class of segments lying between AB and CD and parallel to the bases. An indivisible of the square is any one such segment. The main feature of an indivisible, then, is that its dimension is lower than the figure of which it is a constituent. Thus, points are the indivisibles of line segments, segments of plane figures, and planes of solids. By contrast, an infinitesimal is an infinitely small quantity that has the same dimension of the geometrical object of which it is part. In the case of a segment, an infinitesimal would be an infinitely small linelet; in the case of the square, we could consider the base of the square as being divided into infinitely many small linelets. Thus, the square itself could be seen as being composed of infinitely small rectangles, one of whose sides is an infinitely small linelet and the other is a segment whose length is the same as the side of the square. This notion of infinitesimal can be seen as emerging from the logical difficulties that Cavalieri's indivisibles gave rise to, and it is found in, among others, Isaac Barrow (1630–1677), Blaise Pascal (1623–1662), Gilles Personne de Roberval (1602–1675), and, in particular, in Gottfried Wilhelm Leibniz (1646–1716) as the only possible rigorous reading of the language of indivisibles.

The mathematical fruitfulness of infinitesimals is shown by their role in the Leibnizian calculus. Leibniz published his first results on the calculus in 1684. The central notion of the Leibnizian calculus is that of differential (although in 1684 he still speaks of differences). Leibniz had several, at times conflicting, interpretations of the notion of differential. Sometimes he interpreted differentials as standing for finite quantities; at other times he thought of them as denoting infinitesimal quantities. The first textbook on the calculus, written by Guillaume F. A. de L'Hôspital (1661–1704) in 1696, defines the differential of a quantity x, denoted by dx, as the infinitely small part whereby a variable quantity is continually increased or decreased. By means of infinitesimalist considerations, L'Hôspital systematizes the main results of the infinitesimal calculus as had been developed up to that point by Leibniz and the Bernoulli brothers, Jakob I (1654–1705) and Johann I (1677–1748).

Most of the problems relating to the use of infinitesimals were not of a technical nature but, rather, of a foundational one. The notion of infinitesimal does not fit in the general theory of quantities and ratios inherited from the Greek works. In particular, according to that theory two quantities A and B have a ratio if there is a natural number n such that A added to itself n times is greater than B (or vice versa). Under such a characterization, it is not possible to say that a finite quantity and an infinitesimal can have a ratio. Moreover, a consistent use of infinitesimals seems to defy the usual algebraic laws. For example, one of L'Hôspital's axiom is that $x + dx = x$, but one cannot apply indiscriminately the algebraic law that, if from equals we subtract equals, then the results are equal. That would, in fact, yield that in general $dx = 0$, which contradicts the notion of dx as an infinitely small quantity and, thus, not zero.

The use of infinitesimals in the calculus led to several debates of a foundational nature. Some people simply rejected the notion as inconsistent and even leading to mathematical mistakes. The most powerful attack against the conceivability of infinitesimals from a philosophical point of view was carried out by George Berkeley (1685–1753) in *The Analyst* (1734), which also attacked the Newtonian approach to the calculus. However, even within the camp of those who upheld the use of infinitesimals in mathematics there were disagreements as to their nature. Bernard Nieuwentijt (1654–1718) accepted only first-order differentials and claimed, for example, that products like $dx \cdot dx$ must always be set equal to zero, against the usual practice of Leibnizian analysis. Moreoever, Leibniz found himself in conflict with Jakob Bernoulli, L'Hôspital, and Bernard le Bovier de Fontenelle (1657–1757), who had a stronger commitment to the existence of infinitesimal quantities than Leibniz. The latter often thought of infinitesimals as a way of speaking that could be eliminated in favor of a more rigorous, if less direct, language, something that could not be considered achieved until the end of the nineteenth century. Recent developments, such as nonstandard analysis and results from synthetic differential geometry, have given rigorous and alternative approaches to the notion of the infinitesimal, and much historiographical effort has been devoted to the issue of whether these later developments in some sense "vindicate" the intuitions of seventeenth-century mathematicians.

BIBLIOGRAPHY

Bell, John L. "Infinitesimals." *Synthese* 75 (1988), 285–315.

Bos, Henk J. M. "Differentials, Higher-Order Differentials, and the Derivative in the Leibnizian Calculus." *Archive for History of Exact Sciences* 14 (1974), 1–90.

Boyer, Carl B. *The History of the Calculus and Its Conceptual Development*. New York: Dover, 1959.

Mancosu, Paolo. *Philosophy of Mathematics and Mathematical Practice in the Seventeenth Century*. Oxford: Oxford University Press, 1996.

PAOLO MANCOSU

See also Calculus; Cavalieri, Bonaventura; Infinity, Mathematical; Leibniz, Gottfried Wilhelm

Infinity, Mathematical

Although reflections about the nature of the infinite and the continuum abound in the philosophical and theological literature of previous ages, it was the seventeenth century that witnessed the beginnings of the mathematical treatment of infinity. The infinite appeared in two forms: the infinitely small and the infinitely large. As the former is treated in other entries, only the infinitely large is treated here.

In Galileo Galilei's (1564–1642) reflections on infinity and the continuum, in his *Two New Sciences* (1638), there is a discussion of the paradoxes of the infinite. Some of these paradoxes arise from the fact that there are infinite sets that can be put in one-to-one correspondence and, at the same time, are such that one includes the other (e.g., the set of the natural numbers and the proper subset of it that contains just the perfect square numbers). Since there is a one-to-one correspondence between the natural numbers and the squares (let n be paired with n^2), it seems that there are as many squares as natural numbers. However, since the squares are a proper subset of the natural numbers, one should instead conclude that there are more natural numbers than squares. Galileo's way out of this paradox is to assert that the relations of less than, equal to, and greater than do not apply to infinities. Galileo's reflections, however, are quite close in spirit to the previous philosophical literature on the subject and are still too removed from the actual mathematical practice of his time, in which the infinitely large appeared in a number of different contexts.

In the geometry of indivisibles, Bonaventura Cavalieri (1598–1647) put forward a theory that would allow the consideration of ratios between (infinite) collections of indivisibles. In the demonstration of his main theorems, moreover, he implicitly used infinitary congruency procedures. The summation of infinite series is carried out by Gregory of St. Vincent, Pietro Mengoli (1625–

1686), John Wallis, and later mathematicians. By such means, Gregory of St. Vincent (1584–1667) offered a solution to Zeno's paradoxes. (It is to John Wallis, 1616–1703, that we owe the introduction of the symbol ∞.) In projective geometry, Girard Desargues (1591–1691) introduced points at infinity; postulation of points at infinity can also be found in Johannes Kepler (1571–1630) at the beginning of the century. By far the most shocking result of the period was Evangelista Torricelli's (1608–1647) on the acute hyperbolic solid, an infinitely long figure obtained by rotating a branch of the hyperbola around one of the axes and then cutting the solid obtained by the rotation with a plane perpendicular to the axis of rotation. Torricelli showed that the solid so obtained, which extends indefinitely in the direction of the axis of rotation, has a finite volume. The importance of the result is fourfold. First, the result challenged the Aristotelian dictum that there is no proportion between the finite and the infinite. Second, it showed that the human mind, although finite, can establish nontrivial properties of infinity. Third, it opened the way to similar work on infinite figures by Pierre de Fermat (1601–1665), Wallis, Gottfried Wilhelm Leibniz (1646–1716), and others. Fourth, it constituted the first infinitistic result in mathematics for which a finitistic reading was not readily available. It thus represented a challenge for various empiricist philosophies of mathematics, as evidenced by the debate between Thomas Hobbes (1588–1679) and Wallis.

The infinitely large also appeared in the calculus. In this connection, it is interesting to refer to the debate between Leibniz and Bernard Nieuwentijt (1654–1718). Nieuwentijt believed that there was only one infinite number and, thus, restricted his infinitesimals to those that could be obtained by dividing any finite number by this infinite number. Leibniz, by contrast, believed that the infinite is subject to increase and, thus, admits the existence of different orders of infinity.

BIBLIOGRAPHY

Field, Judith V. "The Infinitely Great and the Infinitely Small in the Work of Girard Desargues." In *Desargues en son Temps,* eds. Jean Dhombres and Joël Sakarovitch. Paris: Blanchard, 1994, pp. 219–230.

Mancosu, Paolo. *Philosophy of Mathematics and Mathematical Practice in the Seventeenth Century*. Oxford: Oxford University Press, 1996.

Mancosu, Paolo, and Ezio Vailati. "Torricelli's Infinitely Long Solid and Its Philosophical Reception in the Seventeenth Century." *Isis* 82 (1991), 50–70.

Moore, Adrian W. *The Infinite*. London and New York: Routledge, 1990.

PAOLO MANCOSU

See also Cavalieri, Bonaventura; Infinitesimals

Infinity of the World

At the start of the seventeenth century, the majority of thinkers concluded, with Aristotle, that the universe as a whole is finite. However, they also denied Aristotle's arguments for the impossibility of plural worlds. They thought that God could create more worlds but that this plurality of worlds might increase continually without ever becoming an actual infinity of worlds. Following Aristotle, they held that actual infinity is absurd. Of course, there were also minority positions on these issues, even schoolmen who denied that God could not create an infinite body. Giordano Bruno (1548–1600) accepted an infinite plurality of worlds. Nicholas of Cusa (1401–1464) and René Descartes (1596–1650) thought the universe itself indefinite in extent. Ultimately, the infinity of the world became the majority position with Gottfried Wilhelm Leibniz (1646–1716) and Isaac Newton (1642–1727).

The question of the infinity or finiteness of the world depends on the resolution of the question of the possibility of infinity itself, a complex topic. Aristotle (384–322 B.C.E.) denied actual infinity, both the infinitely large and the infinitely small. He accepted potential infinities as processes that are finite at every stage but always different. Hence, he affirmed potential infinities such as the infinite in time, in the generations of man, in magnitude by division, and in number but denied actual infinities in them. When he discussed the potential infinite in magnitude by addition in his *Physics,* however, he rejected it for entailing an actuality: "there is no infinite in the direction of increase. For the size which it can potentially be it can actually be. Hence, since no sensible magnitude is infinite, it is impossible to exceed every assigned magnitude; for if it were possible, there would be something bigger than the heavens." Thus, Aristotle's physical world was finite and could not grow, but, in that world, magnitude was continuous, and time and generation were unending.

Inevitably, given that many of Aristotle's doctrines on infinity were in conflict with the conception of an absolutely omnipotent Creator, these doctrines were modified considerably by later Aristotelians. The Roman Catholic Church's condemnation of various propositions in 1277 most likely influenced the discussions of potential and actual infinites in nature. Among the condemned propositions was "That the first cause cannot make more than one world." It directly challenged the Aristotelian doctrines of the singularity of the universe and the impossibility of the potential infinitely large in magnitude.

In general, seventeenth-century Aristotelians accepted the latter infinity but rejected any infinite in actuality; they were also careful to indicate that others had argued that God could create an actual, or "categorematic," infinite. For example, the Jesuit Franciscus Toletus (1532–1596) answered negatively the question whether a body can be actually infinite but referred his readers to Albert of Saxony's (1316–1390) position that God could create an actual, or "categorematic," infinite in nature. Similarly, the textbook writer Charles François d'Abra de Raconis gave references to William of Ockham (ca. 1300–ca. 1349) and Gregory of Rimini (d. 1358), placing them in the camp of those who held that an actual categorematic infinite can be created by divine power. The seventeenth-century Aristotelian world was still finite, but it could grow by God's power; some thought it could grow enough to become infinite (as did Jacques du Chevreul, professor at Paris in the 1620s and 1630s).

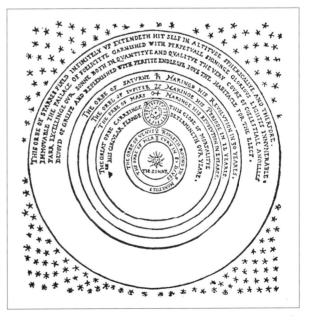

The Copernican system set in an infinite universe, as portrayed by Thomas Digges in a brief work attached to the publication of his father Leonard Digges's A Prognostication Everlastinge *(1576).*

Non-Aristotelians were somewhat bolder in their pronouncements. Nicholas of Cusa maintained that the universe is not finite but indeterminate; that is, it does not have a boundary and it lacks precision (it cannot be determined by us). However, it is also not infinite: only the absolute maximum is infinite, for it alone is everything it can be; the universe includes everything outside God, but it is not God. Descartes agreed. Echoing Cusa, he asserted that God is the only being in whose perfections one notices no limits, and one can see that he is greater than the world, so that the world cannot be called infinite. But it conflicts with one's conception for the world to be finite or bounded. Hence, one calls it indefinite.

On the other hand, the same lack of termination or limits claimed by Cusa and later Descartes prompted Bruno to call the universe infinite. Finitism was no longer the rule. For Platonists or atomists, some aspect of the universe was infinite, whether the universe itself, or space (e.g., Francesco Patrizi's [1529–1597]) infinite, immobile container in which God placed bodies), or void (e.g., Pierre Gassendi's [1592–1655] infinite three-dimensional void space in which God placed a finite world of atoms). Isaac Newton (1642–1727) followed the atomist line, positing an infinite absolute space. Disagreeing about absolute space, absolute time, and the void, Newton and Leibniz would agree about the infinity of the world. On the basis of his principles of plenitude and sufficient reason, Leibniz held the universe to be maximally perfect: the best of all possible worlds is composed of an infinity of living creatures.

BIBLIOGRAPHY

Alexander, H. G., ed. *The Leibniz-Clarke Correspondence.* Manchester: Manchester University Press, 1956.

Duhem, Pierre. *Medieval Cosmoslogy: Theories of Infinity, Place, Time, Void, and the Plurality of Worlds.* Ed. and trans. Roger Ariew. Chicago: University of Chicago Press, 1985.

Grant, Edward. *Planets, Stars, and Orbs.* Cambridge: Cambridge University Press, 1996.

Koyré, Alexandre. *From the Closed World to the Infinite Universe.* Baltimore: Johns Hopkins University Press, 1957.

ROGER ARIEW

See also Aristotelianism; Bruno, Giordano; Descartes, René; Digges, Thomas; Space

Instrument Makers

Current historiography distinguishes between the different levels at which instrument making operates and accepts that science covers a spectrum of interconnected activities embracing the cerebral, the social, and the practical. The craftsman who made everyday devices, such as balances, clocks, compasses, sundials, and drawing and surveying instruments, provided useful artifacts whose design and application was perceived to be founded on scientific principles. That reservoir of technical expertise could be tapped by the natural philosopher wishing to use an existing device in a new way or to create something improved or novel so as to uncover or examine a phenomenon. In time, a new device might become a routine product of a workshop, no longer required for original investigation but cementing the infrastructure of scientific endeavor, used for teaching, or by professional and trade practitioners, or in the social context of the practice of polite science.

In 1471 the much-traveled mathematician and astronomer Johannes Regiomontanus (1436–1476) settled in Nuremburg. Here lived groups of craftsmen whose skill in fine metal work was unrivaled in Europe. By his own account, Regiomontanus chose to live there not only on account of the availability of instruments, particularly the astronomical instruments on which the entire science of the heavens is based, but also on account of the great ease of all sorts of communication with learned men living everywhere, since this place was regarded as the center of Europe because of the journeys of merchants. He set up a workshop to print scientific texts and to make scientific instruments. Nuremburg was not unique in having craftsmen with instrument-making skills, but, as a Free State at the hub of Europe's trade routes, it maintained a preeminence until overtaken by the disruptions of the Thirty Years War (1618–1648).

By 1500 instrument making had become a small but established specialist trade in a number of the larger cities and academic centers in Europe. Master craftsmen such as Lorenzo della Volpaia (1446–1512) in Florence, Hans Dorn (ca. 1430–1509) in Vienna, George Hartmann (1489–1564) in Nuremburg, and Gerard Mercator (1512–1594) in Louvain (Duisberg from 1552) set standards of precision for contemporaries and successors, founding schools and dynasties of skilled workmen. The London trade can be traced to the mid-sixteenth century and the arrival (ca. 1540) of a Flemish immigrant,

Thomas Geminus (ca. 1510–1562), whose skills appeared to have been nurtured in Louvain. Geminus worked as an engraver, printer, and publisher in addition to making mathematical instruments. Humphrey Cole (ca. 1520–1591), map engraver, die-sinker to the mint, and the leading mathematical instrument maker of the Elizabethan Age, was proud to announce that he was English. The style of his engraving betrays the influence of Geminus; thus, the pervading calligraphy of Mercator embraced the growing number of London instrument-making workshops. In France, the social and economic disturbances of generations of religious warfare in the sixteenth century were not conducive to the establishment of the new trade. Significantly, in 1608 three instrument makers were included among the skilled craftsmen whom the enlightened Henry IV established in the Louvre.

By 1600 throughout Europe, mathematical practitioners, men who earned a living as architects, land and quantity surveyors, ship designers, pilots, and navigators, military engineers and gunnery officers, accountants and judicial and medical and general astrologers could acquire the tools of their trade from specialist instrument makers. Teachers of the new sciences could turn to the same men for didactic and demonstration apparatus. Galileo Galilei (1564–1642), when teaching mathematics at Padua, in 1599 provided the instrument maker Marcantonio Mazzolini with both living accommodations and a workshop in his own house, paying him a salary so as to control the manufacture and sale of his newly designed geometrical and military sector.

As the development of the telescope illustrates, the demands of savants were not necessarily met by artisans. Lenses ground by spectacle makers were initially far from adequate for the astronomical applications that Galileo and Thomas Harriot (ca. 1560–1621) pioneered for the new device. In the area of optical instrumentation, the craftsmen of the seventeenth century, with a few notable exceptions, such as Giuseppe Campani (1635–1715) of Rome and Eustachio Divini (1610–1685) of Bologna, were unable to respond to the expectations of astronomers. René Descartes (1596–1650) proposed aspherical lenses (1627) in the hope of improved image quality, but, notwithstanding the technical and financial input of the geometrician Claude Mydorge (1585–1647), the Parisian optician Jean Ferrier could not realize the design. The Huygens brothers, Christiaan (1629–1695) and Constantijn, dissatisfied with commercially available telescopes, designed (ca. 1654) and used their own lens-polishing machinery. The London opticians commissioned (1664–1665) by James Gregory (1638–1675) to realize his design for a reflecting telescope did not persist. Isaac Newton (1642–1727), in Cambridge, taught himself to cast and grind mirrors and so produced the first reflecting telescope (1668). Not until the next century did the trade make a technical and commercial success of the reflector.

As for the microscope, the stimulating investigations of the 1670s and 1680s were made by Antoni van Leeuwenhoek (1632–1723) using high-magnification single-lens instruments that he made himself, with optical performances that no professional instrument maker could match for more than a century.

By 1700 the established instrument-making trade was largely ruled by the financial imperative. Savant and practitioner could buy off the shelf or commission routine apparatus at an agreed price. As ever, some natural philosophers learned, mastered, and extended craft skills. Some artisans had the inclination, the intellect, and the time to develop scientific interests. Partnerships between scholar and craftsman, patron and artisan were particularly fruitful and continued throughout the period, from Georg Peurbach (1423–1461) with Dorn in fifteenth-century Vienna, through Reiner Gemma Frisius (1508–1555) with Mercator and the Arsenius family in the Low Countries from the mid-sixteenth century. Ferdinand II of Tuscany funded the Accademia del Cimento in Florence (1657–1667), making available his glass-blower Andrea Mariani, in whose hands the sealed spirit in the glass thermometer was brought to perfection. Louis XIV and his chief minister, Colbert, funded Gian Domenico Cassini's (1625–1712) purchase of the best Italian telescopes for the Paris Observatory—but no amount of money would persuade Giuseppe Campani to divulge his craft secrets. The economically aware artisan spent his time making marketable products, willing to respond to the demands of scientifically motivated clients, only when adequately rewarded.

BIBLIOGRAPHY

Daumas, M. *Scientific Instruments of the Seventeenth and Eighteenth Centuries and Their Makers*. London: Batsford, 1972. First published as *Les instruments scientifiques aux xviie et xviiie siècles*. Paris: Presses Universitaires de France, 1953.

Taylor, E. G. R. *The Mathematical Practitioners of Tudor and Stuart England*. London: Cambridge University Press for the Institute of Navigation, 1954.

Turner, A. J. *Early Scientific Instruments: Europe, 1400–1800.* London: Sotheby's, 1987.

D. J. BRYDEN

See also Craftsman-and-Scholar Thesis

Intelligencers. See Correspondence Networks

Internalist/Externalist Historiography

Ever since the rise of their discipline in the twentieth century, historians of science have contended over contrasting, often politically charged, interpretations of the Scientific Revolution. Prior to the 1970s, these divergent approaches were represented as deriving from a polar opposition between two schools of interpretation, termed *internalist* and *externalist*. Since that time, historians of the Scientific Revolution have spoken about the triumphant transcendence of the internalist/externalist debate, through the emergence of new forms of social and contextual history of science. Even more recently, it has become clear that this disciplinary folklore needs revision, that the internalist/externalist division was overstated, and that its proclaimed transcendence was not as definitive as had been alleged. This essay first maps the traditional account of the debate before turning to the newer revisionist view.

According to the customary view of the debate, internalists and externalists tended to concentrate, respectively, upon the cognitive and the socioeconomic dimensions of science. Internalists believed that scientific ideas and methods are autonomous, unfolding through the internal dynamics of rational thought and procedure alone, with social and economic circumstances at best affecting the timing or direction of research and at worst hindering progress. Externalists, especially of the Marxist school, held that the content as well as the direction of scientific knowledge was shaped by technological pulls that ultimately depended upon economic and social forces and structures. Cutting across the internalist/externalist clash was a second debate between advocates of continuity on the one hand and advocates of revolution on the other. While one could find internalist explanations of continuity as well as revolution, externalist explanations were confined to tales of revolution. The polar opposition of internalism

and externalism is illustrated by comparing the well-known views of Alexandre Koyré (1892–1964), the most influential internalist in Anglo-American and French historiography of science, with those of Boris Hessen, one of the earliest and most influential of the breed of Soviet Marxist advocates of externalism.

Koyré held that the development of modern science depended upon a revolutionary shift in ideas, the establishment of a new "metaphysics," or set of deep conceptual presuppositions for scientific thought. In his *Études Galiléennes* (1939), the classic internalist study of the Scientific Revolution, Koyré attributed Galileo Galilei's (1564–1642) success in founding the first version of classical mechanics to the fact that he worked within the correct sort of metaphysical framework, a nonmystical "Platonism," the belief that the basic furniture of the world consists in mathematical objects, moved according to simple mathematical laws. For Koyré, this sort of Platonic metaphysics was the only viable framework for scientific advance. In other works, Koyré similarly used close textual analysis of conceptual foundations to explain the rise of Copernicanism and the Newtonian synthesis, thus creating a widely admired model of internalist explanation of the revolutionary origins of modern science.

Hessen's explanation of the Scientific Revolution, set out in his widely discussed 1931 paper on "The Social and Economic Roots of Newton's *Principia*," stimulated a variety of Western Marxist externalists over the next generation. Hessen claimed that Isaac Newton's (1642–1727) physics was a response to practical, economically relevant questions thrown up over the previous century and a half by the development of the fledgling commercial capitalist economy and the early-modern state. He held that problems in mining, shipbuilding, gunnery, navigation, and cartography pertained, in essence, to fundamental areas of physics and that they invited solution in the form of the development of Newtonian physics. In this way, changes in the socioeconomic base produced the greatest and most permanent achievement of the age, Newton's science.

Hessen recognized the theological and philosophical dimensions of Newton's scientific work, and the *Principia mathematica philosophiae naturalis* (1687) as more than a compendium of results in applied physics, but he read these elements, however, as ideological reflections of Newton's class position and, hence, as superfluous to his science. For Koyré, Newton's philosophical and religious conceptions were essential, for they constituted the metaphysics that shaped his science. Koyré, however, refused to address social-historical questions about the metaphysical foundations of scientific theories—questions of how, why, and in whose interest particular pieces of "metaphysics" were deployed constitutively of scientific claims.

To understand the internalist/externalist debate and its fate, one needs to see that internalists and externalists agreed upon a demarcation between the *cognitive* inside of science and its *social* outside. As Hessen illustrates, the cognitive inside of science, scientific method and Newtonian mechanics, was fine as long as it depended upon, and was endemically shaped and sustained by, the "appropriate" sorts of social factors. Conversely, as the case of Koyré illustrates quite well, internalists readily explored the *intellectual* contexts of scientific thought but shunned the institutional, social, political, and economic analysis of those contexts. Contexts were fine as long as they were intellectual, not *social*.

The standard picture of the internalist/externalist debate continues by asserting that the polar positions came into conflict in the 1930s after the dramatic appearance of Hessen's work and that the ensuing debate permeated the emerging profession of the history of science in the 1950s and 1960s, before being resolved in the 1970s with the emergence of post-Kuhnian sociology of scientific knowledge and contextual history of science. However, incisive analyses by Robert Young (1985), Barry Barnes (1974), and Steven Shapin (1992) have revised this standard account. They hold that the internalist/externalist dispute actually ignited in the 1950s rather than the 1930s and that it was very much shaped by Robert K. Merton's (1910–) setting of the problem and by the Cold War ambience of humanities scholarship then prevailing in the United Kingdom and the United States. It turns out that actual practices in the 1950s and 1960s were not as polarized as the covering internalist-versus-externalist rhetoric might suggest and that in the 1970s and 1980s the dispute was not really resolved or transcended in any theoretically significant way.

Merton first addressed the internalist/externalist problem in 1938 in his influential Harvard University dissertation on "Science, Technology, and Society in Seventeenth Century England." His views were later refined in new and revised case studies boasting greater theoretical articulation. His focus on science as a social institution defined the study of scientific communities and institu-

tions as an externalist undertaking: first, because he eschewed all concern with the technical contents of science and, second, because he attempted to discern the social norms that supposedly are functional to healthy science. Merton's historical treatment of the rise of modern science in seventeenth-century England became an exemplary externalist project, in which he sought to identify the larger social conditions, particularly the prominence of Puritanism and the Puritan "ethos," which, in turn, carried and fostered the values necessary for modern science. As for the "inside" of science, Merton posited a cognitive realm defined in positivist terms by the existence of a universal scientific method, arising from a balanced amalgam of the "technical norms" of "rationalism" and "empiricism." Hence, his approach depended upon the expected sort of social/cognitive boundary marking.

However, as Shapin has shown, Merton's significance extends much further than forging a new style of externalism. On a deeper level, Merton was defining the traffic that could pass over the cognitive/social barrier, for he was willing to admit that both internal and external factors played a role in the history of science. He even went so far as to accommodate, or finesse, the Marxist challenge by devoting half of his dissertation to the issue of technological and economic stimuli to scientific achievement in seventeenth-century England.

When the wider debate did ignite in the Cold War atmosphere of the 1950s, the polarized grand rhetoric of internalism versus externalism sat atop more eclectic forms of everyday practice, shaped in large measure by the example of Merton's sophisticated gatekeeping. High-level polar debate was mediated by increasing attention being paid to a middle realm of institutions, communities, groups, and their social norms, just inside of which Merton had placed the social/cognitive boundary. Institutionally and professionally dominant internalists could then concede that both internal and external factors were at work in the Scientific Revolution. The resulting style of Anglo-American history of science during the first generation of the Cold War might be labelled "internalist-biased eclecticism." A "balanced" appeal to external and internal factors was allowed, but exceptional tolerance was always exercised toward internalist work, while no tolerance was extended to Marxist versions of externalism. The polarized, formal positions of internalism and externalism provided the rhetoric for such professional boundary management among historians of science.

I

Nevertheless, in partial correction to Shapin, it needs to be recognized that the extreme poles of the debate did have a continuing and constitutive role in the 1940s and 1950s at the level of grand narratives and explanations of the Scientific Revolution. The cognitive/social boundary agreed by both sides structured an endemic pattern of explanation, shared by both internalist and externalist historians, regardless of whether they advocated a revolutionary or an evolutionary interpretation of the rise of modern science. This pattern had two moments. In the first, the "meaning" of the Scientific Revolution as a historical event was abstracted out in the form of a simple descriptive gloss that presumably bespoke the essential feature(s) of modern "Science." These essences included, for example, "the birth of scientific method"; "the invention of the concept of natural law"; "the establishment of the values necessary for the proper functioning of modern science"; or "the establishment of the mechanistic or Newtonian world-view." In the second explanatory moment, the selected descriptive gloss was subjected to a causal explanation (i.e., the sudden or gradual genesis of the preferred essence was referred to the action of some large internally or externally acting mono-cause. So, for example, externalists such as J. D. Bernal (1901–1971) and Edgar Zilsel focused their narratives of revolution upon the social and economic shaping of the new doctrine of "scientific method." Similarly, in Merton's version of externalism, the rise of scientific method results from the amalgamation of the "technical norms" of rationalism and empiricism, these, in turn, being crystallizations of values carried most efficiently in the period by Protestants. Marxist and Mertonian externalism was contested by internalists such as J. H. Randall (1899–1980) and A. C. Crombie (1915–1996), who offered intellectualist and evolutionary stories of the slow development of scientific method from the Middle Ages through the seventeenth century.

Let us return, finally, to the standard claim that the internalist/externalist debate was successfully transcended in the 1970s. The internalist/externalist debate certainly produced no convincing explanation of how external and internal factors interact in the dynamics of scientific subcultures. However, one may also doubt whether today's post-Kuhnian sensibilities and the rise of contextual and cultural history of science really constitute a definitive advance. Local studies of specific times and places, indebted to the sociology of scientific knowledge, are difficult to link to the long-term dynamics of knowledge-making subcultures or to wider contexts and their dynamics. Similarly, the currently fashionable cultural history of science is characterized by its attention to the immediate imprinting by contexts upon scientific sites and practices. This tends to obscure the fact that knowledge is made in evolving traditions of practice or subcultures that have their own synchronic density and diachronic dynamics. Hence, post-1970s historiography of the Scientific Revolution displays a modern version of eclecticism. A new internalism, grounded in post-Kuhnian sociology of scientific knowledge, is judiciously mixed with a new externalism, grounded in immediate contextual imprinting upon sites and events. The historiography of the Scientific Revolution, therefore, still confronts the problem of theorizing scientific change as part of the wider problem of theorizing the historical dynamics of the West. The internalist/externalist debate has not been solved or dissolved, merely shifted, transformed, and left open.

BIBLIOGRAPHY

Barnes, Barry. *Scientific Knowledge and Sociological Theory*. London: Routledge and Kegan Paul, 1974, pp. 99–124.

Kuhn, Thomas S. *The Trouble with the Historical Philosophy of Science*. (Robert and Maurine Rothschild Distinguished Lecture, November 19, 1991). Cambridge, MA: Department of the History of Science, Harvard University, 1992.

Rossi, P. *Philosophy, Technology, and the Arts in the Early Modern Era*. Trans. Salvatore Attanasio. New York: Harper and Row, 1970.

Shapin, Steven. "Discipline and Bounding: The History and Sociology of Science as Seen Through the Externalism-Internalism Debate." *History of Science* 30 (1992), 333–369.

Young, Robert. "The Historiographic and Ideological Contexts of the Nineteenth-Century Debate on Man's Place in Nature." In Young, Robert. *Darwin's Metaphor: Nature's Place in Victorian Culture*. Cambridge: Cambridge University Press, 1985, pp. 164–247.

JOHN A. SCHUSTER

See also Craftsman-and-Scholar Thesis; Marxist Historiography; Puritanism and Science

J

Jesuits. See Society of Jesus

Journal des sçavans

Published from 1665 to the present (with a hiatus from 1792 to 1816), this was one of the earliest learned periodicals and the first to feature scientific news. As such, it inspired the *Philosophical Transactions* of the Royal Society of London, Pierre Bayle's (1647–1706) *Nouvelles de la République des Lettres,* and other imitators. By exposing the latest discoveries and debates, and by evaluating current books in historical and philosophical context, its pages were witness to the factious unfolding of the Scientific Revolution, albeit from a Cartesian perspective. In the process, the journal helped assimilate scientific writing into broader literary and learned traditions.

Claiming the Republic of Letters as their hereditary domain, the editors strove to supplant rival periodicals and to express critical judgments while giving the appearance of impartiality. Thus, a review not only summarized the contents of a book, but also might point out internal inconsistencies, feature unconventional ideas, or cite different treatments of the same topic. As a result, the journal functioned as a guide to learned controversy, and it instructed the comfortable classes, in France and abroad, in the history of ideas and the strategies of critical reading.

The *Journal des sçavans* served in part as the house organ for the Académie Royale des Sciences (Paris). Both institutions enjoyed the protection of Louis XIV's chief minister, Jean-Baptiste Colbert (1619–1683); indeed, the Abbé Jean Gallois (1632–1707) served simultaneously as

editor (1666–1674) of the journal and as secretary to the Académie. In its pages, academicians published their dissections and eclipse observations, announced inventions and discoveries, and challenged one another's views.

The editors also reported scientific news from Paris, the provinces, and abroad. Gallois's successor, the Abbé Jean-Paul de La Roque (editor, 1675–1687), announced the dates of eclipses and the addresses of instrument makers, related curiosities gleaned from international correspondents, and reported autopsies whose startling finds were authenticated by learned witnesses. From Avignon and other cities, astronomers contributed eclipse observations and methods for making cheap observational apparatus. From London came news of the Royal Society and articles translated from the *Philosophical Transactions,* which repaid the compliment in kind. Summaries of Jan Swammerdam's (1637–1680) views on the metamorphosis of insects (1682) and translations of three letters (1675, 1678, 1679) by Antoni van Leeuwenhoek (1632–1723) briefly acquainted readers with Dutch microscopy. In the 1690s, Gottfried Wilhelm Leibniz (1646–1716) and the Bernoulli brothers, Johann (1667–1748) and Jakob (1654–1705), sent articles for publication, and Leibniz's works were generously reviewed.

The journal's deference to censorship has been exaggerated. From the first issue, it defended heliocentrism and publicized Cartesianism. Successive articles vaunted the power of new telescopes, explained the theoretical implications of astronomical observations, belittled the Catholic Index of Forbidden Books, and emphasized the technical (not theological) questions raised by the plurality of worlds. The policy was instigated by Denis de Sallo (1626–1669, editor in 1665), known for his Gallican sympathies. The long-term effect

LE
IOVRNAL
DES
SÇAVANS

Du Lundy V. Ianvier M. D C. L X V.

Par le Sieur DE HEDOVVILLE.

A PARIS,

Chez I E A N C V S S O N, ruë S. Iacques, à l'Image de S. Iean Baptiſte.

M. D C. L X V.

AVEC PRIVILEGE DV ROY.

The first seven volumes of the earliest scientific journal.

was to make Copernicanism inoffensive and to empha-size reasoned discussion of Cartesian cosmology.

When Gabriel Daniel's (1649–1728) *Voyage au monde de Descartes* (Voyage into the World of Descartes) appeared in 1691, the reviewer could assume familiarity with René Descartes's arguments for the existence of God, his distinction between body and soul, his system of light, his laws of motion and of reflection and of refraction, and his theory of *tourbillons* (celestial vortices). The pros and cons of Cartesian philosophy were recapitulated in notices of theological works by Nicolas Malebranche (1638–1715) and Pierre-Daniel Huet (1630–1721) and systematic treatises by Jacques Rohault (1620–1675), Antoine Le Grand (fl. 1660–1680), and Pierre-Sylvain Régis (1632–1707). While mechanistic physiology became commonplace thanks to summaries of the anatomical work of Giovanni Alfonso Borelli

(1608–1679) and Marcello Malpighi (1628–1694), among others, opponents of the animal-machine fared better than defenders.

By the 1680s, the issue was how to correct and build on the Cartesian legacy, and, while editorial policy favored the Cartesians, cogent criticism got its due; thus, Louis Cousin (1627–1707, editor, 1687–1702) published debates between Nicolas Hartsoeker (1656–1725) and Collège Royal professor La Montre (fl. 1690–1710) over matter theory. Finally, Isaac Newton's (1642–1727) *Principia mathematica philosophiae naturalis* (1687) was favorably received, albeit with the reservation that its speculative assumptions were more appropriate to geometry and mechanics than to natural philosophy properly speaking (1688).

Cousin's policy was to feature the innovative and contentious traits of the new science and mathematics. Bland notices of textbooks in theoretical and practical geometry gave way to challenges to solve mathematical problems, often with prizes attached. In 1695 and 1696, readers learned about the new calculus from notices of works by Leibniz and Guillaume-François-Antoine de L'Hôspital, marquis de Sainte-Mesme (1661–1704). Judicious book reviews were balanced by heated exchanges between the Malebranchists and Régis or Antoine Arnauld (1612–1694).

Taken together, the articles and reviews of the *Journal des sçavans* evoke the values of the Scientific Revolution. By giving space to foreign books and contributions, the editors demonstrated that the Republic of Letters respected neither geographical nor political borders, but also that it flourished under royal auspices. When editors or contributors challenged the disinterestedness of testimonials or debated the reliability of observations, the journal aired the problem of evidence. Utilitarian aspirations found voice in articles about medical treatises and public health, as well as in announcements of new inventions. The complex springs of interest in science—for its curiosity value, theoretical implications, and practical applications—were fed by the journal.

The *Journal des sçavans* reveals scientific thought and writing in flux. Its pages witnessed, but also contributed to, that evolution. First, the editors promulgated and dignified scientific inquiry by including it in a journal concerned with jurisprudence, sacred and profane history, and moral philosophy. Specifically, they nurtured a public for science by making the subject both intelligible and intriguing.

Second, the editors portrayed scientific inquiry not as a positivist but, rather, as a discursive project, an enterprise that was uncertain and controversial but capable of progress. By questioning assumptions and reasoning, they clarified its philosophical aspects. By weighing evidence, they emphasized its empirical obligations. By reporting the quest for more powerful telescopes and microscopes, they recognized its technical concerns. By printing priority disputes and prize announcements, they manipulated the psychology of invention. By eulogizing scientists and mathematicians, they showed that savants as well as princes could earn *gloire* (glory) with their deeds. As an advocate of the Republic of Letters and the New Science, the *Journal des sçavans* enhanced the status of scientists and made their work intelligible to a wide public.

BIBLIOGRAPHY

Eisenstein, Elizabeth Lewisohn. *Grub Street Abroad: Aspects of the French Cosmopolitan Press from the Age of Louis XIV to the French Revolution.* Oxford: Clarendon, 1992.

Hatin, Eugène. "La Presse littéraire aux XVIIe et XVIIIe siècles: Première période, 1665–1730." In *Histoire politique et littéraire de la presse en France.* 8 vols. Paris: Poulet-Malassis et de Broise, 1859–1861, vol. 2, pp. 149–325.

Morgan, Betty Trebelle. *Histoire du Journal des Sçavans depuis 1665 jusqu'en 1701.* Paris: Presses Universitaires de France, 1929.

Table générale des matières contenues dans le Journal des Sçavans de l'édition de Paris, depuis l'année 1665 qu'il a commencé, jusqu'en 1750. 10 vols. Paris: Briasson, 1753–1754.

Trenard, Louis. "Les Débuts de la presse périodique (iv) *Le Journal des Savants.*" In *Histoire générale de la presse française,* ed. Claude Bellanger, Jacques Godechot, Pierre Guiral, and Fernand Terrou. 5 vols. Paris: Presses Universitaires de France, 1969–1976, vol. 1, pp. 124–137.

Vittu, Jean-Pierre. "Journal des Savants (1665–1792, puis 1797 et depuis 1816)." In *Dictionnaire des journaux, 1600–1789,* ed. Jean Sgard. 2 vols. Paris: Universitas; Oxford: Voltaire Foundation, 1991, vol. 2, pp. 645–654.

ALICE STROUP

See also Académie Royale des Sciences; Cartesianism; Correspondence Networks; *Philosophical Transactions*

K

Kabbalah

A commonly used term for the mystical teachings of Judaism from the twelfth century to the present day. The word means "that which is received" or "tradition," and it was generally believed that the Kabbalah represented the unwritten aspect of the divine revelation granted to Moses on Mt. Sinai, which had passed orally from one generation to the next until it was finally written down. The Kabbalah has been studied primarily as a Jewish phenomenon. Only in recent years have scholars begun to recognize its importance for European philosophy and science as a whole.

The two major sources of kabbalistic thought available to Christians before the seventeenth century were the *Sefer Yezirah,* or *Book of Formation,* written between the third and sixth centuries, and the *Zohar,* or [*Book of*] *Splendor,* attributed to the second-century Rabbi Simeon ben Yohai but actually written by Moses de Leon in the thirteenth century. These two works had enormous influence on Jews and Christians in terms of the theories of Creation they present and their vision of the relation between God and man. According to the *Sefer Yezirah,* Creation occurs through the act of divine speech and the manipulation of the Hebrew letters, which are described as the "gates" or "roots" from which all things were formed. In the *Zohar,* Creation is described differently as a process in which the ten *sefirot,* the primordial or ideal numbers (from the Hebrew verb *safor,* "to numerate"), emanate from a primordial, unknowable One (*Eyn Sof*). Since Creation involves the shattering of divine unity and the production of lesser beings, the ultimate cosmic goal is the return of the many to their original divine source through the process or *Tikkun,* or restoration. Kabbalists

were clearly influenced by Neoplatonism in these formulations, but where they differed from Neoplatonists and Christians was in their insistence that human beings played a crucial role in the redemptive process. Because man is made in the image of God and originates from the Godhead itself, he has the power to influence and act in the divine realm. By serving God with appropriate devotion, man becomes an active participant in the "mystery of unification" (*sod ha-yihud*), the process in which the divine forces are united, perfected, and return to their source.

A new form of Kabbalah appeared in the sixteenth century, derived from the teachings of Isaac Luria (1534–1572). Luria built on ideas in the *Zohar,* placing special emphasis on the redemptive process of *Tikkun.* Luria believed that everything in the world is alive and full of souls in different states of spiritual awareness. Through repeated reincarnations (*Gilgul*), every created entity would rise up the ladder of Creation until finally freed from the cycle of rebirth. Luria's teachings were made available to Christians with the publication by Christian Knorr von Rosenroth (1636–1689) of the *Kabbala denudata,* the largest collection of kabbalistic (particulary Lurianic) texts available to the Latin-reading public up to the nineteenth century.

Since the 1970s, there has been increasing willingness to recognize the important ways in which mystical and occult thinking contributed to the development of science and the emergence of toleration. However, at the turn of the twenty-first century, the Kabbalah had not yet been integrated into the new historiography, although it richly deserves to be. The Kabbalah acted as something of a permeable barrier between Christians and Jews, allowing for the circulation of ideas. While scholars have long recognized the influence the Kabbalah had on Christian poets, theologians, and philosophers, they are only beginning to investigate the way in which kabbalistic ideas influenced the thought of key figures in the Scientific Revolution, such as Gottfried Wilhelm Leibniz (1646–1716), John Locke (1632–1704), and Isaac Newton (1642–1727). The kabbalistic vision of a universe restored to its original perfection through human effort provided the basis for a radically optimistic philosophy predicated on the conviction that progress is inevitable, an idea that became a hallmark of both the Scientific Revolution and the Enlightenment. Kabbalistic ideas also influenced the debate about language that preoccupied so many intellectuals in the sixteenth and seventeenth centuries, culminating in the conflict between Leibniz and Locke over the nature of human understanding. The effect of the Kabbalah on Christian religious thought was also signficant. Christians who accepted the kabbalistic notion of universal salvation rejected the concept of an eternal hell and predestination and tended to minimize, or allegorize, the role of Christ in the redemptive process. For these Christians, and Leibniz was among them, doctrinal differences appeared increasingly insignificant. The Kabbalah should be recognized for the contribution it has made to all of these different aspects of modern thought.

BIBLIOGRAPHY

Coudert, Allison P. *Leibniz and the Kabbalah*. Dordrecht and Boston: Kluwer, 1994.

Idel, Moshe. *Kabbalah: New Perspectives*. New Haven, CT: Yale University Press, 1988.

Lachower, Fischel, and Isaiah Tishby, eds. and comms. *Zohar: The Wisdom of the Zohar*. Trans. David Goldstein. (The Littman Library of Jewish Civilization). 3 vols. Oxford: Oxford University Press, 1991.

Scholem, G. *Kabbalah*. New York: Meridian, 1974.

ALLISON P. COUDERT

See also Hermetism; Magic; Neoplatonism; *Prisca theologia;* Religion and Natural Philosophy

Kepler, Johannes (1571–1630)

Born in Weil der Stadt, Germany, he attended the University of Tübingen. Kepler is chiefly remembered for his revolutionary and accurate theory of planetary motions, involving elliptical rather than circular orbits, radii sweeping out areas proportional to times, and periodic times of pairs of planets proportional to the 3/2 power of

their mean distances. His work constituted the first attempt to provide a sound physical basis for astronomy and led to the more successful and comprehensive theory of Isaac Newton (1642–1727). Kepler also made significant contributions to optics and mathematics.

Toward the end of his career, in 1621, Kepler returned to his first publication, *Mysterium cosmographicum* (Cosmographic Mystery, 1596). In his notes to his new edition of this work, he qualified or took issue with nearly every conclusion of the original. Yet, at the same time, he remarked (in the dedicatory letter): "Almost every book on astronomy which I have published since that time could be referred to one or another of the main chapters set out in this little book, and would contain either an illustration or a completion of it."

Viewing Kepler's work as a whole four centuries later, we find ourselves in a somewhat similar position. Despite his substantial contributions to later science, his books are mostly filled with ideas with which we would at least take issue and that often seem odd in the extreme: cosmic dimensions governed by regular geometrical solids and archetypal proportions, celestial music, planetary souls, Aristotelian views on motion, and more. Nevertheless, though we might not accept his conclusions, we can see in the direction that Kepler took, and the lines of thought that he opened up, the beginning of a wholly new approach to astronomy that would culminate in universal gravitation and the development of celestial physics.

Astronomy

At a time when astronomy was classified as a branch of mathematics and was considered incompetent to make judgments about what really goes on in the heavens, Kepler's first publication, *Mysterium cosmographicum,* was characteristically bold and original. It was also not a little confusing to the public. Kepler remarked in a note in the second edition: "the word cosmography is commonly used to mean geography; and that title, though it is drawn from the universe, has induced bookshops and catalogers to include my book under geography." Kepler's aim, from the very beginning, was to bring mathematics, theology, and physical theory together under the umbrella science of cosmology, in which he could deal with the real questions of how the universe is put together and how the celestial bodies are really moving.

The more immediate question Kepler intended to answer in the book was why there are six primary planets

K

Johannes Kepler. From volume 18 of Johannes Kepler, Gesammelte Werke, *ed. Max Caspar (1959). Courtesy Bavarian Academy of Sciences.*

and not more or less than that number. It had occurred to him, in the middle of drawing a diagram in class, that there might be a connection between this number and the number of regular geometrical solids, of which there are five. Might God have determined the spaces between the planets by nesting the regular solids alternately with the planets, so that each solid is between two planetary orbits? A quick calculation showed that the fit was fairly good, and Kepler sent off a series of three letters to his astronomy professor at Tübingen, Michael Maestlin (1550–1631), announcing the discovery and asking for help in improving the fit.

Kepler's first thought was that the discrepancies might have been a result of defects in astronomical theory rather than in his regular solid hypothesis. Nicolaus Copernicus (1473–1543) had determined the dimension of the orbits by referring them to the center of Earth's orbit, not to the center of the Sun. Kepler found, with Maestlin's help, that, if one chose the Sun itself as center and followed the usual procedures for determining the orbit, one would obtain an entirely different orbit, with a different center from the one found by Copernicus. Although the new orbits also did not quite fit into the

nest of regular solids, Kepler believed he was on the right track. He had made the important discovery that physical principle (in this case, the central role played by the Sun) applied to mathematical theory would lead to new predictions that could be observationally tested. "Now, by Hercules," he remarked to Maestlin, "this is the a priori road to correction of the motions; and there is some hope if others, to whom observations are available, try it."

Kepler's emphasis of the Sun's central role arose from his idea, borrowed from the *Timaeus* of Plato (428–348 B.C.E.), that God used his own image as a pattern for the cosmos as a whole. Recasting this Platonic idea in Christian terms, Kepler supposed that the universe must be spherical and that the Trinity is expressed in it as center, circumference, and intervening space. As he put it in a letter to Maestlin: "Accordingly, the Sun in the middle of the movables, being at rest itself and nonetheless the source of motion, bears the image of God the Father, the Creator." This analogy leads to another physical principle, namely that the effect of the Sun upon the planets varies inversely with the distance. In the same letter, Kepler continues: "Now the Sun disperses a moving power through the medium in which the movables are, and in just this way the Father creates through the Spirit or the power of the Spirit. And now, from the necessity of the presuppositions, it follows that the motions are proportional to the distances." Kepler uses this idea in Chapter 22 of *Mysterium cosmographicum* as a physical explanation of Ptolemy's equant point. The second-century Egyptian astronomer Claudius Ptolemy (ca. 100–ca. 170) had allowed planetary speeds to vary by supposing that equal angles are traversed in equal times about a point not at the centers of circles. Later astronomers called this point the *punctum aequans,* or equant in English. Kepler argued that the particular placement of the equant used by Ptolemy resulted in a motion that followed the Keplerian speed rule. "The path of the planet is eccentric, and it is slower when it is further out, and swift when it is further in. For it was to explain this that Copernicus postulated epicycles, Ptolemy equants."

In this early work, we can already discern the radically new approach to astronomy that characterized his mature work. Astronomy is developed in the context of cosmology. In contrast with earlier systems, such as that of Ptolemy, which abandoned physics to give a purely mathematical predictive account of planetary positions, Kepler's aim was to describe what really happens in the heavens. In his system, the Sun plays a dynamically central role in the planetary motions, which are to be explained in terms of physical forces.

When circumstances brought Kepler to Prague to work as an assistant to Tycho Brahe (1546–1601), who had taken up residence there, Kepler found the opportunity he had been awaiting. Brahe's years of systematic observation with superb naked-eye instruments had produced a body of data against which Kepler could—he hoped—test and refine his theories. Of course, it was not quite so simple: Brahe was by no means eager to hand over his treasure to this brash youngster. Nevertheless, Kepler did have limited access to some of the observations and was able to make a good start. He regarded it as divine providence that his assignment was to give an account of the motions of Mars, since that planet's large eccentricity and its proximity to the earth made it the ideal subject for a minute examination of the orbit's shape and position.

Kepler's first attempts, as shown in his working papers on Mars, were characteristically original. Instead of beginning, as most astronomers had, with the longitudinal motions around the Sun, he took up the relatively small latitudinal motions north and south of the plane of Earth's orbit. In previous theories, such as that of Copernicus, these motions had been accounted for by referring the orbit not to the Sun itself but to the center of Earth's orbit. The resultant theory had to allow the plane of the orbit to assume different positions depending upon where the planet was on it. Kepler reasoned, on physical grounds, that the orbit must go through the Sun itself, and he was able to show that, when the orbit is referred to the Sun's true position, the plane of Mars's orbit remains at a small fixed angle to the plane of Earth's orbit. The discovery that the planes of planetary orbits pass through the Sun, which, because of its importance, has been called Kepler's Zeroth Law, confirmed Kepler's trust in his physical ideas and also led to an ingenious way of finding Mars's distances by comparing its apparent latitude with the orbital inclination.

This technique was also important because later, after Kepler had used Brahe's observations to establish a provisional theory of Mars's motion, it let him check the approximate position of Mars's orbit in space. The accuracy of the check was sufficient to show that no circular orbit, with a fixed equant point, could simultaneously put the planet at the right distance and at the right angular position. Thus, although Kepler had found a combination of a circular orbit and a fixed equant that gave accurate longitudes, a theory that would have satisfied any other astronomer, he knew that it could not represent the truth. His next step was to suppose a circular orbit that would satisfy the distances at aphelion and perihelion and see how far off the angular positions would be. The resulting maximum discrepancy of some eight minutes of arc at the octants (i.e., at 45° and 135° on both sides of the orbit) would have been acceptable to earlier astronomers, but with Tycho Brahe's superior observations it was too much. "Now," Kepler remarked, "because they could not have been ignored, these eight minutes alone will have led the way to the reformation of all of astronomy."

This incorrect orbit had been arrived at through two assumptions: an eccentric circular orbit and a fixed equant point. Evidently, at least one of these assumptions must have been wrong, and Kepler had a notion which it was. The Ptolemaic equant was not quite equivalent to Kepler's physical principle that a planet's speed decreases in proportion to its distance from the Sun. It occurred to him that, if the physical principle could be expressed in a mathematically calculable form, it might produce the correct longitudes on a circular orbit that had the correct eccentricity. Here is how Kepler described his procedure:

> I began by dividing the eccentric into 360 parts, as if these were least particles, and supposed that within one such part the distance does not change. I then found the distances at the beginnings of the parts or degrees ... and added them all up. Next, I assigned an artificial round number to the periodic time: ... I set it equal to 360 degrees, or a full circle.... As a result, I have so arranged it that as the sum of the distances is to the sum of the time, so is any given distance to its time. Finally, I added the times over the individual degrees and compared these times with ... the number of parts whose distance was sought.

This is obviously not an easy way to compute eccentric positions—Kepler described it as "mechanical and tedious"—so he looked for a shortcut. A new way soon occurred to him: "since I knew that the points of the eccentric are infinite, and their distances are infinite, it struck me that all these distances are contained in the plane of the eccentric. For I had remembered that

K

Archimedes, in seeking the ratio of the circumference to the diameter, once thus divided a circle into an infinity of triangles."

The idea was to represent the sum of the distances by the areas swept out by the Sun-planet line. These areas would then be proportional to the times. This principle, which Kepler always regarded as a computational shortcut, is what we now call Kepler's second law—a name that it did not acquire until more than a century later. Although it was only qualitatively supported by observations, Kepler had great confidence in it. For it was this area/time proportionality that, more than anything else, convinced him that planetary orbits had to be oval rather than circular. He found that when he applied it to a circular orbit, the planet was slightly too fast at aphelion and perihelion and slightly too slow at the intermediate points. It struck him that this would be corrected if some of the area were moved from the sides of the circle to the region of aphelion and perihelion. As Kepler vividly put it: "The times, when they are abstracted from the plane and adjusted upward and downward, will be accumulated at aphelion and perihelion in much the same manner as, if one were to squeeze a fat-bellied sausage at its middle, he would squeeze and squash the ground meat, with which it is stuffed, outwards from the belly towards the two ends, emerging above and below from beneath his hand." It was only after this realization that he began to take seriously the indications, of which he was already aware, that the distances at the sides of the orbit were slightly shorter than those given by a circle.

The acceptance of an oval shape for the orbit did not immediately lead to a satisfactory conclusion. At every step of the way, Kepler asked how the forces moving the planets (whether guided by living beings or by physical action alone) could produce the orbit. He did not expect the result to be geometrically neat, since, in real life, simple tendencies have a way of interacting to produce complex results (bear in mind that the Galilean and the Cartesian idea that nature is mathematical was yet to come). The elliptical form of the orbit was established only when Kepler realized that it could be produced by a simple oscillation of the planet in and out along the radius to the Sun. This result, together with the area law, was published in the *Astronomia nova* (New Astronomy, 1609).

The relationship between the periodic times of planets and their distances from the Sun eluded Kepler for another decade. He had, indeed, attempted a solution in the *Mysterium cosmographicum* of 1596, but the fit (though good enough to publish) was not exact, and the method of computation was hard to justify. Finally, in 1618, he tried comparing the cubes of the distances to the squares of the periodic times and found a very close agreement. This relationship, which later came to be called Kepler's third law, was of crucial importance to Newton in establishing universal gravitation. However, it had no such implication for Kepler: he regarded it, not as a simple effect of the weakening of the Sun's force but as a divinely contrived coincidence of solar force and planetary density, size, and distance.

A crucial final step in Kepler's astronomical life's work was the computation of usable astronomical tables based on his startlingly new theories. His *Tabulae Rudolphinae* (Rudolphine Tables) appeared in 1627 and were followed in 1630 by ephemerides for 1621 through 1636. In the course of computing the latter, Kepler found that in 1631 both Mercury and Venus should be visible traversing the Sun's disk at inferior conjunction. Although he was wrong about Venus, his Mercury prediction came within 0.25° of the observed position, far closer than any other tables of the day. Such successes soon overcame the understandable reluctance of astronomers to accept Kepler's theories, though a number of attempts were made to improve their accuracy and to make the computations easier.

Optics

Kepler initially took up the study of optics to solve certain problems associated with the nontelescopic astronomical instruments of the day. With characteristic thoroughness, he immersed himself in the study of the perspectivist tradition exemplified by the Arab Alhazen (Ibn al-Haytham, d. 1039) and his thirteenth-century European disciple Witelo. He found that many of his questions had not been adequately answered and set out to develop what he called a "supplement" (*Paralipomena*) to Witelo's work, which he published in 1604. The part of this book that was historically most influential is the theory of vision (Chapter 5), which identified the retina as the place where the image was formed and was transferred to the nerves. It was a great puzzle to him and his contemporaries that, although he showed that the image on the retina is inverted, we nevertheless see the world right side up.

Other notable achievements of the *Optics* were a serviceable (though physically ill-founded) theory of refractions, a succinct treatment of conic sections, and a thorough and accurate account of pinhole images. Although his theory of refractions was soon to be displaced by the work of Willebrord Snel (1580–1626) and René Descartes (1596–1650), it enabled him to develop a theory of lenses and their images that gave the first successful account of how telescopes work (published in the *Dioptrice* of 1611).

Mathematics

In mathematics, Kepler is better known for having proposed problems than for solving them. Because of his intention to provide a physical basis for astronomy, he dealt almost from the beginning with problems of integral and differential calculus that were beyond his or anyone else's ability. Typically, when an integration was called for, Kepler would laboriously calculate the sum of a large number of small elements. An example of this was described above, in his attempt to apply the distance/speed relationship to planetary orbits.

He used this same technique to compute the volumes of curvilinear solids, which he published in his *Stereometria doliorum vinariorum* (Solid Measure of Wine Barrels, 1615). The origin of this work is curious. Kepler had been purchasing wine for his wedding and saw the vintner measure the volume of a barrel by measuring the diagonal from the middle of the belly to one of the ends. Questioning the accuracy of this method, he found that the barrels in that part of Austria had been given proportions that resulted in the maximum volume for a given diagonal. This ensured that small differences in the dimensions of different barrels would have a minimal effect on their volumes. Kepler's method of finding the maximum was similar to that of Pierre de Fermat (1601–1665), though, where Fermat used algebra, Kepler used Euclidean ratios.

BIBLIOGRAPHY

Caspar, Max. *Kepler*. Trans. C. Doris Hellman. New York: Dover, 1993.

Field, J. V. *Kepler's Geometrical Cosmology*. London: Athlone, 1988.

Kepler, Johannes. *Gesammelte Werke*. Ed. Max Caspar et al. 20 vols. Munich: C. H. Beck, 1939–.

———. *The Harmony of the World*. Trans. E. J. Aiton, A. M. Duncan, and J. V. Field. Philadelphia: American Philosophical Society, 1996.

———. *Mysterium cosmographicum: The Secret of the Universe*. Trans. A. M. Duncan. New York: Abaris, 1981.

———. *New Astronomy*. Trans. William H. Donahue. Cambridge: Cambridge University Press, 1992.

Stephenson, Bruce. *Kepler's Physical Astronomy*. Princeton, NJ: Princeton University Press, 1994.

WILLIAM H. DONAHUE

See also Astronomical Tables and Ephemerides; Astronomy; Copernicanism; Keplerianism; Optics

Keplerianism

During Johannes Kepler's lifetime (1571–1630), very few astronomers accepted his basic astronomical ideas, nor, for that matter, were a majority convinced of Copernicus's. Although the leading natural philosophers were aware of Kepler's elliptical planetary orbits, most hardly mentioned them—Galileo Galilei (1564–1642) not at all—or were noncommittal. Mathematical astronomers, to whom Kepler's works were addressed, objected to his novelties for a number of reasons:

1. Celestial motions in circles had behind them the sanction and authority of the greatest philosopher, Aristotle (384–322 B.C.E.), and the greatest astronomer, Ptolemy (ca. 100–ca. 170), of antiquity and were perceived as part of the natural order of things.

2. Keplerian astronomy was a variant of the Copernican theory, which violated the known principles of celestial and terrestrial physics.

3. The calculation of planetary position in an elliptical orbit according to Kepler's rule governing the relation between speed in orbit and distance from the Sun (later called his second law) required difficult and tedious approximations and ill befit the nature of astronomy.

4. Kepler's insistence on physical explanations for the motions of the planets likewise went counter to the nature and purpose of astronomy as well as accepted principles of physics.

5. The use of Tycho Brahe's (1546–1601) observational data was unsupported by Tycho's independent publication of them, nor was there adequate contemporaneous empirical evidence in support of Kepler's novel theories.

A turning point came in 1627 with the publication of Kepler's *Rudolphine Tables*. After Tycho Brahe, as had not been the case for Nicolaus Copernicus (1473–1543), accuracy of prediction became the chief desideratum in the choice among competing astronomical systems. Kepler's tables, beginning with their prediction of the time of the the transit of Mercury across the Sun in 1631, soon began to outshine the rest, Ptolemaic, Copernican, and Tychonian. This did not necessarily persuade astronomers to adopt ellipses and nonuniform motion, as a number of them, while using and constructing tables based on Kepler's, continued to adhere to circles and uniformity; an ellipse can be generated using the traditional epicycle on its deferent moving uniformly. Some, however, did tend to see merit in Kepler's improvements in the relation of the Sun to planetary orbits in Copernicus's system, namely in his placing the Sun in all of their planes and keeping constant the inclinations of the orbital planes, as this yielded definite improvements in observed planetary latitudes. His use of the true Sun rather than Copernicus's mean sun in the calculation of conjunctions and oppositions also gave improved results.

Substantial support for Kepler's elliptical orbits was provided by the work of Ismaël Boulliau (1605–1694), who was convinced of them by the superiority of the *Rudolphine Tables*. Boullian's *Astronomia Philolaica* of 1645 was influential in the middle decades of the century, and a number of astronomical tables were based on it. Boulliau, however, rejected Kepler's second law and his celestial dynamics, opting instead for a purely kinematic geometrical explanation of planetary motion along a conic section. He also made some improvements in Kepler's tables for some of the planets, particularly in a work of 1657, which made slight adjustments to his earlier model. Along with, and in the wake of, Boulliau's publications, a number of astronomers undertook to improve Kepler's tables, now accepted as the best extant.

Most effective in these efforts was Jeremiah Horrocks (1618–1641), in the words of a notable astronomer and historian of astronomy, "Kepler's only true disciple." In the late 1630s, he fully accepted fundamental Keplerian principles: elliptical orbits with the Sun in one of their foci, governing the planets in their nonuniform motions. Although he did not mention Kepler's area rule—a line from an orbiting planet to the Sun sweeps out equal areas in equal times—he clearly was aware of it and developed a procedure of his own for the calculations it required. He was an indefatigable observer, and his precise observations enabled him to obtain more

accurate figures for some of Kepler's parameters. This enabled him to create a lunar theory that was far and away the best up to that time and to be the first to predict and observe a transit of Venus across the face of the Sun. He also stated that he had verified by repeated observation the validity of Kepler's relationship between the squares of the planetary periods and the cubes of their distances from the Sun. His papers were little known until they were published two and three decades after his death; they nevertheless had some influence on astronomical developments.

In the middle years of the seventeenth century, astronomers who accepted Kepler orbits created a variety of mathematical models designed to avoid the difficulties in applying Kepler's area rule. These involved lines from the focus of an ellipse unoccupied by the Sun to the moving planet generating equal angles in equal times. These "empty-focus equant" theories, though sometimes giving good results, were not good enough, according to Nicolaus Mercator (ca. 1619–1687), after whose publications in the 1670s astronomers began to undertake the tedious calculations necessitated by Kepler's area law. Kepler had by this time also come to be praised for dealing with real orbits devoid of such "figments" as complex sets of circles.

Although Kepler's explanation of planetary motion by quasi-magnetic forces from the Sun was increasingly rejected in the course of the century, the fundamental idea of a solar role in moving the planets had been essential to Kepler's discoveries from the very beginning. In the middle decades of the seventeenth century, Kepler's vision of an astronomy embracing both geometrical models and celestial forces slowly came to be accepted. Mechanical principles and analogues were substituted for "magnetic fibers," and centrifugal force and inertia were invoked as causes of planetary motion; a means of propulsion was no longer thought necessary. Important roles were played by Giovanni Alfonso Borelli (1608–1679), Christiaan Huygens (1629–1695), Robert Hooke (1635–1703), and Christopher Wren (1632–1723) in promoting the conception that the physical explanation of planetary motion lay in the principle of inertia and an inverse-square centripetal force.

It was only Isaac Newton (1642–1727) who could provide the desired mathematical demonstration that centripetal force and inertia could yield elliptical orbits and that the assumption of Kepler's laws, in turn, implied the physical principles. Newton does not seem to have acquired his knowledge of Kepler's ideas on planetary motion from Kepler's works directly but from various astronomical textbooks, notably that of Nicolaus Mercator. By 1676 he was aware of empty-focus-equant theories and had computed the areas necessitated by Kepler's second law. However, nowhere in Book I of Newton's *Principia mathematica philosophiae naturalis* of 1687, where Kepler's laws are mathematically demonstrated, does Kepler's name appear; Newton was persuaded that only he had established their validity. Despite that, Kepler's role in transforming his discipline and setting it on a new path is undeniable.

BIBLIOGRAPHY

Applebaum, Wilbur. "Keplerian Astronomy After Kepler: Researches and Problems." *History of Science* 34 (1996), 451–504.

Russell, John L. "Kepler's Laws of Planetary Motion, 1609–1666." *British Journal for the History of Science* 2 (1964), 1–24.

Voelkel, James R. "The Development and Reception of Kepler's Physical Astronomy, 1593–1609." Ph.D. diss. Indiana University, 1994.

Wilson, Curtis A. "From Kepler's Laws, So-Called, to Universal Gravitation: Empirical Factors." *Archive for History of Exact Sciences* 6 (1970), 89–170.

———. "Predictive Astronomy in the Century after Kepler." In *Planetary Astronomy from the Renaissance to the Rise of Astrophysics. Part A: Tycho Brahe to Newton* (The General History of Astronomy, vol. 2), ed. René Taton and Curtis A. Wilson. Cambridge: Cambridge University Press, 1989, pp. 161–206.

                                    WILBUR APPLEBAUM

See also Bouillau, Ismaël; Copernicanism; Horrocks, Jeremiah; Kepler, Johannes

Kinematics

André-Marie Ampère (1775–1836) coined the word *cinématique,* or kinematics, in his classification of human knowledge put forward in *Essai sur la philosophie des sciences* (1834). He divided mechanics into elementary and transcendent. The former consists of kinematics and statics; the latter, of dynamics and molecular mechanics. Kinematics studies motion with no regard to the forces, while statics studies the forces with no regard to motion. Thus, they are presented as complementary. According to Ampère, kinematics dealt mainly with the velocities of different points of a machine or of an arbitrary system of material points (i.e., with the determination of virtual velocities independently of the applied forces). His classification was clearly connected with the type of mechanics practiced in his time. Ampère's new term was accepted by William Whewell (1794–1866) and others later in the century to mean a purely geometrical science of motion considered in abstract terms without reference to the objects moved or to the force producing or affecting motion. The notion of kinematics became particularly popular among those physicists such as Heinrich Hertz (1857–1894) in *Die Principien der Mechanik* (1894), who rejected the legitimacy of the notion of force on philosophical grounds and attempted to construct a new mechanics on more satisfactory principles.

It is now common to use the term *kinematics* for seventeenth-century authors such as Galileo Galilei (1564–1642) or Christiaan Huygens (1629–1695) and even for medieval authors such as William Heytesbury (fl. 1330–1348) and Thomas Bradwardine (ca. 1290–1349) to mean a mathematical science of motion with no regard to its causes. Historians, for example, have used both terms, *kinematics* and *dynamics,* in relation to Galileo's entire contributions to the science of motion. At the outset of the third day of his *Discorsi e dimostrazioni matematiche intorno a due nuove scienze* (1638), however, Galileo named his treatise *De motu locali* (On Local Motion), dividing it into three parts, dealing with equable or uniform motion, naturally accelerated motion, and violent motion or the motion of projectiles. He believed his science of motion to be one of the two new sciences announced in the title, the other being the science of resistance of materials.

In the last two decades of the twentieth century, historians started paying greater attention to changes of disciplinary boundaries and the location of disciplines on the map of knowledge. Doubts have been raised, for example, about the meaning of the term *mechanics* in the sixteenth century, about its extension in meaning at the beginning and at the end of the seventeenth century, and about whether Isaac Newton's (1642–1727) *Principia mathematica philosophiae naturalis* (1687) can be properly considered as a treatise in mechanics. The most radical advocates of such historicist concerns may argue that, strictly speaking, it is anachronistic to talk of seventeenth-century kinematics. Although in some contexts this may appear to be innocuous, in others it may be misleading because kinematics belongs to a different disciplinary matrix from the seventeenth-century science of motion (*scientia de motu*). Those wishing to write about the emergence and transformation of disciplines, taking into account issues such as teaching at the universities and Jesuit colleges, for example, would be well advised to strictly follow practitioners' categories as well as university statutes and the *ratio studiorum* (i.e., the highly structured Jesuit educational program). In such cases, employing nineteenth-century denominations would risk imposing artificial distinctions and creating false problems. For example, one would have to consider whether seventeenth-century authors were consciously providing a geometrical description of motion avoiding a discussion of the causes, or whether, in order to create such an account, the historian needs to extract quotations from a text in which such a clear distinction is not to be found. Other historians more concerned with purely intellectual accounts may reply that this is merely philological pedantry and that kinematics is a perfectly adequate denomination for a mathematical science describing different types of motion. Although it is not possible to predict how these rival tendencies will develop, all scholars of the Scientific Revolution ought to be aware of their scientists' map of knowledge and of the terminology they employed, without taking for granted that it is legitimate to assume that kinematics always existed.

BIBLIOGRAPHY

Ampère, André-Marie. *Essai sur la philosophie des sciences.* Paris, 1834.

Cohen, I. B. *The Newtonian Revolution: With Illustrations of the Transformation of Scientific Ideas.* Cambridge: Cambridge University Press, 1980.

Gabbey, A. "Force and Inertia in Seventeenth-Century Dynamics." *Studies in History and Philosophy of Science* 2 (1971), 1–67.

Westfall, R. S. *Force in Newton's Physics: The Science of Dynamics in the Seventeenth Century.* London: Macdonald; New York: American Elsevier, 1971.

DOMENICO BERTOLONI MELI

See also Dynamics; Force; Mechanics; Motion

Kircher, Athanasius (1602–1680)

A German Jesuit who spent the majority of his life in Rome, Kircher was one of the most prolific Baroque encyclopedists. Originally from Fulda, Kircher entered the Society of Jesus in 1616 and was ordained in 1628 after three years of study in Mainz. Appointed that same year to teach philosophy, mathematics, Hebrew, and Syr-

iac at the University of Würzburg, Kircher began to develop his interest in a wide variety of sciences that would characterize his later career. The disruptions of the Thirty Years War (1618–1648) forced him to flee Germany in 1631, initially for Avignon, where he met the French savant Nicolas-Claude Fabri de Peiresc (1580–1637) and deepened his interest in astronomy and Egyptian hieroglyphics. By 1633 he was in Rome, hard at work deciphering the meaning of the hieroglyphs from a Coptic grammar lent by Peiresc. Shortly thereafter, his position in Rome was secured by appointment as professor of mathematics at the Collegio Romano, succeeding such distinguished Jesuit mathematicians as Christoph Clavius (1538–1612) and Christoph Scheiner (1573–1650) in this post.

The search for ancient truths occupied the next forty years of Kircher's career. Kircher perceived the hieroglyph as a metaphor for all forms of universal knowledge, whether found in languages (Egyptian, Chinese, Hebrew, Aztec) or in the laws of nature. His researches in these fields produced a dazzling array of

From Kircher's Musurgia universalis *(1650).*

treatises on magnetism, acoustics, optics, astronomy, medicine, numerology, ciphers, philology, archeology, geology, and theology—more than thirty encyclopedic volumes in total, designed to contribute to *pansophia* (universal wisdom). Each treatise was an eclectic amalgamation of ancient writings and contemporary observations, an endless procession of experiments culled from virtually every part of the world and placed in the service of Kircher's Neoplatonic theories of wisdom that emphasized the importance of secret correspondences in nature. These occult virtues, according to Kircher, moved the planets; caused the spread of disease; explained the attractive properties of magnets, the force required to produce a volcanic eruption, and the physics of an echo; and revealed why frenzied dancing in Puglia cured the bite of a tarantula. Embedded in these treatises were hundreds of novel and interesting observations that evidenced Kircher's sharp observational powers and his incessant experimental activity with all of the latest instruments of the day (many devised by his Jesuit colleagues and students). At the same time, his conclusions made evident the largely traditional and magical framework within which he viewed the world.

Kircher's intellectual work occurred in two arenas: the museum at the Collegio Romano and his vast correspondence with other scholars. In 1650 a Roman patrician donated his collection of curiosities and antiquities to the Society of Jesus; Kircher was appointed its curator. From the 1650s through the 1670s, the museum became one of the primary intellectual centers in Rome. Kircher drew upon the missionary networks of the Society of Jesus to increase the size and scope of the collection and persuaded princes and scholars to donate gifts as well. It was here that he performed experiments arguing against such theses as the Copernican system, the possibility of a vacuum in nature, and the existence of perpetual motion. In this gallery as in his books, he displayed the fruits of his research, placing Galilean telescopes next to fragments of Etruscan tombs and Chinese scrolls, and chameleons next to magic lanterns in which the Devil danced to amuse visitors.

Kircher's reputation in his own lifetime reflects the transitional state of science in this age. His work was known and discussed by the leading scholars of his day, among them Robert Boyle (1627–1691) and Francesco Redi (1626–1697), and his museum provided an important resource for scholars interested in virtually every aspect of learning. But Kircher's a priori approach to knowledge increasingly made him an object of scorn and derision among those contemporaries who thought that new observations inevitably led to new theories. Thus, while Kircher's *Mundus subterraneus* (Subterranean World, 1664) was eagerly awaited by natural philosophers, most found its contents disappointing. By the late seventeenth century, it was hard to remain entirely committed to ancient learning as the source of all wisdom. Kircher's desire to do so makes him both a fascinating figure to study and one of the last of the great Renaissance humanists.

BIBLIOGRAPHY

Baldwin, Martha. "The Snakestone Experiments: An Early Modern Medical Debate." *Isis* 86 (1995), 394–418.

Findlen, Paula. *Possessing Nature: Museums, Collecting, and Scientific Culture in Early Modern Italy.* Berkeley and Los Angeles: University of California Press, 1994.

Godwin, Joscelyn. *Athanasius Kircher: A Renaissance Man and the Quest for Lost Knowledge.* London: Thames and Hudson, 1979.

Reilly, Conor. *Athanasius Kircher, S.J., Master of a Hundred Arts.* Rome: Edizioni del Mondo, 1974.

PAULA FINDLEN

See also Correspondences; Magic; Museums and Collections; Neoplatonism

L

Laboratories

Manual work carried out in the laboratory stands at the heart of a new approach to the study of nature that emerged in the Scientific Revolution. Like botanical gardens, cabinets of curiosities, and anatomy theaters, the laboratory became emblematic of this new approach because it was a site in which nature was experienced directly rather than through the redaction and consultation of texts.

In antiquity, work with the hands could not lead to "scientific" or theoretical knowledge because manual labor was associated with servile and commercial pursuits. This view was slowly transformed in western Europe as the result of a number of developments, and, by the seventeenth century, the work of the hands, or practice, came to be regarded as necessary to establish principles or laws of nature. Christian attitudes toward manual work as penitential and redemptive emerged in the Middle Ages. With the interest in, and access to, Arabic writings and their redaction of Greek and Roman authors that peaked in Europe in the twelfth century, a new and stimulating attitude toward manual labor emerged, particularly in the work of Arabic alchemical authors. This alchemical tradition was new to European thinkers because it possessed both manual and textual components and thus unified theory and practice in a way that few other areas of study in medieval Europe did; nevertheless, a new experimental philosophy did not come into existence until the late Renaissance.

Important sources for the new attitude toward manual labor and the arts in the Renaissance included the *Hermetic Corpus* that reached western Europe in the early fifteenth century. These texts, of great importance because of their assumed contemporaneity with Moses, gave a central place to technology and the human ability to transform nature by means of "natural magic." The increasing economic and political importance of craftspeople in guild cities further raised the status of artisans and their labor in the workshop at this time, and humanist interest in Roman models of practical activity resulted in a lively interaction between scholarly and artisanal cultures during the fifteenth and sixteenth centuries. These developments led to the legitimation of manual labor as part of the production of scientific knowledge. In the sixteenth century, the word *laboratorium* came to designate a specific site in which (usually chemical) experiments or trials were carried out. Before this time, "laboratories" had been indistinguishable from apothecary shops and the workshops of artisans (indeed, laboratories continued frequently to be called *officinae,* or workshops).

One of the most important sites for the development of this new exchange between scholars and artisans was the noble Court. As territorial principalities all over Europe began to assert themselves beginning in the fifteenth century, princes began to employ artisans in great numbers, especially those connected to warfare, building, the production of territorial income, and display. As artisans competed for the patronage of nobles, they began to publish their techniques, and their activity of authorship created a further link between texts and techniques. Eventually, the publication of replicable processes would become a hallmark of laboratory activity.

Religious reform also gave powerful impetus to the view that direct engagement with nature (as the original revelation of God) was a legitimate, indeed especially holy, way to gain knowledge. This idea was particularly strong in the writings of Theophrastus von Hohenheim, called Paracelsus (ca. 1491–1541), who placed the alchemical laboratory at the center of the redemptive study of nature. Work in the laboratory was a search for the generative spirit in nature, and the ability to imitate natural processes resulted in healing medicaments that would redeem the original sin of the human race.

In the sixteenth and seventeenth centuries, many nobles, including the Medici, the Spanish and Austrian Habsburgs, and the Hohenzollerns, established alchemical laboratories. In these laboratories, they employed alchemists, apothecaries, and artisans (and sometimes labored themselves) to make expensive medicines, to produce gold from base metals, and to seek other valuable products, such as tinted glass and porcelain. Under the influence of Paracelsian ideas, Emperor Rudolf II (1576–1612) and Landgrave Moritz of Hessen-Kassel founded laboratories as part of a material, intellectual, and spiritual reform that might heal the fractures in Christendom. As part of the religious reform of his territory, Landgrave Moritz founded a chair of *chymiatria* at the University of Marburg in 1609 and appointed a Paracelsian who included laboratory training in his courses. From 1609 to 1621, the students were taught laboratory techniques and medicinal preparations. While this is the first record of laboratory instruction within a university curriculum, public courses for apothecaries, which focused on medicinal preparations in the laboratory, existed from the sixteenth century in Paris. This would remain typical of laboratory work up into the nineteenth century; it was most often carried out within the context of medical education and was not explicitly tied to the elaboration of theory.

Many learned academies advocating the reform of letters and the "new method of philosophizing" came into existence in the sixteenth and seventeenth centuries, and they, too, established laboratories. Some of the seventeenth-century academies, such as the Academia Naturae Curiosum (1652) of the German territories, the Accademia del Cimento (1657) of Florence, the Royal Society of London (1660), and the Académie Royale des Sciences (1666) of Louis XIV (1638–1715), were inspired

A chemical laboratory set up by Johann Konrad Barchusen in Utrecht. From Barchusen's Pyrosophia *(1698).*

in part by the utopian writings of Francis Bacon (1561–1626), Tommaso Campanella (1568–1639), and Johann Valentin Andreae (1586–1654). These writers made the laboratory a central part of their reforms, aimed at gaining human dominion over the natural world. In the societies, such a reform was translated into an adherence to the New Philosophy, which, although not spelled out or practiced rigorously, was based upon active practice, including trial and experiment in the laboratory. It was in these academies and in the practices of members of institutions such as the Parisian Jardin Royal des Plantes (founded 1626) that a new conception of replicable experimentation in the controlled space of the laboratory began to be formulated. For example, Thomas Sprat's (1635–1713) *History of the Royal Society* (1667) developed clearly the idea of the laboratory as a place where "matters of Fact" were judged and resolved by demonstration in a public space before reliable witnesses. "Experiment" came to mean more than the simple observation of nature; it took over the rhetoric of chemical assaying, in which nature was tried and tortured in order to give up its secrets. Authors such as Robert Boyle (1627–1691) published works meant to enable the replication of his laboratory experiments. Thus, the chemical laboratory became a model for the unification of theory and practice.

Even after the laboratory came to be regarded as a central locale for the production of new knowledge about nature, it remained, in practice, more often a place of pedagogy, entertainment, and spectacle. Nevertheless, the laboratory was at the heart of a new active mode of pursuing natural knowledge that emerged in the period of the Scientific Revolution.

BIBLIOGRAPHY

Debus, Allen G. *The Chemical Philosophy*. 2 vols. New York: Science History Publications, 1977.

Dobbs, B. J. T. *The Foundations of Newton's Alchemy*. Cambridge: Cambridge University Press, 1975.

Eamon, William. *Science and the Secrets of Nature: Books of Secrets in Medieval and Early Modern Culture*. Princeton, NJ: Princeton University Press, 1994.

Moran, Bruce T. *The Alchemical World of the German Court: Occult Philosophy and Chemical Medicine in the Circle of Moritz of Hessen, 1572–1632*. (Sudhoffs Archiv. Supplement 29.) Stuttgart: Franz Steiner Verlag, 1991.

Rossi, Paolo. *Philosophy, Technology, and the Arts in the Early Modern Era*. Trans. Salvatore Attanasio. New York: Harper and Row, 1970.

Shapin, Steven. "The House of Experiment in Seventeenth-Century England." *Isis* 79 (1988), 373–404.

Smith, Pamela. *The Business of Alchemy: Science and Culture in the Holy Roman Empire*. Princeton, NJ: Princeton University Press, 1994.

PAMELA H. SMITH

See also Alchemy; Books of Secrets; Chemistry; Craftsman-and-Scholar Thesis; Experience and Experiment; Patronage

La Hire, Philippe de (1640–1718)

A member of the Académie Royale des Sciences for forty years, La Hire worked on a variety of subjects, including geometry, astronomy, mechanics, cartography, and physiology.

La Hire's interest in art and mathematics came from his father, Laurent, who was a professor at the Royal Academy of Painting and Sculpture. When his father died in 1660, La Hire went to Venice for four years, where he studied art and geometry, especially the *Conics* of Apollonius (fl. ca. 200 B.C.E.); on his return to Paris, he devoted himself to art and mathematics.

In 1672 Girard Desargues (1591–1661), a mathematician, and Abraham Bosse (1602–1676), an engraver, were working on a treatise on the cutting of stones but felt in need of assistance because of the mathematics involved, so they consulted La Hire, who contributed a discussion of conics. This was his first publication.

The next year he produced a work on geometry, analyzing conic sections, followed in 1676 by one on the cycloid. By 1678 his reputation had grown to the point where he was invited to become a pensioner of the Académie Royale des Sciences as an astronomer. He later published astronomical tables of his observations made from the Paris Observatory. He solidified his reputation the next year with the publication of further works on geometry and conics, developing, for example, some of René Descartes's (1596–1650) ideas.

Louis XIV's chief minister, Colbert, wanted an accurate map of France and engaged Jean Picard (1620–1682) and La Hire, who worked together and then separately to make the observations needed for the map. Among other phenomena La Hire investigated were magnetism, rain, the thermometer, the barometer, and gnomonics, publishing a treatise on the latter in 1682.

After an appointment to the chair of mathematics at the Collège Royal in 1682, he taught various subjects in physics, many of which he dealt with in his *Traité de mécanique* (1695), using a Cartesian, rather than a Newtonian, analysis.

In 1687 he was appointed professor at the Académie Royale d'Architecture, where he lectured weekly until the year before his death.

Bernard le Bovier de Fontenelle's (1657–1757) *eloge* is the major source for information about him and has been drawn upon by various biographers.

BIBLIOGRAPHY

Buti, A., and M. Corradi. "I contributi di un matematico del XVII secolo ad un problema di architettura: Philippe de La Hire e la statica degli archi." *Atti della Accademia Ligure di Scienze e Lettere, Genova* 38 (1981), 303–323.

Fontenelle, Bernard le Bovier de. *Eloges des académiciens,* tome II. La Haye: Isaac vander Kloot, 1740. Repr. Bruxelles: Culture et Civilisation, 1969, pp. 12–34.

Taton, René. "La première oeuvre géometrique de Philippe de la Hire." *Revue d'histoire des sciences et de leurs applications* 6 (1953), 93–111.

WILLIAM LEWIS HINE

See also Académie Royale des Sciences; Geometry; Observatoire de Paris; Picard, Jean

Langren, Michael Florent van (1598–1675)

An astronomer and mathematician with original ideas, including the use of map scales as representative fractions, the introduction of the dateline on globes, and the naming of lunar features. His innovations were not recognized in his lifetime and were reinvented much later.

Born in Amsterdam, the son of engraver and globe-maker Arnold Floris van Langren, he moved to the Spanish-ruled southern Netherlands in 1607 or 1608. On several maps published in the 1620s he introduced map scales as representative fractions: on the wall map of Brabant, he wrote (in French): "the true distances between the places shown on this map are 140,000 times farther than here." Comparable texts are found on his map of the region of Mechelen (1:114,500) and of the Fossa Eugeniana (a planned canal between the rivers Meuse and Rhine) (1:143,000). It took two centuries and the introduction of the decimal system before it became common to express map scales as representative fractions.

Van Langren and his friend, humanist Erycius Puteanus (1574–1645), were both involved in the construction of globes for van Langren's father. The most remarkable change to the terrestrial globe is the addition of the dateline. In 1632 Puteanus proposed to include on the globe a *Circulus Urbanianus,* named after Pope Urban VIII (1623–1644). This circle consisted of the meridian going through Rome and through the antipodal point of Rome. The meridian running through the antipodal point marked the beginning of the day and was called *Linea archimerina* or *Dachbeginsel* (beginning of day). The concept was completely forgotten, and only in 1865/1866 did a map again include a dateline, after its necessity had been recognized in the nineteenth century.

Finally, van Langren worked on a method to establish longitude using the lightening and darkening of the lunar mountains during the waxing and waning Moon. It was, therefore, necessary to identify the lunar features by giving them names. The only results were some pamphlets and two maps of the full Moon. One is an engraved map (1645), which was published as an advertisement for support. It shows the first comprehensive system of the names of lunar features ever published. In 1651 this system was improved upon by that of Giovanni Battista Riccioli (1598–1671).

BIBLIOGRAPHY

Krogt, Peter van der. "Das 'Plenilunium' des Michael Florent van Langren: Die erste Mondkarte mit Namenseinträgen." *Cartographica Helvetica* 11 (1995), 44–49.

———. "Het verhoudingsgetal als schaal en de eerste kaart op schaal 1:10000." *Kartografisch tijdschrift* 21 (1995)/*Nederlands geodetisch tijdschrift/geodesia* 37(1) (1995) [joint issue], 3–5.

———. *Globi Neerlandici: The Production of Globes in the Low Countries.* Utrecht: HES, 1993.

PETER VAN DER KROGT

See also Cartography; Globes, Astronomical and Terrestrial

Laws of Nature

Statements of the regularities observed among natural phenomena that hold for every time and place. In modern physics, they are expressed mathematically and constitute the primary form of explanation. Before the rise of modern physics in the seventeenth century, Aristotelian physics predominated. Following the Greek philosopher Aristotle (384–322 B.C.E.), Aristotelians held that scientific explanation consisted in the identification of a thing's causes. There were four different kinds of causes: the defining properties of a substance, what it was made up of, its purpose, and what triggered its alteration.

René Descartes (1596–1650), one of the founders of modern philosophy and science, first formulated laws that held for all physical phenomena and could be expressed mathematically. His three laws of nature first appear in Chapter 7 of his treatise *The World* (composed from 1629 to 1633): a version of the law of inertia, a law of collision, and the law that each individual part of matter always tends to continue moving in a straight line. Although Descartes's laws contained inaccuracies, he set up a framework for understanding all physical phenomena. Christiaan Huygens (1629–1695) and Gottfried Wilhelm Leibniz (1646–1716), while disagreeing with the content of Descartes's physics, furthered his project of describing physical phenomena in terms of the laws governing matter in motion. By the end of the seventeenth century, Isaac Newton (1642–1727) published his *Mathematical Principles of Natural Philosophy,* and the basic laws of classical physics were in place.

The modern concept of laws of nature was born in the early seventeenth century, but we must go back further to understand its development. Descartes's notion of laws of nature combines two distinct and, until then, opposed elements. The first grew out of the ancient Greek tradition, which regarded nature as inherently rational and used mathematics to predict observed phenomena. The second emerged from the Christian theological tradition, which centered on the idea of God, the all-powerful Creator and Lawgiver. Each tradition contained assumptions that posed a barrier to the development of laws of nature. By combining aspects of both traditions, Descartes removed these barriers.

The first barrier to the development of the notion of laws of nature lay in the separation between the mixed sciences and physics. The laws of the mixed sciences were mathematical, not physical, in nature, and Aristotelians denied that mathematics could describe the essence of substances. By contrast, Descartes claimed that material substance consisted of nothing but geometrical properties, such as size, shape, and motion. This allowed him to describe the physical world in mathematical terms.

Descartes's redefinition of the nature of matter alone was not enough to generate the concept of laws of nature. The idea of law also had important theological connotations that prevented its use in physics. In the Bible, the term *law* is used in reference to the restrictions God imposed on the natural elements, as well as his moral prescriptions. This biblical notion conflicted with the ancient Greek idea of a rational order inherent in nature. For example, the Stoics spoke of fate and

described nature as deterministic, thereby denying the omnipotence of God and the possibility of miracles. Even Aristotle's nondeterministic view of nature posed problems to divine omnipotence. According to Aristotle, things act by their own powers in accordance with their natures, and even aberrations can be explained naturalistically.

Throughout the Middle Ages, theologians had tried to reconcile the fruits of ancient Greek learning with theological doctrine. In his influential synthesis of Aristotle's philosophy and Catholic theology, Saint Thomas Aquinas (d. 1274) reconciled God's power with the powers inherent in Aristotle's natural substances. He claimed that once God had created the world, he was bound by the natural order he had set up, and, although God could perform miracles, they were separate from the order of nature. Several of Saint Thomas's theses were condemned by the Catholic Church in 1277, and later theologians, careful to preserve God's omnipotence, held that God was bound only by the law of noncontradiction. This view, known as voluntarism, ensured God's absolute power, for he could intervene and change the course of nature at will.

Since God's purposes are unknown to humans, the voluntarist could not assume that God would set up the same underlying order in nature tomorrow as he did today. Physicists who adhered to a voluntarist theology were, therefore, unlikely to think of nature in terms of universal laws. However, with the rise of the Jesuit Order, the sixteenth century saw a revival of Saint Thomas's theology. Some Jesuits, among them Francisco Toledo (1532–1596) and Antonio Tubio (1548–1615), even spoke of a fixed order among natural causes, which they called the "order of nature," but they were anxious to distinguish this idea from the Stoic notion of fate. These Jesuits thought that the Stoic "law of fate" negated divine omnipotence and human free will; they therefore emphasized that the order among natural causes was not necessary in itself but dependent on God's power. Furthermore, they used the more neutral term *order,* presumably to avoid the deterministic connotations of the term *law* used by neo-Stoics like Justus Lipsius (1547–1606).

The second barrier to the development of the concept of laws of nature lay in these theological concerns. On the one hand, strict voluntarists did not speak of "laws of nature" because, for them, all laws were direct decrees from God that could change at any moment. On the other hand, those who rejected voluntarism, like the above-mentioned Jesuits, wanted to distinguish their view from the Stoic idea of a deterministic law, so they spoke of an "order of nature" stressing its dependence on God. Descartes agreed that there was a nonfatalistic natural order that was dependent on God, but he did not shy away from calling it "law."

The recovery of ancient Greek scientific texts and medieval scientific developments contributed to the innovations of the Renaissance. Scientific laws were developed at this time, but they were rarely called laws. The best examples are Galileo Galilei's (1564–1642) law of falling bodies and Johannes Kepler's (1571–1630) three laws of planetary motion, all of which could later be derived from Newton's laws of nature. Although these are derivative, not general, laws, it is likely that they inspired Descartes's laws of motion. However, Descartes's use of the term *law* was new, for neither Galileo nor Kepler used the term to refer to their laws. Galileo set out his laws as theorems and propositions in the style of Greek mathematicians (*Discourses on Two New Sciences*). Kepler also used the mathematical term *theorem* instead of the term *law* (*Harmonics of the Universe*, 1619).

Occasionally, the term *law* was employed in medieval and Renaissance texts on optics and astronomy, but there it functioned like *rule* or *proportion*. Ancient and medieval schools treated optics, mechanics, astronomy, and harmonics as part of mathematics, and this tradition continued until the late seventeenth century. These disciplines were known as mixed sciences because they were intermediate between physics, which dealt with real things, and mathematics, which dealt with abstractions. Given that their subject matter was in part mathematical and abstract, the mixed sciences could not investigate the true causes of natural phenomena. Conversely, physics could not employ mathematics, for it dealt with the causes of real things, not abstract mathematical entities.

Francis Bacon (1561–1626) was the only one who spoke of *universal laws* when discussing the methods of physicists (*New Organon*, 1620). However, Bacon was not referring to observed regularities that could be expressed mathematically, for by *law* he meant *form* (i.e., the properties shared by a species of substances). Bacon's concept of universal law has a different content from the modern one. Descartes's laws most resemble the laws of the mixed sciences, for, like Galileo and Kepler, he extended the mathematical methods used in these sciences to the domain of physics.

When Descartes formulated his laws of nature, he not only abolished the separation between physics and the mixed sciences, he also reconciled God's omnipotence with the Greek ideal of an intelligible universe. Descartes derived his three laws of motion directly from God's nature, thus preserving the Judeo-Christian idea of a divine Being who imposes laws on nature. However, since Descartes also rejected the view that God could change these laws at any time, he could posit an orderly, knowable universe in which the mathematical laws of the mixed sciences applied to all physical phenomena. By tracing these laws back to God's nature, Descartes elevated them to "laws of nature" that provided true explanations of all physical phenomena.

Christiaan Huygens and Leibniz accepted this general framework for understanding physical phenomena while criticizing the content of some of Descartes's laws. Huygens corrected Descartes's laws of collision, and Leibniz argued that the correct measure of force was mv^2, not mv, as Descartes had thought. Newton made even more extensive innovations in his *Mathematical Principles of Natural Philosophy* (1687). His three laws of motion still form the backbone of classical physics today. The main difference between Newton's laws of motion and Descartes's is that Newton's laws not only describe the motions of bodies, but also express the mathematical relations between the forces governing these motions. Therefore, using Newton's laws, one can predict every motion, from the fall of an apple to the return of a comet. Newton brought Descartes's vision of explaining all physical phenomena by a few universal laws to its full fruition.

BIBLIOGRAPHY

Funkenstein, Amos. *Theology and the Scientific Imagination.* Princeton, NJ: Princeton University Press, 1986.

Harrison, Peter. "Newtonian Science, Miracles, and the Laws of Nature." *Journal of the History of Ideas* 56 (1995), 531–553.

Knebel, Sven K. "Necessitas moralis ad optimum (III): Naturgesetz und Induktionsproblem in der Jesuitenscholastik während des zweiten Drittels des 17. Jahrhunderts." *Studia Leibnitiana* 24 (2) (1992), 182–215.

Milton, John R. "The Origin and Development of the Concept of the 'Laws of Nature.'" *Archives européennes de sociologie* 22 (1981), 173–195.

Oakley, Francis. "Christian Theology and the Newtonian Science: The Rise of the Concept of the Laws of Nature." *Church History* 30 (1961), 433–457.

Osler, Margaret. *Divine Will and the Mechanical Philosophy: Gassendi and Descartes on Contingency and Necessity in the*

Created World. Cambridge: Cambridge University Press, 1994.

Ruby, Jane E. "The Origins of Scientific Law." *Journal of the History of Ideas* 47 (1986), 341–359.

Zilsel, Edgar. "The Genesis of the Concept of Physical Law." *Philosophical Review* 2 (1942), 245–279.

HELEN HATTAB

See also Demonstration; Descartes, René; Experience and Experiment; Hypothesis; Theory

Leeuwenhoek, Antoni van (1632–1723)

His fame rests solely on his microscopes and the studies he made with them. Leeuwenhoek's handmade microscopes were of the single-lens type and of a quality and maximum magnification of 270 diameters, which was unsurpassed during his lifetime. He blew or ground the lenses himself according to a secret procedure. For each

Antoni van Leeuwenhoek. Courtesy Oklahoma University Library.

preparation he constructed a new microscope. Of the more than five hundred microscopes he left after his death, only ten survive. His manual skill allowed him to make preparations meeting the highest standards, the study of which led to many discoveries.

Leeuwenhoek was born into a lower-middle-class family in the small town of Delft in Holland. He received only a primary education and never mastered Latin, the language of science of the time. He owned a draper's shop, and in 1669 he was named a land surveyor for the city of Delft. He always lived in his native town and died there as a celebrity who had attracted many scientists, politicians, and royalty to the city.

He wrote the results of his researches in more than 350 letters, most of which were sent to the Royal Society of London, which elected him a Fellow in 1680. A substantial number were published in the society's journal, *Philosophical Transactions.* Leeuwenhoek's most important discoveries were the spermatozoa (in humans and all kinds of animals), red-blood cells, and many kinds of what we now call microorganisms. But his interests covered practically all aspects and forms of dead and living nature. So one can find—scattered in his letters—comparative descriptions of the cellular structure of different kinds of wood, of the shape of crystals from salts obtained by burning to ashes various kinds of plants, of bacteria in the dental plaque, of striated muscle cells, and so on. The discovery that satisfied him most was the factual demonstration of the circulation of the blood in the tail fin of a living young eel in 1688.

The great variety and number of Leeuwenhoek's works might obscure the fact that, notwithstanding his lack of scientific training, he was concerned with a few general items: the (microscopical) structure of organisms and the operating mechanisms of reproduction and growth. His starting point was the concept of uniformity in nature, and his instrument for explanation was based upon the Cartesian concept of matter. Leeuwenhoek constructed a theory that all matter consisted of "globules" (small balls). His enduring opposition to the idea of spontaneous generation was founded in the conviction that the Creator had created the world in a uniform and perfect manner; it was supported by the discovery of many very small organisms that normally escaped the eye but that nevertheless appeared to possess a perfection equal to that of higher animals and plants. Leeuwenhoek supported the preformationist theory of generation, especially the animalculistic version: the spermatozoa

L

were preformed organisms, while the female reproductive organs served only to nourish them to maturity. Contrary to some contemporary microscopists, however, Leeuwenhoek never claimed to have seen a miniature organism in the head of a spermatozoon. In his research of the growth and nourishment of plants, he made elaborate studies of sap transport and compared it to the circulation of blood in animals.

Despite the admiration for Leeuwenhoek's often spectacular observations, his influence on the development of scientific ideas and concepts was scant. This was caused partly because Leeuwenhoek was so secretive that his observations could be repeated by others only with great difficulty. The lack of adequate concepts for microscopical structures like cells and their parts was another reason for the oblivion into which his work fell in the eighteenth century.

BIBLIOGRAPHY

Ford, Brian J. *The Leeuwenhoek Legacy*. Bristol: Biopress; London: Farrand, 1991.

Fournier, Marian. *The Fabric of Life: The Rise and Decline of Seventeenth-Century Microscopy*. Baltimore: Johns Hopkins University Press, 1996.

Leeuwenhoek, A. van. *Alle de brieven van Antoni van Leeuwenhoek: The Collected Letters of Antoni van Leeuwenhoek*. Ed. and annotated by a Committee of Dutch Scientists. 19 vols. Lisse: Swets and Zeitlinger, 1939–.

Palm, Lodewijk C., and Harry A. M. Snelders, eds. *Antoni van Leeuwenhoek 1632–1723: Studies on the Life and Work of the Delft Scientist Commemorating the 350th Anniversary of His Birthday*. Amsterdam: Rodopi, 1982.

Wilson, Catherine. *The Invisible World: Early Modern Philosophy and the Invention of the Microscope*. Princeton, NJ: Princeton University Press, 1995.

LODEWIJK C. PALM

See also Generation; Microscopy; Preformation

Leibniz, Gottfried Wilhelm (1646–1716)

One of the greatest philosophers and mathematicians of the Western world, despite the fact that he was neither a professional philosopher like Immanuel Kant (1724–1804) nor a professional mathematician like Isaac Newton (1642–1727). For forty years, Leibniz was employed by the dukes of Hanover for a variety of tasks—legal, technological, historical, diplomatic, and theological—and as a librarian. His writings and activities cannot be easily separated along disciplinary lines because, just to

mention a few examples, his metaphysics of space, time, and matter was related to the problem of transubstantiation and the reunion of the churches, a lifelong concern of Leibniz with profound implications for his views on logic and the problems of freedom and necessity. His theological plans for church reunion had clear political connotations, as did many of his technological projects and historical endeavors, and even his mathematics had connections with his natural philosophy, metaphysics, and theology. His binary system of arithmetic, for example, suggested an analogy with biblical Creation. The most challenging task for the Leibniz scholar is to master several historical disciplines, requiring high technical competence, without losing sight of their connections and of the complexity of the whole.

Leibniz published several works in his lifetime, yet this was only a very small portion of his enormous production. Those who know him only through what he published cannot grasp the depth and complexity of his views. Most of his major works in whole areas, such as logic, for example, remained unpublished until the beginning of the twentieth century. Leibniz often relied on the support of the works of other philosophers in order to put in finished form his original views. Some of his major works are constructed in this way, such as *Animadversiones in partem generalem principiorum Cartesianorum* of the early 1690s; the *Nouveaux essais* of the mid-1700s, containing his response to the philosophy of John Locke (1632–1704); and the anonymous *Essais de théodicée* (1710), based on a comment to Pierre Bayle (1647–1706). Not surprisingly, his epistolary exchanges, too, are exceedingly important, notably those with the Jansenist theologian Antoine Arnauld (1612–1694), the Dutch philosopher Burchard de Volder (1643–1709), the Jesuit Batholomaeus des Bosses (1638–1738), and the mathematician Johann Bernoulli (1667–1748).

Throughout his life, Leibniz was engaged in both highly speculative and eminently practical pursuits. This is symbolized in the motto he chose for the Berlin Academy of Science, which he founded in 1700: *theoria cum praxi*. One of his most representative projects was that of an alphabet of human thought, or *ars characteristica*, which he was hoping to use as a tool for discovery, thus binding again intellectual pursuits with practical purposes.

Leibniz was educated at his hometown university, Jena, and at Altdorf, from which he graduated in law in 1667. His legal training influenced whole areas of his

Gottfried Wilhelm Leibniz. From A. Wolf, A History of Science, Technology, and Philosophy in the Sixteenth and Seventeenth Centuries *(London: Allen and Unwin, 1935).*

thought. He refused a university appointment at Altdorf, opting instead for a more politically active type of intellectual activity. In 1668 Leibniz entered the service of the Elector at Mainz as a judge and adviser, drafting at the same time political, theological, and philosophical projects. In 1671 he published in Mainz *Hypothesis physica nova,* in which he put forward his views on motion. In 1672 Leibniz left Mainz and set out for Paris with a diplomatic mission on behalf of the Elector.

Between 1672 and 1676, Leibniz lived in Paris in contact with some of the most prominent intellectuals of his age, such as Christiaan Huygens (1629–1695), who was his mentor in mathematics, and other members of the Académie Royale des Sciences. Although he was a novice in mathematics when he arrived in Paris, by the time he left he had become one of the leading mathematicians of his time, having invented the differential calculus in 1675. From Paris he traveled twice to England, where he visited the Royal Society, met many of its most prominent members, presented a model of his calculating machine, and was elected a Fellow in 1673. In the

mid-1660s, he had an important correspondence with British mathematicians, including Isaac Newton. Having been dismissed by his Mainz patrons and having failed to gain a position at the Paris Académie, Leibniz reluctantly accepted a position in Germany, stopping on the way in the Low Countries, where he met Jan Swammerdam (1637–1680), Antoni van Leeuwenhoek (1632–1723), and Benedict de Spinoza (1632–1677).

From 1676 until the end of his life, Leibniz lived mostly at Hanover in the employ of three dukes who showed a decreasing appreciation for his services. In his first and probably happiest dozen years there, he was heavily involved in a technological mining project in the Harz region and was in frequent contact with a large number of technicians and inventors of chemical substances and technological devices. In those years, Leibniz published some of his most important works in the recently founded *Acta eruditorum* of Leipzig, notably the 1684 *Nova methodus pro maximis et minimis,* which is the first publication on the differential calculus, and the 1686 *De geometria recondita,* which deals with the inverse problem or integral calculus. In the same year, in *Demonstratio erroris memorabilis Cartesii et aliorum,* he attacked René Descartes's (1596–1650) measure of force and announced his principle of conservation of mv^2, later called *living force,* one of the cornerstones of his system, which he elaborated in metaphysical and mechanical terms for the rest of his life.

From 1687 to 1690, Leibniz traveled through southern Germany, Austria, and Italy on a politico-historical mission on behalf of his duke. His genealogical researches established a link between the houses of Hanover and Este, eventually allowing his duke to gain the title of ninth elector of the Holy Roman Empire. In 1688 Leibniz read Newton's *Principia mathematica philosophiae naturalis* (1687); in 1689 he replied with three articles in the *Acta eruditorum* attacking the philosophical implications of Newtonianism and trying to establish priority in the invention of the calculus. While in Italy he met the main Italian intellectuals, including Vincenzo Viviani (1622–1703) and Marcello Malpighi (1628–1694), composed his bulky *Dynamica,* and intensified his efforts to have the ban against the Copernican system lifted by the Catholic Church.

Back in Hanover in the 1690s, Leibniz was heavily involved in projects for the reunion of the churches and also developed important aspects of his dynamics in the 1695 *Specimen dynamicum* and his metaphysics, elaborating his notion of substance, or monad (from the Greek *monas,* meaning "unity"), a term that entered his vocabulary in the mid-1690s. At the end of the century, the virulent priority dispute with Isaac Newton over the invention of calculus emerged, to subside only after Leibniz's death. At the same time, however, Leibniz was witnessing his own differential calculus being developed by a number of exceedingly able Swiss and French mathematicians.

Leibniz's favor at Court diminished considerably with the accession of Duke Georg Ludwig in 1698, who later, as King George I (1660–1727), forbade him to set foot in England. Leibniz spent more and more time at the Berlin and Vienna courts and, from 1700, grew very close to Sophie Charlotte (1668–1705), queen of Prussia, with whom he maintained an extensive correspondence. He was devastated at her premature death. Her role of political patron and intellectual disciple was taken by Caroline of Ansbach (1683–1737), who later, as princess of Wales, acted as intermediary in the 1715–1716 dispute between Leibniz and Samuel Clarke (1675–1729), acting for Newton, possibly the most famous philosophical dispute of all time, on issues in the relation between theology and natural philosophy. While at Vienna in 1714, Leibniz composed two popular accounts of his philosophy, *Principes de la nature et de la grace, fondés en raison,* published posthumously in 1718, and *La monadologie,* also published posthumously in 1720.

Despite some ferocious satires of his philosophical system, and especially of his belief that we live in the best of all possible worlds, his intellectual legacy dominated eighteenth-century Continental thought and is still an extraordinarily fertile and broad field of research for the historian.

BIBLIOGRAPHY

Aiton, E. J. *Leibniz: A Biography.* Bristol and Boston: Adam Hilger, 1985.

Bertoloni Meli, D. *Equivalence and Priority: Newton versus Leibniz: Including Leibniz's Unpublished Manuscripts on the "Principia."* Oxford: Oxford University Press, 1993.

Bos, H. J. M. "Differentials, Higher-Order Differentials, and the Derivative in the Leibnizian Calculus." *Archive for History of Exact Sciences* 14 (1974), 1–90.

Hall, A. R. *Philosophers at War: The Quarrel Between Newton and Leibniz.* Cambridge: Cambridge University Press, 1980.

Müller, K. *Leibniz-Bibliographie.* Ed. A. Heinekamp. 2nd ed. Frankfurt: Klostermann, 1984.

Rutherford, D. *Leibniz and the Rational Order of Nature.* Cambridge: Cambridge University Press, 1995.

DOMENICO BERTOLONI MELI

See also Calculus; Religion and Natural Philosophy

Lemery, Nicolas (1645–1715)

French author of a popular chemical textbook entitled *Cours de chymie* (1675), which went through many editions and was translated into six languages. Like many chemists of his time, he received chemical instruction in the laboratories of apothecaries. He also worked in the laboratory at the Paris Jardin des Plantes. Later he had a manufacturing laboratory of his own in Paris and gave experimental lectures that made him famous. In 1699 he became a member of the Académie Royale des Sciences in Paris. His *Cours de chymie* is, to a large extent, a book of recipes. Its practical part does not merely describe the preparation of chemical medicines, it also explains many

The first English translation of Lemery's popular Cours de Chemie.

chemical operations. The theoretical part is an amalgamation of mechanical-corpuscular ideas with the theory of natural *mixta* and principles. Lemery admits five principles as constituents of all natural bodies: water, spirit, oil, salt, and earth. In the tradition of Paracelsus (ca. 1491–1541), he conceived of these principles as carriers of sets of qualities that cause the observable properties of bodies. In contrast to Paracelsus, he understood principles as tangible bodies into which natural bodies can be separated by distillation. Lemery gave a mechanical-corpuscular explanation of the creation of salts. He conceived of acids as consisting of agitated and pointed particles, and alkalis and metals as having pores that are penetrated by the acid particles when salts are created. Effervescence, formerly explained in animistic terms as a battle between opposite substances, was now mechanistically reinterpreted as a violent breaking and moving of the penetrated alkaline particles by the pointed acid particles.

BIBLIOGRAPHY

Bougard, Michel. "La Chimie de Nicolas Lemery (1645–1715): Entre l'officine et l'amphitheatre." In *Nouvelles Tendances en Histoire et Philosophie des Sciences,* ed. Robert Halleux and Anne-Catherine Bernes. Bruxelles: Palais des Acdemies, 1993, pp. 167–185.

Metzger, Hélène. *Les doctrines chimiques en France du début du XVIIe à la fin du XVIIIe siècle.* Paris: Presses Universitaire de France, 1923. 2nd ed. 1969, 281–338 and passim.

Partington, J. R. *A History of Chemistry.* 4 vols. London: Macmillan, 1962, vol. 3, pp. 28–41.

URSULA KLEIN

See also Chemistry; Matter; Paracelsus

Leonardo da Vinci (1452–1519)

Trained as a painter and sculptor in the Florentine workshop of Andrea del Verrocchio (1435–1488), Leonardo came to see painting and the investigation of the natural world as intrinsically related activities. One of the greatest painters of the Italian Renaissance, he was also a sculptor, an engineer, an inventor, an anatomist, and an architect. Engineering projects often preoccupied him, as did his investigations into water, flight, optics, anatomy, and mechanics. He viewed the world as a unity in which individual things reflect one another. In voluminous notebooks, he posited hundreds of questions about the natural world, provided numerous explanations, and

executed spectacular drawings of both mechanical and natural phenomena.

After his move to Milan in the early 1480s as a client of Ludovico Sforza (1451–1508), Leonardo undertook work on the Milanese canal system. His project soon included a study of water and how it behaved under a variety of conditions. Another endeavor, a large equestrian bronze statue of Francesco Sforza, involved him in a study of horses and their proportions, in the technical problems of large-scale casting, and in the invention of furnaces. As these projects exemplify, Leonardo's approach to engineering and construction projects often involved him in investigations of natural phenomena.

He inherited and expanded earlier-fifteenth-century Italian knowledge of the painter's perspective, while, at the same time, he studied late-medieval optical treatises in his efforts to understand the phenomena of light and vision. For Leonardo, painting was itself an exploration

Leonardo da Vinci, a self-portrait. From Jean Paul Richter, The Literary Works of Leonardo da Vinci *(1883).*

of vision, of light, and of perspective. Lacking a university education and formal training in Latin, he nevertheless studied Latin treatises on optics. His interest extended to his anatomical studies, which included study of the eye, especially the variable diameter of the pupil. His perspectival studies led him to compare the eye to a camera obscura.

Leonardo's painting—particularly of humans and animals—eventually involved him in the study of anatomy. He undertook the dissection of human and animal bodies and body parts. His interest in the representation of the body in painting transformed itself into a preoccupation with bodily structure, form, and function. In his anatomical drawings, he adopted, and on occasion invented, new techniques of representation—transparent and exploded views and musculature shown from diverse vantage points. Leonardo was the first to thoroughly understand the importance of careful observation and visual depiction to the discipline of anatomy.

His consummate skill in observation and representation is evident in other areas as well. His drawings of plants, of geological formations, and of meteorological events, for example, are exceptional in both accuracy and beauty. His observations of fossils, of water, of storms, and of the flight of birds are astounding in their detail and accuracy.

Leonardo's sense of the unity of the world was based on his assumption that individual objects and persons were microcosms reflecting the macrocosm of the universe. The mutual reflections of the universe and of individual things in it were mediated through mathematical proportions. Both his architecture and his anatomical studies reveal his interest in ratio and proportion. He drew numerous analogies of other kinds as well, both within the natural world and between the realms of nature and human artifice. Yet, his pervasive sense of analogy and proportion did not interfere with his minute observations of the particularities of the things in the world. His notebooks make clear that, as much as he pursued analogy, he also investigated the anomalous, the peculiar, and the grotesque. Leonardo was a technologist and an engineer as much as he was a painter, sculptor, and architect. There is no doubt that he worked on mechanical inventions in material form, and we know that on occasion he employed artisans to help construct machines. Yet, what remains of his inventions and work on machines is in the form of hundreds of notes and brilliantly executed drawings of machines and machine parts,

some taken from examples around him, others newly invented. Machines pertinent to the textile industry, clockworks, cannon, gears, pulleys and lifting machines, flying machines, and many other devices are beautifully drawn in the *Codex Atlanticus,* in the *Madrid Codices,* and in his other notebooks.

The *Madrid Codices* are notebooks that were discovered in the National Library of Madrid in the early 1960s. *Madrid Codex I* is a formal treatise on machines and mechanics in which Leonardo discusses and illustrates numerous mechanisms and describes how they work. He treats, as well, theoretical mechanics, which for him primarily concerned weight, force, impact, and motion. In this notebook, Leonardo brings together two separate traditions. He demonstrates his interest in and knowledge of Aristotelian mechanics and medieval statics and kinematics, on the one hand, and he explicates the workings of machines, on the other.

Traditionally, historians of science have studied Leonardo's notebooks to see if he got things "right" in the areas of mechanics, optics, anatomy, and other disciplines. Finding that often he did not, usually noting that he had no influence anyway because his notebooks remained unpublished, they turn to other subjects. Yet, Leonardo was famous during his lifetime, and his notebooks and drawings were viewed by at least some individuals both while he lived and in the decades after his death.

As much as in any specific discipline, Leonardo's significance lies in his approach to the natural world. He not only asserted the importance of observation, but also provided numerous minutely detailed observational accounts both in writing and in drawing. He developed brilliantly innovative methods of visual representation both for natural phenomena, including the human body, and for machines. Finally, he brought together traditions of theory and of practice that had been separate—theoretically oriented, university disciplines such as mechanics, optics, and anatomy, on the one hand, and mechanical arts, including painting, sculpting, engineering, and machine construction, on the other. Within such amalgamations lies a key to the methodological changes characteristic of the Scientific Revolution.

Bibliography

Ahl, Diane Cole, ed. *Leonardo da Vinci's Sforza Monument Horse: The Art and the Engineering.* Bethlehem, PA: Lehigh University Press, 1995.

Galluzzi, Paolo, ed. *Leonardo da Vinci: Engineer and Architect.* Montreal: Montreal Museum of Fine Arts, 1987.

Kemp, Martin. *Leonardo da Vinci: The Marvellous Works of Man and Nature.* Cambridge, MA: Harvard University Press, 1981.

Pedretti, Carlo. *Leonardo da Vinci on Painting, A Lost Book (Libro A).* Berkeley and Los Angeles: University of California Press, 1964.

Reti, Ladislao, ed. *The Unknown Leonardo.* New York: McGraw-Hill, 1974.

PAMELA O. LONG

See also Art; Craftsman-and-Scholar Thesis; Macrocosm/Microcosm

Libavius, Andreas (1540–1616)

Libavius studied philosophy, history, and medicine in Jena and was a professor of history and poetry and later a physician and a teacher at a gymnasium. From 1607 until his death, he was rector of the gymnasium in Coburg. Libavius published treatises on a broad variety of subjects, among them theology, philosophy, poetry, astronomy, and chemistry. He was a sharp critic of some iatrochemists, who claimed to have found the "universal medicine" and other secret remedies. Libavius was a humanist who disliked the obscure style of these authors and a passionate advocate of scientific openness. He understood "alchemie" not as private and secret but as public knowledge. This attitude was interwoven with his didactic passions. He was not opposed to Paracelsian medicines and the alchemical concept of transmutation in principle. In a 1607 treatise he defended the possibility of the transmutation of metals. He also published polemics (1601–1607) against the prohibition of Paracelsian medicines by the medical faculty of Paris.

Among his chemical books, his *Alchemia* (1597) is the most prominent. This textbook, written in Latin, has a rigidly dichotomized organization. It is divided into two main parts, *Encheria* and *Chymia.* The former means knowledge of the hand. It describes and defines the different kinds of chemical operations and instruments. *Chymia* describes the preparation of individual substances. In the Introduction, Libavius emphasizes that he does not teach his own experiments but only the proved and established ones of the chemical artisans. He also alludes to metallurgy and pharmacy as the main sources of his chemical knowledge. It is apparent from Libavius's definition of chemical operations, as well as from his classification and definition of substances, that he was deeply influenced by the Paracelsian philosophy. The

two main procedures of the *Encheria* are *elaboratio* and *exaltatio.* *Elaboratio* means the separation of the tangible "bodily" part of a natural body from its hidden "essence," conceived as the "subtle" constituent of a body that carries all of its precious qualitites and its healing forces. *Exaltatio* is the enhancement of the qualitites of a body by means of fire or of an added substance ("ferment," "tincture"). It is not clear how influential Libavius's textbook really was. The French chemist Jean Beguin (ca. 1550–ca. 1620), author of a famous chemical textbook, *Tyrochinium chymicum* (1610), derives his division of it into a part on chemical operations and a part with recipes from Libavius's *Alchemia.*

BIBLIOGRAPHY

Hannaway, Owen. *The Chemists and the Word: The Didactic Origins of Chemistry.* Baltimore: Johns Hopkins University Press, 1975.

Partington, J. R. *A History of Chemistry.* 4 vols. London: Macmillan, 1961, vol. 2, pp. 244–270.

URSULA KLEIN

See also Alchemy; Beguin, Jean; Chemistry; Paracelsus

Libraries

Libraries have traditionally played a minor role in the history of the Scientific Revolution. Most definitions of that movement stress its emphasis on experimentation, based on the empirical observation of nature rather than the study of texts—the reading of the "Great Book of Nature" rather than the "little books of men." Thus, laboratories, observatories, and even gardens are more likely than libraries to figure as sites or subjects of scientific activity. Yet, before and after the Scientific Revolution, and particularly in the fifteenth and sixteenth centuries, libraries served both as repositories of scientific learning and as places of scientific inquiry in their own right.

It was through libraries, and the efforts of those who created and maintained them, that the classic mathematical, medical, astronomical, and geographical texts of the ancient world made their way to Renaissance Europe. Many humanists considered the works of Archimedes (ca. 287–212 B.C.E.), Ptolemy (ca. 100–ca. 170), Euclid (fl. 300 B.C.E.), and Hippocrates (ca. 460–ca. 370 B.C.E.) more valuable than their literary and historical counterparts, and they bestowed considerable labor on their recovery and refinement. This, as much as their pioneering experiments, laid the groundwork upon which seventeenth- and eighteenth-century science was built. Ironically, given their resistance to these later developments and their persecution of those who advanced them, the popes proved to be the leading sponsors of this program, and, during the Renaissance, the Vatican Library was Europe's richest collection of scientific texts. One of the first to appreciate these treasures was Cardinal Bessarion, who was responsible for bringing Johannes Regiomontanus (1436–1476)—their leading interpreter—to Rome. Regiomontanus later served the Hungarian King Matthias Corvinus, whom he helped to establish an important library and an astronomical observatory, and he eventually set up his own press, dedicating much of his life to editing, writing, and publishing scientific texts.

The comprehensive experimental project outlined by Francis Bacon (1561–1626) provided a better-known impetus for the birth of modern empirical science, but neither Bacon nor the Baconians left books behind, nor did they focus narrowly on scientific texts. Books from all disciplines played an essential role in Bacon's scientific theories and practices, providing sources, rhetorical models, and institutional bases for the study of nature. For the Baconian circle around Samuel Hartlib (ca. 1600–1662), the advancement of knowledge and its application to the benefit of humanity could proceed only through the collection and analysis of all available information. Through the seventeenth century and into the eighteenth, leading scientists such as Robert Hooke (1635–1703) and Sir Isaac Newton (1642–1727) remained active collectors and readers.

In 1594 Bacon advocated the creation of a scientific institution under royal auspices, containing a library, a garden, a cabinet of curiosities, and a chemical or alchemical laboratory. This has often been taken as a forward-looking proposal, but many of the larger libraries of the period—in private as well as royal hands—were connected to museums and collections of various sorts and formed precisely this kind of research institution. The household of John Dee (1527–1608), one of Tudor England's most notable scientists, contained a large library, which featured a collection of maps, scientific instruments, and natural wonders and opened onto a laboratory he referred to as its "appendix practical." This complex was the center of a loose network of people and projects, which spread from the universities through the mechanical community to the Continental Courts: libraries like Dee's provided channels for

scientific activity not yet fostered by the universities or the state.

For figures like Dee, libraries provided an intellectual and professional base for their careers and influenced the nature of their writings and services. The case of the Swiss physician, naturalist, and bibliographer Conrad Gessner (1516–1565) is exemplary. Gessner began as a teacher of Greek, and he published several dictionaries and linguistic studies, but he became best known as the editor of Galen's (second century) texts, the creator of encyclopedic works on natural history, and the compiler of a universal listing of authors and their works, employing the first major system of bibliographical classification.

In due course, the library itself became subject to scientific methods. Information science was an integral—and ultimately, perhaps, an essential—component of the Scientific Revolution. It would not only help manage the growing body of data being generated by scientific study, but (by extension) also would offer ways of organizing and understanding the natural world itself.

BIBLIOGRAPHY

Eisenstein, Elizabeth. *The Printing Press as an Agent of Change.* 2 vols. Cambridge: Cambridge University Press, 1979.

Grafton, Anthony, ed. *Rome Reborn: The Vatican Library and Renaissance Culture.* Washington, D.C.: Library of Congress, 1993.

Ophir, Adi. "A Place of Knowledge Re-Created: The Library of Michel de Montaigne." *Science in Context* 4 (1991), 163–189.

Sherman, William H. *John Dee: The Politics of Reading and Writing in the English Renaissance.* Amherst: University of Massachusetts Press, 1995.

WILLIAM H. SHERMAN

See also Encyclopedias; Humanism; Illustration; Printing; Translations

Light Transmission

Until the early seventeenth century, the nature of light and its transmission was conceived in a basically Aristotelian fashion. According to Aristotle (384–322 B.C.E.), light is the instantaneous actualization of the transparency of the medium between observer and object. This actualization enables the colors of the object—the actual object of vision—to be transferred through the medium. During the Middle Ages, Roger Bacon (ca. 1220–ca. 1292), in particular, developed the concept of *multiplicatio specierum,* in which light was viewed as the multiplication of properties of an object through the surrounding medium. The sixteenth century saw a revaluation of alternative conceptions like the atomistic theory of light, in which light was regarded as local motion of particles. Theories in which light was conceived as a modification of a medium remained, however, the mainstream.

Johannes Kepler's (1571–1630) successful solving of several problems in optics has been judged in different ways by historians of science. Whereas some have focused on revolutionary aspects of Kepler's optics, David Lindberg (1986) stresses its continuity with medieval optics. In the first chapter of *Ad Vitellionem paralipomena* (Supplements to Witelo, 1604), Kepler put forward a theory of light that was a critical adaptation of Bacon's concept of multiplying virtues. Kepler stressed physical and mathematical aspects of light. Light is an expanding, spherical, two-dimensional surface, devoid of matter and incorporeal. On this theory, Kepler founded the basic principle of optics, that of the rectilinearity of light rays, which his predecessors had merely assumed. He stressed that a ray is only the geometrical line representing the motion of light and not light itself.

René Descartes (1596–1650) put forward the first mechanistic theory of light. Light is not a motion of matter but a tendency to motion transmitted instantaneously through a medium of subtle matter. This tendency to motion is caused by the particles constituting the Sun and the stars, which exert a pressure on the surrounding matter because of their constant motion. Descartes put forward this theory in *Le Monde; ou, Traité de la lumière,* which he wrote in 1633 but withheld for fear of the Inquisition and which was published posthumously in 1664. He did publish *La Dioptrique* (1637), in which he discussed the mathematical properties of light rays: the principle of rectilinearity and the laws of reflection and refraction. In this study, he did not explain his views on the nature of light but used several mechanistic analogies to explain these properties. In fact, these analogies were not fully consistent with his conception of light as a tendency to motion. In his mechanistic theory, for example, light propagated instantaneously, whereas the motion in his analogies had finite velocity. Later textbooks on Cartesian physics, like the popular *Traité de physique* (1671) of Jacques Rohault (1620–1675), did not succeed

in unifying his mechanistic theory of light with the mathematical laws of light rays either.

Descartes's views, although generally criticized, were an important stimulus to the development of mechanistic theories of light. His mechanistic clarification of the sine law (for given media, the sines of the angle of incidence and the angle of refraction are in constant proportion), in particular, was considered problematic. He compared refraction of light to the behavior of a projectile when passing through a surface, and he used the resolution of the motion to derive the sine law. He had to assert that light penetrates more easily though a denser medium and that a tendency to motion has the same properties as motion itself. Pierre de Fermat (1601–1665) rejected Descartes's physical assumptions and at first even the sine law itself. By the time he came to reconsider the law in the 1650s, experimental verifications by Pierre Petit (ca. 1598–1677) and others convinced him to accept it. Moreover, he realized that a convincing mathematical proof of the law was possible by using the principle of least action, that light travels in the shortest time by the shortest path. Others put forward alternative analogies to explain refraction, including Pierre Hérigone (d. ca. 1640), who used the science of statics, and Claude Milliet Deschales (1621–1678), who drew an analogy with a cart pulled through heavy soil.

Another question, which gained new relevance with the emerging mechanistic view on the nature of light, was that of the speed of its transmission. Descartes upheld the Aristotelian view that light propagates instantaneously, although his clarifications on refraction seemed inconsistent with this view. He defended the instantaneous motion of light with the argument that the eclipse of the Moon is always seen in its proper place, without a sensible lapse of time. A similar argument was used in 1676 by Ole Christensen Römer (1644–1701) to prove the opposite. According to Römer, observations of the eclipses by Jupiter of its moon showed that the speed of light is finite. Römer's argument certainly did not settle the case; conceptions of the speed of light were often based on a theoretical decision. This also applied to the question whether the speed of light was greater or smaller in media of higher optical density.

Thomas Hobbes (1588–1679) was the first to base a proof of the sine law on an alternative mechanistic theory of light. He conceived of light as impulses transmitted through a material medium. These pulses produce physical rays of light, three-dimensional rays whose fronts are always normal to their sides. When light is refracted, the front is deviated from its rectilinear path because its speed changes at the interface between two media. The sine law can be derived by assuming that the speed of propagation is smaller when the medium is denser. Hobbes's explanation became known through the works of Emanuel Maignan (1600–1676) and Isaac Barrow (1630–1677), and it was subsequently attributed to them instead of Hobbes. In *Micrographia* (1665), Robert Hooke (1635–1703) used a pulse conception of light to explain the production of colors. He did not elaborate the mechanistic particulars of these pulses, nor did he derive mathematical properties of light rays, like the law of refraction.

During the 1670s, Christiaan Huygens (1629–1695) developed a wave theory of light in which mechanistic and mathematical properties of waves were elaborated and unified. Huygens developed an unpublished theory of Ignace Gaston Pardies (1636–1673), whose manuscripts he had seen. According to Huygens, the virulent

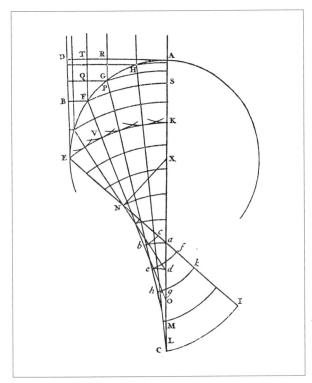

An illustration of Christiaan Huygens's wave theory of light, from his Traité de la lumière *(1690). Parallel light rays falling on a spherical glass surface retain their curved, wavelike character, although they are modified when refracted and generate new curvilinear waves.*

motion of particles in a light source produces spherical pulses of impact in a medium of ether particles. The innovative idea of Huygens was that each point in the medium is, in its turn, the center of a spherical pulse. The superposition of pulses from a series of points he called the *principal wave—wave front,* in modern terms— which produces visible light. With this theory, Huygens derived the basic properties of light rays: rectilinearity, reflection, and refraction. The ultimate proof was, according to him, the successful explanation of the strange refraction in Iceland crystal. He assumed that, in this crystal, light does not propagate with the same speed in each direction, thus producing elliptical instead of spherical wave fronts. In this way, he could explain why perpendicular rays are refracted, contrary to the sine law. Huygens published his theory in *Traité de la lumiere* (1690), more than ten years after he explained strange refraction in Iceland spar.

The principal objection to wave theories was that the propagation of ordinary waves seemed to contradict the rectilinear propagation of light rays. One of the most ardent critics of the wave conception was Isaac Newton (1642–1727), who thought of light as particles emitted by a luminous source. The emission conception of light, part of the revival of ancient atomism, was held by various seventeenth-century scholars, such as Thomas Harriot (ca. 1560–1621), Pierre Gassendi (1592–1655), Francesco Maria Grimaldi (1618–1663), and Robert Boyle (1627–1691). With an emission theory, the rectilinearity of light rays and the reflection of light could be explained in a straightforward way. Newton can be considered to have had the deepest understanding of the consequences of an emission conception. In *Opticks* (1704), he discussed the nature of light and its propagation only in the "Queries," a series of tentative remarks. He thought that light and matter interacted through attractive forces of matter. In his *Principia mathematica philosophiae naturalis* (1687), he derived the laws of reflection and refraction using a model in which small particles are deflected by perpendicular forces on the surface of a medium.

BIBLIOGRAPHY

Lindberg, David C. "The Genesis of Kepler's Theory of Light: Light Metaphysics from Plotinus to Kepler." *Osiris,* 2d ser., 2 (1986), 5–42.

Sabra, A. I. *Theories of Light from Descartes to Newton.* London: Oldbourne, 1967.

Shapiro, Alan E. "Kinematic Optics: A Study of the Wave Theory of Light in the Seventeenth Century." *Archive for History of Exact Sciences* 11 (1973), 134–266.

FOKKO J. DIJKSTERHUIS

See also Descartes, René; Grimaldi, Francesco Maria; Huygens, Christiaan; Optics; Refraction; Snel, Willibrord

Lincei. See Accademia dei Lincei

Lister, Martin (1639–1712)

A physician and naturalist, he is best known for his work and publications on the natural history of invertebrates. After studying medicine at Cambridge (1655–1662) and Montpellier (1663–1666), he opened a medical practice at York. In 1684 he moved to Westminster, London, where his patients included members of the aristocracy. Through the influence of his niece, Sarah Churchill, duchess of Marlborough, he was appointed physician in ordinary to Queen Anne in 1709. Lister was elected a Fellow of the Royal Society in 1671 and became vice president of the society in 1685, when Samuel Pepys was president.

In addition to fifty-two contributions to the society's *Philosophical Transactions,* he published sixteeen books and edited the works of other contemporary writers. Lister made detailed field observations on a number of species and was interested particularly in the life histories, anatomy, and taxonomy of worms, wasps, mollusks, and spiders. His classification of spiders was outstanding for its time, as was his multivolume work on the molluska, illustrated by hundreds of engravings made from drawings by his wife and daughter. He was an eager collector and student of fossil shells and, owing to his religious commitments, believed them to have had geological origins. He noticed a correlation between certain types of shells and the rocks in which they were found.

Following a visit to France, his *A Journey to Paris in the Year 1698* was published in 1699. Another two editions were published the same year; it remains a valuable account of life in Paris at that time.

BIBLIOGRAPHY
Carr, Jeffrey. "The Biological Work of Martin Lister (1638–1712)." Ph.D. diss. University of Leeds, 1974.

Lister, Martin. *Letters and Divers Other Mixt Discourses in Natural Philosophy.* York, 1683.

Parker, J. R., and B. Harley, eds. *Martin Lister's English Spiders.* Trans. Malcolm Davies and Basil Harley. Colchester: Harley, 1992.

JOHN R. PARKER

See also Natural History; Taxonomy; Zoology

Literature

During the Scientific Revolution, literature, history, and science were generally not distinguished from each other as discrete forms of written discourse. Historical chronicles; biographical accounts; personal journals; philosophical essays; treatises of natural philosophy, logic, and rhetoric; and poems, plays, and fables together were recognized as "literature." Some early-modern commentators, notably Philip Sidney (1554–1586) and Thomas Sprat (1635–1713), described how the factual content and practical style of some forms of writing functioned differently from the imaginative art and fanciful artifice of others. For present purposes, "literature" will be employed in this newly nascent sense to signify creative writing—poetry, drama, and fictional narrative. The task at hand is to explore how contemporary poems, plays, and prose—through their literary history, style, and content—provide valuable resources for the historiography of the Scientific Revolution.

Critical biographies and interpretative studies of individual writers who achieved a high degree of scientific literacy and employed sophisticated scientific images and themes in their work are also frequently cited. Full of quotable generalizations about how literature reflects the development of science, such studies have been repeatedly relied upon as evidence of the social and intellectual "crisis" precipitated by the events of the Scientific Revolution, despite the fact that the central theses of their authors often suggested otherwise. New interdisciplinary studies of early-modern literature and science supply sophisticated analyses of literary themes that offer useful interpretations of particular texts and provide strong test cases for new methodologies beyond the traditional history of ideas.

Mastery of the literature of the Scientific Revolution promises ample rewards for historians of science. As in any historical inquiry, firsthand experience with primary materials is indispensable. Reading individual works of creative writing, scholars construct an understanding of the mutual relation and significance of literary forms, themes, imagery, diction, and tropes as they have developed over time. A ready familiarity with the literary history of the Scientific Revolution enables readers to interpret other forms of contemporary discourse with robust sophistication. Formal conventions, motifs, wordplay, and figures of speech encountered in scientific texts and other historical source materials have established patterns of meaning within literary tradition. As one casual example, images describing light beams darting from human eyes frequently occur in early-modern writing of many types. Most of these allusions owe more to their authors' acquaintance with literary conventions in early Renaissance love poetry, especially the Petrarchan tradition, than to their direct knowledge of Islamic optics and theories of vision. Awareness of such cases adds caution to historical conclusions about how particular scientific ideas are transmitted and popularized.

Literary history of the early-modern period maps the range of culturally available meanings of diverse forms, styles, themes, and ideas. These contexts help scholars distinguish when scientific authors are employing original or derivative concepts, establishing an important variation on a theme, or idly repeating a commonplace. Isaac Newton's (1642–1727) famous "If I have seen further, it is by standing on ye sholders (sic) of giants," for instance, accumulates significance both from its allusion to past usages of the image by other writers and by its adaptation of prevailing techniques of *ad hominem* satiric attack.

The literature of the Scientific Revolution provides a complex knowledge base for interpreting the nature and purposes of discursive production within emergent scientific and literary communities. Throughout literature, the meanings of scientific terms and concepts shift as they enter and travel through different intellectual populations and social classes. Fundamental nomenclature and the popular conceptualization of such words as *science, astronomy,* and *force* metamorphose remarkably. The degree of literacy and learning possessed by authors and audiences greatly influences literary references to scientific developments. For example, discussions of Aristotelian-Ptolemaic and Copernican astronomy by popular-almanac writers do not claim that both systems are roughly equivalent as symbols of the limitations of human reason, as in John Milton's (1608–1674) perspective in *Paradise Lost*. Natural philosophers also appropriate or modify language and concepts from literature and other types of writing in the surrounding culture. The influence of religious faith upon the work of Johannes Kepler (1571–1630), Galileo Galilei (1564–1642), and Newton can be analyzed, in part, by determining how their writing draws upon disparate aspects of theological poetics.

Reading the literature of the early-modern period in explicitly literary ways, scholars supplement their knowledge of formal style, rhetorical principles, and their applications. Not all uses of rhetoric go by the book, Aristotelian or otherwise. Then, as now, grammar, rhetorical style, and literary technique were primarily learned through usage rather than university instruction. Through careful attention to the structure of primary texts, and much practice, readers learn to recognize personal trademarks of diction and the jargon of intellectual peers. They discern when nuances of tone indicate genuine emotional response or a quick bow to literary convention—personal regard versus courtly compliment, honest reluctance to publish versus stylish authorial false modesty. Such awareness directly shapes the interpretation of texts because persuasive strategies, argumentative styles, and fashionable forms of irony all exhibit faddish change within intellectual coteries.

In their writing, natural philosophers frequently draw upon literary models outside their own subject matter to engage in debate with their contemporaries and historical predecessors. These dialogues often betray themselves in the subtext (i.e., at the level of tonal echoes, parodic allusion, and imitative formal structures). Subtle analyses of texts often depend upon the recognition of commonalities between literary and scientific discourse. Alexander Pope's (1688–1744) many verse epistles, *Essay on Man,* and *The Dunciad* are brilliant case studies of how men of letters used writing to negotiate complex public and private quarrels, campaigns for and against competing professional styles, and disputes concerning political, social, and moral values. The satiric papers of Jonathan Swift (1667–1745) and others provide profound parodies of how intellectual skirmishes between the "ancients and moderns" and moral and natural philosophers were planned and executed (*Battle of the Books* and *Bickerstaff Papers*). Read in light of literary pyrotechnics, the dark shadows of priority disputes and bitter correspondence between Newton and Robert Hooke (1635–1703), Newton and John Flamsteed (1646–1719), and Newton and Gottfried Wilhelm Leibniz (1646–1716) flash into sharp silhouette.

The enlistment by prominent scientific actors of networks of correspondents and discursive champions who pledged their pens to defend the cause is likewise usefully backlit by the important strategic advantages commanded by literary figures with strong coffeehouse followings and large popular readerships. Applying specialized literary reading skills to historical and scientific texts, scholars gain insight beyond the texts' superficial content that can prove invaluable for understanding the form and function of the verbal assaults natural philosophers launched upon each other.

The appreciable historical benefits of an educated awareness of literary history and literary style have received less direct attention from scholars of the Scientific Revolution than those of literary content. Historically and scientifically germane content is embedded in poetic, dramatic, and fictional forms and subject matter. Historians of the Scientific Revolution can discover within contemporary creative literature evidence to substantiate or contradict the information available from other sources. Literary texts provide insights into the achievements, goals, and interpersonal relationships of scientific actors as individual thinkers and as members of culturally distinct groups. Literary works record, illuminate, and inform the social and political contexts, institutional settings, and popular perceptions of scientific activities. Poets, dramatists, and storytellers express the interests and concerns of the culture at large, and their subjects often directly involve discoveries and developments in natural knowledge. These texts record their authors' awareness of, and responses to, science in general as well as particular developments in a wide range of scientific endeavors, including magic, alchemy, medicine, astronomy, natural history, and experimental science.

Renaissance drama is especially rich territory for exploring social and intellectual attitudes toward the natural sciences as they emerged alongside alchemy, astrology, and magic. In his complex morality play, Christopher Marlowe's (1564–1593) *Dr. Faustus* rejects the limited knowledge of law, philosophy, rhetoric, and theology and aspires, instead, to godlike omniscience and power via demonic conjuring—with damnable results. In William Shakespeare's (1564–1616) *The Tempest,* Prospero proves a better student of nature and human nature than Faustus. As the magician commands the forces of nature, he comprehends the need to temper his natural instinct toward retribution with compassion and to wield self-control rather than power. On a lighter

note in *The Alchemist,* Ben Jonson (1572–1637) satirizes a constellation of dubious sciences through direct contemporary allusions to alchemical language and practices. The play is particularly useful for its depiction of how ignorance of new science and blind faith in the arcane powers of magic, alchemy, and astrology were shared by representatives of many social strata and educational levels, both genders, and those with amorous, economic, political, and religious motivations.

Throughout the Scientific Revolution, literary writers subject the quest for natural knowledge to intelligent, healthy critique. Rarely does a poet or a playwright grant unquestioning acceptance to science or its practitioners. Medicine receives dramatic scrutiny in plays by Thomas Shadwell (ca. 1642–1692), Aphra Behn (1640–1689), and Jean Baptista Poquelin Molière (1622–1673), among others. In a typical treatment, central characters who crave physick or practice medicine are depicted as selfish hypochondriacs or quacks whose involvement in medicine diverts them from fulfilling their normative roles in family and society. This type of warning, directed primarily at male projectors at the beginning of the seventeenth century, targets female virtuosa by century's end.

Metaphysical, cosmological, and physico-theological poetry provides valuable source material for tracing popular understanding of the historical development of astronomy. Virtually every conceivable astronomical phenomenon and theoretical concept is represented. While some early-modern writers looked to ancient and medieval astronomy to supply subjects, themes, and imagery, others were already rapidly adapting the latest astronomical observations and theories. In *La sepmaine; ou Création du monde,* Guillaume de Saluste Du Bartas (1544–1590) follows the lead of medieval encyclopedists to describe a Christianized Aristotelian system that rejected the nonsensical physics of Nicolaus Copernicus (1473–1543). John Donne (1572–1631) uses his knowledge of early-modern astronomy from Copernicus to Kepler to create explicit and structural astronomical analogies that describe human emotion, political intrigue, philosophical dilemmas, and religious faith, as in his "Valediction: Forbidding Mourning"; "Ignatius His Conclave"; "The Anniversaries"; and "Good Friday 1613." Competing seventeenth-century cosmologies are depicted in Henry More's (1614–1687) Platonic poems, *Psychathanasia* and *Insomnium Philosophicum,* and Margaret Cavendish's (1623–1673) Cartesian-atomistic verse. In his Christian epic, *Paradise Lost,* John Milton

(1608–1674) melds his popular knowledge of astronomy and intimate acquaintance with the work of other cosmological poets such as Du Bartas, Aratus (fl. ca. 270 B.C.E.), and Manilius (fl. 9–35) with artistic virtuosity. The astronomy in Books 2, 7, and 8 especially reflects Milton's personal knowledge of Galileo's dialogue on "two" chief world systems and sunspot observations. Newton's achievements in cosmology, optics, and mechanical philosophy are encapsulated in Pope's tour de force two-line epitaph "Nature and Nature's laws lay hid in night./God said, 'Let Newton be!' (and all was Light.)" and recounted at great length in the prefatory ode to the *Principia* by Edmond Halley (ca. 1656–1743) and myriad memorial verses like James Thomson's (1700–1748) *To the Memory of Sir Isaac Newton.* Physico-theological poems describe all aspects of post-Newtonian nature, from microscopic to telescopic levels, drawing upon contemporary natural history for detail.

Despite much literary evidence of strong popular interest and admiration, early-modern astronomy served as a target for satire as well as one of its vehicles. Jonson equated the novelties disclosed by Galileo's telescope with the trivial "new news" of daily headlines and horoscopes: *News from the New World Discovered in the Moon, The Staple of News.* Samuel Butler (1612–1680) lampooned the ambitious scientific efforts of the Royal Society in *Hudibras* and the *Elephant in the Moon,* ridiculing the untrustworthy nature of the human senses (with or without instruments) and the natural philosophers who put fame and greed above truth. Shadwell's *The Virtuoso* and Behn's *Emperor of the Moon* both mocked the preposterous obsessions of mechanical philosophers, astronomers, and projectors of experimental science. Literary treatments of space travel regularly contained social, political, and religious allegory and themes. In *The Description of a New World, Called New Blazing World,* Cavendish combined the cosmic-voyage motif with dialogues on natural philosophy and social and political satire. This medley of forms is put to good use again by Swift in *Gulliver's Travels* to reproach English politics and mores, as well as to chastise the "unnatural" natural investigations of the Royal Society and critique the social and theological implications of Newtonianism.

Whatever their technical subject matter and whatever their methodological approach, internalist or externalist, concerned with ideas or social constructions,

continuity or discontinuity, words or things, historians of the Scientific Revolution can find what they are looking for in literary works produced during the era. It has even happened that all of the above have been located within the same half-dozen poetic lines, the most notorious case being the verses following Donne's too frequently cited "New philosophy calls all in doubt." Indeed, such cases have perpetuated the persistent perception that poems, plays, and fiction are susceptible to a particularly dangerous strain of interpretative free association that renders them unreliable. As suggested above, the interpretative latitude afforded literary works need not be appreciably wider than that granted other types of historical documents or scientific texts. Literary and historical exegetes often assign meaning by working within similar sets of hermeneutic parameters: issues of authorship and audience, biographical detail, professional and personal aims, cultural and technical contexts, and rhetorical and stylistic traditions.

By including creative writing among their source materials, scholars of early-modern science simultaneously extend the range of their research and enrich their repertoire of reading skills. The unpredictable cadences of descriptive prose, the unexpected presence of a narrator's voice, the exotic melodies of poetic prosody—rarely encountered in most academics' research materials—offer a refreshing break from professional reading habits. The versatility and subtle precision with which creative writers employ literary devices remind researchers to actively select and creatively shape the meaning of the literary forms and tropes they use. As writers, historians of the Scientific Revolution have constructed an array of narratives and devised various metaphors to describe and explain the development of medicine, science, and technology between 1543 and 1727. Scholarly reappraisals of the history of the period have included reconsideration of the meaning of the central metaphor of *revolution* and even whether developmental models themselves need reconfiguration or replacement in historical narratives. Attention to how narrative structure, characterization, tone, analogy, and metaphor operate in primary texts—thinking about the words used to write history—literally helps scholars to think about history. Just as important, such knowledge enhances the ability of historians of the Scientific Revolution to communicate and promote their professional goals and epistemological and philosophical values to the general public as well as to others working within the growing—and increasingly diverse—interdisciplinary community.

BIBLIOGRAPHY

Bono, James J. *The Word of God and the Languages of Man: Interpreting Nature in Early Modern Science and Medicine.* 2 vols., vol. 1: *Ficino to Descartes.* Madison: University of Wisconsin Press, 1995.

Eade, J. C. *The Forgotten Sky: A Guide to Astrology in English Literature.* Oxford: Clarendon, 1984.

Gossin, Pamela, ed. *Literature and Science: An Encyclopedic Companion* (forthcoming)

———. *"Poetic Resolutions of Scientific Revolutions: Astronomy and the Literary Imaginations of Donne, Swift, and Hardy."* Ph.D. diss. University of Wisconsin-Madison, 1989.

Markley, Robert. *Fallen Languages: Crises of Representation in Newtonian England, 1660–1740.* Ithaca, NY: Cornell University Press, 1993.

Meadows, A. J. *The High Firmament: A Survey of Astronomy in English Literature.* Leicester: Leicester University Press, 1969.

Mebane, John. *Renaissance Magic and the Return of the Golden Age: The Occult Tradition and Marlowe, Jonson, and Shakespeare.* Lincoln: University of Nebraska Press, 1989.

Moss, Jean Dietz. *Novelties in the Heavens: Rhetoric and Science in the Copernican Controversy.* Chicago: University of Chicago Press, 1993.

Schatzberg, Walter, Ronald A. Waite, and Jonathan K. Johnson, eds. *The Relations of Literature and Science: An Annotated Bibliography of Scholarship, 1880–1980.* New York: Modern Language Association, 1987.

PAMELA GOSSIN

See also Discourse, Styles of; Humanism; Rhetoric

John Locke. From A. Wolf, A History of Science, Technology, and Philosophy in the Sixteenth and Seventeenth Centuries *(London: Allen and Unwin, 1935).*

Locke, John (1632–1704)

Synthesized and popularized arguments for corpuscularianism and an empiricist approach to scientific inquiry. Locke participated directly in England's scientific community by working in the laboratories of Robert Boyle (1627–1691) and Thomas Sydenham (1624–1689), investigating herbal remedies and surgical procedures in his medical studies and practice and sharing his empiricist views with other Fellows of the Royal Society. Yet, his principal contribution to the science of his times is his *Essay Concerning Human Understanding,* in which he endeavors to define the character of warranted empirical belief and highlight those conceptual errors and misuses of language that he believes led scientists in the past to an

unsalutory mix of confusion and hubris. In the "Epistle to the Reader" of the *Essay,* Locke describes his chosen mission as "clearing the ground a little, and removing some of the rubbish, that lies in the way to Knowledge" on behalf of his great scientist contemporaries, like Isaac Newton (1642–1727), Boyle, Christiaan Huygens (1629–1695), and Sydenham.

At the core of this mission is the task of indicating the limits of viable empirical belief. Locke suggests that, while knowledge with certainty of what he calls the "real" essences of substances is outside our grasp, probable understanding of their sensible qualities, or the elements of their "nominal" essences, is not. To grasp such real essences, we would need epistemic access to the "primary" qualities of substances—including their solidity, extension, figure, motion (or rest), number, and position—that underlie the "secondary" qualities that produce in us the ideas we have of their surface-level phenomena. The problem, Locke proposes, is that, from sensory experience, we are limited to only ideas of secondary qualities, and these fail to represent the truly constitutive primary qualities. So, though we might believe we can judge what those primary qualities are, we have no grounds for certainty about those beliefs. Since, for Locke, knowledge requires certainty, he holds that we cannot know the basic constituents and relations of physical objects. Yet, he clearly rejects the anti-empiricist bent of classical skepticism, for he accepts that we learn about the physical world—though acquiring only probable beliefs—through experiment and observation. This balance of doubt about knowledge of underlying essences, and faith in empirical inquiry founded on information from the senses, marks Locke as a proponent—like Pierre Gassendi (1592–1655), Marin Mersenne (1588–1648), and Joseph Glanvill (1636–1680)—of what Richard Popkin has called "constructive scepticism," a limited warrant for empirical belief based on the insight that such belief need not be certain to be justified. On the basis of this limited warrant, Locke develops elements of a scientific method and, in particular, defends the use of hypotheses in science on the ground that probable conjecture is the most we can hope for in empirical judgment.

At some points in the *Essay,* however, Locke appears unhappy about science based on hypotheses. He proposes that we adopt hypotheses about individual substances only after gathering observations and conducting experiments regarding those substances. We can never expect certain demonstration of empirical hypotheses, since certain knowledge of substances lies beyond our reach, nor will inferences from hypotheses yield anything more than probabilistic judgment. Locke clearly is not a proponent of classical hypothetico-deductivism, insofar as he rejects certain knowledge *from* (as well as *of*) hypotheses. At other points, however, he unequivocally promotes the utility of hypothetical reasoning in the pursuit of empirical inquiry. Regardless of his polemics, it must be that Locke accepts such reasoning simply because he reasons from hypotheses throughout his writings.

The hypothesis Locke most clearly and frequently promotes, in his philosophical as well as scientific writings, is the corpuscularian proposal that matter is composed of microsize particles, the actions and combinations of which explain the character of macrosize objects and phenomena. Like many of his contemporaries, Locke embraces this hypothesis as a central element of the mechanist picture and the best available account of the underlying structure of the world. One of the more compelling applications of this hypothesis for Locke is in a causal account of perception. He suggests that perception takes place when an external body's corpuscles impact upon our receptor organs, thereby producing distinct sensations in us corresponding to, though not directly representing, the underlying qualities and relations of the corpuscles. What we perceive, rather, are those of the body's phenomenal qualities produced by that underlying corpuscular structure.

While Locke hopes for experimental confirmation of a corpuscularian science, he doubts it will ever have sure, broad foundations—and with good reason, given the paucity of direct evidence in his times. In an even more quixotic vein, he suggests that we could get ideas of the real essences of bodies if only we had access to their corpuscular "inner constitutions," such that advances in microscopy would push metaphysics along, too. But as we have seen, he also thinks it impossible in principle to have empirical knowledge of real essences, so it cannot be that we would gain it by knowing inner corpuscular constitutions. In the end, Locke's corpuscularianism is less successful as support for his metaphysics than as an instance of his proposal that, lacking "certainty and demonstration" about our ideas of bodies, we fruitfully use hypotheses to tell coherent stories about our diverse experiential data.

BIBLIOGRAPHY

Alexander, Peter. *Ideas, Qualities, and Corpuscles: Locke and Boyle on the External World.* Cambridge and New York: Cambridge University Press, 1985.

Downing, Lisa. "Are Corpuscles Unobservable in Principle for Locke?" *Journal of the History of Philosophy* 30 (1992), 33–52.

Laudan, Laurens. "The Nature and Sources of Locke's Views on Hypotheses." *Journal of the History of Ideas* 28 (1967), 11–223.

Locke, John. *The Conduct of Human Understanding.* 2nd ed. of 1706 ed., corr. and rev. New York: B. Franklin, 1971.

———. *An Essay Concerning Human Understanding.* Ed. Peter H. Nidditch. 4th ed. of 1700 ed. Oxford: Clarendon, 1975.

Mandelbaum, Maurice. *Philosophy, Science, and Sense Perception: Historical and Critical Perspectives.* Baltimore: Johns Hopkins University Press, 1964.

Woolhouse, Roger S. *Locke's Philosophy of Science and Knowledge*. Oxford: Blackwell, 1971.

Yolton, John W. *John Locke and the Way of Ideas*. Oxford: Clarendon, 1956. 2nd ed. 1968.

SAUL FISHER

See also Atomism; Empiricism; Hypothesis; Qualities

Logarithms

The word in the current sense is John Napier's (1550–1617), meaning number ratio or something similar; logarithms are the inverse of exponents, an idea known in the West at least since the time of Archimedes (ca. 287–212 B.C.E.). The relation is that of a geometric to an arithmetic sequence (e.g., if y equals 2^x, where 2 is the "base," then x is the logarithm of y to that base). There are some numerical traces of this in Old Babylonian astronomical work. Medieval mathematicians had struggled with the ideas of exponents and roots, but computational logarithmics began with Thomas Harriot (ca. 1560–1621), Napier, and Henry Briggs (1561–1631). Joost Bürgi's (1562–1632) *Progress Tables* (1620), simple powers of 1.0001, give only a partial improvement on direct methods. Medieval compound-interest results, as in Luca Pacioli (1494), provide a shadowy background.

In the 1590s, two distinct problems, one kinematical and one geometrical, led independently to the concrete solution of the inverse problem in the form of extensive practical tables. The geometrical problem, stated in 1569 by Gerard Mercator (1512–1594), was to map a spherical surface onto a plane while maintaining angles. Two types of solution arose, one by the addition of secants, a numerical quadrature, the other by inverting exponentials. John Dee (1527–1608) in ca. 1558, Harriot in 1584, and Edward Wright (1558–1615) in 1599 gave the first; Harriot, from 1594, the second (logarithmic) solution.

By stereographic projection of a spherical loxodrome, Harriot showed that $\tan(1/2 \; \lambda \; (n)) = \tan^n(1/2 \; \lambda \; (1))$, where $\lambda \; (n)/\lambda(1)$ is the ratio of colatitudes for which the longitude-line extension on the map is $n/1$. This gives $\lambda(n)$ in terms of n, but the cartographer needed, inversely, to express n in terms of $\lambda(n)$. Original results on the equiangular (logarithmic) spiral and interpolation led Harriot to a brilliant solution; the resultant logarithmic tangents, accurate to 1 in 10^9 or better, except for very high angles, were ready in 1614, the year Napier's tables appeared.

Napier's ideas were developed kinematically, not by geometry, and involved calculating the instantaneous speed of a particle which is directly proportional to a decreasing distance to be traveled. Numerically, such work depends on finite intervals and averaging, so the level of accuracy is difficult to control, and Napier was a little unlucky here, his results being unreliable in the final figure of seven. Both he and Harriot realized this; it was removed in the 1616 edition. Napier's logarithms are of sines and cosines at one-minute interval, not of natural numbers. They facilitate trigonometric, navigational, and astronomical calculations, which are explained in a detailed Introduction. Napier also gave differences between his logsine and logcosine, which are thus logtangents and directly proportional to Harriot's results, a fact that became generally known only after 1645.

Napier's own account of his construction (1619) was overtaken by Briggs's calculation of the more convenient common logarithms, giving fourteen figures to base 10 and effectively up to 101,000, published in 1624 (a brief table in 1617). Briggs explained his own quite different and more powerful methods, involving repeated square-rooting, binary decomposition of exponents, and interpolation by differences. Napier's logarithms implicitly have a base, very close to $1/e$, but their calculation did not involve that. Harriot and Briggs were closer in both using a base, Harriot's equal to $\exp(-2\pi/360 \times 60)$ to the twelfth figure, and in forming their final tables from similar decompositions.

Dozens of sets of tables were published in the seventeenth century. Few, unlike Johannes Kepler's (1571–1630), published in 1624, were in Napier's form or the result of a full recalculation. Adrian Vlacq's (1600–ca. 1667) tables, published in 1628, had the longest life, being reprinted frequently from 1794 until 1958 in the form given by Georg von Vega (1756–1802). In 1667, James Gregory (1638–1675) gave the quadrature of the hyperbola, whose relation to logarithms had been noticed by by others.

For 350 years, the use and development of logarithms dominated the computational scene. All this, including slide rules, vanished with the advent of digital computing, A. J. Thompson's twenty-figure tables of 1952 their last monument. Despite the advent of modern

L

computing, the logarithm will always retain its theoretical place in the mathematical theory of functions.

BIBLIOGRAPHY

Shirley, John W. *Thomas Harriot: A Biography.* Oxford: Clarendon, 1983.

Whiteside, D. Thomas. "Patterns of Mathematical Thought in the Later Seventeenth Century," *Archive for History of Exact Sciences* 1 (1961), 179–388.

JON V. PEPPER

See also Briggs, Henry; Napier, John; Slide Rule

Logic

The sixteenth and seventeenth centuries saw profound changes in views about the nature and uses of logic. Logic was the main subject of study for beginning undergraduates throughout this period, and it is important to bear in mind that, through all of these changes, the study of valid syllogistic arguments formed a common core to the textbooks of the time, whatever the philosophical views of their authors. Outside of this common core, the seeds were sown for the rise of a certain eighteenth-century view of logic that, to present-day logicians, looks to be an unfortunate mixture of psychology and epistemology with logic. At the same time, some of the developments taking place in mathematics were prerequisites for the beginnings of modern mathematical logic in the nineteenth century.

The study of logic in medieval universities can be regarded as having two parts. First, there was a focus on Aristotelian logic, both in comprehensive logic textbooks such as the *Summulae logicales* of Peter of Spain (ca. 1210–1277) and in commentaries on Aristotle's (384–322 B.C.E.) *Organon,* his logical treatises. Second, there were treatises dealing with a variety of particular, often non-Aristotelian, topics having to do with, for instance, the properties of terms (such as their reference in various contexts) or the nature of propositions and the relations between them (such as the consequence relation). These writings often featured an almost obsessive concern for the effects of changes in word order, heavy use of specially constructed problematic sentences (the so-called *sophismata*), and use of an unnatural and technical Latin.

Changes to all of this can be attributed, in large part, to the rise of humanism. During the sixteenth century, many ancient Greek commentaries on Aristotle's logic became available for the first time, as did new and better translations of Aristotle's own work. The result was that logic texts more closely followed the *Organon*—the categorical syllogism became the focus of study, and strictly medieval subjects largely disappeared. The emphasis of the humanists on simple and elegant prose and their attacks on the barbaric language of the Scholastics were also important. Latin ceased to be tortured into use as a technical tool, *sophismata* disappeared completely, and the obsessive concern with word order was replaced by the use of straightforward examples that dodged such difficulties.

This period also saw the rise of humanist logic. Humanist logicians wanted a theory of persuasive discourse in general, and, since one cannot expect to establish conclusions with certainty in, for example, a legal dispute, this meant that they needed a theory able to deal with reasoning about probabilities. Many called their subject *dialectic,* which was the Aristotelian name for reasoning about probabilities. While some humanist logicians, such as Rudolph Agricola (ca. 1443–1485), were aware that probabilistic reasoning might have to do with arguments in which the truth of the premises would make the conclusion probable, even though the argument was not deductively valid (i.e., the truth of the premises did not *guarantee* the truth of the conclusion), the study of such arguments was not systematically pursued. Instead, they read "probable" epistemically and so concerned themselves with the use of deductively valid arguments for which one has only probable grounds for the premises, hence only probable grounds for the conclusion. Thus, Peter Ramus (1515–1572) could identify dialectic with logic, since the argument patterns were the same in each. Nonetheless, the official subject matter of dialectic was the art of persuasive discourse in general, so many of the subjects that were part of *rhetoric* in the traditional curriculum were absorbed into Ramist logic, with the result that rhetoric was left as merely the study of ornamenting discourse and of nonargumentative methods of persuasion.

It was common for the humanists and those influenced by them to describe logic as being in the business of organizing and presenting knowledge. Meanwhile, though, many Aristotelian logicians, such as Jacopo Zabarella (1533–1589), were attempting to develop an account of scientific methodology based on the syllogism. It was in this context that René Descartes (1596–

1650) launched an influential attack on formal logic: as a method of discovery, formal logic is circular, since we would need to appeal to the conclusion as evidence for the premises before we could accept any deductive argument as conclusive, and so the argument could not have helped us discover the conclusion after all. Formal logic is, Descartes argued, at best an expository tool. This is also the humanist view, and one sees the difference between a concern with the recovery of ancient wisdom and the concerns of someone in the vanguard of the new science in the fact that Descartes saw this as constituting an attack on formal logic.

Descartes offered his own account of inference. Certainty is conferred, according to Descartes, by the "natural light of reason" when one perceives ideas clearly and distinctly. Correct inference is a matter of careful comparison of propositions to ensure that we clearly and distinctly perceive that they are appropriately related. Thus, "none of the mistakes which men can make are due to faulty inference," and stringing together propositions into extended arguments is only a means to comparing the premises and conclusion directly. In this process, syllogism is unnecessary and might even distract one from exercising sufficient caution.

In *An Essay Concerning Human Understanding,* John Locke (1632–1704) refers to "native rustic reason" rather than the "natural light of reason" but otherwise adopts, essentially unchanged, both Descartes's criticism of formal logic and his account of inference. Knowledge is defined in the *Essay* to be "the perception of the agreement or disagreement of our ideas," and the book has as its goal the detailing of the various faculties of the mind in order to show how these faculties can be correctly employed in the search for such knowledge. Locke's work was immediately accepted by many as a new and better sort of logic, and, in the eighteenth century, the business of logic was often taken to be the provision of rules for making the best use of our intellectual faculties.

Somewhat ironically, Descartes is also at the center of mathematical developments that were necessary for the eventual development of modern logic. In his *Geometry,* he developed methods that solved some ancient problems, but his methods constitute solutions only if one is willing to drop constraints that ancient mathematicians would have insisted on—for example, one must be willing to accept negative numbers, irrationals, and negative and imaginary roots as solutions to equations.

Descartes justifies this by arguing that algebra is not concerned with "useless numbers" (i.e., with particular solutions to equations) but with systematic relations between "magnitudes." But Descartes did not recognize his procedure as in any way a deductive one, nor did he recognize the possibility of similarly abstracting from particular cases to investigate systematic relations between propositions. While there are some tantalizingly suggestive passages in the writings of Gottfried Wilhelm Leibniz (1646–1716), especially those concerned with the possibility of a universal language, a properly algebraic approach to logic had to wait until the nineteenth century.

BIBLIOGRAPHY

Ashworth, E. J. *Language and Logic in the Post-Medieval Period.* Dordrecht and Boston: Reidel, 1974.

———. "Traditional Logic." In *The Cambridge History of Renaissance Philosophy,* ed. Charles B. Schmitt, Quentin Skinner, and Eckhard Kessler. Cambridge: Cambridge University Press, 1988, pp. 143–172.

Gaukroger, Stephen. *Cartesian Logic: An Essay on Descartes's Conception of Inference.* Oxford: Clarendon, 1989.

Jardine, Lisa. "Humanistic Logic." In *The Cambridge History of Renaissance Philosophy,* ed. Charles B. Schmitt, Quentin Skinner, and Eckhard Kessler. Cambridge: Cambridge University Press, 1988, pp. 173–198.

Mack, Peter. *Renaissance Argument: Valla and Agricola in the Traditions of Rhetoric and Dialectic.* Leiden and New York: Brill, 1993.

DAVID DE VIDI

See also Demonstration; Dialectic; Resolution and Composition; Rhetoric; Zabarella, Jacopo

Longomontanus. See Severin, Christian

Lower, Richard (1631–1691)

His researches and experiments in anatomy, cardiopulmonary function, and blood transfusion enlarged upon the work of William Harvey (1578–1657) on the circulation of the blood. A number of his researches were carried out in collaboration with Thomas Willis (1621–1675), Robert Hooke (1635–1703), and Robert Boyle (1627–1691) at Oxford and London and were aided by his great skill as a vivisectionist. Lower received his arts and medical degrees from Oxford and served for a time as Willis's research assistant. He became a highly

William Lower. From A. Wolf, A History of Science, Technology, and Philosophy in the Sixteenth and Seventeenth Centuries *(London: Allen and Unwin, 1935).*

successful physician and a member of the Royal College of Physicians and the Royal Society of London.

Lower challenged the doctrine that the role of the heart was to impart "vital spirits" and heat to the blood by "ebullition" or "fermentation." A series of experiments designed to clarify the reasons for the pronounced difference in color and other characteristics of the blood in arteries and in veins led him to conclude that the lungs functioned in the course of respiration alternately to discharge waste from the blood and to absorb a "nitrous spirit of the air" necessary for life. He also added to knowledge of heart function by investigating the anatomy of heart muscle and the arrangement of its fibers.

Lower conducted a number of experiments on dogs to develop and test his conclusions and to explore the possibility of transfusion. With Willis, he injected various liquids into blood vessels to trace the paths of blood flow and its speed; he concluded from the results that the blood completely passed through the heart thirteen times per hour. He later conducted experiments in blood transfusion from dog to dog and successfully performed a human transfusion, but he ceased such experiments when he became aware of the likelihood of resulting fatality. He published the details of his experiments and work on transfusion and the anatomy and physiology of the heart in *Tractatus de corde* (Treatise on the Heart, 1669).

BIBLIOGRAPHY

Frank, Robert G., Jr. *Harvey and the Oxford Physiologists: Scientific Ideas and Social Interaction.* Berkeley and Los Angeles: University of California Press, 1980.

Hoff, Ebbe C., and Phebe M. Hoff. "The Life and Times of Richard Lower, Physiologist and Physician." *Bulletin of the History of Medicine* 4 (1936), 517–535.

Lower, Richard. *Tractatus de corde,* facs. reprint, trans. K. J. Franklin. In *Early Science in Oxford,* ed. R. T. Gunther. Oxford: privately printed, 1932, vol 9.

Wilson, Leonard G. "The Transformation of Ancient Concepts of Repiration in the Seventeenth Century," *Isis* 51 (1960), 161–172.

ELSA L. GONZALEZ

See also Fermentation; Harvey, William; Mayow, John; Physiology; Willis, Thomas

M

Macrocosm/Microcosm

The ancient Chaldean priests and sages ca. 850 B.C.E. were presumably the first to establish the concept that the earth, or, more specifically, man, mirrors the whole of Creation. This microcosm/macrocosm analogy consequently led to the conclusion that what happened in the celestial sphere was of importance for human life and destiny; astrology was born. The Chaldeans did not consider the planets and stars gods or goddesses themselves but, rather, embodiments of the heavenly powers that could indicate the will of the gods. The assumed relation between macrocosm and microcosm became important for astrology and would, as well, for alchemy and for Western metaphysics as a whole.

During the first centuries of the Christian era, alchemy was developed in Hellenistic Egypt, and the analogy of microcosm and macrocosm was part of it from the beginning. In alchemy, old Egyptian traditions of chemical and technological knowledge, kept by the Pharaonic priests, converged with Jewish and Greek ideas: the latter source mainly contributed Stoic, Neoplatonic, and Neopythagorean wisdom; the former, kabbalistic and Christian beliefs. The biblical notion that God created man in his own image was of particular importance for keeping the microcosm/macrocosm analogy in Christian occidental culture as well.

The importance for alchemy of the metaphysical connection between the small and the large world can be easily seen in the *Emerald Tablet,* said to have been bestowed on mankind by the mythical founding father of alchemy, Hermes Trismegistus, and to contain all alchemical wisdom in a nutshell. There it is said: "it is true, no lie and absolutely certain. What is below resembles that which is above, and what is above resembles which what is below. Thus one can comprehend the wonder of the One Thing." The One Thing, the Stone of the Sages, also called the Philosopher's Stone, contains and reconciles in itself opposites: above and below, man and woman, even and odd, light and dark. This is the main characteristic of the Stone but also of God. "Above" and "below" stand for macrocosm and microcosm, respectively. Only Latin versions of the text are known, dating from ca. 1200; it seems likely, however, that it is based on early Greek texts.

The Muslim author Jabir Ibn Hayyan (fl. ca. late eighth and early ninth centuries) explains in his *Book of Compassion* that, in principle, all material substances can be used as a source, *prima materia,* for the preparation of the Stone because of the complete analogy of microcosm and macrocosm, although some substances relate more closely to the matter of the Stone than others. He furthermore cites Plato (428–348 B.C.E.) as saying that the Stone can be seen as a "third world," connecting macrocosm and microscosm. Although this reference is correct at best in regard to Neoplatonic thought, it demonstrates the close relationship of alchemy to the macrocosm/microcosm analogy.

The highly important scriptures of the so-called True Brotherhood, written in Iraq during the late tenth century, also stress the importance of celestial influences on earthly beings as well as substances. The planets, Sun, and Moon not only indicate changes on earth, but also cause them, acting as mediators between the divine celestial sphere and the crude, material earth, thus connecting macrocosm and microcosm. The seven main celestial bodies (five planets, Sun, and Moon) are connected to the seven metals (Sun and gold, Moon and silver, Venus and copper, Mercury and mercury, Mars and iron, Jupiter and tin, Saturn and lead) as well as to certain parts of the human body.

In medieval Europe, the macrocosm/microcosm analogy was well established not only in alchemy, but also in theological mysticism and in astrology. Besides a microcosm centered on man, other entities for the role of microcosm were also conceivable. One was the interior of the earth, with the metals and minerals growing like the flowers or grain on the surface and inhabited by gnomes or elves instead of humans. An example of a late form of this subterranean world is Athanasius Kircher's (1602–1680) *Mundus subterraneus* (Subterranean World, 1664). Another sort of microcosm was the alchemist's flask itself, the *vas hermeticum* (hermetic flask). In it, the process of Stone-making occurred, which, in turn, was a kind of second creation of the world. The hermetic flask was also called the philosopher's egg and symbolized the world *in statu nascendi* (in the state of being born), because the egg includes all of the necessary ingredients to make a complete creature, similar to the creation of the Stone out of the prime matter. Even the Stone itself was believed to be a perfect small world, a microcosm created by the adept.

In all of these conceptions is the idea of a universal, "sympathetic" relation between seemingly independent entities like heaven and earth. This idea is still powerful in early-modern times, as can be seen in the writings of Basil Valentine and Robert Fludd (1574–1637). Valentine was a highly influental pseudonymous author living around the turn of the sixteenth to the seventeenth century, whose identity is not yet known beyond doubt. He published a tract in 1602, following the thought of Paracelsus (ca. 1491–1541), in which he describes the body as a model of the macrocosm. His concept is visualized in a plate representing the relationship between humanity and astrology, the alchemical and Aristotelian elements, and God's creation of the universe. Fludd was also influenced by Paracelsus. His *Utriusque cosmi historia* (History of the Two Cosmoses, 1617) contains a number of complicated allegorical plates, also illustrating the relation among God's universe, humans, and knowledge.

The concept of an inner relationship between macrocosm and microcosm has a very long tradition, dating from the early stages of human civilization. While not a rational concept, it was not unreasonable, since it explained and ensured the unity of God with his Cre-

ation. Man did not, therefore, need to feel exposed to the blind, impersonal rule of natural law.

BIBLIOGRAPHY

Lippmann, Edmond O. von. *Entstehung und Ausbreitung der Alchemie*. Berlin: Springer Verlag, 1919, passim.

Partington, J. R., *A History of Chemistry*. 4 vols. London: Macmillan; New York: St. Martins, 1961–1964, vol. 2, passim.

Titley, A. F. "The Macrocosm and the Microcosm in Medieval Alchemy." *Ambix* 1 (1937), 67–69.

CLAUS PRIESNER

See also Alchemy; Astrology; Correspondences; Fludd, Robert; Hermetism; Kircher, Athanasius; Paracelsus

Maestlin, Michael (1550–1631)

A German astronomer, and early Copernican, he contributed to the demise of Aristotelian cosmology in his own right and through his student Johannes Kepler (1571–1630). Unlike many early Copernicans, he spent most of his life in a university.

Maestlin was persuaded by his own observations of the 1572 nova that Aristotle (384–322 B.C.E.) was wrong to deny change in the heavens. In 1578 Maestlin announced that the bright comet of the previous year must also be above the Moon, and he offered figures for its distance from the earth that would have taken it through several of Aristotle's spheres. Instead of concluding that there were no celestial orbs, Maestlin made the startling suggestion that the comet itself had an orb—a Copernican one, outside the orb of Venus and inside the orb of the earth.

Kepler received his training in astronomy from Maestlin and emphasized Maestlin's role and the work on comets as factors in his own conversion to Copernicanism. When Kepler hit upon the polyhedral construction as an explanation for the spacing of the planetary orbs, he called on Maestlin's technical expertise to calculate Copernican planetary distances. Maestlin's contribution to this research appeared as an addendum to the first edition of Kepler's *Mysterium cosmographicum* (The Cosmographic Mystery, 1596). Maestlin also helped get the book published and remained in sporadic contact with Kepler for the rest of his life.

Although there are clear indications that he was a convinced Copernican by 1580, the introductory astronomy courses he was obliged to teach constrained Maestlin to present traditional ideas with a bare mention of Nicolaus Copernicus (1473–1543). Significantly, he failed to adopt the usual Lutheran reading of Copernicus, which accepted the equantless models but rejected the cosmology. In its place, Maestlin taught Ptolemaic models with equants to his beginning students and, presumably, Copernican models to his advanced students.

In later years, Maestlin became embroiled in a polemic against the new Gregorian calendar. An ambitious program of work outlined in the 1580s was never completed, beyond a textbook of astronomy (first published 1582) that combines in a single volume the material previously presented in separate *sphaerae* and *theoricae,* introductions to spherical astronomy and techniques for predicting planetary positions. The first English-language *theorica,* Thomas Blundeville's *Theoriques of the Seuen Planets* (1602), borrows extensively from Maestlin. The content of Kepler's later publications bears a striking resemblance to Maestlin's uncompleted program.

BIBLIOGRAPHY

Jarrell, Richard A. "Maestlin's Place in Astronomy." *Physis* 17 (1975), 5–20.

Methuen, Charlotte. "Maestlin's Teaching of Copernicus: The Evidence of His University Textbook and Disputations." *Isis* 87 (1996), 230–247.

PETER BARKER

See also Copernicanism; Kepler, Johannes; Reinhold, Erasmus

Magic

The role of magic in the Scientific Revolution has been vigorously contested. While a number of scholars have forcefully pointed to a number of ways in which magical ideas and traditions might be said to have influenced Renaissance and early-modern ways of understanding the physical world, others have denied the relevance of all such studies to an understanding of the development of the natural sciences. It seems clear, however, from the best historical studies of magic in the Scientific Revolution that the rational precepts upon which magic was based replaced a number of the precepts of traditional natural philosophy and gave rise to approaches to the study of the physical world that were closer to the approaches of modern science than anything that had gone before.

For example, a great deal of work has gone into establishing the magical origins of an important role for experimentation. Traditional natural philosophy was concerned with explanation of phenomena in terms of causes. But this meant that all things were to be explained by recourse to the four Aristotelian causes: material, efficient, formal, and final. Explanations of this kind tended to be speculative rather than empirically based—particularly as it was believed that true causal explanations should all be based upon manifestly true premises. An explanation of why oil floated on water, for example, would rest on the argument that oil contains fire and fire is lighter than water and will not mix with it. There would be no need to empirically test this explanation. Part of the point of the explanation would be that everyone knows oil contains fire, since it is used as an easily ignitable source of fire, and everyone knows that fire cannot mix with water without the destruction of one or the other.

In the magical tradition, however, there was no such concern with causal explanations. What was important was practical success in bringing about a desired outcome. If a magical technique worked, it was exploited; explanations were an optional extra. As Francis Bacon (1561–1626) acknowledged: "Magic proposes to recall natural philosophy from a miscellany of speculations to a magnitude of works." Perhaps the most obvious manifestation of empiricism in the magical tradition is alchemy, but there was a general consensus amongst practitioners or advocates of magic that it was based on the careful observation and experience of natural phenomena. Cornelius Agrippa (1486–1535), for example, insisted that "magicians are careful explorers of nature." It followed from this more pragmatic approach that so-called occult qualities became more and more prominent in explanations.

Scholastic natural philosophers wished to avoid recourse to occult qualities in their explanations. Proper explanation was supposedly based on what was manifestly true and should, therefore, rely on the manifest qualities, directly accessible to the senses: hotness, coldness, wetness, dryness, and the other sensible qualities that were held to derive from these, such as smoothness, hardness, and the like. Developments in pharmacy and chemistry, however, resulted in increasingly frequent recourse to occult qualities. There had always been drugs that did not seem to operate on the body in the manifest ways of raising or lowering body heat, or through retaining or expelling fluid, and the great medical authority Galen (second century) had referred to these as working in some occult way on "the whole substance" of the body. The introduction of new drugs during the Renaissance, particularly from the New World but also from the Far East, to say nothing of the efforts of the Paracelsians and other iatrochemists to introduce mineral, as opposed to botanical, drugs, led to a vast increase in the number of drugs that were acknowledged to operate by occult means.

Embarrassing as this was to Scholastic philosophers, it led others to criticize the Aristotelian tradition. One major result of these criticisms was a completely new attitude toward occult qualities. Going hand in hand with developments in matter theory, which supposed that all bodies were composed of invisible particles of matter, occult qualities were explained either by making assumptions about the efficient capabilities of the invisible particles or by taking for granted their empirically established effects. On the former assumption, for example, a magnet was said to attract because of the behavior of invisible particles given off by the magnet. On the latter assumption, the abilities of magnets to attract other pieces of iron, to orient themselves, and so forth were acknowledged as properties that, though occult in operation, were entirely manifest to the senses. Meanwhile, the supposed obviousness of the traditional manifest qualities was denied. It was no longer accepted as a real explanation to say that fire burns because it is hot. Fire had to be explained either in terms of the inferred behavior of the invisible particles of fire (which were assumed to be very small and very fast moving to make them highly penetrative) or by recourse to its empirically demonstrated effects. While the explanation of magnetism divided opinion, fire was usually explained in terms of the behavior of its particles. It is important to note, however, that fire was explained in terms of the behavior of invisible particles, which were completely inaccessible to empirical confirmation. Whichever explanatory assumption was made, therefore, it derived from the occult tradition.

The magical tradition, therefore, with its easy acceptance of occult qualities, can be seen to have played a major role in the development of the experimental method and of the so-called mechanical philosophies that were so characteristic of the Scientific Revolution. Similarly, the new emphasis on the role of mathematics in the understanding of the physical world, another characterizing feature of the Scientific Revolution, can also be shown to owe something to the magical tradition. Certainly, Pythagoras (fl. sixth century B.C.E.), who was associated throughout the Middle Ages with the belief that mathematics could be used to represent and explain phenomena in the real world, was regarded as a great ancient magus. Mathematics was regarded, therefore, as a branch of magic or, as Agrippa declared, as "necessary and cognate to magic." Thinkers with reputations as mathematicians, from Roger Bacon (ca. 1214–1292), John Dee (1527–1608), and John Napier (1550–1617) to John Flamsteed (1646–1719), were regarded as magicians, and this was not just because they cast astrological charts. Mechanical devices that produced great power or motion or kept time were also regarded in the popular consciousness as magical in their operation. This was not because the machines were believed to contain demons, but simply because they were designed and produced with the aid of mathematical skill.

Finally, it is not difficult to establish that magic also played an important role in the new concern for the pragmatic benefits of natural knowledge. Unlike contemplative natural philosophers, magicians were always concerned to bring about desired effects. This is one reason why mechanical devices were seen as the province of the magician. Francis Bacon undoubtedly derived his own concern for the usefulness of natural philosophy from the magical tradition. When he wrote that human knowledge should be used to extend "the bounds of Human Empire, to the effecting of all things possible," he was writing like a magus. Even René Descartes (1596–1650), whose mature philosophy eschewed all notions of occult powers (though its explanations in terms of the unobservable and untestable behavior of invisible particles can be seen to derive from earlier occultist critiques of Scholasticism), wished, early on in his career, to make contact with the supposedly reformist Rosicrucian brotherhood because of his desire to make the philosophy of nature more beneficial to mankind.

Magic can be shown, therefore, to have played some role in the mathematization of the world picture, in the development of experimental method, in the new emphasis on the pragmatic usefulness of the natural sciences, and in the epistemological justification of the matter theories of the new mechanical philosophies. Moreover, the individual contributions of a number of leading thinkers can also be shown to have owed a great deal to magical traditions. Salient among such thinkers are Paracelsus (ca. 1491–1541), Johannes Baptista van Helmont (1579–1644), Johannes Kepler (1571–1630),

Pierre Gassendi (1592–1655), William Gilbert (1544–1603), Francis Bacon, Robert Boyle (1627–1691), Gottfried Wilhelm Leibniz (1646–1716), and, perhaps most famous of all, Isaac Newton (1642–1727).

It is easy to suggest, even in a very brief survey like this, the importance of magic in the shift from traditional natural philosophy to something closer to our modern conception of science. But we still need to know why it was that magic had this great impact. Part of the explanation lies in the fact that newly recovered ancient magical texts, particularly the writings attributed to Hermes Trismegistus, provided a new understanding of the theory of magic and persuaded many intellectuals that here was the key to the most ancient wisdom known to man. But we also need to know what it was about this newly recovered magic that made it seem so useful for the new philosophers. How was it that magical traditions inspired such new approaches to the understanding of the natural world? In short, what was magic?

Magic then was clearly different from magic now. Moreover, the crucial difference was, arguably, the dominant aspect of premodern magic. It was the tradition known as *natural magic*. In this tradition, it was assumed that there were hidden connections linking each thing to a variety of other things. These were the "correspondences," and, in the right circumstances, an entity might be made to influence or act upon one or all of its corresponding entities. Underwriting this assumption was the belief that God had created the world in accordance with a hierarchically ordered pattern and had built the correspondences into the system, so that a lower creature might influence a higher, a planet might influence a plant, a specially constructed amulet might affect a human, or the stars might affect a political event. The trick, for the magus, was to know the correspondences and how to exploit them to bring about particular ends. This required vast experience of the physical world and all of its creatures (though in practice, of course, as critics of magicians, if not of magic, often pointed out, magicians too often relied upon supposedly authoritative books, rather than the study of nature itself). It is this that made magic an essentially empirical pursuit. The hidden correspondences could be discovered only by trial.

There were, however, two main means of cutting corners, if you aspired to be a powerful magus. One was to rely upon the interpretation of signatures. It was assumed that God had provided clues to the correspondences. A yellow flower might signify a cure for jaundice; surely it is significant that the flesh of the walnut in its shell looks just like the human brain in the skull. Even with these clues, empirical checking was not entirely avoided, but at least the magus was provided with a likely place to start. Alternatively, and more efficiently, if more dangerously, one could bring about a desired end by summoning a demon and commanding the demon to bring it about. It is important to note here, if only to grasp the full importance for pre- and early-modern thinkers of natural magic, that a demon, even the Devil himself, could bring about magical effects only by exploiting the correspondences of things. At this time, it was believed that only God could perform supernatural acts. The Devil, being God's creature, was subject to nature and natural laws, but, because of his longevity and his once-angelic status, he was a supreme natural magician and knew how to accomplish anything that was naturally possible.

It was the connection with demonology, of course, which drew down upon magic the *odium theologicum* from which it always suffered. Moreover, it was always assumed by theologians that the Devil and his demons were clever enough to be able to deceive people into thinking they were bringing something about in one way, while actually accomplishing it in another way. A witch might believe that she is able to fly due to a magical ointment, but, in fact, the Devil uses some other natural means to enable her to fly. In such cases, the ointment is not naturally efficacious but is merely a "sign" that the witch has made a compact with the Devil and is, therefore, guilty of the worst kind of heresy. The period of the Scientific Revolution was also the period of the European witch crazes, and it was very important for the new philosophers to ensure that they were exploiting genuine natural effects and not being unwittingly deceived by mere "signs" provided by the Devil. It was during the process of deciding which were genuinely natural effects and which were unsubstantiated superstitious beliefs that natural magic became fragmented—much of it being absorbed into the new philosophy and the rest rejected. The end result was that natural magic lost its identity, and those parts of the magical tradition that were not absorbed into the new science came to be representative of magic as a whole. Our image of magic today contains some important (rejected) aspects of what was once the natural-magic tradition, such as astrology, but nothing that fully corresponds to natural magic, which is why we find it hard to understand the link between magic and empiricism. The natural magic that was once the predominant aspect of the magical tradition has largely been absorbed into the scientific worldview, leaving demonology to become dominant in our image of magic. This is why it is anachronistic to assume that, because magic now is entirely irrational and superstitious, it must always have been so.

BIBLIOGRAPHY

Copenhaver, Brian. "Astrology and Magic." In *The Cambridge History of Renaissance Philosophy,* ed. C. B. Schmitt and Q. Skinner. Cambridge: Cambridge University Press, 1988, pp. 264–300.

———. "Natural Magic, Hermeticism, and Occultism in Early Modern Science." In *Reappraisals of the Scientific Revolution,* ed. D. C. Lindberg and R. S. Westman. Cambridge: Cambridge University Press, 1990, pp. 261–302.

Rossi, Paolo. "Hermeticism, Rationality, and the Scientific Revolution." In *Reason, Experiment, and Mysticism in the Scientific Revolution,* ed. M. L. Righini Bonelli and W. R. Shea. London: Macmillan, 1975, pp. 247–273.

Thorndike, Lynn. *A History of Magic and Experimental Science.* 8 vols. New York: Columbia University Press, 1923–1958.

Vickers, Brian, ed. *Occult and Scientific Mentalities in the Renaissance.* Cambridge: Cambridge University Press, 1984.

Webster, Charles. *From Paracelsus to Newton: Magic and the Making of Modern Science.* Cambridge: Cambridge University Press, 1964.

JOHN HENRY

See also Correspondences; Hermetism; Iatrochemistry; Kabbalah; Macrocosm/Microcosm; Magic and the Scientific Revolution; Rosicrucianism; Witchcraft

Magic and the Scientific Revolution

The role of magic in the Scientific Revolution is a controversial matter, upon which there is no consensus. A traditional and surely familiar view sharply distinguishes magic from modern science and sees this contrast as one of the major characteristics of western European culture. Its supporters portray the Scientific Revolution as an unequivocal suppression of earlier magical traditions. Others argue that magical attitudes were an important motivating factor in the Scientific Revolution, stimulating interest in the mathematization of nature, for example; or, further, a vital source for some major steps in it, like Isaac Newton's (1642–1727) reintroduction of "active principles"; or, finally, that modern science derives some

of its essential components from the premodern magical worldview.

The traditional interpretation sketched above presumably dates back to the Enlightenment and that era's notion that Europe had finally freed itself from the superstition, and closely attached clericalism, of the Middle Ages. It is also closely associated with a contrast traditionally perceived between the rational and progressive culture of western Europe and the irrational and bankrupt culture on non-European "primitives"—for much colonialism was rationalized in terms of the benefits provided by the associated diffusion of an allegedly superior culture. Accordingly, anthropological literature frequently classifies the beliefs and practices outside the Western cultural sphere in terms of medieval European categories like "witchcraft" and "magic," although protests against this are routine. Clifford Geertz sees this question as going "to the heart of cultural anthropology," but others posit that the European categories may be themselves part of some broader cross-cultural schema. Conversely, there is a deeply ingrained tendency for historical and philosophical discussions of the European magical tradition to make overt references to anthropology and to that discipline's analyses of the way "primitive mentality" differs from that of the modern West.

There is, however, no trace of this anthropological contrast in Lynn Thorndike's monumental *History of Magic and Experimental Science* (1923–1958), but the hostility to religion is evident, and one of the aims of the study was apparently to place blame upon the Catholic Church for its role in sustaining the sort of irrational worldview in which witch persecutions and the like could flourish. Along the way, Thorndike came to change his mind and realized that the traditional contrast between magic and rationality had been too sharply drawn, for the experimental humility of some magic was analogous to that of post-seventeenth-century European science and, perhaps, a source for it. Edwin A. Burtt took quite a different and far more revisionist view in his *Metaphysical Foundations of Modern Physical Science* (1924): some heroes of the Scientific Revolution, he observed, were motivated by seemingly mystical considerations. Many writers since Thorndike and Burtt have extended this retreat from the traditional view.

In our postcolonial world, explicit opposition would be unfashionable, but it can certainly be found. Brian Vickers (1984) opposes it directly, while A. R. Hall (1975) declared that the whole history of science would be "a tale told by an idiot" if magic had a significant place in it. Both insist that occultist thinking is radically different from that of science, but they leave it quite unclear why entities that are radically different cannot be vital to each other's histories. Implicit opposition is more common. Carolyn Merchant (1980) is not alone in taking the view that something extremely valuable was lost in the Scientific Revolution, and thus she agrees with many of her opponents that some major disenchantment of the world did, indeed, take place. Much literature has similarly taken the view that the occult powers that magicians believed ran the world were one of the principal targets of seventeenth-century philosophical polemic and were irrational and, therefore, rightly rejected.

There can be no doubt at all that premodern magic often portrayed itself as beyond reason and that much seventeenth-century rhetoric focused on occult powers. But there is still a shortage of studies that seek to explore these questions in detail and, more generally, to sort out the conceptual framework here. What is the connection between magic and demonism? What constituted a supernatural cause and how did it relate to an occult cause? Was there a uniform view on these questions in Renaissance Europe? Keith Hutchison has explored some answers to these questions in five short studies, while Wayne Shumaker's *Occult Sciences* (1972) remains useful for the details of magical belief, as do Daniel Walker's *Spiritual and Demonic Magic* (1958), Stuart Clark's essay on the scientific status of demons in Brian Vickers's *Occult and Scientific Mentalities* (1984), and the surveys of earlier European magic by Brian Copenhaver (1990) and Bert Hansen (1978).

By far the most noteworthy statement of the revisionist view occurs in Frances Yates's difficult writings, especially the classic *Giordano Bruno and the Hermetic Tradition* (1964). Like Vickers and Hall, Yates accepts that there is a dramatic contrast between magic and modern science, but she insists that the latter was historically influential in generating the shift away from Scholastic Aristotelianism, in preparing the way, as she puts it. One of the critical factors here was the mid-fifteenth-century translation of the *Corpus Hermeticum*. Since texts claiming the same author were patently magical, the patent piety of these texts defused the old fear that magic was incompatible with Christianity. Keith Thomas, by contrast, observes in his *Religion and the Decline of Magic* (1971) that sixteenth-century Protestants saw Catholic ceremony as being too close to magic

and suggests that the Reformation was a major factor in explaining the latter's decline. With its new respectability, says Yates, magic brought a confidence that the universe contained novel powers ready for human exploitation and, accordingly, strengthened the rejection of an inherited Hellenic presumption that philosophy was to be disengaged from action. It also increased concern to reveal the hidden harmony of the cosmos and emphasized the symbolic importance of the Sun, thus hastening the Copernican transformation of the universe so central to the new worldview. So for Yates, the Scientific Revolution is portrayed as a two-stage process, in which magic first disarmed Aristotelianism, then joined it in being defeated by mechanism and experimentalism.

Such a view certainly survives the various attacks on Yates. Despite her immense influence and popularity, Yates laid herself open to numerous complaints, in part because of her unwillingness to state her theses clearly, or to marshal the evidence for them in a systematic and convincing fashion. But from the perspective of the present discussion, many objections to the claims have been primarily a matter of dotting "i"s and crossing "t"s. "Was it really the *Corpus Hermeticum* that exerted the influence or some more general Neoplatonism?" is a question justly posed by J. E. McGuire, Robert Westman, and Copenhaver. Yet, radical correction of Yates here can still leave her view of the role of magic in some more general sense relatively unaffected.

Far stronger claims for the role of magic have, however, been made by others, with particular reference to Newton (though a contending literature is growing up around these claims and suggesting that Newton's apparent activation of matter was not unique). Betty Dobbs has taken a Burtt-like view of Newton's internal motivation, arguing that alchemy and the like were both an important motivation for his basically theological quest and essential to the way Newton departed from the mechanical philosophy in introducing gravitational forces that seemed to act at a distance. Richard S. Westfall has taken a similar view on this last point, but neither Dobbs nor Westfall really establish that active principles could not have been provided by the main Aristotelian tradition. What magic provided was *occult* powers, generally excluded from the Scholastic universe—yet fully accommodated by the new science, at first in their universal forms but much later with their idiosyncrasy as well. According to this view, what magic passed on to science was the idea that the fundamental operations of the

M

universe are profoundly invisible, yet still accessible to the human intellect, albeit with major limitations. Much that the magicians believed was rejected, indeed, but some of it survived. But what survived was central to the defeat of Scholasticism and to the new epistemology that replaced it.

BIBLIOGRAPHY

Copenhaver, Brian. "Natural Magic, Hermetism, and Occultism in Early Modern Science." In *Reappraisals of the Scientific Revolution,* ed. David Lindberg and Robert Westman. Cambridge: Cambridge University Press, 1990, pp. 261–301.

Hall, Alfred Rupert. "Magic, Metaphysics, and Mysticism in the Scientific Revolution." In *Reason, Experiment, and Mysticism in the Scientific Revolution,* ed. M. L. R. Bonelli and W. R. Shea. New York: Science History Publications, 1975, pp. 275–282.

Hansen, Bert. "Science and Magic." In *Science in the Middle Ages,* ed. David Lindberg. Chicago: University of Chicago Press, 1978, pp. 483–506.

Merchant, Carolyn. *The Death of Nature: Women, Ecology, and the Scientific Revolution.* San Francisco: Harper and Row, 1980.

Shumaker, Wayne. *The Occult Sciences in the Renaissance: A Study in Intellectual Patterns.* Berkeley and Los Angeles: University of California Press, 1972.

Thomas, Keith. *Religion and the Decline of Magic.* London: Weidenfeld and Nicolson, 1971.

Thorndike, Lynn. *A History of Magic and Experimental Science.* 8 vols. New York: Macmillan and Columbia University Press, 1923–1958.

Vickers, Brian, ed. *Occult and Scientific Mentalities in the Renaissance.* Cambridge: Cambridge University Press, 1984.

Yates, Frances. *Giordano Bruno and the Hermetic Tradition.* London and Cambridge: Cambridge University Press, 1964.

Walker, Daniel. *Spiritual and Demonic Magic from Ficino to Campanella.* London: Warburg Institute, 1958.

KEITH HUTCHISON

See also Correspondences; Hermetism; Kabbalah; Magic

Magini, Giovanni Antonio (1555–1617)

A professor of mathematics and astronomy at the University of Bologna, he was perhaps better known in his day as an astrologer. In 1582 he published the first of a series of ephemerides, which he intended for both astrological and astronomical purposes. In them he used Copernican observations, as well as the *Prutenic Tables,* based on Nicolaus Copernicus (1473–1543), and ad-

justed them for the Gregorian calendar. He followed this with other works on astronomy and astrology. As a result of his publication record, in 1588 Magini was appointed to the University of Bologna to teach astronomy and mathematics instead of Galileo Galilei (1564–1642), who had also applied for the position.

Although he rejected the Copernican cosmology, preferring the Ptolemaic, Magini did modify his ideas by adopting some Copernican innovations. He made use of Copernicus's observations and mathematical techniques, adapting Copernicus's theory of precession of the equinoxes and adding additional spheres, and replaced the "trepidation" theory (a variable precession of the equinoxes) of medieval Ptolemaic astronomy with Copernicus's version ("libration"). His work on astronomy enabled some of those with geostatic convictions to appreciate parts of Copernicus's work. He corresponded with a number of outstanding astronomers, including Johannes Kepler (1571–1630), who at Magini's death was offered, but did not accept, his vacant chair of mathematics at the University of Bologna.

Giovanni Antonio Magini. From Paul Freher, Theatrum virorum eruditione clarorum *(1688).*

Despite his interest in astronomy, Magini was known chiefly for his astrology and was employed by the nobility for his astrological predictions. However, he also published treatises on trigonometry and tables on square numbers and square roots and on the properties of spherical mirrors; his interest in geography is evidenced by his publication of an edition of Ptolemy's (ca. 100–ca. 170) *Geography* with commentary and an atlas of Italy containing maps of the various regions, which was completed only after his death.

Relatively little research has been done on Magini since Antonio Favaro's rather lengthy work on him in 1886. He has, however, been considered less anti-Galilean than was once thought.

BIBLIOGRAPHY

Baffetti, Giovanni. "Il *Sidereus nuncius* a Bologna." *Intersezioni: Rivista di storia della idee* 11 (1991), 477–500.

Clarke, A. G. "Giovanni Antonio Magini (1555–1617) and Late Renaissance Astrology." Ph.D. diss. Warburg Institute, London, 1986.

Favaro, Antonio. *Carteggio inedito di Ticone Brahe, Giovanni Keplero e di altri celebri astronomi e matematici dei secoli XVI e XVII con Giovanni Antonio Magini*. Bologna: Nicola Zanichelli, 1886.

WILLIAM LEWIS HINE

See also Astronomical Tables and Ephemerides; Copernicanism; Copernicus, Nicolaus

Magnetism

Magnetism became the subject of a genuinely new physical science during the Scientific Revolution. As is rarely the case, it was established by one book, the *De magnete* (1600) of William Gilbert (1544–1603). "New philosophers" of the next generation frequently presented magnetic science as a symbol of their post-Renaissance progress. Traditional treatises confined discussion to the lodestone, considered as an unusual species of mineral. Its attraction of iron, north-south polarity, and use in compasses was well known. Aristotelians classified it as an occult quality, produced by the lodestone's specific form and propagated like light through a medium.

Interest in magnetism grew throughout the sixteenth century. Renaissance occultists cited it as evidence of sympathetic forces supposedly linking terrestrial objects with celestial virtues. A popular theory held that magnets drew down powers from the North Star. *Magnetismus* was a Paracelsian medical term for the capacity

of magical medicines to draw poisons out of the body. The first compendium of magnetic phenomena was a chapter "On the Lodestone" in Giambattista della Porta's (1535–1615) *Magia naturalis* (1558). It combined basic observations with gentlemanly amusements and oft-repeated errors, such as garlic's antimagnetic property. More significantly, European voyages of trade and colonization made urgent a better understanding of the magnetic compass. Dealing with magnetic variation was a particular problem, motivating secret, state-sponsored research in Spain and Portugal. When England became an imperial power under Elizabeth I, it developed its own experts. By 1600 they realized that their practical expertise in geomagnetism outstripped the explanations of natural philosophers.

William Gilbert, a London physician, dismissed all existing explanations. In their place he proposed a "magnetic philosophy," which contradicted orthodox natural philosophy at many points. For him, the entire earth was distinguished by its possession of a quasi-animate magnetic virtue, the terrestrial counterpart to the Sun's light. As a magnetic sphere, lodestone was its true elemental substance, and its geographical poles and axis were magnetically produced. Its virtue controlled the motion of "earthy" bodies, such as lodestones, iron, and compass needles. Gilbert argued that the force binding the earth and the Moon was magnetic and caused the tides; he hinted that gravity, too, was magnetic. Indeed, he proposed the earth's magnetic virtue as the answer to many of the dynamic problems of Copernican astronomy: it both rotated the earth and stabilized it in space. In short, Gilbert elevated magnetism into an immaterial, cosmic, law-bound, and measurable force.

De magnete commanded immediate respect because its conclusions were built upon thorough and persuasive magnetic experiments, which provided a corpus of phenomena. The most important established the central principle of the new science: that spherically shaped lodestones, manipulated in the laboratory, behaved analogously to the earth. Other experiments distinguished magnetism from *electricitas* (Gilbert's neologism for electrostatic attraction), which he displayed as dependent upon a material medium.

It is possible that *De magnete*'s experimental style grew out of Gilbert's contacts with London's maritime community, notably with Edward Wright (1558–1615). Wright's influence lay behind the discovery of a mathematical correlation between latitude and magnetic

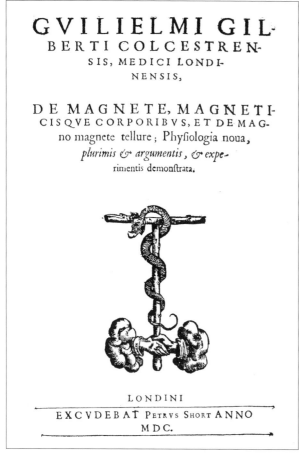

GVILIELMI GIL-
BERTI COLCESTREN-
SIS, MEDICI LONDI-
NENSIS,

DE MAGNETE, MAGNETI-
CISQVE CORPORIBVS, ET DE MAG-
no magnete tellure; Phyſiologia noua,
plurimis & argumentis, & experimentis demonſtrata.

LONDINI
EXCVDEBAT PETRVS SHORT ANNO
MDC.

Title page of the first edition of William Gilbert's work on the magnet.

inclination, a laboratory result transformed into a position-finding technique. *De magnete*'s influential explanation of variation—that it was caused by the earth's deviations from a perfect sphere—reinforced Wright's preferred answer to the pressing problem of finding longitude at sea. If variation was a function of geology, its complex global patterns would, in principle, permit sailors to know when and where they were approaching a landmass.

The new magnetic philosophy, therefore, was an early result of the new relationship forged in the Scientific Revolution between natural philosophy and technical practice. It was taken up in new locations sponsored by the state or entrepreneurial elites. One was London's Gresham College (founded 1597), which trained navigators. Work by a succession of its professors and naval experts culminated in the discovery that variation changed with time. Secular variation, announced by Henry Gellibrand (1597–1636) in 1634, challenged the classical Gilbertian paradigm both philosophically and practically. It questioned whether the earth was a simple magnetic sphere, and variation patterns a simple answer to the longitude problem. Magnetic philosophy became more complex and ad hoc. By 1700 theories of separate magnetic poles, or even pairs of poles, had been proposed (notably by Edmond Halley, ca. 1656–1743), together with numerous magnetic navigation schemes that vied for lucrative financial rewards. Throughout the period, geomagnetic data were, in fact, unreliable and contradictory. This lent credence to the anti-Gilbertian theory of the Jesuit Athanasius Kircher (1602–1680). He restricted magnetic earth to a shallow layer of subterranean fibers, so that local geological disturbances produced unpredictable local changes in variation.

Kircher's opposition arose from his objections, as an official Catholic intellectual, to magnetic Copernicanism. Johannes Kepler (1571–1630) and Simon Stevin (1548–1620) had both extended Gilbert's cosmology to the whole solar system by 1609, and Kepler had inferred complex magnetic interiors for each planet from the elliptical orbits he had calculated. The resultant attractive and repulsive forces provided a plausible physical cause of the ellipses. Galileo Galilei (1564–1642) also commended aspects of Gilbert's theory, which ensured that *De magnete* was censured in Catholic condemnations of Copernicanism. Magnetic philosophy became a cosmic battlefield. A succession of Jesuit philosophers, beginning with Niccolo Cabeo (1586–1650) in his *Philosophia magnetica* (1648), recast Gilbert's experimental corpus with ingenious Aristotelian explanations. Cabeo made magnetism a new prime quality of earth. In 1644 Jacques Grandami (1588–1672) announced that his *terrellae* always came to rest in a fixed East-West orientation, which confirmed the Aristotelian principle that all moving bodies, including magnetic ones, come to rest in their natural place. This experimental claim was never challenged. New philosophers began to concede the central principle, now arguing that all terrestrial magnets were overpowered by the earth's sphere of magnetic influence and, hence, had no cosmological significance.

The concession was made easier by the rise of the mechanical philosophy, for René Descartes's (1596–1650) model of the solar system as a fluid vortex had largely replaced magnetic conceptions.

Magnetic and mechanical philosophies coexisted in creative tension in the latter stages of the Scientific Revolution, by which time Gilbert's and Kepler's immaterial magnetic forces looked like dated, even dangerous, occultism. Indeed, Robert Fludd's (1574–1637) *Philosophia Moysaica* (1631) had presented Gilbert's work as experimental proof of cosmic sympathies. By contrast, Descartes's characteristically ingenious explanation used only contact forces. He proposed that magnetic bodies were distinguished by an internal structure of parallel channels, half with left-handed and half with right-handed threads. Two streams of screw-shaped particles, of opposite handedness, flowed around and through the magnet in two opposite vortices linking pole to pole. If, upon leaving a pole, they encountered a ferrous body, they screwed their way through its channels, thereby moving it into alignment with the particulate lines of magnetic force and pulling it back toward the pole. Although he eliminated Gilbert's immaterialism, Descartes maintained magnetism's cosmic dimension. His magnetic vortex was the model for the earth's own vortex and even the Sun's.

But mechanical philosophers like Descartes, Pierre Gassendi (1592–1655), Kenelm Digby (1603–1655), Gottfried Wilhelm Leibniz (1646–1716), and Robert Boyle (1627–1691) basically reduced magnetism from a cosmic force to just another kind of matter-in-motion, albeit a peculiar one. For Boyle, streams of magnetic effluvia jostled, in the world and for his attention, alongside the subtle effluvia of heat, electricity, numerous atmospheric and subterranean "streams," and "exotic" planetary effluvia. By the 1680s, magnetic philosophy persisted in name only, its central, analogical principle abandoned, cosmic magnetism dismantled, and hopes for navigational applications waning. And by imagining an effluvium for every phenomenon that was not obviously mechanical, mechanists returned magnetism to the company of natural oddities from which Gilbert had promoted it. Theoretical work on magnetic streams also ran into dead ends.

Gilbertian magnetism had one further role in the Scientific Revolution. It offered an alternative dynamic model to the micromechanical paradigm. A few nonconformists, like Gilles Personne de Roberval (1602–1675) at the Paris Académie Royale des Sciences, continued to believe in real attractions. Others, like Robert Hooke (1635–1703) and Christopher Wren (1632–1723) at the Royal Society of London, used magnetism heuristically to understand planetary forces. Hooke measured the force-distance relation in magnets as he investigated inverse-square laws of force. These were important resources as Isaac Newton (1642–1727) began to think about gravity as a real attraction. Early-eighteenth-century Newtonians occasionally studied magnetism as an example of Newton's "active principles" but were now more interested in the latest new science of electricity.

BIBLIOGRAPHY

Ariotti, Piero E. "Benedetto Castelli's Discourse on the Loadstone (1639–1640): The Origin of the Notion of Elementary Magnets Similarly Aligned." *Annals of Science* 38 (1981), 125–140.

Baldwin, Martha R. "Magnetism and the Anti-Copernican Polemic." *Journal for the History of Astronomy* 16 (1985), 155–174.

Gilbert, William. *De Magnete*. Trans. P. Flleury Mottelay. New York: Dover, 1958. Repr. of 1st ed. 1893.

Pumfrey, Stephen. "Magnetical Philosophy and Astronomy, 1600–1650." In *The General History of Astronomy,* ed. R. Taton and C. Wilson. Cambridge: Cambridge University Press, 1989, vol. 2A, pp. 45–53.

———. "William Gilbert's Magnetical Philosophy, 1580–1674: The Creation and Dissolution of a Discipline." Ph.D. diss. Warburg Institute, London, 1987.

STEPHEN PUMFREY

See also Attraction; Compass, Magnetic; Gilbert, William

Malebranche, Nicolas (1638–1715)

A French philosopher and Oratorian priest, he integrated the Cartesian heritage into an original and rationalist speculative system, which he elaborated on theological foundations. Malebranche considered the universe similar to the mechanism of a clock, regulated by the continuing action of God; he denied the existence of inherent forces in bodies. The collision of two bodies is, thus, the occasion for God's intervention to effect the changes in motion in the simplest manner; in similar situations, God effects the same changes. This approach is known as Malebranche's *occasionalism*.

Malebranche's interest in mathematics and the sciences flows directly from his rationalist philosophy, which insists on the necessity for an experimental philosophy of nature. The successive editions of *La recherche de la vérité* (Researches on Truth, 1674–1712), begun in 1668, testify to the extent and evolution of his scientific studies. In 1690 Malebranche began the study of the mathematics of the infinite in the company of a group of mathematicians assembled about the Marquis de l'Hôspital and oriented toward a synthesis of the tradition stemming from the mathematics of Pierre de Fermat (1601–1665) and the methods of the English school, as expressed in the work of Isaac Barrow (1630–1677) and John Wallis (1616–1703). In 1691, however, his meeting with Johann I Bernoulli (1667–1748) and the introduction of the differential calculus resulted in dropping the initial projects. The group opened itself to the new Leibnizian analysis and made itself its disseminator and soon its advocate in France. The mathematicians of Malebranche's circle (L'Hôspital, Louis Carré, Charles-René Reyneau) were also the first to write textbooks of the infinitesimal calculus. Thus, Malebranche was at the center of intense mathematical activity, for which he received full recognition through his nomination in 1699 as an honorary member of the Académie Royale des Sciences of Paris.

After that date, Malebranche greatly emphasized the importance of experimental method and engaged in experimentation himself. His observations of chicken embryos in eggs incubated in a stove confirmed him in the validity of ovist theory, of which he was an advocate. In optics, he provided experimental evidence for the near-equivalence of the air and of the void in the air pump as media for the propagation of light. For Malebranche, light is like a vibration in a medium under pressure, whose frequency is characteristic of its color, an idea taken up again and elaborated in the nineteenth century. His conception of matter and his researches on elasticity led him to formulate, after some inconsistent results and ensuing debates, the correct laws of collision of elastic bodies. This was his most original contribution to the scientific movement of the era.

BIBLIOGRAPHY

Centre International de Synthèse. *Malebranche, l'homme et l'oeuvre, 1638–1715*. Paris: Vrin, 1967.

Malebranche, Nicolas. *Oeuvres complètes*. Ed. André Robinet. 23 vols. Paris: Vrin, 1958–1968.

Mouy, Paul. *Les lois du choc des corps d'après Malebranche*. Paris: Vrin, 1927.

JEANNE PEIFFER
TRANS. WILBUR APPLEBAUM

See also Arnauld, Antoine; Calculus; Cartesianism; Infinity, Mathematical; Religion and Natural Philosophy

Malpighi, Marcello (1628–1694)

One of the greatest anatomists of all time. His skill in microscopy in developing and inventing several observation techniques led him to discover many previously unknown microstructures in plants and animals.

Malpighi was born at Crevalcore near Bologna. Apart from a brief period at Mantua, he studied at Bologna University with Francesco Natali (d. 1675), Bartolomeo Massari (1603–1655), and Andrea Mariani (1593–ca. 1661), graduating in philosophy and medicine in 1653. He assisted Massari and Mariani in the practice of medicine and started teaching logic at Bologna University in 1656. Together with Carlo Fracassati (d. 1672), he was one of the nine members of the Coro Anatomico, an informal gathering established ca. 1650 by Massari and continued by Mariani to perform dissections and vivisections and to investigate recent anatomical findings, such as William Harvey's (1578–1657) circulation of the blood. This anatomical apprenticeship was a major component of his training.

At the end of 1656, Malpighi was called to teach medicine at Pisa University, where he remained until 1659. During those years, he established strong links with Giovanni Alfonso Borelli (1608–1679), who instructed him in the corpuscular and mechanical philosophy. Probably in those years they started microscopic investigations with the instruments available at the Tuscan Court. Their intellectual links and friendship remained profound for a decade but cooled down ca. 1665 until, in 1668, Malpighi interrupted his correspondence with Borelli for personal and intellectual reasons.

In 1659 Malpighi returned to Bologna University and soon published his first, and possibly most important, works, two *Epistolae de pulmonibus* (1661), dedicated to Borelli. On the basis of microscopic observations reproduced in influential illustrations, he was able to establish that the lungs were not fleshy viscera but consisted of a series of thin membranes separating progressively smaller cavities. Malpighi was also able to detect the anastomoses, or junctions, of arteries and veins in the lungs of frogs, as well as the blood moving in opposite directions in the two types of vessels, an observation hailed by Borelli as decisive in favor of Harvey's views. Malpighi inferred a similar structure in the lungs of higher animals. Despite his success with the structure of lungs, he was uncertain as to their function, arguing that they served to mix the blood. The problematic tension between structure and function remained a constant feature of his contributions.

In 1662, thanks to Borelli's influence on the Messina Senate, Malpighi was called to the first chair of medicine at the university. At Messina he composed *De lingua* and *De cerebro* (1665, published together with works by Fra-

Marcello Malpighi. From Fielding H. Garrison, An Introduction to the History of Medicine, *3rd ed. (Philadelphia and London: Saunders, 1921).*

cassati on the same subjects), *De omento, pinguedine et adiposis ductibus* (1665), and *De externo tactus organo* (1665). *De lingua* and *De externo tactus organo* were closely linked in subject matter and investigation techniques. They deal with the anatomical basis for the sense of taste and touch and are inspired by some passages by Galileo Galilei (1564–1642). *De cerebro* deals with sense perception, namely sight, and contains a refutation of René Descartes's (1596–1650) theory of vision; it is based on the peculiar structure of the optic nerve of the swordfish and is illustrated with a beautiful copperplate.

On his return to Bologna in 1666, Malpighi started collecting postmortem reports and other anatomical observations, which found their way into his later publications. In *De viscerum structura* (1666), containing *De hepate, De cerebri cortice, De renibus, De liene,* and *De polypo cordis,* Malpighi identified in the gland the fundamental structure of the liver, the cerebral cortex, the kidneys, and the spleen. His findings on the cerebral cortex were an artifact of his observation techniques, such as ink staining, which could produce stunning results in one case and be deceptive in others. Following the works

of Franciscus Sylvius (1614–1672) and Nicolaus Steno (Niels Stensen, 1638–1686), Malpighi conceived glands as mechanical machines capable of filtering the blood and producing different fluids (bile in the liver, nervous juice in the cerebral cortex, and urine in the kidneys) according to their peculiar conformations. Although the microstructure of major organs was in this way associated with their functions, Malpighi was unable to see how glands work. Even in *De structura glandularum* (1689), after having identified a common structure in all glands, namely a central follicle with blood and nervous vessels and an excretory duct, Malpighi shifted the problem to the structure of the follicle. This example instantiates the problem of the machine within the machine that plagued seventeenth-century iatromechanics. In *De polypo cordis,* Malpighi investigated the composition of the blood on the basis of experiments, microscopy, and postmortems.

Following a letter by Henry Oldenburg (ca. 1619–1677), Malpighi published a major work on the silkworm, *De bombyce* (1669), and was elected a Fellow of the Royal Society. For a decade he focused on lower animals, plants, and the problem of generation. These themes were related by the belief that their supposed simplicity would help him understand structures and their functions in higher animals. *Anatome plantarum* (1675, 1679) relies heavily on the analogy between plants and animals. *De formatione pulli in ovo* (1673) and *Appendix de ovo incubato* (1675) contain major microscopic investigations of the problem of generation. Malpighi published miscellaneous anatomical observations in the form of a letter in the *Philosophical Transactions* for 1684.

Throughout his career, Malpighi was a physician, and in 1691 he was called to Rome by Innocent XII (1615–1700) to be pontifical archiater (chief physician). Malpighi, however, wished to be remembered as an anatomist, and he prevented his disciples from publishing his writings on medical practice, which nonetheless appeared as *Consultationes* (Padua, 1713; Venice, 1747). By contrast, he arranged for his autobiography to appear posthumously (1697). In more than one hundred folio pages, he replied to all of his critics, even over matters dating to his youth. His *Opera posthuma* also includes his 1665 reply to Michele Lipari (d. 1676) and rebuttal of an attack in 1689 by Gerolamo Sbaraglia (1641–1710). Both are invaluable for the connections they establish between anatomy and medical practice.

BIBLIOGRAPHY
Adelmann, H. B., ed. *The Correspondence of Marcello Malpighi.* 5 vols. Ithaca, NY: Cornell University Press, 1975.
———. *Marcello Malpighi and the Evolution of Embryology.* 5 vols. Ithaca, NY: Cornell University Press, 1966.
———, Bertoloni Meli, D., ed. *Marcello Malpighi: Anatomist and Physician.* Firenze: Olsckhi, 1997.

DOMENICO BERTOLONI MELI

See also Anatomy; Dissection; Embryology; Generation; Iatromechanics; Microscopy; Physiology

Mapmaking. See Cartography

Mariotte, Edmé (ca. 1620–1684)

An early member of the Académie Royale des Sciences in Paris, Mariotte was known for his work in physics, optics, and mechanics. His experimental skill drew together diverse disciplines, and his leadership abilities helped establish cooperation among early members of the academy.

Born to an administrative family from Burgundy, Mariotte left little record of his early life and education; it appears that he was tonsured in 1634 and that his science was self-taught. It is not known when or why he came to Paris, though his work on plant physiology was known to members of the academy by 1666, and in the following year he was inducted representing physics. Condorcet, in the eighteenth century, identified Mariotte as the first among the French to embrace "experimental philosophy," clearly in evidence in the "singular doctrine" that sap in plants circulates in analogy to blood in animals (*De la vegétation des plantes,* 1679). Mariotte's scientific activities in the academy were diverse, ranging through physics, mathematics, geometrical optics, botany, meteorology, navigation, instrumentation, and hydrostatics. The crucial link was experiment. Among his earliest and most sustained interests was vision. Mariotte moved a white circle in front of one eye until its image in the eye covered the entrance of the optic nerve; he is credited with discovering the "blind spot." Mariotte engaged in an extended dispute on the seat of vision, arguing that it was not the retina but the choroid layer that lay behind it. His theory was widely opposed.

Mariotte's other work was characteristically experimental, including his *Traité de la percussion ou choc des corps* (1673), on laws of impact; *De la nature de l'air* (1679), in which Mariotte's Law on the relation between pressure and volume in a gas is stated, independently of Boyle (1676); *De la nature des couleurs* (1681), which describes his failure to repeat Isaac Newton's (1642–1727) so-called *experimentum crucis* on the dispersion of white light through a prism; and his posthumous *Traité du mouvement des eaux et des autres corps fluides* (1686), on the motion of fluids and bodies in resisting media.

BIBLIOGRAPHY
Mariotte, savant et philosophe (d. 1684): Analyse d'une renommée. Preface by P. Costabel. Paris: Vrin, 1986.
Sturdy, David J., *Science and Social Status: The Members of the Académie des Sciences, 1666–1750.* Woodbridge: Boydell, 1995.

ROBERT A. HATCH

See also Pneumatics; Vision

Marxist Historiography

Karl Marx (1818–1883) read history by means of his notion of the *mode of production*. According to this reading, the way a people provided for themselves or produced their means of subsistence gave shape to other social and cultural aspects of life. This production, furthermore, took place within specific sets of relations, relations between persons in society (division of labor, classes) and relations to nature (crop rotation, strip mining). Relations in society influence the specific way of laboring upon the materials of nature, and the way of directing activity toward nature shapes the specific relations in society. Marx periodized history into several historically specifiable sets of these relations, called modes of production. Labor is usually bound or unfree in each period, but the precise way in which it is bound distinguishes one mode of production from another. When we engage in a historically specific form of direct, productive, laboring activity, we not only produce the material products necessary for life in our society, we also reproduce the social apparatus in which all of this production takes place. The specific form and social organization of our activity mediate the way in which we are conscious of our world, both material and social. The way people think and perceive is not unrelated to the way they live. There is no such thing as "pure" consciousness; it is always *someone's* consciousness. The philosophy, law, religion, or science of a people also arises in the context of these kinds of relations. The various Marxist contributors to the historiography of the Scientific Revolution place greater emphasis either on the means or on the relations of production.

According to Marx, "The hand-mill gives you society with the feudal lord; the steam-mill gives you society with the industrial capitalist." Orthodox Marxists tend to interpret this kind of comment as suggesting that means of production (the specific productive techniques and their attendant technological problems) direct intellectual attention to nature as revealed by that set of problems. If a productive solution results from this intellectual appropriation, the theoretical understanding of nature embodied in that solution counts as objective, systematic, scientific knowledge. If working people (direct labor) are serfs producing with hand mills, no such propitious problems face well-positioned intellectual laborers. The ruling intellect in a society with hand mills resides in Scholastic philosophers whose task is to legitimate the positions of feudal lords and Church officials. The productive needs of the dominant class present no scientifically or industrially fruitful problems to intellectual laborers in the employ of the dominant class of feudal lords.

The industrial capitalist and the steam mill, however, according to this Marxist view, present a different picture. The industrial capitalist has productive needs, initially in transportation, navigation, mining, and ballistics, which call for immediate intellectual attention. Those who labor with more complex machines producing commodities for exchange are free of explicit bondage and have a hand in presenting exactly the right problems to intellectual laborers.

Marx's colleague Frederick Engels (1820–1895) said that a technological requirement of society helps science more than ten universities. A revolutionary bourgeoisie, in overthrowing feudalism, prepared the ground, at the same time, for a scientific, intellectual appropriation of nature. Some Marxists who followed Engels's lead decided that this line of thought had two advantages: it related scientific thought to the class structure of society, and it preserved the empirical-truth claim of those features of modern science that appeared to have incontrovertibly fruitful industrial application.

Various Marxist analysts have emphasized different features of the Marxian legacy. Those following Engels have emphasized means of production, the overthrow of Scholastic philosophy and theology, and the preservation of the empirical validity of the resulting science. Others have emphasized relations of production and the precise position of intellectual laborers as affecting the content of science; they view social relations as projected onto nature (i.e., relations in society mediate the intellectual appropriation of nature even in the context of bourgeois productive needs).

Although it is no accident that the emergence of capitalism is coincident with the Scientific Revolution, there is more than one way to articulate the relationship between them within a Marxian framework. One of the earliest formulations of the means-of-production position appears in the work of Boris Hessen in 1931. According to Hessen, it was a set of productive, economic needs of the bourgeoisie that presented the appropriate experts with a set of technical problems. These investigators uncovered the physical bases of such problems, and these solutions led, in turn, to advancement in the productive forces. At the same time, those such as Isaac Newton (1642–1727) who were at the forefront of theorizing about such forces could not complete the mechanistic-materialistic world picture because of idealistic/theological elements of their worldview that were owing to class position. Productive need accounts for truth production, ruling-class position, for error. This completion, according to Hessen, had to await further developments in productive forces. The later development of the steam engine and its attendant problems led to the development of thermodynamics from James Watt to Sadi Carnot.

Henryk Grossmann refines Hessen's thesis by suggesting that it was actually the machinery employed in production that provided the object of analysis and that was, thereby, also made more productive. The concept of mechanical "work" was created in this way. According to Grossmann, this development begins with Leonardo da Vinci (1452–1519) and grows with the productive problems presented by early mercantilism.

J. D. Bernal claims, further, that the rise of capitalism necessitated the rise of science. Science's productivity, in Bernal's view, will eventually make capitalism unnecessary. Bernal eschews the ancient heritage entirely, since the commodification of goods and labor led eventually to a heightened conflict between ancients and moderns. Craft experts were now necessary for the making, as well as the spending, of money.

Alfred Sohn-Rethel gives expression to the role of social relations as concerns the development of mathematics but asserts the more immediate appropriation of nature's physical properties. Relations, in his view, influence the form of thought but not its content. Gideon Freudenthal (1986) attempts to relate the content of mechanistic science to socially constituted categories, but he does so in a way that argues for the scientific, objective status of those categories themselves. Freudenthal's argument is that relations of social contract, mediated by social philosophy and first principles, find expression in Newton's physics. For Freudenthal, nonetheless, the first principles derived from social philosophy have an objective, immediate character. Thomas Hobbes's (1588–1679) ascription of qualities to the natural human individual (although it takes place by the social-philosophical mediation of contractual relations) is scientifically correct; it adequately describes an empirical state of affairs. Just as for Hobbes humans have properties that belong to them independently of their relations with others, so for Newton do bodies have similarly essential properties. Newton argues that space is absolute by observing the curving surface of water in a rotating bucket and the extension of a spring rotating about its midpoint with bodies attached at either end. This is evidence for the absolute character of space, Freudenthal points out, only if one makes the assumption that the properties of bodies belong to them essentially and not as the result of their relations to one another in a system. Hobbes, Newton, and numerous successors proceeded to view systems of all sorts as composed of equal elements whose properties belong to them essentially.

Freudenthal represents the current end point of what he terms "the Hessen-Grossmann thesis"—that economic/technical problems provided the impulse for the investigation of physical problems—and eschews the sociology-of-knowledge perspective on the role of relations of production. On this view, machines provided the subject matter of mechanics. The machine is both a human product and a natural object obeying laws of nature, and the mechanics of the Scientific Revolution result directly from its analysis.

Franz Borkenau was the first to appropriate systematically Marx's discussion of the social relations of capitalism for a sociology of mechanistic thought. According to Borkenau, not only the institutional supports of science, but also the form of human thought appropriate to it, is a product of history. He draws on Marx's suggestion that René Descartes (1596–1650) had viewed the world through the eyes of the era of manufacture. When Descartes suggests that we can know the nature of things

as we know the different crafts of our artisans, Borkenau claims, he is invoking the analogous character of two reductions or abstractions: the social process of the reduction of labor to simple movement and of its substrate to homogeneous matter and the reduction of nature to body in motion. The calculability of both the usefulness and the exchange value of things is a socially produced feature that mechanistic thinkers extend to nature by interpreting phenomena as the calculable result of bodies in motion.

Like other Marxists, Borkenau does believe that technology provides the material for intellectual appropriation. Unlike the others, however, Borkenau does not think that a transcendant human *ratio* performs universally valid operations upon that technologically delivered thought material. What happens to this material in terms of theoretical generalizations depends not on the technology itself but, rather, on the relations between persons in society. Borkenau examines the role of class relations in determining the meaning of "natural law" in the thought of many exemplars of mechanistic thought.

According to Edgar Zilsel, modern science owes its origin to a set of relations wherein labor is formally free. The merger of hand and brain, which was necessary for the Scientific Revolution, occurred when upper-class, academically trained scholars and humanists paid attention to the practical thought of artisans. Robert Norman's (fl. 1581) work on compasses provided the basis for William Gilbert's (1544–1603) work on magnetism. The freeing of manual labor after the decay of the medieval guilds allowed "free artists" to emerge from the ranks of superior craftsmen. These people did the work required in early experimentation, and some acquired the academic training for scientific thought. The new society of the sixteenth century had grown to demand calculation and measurement and, thus, the work of Robert Recorde (1510–1558), Thomas Digges (ca. 1546–1595), Luca Pacioli (ca. 1445–1517), and Niccolò Tartaglia (1499–1557) mathematized nature.

Michael Wolff also draws on Marx's theory of value in a way reminiscent of Borkenau. As early as Philoponos's (sixth-century) critique of Aristotle (384–322 B.C.E.), claims Wolff, we can witness, in an urban, free-artisan setting, a similar appropriation of nature in terms of "impetus." The transfer of force or value from producer to object "worked" in this setting economically, physically, and theologically. The parallels are these: God transfers his nature to the human, the worker transfers value to the product, the thrower transfers impetus to the projectile. Each of these was a contested claim in sixth-century Alexandria. Wolff also argues that, in the fourteenth century, economic thinkers like Olivi (fl. 1304) saw money as a carrier of industry just as natural philosophers saw impetus as mechanically transferred.

A recent extension of Borkenau's argument is that of Richard Hadden. He argues that social relations of commodity exchange and their attendant practices of calculation provided for changes in theoretical mathematics, which, in turn, helped define the appropriate, commensurable, physical objects for mathematical mechanics. When social relations are such that commodity exchange becomes established as the dominant means of satisfying wants and needs, the means of calculating the commensurate value of dissimilar goods affects number theory and algebra. Commercial reckoners prepare the way for a mechanics of body in which qualitative distinctions become irrelevant; nature and natural phenomena receive a treatment in terms of calculable matter and motion.

Such mathematical changes arise in the work of Thomas Bradwardine (d. 1349), Nicole d'Oresme (d. 1382), Pacioli, Recorde, John Dee (1527–1608), Rafael Bombelli (1526–1572), Tartaglia, François Viète (1540–1603), Simon Stevin (1548–1620), and Descartes. The attendant mechanical developments arise in the work of Tartaglia, Stevin, Descartes, Galileo Galilei (1564–1642), and members of the Royal Society of London. These thinkers rely on ancient resources like Euclid (fl. 300 B.C.E.) and Archimedes (ca. 287–212 B.C.E.) but change their mathematical meaning because of theoretical generalizations owing to social relations of commodity production and exchange in early-modern European societies.

A means-of-production focus traces the development of topics of investigation provided by advances in productive need and a technological framing of questions. It accounts for specific topics of investigation in terms of the needs of the dominant class. This is bought at the price of assuming a universal *ratio* and historically unproblematic criteria of objectivity. Does the production of truth demand a classless society or simply a proletarian direct producer? A relations-of-production focus traces the social context of intellectual labor in its varying interpretation of technologically produced questions. It accounts for mechanistic interpretation in terms of class relations. This is bought at the price of an account of the possible intellectual bases for practical, historical progress.

BIBLIOGRAPHY

Engels, Frederick. *Dialectics of Nature.* Ed. and trans. Clemens Dutt. New York: International Publishers, 1940.

———. "To H. Starkenburg." In *Selected Correspondence, 1846–1895.* Trans. Dona Torr. New York: International Publishers, 1942.

Freudenthal, Gideon. *Atom and Individual in the Age of Newton.* Trans. Peter McLaughlin. Dordrecht and Boston: Reidel, 1986.

———. "Towards a Social History of Newtonian Mechanics: Boris Hessen and Henryk Grossmann Revisited." In *Scientific Knowledge Socialized,* ed. Imre Hronszky, Marta Feher, and Balazs Dajka. Dordrecht and Boston: Kluwer, 1988.

Hadden, Richard W. *On the Shoulders of Merchants: Exchange and the Mathematical Conception of Nature in Early Modern Europe.* Albany: State University of New York Press, 1994.

———. "Social Relations and the Content of Early Modern Science." *British Journal of Sociology* 39, (1988), 255–280.

Hessen, Boris. "The Social and Economic Roots of Newton's *Principia.*" *Science at the Cross-Roads.* London: Kniga, 1931.

RICHARD W. HADDEN

See also Craftsman-and-Scholar Thesis; Ideology, Science as; Social Class and Science

Mass

No definition of mass, usually rendered in Latin as *massa* or *moles,* can be given outside a framework involving the definitions of other entities and their relations. Since this broader framework was in a state of flux in the seventeenth century, no universally valid definition of mass can be given at the time of the Scientific Revolution without taking into account the specific ways in which historical actors used this term. Take, for example, Isaac Newton's (1642–1727) *Principia mathematica philosophiae naturalis* (1687).

Definition 1 in Book I states that the quantity of matter, or mass, arises from density and bulk taken conjointly. In Book III, Propositions VI and VII, Newton argued that all bodies gravitate toward each other and that the power of gravity is proportional to the quantity of matter they contain. He claimed to have established this proportionality, or rather equivalence, on the basis of remarkably accurate pendulum experiments. Thus, in principle, mass could also be defined on the basis of the gravity it produces, because quantity of matter and gravitational mass, though conceptually different, are equivalent. If one, following most seventeenth-century natural philosophers, did not accept the notion of universal gravity, however, the very notion of gravitational mass would make no sense. Gottfried Wilhelm Leibniz (1646–1716), for example, believed gravity to be caused by a subtle fluid that could not be itself endowed with gravity since it was the cause of gravity in the bodies of our common experience. Frequently, however, gravity or weight were considered to be related or proportional to the mass of a body, and the terms *moles, gravitas,* and *pondus* were used interchangeably.

During the seventeenth century, mass was often given an intuitive definition as quantity of matter or bulk. As such, it was related to extension and, in a more problematic fashion, to density. The relation to density was problematic because some philosophers, such as Christiaan Huygens (1629–1695), believed mass to be homogeneous and density constant. Apparent differences in density depended on the existence of pores in matter, whereby all objects were conceived to be conceptually analogous to sponges. The pores were filled with ethereal particles, effluvia, and other subtle fluids, raising the issue of whether they had to be considered in the definition and calculation of the mass of a body. Newton, for example, in the Definition 1 referred to above, stated that he was not considering a medium pervading the interstices of bodies, if such a medium existed at all.

Besides extension and density, impenetrability also was a property often associated with mass, meaning impenetrability to the matter of bodies of our experience as opposed to subtle fluids. In this regard, mass was linked to the problem of impact, notably to the impact laws and the conservation of quantity of motion (i.e., mass times velocity). The impact laws entered the intellectual arena of the seventeenth century with René Descartes's (1596–1650) *Principia philosophae,* first published in 1644. Several philosophers and mathematicians discussed them in the third quarter of the seventeenth century, including John Wallis (1616–1703), Christopher Wren (1632–1723), and Huygens, whose papers were published by the Royal Society in 1669. In the phenomenon of impact, the same impelling body, approaching with the same velocity, transmits different velocities on bodies at rest depending on their masses. The larger the mass, the smaller the velocity they would acquire. Thus, besides extension, density, and impenetrability, reluc-

tance to being set in motion also was associated with the notion of mass. This reluctance was at times called *inertia,* though this term had other meanings as well and, much like the notion of mass, has to be considered on a case-by-case basis.

The notion of the reluctance of mass to be set in motion should not lead one to think that the notion of mass was associated with that of passivity. Several philosophers conceived mass, or at least a portion of it, to be endowed with activity, thus emphasizing the reluctance of mass to be brought to rest once it is set in motion. Leibniz, for example, believed matter or mass to be endowed with both activity and passivity, manifesting themselves in different ways in different phenomena.

In conclusion, the scholar of the Scientific Revolution cannot rely on a simple and univocal definition of mass, including Newton's. Rather, it is necessary to gain familiarity with the conceptual and philological maze within which the notion of mass evolved, taking into account the relevant disciplines and specific areas. Moreover, it would be generally anachronistic to impose definition criteria and charge seventeenth-century actors with lack of precision or confusion in their terminology, because those very criteria emerged in the course of the century in connection with the transformation of a cluster of disciplines, including metaphysics, mechanics, the science of motion, and natural philosophy.

BIBLIOGRAPHY

Cohen, I. B. *The Newtonian Revolution: With Illustrations of the Transformation of Scientific Ideas.* Cambridge: Cambridge University Press, 1980.

Jammer, M. *Concepts of Mass.* Cambridge, MA: Harvard University Press, 1961.

Westfall, R. S. *Force in Newton's Physics: The Science of Dynamics in the Seventeenth Century.* London: Macdonald; New York: American Elsevier, 1971.

DOMENICO BERTOLONI MELI

See also Dynamics; Force; Inertia

Mathematical Practitioners. See
Instrument Makers

Mathematics

The flowering of early-modern mathematics in the sixteenth and seventeenth centuries may be understood as a process in which formerly distinct domains are partly unified by means of fruitful analogies, often guided by abstract structures. The process of partial unification gives rise to novel problems, objects of study, and, indeed, to whole domains, like that of the infinitesimal calculus. Perhaps the most dramatic and thought-provoking episode in this process is the combination of mechanics, geometry, arithmetic, and algebra that culminates in Isaac Newton's (1642–1727) *Principia mathematica philosophiae naturalis* (1687) and the work of Gottfried Wilhelm Leibniz (1646–1716) and the Bernoulli brothers, Jakob I (1654–1705) and Johann I (1667–1748), at the end of the seventeenth century.

The historical conditions for this flowering include the fall of Constantinople in 1453, which created a diaspora of scholars from Asia Minor to western Europe, some of whom were learned in the Greek and Arabic mathematical traditions. This stream of scholars (and manuscripts) arrived in Italy about the same time as the invention of the printing press and the Renaissance fascination with classical antiquity. A little more than a hundred years later, through the edition and translation of manuscripts and the diffusion of printed texts, western Europe had recovered most of the major mathematical works of antiquity, including the difficult and still imperfectly understood works of Archimedes (ca. 287–212 B.C.E.) and Apollonius (fl. ca. 200 B.C.E.).

In sixteenth-century Italy, the works of Archimedes that geometrize statics (*On Plane Equilibrium* and *On Bodies in Water*) influenced two important schools of mechanics, that of Niccolò Tartaglia (1499–1557) and Girolamo Cardano (1501–1576) in the north, oriented toward practical problems, and the more theoretical school of Federico Commandino (1509–1579) and Guidobaldo del Monte (1545–1607) in central Italy. Tartaglia published the first Italian translation of Euclid (fl. 300 B.C.E.) and the first Latin translation (perhaps executed by William of Moerbeke) of the two treatises of Archimedes. He and Cardano speculated on projectile motion and free fall in ways that threw certain central Aristotelian assumptions sharply into question. Commandino undertook the reconstruction and translation of a series of ancient texts by Archimedes, Apollonius, Pappus (fl. 300–350), and Ptolemy (ca. 100–ca. 170), as well as a new Latin translation of Euclid. His student Guidobaldo del Monte published works on perspective, astronomy, and theoretical mechanics that show a devotion, inspired by Archimedes, to mathematical rigor. Galileo Galilei (1564–1642) profited from and synthesized the results of

both schools, setting the stage for a new science in the seventeenth century that would be at once efficacious and explanatory, and highly mathematized.

Profiting from the works of Diophantus (fl. 250), results stemming from the medieval Arabic tradition, and the German "cossist" art of computation, three Frenchmen jointly developed modern algebra in the first half of the seventeenth century. François Viète (1540–1603) devised a partly symbolic algebra that was freed for the first time from its traditional interpretation in terms of numbers. René Descartes (1596–1650) and Pierre de Fermat (1601–1665) applied algebra to geometrical problems. Fermat, primarily concerned with geometrical locus problems, first enunciated the central insight of analytic geometry that plane curves are correlated with algebraic equations in two unknowns.

Descartes's contribution to analytic geometry had the most widespread effect through the publication of his *Géométrie* (1637) and the subsequent Latin translation with commentary published by Frans van Schooten (ca. 1615–1660) in 1649 and 1659–1661. Johann Hudde (1629–1704), Jan De Witt (1625–1672), and René-François de Sluse (1622–1685) also made important contributions to the development of analytic geometry following Descartes. Hudde explored the extension of analytic geometry to the study of surfaces; De Witt showed how to reduce all second-degree equations in two unknowns to canonical form; and Sluse discovered a method for finding the tangent to a curve whose equation is a polynomial in two unknowns set equal to zero.

In the *Géométrie,* Descartes proposed a generalization of a problem taken from the *Synagoge* (Collection, 320) of Pappus of Alexandria, a locus problem that implies a whole new class of curves. The problem requires one to find a set of points, each of which satisfies a condition vis-à-vis a set of fixed lines; this condition is expressed as a proportion. Descartes showed how to convert the condition from a proportion to an equation in two unknowns by establishing a coordinate system and employing the new algebra. The equation is then treated by plugging in values for one of the unknowns and constructing the other unknown geometrically, generating the locus in a pointwise fashion. In principle, this procedure works for equations of any finite degree, so, despite certain technical difficulties, Descartes here opened up the study of higher algebraic curves.

Because algebra was initially devised to represent relations among numbers, the work of Descartes is generally regarded as establishing a new analogy between geometrical items and numbers, based on the correlation of a point on the plane with a pair of real numbers. However, the algebra of line segments presented in the *Géométrie* does not concern itself with the realm of number; it leaves unspoken the various extensions of the number system that the algebraic yoking of number and geometry promises. In Greek mathematics, number was limited to the positive rational numbers; the Greek theory of proportions carefully segregated arithmetical and geometrical magnitude. A deeper exploration of the analogy that Descartes's analytic geometry made possible between geometry and the realm of number was left to his successors, most importantly John Wallis (1616–1703) in England and Gottfried Wilhelm Leibniz in Germany. (Indeed, an adequate understanding of the real and complex number systems was not achieved until the nineteenth century.)

In his *Tractatus de sectionibus conicis* (1655), Wallis revisited the problems concerning conic sections around which analytic geometry was formulated, replacing geometrical concepts by numerical ones wherever possible. Even more important was his *Arithmetica infinitorum,* which arithmetized the work of Bonaventura Cavalieri (1598–1647), or, more precisely, that of Evangelista Torricelli (1608–1647), through whose *Opera geometrica* (1644) Wallis probably learned most of what he understood of Cavalieri's *Geometrica indivisibilibus* (1635). Though Descartes banished the study of infinitesimals from geometry, his contemporaries in Italy were investigating processes of quadrature (integration) using infinitesimalistic methods. Wallis recast these methods in an arithmetical idiom, associating with numerical values the infinitely many "indivisibles" taken to compose the geometrical figures whose quadratures were being sought and expressing his solutions in algebraic form.

During a stay in Paris (1672–1676) as a young man, Leibniz recapitulated the history of mathematics, moving from the study of Euclid to the discovery of the infinitesimal calculus. Under the tutelage of Christiaan Huygens (1629–1695), he studied the work of Blaise Pascal (1623–1662) and became fascinated by the sequences of numbers flanked by difference sequences and sum sequences that compose "Pascal's triangle": the operation of forming differences is the inverse of forming sums, in the sense that the sum sequence of the difference sequence of a sequence is just that sequence. Leibniz's exploration of the analogy between these arith-

metic sequences, and sequences of points on curves and their associated difference and sum sequences, led him to the basic algorithms of the infinitesimal calculus and its fundamental theorem. Like Viète, Leibniz had a thoroughly modern sense of the power of abstract structures, expressed in formal languages capable of being detached from the models that gave rise to them, to further mathematical discoveries.

Considered as models of the new algebra, the domain of number and geometry are brought into a novel analogy that alters and extends both: the domain of number begins to include (systematically) negative, imaginary, irrational, and complex numbers, and geometry begins to include (systematically) higher algebraic and even transcendental curves as well as problems of tangency and integration. Indeed, algebra itself changes as these domains expand: the algorithms of the calculus, for example, extend algebraic notation by new operators for forming differentials and for summing infinite collections of differentials. In the midst of these dramatic new configurations in mathematics, another domain impinges, as it were, from outside and profoundly changes human understanding of both mathematics and nature. That domain is mechanics.

In the works of Archimedes mentioned above, mathematics and mechanics were brought into conjunction, but mechanics was limited to statics, and machines were understood solely as human artifacts. The natural philosophy of Aristotle (384–322 B.C.E.), by contrast, offered causal explanations of phenomena but no precise mathematical rendering of them. The link that had to be developed between mathematics and mechanics was, first of all, motion—motion no longer understood as an inherent property of bodies but understood for the first time as a computable trajectory. Thereafter, a place had to be found for the notions of time and force in a mathematical mechanics that had dynamic, as well as kinematic, import.

Two of the most important early figures to reconceptualize motion, Galileo and Descartes, left aside considerations of force in their treatment of mechanical motion. In his *Discorsi intorno a due nuove scienze* (Discourses on Two New Sciences, 1638), Galileo entertained a version of the principle of inertia and provided a precise geometrical description of free fall and of projectile motion as the compounding of inertial motion and free fall. He showed that the velocity of a body in free fall is proportional to the time elapsed and that the distance fallen is proportional to the square of the time elapsed; he also showed that the trajectory of a projectile is a parabola. He abstained from speculating about the ultimate causes of these motions (i.e., the forces that produce them).

Descartes also formulated (more correctly) a principle of inertia: a body is indifferent to its state of uniform rectilinear motion or rest. For Descartes, all physical interaction is the result of the collision of corpuscles of matter, governed by his rules of impact. In the Cartesian model of impact, bodies move toward each other in a straight line at constant velocity and then, upon impact, change velocity instantaneously; there is no process of deceleration or acceleration, and time as a parameter is all but absent from Cartesian mechanics. (Galileo, by contrast, had the insight to formulate his rules of motion in terms of the parameter of time rather than distance.) Cartesian metaphysics also shatters the Archimedean segregation of machines from the things of nature: Descartes claimed that the natural world, with the exception of human souls, is a collection of more or less complex machines.

The role of Descartes in the unification of mathematics and mechanics is hard to evaluate. On the one hand, he posited that mechanics is inherently and thoroughly mathematical, gave mathematical rules so that the outcome of all mechanical interactions could be computed from their ingredient events (at least in principle), and offered the metaphysical claim that all of nature is made up of machines. On the other hand, he banished "mechanical" (transcendental) curves from mathematics—curves whose definition promotes a properly mathematical motion in analytic geometry that proves crucial to its unification with mechanics. Moreover, he neglected the infinitesimalistic methods that would be the key to the representation of nonuniform motion and the forces that produce it. In his *Principia philosophiae* (1644), the mathematization of mechanics and the proposal of explanatory mechanisms are two rather disjunct projects.

The figures of Huygens, Cavalieri, and Torricelli are especially prominent in the transition from Galileo and Descartes to Leibniz and Newton. The greatest exponent of the school of Cartesian mechanics (vortex theory), Huygens shared with Galileo the ability to subject motion to precise mathematical description. His *Horologium oscillatorium* (1673) contained a thoroughgoing treatment of problems involving pendula. It united a practical concern for the accurate construction of clocks with a highly theoretical treatment of the cycloid, a transcendental curve, and offered a definitive account of the notions of radius of curvature and of involutes and evolutes. His *De vi centrifuga* (1703) presented the law of centripetal force for circular motion, though Huygens understood it as centrifugal force, due to his allegiance to Descartes's vortex theory. Analyzing this force in terms of impeded motion, Huygens evaluated it as a function of the velocity of rotation and the size of the circle traversed.

Taking off from Galileo's discussion of indivisibles in the *Discorsi,* Cavalieri attempted to give these problematic entities a logically rigorous treatment that avoided the question of whether continuous magnitudes are made up of indivisibles. He carefully avoided equating, for example, a plane figure with the aggregate of lines that can be cut from it; rather, his demonstrations rested on an assumption of proportionality: continuous magnitudes are related to each other in the same way as the aggregates of indivisibles that can be cut from them. Indeed, Cavalieri paid so much attention to rigor in his *Geometria indivisibilibus* that the book is almost unreadable.

By contrast, the presentation of indivisibles in Torricelli's *Opera geometrica* is direct and natural, though Torricelli was not faithful to Cavalieri's principles: his indivisibles do constitute continuous magnitudes. Torricelli's bold and fruitful methods produced a series of new results in the rectification of curves, most importantly the comparison of an arc of a spiral and an arc of a parabola. By the mid-seventeenth century, the use of mathematical indivisibles was widespread; in particular, it was transmitted to Newton through his teacher, the geometer Isaac Barrow (1630–1677), and to Leibniz through Huygens and the work of Pascal.

In his *Principia mathematica philosophiae naturalis* (Mathematical Principles of Natural Philosophy, 1687), Newton combined geometry and mechanics. He brought Euclidean geometry into the service of mechanical problems but, in so doing, transformed it. He made use of a seventeenth-century tendency to conceptualize geometrical items as generated by "motion" in "time"; his theory of fluxions was based on the notion of velocity of increase of all kinds of geometrical magnitudes and a unique infinitesimal that is an interval of time. Likewise, his method of ultimate ratios made possible the comparison of ratios between finite magnitudes and ratios between infinitely small elements of figures—elements that are just on the point of vanishing altogether.

Newton also brought to a novel culmination a tradition of understanding mechanical processes in geometrical terms, synthesizing Johannes Kepler's (1571–1630) law of areas, Galileo's characterization of free fall, Descartes's notion of inertial motion, and Huygens's law of centrifugal (centripetal) force in his masterful treatment of central forces. The theorems of Book I that establish the inverse-square law for a center of force about which a body describes an elliptical orbit put geometry to powerful and subtle new uses, representing time, velocity that varies at every instant, virtual trajectories, and force directly by means of elements of the diagram.

Book III of the *Principia,* which brings the theoretical apparatus of the earlier two books into connection with "the System of the World," also permanently changed the modern understanding of mathematics, transforming it into an inductive tool and conferring upon it explanatory power. Henceforth, the invisible causes of nature would be assumed to conform to the precise descriptions afforded by a mathematics that evolved partly in response to the demands of science. And although those causes might be the source of endless metaphysical speculation and might elude human perception (even aided by increasingly sophisticated instrumentation), they could be rationalized and made tractable by the neutral language of mathematics.

Leibniz's approach to problems of mechanics stood in strong contrast to that of Newton, since, for him, abstract structure, the "universal characteristic" that formally records the rational structure of the world, was central. Leibniz's exploration of the new algorithms of the infinitesimal calculus, first announced in the *Nova methodus pro maximis et minimis* (1684) and *De geometria recondita et analysi indivisibilium atque infinitorum* (1686), quickly led him to the study of a whole host of transcendental curves as solutions of differential equations. These curves, generated by various kinds of idealized motion and arising in problems that, in a broad sense, were mechanical, inhabited a fertile middle ground between geometry, algebra, and mechanics. They included the brachistochrone or cycloid, the catenary, the tractrix, the isochrone, trigonometric functions, and curves related to the logarithms first set forth by John Napier (1550–1617) in his *Mirifici logarithmorum canonis descriptio* (1614).

Leibniz's researches into the celestial mechanics of the solar system, guided by the vortex theory of Descartes and Huygens, sought appropriate differential equations that would capture the constraints that determine the motion of the planets. His investigation of the new domain of differential equations was taken over by brothers Jakob and Johann Bernoulli. It was Johann who, profiting from the work of both Newton and Leibniz, finally offered the correct analytic expression of the solution to the problem, how to characterize the orbit of a body around a center of force obeying the inverse-square law. Their investigation of transcendental curves and of methods of solution for differential equations prepared the way for the accomplishments of Leonhard Euler (1707–1783), who was to dominate mathematics in the eighteenth century.

BIBLIOGRAPHY

Blay, M. *La naissance de la mécanique analytique.* Paris: Presses Universitaires de France, 1992.

Bos, H. J. M. "Differentials, Higher-Order Differentials, and the Derivative in the Leibnizian Calculus." *Archive for History of Exact Sciences* 14 (1974–1975), 1–90.

Boyer, C. B. *A History of Mathematics.* Princeton, NJ: Princeton University Press, 1985, chs. 16–19.

De Gandt, F. *Force and Geometry in Newton's Principia.* Princeton, NJ: Princeton University Press, 1995.

Drake, S., and I. E. Drabkin. *Mechanics in Sixteenth-Century Italy.* Madison: University of Wisconsin Press, 1969.

Parmentier, M. *G. W. Leibniz: La naissance du calcul différentiel.* Paris: Vrin, 1989.

Struik, D. J., ed. *A Source Book in Mathematics, 1200–1800.* Cambridge, MA: Harvard University Press, 1969.

Whiteside, D. T. "Patterns of Mathematical Thought in the Later Seventeenth Century." *Archive for History of Exact Science* 1 (1961), 179–388.

EMILY GROSHOLZ

See also Algebra; Analytic Geometry; Calculus; Infinitesimals; Infinity, Mathematical; Mechanics; Series, Mathematical

Matter

In modern parlance, matter is the stuff of which bodies are made, but this is a legacy of the Scientific Revolution. Before the wide-reaching intellectual changes of the period known as the Scientific Revolution, bodies were more usually held to be made of matter and form. Matter without form was held to be inconceivable; only by being enformed could a portion of matter be said to become some definite thing. Matter and form, therefore, were an inseparable unity that together constituted a particular body. This concept of body was first developed by Aristotle (384–322 B.C.E.) as a response to what he saw as the excessive materialism of the atomists and the excessive idealism of Plato (ca. 428–348 B.C.E.). The atomists, according to Aristotle, neglected the role of form, while Plato neglected matter at the expense of form.

Notwithstanding Aristotle's immense influence throughout the High Middle Ages, his theory of hylomorphism, as it was called (*hyle,* from the Greek "matter," and *morphe,* "form"), was always a source of dispute. A number of commentators thought that, in spite of Aristotle's insistence that prime, or unformed, matter became substantial only when it was made into a particular body by a specific form being imposed upon it, there was a case to be made for the belief that prime matter itself might have its own inbuilt "form of corporeity" or "material form." So, while Aristotle argued that a substance must consist of matter and form and that matter could have only a "potential" existence until it was enformed, many of his followers found it impossible to deny that matter itself had its own real existence and substantiality. If Aristotelian hylomorphism raised skepticism among natural philosophers, it almost entirely failed to convince those, like alchemists, who were practically engaged in the manipulation and transformation of substances in the pursuit of their art. Their empirical familiarity with the ways in which substances could react to give new substances and then be resolved back into the originals again—which led to intractable problems for Aristotelians as to whether the original substances were present in the compound or not—led them to opt instead for a particulate theory of matter in which the combination and separation of substances could be envisioned in an entirely unproblematic way. These particulate theories were closer to the ancient atomist emphasis on matter as essentially sufficient to constitute bodies, but they are usually referred to as *corpuscular* rather than *atomist* theories because, unlike atomism, they do not depend upon assumptions about the finite divisibility of matter or the existence of void space.

Such chemical or alchemical ideas, together with an Aristotelian reformist tradition that emphasized the existence of so-called *minima naturalia* in the constitution of bodies and the revival of ancient atomism in the Renaissance, have all been shown to have led to the new matter theory of the seventeenth-century mechanical philosophy. In this newly triumphant theory of matter, bodies could be said to be constituted exclusively of matter. Certainly, this matter was regarded as having its own corporeal form, and the precise ways in which the particles of matter were individually shaped and collectively arranged in space were always recognized as important defining features of any given body, but beyond that there was no longer any perceived need for a metaphysical principle of form to make a body what it was.

One of the major sources for the corpuscular tradition of alchemy was the *Summa perfectionis* attributed to the Arabic alchemist Jabir ibn Hayyan (fl. eighth century), known in the Latin West as Geber, but almost certainly written by a Christian alchemist toward the end of the thirteenth century. The *Summa,* borrowing from Arabic alchemy, gives entirely corpuscularian accounts of the chemical processes of calcination, sublimation, and transmutation. The fact that it was immensely influential throughout the Middle Ages and the Renaissance ensured that a corpuscularian alternative to Aristotelian hylomorphism was always available to intellectuals, particularly those more pragmatically engaged in attempts to understand the nature of matter. During the Scientific Revolution, the influence of alchemical corpuscularism can be discerned in the work of Daniel Sennert (1572–1637), Johannes Baptista van Helmont (1579–1644), Pierre Gassendi (1592–1655), Kenelm Digby (1603–1665), Walter Charleton (1620–1707), Robert Boyle (1627–1691), and others.

Even within the more orthodox tradition of Scholastic Aristotelianism, it was recognized that hylomorphism had to be refined to take account of chemical phenomena. The concept of *minima naturalia* was developed in order to draw distinctions between a true mixture (we would say a chemical compound) and an ordinary mixture. If iron and sulfur are heated together, the resulting substance is neither iron nor sulfur; the matter may be the same (presumably), but the form has certainly changed. What then has happened to the original substances? Have they disappeared or are they still present in the "mixture"? Do the original forms of the separate ingredients somehow persist, and, if so, how? To provide answers to these questions, a number of Scholastics, adapting another of Aristotle's arguments, suggested that, although bodies are infinitely divisible in principle, in practice the form of a body must have a minimum size, beyond which the hylomorphic identity of the body could not be sustained. All bodies, therefore, have natural minimal sizes. In a chemical combination, as opposed to an ordinary mixture, it was supposed that the ingredients mixed with one another at the level of their *minima naturalia* and that the *minima* were able to act upon one another to give rise to the new form of the compound, while the forms of the separate *minima* persisted far below the sensory level. It should be noted that, on this account, there is a plurality of forms in the compound body. Some Aristotelians resisted this pluralistic development, but others had no difficulty in pointing to other reasons to suppose that a plurality of forms in any given body must be the norm.

The obvious case is that of a human being. The orthodox Scholastic view held that a man is a parcel of prime matter given individual identity by a single substantial soul imposed upon the matter. Others argued that the substantial soul of any individual being must be regarded as the ultimate form in a hierarchy of many forms. To say that a man has only one substantial form that makes him what he is (and that form was, therefore, identified with the concept of the personal immortal soul) seems to imply that his blood, his bones, his flesh, and other attributes common to all humans (and many animals) are unique products of that substantial form. Aristotle himself insisted, however, that the form of a thing is the form of the *species*, so one person's blood differs from another's not by virtue of the form of blood, which is the same for both, but by virtue of the matter. It was easy, therefore, for some thinkers to insist, upon Aristotle's authority, that a complex creature like a man must be a composite of many different forms—the forms of blood, of bone, and so forth—united as one unique individual by the ultimate "substantial" form.

Daniel Sennert, professor of medicine at Wittenberg and an important figure in the history of the development of the new matter theory of the Scientific Revolution, adopted these views and extended them by applying them to the understanding of chemical compounds. By the time he came to write his *Hypomnemata physica* of 1636, Sennert wrote of atoms rather than *minima naturalia*, although his atoms still bore many of the hallmarks of their origin in Aristotelian theory. In particular, he declared that each atom had its own substantial form, and, therefore, its own set of qualities, unlike the atoms of the ancient Greek atomists, which were characterized only in terms of size, shape, and motion.

Recent research has uncovered yet another Aristotelian source of corpuscularist ways of thinking about the constitution of body, which derives from a new em-

phasis in the late sixteenth century upon Aristotle's speculations in Book IV of his *Meteorology*. The explanations of physical phenomena in this book seem so atomistic that a number of eminent modern Aristotelian scholars have dismissed the book as spurious. There were evidently no such doubts among earlier thinkers, but it seems that Aristotle's exposition of hylomorphism and his objections to atomism in the *Physics* were sufficient to overshadow the corpuscularism of *Meteorology* IV in mainstream Scholasticism, though it was influential in the medieval alchemical tradition. The culmination of its influence in alchemy can be seen in Andreas Libavius's (1540–1616) *Alchemia* of 1606, which links Aristotle's views in the *Meteorology* to the iatrochemical speculations of Paracelsus (ca. 1491–1541). Libavius's book, in turn, influenced Sennert, Joachim Jungius (1587–1657), and others.

Some aspects of ancient atomism were known throughout the Middle Ages as a result of Aristotle's attempts to refute it, but the real revival of atomism began after 1473 with the discovery of *De rerum natura*, an exposition in hexameter verse of Epicurean atomism written by the Roman poet Titus Lucretius Carus (ca. 99–55 B.C.E.), and the discovery in 1475 of Diogenes Laertius's (fl. second century) *Lives of the Philosophers*, which included three letters by Epicurus (341–270 B.C.E.). Hampered at first by Christian disapproval of Epicureanism as a licentious and atheistic philosophy, and by confusion between notions of mathematical and physical indivisibility, it had to await the careful and apologetic exposition of Pierre Gassendi before it could begin to be taken seriously. Galileo Galilei (1564–1642), for example, tried to develop an atomist account of bodies in which atoms were held to be indivisible because they were partless mathematical points. This runs head first, however, into many of Aristotle's criticisms of atomism, which insist that partless points cannot be laid side by side to build up a line or a body since sides imply distinguishable parts. Partless points can only be superimposed, whole to whole, and, no matter how many are superimposed, the accumulation is no bigger than a single partless point. Galileo's attempts to avoid this problem by supposing the points of matter to be separated in space by intervening indivisible mathematical points of vacua looks like a lamentable failure to understand the issue. Moreover, as recent research has uncovered, Galileo's attempts to revive atomism drew the attention of the Inquisition because of its irreligious associations. Gassendi, to some extent at least, was able to deal with these and other problems associated with Epicurean atomism by dismissing mathematical atomism in favor of a physicalist account in which atoms were simply held to be physically indivisible and by providing an apologetic reinterpretation of Epicurean religious and moral beliefs.

In practice, of course, alchemical corpuscularism, the doctrines of *minima naturalia,* and the revival of atomism went hand in hand with one another, each reinforcing the other in the thought of the various reformers of matter theory. They also had a clear influence upon the development of the new matter theories of the mechanical philosophy. Essentially, the various versions of the mechanical philosophy relied upon a matter theory that was very close to ancient atomism, although the indivisibility of the ultimate particles was often rejected, and an interparticulate void space was sometimes denied. The most original of the new mechanical theories of matter was that of René Descartes (1596–1650), which was extremely sparse and abstracted, matter being equated with extension. It followed that matter (extension) was entirely passive (although this was a claim that was vigorously contested by his contemporaries) and that the notion of vacuum, or empty extension, was a contradiction in terms. It also followed, of course, that there was only one kind of matter, but Descartes was led by his cosmogonical scheme to suppose that matter appears in three major forms, which he refers to as *elements.* The third element consists of (comparatively) large particles with innumerable irregular shapes. These particles make up most of the bodies of the world. The particles constituting the second element are smaller and spherical, or nearly spherical, in shape. This kind of matter fills most of the visible world and constitutes any subtle fluid, such as "air" or "fire"; it is also referred to as *celestial matter.* Spherical particles, however, cannot be close packed to leave no empty space between, so Descartes had to suppose that the extension between the particles of the second element, which would always be changing due to the rapid movements in all directions of those particles, had to be filled with an even more subtle and infinitely changeable form of matter, which he called the *first element.* The first element, too, was conceived as particulate, but these particles were the smallest of all, appearing in many shapes, and were easily changed by collisions and jostlings together. Primarily, these particles were required to ensure that, no matter how the other two elements moved, empty space could not be said to result; the particles of the first element were so pervasive and fast moving that they would instantly fill any would-be gaps. In Descartes's cosmology, the first element constituted the matter of the Sun, the stars, and other shining bodies; the second element constituted the matter of the heavenly spaces; and the third element composed the dull opaque bodies like the planets and the earth. At a more down-to-earth level, Descartes believed he could explain all physical phenomena in terms of the collisions, conglomerations, and separations of these particles of matter, which were held to be entirely passive apart from the force of impact they had as a result of their motions.

Descartes was undoubtedly the single most influential mechanical philosopher, his ideas being particularly dominant in Continental Europe. Gassendi was more influential in England, however, having been introduced to English readers in 1654 by the translation and paraphrase of his ideas published by Walter Charleton, a medical writer who had previously translated works by van Helmont and who had clearly been influenced by alchemical corpuscularism. Gassendi's system, which was itself influenced by alchemical corpuscularism, was less strictly mechanistic than the Cartesian system and seems to have appealed more to English natural philosophers. It was less strictly mechanistic in the sense that it did not profess to rely simply upon the intermeshings of inert matter. On the contrary, Gassendi wrote of atoms with "natural impulses," "internal faculties" or "forces," and "seminal powers."

The only major system of the new philosophy that endeavored to be as strictly mechanical as Descartes's was that of Thomas Hobbes (1588–1679). Since Hobbes was regarded by most English thinkers as a materialist and an atheist, there was always a similar suspicion attached to the Cartesian system. The versions of the mechanical philosophy that were most influential in England, therefore, were less strict in their mechanicism and allowed greater scope for the action of unexplained occult qualities, such as attraction, repulsion, inherent self-motion, and the self-organizing powers of so-called seminal particles. The methodological justification for the recourse to such unexplained phenomena was based entirely upon an empirical phenomenalism: if the carefully observed behavior of bodies seemed to imply that they attracted one another, and if experimental efforts to determine a strictly mechanical cause of the attraction (such as the emanation of streams of particles) failed, it was simply assumed that the bodies must attract one another.

The acceptance of occult qualities may have been justified on methodological grounds, but theoretical explanations of their existence seem to have stemmed largely from theological and religious concerns. The strength of the Calvinist tradition in English Protestantism ensured that virtually all of the leading natural philosophers subscribed to a voluntaristic theology— that is to say, a theology that emphasized God's absolute omnipotence by insisting that he (as they all thought of God) created the world and all of its creatures by the unconstrained use of his will. Within this theological tradition, it was blasphemous to suggest that the omnipotent God could not create matter that was inherently active in various ways and heretical to claim that God's will was constrained to create things in accordance with what, in spite of our rational convictions, might prove to be nothing more than humankind's conventional expectations. For English voluntarists, the Cartesian system was far too rationalist, seeming to imply that God had had to create the world in accordance with the methodical analysis to which Descartes had arrived. Moreover, the notion of matter as completely inert, devoid of all properties except its three-dimensionality, not only failed to match up to various empirical facts about the behavior of matter, but seemed to imply (because of the rationalist way in which Descartes asserted the passivity of matter) that not even God could endow a passive principle like matter with activity. Accordingly, Walter Charleton, for example, insisted that "the matter of bodies is not idle and unactive . . . but uncessantly operative; and that, not by impression but by inhaerency," while Robert Boyle suggested that every atom might have "an innate and unloseable mobility"; in each case, the writer linked the activity of matter to the omnipotence of God. In the last of the "Queries" appended to his *Opticks* (1717), Isaac Newton put the point succinctly: "God is able to create Particles of Matter of several Sizes and Figures, . . . and perhaps of different Densities and Forces, and thereby to vary the Laws of Nature, and make Worlds of several sorts in several Parts of the Universe. At least, I see nothing of Contradiction in all this." The message is clear: God can do as he pleases, irrespective of what Descartes, or anybody else, might say about how the world must be.

It should be borne in mind that, in a general sense, natural philosophy was regarded throughout the pre-modern period as a "handmaiden" to theology and, more specifically, that the Aristotelian theory of matter had, ever since the thirteenth century, played an important role in explaining the Eucharist. In the miracle of the Eucharist, it was held that the essential properties of the bread and wine were completely changed into the body and blood of Jesus Christ but that the accidental properties of the bread and wine—its appearance, texture, and taste—were preserved.

As far as Catholics were concerned, the Eucharist was a major stumbling block for atomist theories. Built into atomism was the distinction between what were called *primary* and *secondary* qualities. The primary qualities were held to be the real properties of bodies, including the atoms or corpuscles that constituted them; usually these were taken to be shape, size, arrangement, and motion. The secondary qualities of a body, by contrast, were held to be merely the result of the effects of the constituent parts of that body on the senses (individual atoms or corpuscles, therefore, had no secondary qualities). So, the color of a body was simply the result of the way its particles reflected or absorbed the light that fell upon it; its texture was due to the arrangement of the particles, giving rise to a sensation of roughness or smoothness when felt by the fingers; its taste was due to the way the shape and motions of the particles affected the tongue. It followed that a wafer of bread could not be changed into flesh without some concomitant change in the sensory effects of the wafer. Since there was no "form" bestowing properties onto the body, the change could be effected only by rearranging the particles, altering their shapes, sizes, or motions. Any or all of these changes would necessarily incur a change in the secondary, sensible, qualities of the body; the wafer could not continue to look, feel, and taste like bread. Descartes tried to circumvent these difficulties, but it seems fair to say that he could do so only by betraying his own principles. His efforts proved ineffective anyway, since his works were put on the Index of Forbidden Books in 1663, and, in 1671, the teaching of Cartesianism was banned in French universities.

Another, more general, reason for the association of ideas on the nature of matter with religious concerns stems from the traditional dualism of matter and spirit. It was a common boast of the early mechanical philosophers that, by showing the extent of the powers of matter, they were clearly indicating where and when immaterial spiritual entities must be invoked to account

M

for the remainder of natural phenomena. Natural philosophers tried to strike a balance between a system of mechanical philosophy that explained everything in materialist terms and one that involved God too directly in the mundane workings of even the vilest of natural phenomena, as was the case with some followers of Descartes. The favored stratagem among English natural philosophers was to suppose that matter was endowed with various active powers at the Creation by God, but here again it was important to limit the number and scope of these active powers. If matter was too active, it would be too easy to conclude that spiritual entities were surplus to requirements. If matter was considered to be too inactive, however, it left too much scope for supernaturalistic accounts that undermined the principles of natural philosophy, or, as in the case of the philosophies of the Cambridge Platonists, who invoked an immaterial "Spirit of Nature" as the vicarious power of God in the world, it undermined the principles of Calvinist voluntarist theology by insisting that not even God could create active matter.

It should be clear that there were numerous different versions of the mechanical philosophy, each with its own particular theory of matter, depending not only upon whether their authors were influenced by alchemical corpuscularism, the Aristotelian *minima* tradition, revived ancient atomism, or more recent mechanical philosophies, but also upon the methodological, philosophical, and theological concerns of their authors. The result was a rich array of alternative schemes to replace Aristotelian hylomorphism. One of the most significant and far-reaching differences among mechanical philosophers was in their approach to occult qualities. In the Aristotelian tradition, which endeavored to explain things in terms of irrefutable knowledge, a valid explanation was supposed to be couched in terms of the so-called manifest qualities (hot, cold, dry, and wet). Inexplicable occult qualities, therefore, were something of an embarrassment, and, yet, increasingly throughout the Renaissance, more and more phenomena were discovered that had to be attributed to the operation of such unknown qualities. It was one of the major advantages of the mechanical philosophy that it could give as satisfactory an account of occult qualities as it could of manifest qualities. There were, however, two radically different approaches. The strict mechanical approach was to explain occult phenomena like magnetism, gravitational attraction, various pharmacological and chemical phenomena, and even vital processes in terms of the putative behavior of invisibly small corpuscles or atoms. The alternative approach was to provide a rigorous empirical analysis of the modus operandi of such occult properties to put them on the same footing as the supposedly manifest qualities, which, it was pointed out, were also understood only in terms of their empirically determined behavior.

Strict versions of the mechanical philosophy never overcame the scientific and religious objections that were raised against them, and it was the characteristically English version of the mechanical philosophy developed by Isaac Newton, occult qualities and all, that had the greatest influence beyond the Scientific Revolution. In the Preface to his *Mathematical Principles of Natural Philosophy* (1687), Newton expressed his belief that all of the phenomena of nature may be explained upon the assumption of invisibly small particles of matter endowed with attractive and repulsive forces. Later, in response to charges of excessive materialism from Gottfried Wilhelm Leibniz (1646–1716), Newton hinted that matter was the least considerable thing in the universe and set in train speculations that resulted in what has been called the "nut-shell" theory of matter—summarized in Joseph Priestley's (1733–1804) comment that "all the solid matter in the solar system might be contained within a nutshell," emphasizing the interparticulate forces at the expense of the particles of matter that were meant to be their source. Not all Newtonians took their mentor's ideas about the nature of matter quite so far, but there can be no doubt that the Newtonian theory of matter played a major role in eighteenth-century developments.

BIBLIOGRAPHY

Clericuzio, Antonio. "A Redefinition of Boyle's Chemistry and Corpuscular Philosophy." *Annals of Science* 47 (1990), 561–589.

Dijksterhuis, E. J. *The Mechanization of the World Picture.* Oxford: Oxford University Press, 1961.

Emerton, Norma E. *The Scientific Reinterpretation of Form.* Ithaca, NY: Cornell University Press, 1984.

Gabbey, Alan, Daniel Garber, John Henry, and Lynn Joy. "New Doctrines of Body and Its Powers, Place, and Space." In *The Cambridge History of Seventeenth-Century Philosophy,* ed. M. Ayers and D. Garber. Cambridge: Cambridge University Press, 1998.

Henry, John. "Occult Qualities and the Experimental Philosophy: Active Principles in Pre-Newtonian Matter Theory." *History of Science* 24 (1986), 335–381.

Hutchison, Keith, "What Happened to Occult Qualities in the Scientific Revolution?" *Isis* 73 (1982), 233–253.

Meinel, Christoph. "Early Seventeenth-Century Atomism: Theory, Epistemology, and the Insufficiency of Experiment." *Isis* 79 (1988), 68–103.

Michael, Emily. "Daniel Sennert on Matter and Form: At the Juncture of the Old and the New." *Early Science and Medicine* 2 (1997), 271–298.

JOHN HENRY

See also Active Principles; Atomism; Elements; Epicureanism; Gassendi, Pierre; Mechanical Philosophy; Qualities

Maurolico, Francesco (1494–1575)

Born in Sicily to a Greek family, he was one of the foremost mathematicians of the sixteenth century. His continuous efforts to compose mathematical, astronomical, and optical works resulted in an enormous production, the greatest part of which was devoted to the reconstruction of a corpus of the major ancient Greek mathematicians: Euclid (fl. 300 B.C.E.), Archimedes (ca. 287–212 B.C.E.), Apollonius (fl. ca. 200 B.C.E.), Theodosius (fl. ca. 100 B.C.E.), Menelaus (fl. ca. 100), and Autolycus (fl. ca. 300 B.C.E.). The quality of his work and his method of approaching mathematical ideas made him a first-rate student and interpreter of the ancients during the most crucial century for the transmission of the Greek scientific thought to the Latin West. Primarily interested in the best mathematical manner of presentation, he scarcely prepared literal versions. Further, he never hesitated to reorganize his material and correct the text by adding or replacing propositions and lemmas (subsidiary propositions) and even by adopting methods that he judged to be better than the originals.

The geographical isolation of Sicily was an obstacle for the diffusion of his work, which in most cases was published after his death. Thus, Maurolico's *Emendatio et restitutio conicorum Apollonii Pergaei,* containing an important reconstruction of Books V and VI of Apollonius's *Conics,* lost at that time, appeared in 1654, while his *Admirandi Archimedis Syracusani monumenta omnia* was published in 1685. His versions of Theodosius's, Menelaus's, and Autolycus's treatises on the sphere, having been related to astronomical research, were included in the omnibus edition of 1558 under the title *Theodosii sphaericorum.* . . . His original treatise *Arithmetica,* which was contained in the edition of another important collection entitled *Opuscula mathematica* of 1575, allowed some historians to suppose that Maurolico had utilized a premature form of mathematical induction.

The contributions of Maurolico to the field of astronomy are numerous, among them one of the earliest observations of the new star near the constellation of Cassiopeia in 1572. In optics, his *Photismi de lumine et umbra* (1611) is considered one of the most important works in this field up to his time.

BIBLIOGRAPHY

Clagett, Marshall. "Francesco Maurolico and the Medieval Archimedes." In Clagett, Marshall. *Archimedes in the Middle Ages.* 5 vols. Philadelphia: American Philosophical Society, 1964–1984, vol. 3, ch. 5, pp. 749–1053.

———. "The Works of Francesco Maurolico." *Physis* 16 (1974), 174–198.

Lindberg, David C. "Laying the Foundations of Geometrical Optics: Maurolico, Kepler, and the Medieval Tradition." In *The Discourse of Light from the Middle Ages to the Enlightenment: Papers Read at a Clark Library Seminar.* Los Angeles: Clark Memorial Library, University of California, 1985, pp. 3–65.

Moscheo, Rosario. *Francesco Maurolico tra Rinascimento e scienza galileiana: Materiali e ricerche.* Messina: Società messinese di storia patria, 1988.

IOANNA MOUNTRIZA

See also Optics; Translations

Mayow, John (1641–1679)

English physician, one of a group of Oxford physiologists who applied the New Science to medical phenomena. Respiration was a problem that was thought to be particularly suited to the new experimental and chemical medicine. Mayow drew upon the work of Robert Boyle (1627–1691) on the elastic properties of air to explain how air entered the lungs during inspiration; he then asserted that the air communicated some life-giving particles to the blood and that, when these were used up or exhausted from the air, the air could no longer serve for respiration. In support of this latter view, he cited Robert Hooke's (1635–1703) experiment that demonstrated that, if the lungs moved but no air was allowed to enter them, then life ceased, indicating that the essence of respiration did not involve the agitation of blood; instead, what was crucial was that something entered the lungs and, in them, was communicated to the blood.

Mayow believed that the life-giving matter in the air was composed of the by now popular "nitrous particles," and, like other members of the Oxford group, he argued that niter from the air mixed with sulfur in the blood to produce a ferment or combustion, accounting for the body's heat, which was equated with its life. The fermentation took place in the pulmonary blood vessels and in the arteries, not just in the heart. Mayow, like his Oxford colleagues, followed in William Harvey's (1578–1657) footsteps and stated that the active phase of the heartbeat was in systole and not in diastole, rejecting the Cartesian view, which held that the heart acted in diastole when it expanded because the blood evaporated or fermented. Mayow also argued, using a modified version of Thomas Willis's (1621–1675) views, that muscular contraction occurred by means of a series of minute explosions produced by the meeting of nitrosaline particles located in the muscles and volatile spiritous particles associated with the "animal spirits" produced in the brain.

In 1674 Mayow developed the chemical aspects of an earlier treatise on respiration and used nitro-aerial particles as the basis for a natural philosophy that accounted for the properties of fire, the elasticity of air, and the "goodness" of air (seen by some historians as an anticipation of the concept of oxygen), as well as the fermentation of the blood and the body's heat.

John Mayow. From Fielding H. Garrison, An Introduction to the History of Medicine, *3rd ed. (Philadelphia and London: Saunders, 1921).*

Mayow integrated the views and experiments of the Oxford circle of physiologists with his own to produce an experimental philosophy that united chemistry, air, combustion, and life in one system. However, the gatekeepers of reputations in the New Science, Robert Hooke and Henry Oldenburg (ca. 1619–1677), the secretary of the Royal Society, did not receive Mayow's later work with any enthusiasm.

BIBLIOGRAPHY

Frank, Robert. *Harvey and the Oxford Physiologists*. Berkeley and Los Angeles: University of California Press, 1980.

Partington, J. R. *A History of Chemistry*. 4 vols. London: Macmillan, 1961–1964, vol. 2.

———. "The Life and Work of John Mayow (1641–1679)." *Isis* 47 (1956), 217–230, 405–417.

ANDREW WEAR

See also Harvey, William; Lower, Richard; Physiology; Willis, Thomas

Measurement

In the context of the Scientific Revolution, measurement came to be the use of mathematical units to supply data and information about a range of features of the universe. In the minds of some, the introduction of the use of mathematics, not only for scientific measurement but also in the creation of mathematical physics, is the hallmark of the revolution. The importance of the introduction of measurement as a key aspect of science is even more fundamental than that, for it must be understood in the context of a battle over the very concept of nature itself. It should not be assumed, however, that the rise of measurement as a serious dimension of human activity was merely the result of theoretical considerations; theoretical battles notwithstanding, the world of the practical had a significant impact as well.

In the fifteenth century, the prevailing conceptual system was Aristotelian, with its insistence of the primacy of first principles. In this sense, the discovery of truths about nature involved proper deductions from these principles. As a specialized form of deduction, syllogistic reasoning contained at its heart the idea that, once the first principles were known, all there was to know about nature was deducible from them. In short, there was nothing new to be discovered about nature by way of observation through measurements or other means. This view of what could be known about nature and how it was to be known was institutionalized in the characterization of what were then called the "sciences" in the major intellectual centers of Europe (i.e., the Jesuit universities).

The status of geometry in the Jesuit hierarchy of the sciences presented a problem for those who would use such techniques to investigate nature for two distinct reasons. First, the sciences, properly called, were circumscribed by their use of demonstration: demonstrations were primarily arguments employing syllogisms. Thus, specific terms and their definition played key roles, since demonstration was primarily a matter of keeping the terms straight in their relationships to one another. On this account, there were five sciences: of God, (Aristotelian) intelligences, being, natural bodies, and quantity. Mathematics, including geometry, was the accepted means for studying quantity. In the context of Jesuit scholarship, such as would be found at universities where Galileo Galilei (1564–1642) studied and taught (e.g., Pisa and Padua), it differed in a profound way from the other four sciences. Quantity can be analyzed without relation to any material or substance, whereas the other sciences necessarily are tied to some substance or other—that is, quantity, by not being associated with a substance, could not be used to measure anything about the world. The relations among bodies and other natural phenomena were already the property of other, nonmathematical science. Second, there was an order to these sciences according to their degree of certainty. Mathematics provides the greatest certainty because it does not use probable arguments. However, it is the least noble of the five because its central terms could not be shown to be true and it did not deal with causes and effects. What mathematics proves, it proves well, but the truth of its premises was in constant doubt. So, on Aristotelian grounds, the use of measurements to provide new insights into the world was problematic at best.

But, while Aristotelianism was the dominant philosophical worldview at the beginning of the Scientific Revolution, there were competing points of view active as well. In particular, the Neoplatonists posed a serious challenge to the view of the sciences and the role of mathematics in reasoning about the world. Just as there were many Aristotelianisms, there were several varieties of Neoplationism at the time. The one that served as the major challenger to the Aristotelian view of nature was committed to the position that the use of mathematics leads to truths about reality. In this view, nature is not a

systematic whole, penetrable through a priori insight. Rather, it is a complex collection of innumerable things and relationships to be discovered. The heart of the Neoplatonic ideal was that nature was mathematically structured and its secrets could be uncovered by studying its essential mathematical relationships.

The contrast could not be clearer. In the Aristotelian view, nature is a coherent system whose inner workings could be deduced from first principles. In the Neoplatonic view, nature is a collection of things to be discovered by the use of mathematics. It would be misleading, however, to assume that the contrast is as clean as just stated. Just as the many Aristotelian points of view suffered from the difficulties of providing adequate definitions and demonstrations to cover all cases, Neoplatonism carried a certain occult baggage that was associated in the minds of some with a nonempirical approach.

Conceptual battles notwithstanding, nothing succeeds like success. Thus, while it is true that arguments over whether it was proper to apply mathematics to the process of exposing the plenitude of nature were to be heard, especially in academic environments, employing mathematics and derivatively discrete units of measurement went on long before these arguments were resolved. This was particularly the case in the *media scenzia,* the middle sciences, or what eventually came to be known as engineering. It is here that measurement makes its first serious impact.

The newly important or emerging techologies of the Renaissance—gunnery, navigation, cartography, surveying, and architecture, among others—led a number of natural philosophers to stress the importance of mathematics and measurement in investigations of natural phenomena and to create new instruments for that purpose. Thus, it may be no accident that Galileo, the great theoretical scientist, was first a very practical inventor concerned with creating machines with real-world application. Galileo's first invention was the military compass, a device used to figure the proper angle for a cannon shot to reach its target. His first published work was an account of how to use the compass. The crucial point here is that, in 1596, Galileo introduced a method of calculating by the measurement of distances and altitudes based on sighting and triangulation. An earlier version of the compass had been around for some time, with scales marked only on the arc. Galileo introduced scales of various kinds elsewhere in the device, making it of great use to artillerymen as well as military engineers. By 1599, Galileo had turned the military compass into a general calculator that could be used to solve just about any general problem.

A similar device was also independently developed by Thomas Hood (ca. 1557–1620) in 1598, which he called the *sector*. Using Galileo's book, Hood wrote, anyone interested could do surveying and other terrain-mapping activities. Whether or not Galileo's success with the military compass was the source of his commitment to replacing metaphysical presuppositions about the world with exact measurement cannot be concluded with any degree of certainty. But the introduction of precise means of making measurements in the arena of practical activity by the same person who later championed the replacement of Aristotelian verbal jousting with measurable quantities should not be overlooked.

The science of astronomy had always used measurement for its chief purpose of predicting the future positions of celestial bodies. In the latter part of the sixteenth century, astronomers, notably Tycho Brahe (1546–1601), came to recognize that the desired renovation of astronomy required significant improvement in observational precision. Observation with improved methods and instruments, as well as new ones, over the next century challenged Aristotelian principles and methodology at their foundations. Measurements of the nova and comet of the 1570s, Johannes Kepler's (1571–1630) discoveries concerning the motions of the planets, and Galileo's measurements of the height of the lunar mountains in the first decade of the seventeenth century called into question the traditional distinction between the celestial and terrestrial regions.

In the seventeenth century, measurement came to be applied over a range of traditional and newly discovered natural phenomena, and experiments were designed to yield measurable results. Among them were Galileo's efforts to determine the rate of acceleration in free fall, William Harvey's (1578–1657) estimate of the quantity of blood moved by the beating heart, Blaise Pascal's (1623–1662) investigation of the height of mercury in the barometer at different altitudes, and Robert Boyle (1627–1691) and Edmé Mariotte's (ca. 1620–1684) determination of the relation of volume to pressure in a gas. More accurate means of gauging weights, angles, distances, times, volumes, and heat, as well as discriminating betweeen increasingly smaller units, were sought and found. To the odometer, military compass, pendulum clock, and thermometer were added a cluster of new devices and mathematical techniques to ease and expedite calculation: the calculating machine, the slide rule, logarithms, the decimal system, and trigonometrical tables for ever smaller angles.

The increasing importance of measurement in the Scientific Revolution also had as a consequence the solution of what was thought to be a theoretical problem by the development of a practical method of taking measurements. A long-standing theoretical issue in astronomy concerned the relative sizes of the planets. Prior to the development of the telescope, a variety of schemes based on assumptions about harmonic relations produced inconclusive results. The solution to determining the relative size of the planets required two significant developments: the invention of the telescope and its improvement by allowing the insertion of a micrometer with a graduated scale so that the diameter of a planet could be directly measured.

The use of the telescope to observe the transits of Venus and Mercury in the first half of the century produced observable results that varied considerably from predictions based on various proportionality schemes developed to order the planets in terms of size as against their distances from the Sun. The use of the micrometer in improved telescopes about mid-century settled the question of the relative size of the planets (except for that of the earth) by the mid-1670s. What we see here is the practical need for a solution simply taking over the theoretical problems when a solution was at hand.

The introduction of the methodological principle that the taking of measurements could provide genuine knowledge of nature involved a transformation in our understanding of nature. It also seems to have reflected the fact that, in a number of areas in which there were real-world issues to be solved, from sighting a cannon to providing a hands-on solution to what was initially thought to be a theoretical issue, measurement was a key feature in marking the Scientific Revolution as a transformation in both how we think and how we deal with the world.

BIBLIOGRAPHY

Bennett, J. A. "The Mechanics' Philosophy and the Mechanical Philosophy." *History of Science* 24 (1986), 1–28.

Dear, Peter. *Discipline and Experience: The Mathematical Way to the Scientific Revolution*. Chicago: University of Chicago Press, 1995.

Galilei, Galileo. *Dialogue on the Two Chief World Systems*. Trans. Stillman Drake. Berkeley and Los Angeles: University of California Press, 1967.

———. *Operations of the Geometric and Military Compass, 1606.* Trans. with an Introduction by Stillman Drake. Washington, D.C.: Smithsonian Institution Press, 1978.

Pitt, Joseph C. *Galileo, Human Knowledge, and the Book of Nature.* Dordrecht: Kluwer Academic, 1992.

Taton, R., and C. Wilson, eds. *Planetary Astronomy from the Renaissance to the Rise of Astrophysics.* (The General History of Astronomy, vol. 2A.) Cambridge: Cambridge University Press, 1989.

JOSEPH C. PITT

See also Barometer; Cross-Staff; Experience and Experiment; Instrument Makers; Mixed Sciences; Proportional Dividers; Quadrant; Surveying; Thermoscope/Thermometer

Mechanical Philosophy

The Scientific Revolution of the seventeenth century fashioned a new philosophic framework as it proceeded. When new conclusions in astronomy and mechanics had rendered Aristotelian natural philosophy untenable, a radically different view of physical reality, which saw it in quantitative rather than qualitative terms, furnished the generally accepted set of assumptions that bound the disparate conclusions in a number of fields of study into a reasonably coherent whole. Although it has been modified almost beyond recognition, the natural philosophy elaborated during the seventeenth century was the starting point from which all subsequent natural philosophy in the West has proceeded.

From the time of the revival of learning in western Europe in the twelfth and thirteenth centuries, Aristotelian philosophy had dominated every field of thought, almost to the extent of excluding any alternative. The corpus of Aristotle's (384–322 B.C.E.) writings had been among the early works that Europe recovered from antiquity. His logic provided Christian theology with a vehicle to elaborate doctrine more powerful by far than anything available before, and logic paved the way for the rest. The creation of universities saw Aristotelian philosophy, with special emphasis on his natural philosophy, acquire an institutional base; three centuries later, it was still going strong. By the sixteenth century, it was beginning to seem a bit stale, and the more daring leaders of thought began to propose alternative philosophies, all calling upon some other ancient model, most of them derivatives from Plato (428–348 B.C.E.).

Nevertheless, it was not the competing naturalistic philosophies but the appearance of Copernican astronomy that doomed Aristotelian natural philosophy. Aristotle had built his system on the assumption, almost unchallenged in the ancient world, that the earth is the unmoved center of the universe. There was no way that geocentrism could be removed and the system left standing. To be sure, the progress of heliocentrism was slow, but a number of factors seemed to work in its favor. Observations demonstrated that the new stars (supernovae, as we now call them) of 1572 and 1604 and the comet of 1577 were high in the heavens. Aristotelian philosophy demanded that they be below the Moon, and again this was a facet of Aristotle's thought that could not be amended without calling into question his view of the cosmos and of natural philosophy. Phenomena discovered with the telescope after its invention in 1609, such as the host of hitherto unknown stars, sunspots and the likely rotation of the Sun on an axis inclined to the ecliptic that sunspots revealed, the phases of Venus, and the satellites of Jupiter, all raised acute problems for geocentric systems, while they fit smoothly into the heliocentric and even enriched it. If there had been few Copernicans before 1600, by 1650 there was no one well informed in astronomy and free to follow where his intellect led who was not a heliocentrist.

The science of mechanics, intimately involved in the New Astronomy, further shook the foundations of Aristotelian philosophy. Phenomena of motion, such as the vertical fall of bodies, could not take place on a moving earth, as they are universally observed to do, if Aristotle's analysis of motion were correct. This problem, the major objection to heliocentric astronomy, called a new conception of motion, substantially identical to the principle of inertia, into being. It was the work of Galileo Galilei (1564–1642) more than anyone else, and, like heliocentric astronomy with which it was closely allied, it was widely influential throughout the nascent scientific community. It also drove another stake into the heart of Aristotelian natural philosophy, for the analysis of motion was a central member of it.

By the fourth decade of the seventeenth century, for anyone who cared to look, the Aristotelian system had been reduced to a shambles. Whatever the appeal of the philosophies prominent in the sixteenth century, a vigorous scientific life was not one, for they do not appear likely to have promoted such. In fact, those philosophies waned as the seventeenth century progressed, and the mechanical philosophy filled the void left by the collapse of Aristotelianism. About the fourth decade of the century a number of philosophers were turning toward mechanistic modes of thought influenced by ancient atomism. None of them were as influential as the French philosopher René Descartes (1596–1650).

In Part I of his *Discourse on Method,* one of the revealing texts from the early seventeenth century, Descartes described his education. He had attended the Jesuit school at La Flèche, reputed to be the best school in France. He had gone there with the promise of learning truth; he had emerged filled with doubt. Nothing appeared to have been settled with certainty. He was impressed by mathematics, to be sure, but surprised to find how little had been built upon its foundation. Philosophy offered a medley of conflicting opinions. "There is nothing imaginable so strange or so little credible that it has not been maintained by one philosopher or other." Take Descartes's reaction to his education as the response of a generation to the collapse of Aristotle. His conclusion, that the only avenue of escape from this impasse was to purge his mind of the accumulated errors of the past and to start anew, consciously rejected the whole structure of received learning.

Descartes put himself through a process of systematic doubt, refusing to accept as true anything he could find the least reason to doubt, in the hope that he would find some proposition beyond doubt that would serve as a basis for certainty. Almost the first thing that went was belief in the existence of the external world. Evidence of the senses had led men to believe in its existence. The senses sometimes err, however, and the existence of the external world cannot be beyond doubt. Once he had found his rock, the certainty that was beyond the possibility of doubt—the proposition *cogito ergo sum* (I think, therefore I am)—Descartes proceeded to build a new structure of knowledge on its foundation, and he restored the external world to being, now as a demonstrated truth rather than an unexamined assumption.

The world he restored differed, however, by conscious intent from the Aristotelian world he had doubted away. Aristotle had assumed a one-to-one correspondence between appearance to a healthy observer and external reality; his world had been inherently qualitative. Descartes concluded that, if the external world necessarily exists, there is no necessity that it be in any way similar to the world our senses depict. We see about us a world filled with life and with qualities. They are only illusions; there is nothing out there but particles of matter in motion. Descartes's clear and distinct proposition—

I think, therefore I am—became his definition of mind as thinking substance, one half of a dualistic metaphysics. The other half was supplied by a second clear and distinct idea, extension. Cartesian dualism excluded mind from the domain of physical nature. The activity of thinking, and the activity of thinking alone, characterizes mind. You must not ascribe to mind size or location, or any physical property; the essence of mind is thinking. Correspondingly—and this was the issue of importance for the new natural philosophy—you must not ascribe to matter anything pertaining to thought or any source of spontaneous activity such as thought is. Extension in three dimensions, and extension alone, characterizes matter. Descartes always used the past passive participle *extensa* to describe matter. The external world consists solely of particles of this passive matter, moved where mechanical necessity forces them to move.

Although only a few accepted the full rigor of Cartesian metaphysics, one or another rendition of Cartesian dualism appeared in every version of the mechanical philosophy and dominated European thought by the second half of the century. Concepts such as teleology, implying the presence of consciousness or thought in material objects, were generally excluded. So were active principles, though among less rigorous metaphysicians they frequently crept back in under various guises. In general, by excluding mind from the operation of nature, Cartesian dualism presented the world as an arena in which mechanical necessity alone prevailed.

In defining matter as extension, Descartes identified mathematical with physical division, and, because every mathematical extension can be divided, he denied that there can be such a thing as an ultimate particle, or atom. Whether ultimate or not, however, particles made up nature as he conceived of it. Because matter cannot move itself, he ascribed to God an initial impulse that set the world in motion. The first effect of motion was to shatter the crystalline purity of extension into a myriad of particles, and the whole of Descartes's natural philosophy consisted of describing the mechanisms of moving particles conceived to produce the phenomena of nature. This was the essence of the mechanical philosophy, whether in its Cartesian form or another—the assertion that particles of matter, moved solely by mechanical necessity, produce all of the phenomena of nature.

Unlike Aristotelian philosophy, the mechanical philosophy was at ease with the new conception of motion. Indeed, it was inconceivable without it. To set passive matter in motion in the first place, some principle external to nature was required; in the seventeenth century, this could only be God. Once matter was set in motion, however, no continued source of motion was required because it is the nature of motion to persevere. In Cartesian terms, the quantity of motion in the universe is constant. Those particles in motion that made up the new nature remained in motion under the principles of the new mechanics.

For Descartes, the universe was a plenum. Extension was literally identical to matter, and the notion of even a scruple of empty space was a contradiction in terms. How was motion possible in a plenum? Only if an entire closed circuit of matter moved together, like the rim of a wheel rotating on its axis. Hence, of necessity, Descartes's universe had divided itself into a number—a very large, indeed unlimited, number—of huge whirlpools, which he called *vortices*. At the center of each was a luminous body. Around it, as in our system, there might be a number of planets, carried along by the vortex like pieces of wood floating in a river. Descartes conceived of the vortices as immense; the orbit of Saturn, for example, was no more than a point in comparison to the extent of our vortex. In so doing, he accommodated his philosophy to the vast distances demanded by the New Astronomy. By treating the system of vortices as a dynamic equilibrium in constant flux, he accepted the appearance of new stars. He saw comets as celestial bodies, like planets in structure but not in stable orbits about a sun. Above all, the system was necessarily heliocentric, and it offered an explanation of why the planets move in the same direction in the same plane about a central Sun. All mechanical philosophies were heliocentric, and all accepted the concept of a vortex, though not necessarily Descartes's plenum, to explain the planetary system. Unlike Aristotle's philosophy, which was radically incompatible with the early achievements of the Scientific Revolution in astronomy and mechanics and was, therefore, doomed, the mechanical philosophy built those achievements into its very structure.

The mechanical philosophy set out to account for all of the phenomena of nature in terms solely of particles of matter in motion. Qualities in general offered little difficulty. In asserting that nature need not be similar to what our senses depict, Descartes distinguished between *sensations* and *qualities*. Particles of matter impinge on the nerves of sentient beings, causing sensations. Mankind has mistakenly projected the sensations onto nature and

treated qualities as existent realities. Take heat and cold as examples. For Descartes, the physical reality of heat was particles in rapid motion. A motion sufficiently violent damages what its touches; that is, it burns. A gentle motion pleasantly warms. Little motion we feel as cold. Cold ceased to be a positive quality with Descartes and became merely a low degree of heat. In a similar manner, qualities paired as opposites by Aristotle, such as heavy and light and wet and dry, were reinterpreted as different degrees on a single scale, the physical reality of which was particles of some particular size and shape in some particular motion. The kinetic theory of heat, one of Descartes's most prescient insights, proved difficult for many seventeenth-century thinkers to accept, and other versions of the mechanical philosophy frequently incorporated a special matter of heat and fire—still particles in motion, but, nevertheless, compromises with qualitative philosophy.

Gravity, which in the pre-Newtonian age meant heaviness, the downward tendency of bodies, is a prominent phenomenon that any natural philosophy must deal with. Descartes explained it as a consequence of vortical motion, in this case a special vortex that circles the earth as its center. Although circular motion (i.e., motion in a closed orbit) is necessary, it is unnatural, because motion is rectilinear in nature. If bodies in a plenum must move in closed circuits, they nevertheless strive at every moment to move in straight lines and, thus, to recede from the center. In a plenum, one body can move away from a center only if an equal one moves toward it. What we experience as heaviness in bodies is their deficiency in centrifugal tendency in comparison to the invisible matter in the vortex that we do not observe directly. Other mechanical philosophies frequently postulated an invisible matter they called an *ether* that streams down toward the earth bearing bodies it strikes with it.

Magnetic phenomena were of great interest in the early seventeenth century. The selectivity of magnetism—the capacity of a magnetized needle to distinguish direction, and the attraction of a magnet for iron but not for other substances—had made it the very symbol of the mysterious influences earlier philosophies had deemed to pervade the universe. It was essential that Descartes reduce magnetism to matter in motion. He explained how the turning of the vortex on its axis generates little screw-shaped particles, both right-hand threads and left-hand threads, from the two different ends of the vortex's axis, corresponding to the two magnetic poles, and how these particles, pressed down along the axis, bore corresponding pores in the matter on the surface of the sun, which is iron in the process of formation. Because the earth was once a sun that crusted over, it contains a great deal of iron with these pores, and Descartes proceeded to explain all of the magnetic phenomena by the motions of the screw-shaped particles through the screw-shaped pores in iron.

Light does not appear as a likely topic to explain in Descartes's terms. Part of the success of his philosophy rested on his success in optics. Light, he said, was a pressure transmitted through a transparent medium—not a motion but a tendency to motion. His explication of gravity had made use of the tendency of bodies constrained to move in a close circuit to recede from the center. Inevitably, there is a pressure out from the center of every vortex. It is not by accident that vortices have luminous bodies at their centers. In his essay *Dioptrics,* Descartes offered three analogies for the understanding of light. The first was a blind man's stick. As a blind man walks, the end of his stick strikes objects in his path, and he "sees" them through the pressure transmitted to his hand. In the same way, pressure transmitted through transparent media pushes on the retina; the optic nerve transmits the stimulus to the brain, and we say that we see. The second analogy, the motion of juice toward the hole in the bottom of a vat of grapes, explained how light can be transmitted in straight lines through media such as glass. Because of the solid matter of the grapes in the way, the juice cannot flow in a straight line toward the hole. Nevertheless, every particle of juice tends toward the hole in a straight line. The third analogy made use of the motion itself of a tennis ball striking a surface. When the surface is solid, the ball rebounds at an angle equal to the angle of incidence. Descartes represented a refracting surface by a stretched piece of cloth that the ball breaks through, and, pursuing an argument about how its velocity is altered, he derived for the first time in print the sine law of refraction. The three analogies hardly agreed with one another. Descartes believed that the pressure we call light moves instantaneously, but his third analogy used the altered velocity of the tennis ball to derive the sine law of refraction. Never mind; all three were mechanical and expressed the conviction that light must be a mechanical disturbance in a mechanical universe.

Life was more difficult still than light. Descartes was convinced that animals are merely complex automata. If we could build a machine, he said, that does all of the things a monkey does, we should have no way to distinguish it from a monkey—that is, a monkey, like other animals, is such a complex machine. Mankind is different, because in each human being a thinking soul is united to a body, but even in the case of human beings the great majority of our actions are purely mechanical. Hearts beat and blood circulates without any conscious effort on our parts. We digest food and grow, and we respond reflexively to stimuli without thought. In his essay *Man,* Descartes described a machine that did all of these things, that did everything but think, which he did not consider an organic activity. To explain all of the functions of the human body, he concluded, "it is not necessary to imagine a vegetative or sensitive soul in the machine, or any other principle of movement and life other than its blood and spirits agitated by the fire which burns continually in its heart and which differs in nothing from all the fires in inanimate bodies."

The mechanical philosophy was a program of explanation, not a program of investigation. In the case of physiology, Descartes accepted William Harvey's (1578–1657) discovery of the circulation of the blood. Blood circulating in a closed system precisely exemplified the conditions Descartes considered necessary for any motion in a plenum. The fire without light in the heart was entirely a product of his imagination to explain the motion of the blood. In a similar way, he explained the known phenomena of magnetism by inventing the complex machinery of screw-shaped particles and pores, which had no empirical foundation beyond the magnetic phenomena they served to explain. Descartes did not exercise great skepticism in regard to the phenomena he chose to explain. It was widely accepted in the early seventeenth century that the blood of a murdered man runs if the murderer approaches the body; Descartes imagined a mechanism of invisible particles of given shapes and motions that causes this to happen. Behind the mechanical philosophy stood the unstated assumptions that microscopic mechanisms are identical to macroscopic ones we observe and that nature is essentially transparent to the human understanding so that we can confidently imagine mechanisms that must exist. Mechanical philosophers turned out to have fertile imaginations for the unobservable particles.

Descartes's was not the only mechanistic system. About the same time that he was composing his system, another French philosopher, Pierre Gassendi

(1592–1655), was also at work. The two differed in many respects. Where Descartes set out consciously to reject the past and build anew on the authority of his own clear and distinct ideas, Gassendi was a scholar who pored over the history of philosophy, selecting out what seemed best. What seemed best was the atomist tradition, and this, too, led to differences with Descartes. Gassendi believed that there are ultimate, undivided particles—atoms—and that void spaces separate them. The differences between the two men involve profound philosophical issues, but, paradoxically, they ended up with systems of natural philosophy that were remarkably similar. For both, physical nature consisted solely of particles of inert matter controlled in their motion by mechanical necessity alone. They might differ in the details of their explanations, but the principles of their explanations were the same.

Nor were Descartes and Gassendi the only ones. In England, Thomas Hobbes (1588–1679) elaborated a similar system of natural philosophy at much the same time, and we can find tendencies in the same direction, though not fully developed systems, in a number of others. When young Robert Boyle (1627–1691) began seriously to read natural philosophy ca. 1650, he concluded that what the systems held in common greatly outweighed the points on which they differed, and he coined the name, *mechanical philosophy,* that historians continue to employ to describe a natural philosophy dedicated to the proposition that all of the phenomena in nature, aspects of mankind alone excepted, are produced by inert particles characterized solely by size and shape and moved according to the laws of mechanics.

As in the case of Boyle, ca. 1650 the mechanical philosophy became the reigning orthodoxy. Christiaan Huygens (1629–1695), one of the leading scientists of the century, expressed its authority when he said that we must seek mechanistic explanations "or wholly renounce all hope of ever understanding anything in nature." In the years when it was being formulated, issues that centered on the barometer, invented in 1642, stood at the center of scientific debate. They served to focus the differences between the Aristotelian philosophy and the mechanical. Aristotelians, forced to deal with a phenomenon unknown to Aristotle himself, called upon nature's abhorrence of a vacuum, a concept redolent with teleological overtones. Mechanical philosophers explained the column of mercury in the tube by reference to an equilibrium of opposed weights. The mechanism in play

here was not of microscopic particles, but philosophers convinced that microscopic mechanisms are identical to macroscopic ones saw no distinction. As the debate progressed, it produced the most famous experiment of the century, the experiment of Blaise Pascal (1623–1662) with a barometer carried to the top of a mountain, and then a new instrument of investigation, the air pump. With the air pump, the concept of pressure came to the fore, and an equilibrium of pressures replaced an equilibrium of weights. The end product of the debate, a vindication of the mechanical philosophers, was Boyle's Law relating the pressure and volume of gases, one of the early mathematical laws of modern science and an expression of the mechanistic insight into nature.

From the middle of the century, the mechanical philosophy dominated optics. In a mechanistic universe, light could be only one of two things: a disturbance of some sort transmitted through a material medium, or tiny bodies in motion. The wave theory of light developed out of Descartes's conception. His pressure of light, which he had treated as a vectorial quantity, became pulses of motion in Robert Hooke's (1635–1703) discussion of light and, eventually, waves. The principal objection to the wave theory was the fact that light does not bend into shadows, as waves on a surface of water do. In his *Treatise on Light* (1691), Christiaan Huygens, the most important exponent of the wave theory in the seventeenth century, solved the problem of rectilinear transmission with the concept of a wave front.

The champion of the corpuscular conception was Isaac Newton (1642–1727), who was convinced of the necessity of corpuscles both by the rectilinear transmission of light and by the phenomena of colors. His discovery of the heterogeneity of light adjusted immediately to the notion of corpuscles of different sizes. Where phenomena of colors had been explained by a modification of light in reflection and refraction, Newton showed that they arise when the heterogeneous mixture in sunlight is separated into its components, and he was convinced that all wave theories were inherently inclined to the idea of modification. There were other discoveries in optics. The velocity of light was measured from astronomical phenomena. Both Huygens and Newton were committed to a finite, though immense, velocity of light, and this discovery fitted well with both mechanical conceptions of light. Other discoveries fitted with neither—periodicity of some optical phenomena (Huygens's waves were not periodic), polarity of some phenomena, and diffraction.

All remained problems for optics until a more sophisticated wave theory appeared in the nineteenth century.

The mechanical philosophy transformed the way chemistry was explicated. The two leading chemists of the second half of the seventeenth century, Robert Boyle and the Frenchman Nicolas Lemery (1645–1715), both espoused the mechanical outlook and devoted their writings to expressing chemistry in mechanistic terms (i.e., explaining reactions in terms of particles of different shapes). It has been argued that mechanical chemistry destroyed the hold of earlier qualitative concepts and, thus, prepared the way for a revolution in chemistry. No one has claimed anything more for mechanical chemistry, and all are agreed that the revolution that Antoine Lavoisier (1743–1794) brought to chemistry in the late eighteenth century is not to be understood as a manifestation of the mechanical philosophy.

The influence of the mechanical philosophy extended also to the life sciences. Early in the century, before Descartes and Gassendi published their systems, William Harvey discovered the circulation of the blood. Harvey was anything but a mechanist; nevertheless, his willingness to consider mechanical constraints in the motions of the heart and the blood led him to realize that blood must circulate. Later in the century, the circulation of the blood, now seen as the archtype of organic processes, became the centerpiece of a school of physiology known as *iatromechanics*. Its most influential exponent, the Italian Lorenzo Bellini (1643–1704), extended the circulation of the blood into a general theory of secretions that filled the body with filters to separate out particles from the various fluids. As one of his English followers put it, the body "is a hydraulic machine of the most exquisite art, in which there are numberless tubes properly adjusted and disposed for the conveyance of fluids of different kinds. Upon the whole, health consists of regular motions of the fluids, together with a proper state of the solids, and diseases are their aberrations." An analogous theory of vegetable physiology was also worked out. Iatromechanics, devoted, as most work in the life sciences was in the seventeenth century, to medicine, did not yield any improvement in therapeutics, and it gradually died out during the eighteenth century. As with mechanical chemistry, its importance lies in the revelation it provides of the widespread influence the mechanical philosophy exercised.

Ca. 1664, Isaac Newton, then an undergraduate in Cambridge, discovered the mechanical philosophy in the writings of Descartes and forthwith abandoned the Aristotelian curriculum still prescribed in the universities to enroll under its banner. Newton soon began to have second thoughts, however. Some of them had to do with religion; he became convinced that the mechanical philosophy was a prescription for materialism and atheism, and he wanted to ensure the dominance of spirit in nature. Other problems had to do with the natural philosophy itself. A number of phenomena did not, in his eyes, readily reduce to particles of matter in motion. Especially in chemical reactions, those that generate heat and those that display elective affinities, he seemed to be observing sources of activity that the mechanical philosophy denied could exist. Gradually, Newton convinced himself that the ontology of nature contains more than inert particles in motion. It appeared to him that there are forces of attraction and repulsion, which he sometimes referred to as *active principles,* between particles of matter.

For a mathematical scientist, as Newton was, forces defined mathematically held great promise. The mechanical philosophy generated visual images of micromechanisms that were almost invariably in conflict with the early mathematical laws of science. No imagined vortex could yield the precise relations of Johannes Kepler's (1571–1630) three laws of planetary motion. No imagined mechanism to explain the heaviness of bodies could yield the two central propositions of Galileo's kinematics of free fall—that bodies fall with a uniformly accelerated motion and that the acceleration for all bodies, whatever their size and substance, is identical. A force of attraction could solve these problems.

Newton convinced himself that there is a range of different forces in the universe—magnetic force, electric force, atomic forces that hold bodies together and give rise to chemical reactions, and gravity. Because he saw forces as a direct action of God in the Creation, they removed the danger of materialism. Although he tried, most of the forces did not yield to his efforts to mathematize their effects. Gravity was different, for in its case he could call upon the large body of data that astronomy had collected. In *The Mathematical Principles of Natural Philosophy* (or *Principia* from its Latin title), published in 1687, Newton demonstrated that Kepler's three laws follow necessarily from an attraction toward the Sun that varies inversely as the square of the distance. In the narrow zone around the earth where the attraction toward the earth is essentially constant, it entails Galileo's

M

kinematics of free fall; in the broader zone that embraces the Moon, the attraction of the earth, decreasing in intensity in proportion to the square of the distance, correlates the measured acceleration of gravity at the surface of the earth with the observed orbit of the Moon. The *Principia* did much more as Newton explored the mathematical consequences of the universal force of attraction. It explained the tides and a conical motion of the earth's axis that generates an appearance called the *precession of the equinoxes* from the combined attractions of the Moon and the Sun on the earth, and it explained the observed inequalities of the Moon as perturbations caused by the attraction of the Sun. Treating the great comet of 1681–1682 as a planetlike body, it succeeded in showing that, under the attraction of the Sun, it had followed a path that was a conic curve. All this it did with exquisite mathematical precision that left no room for doubt.

That is, to us, three centuries later, it appears to have left no room for doubt. Mechanical philosophers, to whom the denial of action at a distance was a matter of principle, found plenty of room to doubt, and for several decades, until a new generation swayed by the power of Newton's mathematics grew up, a debate raged among natural philosophers. Nevertheless, Newton must be seen as a mechanical philosopher also. Like the nature that Descartes and Gassendi presented, Newtonian nature consisted of particles of matter, and all of the phenomena of nature followed from their motions, aggregations, and separations. He did, of course, alter the original mechanical philosophy by expanding its ontology to include forces of attraction, and this alteration opened the way to the mathematization of science. Modern science has moved down that path ever since.

BIBLIOGRAPHY

Burtt, E. A. *The Metaphysical Foundations of Modern Physical Science*. London: K. Paul, Trench, Trubner, 1925. Rev. ed. Garden City, NY: Doubleday, 1955.

Butterfield, H. *The Origins of Modern Science, 1300–1800*. London: Bell, 1950.

Hall, A. R. *The Revolution in Science, 1500–1750*. London: Longman, 1983.

Hall, Marie Boas. "The Establishment of the Mechanical Philosophy." *Osiris* 10 (1952), 412–541.

Harré, R. *Matter and Method*. London: Macmillan, 1964.

Osler, Margaret. *Divine Will and the Mechanical Philosophy: Gassendi and Descartes on Contingency and Necessity in the Created World*. Cambridge: Cambridge University Press, 1994.

Shea, W. R. *The Magic of Numbers and Motion: The Scientific Career of René Descartes*. Nantucket, MA: Science History Publications, 1991.

Yoder, Joella G. *Unrolling Time: Christiaan Huygens and the Mathematization of Nature*. Cambridge: Cambridge University Press, 1988.

RICHARD S. WESTFALL

See also Active Principles; Aristotelianism; Atomism; Cartesianism; Clockwork Universe; Descartes, René; Gassendi, Pierre; Iatromechanics; Matter

Mechanics

A new science of motion stood at the heart of the Scientific Revolution. The work of the entire seventeenth century, it began with Galileo Galilei (1564–1642) and found, not its conclusion, but its highest expression during that period in the *Principia mathematica philosophiae naturalis* (The Mathematical Principles of Natural Philosophy, 1687) of Isaac Newton (1642–1727). Important in itself because of the centrality of motion in most natural philosophies, it also provided the paradigm of what science in the West has been attempting to be ever since.

Aristotelian science included a system of mechanics. Its fundamental premise was the assertion, seemingly ratified by daily experience, that the constant exertion of force is necessary for a body to be in motion. To move is to be moved; when the cause is removed, the effect ceases. To a society accustomed to seeing carts drawn by oxen and ships propelled by oars, no proposition about motion could have seemed more self-evident. When equal bodies are moved under the same conditions, the velocities are proportional to the forces applied and inversely proportional to the resistance of the medium through which they move. Although the proportions sound mathematical and the word *force* that we impose on Aristotle's (384–322 B.C.E.) Greek has a modern ring, we must not allow ourselves to imagine that an elaborated mathematical system of dynamics existed. Nevertheless, during the flowering of medieval science, the concept of motion received much attention. Medieval philosophers emended the weakest aspect of Aristotle's mechanics, its explanation of projectile motion, and proposed the concept of a force, or *impetus,* impressed on a body set in motion, that sustains its motion. One school of medieval philosophers, the Oxford Calculators, developed a sophisticated mathematics of motion that was consistent with Aristotle's dicta. Despite the emendations, Scholastic mechanics remained within the precincts of Aristotelian philosophy, and, what was of greatest importance, it did not question the proposition that a body cannot move without the continued exertion of a force.

With Galileo, early in the seventeenth century, the science of mechanics took a decisive new turn. We know from his manuscripts that Galileo worked intensively on problems of motion in the last decade of the sixteenth and the first decade of the seventeenth century, and we know that he then arrived at many of the new conclusions that made up his mechanics (i.e., this occurred before the telescope and his fervent commitment to Copernicanism). Nevertheless, that commitment, which came long before he published anything on mechanics, gave his work on motion a pressing relevance that it did not have before. The great objection to Copernicanism rested on observed phenomena of motion, especially the vertical fall of bodies. In terms of Aristotle's analysis of motion, bodies cannot fall vertically on an earth that is turning on its axis. Falling bodies, separated from any source of motion, would be left far behind.

The essence of Galileo's response, which was also the foundation of his mechanics, was a new conception of motion that denied the necessity of a cause. For Aristotle, motion had included much more than it does for us. Motion, or perhaps change, included such examples as acorns growing into oak trees and boys being educated. Motion in these terms was an ontological process in which bodies realized their potentiality—the acorn as an oak tree, the boy as a rational man. So also an object falling was realizing its essence as a heavy body to be near the center of the universe. Motion as an ontological process required a cause. Galileo narrowed down the conception of motion to much the meaning it has for us: movement from here to there. He denied that anything essential to a body was involved in its motion. As he put it, a body is indifferent to motion or rest. It is no wonder that we do not perceive our uniform motion from west to east, which has always been a condition of our existence and affects nothing vital to us. Uniform motion does not require a cause; a body in uniform motion on a horizontal plane will continue until something external stops it.

In answering the objection to Copernicanism, Galileo called repeatedly on experience in ships. One example concerned a stone dropped from the top of the mast of a moving ship. Galileo was not the first to see that the case was exactly analogous to dropping a rock from a tower on a turning earth. Opponents knew very well that a stone dropped from the mast of a ship falls to the rear of the ship; because stones dropped from towers do not similarly fall to the west, the earth cannot be turning on its axis. Galileo knew even more certainly that a stone falls at the foot of the mast, but it appears that, nevertheless, he did try it on a galley in the sea off Pisa. Does anything at all happen differently when the ship is at rest than when it is moving uniformly? This argument and all of Galileo's arguments do not prove that the earth is in motion, of course. They do demonstrate that the standard objection against Copernicanism rests on no foundation at all.

It is not precisely correct to equate Galileo's conception of motion with the principle of inertia. He spoke always about uniform motion on a horizontal plane. Obsessed as he was with the Copernican issue, he equated the surface of the earth with a horizontal plane. Although Galileo formulated the concept that a uniform motion on a frictionless horizontal plane will continue indefinitely, he never arrived at the rectilinearity that is a necessary aspect of our principle of inertia.

Vertical motion also played a major role in Galileo's mechanics. Although it is unlikely that he performed the famous experiment at the tower of Pisa, he concluded early that bodies do not fall with velocities proportional to their weights, as Aristotle's mechanics demanded. Before long, he concluded that all bodies of whatever size and substance fall through equal distances in the same time, allowance being made for the resistance of the air. Equal velocity was not the phrase to apply to them, however, for their velocity changes continuously. Bodies fall, rather, with a *uniformly accelerated motion*. What did he mean by uniformly accelerated motion? At first, he meant that velocity increases in proportion to the distance fallen. In a well-known document, he reasoned from this premise, via fallacious logic, to a conclusion he had already reached, that the distance traveled in free fall increases in proportion to the square of elapsed time. Galileo did correct himself, however, by contemplating what he called the supreme affinity between motion and time. In uniformly accelerated motion (the motion with which bodies fall everywhere on the earth), velocity increases in proportion to the elapsed time. All bodies fall with the same uniform acceleration, allowance again being made for the resistance of the medium.

M

From the concept of uniformly accelerated motion, Galileo went on to deduce mathematically consequences that follow from it. The increase of distance in proportion to the square of time, deduced now without the earlier fallacy, was one of them. Equal times of descent along all chords from the uppermost point of a circle in a vertical plane was another. There were many more, and it is well to pause with them. Astronomy had always been a geometrical science, and Johannes Kepler (1571–1630) was making it more geometrical at the very time Galileo was at work on terrestrial mechanics. Galileo's kinematics of uniformly accelerated motion, in which he worked out the various relations of velocity, distance, and time in such motion, brought mathematics down from the heavens. Perhaps the central strand of science since that time has been the steadily expanding role of mathematics.

Galileo added one further major conclusion to mechanics. He treated projectile motion as a composition of uniform horizontal motion and uniformly accelerated motion. Because bodies are indifferent to motion, the two component motions do not interfere with each other, and Galileo demonstrated that the resultant trajectory is a parabola.

A circle of young followers of Galileo in Italy carried on the teaching of their master. The most important of them, Evangelista Torricelli (1608–1647), developed further demonstrations about projectile motion and sketched out a system of dynamics compatible with uniformly accelerated motion in a straight line, though it fell on deaf ears at the time. In Italy, however, the science of motion did not advance far beyond the point to which Galileo brought it. This was not the case in northern Europe.

Influenced by the Dutch natural philosopher Isaac Beeckman (1588–1637) in the 1620s, perhaps two decades later than Galileo but before Galileo had published his mechanics, René Descartes (1596–1650) arrived at a similar conception of motion. In his *Principles of Philosophy,* he offered the best philosophical explication it received. Aristotle's definition of motion (the act of a body in potency insofar as it is in potency) seemed completely meaningless to Descartes. Motion is simply the transference of a body from the vicinity of those next to it to the vicinity of others. It is not an act or a process but, rather, a state in which a body finds itself, like its shape or size. A body cannot, by itself, change its shape or size. If it is at rest, it cannot put itself in motion. Why should motion alone of all the states of a body have as its

end its own extinction? No, a body in motion will continue in motion until something external stops it. Philosophers have been asking the wrong question, Descartes concluded. They have been asking what keeps a body in motion. They should ask what causes it to stop. Essentially, this was Galileo's conception of motion stated in different words. Descartes did not work out a mathematical kinematics as Galileo did, but he went beyond Galileo in one important matter. Quite explicitly, he asserted that motion, the state that continues without the exertion of any force, is rectilinear in nature.

Descartes also defined two problems that continued to command the attention of the science of mechanics. In his mechanical philosophy of nature, the sole agent of causation was the impact of one body on another. It is not surprising, then, that he set the problem of how two bodies in impact affect each other's motion. As a general principle of natural philosophy, he concluded that, because of the immutability of God, the total quantity of motion in the universe remains constant; the same principle governs the impact of two bodies. The principle sounds like our principle of the conservation of momentum. In the details, because of his concept of velocity and because of his lack of a concept of mass, the two differ greatly, and, of the seven cases of impact that Descartes analyzed, we consider his results correct only in one. Somewhat the same can be said of his analysis of circular motion. Again, he was the one who first set the problem. Circular motion became an issue in dynamics when inertial motion became rectilinear. And, once again, we find his solution imperfect. Instead of concentrating on the force that turns a body from its rectilinear path into a curved one, he focused on the endeavor of a body constrained to move in a circle to follow the tangent and, hence, to recede from the center. Christiaan Huygens (1629–1695) later dubbed the tendency to recede *centrifugal force,* and it dominated all approaches to circular motion for another generation.

Between Galileo and Descartes near the beginning of the century and Newton near the end, no one contributed so much to mechanics as Huygens. Embracing the new conception of motion and Galileo's vision of a mathematical mechanics, he demonstrated that all oscillations of a pendulum swinging in a cycloidal path, whatever their amplitude, are isochronous. He demonstrated as well how to make a pendulum swing in a cycloidal path, and he used the demonstration in his construction of the first truly precise clock. Huygens used the principle of relativity implicit in the new conception of motion to correct Descartes's analysis of impact. Imagine a barge coasting smoothly down a Dutch canal. As it moves, a man on the barge joins hands with a man on the bank, and the two together, setting two balls in motion, perform one and the same experiment in impact. Friction is imagined away, and the balls are, by definition, perfectly hard, which we can take as perfectly elastic. Let the men set two equal balls moving toward each other with speeds equal to that of the barge. From principles of symmetry, Huygens assumed that two perfectly elastic balls of equal size moving with equal and opposite velocities rebound from impact with velocities exactly reversed. This is what the man on the barge sees. The man on the shore sees a body with a velocity twice that of the barge strike another at rest, setting it in motion with a velocity twice that of the barge while the first comes to rest. Huygens assumed again that a larger body striking a smaller one at rest will always put it in motion and lose some of its own motion. By means of the barge, he reversed the two and concluded, correcting one of Descartes's errors, that, when a smaller body strikes a larger one, no matter how great the disparity of their sizes, it always effects some change in the rest or motion of the larger. Proceeding in this manner, Huygens worked out all of the situations of impact of perfectly elastic bodies, concluding that the common center of gravity of two such bodies in impact remains in a state of rest or of uniform motion in a straight line. Here was the ultimate justification of the principle of inertia—that an isolated system of bodies in impact can be considered as a single body, concentrated at the system's center of mass, which also conforms to the principle of inertia. Huygens deduced as well that a mathematical quantity proportional to what we now call kinetic energy is conserved in every perfectly elastic impact.

Huygens also addressed the mechanics of circular motion. He remained within Descartes's conceptual framework, the endeavor of a body constrained in circular motion to recede from the center, to which he gave the name, as already indicated, centrifugal force. He not only named it, but, in keeping with the direction of seventeenth-century mechanics, he submitted it to mathematical calculation. The centrifugal force of a body in uniform circular motion is equal to its weight when its velocity is equal to what it would acquire in falling from rest through a distance equal to half its radius. Mathe-

matically, this is equivalent to the formula we still use for the radial force in circular motion.

Although Huygens coined the phrase centrifugal force, his work in mechanics was primarily kinematical. It remained for Isaac Newton to formulate a system of dynamics that underlay established kinematics, both celestial and terrestrial, and bind them all together in one mathematical science of mechanics. Newton first confronted the science of motion when he began to read Descartes toward the end of his undergraduate career in the early 1660s. Like Huygens, he attacked the two problems Descartes had posed but failed to settle, and, by different routes, he arrived at the same conclusions Huygens reached. Soon thereafter, Newton turned away from mechanics, which he largely ignored for the following two decades, and his early work remained unknown to anyone except himself. He even abandoned the principle of inertia in a religiously motivated revulsion from what he viewed as the materialism of Descartes's philosophy. In 1684–1685, when a visit from Edmond Halley (ca. 1656–1743) turned him back from other pursuits to problems of orbital dynamics, Newton seriously addressed the construction of a mathematical dynamics.

When he began work on what became *The Mathematical Principles of Natural Philosophy,* Newton held a conception of motion akin to the medieval doctrine of impetus. His initial formulation of the first law of motion stated that a body perseveres in its uniform motion by its inherent force. Central to the treatise he was writing was the problem of orbital motion, however, and a dynamics that treated orbital motion as an accelerated motion precisely analogous to free fall proved impossible to build on such a concept of inherent force. As he worked, Newton embraced the principle of inertia anew, and, in his final formulation of the first law of motion, he gave the statement of the principle that has remained definitive ever since.

The first law demanded a second one that defined what happened when an external agent acts to change a body's inertial motion. From the welter of terms, such as power, energy, impetus, and momentum, used interchangeably by seventeenth-century writers on mechanics, Newton singled out *force,* and, though he experimented with a variety of wordings, he never wavered from the notion that the measure of force is the change of motion it generates. Contrary to the wording of the second law one finds in textbooks of physics today, the *Principia* asserts that the change of motion, not the rate of change of motion, or acceleration, is proportional to the force impressed. Strictly speaking, this is the concept we now call impulse (force applied over an interval of time), though it seems clear from usage in the *Principia* that Newton understood his statement of the law to embrace both impulse separated by tiny increments of time and the instantaneous action of force and that he used the law correctly in both senses as the situation demanded one or the other.

The concept of force, in its turn, demanded a concept of *mass,* which had not been present in physics before the *Principia* in any precise form. A later age has found Newton's definition of quantity of matter, or mass, in terms of volume and density circular, because we define density in terms of volume and mass. The seventeenth century, with its picturable image of corpuscles packed more or less tightly, found no problem with the definition. More than simply density and volume were involved in Newton's conception of mass. It involved as well an idea of resistance to changes of motion, which establishes a proportion between a force and the change of motion it produces. Inherent force, which he eliminated from his notion of inertial motion, transformed itself in his concept of mass into a latent resistance called into action whenever an external force operates to change a body's state of uniform motion or rest. The third law of motion, the equality of action and reaction, both codified earlier perceptions of the equal and opposite changes of motion that two bodies experience in impact and drew upon the idea of an inherent force in bodies by which they resist changes in their state.

The success of Newton's dynamics lay in its capacity to deal with both rectilinear and curvilinear accelerations in the same terms. Orbital dynamics were central to the *Principia.* When Newton had first attacked circular motion, he had thought in Cartesian terms of an endeavor to recede from the center—Huygens's centrifugal force. It was Robert Hooke (1635–1703) who transformed the conceptualization of circular motion. If inertial motion is rectilinear, then the operation of a force toward the center, continuously pulling a body away from its tangential path, is necessary for a body to move in a circle. In correspondence (1679–1680) about the path of fall of a body on a turning earth, in which the path was treated as a segment of an orbit about the center of the earth, Hooke taught this lesson to Newton. Not least because of the lesson, Newton hated Hooke and did not acknowledge

the debt. Once he had seized the new conceptualization of circular motion as uniformly accelerated, however, the path was open to a successful celestial dynamics. In conscious parallel to Huygens's term, Newton coined the name *centripetal force,* force seeking the center, and derived anew its quantitative measures.

In the *Principia,* Kepler's laws functioned as quasi-empirical constraints on the new dynamics. Proposition I demonstrated that Kepler's second law, the proportionality of area to time, follows for any centripetal force, whatever its variation with distance. An elliptical orbit about a center of force at one focus entails an inverse square force, and when a number of planets revolve around the center of an inverse-square force field, they must obey Kepler's third law.

The *Principia* went on to employ the dynamics spelled out in its early pages to demonstrate mathematically an incredible array of propositions concerning natural phenomena—mostly, but far from exclusively, celestial phenomena. The success of every proposition became another argument for the validity of the system of dynamics. It continues to be taught today as the foundation of the structure of physics. The essence of its success lies in its uniform application to all motions, celestial and terrestrial. Early in the seventeenth century, Kepler's kinematics of celestial motions and Galileo's kinematics of terrestrial motions emerged as triumphs of a new science. Newton's dynamics provided a common foundation for both, tying heaven and earth together in one mathematical science.

BIBLIOGRAPHY

Barbour, Julian. *Absolute or Relative Motion?* 2 vols. Cambridge: Cambridge University Press, 1989, vol. 1: *The Discovery of Dynamics.*

Clavelin, M. *The Natural Philosophy of Galileo: Essays on the Origins and Formation of Classical Mechanics.* Trans. A. J. Pomerans. Cambridge, MA: MIT Press, 1974.

Dugas, René. *Mechanics in the Seventeenth Century (From the Scholastic Antecedents to Classical Thought).* Trans. Freda Jacquot. New York: Central Book Company, 1958.

Gabbey, A. "Force and Inertia in Seventeenth Century Dynamics." *Studies in the History and Philosophy of Science* 2 (1971), 1–67.

Herivel, John. *The Background to Newton's "Principia."* Oxford: Oxford University Press, 1965.

Koyré, A. *Galileo Studies.* Trans. John Mepham. Atlantic Heights, NJ: Humanities Press, 1978. French ed. Paris: Hermann, 1939.

McMullin, E., ed. *Galileo: Man of Science.* New York: Basic Books, 1967.

Westfall, Richard S. *Force in Newton's Physics: The Science of Dynamics in the Seventeenth Century.* London: Macdonald, 1971.

Yoder, Joella G. *Unrolling Time: Christiaan Huygens and the Mathematization of Nature.* Cambridge: Cambridge University Press, 1988.

RICHARD S. WESTFALL

See also Aristotelianism; Dynamics; Force; Inertia; Kinematics; Mass

Medical Education

In order to situate historically the development of medical education during the Renaissance and the seventeenth century, one must remember that, at that time, medicine was the only scientific type of occupation that had been professionalized. Qualifications had begun to be regulated in the twelfth century, and in the thirteenth century so was the education to be received by those wishing to qualify as physicians. In the regulations promulgated by Frederick II in 1240 for the kingdom of Sicily, universities were already the institutions where such studies were taught. This model of medical teaching, practiced at the principal universities of the late Middle Ages, led by Bologna, Padua, and Montpellier, was limited to physicians, strictly speaking. Surgeons were excluded from university education, their exclusion influenced by the negative appraisal of manual work and techniques as tasks of a lower category, stemming from the works of Plato (428–348 B.C.E.) and Aristotle (384–322 B.C.E.). The training received by surgeons continued to consist basically of a craft apprenticeship with its own teaching institutions in certain countries from the fourteenth century onward.

The regulations governing the university education of physicians were consolidated and developed during the Renaissance. Generally, it was necessary to study first in the arts faculty and graduate as Bachelor of Arts or with an equivalent qualification. This was followed by an average of three or four years in the faculty of medicine, culminating in the Bachelor of Medicine, which was normally required to be a practicing physician. To receive the title of licenciate or doctor, however, just required the successful defense of theses on specific subjects. The didactic method was Scholastic, based on *lectio*: texts by classic authorities were read and interpreted, with difficult or obscure passages giving rise to problems (*quaestiones*) forming the object of discussion (*disputatio*).

Up to the ascendancy of the humanist movement, during which the original texts in Greek and their Latin versions were published in translations made directly from the medical works of classical times, the texts used in *lectiones* were the Latin versions translated from Arabic translations of some of these ancient works and of others by Muslim authors from the late Middle Ages. Direct, polished translations by humanist physicians were introduced into certain universities in the mid-sixteenth century and into most of them several decades later.

Some universities also introduced innovations modifying traditional Scholastic teaching. These changes were strongly influenced by the position of the faculty of medicine in each university, which was generally subordinate to that of the faculties of theology and canon and civil law. The faculty of medicine was given preferential treatment by the authorities at only a few universities. The best example is the encouragement given by the Venetian Senate to the faculty of medicine at the University of Padua, which made a decisive contribution to it becoming the most important in Europe at that time. Other similar cases include the University of Valencia, whose

An anatomical theater, with students observing a professor and his assistant dissecting a cadaver. From Barthélemy Cabrol, Ontleeding des menscelycken lichaems *(1633).*

faculty of medicine was the most prestigious and best equipped of the Hispanic kingdoms, thanks to the support received from the municipal urban oligarchy on which it depended.

The most outstanding innovation concerned how anatomy was taught. The practice of dissecting human cadavers had begun at the University of Bologna in the early fourteenth century, spreading later to the Universities of Padua, Montpellier, Lerida, and others, mainly in Italy, France, and Spain. Usually, however, there would be one autopsy at the most during the winter months, and the autopsy would be designed, moreover, to exemplify Galenist doctrines. As Andreas Vesalius (1514–1564) was to say later in the Preface to his *De humanis corporis fabrica* (On the Structure of the Human Body, 1543), the professor remained seated in his cathedra "reciting information about facts he had never seen personally but had learnt by memory from books," while someone else, "incapable of explaining the dissection to the students," carried out the autopsy, "destroying what he was supposed to show." Vesalius himself, after being appointed professor of surgery in 1537 at the University of Padua, revolutionized how anatomy was taught by coming down from his cathedra and approaching the dissection table, where he carried out the autopsies personally and showed the parts of the cadaver to his students.

This innovation was quickly adopted by the Universities of Bologna, Rome, Pisa, Pavia, Ferrara, and Naples, which, together with the University of Padua, employed the most prominent anatomy professors of the time. This method was also adopted at an early date at the University of Valencia following its introduction in 1547 by disciples of Vesalius, and this converted Valencia into the heart of the Spanish Vesalian movement, which saw chairs of anatomy established at the Universities of Alcalá (1549) and Salamanca (1551). This New Anatomy was warmly received in France at the University of Montpellier, although the chair was not established until 1593. The University of Paris, on the other hand, became the major center of opposition to this reform and was the base from which Jacques du Bois (Sylvius, 1478–1555), a former professor of Vesalius, launched his scathing criticism. In the German-speaking world, the University of Basel was the first participant in the Vesalian movement (1570). In England, the Tomlins Readership in Anatomy of the University of Oxford was not set up until 1624.

Another important innovation was that related to the teaching of *materia medica*. Mention is often made of

botany chairs being established, but in fact these were chairs of "simple medicines," most of which were vegetable with a few of animal and mineral origin. The first of these was created at the University of Padua (1533), and, as in the case of the chairs of anatomy, others were set up at various Italian universities and at universities in countries more directly influenced by the Italian Renaissance schools of medicine. These were sometimes chairs of "anatomy and simples," teaching anatomy in the autumn and winter and *materia medica* during the spring and summer, although these were split into two separate chairs at a later date. Their functions were not merely of a Scholastic nature, since students were directly involved in handling and collecting the plants on outings, and plants were planted in different areas close to the cities where the universities were found. The utility of medicinal-plant gardens was obvious, so the Venetian Senate set up one at the University of Padua in 1545. The one belonging to the faculty of medicine at the University of Pisa was created at virtually the same time, followed by those at Valencia (1567), Bologna (1568), Leipzig (1579), Leiden (1587), Paris (1591), Montpellier (1598), and others. These were not botanical gardens in the strict sense of the word; the aim was simply to collect as many medicinal plants as possible to enable students of simple medicines and physicians to become familiar with them. This did not prevent some of them making a considerable contribution to botanical research.

Clinical teaching was the third noteworthy Renaissance innovation. In most countries, in order to be allowed to enter medical practice, after qualifying as a Bachelor of Medicine, it was normal to require a certain period of clinical training in a hospital or as an assistant to a qualified physician. Such regulations must not be confused with the practice of teaching at the patient's bedside being introduced into university medical education. This decisive innovation also began at the University of Padua. Although there is evidence that it began at an earlier date, the person largely responsible for its introduction was Giambattista Da Monte (Montanus, 1498–1551) upon being appointed professor in 1539. In a ward of the San Francesco Hospital of Padua, students prepared the anamnesis (case history) of a patient, observed him, and took his pulse to draft his clinical history. This was read out to Da Monte, who then commented on the case in public. These clinical lessons stopped at the death of Da Monte but were taken up again at the end of the sixteenth century by Albertino

Bottoni (d. 1596), who also brought students into the autopsy room to show them the anatomical lesions on the bodies of deceased patients.

Surgeons continued to be excluded from university medical education throughout the Renaissance in most parts of Europe. In Italy, however, several universities had chairs of surgery, the first of which was established in the late thirteenth century in Bologna. The most prestigious chair of surgery in the sixteenth century was that of Padua, where Vesalius introduced his innovations in the teaching of anatomy. Surgery had also been taught in Montpellier, in association with the university there, since the late Middle Ages. The Italian influence led to several Spanish universities establishing chairs of surgery, the first being that of Valencia (1502).

The picture of medical education was completely different during the seventeenth century. Although Italy retained a prominent position, it was no longer the principal center, being overtaken by Holland and England. Generally, universities were left behind as a medical revolution was taking place in new academic institutions and in certain professional guilds. The University of Paris continued to be the main redoubt of radically anti-innovative Galenism, a viewpoint shared by many other universities, including those in Spain and even that of Valencia, which had been a prominent seat of innovation during the Renaissance. Some universities permitted innovation to a certain extent (e.g., the Universities of Montpellier and Padua and others in Italy and Germany, such as those of Marburg and Wittenberg, where the teaching of *chymiatria* [medical chemistry] was introduced as part of the Paracelsian movement).

The university committing itself totally to innovation was Leiden, whose faculty of medicine was the most important in Europe from the second half of the seventeenth century onward. Leiden had been providing a high standard of teaching in normal and pathological anatomy and in simple medicines, or medicinal botany, from the end of the previous century. In addition, Jan van Heurne (1543–1601) introduced clinical teaching, which was systematized by his son Otto van Heurne (1577–1652). These improvements were consolidated in 1658 by the professorship of Franz de le Boë (Franciscus Sylvius, 1614–1672). In addition to converting clinical teaching into a fundamental method of medical education, Sylvius created a chemical laboratory for "practicals," the first of its kind in the world, where analytical *demonstrations,* as they were known, concerning mainly

physiology and other topics of medical interest were presented. The prestige of the Leiden faculty of medicine peaked in 1701 when Hermann Boerhaave (1668–1738) was appointed professor. Boerhaave came to be known as *communis Europae praeceptor* (the teacher of all Europe). His *Institutiones medicae* (1708) was the text that made the greatest contribution toward superseding the Galenic handbooks used in medical schools. Through his pupils, Leiden's educational model spread to other universities, notably those of Vienna, Göttingen, and Edinburgh.

Along with the important changes introduced and consolidated by Sylvius and Boerhaave, in Mediterranean Europe an important role was played by Marcello Malpighi (1628–1694). Generally remembered as a great classic microscopist, he propounded a program in 1689 to base university medical education on the new basic disciplines. This program was put into practice in Rome and Padua.

The new institutions of the Scientific Revolution themselves, such as the Royal Society of London, the Académie Royale des Sciences of Paris, and other academies, made decisive contributions to scientific communication and research and, to a lesser extent, to teaching. Professional guilds played a more important role in renovating the teaching of medicine. In Paris, for example, in comparison with the stagnation taking place at the university, the Fraternity of Saint Côme became an authentic École de Chirurgie (school of surgery), while in Amsterdam, Nicolas Tulp (1593–1674), the anatomy teacher in the guild of surgeons, who was immortalized in a famous painting by Rembrandt, was one of the first to describe the chyliferous vessels and was also the author of extensive work on pathological anatomy. The professional guild most active in renovating the teaching of medicine, however, was that of the Royal College of Physicians of London, whose influence can only be compared to that of the University of Leiden. This point is underlined by the lectures given there by some of the most prominent figures of the Scientific Revolution, such as William Harvey (1578–1657) and Francis Glisson (1597–1677).

BIBLIOGRAPHY

Brockliss, L. "Medical Teaching at the University of Paris, 1600–1720." *Annals of Science* 35 (1978), 221–251.

Bylebyl, J. J. "The School of Padua: Humanistic Medicine in the Sixteenth Century." In *Health, Medicine, and Mortality in the Sixteenth Century,* ed. C. Webster. Cambridge: Cambridge University Press, 1979, pp. 335–370.

López-Piñero, J. M. "The Vesalian Movement in Sixteenth Century Spain." *Journal of the History of Biology* 12 (1979), 45–81.

Ogawa, T., ed. *History of Medical Education: Proceedings of the Sixth International Symposium on the Comparative History of Medicine.* Tokyo: Saikon, 1983.

O'Malley, C. D., ed. *The History of Medical Education.* Los Angeles: University of California Press, 1970.

Reeds, K. M. *Botany in Medieval and Renaissance Universities.* New York and London: Garland, 1991.

JOSÉ M. LÓPEZ-PIÑERO

See also Anatomy; Colleges of Physicians; Dissection; Galenism; Medicine; Paracelsus; Pharmacology; Surgery

Medicine

Medicine played a minor, but important, role in shaping the New Science, its influence being diffuse and in the background rather than direct. On the other hand, the changes in natural philosophy and chemistry that were integral to the Scientific Revolution had profound effects on some, but not all, parts of medicine.

The mastery of Greek knowledge was an essential preliminary stage of the Scientific Revolution, and medicine was fully involved in the enterprise. In the early sixteenth century, medical writers were concerned with retrieving Greek medical knowledge. They viewed the extensive medieval medical collection of classical texts as "corrupt" and "barbarous" and wished, instead, to re-create the original pure form of Greek medical knowledge. A result of this endeavor was that the complete works of Galen (second century) were printed in Greek in 1525 and those of Hippocrates (ca. 460–ca. 370 B.C.E.) in the following year. A critical, but not revolutionary, attitude toward Greek medicine emerged in the sixteenth century out of the scholarly work of the medical humanists. It was largely contained, however, within the bounds of orthodox learned medicine (the medicine taught in the universities and based on Greek and, to a lesser extent, on Arabic writers). It is most clearly present in anatomy and medical botany.

The rise of anatomy in the sixteenth century as an important medical discipline (in the Middle Ages it had been an adjunct of surgery), following largely upon the work of Andreas Vesalius (1514–1564) and his successors in Padua, introduced into learned medicine a new critical attitude to the past and a renewed emphasis on the decisive nature of direct visual observation as the cri-

terion of truth. This skepticism and the belief in the validity of empirical knowledge seeped into the wider learned culture of the time and forms part of the background for the radical changes in natural philosophy of the seventeenth century. However, the skepticism of the anatomists was limited to matters of observation and did not extend to theory.

The Aristotelian-Galenic synthesis of qualities, elements, and humors, and the associated belief in teleological reasoning (i.e., that everything has a purpose and that the end of philosophy is to discover what it is), remained intact. For instance, the discovery of the circulation of the blood by William Harvey (1578–1657) in 1628 was seen in the later seventeenth century as one of the great achievements of the New Science. But Harvey, who was trained in the Paduan anatomical tradition, was deeply conservative in matters of theory and strongly disapproved of the new mechanical philosophies. His image of the body was not mechanical but vitalistic, and he still accepted teleological reasoning, though he did not think of it as having the same certainty as that derived from observation.

If the knowledge of the body was reformed, so was that of plants, which formed the backbone of classical therapeutic medicine. It became apparent in the sixteenth century that the plants of Asia Minor and Greece described by Dioscorides and Galen in antiquity often could not be found north of the Alps. North European (and also American, East Indian, and Indian) plants were described and integrated into learned medicine by writers such as Leonhart Fuchs (1501–1566), William Turner, and Gaspard Bauhin (1560–1628) (for north Europe), Nicolas Monardes (for America), and Garcia d'Orta and Christovao da Costa (for India and the East Indies). Greek plant knowledge was seen as geographically limited, and a new worldwide *materia medica* emerged, but, as with the new discoveries in anatomy, it did not threaten the theoretical basis of medicine. However, from within orthodox learned medicine there emerged by the end of the sixteenth century newly observed versions of the body and of the plant world that conveyed the unmistakable message that the moderns had observed many more phenomena and more accurately than had the ancients.

Revolutionary ideas did enter the world of medicine and well before the Scientific Revolution of the seventeenth century. In the first half of the sixteenth century, Paracelsus (ca. 1491–1541) rejected the philosophy of

Aristotle and the medical systems of Galen and the Arabic writers. He attacked the theoretical foundations of learned medicine and also created a new type of therapeutics. Chemical principles and substances formed the basis of Paracelsian medicine, especially the *tria prima* of solidity (salt), inflammability (sulfur), and spiritousness (mercury). The body was perceived as working along chemical lines, with *archei,* or "alchemists within the body," controlling processes such as digestion. Chemistry was also seen as the key to treating diseases, with remedies such as mercury and arsenic being recommended by Paracelsus. Paracelsian medicine represents the first systematic rejection of the Aristotelian-Galenic synthesis, and it reached beyond classical medicine to natural philosophy. However, although chemistry was an integral part of the Scientific Revolution, and the ideas of Paracelsus undoubtedly brought it to prominence, the influence of Paracelsian medicine upon the Scientific Revolution is a matter of debate.

Paracelsus's world was a vitalistic one in which the stars could send down seeds of disease, and God was the great magician, or magus, who directed nature. The powers of nature were hidden, or occult, understood only by those endowed with knowledge by God and who were students of the Book of Nature rather than university texts. Although recognition of occult powers can be found in the foundations of the Scientific Revolution, they officially lay outside of acceptable knowledge as defined by writers like Robert Boyle (1627–1691). Moreover, the universe of the New Science was largely a mechanical rather than a vitalistic one. Nevertheless, by his rejection of Aristotle and Galen and his stress upon the value of personal experience and that of ordinary people like the miners and peasants of his native Switzerland, Paracelsus anticipated some of the most powerful beliefs that underlay the Scientific Revolution. Moreover, his radical social views (unlike Martin Luther, 1483–1546, he supported the German peasants against their rulers) and his millenarian prophecies were congenial to the English reformers in the Civil War (1642–1646) period who were laying down some of the groundwork for the New Science that emerged with the Restoration of Charles II.

If the influence of Paracelsianism upon the Scientific Revolution is complex, its influence upon medicine is easier to discern. The writings of Paracelsus took a long time to be published, and it was only in the last quarter of the sixteenth century that Paracelsian medicine began to spread through Europe. It did so in the royal courts of Europe, first among those of the German princes and the Danish king and then at the Court of Henri IV of France, but, except for isolated universities such as Montpellier, it did not supplant Galenic medicine in the universities. However, royal courts were also patrons of many aspects of the New Science, and their support of Paracelsianism provides another link between it and the Scientific Revolution.

Although some medical writers like Peter Severinus (1542–1602) and Oswald Crollius (ca. 1560–1609) publicized Paracelsus's philosophy and cosmology alongside his chemical remedies, a more dilute form of Paracelsianism became common in which the philosophy was largely ignored and the chemical remedies were emphasized. Since chemical remedies were, in any case, known to the Greeks and Arabs, and since herbs had routinely undergone the chemical process of distillation in the Middle Ages, it was easy for a number of Galenic physicians to include chemical drugs among their remedies. Many, on the other hand, did feel under pressure from a variety of chemical physicians who might or might not subscribe to the ideas of Paracelsus or of his disciple, Johannes Baptista van Helmont (1579–1644). Galenic institutional strongholds, such as the faculty of medicine at the University of Paris, gave in to chemical medicine by the 1660s and admitted it alongside the learned medicine of the Greeks.

Chemical medicine underwent a theoretical transformation as writers like Robert Boyle brought chemistry within the compass of the mechanical philosophy in the form of the corpuscular philosophy. In relation to medicine, the New Chemistry meant an interest in specific chemical remedies for particular diseases, thus making the empirics and the quacks more respectable and eroding the traditional belief of learned medicine that treatment had to be tailored to the individual patient, rather than all patients with the same disease being given the same treatment. Taken together with the commercialization of the drugs trade, which occurred at the same time as the change to treating the disease rather than the patient, the prescribing of medicines looks forward to the modern pharmaceutical industry and modern medical practice, in which it is seen as most cost effective to provide one remedy for many people; and nowadays concern with the individual patient and with treating his or her whole constitution is no longer the focus of elite establishment medicine as it was in the sixteenth century but is part of alternative "holistic" medicine.

The new mechanical and corpuscular philosophies undermined the foundations of learned medicine. Classical and Renaissance medicine was based upon the natural philosophy of Aristotle, and the former did not long survive the latter's demise. The most fundamental change as it affected medicine was René Descartes's (1596–1650) assertion in the *Discourse on Method* (1637) that the body was like the rest of the world, mechanical in nature, and that it was separate from the soul (except for a tenuous link by means of the pineal gland). Rather than the body being kept alive by the vital powers of the soul, the body was seen like a clock that stops when one of its mechanical parts breaks down. Descartes's philosophy reduced the body to a machine and excluded vitalistic explanations; although the soul was recognized to exist, it did so as an immaterial entity. In the new vision of the body, the qualities, elements, and humors of the old philosophy and medicine were replaced by Descartes's explanation for the world: matter in motion. The traditional link between macrocosm and microcosm remained, as did the view that a single explanatory theory should apply to both.

Although Descartes began from first principles rather than from observation and experimentation, he did some dissection and supported Harvey's view on the circulation of the blood, though not on the action of the heart, which he saw as acting in diastole rather than in systole and not as a muscle activated by vital forces as Harvey believed but, to use an anachronistic term, as a combustion engine, the heat in the heart vaporizing drops of blood and ejecting them from the heart as fine particles. On the matter of the detail of the action of the heart, the English mechanical and corpuscular philosophers sided with Harvey, not only because of patriotism but also because men like Richard Lower (1631–1691), John Mayow (1641–1679), Robert Hooke (1605–1703), and Thomas Willis (1621–1675) were much more experimental than a priori philosophers, being more in the Baconian than the Cartesian mold.

New medical systems built upon the new philosophies came and went. Boyle's corpuscular philosophy underpinned the chemical medicine or physiology of Lower and Mayow, who, together with Hooke, Christopher Wren (1632–1723), and Boyle, explored the problem of respiration and how "nitrous spirit" or "nitro-aerial" particles in the air combined in the blood. Iatromechanics also became popular. In Italy, Giovanni Alfonso Borelli (1608–1679), in his *De motu animalium*

(1680–1681), calculated the power exerted by different muscles, comparing the body to a machine whose parts have to be analyzed geometrically. In England, a "Newtonian medicine" came to prominence at the end of the seventeenth century that gave the appearance of being highly mathematical and mechanical. Archibald Pitcairne and David Gregory (1659–1708) led a group of physicians, amongst whom were Richard Mead, George Cheyne, John Freind, and James and John Keill, who considered Isaac Newton (1642–1727) to be their patron. They viewed the body as acting hydraulically, with fluids being impelled by quantifiable forces through the vessels of the body. They placed little emphasis on Newton's views on attraction at a distance, considering them to be close to the occult forces that the New Science was banishing from philosophy. However, in the second edition of the *Principia mathematica philosophiae naturalis* (1713) and the 1717 edition of the *Opticks,* Newton announced the *ether,* "a most subtle fluid," and this introduced for Newtonian physicians a nonmathematical element at the center of Newton's physics and made their medical systems less starkly mathematical in form.

Much of the New Medicine, however, was about principles and expectations rather than precise results. Often, the new systems of chemical/corpuscular and mechanical medicine were qualitative rather than quantitative. The analogies between the parts of the body and contemporary machines were often crude and, as physicians in the eighteenth century realized, did not capture the nature of living activity (what we now call biology). The discovery of the microscope in the early seventeenth century was giving hope by the 1660s that a new world of microphenomena would be discovered analogous to the world opened up by the telescope. The effective magnification of the compound microscope, however, was limited to about twenty diameters, and, although the self-taught Dutchman Antoni van Leeuwenhoek (1632–1723), using a simple lens, achieved magnifications of up to four hundred diameters, it was not until the nineteenth century that essentially "biological" building blocks of the body such as cells came to replace the "particles" derived from physics.

By the end of the seventeenth century, all supporters of the New Science were agreed that the body had to be viewed in chemical and/or mechanical terms. In medicine as a whole, as opposed to physiology and anatomy, the New Science was most thoroughly put into effect in Leiden, which replaced Padua in the second half of the seventeenth century as the leading European medical school. At Leiden, Franciscus Sylvius (1614–1672) based his medical teaching around a chemistry of acid-alkali reactions, and Hermann Boerhaave (1668–1738), the greatest of the Leiden medical professors, who exerted a lasting influence on the Scots who were to become the early teachers of the Edinburgh school of medicine, asserted an epistemology of medicine based on experimentation rather than on hypotheses.

Although explanations of the body, of the powers of remedies, and of the causes of disease were radically changed, much remained unaltered. Preventive medicine or regimen was still structured along traditional lines and took into account factors such as diet, environment, and amount of exercise; in other words, the emphasis on the individual was retained. In therapeutics, although chemical remedies were common, herbal ones were not ignored, and many procedures such as bleeding, purging, vomiting, and blistering continued to be used. Indeed, one might argue that the rationale underlying the new therapeutics was the same as that of the old: getting rid of a malign or noxious substance in the body.

Although medicine underwent a revolution, it was only a partial one. The lack of consensus in the eighteenth century on a single medical system is an indication of this and contrasts with the settled view among physicists of the nature of their subject. On the other hand, the clear dependence of medicine on natural philosophy for its fundamental theories was as clear in the late seventeenth century as in the classical period.

BIBLIOGRAPHY

Conrad, Lawrence I. et al. *The Western Medical Tradition.* Cambridge: Cambridge University Press, 1995.

Cook, Harold J. *The Decline of the Old Medical Regime in Stuart London.* Ithaca, NY, and London: Cornell University Press, 1986.

———. "The New Philosophy and Medicine in Seventeenth-Century England." In *Reappraisals of the Scientific Revolution,* ed. David Lindberg and Robert Westman. Cambridge: Cambridge University Press, 1990, pp. 397–436.

Debus, Allen. *The French Paracelsians.* Cambridge: Cambridge University Press, 1991.

Frank, Robert. *Harvey and the Oxford Physiologists.* Berkeley and Los Angeles: University of California Press, 1980.

French, Roger, and Andrew Wear, eds. *The Medical Revolution of the Seventeenth Century.* Cambridge: Cambridge University Press, 1989.

Reeds, Karen M. *Botany in Medieval and Renaissance Universities.* New York: Garland, 1991.

Webster, Charles. *The Great Instauration: Science, Medicine, and Reform, 1626–1660.* London: Duckworth, 1975.

ANDREW WEAR

See also Anatomy; Colleges of Physicians; Etiology; Galenism; Medical Education; Paracelsus; Pharmacology; Physiology

Medieval Science and the Scientific Revolution

The idea of a Scientific Revolution in the seventeenth century implies the overthrow of an older order of knowledge about nature and the world, usually identified as medieval. Through the nineteenth century, it was fashionable, and is still among some popular writers, to dismiss the entire period between the end of antiquity and the beginning of the modern age—ca. 400–1500—as benighted, superstitious, and scientifically sterile. Such an assessment is no longer tenable. In the early twentieth century, the question of the origins of the Scientific Revolution led historians back into the Middle Ages in search of the roots of early-modern science and the supposed sources of Leonardo da Vinci (1452–1519), Galileo Galilei (1564–1642), and Isaac Newton (1642–1727). Their research has revealed that the Middle Ages, especially 1100–1400, was a period of intense and vigorous intellectual development, in the sciences as well as in philosophy, theology, and law. But before one considers what relation this bears on the Scientific Revolution, it would be well briefly to consider the nature and scope of science in the Middle Ages.

The history of Western science through the Middle Ages and up to the time of the Scientific Revolution is largely the history of the gradual recovery and assimilation of ancient Greek science, first by the Romans, then by Islam, and finally by medieval Christians. What remained as almost the sum total of learning in the Latin West were the encyclopedic works of the Roman popularizers.

If advanced Greek philosophy, mathematics, and medicine had disappeared in the Latin West with the fall of Rome, they soon thrived within the newly expanded Islamic world. When Islam burst out of the Arabian Peninsula in the seventh century, it acquired all of the learning of Athens and Alexandria. The works of Aristotle (384–322 B.C.E.) on logic, natural philosophy, metaphysics, and ethics; of Euclid (fl. 300 B.C.E.) on geometry and optics; of Archimedes (ca. 287–212 B.C.E.) on statics, hydrostatics, and conic sections; of Ptolemy (ca. 100–ca. 170) on astronomy; and of Galen (second century) on medicine were translated into Arabic, commented on, and extended in independent works. By the end of the twelfth century, the creative period of Islamic science, mathematics, and philosophy had ended, but its legacy to the Latin West was just beginning. This "Renaissance of the Twelfth Century," as it is usually called, was at first entirely Latin in character, drawing only on the old sources of Latin learning that had always been available. In the course of the century, most of what remained of Greek science, mathematics, and philosophy was translated from Arabic and Greek, together with Arabic commentaries and additions.

By ca. 1270, the entire corpus of Aristotle's works, along with commentaries by the Arabs Avicenna (980–1037) and Averroës (1126–1198), was available in Latin, as were Euclid's *Elements* and *Optics,* Alkindi's and Alhazen's works on optics, most of Archimedes's and a number of derivative Arabic works on statics and hydrostatics, Ptolemy's *Almagest* (on mathematical astronomy), Galen's works on medicine, and Avicenna's *Canon* (a textbook reworking of Galenic medicine). By this time, too, Aristotle's works had become the core of logic, natural philosophy, metaphysics, and moral philosophy at the newly formed universities, while the other new works introduced whole new areas of study, such as optics (called then *perspectiva*), the science of weights (roughly, statics), and algebra. The new learning was assimilated into standard textbooks composed on each of the mathematical sciences for use in the schools.

The Scholastic method of instruction was the detailed and critical examination of authorities and the subjection of their teachings to the minutest rational inquiry. This tendency to subject all authorities—from Aristotle to the Bible—to the searching scrutiny of reason culminated in the Christian philosophy and rational theology of Thomas Aquinas (d. 1274). For Thomas, there is but one truth and one source of truth, and philosophy (or reason) is not contradicted by faith but completed by it. But some Masters of Arts at the University of Paris took as their mandate the explication of Aristotle's thought even where it contradicted the articles of Christian faith, such as concerning the mortality of the human soul, the eternity of the world, and the possibility of earthly happiness. Conflicts over the proper scope of philosophy and its independence from faith and theology came to a head in 1277, when the bishop of Paris

condemned 219 propositions said to be taught in the faculty of arts at the university.

After 1277, philosophy and theology generally took a turn toward skepticism and an increasing recourse to God's omnipotence, represented especially in the nominalist philosophy and voluntarist theology of William of Ockham (ca. 1285–1349). Ockham and his contemporaries explored the limits of philosophy and theology by inquiring not how things, in fact, are but how they might be, given God's omnipotence. The consideration of hypothetical and counterfactual cases could hardly yield much knowledge about the real world, but it did allow philosophers to consider as possibilities what Aristotle had deemed impossible: the motion of the earth, multiple or even infinite worlds, void space, and the like.

While Aristotelian works continued to form the core of late-medieval natural philosophy, in the fourteenth century Aristotle's doctrines were extended in many surprising and novel ways. At Oxford, the so-called Calculators, many of them associated with Merton College, devised a number of quantitative methods for the logical examination and description of qualitative change and motion. One remarkable result was Bradwardine's Rule, named for the theologian and later Archbishop of Canterbury Thomas Bradwardine (ca. 1295–1349), who related the speed of a moving body to motive powers and resistances in what was almost an exponential function. Another was the mean-speed theorem, which equated the overall speed of a uniformly accelerated motion to its mean, or middle, degree of speed. Usually attributed to William Heytesbury (fl. 1335), the mean-speed theorem was widely used and is found in the works of other fourteenth-century Mertonians.

The quantitative treatment of motions and qualities begun at Oxford was extended by the Parisian master Nicole Oresme (ca. 1320–1382), who devised a graphical representation of speeds and qualities. Oresme also extended the mathematics of Bradwardine's Rule to include fractional and irrational exponents. And, finally, in one of the most remarkable developments in medieval science, the Parisian master Jean Buridan (ca. 1295–1358) rebutted Aristotle's theory that projectiles continue in their motion because they are moved by the medium through which they pass and suggested instead that the original mover imparts a temporary power—impetus—to the projectile, which causes it to keep moving. Buridan then went on to apply impetus theory to one of the most vexing questions in Aristotelian physics:

he argued that a body continually speeds up as it falls because, in falling, it continually accumulates impetus.

These fourteenth-century ideas continued to be taught in various forms through the sixteenth century, when they finally fell under the criticism of the humanists, who ridiculed them for their trivial logic-chopping and their authors for their barbarous Latin and bizarre names. Their works lay unread until the French physicist and historian of science Pierre Duhem (1861–1916) rediscovered them at the end of the nineteeenth century in his search for the medieval "precursors" of Leonardo da Vinci and Galileo. In the medieval science of weights, Duhem saw the origins of modern statics. In Heytesbury's mean-speed theorem and Buridan's impetus theory, he saw the essential ideas of modern dynamics: the laws of free fall and of inertia. And in Oresme's configuration of qualities, he saw premonitions of René Descartes's (1596–1650) analytical geometry. Further, Duhem saw the general fourteenth-century treatment of hypothetical and counterfactual cases, such as the motion of the earth and infinite worlds, as the overthrowing of Aristotle's stifling authority, and he attributed this new freedom, ironically, to the condemnations of 1277. The birth of modern science, according to Duhem, occurred in 1277, when the bishop of Paris replaced the authority of Aristotle and Averroës with the omnipotence of God. This thesis was immediately attacked by Antonio Favaro, the great Galileo scholar, who would allow no predecessors any credit for Galileo's genius except Archimedes in method and Plato in philosophy. Favaro's opinion of the Duhem thesis was generally shared by historians of early-modern science, most notably by Alexandre Koyré, the first great historian of the Scientific Revolution.

Despite these criticisms from historians of early-modern science, Duhem had opened up the history of medieval science as a whole new field of scholarly interest. Those who pursued it, however, inevitably challenged and qualified his conclusions. Anneliese Maier, writing in the 1940s and 1950s, showed that impetus was philosophically different from inertia and so was not a medieval precursor to it. She also discovered the full meaning of Bradwardine's Rule as an exponential or a logarithmic function, which Duhem had missed, and in a famous sentence suggested that Bradwardine had wanted to write the *Mathematical Principles of Natural Philosophy* of his age. Maier identified the idea of the mathematical function, which she found in Heytesbury,

Bradwardine, Oresme, and the other Mertonians and Parisians, as the most significant medieval contribution to science. But, especially in her later writings, she was cautious in seeing adumbrations of Galileo and Newton in the medieval Scholastics and was especially alert to the very different philosophical and metaphysical assumptions that underlay medieval and early-modern science.

Subsequent scholars often tacitly assumed some degree of continuity between late-medieval and early-modern science without necessarily adhering to the whole Duhem thesis. In his influential *Science of Mechanics in the Middle Ages* (1959), Marshall Clagett included passages from Galileo's works for comparison with those of Bradwardine and Heytesbury; the similarities thus revealed—especially Galileo's use of the mean-speed theorem—implied a continuity. Ernest A. Moody, however, suggested that Galileo's early ideas concerning motion were not derived from the fourteenth-century Mertonians and Parisians but from anti-Aristotelian alternatives reported in the sixteenth-century sources that Galileo is known to have read. Since these sources contained little about such fourteenth-century developments in physics as the mean-speed theorem, Moody suggested that Galileo later rediscovered them on his own. This suggestion was later corroborated by Christopher Lewis, who found that the sources for fourteenth-century innovations in physics available in the sixteenth century were generally too garbled to have been of much use to Galileo, even if he had read them. In sum, Duhem's thesis—that there was a direct continuity between late-medieval and early-modern science and that modern science was born with the condemnations of 1277—is now held by only a few historians of medieval science, notably Edward Grant (1994), albeit in a very qualified form. Most historians since Anneliese Maier have been concerned more with the context and purpose of medieval science in its own time than with its possible influence in a later age.

But if the actual content of medieval science now seems an unpromising source for early-modern science, medieval scientific method is not. A. C. Crombie (1953) traced what he saw as the two chief characteristics of the method of early-modern science—the appeal to experiment and the use of mathematics—back to Robert Grosseteste in the thirteenth century, who (he claimed) developed an experimental and mathematical scientific method, especially in optics, out of Aristotle's logical treatises. Other historians, in contrast, notably James A.

M

Weisheipl, have seen Grosseteste's use of mathematics as a form of mathematical Platonism and instead have attributed the rise of modern scientific method to the authentic Aristotelianism recovered and then modified by Albertus Magnus (ca. 1200–1280) and Thomas Aquinas, in which is set out the proper search for the real causes of natural things. The modern mathematical sciences, for Weisheipl, have not replaced the whole of natural philosophy, but they are, rather, additions to what Aquinas had called the "middle sciences" (*scientiae mediae*), which in his time included astronomy, harmonics, optics, and the science of weights but which were later extended by Galileo and others to include motion and mechanics. Newton's *Mathematical Principles of Natural Philosophy* (1687) expounds, according to Weisheipl, such a middle science.

John Herman Randall (1961) also saw Galileo's scientific method as essentially Aristotelian rather than Platonic, especially in what he saw as Galileo's use of the twofold method of resolution and composition. Randall found the origins of this method, called the *regressus* or *demonstrative regress,* in Aristotle's *Posterior Analytics* as it was interpreted and applied by a series of Paduan logicians, natural philosophers, and physicians from the thirteenth century to the sixteenth. There is no evidence, however, that Galileo was famliar, either directly or indirectly, with any of these works. Randall's thesis was revived in somewhat different form when A. C. Crombie and Adriano Carugo discovered in the 1970s the immediate sources of Galileo's early Scholastic works, previously dismissed by Favaro and others as student exercises, in the published lectures of Jesuit professors at the Collegio Romano, the Jesuit college in Rome. William A. Wallace later uncovered even more sources in the unpublished lecture notes of the Jesuits and then attempted to trace their essentially Aristotelian and Thomistic ideas of scientific method and scientific demonstration right through Galileo's mature scientific works.

If the question of the medieval origins of the Scientific Revolution is still open, it is due not only to our imperfect knowledge of medieval science, but also to general disagreement over the essential nature of early-modern science itself. Was it chiefly mathematical or empirical, theoretical or experimental, Platonic or Aristotelian or Archimedean? Did it involve a radical change in philosophical assumptions or in scientific methodology or in both? The origins one finds for it will depend largely on which, from among all of these, one chooses.

While inconclusive itself, then, the search for the medieval origins of the Scientific Revolution has opened up the history of medieval science as a whole new branch of study, adding immeasurably to our knowledge of a previously neglected and maligned period; it has also prompted a reassessment of the main features of that revolution itself.

BIBLIOGRAPHY

Crombie, A. C. *Robert Grosseteste and the Origins of Experimental Science, 1100–1700.* Oxford: Clarendon, 1953.

Duhem, Pierre. *Medieval Cosmology: Theories of Infinity, Place, Time, Void, and the Plurality of Worlds.* Ed. and trans. Roger Ariew. Chicago: University of Chicago Press, 1985.

Grant, Edward. *Planets, Stars, and Orbs: The Medieval Cosmos, 1200–1687.* Cambridge: Cambridge University Press, 1994.

Lindberg, David C. *The Beginnings of Western Science: The European Scientific Tradition in Philosophical, Religious, and Institutional Context, 600 B.C. to A.D. 1450.* Chicago: University of Chicago Press, 1992.

Maier, Anneliese. *On the Threshold of Exact Science: Selected Writings of Anneliese Maier on Late Medieval Natural Philosophy.* Ed. and trans. Steven D. Sargent. Philadelphia: University of Pennsylvania Press, 1982.

Randall, John Herman, Jr. *The School of Padua and the Emergence of Modern Science.* Padua: Antenore, 1961.

W. R. LAIRD

See also Aristotelianism; Demonstration; Impetus; Logic; Motion; Resolution and Composition

Menageries

Collections of live animals, usually including exotic species, existed throughout early-modern Europe. They included fixed menageries maintained by monarchs, municipalities, or wealthy individuals and roving menageries whose proprietors showed animals for a fee. Some of the former eventually became today's zoos.

The most common species—bears, lions, leopards, monkeys, ostriches, and camels—came from Europe, the Near East, and north or central Africa. Expanding maritime commerce, particularly with the East and West Indies, increased the number of available species. Animals were acquired primarily through purchase from sailors or merchants or as gifts from dignitaries. The animals were usually kept in cages, sometimes around an arena or a courtyard, sometimes in separate structures dispersed through the grounds of an estate. Some menageries (e.g., the Tower of London and Versailles) were open to the public, who could also view strange animals at inns or fairs.

Menageries served many purposes, from symbols of domestic or international power, to entertainment, to scientific study. Exotic animals made dramatic diplomatic gifts. Entertainment frequently took the form of animal combats; Louis XIV (1638–1715), for example, treated the ambassador of Persia to a fight to the death between an elephant and a tiger in 1682.

Although not established for scientific goals, menageries were increasingly used by scholars to learn about animal behavior and anatomy. In late-seventeenth-century Paris, Claude Perrault (1613–1688) and his colleagues of the Paris Academy of Sciences dissected and described many species from the king's menagerie—including the tiger killed in the fight just described.

Menageries existed in almost all European countries; their fortunes generally paralleled the country's success in world trade. Sixteenth-century Italy boasted impressive menageries in Venice, Florence, and Rome. Pope Leo X (1475–1521) filled the Vatican menagerie with rarities, including an elephant given by the king of Portugal.

Early-seventeenth-century Holland swelled with animals arriving from the East and West Indies on merchant ships. Stadtholder Frederik Henry (1584–1647) collected animals at his palace Honselaarsdijk. He acquired the first live chimpanzee in Europe, which was described and illustrated by the physician Nicolaas Tulp (1593–1674). Succeeding rulers continued to expand the animal collections. The public enjoyed viewing exotic animals and birds at a commercial menagerie begun at an inn in Amsterdam in the 1690s.

In England, the Tower of London menagerie dated back to the thirteenth century. Elizabeth I (1533–1603) and James I (1566–1625) both staged animal fights there. In 1708 the residents included eleven lions, two leopards, three eagles, and two owls. Traveling menageries were also common sights at annual fairs.

French royalty, too, had a long tradition of keeping wild animals. In the late sixteenth century, the Louvre housed the royal menagerie; the collection was decimated in 1583 by Henry III (1551–1589), however, after he dreamed that the animals had attacked him. In 1664 Louis XIV constructed the largest menagerie in Europe, at Versailles. The Sun King's power had attracted to his menagerie, by 1700, fifty-five mammal and more than one hundred bird species.

BIBLIOGRAPHY

George, Wilma. "Alive or Dead: Zoological Collections in the Seventeenth Century." In *The Origins of Museums: The Cabinet of Curiosities in Sixteenth- and Seventeenth-Century Europe,* ed. Oliver Impey and Arthur MacGregor. Oxford: Clarendon, 1985, pp. 179–187.

Hoage, R. J., Anne Roskell, and Jane Mansour. "Menageries and Zoos to 1900." In *New Worlds, New Animals: From Menagerie to Zoological Park in the Nineteenth Century,* ed. R. J. Hoage and William A. Deiss. Baltimore: Johns Hopkins University Press, 1996, pp. 8–18.

Loisel, Gustave. *Histoire des ménageries de l'antiquité à nos jours.* 3 vols. Paris: Octave Doin et Fils, 1912.

Mullan, Bob, and Garry Marvin. *Zoo Culture.* London: Wiedenfeld and Nicolson, 1987.

LOUISE E. ROBBINS

See also Museums and Collections; Zoology

Mercator, Gerard (1512–1594)

Born in Rupelmonde, Flanders, to German parents, he was one of the most important mapmakers of the Renaissance. Until ca. 1552 Mercator worked at Louvain, then he moved to Duisburg, remaining there for the rest of his life.

In Louvain, Mercator was not only educated as a scholarly cartographer, but also became skilled in copper engraving. He cooperated in 1536 in engraving the maps of the globes designed by his teacher Reiner Gemma Frisius (1508–1555). One of the first maps he published himself is the *Orbis imago* (1537), a folio-size world map in a double-cordiform map projection. This map is the first widely distributed map to use the term *America* and the first map to divide the New World into North America and South America. In 1540 he published a manual on the italic lettering of maps, which became the standard for map lettering for centuries.

In 1541 he published a terrestrial globe 41 cm in diameter. Dissatisfied with the manner in which the discoveries in the East Indies were incorporated into the Ptolemaic world image, Mercator cast aside Ptolemy's (ca. 100–ca. 170) maps. Denying that Ptolemy's image of the world was wrong, however, Mercator indicated (erroneously, it turned out) that the new discoveries could be incorporated in it. The addition of loxodromes made the globe usable for navigation. The scale of ca. 1:300 million was, however, too small to be of practical use aboard ship. In 1551 Mercator published a companion celestial globe. Through the commercial success of

ATLAS
SIVE
COSMOGRAPHICÆ
MEDITATIONES
DE
FABRICA MVNDI ET
FABRICATI FIGVRA.

Gerardo Mercatore Rupelmundano,
Illustrissimi Ducis Juliæ Clivie & Mõ-
tis &c.ᵃ Cosmographo Autore.
Cum Privilegio.

DVISBVRGI CLIVORVM.

Title page of Mercator's atlas.

The last twenty-five years of his life, Mercator applied his efforts to what had to become his magnum opus: a multivolume cosmography describing the origin and history of everything created. Published were the chronology (1569), Ptolemy's maps (1578), and four sections with modern maps (1585 and 1589). At his death in 1594, he left a manuscript with the story of the Creation and a fifth section of modern maps. In 1595 his son, Rumold Mercator, published a single volume with the title his father wanted to give to the complete cosmography: *Atlas sive cosmographicae meditationes de fabrica mundi et fabricati figura,* containing as Part I the story of the Creation and as Part II all modern maps. *Atlas* then became the generic term for a book with maps.

BIBLIOGRAPHY

Averdunk, H., and J. Müller-Reinhard. *Gerhard Mercator und die Geographen unter seinen Nachkommen.* Gotha: Justus Perthes, 1914. Repr. Amsterdam: Theatrum Orbis Terrarum, 1969.

Blotevogel, Hans Heinrich et al., eds. *Mercator-Symposium.* (Proceedings Published in the Series Duisburger Mercator-Studien). 4 vols. Bochum: Universitätsverlag Dr. N. Brockmeyer, 1993–1996.

Krogt, Peter van der. *Globi Neerlandici: The Production of Globes in the Low Countries.* Utrecht: HES, 1993.

———. *Koeman's Atlantes Neerlandici,* vol. 1: *The Folio Atlases Published by Gerard Mercator, Jodocus Hondius, Henricus Hondius, Johannes Janssonius, and Their Successors.* 't Goy-Houten: HES, 1997.

Watelet, Marcel, ed. *Gerardus Mercator Rupelmundanus.* Antwerp: Mercatorfonds Paribas, 1994.

PETER VAN DER KROGT

See also Cartography

Mercator, Nicolaus (ca. 1619–1687)

Born in Holstein, he taught at the University of Rostock, his alma mater, and at the University of Copenhagen until he left to reside in England ca. 1653. His interests included mathematics, astronomy, astrology, calendar reform, cartography, and other mathematical sciences and technology. Upon presenting his invention of a marine chronometer to the Royal Society of London, he was elected a Fellow in 1666. He wrote textbooks on astronomy and mathematics and worked as a mathematical tutor. Ca. 1683 he was invited to France to help design the waterworks at Versailles.

his globes, the concept of a pair of globes became so established that globes were sold in pairs up to the nineteenth century.

Mercator made scientific instruments for Emperor Charles V (1500–1558) in the 1540s, which were subsequently destroyed. In the 1990s, three astrolabes were identified that could be confidently attributed to Mercator, one bearing his monogram.

After his move to Duisburg, Mercator created various important wall maps: Europe (1554, fifteen sheets, 132 × 159 cm) and the large world map in what has come to be known as the Mercator projection (1569, twenty-one sheets, 134 × 212 cm). Mercator spent much time and energy in collecting the most reliable data for his maps. The result was a lengthy production time but the creation of outstanding maps that constituted an enormous improvement in the mapping of the world.

He was acquainted with the leading mathematicians in England, including Isaac Newton (1642–1727), with whom he corresponded on lunar theory, and who learned some of the fundamentals of Keplerian astronomy from his writings. A textbook on spherical trigonometry provided logarithmic solutions for right and oblique triangles and gave the logarithms of sine, cosine, tangent, and cotangent functions for each minute. In his *Logarithmotechnia* (1668) and other work, he used novel means for the calculation of logarithms, including series expansions, independently of the work of Newton and others.

In *Hypothesis astronomia nova* (1664), Mercator accepted the fundamental principles of Keplerian astronomy, but, instead of Johannes Kepler's (1571–1630) area rule, he presented his own mathematical model to account for the nonuniform motions of the planets in elliptical orbits. This was a unique variation of efforts by contemporaries to avoid the difficulties in applying Kepler's second law. It involved a line from a moving planet to the empty focus of the ellipse generating equal angles in equal times.

In 1670, however, in an article in the *Philosophical Transactions of the Royal Society of London,* Mercator presented a correct statement of Kepler's area law and affirmed that it agreed best with observation. A few years later, in his *Institutionum astronomicarum libri duo* (1676; republished 1685; English ed. 1690), he described Kepler's methods of approximation required for the application of the area law. This proved a turning point in the acceptance by astronomers of the need for such approximations and their abandonment of Keplerian "empty-focus" theories.

BIBLIOGRAPHY

Applebaum, Wilbur. "A Descriptive Catalogue of the Manuscripts of Nicolaus Mercator, F.R.S. (1620–1687), in Sheffield University Library." *Notes and Records of the Royal Society of London* 41 (1986), 27–37.

Hofmann, Joseph E. "Nicolaus Mercator (Kauffman) sein Leben und Wirken, verzugsweise als Mathematiker." In *Abhandlungen der Academie der Wissenschaften und der Literatur zu Mainz: Mathematisch-Naturwissenschaftliche Klasse,* 3. Wiesbaden: Steiner Verlag, 1950.

Wilson, Curtis A. "From Kepler's Laws, So-Called, to Universal Gravitation: Empirical Factors." *Archive for History of Exact Sciences* 6 (1970), 128–133.

WILBUR APPLEBAUM

See also Kepler, Johannes; Keplerianism; Logarithms; Series, Mathematical

Mersenne, Marin (1588–1648)   M

The chief philosophical intelligencer of his time, conducting a wide correspondence that spanned Europe. His interests lay in many areas of natural philosophy as well as in mathematical sciences such as astronomy and mechanics; he was especially active in writing on another mathematical science of the period, music.

He entered the Jesuit college of La Flèche in northern France soon after its founding in 1604, leaving in ca. 1609 to study in Paris at the Sorbonne and the Collège de France. In 1611 he ceased formal schooling and entered the austere Catholic order of Minims. In 1619 he entered the Minim convent in Paris, where he lived for the rest of his life.

Mersenne's publications began appearing in the early 1620s. The first of his works to focus on the sciences of nature was *Quaestiones in Genesim* (1623), a large commentary on the Book of Genesis that dwelt on philosophical and mathematical matters. One of his most important books, *La verité des sciences,* appeared in 1625. In it, he attempted to combat philosophical skepticism, recently revived on the basis of ancient Greek sources. Skepticism threatened established philosophical systems by challenging their characteristic assertions of certainty for many of their conclusions. Mersenne's strategy was to accede to many classical skeptical arguments but to draw a sharp line around certain kinds of knowledge. Ordinary sense perception was to be trusted (taking appropriate precautions against the illusions beloved of the skeptics). Above all, the demonstrations of the mathematical sciences, starting with the pure branches, arithmetic and geometry, were to be seen as unquestionable. Mersenne attempted to refute skepticism by pointing to areas of knowledge that he thought could not reasonably be doubted. He committed himself to the mathematical sciences as the most reliable kind of knowledge available to the limited human intellect; only in heaven would we know things in themselves, as God knows them.

His subsequent publications concentrated on expositions of mathematics in most of its then-recognized branches, including such topics as mechanics and optics. His special interest lay in music, then regarded as one of the mathematical sciences, being closely associated with arithmetic because of its use of number-ratios in determining consonances. Mersenne's most important work on music was the *Harmonie universelle* (1636–1637), in which he surveyed the whole contemporary field of music, from musical instruments to music theory, and discussed, in digressions on motion and falling bodies, the relevance of the mathematics of music to the understanding of other areas of the natural world.

At least as important as these books, Mersenne's extensive correspondence linked together, from the 1620s onward, a considerable network, covering most parts of Europe, of people, both Catholic and Protestant, with philosophical interests. His single most important correspondent was René Descartes (1596–1650). In the 1630s and 1640s, Mersenne acted as Descartes's main link to the rest of the learned world. Although he did not commit himself to Descartes's ideas, Mersenne's interest in them led him to assist in publication of the *Discourse on Method* (1637) and in the solicitation of the lengthy "Objections" published with Descartes's replies in the *Meditations* (1641). Another important figure whose work Mersenne helped publicize through correspondence and publications was Galileo Galilei (1564–1642). In addition to his discussions in other works, *Les méchaniques de Galilée* (1634) was Mersenne's French paraphrase of a Galilean manuscript dating from the beginning of the century, while *Les nouvelles pensées de Galilée* (1638–1639) presented material from Galileo's *Discourses and Demonstrations on Two New Sciences* (1638).

Doctrinally, Mersenne tended to be pro-Copernican; he also viewed Galileo's ideas on falling bodies and mechanics sympathically, although by no means uncritically. In the 1630s and 1640s, he questioned some of Galileo's claims about uniform acceleration during fall on the basis of his own experiments, concluding that scientific certainty could not be had in such matters. A similar reluctance to commit himself dogmatically to any particular set of docrines concerning the behavior and causes operative in nature showed itself in his attitude toward Descartes's philosophy, with its causal mechanical picture of the physical world. In the cases of both Galileo and Descartes, it was clearly the mathematical possibilities of their work that appealed to Mersenne, in keeping with the methodological predilections expressed in *La verité des sciences*.

Mersenne published three major compendia during the 1640s. Two appeared in 1644 and one in 1647, perhaps the most notable being the *Cogitata physico-mathematica* (1644); all three presented material on the mathematical sciences, especially areas related to mechanics and motion. In 1645 he returned from a trip to Italy carrying news of Evangelista Torricelli's (1608–1647) experiment of the mercury barometer. His report encouraged others in France, most notably Blaise Pascal (1623–1662), to repeat it and similar trials, which were taken to relate to the possibility of a vacuum in nature.

BIBLIOGRAPHY

Dear, Peter. *Mersenne and the Learning of the Schools*. Ithaca: Cornell University Press, 1988.

Duncan, David Allen. "The Tyranny of Opinions Undermined: Science, Pseudo-Science and Scepticism in the Musical Thought of Marin Mersenne." Ph.D. diss. Vanderbilt University, 1981.

Lenoble, Robert. *Mersenne ou la naissance du mécanisme*. Paris: Vrin, 1943/1971.

PETER R. DEAR

See also Correspondence Networks; Demonstration; Descartes, René; Galilei, Galileo; Music/Harmonics; Pneumatics; Skepticism

Meteorology

In his *Meteorologica,* Aristotle (384–322 B.C.E.) considered a vast range of phenomena as embraced by this science. Since antiquity, meteorological phenomena were thought to take place inside the earth and in the space extending from our planet to the Moon. As a subject, meteorology had not the specific boundaries associated with it today and, as it included not only various aspects of the weather, but also rainbows, comets, and meteors, Aristotle regarded meteorological studies as a sort of bridge between his *De caelo* (On the Heavens) and his *De generatione et corruptione*. In his *Meteorologica,* he used the theory of the four elements, that all matter is composed of the principles of earth, air, fire, and water in varying degrees, and assumed two exhalations (one damp and the other dry, similar, respectively, to vapor and smoke) for explaining the effects in what could be called the atmosphere.

In the Renaissance, many philosophical, poetic, and literary works were dedicated to the topic of "meteors," various appearances in the atmosphere. Interest in this subject was also stimulated by reports of the oceanic voyages, which enlarged knowledge of the variety of atmospheric phenomena, and by new developments in disciplines such as geography and the study of crystals. Until the seventeenth century, Aristotle's *Meteorologica* was considered *the* text on the subject, and it continued to exert a strong influence.

In 1637 René Descartes (1596–1650) published his *Essays* containing the *Météores* (i.e., the attempt of the French philosopher to take the place of Aristotle in the meteorological field). Descartes's treatise was similar to a late-Scholastic commentary; it did not contain revolutionary explanations, except for the discourse on the rainbow, but it constituted a genuine philosophical novelty. Descartes focused on the genesis of phenomena, did not classify "meteors" according to the four elements, and identified clouds as the most important meteorological phenomenon. In sum, Descartes favored a purely mechanical approach to meteorology, opposed to Aristotelian naturalism and to Renaissance eclecticism.

During the seventeenth century, a new experimental meteorology started to develop outside the universities. In Italy, at the University of Padua—the center of Renaissance Aristotelianism—teachers continued to lecture on the text of *Meteorologica*, while, at the same time, at the Medici Court in Florence, a new scientific meteorology was being born. In the Accademia del Cimento, natural philosophers started to engage in research in a new way. Two factors allowed meteorology to limit its subject matter more narrowly and to improve its methods and scientific status: the invention and use of new instruments and the accumulation of systematic observations. Thanks to the patronage and support of Grand Duke Ferdinand II (1610–1670), in 1654 a network of stations, charged with collecting metereological observations and data, was established. This "Medicean network," which lasted until 1667, was extended to various European cities, such as Paris and Warsaw.

The use of the barometer and the thermometer, respectively, permitted the quantification of atmospheric pressure and the measurement of temperature, while the hygrometer, the anemometer, and the pluviometer favored new approaches to the phenomena of water vapor, winds, and rain. Observation, experimentation, and quantification became the trends in the New Meteorology.

Only in the nineteenth century did meteorology find its identity as the science that studies the physical and dynamical properties of the atmosphere. During the Scientific Revolution, however, meteorology, as well as other sciences, started searching for its proper thematic field as a newly developing branch of knowledge. To construct its identity as a science, it had to destroy the Aristotelian tradition, to create a new image, and to invent new methods and new tools for investigation.

BIBLIOGRAPHY

Brenni, Paolo, and Stefano Casati. "I filosofi e le meteore." In *Museo di Storia della Scienza Catalogo,* ed. Mara Miniati. Florence: Giunti, 1991, pp. 148–175.

Middleton, W. E. Knowles. *A History of the Theories of Rain and Other Forms of Precipitation.* New York: Franklin Watts, 1966.

———. *Invention of the Meteorological Instruments.* Baltimore: Johns Hopkins University Press, 1969.

FERDINANDO ABBRI

See also Accademia del Cimento; Aristotelianism; Barometer; Descartes, René; Thermoscope/Thermometer

Microscope

It is not known where, or by whom, the microscope was invented, but it would have been shortly after the invention of the telescope in 1608. It was named *microscopium* in 1625 at Florence, and its earliest representation is in a drawing of 1631.

The early development and use of the microscope were shaped by the quality of glass available, which was poor by modern standards, and by aberrations of the image. Chromatic aberration was caused by unequal refraction of light rays, producing a colored edge to the image. This was corrected at the end of the eighteenth century by the Amsterdam instrument maker Harmanus van Deijl (1738–1809). The other aberration resulted from the spherical curvature of lenses, producing a blurred image. Spherical aberration was not solved until 1830, with the work on lens combinations of Joseph Jackson Lister (1786–1869). What improved slowly over two centuries was the design of the microscope stand and the methods of illumination and specimen preparation.

Because of the distortions of the image affecting combinations of lenses, the simple, single-lens microscope was, during at least the first century after invention, the more effective in achieving high resolution. Success was dependent upon the skill of the observer. The most notable seventeenth-century microscopist was Antoni van Leeuwenhoek (1632–1723), a merchant in Delft. He used a tiny bead lens that he made himself, contained in a metal plate with a spike to hold the specimen; he achieved a resolution of ca. two micrometers. His research, particularly into the reproductive system, was embodied in a series of letters to the Royal Society of London.

Other notable users of the simple microscope in the early period included the Italian Marcello Malpighi (1628–1694), who discovered the capillary circulation of the blood; Jan Swammerdam (1637–1680) of Amsterdam, whose observations refuted the concept of metamorphosis in insects; and Nehemiah Grew (1641–1712), secretary of the Royal Society of London, who revealed the cellular structure of plants.

The compound microscope achieved instant popularity through the publication in 1665 of the best-selling *Micrographia* (1665) by Robert Hooke (1635–1703). He devised a side-pillar microscope on a solid base that could be used on a table and tilted at the convenience of the user. His book described and illustrated the design, with an illuminating arrangement of lamp and bull's-eye lens, and then recounted a sequence of fifty-seven microscopical observations.

All of Hooke's observations were of solid objects by reflected light. The adaptation of the side-pillar microscope for use with transmitted light was made ca. 1693 by the London instrument maker John Marshall. He invented the fishplate to demonstrate the circulation of the blood, an accessory that remained standard for the next two centuries.

Henry Baker's *The Microscope Made Easy* (1742), provided a further impetus to microscopy. He, like Hooke, improved the design and convenience of the microscope stand with an all-brass microscope that was made and sold by John Cuff (1708–1772) in London. Throughout the eighteenth century, the compound microscope continued to be the popular tool of naturalists, the majority of whom were satisfied to examine the standard specimens.

The early nineteenth century was filled with attempts to solve spherical aberration. None, however, was successful until Joseph Jackson Lister succeeded empirically in devising a lens pair that eliminated the fault, a breakthrough that heralded the great age of the optical microscope.

BIBLIOGRAPHY

Turner, G. L'E. *Collecting Microscopes*. London: Studio Vista, Cassell, 1981.
——. *Essays on the History of the Microscope*. Oxford: Senecio, 1980.
——. *The Great Age of the Microscope: The Collection of the Royal Microscopical Society Through 150 Years*. Bristol, England, and New York: Adam Hilger, 1989.

G. L'E. TURNER

See also Grew, Nehemiah; Hooke, Robert; Leeuwenhoek, Antoni van; Malpighi, Marcello; Microscopy; Swammerdam, Jan

Microscopy

Microscopes together with other optical instruments played a significant role in the evolution of seventeenth-century science. Johannes Kepler (1571–1630) was able to state the main optical theorems in 1611, and knowledge of the refractive power of lenses of various shape and curvature was acquired both by a priori methods—notably by René Descartes (1596–1650)—and by experimentation. Optical instruments lost their association with natural magic: those instruments that improved normal human vision or that compensated for its deficiencies (telescopes, microscopes, eyeglasses) came to be distinguished from other devices for the creation of multiple or distorted mages. Although the mere creation of a novel visual display at times seems to be the only aim of early microscopy, microscopes acquired a recognized role in knowledge acquisition, along with other machines and instruments of the Scientific Revolution.

Despite tantalizing or merely puzzling comments suggesting that ancient and medieval writers had some experience with magnifying lenses, there is no accepted evidence for the existence of telescopes or of compound

Robert Hooke's microscope. From Hooke's Micrographia *(1665).*

microscopes before the early 1600s. It is generally agreed that the compound microscope was a by-product of the invention of the telescope, while the single-lens microscope was an evolved version of the hand magnifiers that had been used much earlier for reading small print or performing other delicate tasks. The first reports of the instrument stem from Holland ca. 1610, and, by mid-century, pocket microscopes, "flea glasses," and compound instruments seem to have been widely available and to have been manufactured in a number of European countries, including Italy, (home of the appropriately named Accademia dei Lincei) Austria, England, France, and Holland. The compound instruments of the seventeenth century with two or more lenses typically magnified with good resolution from ten to fifty times; above this range, illumination became a serious problem, for the light transmitted by a lens decreases with its power. The microscope might be held against the light like a telescope or the specimen illuminated by a candle and a condenser, as in Robert Hooke's (1635–1703) design. Single-lens microscopes, though more awkward, had greater capacity for magnification: Antoni van Leeuwenhoek's (1632–1723) best microscopes were able to magnify 200–300 diameters.

The earliest and most popular subjects of seventeenth-century microscopy were insects. Galileo Galilei (1564–1643) made observations of flies in 1610, and a microscope-based study of the anatomy of the bee was produced by Francesco Stelluti in Florence in 1625. The eye of the fly was described and illustrated by Giovanni Hodierna in Palmermo in 1644. Other early initiatives included Pierre Borel's *Centuria observationum microscopicaricum* (1655–1656), which contained descriptions and simple illustrations of seeds, insects, human glands, tissues, and secretions. Hooke's *Micrographia* (1665), with its beautiful engravings, examined a variety of man-made and natural objects and phenomena—including molds, hair, slices of cork, and sparks struck from flint—affording Hooke the opportunity to speculate on the causes of various phenomena. Between 1660 and 1720, the compound instrument was subject to notable improvements and design variations: these included interchangeable lenses of various powers, the introduction of a substage mirror and diaphragm, focusing mechanisms, and fitting it with mica "sliders" containing mounted specimens. The microscope acquired its stable tabletop design, which left the arms free for maneuvering the specimen. Techniques of preparation for specimens, in-

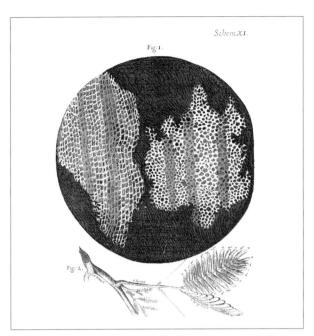

A slice of cork under the microscope showing its structure as composed of what would later be called cells. From Robert Hooke's Micrographia *(1665).*

cluding dessication, insufflation, wax injection, boiling, freezing, and dyeing, were developed simultaneously.

Fine anatomy and minute natural history made remarkable progress during the first, curiosity-driven period of microscopical research. Antoni van Leeuwenhoek described a variety of plant and animal structures, including muscle fibers, blood corpuscles, and pores and channels in plant tissue, as well as microorganisms in stagnant water, human and animal spermatozoa, and bacteria. Marcello Malpighi (1628–1694) investigated the fine anatomy of plants and animals, including the brain, sensory organs, lungs, and glands, which he construed as sieves and filters for the production of vital fluids. Jan Swammerdam (1637–1680) examined insects and reproductive organs of males and females and developed important techniques for stiffening and preserving tissues for microscopic examination. The use of natural dyes (e.g., ink and saffron) was essential in much fine work, as many plant and animal sections appear transparent or undifferentiated under the microscope. The fifth of the "classical microscopists," the clergyman Nehemiah Grew (1641–1712), made numerous illustrated studies of plants and seeds.

Advances in theory, as opposed to descriptive natural history, were several. The demonstration of the previously invisible capillaries confirmed William Harvey's

(1578–1657) theory of the circulation of the blood. Many aspects of the fascinating phenomenon of generation were addressed by the microscope, and speculations about the role of microorganisms in the generation of disease were aired, though not well established. Optical deficiencies and distortions have been blamed for fanciful theories involving diseases caused by "worms in the blood," though the deficiencies of early microscopes and their contribution to error are sometimes exaggerated.

Wider theoretical contributions were not lacking. The microscope contributed to the downfall of Aristotelian conceptions of qualities, substances, and change. On the one hand, the new natural history of small objects challenged, as the new astronomy associated with the telescope had, the reliability of ordinary human sense perception as a guide to nature and established the fruitfulness of knowledge mediated by artificial devices. On the other hand, optical instruments supported empiricist conceptions of science over speculative rationalist conceptions. Observers in the mid-seventeenth century hoped to be able to "see" the atoms merely posited by philosophers and to gain an understanding of, and control over, atomic combination. This hope, however, proved vain; rather than uniform particles possessed only of the "primary" qualities, observers glimpsed ever more complex structures before losing sight of their specimens beyond the limits of illumination and resolution. The ubiquity of living forms dealt a blow to simple mechanical theories of nature, and especially to Cartesian epigenesis. The true complexity of vital phenomena—muscular contraction, respiration, and secretion, as well as nutrition, generation, and sensation—became discouragingly evident.

After the 1690s, scientific microscopy appeared to go into a temporary decline, though, for the purpose of public and private amusement, microscopy continued to flourish. Stalled in repetitive observations and their hopes for Baconian wealth-creation through the rearrangement of underlying form dashed, natural scientists turned to other research programs. Few real advances either in power of resolution or freedom from distortion were made before the second half of the eighteenth century, and, even with good microscopes, the study of living organisms and microorganisms did not progress significantly beyond what had been accomplished in the classical period until the beginning of the nineteenth century.

BIBLIOGRAPHY

Bracegirdle, Brian. "The Performance of Seventeenth and Eighteenth Century Microscopes." *Medical History* 22 (1978), 187–195.

Dobell, Clifford. *Antoni van Leeuwenhoek and His "Little Animals."* New York: Harcourt Brace, 1932. Repr. New York: Dover, 1960.

Fournier, Marian. *The Fabric of Life: Microscopy in the Seventeenth Century.* Baltimore: Johns Hopkins University Press, 1996.

Turner, G. L'E. *Essays on the History of the Microscope.* Oxford: Senecio, 1980.

Wilson, Catherine. *The Invisible World.* Princeton, NJ: Princeton University Press, 1995.

CATHERINE WILSON

See also Epigenesis; Generation; Hooke, Robert; Leeuwenhoek, Antoni van; Malpighi, Marcello; Microscope; Swammerdam, Jan

Mining and Metallurgy

From ca. 1470 to 1550, a mining boom occurred in central Europe. Driven by the demand for metals needed for both specie and guns, deeper mines were excavated, resulting in an increase in the production of copper, tin, lead, iron, silver, gold, and substances such as saltpeter (an essential ingredient in gunpowder), alum (needed to stabilize dyes used in the textile industries), and, especially from the sixteenth century, coal. In this period, production of metals increased several times over, sometimes fivefold. Deeper, more costly mines required large outlays of capital. Gradually, small cooperative groups of miners gave way to wage earners paid by absentee shareholders who provided capital and reaped profits along with the princes and others who held regalian rights over the land. The boom ended during the second half of the sixteenth century as a result of depletion of the richest veins, oversupply exacerbated by a flood of precious metals from the New World, and the disruptions of war. Yet, mining remained one of the earliest examples of industrial capitalism. It effected the reorganization of labor and capital, produced new technologies and techniques, and, on a more abstract level, influenced the development of knowledge.

Mining and metallurgy in the sixteenth and seventeenth centuries is characterized by increasing mechanization. Practitioners made improvements in mine shafts, hoists, ventilators, stamp mills, and water-powered

By the sixteenth century, assayers practiced a highly skilled craft that primarily involved evaluating ores and testing coinage and jewelry for fraud. The latter task, connected with minting, was a complex, ongoing enterprise complicated by the production of hundreds of different kinds of specie minted by the numerous princes and rulers of early-modern Europe. Assayers utilized wind and muffle furnaces, forge fires adapted for melting metals in crucibles, cupels, balances, and weights. Cupellation became particularly important as an accurate method of assaying. As an aid to exact measurement, one assayer, Ciriacus Schreittmann (fl. 1550s), devised a strikingly innovative decimal system of weights and measures.

Beyond material practice, mining and metallurgy became the focus of numerous treatises in the sixteenth century. There were a few precedents, such as Pliny the Elder's (23/24–79) treatment of metallurgy in the *Natural History,* relevant material in recipe books, Albertus Magnus's (ca. 1200–1280) treatise on mineralogy, and the extensive writings of the alchemical traditions. However, sixteenth-century authors on mining and metallurgy often dissociated themselves from alchemy. They condemned alchemical obscurity and pointed to the fraudulent activities of the alchemists—and to their basic lack of skill. Meanwhile, metallurgists, assayers, and even learned humanists produced a rich tradition of exoteric writings destined for patrons and interested investors, among others.

These writings include small vernacular pamphlets such as the *Bergbüchlein* by Calbus of Freiberg (d. 1523) and major treatises such as the *Pirotechnia* by the Sienese Vannoccio Biringuccio (1480–ca. 1540), the famous *De re metallica* by Georgius Agricola (1494–1555), and the books of Lazarus Ercker (ca. 1530–1594), including his masterpiece, *Beschreibung der allervornehmsten mineralischen Erze und Bergwerksarten* (1574). Mining and metallurgical authorship continued into the seventeenth century and beyond. Written in Latin and in vernacular languages, such books treated numerous aspects of mining, ore processing, assaying, and metallurgy. Many authors were skilled practitioners, mint masters, and overseers; others were university educated. Most advocated the openness of technical knowledge. Their books facilitated the development of precise technical language and, in some cases, technical illustration. Mining and metallurgical authorship transformed local craft practices into rational disciplines for a readership that included the learned and the well born.

The preparation of lead. From Georgius Agricola, De re metallica *(1556).*

apparatus for crushing, jigging, sieving, and roasting. The waterwheel became centrally important, especially for draining deep mines. Metallurgists produced numerous alloys, including those of copper and zinc to make brass, copper and tin for bronze, tin and various other metals (copper, bismuth, antimony) for pewter, and alloys of gold, silver, and copper for specie. They used furnaces to reduce ores and to remelt metals for casting and making alloys. They also developed the important innovation of the blast furnace, using it for the smelting of nonferrous metals. As they increasingly utilized cast iron, they replaced open-hearth furnaces (bloomeries) with blast furnaces for iron production as well. For another operation, the large-scale melting needed for making cannon and bells, they employed reverberatory furnaces.

Agricola, the most prominent and influential of all metallurgical authors, was a learned humanist and physician who had spent some years assisting the humanist Aldine Press in Italy and who wrote his books while practicing medicine in the mining regions of central Europe. Agricola's first metallurgical book, *Bermannus sive de re metallica* (1530), was a dialogue concerning regional ores and those mentioned in ancient writings. He wrote a number of other treatises on metals and mineralogy. His masterpiece *De re metallica,* published posthumously in 1556, is a comprehensive, elaborately illustrated treatise on mining, ore processing, and assaying. Agricola begins with a defense of mining. He also advocates openness and struggles to create precise technical language, inventing numerous Latin terms as he explicates technical processes in a language poor in technical vocabulary. In addition, he describes the instruments and machines needed to carry out the processes of mining, ore processing, and assaying.

Mining and metallurgical authorship made the details of practice available for use and appropriation by experimental philosophers in the seventeenth century. To give just one example, in proposing queries for miners and metallurgists for a history of trades, Robert Boyle (1627–1691) formulated his questions by changing Agricola's statements in the *De re metallica* into interrogative form. Metallurgical authors had already displayed the value of the open discussion of technical subjects and often explicitly advocated such openness. They had advocated aggressive mining as well. As mining expanded and became organized as a discipline of knowledge, ancient prohibitions against the excavation of metals and other substances, seen as a violation of Mother Earth, also fell away. At the same time, new methods of ore processing and assaying were developed. Mining and metallurgy encompassed complicated large-scale operations, precise quantitative evaluation, and written explication within an exoteric tradition of authorship. They became rationalized disciplines described in books, just as they also constituted technological practices that formed the economic base for many of the states of Europe. As such, they provided significant models for Baconian utilitarianism in the seventeenth century.

BIBLIOGRAPHY

Agricola, Georgius. *De re metallica.* Trans. Herbert Clark Hoover and Lou Henry Hoover. 1912. Repr. New York: Dover, 1950.

Hatcher, John. *The History of the British Coal Industry.* 2 vols. Oxford: Oxford University Press, 1993.

Long, Pamela O. "The Openness of Knowledge: An Ideal and Its Context in Sixteenth-Century Writings on Mining and Metallurgy." *Technology and Culture* 32 (1991), 318–355.

Merchant, Carolyn. *The Death of Nature: Women, Ecology, and the Scientific Revolution.* New York: Harper and Row, 1983.

Nef, John U. "Mining and Metallurgy in Medieval Civilisation." In *The Cambridge Economic History of Europe,* vol. 2: *Trade and Industry in the Middle Ages,* ed. M. M. Postan and Edward Miller, assisted by Cynthia Postan. 2nd ed. Cambridge: Cambridge University Press, 1987, pp. 691–761, 933–940.

Smith, Cyril Stanley and R. J. Forbes. "Metallurgy and Assaying." In *A History of Technology,* ed. Charles Singer, E. J. Holmyard, A. R. Hall, and Trevor I. Williams, vol. 3: *From the Renaissance to the Industrial Revolution c. 1500–c. 1750.* New York: Oxford University Press, 1957, pp. 27–71.

PAMELA O. LONG

See also Agricola, Georgius; Biringuccio, Vannoccio; Ercker, Lazarus; Histories of Trades

Mixed Sciences

The name often used from the sixteenth century onward for those sciences that apply mathematics to nature, especially astronomy, harmonics, optics, and mechanics; later also included practical mathematics, such as navigation, surveying, mapmaking, fortification, dialing, the design of mathematical instruments, and the like.

In the early Middle Ages, arithmetic, geometry, astronomy, and music constituted the *quadrivium* ("fourfold way") among the seven liberal arts (the other three liberal arts—grammar, logic or dialectic, and rhetoric—formed the *trivium*). The quadrivial arts were distinguished from the others in that they were about real things rather than about words. For this reason, all or some of them were sometimes identified as natural philosophy, though they were more often seen as forming a distinct part of philosophy called *mathematica* (the other parts of philosophy were usually divine philosophy, or metaphysics, and natural philosophy, or *physica*). Within the quadrivium, astronomy, which concerns the magnitudes of the motions of stars and planets, and music, which concerns the numbers and ratios in sounds, were generally seen as coming after or depending on arithmetic.

By the thirteenth century, *mathematica* had been expanded beyond the four quadrivial arts with the addition of optics (*perspectiva*) and, for some authors, the science of weights (*scientia de ponderibus,* roughly, statics), the science of machines (*scientia de ingeniis*), and the science of the moved sphere (*scientia de sphaera mota*). From Aristotle's (384–322 B.C.E.) discussions of them, especially in the *Posterior Analytics,* astronomy, music, and optics came to be considered subordinate or subalternated to either arithmetic or geometry in that they applied mathematical principles from arithmetic or geometry to some aspect of physical reality. Because they were seen as neither wholly mathematical nor wholly physical, but in between mathematics and physics, they were usually called the "middle sciences" (*scientiae mediae*), a term coined by Thomas Aquinas (d. 1274). Some medieval authors went on to assert that the middle sciences were also subalternated to physics as well as to arithmetic or geometry.

Under the theoretical and mathematical middle sciences, there were ranged, in turn, a number of more practical mathematical sciences and arts, such as practical geometry (surveying and range-finding), practical arithmetic (calculation), judicial astrology, and the like. Practical arts in general—called sellularian or mechanical arts—whether mathematical or not, were considered ignoble or illiberal in the Middle Ages, since their purpose was to supply the physical necessities of fallen man.

The mathematical sciences and arts were conceived of as a hierarchy, then, with arithmentic and geometry—the pure sciences—at the top, the middle sciences subalternated to them, and the practical mathematical arts at the bottom. There was considerable debate, however, over the nature of subalternation and its effect on the demonstrative status of the subalternated sciences, and the general notion of subalternation was extended to practical mathematical arts, to nonmathematical sciences and arts, and to philosophy and theology generally. The medieval tradition of the middle sciences continued unbroken into the sixteenth century, though the term "mixed" (*mixta* or *mista*) began to appear as an alternative to "middle." The Paduan Aristotelian Jacopo Zabarella (1533–1589), for instance, offered a particularly precise account of what he now called the mixed sciences, which for him included only theoretical sciences—astronomy, optics, harmonics, and mechanics—

and explicitly excluded practical arts such as navigation and "accoustical" (i.e., performed, as opposed to mathematical) music. Mechanics was rescued from its ignoble and illiberal medieval reputation and joined his list of theoretical sciences largely through the influence of the Pseudo-Aristotelian *Mechanical Problems,* which was recovered in the early sixteenth century, translated into Latin, and was the subject of a number of commentaries.

By the late sixteenth century, however, Scholastic and Aristotelian theories of subalternation and the middle sciences were becoming increasingly irrelevant as mathematicians looked for method and certainty in the ancient mathematicians, especially Euclid (fl. 300 B.C.E.), Pappus (fl. 300–350), and Archimedes (ca. 287–212 B.C.E.). The mixed-mathematical works of Archimedes in particular—on statics, hydrostatics, and the like—were especially admired and imitated. Niccolò Tartaglia (1500–1557) developed what he called his New Science, a mathematical treatment of artillery and projectiles, clearly inspired by Archimedes and by the medieval science of weights. Similarly, the accomplishments of Galileo Galilei (1564–1642) in astronomy and in various branches of what is now called physics—concerning statics, hydrostatics, falling bodies, projectile motion, and impact—were more in the tradition of mixed mathematics than of natural philosophy, despite Galileo's famous claim that he had spent more years studying natural philosophy than months studying mathematics. In his last and greatest work, *Discourses on Two New Sciences* (1638), the two new sciences of the title were his mathematical treatment of the strength of materials and his new, mathematical science of motion. Motion in its nonmathematical aspects had long been a central topic of Aristotelian natural philosophy: Galileo's achievement was to create an entirely new science of motion by treating it mathematically, a science that he modeled explicitly after astronomy, optics, and mechanics—the classic mixed sciences.

Like Tartaglia and Galileo, many sixteenth- and seventeenth-century mathematicians increasingly applied their skills to practical mathematics, to geography (including navigation, surveying, cartography, and the like), fortification, gunnery, chronology (especially for calendar reform), hydraulics, dialing or gnomics (designing sundials), and the making of other mathematical instruments. Their concern with the design of mathematical instruments, notably, was an important link between

M

mathematics, natural philosophy, and practical utility, and it perhaps contributed to the rise of the mechanical philosophy. In the course of the seventeenth century, the mixed sciences generally came to include any mathematical science—whether applied or practical—other than pure geometry and arithmetic, and collectively they represented a significant proportion of scientific activity. Papers on mixed mathematics of various sorts constitute more than 20 percent of the contents of the *Philosophical Transactions of the Royal Society of London* in the eighteenth century, exceeding experimental and mathematical or speculative natural philosophy and pure mathematics combined and exceeded, in turn, only by natural history.

BIBLIOGRAPHY

Bennett, J. A. "The Mechanics' Philosophy and the Mechanical Philosophy." *History of Science* 24 (1986) 1–28.

Freedman, Joseph S. "Classifications of Philosophy, the Sciences, and the Arts in Sixteenth- and Seventeenth-Century Europe." *Modern Schoolman* 72 (1994), 37–64.

Laird, W. R. "The Scope of Renaissance Mechanics." *Osiris,* 2d ser., 2 (1986) 43–68.

Rose, Paul Lawrence. *The Italian Renaissance of Mathematics.* Geneva: Librairie Droz, 1975.

Weisheipl, James A. "Classification of the Sciences in Medieval Thought." *Mediaeval Studies* 27 (1965), 54–90.

W. R. LAIRD

See also Classification of the Sciences; Zabarella, Jacopo

Monte, Guidobaldo del (1545–1607)

One of the leading mathematicians of his age and an influential patron and correspondent of young Galileo Galilei (1564–1642). Del Monte was born into a noble family. His father, Raniero, knowledgeable in architecture and astrology, was rewarded for his military services by the duke of Urbino with the fief of Montebaroccio, near Pesaro, which was inherited by his son. In 1564 Del Monte studied philosophy at Padua without taking a degree; on his return to the Duchy of Urbino, he was instructed in mathematics by Federico Commandino (1509–1579).

In 1577 he published at Pesaro his masterpiece, *Liber mechanicorum,* in which he brought together the science of machines and Archimedean statics. He greatly admired Greek mathematics for its rigorously deductive formulations, while despising the medieval tradition of Jordanus de Nemore (fl. ca. 1220) and the practical mathematics of Niccolò Tartaglia (1500–1557). His obsession with rigor led him to believe that the perpendiculars to the arms of a balance were not parallel, since they converge to the center of the earth. He even tried to display the consequences of these views with a balance built for the purpose by the Urbino instrument maker Simone Barocci (d. 1608). His collaboration with Barocci involved many instruments, including a reduction and proportional compass, which he improved over earlier designs.

At Pesaro in 1588, Del Monte published a version of Archimedes (ca. 287–212 B.C.E.)—*In duos aequiponderantium libros paraphrasis*—and saw through the press Commandino's edition of Pappus, *Mathematicae collectiones,* one of the most influential works of the time. Thanks to Del Monte and his brother, Cardinal Francesco Maria, Galileo obtained the chairs of mathematics at Pisa in 1589 and Padua in 1592. Galileo announced in his correspondence with Del Monte his discovery of the isochronism of pendular oscillations, a claim received with skepticism by Del Monte, who believed motion not to belong to the mathematical disciplines. In Galileo's *Discourses on Two New Sciences* (1638) are several statements that can also be found in Del Monte's manuscripts, notably the claim that an inked ball rolled with a sideways impulse on an inclined plane describes a parabola, though it is not clear whether this idea originated with Del Monte or Galileo. Unlike Galileo, however, Del Monte did not have a correct theory of motion along inclined planes.

After having published *Planisphaeriorum universalium theorica* (1579), Del Monte produced *Perspectiva libri sex* (1600), a major work expanding on previous treatises on perspective and including a general theory of vanishing points. His *Problemata astronomica* (1609) and *De cochlea* (1615) were published posthumously.

Unlike other sixteenth-century mathematicians, Del Monte did not see the emergence of the mathematical disciplines as a challenge to philosophy. He refused to accept with Christoph Clavius (1538–1612) and Galileo that the 1604 nova was beyond the sphere of the Moon, for example, on the ground that the heavens were incorruptible.

BIBLIOGRAPHY

Bertoloni Meli, D. "Guidobaldo dal Monte and the Archimedean Revival." *Nuncius* 7 (1992), 3–34.

Drake, S., and I. E. Drabkin. *Mechanics in Sixteenth-Century Italy.* Madison: University of Wisconsin Press, 1969.

DOMENICO BERTOLONI MELI

See also Commandino, Federico; Galilei, Galileo; Mechanics

Montmor Academy

Situated at 79, rue du Temple (rue Sainte-Avoye), the Hôtel de Montmor was an important site of scientific activity during the years 1653–1664. There, in the course of a decade, a small circle of friends came to identify itself as a scientific academy boasting some thirty members, a constitution, rules, admission criteria, and a working agenda. By one tradition, the private patronage of H-L. Habert de Montmor (ca. 1600–1679) was the "birthplace" of state-sponsored science.

While the origins of the Montmor group remain obscure, the role of "Montmor le Riche" as private patron clearly began in the 1630s. But there is little evidence of a "Montmor group" at the hotel before May 1653, when Pierre Gassendi (1592–1655) began to lodge on the second floor. The group that gathered here signaled the beginning of the Académie Montmor. It likely drew members from the earlier assemblies of Marin Mersenne (1588–1648) and Jacques Le Pailleur (d. 1654).

Core members of the Gassendi Circle (1653–1655) were mathematicians and medical men. In addition to Gassendi and Montmor, the group likely included Ismaël Boulliau (1605–1694), Charles du Bosc (d. 1659), Pierre Carcavi (ca. 1603–1684), Claude Clerselier (1614–ca. 1686), Gérard Desargues (1593–1662), Guy Patin (1601–1672), Blaise Pascal (1623–1662), Pierre Petit (ca. 1598–1677), Abraham du Prat (1616–1660), Gilles Personne de Roberval (1602–1675), J-R de Segrais (1624–1701), and perhaps Jean Chapelain (1595–1674). Early visitors included Michel de Marolles (1600–1681) and Balthazar de Monconys (1615–1665).

But if the Académie Montmorienne, as it came to be named in 1657, grew by stages, the critical phase was underway by December 1657. At the request of Montmor, Samuel Sorbière (1615–1670) and Abraham du Prat drafted a short constitution consisting of nine rules. The goal of the nascent academy was clear knowledge of nature not a "parade of wit over useless subtleties." Meetings would have a moderator, weekly topics, precirculated papers, and discussion guidelines; admission and attendance would be regulated.

With these rules, the small group once surrounding Gassendi was slowly transformed into a semiprivate Académie. Even after his death, Gassendi's spirit was invoked to "reign over our Assembly" in order that a "true method of philosophizing" be followed. Weekly meetings (Fridays, then Tuesdays) were attended by an illustrious assembly, including secretaries of state, cordons bleus, and parliamentarians. Sorbière boasted that it would be difficult to compose a comparable group anywhere.

But personal bickering and doctrinal disputes soon disrupted the meetings. In December 1658, a legendary clash occurred between Montmor and Gilles Personne de Roberval, ostensibly over a doctrine of René Descartes (1596–1650). The dispute stymied activity for eight months. If the problem was a tendency to speechify, the solution was to emphasize experiment. After the summer of 1659, meetings resumed more or less weekly until June 1664, when Christiaan Huygens (1629–1664) pronounced that the academy had "ended forever."

Documentary evidence concerning weekly meetings, membership, and discussion topics is scarce. But old problems clearly accompanied continued formalization. Two examples suffice. In the summer of 1661, Montmor's wife fell ill, and, as a consequence, no meetings were held for three months. Throughout its existence, the Académie remained a private assembly, not a public institution; if its patron suffered, so did its members. But "membership" took on new meaning during these years. Close reading of correspondence during the period shows subtle shifts of reference, as early mentions of "our friends" and "our other experts" change to more formal reports on topics and group activities. Comportment was a constant concern.

By 1658 membership in the Académie Montmor (access, attendance, participation) had achieved greater regularity. Organizational leaders of the group included Sorbière and Abraham du Prat, while behind the scenes Jean Chapelain was a constant promoter.

Although little is known of specific discussion topics, a general picture has emerged. There was concern to avoid the "vain exercise of the mind on useless subtleties; rather, one should always propose the clearest knowledge of the works of God and the advancement of the conveniences of life, in the arts and sciences that best serve to establish them." Contemporary correspondence shows that discourses were read and discussed and that the tenor of meetings was often shrill.

Although medical and physical demonstration was often discussed, we know little about what experiments were made or how they were performed. Topics of record include Jacques Rohault's (1620–1675) experiments with the magnet; Thévenot's presentation of his "tubes"; Huet's discourse on the shattering of glass drops brought from Germany, which had been formed from molten glass and thrown into cold water; Huygens's work with the air pump; Pierre Guisony's work on vegetation; and Pecquet's dissections. Specific discussion topics include Chapelain's announcement of Huygens's discoveries on the pendulum clock, Saturn's moon Titan, and Saturn's rings, as well as formal exchanges on such topics as the science of motion, rarefaction and condensation, and the limits of natural knowledge and sources of error. Foreign correspondence was read and discussed at the close of each session.

The Hôtel Montmor represents in microcosm a critical transition in the organization of science. Yet, while several members of the group—the "Montmoriens dissidents"—called for royal patronage, it would be a mistake to see the Académie Montmor as the "birthplace" of the Académie Royale des Sciences. If an impetus for royal favor was felt in France, it likely came from the Royal Society of London (1662), while questions of ancestry—or at least family resemblance—clearly point to the French civil service.

BIBLIOGRAPHY

Bigourdan, Guillaume. *Les premières sociétés de Paris et les origines de l'Académie des Sciences*. Paris: Gauthier-Villars, 1919.

Brown, Harcourt. *Scientific Organizations in Seventeenth Century France*. Baltimore: Johns Hopkins University Press, 1934.

Sturdy, David. *Science and Social Status: The Members of the Académie des Sciences, 1666–1750*. Woodbridge: Boydell, 1995.

ROBERT A. HATCH

See also Académie Royale des Sciences; Correspondence Networks; Gassendi, Pierre; Mersenne, Marin

More, Henry (1614–1687)

Graduated B.A. at Christ's College, Cambridge, in 1636, he became a Fellow of the college in 1639. His first publication, *Psychodia Platonica,* four philosophical poems on the nature of the soul, appeared in 1642, and he continued to publish regularly until his death. He refused all

Henry More. From A. Wolf, A History of Science, Technology, and Philosophy in the Sixteenth and Seventeenth Centuries *(London: Allen and Unwin, 1935).*

preferment throughout his career but did take a D.D. in 1660. More was known as one of the leading members of the Cambridge Platonists; his theological works proved highly influential in the eighteenth century, but his more philosophical works, particularly *An Antidote Against Atheisme* (1653), *The Immortality of the Soul* (1659), and *Enchiridion metaphysicum* (1671), can be seen as early essays in natural theology.

Together with his colleague at Christ's College Ralph Cudworth (1617–1688), More was the first to teach Cartesian mechanical philosophy in England. From 1648 he exchanged a number of important philosophical letters with René Descartes (1596–1650) that dealt mainly with the nature of substance, space, and causality; they show that More was never a fully committed Cartesian.

Principally concerned to use Cartesian mechanism to show the limitations of materialist explanations of physical phenomena, More believed that the mechanical philosophy made plain the necessary role of active spirits in the world system and so provided an antidote against atheism. By the late 1660s, More was beginning to realize that by no means did everyone agree with what he took to be this obvious lesson of Cartesianism, and, dismissing it as atheistic, he began to promote his own philosophy more vigorously. More's natural philosophy was a radically dualist mechanical philosophy in which particles of matter were necessarily completely inert, all of their interactions, motions, and other activities being brought about by the operation of an active Spirit of Nature. The Spirit of Nature was the vicarious power of God, blindly enacting the laws of nature established by God, but ensuring that God was not directly concerned with mundane things and so not directly responsible for all that takes place. More came into conflict with Robert Hooke (1635–1703) and Robert Boyle (1627–1691) after 1671, when he tried to use the experimental results of their air-pump trials as evidence for the existence of the Spirit of Nature. Later still (1679), he attacked in print the philosophies of Benedict de Spinoza (1632–1677) and of Francis Glisson (1597–1677), both of whom threatened his categorical distinction between passive matter and active spirit by allowing activity in matter itself.

BIBLIOGRAPHY

Gabbey, Alan. "Philosophia cartesiana triumphata: Henry More (1646–1671)." In *Problems of Cartesianism,* ed. T. M. Lennon, J. M. Nicholas, and J. W. Davis. Kingston and Montreal: McGill-Queen's University Press, 1982, pp. 171–250.

Hall, A. Rupert. *Henry More: Magic, Religion, and Experiment.* Oxford: Blackwell, 1990.

Henry, John. "Henry More and Newton's Gravity." *History of Science* 31 (1993), 83–97.

Hutton, Sarah, ed. *Henry More (1614–1687): Tercentenary Studies.* Dordrecht: Kluwer, 1990.

JOHN HENRY

See also Active Principles; Cambridge Platonists; Physico-Theology; Religion and Natural Philosophy

Motion

The concept of motion underwent great changes from the end of the sixteenth century to the end of the seventeenth. The dominant view for much of the period was the Aristotelian concept and its associated doctrines as represented in the textbooks of the Collegio Romano; late Scholasticism already countenanced important departures from Aristotle's (384–322 B.C.E.) views—the addition of *impetus* theory in particular. But the work of Galileo Galilei (1564–1642), René Descartes (1596–1650), and others resulted in further significant alterations, encapsulated in the principle of inertia, which ultimately led to Isaac Newton's (1642–1727) account. However, not all issues resulted in consensus: for instance, Newton's views on absolute accelerations were disputed by Gottfried Wilhelm Leibniz (1646–1716).

Aristotle defined motion as the actualizing of what is in potentiality insofar as it is in potentiality. This definition was celebrated by the Scholastics but ridiculed by the moderns. Pierre Gassendi (1592–1655) defied anyone to make it intelligible, and Descartes complained that its "words are so obscure that I am compelled to leave them in Latin [the language of Scholasticism] because I cannot interpret them." For Descartes, the nature of motion is simpler and more intelligible than the nature of other things. It is used to explain other things instead of being explained by them—for example, lines are explained as the motion of a point and surfaces as the motion of a line. But as obscure as the definition of the Scholastics was, it was not so obscure that Descartes could not contrast his own definition with that of the Scholastics: the Scholastic definition had genuine consequences that moderns would dispute. Among these was the principle that everything that is moved is moved by some other thing.

Motion, according to its Aristotelian definition, is an imperfect actuality, the actuality of a being whose potentiality is being actualized, while still remaining in potency to further actualization. In this terminology, an actuality is an accidental or a substantial form, in succession or enduringly, and, thus, to be in actuality is to participate in a form. As a result, motion for an Aristotelian is a much broader concept than for a modern (for whom it is roughly equivalent to Aristotelian local motion, only one of the kinds of motion). However, motion is not just any mutation or change. It is to be distinguished from generation and corruption, which is a change in the substance of a thing: the substance acquiring a substantial form. Substantial forms are said to be indivisible, not capable of more or less, and not possessing contraries, and, thus, they cannot be acquired successively and piecemeal. Motion, in contrast, occurs successively between contraries;

motion must pass from one contrary as the term from which (*a quo*) to the other contrary as the term to which (*ad quem*). Forms in the categories quantity, quality, and place have contraries, or positive opposite terms. Thus, true motion is only in those three categories, which entails that there are three kinds of motion: augmentation and diminution (in the category of quantity), alteration (in quality), and local motion (in place). A being changes or moves, then, by virtue of the successive acquisition of places or of qualitative or quantitative forms. For example, water becomes hot by the acquisition of heat, which it has the potential for acquiring. But, since a thing cannot be in both actuality and potentiality at the same time with respect to the same form, no object undergoing change can be the active source of its own change or motion; rather, it would have to be moved by an agent already possessing the actuality it itself lacks. That which moves, the agent that introduces a form, must possess the form or actuality; that which is moved has the power or potentiality for receiving the form. Water, for example, cannot be the active cause of its own heating, whereas fire can be the cause of the water's heating, given that fire is actually hot and can turn the water's potentiality for heat from potency to act. Therefore, the thing that moves and the thing that is moved are not the same. Another consequence of the definition of motion is that rest is opposed to motion; it is the privation of motion in the thing that is naturally capable of motion.

Having accepted the basic tenet of the Aristotelian theory of motion, there are further distinctions to be made. Obviously, living things are also moved by an internal principle of motion; there is no separation in animals between mover and moved thing (though as inert bodies, they are also subject to the principle of motion). Similarly, the elements (i.e., the simple bodies) are carried to their natural places by their forms, which tend to their places—the natural place of earth being in the center of the universe, surrounded, in order, by the natural places of water, air, and fire—and natural motion comes in two kinds: downward for heavy bodies because of gravity and upward for light bodies because of levity. Thus, there is a distinction between natural and violent motion in the Aristotelian theory, and the principle of motion needs to be restricted to violent motion, or motion by impact.

Two notorious difficulties with the principle of motion concerned projectile motion and acceleration. Aristotle had argued not only that everything in motion is moved by something else, but also that the mover must be in contact with the moved thing. In the case of projectile motion, the only thing in contact with the moving object is the medium through which it moves (usually the air). Aristotle's solution to the continued lateral motion of the projectile was that the mover of the projectile gives the air immediately surrounding it the power to move the projectile further and that this power is passed on through the medium with the projectile. Aristotle distinguished his solution from another, often called *antiperistasis,* in which the air ahead of the projectile moves out of the way and rushes around behind the projectile, pushing it forward.

Scholastics such as John Buridan (ca. 1295–1358) rejected both of these solutions and proposed instead that, when a projectile is thrown, the mover transmits an *impetus* to it, which then continues to act as an internal cause of its continued motion. Buridan treated the *impetus* as a quality inherent in the moving body, proportional both to the quantity of matter of the moving body and to its speed. He believed *impetus* to be a quasi-permanent quality; consequently, he inferred that, once the moving body is set into motion, it would tend to continue to move under the direction of the *impetus* until some counteracting cause or resistance intervened. Buridan also used *impetus* to resolve the other difficulty in Aristotle's theory, that of the acceleration of bodies undergoing natural motion. Any increase in the speed of a falling body would be extremely difficult for an Aristotelian to explain, given that there appears to be no external cause for the added motion. Buridan's solution was that the *gravity* of the body is continually impressing more *impetus* in the body, producing a constantly growing speed.

Buridan's theories were discussed in the late sixteenth century by the Jesuits of the Collegio Romano, including Toletus, who (along with Julius Scaliger) was usually cited as the authority in favor of *impetus* by textbook authors in the seventeenth century (e.g., Charles François d'Abra de Raconis, a textbook writer who taught at the University of Paris). The Jesuits credited Buridan, Albert of Saxony, Scaliger, and Domingo de Soto with these doctrines, thereby giving a sketch of their line of descent. They accepted the basic tenets of the Aristotelian account of motion, adding *impetus* to it; some even accepted Aristotle's solution (about the power of the mover being passed on with the medium) as probable, with *impetus* as simply more probable. The *impetus* theory of the Jesuits was similar to the one advanced by Galileo in his early work.

There were, however, other lines of descent for such ideas. Buridan's suggestion that the acceleration in the motion of falling bodies might be accounted for by the steady increase in impetus can be found in the work of Giovanni Battista Benedetti (1530–1590), a Venetian mathematician. Benedetti's work likewise contains an argument, later found in Galileo, that the speed of bodies of equal specific gravity falling in a vacuum cannot be proportional to their weight. Benedetti also rejected the distinction between heavy and light bodies, arguing that all bodies are heavy.

In his mature work, Galileo defined uniformly accelerated motion as one in which, starting from rest, a body acquires equal moments of speed during equal time intervals; he had overcome the prior tendency to think that acceleration is change of speed with respect to distance. Galileo also developed the notion of (circular) inertia and the parabolic analysis of projectile motion. According to Galileo, any degree of speed will be, by its nature, indelibly impressed on a moving body, provided that external causes of acceleration or retardation are removed. This situation, however, occurs only on a horizontal plane. Therefore, motion on the horizontal is eternal: if the plane slopes downward, a cause of acceleration is present; if upward, a cause of retardation; and if neither, the motion must be uniform. Galileo handles projectile motion as the compounding of two displacements, one uniform and the other naturally accelerated. The uniform displacement is that of the body projected along the horizontal plane, conceived as lacking any obstacles, hence remaining uniform indefinitely, if the plane is extended to infinity. If the plane is limited and elevated, then a heavy body passing over its edge also acquires a downward propensity caused by its own weight. The resulting motion is composite; such a motion follows the path of a semiparabola. Thus, for Galileo, once the plane is removed and no longer supports the body, the body falls. Its motion continues in a straight line as long as it remains on the horizontal plane, but the body does not move in a straight line by itself once it is no longer on the horizontal plane.

Descartes elaborated upon and extended some of these themes. The basic principle of Descartes's metaphysics is the real distinction between mind and body. Body is simply extension. Descartes, in this way, dismantled the Scholastic apparatus of forms and qualities, with the consequence that all change must be grounded in change of place; the Aristotelian account of motion must, therefore, make way for the modern account of local motion. Descartes contrasted the ordinary sense of the word *motion*: "the action by which some body passes from one place to another," with its strict sense: "the transference of one part of matter or of one body from the neighborhood of those bodies that immediately touch it and are regarded as at rest, into the neighborhood of others." The difference between the two senses is the one holding between an action and a transference. According to Descartes, if one thinks of motion as an action, then one is immediately led to think of rest as the lack of action. And Descartes believed this to be a mistake: "no more action is required for motion than for rest." He argued that the action necessary to put a body at rest into motion is no greater than the activity necessary to stop it. Moreover, for Descartes, motion as transference is not in the thing that moves but in the moving object; hence, motion "is a mode of a thing and not some subsisting thing, in just the same way that shape is a mode of a thing with shape, and rest is a mode of a thing at rest." These perspectives, together with some considerations about the ultimate cause of motion, suggested to Descartes his first law of motion: "Each and every thing, insofar as it is simple and undivided, always remains, insofar as it can, in the same state, nor is it ever changed except by external causes. . . . And, therefore, we must conclude that whatever moves always moves insofar as it can." Descartes's law (generally attributed to Galileo) received its canonical statement as Newton's first law or axiom of motion in Book I of the *Principia mathematica philosophiae naturalis* (1687): "Every body continues in its state of rest or of uniform motion in a straight line, unless it is compelled to change its state by forces impressed upon it." This law, the principle of *inertia,* is the foundation of the modern concept of motion. The new concept asserts that motion is a state, and, although it contrasts motion with rest, it locates them both at the same ontological level. It asserts the equivalence of hypotheses for uniform straight-line motions—the body is unaffected by whether it is at motion or rest, and it is impossible to attribute the state of rest or of motion to a given body except in relation to another body, which is taken to be at rest or in motion. However, the principle of inertia does not assert the eternal persistence of all motions, but only of uniform straight-line motion. Newton did not recognize the equivalence of hypotheses in the case of circular or rotational motions.

In the Scholium to Definition 8 (*Principia,* Book I), Newton considered a twirling bucket filled with water hanging by a long cord. At the beginning, before the motion of the bucket, the surface of the water is flat, but, after the bucket begins to rotate, the water withdraws from the middle and climbs up the sides, adopting a concave shape. According to Newton, the motion of the water, its acceleration or change of motion directed toward the center, must result from a real cause (i.e., a real force), as calculated by the second law of motion: "the change of motion is proportional to the motive force impressed and is made in the direction of the right line in which that force is impressed." The way the water climbs the sides of the bucket shows that it is the bucket that is moving in a universe at rest, not the universe twirling around a bucket of water: "This ascent of the water shows its endeavor to recede from the axis of its motion; and the true and absolute circular motion of the water, which is here directly contrary to the relative, becomes known and may be measured by this endeavor."

Leibniz, who rejected Newton's concept of absolute space and time, also rejected this argument, which entails absolute motion for accelerations. His basic idea was that accelerated or non-straight-line motions are made up of very short segments of uniform straight-line motions. Insofar as the equivalence of hypotheses holds for uniform straight-line motions, it should also hold for accelerated or non-straight-line motions: "It is a wonderful law of nature that no eye, wherever in matter it might be placed, has a sure criterion for telling from the phenomena where there is motion, how much motion there is and of what sort it is, or even whether God moves everything around it, or whether he moves that very eye itself" (*On Copernicanism and the Relativity of Motion*). According to Leibniz, not even an angel could discern whether the earth moves around the Sun or the Sun moves around the earth.

Obviously, in a short time, significant changes were made in the account of motion, from the distinctions between natural and violent motion, and motion and rest, and the axiom "whatever is moved is moved by another," to the principle of inertia and the relativity of rectilinear motion, and, ultimately, to the relativity of curvilinear motion.

BIBLIOGRAPHY

Alexander, H. G., ed. *The Leibniz-Clarke Correspondence.* Manchester: Manchester University Press, 1956.

Descartes, René. *Principles of Philosophy.* Trans. V. R. Miller and R. P. Miller. Dordrecht: Reidel, 1983.

Des Chene, Dennis. *Physiologia, Natural Philosophy in Late Aristotelian and Cartesian Thought.* Ithaca, NY: Cornell University Press, 1996.

Galilei, Galileo. *Dialogue on Two New Sciences.* Trans. S. Drake. Madison: University of Wisconsin Press, 1974.

Garber, Daniel. *Descartes' Metaphysical Physics.* Chicago: University of Chicago Press, 1992.

Grant, Edward. *The Foundations of Modern Science in the Middle Ages.* Cambridge: Cambridge University Press, 1996.

Koyré, Alexandre. *Galileo Studies.* Trans. J. Mepham. Atlantic City, NJ: Humanities Press, 1978.

Wallace, William A. *Galileo and His Sources: The Heritage of the Collegio Romano in Galileo's Science.* Princeton: Princeton University Press, 1984.

ROGER ARIEW

See also Aristotelianism; Benedetti, Giovanni Battista; Descartes, René; Galilei, Galileo; Impetus; Inertia; Newton, Isaac

Museums and Collections

Museums and collecting became a standard feature of early-modern science by the middle of the sixteenth century. During that period, the first museums of natural history, instrument collections, and botanical gardens appeared in Europe. Initially housed in the studies of late-Renaissance humanists, courtiers, and princes, scientific collections mingled with growing collections of books to create rooms that ideally contained all of the knowledge of the world through its objects. Described by contemporaries as "theaters of nature," "wonder rooms," and "cabinets of curiosities," these early museums reflected the growing interest in material culture among physicians, apothecaries, mathematicians, and natural philosophers of this period. They also demonstrated the importance of the unity of all knowledge as a philosophical goal: what made these collections curious and wondrous was the mingling of objects all in one place. Paintings, antiquities, books of dried plants, exotic animals, and fossils cohabited with armillary spheres, Galilean telescopes and microscopes, perpetual-motion machines, and pneumatic air pumps; Egyptian mummies and Chinese scrolls surrounded an exhibit of a mermaid, all overseen by a crocodile hanging from the ceiling. In the early-modern museum, virtually every form of knowledge was represented by at least one object.

Museums initially appeared in the homes of private scholars who turned their studies into theaters of knowledge. While the first museums may initially have arisen from a desire to possess the natural objects and scientific instruments described in ancient texts, such as Pliny the Elder's (23/24–79) *Natural History* and Ptolemy's (ca. 100–ca. 170) *Geography,* later museums surely arose due to the popularity of these sites as centers for learned conversation. As travel became a more common feature of scientific life in the late sixteenth century, scholars began to visit each other's museums and describe them in letters and published travel diaries; in turn, collectors publicized their acquisitions through museum catalogs, a new genre of writings that first appeared in 1565. Soon, no scholar could appear at a museum without bearing a new object for the collection, and no participant in this collecting culture could write a scientific book without referring to the prize objects in his collection, whether they were rare plants from the Americas, such as tobacco and corn, or important instruments, such as a surveying device and an achromatic lens. By the seventeenth century, objects had become an essential point of reference for the empirical work of science; without them, many philosophers believed, all conclusions were mere speculations subject to doubt.

The emphasis on material culture heralded by the museum was particularly important to the field of natural history. Throughout Europe, physicians, surgeons, and apothecaries collected specimens in order to create better medicines and to satisfy their curiosity about the strange facts of nature (such as whether a bear licked its cubs into shape after their birth). For instance, the French surgeon Ambroise Paré (ca. 1510–1590) created a cabinet of medical oddities to remind himself about the more unusual things produced by, and found in, the human body, from monstrous births and human horns to intestinal worms and nails found in the stomachs of his patients. Such objects made the human body comprehensible within a larger system of understanding that imagined nature to be a constantly creative force that could produce images at will wherever it pleased this deity (or God through nature) to leave its mark. Thus, collecting provided a means of understanding and even displaying natural knowledge in its broadest sense.

Collecting also provided a focal point for the revitalization of natural history as a discipline. In Bologna, Ulisse Aldrovandi (1522–1605) attempted to write a new natural history to rival those of Aristotle (384–322 B.C.E.) and Pliny, using the objects in his collection; in Rome, the pope encouraged his Court physician Michele Mercati (1541–1593) to create a Vatican mineralogical collection to perfect the study of this part of nature. Both men were products of the training offered by a generation of medical professors, from Rabelais's teacher Guillaume Rondelet (1507–1566) in Montpellier to Luca Ghini (ca. 1490–1556) in Bologna and later Pisa, who gradually introduced natural history into the medical curriculum. By the seventeenth century, several generations of medical students had helped their professors describe, depict, and collect specimens on field trips; they had witnessed anatomies in museums and memorized plants in the great university botanical gardens at Padua, Pisa, Bologna, Basel, Montpellier, and Leiden. Some, like the Spanish Court physician Francisco Hernández (1514–1587), had even committed themselves to writing natural histories of regions unknown to the ancients, such as Mexico, spending years in great physical discomfort attempting to interview natives about indigenous flora and fauna. They understood natural history as a fully empirical enterprise.

Prior to the seventeenth century, very few museums had any sort of institutional identity, save for collections associated with university botanical gardens and anatomy theaters. With the growth of scientific societies in the 1630s through the 1660s, museums became more firmly associated with scientific institutions, appearing in Jesuit colleges throughout Europe, in settings such as the Royal Society of London and the Paris Académie Royal des Sciences, and in the meeting houses for colleges of physicians and of surgeons in such cities as Amsterdam and Delft. The development of such instruments as the telescope, the microscope, the barometer, and the air pump during this period gave new significance to the activities within a museum: rather than emphasize the accumulation of novel objects, unknown to the ancients, scholars highlighted the novelty of the procedures with which they investigated nature. By the late seventeenth century, the museum had become a site for heated scientific debates on virtually every imaginable subject; they gave physical reality to the Republic of Letters, which otherwise existed only on paper and defined the early-modern scientific community. Traveling among collections and witnessing experiments, the learned world imagined the museum as an ideal setting in which to test assumptions about nature in front of an audience.

Early in the seventeenth century, natural philosophers hoped that the museum would provide the necessary materials out of which to create a new, more empirically grounded theory of knowledge. Most famously, the English statesman and philosopher Francis Bacon (1561–1626) suggested that a museum would be the place in which to deposit all of the facts of nature and all of the useful inventions of humankind. Bacon hoped that new objects would reveal new facts, and he imagined physical possession of nature to be a necessary step in its intellectual mastery. Other philosophers, such as René Descartes (1596–1650), overwhelmed by the sheer quantity of information that poured into museums, suggested that the search for complete knowledge was a fruitless endeavor; it was better to have one well-reasoned thought. In short, the act of collecting nature provided a focal point for debates about the importance of induction versus deduction, in which the collectors themselves obviously sided with Bacon. By the end of the seventeenth century, the museum had become the most important place within which to contain and make new knowledge. The continued existence of science museums as both research sites and as centers for public education testifies to the significance of the early-modern obsession with the objects of science.

BIBLIOGRAPHY

Findlen, Paula. *Possessing Nature: Museums, Collecting, and Scientific Culture in Early Modern Italy.* Berkeley and Los Angeles: University of California Press, 1994.

Impey, Oliver, and Arthur MacGregor. *The Origins of Museums: The Cabinet of Curiosities in Sixteenth- and Seventeenth-Century Europe.* Oxford: Clarendon, 1985.

MacGregor, Arthur, ed. *Tradescant's Rarities: Essays on the Foundation of the Ashmolean Museum 1683.* Oxford: Clarendon, 1983.

Olmi, Giuseppe. *L'inventario del mondo: catalogazione della nature e luoghi del sapere nella prima età moderna.* Bologna: il Mulino, 1992.

Pomian, Krzysztof. *Collectors and Curiosities: Paris and Venice, 1500–1800.* Trans. Elizabeth Wiles-Portier. London: Polity, 1990.

PAULA FINDLEN

See also Botanical Gardens; Menageries

Music/Harmonics

Up to the eighteenth century, music was a science (*musica theorica*) and a practice (*musica practica*). The latter included composition and its rules, which musicians wrote mainly for musicians. At the beginning of the seventeenth century, a distinction existed between the *Prima* and the *Seconda prattica*. The first was the practice of counterpoint introduced in the twelfth century, the rules of which Gioseffo Zarlino (1517–1590) codified in the sixteenth century. The second was a freer approach to contrapuntal writing, which paved the way for the chordal structure of Baroque music. Philosophers wrote *musica theorica* mainly for philosophers. Its object was harmony, understood as order and proportion among the different parts of a whole. Its scope ranged from the narrow sphere of the rules of composition and of tonal relationships to the larger ones of cosmology, mathematics, and natural philosophy. Its model was, for long, the Boethian tripartition of music into *mundana, humana,* and *instrumentalis* (harmony of the cosmos, of the mind-body relationship, and of sounds and voices), which reflected musically the classic tripartition of theoretical philosophy into metaphysics, mathematics, and physics. The distinction between *musica theorica* and *musica practica* reflected the distinction between reason and experience. Pythagoras (fl. sixth century B.C.E.) had introduced into music the dominion of *ratio* over *sensus,* rationalizing a numerical limit for consonance: the numbers one to four, which defined unison (1:1), octave (1:2), fifth (2:3), and fourth (3:4).

The origin and foundation of harmony was the *sounding number,* the subject of the age-old intellectual tradition of the science of music. The Pythagorean consonances had been the cornerstones of musical composition up to the twelfth–thirteenth centuries. Polyphonic music in the thirteenth century led to the introduction of not just successive, but simultaneous, voices, involving the use of intervals, such as the major and minor thirds (4:5 and 5:6, respectively), which did not fit with the Pythagorean tuning synthesized by Boethius (480–524). Theorists had to come up with a new system of consonance and intonation, and this was the achievement of Renaissance musical thought. The men of the sixteenth century were the first to intuit the continuity of *musica theorica,* which stretched back before Boethius to the Greco-Latin musical sources they had rediscovered. They also understood that the very continuity of *musica*

The first edition of Gioseffo Zarlino's work on the science of music.

theorica depended on its exact position in the classification of knowledge, in which music was a theoretic discipline that stood alongside arithmetic, geometry, and astronomy. More than in previous times, the sixteenth century saw a much greater integration between music and science, especially mathematics and cosmology, than it had had since Plato's (428–348 B.C.E.) time. The speculative musical treatise revived and, until the eighteenth century, remained the basic scientific-musical genre. Other Renaissance musical writings imitated the literary genres of the humanists, notably the dialogical one. Earlier editions of previously neglected ancient musical sources were published. Music became a theoretical subject in the books of magic and natural philosophy, of mathematics, of cosmology, of architecture, and of medicine.

It was in the context of the "Music Renaissance" that Gioseffo Zarlino's reform of the Pythagorean-Boethian theory of consonance and intonation took place. In his *Istitutioni harmoniche* (1558), Zarlino was the first to challenge the authority of Pythagoras and Boethius with a view to adapting the science of the "sounding number" to the musical practice of the time.

Zarlino reaffirmed the priority of *ratio* over *sensus* but defined a new numerical limit for consonance, the *senario,* or numbers one to six, which took in the thirds (4:5, 5:6) and the major sixth (3:5). He also put forward a "natural" tuning, where all the consonances were "just." Besides reforming tradition, Zarlino reformed its scientific genre, the speculative musical treatise. In his *Dimostrationi harmoniche* (1571), he linked the dialogical genre of the humanists to the geometrical demonstration that Euclid's (fl. 300 B.C.E.) *Elements* and its Neoplatonic commentaries had placed at the center of the Renaissance debate on scientific method. The passage from arithmetic to geometry changed the place of music in the realm of mathematics. The "sounding number" no longer had a meaning of its own, independent of the musical continuum, and music grew away from arithmetic toward the sciences of continuous quantity, as in geometry, astronomy, and cosmology.

The geometrical grounding of *musica theorica* continued with René Descartes (1596–1650) and Johannes Kepler (1571–1630). In Descartes's *Compendium musicae* (written 1618, edited 1650), the musical continuum generated the numerical values of duration and pitch of the voices deduced by a simple geometrical magnitude, the line, spatial representation of musical sound. In the third book of his *Harmonices mundi libri V* (1619), on the other hand, Kepler worked out the consonances from the regular polygons inscribed in the circle and applied them to the motions of voices, to the motions of sublunar nature, and to the motions of the heavens. Kepler united geometry, music, and astronomy, linking the polyphonic revolution unknown to the ancients to the astronomical revolution of the moderns. Descartes combined geometry, music, and arithmetic, simplifying Zarlino's *senario* and grounding harmony in the "sounding numbers" two, three, and five. Music led Descartes, inspired by Zarlino and Proclus's (410–485) *Commentary on Euclid,* to "universal mathematics"; it led Kepler, inspired by Zarlino and Proclus's *Commentary* on Plato's *Timaeus,* to the laws of planetary motion.

Until this time, *musica theorica* had explained harmony through a mathematical paradigm far removed from the physical nature of sound. Musical harmony sprang from the harmony in the mind of the "geometrizing God," who had located number, weight, and measure in the Creation. Seventeenth-century musical science, in contrast, sought harmony in the physical laws of the "sounding body." In the tradition of Aristotelian natural philosophy, sound was already viewed as a sensible quality that was the object of hearing, and music was a discipline that brought natural explanations to investigations into the nature, propagation, and reception of sound.

In the second half of the sixteenth century, Giovanni Battista Benedetti (1530–1590) had applied the Aristotelian theory of time as measure of motion to vibrations produced in the air by the sounding source. The proportion between the times of the vibrations quantified musical consonances, which were now accounted for physically by the periodic motion of sounds. The attack on the "arithmetical universals" in music was then continued by Vincenzo Galilei (1520–1591), the father of Galileo Galilei. Like Benedetti, Vincenzo Galilei criticized the syntonic diatonic tuning of Zarlino and set against the perfection of the "sounding number," the *"esperienza delle cose maestra."* This proved to him how the "sounding number" depended on the material constituents of the "sounding body": tension of strings, cross-section area, mass of the material, volume of pipes. The primacy afforded motion and matter over number was the premise of seventeenth-century musical science. In his *Harmonie universelle* (1636–1637), Marin Mersenne (1588–1648) translated the Augustinian concept of universal harmony into the language of Archimedean mechanics. Mersenne's definition of the first mechanical law of the vibrating string still intersected the two levels of musical discourse, metaphysical and natural, but, for the first time in a musical treatise, the experimental study of sound introduced the study of musical theory. Mersenne's interweaving of the science of sound and the Platonic-Christian idea of universal harmony gave rise to two modern traditions of writings on music: on the one hand, the experimental genre, which expanded in the European academies of science up to the eighteenth century, on the other hand, the encyclopedic genre, from Athanasius Kircher (1602–1680) to Caramuel de Lobkowitz (1606–1682), which, under the influence of the universal-language tradition, inspired Gottfried Wilhelm Leibniz's (1646–1716) metaphysics of harmony. More decidedly than Mersenne, Galileo Galilei (1564–1642), in his *Discourses on Two New Sciences* (1638), recycled the theory of consonance in his new sciences of elasticity and kinematics. Galileo assimilated the law of the simple harmonic motion of an ideal pendulum to the kinematics of the vibrating string and

proved experimentally that the frequency of the periodic motions of the string was the physical cause of the pitch of sounds. The kinematics of consonance laid the basis for a physiology of sound perception that Galileo limited to the tympanic membrane, which he compared to a deformable body capable of oscillating in synchrony with the regular impulses transmitted in the air by the resonator. Music became a chapter of the mechanics of elastic bodies, and the new paradigm changed the contents and the lexicon of musical science.

Speculative music treatises recorded these changes. In Pietro Mengoli's (1625–1686) *Speculationi di musica* (1670) and in four treatises by Daniello Bartoli (1608–1685), the search for the physical basis of music went hand in hand with the search for its anatomical and physiological basis, in line with the musical studies carried out by the scientists of the Royal Society of London and the Académie Royale des Sciences in Paris. Between the late seventeenth century and the early eighteenth, experimental philosophy showed that a string vibrates in many ways at the same time and, by virtue of its own fundamental sound, generates the series of its concomitant harmonic sounds. "Perfect harmony" existed in nature as a physical law of the "sounding body." The discovery of the "natural" principle of harmony, hidden away for two millennia in nature's womb, became a part of the music theorist's cultural baggage only in the years following. For more than a century after introduction of the physico-mathematical paradigm, the search for the "natural" principle of harmony had been separated from the search of its "musical" principle. It was not until the early eighteenth century that the modern theory of harmony and the experimental science of sound converged.

BIBLIOGRAPHY

Christensen, T. *Rameau and Musical Thought in the Enlightenment.* Cambridge: Cambridge University Press, 1993.

Cohen, H. F. *Quantifying Music: The Science of Music at the First Stage of the Scientific Revolution.* Dordrecht: Reidel, 1984.

Gozza, P., ed. *La musica nella Rivoluzione Scientifica del seicento.* Bologna: il Mulino, 1989.

Palisca, C. V. "Was Galileo's Father an Experimental Scientist?" In *Music and Science in the Age of Galileo,* ed. V. Coelho. Dordrecht: Kluwer, 1992, pp. 143–151.

Walker, D. P. *Studies in Musical Science in the Late Renaissance.* London: Warburg Institute, 1978.

PAOLO GOZZA

See also Acoustics

N

Napier, John (1550–1617)

A Scottish landowner (not a peer), he was educated at St. Andrews University and possibly abroad. Although known principally for his development and publication in 1614 of logarithms (the word, meaning "ratio or reckoning number," was not new, but Napier's specific meaning was), which soon led to a computational aid dominant for 350 years, Napier showed many of the more usual enthusiasms of his class and time, such as agricultural development, a strong Protestantism, and military invention.

In mathematics, Napier gave rules suitable for logarithmic use and, still known as *Napier's analogies,* for solving right-angled spherical triangles (1614) and publicized in his *Rabdologiae* (1617) both his popular elementary calculating rods and a "promptuary," which is a more involved form of calculating machine. Earlier work on arithmetic and algebra remained unpublished until 1839.

Arising from medieval kinematical notions, Napier's logarithmic calculations seem to have been developed from the early 1590s up to their publication, complete with tables and a text showing their use in facilitating trigonometric calculations in astronomy, surveying, and navigation. Logarithms in Napier's own form, where neither $\log xy = \log x + \log y$ nor $\log 1 = 0$ applies, were short lived and were soon replaced by those of Henry Briggs (1551–1631), who discussed improvements with Napier and produced better-constructed short tables in 1617 and extensive tables in 1624. Irrespective of its practical use in calculations, the notion of logarithm, which is inverse to that of an exponential, remains a fundamental of mathematical theory.

BIBLIOGRAPHY

Bryden, D. J. *Napier's Bones: A History and Instruction Manual.* London: Harriet Wynter, 1992.

Coolidge, Julian L. *The Mathematics of Great Amateurs.* Oxford: Oxford University Press, 1949. Repr. New York: Dover, 1963.

JON V. PEPPER

See also Briggs, Henry; Logarithms

Natural History

As a field of inquiry, natural history has commonly been defined in one of two ways: by its objects and by its methods. First, it has been used to refer to the study of all natural objects, whether animal, vegetable, or mineral; in this sense, natural history might be seen as an umbrella discipline encompassing zoology, botany, and mineralogy, together with other subdisciplines dealing with natural phenomena (e.g., meteorology). Second, *natural history* has also been used to refer to empirical or descriptive modes of investigation, to be contrasted with the more theoretical or mathematical methods of *natural philosophy.* Both of these senses of the term suggest the breadth of areas that have been considered to be natural history over time. Though the ancients wrote *natural histories,* and most societies throughout the world have acquired extensive knowledge of their local environments, natural history as a discipline rose to particular prominence during the Scientific Revolution, when it captured the attention of scholars, physicians, virtuosi, and members of the new scientific societies alike. What had, in antiquity, been primarily a literary tradition became one of the major focuses of scientific activity during the early-modern period.

Several traditions met to form the natural history of the sixteenth and seventeenth centuries. Pliny the Elder's (23/24–79) *Natural Histories,* dating from the first century, was to prove enormously influential. Pliny regaled his Roman readers with "natural histories," stories of the strange forms and wonderful powers of peoples, creatures, and objects of the Mediterranean and beyond. For him, as for many of the ancients, a natural history was a story or narrative illustrating the basic qualities, or nature, of an object or a creature. While the Greek philosophers Aristotle and Theophrastus shared this basic understanding, they developed natural history in a different direction, one that would prove equally influential. With Aristotle's (384–322 B.C.E.) writings on animals (*History of Animals* and *On the Parts of Animals,* fourth century B.C.E.) and Theophrastus's on plants and minerals (*History of Plants, Causes of Plants,* and *On Rocks,* third century B.C.E.), zoology, botany, and mineralogy were treated systematically, as attempts to understand the variety of natural forms at a deeper, more fundamental level. Outlining the various *differentiae* (differences) that separated the appearance and other features of a natural object, the two Peripatetic philosophers attempted to formulate logical divisions structuring the natural world. Still another direction was taken by Dioscorides, whose first-century collection of *materia medica* (medicinal substances) was preserved in numerous forms and came to be one of the key sources of information on ancient natural history. During the Middle Ages, bestiaries and encyclopedic compendia offered readers Christian interpretations of the natural world's moral meanings.

The Renaissance saw the awakening of varied forms of interest in natural history. An influx of strange new natural objects from the Americas, Africa, and Asia, together with the invention of printing and a host of other factors, led Europeans to widespread interest in the close investigation of all things "natural." Numerous histories of plants, animals, and other natural phenomena were compiled, and new techniques of observation, illustration, and identification were developed to analyze specimens.

In the early years of the seventeenth century, the English philosopher Francis Bacon (1561–1626) gave natural history a crucial status in his project for the reorganization of science. In *The Advancement of Learning,* as well as in *New Organon,* Bacon laid out a set of ambitious proposals for the collection of knowledge about the natural world, with this natural history to serve as a foundation for the natural philosophy to be derived inductively from it. Bacon's conception of natural history lent yet another powerful impetus to empirical studies of the natural world. Upon the foundation of the Royal Society of London in 1660, for example, its members undertook natural histories of entities ranging from air, nitre, and fire, to entire countries. Elsewhere in Europe and the colonies, naturalists rushed to accumulate information about species and natural objects of all kinds, often drawing on the knowledge of indigenous peoples. They wrote up their findings in the form of travel reports, local floras, and contributions to the scientific journals then emerging. By the early eighteenth century, numerous systems for classifying this information had come into existence; the botanical one proposed by the Swedish professor Carl Linnaeus (1707–1778) standardized nomenclature and eventually won the day.

Natural history may have been prominent in the Scientific Revolution, but was there a scientific revolution *in* natural history (i.e., did the discipline itself undergo significant transformation?). The answer seems to be yes. Over the course of the sixteenth and seventeenth centuries, approaches to the description of natural objects changed greatly. The period saw a shift from the emblematic style of the sixteenth century, in which all of a natural object's various names, properties, symbolic associations, mythological connotations, folk uses, and so forth would be recounted in full, to a bare or plain style in the seventeenth century, focusing solely on physical appearance. Authors of natural histories developed techniques for the handling and analysis of natural objects unknown in antiquity. And conceptions of nature itself shifted, from the playful Renaissance goddess Natura, occasionally generating "jokes of nature," to the stern Enlightenment conception of a rationally comprehensible world that obeyed a series of natural laws. These changes were reflected in the very processes of conducting and writing up investigations in natural history. In short, the Scientific Revolution may no longer be viewed as a set of transformations solely in physics and astronomy; natural history played a crucial role in the early-modern revisioning of the natural world.

BIBLIOGRAPHY

French, Roger. *Ancient Natural History.* London: Routledge, 1994.

Jardine, N., J. A. Secord, and E. C. Spary, eds. *Cultures of Natural History.* Cambridge: Cambridge University Press, 1996.

Levine, Joseph M. "Natural History and the History of the Scientific Revolution." *Clio* 13 (1983), 57–73.

Park, Katharine, and Lorraine Daston. *Wonders and the Order of Nature, 1150–1750.* New York: Zone Books, 1997.

Shapiro, Barbara. "History and Natural History in Sixteenth- and Seventeenth-Century England: An Essay on the Relationship Between Humanism and Science." In *English Scientific Virtuosi in the Sixteenth and Seventeenth Centuries,* ed. Barbara Shapiro and Robert G. Frank, Jr. Los Angeles: William Andrews Clark Memorial Library, 1979, pp. 1–55.

ALIX COOPER

See also Baconianism; Botany; Emblematics; Empiricism; Zoology

Natural Laws. See Laws of Nature

Natural Theology. See Physico-Theology

Navigation

As Portuguese sailors made their way down the West African coast into unknown waters during the fifteenth century, they found traditional methods of location of little use. The compass had imposed a sense of direction more precise than the winds, while mariners already used the Moon to know the establishment of the tides, and the Guards around the Pole Star to mark the time, so now they would look to the sky for answers. In antiquity, Ptolemy (ca. 100–ca. 170) and others had shown how the location of places on earth could be identified by coordinates of latitude and longitude. Even if coastlines and islands were hard to pinpoint, with the aid of celestial observation it would be worth trying. New instruments would be needed, simplified from those of astronomers, to study the sky from a ship at sea.

To find the latitude, the navigator had to know how to handle the cross-staff and the quadrant so he could read the altitude of the Pole Star above the horizon, from which the latitude could easily be calculated. True, the Pole Star was known not to be exactly at the celestial pole, so astronomers would have to work out the precise angular distance at any given time, knowing the secular change of this value, on account of precession. In lower latitudes, an alternative method is needed. The movement of prominent stars, as they crossed the meridian might be noted—not an easy procedure for sailors, who

Title page of the fifth edition of John Seller's Practical Navigation *(1683), a popular English manual. Some of the instruments used in navigation are illustrated.*

preferred to take the altitude of the Sun itself. Since that changes through the year, and slightly year by year, they also needed tables of the Sun's noon altitude through a period of years. For this difficult observation, Portuguese and Spanish sailors used a simplifed astrolabe. The Sun's rays were to pass through pinholes on the alidade to produce a spot of light on the rim.

Longitude, however, was a more difficult problem. Ancient authorities used the times when lunar eclipses are observed in different places to establish their respective meridians. Christopher Columbus (1451–1506) tried this, although his results were very far from accurate, and such eclipses are too infrequent to be useful anyway. Another method depends on the movement of the Moon against the background of the fixed stars as it travels around the earth. This, too, could really only be used ashore, by trained professionals, who, indeed, sometimes achieved quite good results. However, these techniques required detailed tables of the Moon's motion over quite long periods, as well as precise locations for the stars.

Some mathematician-astronomers put their minds to solving this question. Reiner Gemma Frisius (1508–1555) in 1553 suggested that, if proper tables were available, a voyager would only have to observe the time at a given location and compare that with a clock that would keep the exact time of his home port. Although there were some remarkable refinements in clockmaking in his lifetime, portable clocks and watches were certainly not accurate enough for his purpose. So the only method recommended by the first handbooks of mathematical navigation was to take the desired latitude as far as might be feasible; and then take a second latitude observation after a few days, having noted the direction from the compass, including any changes imposed by the wind; and then estimate the distance covered, from the ship's speed. Where this line cut the second parallel would be your new longitude.

Seamen had traditionally assumed that a constant compass bearing would be the shortest route to any particular destination. Then, in 1537, Pedro Nuñes (1502–1578) pointed out that, since a great circle route is the shortest, they were mistaken. On a simple two-dimensional chart, meridians can be treated as parallel, but on a spherical earth, they converge toward the poles. Besides, wind and current usually prevented sailing ships from following such a route, and, over shorter distances, a constant bearing would at least get you close to where you wanted to go.

Meanwhile, it had become clear early in the sixteenth century that the compass was not pointing to true north after all; it varied, nor'easting or nor'westing in an irregular manner. At first, the learned world hoped this anomaly would prove to be the consequence of impurities in the lodestone used to magnetize the needle or in the needle itself. But by mid-century, it had become clear this was not so. It might be that the variation was at least constant for a given position, and that might help fix the longitude. Such was the claim of William Gilbert (1544–1603) in his *De magnete* (1600). He argued that the variation was the effect of the pull of the continents. A table of this declination would then inform the traveler of his exact position. The needle's dip below the horizontal plane, Gilbert thought, increased in direct relation to the latitude, and precise measurement would give this value without any celestial observations. Several dip circles to measure this effect were made. Unfortunately, the earth's magnetic field is not so neat in its conduct. Meanwhile, in 1635 Henry Gellibrand (1597–1636), comparing his values for London with those of his predecessors, claimed that the declination is not constant for a given latitude but varies with time. Within a few decades, evidence accumulated to show that he was right as to the fact, although an explanation was long in coming.

In 1610 Galileo Galilei (1564–1642) discovered four of Jupiter's satellites, which he hoped would provide an alternative to older astronomical techniques, since they are eclipsed much more frequently than is our one Moon. From time to time during the seventeenth century, this idea was taken up, and, indeed, while observing to this purpose Ole Christensen Römer (1644–1710) noted a brief delay in the arrival of one of the satellites. Concluding that their light must take that much longer to reach us, he arrived at the first, fairly accurate, estimate of the velocity of light. National observatories were founded in consequence of these navigational problems, as neither a precise-enough theory of the Moon's motion nor knowledge of the positions of the stars existed as yet. As Isaac Newton (1642–1727) noted in 1714, Galileo's method was impractical, too. As for the timekeeping method, clockmakers continued to try to make an accurate timekeeper that would be unaffected however much the ship pitched and rolled or whatever the variations of temperature and humidity. It was hoped that the pendulum clock would be the answer, but the pendulum clock had another flaw in that a pendulum that kept seconds perfectly at, say, 50° north latitude did not do so at the equator.

Some of Newton's optical discoveries were now incorporated in such instruments as the first practical "octants" using reflection to combine observations, which were invented by Thomas Godfrey (1704–1749) in Philadelphia in 1730 and then by John Hadley (1682–1744) in London. From the middle of the century onward, they were usually fitted with telescopic sights, and this became the standard form of sextant.

Meanwhile, men were still working on a watch to keep time exactly. The most successful were Pierre Le Roy (1717–1785) in France and in England John Harrison (1698–1776), who spent many years improving his chronometer, with bimetallic gridiron pendulums to compensate for changes in their immediate environment and damp the effects of the ship's motion. With their efforts, the search of two centuries for a timekeeper was ended, and chronometers, too, became regular equipment on shipboard.

BIBLIOGRAPHY

Hewson, J. B. *A History of the Practice of Navigation.* Glasgow: Brown, Son and Ferguson, 1951. 2nd ed., 1983.

Howse, Derek. *Greenwich Time and the Discovery of the Longitude.* Oxford: Oxford University Press, 1980.

Randles, W. G. L. "Portuguese and Spanish Attempts to Measure Longitude in the Sixteenth Century." *Mariner's Mirror* 81 (1995), 402–408.

Taylor, Eva. *The Haven-Finding Art.* London: Hollis and Carter, 1956.

Waters, David. "Columbus's Portuguese Inheritance." *Mariner's Mirror* 78 (1992), 385–405.

———. *Science and the Techniques of Navigation in the Renaissance.* (National Maritime Monographs and Reports). London: National Maritime Museum, 1974.

ALEX KELLER

See also Casa de la Contratación; Compass, Magnetic; Cross-Staff; Nuñes, Pedro; Quadrant

Neoplatonism

A term coined in modern times to distinguish an eclectic form of Platonism incorporating Aristotelian, Stoic, and Pythagorean elements; it was inaugurated by Plotinus (205–270) and developed by subsequent philosophers, most importantly by Porphyry (232–305), Iamblichus (ca. 250–ca. 330), and Proclus (410–485). Neoplatonism was the dominant philosophy in the Greco-Roman world between the third century and the sixth, and the movement as a whole had a profound influence on Judaism, Islam, and Christianity and, consequently, on the history of religion and philosophy in Europe and the Near East well into the early-modern period and beyond. (Neoplatonism also influenced Eastern religions, a subject beyond the scope of this article.) The significant impact that Neoplatonism had on Jewish and Islamic scholars reverberated in the West, since it was largely through the translations and commentaries of these scholars that the West recovered lost classical texts.

The Neoplatonists would have been unhappy to think there was anything "new" about their philosophy, because they believed that they were simply passing on authentic Platonic and Pythagorean teaching, which in their view was the *prisca theologia* (ancient theology) par excellence and, consequently, the purest, truest philosophy ever to exist. Yet, the distinction between Platonism and Neoplatonism is legitimate because the teachings of

Plotinus and his followers were distinctive and original. They arose in large part as a reaction against both the skeptical tradition and Aristotelianism and Epicurean materialism, which rejected the immortality of the human soul. But however critical Plotinus and later Neoplatonists were of Aristotle (384–322 B.C.E.), elements of his thought, especially relating to epistemology and logic, were accepted into Neoplatonism, thus paving the way for the eclectic mixture of Aristotelian, Neoplatonic, and Platonic ideas characteristic of many subsequent philosophers.

Although Neoplatonists disagreed on many issues, they shared the following distinctive doctrines: (1) the first principle and source of reality, described by Plotinus as The One, is utterly transcendent and unknowable; (2) every created entity has its source in The One and emanates from it, creating a Great Chain of Being linking the highest spirituality to the lowest corporeal objects; thus, Neoplatonism is, at heart, a monist philosophy; (3) although creation is a necessary process, inasmuch as The One must communicate its goodness to the greatest degree possible, it brings into existence imperfect, lesser beings, since whatever is created is naturally inferior to its creator (a basic Neoplatonic assumption); and (4) the ultimate goal of each created soul is to return to The One. Neoplatonism is, therefore, both a philosophy and a religion. It attempts to answer the perennial questions as to how and why The One, or God, gave rise to the many; how and why matter and evil could exist in a world emanating from a perfect, spiritual One; and what the ultimate goal of human life should be. Although Neoplatonists were extremely hostile and critical of Christians—Porphyry, for example, wrote a treatise against them—Neoplatonism had a profound influence on the early Eastern Church through the work of Basil of Cesara, Gregory of Nyssa, Synesius of Cyrene, and Nemesius of Emesa, and later through Psellus (eleventh century) and Gemistos Plethon (fifteenth century), who emigrated to Italy and influenced the scholars and philosophers at the Medici Court. Neoplatonic influence was equally strong in the Western Church, leaving its mark on Ambrose, Augustine (354–430), Pseudo Dionysius, Boethius, Calcidius, Macrobius, and Erigena, from which sources it passed into the work of Suso, Tauler, Ruysbroeck, Cusa, Boehme, and the Cambridge Platonists. The intertwining of Neoplatonism and Christianity provided an ongoing source for the heretical idea that human beings were potentially, if not actually, divine and, therefore, capable of achieving their own salvation without the intercession of Jesus Christ.

In explaining how The One became the many, Plotinus introduced the concept of the three *Hypostases,* a Greek term interpreted as meaning "origin," "substance," "real nature," or "first principle." According to Plotinus's formulation in his great work *The Enneads,* the first of these *Hypostases* was The One (*to hen*); the second, Intellect or Mind (*nous*); and the third, Soul (*psuche*). While Plotinus saw these as three separated entities, each one emanating from the previous one, Proclus tended to abolish any absolute distinction between them and telescoped them into one. Christians were happy to see prefigurations of the Trinity in these triadic formulations (Proclus was especially helpful in this respect), and, indeed, it has been suggested that Neoplatonic philosophy helped Christian theologians formulate the doctrine of the Trinity. Such triads made their way into Judaism and Islam through the infiltration of Neoplatonic ideas, thus opening the way for Trinitarian interpretations of these rival religions by proselytizing Christians. Plotinus's emphasis on the unknowableness of The One was the source for what has become known as Negative Theology, which made its presence felt in Judaism (especially in the Kabbalah), in Islam (Sufism), and in the writings of Christian mystics such as Meister Eckhardt (1260–1327) and the anonymous masterpiece *The Cloud of Unknowing* (fourteenth century) to give just two of many possible examples.

While the crosscultural religious and philosophical influence of Neoplatonism has been long recognized, its role in the development of Western science has become a subject of debate only within recent years. One reason for the delay was that the extent of Neoplatonic influence on interpretations of both Plato (428–348 B.C.E.) and Aristotle was not fully appreciated. However, as historians have increasingly realized, Plato was seen through Neoplatonic eyes up to the nineteenth century, and the Aristotelianism long recognized as a mainstay of the Christian religious and scientific worldview was thoroughly Neoplatonized. Several influential books attributed to Aristotle were actually by Neoplatonists. For example, the *Theologia Aristotelis,* originally written in Arabic and translated into Latin, was a paraphrase of the fourth, fifth, and sixth *Enneads* of Plotinus, and the *Liber de causis* originated as an Arabic interpretation of Proclus's *Elements of Theology.* This last book was a primary

source for the strong Neoplatonic strain in the thought of Saint Thomas Aquinas (d. 1274).

The importance of Neoplatonism for Western science emerged with the demise of the so-called Whig view of the history of science, according to which genuine science gradually triumphed over the irrational forces of religion and occultism. Frances Yates (1964) was one of the first to argue the case for occultism. Yates contended that the idea so basic to modern science, namely that man can change his environment for the better and harness the powers of nature to his own advantage, had its roots in the occult world of Renaissance Hermetists, like Marsilio Ficino (1433–1499) and Giovanni Pico della Mirandola (1463–1494), who were deeply influenced by the *Corpus hermeticum,* a miscellany of texts produced between the second and fourth centuries but erroneously thought to be pre-Christian and written by a contemporary of Moses, Hermes Trismegistus.

While Yates's claim that Hermetism was an all-important force in the development of modern science has been judged erroneous, her basic insight into the manifold connections between occultism and science is beyond dispute. Mounting evidence has conclusively shown that the ideas of the major thinkers in the scientific pantheon, such as Nicolaus Copernicus (1473–1543), Johannes Kepler (1571–1630), Giordano Bruno (1548–1600), Paracelsus (ca. 1493–1541), and Johannes Baptista van Helmont (1579–1644), were influenced by occultism; but instead of occultism being defined as Hermetism, it is increasingly defined under the broader rubric of Neoplatonism. Walter Pagel (1985) spent a lifetime describing the way occult and Neoplatonic ideas influenced developments in science and medicine in the early-modern period. The influence of alchemy on even the most apparently rational of seventeenth-century philosophers and scientists, such as Robert Boyle (1627–1691), John Locke (1632–1704), Gottfried Wilhelm Leibniz (1646–1716), and Isaac Newton (1642–1727), has been increasingly pointed out by scholars, and the theoretical basis of alchemy lay largely in Neoplatonism. At the heart of the extensive debate over language that began in the Renaissance and played a fundamental part in both the Scientific Revolution and the controversy between Leibniz and Locke on the nature of human understanding lay the Neoplatonic concept of innate ideas and the Neoplatonic view of the cosmos as a Great

Chain of Being in which every level mirrored the preceding one on a diminished level. Locke rejected both of these basic Neoplatonic concepts and, as a result, created a crisis in epistemology that was not healed until it was addressed by Immanuel Kant (1724–1804)—for how could anyone be certain that his ideas reflected reality if their source lay in sensations alone? Neither Benedict de Spinoza's (1632–1677) monism nor Leibniz's monadism can be understood without appreciating the indebtedness of these two philosophers to Neoplatonic monism. Neoplatonism is a prime component in the various idealistic and vitalistic philosophies that appeared from the eighteenth to the twentieth centuries in the work of such philosophers and scientists as Berkeley, Schelling, Hegel, Mesmer, and Bergson.

The impression should not be left, however, that Neoplatonism exerted a wholly positive force on the development of modern science. Those intellectuals who concentrated on Plotinian metaphysics and endeavored to attain mystical union with The One, or God, tended to dismiss science as a lesser activity because it dealt with the impermanent world of vile matter rather than the spiritual world of eternal forms. The Cambridge Platonist Henry More (1614–1687) provides a good example of a Neoplatonic philosopher who dismissed the activities of contemporary scientists as unworthy of a true philosopher. Thus, the very eclecticism of Neoplatonism made it both a positive and a negative force in the development of modern science, as well as in shaping attitudes toward the physical world. Those who saw created things as reflections of the divine One considered science a noble pursuit, while those who emphasized the distance between the One and the many dismissed this world as inferior and yearned for spiritual fulfillment in the world above.

BIBLIOGRAPHY

Armstrong, A. H., ed. *The Cambridge History of Later Greek and Early Medieval Philosophy*. Cambridge: Cambridge University Press, 1967. Repr. 1970.

Goodman, Lenn E., ed. *Neoplatonism and Jewish Thought*. (Studies in Neoplatonism: Ancient and Modern 7). Albany: State University of New York Press, 1992.

Morewedge, Parviz, ed. *Neoplatonism and Islamic Thought*. (Studies in Neoplatonism: Ancient and Modern 5). Albany: State University of New York Press, 1992.

O'Meara, Dominic, ed. *Neoplatonism and Christian Thought*. (Studies in Neoplatonism: Ancient and Modern 3). Albany: State University of New York Press, 1982.

Pagel, Walter. *Religion and Neoplatonism in Renaissance Medicine*. Ed. Marianne Winder. London: Variorum Reprints, 1985.

Yates, Frances A. *Giordano Bruno and the Hermetic Tradition*. London: Routledge and Kegan Paul, 1964.

ALLISON P. COUDERT

See also Cambridge Platonists; Hermetism; Kabbalah; Religion and Natural Philosophy

Neopythagoreanism

Pythagoras (fl. sixth century B.C.E.) was a shadowy figure even to Plato (428–348 B.C.E.) and Aristotle (384–322 B.C.E.), who knew him only through the works of his spiritual heirs, because none of his own works survived. Tradition linked Pythagoras to the foundation of a religio-ethical society that taught metempsychosis and developed ideas of mathematical harmonies. Pythagoreanism also applied numerical and geometrical harmonies to speculation about the composition of the cosmos. Plato in his *Republic* and Aristotle in his *De caelo* discuss Pythagoreanism's "harmony of the spheres," the idea that the intervals between the celestial spheres correspond to the relative lengths of musical strings. Plato's discussions in the *Timaeus* of the numerical basis of matter and the cosmological significance of the geometrical solids are Pythagorean in nature.

In late antiquity, Pythagorean mathematical doctrines were praised, developed, and passed on by Neopythagoreans, who were also usually Neoplatonists. Influential Neopythagoreans of that era included Nicomachus of Gerasa (fl. late first century), famed for his *Introduction to Arithmentic* and *Manual of Harmonics;* Iamblichus of Chalcis (ca. 250–ca. 330), noted for developing the mystical and magical aspects of pagan Neoplatonism; Proclus (410–485), head of the Academy, Neoplatonic systematizer and commentator, and source of much of the medieval knowledge of Plato; and Boethius (ca. 480–525). Boethius's *De arithmetica,* based on the work of Nicomachus, was a standard text, carrying Pythagoreanism through the Middle Ages into the Renaissance. Boethius expressed the essence of Pythagorean mathematical theory: "All things appear to be formed by numbers, for this was the principal pattern in the Creator's mind."

The belief that number and harmony are the basis of the material world became commonplace. The *quadrivium,* so central to medieval and Renaissance education, and consisting of arithmetic, geometry, astronomy, and harmonics, fostered a Neopythagorean worldview. Popular games, such as *rithmomachia,* played from the tenth through the sixteenth centuries, reinforced Pythagorean arithmetic and its relationship to the structure of the elements. In the fifteenth century, Nicholas of Cusa (1401–1464) developed the idea found in Plato that mathematics, especially geometry, is intermediary between God and the created world. Mathematics, like God, is unchanging and is fundamental to the formation of the world. Such a perception was reinforced by the development of perspective art, which could re-create the world using number and proportion.

In the Renaissance, Neopythagoreanism was linked to the newly emerging emphasis on Platonism. The great translator and commentator on Plato, Marsilio Ficino (1433–1499), demonstrated the agreement of Plato, Pythagoras, Moses, Zoroaster, and Hermes Trismegistus in their doctrines of Creation. The world is patterned after the eternal forms in God's mind. This connection between the masters of the past was extended by Giovanni Pico della Mirandola (1463–1494) and Johannes Reuchlin (1455–1522) in developing a Christian Kabbalah. Kabbalah, with its number-letters transmitted from Sinai, agreed not only with the traditional Biblical text, but also with Neopythagoreanism and Neoplatonism. Not only the pagans, but also God himself, gave authority to the concept that number is the creative unit and holds the key to understanding the universe.

The extensive possibilities of Neopythagorean applied mathematics were suggested by John Dee (1527–1608) in his "Mathematicall Praeface" to *The Elements of Geometrie of Euclid,* translated by H. Billingsley (1570). The "Praeface," which was reprinted for more than a century, called for the mathematical reform of practically everything, from astronomy and architecture to the theater. Some of the first fruits of the modern Neopythagorean fusion with Platonism appeared in cosmology. Plato had believed that mathematics could produce a physical model of the cosmos. The mathematical models employed by astronomers to predict planetary positions, however, could not be made to conform to certain observations and long-accepted cosmological axioms. For practical purposes, Ptolemy's (ca. 100– ca. 170) computational system of epicycles, tangents, equants, and the like was kept in a separate intellectual compartment from the physical model of the universe

required by Aristotle's cosmological principles. In the 1520s and 1530s, Giovanni Battista della Torre (fl. 1520), Girolamo Fracastoro (ca. 1478–1553), and Giovanni Battista Amici (d. 1538) proposed homocentric astronomical models, but none were worked out in detail, and they would have been computationally inadequate in any case. Nicolaus Copernicus (1473–1543) put forth heliocentrism as an astronomical system that could solve both physical and computational problems. Johannes Kepler (1571– 1630), after calling Copernicus "Pythagoras reborn" in his *Mysterium cosmographicum* (1596), later remedied the computational problems of Copernicanism with his discovery of elliptical orbits. Kepler was a dedicated Neopythagorean who wrote in his *Harmonice mundi* (1619) that "geometry existed before the creation, is co-eternal with the mind of God." His own discoveries grew out of his search for the harmony of the celestial spheres.

Kepler's Neopythagoreanism was, in great measure, linked to observation. This put him at odds with another stream of Neopythagoreanism represented by Robert Fludd (1574–1637). Fludd speculatively suggested in 1617 that the harmony of the universe could be described using a single string—a divine monochord. Kepler mocked mathematics divorced from observation as creating incomprehensible picture puzzles, and Fludd's heirs have been considered mystics rather than "scientists."

The enduring importance of Renaissance and early-modern Neopythagoreanism is seen in the "classical" scholia that Isaac Newton (1642–1727) prepared in the 1690s for addition to his *Principia mathematica philosophiae naturalis* (1687). Newton there expressed his belief that Pythagoras and other ancients knew the newly rediscovered secrets of the heavens but had hidden them from the vulgar by couching them in discussions of harmony. These scholia were not published in Newton's lifetime; perhaps they already seemed old-fashioned. Nonetheless, Neopythagoreanism had served a crucial function by establishing mathematics as descriptive of reality. Observation firmly entrenched the idea, and, by the eighteenth century, the mathematical study of nature no longer needed the warrant of sacred tradition.

BIBLIOGRAPHY

Clulee, Nicholas H. *John Dee's Natural Philosophy.* London: Routledge, 1988.

Dreyer, J. L. E. *History of the Planetary Systems from Thales to Kepler.* Cambridge: Cambridge University Press, 1906.

Repr. as *A History of Astronomy from Thales to Kepler*. New York: Dover, 1953.

Godwin, Joscelyn. *Robert Fludd: Hermetic Philosopher and Surveyor of Two Worlds*. Boulder, CO: Shambala, 1979.

McGuire, J. E., and P. M. Rattansi. "Newton and the 'Pipes of Pan.'" *Notes and Records of the Royal Society of London* 21 (1966), 108–143.

Westman, Robert S., and J. E. McGuire. *Hermeticism and the Scientific Revolution*. Los Angeles: University of California Press, 1977.

MICHAEL T. WALTON

See also Fludd, Robert; Hermetism; Kabbalah; Music/Harmonics; Neoplatonism

Newcastle, Duchess of. See Cavendish, Margaret

Newton, Isaac (1642–1727)

Isaac Newton. Courtesy Whipple Museum of the History of Science, Cambridge, England.

The posthumous and only child of a prosperous yeoman farmer possessed of a small manor was born in the manor house of Woolsthorpe near the village of Colsterworth, Lincolnshire, on Christmas Day. As many have noted, Galileo Galilei (1564–1642) died earlier that same year. Between them, these two long-lived men spanned virtually the entire Scientific Revolution, to which their combined work was central.

During his formative years, Newton lived with his maternal grandparents. When he was three years old, his mother had remarried and gone to bear three additional children in the parsonage in nearby North Witham, leaving her first son with her parents in the Newton family house in Woolsthorpe. It was not a harmonious arrangement. The grandfather later pointedly omitted Newton from his will, and for his part Newton never mentioned the grandfather. He mentioned the grandmother only once. For that matter, there is evidence to suggest that he hated his stepfather as well. It is not impossible that the evident strains in Newton's personality stemmed from this difficult period of his life.

His stepfather, the Rev. Barnabus Smith, died when Newton was ten, leaving his mother a relatively wealthy widow, and, for a short period, the now-expanded family was reunited in Woolsthorpe. However, his mother soon sent him to Grantham, six miles to the north, to attend grammar school. It was his mother's intention that Newton manage her now-considerable estate, and, with that in mind, she brought him home as he approached the age of seventeen. After nine apparently stormy months, it was decided that his destiny lay in learning rather than rural pursuits. He returned to Grantham for a final year and enrolled in Trinity College, Cambridge, in the summer of 1661.

In Cambridge, Newton met the traditional university curriculum, which, despite the changes wrought by the English Civil War (1642–1646) and the Commonwealth, was still largely intact. His introduction to the world of science, therefore, was Aristotelian natural philosophy. Because Newton seldom threw a paper away, we have the notes from his student reading, and we know that, during his undergraduate years, probably during 1664, he discovered for himself a new body of reading and, simply abandoning the established curriculum, surrendered to the new reading entirely. It marked the beginning of the career we associate with him and his outstanding role in the Scientific Revolution.

His first major passion was mathematics. More than sixty years later, near the end of his life, Newton recalled his introduction to mathematics. As John Conduitt, the husband of Newton's niece, recorded the story:

> He bought Descartes's Geometry & read it by himself when he was got over 2 or 3 pages he could understand no farther than he began

again & got 3 or 4 pages farther till he came to another difficult place, than he began again & advanced farther & continued so doing till he made himself Master of the whole without having the least light or instruction from any body.

In the space of less than a year, working by himself, Newton mastered the whole achievement of seventeenth-century mathematics up to his time. He did not allow himself to be confined to René Descartes (1596–1650), although Frans van Schooten's (ca. 1615–1660) great edition of the *Geometry,* with a wealth of commentaries, was perhaps foremost among his sources. From the works of François Viète (1540–1603), he digested algebra, from those of John Wallis (1616–1703), the application of infinitesimals to determining areas under curves. Gradually, reading notes transformed themselves into original investigations, and, during the winter of 1664–1665, he achieved his first major success, the binomial expansion, which made it possible to evaluate areas under curves not amenable to the established algorithms and, thus, constituted a major step toward a universal method of what were then called *quadratures* and we call integration.

He had been working as well, following Descartes's lead primarily, at finding the tangents to curves at given points, something similar to what we know as differentiation. During the spring of 1665, in a context that considered curves as the paths of points moving under defined conditions and similarly thought of areas, not as created by stacking up static infinitesimals but as generated by a moving line, he perceived related but inverse patterns in the algorithms for finding tangents and those for determining areas. Newton would ultimately call the method that emerged from this insight the *fluxional method,* from the past participle of the Latin verb *fluere* (to flow). We know it as the calculus. Working with incandescent intensity, Newton consolidated the insight during the coming months, and, finally, in October 1666, he composed what we recognize today as a definitive statement of the method. As far as we know, he did not show it to anyone at the time. Years later, his failure to publish his method would lead to a bitter controversy with Gottfried Wilhelm Leibniz (1646–1716) over priority. With the solution of the problems he had initially confronted, Newton found that his interest in mathematics quickly ebbed. In the years ahead, he often returned to mathematics, though less and less frequently and increasingly

as a result of some external impetus. Command of the fluxional method would, in time, profoundly influence his achievement in physics.

When we consider the intensity and the extent of his work in mathematics, it is difficult to believe that Newton had time for anything else during the period 1664–1666. As his papers reveal, however, he also discovered the New Science, as he found it first of all in the writings of Descartes, but also in those of Pierre Gassendi (1592–1655), Robert Boyle (1627–1691), and a number of others, who were generally exponents of what is called the *mechanical philosophy,* which had by that time supplanted Aristotelian natural philosophy among leaders of thought. Newton's notes on his reading, recorded in a notebook under the general heading *Quaestiones quaedam philosophicae* (Certain Philosophical Questions, 1661–ca. 1664), witnessed his first encounter with issues of motion, gravity, and light.

He soon made significant progress in all three. In the science of mechanics, he pursued the problem of impact to the conclusion that the common center of mass of two isolated bodies in impact remains at rest or in uniform motion in a straight line. This is equivalent to the conservation of momentum. He investigated circular motion and arrived at a formula for the radial component identical to the one we continue to employ. It is necessary to note, however, that, like every early student of circular motion, he at that time conceived of the radial component as centrifugal rather than centripetal. In a separate paper, he applied the measure of centrifugal force to an imagined conical pendulum equal in height and period to an ordinary pendulum whose period he had carefully measured and arrived at an accurate determination of the acceleration of gravity. He then tested one of the common objections to the Copernican system, that bodies would be flung off a rotating earth, by comparing his measure of g with the centrifugal tendency of a body on the equator of a rotating earth. He found g to be about three hundred times greater (i.e., the objection to a rotating earth had no substance). Another paper substituted Kepler's third law into the formula for centrifugal tendency, and Newton found that the centrifugal force varied inversely as the square of the distance from the Sun. In the same paper, he also compared the centrifugal acceleration of the Moon in its orbit with the measured acceleration of gravity. Because the figure he used for the radius of the earth was too small, he found only a very rough approximation to the inverse-square relation in this case, though he would later remember that, as he put it, they answered "pretty nearly." All of this was highly suggestive, and Newton would later recall it as a significant step forward. Nevertheless, it was a far cry from the concept of universal gravitation, especially in its use of centrifugal tendencies.

In his investigation of light and colors, Newton advanced much further. The established theory of color held that light, thought to be uniform and white in its pristine form, is modified in some way in processes of refraction and reflection to produce colors. Already in the *Quaestiones quaedam,* Newton began to entertain the idea that light as it comes from the Sun is a heterogeneous mixture and that each ray is immutably associated with one color. Here the influence of the mechanical philosophy asserted itself definitively. The mechanical philosophy argued that physical nature consists solely of particles of matter in motion, particles that are qualitatively neutral and characterized by size and shape alone. Qualities such as heat, hardness, and color do not exist as such; rather, they are sensations caused by the impact of particles on the nerves of sentient beings. From the beginning, Newton held a corpuscular conception of light: a ray of light consists of tiny particles moving with enormous velocity. The different rays are not colored; rather, when they impinge on an optic nerve, different rays generate unique sensations of color. White is the sensation caused by the heterogeneous mixture. Phenomena of colors arise not from the modification of white light but from its separation into its components.

The bands of color that appear to surround bodies viewed through a prism had initially suggested the new theory of colors to Newton. He proceeded to test it with an experiment. It is well to pause here for a moment. Neither Newton nor the seventeenth century at large invented the concept of experimentation. Nevertheless, experimentation was not seen as the characteristic procedure of scientific investigation when the seventeenth century opened. Aristotelian natural philosophy had been empirical; it had insisted on the primacy of observation as the source of knowledge. Only rarely, however, had philosophers intervened actively to query nature by manipulating the conditions under which the phenomena they observed would appear. During the seventeenth century, active interrogation of nature through experimentation became increasingly common. Newton seized upon experimental procedures as though by instinct. His work in optics was an experimental investigation of the allied concepts of the heterogeneity of light and the production of colored phenomena by the analysis of the heterogeneous mixture into its components. At the very least, it was one of the outstanding experimental investigations of the century, which did much, when it was published, to permanently establish the role of experimentation in modern science from that time forward.

His first experiment was a simple one. Red and blue were universally taken as the extremes of the spectrum of colors. If the colors seen through a prism arise from the unequal refractions of rays of light, and if he colored one end of a thread red and the other blue and viewed the thread through a prism, then he should see the two ends disjoined. He tried it, and he saw the result his theory predicted. Here, for the time being, he paused. Somewhat later, probably early in 1666, he was trying to grind lenses of elliptical and hyperbolic cross-section. Recall that the telescope was a sensational new instrument in the seventeenth century and that no early telescope gave a perfect image. Lenses had spherical cross-sections because that symmetric shape automatically appears from a carefully controlled process of grinding, and Johannes Kepler (1571–1630) had demonstrated that spherical lenses do not refract parallel rays—from a star, for example—to a perfect focus. In one of the triumphs of his new method in mathematics, Descartes had demonstrated that lenses of elliptical and hyperbolic cross-section would refract parallel rays to a perfect focus. Unaware even that it was an assumption, Descartes had proceeded under the conviction that light is uniform. As Newton worked at grinding lenses of conical sections, he recalled his experiment with the thread. What if he did succeed in producing a conical cross-section? He would still not achieve a perfect focus because different rays in the heterogeneous mixture of white light are refracted at different angles. Later, Newton would demonstrate that chromatic aberration introduces far greater problems in telescopes than spherical aberration. In early 1666, the realization of the problem led to an elaborated experimental investigation of light and colors.

His basic tool was the prism, and his basic experiment the projection of a narrow beam of light through a prism onto a wall twenty-two feet away, where he found that the round beam produced an elongated spectrum. Later, in what he called the *experimentum crucis* (crucial experiment), he introduced a second prism that refracted beams isolated in the initial spectrum; the blue rays were refracted more than the red, but no further dispersion

N

occurred. Another experiment used a lens to bring the diverging spectrum back to a focus, which appeared white. As he pursued the investigation, Newton was ingenuity itself in thinking up consequences that ought to follow if his theory were correct and in imagining experimental arrangements that put them to the test. Drawing on Robert Hooke's (1635–1703) observations of colors in thin transparent films, he measured the alternating dark and light rings—*Newton's rings,* as we still call them—in the film of air between a lens of known curvature and a flat sheet of glass. For Newton, these experiments completed the theory of colors by showing that reflections as well as refractions could separate light into its components, and they became the basis of his explanation of colors in solid bodies. The experiments with Newton's rings also first established the periodicity of an optical phenomenon.

His experiments with light and color introduced Newton to the scientific community. He chose the subject for his first lectures as Lucasian Professor of Mathematics at Cambridge University, a chair to which he was appointed in 1669. It was then that he polished his still rough notions into the finished theory, which, in turn, led him to build a reflecting telescope to avoid the problem of chromatic aberration. When the Royal Society in London heard about the telescope, they asked to see it, and its enthusiastic reception, accompanied by Newton's election to the body, encouraged him to summarize the theory in a paper sent to the Royal Society early in 1672 and published in the *Philosophical Transactions.* The paper led to a personal crisis. Though generally well received, it was not universally well received, and Newton proved unable to handle objections rationally. First, Robert Hooke saw a connection between Newton's theory and his own work in optics and rejected what he saw as primarily a defense of the corpuscular conception of light. Newton's excessive, furious response to Hooke initiated three decades of animosity between the two men, which ended only with Hooke's death. Then a group of English Jesuits in Liège challenged the experiments themselves, ultimately driving Newton to distraction with their letters and leading him to sever correspondence with the Royal Society and withdraw into himself. It was nearly thirty years later when, crowned by the success of the *Principia mathematica philosophiae naturalis* (Mathematical Principles of Natural Philosophy, 1687) and elected president of the Royal Society, Newton published his theory in full in the *Opticks* (Opticks, 1704).

Meanwhile, his attention had shifted to other topics. Ca. 1670 he discovered alchemy, and he plunged into it without reserve. He devoured the traditional literature of alchemy; the leading authority on this subject asserts that no one had ever mastered this literature to the same extent. Nor did he ignore more recent alchemists; his favorite author was Eirenaeus Philalethes, the pseudonym of the American colonist George Starkey (1628–1665), who was still active in England when Newton began to read his works. Newton eventually assembled an extensive collection of alchemical works, which formed a considerable proportion of his personal library. He did more than read; he wrote alchemical tracts himself. He experimented in a laboratory erected in the garden outside his chamber in Trinity College. Over a period of twenty-five years, he devoted well over a million words to alchemy.

With Newton, alchemy was not focused on making gold. Rather, it was an aspect of natural philosophy, an attempt to probe the functioning of nature. There is good reason to think that alchemy influenced a fundamental transformation in his conception of nature that took place in the late 1670s or early 1680s. He had become increasingly concerned that the mechanical philosophy, with its bare ontology of inert particles in motion, was a vehicle for atheism. In alchemical theory, he found active principles, which he associated with the primacy of spirit in nature; in his chemical experiments, he seemed to perceive active principles at work. Newton eventually transformed these active principles into forces of attraction and repulsion between particles of matter. Query 31, published with the Latin edition of the *Opticks* in 1706 but sketched originally in 1686 to accompany the *Principia,* most fully expressed the program of Newton's dynamic mechanical philosophy, in which forces between particles became the central explanatory agent in science. In Query 31, Newton justified the existence of such forces primarily by reference to chemical phenomena, but it was a different force, found in the cosmic order, that converted the scientific community to his view.

Meanwhile, Newton had taken up a second field of study—theology. Perhaps it was the requirement of Trinity College that Fellows be ordained to the Anglican clergy within seven years of undertaking the M.A. degree that initially stimulated him. Whatever the cause, his papers leave no doubt that he began serious reading in theology ca. 1672. He digested the Bible to the extent that more than one of his contemporaries envied his command of Scripture. He plunged into the writings of the early Fathers of the Church. Before he was done, Newton composed, both then and later in his life, a corpus of theological papers more extensive by far than those devoted to alchemy. And he quickly read himself into heresy. Newton became absorbed in, and ultimately obsessed with, the Arian controversy of the fourth century. He came to see Athanasius, the most important author of the doctrine of the Trinity, as an evil genius who had perverted Christian truth for personal ends. Newton identified with Arius, who held that Christ was a created intermediary between God and man, a position similar to, but not identical with, modern Unitarianism.

Interest in the biblical prophecies went hand in hand with his interest in theology. During the early 1670s, Newton began to elaborate an interpretation of the prophecies that hinged on Arianism. Central to his interpretation was the notion of the Great Apostasy, Trinitarianism. The vials of wrath and plagues of the Book of Revelation were God's punishments on a stiff-necked people who had gone whoring after false gods. Newton's idea of successful biblical interpretation was an exact correspondence between the revealed prophecy and the events of history. To this end, he established the text of Revelation by collating multiple manuscript versions, and he pored over ancient sources to establish the facts of history.

Newton never altered the theological stance he had taken in the early 1670s. It did much to shape his life, for his views were anathema to the great majority of his compatriots, and the necessity to keep them secret never evaporated. Had they been known, they would have led to his instant dismissal from Cambridge and later, when he moved to the mint in London, to discharge from governmental service. In London, Newton did form a small circle of men who either shared or were taught to share his views. Outside that circle, silence prevailed, and we learned the full extent of Newton's heterodoxy only in the twentieth century.

For nearly fifteen years, from ca. 1670 until late in 1684, alchemy and theology furnished the principal content of Newton's intellectual life. Late in 1679, he engaged in a short correspondence with Hooke about the path of fall of a body released from a tower on a rotating earth, which became a disguised discussion of orbital motion. The correspondence did nothing to resolve the tension between the two men, but it did

introduce Newton to a new conceptualization of circular motion that focused not on the centripetal tendency of a body constrained in circular motion but on the force toward the center, which Newton soon named *centripetal,* that diverts a body from its tangential path and holds it in a circular one. As a result of the correspondence, Newton demonstrated to himself that the centripetal force toward one focus necessary to hold a body in an elliptical path varies inversely as the square of the distance. Five years later, Edmond Halley (ca. 1656–1743) traveled to Cambridge to question Newton about nearly the same problem. The visit from Halley drew Newton back to the physical studies he had virtually abandoned, and out of it grew the *Principia.*

The immediate aftermath of Halley's visit was a short tract named *De motu,* which he sent to Halley. It was an exercise in orbital dynamics, which took up and expanded the demonstration on motion in an elliptical orbit he had worked out earlier. This time the problem seized Newton and would not let him go. Two and a half years of intense labor, during which he excluded everything else from his life, elaborated *De motu* into the *Principia.*

His first task was to formulate a science of dynamics. Early in the century, Galileo Galilei (1564–1642) had developed the kinematics of uniform motion in a horizontal plane and of uniformly accelerated motion, as in freely falling bodies, but no one had succeeded in producing a corresponding science of dynamics. This Newton achieved during the early months of 1685. Twenty years after he seemingly accepted the principle of inertia, but then began to hesitate, he embraced it definitively and made it his first law of motion. His second law added the principle that force is proportional to the change in motion it produces. A good part of its explanatory success was the recognition that a change of direction is as much an acceleration as a change of speed. In the *Principia,* Newton defined the concept of centripetal force; the problem central to the whole work was the operation of centripetal force in holding the solar system together. Newton's third law stated in dynamic terms the recognized principle that the changes of motion of two bodies in impact are equal and opposite to each other. The system of dynamics that opens the *Principia* was one of the culminating triumphs of the Scientific Revolution. Its success lay in its synthesis of the achievements of Galileo and Kepler in terrestrial and celestial motion, both of which emerged as necessary consequences of Newton's three laws of motion.

N

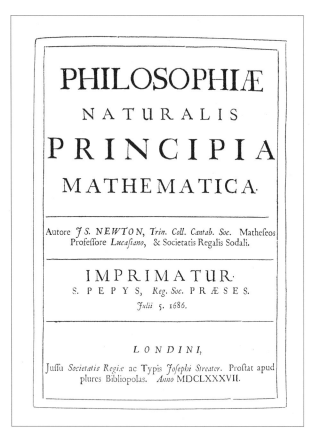

PHILOSOPHIÆ

N A T U R A L I S

PRINCIPIA

MATHEMATICA.

Autore JS. NEWTON, Trin. Coll. Cantab. Soc. Mathefeos
Profeffore Lucafiano, & Societatis Regalis Sodali.

IMPRIMATUR.
S. P E P Y S, Reg. Soc. P R Æ S E S.
Julii 5. 1686.

L O N D I N I,

Juffu Societatis Regiæ ac Typis Jofephi Streater. Proftat apud
plures Bibliopolas. Anno MDCLXXXVII.

First edition of Newton's masterpiece.

Newton devoted Book I of the *Principia* primarily to the motion of bodies, mostly orbiting bodies, under conditions of no resistance. Having dealt with single bodies orbiting hypothetical centers of force, Newton considered the problems introduced by mutual attractions: first, the two-body problem, in which the orbiting body also attracts the body at the center of force, then, the three-body problem, made to stand as a means of analyzing the perturbations arising from the mutual attractions of many bodies. Proposition 66, the three-body problem, with twenty-one corollaries, became the foundation for the treatment of multiple complex problems, such as lunar theory, the tides, and precession of the equinoxes in Book III. Proposition 71, not strictly on orbital motion, demonstrated that a homogeneous sphere, composed of particles that attract with an inverse-square force, also attracts with an inverse-square force directed to its center. One of the key propositions in the *Principia,* Proposition 71, allowed the correlation of the acceleration of gravity of bodies near the surface of the earth with the centripetal acceleration of the Moon in its orbit, the key step in the argument for universal gravitation.

Book II takes up the motion of bodies through resisting media and the motions themselves of such material media. Aspects of the book, especially its theory of the source of resistance in the inertia of the particles that compose material media, have not survived. For all that, Book II was a pathbreaking endeavor that initiated mathematical treatment of issues hitherto beyond the scope of quantitative physics. It culminated in a devastating assault on Cartesian natural philosophy by demonstrating, first, that vortical motion in a material medium would not yield the relations of Kepler's three laws and, second, that vortical motion cannot sustain itself without the constant input, in modern terminology, of energy. As Newton concluded: "the hypothesis of vortices is utterly irreconcilable with astronomical phenomena, and rather serves to perplex than explain the heavenly motions."

Book III applied the demonstrations of Book I to achieve what the hypotheses of vortices could not: an account of the heavenly motions based on the proposition that the planets move without resistance through empty space under the control of forces of attraction that hold them in closed orbits. The observed phenomena of closed orbits showed the necessity of centripetal forces. Kepler's third law showed that the force directed toward the Sun varies inversely as the square of the distance. The same law observed among the satellites of Jupiter showed an inverse-square attraction toward that planet. Because the Moon orbits the earth, some attraction toward the earth must hold it in orbit, but we cannot apply Kepler's third law to a single satellite. However, we can compare the acceleration of gravity at the surface of the earth with the centripetal acceleration of the Moon in its measured orbit. When Newton had attempted this correlation in 1666, he had not had an accurate measurement of the size of the earth. In 1687 he did, and the correlation now answered with high precision. Thus, he could apply the ancient word *gravitas* to the cosmic inverse-square force and derive the law of universal gravitation.

The rest of Book III then applied the concept of universal gravitation to the explanation of a number of phenomena not called upon in its derivation. A lunar theory traced perturbations observed by astronomers to the attraction of the Sun. The book offered the first successful explanation of the tides, carried out, of course, in quantitative terms. It demonstrated that the attractions of the Moon and the Sun generate a slow, conical motion of the earth's axis, giving rise to a phenomenon known as *precession of the equinoxes*. And, in the final triumph of the work, Newton reduced the observed positions of the great comet of 1680–1681 to a conical section in orbit around the Sun.

The publication of the *Principia* in the summer of 1687 transformed Newton's life. Received instantly in Britain as a master work, it vaulted Newton to the forefront of British scientific life and made it impossible that he ever withdraw again into the privacy of his study as he had ten years earlier. Mechanical philosophers on the Continent vehemently rejected the book's conception of attractions at the distance. For all that, they could not ignore the immense technical power of the book, so that Newton's reputation on the Continent was scarcely lower than it was at home. For example, upon its reorganization in 1699, the French Academy of Sciences elected him as one of eight foreign associates.

Events of a totally different nature also worked to ensure his prominence. In 1687, just as Newton completed the *Principia,* James II initiated an effort to Catholicize the English universities. In Cambridge, Newton, now freed from the absorbing concentration on his work, spoke out his opposition to the king's intent and immediately found himself a leader among the dons. When the Glorious Revolution validated his courage, the university elected Newton as one of its representatives to the Convention Parliament, where, to be sure, he did not become a leader.

Eventually, in 1696, Newton chose to abandon Cambridge for a governmental appointment in London, first as warden and then as master of the mint. He turned out to be an outstanding administrator. As warden, he played a prominent role in the great recoinage and contributed markedly to its success. As master, he oversaw all of the operations of the mint and advised the government on monetary policy. He also earned a handsome income. Newton continued as master of the mint until his death, and, though he was far from the wealthiest man in London, there is no way to avoid applying the adjective "wealthy" to him during his final quarter of a century.

Vaulted to prominence by the *Principia,* Newton now became the doyen of British science. In 1703, the Royal Society elected him president, another position he held until his death and another manifestation of his administrative talents. At the time of his election as president, the Royal Society was floundering, through the disinterest of the prominent politicians chosen as presidents, tottering on the verge of bankruptcy, and wanting in serious scientific activity. All of this Newton changed. He took leadership firmly into his own hands and seldom failed to be present at a meeting either of the society or of its council. He put the finances on a sound footing, so that the society was even able to purchase a building of its own and move out of its first home, Gresham College. He also brought to its meetings a demonstrator of outstanding ability, Francis Hauksbee (ca. 1666–1713), who provided the sort of substance that Robert Hooke had once furnished. A society on the verge of collapse quickly righted itself and resumed the career of scientific leadership that it has followed ever since.

Newton's years of scientific productivity were over but not his years of publication. Almost immediately upon assuming the chair, he presented the society with his *Opticks* (1704), which expounded theories of light and color worked out thirty-five years earlier. A Latin edition and two further English editions of the *Opticks* followed. So also did a second edition of the *Principia,* which embodied some serious emendation of detail, though no fundamental alteration of substance, and later a third edition. In mathematics, he allowed himself to engage in an unfortunate, bitter dispute with Leibniz over priority in invention of the calculus, a dispute in which neither man distinguished himself. Most of his time, however, Newton devoted to theology, though here, too, he confined himself to reshuffling earlier ideas.

Until well past eighty, Newton's health remained strong. Toward the end, he did inevitably decline and ceased largely to attend either to the mint or to the Royal Society. Both his own prominence and the prominence that science had gained during the seventeenth century are demonstrated by the pomp of his funeral, with leading figures of the land bearing the pall, and by his burial in Westminster Abbey.

BIBLIOGRAPHY

Cohen, I. Bernard. *The Newtonian Revolution.* Cambridge: Cambridge University Press, 1980.

Dobbs, B. J. T. *The Janus Faces of Genius: The Role of Alchemy in Newton's Thought.* Cambridge: Cambridge University Press, 1991.

Koyré, Alexandre. *Newtonian Studies.* Cambridge, MA: Harvard University Press, 1965.

Manuel, Frank. *A Portrait of Isaac Newton.* Cambridge, MA: Harvard University Press, 1968.

McGuire, J. E., and Tamny, M. *Certain Philosophical Questions: Newton's Trinity Notebook.* Cambridge: Cambridge University Press, 1985.

McMullin, E. *Newton on Matter and Activity*. Notre Dame, IN: University of Notre Dame Press, 1978.

Palter, Robert, ed. *The 'Annus Mirabilis' of Sir Isaac Newton*. Cambridge: MIT Press, 1970.

Turnbull, H. W. et al., eds. *The Correspondence of Isaac Newton*. 7 vols. Cambridge: Cambridge University Press, 1959–1977.

Wallis, Peter, and Ruth Wallis. *Newton and Newtoniana, 1672–1975*. Folkestone: Dawson, 1977.

Westfall, Richard S. *Never at Rest: A Biography of Isaac Newton*. New York: Cambridge University Press, 1980.

RICHARD S. WESTFALL

See also Active Principles; Calculus; Color; Dynamics; Force; Mechanical Philosophy; Optics

Novae

In the Aristotelian universe of the sixteenth century, stars were not supposed to appear and disappear. The stars had never been known to change, and their motions were explained by the supposition that the stars and the heavens as a whole are made of an eternal and unchangeable substance whose natural motion is circular. Nevertheless, a few authors, such as Girolamo Cardano (1501–1576), were beginning to question the absoluteness of this distinction, particularly in the region just above the Moon. They believed that comets, considered atmospheric by Aristotle (384–322 B.C.E.), might exist in the celestial region. But (apart from a few obscure ancient reports) changes in the fixed stars were unheard of.

It was, therefore, a great surprise when, in 1572, a very bright new star suddenly appeared in the constellation of Cassiopeia. The discussions about the place of comets had suggested the idea of using parallax measurements to estimate altitude, so a substantial number of astronomers applied this technique to the nova. Many of these observations were collected and published by the Danish astronomer Tycho Brahe (1546-1601), who also made his own observations. The best observations showed little or no parallax, so Brahe concluded that the apparition was really a star, above the planetary region. He also found that it was in a position not previously occupied by any known star and, thus, appeared to be a new creation. Although there was much discussion of its origin, and several theories were proposed to explain it, most observers agreed with Brahe that it was a new and miraculous work of God, outside the ordinary course of nature. This explanation had the advantage of keeping the heavens unalterable in their own nature.

Nevertheless, it did occur to Brahe at the same time that new stars might not be all that unusual. The 1572 nova was unusually bright: might not others have appeared that, being dimmer, escaped notice? Astronomers of the following decades who shared this suspicion were gratified when, by a remarkable coincidence, another new star, nearly as bright, appeared in Ophiuchus in 1604. In the meantime, there had been three other reports of new stars: one seen only by Johannes Kepler (1571–1630) while observing the Moon in 1602, one observed by David Fabricius (1564-1617) in 1596 in Cetus (that was later identified as the variable star Mira Ceti), and one, first observed by Willem Janszoon Blaeu (1571-1638) in 1600, that was visible until some time in the 1620s. New stars seemed to be popping up everywhere, and their number was increased by others, purportedly from historical accounts, that were announced by opportunistic authors.

Therefore, after Kepler observed the 1604 nova, he thought it time for a thorough reassessment of the origin and nature of such stars. In his book *De stella nova* (1606), he pointed out that, to ascribe a miraculous origin to these stars is to abandon any attempt to explain them. There were, on the other hand, plenty of possible explanations at hand, so the question was not whether they could be explained but which explanation seemed most plausible. Kepler's own account was that the matter for the new star was gathered by an excretory faculty of the transparent, space-filling celestial substance, which serves to maintain the heavens' clarity. This matter then ignited to form the star.

This explanation, thoroughly argued, served to explain all of the phenomena and so won widespread approval. By the mid-1620s, even some of the most opinionated Aristotelians had accepted an account that generally followed Kepler's. It also seemed that celestial change had abated: evidently, the great novae of 1572 and 1604 had burned all of the available celestial excreta.

Later in the seventeenth century, accounts of new stars were influenced by the discovery of variable stars, which raised the question of whether the novae were, in fact, long-period variables. In 1665 the French astronomer Ismaël Bouillau (1605-1694) proposed an explanation, which was sometimes applied to novae, that involved a rotating star with a dark side and a bright side. From this time on, in the absence of further novae and the discovery of more variables, attention was focused on explaining the latter.

BIBLIOGRAPHY

Grant, Edward. *Planets, Stars, and Orbs: The Medieval Cosmos, 1200-1687*. Cambridge: Cambridge University Press, 1994, pp. 210-219.

Hellman, C. Doris. *The Comet of 1577: Its Place in the History of Astronomy*. New York: AMS, 1971, pp. 111-117.

WILLIAM H. DONAHUE

See also Brahe, Tycho; Celestial Spheres; Kepler, Johannes; Parallax

Nuñes, Pedro (1502–1578)

Born near Lisbon, Nuñes studied medicine and mathematics at Salamanca. Back in Portugal, he was appointed royal cosmographer in 1529, professor of mathematics at Coimbra in 1544, and chief cosmographer in 1547. He published *Libro de algebra en arithmetica y geometria* (1567), a good algebra book that influenced Simon Stevin's (1548–1620) work, but he is mostly remembered as the founder of scientific navigation. As the leading mathematician of the Portuguese Court, Nuñes played a crucial role in gathering new geographical information, such as Joao de Castro's (1500–1548) first study of magnetic declination. He designed new astronomical and nautical instruments needed for oceanic (as opposed to coastal and Mediterranean) navigation, including instruments for measuring magnetic declination and the Sun's altitude and also the *nonius* (after his Latinized name, Petrus Nonius), which accurately measures small portions of arc. Transoceanic travel made it apparent that sailing on a "straight" track—keeping the rudder steady with constant wind and no sea currents present—is not equivalent to steering a constant course—one in which the magnetic needle keeps pointing in the same direction. Correctly interpreting it as an effect of the earth's curved surface, Nuñes studied the track that would result from sailing on a constant course. He developed methods to keep a ship on great circles, or tracks of shortest distance, and showed that a constant-course track, making a constant angle with all meridians it crossed, would be a sort of spiral that would turn around and around one of the earth's poles, getting ever closer but never reaching it. He designed an instrument for visualizing such spiral lines, now called *loxodromes,* and suggested that marine charts would be most useful if the curved surface of the earth were projected on them so that loxodromes appear as straight lines. His main contributions, first published in Portuguese in 1537, appeared enlarged and improved in the Latin *Opera* (1566). They were probably used by Gerard Mercator (1512–1594) and developed by Edward Wright (1558–1615) and Stevin.

BIBLIOGRAPHY

Costa, A. F. da. *A marinharia dos descobrimentos*. Lisbon, 1933.

Randles, W. G. L. "Pedro Nuñes and the Discovery of the Loxodromic Curve." *Revista da Universidade de Coimbra* 35 (1989), 119–130.

Sousa Ventura, M. *Vida e obra de Pedro Nunes*. Lisbon: Instituto de Cultura e Língua Portuguesa, 1985.

ANTONI MALET

See also Cartography; Geography; Mercator, Gerard; Navigation; Stevin, Simon; Wright, Edward

Observatoire de Paris

The decision to build an official observatory in Paris was contemporaneous with, and equal in importance to, the organization of the Académie Royale des Sciences in 1666. The structure was even initially intended to serve not only for astronomical observation, but also as a place of assembly and experiment, as a chemical laboratory and a depository for the natural history and mechanical collections of the Académie. Although the astronomical function rapidly prevailed, the observatory remained under the supervision of the Académie until 1711.

A site was selected outside the city gates, and the grounds were acquired on March 7, 1667. On June 21, 1667, the day of the summer solstice, the astronomers of the Académie determined the meridian of the place on which the structure was to be centered. Claude Perrault (1613–1688), a member of the Académie, designed the building. His colleagues Adrien Auzout (1621–1691) and Jean Picard (1620–1682), and afterward Jean-Dominique Cassini (1625–1712), demanded and obtained some modifications to facilitate its use in observation. The bulk of the work was completed by 1672. The fitting out of the observatory, however, continued beyond the visit of Louis XIV and a party of the Court on May 1, 1682. In total, it cost the royal Treasury (between 1667 and 1677) a little more than 700,000 livres, a sum to which it was necessary to add several tens of thousands of livres to acquire the various instruments.

For zenithal observations, a 55-meter channel extended from a well cut in the stone floor of the foundation through the middle of the structure to the roof. From the early years of the use of the structure, a gnomon, together with an opening high on the south wall and a meridional line traced along the length of the ground in the great hall of the second floor, was put in place, thereby permitting precise observation of the Sun at noon. At the end of 1685, the Marly tower, a wooden tower 120 feet (ca. 39 m) high, initially constructed for the water supply at Versailles, was installed in the garden for the use of the great telescopes "without tubes."

Designed and built when observational techniques were in flux, the observatory was ill suited to astronomical work. During construction, moreover, the decision was taken to leave the Académie's headquarters, including the chemical laboratory and dissecting room in Paris, instead of moving them to the observatory as originally planned. That is why, other than a chamber reserved as a repository for machines, a great part of the structure was converted into accommodations for the astronomers and their assistants.

The astronomers began using the building even as it was being constructed. From September 14, 1671, Cassini moved to the observatory and began to work there, coordinating his observations with those of Picard and Jean Richer (1630–1696) in Denmark and Cayenne, respectively.

Inauguration of the Observatoire de Paris marks the start of a new era in astronomical precision. Only the most up-to-date instruments conceived and constructed within the last five years were used, improving in a spectacular manner the precision of measurement: the filar micrometer of Auzout and Picard, shortly to be perfected by Ole Christensen Römer (1644–1710); quadrants and other sectors equipped with optical sights, steadily improved by Picard; Huygensian pendulum clocks in their latest state of perfection; telescopic lenses

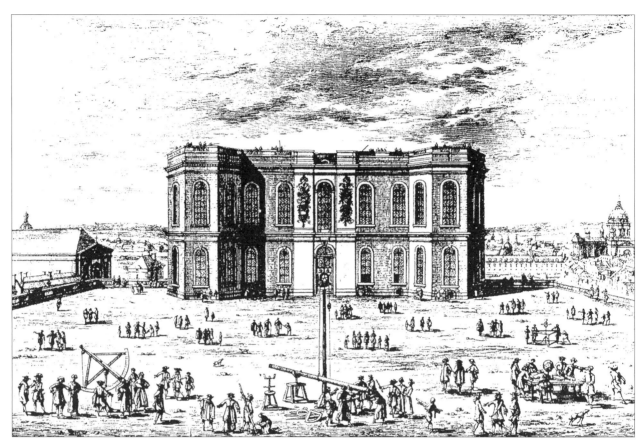

The Paris Observatory. From Les places, portes, fontaines, églises, et maisons de Paris.

cut and polished by the best Italian and French makers (Campani, Divini, Lebas, Ménard, Borelly); and so forth. These instruments were then put to work by very active, excellent astronomical observers: Cassini, Picard, Römer, and Philippe de La Hire (1640–1718). Further, they strove to coordinate their labors and to apportion the tasks within the framework of effective programs of research, in particular a comprehensive program for the determination of longitudes made possible by Cassini's tables of the motions of the satellites of Jupiter; expeditions to Uraniborg, Cayenne, the French coasts, Cape Verde, and the Antilles; collaboration with Jesuit missionaries; and establishment of a wide network of correspondents in France and abroad.

It is not surprising that, under these conditions, remarkable results were obtained within a few years by the observatory: discovery and measurement of the annual displacement of the Pole Star; discovery of four new satellites of Saturn; determination of the parallax of Mars and indirectly of the dimensions of the solar system; discovery of the flattening of Jupiter, making clear the finitude of the speed of light and the division of the ring of Saturn; establishment of a precise map of the Moon; and discovery of the zodiacal light improved knowledge of the fundamental elements of astronomy. Finally, the astronomers systematically corrected terrestrial longitudes: using a large world map delineated on the pavement in the west room of the first (i.e., second in American usage) floor, they recorded the findings of the geodesic expeditions and observations communicated by their correspondents around the world.

It may also be noted that it is at the Observatory of Paris that works were conceived that were also useful to astronomers, such as the tables of La Hire and the *Connaissance des temps* (regularly issued astronomical tables), and that many French and foreign observers, who were not members of the Académie, received from it practical orientation in the latest techniques before exercising their talents elsewhere.

Bibliography

Armitage, Angus. "Jean Picard and His Circle." *Endeavour* 13 (1954), 17–21.

Boquet, F. "Fondation de l'Observatoire de Paris." *Astronomie* 27 (1913), 95–115.

Débarbat, Suzanne. "Newton, Halley et l'Observatoire de Paris." *Revue d'histoire des sciences et de leurs applications* 39 (1986), 127–154.

Taton, René. L'Observatoire de Paris à l'époque de Roemer." In Taton, René. *Roemer et la vitesse de la lumière.* Paris: Vrin, 1978, pp. 99–112.

Wolf, C. *Histoire de l'observatoire de Paris de sa fondation à 1793.* Paris: Gauthier-Villars, 1902.

GUY PICOLET
TRANS. WILBUR APPLEBAUM

See also Académie Royale des Sciences; Cassini, Gian Domenico (Jean-Dominique); La Hire, Philippe de; Picard, Jean; Richer, Jean; Römer, Ole Christensen; Royal Observatory at Greenwich

Oldenburg, Henry (ca. 1619–1677)

As first secretary of the Royal Society of London, he ably developed the art of scientific communication to a high degree and virtually invented the practice of scientific administration. For fifteen years, he represented the Royal Society in the eyes of the learned world, upholding and publicizing the society's ideals.

Born in Bremen, with a Master's degree in theology, he acquired linguistic skill traveling as a tutor. In 1653 he came to England as an emissary of the Senate of Bremen to Oliver Cromwell. He became friendly with the family of Robert Boyle (1627–1691) and with many practitioners of the new English experimental philosophy, typifying the Scientific Revolution. As tutor to Boyle's nephew, he traveled in France and Germany, meeting scientists everywhere, as he wrote to Boyle and Samuel Hartlib (ca. 1600–1662). In 1660 he was invited to join the group that founded the Royal Society, and in 1662 he became one of its two secretaries, in effect the only active one. As secretary he attended all regular and council meetings, taking careful minutes and seeing to their entry into bound *Journal Books.* He had papers read at meetings copied into the *Register Book.* He read to meetings letters addressed to the society or to himself and replied to them either as directed or on his own initiative. He met regularly with other officers to discuss and organize society business. He thus played a key role in keeping the society running smoothly.

As a letter writer he was unique. He gradually built up the number of his correspondents, both domestic and foreign, until they numbered hundreds, writing in English, French, Latin, Dutch, and Italian (German was as yet hardly a scientific language). He even wrote to the Americas. What made his correspondence particularly important was that he learned how to elicit information from men often reluctant to publish, partly by encouragement, telling one man what another was doing, acting as a link between men working on the same subject, always urging replies. This only occasionally produced ill feeling—fortunately, seldom directed against Oldenburg himself. Without him, much important scientific work of his time would never have seen the light of day. Best known is his share in persuading Isaac Newton (1642–1727) to publish his early papers on light and colors as well as allowing communication of some of his early mathematical work to René-François de Sluse (1622–1685) and Gottfried Wilhelm Leibniz (1646–1716). He encouraged many, like Marcello Malpighi (1628–1694), whose letters he collected and published; Antoni van Leeuwenhoek (1632–1723), whose published work was only in the form of letters; and young men like John Flamsteed (1646–1719) and Martin Lister (1639–1712).

Equally important was his founding of the *Philosophical Transactions* in 1665, which published and so disseminated so much of scientific importance during his editorship. His own interest lay in gathering information for a universal natural history, as Francis Bacon (1561–1626) had advised.

Thanks to his conscientious energy, the Royal Society possesses a unique archive of seventeenth-century documents and letters, for most incoming letters were preserved by Oldenburg. His surviving correspondence is a monument to his skill, diligence, and authority.

BIBLIOGRAPHY
Hall, M. B. "Oldenburg and the Art of Scientific Communication." *British Journal for the History of Science* 2 (1965), 277–290.

Oldenburg, Henry. *The Correspondence of Henry Oldenburg.* Eds. and trans. A. R. Hall and M. B. Hall. 13 vols. Madison and Milwaukee: University of Wisconsin Press; London: Mansell; London: Taylor and Francis, 1963–1986.

MARIE BOAS HALL

See also Correspondence Networks; *Philosophical Transactions;* Royal Society of London

Optics

Whether optics experienced a revolution during the sixteenth and seventeenth centuries has been subject to historical analysis and discussion. The seventeenth-century transformation of natural philosophy also affected the study of light: scholars increasingly explained the nature of light and its propagation in mechanistic fashion. Natural-philosophical accounts of light remained, however, closely connected to ontological and epistemological questions. In particular in Cartesian physics, as exemplified by the *Traité de physique* (1671) of Jacques Rohault (1620–1675), accounts of the nature of light were interwoven with natural philosophy as a whole. Generally, the organization of the science of optics did not change fundamentally during the seventeenth century. Geometrical optics experienced profound changes in content and extension of its subject matter but continued to constitute an independent field of study throughout the seventeenth century. In the methodology of optics, the most drastic changes took place during the second half of the seventeenth century. New ways to account for the nature of light emerged in which experimental and mathematical aspects were integrated. An important impulse for this development came from experimental research, which led to the discovery of several new properties of light.

In the first decade of the seventeenth century, Johannes Kepler (1571–1630) innovated geometrical optics by introducing a new concept of image formation. The principal problem of image formation was how an unambiguous image can be formed when each point of an object emits rays in every direction. In medieval optics, a one-to-one correspondence between an object point and its image was assured by explaining how refraction in the eye weakened all rays but one, the ray that produced the image. According to Kepler, the contributions of the other rays cannot be ruled out, and the image must in some way be formed by a pencil of rays emitted by the object point. In his view, a sharp image is produced when the rays emitted from one point of the luminous source are brought to a focus in a point of the image. Kepler published this new concept of image formation in *Ad Vitellionem paralipomena* (Supplements to Witelo, 1604).

In *Paralipomena,* Kepler applied his conception of image formation to various questions concerning reflection and refraction, including atmospheric refraction. He refuted the Cathetus Rule, the central principle of geometrical optics used to determine the position of the image of objects. The cathetus is the line through the object that is perpendicular to a reflecting or refracting surface. The Cathetus Rule implies that the image of the object is perceived at the intersection of the cathetus and the rays that enter the eye. This rule is only correct in

some particular cases. Kepler's conception of image implies that the position of an image cannot be determined by one ray alone; the position of the image is the place where the eye perceives the intersection of the rays entering it. In the last chapter, he explained image formation in the eye. He adopted new views on the anatomy of the eye, in which the retina, instead of the lens, was considered to be the sensitive organ. In the eye, the cornea, the lens, and the vitreous humor between them refract rays in such a way that they focus on the retina, and a sharp, reversed image is formed.

The impulse toward Kepler's optical studies had been an anomaly in astronomical observation encountered by Tycho Brahe (1546–1601). When the eclipsed Sun is projected through a small aperture, the diameter of the Moon appears smaller than it ought to be. The background to this anomaly is the problem of pinhole images, which had puzzled medieval writers on optics. Regardless of its shape, a small aperture projects a circular image of the Sun (e.g., a triangular aperture produces a circular instead of a triangular image). This phenomenon seems to contradict the principle of rectilinear propagation of light rays, which was fundamental to geometrical optics. The correct explanation of it was given in 1600 by Kepler, who explained that, in the case of a triangular aperture, multiple triangular images of the Sun are superimposed and produce a circular image with a blurred, penumbral circumference. In 1521 Francesco Maurolico (1494–1575) had been the first to acquire a full understanding of penumbral shadows, in his *Photismi de lumine et umbra* (Some Enlightenment on Light and Shadow). He had given a nearly correct solution to the problem of pinhole images, but the work remained unpublished until 1611. Kepler's solution of the problem of pinhole images explained why the image of the eclipsed Sun produces an anomalous value for the diameter of the Moon: a blurred image of the visible parts of the Sun covers the borders of the image of the Moon.

Kepler's concept of image formation was adopted rather quickly. His explanation of the retinal image exerted a profound influence on seventeenth-century optics in general. In his *Oculus hoc est: Fundamentum opticum* (The Eye; or, The Foundation of Optics, 1619), Christoph Scheiner (1573–1650) described experiments verifying the existence of the retinal image and discoveries of new properties of perception. René Descartes (1596–1650) combined Kepler's theory of the retinal image with his own mechanistic explanation of vision.

Investigations into the anatomy and physiology of the eye, as well as mechanistic explanations of them, remained a substantial part of optics throughout the seventeenth century. In geometrical optics, James Gregory (1638–1675) and Isaac Barrow (1630–1677) extended Kepler's analysis of reflected and refracted images.

In *Paralipomena,* Kepler did not succeed in finding an exact law of refraction. In *Dioptrice* (1611), he developed a theory of the newly invented telescope using an approximate rule for refraction. During the first quarter of the century, several scholars discovered the law of refraction. The sine law remained unpublished until Descartes published it in *La Dioptrique* (1637). In addition to Kepler's contributions to optics, the discovery of the sine law was an important stimulus to seventeenth-century optics. The mechanistic explanation of this law became an important topic of seventeenth-century optics, which induced theoretical and experimental studies of light. The sine law enabled the development of an exact theory of lenses and their configurations and the quantitative study of the refraction of light in general. By a revolutionary reinterpretation of the law, Isaac Newton (1642–1727) laid the foundations of his mathematical theory of colors, which he announced in 1671.

In the second half of the seventeenth century, several new properties of light were discovered, which posed problems for theoretical accounts of the nature of light. In *Physico-Mathesis de lumine, coloribus et iride* (The Physico-Mathematical Treatment of Light, 1665), Francesco Maria Grimaldi (1618–1663) described a phenomenon that is nowadays called *diffraction*. When he let a narrow beam of light fall on a small, opaque object, he saw colored bands on both the inside and the outside of the shadow. This phenomenon seemed to contradict the principle of rectilinearity of light rays. Grimaldi explained the apparent bending of the rays by considering light to be a fluid substance emitted by a light source, which produces colors when obstacles are encountered. Robert Hooke (1635–1703) independently discovered the same phenomenon somewhat later and called it *inflection*. Hooke compared inflection to atmospheric refraction, the multiple refraction of light traveling through a medium of gradually changing density. Hooke did not, however, mention colors but only lighter and darker bands. Toward the end of the 1660s, members of the Académie Royale des Sciences in Paris were not able to repeat Grimaldi's observations and rejected them. Isaac Newton discussed diffraction for the first time in 1675, in a paper read to the Royal Society of London. In the 1690s, he tried to discover the mathematical properties of the phenomenon, but he broke off his investigations dissatisfied.

In 1665, Robert Hooke published *Micrographia*. Apart from many observations and experiments, the book contained a description of the colors produced by thin films of transparent material, nowadays explained by interference. Hooke explained the phenomenon by his pulse theory of light. He noticed that the colors are related to the thickness of the film and supposed that the colors vary periodically with it. Contrary to Hooke, Christiaan Huygens (1629–1695) could determine the thickness of the film exactly. By pressing two convex lenses together, he produced colored rings. The spherical shape of the lenses produced a thin film of air of determinate shape, the thickness of which Huygens could easily derive. Newton performed a similar experiment in the early 1670s, independently of Huygens and with much greater precision. He proved the periodicity of the colored rings, which are nowadays called *Newton's rings*. Newton went much further than Huygens and performed extensive experiments with the colored rings. By using monochromatic light, he showed that light of a specific color is reflected or transmitted at certain thicknesses. This property was an important underpinning of his theory of the compound nature of white light. Newton's discussion of colors in thin films formed a crucial part of his *Opticks* (1704).

In 1669 Erasmus Bartholin (1625–1698) published *Experimenta crystalli Islandici disdiaclastici* (Experiments on Birefringent Icelandic Crystal), in which he described the uncommon refractional properties of Iceland crystal. In addition to the double refraction this crystal produces, one of these refractions contradicts the sine law of refraction. By this so-called *strange refraction,* perpendicular rays are refracted. Bartholin's explanation of the strange refraction was a geometrical one. He said that the sine law holds, not in respect to the perpendicular of the refracting surface but to a line obliquely to it. Christiaan Huygens explained the strange refraction in 1678 by means of his wave theory of light. He considered his explanation to be the cornerstone of the theory he published in *Traité de la lumière* (Treatise on Light, 1690). Isaac Newton discussed the strange refraction in one of the Queries, his tentative remarks at the end of the *Opticks*.

Newton's primary interest in Iceland crystal concerned another property of light, described but not

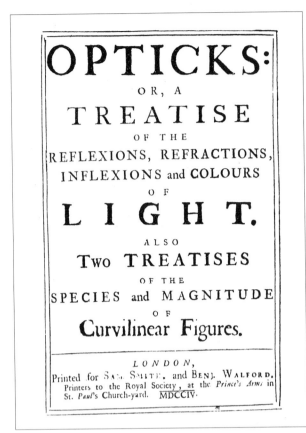

The first edition of Isaac Newton's Opticks *of 1704.*

explained by Huygens in *Traité de la lumière*. Newton placed a crystal behind another and conducted a beam of light through them. He noticed that the orientation of the crystals to each other affected the refraction of light in the second crystal. For example, only when all faces of both crystals are parallel is the ray normally refracted by the first refracted normally by the second. According to Newton, this phenomenon indicated a new, distinct property of light. In the concluding Queries of the *Opticks,* he suggested that rays have "several sides," each with its own properties. The phenomenon Huygens described is nowadays called *polarization.*

The optics of Hooke, Huygens, and Newton was methodologically innovative. They treated physical aspects of light independently from ontological and epistemological questions. They used—in varying degree—experimental and mathematical means to develop their theories of light. In all cases, some new property of light was central to their theories. Hooke founded his theory of color on experiments with thin films. The core of Huygens's theory of light consisted of a mathematical model of the propagation of light from which the laws of

optics could be derived. It was based on a mechanistic account of the propagation of waves through a medium of colliding particles. According to Huygens, his explanation by means of this model of the strange refraction in Iceland crystal constituted the verification of his theory of light. Newton tried to found a quantitative science of colors on his experiments with prisms and Newton's rings. He did not succeed entirely, and the *Opticks* contained a primarily experimental theory of light and color. Toward the end of the seventeenth century, a new approach to optics was emerging, in particular in the work of Hooke, Huygens, and Newton.

BIBLIOGRAPHY

Buchwald, Jed Z., and Kurt M. Pedersen. "Bartholin, His Discovery, and Its Significance." *Acta historica scientiarum naturalium et medicinalium* 40 (1991), 9–29.

Hall, A. R. "Beyond the Fringe: Diffraction as Seen by Grimaldi, Fabri, Hooke, and Newton." *Notes and Records of the Royal Society of London* 44 (1990), 13–23.

Lindberg, David C. "Laying the Foundations of Geometrical Optics: Maurolico, Kepler, and the Medieval Tradition." In *The Discourse of Light from the Middle Ages to the Enlightenment: Papers Read at a Clark Library Seminar, April 24, 1982,* ed. David C. Lindberg and Geoffrey Cantor. Los Angeles: William Andrews Clark Memorial Library, University of California, 1985, pp. 3–65.

———. *Theories of Vision from Al-Kindi to Kepler.* Chicago: University of Chicago Press, 1975.

Sabra, A. I. *Theories of Light from Descartes to Newton.* London: Oldbourne, 1967.

Westfall, Richard S. *Never at Rest: A Biography of Isaac Newton.* Cambridge: Cambridge University Press, 1980.

FOKKO J. DIJKSTERHUIS

See also Color; Diffraction; Light Transmission; Reflection; Refraction; Vision

Ortelius, Abraham (1527–1598)

The maker of the first atlas, the *Theatrum orbis terrarum* (1570). He started his career as a colorist of maps. Later he became a trader in books, prints, and maps. His scientific and collecting interests developed in harmony with those of a trader, and he traveled extensively all over Europe. He was, in the first place, a historian. Geography for him was the "eye of history." This may be why Ortelius, in addition to coins and historical objects, also collected maps. Through his travels throughout Europe and with the help of his international circle of friends, Ortelius was able to build a collection of the most modern maps available. This collection formed the starting

The first atlas, published in 1570.

point for his *Theatrum,* an important aspect of which is its being the first of its kind to reduce the best available maps to a uniform format. In selecting maps for his compilation, Ortelius was guided by his critical spirit and his encyclopedic knowledge of maps.

The *Theatrum orbis terrarum* was an instant success. It was the most expensive but also the best-selling book produced in the second half of the sixteenth century. The *Theatrum* was published in more than thirty editions in different languages, and the number of maps increased from 53 in 1570 to 165 in the 1612 editions. After 1579 he included a section, increasing in size with subsequent editions, of historical maps, the *Parergon.*

In his *Theatrum,* Ortelius listed the names of the authors of the original maps and added the names of a great many other cartographers and geographers to it. This *Catalogus auctorum tabularum geographicarum* is now one of the major sources for our knowledge of sixteenth-century cartography.

During the last years of his life, he prepared a reproduction edition of the so-called Peutinger map for publication. He was never to see its appearance, however, for he died at Antwerp on July 4, 1598. This reproduction was included in the final and most complete edition of Ortelius's historical atlas, the *Parergon,* posthumously published in 1624.

BIBLIOGRAPHY

Broecke, Marcel van den. *Ortelius Atlas Maps: An Illustrated Guide.* `t Goy-Houten: HES, 1996.

Broecke, Marcel van den, Peter van der Krogt, and Peter Meurer, eds. *Abraham Ortelius and the First Atlas: Essays Commemorating the Quadricentennial of His Death, 1598–1998.* `t Goy-Houten: HES, 1998.

Koeman, C. The *History of Abraham Ortelius and His "Theatrum Orbis Terrarum."* Lausanne: Sequoia S.A., 1964. (Accompanying English and French eds. of the facs. ed. of Ortelius's *Theatrum*).

Meurer, Peter H. *Fontes cartographici Orteliani: Das "Theatrum Orbis Terrarum" von Abraham Ortelius und seine Kartenquellen.* Weinheim: VCH-Acta Humaniora, 1991.

PETER VAN DER KROGT

See also Blaeu, Willem Janszoon; Cartography; Mercator, Gerard

Oughtred, William (1575–1660)

One of the most influential English mathematicians of his generation, Oughtred began teaching mathematics as a Fellow of King's College, Cambridge. On leaving the university in 1605, he became vicar of Shalford and, soon afterward, rector of Albury, both in Surrey; he retained the latter benefice until his death. His *Arithmeticae in numeris et speciebus institutio: Quae . . . totius mathematicae quasi clavis est* (1631) was compiled, he said, while he was tutor to one of the sons of Thomas Howard, second earl of Arundel (1586–1646). It took algebraic methods from Continental sources, especially from François Viète (1540–1603), and presented them in an unusually concise form. An English edition appeared in 1647, and second and third Latin editions, under the title *Clavis mathematica[e]* (A Mathematical Key), in 1648 and 1652. The last was produced in Oxford by a group including John Wallis (1616–1703), Seth Ward (1617–1689), and the young Christopher Wren (1632–1723). It reflects the unique status Oughtred had by then attained as a figurehead for contemporary English mathematicians.

Despite the later stress on Oughtred's achievements as a theoretician, there is evidence that he taught a full

William Oughtred.

range of mathematical subjects, including the practical; he also collaborated closely with the instrument maker Elias Allen. Competition over priority with respect to an instrument led him to publish a furious attack to his ex-pupil Richard Delamain (fl. 1625–1633) in *The Just Apologie* (1633); here and elsewhere he defended the unity of mathematics, deploring the "superficiall scumme and froth of Instrumentall tricks and practices" that emerged when practice was not based upon sound theoretical understanding.

BIBLIOGRAPHY

Aked, C. K. "William Oughtred: An Early Horological Expositor." *Antiquarian Horology* 13 (1981), 192–201.

Cajori, Florian. *William Oughtred.* Chicago: Open Court, 1916.

Willmoth, Frances. *Sir Jonas Moore: Practical Mathematics and Restoration Science.* Woodbridge: Boydell, 1993, ch. 2.

FRANCES WILLMOTH

See also Algebra; Viète, François

Oxford Philosophical Society

A group of natural philosophers meeting in Oxford from ca. the late 1640s to the early 1690s. The society went through several phases, beginning as an informal group known as the Philosophical College or the Experimental Philosophy Club, meeting under the leadership of John Wilkins (1614–1672). It originated as a combination of London-based natural philosophers—including Robert Boyle (1627–1691) and John Wallis (1616–1703), who relocated to Oxford as a consequence of the Puritan reforms of the university—and the remnants of William Harvey's (1578–1657) circle at Oxford. By 1651 the group had a formal basis, with written by-laws calling for weekly meetings, although the meetings themselves were irregular. The society lapsed with the Restoration, when Wilkins removed to Cambridge and several other members to London, where they formed part of the nucleus of the Royal Society.

Natural-philosophical meetings resumed in Oxford in 1665, when the plague of London caused many virtuosi to leave that city. Those at Oxford held meetings with local natural philosophers. These meetings continued after the plague and the departure of the Londoners, the Oxford Philosophical Society taking shape as a regional society corresponding with the Royal Society and the Dublin Philosophical Society. Leading lights of the society included Wallis, its chairman; the local natural historian Dr. Robert Plot (1640–1696), author of two influential studies, *The Natural History of Oxfordshire* (1677) and *The Natural History of Staffordshire* (1686); and the botanist and antiquarian Edward Lhwyd (1660–1707). From 1683 the society met weekly in the Ashmolean Museum, of which Plot was keeper. Papers read and topics discussed covered such standard areas as monsters, magnetic experiments, dissections, and antiquities. With the removal of Plot to London, where he became secretary of the Royal Society in 1682, and the general waning of interest in natural philosophy at Oxford, the society dissolved by the early 1690s.

BIBLIOGRAPHY

Gunther, R. T. *The Philosophical Society: Early Science in Oxford,* vol 4. Oxford: privately printed, 1925.

Webster, Charles. *The Great Instauration: Science, Medicine, and Reform, 1626–1660.* London: Duckworth. 1975.

WILLIAM E. BURNS

See also Academies; Royal Society of London; Virtuosi

P

Pacioli, Luca (ca. 1445–1517)

His life and work epitomize the new role mathematics came to occupy in Renaissance society. A Franciscan friar, he moved easily both geographically—from Florence to Rome, from Milan to Venice—and socially—from Courts to the houses of merchants, from universities to the workshops of painters and architects. His most well-known work is *De divina proportione* (1509), which includes sixty engravings drawn by his friend Leonardo da Vinci (1452–1519), but he is also the author of the six-hundred-page *Summa de arithmetica geometria proportioni et proportionalità* (1494), the first and one of the most influential mathematical encyclopedias of the Renaissance.

De divina proportione is devoted to the proportion between the segments obtained cutting a straight line of length a in two parts, x and $a - x$, such that $a : x :: x : a - x$. It was called "divine" from the notion, of Neoplatonic and Pythagorean origins, that it was one of the "highest" and "strongest" proportions. Endowed in classical antiquity and again in the Renaissance with aesthetic and philosophical meanings, it was widely used in architecture and the fine arts. It was assumed to be the key to the geometrical relationships among the five Platonic solids and also to the Platonic form of the quintessence. The 1494 *Summa* (reprinted in 1523) teaches the use of Hindu-Arabic numerals in basic arithmetic computations, including extraction of square roots and fractions. It deals with the rule of three (a means of finding an unknown term in a simple proportion) and how to apply it and also includes a good account of the rules for solving quadratic equations—the only ones that could be solved then through rules equivalent to our modern formulas. Pacioli's *Summa* was intended for a public that used mathematics primarily in a commercial context. It contains tables of units of money, length, and so on and problems showing how to calculate in different units and pass from one system to another. A great number of problems deal with computation of interest, barters, alloys, and the like. It devotes twenty-five pages to the first printed treatise on double-entry bookkeeping.

BIBLIOGRAPHY

Franchi, R., and L. Toti Rigatelli. "Towards a History of Algebra from Leonardo of Pisa to Luca Pacioli." *Janus* 72 (1985), 17–82.

Giusti, E., and C. Maccagni, eds. *Luca Pacioli e la matematica del Rinascimento*. Firenze: Giunti, 1994.

Speziali, P. "Luca Pazioli et son oeuvre." In *Sciences de la Renaissance: VIIIe Congrès International de Tours*. Paris: Vrin, 1973, pp. 93–106.

ANTONI MALET

See also Algebra

Paracelsus (ca. 1493–1541)

Theophrastus Philippus Aureolus Bombastus von Hohenheim, before he became known as Paracelsus, is remembered as an iconoclastic physician from an age of reformation and rebellion, an innovative healer who shunned the medical guilds and enraged the apothecaries by denouncing their practices and urged physicians to make their own remedies.

Paracelsus was a rustic. His manner of presentation was rough and filled with disdain for anything foreign or bearing the marks of arrogant intellectual artifice, and he readily alienated the medical establishment. When briefly employed as city physician in Basel, a position

Paracelsus. Courtesy Oklahoma University Library.

that permitted him to lecture publicly, he preached against academic medicine and the pagan philosophy upon which it was founded. He thought that, instead of learning medicine from books, the physician should "overhear" the secrets of nature and discover through personal observation and experience how they apply to medicine.

Paracelsus's chronic penury and proclivity for making influential enemies wherever he resided discouraged publication of his abundant writings. Only a couple of volumes appeared during his lifetime, but he left a trail of manuscripts behind him as he restlessly moved from one town to another. After his death, his treatises were collected and copied by a growing number of adherents, who were drawn to his reputation as a healer of incurable diseases, such as epilepsy and arthritis. The medical and philosophical tracts were edited and published beginning in the 1560s, and the first collected works, the Huser edition, came out in 1589–1591. These texts, and the Paracelsian studies based on them, put forth a world-

view that was radically different from the accepted Aristotelian natural philosophy and denied the fundamentals of Galenic medicine, which viewed disease as an intemperate mixture of the body's four basic fluids. Opposing this materialist and qualitative theory, Paracelsus argued that the real causes of organic phenomena, including diseases, were spiritual. These spiritual powers, which in their simplest form reduced to the three principal spirits of Salt, Sulfur, and Mercury, manifest themselves in the laboratory and in the body as chemical properties or signatures. He even interpreted the Creation of the world, as told in Genesis, in terms of chemical philosophy. His approach was antimaterialist inasmuch as chemical philosophy was "vital philosophy" and entailed understanding what the Paracelsians called "the anatomy of the world." According to this theory, the fundamental creative process is separation; species and individuals come into existence as specifics when they are separated or distinguished from the more general.

For Paracelsus, true medicines were also essentially spiritual and must be freed from the gross matter in which they occur in nature before they can most effectively be used to treat diseases. Such separations are accomplished by means of fire, which Paracelsus elevated from its Aristotelian status as one of the four terrestrial elements, blurring the distinction between it and the quintessence, which the Aristotelians supposed to constitute the celestial region. The Paracelsians, however, considered fire to be present wherever there was activity—vitality—and spoke of "stars" or stellar matter (*astrum*) mixed in with the terrestrial elements. Thus, living organisms, minerals included, possess a spiritual vitality that can be used to heal.

Paracelsus called chemistry one of four pillars upon which true medicine is supported, and he separated its legitimate medical use—iatrochemistry—from esoteric efforts to transmute base metals into gold for personal gain. He believed that human metabolic processes were chemical digestions, separations, and exaltations conducted by spiritual efficient agents that he likened to alchemists and named *archei*. The failure of an *archeus* led to a local buildup of toxic impurities, which constituted a specific disease. To cure the most difficult diseases, Paracelsus recommended potent, mineral-based, and sometimes highly poisonous drugs that could destroy or expel the morbific impurities. These he prepared by high-temperature distillations and other techniques adapted from medieval alchemy, which were intended to remove their toxicity while retaining their spiritual powers.

Critics of Paracelsian medicine decried the use of "poisons" as medicaments and maligned Paracelsus's rejection of the time-tested Galenic therapy, which sought to reestablish the patient's proper qualitative balance through contrary indications—a patient who was too hot needed to be bled or given an emetic to remove excess blood and "choler" (yellow bile), the two "hot" constituent fluids. Instead of this method of applying contraries (*contraria contrariis*), Paracelsus argued that, since diseases were spirits, they needed to be cured by applying similar spirits (i.e., medicines possessing chemical characteristics that produced symptoms similar to those caused by the morbific agents). For this reason, the Paracelsian theory of similars (*similia similibus*) is sometimes viewed as a forerunner of homeopathic medicine.

The chemical characteristics exhibited by all natural phenomena reflected the underlying system of correspondences and harmonies that the Paracelsians believed knitted together the cosmos. Humans, who possessed a unique status as semidivine images of God, reflected the entirety of the greater world, or macrocosm, for which reason man was called the microcosm. Consequently, Paracelsus viewed human symptoms as correlating with observed phenomena: paroxysms were the same as earthquakes, for example.

The Paracelsian "macrocosm/microcosm correspondence," as it is called, was an elaboration of the medieval Hermetic belief that the seven planets had specific affinities with the seven principal organs and the seven metals. According to this theme, a given disease would naturally be specific to a particular organ; a medicine with the corresponding chemical signature would naturally be attracted to that particular organ and be the appropriate treatment. Therefore, the chemical identity of diseases and proper preparation of specific drugs was a salient characteristic of Paracelsian pharmacology.

Paracelsian theory offered a new, chemical vision of nature's operations and the relation of humans to the cosmos and also provided a doctrinal base for the use of chemically prepared medicines, the popularity of which grew apace in the second half of the sixteenth century. In the seventeenth century, these drugs were incorporated into the official pharmacopoeias and formularies, and courses in chemical methods were offered—sometimes within the universities but more often privately or at competing institutions. By the middle of the century,

both laboratory techniques and iatrochemical theory were far more sophisticated and coherent than anything Paracelsus had described, but his name persisted as a unifying symbol in the professional and rhetorical struggle between the established Galenists and the Chemical Physicians, who clamored for educational reform. For this reason, he is hailed as a pioneer in pharmaceutical chemistry.

Piety, or virtue, was another pillar of Paracelsus's medicine. Although he was summoned to treat the wealthy and powerful, he was most at home among peasants and miners, where his duty as a Christian healer was clear. He was as much a lay religious reformer as he was a physician. His religious writings, however, remained unpublished until the twentieth century, leaving the historian the difficult task of assessing the importance of a shadowy manuscript tradition. The emerging picture of Paracelsus is one of a provocative, impatient, and brilliant theoretician who put forth a unified but poorly articulated worldview, which was, by the standards of his own time, doctrinally heterodox and dangerously radical. His suppositions about the astral body and the divinity of the human essence are integral parts of his natural philosophy, which influenced the mysticism of Valentin Weigel (1533–1588) and Jacob Boehme (1575–1625) and left Paracelsian medical ideas vulnerable to attack on religious grounds.

Paracelsian medical and religious doctrines came under severe censure in a 1572 treatise written by Thomas Erastus (1523–1583), who regarded Paracelsus as a magician and drunkard who trafficked with brute peasants and Jews and maintained views that were unacceptable to orthodox Protestants. A quarter of a century later, Andreas Libavius (1540–1616) chastised the Paracelsians for their impiety, their unrepentant confusion of categories (illogical thinking), and their propensity for obscuring the truth rather than teaching it openly. Indeed, Paracelsus rejected the traditional categories of medieval Aristotelian philosophy and embraced a Neoplatonic holism. Although he regarded knowledge of nature's innermost secrets as best reserved for illuminati who had become adept through long apprenticeship in nature's workshop, he despised hierarchies that kept medical and spiritual service from those who most needed it. This kind of thinking naturally brought into question the medieval social, religious, and political structures, residues of which persisted in early-modern Europe, and consequently made

P

Paracelsus's writings attractive to diverse audiences. His views on popular piety, private property, usury, and capitalist monopoly—ideas that found him followers among the Anabaptists, Rosicrucians, and Puritans in early-modern Europe—also gave him appeal, successively, to nineteenth-century occultists, Nazi ideologists, and their Communist successors. In our own time, the specter of Paracelsus lives on in a play by George Ryga, in which he stands as a timeless warning against the hubris of scientific medicine.

BIBLIOGRAPHY

Debus, Allen. *The Chemical Philosophy: Paracelsian Science and Medicine in the Sixteenth and Seventeenth Centuries.* 2 vols. New York: Science History Publications, 1977.

Pagel, Walter. *Paracelsus: An Introduction to Philosophical Medicine in the Era of the Renaissance.* 2nd rev. ed. Basel: Karger, 1982.

Paracelsus. "The Herbarius of Paracelsus." Trans. with Introduction by Bruce Moran. *Pharmacy in History* 35 (1993), 99–127.

Trevor-Roper, Hugh. "The Paracelsian Movement." In *Renaissance Essays,* ed. Hugh Trevor-Roper. London: Secker and Warburg, 1985, pp. 149–199.

                                          JOLE R. SHACKELFORD

See also Alchemy; Chemical Philosophy; Correspondences; Galenism; Iatrochemistry; Libavius, Andreas; Macrocosm/Microcosm; Pharmacology

Parallax

The angular difference in the apparent position of a celestial object when viewed from two different locations. Using the known values for the baseline (the linear distance between the two observation points) and angular directions of the object from each point, one can determine both the apex angle of the resulting triangle—the parallax—and the distance of the object from the earth.

Although it had been described by the Greek astronomer Hipparchus, parallax theory had not proved very useful to astronomers prior to the sixteenth century. In 1471, Johannes Regiomontanus (1436–1476) became the first to devise a way to accurately determine the parallax and the distance of celestial objects in general and comets in particular, which was quickly adopted by the astronomical community when it was finally published in 1531. Combined with improvements in astronomical instrumentation, Regiomontanus's method soon cast doubts on fundamental aspects of the prevailing Aristotelian cosmology.

For Aristotle (384–322 B.C.E.), the heavens above the sphere of the Moon were immutable and eternal; comets and other "new" phenomena in the heavens were considered atmospheric disturbances. For the most part, his conclusions were not seriously challenged until a "new star"—now thought to be a supernova—appeared in the vicinity of the constellation Cassiopeia in 1572. Various astronomers, including Michael Maestlin (1550–1631) and a young Tycho Brahe (1546–1601), used Regiomontanus's technique and could not discern any parallax, leading them to believe that the "new star" was not sublunar. When a spectacular comet appeared five years later, they used the same methods they had employed in 1572 and concluded that it was moving somewhere in the vicinity of the sphere of Venus. When Brahe published his results, he asserted that the positions he had calculated for the comet and for the "new star" five years earlier proved that the heavens did exhibit change. While most philosophers rejected Brahe's conclusions, others sought different ways to explain the appearance of new phenomena while preserving celestial immutability. Some appealed to miracles, and others to the chance condensation and rarefaction of celestial matter. In different guises and with different historical actors, the debate between astronomers and philosophers over the validity of parallax continued well into the seventeenth century.

While the debate remained unresolved, astronomers began to turn their ever-improving instruments to the search for the parallax of a fixed star. In 1543 Nicolaus Copernicus (1473–1543) had hypothesized that the parallax of a star should be detectable as earth moves around the Sun. However, even with the sophisticated telescopes of the eighteenth century, all attempts to detect any stellar parallax failed. As a consequence, astronomers were forced either to reject the Copernican hypothesis or to radically increase the distance between the earth and the stars and, thereby, the dimensions of the universe. In the end, confirmation of the Copernican hypothesis by observation of stellar parallax would have to wait for almost three hundred years, until it was finally detected in the 1830s.

BIBLIOGRAPHY

Barker, Peter, and Bernard R. Goldstein. "The Role of Comets in the Copernican Revolution." *Studies in the History and Philosophy of Science* 19 (1988), 299–319.

Grant, Edward. *Planets, Stars, and Orbs: The Medieval Cosmos, 1200–1687*. Cambridge: Cambridge University Press, 1994.

Martin, Douglas R. "Status of the Copernican Theory Before Kepler, Galileo, and Newton." *American Journal of Physics* 52 (1984), 982–986.

GARY MCINTYRE

See also Celestial Spheres; Comets; Novae

Paré, Ambroise (ca. 1510–1590)

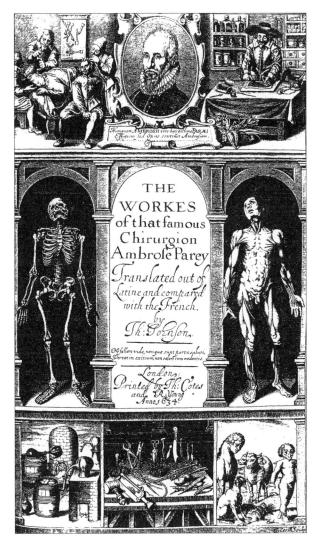

In addition to Paré's portrait, the title page of this translation shows the tools of his trade as well as Paré at work as a surgeon.

A military surgeon, he gained practical experience and developed his novel methods on the battlefields of France. His achievements in the treatment of wounds, particularly gunshot wounds, involved the control of hemorrhage, pain, and infection. He had been apprenticed to a barber-surgeon and studied anatomy as a surgical student at a Paris hospital. His successes as a surgeon led to his appointment as surgeon-in-ordinary to the French king and to the position of master chirurgion at the Collège de Saint-Come despite his lack of Latin.

The standard treatment of gunshot wounds, considered as having been poisoned, was to cauterize them with boiling oil. Paré instead initially used a dressing made with egg yolk, attar of roses, and turpentine. He experimented with various dressings and concluded that the wounds were not poisoned and that cautery was not required. The use of his method, he noted, resulted in more rapid healing and less pain. Paré also discarded cautery as the preferred means to control bleeding from severe wounds or amputation, opting instead for use of the ligature. He also invented a clamp to halt blood flow from ruptured vessels. Among the problems requiring surgery to which he gave his attention were fractures, cataracts, aneurisms, kidney stones, and hernias.

Paré was reputed to be a caring and considerate surgeon and was eager to see surgeons instructed in anatomy. He became acquainted with Jacques Dubois, who had been Andreas Vesalius's (1514–1564) teacher, and was encouraged by him to write a book, published in 1545, describing his methods of treatment for various wounds. In 1564 he published another work on other surgical procedures. In an era before the discovery of the circulation of the blood and dominated by the teachings of Galen (second century), Paré came under persistent attack by members of the medical faculty of the University of Paris. His ideas were very influential, but, after half a century, surgery reverted for a time to its pre-Paré less enlightened past.

BIBLIOGRAPHY

Crenn, Bernard, ed. *Ambroise Paré et son temps: Actes du colloque international, 24 et 25 novembre 1990 à Laval (Mayenne)*. Laval: Association de Commémoration du Quadricentenaire de la Mort d'Ambroise Paré, 1990.

Paré, Ambroise. *The Apologie and Treatise of Ambroise Paré, Containing the Voyages Made into Diverse Places with Many of His Writings upon Surgery*. Ed. and with an Introduction by Geoffrey Keynes. Chicago: University of Chicago Press, 1952.

———. *Ten Books of Surgery, with the Magazine of the Instruments Necessary for It*. Trans. Robert W. Linker and Nathan Womack. Athens: University of Georgia Press, 1969.

ELSA L. GONZALEZ

See also Medical Education; Surgery

Pascal, Blaise (1623–1662)

A mathematician, physicist, and theologian, he was born at Clermont in Auvergne. From the age of eight he was raised and educated by his father, Étienne, in Paris. In 1640 he moved to Rouen in Normandy with his father, returning to live in Paris in 1647.

Pascal's scientific importance relates especially to two areas of his work. As a pure mathematician, still under the tutelage of his father, he showed early promise with a treatise on conic sections; his most important subsequent mathematical work was, perhaps, that on projective geometry, building on the work of his fellow countryman Girard Desargues (1591–1661). As a philosopher of nature, he is most famous for his work on barometric effects and the void. It is impossible, however, to cleanly separate his scientific work from his religious beliefs and sensibilities or from his methodological ideas.

Indeed, in the 1650s, Pascal—like the microscopist Jan Swammerdam (1637–1680) two decades later—was to abandon his inquiries into nature as an unworthy exercise of pride and ambition. His energies, he decided, should be devoted to the welfare of his soul. The spiritual crisis thus created resulted in his most famous work, the posthumously published *Pensées,* which contain his sometimes agonized musings and reflections on theological issues. By the early 1650s, however, Pascal had already completed a considerable amount of significant work on hydrostatics and pneumatics that grew out of his concerns in the mid-1640s with the vexing question of the void.

According to orthodox Aristotelian thinking, there could be no void, or true vacuum, in nature. A number of quite fundamental philosophical arguments were implicated in this position, but most centrally the problem revolved around questions of place and space. Aristotle (384–322 B.C.E.) had regarded the "place" of a material body as being defined by its enclosing surface (think of an object immersed in water). Such an enclosing surface could, therefore, by definition, not be the place of *nothing;* a place always necessarily implied a body occupying that place. This nontrivial argument involves basic definitional notions of the nature of space, rather than empirical issues of whether or not a given region of space can be emptied of all matter. It therefore placed the question of the void on an abstract philosophical level that appeared to distance it from the domain of experimental inquiry. Yet, it was into the latter that Pascal attempted to place it, with the help of methodological arguments.

When Marin Mersenne (1588–1648) brought back firsthand knowledge of the mercury barometer to Paris from his trip to Italy in 1645, there ensued a number of attempts at replication of the phenomenon. Evangelista Torricelli (1608–1647) had discovered, during the preceding year, a means of supporting in a vertical glass tube, closed at the top but open at the bottom, a column of mercury (quicksilver). If the tube were more than ca. 31 inches tall, the mercury would initially drop down the tube, the excess flowing out at the bottom into a dish of mercury in which the end of the tube was immersed. But it would not entirely flow out of the tube; instead, it descended only as far as would leave the column elevated by the magical 31 inches. Torricelli interpreted the suspension of the mercury as being due to the weight of the air pushing on the mercury in the dish. But the central question that many in France asked had to do less with that point than with the space left in the tube above the mercury after its descent. Did it represent an anti-Aristotelian anomaly, a true void in nature?

Initially, the Parisian investigators had difficulty reproducing the phenomenon. The first successful French replication took place in Rouen, still the place of residence of the Pascals, in 1646. Pierre Petit (ca. 1598–1677), together with Blaise Pascal, was able to produce the mysterious space not only atop a column of mercury, but also, in a much longer tube, above a column of water. Pascal published a brief pamphlet in 1647, *Expériences nouvelles touchant le vide* (New Experiments Concerning the Void), which detailed the inferences that he thought these experiments sustained.

Pascal attempted to contain the scandal (as it seemed to some Aristotelian philosophers) of alleging a true void in nature by building a careful methodological protection of the experimental conclusions. In this work, he refused to characterize the space above the mercury as a truly void space—a vacuum. Instead, he spoke in his title of showing that a vessel, however large, "can be emptied of all matter known in nature and which falls under the senses"—he would not assert unequivocally that the space was truly, metaphysically empty, only that it was empty of any matter that could be physically detected. There followed an exchange of letters with an Aristotelian philosopher, the Jesuit priest Étienne Noël (1581–1659), who vigorously denied the possibility of a

Blaise Pascal. Courtesy Oklahoma University Library.

column's reliance on air pressure by arranging that his brother-in-law, Florin Périer, back home in Clermont, carry the apparatus up a nearby mountain, the Puy-de-Dôme. Périer responded with a letter, dated September 22, 1648, that described his ascent of the mountain in the company of named witnesses. The result was as Pascal had anticipated: the higher on the mountainside the apparatus was deployed, the lower the mercury column rested.

In the early 1650s, Pascal wrote two treatises, on hydrostatics and on the weight of the air. These showed how the behavior of enclosed liquids demonstrates the balance or imbalance of pressures between bodies of those liquids (as with siphons) and between them and the surrounding air (as in the cases of barometers or syringes). These were published for the first time only after Pascal's death, as *Traités de l'équilibre des liqueurs et de la pesanteur de la masse de l'air* (1663). Pascal's own failure to publish them signals his shift away from the sciences of nature toward religious and theological concerns.

Pascal began to compose a number of writings of religious import in the 1650s, most notably the *Lettres provinciales,* which were printed in 1656 and 1657. These were propagandistic tracts directed especially against the Jesuits, who were the enemies of the Jansenists, an unorthodox, quasi-reformist religious movement within French Catholicism. Pascal was of the Jansenist party, an ally of the so-called Port-Royalists (named after the center of Jansenism in France). Apart from this intervention in the religious disputes of his time, Pascal also wrote a large number of pieces concerned with theological problems, as well as the state of his own soul. His *Pensées* were first pulled together from the miscellany of material that he had left unpolished and unsystematized at his death in an incomplete edition published at Port-Royal in 1670.

Although such interests pulled Pascal away from scientific matters in his last years, his conception of the natural world around him itself colored his religious sentiments. He was in sympathy with the new mechanistic and mathematical approaches to nature—although he distrusted the dogmatism of René Descartes (1596–1650). His associated belief in an indefinitely large universe led him in his *Pensées* to his famous cri de coeur, fundamentally an expression of the ineffability of religious experience: "The eternal silence of these infinite spaces terrifies me."

vacuum in nature. Pascal's response involved giving Father Noël a lecture on philosophical demonstration, a formalized, elaborated version of the point that he had made in his pamphlet. He used the tools of formal logic to make points about valid and invalid inference that would show his opponent to be begging the question in dogmatizing about Pascal's experiments and their meaning.

Pascal's understanding of the apparatus, however, also required support for the claim that the mercury was supported, as Torricelli thought, by the "weight and pressure" of the air. He opposed the alternative suggestion that an imperfect Aristotelian "fear of the void," whereby nature endeavored to prevent a void's formation, was instead responsible. Again, Pascal's opposition was in part methodological: a "fear of the void" imputed rationality to inanimate nature. Accordingly, Pascal arranged for a dramatic demonstration of the mercury

BIBLIOGRAPHY

Akagi, Shozo. "Pascal et le problème du vide." *Osaka Daigaku. Kyoyobu. Kenkyu Shoroku: Gaikokugo Gaikoku Bungaky* 3 (1967), 185–202; 4 (1968), 170–184; 5 (1969), 109–149.

Bold, Stephen C. "Pascal Geometer." Ph.D. diss. New York University, 1993.

Dear, Peter. "Miracles, Experiments, and the Ordinary Course of Nature." *Isis* 81 (1990), 663–683.

Harrington, Thomas More. *Pascal philosophe: Une étude unitaire de la pensée de Pascal.* Paris: Société d'édition d'enseignment supérieur, 1982.

Pascal, Blaise. *The Physical Treatises of Pascal: The Equilibrium of Liquids and the Weight of the Mass of the Air.* Trans. I. H. B. Spiers and A. G. H. Spiers, with Notes and Introduction by Frederick Barry. New York: Columbia University Press, 1937.

PETER R. DEAR

See also Analytic Geometry; Barometer; Pneumatics; Void

Pathology. See Etiology

Patronage

While not linked exclusively to aristocratic centers, scientific patronage in the sixteenth and seventeenth centuries followed in large part from the cultural and practical interests of European Courts. Royal, princely, and imperial Courts differed widely with respect to specific patronage styles. Patronage varied as well according to the interests of particular patrons and the degree of the patron's personal participation in the design and/or pursuit of individual projects. Regional distinctions also affected patronage typology. The interests of territorial rulers and ecclesiastical officials sometimes reflected practical political ambitions or took shape within specific political environments. Whatever the circumstances, relationships between patrons and clients were inevitably personal and usually dominated by the dynamics of competition, ambition, and dependence current within hierarchical and status-oriented Court societies. Patronage rewards could include grants of money or lands, pensions, and educational positions, as well as appointments, honors, and titles. These might be dispensed by a prince who sought the aid of a particular client or could evolve from a client's own petition for support.

For the most part, studies of scientific patronage have fallen within the realm of the social history of the Scientific Revolution. An emphasis upon clarifying the various and changing roles of both patrons and clients has led to important insights concerning the social foundations of new discoveries and the criticism of older ideas. Learned patrons pursued special interests, supporting projects as collectors, practitioners, and savants. At some Courts, clients accepted a combination of roles in pursuit of utilitarian goals. In such instances, collaborative efforts sometimes joined together the talents of scholars and artisans (e.g., mathematicians and instrument makers) while bestowing prestige upon those active in the laboratory or workshop. Among scholars as well, roles began to change with a shift from university to Court environments. Astronomers, for instance, when released from the pedagogical constraints of the university and confronted by the need to glorify specific patrons, altered traditional occupational patterns centered on the teaching of mathematics and the casting of horoscopes to involve themselves more directly in observational programs, instrument building, and the critical discussion of natural philosophy. Hapsburg imperial patronage, especially during the period of Rudolf II at Prague (1576–1612), has been especially noted in this regard, as have also the mathematical undertakings of Spanish King Philip II and the projects oriented toward geographical exploration associated with the Court of the young English prince, Henry, prince of Wales.

At the imperial Hapsburg Court, science, technology, humanism, and art intertwined. Mathematician-astronomers like Paul Fabritius and Thaddeus Hayek joined others there in making astronomical observations, composing astronomical works, and discussing novel theories. There, also, Tycho Brahe (1546–1601) and Johannes Kepler (1571–1630) were appointed, in succession, imperial astronomers.

Brahe was himself a nobleman who, prior to arriving in Prague, had been granted an island by the king of Denmark, Frederick II, "for all the days of his life, and as long as he lives and likes to continue and follow his *studia mathematices.*" Both in Denmark and at the imperial Court, he bestowed aristocratic status upon activities associated with the study of astronomy. He also offered a source of potential patronage to others, and it was this, along with Tycho's observational data, that Johannes Kepler sought in coming to Prague in 1600. What each would provide the other required negotiation. Nevertheless, while staying at Tycho's residence in Prague, and although refusing to embrace Tycho's cosmology, Kepler

One of the best examples of projects undertaken by an astronomer-prince is the Court of German Landgrave Wilhelm IV of Hesse-Kassel (1532–1592). Wilhelm was a true prince-practitioner, contributing to the design of instruments, making astronomical observations, and emphasizing the value of technical and observational precision. The Kassel Court became, at the end of the sixteenth century, a locus for serious projects of observational astronomy. Those who contributed to the Kassel effort, such as the mechanician Joost Bürgi (1552–1632) and the astronomer-mathematician Christoph Rothmann (fl. 1555–1597) were not supported at Court for their entertainment value but as serious collaborators with the prince in pursuit of the observational reform of the heavens.

In northern Europe, where the consolidation of regional power gained new vigor in the sixteenth century, political and economic motives dominated in turning the attention of princes toward the patronage of practical mathematics and the mechanical arts. The identification of new sources of wealth required an exact knowledge of the prince's own sphere of political and economic influence. In this regard, mapmaking and the design of surveying instruments became important elements in defining the regional extent of the Court's legal jurisdiction and economic privileges. Navigational instruments, proportional compasses, triangulation instruments, mining machinery, and cartographic tools became instruments of state, and the manufacture of such instruments tended to become state of the art.

The aggrandizement of personal wealth led some patrons to support alchemical projects. In fact, the late sixteenth and early seventeenth centuries may be considered the heyday of alchemical patronage, especially in northern Europe. In some instances, alchemical interests combined with interests in magic and the occult arts and led to the support of nontraditional medical ideas and practices. Paracelsian physicians, particularly, seem often to have relied upon Court positions to establish the acceptability of their medical theories and practices. The physician Adam von Bodenstein and the chemist Hans Kilian, both employed at one time or another by the Palatine Elector Ottheinrich, were among the first to collect the manuscripts of Paracelsus (ca. 1493–1541). Another court physician, Johann Huser (ca. 1545–ca. 1600), published a major collection of Paracelsus's writings at Basel in 1589–1590 with the financial aid of his prince, Ernst, elector of Cologne.

The frontispiece of Thomas Sprat's History of the Royal Society *(1667) shows a bust of King Charles II as founder and patron of the Royal Society of London. On the left is the society's first president, William Brouncker, pointing to the king's name; on the right is Francis Bacon, inspiration for the society's goal of bringing new knowledge and practical benefits to mankind.*

defended his benefactor's claims in a priority dispute with Nicholas Raimarus Bär (Ursus) (1551–1600), a mathematician who also could boast of strong supporters, including the governor of Holstein, Heinrich Rantzov, the Danish nobleman Erik Lange of Engelholm, and Emperor Rudolf II.

From a cognitive point of view, Kepler's years at Prague were among his most creative, witnessing the refinement of his laws of planetary motion. The *Astronomia nova,* which appeared in 1609 and described his first and second laws, was dedicated to the emperor. Yet, while Rudolf II stands out personally in this respect, Kepler counted other figures as well within the imperial circle, especially Baron Ferdinand Hofman and Johann Matthias Wackher von Wackenfels, among his patrons and friends.

Besides the Courts of emperors and kings, smaller Courts can also be found supporting astronomical activities and manufacturing sophisticated mechanical devices with the aid of well-trained mathematical appointees.

P

Patronage, at times, could lead to controversy and inspire the further refinement of intellectual positions. The French King Henry IV, for instance, maintained at his Court three Paracelsian physicians—Jean Ribit, Sieur de la Rivière (ca. 1571–1605), Joseph du Chesne (Quercetanus) (ca. 1544–1609), and Theodore de Mayerne (1573–1655). Their presence so near the person of the king, and their religious ties to the Huguenots, led to a bitter debate over medical theory and practice with the faculty of medicine at the University of Paris, a debate that also involved the German chemist and schoolmaster Andreas Libavius (1540–1616). The outcome distanced Paracelsians from Court but left in place a middle road that accepted the utility of chemistry in medicine. For Libavius, who, despite his outspoken anti-Paracelsianism, defended the chemical doctors against the Paris faculty, the debate helped clarify his personal position within the contexts of Galenic, Hippocratic, and Hermetic medical philosophies.

The social, economic, and cultural functions of scientific patronage varied considerably from Court to Court, and, within certain settings, clients themselves attempted to influence patronage decisions or to alter preferred patronage patterns. Success in one area could prompt attention to another or, by means of Court authority, bring about new projects. Recent studies centered on the Court physician and mathematician Johann Joachim Becher (1635–1682), for instance, have underscored the efforts of a specific client to shift the attention of the prince from one type of project to another—in this case, from alchemical and chemical endeavors to commercial and technical concerns.

Patrons often depended upon brokers to bring to them worthy clients. Sometimes, however, patrons and brokers were one and the same. The early-seventeenth-century French scholar and patron Nicolas-Claude Fabri de Peiresc (1580–1637), while not a territorial ruler, nevertheless made use of his personal social status and strong ties to the French Court (as well as his own wealth) to help advance the prospects of many well-known supporters of experimental science, among them Tommaso Campanella (1568–1639), Marin Mersenne (1588–1648), Galileo Galilei (1564–1642), and Pierre Gassendi (1592–1665). Peiresc was a member of the nobility of the robe and held a public office as councillor to the king in the Parlement of Aix, an office that had been held in his family for four generations. He also maintained an extensive correspondence and provides a good example of a patron whose relationships stand outside the courtly structure of the patron-client type. His associations have been referred to in terms of a "dyadic alliance" (i.e., as relationships more or less between equals based upon an emotional commitment of friendship and loyalty and cemented by ritualistic exchanges of gifts and favors). Patronage of this sort made allies of friends and sometimes required of the patron a choice of sides when friends disagreed. Such was the peculiar position in which Peiresc found himself when two natural philosophers within his patronage circle, Galileo and Mersenne, disagreed in their experimental results.

The client as courtier has emerged as a major theme in the study of scientific patronage. None other than Galileo has been described as a brilliant Court strategist who made use of the opportunities and social connections afforded by the Medici Court to communicate and validate his discoveries and to promote the credibility of his intellectual claims. By naming the four moons that he had observed orbiting Jupiter after the Tuscan grand duke and his brothers, and by earmarking other European Courts to receive telescopes for purposes of observing his discoveries, Galileo constructed a powerful social tool of observational verification and thereby stimulated discussion of cosmological issues. Beyond the obvious social maneuvering, however, there has arisen an even stronger argument regarding the effect of social influences upon Galileo's interpretation of his own astronomical discoveries. In this regard, some view Galileo's increasing commitment to Copernicanism, as well as the style and content of the scientific disputes in which he became involved, as partly dependent upon the dynamics of Court patronage.

Naturalists, as well, benefited from the cultivation of princely patronage. Many Courts throughout Europe gathered together, in museums or cabinets of curiosities, curious and rare natural objects together with works of art and examples of fine mechanical engineering and scientific technology. Not all collections were alike. Some emphasized man-made objects over natural wonders, while others combined *artificialia* and *naturalia* in encyclopedic attempts to represent different parts of human knowledge. Motives for collecting also varied. Some collections attempted to draw attention to princely wealth and power by embracing the natural world in all of its dimensions. However, collecting also arose at some Courts as part of a serious philosophical or educational enterprise in which the museum itself functioned as a tangible reminder of the relation among politics, power, and learning. Whatever the motive, such collections focused attention upon the particulars of nature and offered opportunities for artists and naturalists alike to come face to face with the discontinuities of a presumed natural order. Naturalists like Ulisse Aldrovandi (1522–1605) and Athanasius Kircher (1602–1680) helped promote a new attitude toward nature as a collectible entity while fashioning an image of collecting itself as an activity based upon learning and privilege. Such collectors came to possess, through gifts and publication subsidies, the tangible favor of their patrons. In return, naturalists included their patrons in the lists of those who had helped their studies and proudly displayed the portraits of their benefactors in their own museums.

Scientific patronage did not exist in an institutional vacuum, and lines previously thought to have separated Courts from other institutions, and from the development of scientific organizations themselves, have lately come under increasing scrutiny. Good routes of communication are known to have existed between universities and Courts, allowing some to join together university and Court responsibilities. At the German Court of Moritz of Hesse-Kassel (1572–1632), the prince also made room for his own patronage tastes relating to alchemy and occult philosophy at the University of Marburg, where he created the new professorship of chemical medicine (*chymiatria*). For the post, Moritz chose Johannes Hartmann (1568–1631), a professor of mathematics at Marburg who had turned his attention to medicine and chemistry in line with the Kassel prince's patronage interests.

Patronage also relates to the emergence of new institutions with a more purely scientific focus. Contrary to views that have insisted upon the failure of private patronage as the primary rationale for Louis XIV's (1638–1715) chief minister, Colbert's, founding of the Académie Royale des Sciences, for instance, evidence now suggests that a viable center of private patronage continued to exist at Paris, and a network of private-patronage organizations continued to support scientific endeavors in France, up to the moment plans were announced for the new royal institution. Colbert himself experimented with traditional patronage, offering gifts to scholars across Europe. Glorifying the French king was part of Colbert's original intent in supporting the idea of an academy. Thus, recent scholarship has reversed the direction of older descriptions and now regards the creation of the Parisian academy not as the replacement of one sort of scientific organization by another but as a shift of patronage from individuals to more efficient and productive institutions.

Scientific patronage as variously defined within the context of European Courts accorded social legitimacy to the person and a measure of trustworthiness to the claims of clients and protégés. It promoted the procedural values of technical precision, collection, description, and measurement and emphasized the utilitarian aspect of inquiring into and, at times, manipulating nature. The patronage of princes opened up social spaces outside the confines of traditional educational institutions and redefined professional roles while, occasionally, offering opportunities for novel sorts of collaboration. In the aristocratic marketplace, new discoveries, inventions, and descriptions of nature came increasingly to be valued as signs of prominence, distinction, and social wealth. By offering advantages to both patrons and clients, patronage enhanced the connection between science and the state, linking claims to power and the enshrinement of personal glory with the survey and control of nature.

BIBLIOGRAPHY

Biagioli, Mario. *Galileo Courtier: The Practice of Science in the Culture of Absolutism.* Chicago: University of Chicago Press, 1993.

Findlen, Paula. *Possessing Nature: Museums, Collecting, and Scientific Culture in Early Modern Italy.* Berkeley and Los Angeles: University of California Press, 1994.

Lux, David S. *Patronage and Royal Science in Seventeenth-Century France: The Académie de Physique in Caen.* Ithaca, NY: Cornell University Press, 1989.

Moran, Bruce T. *The Alchemical World of the German Court: Occult Philosophy and Chemical Medicine in the Circle of Moritz of Hessen (1572–1632).* Stuttgart: Steiner Verlag, 1991.

———. "German Prince-Practitioners: Aspects in the Development of Courtly Science, Technology, and Procedures in the Renaissance." *Technology and Culture* 22 (1981), 253–274.

———, ed. *Patronage and Institutions: Science, Technology, and Medicine at the European Court, 1500–1750.* Woodbridge: Boydell, 1991.

Sarasohn, Lisa T. "Nicolas-Claude Fabri de Peiresc and the Patronage of the New Science in the Seventeenth Century." *Isis* 84 (1993), 70–90.

Smith, Pamela H. *The Business of Alchemy: Science and Culture in the Holy Roman Empire.* Princeton, NJ: Princeton University Press, 1994.

P

Stroup, Alice. *A Company of Scientists: Botany, Patronage, and Community at the Seventeenth-Century Parisian Royal Academy of Sciences*. Berkeley and Los Angeles: University of California Press, 1990.

Westman, Robert S. "The Astronomer's Role in the Sixteenth Century: A Preliminary Study." *History of Science* 18 (1980), 105–147.

BRUCE T. MORAN

See also Académie Royale des Sciences; Academies; Alchemy; Government and Science; Museums and Collections; Peiresc, Nicolas-Claude Fabri de

Peiresc, Nicolas-Claude Fabri de (1580–1637)

Held a unique position in the development of the natural and physical sciences in the early seventeenth century. He was Consilleur du Roi in the Parlement of Aix and was a noted humanist and naturalist, but his chief importance was as a patron of the arts and sciences. All of the notable intellectuals of the time either visited him at Aix or corresponded with him. Peiresc facilitated scientific activity by creating networks of intellectual discourse, funneling books and manuscripts to appropriate readers, organizing experiments in optics and observational astronomy, and obtaining financial aid and advancement for his clients.

Peiresc's clients included some of the most important figures of the emerging Scientific Revolution: Galileo Galilei (1564–1642), Marin Mersenne (1588–1648), and Pierre Gassendi (1592–1655). His network of savants spanned other fields as well, including such luminaries as Hugo Grotius (1583–1645) and Peter Paul Rubens (1577–1640). Peiresc did not hesitate to intervene for his friends and clients whenever it seemed necessary. He used his contacts in the Roman Curia, for example, to attempt to have Galileo's punishment ameliorated after 1633. His support was crucial in encouraging Gassendi's rehabilitation of Epicurean atomism.

Peiresc acted as an intermediary in many different ways. His broad scholarly interests linked together the late humanists of the sixteenth century and the *libertins érudits* (learned freethinkers) of the seventeenth century. His wide correspondence united intellectuals from different regions, who professed different faiths and adhered to different philosophic schools. Peiresc did not hesitate to intervene between the passionate personalities of his time. Gassendi's famous *Life of Peiresc* (1641)

From Isaac Bullart, Académie des sciences et des arts *(1682).*

indicates that Peiresc acted as a conciliator, who perhaps did not understand that some scientific disagreements were impossible to reconcile.

Peiresc's own work was chiefly as a bibliophile, historical philologist, and collector of coins and inscriptions. He was not merely an antiquarian, however, but instead had a sophisticated understanding of how auxiliary disciplines could aid historical understanding. In the sciences, Peiresc and the Provençal astronomer Joseph Gaultier (1564–1647) were the first Frenchmen to observe the four moons of Jupiter, in 1610. Through astronomical observations, Peiresc and Gassendi were able to determine the length of the Mediterranean Sea with great accuracy. Biological dissections led to the discovery of the lacteal vessels in men. Peiresc never published the results of his own studies, perhaps because they were too eclectic, and he was modest and unassuming about his own accomplishments.

Peiresc's accomplishments as a savant, natural philosopher, and patron led Gassendi to characterize him as a "prince of learning." His court truly was the community of natural philosophers and humanists of the early seventeenth century.

BIBLIOGRAPHY

Hellin, Jacqueline. *Nicolas-Claude Fabri de Peiresc, 1580–1637*. Brussels: R. Lielens, 1980.

Reinhold, Anne, ed. *Peiresc, ou la passion de connaitre: Colloque de Carpentras, novembre 1987*. Paris: Vrin, 1990.

Sarasohn, Lisa T. "Nicolas-Claude Fabri de Peiresc and the Patronage of the New Science in the Seventeenth Century." *Isis* 84 (1993), 70–90.

LISA T. SARASOHN

See also Correspondence Networks; Patronage

Perspective

A pictorial method for creating the illusion of three-dimensionality on a flat surface. Filippo Brunelleschi (1377–1446) is credited with devising the first perspective pictures in linear perspective. In 1425 he painted two small panels depicting the Church of San Giovanni and the Piazza della Signoria in Florence. These small paintings—products of an attempt to record what the painter's eye takes in from a fixed vantage point—ushered in a mode of representation that was profoundly satisfying to Renaissance sensibilities and that has had consequential influence on subsequent experiments in conveying visual knowledge.

Antonio Manetti, writing some time after Brunelleschis's death when perspectival painting had become established, described perspective as "a part of that science, which is in effect to put down well and with reason the diminutions and enlargements which appear to the eyes of men from things far away or close at hand . . . in that measurement which corresponds to that distance which they show themselves to be." Manetti here recognizes and adumbrates the important points about perspective: it aims to be rational, based on mathematical principles; it concerns itself with establishing correct relations between objects in space based on the fixed gaze of a static observer; and it is illusionistic. In *Della pittura*, the first formal exposition of perspectival theory (1435), Leon Battista Alberti (1404–1472) clarified the nature of perspectival construction when he described the painter's task. That task was "to represent with lines and color with pigment any given panel or wall in such fashion that, at a certain distance and in a certain position from the center of vision, it appears as though in the round and will closely resemble the object." Erwin Panofsky's (1991) idea of symbolic form no longer holds sway, and the idea that sustains perspectival construction is that of the picture as a kind of window through which the viewer gazes. This implies that the viewer is a kind of virtual witness to what the artist has seen or imagined: the viewer stands in the artist's shoes. The spatial homogeneity and centralized composition based on a vanishing point (or points) are crucial not only to creating the illusion of reality, but also to satisfying the expectation that the laws of optics have been obeyed. Thus, perspective appears to obey Alberti's dictum that the artist should adhere to the rules of mathematics and the principles of nature. Once the technique for creating linear perspective had been mastered, artists expanded their experiments to other aspects of optical illusionism. Notable is the effort of Leonardo da Vinci (1452–1519) to explore the effects of light and distance on the perceptive of objects in space. His experiments with *sfumato,* a blurring of outline to achieve the illusion of objects enveloped in atmosphere, added another layer of understanding.

Although emphases vary, scholars accept that there is some relationship between late-medieval piety and the drive toward verisimilitude in the visual arts. In particular, the popular desire for more intimate connection with sacred figures and a more immediate realization of sacred stories impelled painters to seek new ways, even more inventive means, for visualizing the events in Scripture and legend. They used naturalism to domesticate the mysterious: Giotto's (ca. 1266–1337) experiments with spatial construction are an important exemplar of the prehistory of perspective.

Another factor in the development of perspective is the work of humanist scholars, with its focus on the recovery of classical texts, its search for apt classical models, and its emphasis on rhetoric. All artifacts of antiquity received new scrutiny and provided artists with a new pictorial language based on a naturalistic approach to space and atmosphere.

A third factor is Renaissance mercantile culture's interest in the practical application of mathematical principles, especially as they applied to surveying, engineering, and architecture. This interest appears in the context of general attempts to rationalize society. It is probably no accident that both Brunelleschi and Alberti were involved in architectural projects. This practical interest, in turn, allied with a long-standing interest in the more theoretical aspects of geometry and optics.

P

Brunelleschi's experiment in 1425 was followed, first, by the work of artists—Masaccio's (ca. 1401–ca. 1429) *Trinity* in the Church of Santa Maria Novella in Florence is the first example—and then with descriptive theoretical treatises. Alberti's *Della pittura* was followed by Lorenzo Ghiberti's (1378–1455) *Commentaries* (1450s), Piero della Francesca's (ca. 1420–1492) *De prospectiva pingendi* (ca. 1474), Viator's (Jean Pélerin, d. 1524) *De artificiali perspectiva* (1505), and Albrecht Dürer's (1471–1528) *Unterweysung der Messung* (1525). In general, artists of the sixteenth century concerned themselves less with the proper relationship between art and nature and more with developing theories of the proper role of the artist and with the problems of art itself. Artists sought to supersede the craft tradition with an artistic practice based on scientific principles—hence, such introspective and theoretical works as Leonardo da Vinci's notebooks and Albrecht Dürer's studies in measurement and human proportion.

Linear perspective had become the common pictorial language by the end of the sixteenth century, partly as the result of the factors enumerated, partly because it was a method easy to teach, and partly due to the relatively wide dissemination of theoretical works through printing. Printing and linear perspective were dual contributors to the history of science. The first contributed by allowing a large number of exact duplicate copies of texts and illustrations; the second, by providing a pictorial reportage of scientific observations. The perspectival mode, by placing the viewer in the place of the artist, allows that viewer to virtually share those detailed observations.

BIBLIOGRAPHY

Dunning, William V. *Changing Images of Pictorial Space: A History of Spatial Illusion in Painting.* Syracuse, NY: Syracuse University Press, 1991.

Edgerton, Samuel Y., Jr. *The Heritage of Giotto's Geometry: Art and Science on the Eve of the Scientific Revolution.* Ithaca, NY: Cornell University Press, 1991.

———. *The Renaissance Rediscovery of Linear Perspective.* New York: Basic Books, 1975.

Kemp, Martin. *The Science of Art.* New Haven, CT: Yale University Press, 1990.

Kubovy, Michael. *The Psychology of Perspective and Renaissance Art.* London: Cambridge University Press, 1976.

Panofsky, Erwin. *Perspective as Symbolic Form.* Trans. S. Christopher. New York: Zone Books, 1991.

MARY G. WINKLER

See also Art; Dürer, Albrecht; Illustration; Leonardo da Vinci

Petit, Pierre (ca. 1598–1677)

A military engineer, he was an active figure in French science for half a century. A skillful experimenter, he became known in 1625 for designing an original proportional compass and also for some determinations of specific weights and comparisons of standards of length and weight, which were valued by his contemporaries. His experiments on the fall of heavy bodies and the motion of pendulums were cited with praise by Marin Mersenne (1588–1648) and Pierre Gassendi (1592–1655). Petit was equally credited for his assiduous experiments on the declination of the magnetic needle and his observations on comets and eclipses of the Sun and the Moon, which resulted in many useful publications. Above all, he was the first to repeat in France Evangelista Torricelli's (1608–1647) experiment on the barometric vacuum, particularly at Rouen in October 1646 in the presence of Blaise Pascal (1623–1662), which marked the starting point for the work of the latter on the weight of the air. If he preceded Adrien Auzout (1622–1691), as is probable, in the invention of the filar micrometer, he did not make one of the first usable models.

Although an engineer by profession and directed, above all, toward experiments and practical results, Petit was not uninterested in theory, as is shown, for example, by the virulent criticisms he directed in 1638 at René Descartes's (1596–1650) *Discourse on Method* and *Essays.*

An active member of several Parisian scientific circles, which were a prelude to the Académie Royale des Sciences, Petit, to his great disappointment, was not among those chosen as a member of the core group of the academy organized in 1666. On April 24, 1667, however, he was one of the first foreigners to be elected to the Royal Society of London.

BIBLIOGRAPHY

Brown, Harcourt. *Scientific Organizations in Seventeenth Century France.* Baltimore: Johns Hopkins University Press, 1934.

Waard, Cornelis de. "Les objections de Pierre Petit contre le 'Discours' et les 'Essais' de Descartes." *Revue de métaphysique et de morale* 32 (1925), 53–89.

GUY PICOLET
TRANS. WILBUR APPLEBAUM

See also Académie Royale des Sciences; Barometer; Pascal, Blaise; Pneumatics

Petty, William (1623–1687)

Physician, professor, surveyor, merchant, and charter member of the Royal Society of London. Karl Marx (1818–1883) labeled him "the founder of political economy." Like many of the educated middle class in England, Petty aspired to the scientific ideals of Francis Bacon (1561–1626) and sought to extend his empirical method to all fields of study. In particular, Petty wanted a more scientific way to treat economic and political policy issues being debated in mercantilist pamphlets.

Petty's education was as diverse as his interests. At age fifteen he entered a French Jesuit college in Caen, where he focused on mathematics, astronomy, and navigation; afterward he joined the Royal Navy. In 1643 he left for the Netherlands and a medical education; he then went to Paris to specialize in anatomy and to study with Thomas Hobbes (1588–1679). In 1650 he completed his studies at Oxford and became its professor of anatomy.

In 1654 Petty took charge of the Down Survey of Ireland. The purpose of the survey was to facilitate the distribution of confiscated rebel lands to English soldiers; so, in addition to mapping most of Ireland, Petty had to invent ways of determining land values in a country with little currency. His solution was to follow an approach analogous to recent work in cartography, which had already become a relatively sophisticated numerical discipline. Thus, he sought to "measure" the value of land indirectly, by establishing natural, mathematical relations between it and the price of the agricultural products yielded.

Later he collaborated with John Graunt (1620–1674) in the founding and development of statistics. Petty's statistical method had two parts. *Political Anatomy* (1691) focused on the collection and organization of numerical data, such as number of acres and amount of taxes collected. In this regard, he advocated the founding of a central statistical office. *Political Arithmetic* (1690), a mix of economic theorizing and statistical inference, algebraically manipulated these data to provide estimates for more abstract figures and conclusions. Again, the search was for quantitative relationships. For example, Petty theorized that the comparative wealth and power of nations could be determined numerically on the basis of the value of their lands, total rents on housing, and the number and wages of laborers in each. Petty's work in political arithmetic was carried on by Charles Davenant, Gregory King, and others.

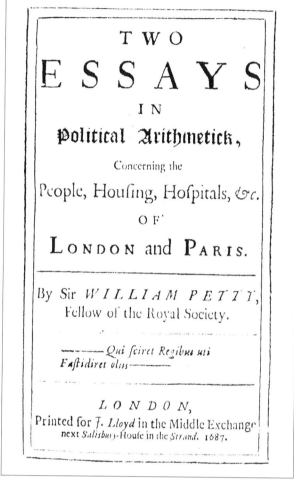

The title page of this portion of Petty's Political Arithmetick *was printed in 1687, before the entire work was published in 1690.*

BIBLIOGRAPHY

Kargon, Robert. "William Petty's Mechanical Philosophy." *Isis* 56 (1965), 63–66.

Petty, William. *The Economic Writings of Sir William Petty.* Ed. Charles Henry Hull. 2 vols. London: Cambridge University Press, 1899.

———. *The Petty Papers: Some Unpublished Writings of Sir William Petty.* Ed. H. Lansdowne. New York: Sentry, 1967.

Strauss, Erich. *Sir William Petty: Portrait of a Genius.* London: Bodley Head, 1954.

TIMOTHY J. TAYLOR

See also Agriculture; Measurement; Statistics

Peurbach, Georg (1423–1461)

This prominent astronomer-astrologer of the fifteenth century was originally named Georg Aunpech of Peuerbach

spawned several commentaries and introduced such students as Nicolaus Copernicus (1473–1543), Galileo Galilei (1564–1642), and Johannes Kepler (1571–1630) to an elementary but updated version of Ptolemaic astronomy. Its woodcut illustrations depict eccentric planetary models imbedded within thick, spherical shells with surfaces concentric with the earth. Peurbach also calculated eclipse tables, *Tabulae eclipsium* (ca. 1459; printed 1514), which he organized in an innovative fashion, and composed treatises on the construction of various instruments and calculating devices. In 1460 Peurbach began an *Epitome* of Ptolemy's (ca. 100–ca. 170) *Almagest,* which was only half finished when he died of the plague in 1461. His colleague Regiomontanus completed the work the following year.

BIBLIOGRAPHY

Aiton, E. J. "Peurbach's Theoricae novae planetarum: A Translation with Commentary." *Osiris,* 2nd ser., 3 (1987), 5–43.

Grössing, Hekmuth. *Humanistische Naturwissenschaft: Zur Geschichte der Wiener mathematischen Schulen des 15. und 16. Jahrhunderts.* Baden-Baden: Valentin Koerner, 1983, pp. 79–116.

MICHAEL H. SHANK

See also Ptolemaic Astronomy; Regiomontanus, Johannes

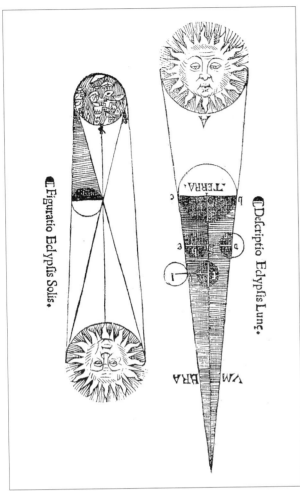

Diagrams of lunar and solar eclipses. From Peurbach's Theoricae novae planetarum *(1525).*

(his birthplace in Upper Austria). He studied at the University of Vienna, where, after several years of travel, he became a Master of Arts in 1453. Although he lectured primarily on classical Latin literature, such as Virgil and Horace, and wrote some florid Latin poetry extolling his love for a monastic novice who later became a priest, astronomy and astrology were his forte. In this capacity, he interspersed academic duties with courtly service, first with the young Ladislaus V. Posthumus, ruler of Lower Austria, Bohemia, and Hungary, and later with the Habsburg Court of Emperor Frederick III in Wiener Neustadt, near Vienna. His best-known work, *Theoricae novae planetarum* (New Theories of the Planets, 1454), was first printed posthumously ca. 1472 by his student and colleague Johannes Regiomontanus (1436–1476). This influential university text had appeared in more than fifty editions by the late seventeenth century. It

Pharmacology

Encompasses the study of the effects of drugs, their therapeutic efficacy, and their fate in the body. When the word gained currency in the 1680s, it also included the art of preparing drugs.

Throughout the previous two centuries, physicians and apothecaries had been adding to and modifying the ancient humoral pharmacological principles codified in herbals, practical guides to botanical identification that also assessed the therapeutic value of plants. This format declined after 1640 as pharmacopoeias began to establish standards for drug preparation and dosage and as botanists began to describe plants in nonmedical contexts.

Many of the new pharmacological concepts originated with Paracelsus (ca. 1493–1541). He argued that disease represents not imbalances among the classic four humors (blood, phlegm, yellow bile, and black bile) but disturbed interactions among their corresponding elements (air, water, fire, and earth) and his *tria prima,* the saline, mercurial, and sulfurous principles he said resided in all matter, including plants. This permitted him, for example, to correct putative abnormal acid-base balances with antacid and antalkaline drugs.

In contrast to traditional medicines compounded of many ingredients, Paracelsus favored drugs made of single substances. For instance, he introduced metallic mercury, tartar emetic (antimony potassium tartrate), and ether, the latter because, he said, it allayed pain and induced sleep in his experiments with chickens. Although he also described curious treatments, such as a salve he claimed would cure a wound when applied to the weapon that had caused the injury, such magical remedies were widely discussed, but they never gained the widespread professional acceptance accorded his simpler remedies, some of which survived into the nineteenth century.

The chemical approach to therapy helped change pharmacological thinking largely because Paracelsus demonstrated the value of a close alliance between medicine and chemistry through the latter's value in preparing effective and safe remedies, such as the chemically purified distilled oils he developed. This prompted European universities to include chemistry courses within their medical curricula, beginning at Marburg, where Johannes Hartmann (1568–1631) was appointed professor of *chymiatria* (chemical medicine) in 1609. However, his curriculum was not all rational chemistry; it also included the preparation of the wound salve and alchemically derived impossibilities such as "potable gold."

Paracelsus had argued that medical cures were properly assessed by observation, not by reliance on theory alone. Investigators such as Robert Boyle (1627–1691) and Francesco Redi (1626–1697) agreed on the appropriateness of experimental trials of new medicines and on the value of animals for testing new drugs, but such methods were not widely accepted for more than 250 years.

Those who explicitly rejected Paracelsian concepts included Johann Joachim Becher (1635–1682), who substituted three putative earths for the *tria prima,* and Georg Ernst Stahl (1660–1734) repudiated iatrochemistry altogether. He gave the name *phlogiston* to Becher's *terra pinguis,* an aspect of combustibility, and promoted antiphlogistic remedies to treat fevers, the most common illnesses of the time. Friedrich Hoffman (1660–1742) favored iatromechanical principles predicated on the assumption that motion is the primary principle of life.

He argued that drugs should either strengthen weak fibers in the body or relax excessively rigid fibers.

Followers of Paracelsus contributed other new chemical ideas to pharmacology. Johannes Baptista van Helmont (1579–1644) developed the concept of therapeutic gases, primarily carbon dioxide. Franciscus Sylvius (Franz de la Boë, 1614–1672) systematized Paracelsus's concepts, focusing increased attention on antacid and antalkaline remedies, while Boyle described chemical indicators of acidity and alkalinity. Johann Rudolf Glauber (1604–1670) developed chemical remedies, such as sodium chloride and magnesium sulfate, that fit within humoral, chemical, and antiphlogistic therapeutic frameworks simultaneously, as did Thomas Sydenham's (1624–1689) stronger—and cheaper—opium preparation. Although most physicians came to recognize the medical value of the new chemicals, they continued to prescribe botanical drugs while slowly rejecting complex polypharmaceuticals from magical and alchemical traditions.

Trade with the East and West Indies led to the introduction of exotic new drugs, especially the American products publicized by Nicolas Monardes (1493–1588). However, most American drugs offered nothing more than those ensconced in the humoral and chemical traditions, and only a few entered European herbals and pharmacopoeias. They included ipecac and cinchona (or Peruvian bark), first used for treating malaria (it is now known to contain quinine) and then for virtually all fevers. Guaiac, sassafras, and sarsaparilla were promoted for treating syphilis, which Europeans believed had been imported from the New World and was, therefore, amenable to treatment with drugs from that area, just as Paracelsus believed that German plants were the best remedies for the diseases of German people.

BIBLIOGRAPHY

Baldwin, Martha. "The Snakestone Experiments: An Early Modern Medical Debate." *Isis* 86 (1995), 394–418.

Debus, Allen G. *The Chemical Philosophy: Paracelsian Science and Medicine in the Sixteenth and Seventeenth Ceturies.* 2 vols. New York: Science History Publications, 1977.

———. The *English Paracelsians.* New York: Franklin Watts, 1966.

Estes, J. Worth. "The European Reception of the First Drugs from the New World." *Pharmacy in History* 37 (1995), 3–23.

———. "John Jones' *Mysteries of Opium Reveal'd* (1701): Key to Historical Opiates." *Journal of the History of Medicine and Allied Sciences* 34 (1979), 200–209.

P

Moran, Bruce T. *Chemical Pharmacy Enters the University*. Madison, WI: American Institute of the History of Pharmacy, 1991.

J. WORTH ESTES

See also Chemical Philosophy; Iatrochemistry; Paracelsus; Pharmacy

Pharmacy

The pharmaceutical art, which since the thirteenth century had been represented through the professional status of the apothecary, changed in manifold ways in the course of the sixteenth and seventeenth centuries. This affected, in the first place, *materia medica* itself, which became substantially enriched through the increase in the importation of vegetable drugs from the Far East and especially from America and, in the wake of Paracelsus (ca. 1493–1541), through increased use of chemical medications, above all mercury and antimony. As iatrochemistry increasingly became the foundation for the preparation of medicines, new manufacturing processes, such as differentiated distillation techniques, were developed, along with new medicinal forms, such as tinctures and extracts, so that the place and nature of the apothecary's work shifted more and more to the laboratory and to chemical operations. In the seventeenth century, this gradual modification of the nature of the original vegetable- (and to a small degree also animal-) based *materia medica* not only resulted in persistent disputes between progressive Paracelsians and conservative Galenists, but also brought forth a new type of chemical literature on the subject by, among others, Andreas Libavius (1540–1615), Oswald Crollius (ca. 1560–1609), Jean Beguin (ca. 1550–ca. 1620), Johannes Baptista van Helmont (1579–1644), and Nicolas Lemery (1645–1715).

Moreover, from the middle of the sixteenth century, official pharmacopoeias in a number of cities standardized the preparing of compounds and assured thereby a therapy of greater reliability, first in Nuremberg in 1547, with the *Dispensatorium* of Valerius Cordus, and later in Augsburg (1564), Cologne (1565), Florence (1567), and, finally, Rome (1583). The Nuremberg and Augsburg pharmacopoeias, in particular, went through many editions well into the eighteenth century.

These works, almost all prepared by individual physicians or colleges of physicians, such as the London *Pharmacopoeia* of 1616, possessing legal standing, were eventually extended to embrace regional and territorial areas. They were joined by relevant textbooks, of which Jean de Renou's *Institutionum pharmaceuticarum libri V* (1608) deserves special mention. The increased demands on apothecaries led also—although only in isolated cases, for example, in Montpellier—to the beginnings of an academic training in pharmaceutics, which until then had been based on pure craftsmanship.

Despite all of the differences in individual European countries regarding relations between apothecaries and doctors concerning the creation of special, more-or-less autonomous corporations—as, for example, the founding of the Worshipful Society of Apothecaries of London in 1617—and with respect to magisterial regulations, pharmacies everywhere, by the end of the sixteenth century, had become indispensable institutions of the public-health system, and the majority of apothecaries had gained a respected social position. A qualified professional practice was overseen, above all in the German territories, through strict official supervision, so that, toward the end of the seventeenth century, more than two hundred cities possessed their own apothecary regulations, often combined with an official list of fixed selling prices for medicines. These regulations, among other things, provided the grant of a privilege as a means of control of the basic prerequisites for the establishment of a pharmacy.

Through the increased reception of chemical substances in the *materia medica,* and promoted through a corresponding specialized literature, pharmaceutical art in this period eventually developed into an increasingly chemically oriented profession and thereby prepared the path for the scientific achievements attained by apothecaries from the middle of the eighteenth century, especially in the analytical field.

BIBLIOGRAPHY

Cowen, David L., and William Helfand. *Pharmacy: An Illlustrated History*. New York: Abrams, 1990.

Kremers, Edward, and Georg Urdang. *Kremers and Urdang's History of Pharmacy*. 4th ed., rev. Glenn Sonnedecker. Philadelphia and Toronto: Lippincott, 1976.

Schmauderer, Eberhard. "Entwicklungsformen der Pharmakopöen." In *Buch und Wissenschaft: Beispiele aus der Geschichte der Medizin, Naturwissenschaft und Technik,* ed. E. Schmauderer. Düsseldorf: VDI-Verlag, 1969, pp. 187–287.

Schneider, Wolfgang. *Geschichte der Pharmazeutischen Chemie*. Weinheim: Verlag Chemie, 1972.

PETER DILG

TRANS. WILBUR APPLEBAUM

See also Iatrochemistry; Paracelsus; Pharmacology

Philosophical Transactions

The oldest scientific journal in the world was founded in 1665 as a private venture by Henry Oldenburg (ca. 1619–1677) to be, as he stated, an account "of the ingenious in many considerable parts of the world." It was licensed—all printed books then required licensing—by an officer of the Royal Society and printed by the society's official printer. Each monthly issue was dated, and there were to be twelve issues to each volume, for which Oldenburg wrote a preface and a dedication and to which he added an index. In fact, because of external events (the plague in London in 1665, the Great Fire of London in 1666, the Anglo-Dutch War of 1667, and printers holidays), there were 142 issues in twelve volumes between 1665 and 1679, the final issues being completed after Oldenburg's death in 1677.

The journal had become so popular and so closely associated with the Royal Society that the society persuaded its successive secretaries to continue it as their private venture. Nehemiah Grew (1641–1712) completed volume twelve. Robert Hooke (1635–1703), also a secretary, in 1679 refused to continue Oldenburg's journal but published seven issues of his similar *Philosophical Collections* between 1679 and 1682. His place as secretary and publisher of the *Philosophical Transactions* was taken by Francis Aston (ca. 1645–1715), when the society promised to buy sixty copies as a subsidy, with Robert Plot (1640–1696) to assist; they declared that what they published was "not to be looked upon as the Business of the Royal Society," although most items had been read at meetings. Except for the years 1686–1690, the journal was published by individuals, usually a secretary, until, finally, in 1752 it became the official publication of the society and contained only papers read at its meetings.

To the world at large, the *Philosophical Transactions* seemed to be the Royal Society's official journal and, therefore, authoritative, as it was certainly informative and up-to-date. The contents of each issue varied greatly, dependent upon what letters were received, what extracts could be made from foreign journals, what papers were read at meetings, and what books were available for review. Each issue concluded with book reviews, and each volume with an index. Nowhere else could news of inventions and discoveries be published so quickly, effectively, and reliably; nowhere else could scientific controversy be carried on so effectively, since the editor could

refuse to publish intemperate attacks and was not himself involved. Very few of the important scientific discoveries of the age escaped being noticed in the *Philosophical Transactions*. Subjects ranged from a little pure mathematics to a considerable quantity of natural history and what were known as "curiosities" and included much astronomy, geology, optics, pneumatics, mineralogy, meteorology, botany, agriculture, medical and physiological topics, and mechanics but not alchemy or astrology. The journal gained importance by the announcement of Isaac Newton's (1642–1727) construction of his reflecting telescope and his optical papers as it did for the publication of Antoni van Leeuwenhoek's (1632–1723) microscopical discoveries beginning in 1673. Other names to be found there are those of Robert Boyle (1627–1691), John Wallis (1616–1703), Richard Lower (1631–1691), John Flamsteed (1646–1719), Edmond Halley (ca. 1656–1743), Christiaan Huygens (1629–1695), Johannes Hevelius (1611–1687), Adrien Auzout (1622–1691), Ismael Bouilliau (1605–1694),

PHILOSOPHICAL
TRANSACTIONS:
GIVING SOME
ACCOMPT
OF THE PRESENT
Undertakings , Studies , and Labours
OF THE
INGENIOUS
IN MANY
CONSIDERABLE PARTS
OF THE
WORLD.

Vol I.
For *Anno* 1665, and 1666.

In the *SAVOY*,
Printed by *T. N.* for *John Martyn* at the Bell, a little without *Temple-Bar* , and *James Allestry* in *Duck-Lane*,'
Printers to the *Royal Society.*

Jean-Dominique Cassini (1625–1712), Gottfried Wilhelm Leibniz (1646–1716), Marcello Malpighi (1628–1694), René François de Sluse (1622–1685), and many more. Minor contributors were delighted to find themselves appearing there, regarding publication as equivalent to commendation by the Royal Society, however much the current editor might declare that he alone chose the papers printed—although, in fact, when interesting papers were read at meetings, it was often recommended that they be published.

There is no way of knowing how many copies of the *Philosophical Transactions* were printed or distributed. Many were given away—to the editors of foreign journals and in response to requests; what is certain is that Oldenburg never made more than forty pounds a year from its sale, although he had hoped for more, and that in the 1680s the sale of sixty copies would cover the cost of printing. What is certain also is that its influence was far greater than this might suggest, especially since foreign journals printed extracts from it.

The one complaint by foreigners was that most of the *Philosophical Transactions* was in English; in the early issues, even Latin extracts were translated, as were those originally in vernacular languages. Later communications written in Latin, still the universal learned language of the European world, were left in the original, especially those in astronomy, mathematics, and medicine. There was a considerable demand for a Latin translation of the whole, as Oldenburg was urged; he was forestalled in the 1670s, first by an incompetent translator, John Sterpin, physician of Copenhagen, then by the more competent Christoph Sand (1644–1680), a German who worked in Holland as a press corrector and consulted Oldenburg about English technical words. These translations, mostly printed in Holland, mostly ascribing the journal to the Royal Society, were widely welcomed and reprinted, but there were never more than six volumes. There were partial translations into French, some made for the Académie Royale des Sciences in Paris, which remained in manuscript. But, assisted by extracts in journals printed in their own languages, foreign natural philosophers gained a very good idea from the *Philosophical Transactions* of what was being done in English science and also secured an audience for their own work well into the eighteenth century.

The *Philosophical Transactions* remained so popular that there were in the eighteenth century numerous abridgements, omitting book reviews and what was regarded as trivia, and translating the Latin. Of these, which preserved much of the best work of the Scientific Revolution, the best known are those of the first twenty-one volumes (to 1700), approved by the society and published in 1705 by John Lowthorp (F.R.S. 1702), and by John Martyn (1699–1768), professor of botany at Cambridge (F.R.S. 1727), who carried the work forward to 1750. There was a French abridgement (published in the years 1787–1791), which was translated into Italian (published 1793–1798); an Italian translation of Lowthorp's abridgement (published 1729–1734); and a German translation of the first fourteen volumes (to 1693) (published 1779–1780). In 1787 P. H. Maty (1745–1787), a librarian (F.R.S. 1771) and foreign secretary, published the *General Index to the Philosophical Transactions,* volumes 1–70 (1665–1780); in 1812 Thomas Thomson (1773–1852), chemist and physician (F.R.S. 1811), published the *History of the Royal Society from Its Institution to the End of the Eighteenth Century,* which is a survey of the *Philosophical Transactions* and an analysis of its contents. All of these works and translations amply demonstrate the importance of the *Philosophical Transactions* as published during the period of the Scientific Revolution, an importance still alive for the scientific world of the eighteenth century and beyond. It has been stated, truly enough, that a very fair picture of seventeenth- and eighteenth-century science can be gathered from reading the *Philosophical Transactions* alone.

BIBLIOGRAPHY

Hall, Marie Boas. "Oldenburg, the *Philosophical Transactions,* and Technology." In *The Uses of Science in the Age of Newton,* ed. J. G. Burke. Berkeley and Los Angeles: University of California Press, 1983, pp. 21–47.

Kronick, David A. "Notes on the Printing History of the Early *Philosophical Transactions.*" *Libraries and Culture* 25 (1990), 243–267.

MARIE BOAS HALL

See also Correspondence Networks; Oldenburg, Henry; Royal Society of London

Physico-Theology

Physics, or natural philosophy, was traditionally an integral part of philosophy as a whole and, as such, closely linked with metaphysics and natural theology. Still, medieval natural theology had little recourse to the investigation of nature. Arguments that we would call religious were regarded as valid in physics. The various alternatives proposed from the sixteenth century onward to replace traditional Aristotelian natural philosophy were at least partly religiously inspired. On the other hand, the impact of physics on religious thinking was initially fairly limited. During the Scientific Revolution, however, natural philosophy developed into a discipline with a program of its own. This made the religious aspects of natural knowledge a pressing problem and led to a reformulation of the relation between science and religion. The several attempts in this field varied widely and made use of heterogeneous elements, so that only the bare outlines can be sketched here.

By the middle of the seventeenth century, the mechanical philosophy became the dominant view of nature, with important consequences for natural theology. The mechanical philosophy presupposed a God who was truly universal and acted in a constant way. God was known not so much by acts of providence, miracles, or telling events but by fixed laws. He was the greater, because he could produce an immense variety of things by a set of simple rules. God's greatness and universality were stressed over his providence. This tendency itself was not new. It had gained increasing strength during the sixteenth century. In the seventeenth century, however, it became dominant. Old ideas on natural theology needed to be adapted to this new general framework. This task was carried on by different philosophers in different ways.

By far the most influential philosopher was René Descartes (1596–1650), who took a rather radical stance. Descartes banned all final causes from nature, allowing only mechanical, causal relations. Thereby, he shook the very foundations of traditional proofs of God's existence from the order of nature—the world as God's Creation showing the marks of its maker. Indeed, Descartes rejected all arguments for God's existence drawn from the Creation and accepted only those based on pure reason.

This image of God was at the background of a fierce theological and philosophical struggle in the seventeenth century. Disputes arose not just on abstract philosophical questions, such as the correct interpretation of nature or the occurrence of active principles, but also on the interpretation of comets and similar phenomena. Traditionally, these were seen as special warnings sent by God, but the New Philosophers interpreted them as fortuitous events, resulting from the laws of nature. Traditionally

minded theologians regarded this interpretation as blasphemous. Still, as long as only the interpretation of nature generally was at stake, the New Philosophers could feel perfectly orthodox. The new mechanical universe was seen as displaying God's majesty and, as such, inspired awe and wonder. In fact, many mechanical philosophers, such as Nicolas Malebranche (1638–1715) and Robert Boyle (1627–1691), saw their philosophy as supporting Christian religion rather than opposing it.

In the course of time, however, people became aware of consequences that were regarded as totally unacceptable from a religious point of view. As long as philosophers argued just about God's acting in nature, all was well. But matters were different when they started to ponder the acts of God as related in the biblical narrative. Benedict de Spinoza (1632–1677) used the principles of the mechanical philosophy to deny not just the possibility of divine miracles in general, he specifically attacked the biblical miracles as well. Therewith, he struck at the heart of seventeenth-century religiosity. This alerted even moderate theologians to the dangers inherent in the New Philosophy. It became urgent for natural philosophers to demonstrate that their view of nature in no way contradicted accepted interpretations of the Bible and was, in fact, completely in agreement with traditional religious values.

The last decades of the seventeenth century saw some major theological controversies that settled the relation between philosophy and the Bible. In England, Thomas Burnet (ca. 1635–1715) proposed a natural philosophical interpretation of the biblical Flood; on the Continent, Balthasar Bekker (1634–1698) brought the biblical sentences on the Devil in line with his Cartesian convictions. Nominally, the ensuing debates were on the mere interpretation of the texts involved; actually, it was the very status of the Bible that was at stake. In both cases, the majority of theologians proved unwilling to adapt their interpretation of the Bible in the light of new philosophical insights. Henceforth, natural philosophers, while still accounting for the new philosophical and scientific insights, would take greater care of religious sensibilities.

The reaction depended greatly on local circumstances. In England and some other countries where political circumstances seemed to make philosophically radical opinions especially menacing, there was a deliberate disavowing of mechanism, in particular Cartesianism. On the other hand, in most parts of Germany, where orthodoxy reigned undisturbed and Cartesianism itself had been admitted only piecemeal, the transition was more gradual. In the long run, the British ideas had the greater impact, but they never dominated the scene completely. The new natural theology can be dealt with under three headings: experimental philosophy, physico-theology, and Newtonian philosophy. These were really three aspects of one powerful movement, although emphasis shifted. Common to the new ideas is that they allowed more scope for God's providence than the earlier mechanical philosophy. Principles of physics or philosophy were not allowed to affect traditional religious ideas.

Experimental Philosophy

Experiments had become ever more important in scientific investigations. The new experimental philosophy, however, was not as much a scientific method (as such, it was hardly new) as a religious and epistemological stance. In this form, it arose mainly in England, largely under the influence of Robert Boyle. What was at stake was not so much the empirical basis of physics (although this aspect was understandably emphasized in contemporary polemics) as the more general claims and intellectual pretensions of Cartesian philosophers. By stressing that all philosophical statements should be based in experimental facts, the experimental philosophers were able to reject any opinion that was unwelcome from a religious point of view as a mere "hypothesis." In practice, the question of where to put the boundary between "fact" and "hypothesis" was answered largely according to one's preconceived religious ideas. Boyle was quite willing to accept ghost stories as empirical evidence for the power of the Devil. He considered the refusal of the Cartesians to believe in any supernatural apparitions as based on wanton philosophical speculation. On the Continent, Bernard Nieuwentijt (1654–1718) used Boyle's arguments to suspend judgment on the Copernican system. However, this radical use of empiricism remained largely restricted to the British Isles. In a sense, the British deliberately cultivated it as a national, "Baconian" tradition. In Germany, under the influence of Christian Wolff (1679–1754), natural philosophy kept professing rationalism, although at the same time recognizing the importance of experimentation. In the Catholic world, Thomism remained the norm.

Newtonian Philosophy

Cartesianism supposed that the whole world consisted of matter in motion. This idea had largely been discredited by the polemical use made of it by radicals proclaiming materialism and attacking religion. An alternative, which argued authoritatively that mere materialism did not suffice to explain natural phenomena but was in accord with modern science, was, therefore, very welcome. This alternative was offered by Isaac Newton's (1642–1727) theory of gravitation. Newton argued that gravity, as not reducible to any mechanical principle, proved that the universe was governed by a power that superseded the principles of mechanics. As a popular theory, it sprung largely from the general scholium appended to the 1713 edition of Newton's *Principia mathematica philosophiae naturalis* (Mathematical Principles of Natural Philosophy), as well as from Roger Cotes's (1682–1716) Preface to the same edition. It was further popularized by Richard Bentley (1662–1742) and others in the lectures endowed by Robert Boyle and by journalists such as Jean le Clerc (1657–1736).

Physico-Theology

The old argument, rejected by Cartesian philosophers, of demonstrating God's attributes from the order of Creation, was taken up afresh by the end of the seventeenth century. By this time, its tone had distinctly changed. Earlier, the argument had been based mainly on contemplation and admiration. But now the argument was based on the empirical investigation of nature, which laid bare the inner working of things and thus showed that they were the result of a designing agent, not of blind natural forces. It was not so much a "theology of nature" as a "science of God's works." Nature was studied as the workmanship of the all-wise God. Final causes were certainly part of the researcher's domain.

In the eighteenth century, the genre became immensely popular in the whole of Europe, with a flood of publications, re-editions, and translations, but it obtained its most influential form in England, where it had been worked out and put into practice in the seventeenth century by people like Robert Boyle and John Ray (1620–1705). However, the genre really established itself only after the publication in 1713 of the second edition of Newton's *Principia*. It was foremost William Derham (1657–1735) who set the trend with his *Physico-Theology* (1713) and *Astro-Theology* (1715). In England, it appears closely linked with Boyle's program of experimental philosophy: the physico-theologists showed God's wisdom, greatness, and goodness not by reason but by empirical facts. It was a means of expounding natural theology by citing experimental observations. The British model was imitated abroad as well. The link with Boyle's program can be discerned also in the Dutch Republic in the work of Bernard Nieuwentijt (1715), although his physico-theology shows distinct traits as well. He wanted not just to demonstrate God's wisdom, power, and goodness, but also tried to find empirical arguments for the divinity of the Bible. Wholly under British influence are the works in Hamburg by Johann Albert Fabricius (1668–1736), who was one of the main propagators of the genre in Germany.

At other places in Germany, physico-theology sprung from existing soil. Conrad Mel's (1666–1733) *Schaubühne der Wunder Gottes* (1714) still largely identified the New Philosophy with Cartesianism. The Swiss physician Johann Jacob Scheuchzer (1672–1733), whose *Physica sacra* (1731–1733) was one of the most conspicuous works in its genre, seems most influenced by the eclecticism of Johann Christoph Sturm (1639–1703). The philosopher Christian Wolff published a physico-theology in 1724. The new genre also spread into France. François de Fénelon's (1651–1715) *Démonstration de l'existence de Dieu, tirée de la connoissance de la nature, et proportionnée à la foible intelligence des plus simples* (1715) regarded the physico-theological argument as unphilosophical but still useful for the instruction of the uneducated. One of the best-selling works of the century was *Le spectacle de la nature* (1732–1750) by Noël-Antoine Pluche (1688–1761). Pluche's example shows that Catholics, too, wrote physico-theology. Most authors, however, were Protestants.

Physico-theology was no part of academic learning, in either theology or physics, but aimed at the lay public. The first works often had a clear apologetic intention. They combated rationalist philosophy and irreligion in general and demonstrated how nicely the results of modern science agreed with traditional religious truths. After their success had established the genre, such apologetics became less necessary. Physico-theology remained popular, however, as an educational and edifying genre. Some of the most popular works, as the one by Pluche, originally aimed at the instruction of the young.

The various strategies for accommodating science and religion remained noncommittal about all but the most general religious dogmas. Physico-theology, experimental philosophy, and Newtonian philosophy are commonly associated with a latitudinarian view in theology. They try to show the agreement of faith and reason, faith being interpreted in terms of established religion, without taking a dogmatic stance. Nor did these strategies serve a rigorous investigation of truth; the philosophical significance of the whole movement is fairly limited. The various works are there just for reassuring the believers that modern science is a religiously harmless, even an edifying, occupation. It was the accepted framework wherein people could contemplate nature in a scientific way without feeling uncomfortable about religious implications of the new science. The literature certainly served its purpose. Natural philosophy quickly lost its controversial character and became one of the century's favorite hobbyhorses.

BIBLIOGRAPHY

Brooke, J. H. *Science and Religion: Some Historical Perspectives.* Cambridge: Cambridge University Press, 1991, chs. 4–6.

Funkenstein, A. *Theology and the Scientific Imagination from the Middle Ages to the Seventeenth Century.* Princeton, NJ: Princeton University Press, 1986.

Gascoigne, J. "From Bentley to the Victorians: The Rise and Fall of British Newtonian Natural Theology." *Science in Context* 2 (1988), 219–256.

Gillespie, N. C. "Natural History, Natural Theology, and Social Order: John Ray and the 'Newtonian Ideology.'" *Journal for the History of Biology* 20 (1987), 1–49.

Philipp, W. "Physicotheology in the Age of Enlightenment: Appearance and History." *Studies on Voltaire and the Eighteenth Century* 57 (1967), 1233–1267.

Westfall, R. S. *Science and Religion in Seventeenth-Century England.* New Haven, CT: Yale University Press, 1958.

RIENK VERMIJ

See also Active Principles; Biblical Interpretation; Mechanical Philosophy; Religion and Natural Philosophy

Physics

A number of physical sciences constituted the heart of the Scientific Revolution. Although at that time there were probably more investigators engaged in the life sciences, whose efforts were by no means in vain, it was not from these sciences that the revolutionary theories that transformed the scientific enterprise emerged. Of central importance for the transformation were changes that occurred in mechanics, the science of motion, and, to a lesser extent, in optics.

The word *physics* was not much used by the men who made the Scientific Revolution. *Physics* was the title of Aristotle's (384–322 B.C.E.) general introduction to natural philosophy, and physics in the Aristotelian tradition included much more than physics today. It included astronomy. It included questions about the composition of bodies that we would now find in chemistry. Above all, it included various branches of what we call biology, such disciplines as taxonomy and physiology. And with the life sciences, it included psychology. All of these topics Aristotelian physics treated in a qualitative way antithetical to the outlook coming to prevail. To the leaders of the New Science, the word *physics* denoted all that they understood themselves to be rejecting. During the Scientific Revolution, a number of men composed systematic natural philosophies that embraced as much as Aristotelian physics, but none of them attached the name *Physics* to their works.

To be sure, the word did not disappear. It continued among Scholastic philosophers, who dominated the universities through most of the century. Perhaps Honoré Fabri (1607–1688), who was more than merely touched by the outlook of the Scientific Revolution, should not be considered a Scholastic philosopher. He was a Jesuit, however, and Aristotelian philosophy was prescribed to Jesuits. It was probably to indicate adherence to the tradition that he published *Physica* in four volumes (an intended fifth was never added) in the period 1669–1671, even if the contents of the volumes contained much that was taken from seventeenth-century science. Fabri's subtitle, *The Science of Corporeal Things,* suggested the Aristotelian scope that physics still embraced. His *Physica* did not include either optics or mechanics, though Fabri, in the spirit of Aristotelian physics, treated both in other treatises. Another *Treatise on Physics* was published in 1671 by Jacques Rohault (1620–1675), a fervent Cartesian. In his case, the whole point was to stress how the new program of mechanical philosophy had taken over the territory. Much like the *Principles of Philosophy* of René Descartes (1596–1650), Rohault's *Physica* ran through most of the issues one expected to find in a book on physics. Though he did not touch on the taxonomic problems that formed part of Aristotelian physics, he did deal with the composition of bodies (in a manner much closer to what we would call chemistry), and he devoted the whole of one of the four parts of his *Physics* to human and, by implication, animal physiology. Throughout the work, of course, he was concerned to show, in the spirit of the new natural philosophy, how particles of matter in motion explained all phenomena of nature.

Although it was not in books with the title *Physics,* what we call physics today constituted the very core of the Scientific Revolution. With the exception, of course, of anything connected with nuclear physics, most of the disciplines that compose physics in our sense of the term were pursued during the Scientific Revolution, some with great vigor and consequence.

Of nothing was this more true than the science of mechanics. From medieval philosophers, the Scientific Revolution inherited principles of statics. Both Galileo Galilei (1564–1642) and Descartes, to mention no others, wrote brief treatises on the simple machines, but it was not works of this sort that turned the world of science inside out. Motion, both kinematics and dynamics, was another matter. Already, realities such as cannon had raised the issue of motion. Now the Copernican system posed it in a way that philosophers could not avoid. The crucial problem was the diurnal rotation of the earth that heliocentric astronomy asserted. If that were true, people in western Europe were moving from west to east at a rate of about one thousand miles per hour, which is more than a thousand feet per second. On the one hand, no one perceived such a motion, though no one failed to perceive far slower ones common in daily life. On the other hand, according to the received conception of motion, it is quite impossible that we can be moving in this way. The received conception of motion came from Aristotle. It asserted that nothing moves unless something moves it; in the language we now employ, motion requires the constant application of force. Since bodies fall vertically, though no moving force is evident after the moment of release, is it not then impossible that the earth is turning on its axis? During a fall of only sixteen feet, the point of release moves east more than a thousand feet. Objects should appear to fall far to the west. This objection could be elaborated in a number of ways (e.g., with cannons that hurled their balls equal distances both east and west). It constituted the major obstacle to the acceptance of heliocentric astronomy.

Galileo effectively removed the objection by reformulating the conception of motion. In the process, he inaugurated the modern science of mechanics. He concluded that uniform motion on a horizontal plane requires no cause. If we can imagine a frictionless plane, a body placed in motion on it will persevere in its motion as far as the plane continues. As Descartes, who shared the new conception of motion, put it, philosophers have been asking the wrong question. They have asked what keeps a body moving; they should ask what makes it stop. We know this conception of motion as the principle of inertia. It effectively removed the Aristotelian objection against the movement of the earth. More than this, it became the foundation of the new science of motion. Philosophers today consider it the cornerstone of the whole of modern science.

Galileo did not confine himself to horizontal motion. Against the Aristotelian conviction that heavy bodies fall faster than light ones because the force moving them is greater, he asserted that all bodies fall through the same distance in the same time. It is not proper, however, to say that they fall with the same velocity, because they fall with constantly increasing velocity. Galileo defined the concept of uniformly accelerated motion—again, he imagined ideal conditions of no resistance—and identified the fall of bodies as such. Contrary to Aristotle, there is no such thing as a positively light body. All bodies are heavy, and, whatever their size and composition, they all fall with the same rate of acceleration. Uniformly accelerated motion is a mathematical concept, and Galileo proceeded to deduce from it the relations of distance, velocity, and time that have constituted the core of kinematics ever since. He also perceived that, in projectile motion, uniform horizontal motion compounds with uniformly accelerated motion in the vertical plane, and he demonstrated that the trajectory of a projectile is a parabola.

During the 1650s and 1660s, the Dutch scientist Christiaan Huygens (1629–1695) took up mechanics and extended it successfully to further problems. Pursuing the kinematics of uniformly accelerated motion, he demonstrated that, when a body oscillates in a cycloidal path, all oscillations of whatever amplitude are isochronous; discovering further how to make a body oscillate in a cycloidal path, he used the demonstration to construct the first precision clock. Huygens exploited the relativity of uniform motions implicit in the New Mechanics to analyze the impacts of what he called perfectly hard bodies, showing that the common center of gravity of two isolated bodies in impact remains in an inertial state of rest or of uniform motion. He also analyzed the mechanics of circular motion and arrived at the mathematical formula for its radial component. For that component, Huygens coined the phrase *centrifugal force,* by which he

meant the endeavor of a body constrained to move in a circle to recede from the center.

Although he did speak of centrifugal force, Huygens's work in mechanics was primarily kinematical. It remained for Isaac Newton (1642–1727), at the end of the seventeenth century, to work out the dynamical principles that stood behind the kinematics. Newton started with inertia as his first law of motion: a body remains in its state of rest or of uniform motion in a straight line until something external acts upon it. In his second law, he applied the generic word *force* to whatever acts to change a body's inertial state, setting a strict proportionality between force and the change of motion it generates. The proportionality demanded a measure of the quantity of the body acted on. For that purpose, Newton defined the concept of mass, which entered physics at this point. His third law stated the equality of action and reaction whenever a force acts on a body. From the three laws of motion, proclaimed in *The Mathematical Principles of Natural Philosophy* (1687), Galileo's kinematics followed as a necessary consequence.

The strength of Newton's dynamics lay in the fact that it applied with equal mathematical rigor to changes of direction, seen as accelerations, and, thus, to orbital motion. The problem inevitably accompanied heliocentric astronomy, especially in its Keplerian form. Whereas earlier astronomy, even in its Copernican form, had approached planetary motions by adding up uniform circular motions, Johannes Kepler (1571–1630) objectified the orbit as a line through space, and his three laws of planetary motion inaugurated modern celestial kinematics at the same time that Galileo was founding terrestrial kinematics. Kepler approached his problem in explicitly dynamic terms. The dynamics he was using, however, was Aristotelian dynamics. Only the kinematics survived. In Newtonian dynamics, however, Kepler's three laws of planetary motion emerged as consequences that were equally necessary as Galileo's kinematics. The concept of a Newtonian synthesis refers primarily to this level of mechanics, to the completion of a science of motion that bound heaven and earth together, treating all phenomena of motion in the universe in the same terms with equal mathematical precision.

Mathematical precision was an essential aspect of the New Mechanics. More than anything else, it marks the change from Aristotelian physics to modern science. Although much of seventeenth-century mechanics was primarily mathematical, a matter of deducing the consequences that followed from the new principles of motion, it understood itself to apply to real motions in the real world, and its ultimate appeal for justification was to observation and experiment. For celestial motions, rapidly improving instruments made the observations ever more precise. Analogous changes occurred in experiments that pertained to terrestrial mechanics. Galileo justified his concept of uniformly accelerated motion by experiments with balls rolling down inclined planes. In his *Principia,* which was primarily a work of mathematics, Newton referred to many experiments (e.g., the demonstration that weight is proportional to mass by means of pendulums). Instruments of greater precision appeared here as well. The pendulum was one of them. Newton especially recognized how its capacity to add up tiny increments in repeated oscillations made more exact measurements possible. With the pendulum clock, it became possible, as it had not been before, to measure time accurately. Take all of these characteristics together—quantitative nature, mathematical precision, measurement, experimentation—and seventeenth-century mechanics emerges as the prototype not only of modern physics but of modern science as a whole.

Fluid mechanics also received attention during the Scientific Revolution. It could scarcely have failed to, for practical needs such as flood control, reclamation, and irrigation forced men competent in similar affairs to attend to it. Hydraulics, which had been managed heretofore by empirical, rule-of-thumb procedures, began to transform itself into a science. The book *On the Measure of Running Waters* (1628) by Benedetto Castelli (1577–1643), Galileo's student and follower, is universally received as the source of the modern science of hydraulics. In it, Castelli enunciated the principle of continuity—as Castelli put it, the cross-section of a river does not measure the quantity of water it carries without the third dimension, velocity. In Italy, a tradition of hydraulics that built on Castelli continued through the century. The inherent complexity and difficulty of fluid dynamics, however, did not at that time permit results comparable to those achieved in the mechanics of solid bodies.

Fluid statics did arrive at a major generalization. Problems with pumps and siphons led a group in Rome to experiment with columns of water. Evangelista Torricelli (1608–1647) tried the same experiment with a heavier fluid and invented the mercury barometer. The questions the barometer posed—Was the space above the mercury really a vacuum? What held the column of mercury up?—stood at the center of scientific discussion during the middle decades of the seventeenth century. As the discussion proceeded, terms were refined. The concept of pressure replaced the cruder weight of fluid columns. The invention of the air pump allowed more sophisticated experimentation. Out of it all came Boyle's Law, relating the pressure and the volume of gases, another of the early mathematical laws of modern science and another founded on experimentation.

The science of optics was scarcely less central to the Scientific Revolution than mechanics. Like mechanics, optics had a long tradition that stretched back beyond medieval Europe to classical Greece. One of the triumphs of medieval science had been the explanation of the rainbow in terms of reflections from innumerable droplets of atmospheric moisture. The primary problem of earlier optics had been the understanding of sight. Early in the seventeenth century, in *The Optical Part of Astronomy* (1604), Kepler settled the question as far as it pertains to optics once and for all with the concept of the retinal image and, in the process, transformed optics as much as he transformed astronomy. Seventeenth-century optics was then, to some degree, a new enterprise. Its concern was light rather than sight. Startling new instruments that appeared soon after Kepler's publication—first the telescope and then the microscope—ensured that optics would remain a center of attention.

The mechanical philosophy of nature set the terms in which light was considered; it could be either a disturbance of some sort transmitted through a material medium or tiny particles of matter moving with immense velocity. Descartes, who first posed the issue of light in a mechanical universe, maintained that it was a pressure transmitted through what he called the second element. This view gradually transformed itself into the wave conception of light, which found its most persuasive champion in Huygens. Such facts as the capacity of a match to illuminate a large sphere of space and the capacity of the Sun to illuminate the whole solar system over thousands of years without being consumed convinced Huygens that it was not possible for light to be material. Newton, the leading exponent of the corpuscular view, also had his reasons. Light throws shadows in straight lines, whereas waves bend behind obstacles. Moreover, all motions change, but he had demonstrated to his own satisfaction that the difform rays that make up light are immutable, implying a material base similar to atoms.

Not until the nineteenth century did a seemingly crucial experiment determine the wave theory; twentieth-century physics showed that the experiment was less decisive than once thought and that light apparently consists of corpuscles and waves at the same time.

Meanwhile, behind the philosophic debate about the nature of light, continued investigation uncovered a considerable range of hitherto unknown regularities and properties. The ancient Greeks had known that, in reflection, the angle of incidence equals the angle of reflection. Refraction was a more difficult matter, but telescopes and lenses urgently required that the law governing refraction be found. The Dutch scientist Willebrord Snel (1580–1626) did so, though Descartes was the first to publish it. The sine law of refraction states that, for an interface between two given media, the ratio of the sine of the angle of incidence to the sine of the angle of refraction is a constant. Optics had been a mathematical science in antiquity; one of its first steps in the seventeenth century was the announcement of another mathematical law of nature.

Experimentation kept revealing new properties. In observing shadows cast by a narrow beam of light, an Italian Jesuit, Francesco Maria Grimaldi (1618–1663), discovered diffraction. Through experiments with a prism, Newton established that light, hitherto considered homogeneous, consists of rays that differ from one another. Sunlight, a heterogeneous mixture, appears white; phenomena of color arise when the mixture is analyzed or separated into its components, each of which provokes a distinct sensation. In experiments intended to explain the colors of solid bodies by showing how reflections can separate rays, Newton first observed and measured the periodicity of an optical phenomenon, though he did not believe that light itself, particles in motion, could be periodic. Periodicity, established for a single phenomenon in the seventeenth century, would in the future dominate the understanding of light. A Danish investigator, Erasmus Bartholin (1625–1698), uncovered another phenomenon that later assumed importance with periodicity. This was a strange double refraction in a natural crystal called Iceland spar. The incident beam was split in two, each of which underwent a different refraction. The phenomenon is an aspect of polarization; although that word was not used in the seventeenth century, experimenters did establish that the perpendicularly opposed sides of a ray that has passed through Iceland spar have different properties.

Another Dane, Ole Christensen Römer (1644–1710), definitively settled the long dispute about the velocity of light. Is it transmitted instantaneously, as most believed, or with a finite velocity? Römer noticed that the periods of the satellites of Jupiter lengthen as the planet recedes from the earth and then shorten as it approaches. He interpreted the data as an appearance caused by the finite velocity of light, and, from the accepted dimensions of the solar system, he measured the velocity. His figure was too small, about 70 percent of the one we now accept. It was of the right order, however, and the finite, though very swift, velocity of light has remained a basic datum of science ever since.

As has been evident, many of the same names that dominated the history of mechanics appeared prominently in the history of optics during the seventeenth century. It was hardly by accident that the optical science they created was no less mathematical than mechanics. Nor was it by accident that it proceeded by experiment and demanded quantitative precision. With mechanics, optics was a powerful force in determining the nature of all subsequent physics.

Only part of these things can be said about other disciplines in what we call physics that the seventeenth century pursued. As the century opened, an English doctor, William Gilbert (1544–1603), published *Concerning the Magnet* (1600), a book generally held to be the fountainhead of the science of magnetism. That is not entirely just. The ancients had known about the lodestone; our word *magnet* comes from the name of a Greek city where lodestones were found. The compass needle revolutionized navigation in the thirteenth century, and there was a major medieval treatise on magnetism. In the sixteenth century, the features of the magnet that suggested consciousness, its directive capacity, and the specificity of its attraction for iron alone made magnetism the archetype of the mysterious powers that natural philosophies of the time thought permeated the universe. Gilbert's book undertook to examine the mythology of magnetism by experimental enquiry, and it is often held up as the first exemplar of experimental physics. It contained very little of the quantitative, mathematical nature of seventeenth-century mechanics and optics, however, and the science of magnetism did not acquire this characteristic during the Scientific Revolution.

Concerning the Magnet set out deliberately to examine the lore of magnetism experimentally. Is it true that diamonds can magnetize iron? Seventy-five diamonds

P

later, Gilbert felt ready to deny it. In the process of similar investigations, he set magnetism on a new footing, systematizing and extending the established knowledge of its effects. He distinguished five magnetic effects, or motions, as he called them: attraction, direction, variation (declination in our present vocabulary), dip, and revolution. We regard the last of these, the asserted capacity of a round lodestone (a *terrella*, as he called it, a little earth) to rotate on its axis when it is in a magnetic field, as Gilbert's own mythology. Indeed, when his book is read closely, it appears far less familiar than one expects the first exemplar of experimental physics to be. What we name attraction, he refused to call by that name. Attraction implied coercion. Gilbert insisted that the magnet and iron come together by mutual consent. He used the language of sexual union in discussing this effect. His universe was animistic and alive rather than mechanical. Magnetic motions, with their inherent order, arrangement, and limits, implied rational choice, and he did not fail to identify magnetism as the soul of the magnet. Because the earth is a great magnet, it, too, has a soul, and the rotation of the earth on its axis in the field of the Sun is, in Gilbert's view, almost a rational decision lest one side of the earth roast while the other freezes. If Gilbert set the knowledge of magnetic effects on a new footing, he still lived in the animistic world of sixteenth-century philosophy.

With Gilbert's book known and read, the mechanical philosophy of the seventeenth century could not ignore magnetism. One of its primary tasks was to explain these peculiar effects in terms of inert particles of matter in motion. Descartes led the way by imagining an elaborate machinery of tiny screw-shaped particles, left-hand threads and right-hand threads for the two poles, with corresponding pores in iron to receive them. The mechanical philosophy produced no exercise in imaginary physics that was more fantastic. Meanwhile, the effects were there. They could not be denied. With one adjustment or another, mechanical philosophers through the century continued to subscribe to similar devices.

Gilbert was more fully the father of another science that also remained experimental and nonmathematical during the seventeenth century, the science of electricity. Before him there was knowledge of an amber effect, the capacity of amber to attract bits of chaff. Gilbert coined the word *electric* from the Greek word for amber and devoted a chapter of *Concerning the Magnet* to the subject. He distinguished electricity from magnetism by a number of characteristics, especially the matter that exhibits the two different effects. While magnetism is the effect of iron, or genuine telluric matter, electricity pertains to the moisture that is the cement binding bodies together. It should, then, not be confined to amber. Gilbert identified twenty-three other electric substances, including glass, sealing wax, and sulfur. It is not too much to say that Gilbert created the science of electricity. Although for a long time far from the focus of scientific interest, it thenceforth maintained existence as a separate subject of investigation.

Gilbert also established the explanatory principle that dominated electricity through the century: the concept of an effluvium, excited by friction, that streams out from electric bodies and carries back bits of chaff and the like when it returns. Though formulated by one who predated the mechanical philosophy, the explanation made ready harmony with mechanistic concepts. As a new subject, electricity did not conflict with established philosophies or with theology, and Jesuit investigators did more than anyone else to keep interest in electricity alive during the century. Its unexpected effects provided substance for courtly demonstrations that helped sustain interest. Through the century, the number of materials known to exhibit electric effects steadily expanded, but, at the end of the century, electricity, which bulks so large on our scientific horizon, still referred only to a small number of static electric attractions. The eighteenth century would witness a great expansion in the effects, including a demonstration that electricity is present throughout nature. And in the nineteenth century, electromagnetism would take on the quantitative, mathematical garb that, with other subjects, had begun to distinguish physics during the Scientific Revolution.

BIBLIOGRAPHY

Cohen, I. Bernard. *The Birth of a New Physics*. Garden City, NY: Anchor Books, 1960. Rev. ed. New York: Norton, 1985.

Hall, A. R. *The Revolution in Science, 1500–1750*. London: Longman, 1983.

Heilbron, John. *Electricity in the Seventeenth and Eighteenth Centuries: A Study of Early Modern Physics*. Berkeley and Los Angeles: University of California Press, 1979.

Koyré, Alexandre. *Newtonian Studies*. Cambridge, MA: Harvard University Press, 1965.

Roller, Duane H. D. *The De Magnete of William Gilbert*. Amsterdam: Hertzberger, 1959.

Sabra, A. I. *Theories of Light from Descartes to Newton*. London: Macdonald, 1967.

Shapiro, A. *Fits, Passions, and Paroxysms: Physics, Method, and Chemistry and Newton's Theories of Colored Bodies and Fits of Easy Reflection*. Cambridge: Cambridge University Press, 1993.

———. "Kinematics Optics: A Study of the Wave Theory of Light in the Seventeenth Century." *Archive for History of Exact Sciences* 11 (1973), 134–266.

Shea, W. R. *The Magic of Numbers and Motion: The Scientific Career of René Descartes*. Nantucket, MA: Science History Publications, 1991.

Yoder, Joella G. *Unrolling Time: Christiaan Huygens and the Mathematization of Nature*. Cambridge: Cambridge University Press, 1988.

RICHARD S. WESTFALL

See also Aristotelianism; Experience and Experiment; Force; Hydraulics and Hydrostatics; Magnetism; Mechanical Philosophy; Mechanics; Mixed Sciences; Motion; Optics; Pneumatics

Physiology

The study of the activities characteristic of living things and the function of their parts has always been associated with several related areas of investigation: anatomy, medical practice, pathology, and speculation on the nature of living matter. There were few works devoted to the subject as a distinct area of study until the early-modern period. The traditions stemming from antiquity were, for the most part, based on passages in Aristotle (384–322 B.C.E.) and Galen (second century) and their treatment by medieval Arabic authors, notably Avicenna (980–1037). A partial questioning of Galen, based on anatomical research with close observation utilizing dissection and vivisection, began in the sixteenth century. Further challenges to ancient authority came from Paracelsus (ca. 1493–1541) and his followers and, in the seventeenth century, from the mechanical philosophers. The work of William Harvey (1578–1657), although he was not a mechanical philosopher, constituted a sharp break with important aspects of Galenic physiology and opened paths leading to new knowledge and a profound transformation of the nature and methods of physiological investigation.

Galenic physiology and its early-modern modifications and variants was founded on the assumption that there are three significant areas of the body, each associated with a particular organ responsible for important functions in the maintenance of life. These organs and subsidiary structures possess certain powers or "faculties"—attraction, repulsion, retention, and alteration—that are the means for carrying out basic activities such as the maintenance of body heat, digestion, gestation and development, movement, volition, and sensation. Four fundamental fluids, the humors, are also associated with distinct organs and have a role in the maintenance of health.

The liver transforms chyle, the nutritive material of the ingesta, brought to it through the portal and mesenteric veins from the stomach and intestines, into blood, which it sends via the veins throughout the body. The heart is the source of innate heat and vital spirits, which it distributes to all parts of the body; diastole and systole are equally active, the latter responsible for the pulse in the arteries, which also carry blood with waste products to the lungs. The blood also nourishes the lungs, is cooled by them in the maintenance of body heat, and is provided an essential ingredient in the air necessary for the functioning of the heart. Arteries and veins, in which the blood ebbs and flows, have different functions and are joined only at the heart. The brain, responsible for the mental faculties, movement, and sensation, converts the blood's vital spirits into animal spirits for distribution through the nerves.

There were some differences between Aristotelian and Galenic approaches to physiology, and each had its partisans and variations in the sixteenth and seventeenth centuries. Bernardino Telesio (1509–1588), seeking to distinguish the Christian concept of the soul from the Aristotelian soul as the form of the body, held that "spirit," residing in the brain, governed the bodily functions. Jean François Fernel (1497–1558) likewise denied the Aristotelian vegetative, sensitive, and rational souls and held spirit as the mediator between the soul and the body in carrying out the latter's functions. He rejected innate heat as analogous to combustion, seeing its source as divine, but, as in Galen, requiring nourishment and cooling. The four classical humors he held to be derived from chyle, rather than separated from it, along with additional humors from which the tissues were formed, and an essential "radical," or fundamental, humor characteristic of life.

Some saw bodily function as analogous to chemical operations. For Paracelsus, innate heat is analogous to fire. There is an internal "alchemist" in the stomach who differentiates good from bad nutriment and helps transform the good into flesh and blood. There is an *archaeus* (a shaping or formative principle) with subordinate forms in the organs. Johannes Baptista van Helmont (1579–1644) rejected the Aristotelian formal and final causes in favor of the material and efficient alone, as well as the four humors and the three Paracelsian principles. He retained, however, the Paracelsian *archaeus* and its guidance of the sub-*archei* but located it in "seeds," precursors of living matter, that had been converted from water by a process of fermentation.

A decisive turning point in physiology came with Harvey's discovery of the circulation of the blood. Its way was paved by the challenges to Galenic anatomy begun by Andreas Vesalius (1514–1564) and the discovery of pulmonary circulation by Realdo Colombo (ca. 1510–1559) and of the valves in the veins by Girolamo Fabrici (1533–1619). Harvey's achievement was made possible by his extensive experience in the dissection and vivisection of a number of species, his close observation of the stages in the beating of the heart, and his ingenious methods and experiments designed as aids to observation and tests of his hypotheses. As a result of Harvey's conclusions, Galenic conceptions of the nature of the blood, its role in life processes, and its relation to the functions of various organs would come under detailed scrutiny by his successors.

Shortly after the publication of Harvey's *On the Motion of the Heart and Blood* (1628), the mechanical philosophy, with its principle that all action takes place by contact, began, along with Harvey's work, to influence the direction of physiological thinking and research. René Descartes (1596–1650) saw the body as a machine with parts analogous to mechanical devices. Human souls resided in the pineal gland, the locus of their interaction with the body-machine. He accepted Harvey's circulation of the blood but differed from him on the cause of innate heat and the active phase of the heart. For Descartes, the heat in the heart, analogous to fire, is sustained by the blood and caused by the rapid motion of invisible particles. This causes the blood to expand and send heat to the rest of the body. In similar manner, Descartes described functions associated with, among other activities, digestion, respiration, generation, and nervous activity.

The work of both Harvey and Descartes was influential in different ways in shaping subsequent physiological inquiry. Experimental investigations into the cardiopulmonary system in England by Robert Boyle (1627–1691), Robert Hooke (1635–1703), Thomas Willis (1621–1675), John Mayow (1641–1679), and Richard

Lower (1631–1691) resulted in the conclusion that "niter," a substance in the air, sustained both life and the "fire" responsible for internal heat and was responsible for the difference in color, density, and function between arterial and venous blood. Marcello Malpighi (1628–1694), using the microscope, discovered the invisible anastomoses (or capillaries) postulated by Harvey as uniting arteries and veins at the body's extremities. Giovanni Alfonso Borelli (1608–1679) and others developed mechanical models to explain muscle action and other activities, as well as pathological conditions. Souls, spirits, and vitalist explanations were now generally out of favor or much reduced in the search for physiological understanding.

BIBLIOGRAPHY

Debru, Claude, ed. *Lectures on the History of the Physiological Sciences.* Amsterdam: Rodopi, 1995.

Descartes, René. *Treatise on Man.* Trans. with an Introduction by Thomas S. Hall. Cambridge, MA: Harvard University Press, 1972.

Foster, Michael. *Lectures on the History of Physiology During the Sixteenth, Seventeenth, and Eighteenth Centuries.* Cambridge: Cambridge University Press, 1924.

Frank, Robert G. *Harvey and the Oxford Physiologists: Scientific Ideas and Social Interaction.* Berkeley and Los Angeles: University of California Press, 1980.

Hall, Thomas S. *History of General Physiology: 600 B.C. to A.D. 1900.* 2 vols. Chicago: University of Chicago Press, 1969, vol. 1, part 2.

ELSA L. GONZALEZ

See also Anatomy; Galenism; Harvey, William; Iatromechanics; Mayow, John; Willis, Thomas

Picard, Jean (1620–1682)

An important figure in the passage from the world of the "pretty nearly" to the universe of precision. Thanks to his exceptional aptitude for observation, his ingenuity in improving his instruments and observational procedures, and his persistent quest for precision, he contributed to the progress of many branches of science, most particularly astronomy and geodesy.

He played a decisive role in the conception, realization, and perfection—sometimes in collaboration with his colleagues at the Académie Royale des Sciences in Paris, sometimes alone—of new astronomical and topographical instruments, such as the filar micrometer, sectors equipped with optical sights, and the telescopic level, instruments that immediately became classic and were imitated all over Europe. Picard also conceived the procedures for use and control that these instruments required and invented a great many novel devices and observational techniques. In particular, he first introduced in the practice of astronomy the method of corresponding altitudes, and also the determination of right ascensions of stars by the time of their passage across the meridian.

In addition to the first series of regular and systematic observations made with the instruments and techniques that he had developed, he also demonstrated the influence of temperature on refraction, conducted the first observation of stars carried out in daylight, determined the annual displacement of the Pole Star, and discovered the flattening of Jupiter. To him, too, we owe the contents of the first five volumes of *La connaissance des temps* (1679–1683), the first nautical almanac.

The best-known scientific result of Picard, however, rests on his precise measurement of a meridional arc (1688–1670), of which he gave an account in his *Mesure de la terre* (1671), a work that exercised considerable influence on the development of geodesy, celestial mechanics, and cartography. If the methods he employed were not new, the new instruments and techniques utilized, as well as the great care employed in the operations, permitted a determination of a degree of the terrestrial meridian with remarkable exactitude, which Isaac Newton (1642–1727) made use of in the first edition of his *Principia mathematica philosophiae naturalis* (Mathematical Principles of Natural Philosophy, 1687).

The mission that Picard carried out in Denmark (1671–1672) to determine the exact coordinates of the former observatory of Tycho Brahe (1546–1601) at Uraniborg and of the astronomical tower of Copenhagen and then to compare their longitudes with that of the royal observatory in Paris is equally noteworthy. It inaugurated a lengthy series of astronomical voyages and expeditions under the aegis of the Académie Royale des Sciences to improve terrestrial cartography, notably by the observations of eclipses of the satellite of Jupiter, for which Jean-Dominique Cassini (1625–1712) had calculated ephemerides.

Picard, who was more a man of the field than of the study, carried out numerous missions in France itself, leading to sensible improvements in the mapping of France. In 1681 he presented to the chief minister, Colbert, a project for establishing the "general framework"

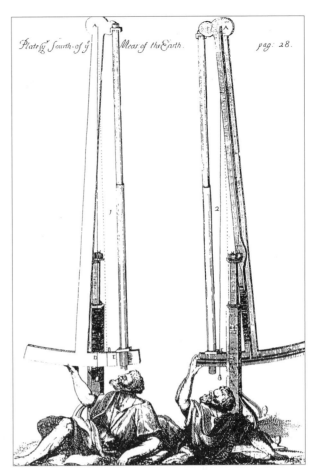

A device for making precise meridianal measurements to determine the size of the earth. From Picard's The Measure of the Earth, *trans. Richard Waller (1688); 1st French ed. (1671).*

of linked triangles for a new map of France, which afterward would be easy to fill in, a program that was finally realized in the following century.

The other missions of Picard related chiefly to the bringing of water to Versailles (1674–1678). They gave him the opportunity to improve the use of the level in surveying. His treatise on surveying, posthumously published in 1684, remained the reference work in that domain until the end of the following century.

Among his other important contributions were his work in meteorology, his exact determination of the length of a pendulum beating seconds at the latitude of Paris, and his discovery of phosphorescence in the void part of the barometer, the first observation of electrical discharge in a highly rarefied gas.

BIBLIOGRAPHY

Armitage, A. "Jean Picard and His Circle." *Endeavour* 13 (1954), 17–21.

Le Vallois, J. J. "La détermination du rayon terrestre par J. Picard en 1669–1671." *Bulletin Géodésique: The Journal of the International Association of Geodesy* 57 (1983), 312–331.

Olmstead, J. W. "Recherches sur le biographie d'un astronome et géodésien méconnu: Jean Picard (1620–1682)." *Revue d'histoire des sciences et de leurs applications* 29 (1976), 213–222.

Picolet, Guy, ed. *Jean Picard et les débuts de l'astronomie de précision au XVIIe siècle: Actes du colloque du tricentenaire.* Paris: Centre National de la Recherche Scientifique, 1987.

GUY PICOLET

TRANS. WILBUR APPLEBAUM

See also Académie Royale des Sciences; La Hire, Phillippe de; Observatoire de Paris

Pico della Mirandola, Giovanni (1463–1494)

This Renaissance humanist studied Aristotelian philosophy from 1480 to 1482 at the University of Padua, where he came under the influence of the Jewish Averroist Elia del Medigo and began the study of Jewish mysticism—the Kabbalah. By the time he became a friend and associate of the Plato scholar Marsilio Ficino (1433–1499) in 1484, Pico was well versed in Scholastic philosophy and Kabbalah and familiar with the Greek philosophers. In 1486 Pico published for debate nine hundred statements on such diverse ideas and thinkers as Plato (428–348 B.C.E.) and Aristotle (384–322 B.C.E.), Avicenna (980–1037) and Averroës (1126–1198), Pythagoras (fl. sixth century B.C.E.), Orpheus, Hermes Trismegistus, and Kabbalah. His "Oration on the Dignity of Man," which was meant as an introduction to the theses, has become a classic statement of the intellectual ambitions of the Renaissance humanist. Pico's continuing interest in Jewish mysticism led to the beginnings of Christian Kabbalism, and in 1487 he published a kabbalist interpretation of the Creation story titled *Heptaplus.* He also intended to write a work reconciling the philosophies of Plato and Aristotle but published only one part, in 1491, *On Being and the One.*

Pico's earlier works show that he accepted the validity of astrological claims that the heavens were a source of knowledge about human personalities and events, but, like many of his contemporaries, he was uncomfortable with the way predictability through astrology threatened human free will. Toward the end of his life, he decided that astrology was irreconcilable with Christianity, possibly because of the influence of the Dominican friar Girolamo Savonarola (1452–1498), and wrote a massive work in 1494, *Disputations Against Judicial Astrology,* denouncing all attempts at understanding human affairs through the study of the heavens. Pico died before he could edit it, and it was published without necessary major revisions by his nephew, the scholar Gianfrancesco Pico. As a result, the work is cumbersome and repetitive. It is also primarily a compilation of Pico's extensive reading on astrology and adds little new material to the debates in the fifteenth century. Pico was not an astronomer or a mathematician, and all of his knowledge of natural philosophy came from reading accepted authorities on the subject. Nevertheless, the reputation of the author as a major scholar and thinker and the weight of the argumentation because it included so much important information and scholarly opinion made his *Disputations Against Judicial Astrology* the most widely debated work on the subject of astrology for the century and a half after it was written.

BIBLIOGRAPHY

Garin, Eugenio. *Giovanni Pico della Mirandola: Vita e dottrina.* Florence: Monnier, 1937.

Pico della Mirandola, Giovanni. *On the Dignity of Man, On Being and the One, Heptaplus,* trans. Charles Glenn Wallis. Indianapolis and New York: Bobbs-Merrill, 1965.

Wirszubski, Chaim. *Pico della Mirandola's Encounter with Jewish Mysticism.* Cambridge, MA, and London: Harvard University Press, 1989.

SHEILA J. RABIN

See also Astrology; Humanism; Kabbalah

Platonism. See Neoplatonism

Plurality of Worlds

The term historically used for the concept of other worlds, possibly inhabited, beyond the earth. The concept had its origin with the ancient Greek atomists Leucippus (fl. 5th century B.C.E.), Democritus (fl. late 5th century. B.C.E.), and Epicurus (341–270 B.C.E.), who held that an infinite number of *kosmoi* existed, while Aristotle (384–322 B.C.E.) argued for a single *kosmos,* with *kosmos* defined as everything in the visible world, including all celestial bodies. For both Aristotle and the atomists, their diametrically opposed conclusions were based on the physical principles of their cosmologies. An entire medieval tradition of *plures mundi* was generated based largely on commentaries on the relevant portions of Aristotle's *De caelo* (On the Heavens). By the end of the fourteenth century, these commentaries had transformed Aristotle's conclusion of a single world to a position more in accord with Christianity: God could create many worlds if he wished, without suspending the laws of nature. But, in fact, the Scholastics inevitably concluded, God had not created more than one world.

The transformation in the sixteenth and seventeenth centuries to a plurality-of-worlds tradition, in which *world* meant an inhabited earthlike planet, was not achieved by successive rebuttals of Aristotle, even though the later writers were aware of the older tradition. Rather, the idea of inhabited planets stemmed from the Copernican revolution, in which the planets became earths and Earth a planet. Just as the heliocentric theory implied a new physics of motion—worked out by Galileo Galilei (1564–1642), Johannes Kepler (1571–1630), Isaac Newton (1642–1727), and their successors and examined in detail by historians of science as one of the hallmark achievements of the Scientific Revolution—so it also implied a new conception of the physical nature of the planets. This new conception—extended also to the possible planets of other stars—was the essence of the renewed plurality-of-worlds tradition. But, while the motions of celestial bodies could be relatively easily observed, the physical nature of the planets and the existence of other planetary systems were not so amenable to observation, even after the invention of the telescope. It is this aspect that gives the subject added interest for the history of science, since the dearth of observational data led to an interesting interplay of philosophy, religion, metaphysics, and empiricism, driven by the Copernican theory.

The idea of a plurality of inhabited earthlike planets began even before the telescope. Giordano Bruno (1548–1600), a dedicated but metaphysical Copernican, professed belief in an infinite number of worlds, based more on his philosophy than his Copernicanism. Kepler, too, in his *Astronomiae pars optica* (The Optical Part of Astronomy, 1604) and *Somnium* (The Dream, begun in the 1590s), speculated on the Moon as an inhabited world. But the telescope gave impetus to the idea that the planets were worlds similar to the earth, and Galileo's

observations, as well as Kepler's speculations in his *Dissertatio cum nuncio sidereo* (Dissertation on [Galileo's] Sidereal Messenger, 1610), began a line of research leading to the present day. This Copernican implication, however, required great caution in the Christian milieu. Galileo himself, while arguing that the Moon was a world, held that any lunar life would be far beyond our imaginings.

In contrast to Bruno, and despite Galilean caution, the Copernican theory was a crucial underlying concept that Kepler and others explicitly related to their belief in a plurality of worlds. John Wilkins's (1614–1672) *Discovery of a World in the Moone* (1638) set forth all of the arguments for an inhabited Moon and answered scriptural objections. Bernard le Bovier de Fontenelle's (1657–1757) extremely popular *Entretriens sur la pluralité des mondes* (Conversations on the Plurality of Worlds, 1686) used the Cartesian vortex cosmology to argue for the plurality of solar systems. And Christiaan Huygens's (1629–1695) *Cosmotheoros* (1698) illustrated the appeal of these ideas to one of the century's most important scientific figures. The success of the idea of other worlds, however, was assured only when Newton's successors made it an integral part of Newtonian natural theology. For most, the usefulness of inhabited worlds in manifesting the magnificence and omnipotence of God overcame all scriptural objections—at least for a while.

The plurality of worlds was a compelling problem given serious and persistent attention in the seventeenth century. Although empirically beyond the limits of seventeenth-century science, it should be seen as an integral part of the Scientific Revolution, a completion of the process that began with the decentralization of the earth and the subsequent shift from the closed world to the infinite universe. The projection of mind into space, even if still unproved, was a watershed in the history of thought, which transformed the divine celestial regions of the medieval worldview into a universe filled with the rational intellect formerly reserved for man. The implications have since echoed through philosophy and theology, and, in the second half of the twentieth century, the idea of inhabited worlds led to major endeavors in astronomy and biology. Even though still unproved, it is a kind of "biophysical cosmology" that is increasingly testable, and whose final proof is even today viewed by many scientists as a completion of the Copernican revolution.

P

BIBLIOGRAPHY

Dick, Steven J. "The Origins of the Extraterrestrial Life Debate and Its Relation to the Scientific Revolution." *Journal of the History of Ideas* 41 (1980), 3–27.

——. *Plurality of Worlds: The Origins of the Extraterrestrial Life Debate from Democritus to Kant*. Cambridge: Cambridge University Press, 1982.

Guthke, Karl S. *The Last Frontier: Imagining Other Worlds from the Copernican Revolution to Modern Science Fiction*. Ithaca, NY, and London: Cornell University Press, 1990.

Lovejoy, Arthur O. *The Great Chain of Being*. 2nd ed. Cambridge, MA: Harvard University Press, 1971. 1st ed. 1936.

STEVEN J. DICK

See also Bruno, Giordano; Infinity of the World; Literature; Wilkins, John

Pneuma

The fundamental substance of the Stoic cosmos, described by the founder of the school Zeno of Citium (ca. 335–263 B.C.E.) as "a craftsmanlike fire, proceeding methodically to genesis" and the life-giving ingredient in air. The pneuma is a world soul, conceived as material thing capable of pervading material bodies. It controls the structure and development of both living and non-living systems (which are not sharply distinguished) and the evolution of the cosmos as a whole. In antiquity, it was regarded as the origin of the intelligence and vital heat in living creatures. During the Scientific Revolution, early neurophysiologists and psychologists appealed to similar fluids. Variations on the Stoic pneuma also provided an alternative to Aristotle's account of the substance of the heavens.

The pneuma is responsible for the unity and cohesion of noncomposite bodies and pervades all natural objects (walls transmit sound because of the pneuma they contain). The pneuma is in tension, which may be understood as the flow of pneuma from place to place or as a change in the internal pressure of a stationary pneuma. Variations in tension explain the variety found in everday objects and the changes that they undergo. Currents of pneuma with different tensions are responsible for one object being redder or harder than another. Each object has a core of pneuma, its seed or "seminal reason," that directs its growth and decay. For the Stoics, there is no sharp separation between living and nonliving matter. All objects change as directed by their seminal reasons and in concert with a broader plan directed by the universal pneuma. Modern readers may regard the entire Stoic cosmos as alive and treat "cosmology" as "cosmobiology."

The pneuma found immediate applications in medicine. In the generation after Aristotle (384–322 B.C.E.), Eristratus of Chios taught that the pneuma was first inhaled into the lungs, then drawn from the lungs into the left ventricle as the heart expanded, and driven out again into the arteries as it contracted. The arteries distributed pneuma to all parts of the body, while the veins carried blood. When an artery was punctured, the pneuma rushed out, leaving a partial vacuum that was filled by blood drawn in from the veins, which, in turn, flowed from the wound. The denial that arteries contain blood was severely criticized by Galen (second century), who, however, still felt the necessity to distribute pneuma throughout the organism. Galen concluded that the arteries carry both blood and pneuma, the latter absorbed both through the lungs and through pores in the skin. To provide blood to mix with the pneuma from the lungs in the left ventricle, Galen introduced minute holes in the wall separating the ventricles. For Galen, the pneuma served both intellectual and physical functions. The most important of the latter were to provide fuel for the inner fire of living organisms and to provide cooling that prevented the innate heat becoming dangerously intense.

Although Galenic medicine was criticized during the Scientific Revolution, "spirits" descended from Galen's pneuma continued to play a role in neurophysiology and early psychology. René Descartes (1596–1650) regarded the brain as a hydraulic system with "animal spirits" as its working fluid. In England, Thomas Willis (1621–1675) taught that arterial blood passing through the cerebrum generated animal spirits in the cerebral cortex, which then divided among different brain structures devoted to sensation, imagination and intelligence, and memory. On this basis, Willis proposed physiological explanations of headaches, nightmares, and paralysis. His analysis of sensations influenced John Locke (1632–1704) and later associationist psychologists.

BIBLIOGRAPHY

Bono, James J. "Medical Spirits and the Medieval Language of Life." *Traditio: Studies in Ancient and Medieval History, Thought, and Religion* 40 (1984), 91–130.

French, Roger K. "Ether and Physiology." In *Conceptions of Ether*, ed. G. N. Cantor and M. J. S. Hodge. Cambridge: Cambridge University Press, 1982, pp. 111–134.

Hahm, David E. *Origins of Stoic Cosmology.* Columbus: Ohio State University Press, 1977.

PETER BARKER

See also Ether; Galenism; Stoicism

Pneumatics

The study of the mechanical properties of air sparked many lively debates during the Scientific Revolution, including speculation about alternatives to Aristotelian matter theory and the possible existence of void space in nature. The term originates from the Greek pneuma, meaning air, breath, or soul.

Air was considered by Aristotle (384–322 B.C.E.) to be one of the four basic elements making up the material world, and the idea that air had weight was part of the Aristotelian doctrine. Accounts of pneumatical phenomena, such as those created by siphons and cupping glasses, were used by Aristotle to prove that a vacuum could not occur in nature. In this view, water moved upward in a siphon-tube and against its natural tendency, so that the air removed at the top would not leave a void space.

Many of Aristotle's successors, including Strato of Lampsacus (d. ca. 268 B.C.E.) and John Philoponus (first half of the sixth century), wrote on air and suggested the possibility of a vacuum disseminated throughout it to explain its condensation and expansion and variations in the densities of matter.

The treatise *Pneumatica,* written by Hero of Alexander (fl. first century), is perhaps the best extant document from classical times dealing with the properties of air. Hero presented theoretical arguments for its atomic structure and the presence of interspersed vacua, as well as precise directions on how to construct intricate devices powered by either air or water. Most of the devices he described are whimsical toys, such as tin birds that whistle or spout water from hidden siphoning devices. These devices display a fascination with technical expertise typical of that time. Although no Greek original of this work survives, it was translated into Arabic in the ninth century. It became a popular example of ancient technological expertise in the Renaissance, was first translated into Latin in 1575, and was copied and translated many times in the seventeenth century.

Early-medieval discussions of the nature of air acknowledged it as corporeal and debated whether empty spaces were scattered through it. Reference was made to many of the same experiments used by the ancients to uphold the impossibility of a vacuum in nature. All of these phenomena, such as water not running out the bottom holes of a water clock, or clepsydra, without an unplugged hole at the top, were explained in several ways, but not, however, in terms of the pressure of the air. Albertus Magnus (ca. 1200–1280) explained this phenomenon in terms of nature's abhorrence of vacuum (*horror vacui*). In his view, water remains in the clepsydra rather than drain out and leave a vacuum behind. Roger Bacon (ca. 1214–1292) explained the same phenomenon in slightly different terms, emphasizing the preservation of the natural order of the universe, rather than the abhorrence of vacuum: the water stays in the clepsydra because of its universal tendency to preserve continuity among all parts of the universe.

Galileo Galilei's (1564–1642) early speculations about why water never rose above ca. thirty feet in a water pump continued the medieval notion of a limited abhorrence of vacuum in nature. By 1638, however, Galileo surmised, in his *Discourses on Two New Sciences,* that water was held at this height by the equilibrium it reached with the force exerted by the weight, or pressure, of the surrounding air. Early experiments in Italy to study Galileo's speculations included those by Giovanni Battista Baliani (1582–1666), who accepted the air's weight based on his experiments conducted with siphons at high altitudes. Believing that the air's weight decreased as elevation increased, Baliani found that siphons operating at higher elevations could not draw water as high as siphons at lower elevations. The lower, or weaker, air pressure at higher altitudes could not support a column of water to the same height as it could at lower elevations when its weight, or pressure, exerted a greater force. This was not an entirely new idea, for Aristotle had acknowledged that air is heavy. Baliani, however, for the first time, linked the air's weight to the nonoccurrence of vacuum. Any abhorrence of vacuum that nature has is not, therefore, an essential tendency but is the mechanical consequence of the air's weight, which prevents the occurrence of empty spaces.

In Holland, Isaac Beeckman (1588–1637), who accepted that air had weight and elasticity, provided a model to explain why air pressure was higher at lower elevations. Beeckman compared the air surrounding the earth to a giant sponge that was more compressed in its lower layers because of its elastic nature. This model

P

assumed air to be both elastic and compressible, as well as heavy.

Further testing of the theory of air pressure led to the construction, sometime in the early 1640s, of the device, later to be called a barometer, the first of many instruments developed as a direct result of studies of the air. This early device was a long vertical tube with a bulb and a valve at the top, filled with water and immersed at the bottom in a vessel, partly filled with water. When the valve was opened, the water dropped to a little more than thirty feet. Experiments with this device were carried out by Gasparo Berti (ca. 1600–1643) in Rome to clarify the status of what remained over the water after its descent. In his *Discourses,* Galileo had also proposed the existence of interspersed vacuities as an explanation of cohesion. He added theoretical weight to his proposal for the existence of vacuum by arguing that, since a line could be divided infinitely, so a body could be divided into atoms, surrounded by empty space.

The experimental device was further refined by one of Galileo's students, Evangelista Torricelli (1608–1647), who first used it in Florence in June 1644 to study the nature of air. Torricelli accepted Galileo's hypothesis of the weight of the atmosphere rather than the ancient *horror vacui* to explain the standing height of the barometer's water. Reasoning that a fluid heavier than water could not be sustained to the same level, Torricelli filled a glass tube with mercury, inverted it in a dish of mercury, and watched the level drop to ca. twenty-nine inches. Following Galileo, Torricelli explained this height in terms of the pressure or weight of the ambient air, claiming that "this force is external and that it comes from outside," rather than being caused by a principle internal to matter. His explanation, which instead explained the phenomenon in terms of the force exerted by the weight of the external air, was strengthened by the accurate prediction that a heavier liquid would drop to a lower level than water.

This kind of explanation was certainly anti-Aristotelian. The liquid was held at a certain level not because of any animistic or teleological preservation of material continuity in the world but, rather, for passively mechanical reasons. The ocean of air surrounding the earth pressed downward, and one effect of this weight, or pressure, was to hold the liquid at a constant level, in equilibrium with the weight of the air.

News of these experiments spread quickly throughout Europe. Marin Mersenne (1588–1648) is credited with carrying news of the Torricellian experiment from Italy back to France in early 1645. The experiment was repeated in the late 1640s by Mersenne, Étienne Noël (1581–1659), Gilles Personne de Roberval (1602–1675), and Blaise Pascal (1623–1662). By 1646, variations of the mercury experiment were performed in France by Pierre Petit (ca. 1598–1677), mathematician and astronomer at the Montmor Academy, although Petit reported the difficulty of acquiring the kind of glassware necessary to conduct pneumatic experiments properly. He performed the Torricellian experiment for the young Blaise Pascal and his father, Étienne, in 1646 at Rouen. Blaise Pascal initially believed the mercury column to be held up by a limited horror of vacuum, since he held the underlying assumption that bodies strive to maintain contact with each other. He subsequently explained the phenomenon entirely in terms of air pressure.

Pascal undertook further experiments of his own and published *Expériences nouvelles touchant le vuide* in 1647. Accepting that air has weight, Pascal predicted that the height of mercury in the Torricellian experiment would be greatest at sea level and would gradually decline if moved upward through the atmosphere. The Puy-de-Dôme experiment, performed by Pascal's brother-in-law, Florin Périer, in 1648, substantiated this theoretical supposition. When the mercury column was carried up the mountain, its level dropped as the surrounding air pressure dropped. There is some evidence suggesting that it was Descartes who suggested this experiment to Pascal. In an additional series of experiments, however, Pascal provided further convincing support for the idea of the weight and pressure of the air as cause of the behavior of the mercury in the Torricelli tube. Notable among these was the "void in the void" experiment, in which a barometric tube was placed in a large chamber at the top of another, longer tube filled with mercury. When the mercury in the latter, controlled by a valve, was allowed to fall below the level of the enclosed device, air admitted by degrees into the chamber at its top produced a corresponding rise of the mercury in the interior barometer.

News of the experiments on air reached England quickly, and it was not long before similar tests were being performed there. Knowledge of the experiments is thought to have passed from Mersenne to Theodore Haak (1605–1690), through their correspondence or during Haak's personal travels to the Continent. By the spring of 1648, Haak reported interest in the experiment in England to Mersenne, remarking that it had already been tried two or three times.

Robert Boyle (1627–1691) heard about these experiments from Samuel Hartlib (ca. 1600–1662) as well, who wrote to Boyle in the spring of 1648 with information about the experiment that he had received from the English exile Charles Cavendish. Boyle learned of pneumatic experiments done with an air pump from Gaspar Schott's *Mechanica hydraulico-pneumatica,* published in 1657, which related the experiments of Otto von Guericke (1602–1686), the mayor of Magdeburg, Germany. Von Guericke is credited with the first construction of another of the instruments associated with seventeenth-century studies of the air: the air pump. The effects of atmospheric pressure afforded by the devices of Pascal and Torricelli were relatively small compared with those built by von Guericke. As public spectacle, his experiments were much more dramatic. After he clamped together the two halves of a large brass globe and emptied it of air, two teams of six horses were unable to pull the globe apart. Von Guericke's explanation of this experiment confirmed speculations about air pressure rather than a universal horror of vacuum.

The air pump used for Boyle's experiments was built by Robert Hooke (1635–1703) and could pump out air more efficiently than von Guericke's machines. Boyle worked, perhaps continuously, with his technicians at Oxford for six months to a year carrying out the forty-three experiments that he published in 1660 as *New*

Otto von Guericke's demonstration that two teams of eight horses each could not separate a pair of joined hemispheres from which the air had been exhausted. From Guericke's Experimenta nova (ut vocantur) Magdeburgica de vacuo spatio *(1672).*

Experiments Physico-Mechanical, Touching the Spring of the Air and Its Effects. Boyle's air pump consisted of a glass chamber, with a thirty-quart volume, sitting atop a pump. This pump apparatus, consisting of a wooden piston within a brass cylinder, operated by a rack-and-pinion device, drew out air from the glass receiver, creating a partial vacuum. The publication of these air-pump experiments was presented as evidence for the notion that air has a spring, or pressure. Later work by Boyle and other natural philosophers, such as Richard Towneley (1629–1707) and Edmé Mariotte (ca. 1620–1684), led to Boyle's Law, which states that the pressure and the volume of a gas are inversely proportional. This law was formally presented in an appendix to the second edition, published in 1662, of *New Experiments.*

Boyle's experiments and the earlier ones raised questions about the nature of air and the status of the seemingly empty space left in the pump. Many philosophers, such as Christiaan Huygens (1625–1695) and members of the Accademia del Cimento in Florence, focused attention and praise on Boyle's description of the weight, or pressure, of air. Others, such as Franciscus Linus (1595–1675) and Thomas Hobbes (1588–1679), challenged Boyle's theory.

Boyle studied other phenomena associated with air, including combustion, respiration, and the transmission of light, sound, and magnetic effects. He also investigated the chemical nature of air, convinced that there was some aspect of air that, when absent, hindered combustion and respiration but not its pressure.

The Royal Society of London accepted Boyle's explanation of the Torricellian experiment in terms of the weight of the air. Much attention was focused on Boyle's new air-pump experiments, which were considered interesting because of what they could teach about the nature of air rather than be used only a means to resolve arguments concerning the nature of vacuum. Pneumatical experiments also served to impress visiting dignitaries, including King Charles II, the Danish ambassador, and Margaret Cavendish (1623–1673). In 1660 Christopher Wren (1632–1723) remarked that "it is not every year [that] will produce such a master experiment as the Torricellian." It was such a "master experiment" because it could "open new light into the principles of philosophy," while, at the same time, it had "something of pomp" about it. Much time was spent examining the effects of reduced or increased air pressure on a variety of subjects, both living and nonliving. Experiments on live subjects were described in a ballad written in 1663 by Joseph Glanvill (1636–1680):

> *To the Danish Agent late was showne*
> *That where noe Ayre is, there's noe breath.*
> *A glasse this secret did make knowne*
> *Where in a Catt was put to death.*
> *Out of the glasse the Ayre being screwed,*
> *Pusse dyed and ne're so much as mewed.*

Studies were not established in a programmatic fashion until Robert Hooke in 1663 suggested an orderly investigation to discern the true nature of air that would involve an examination of what kind of particles air consisted of and whether it was infinitely fluid or definitely solid. However, no systematic study of air was ever carried out, and, by the winter of 1666, pneumatic experiments no longer took center stage at Royal Society meetings, where interest was now focused instead on anatomy, blood transfusion, and tidal movements.

Subsequent studies on air seemed to follow the conclusions of Boyle's early experiments. This is reflected in Charles II betting confidently that air could be compressed by water. He bet fifty pounds to five that such was the case and won. Attention to pneumatic experiments was directed at confirming Boyle's claim about the weight of air. In early March 1670, Boyle performed just such an experiment to show that water dropped in an evacuated tube, "like a metallic body," there being no air to break the fall. Perhaps the most unique and interesting experiment of the year, again perpetrated by Hooke's enthusiasm, involved an air pump large enough to accommodate a person. On March 23, 1671, Hooke sat in a large "air-vess" while one-quarter of the air was pumped out. He remained inside for fifteen minutes and felt fine except for some pain in his ears. By this time, it was known that air is necessary for respiration and plant growth. By 1679, John Mayow (1641–1679) had shown that air is necessary for combustion as well as respiration. It was not until the mid-eighteenth century that natural philosophers acknowledged that air is a compound. By the late-eighteenth century, Antoine Lavoisier (1743–1794) exploded the phlogiston theory and demonstrated that air is a composite of oxygen and hydrogen.

BIBLIOGRAPHY

Helden, Anne C. van. "The Age of the Air-Pump." *Tractix 3* (1991), 149–172.

Koyanagi, Kimiyo. "Pascal et l'expérience du vide dans le vide." *Japanese Studies in the History of Science* 17 (1978), 105–127.

Pighetti, Clelia. "L'opera pneumatica di Robert Boyle." *Cultura e scuola* 20(80) (1981), 244–251.

Shapin, Steven, and Simon Schaffer. *Leviathan and the Air-Pump: Hobbes, Boyle, and the Experimental Life*. Princeton, NJ: Princeton University Press, 1985.

Waard, Cornelis de. *L'expérience barométrique: Ses antécédents et ses explications*. Thouars (Deux-Sèvres): Imprimerie nouvelle, 1936.

Webster, Charles. "The Discovery of Boyle's Law, and the Concept of the Elasticity of Air in the Seventeenth Century." *Archive for History of Exact Sciences* 2 (1965), 441–502.

JANE JENKINS

See also Academia del Cimento; Air Pump; Boyle, Robert; Guericke, Otto von; Pascal, Blaise; Torricelli, Evangelista; Towneley, Richard; Void

Political Economy. See Petty, William

Political Theory

Prior to the early sixteenth century, virtually all discussions of politics and government derived from two closely related classical traditions, and virtually all had large normative elements, in the sense that they focused on questions of how political institutions ought to be structured. The first, derived from Aristotle (384–322 B.C.E.), assumed, first, that knowledge of human political activities differed radically from knowledge of nature because natural events were determinate, whereas human events involved choice. For this reason, political knowledge was about what usually happens, whereas natural knowledge was about what always happens. Aristotelian theory also presumed that all political entities involved a balance among three elements: the one, the few, and the many. In legitimate governmental systems dominated by the one—monarchies—the monarch is forced to govern in the interest of all citizens, rather than in his own private interest, because his power is balanced by the combined forces of the aristocracy and the demos, or common citizens. When, however, the aristocracy or the common citizens fail to live up to their obligations, the monarchy may degenerate into its corrupt counterpart, a tyranny. By the same token, the legitimate form conforming to the dominance of the few—an aristocracy—may degenerate into an oligarchy when the prince or the people fail to enact their appropriate roles; and the legitimate form corresponding to the dominance of the many—a democracy—may degenerate into anarchy when the few and the one are not appropriately represented. Political theory grounded in these assumptions almost always admitted that the corruption of legitimate governments was ultimately inevitable, and it focused on how appropriate balances of power could be maintained so as to maximize the duration of legitimate regimes.

During the Roman Republic, under the combined influence of Stoic philosophy and Roman jurisprudence, a parallel to this Aristotelian-grounded theoretical tradition emerged. According to this tradition, some laws regarding human institutions are universal and derived from the nature of human beings. These *natural laws* are, thus, the same everywhere and for all time. On the other hand, some laws derived from the particular ways of life adopted by specific societies, and, while the *positive laws* so derived should not violate natural laws, neither do they follow of necessity from human nature. Under Christian influences, a level of divine law, presumed to take precedence over both natural and positive law, was incorporated into late-medieval discussions of politics.

Beginning with the writings of Niccolo Machiavelli (1469–1527), normative political theory came under attack on the ground that it was more important for political actors to understand how people do behave than how they ought to act. Those who adopted a more descriptive political theory also tended to assume that the methods of the natural sciences could be applied to obtain complete causal knowledge of human institutions. In Jean Bodin's (1530–1596) *The Six Bookes of a Commonweale* (1604, from the 1576 French original), for example, local variations in customs and laws were explained in terms of humoral differences in peoples produced by differences in environment; in James Harrington's (1611–1677) *The Commonwealth of Oceana* (1656), the dominant form of government was explained in terms of the distribution of land ownership.

Parallel to the tradition that focused on local variations in human interactions, a modern "natural law" tradition that sought to account for virtually all human interactions in terms of human nature emerged in connection with Hugo Grotius (1583–1645) in *The Law of War and Peace* (1623) and the writings of Thomas Hobbes (1588–1679), whose *Leviathan* (1651) was probably the most influential of all seventeenth-century trea-

tises in political theory. Hobbes drew his understanding of human nature from contemporary mechanistic theories of physiology and sensation, especially those connected with William Harvey (1578–1657) and Pierre Gassendi (1592–1655). He then argued that all human actions are grounded in the need to preserve one's vital motions by aquiring wealth and power; that, in the absence of a sufficiently powerful state, humans will necessarily be engaged in a state of violent warfare; and that the only path to safety lies in the creation of a *social contract* in which all persons give up every right except self-defense to a single sovereign authority with the power to impose peace. It should be clear that Hobbes returned to a pattern in which descriptive political theory merged self-consciously back into normative theory. Most subsequent seventeenth-century works in political theory, including those of Benedict de Spinoza (1632–1677) and John Locke (1632–1704), involved attempts to develop, modify, or attack *Leviathan*.

BIBLIOGRAPHY

Kelley, Donald R. *The Human Measure: Social Thought in the Western Legal Tradition*. Cambridge, MA: Harvard University Press, 1990.

Olson, Richard. *The Emergence of the Social Sciences, 1642–1792*. New York: Twayne, 1993.

Pocock, J. G. A. *The Machiavellian Moment: Florentine Republican Thought in the Atlantic Republican Tradition*. Princeton, NJ: Princeton University Press, 1975.

RICHARD OLSEN

See also Government and Science; Hobbes, Thomas; Humors; Mechanical Philosophy

Popularization

Vastly increased efforts to communicate science to non-scientists accompanied the creation of science as a cultural phenomenon during the Scientific Revolution. Popularization was aimed at a number of audiences but excluded the poorest elements of European society, peasants and illiterate laborers. Instead, scientific popularization was directed at men and, to a lesser degree, women educated at least to the level of literacy and having some disposable income. Popularization operated for different motives, through a number of vehicles, and increased in scope during the Scientific Revolution.

The literate lower class was not a blank slate for natural knowledge but had long had sources of scientific and magical information in such popular reading matter as almanacs, cheap medical manuals, and books of secrets. During the sixteenth century, the volume and availability of this material exploded as a result of the dissemination of printed matter. By the late sixteenth and early seventeenth centuries, learned men such as Ambroise Paré (1510–1590) and Sir Thomas Browne (1605–1682) stigmatized much of this demotic knowledge as "vulgar errors" or "old wive's tales," but demotic forms were potential vehicles of popularization of elite science. During the Scientific Revolution, writings directed at a broad popular audience increasingly used scientific concepts. As early as the beginning of the seventeenth century, some almanacs endorsed the Copernican system, and later some communicated the new discoveries and (in a simple form) the theoretical innovations of Galileo Galilei (1564–1642), Johannes Kepler (1571–1630), and Isaac Newton (1642–1727). There was also a growing tendency to use science in such popular entertainments as monster shows and exhibits of curiosities, as well as in works of literature.

Another form of early scientific popularization was the teaching of practical skills. Vernacular treatises on mathematics for merchants and business people went back to fifteenth-century Italy. In the sixteenth century, works of science and mathematics were aimed at others who used them professionally, particularly navigators and agriculturalists. This tradition was especially strong in the Dutch Republic and England, where it involved such leading natural philosophers as John Dee (1527–1608). Gresham College, established in 1597, offered English-language lectures on mathematical and natural-philosophical topics to the general London public. The Collège Royal in France, founded by the king in 1530, also offered lectures in mathematical and scientific subjects.

Despite Francis Bacon's (1561–1626) own elitist concern with the possible dangers of extending natural knowledge beyond a state-aligned group of wise men, early attempts to put Baconianism into practice involved scientific popularization. The French civil servant Theophraste Renaudot's (1583–1653) Bureau d'adresse, active in Paris during the 1630s, brought together noblemen and middle-class Parisians to discuss a number of subjects, including natural philosophy, and published the proceedings. The period of Puritan rule in mid-seventeenth-century England was marked by efforts at popularization motivated by Baconianism and millenarian belief in the increase of knowledge before the Last Days. These plans included educational reform and cooperative projects such as an office to circulate useful information, although few of these efforts were successful.

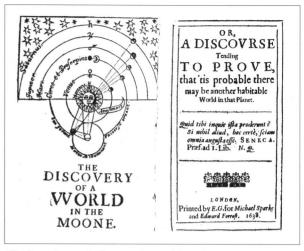

The first of several editions of a work by John Wilkins—based on Johannes Kepler's Somnium (The Dream)—*which details an imaginary voyage to the Moon, designed to illustrate the principles of Copernican astronomy.*

Few leading natural philosophers themselves wrote for a popular audience, although there were exceptions, Many of Galileo's vernacular writings were aimed at a broad literate audience, and Robert Boyle (1627–1691) published a collection of simple medical recipes, *Medicinal Experiments* (1692). John Wilkins (1614–1672) authored several scientific works aimed at the general educated public, including an influential primer of mechanics, *Mathematical Magick* (1648). But most effective popularizers had a foot in the camps of both natural philosophy and literature or journalism, striving for literary polish and often presenting their works in dialogue form. The Frenchman Bernard le Bovier de Fontenelle's (1657–1757) *Entretiens sur la pluralité des mondes* (Conversations on the Plurality of Worlds, 1686) was the most internationally popular and successful work of popularization of the late seventeenth century, going through five editions in the four years after its publication, and was translated into several languages. Like many later popularizations, such as Francesco Algarotti's (1712–1764) very successful *Newtonianismo per le dame* (1737), Fontenelle's was aimed at women, with the interlocutors a learned male Cartesian natural philosopher and a noblewoman.

By the late seventeenth century, the periodical press was another vehicle of scientific popularization. The Englishman John Dunton's (1659–1733) *Athenian Mercury* ran from 1691 to 1697 and consisted of questions sent in by readers with the replies of the editors. The volume of inquiries to the *Mercury* on scientific subjects indicates wide popular interest. Dunton employed, among others, Richard Sault (d. 1702), a contributor to the *Philosophical Transactions* and author of an algebra textbook, to answer inquiries covering a wide range of natural-philosophical issues, such as the nature of eclipses, the reasons for monstrous births, the circulation of the blood, and the humming of bees. Internationally, the French-language periodicals published in the Netherlands by Huguenot exiles also circulated scientific information to nonscientists, playing a particularly important role in disseminating Newtonianism on the Continent.

In addition to printed texts, science was also exhibited in public and semipublic venues, such as coffeehouses and, by the early eighteenth century, Masonic lodges. Some of the most eminent English scientists, such as William Whiston (1667–1752), supported themselves by charging admission to coffeehouse Newtonian lectures. Other lecturers, such as the Huguenot, Anglican clergyman, and Freemason Jean Desaguliers (1683–1744), active in London, the English provinces, and the Continent, were essentially professional popularizers. Lectures were frequently connected with recent dramatic celestial events, such as eclipses, or involved spectacular or entertaining experiments. English lecturers related their presentations more closely to business than did French or Dutch. Lectures and other forms of scientific and mathematical popularization in England led to an increased tendency to think in terms of Newtonian mechanics among people of all classes above the poorest, thereby contributing to the Industrial Revolution. In the highly literate Dutch Republic, where a voluminous vernacular literature debating Cartesianism had been available from the mid-seventeenth century, lectures shifted from a Cartesian emphasis to a Newtonian one by the early eighteenth century.

In France, where the Church often viewed them with suspicion, public scientific lectures were mostly Cartesian and less common than in England. The principal arena for scientific display in France was the more socially exclusive salon, where dramatic experiments or demonstrations were common. The idea of science as a civilized diversion was especially strong in France and in the Italian Courts, particularly Tuscany, where the ideal of the civilized person now included the ability to discourse knowledgeably on the science of the day.

In addition to business and entertainment, science was often popularized for religious reasons, particularly during the vogue for natural theology in the late seventeenth and early eighteenth centuries. It was believed that popularizing science and natural history would effectively combat atheism. In England, the Boyle Lectures, founded by Boyle's will in 1692 and given by liberal Anglican divines, were dedicated to demonstrating a design in nature and thereby establishing the existence of a Designer. Boyle Lectures were often published, and some sold very well. Some popularizers of natural philosophy also wanted to combat potentially destabilizing "enthusiastic" or superstitious understandings of natural phenomena with politically harmless scientific ones. Edmond Halley's (ca. 1656–1743) broadside illustrating the cause of a great eclipse in 1715 by the Moon's blocking the light of the Sun had the stated purpose of refuting those who interpreted the eclipse as a divine condemnation of the recently crowned King George I. As Europe entered the Enlightenment, political and theological reasons for popularization were largely supplanted by economic ones relating to industrial development.

BIBLIOGRAPHY

Jacob, Margaret. *The Cultural Meaning of the Scientific Revolution.* Philadelphia: Temple University Press, 1988. 2nd ed. New York: Oxford University Press, 1995.

McEwen, Gilbert D. *The Oracle of the Coffee House: John Dunton's Athenian Mercury.* San Marino, CA: Huntington Library, 1972.

Stewart, Larry. *The Rise of Public Science: Rhetoric, Technology, and Natural Philosophy in Britain, 1660–1750.* Cambridge: Cambridge University Press, 1992.

Sutton, Geoffrey V. *Science for a Polite Society: Gender, Culture, and the Demonstration of Enlightenment.* Boulder, CO: Westview, 1995.

WILLIAM E. BURNS

See also Almanacs; Baconianism; Books of Secrets; Bureau d'adresse; Collège Royale; Fontenelle, Bernard le Bovier de; Gresham College; Wilkins, John

Porta, Giambattista della (1535–1615)

Born in Vico Equense, near Naples, he was the son of a minor nobleman, Nardo Antonio Della Porta. He was influenced by the philosophical naturalism that derived from the teachings of Bernardino Telesio (1509–1588) and flourished in the Neapolitan academies. While still

Frontispiece of Porta's De distillatione *(1608).*

in his teens, he founded an academy (the Academia Secretorum Naturae) modeled on the Academy of Secrets described by the humanist Girolamo Ruscelli (1500–1566). Della Porta's academy met regularly to conduct experiments on "occult secrets of nature." His first and most famous work, *Magia naturalis* (1558), contained the results of the academy's investigations. An encyclopedic hodge-podge of marvelous phenomena, it was an earnest attempt to give rational and experimental grounds to magic. Della Porta denied that magic was demonic and insisted that magical events were purely natural. His magical investigations caused him trouble with the Inquisition, which questioned him on two separate occasions.

Della Porta applied his method to a wide variety of subjects. His other works on natural philosophy and natural magic included books on human and plant physiognomy, distillation, cryptography, the art of memory, and optics. He wrote on the camera obscura and claimed priority for the invention of the telescope. His services were eagerly sought by princes, including the duke of Ferrara and the Holy Roman Emperor Rudolf II, to whom Della Porta dedicated his unfinished and unpublished magnum opus on magic, *Taumatologia*. He continued to be

an active member of Neapolitan intellectual life until his death. He was one of the early members of the Accademia dei Lincei, which derived its symbol of the lynx and its motto, *Auspicit et Inspicit* ("urging observation and investigation"), from Della Porta's *Phytognomonica* (1588). An important figure in Renaissance Italian literature, he wrote more than a dozen comedies that were popular in Court circles.

BIBLIOGRAPHY

Eamon, William. "Natural Magic and Utopia in the Cinquecento: Campanella, the Della Porta Circle, and the Revolt of Calabria." *Memorie Domenicane* 26 (1995).

———. *Science and the Secrets of Nature: Books of Secrets in Medieval and Early Modern Culture*. Princeton, NJ: Princeton University Press, 1994.

Muraro, Luisa. *Giambattista Della Porta mago e scienzato*. Milan: Feltrinelli, 1978.

Porta, Giambattista della. *Natural Magick*. Ed. Derek Price. New York: Basic Books, 1957. Orig. trans. 1658.

WILLIAM EAMON

See also Accademia dei Lincei; Books of Secrets; Camera Obscura; Magic; Secrets of Nature; Telesio, Bernardino

Positivist Historiography

The traditional picture of the Scientific Revolution, still surviving in textbooks and popular accounts, is indebted to nineteenth-century philosophers and historians of a positivist inclination. Although these writers differed considerably in their philosophical outlooks and historiographical practices, they had in common views about the development of science that belong to the positivist tradition. These views have been severely criticized by later scholars, but they were influential for more than a century and formed the background of later conceptions of the Scientific Revolution.

There is not, and has never been, a positivist school of historiography of science characterized by a shared view of how to understand past science and write its history. Rather, positivist historiography is a label loosely covering a broad spectrum of views that have only little in common except certain general ideas concerning the development of science. Moreover, the connection to (philosophical) positivism is far from unambiguous. The kind of positivism that influenced the history of science was the classical positivism associated with, for example, Auguste Comte (1798–1857) and Herbert Spencer (1820–1903); the logical positivism that emerged in the

1920s was largely ahistorical and, hence, of no relevance to the history of science. In general history, a positivist trend emerged in the mid-nineteenth century, led by Leopold von Ranke (1795–1886) in Germany. According to Ranke and his followers, the prime task of the historian was to unearth facts about the past and use these in building a precise and objective historical account; interpretations and broader generalizations, on the other hand, were held to be avoidable if not harmful. However, science was not considered part of history, and the more sophisticated positivism of the professional historians had little influence on the history of science.

Even though positivist historiography of science is ill defined, it is possible to characterize the position by means of a few minimal conditions: (1) science is held to have progressed unilinearly toward the present state of knowledge in what is, in effect, a teleological process; (2) progress is cumulative and secured by following the proper scientific methods (i.e., empirical results ordered inductively); (3) the accumulation of facts results in scientific progress being continuous once it has taken off; and (4) the historian should evaluate past science—judging it good or bad, true science or pseudoscience—and do so by means of presently accepted knowledge and criteria. Among positivist historians, as among most other historians of science, the Scientific Revolution has been of prime importance, but there is no simple answer, common to all of them, of what constituted the Scientific Revolution or how to assess it historically. In fact, positivist historians have even disagreed as to the very existence of the Scientific Revolution.

The concept of the Scientific Revolution, as a radical redirection of philosophical and scientific activity as well as a repudiation of the ancients and their humanist followers, emerged during the eighteenth century. Long before positivism had been established as a philosophical theory, French philosophers of the Enlightenment, including Voltaire (1694–1778) and Condorcet (1743–1794), described the seventeenth century as the watershed during which the new empirical and rational methods secured perpetual scientific progress. According to these thinkers, the theological domination and lack of empirical concern characterizing the dark Middle Ages made progress impossible until the late sixteenth century. But, with Francis Bacon's (1561–1626) inductive-empirical methodology and its practical use by Galileo Galilei (1564–1642), René Descartes (1596–1650), and others, the New Science was born, and light was brought to humankind. The picture that Voltaire and his allies painted of the Scientific Revolution contained many aspects that would later be adopted by positivist historians of science.

According to Comte, who launched modern positivism in a series of lectures in the 1830s, knowledge develops through different stages, from the mythical to the metaphysical to the "positive," or scientific, stage. In the case of physics, the latter transition had irrevocably occurred during the Scientific Revolution, which saw the final decline of the metaphysical conception of the natural sciences. Comte believed that metaphysics and speculation about the inner reality of the world were not only the main obstacles to positive science, but also characteristic features of Scholastic learning; therefore, what happened ca. 1600 owed nothing to the Scholastic and Renaissance traditions but was a genuine birth of modern science. Comte's idea of a positive history of science has often been ridiculed as primitive and ahistorical in its celebration of progress and fixation on modern knowledge, but it includes a proper historical perspective unusual for his time; for example, in spite of depicting the Middle Ages as "dark" and unscientific, Comte realized that the centuries before 1600 had their own, rich intellectual life that formed the background for the Scientific Revolution. His British contemporary William Whewell (1794–1866) maintained the periodization of a dark age followed by a radically new conception and practice of science, and, like Comte, he believed that the progress in the sixteenth and seventeenth centuries was based on the application of new—Baconian and Cartesian—methods of science. However, he did not share Comte's contempt for metaphysics and speculation, which he considered necessary elements in scientific discoveries: the difference between the sterility of Scholasticism and the dynamics of the New Science was not a question of metaphysics or not, but of Galileo and his generation having a better metaphysics than the schoolmen. With regard to the revolutionary nature of the seventeenth-century transformation, Whewell agreed with Comte and the Enlightenment philosophers while, at the same time, indicating that the Scientific Revolution was preceded by a trend toward clearer and more independent thought in the Renaissance era. Comte and Whewell represented two different strands in early positivist thought and also differed considerably in the quality of their actual historical work, but both considered the history of science to be of interest primarily as a collection of case studies in support of their philosophical views. The most important of these cases was the Scientific Revolution, which they reconstructed in accordance with their philosophical preferences.

The Austrian physicist and philosopher Ernst Mach (1838–1916) also turned to history of science to develop and exemplify his own version of positivistic epistemology and methodology. This included an extreme form of empiricism and a crusade against metaphysical notions in science. In his influential *The Science of Mechanics* (1883), Mach presented Galileo as the archetypal positivist scientist, who, almost single-handedly, had founded mechanics on a few laws of motion deduced by generalization from empirical data. Galileo's feat was a radical break with the past made possible by his adoption of a completely new method: to investigate *how* bodies move rather than *why* they move. Mach's Galileo was a pioneer experimentalist who allowed his preconceived ideas of simplicity and thought economy to guide his experiments. Thus, while abstraction and idealization were important elements in the Galilean revolution, Mach did not assign mathematics a prominent role in the creative process. Mach's view on the Scientific Revolution, and on the history of science in general, was very influential, if more among physicists and philosophers than among historians. For example, Albert Einstein (1879–1955) considered *The Science of Mechanics* the ideal exposition of the history of physics.

The French chemist and physicist Pierre Duhem (1861–1916) was an advocate of a positivist philosophy of science broadly related to the versions found in Comte, Whewell, and Mach. But, as a historian, he differed considerably from his positivist colleagues and represented new ideas that cannot, as a matter of course, be labeled as belonging to positivist historiography. First of all, Duhem argued forcefully against the traditional notion of the seventeenth-century Scientific Revolution, which he showed had important predecessors in the late Middle Ages. The work of Galileo was not the starting point of an entirely new science but the culmination and natural extension of theories and methods that had already been developed by medieval scholars. This is not to say that Duhem denied that something new took place ca. 1600, but he saw the Scientific Revolution as a link in a chain that started three hundred years earlier and not as a discontinuity. In sharp contrast to other historians, positivists or not, he stressed the decisive contributions of Christian scholars such as Jean Buridan (ca. 1295–

1358) and Nicole Oresme (ca. 1320–1382); on the other hand, he saw the Renaissance as a relatively barren period, contrary to what the Swiss historian Jacob Burckhardt (1818–1897) had argued in a work of 1860. In spite of this wholesale refutation of a dogma cherished by positivist historians of science, Duhem's historiography has at least one leg in the positivist tradition. For example, he used the history of science in support of his philosophical ideas and argued, like Comte and Mach, that metaphysics and the search for hidden causes were detrimental to scientific progress; he also considered mathematical formulations to be less important than qualitative insight in the creative process. Neither did his emphasis on continuous progress obtained by the accumulation of empirical knowledge and gradual refinements of concepts go against the positivist tradition. His continuity thesis was certainly radical, but Duhem also believed that the start of modern science could be located in space and time. Only the crucial period was not ca. 1600 but, rather, ca. 1300, when Christian scholars began to attack Aristotelian orthodoxy and form their own ideas of nature.

When positivist historiography of science came under attack beginning in the 1920s, Duhem's continuity thesis was among the targets. A new generation of historians argued that the Scientific Revolution was real and all important, that mathematization was crucial to the revolution, and that philosophical and metaphysical beliefs were part and parcel of the new science. But the new historians did not form a united front, and they did not simply revolt against any kind of positivism. For example, the Dutch historian Eduard Dijksterhuis (1892–1965) placed great emphasis on the role of mathematics, which may be taken as a nonpositivistic feature. But he also followed Duhem some of the way in his evolutionary view and never referred to the seventeenth century as a "revolution," and his view on what constitutes true scientific knowledge agreed fully with that of the positivists, namely that it is the quantitative relationships between measurable quantities and not statements about the real constituents of nature. Alastair Crombie (1915–1996) also defended a version of Duhem's thesis: a methodological continuity from the schoolmen to the scientists of the seventeenth century.

Even more than Dijksterhuis, and in a very different way, was George Sarton (1884–1956) influenced by positivism, especially in its Comtean version. For Sarton, the history of science was the history of "systematized positive knowledge," and he believed that the study of the development of such knowledge would contribute to modern research as well as serve higher, moral purposes. He was not especially interested in the Scientific Revolution, but his great emphasis on progress through accumulation of knowledge—he considered science to be uniquely defined as a cumulative enterprise—led him to rate Greek science as cumulative and to an evolutionary, rather than revolutionary, view. The Scientific Revolution was not the birth of science, but neither was it a myth; it marked the beginning of a phase of vigorous acceleration that has proceeded to our time. For Sarton, the history of medieval learning had no justification in itself, but, by contrasting this "history of errors" with real science, it could serve a moral purpose.

Positivist historiography long ago ceased to be a force in academic history of science. Indeed, and somewhat unfairly, it is often identified with "bad history of science." Yet, vulgar versions of positivism continue to play a role in more popular expositions and in historical work written by, or aimed at, scientists. In such work, the Scientific Revolution is pictured in the same black-and-white colors that Comte and Mach used.

BIBLIOGRAPHY

Agassi, Joseph. *History and Theory,* vol. 2: *Towards an Historiography of Science.* 's-Gravenhage: Mouton, 1963.

Cohen, H. Floris. *The Scientific Revolution: A Historiographical Inquiry.* Chicago: University of Chicago Press, 1994.

Eastwood, Bruce S. "On the Continuity of Western Science from the Middle Ages: A. C. Crombie's Augustine to Galileo." *Isis* 83 (1992), 84–99.

Frängsmyr, Tore. "Science or History: George Sarton and the Positivist Tradition in the History of Science." *Lychnos* (1973–1974), 104–144.

Kragh, Helge. *An Introduction to the Historiography of Science.* Cambridge: Cambridge University Press, 1987.

Lindberg, David C. "Conceptions of the Scientific Revolution from Bacon to Butterfield: A Preliminary Sketch." In *Reappraisals of the Scientific Revolution,* ed. David C. Lindberg and Robert S. Westman. Cambridge: Cambridge University Press, 1990, pp. 1–26.

HELGE KRAGH

See also Medieval Science and the Scientific Revolution; Scientific Revolution

Power, Henry (1623–1668)

Physician and Fellow of the Royal Society, Power was a Cambridge graduate and a friend and admirer of Sir Thomas Browne (1605–1682). He published the first English, and one of the first European, books of microscopical observations and experiments, *Experimental Philosophy in Three Books: Containing New Experiments Microscopial, Mercurial, Magnetical* (1664), which included in Book I descriptions of small animals, such as fleas and cheese mites, as well as seeds and pollen and other living and nonliving things. It also described experiments on these creatures, such as the freezing and thawing of nematodes. Power was a great enthusiast of the microscope, believing that it made the previous writings of ancients on small things obsolete. He claimed that the microscope would help demonstrate the atomic nature of matter and, by laying bare the exquisitely precise arrangements of the tiniest living things, would show the glory of God. Power even wrote a poem praising the microscope. Books II and III of *Experimental Philosophy,* the only book he published during his life, were less original and included experiments on air pressure and on magnetism.

Power was one of the first class of members elected to the Royal Society after its founding, and from his home in Yorkshire he carried out observations for the society on topics such as the weather and the behavior of gases in coal mines. *Experimental Philosophy* was soon overshadowed by Robert Hooke's (1635–1703) *Micrographia,* published the following year and, unlike Power's book, containing elaborate illustrations.

BIBLIOGRAPHY

Cowles, Thomas. "Dr. Henry Power, Disciple of Sir Thomas Browne." *Isis* 20 (1934), 344–366.

Hall, Marie Boas. "Introduction." In Power, Henry. *Experimental Philosophy in Three Books: Containing New Experiments Microscopial, Mercurial, Magnetical.* Repr. with additional material. New York: Johnson Reprint, 1966, pp. ix–xxvii.

Webster, Charles. "Henry Power's Experimental Philosophy." *Ambix* 14 (1967), 150–178.

WILLIAM E. BURNS

See also Microscopy

Praetorius (Richter), Johannes (1537–1616)

Astronomer, instrument maker, and mathematician, he was born in Joachimsthal and studied at the University of Wittenberg, probably under Caspar Peucer (1525–1602). In 1562 he moved to Nuremberg, where he made astronomical instruments. In 1569 he became closely associated with Georg Joachim Rheticus (1514–1574). In 1571 Peucer and the university senate called him to Wittenberg, where he taught higher mathematics until 1576, when he assumed a position at the newly founded Altdorf Academy near Nuremberg, where he taught astronomy, mathematics, and instrument making until his death.

Apart from prognostications and calendars, Praetorius published only a tract on the comet of 1577 and one mathematical work, but he corresponded widely and was highly regarded. Tycho Brahe (1546–1601) called him "one of the leading *mathematici*."

Praetorius was representative of the "Wittenberg interpretation" of Nicolaus Copernicus (1473–1543). He knew that Andreas Osiander (1498–1552) was the author of the fictionalist Preface of Copernicus's *De revolutionibus* (1543) but did not entertain the reality of heliocentrism. His manuscripts show that, in attempting a sophisticated accommodation of Copernican theory to a stationary earth, he approached a Tychonic system with the planets circling the Sun, which, in turn, revolved about the stationary earth. He retreated, however, when faced with the presumed discovery of the intersection of the solar and Martian spheres. His view of the relationship between mathematical astronomy and physics is embodied in his assessment of Johannes Kepler's (1571–1630) *Mysterium cosmographicum* (Cosmographic Mystery, 1696) as tedious and pointless.

His library and manuscripts became the core of the Praetorius-Saxonius-Bibliothek, now in Erlangen, Schweinfurt, and Munich. A number of splendid instruments he made in collaboration with the goldsmith Hans Epischofer are preserved at the Germanisches Nationalmuseum in Nuremberg.

BIBLIOGRAPHY

Müller, Uwe, ed. *"450 Jahre Copernicus revolutionibus": Astronomische und mathematische Bücher aus Schweinfurter Bibliotheken: Ausstellung des Stadtarchivs Schweinfurt in Zusammenarbeit mit der Bibliothek Otto Schafer, 21. November 1993–19. Juni 1994.* (Veröffentlichungen des Stadtsarchivs Schweinfurt, 9). Schweinfurt: Stadtarchiv Schweinfurt, 1993.

Westman, Robert. "Three Responses to the Copernican Theory: Johannes Praetorius, Tycho Brahe, and Michael Maestlin." In *The Copernican Achievement*, ed. R. S. Westman. (Contributions of the UCLA Center for Medieval and Renaissance Studies 7). Berkeley and Los Angeles: University of California Press, 1975, pp. 285–345.

Willers, Johannes, and Karin Holzamer. "Katalog und Ausstellung," *Schätze der Astronomie: Arabische und deutsche Instrumente aus dem Germanischen Nationalmuseum,* ed. Gerhard Bott. Nuremberg: Germanisches Nationalmuseum, 1983, pp. 78–93.

JAMES R. VOELKEL

See also Celestial Spheres; Copernicanism; Geoheliocentrism; Rheticus, Georg Joachim

Precession

The slow westward motion of the equinoctial points along the ecliptic, whose effect is to make the tropical year (the Sun's passage from one vernal equinox to the next) slightly shorter than the sidereal year (one circuit of the Sun with respect to the fixed stars). Precession was first noted by Hipparchus (fl. 127 B.C.E.). Ptolemy (ca. 100–ca. 170), employing earlier observations, accepted an annual rate of 36 arc-seconds. During the tenth century, Arabic astronomers believed that the rate was variable and that precession reversed itself periodically. This so-called trepidation (*trepidatio*) became a standard feature of later Islamic astronomy. A ninth sphere was required to account for the motion. In the thirteenth century, Nasr Eddin, who doubted trepidation, calculated the precessional rate at 51 arc-seconds, close to the modern 50.3 arc-seconds.

Precession with trepidation passed into the European tradition. Johannes Werner (1468–1522) published a book on precession and trepidation in 1522, to which Nicolaus Copernicus (1473–1543) responded. Later, in his *De revolutionibus* (1543), Copernicus explained precession—which he fixed at 50.2 arc-seconds—as the slight difference between Earth's annual motion and the (spurious) "third motion" of the earth's axis. Unfortunately, he not only accepted the idea of trepidation, he also assumed periodic changes in the obliquity of the ecliptic. These complications required further motions later shown to be unnecessary.

Tycho Brahe (1546–1601) dismissed trepidation and changes to obliquity but, having a geoheliocentric model of the universe, could rely upon the traditional mechanism to account for precession. Johannes Kepler (1571–1630) was not so confident, but some Copernicans, such as Philip van Landsberge (1561–1632), who produced planetary tables in the early seventeenth century, followed Copernicus uncritically.

Until Isaac Newton (1642–1727), no one provided a convincing physical explanation of precession. In Book III of the *Principia mathematica philosophiae naturalis* (1687), Newton argued that the combined gravitational effects of the Sun and Moon on a spheroidal earth with flattened poles would result in a slow revolution of the axis of rotation every twenty-six thousand years. Although some of his assumptions were incorrect, he was able to calculate a precessional rate almost identical with the observed rate.

BIBLIOGRAPHY

Taton, R., and C. Wilson, eds. *Planetary Astronomy from the Renaissance to the Rise of Astrophysics.* Part A: *Tycho Brahe to Newton.* Cambridge: Cambridge University Press, 1989, passim.

RICHARD A. JARRELL

See also Astronomy; Brahe, Tycho; Copernicus, Nicolaus; Kepler, Johannes; Newton, Isaac; Ptolemaic Astronomy

Preformation

The theory that the unborn organism preexists in the seed of the parent with all of its limbs, organs, and tissues present is often regarded as a an example of scientific delusion fostered by primitive early microscopes. However, few if any preformationists thought that complete miniaturized organisms preexisted. The sense in which the parts of the animal were held to be "present" was accordingly elusive and philosophical rather than observational.

Aristotle (384–322 B.C.E.) had denied that the parts were present from the time of conception, arguing that they were formed simultaneously but gradually. Although preformation had been suggested by some ancient and medieval writers, it came into prominence in the seventeenth century as a theory properly in keeping with the mechanical world picture and the Christian doctrine of Creation. By understanding generation as essentially a process of growth, which was imagined, in turn, as explicable by reference to mechanical processes of filtering and accretion, references to souls, forms, and forces could be eliminated, and God's Creation remained a unique act. Jan Swammerdam (1637–1680) proposed that Eve had contained in her loins all future generations encapsulated within each other, and this doctrine was popularized and generalized by Nicolas

Malebranche (1638–1715). Albrecht Haller (1708–1777) and Charles Bonnet (1720–1793) were its last important representatives.

To preformationists, William Harvey's (1578–1657) idea that a beating heart and vascular system could exist in the embryo without a brain and nervous system seemed incredible. Observational evidence in favor of preformation supplemented a priori considerations. It had long been observed that the buds, bulbs, and seeds of plants may contain furled blossoms, stems, and leaves. Swammerdam demonstrated furled wings and legs in pupating insects that were formerly "worms." Observers armed with the microscope reported that they could see recognizable structures present in the wormlike mammalian embryo within a matter of days or weeks after fertilization. However, preformation was difficult to reconcile with Harvey's studies of the hen's egg in its sequential phases of development; it became further evident in the researches of Marcello Malpighi (1628–1694) that form emerged from a state of relative formlessness, and dissection and unwrapping could reveal little in the way of further structure. Hopes, and, indeed, expectations were disappointed, though not extinguished. When Nicolaas Hartsoeker (1656–1725) published a celebrated drawing of a tiny fetus curled up in the head of a spermatozoon, he was careful to say that the drawing represented only what we ought to be able to see, not what he had seen with a microscope.

It became increasingly evident that a paradox was at work in the theory of preformation. Unless, as some theorists believed, unknown techniques of preparation and better microscopes would eventually reveal completely formed organisms, discarded vital forces had to be reintroduced to explain how the visible organism emerged from its theoretically preformed but observationally amorphous state.

BIBLIOGRAPHY

Roe, Shirley. *Matter, Life, and Generation.* Cambridge: Cambridge University Press, 1981.

Ruestow, Edward. "Piety and the Defense of the Natural Order: Swammerdam on Generation." In *Religion, Science, and Worldview,* ed. Margaret J. Osler and Paul Farber. Cambridge: Cambridge University Press, 1985, pp. 217–241.

CATHERINE WILSON

See also Generation; Malpighi, Marcello; Microscopy

P

Printing

A technique for producing books and other textual artifacts by means of reusable metal characters, which, when inked and employed in a press, are used to create impressions on paper. Printing permits the reproduction of multiple copies without the degradation seemingly inevitable to any process of written copying. Many scholars, therefore, suggest that it provided the foundation of textual reliability on which a Scientific Revolution could be built in early-modern Europe.

For a technique supposedly providing such reliability, theories about the origin of printing itself were for a long time disconcertingly uncertain. When, where, and by whom it had been invented remained unclear for hundreds of years. Only in the nineteenth century was agreement largely attained that the inventor had been one Johann Gutenberg (ca. 1398–1468), a goldsmith

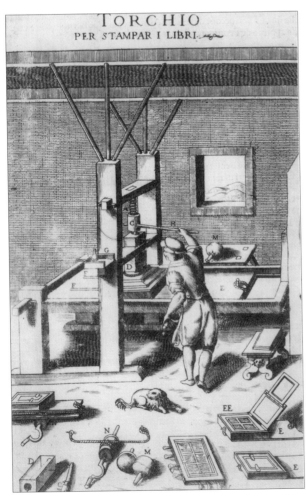

The printing press and the tools of the printer's trade. From Vittorio Zonca, Novo teatro de machine et edicii *(1607).*

from the Rhineland town of Mainz. In the meantime, this uncertainty reflected a more profound confusion over the nature and consequences of the craft. How was it properly to be used, by whom, and to what ends? In short, what *was* printing?

These were urgent questions. Within a generation of Gutenberg, printers had appeared in a score of German, Dutch, Italian, and French cities. William Caxton (ca. 1422–1491) set up his printing house in London at the end of this first wave of expansion. With each press, a pair of workers could produce perhaps a thousand sheets of printed paper every day. These were unprecedented quantities. It was not long before the number of printed books available exceeded, in all probability, the number ever produced in manuscript up to that time. Lucien Febvre and Henri-Jean Martin (1984) estimate that by 1500 there was already a printed book in existence for every five living Europeans.

Sheer quantity had its consequences. Books were suddenly available in unprecedented numbers, in more places, and at lower costs. Literacy increased and spread through social ranks, as people—especially town dwellers—made these new objects their own. But numbers alone cannot explain their specific effects. More important for the history of science were the substantial *qualitative* changes brought about by print. These were of two major kinds: transformations in the making and appearance of the page and innovations in the uses of books by readers.

After a brief period of imitation, the printed page began to look different from its manuscript equivalent. Typefaces and layouts slowly became standardized, and the use of cross-referencing, indexes, errata, and notes grew common. Woodcuts and engravings allowed the use of repeatable images, giving rise to the diagram, the accurate chart, and the scientific illustration. Hitherto, it had been virtually impossible to express knowledge claims in such pictorial forms, so rapidly did images degrade in the hands of copyists; the many images in manuscripts had had other purposes, less characteristic of reproducibility. But verisimilitude nevertheless remained thoroughly conventional in character. It depended on a visual craft that had to be learned. Galileo Galilei's (1564–1643) pioneering images of the Moon, for example, printed in his *Sidereus nuncius* (1610), appear to us "realistic," yet they conveyed a general impression of the Moon's nature rather than aspire to topographical veracity. Nonetheless, the possibilities raised by print transformed the chances of making accurate, trustworthy, and enduring records of claims. As Elizabeth Eisenstein (1979) argues, the simple ability to juxtapose and compare reliable representations of competing theories revolutionized the possibilities for learned work.

Scientific enterprises could only really be transformed, however, when such resources were put to use. The "printing revolution" was, most importantly, a revolution in practices. It witnessed the advent of conventions of openness, intellectual property, authorship, and collaboration. These, indeed, rested on the use of printed materials for recording and communicating knowledge, but natural philosophers themselves had to *make* print into a useful medium. The press was rich in potential for many different uses, including piracy and plagiary, as well as openness and discovery. Which of these possibilities would be realized long remained in doubt. In putting it to use as they did, men like Galileo not only advanced significant new knowledge, they also helped make modern print culture itself.

Among the most determined in his efforts to exploit print was the Danish astronomer Tycho Brahe (1546–1601). Brahe embedded a printing house in the very walls of his palatial observatory of Uraniborg. He used it to produce books recording his achievements, which he then distributed among the Courts and learned men of Europe. An important element in his success was that Brahe himself remained master of the processes of production and distribution. No other scientific figure—with the notable exception of Johannes Hevelius (1611–1687)—came close to asserting this degree of control. Others had to negotiate a commercial book trade. This might be no easy matter. Even Brahe continued to experience problems, in fact, to the extent that his prized star catalog remained in manuscript at his death.

Collectives had a greater chance of success than individuals—even individuals as privileged as Brahe—in mastering such an environment. The Royal Society of London and the Académie Royale des Sciences in Paris pioneered strategies for managing the press and for using its products. The former became part of the English government's licensing system for regulating the book trade and gained the legal right to give specific printers monopoly rights to the texts of its Fellows as an incentive to publish works that would, after all, have limited markets. Such societies and academies were instrumental in developing new forms of publication, in particular the

learned periodical, and new kinds of authors. At the same time, they developed practices of criticism and conversation useful in assessing printed materials received from elsewhere. These practices were productively creative but bound by conventions of civility. Together, they were fundamental to the making of learned communities, and they could be of profound consequence for the fortunes of particular authors and their claims. Isaac Newton (1642–1727) was able to use the Royal Society's mechanisms, for example, both to produce his own work and to condemn Gottfried Wilhelm Leibniz (1646–1716) as its plagiarist.

The conventions of reading and publishing inaugurated in such settings relatively quickly became norms. It was this standardization, as much as the fixity of printed texts themselves, that distinguished the contribution of printing to the scientific enterprise. It reached fruition in the Enlightenment. The coming of a new kind of public was now widely forecast. Defined by its common readership of periodicals such as the *Philosophical Transactions* and the *Journal des sçavans,* this public would, with Baconian ambition, take all knowledge to be its province. It asserted its right to judge all claims, be they political, religious, or scientific. As the editor of the *Philosophical Transactions* put it, readers now asserted "an absolute and indisputable power over all that appear in print." Aspirant authors—"even those Wonders of Nature, the Newtons and the Halleys"—must pass muster before "this great Judge of them all." Natural philosophy thus became an enterprise defined by its embrace of public communication. Its explanatory resources and conclusions alike rested on their visibility before audiences and readers. Claims were allegedly ratified by this dispersed, international community. Chemists, for example, repudiated the private epistemologies associated with alchemy in favor of accountable methods open to public scrutiny via the medium of print. The viability of this forum clearly depended on the representation of print as providing for the unimpeded circulation of identical texts across national and confessional rifts. This representation had evident problems, not least the interventions of censorship. Nonetheless, its effects have lasted. They include our own notions of scientific openness and objectivity.

BIBLIOGRAPHY

Chartier, Roger, and Henri-Jean Martin, eds. *Histoire de l'édition Française.* 4 vols. Paris: Promodis, 1982–1986. 2nd ed. 1990–1991.

Eisenstein, Elizabeth L. *The Printing Press as an Agent of Change: Communications and Cultural Transformations in Early-Modern Europe.* 2 vols. Cambridge: Cambridge University Press, 1979.

Febvre, Lucien, and Henri-Jean Martin. *L'apparition du livre.* Paris: Michel, 1958. D. Gerard, trans. *The Coming of the Book: The Impact of Printing, 1450–1800.* London: Verso, 1984.

Ivins, William M. *Prints and Visual Communication.* Cambridge, MA: Harvard University Press, 1953. 2nd ed. 1969.

Johns, Adrian. "History, Science, and the History of the Book: The Making of Natural Philosophy in Early Modern England." *Publishing History* 30 (1991), 5–30.

ADRIAN JOHNS

See also Académie Royale des Sciences; Emblematics; Illustration; *Journal des sçavans;* Libraries; *Philosophical Transactions;* Royal Society of London

Prisca theologia

This Latin term, meaning ancient theology, refers to non-Jewish, pre-Christian religious traditions that Christian apologists believed shared some elements of Christian doctrine (e.g., monotheism, the Trinity, the immortality of the soul, and the Last Judgment). In the fifteenth and sixteenth centuries, interest in and respect for the *prisca theologia* increased dramatically, and *prisca theologia*'s effect on some of the most important theologians and philosophers of the period made it a seminal influence on the Renaissance and the Scientific Revolution.

The Renaissance veneration of the *prisca theologia* was based, to a large extent, on the availability of a substantial number of new sources unknown to medieval scholars. These were acquired primarily from the Byzantine East and introduced to the Latin West by Marsilio Ficino (1433–1499) and the members of the Platonic Academy of Florence. Many theologians and philosophers who studied the new texts became convinced that ancient theologians (*prisci theologi*) like Plato (428–348 B.C.E.), Pythagoras (fl. sixth century B.C.E.), Orpheus, Zoroaster, and Hermes Trismegistus were recipients of a pure, complete, uniform revelation regarding the Creation of the world and humanity's role in God's providential plan.

Today scholars know that the *prisca theologia* tradition is made up of a highly eclectic and even contradictory collection of esoteric religions and occult sciences. Moreover, the "ancient" theology was not nearly as old as Renaissance thinkers believed, and the parallels with Christianity were due to the fact that much of the *prisca theologia* tradition was post-Christian and often incorporated elements of it. But this modern understanding is not the perspective of the Renaissance. In that time, the *prisca theologia* was believed to have originated in an age before Moses and sometimes was traced back to Adam before the Fall. In the Renaissance view, the recovery of the *prisca theologia* opened the prospects of a deeper, fuller understanding of God's intent and purpose in creating humanity and the world. It, therefore, did not merely complement Christian dogma, it offered the possibility of gaining a deeper, full understanding of divine truth.

The impact of the *prisca theologia* tradition on the Renaissance concept of nature and human nature can be seen in Ficino's writings. In *De vita triplici libri* (Three Books on Life), Ficino provides a detailed description of the ordering principles that govern the created world. According to Ficino, the cosmos is composed of inert, formless matter (*prima materia*), which is given order and beauty through divine creative activity. The agent for this divine activity is the *spiritus mundi* (world spirit), which channels celestial spiritual power into matter. In the De vita, Ficino explains that the wise man (*magus*), who has fully developed his God-given intellect, is able to draw upon the spiritual forces governing the world in order to cure disease, prolong life, increase intelligence, and restore nature to its original perfection. These themes are repeated in another of his major works, *Theologia Platonica*. Here Ficino purports to offer a new understanding of human nature. He argues that the soul is the point of intersection between the material world and the divine creative intelligence that gives order, meaning, and purpose to the world. By fully actualizing the divine intellect in soul, man can learn to master nature and create a world of peace, harmony, and prosperity.

The recovery of the *prisca theologia* by Ficino and the Renaissance Neoplatonists affected the Scientific Revolution in two fundamental ways. First, as Ficino's *De vita* suggests, it was a direct stimulus to the search for the ordering principles and shaping forces that govern both the celestial and the terrestrial orders. It also contributed to the investigation of material compounds in an effort to discover their formative spiritual or vital properties. This search is clearly an integral part of the Paracelsian Revolution in medicine and chemistry. The second way the *prisca theologia* influenced the Scientific

Revolution was by introducing an epistemology in which knowledge of nature becomes knowledge of how to control nature and make it serve human purpose. This dimension is clearly present in Francis Bacon's (1561–1626) programs for the advancement of learning that would bring relief to "man's estate."

Recognition of the role of the *prisca theologia* in the extraordinary advances in astronomy, medicine, chemistry, and physics is a relatively recent development. George Sarton and early historians of science drew a sharp distinction between seventeenth-century science and pseudosciences, like magic and alchemy, that preceded it. Recent research, however, makes this bifurcation untenable. For many early-modern natural philosophers, including Bacon and Isaac Newton (1642–1727), magic and alchemy were not "pseudosciences"; they were components of the truest understanding of Creation, the *prisca theologia*.

BIBLIOGRAPHY

Debus, Allen. *The Chemical Philosophy: Paracelsian Science and Medicine in the Sixteenth and Seventeenth Centuries.* 2 vols. New York: Science History Publications, 1977.

McKnight, Stephen A. *The Modern Age and the Recovery of Ancient Wisdom.* Columbia: University of Missouri Press, 1991.

———. "Science, the Prisca Theologia, and Modern Epochal Consciousness." In *Science, Pseudoscience, and Utopianism,* ed. Stephen A. McKnight. Columbia: University of Missouri Press, 1992, pp. 88–117.

Walker, D. P. *The Ancient Theology.* Ithaca, NY: Cornell University Press, 1972.

———. *Spiritual and Demonic Magic from Ficino to Campanella.* London: Warburg Institute, 1950. Repr. South Bend, IN: University of Notre Dame Press, 1975.

Yates, Frances. *Giordano Bruno and the Hermetic Tradition.* Chicago: University of Chicago Press, 1964.

STEPHEN A. MCKNIGHT

See also Hermetism; Neoplatonism; Paracelsus; Religion and Natural Philosophy

Probability

Mathematical probability, a new style of engagement with uncertainty, began in the second half of the seventeenth century. An uninterrupted line of mathematicians, from Blaise Pascal (1623–1662), Pierre de Fermat (1601–1665), and Christiaan Huygens (1629–1695) to Jakob Bernoulli (1654–1705), contributed to this new style. Prior to the seventeenth century, *probable* had a

range of qualitative senses—resonating with approvable, provable, and probationary—some of which have since become obsolete. The things of which it was predicable included events that usually happen (Aristotle, 384–322 B.C.E.), statements having the semblance of truth (Cicero, 106–43 B.C.E.), opinions deserving approval by authority (Thomas Aquinas, d. 1274), and persons or deeds worthy of approval. The intellectual experience designated by probability was transformed radically when Bernoulli characterized probability as a "degree of certainty" and aligned its degrees with the continuum between zero and one. The mathematics of probability was constructed upon the assumption that, when personal uncertainties were apportioned to evidence, they could be rendered commensurable, quantitative, and computable.

The first calculations were on games of chance. In 1654 Pascal and Fermat exchanged their solutions to the problem of dividing stakes in an interrupted game. This problem has affinities with aleatory contracts, the equity of which was a topic of controversy among jurists in the sixteenth and seventeenth centuries. There were a few quantitative treatments of games of chance before the Pascal-Fermat correspondence, most notably by Girolamo Cardano (1501–1576) and Galileo Galilei (1564–1642). Cardano's *Liber de ludo aleae* (Book of Games of Chance, composed ca. 1560, published in 1663) was a gambling manual in which dice games were considered at some length. However, neither Cardano nor Galileo aspired to provide a "geometry of chance," which was Pascal's project.

The Pascal-Fermat correspondence attracted the attention of mathematicians such as Huygens and Gottfried Wilhelm Leibniz (1646–1716). Huygens's *De ratiociniis in ludo aleae* (1657) was the first published outcome of the new interest in the mathematics of games. Huygens underscored the fundamental concept of these earlier calculations, the fair price of a game, by christening it *expectation*. Huygens's notion of expectation figured prominently in the efforts of Jan Hudde (1628–1704) and Jan de Witt (1625–1672) in the 1670s to compute the fair prices of annuities and life-insurance policies on the basis of statistical considerations. The concept of probability, conceived in terms of reasonable assent, was brought to bear on games of chance in *La logique; ou, l'Art de penser* (1662), written by Antoine Arnauld (1612–1694) and Pierre Nicole (1625–1695). *La logique* advanced precepts for good judgment and correct reasoning, mostly demonstrative, aiming to instruct in "the art of thinking." The same work contained what came to be known as "Pascal's wager," the argument for piety based on an analogy between religious choice and games of chance.

Writing in the last decades of the seventeenth century, Jakob Bernoulli drafted his work as a sequel to the *La logique,* naming it *Ars conjectandi* (1713). Bernoulli sought to cultivate sound conjecturing, an undertaking that took on significance when the traditional ideal of certain knowledge came to be seen as unattainable. The roots of the erosion of the domain of demonstrative knowledge can be traced back to the sixteenth-century Reformation controversies and to the revival of skeptical philosophy. Bernoulli recommended probabilistic reasoning as a middle course that circumvented both skepticism and dogmatism, the two extreme positions in the earlier controversies. Embedding Huygens's treatise as a chapter, Bernoulli aimed to broaden the applications of the previous calculations to all kinds of nondeductive inference. To this end, he formulated his famous theorem, a version of which we now call the weak law of large numbers. The theorem linked probability to relative frequencies, asserting that, with moral certainty, the probability of an event can be approximated by the relative frequency with which it occurs after a finite number of observations.

The mathematical probability that emerged in the seventeenth century had both objective and subjective features. Probability was subjective, because the uncertainties it quantified were not perceived to be due to an indeterminacy in the world. Most of the seventeenth-century natural philosophers, including Bernoulli, were convinced determinists. In a world that was fully determined by divine Creation, Bernoulli maintained, contingency resulted only from the incompleteness of human knowledge. On the other hand, probability was not an expression of uninformed personal conviction, varying from person to person. The practitioners of mathematical probability assumed that there were standards of reasoning to be emulated by all reasonable men. Those standards were derived, for the most part, from the symmetries of gambling devices or from statistical frequencies. Thus appeared the classical concept of probability and its claim to model rational decision under uncertainty, both descriptively and prescriptively.

BIBLIOGRAPHY

Byrne, Edmund F. *Probability and Opinion: A Study in the Medieval Presuppositions of Post-Medieval Theories of Probability.* The Hague: Nijhoff, 1968.

Daston, Lorraine. *Classical Probability in the Enlightenment.* Princeton, NJ: Princeton University Press, 1988.

Hacking, Ian. *The Emergence of Probability: A Philosophical Study of Early Ideas About Probability, Induction, and Statistical Inference.* Cambridge: Cambridge University Press, 1975.

Krüger, Lorenz, Lorraine J. Daston, and Michael Heidelberger, eds. *The Probabilistic Revolution,* vol. 1. Cambridge, MA: MIT Press, 1987.

Shapiro, Barbara J. *Probability and Certainty in Seventeenth-Century England: A Study of the Relationships Between Natural Science, Religion, History, Law, and Literature.* Princeton, NJ: Princeton University Press, 1983.

BERNA KILIÇ EDEN

See also Arnauld, Antoine; Bernoulli, Jakob I; Cardano, Girolamo; Statistics; Witt, Jan de

Progress. See Positivist Historiography

Proof. See Demonstration

Proportional Dividers

Known also as proportional compasses, they are instruments used to enlarge or reduce drawings, consisting of two crossed arms with sharp points at each end. The arms are held together by a pivot. The position of the pivot determines the ratio of the separation of the points at opposite ends of the instrument. Proportional dividers with a fixed pivot have been known since antiquity; an example survives that was excavated from the ruins of Roman Pompeii.

In a notebook ca. 1495, Leonardo da Vinci (1452–1519) sketched and described proportional dividers in which the position of the pivot could vary. In 1569 Jacques Besson (fl. 1550–1570) described, in his *Theatrum instrumentorum,* an instrument for enlarging and reducing drawings that had two slotted arms and an adjustable pivot. The arms of Besson's instrument were not pointed. A surviving example much like the present form of the instrument was made ca. 1590 by Joost Bürgi (1552–1632), a native of what is now Liechtenstein and the instrument maker in the observatory of Duke Wilhelm IV in Kassel. Bürgi's instrument has slotted, pointed arms with a pivot that slides along the slots and is fixed by a screw. A scale along the edge of one slot indicates the ratio of separation of the points.

In English instruments, this scale would be labeled "lines." A second scale is used to inscribe regular polygons with six or more sides in a circle. One sets the pivot next to the mark for the number of sides in the polygon and separates the longer arms to the radius of the inscribing circle. The separation at the opposite end is the length of the side of the desired polygons. This scale would be labeled "circles." Proportional dividers of this form became common and were sold both individually and in sets of drawing instruments well into the twentieth century. They were made of brass, or silver, or stainless steel, often with steel points. Authors and instrument makers have proposed diverse scales, and diverse uses of proportional dividers, including computing squares and cubes of numbers. Instruments with logarithmic scales, such as the slide rule, proved more popular for such computations.

BIBLIOGRAPHY

Hambly, Maya. *Drawing Instruments, 1580–1980.* London: Sotheby's Publications, 1988.

Zinner, Ernst. *Deutsche und Niederländische astronomische Instrumente des 11.–18. Jahrhunderts.* Munich: C. H. Beck-'sche Verlag, 1956, pp. 268–276.

PEGGY ALDRICH KIDWELL

See also Bürgi, Joost; Instrument Makers; Slide Rule

Protestantism. See Reformation, Protestant

Providence, Divine

God's foresight in designing and caring for his Creation. Traditionally, the concept was divided into general providence—the order and foreknowledge God implanted in the original Creation—and special providence—his concern for humankind. Seventeenth-century thinkers also distinguished between ordinary providence—God's design of the Creation—and extraordinary providence—his miraculous intervention in the natural order. Two issues about divine providence were of particular concern during the Scientific Revolution: to ensure that God's care for, and interaction with, the Creation retained a central role in any new philosophy of nature, and to understand just how that role might be understood. The first issue was entangled with controversies about the nature of matter and its properties; the second, with debates about the status of the laws of nature.

In the aftermath of the Copernican revolution and the subsequent erosion of Aristotelianism, European natural philosophers sought a new philosophy of nature to provide metaphysical foundations for their endeavors. Two prominent candidates were the mechanical philosophy, articulated by Pierre Gassendi (1592–1655) and René Descartes (1596–1650), and the so-called chemical philosophy, which derived from the work of Paracelsus (ca. 1493–1541). Both of these philosophies were perceived to challenge the traditional Christian doctrine of providence, largely because their respective theories of matter seemed to exclude God from having an active role in nature. The mechanical philosophers postulated a sharp demarcation between matter and spirit. For Descartes, matter (*res extensa*) was essentially distinct from the incorporeal entities, mind (*res cogitans*) and God. Similarly, though less elegantly, Gassendi's Christianized atomism embodied a sharp division between the corporeal (composed of indivisible atoms) and the incorporeal (including the rational soul, God, angels, and demons). The total exclusion of spirit from the material world rendered the mechanical philosophy susceptible to the twin dangers of materialism and deism, if not outright atheism. While the chemical philosophy did not stipulate such a radical separation of body and spirit, and incorporated active and spiritual properties into matter, it, too, was thought to pose the danger of excluding God from the natural world since active matter alone seemed able to account for all of the phenomena in the world without recourse to separate, spiritual agents.

The antiprovidential implications of the mechanical philosophy were seen as realized in the philosophy of Thomas Hobbes (1588–1679), whose materialism and determinism became symbolic of the dangers posed by the mechanical philosophy. Fear of "Hobbism" led other thinkers to insist on providential interpretations of the mechanical philosophy. Gassendi, who modified atomism to rid it of the materialistic and atheistic associations with Epicureanism, explicitly incorporated divine providence into his version of the mechanical philosophy. Making extensive appeal to the argument from design, he reasoned that the world must be the product of intelligent design rather than the chance collision of atoms, as both the ancient atomists and Hobbes believed. Denying both the Epicurean doctrine of chance or fortune and the Stoic doctrine of fate, Gassendi redefined these notions providentially, interpreting fortune as an expression of divine foresight and providence and fate as divine decree.

P

Henry More (1614–1687), an influential Cambridge Platonist, was initially attracted to Cartesianism, particularly because Descartes considered spirit to have the same ontological status as matter. He subsequently grew very critical of it, fearing that it would easily slip into materialism. To avoid this danger, he enriched Descartes's mechanical philosophy by adding another nonmaterial entity to the world. More argued that all sorts of phenomena are impossible to explain simply in terms of "the jumbling together of the *Matter*." Resisting purely mechanical explanation and indicating the actions of a wise providence, he introduced the Spirit of Nature, which is incorporeal, extended, and "indiscerpible," a causal agent, carrying out God's providential plan for the Creation.

Isaac Newton (1642–1727) also found it necessary to modify the mechanical philosophy in ways that would ensure an important role for providence and divine activity in the world. From his early forays into natural philosophy in the 1660s, Newton found that many phenomena resisted purely mechanical explanation. These "difficult" phenomena included gravitation, the reflection and the refraction of light, the cohesion of bodies, and the processes of living bodies. This limitation of the mechanical philosophy was exacerbated by the dangers it posed for a providential view of the world. As a theological Arian, Newton held a conception of a God who was extremely transcendent, and he faced the important problem of securing a central place for divine activity in the world. Newton preserved his providential worldview by supplementing the mechanical philosophy with active principles drawn from his extensive alchemical studies. These active principles enabled him to explain the recalcitrant phenomena and to develop his theory of universal gravitation. He explained the passive and active forces with which he enriched the mechanical philosophy as resulting directly from divine activity, thus ensuring a central role for providence in his cosmology. God was literally present everywhere in Newton's universe, and the study of natural philosophy became a massive argument from design.

Ensuring a role for providence in the world was one problem. The interpretation of God's relationship to the Creation was another, and it had major implications for understanding the metaphysical and epistemological status of the laws of nature. Is God bound by his Creation, or is he always free to change whatever he created in the world? The seventeenth-century answers to this question originated in thirteenth- and fourteenth-century discussions following the introduction of Aristotle's (384–322 B.C.E.) philosophy into mainstream European thought. There was a delicate balance in medieval theology between the rationality of God's intellect and his absolute freedom in exercising his power and will. In the seventeenth century, these ideas about God's relationship to the Creation were transformed into views about the metaphysical and epistemological status of human knowledge and the laws of nature. For intellectualists, the laws of nature describe the essences of things and can be known a priori, while the empiricist and probabilist interpretations of scientific knowledge provided a way of thinking about the contingency of a world that no longer contained essences in a Platonic or an Aristotelian sense.

Gassendi, who was a voluntarist, described a world utterly contingent on divine will. This contingency expressed itself in his conviction that empirical methods are the only way to acquire knowledge about the natural world and that the matter of which all physical things are composed possesses some properties that can be known only empirically. The laws of nature, according to Gassendi, are simply empirical generalizations that embody no necessity. God can change them at will, a fact to which miracles attest. Descartes, as an intellectualist, described a world in which God had embedded necessary relations, some of which enable us to have a priori knowledge of substantial parts of the natural world. The capacity for a priori knowledge extends to the nature of matter, which, Descartes claimed to demonstrate, possesses only geometrical properties. According to Descartes, the laws of nature are necessary truths that follow directly from divine immutability. The Cambridge Platonists, like Henry More, adopted an even more extreme form of intellectualism, according to which God's freedom is limited by absolute standards of goodness that exist independently of him.

The famous controversy in 1715–1716 between Newton's spokesman Samuel Clarke (1675–1729) and his rival Gottfried Wilhelm Leibniz (1646–1716) hinged on the debate between voluntarist and intellectualist interpretations of providence. Leibniz, an intellectualist, argued that the Newtonian insistence on divine activity implies that God's workmanship is so imperfect that he must constantly intervene in nature and repair his work. A better workman would create a world that would run smoothly forever, without the need for intervention. Clarke, replying as a voluntarist, argued that Leibniz's account implies an unacceptable limitation on God's freedom and power.

BIBLIOGRAPHY

Alexander, H. G., ed. *The Leibniz-Clarke Correspondence.* Manchester: Manchester University Press, 1956.

Dobbs, B. J. T. *The Janus Faces of Genius: The Role of Alchemy in Newton's Thought.* Cambridge: Cambridge University Press, 1991.

Funkenstein, Amos. *Theology and the Scientific Imagination from the Middle Ages to the Seventeenth Century.* Princeton, NJ: Princeton University Press, 1986.

Oakley, Francis. *Omnipotence, Covenant, and Order: An Excursion in the History of Ideas from Abelard to Leibniz.* Ithaca, NY: Cornell University Press, 1984.

Osler, Margaret J. *Divine Will and the Mechanical Philosophy: Gassendi and Descartes on Contingency and Necessity in the Created World.* Cambridge: Cambridge University Press, 1994.

Westfall, Richard S. *Science and Religion in Seventeenth-Century England.* New Haven, CT: Yale University Press, 1958.

MARGARET J. OSLER

See also Active Principles; Book of Nature; Cambridge Platonists; Physico-Theology; Religion and Natural Philosophy

Psychology

Although the term *psychologia* was first used in the sixteenth century, the phenomena of psychology had made up a distinct field of study since classical antiquity. In the sixteenth and seventeenth centuries, the same confluence of ideas that revolutionized the physical sciences also challenged the hegemony of the Aristotelian concept of the soul. The phenomena of psychology, however, both human and animal, and the theological necessity that each human possess an immortal, hence immaterial, portion, confounded naive mechanistic theorists and permitted the retention of Aristotelian elements well into the modern era.

Aristotle (384–322 B.C.E.) had recognized, and his medieval commentators had accepted, that the intellect was entirely dependent upon the senses for its input in the common course of nature. Theories of perception called for the qualities received from an object by the external senses to combine in the internal "common sense" and form an image of the sensed object. For Renaissance psychologists, the common sense was the first of as few as three or as many as five internal senses, always including imagination and memory, the workshop and storehouse, respectively, of images. Imagination served two functions: it was capable of dismantling images of perceived objects and reassembling the parts into new images of objects that did not exist in nature, such as images of golden mountains, and it also functioned as a stage upon which images, once placed, were subjected to the action of an active intellect capable of stripping away the last vestiges of individuality from the image and extracting its universal nature.

Philosophers believed that the apprehension of universals could not depend on individual organs. Physicians, on the other hand, had always believed that the function of intellect was closely tied to the complexion of the body in which it was located. As far back as Hippocrates (ca. 460–ca. 370 B.C.E.), intellectual ability was related to the body's humoral constitution. Traditionally, those persons of a cool and dry temperament (melancholics) were thought best suited to intellectual activity.

The danger inherent in allowing reliance on organs for intellectual function was that the immortal human soul would be left with no role to play in the person's daily life. The willingness of physicians to subsume the intellect under physiology and the enthusiasm of mechanical philosophers to reduce physiology to complicated arrangements of matter and motion posed a threat to the immortal soul of humans, a threat that René Descartes (1596–1650) tried in vain to meet. Descartes proposed that each human can, by introspection, prove that he or she is essentially an entity capable of doubt and that, because doubt appeared to use no organ, the essential person was not organic. The consequent duality of extended stuff (*res extensa*) and thinking stuff (*res cogitans*) pleased those who feared a rising tide of rational atheism because it seemed such a persuasive argument for the immateriality, hence immortality, of the intellect. Yet, atheists and materialists enthusiastically extended physiology from the vegetative and sensitive powers to the intellect. Cartesian dualism failed to satisfy those who could not accept Descartes's explanation of how the extensionless soul interacted with the extended body. The response of Gottfried Wilhelm Leibniz (1646–1716) and others was to propose a monism that attributed both mind and extension to all matter, with the consequence that minerals, plants, and animals differed only in quantitative terms.

BIBLIOGRAPHY

Harvey, E. Ruth. *The Inward Wits: Psychological Theory in the Middle Ages and the Renaisssance.* London: Warburg Institute, 1975.

P

Jolley, Nicholas. *The Light of the Soul: Theories of Ideas in Leibniz, Malebranche, and Descartes.* Oxford: Clarendon, 1990.

Michael, Emily. "The Nature and Influence of Renaissance Paduan Psychology." *History of Universities* 12 (1993), 65–94.

Summers, David. *The Judgment of Sense: Renaissance Naturalism and the Rise of Aesthetics.* Cambridge: Cambridge University Press, 1987.

PETER G. SOBOL

See also Descartes, René; Humors; Leibniz, Gottfried Wilhelm; Soul

Ptolemaic Astronomy

The term *Ptolemaic Astronomy* is used in two senses. In the general sense, it refers to the geocentric system of the world in which the Sun, the Moon, the planets, and the stars move about about a central, fixed earth. In the specific sense, it refers to the astronomy of Ptolemy (ca. 100–ca. 170) as set out in the *Almagest* and other works. Both are of great importance in the period of the Scientific Revolution—the general as one of the three systems of the world: Ptolemaic, Copernican, and Tychonic; the specific as the principal source for the techniques of mathematical astronomy. The Ptolemaic system was predominant until ca. 1600; during the first half of the seventeenth century, all three systems were considered, after which the Copernican prevailed, although, for theological reasons, the Ptolemaic and the Tychonic systems had advocates among Catholics, particularly those in orders, even into the eighteenth century.

Claudius Ptolemaeus lived in Alexandria in the second century and wrote on nearly every branch of applied mathematics known in antiquity (i.e., astronomy, optics, harmonics, and cartography), omitting only mechanics. His most important astronomical work, originally called *Mathematical Treatise* or *Mathematical Collection,* is known from the Arabic contraction of its title as the *Almagest.* It treats in detail all parts of mathematical astronomy: spherical astronomy, solar and lunar theory and eclipses, the fixed stars, and the theory of the planets in longitude and latitude. Among his other astronomical works are the *Planetary Hypotheses,* concerned with analogue computational models of the motions of the Sun, the Moon, and the planets and with physical models composed of spheres, or equatorial sections of spheres, that account for the motions of the bodies in the heavens; the *Handy Tables,* intended for practical computation and the prototype of astronomical tables, at least until the time of Johannes Kepler (1571–1630); and the *Tetrabiblos,* the most important treatise on astrology ever written.

Most of Ptolemy's works were translated into Arabic in the ninth and tenth centuries and, in the following centuries, were the foundation of highly original work in Arabic. The *Almagest* was translated into Latin twice in the late twelfth century, an anonymous version from the Greek made in Sicily, which had little distribution, and a widely known version from the Arabic made by Gerard of Cremona (ca. 1114–1187) in Spain. The *Tetrabiblos* was translated twice from Arabic and also became widely known. Neither the *Planetary Hypotheses* nor the *Handy Tables* was translated into Latin, but Arabic writings based upon the *Hypotheses* were translated, and tables ultimately based upon the *Handy Tables,* namely the *Toledan Tables* and the *Alfonsine Tables,* both made in Spain, in the eleventh and the thirteenth centuries, respectively, were widely distributed in Latin versions. Hence, Ptolemy's works were also the foundation of late-medieval European astronomy.

But it must be confessed that not a lot was done with them until the second half of the fifteenth century, when they were taken up as part of the new recovery of ancient learning. Around the middle of the century, Giovanni Bianchini, a fiscal and government official in Ferrara, wrote an extensive exposition of Books I–VI of the *Almagest,* and George Trebizond, then in Rome, made a new translation from the Greek and a commentary on all thirteen books. In the years 1460–1463, at the request of Cardinal Johannes Bessarion, Georg Peurbach (1423–1461) and Johannes Regiomontanus (1436–1476) wrote an excellent abridgment in a rigorously mathematical form called the *Epitome of the Almagest,* which was printed in 1496, 1543, and 1550 and was the standard advanced textbook of mathematical astronomy throughout the sixteenth century. Peurbach had earlier written the *Theoricae novae planetarum* (1454), a description of Ptolemy's solar, lunar, and planetary theory in their physical form as spheres (as in Figure 4), along with explanations of technical terms, application to tables, and phenomena such as eclipses, heliacal risings and settings, and stations. This also became a standard work and, after its first printing by Regiomontanus ca. 1474, was printed more than fifty times, sometimes with substantial commentary, most notably one by Erasmus Reinhold (1511–

P

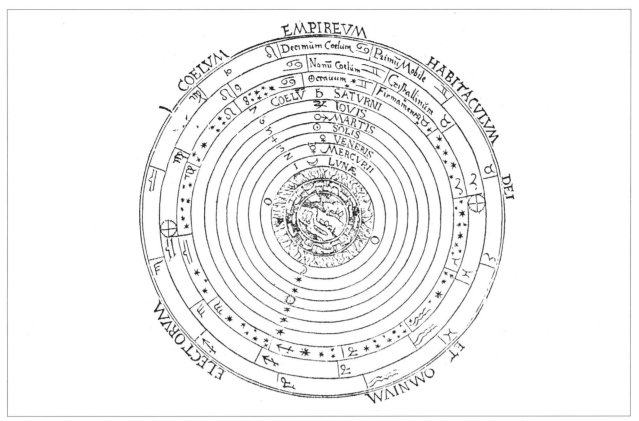

The Ptolemaic system with the Sun and three celestial bodies on either side of it revolving about the stationary earth. This is a late medieval adaptation of Ptolemaic astronomy in an Aristotelian context, showing the four terrestrial elements surrounding the earth and the sphere of the stars in a finite universe. From Peter Apian, Cosmographia *(1539).*

1553) that first appeared in 1542. Gerard of Cremona's translation of the *Almagest* was printed in 1515 and George Trebizond's in 1528 and in later editions; the Greek text with Theon of Alexandria's (fl. second half of fourth century) commentary appeared in 1538. Through these publications, Europeans could at last learn Ptolemy's astronomy from the elementary to the most advanced level; the succeeding work of Nicolaus Copernicus (1473–1543), Tycho Brahe (1546–1601), and Kepler is built upon the foundation provided by Ptolemy—indeed, is unintelligible without an understanding of Ptolemy.

Ptolemy's method may be characterized simply: it is rigorously empirical and rigorously mathematical. Every model is either derived from or confirmed by observation, although not all of the observations are presented in the text, and every numerical parameter is derived from observation by strict mathematical procedures. This was the most important lesson in method that Ptolemy taught to later astronomers, although very few applied it as strictly and comprehensively as he did. There is, how-

ever, a large range of precision in his observations, from positions and times measured to within a few minutes for the derivation of parameters—although their accuracy is more variable, and there are systematic errors—to rough, even qualitative observations for demonstrating the properties of models.

It is observations of the qualitative sort that support his description of the world. Thus, that the heavens may be regarded as a rotating sphere is shown by the circular arcs of stars as they rise and set or move about the pole. Other models are refuted as contrary to observation (e.g., that the stars do not move in straight lines is shown by the fact that their sizes do not diminish as they approach the horizon). The sphericity of the earth is proved by the difference in time of lunar eclipses observed in locations to the east or west, showing curvature in longitude, and by the difference in the elevation of the celestial pole in locations to the north or south, showing curvature in latitude: hence, the earth must be spherical. Were it, say, flat, stars would rise and set at the same time for all locations, which is not what is seen.

That the earth is located in the middle of the heavens is shown by what would be seen if the earth were not so located: the equinoxes would not occur when the Sun is a quadrant from the solstices, which they do, and the horizon would not bisect the heavens, which it does since six zodiacal signs are visible and six invisible at all times and at all places on the earth. For the same reasons, the earth does not move out of the center of the world. Note that these demonstrations, empirical and based upon observations anyone can make, are quite different from the Aristotelian arguments for the same conclusions, which are physical and based upon the properties of the substances that make up the heavens and the earth. Even Ptolemy's arguments that the earth cannot have a diurnal rotation—the appearances of the heavens are the same whether the earth rotates or the heavens do—are principally observational, based upon what would be seen near the earth if the earth did rotate: clouds, birds, and projectiles left behind to the west as the earth turned toward the east, or, if the air moved along with the earth, the same clouds, birds, and projectiles remaining fixed in place since they could not move independently against the rapid motion of the air; since neither is seen, the earth does not rotate.

These empirical arguments, along with Aristotle's (384–322 B.C.E.) physical arguments concerning the natural place and motion of the elements, are the principal evidence for the Ptolemaic theory in the sense of the geocentric system of the world. They are very strong arguments since they are supported by every observation that could be made, and they placed a great burden on supporters of the heliocentric theory, such as Copernicus, Kepler, and Galileo Galilei (1564–1642), to argue that, even though supported by observation, the geocentric theory is false, and even though not supported by observation, the heliocentric theory is true. In defense of the geocentric theory, the arguments against the motion of the earth were multiplied with many examples of what would be observed if the earth rotated, such as the paths of objects dropped from towers or even from the Moon and cannons fired to the east or west—what a pity there were no cannons in Aristotle's time, Galileo remarked—and in the seventeenth century these arguments became more Aristotelian and Scholastic than astronomical as the astronomers increasingly went over to Copernicus, leaving principally philosophers to defend Ptolemy and Aristotle. Among the notable defenders were Christoph Clavius (1538–1612), perhaps the last competent Ptole-

maic astronomer, and the philosopher Scipione Chiaramonti (1565–1652), called the "Aristotle of our age," who violently attacked Copernicus, Brahe, Kepler, and Galileo. Aside from those few immortalized by Galileo's criticism, most defenders of the immobility of the earth are totally forgotten today, not just because history is written by the victors but because there was really little more to say beyond elaborating what Aristotle and Ptolemy had said in the first place.

We return to Ptolemy. On the basis of the spherical heavens and the central, spherical earth, Ptolemy first develops spherical astronomy, concerned with the geometry and apparent motions of the celestial sphere (i.e., the relation of the fundamental circles of the sphere and the rising and setting of points located by their coordinates), all through a rigorous application of spherical trigonometry. The diurnal motion of the heavens, as seen in the rising and setting of the fixed stars, is uniform and circular. It was, therefore, only reasonable to assume that, as part of the heavens, the motions of the Sun, the Moon, and the planets, although apparently nonuniform, must also be uniform. The problem was to discover models by which apparent inequalities of motion may be produced by uniform, circular motion. Such an analysis has the mathematical consequence of dividing apparent motion into a uniform, "mean" motion, a linear function of time, and one or more variable corrections or "equations."

In the case of the Sun, there is a single inequality most evident in observations, showing that the intervals of time between the equinoxes and the solstices, although separated exactly by quadrants, are unequal, meaning that the apparent motion of the Sun is nonuniform. Ptolemy accounts for this inequality by letting the motion of the Sun take place on a circle eccentric to the earth, a model earlier used by Hipparchus, and an equivalent epicyclic model may also be used. In Figure 1, the equinoxes and the solstices seen from the earth at O are separated by quadrants, but the arcs of the Sun's motion on an eccentric circle about C are greater or less than quadrants. The motion of the Sun S may thus be considered as a uniform motion $\bar{\kappa}$ about C and a variable correction c, resulting in a nonuniform apparent motion $\bar{\kappa} = \kappa \pm c$ about O. The mean anomaly $\bar{\kappa}$, the eccentricity e as a fraction of the radius R of the eccentric, and the direction of the apogee A and the perigee B may be derived from the very observations of intervals of time between the equinoxes and the solstices that showed the Sun's inequality. Although later astronomers found improved

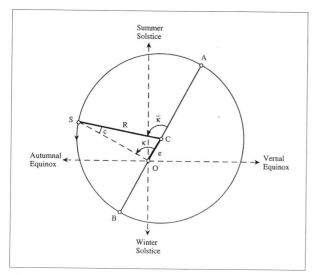

Figure 1.

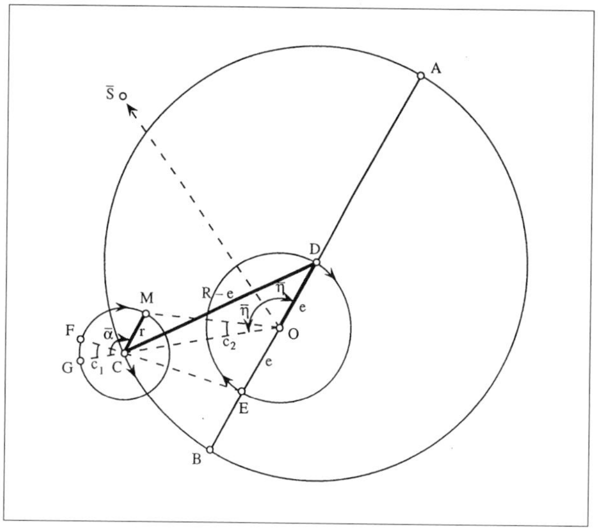

Figure 2.

values of these parameters, the solar model itself received no improvement prior to Kepler.

The theory of the Moon is considerably more complex as Ptolemy found that it displayed two inequalities, the first with a period of the anomalistic month, in which the Moon returns to the same point in its (moveable) orbit, already known to Hipparchus, and the second, which modifies the first, with a period of one-half a mean synodic month, in which the Moon returns to conjunction with, or opposition to, the "mean sun" (i.e., the Sun with only its mean motion [$\bar{\kappa}$ in Figure 1]). He accounted for the first inequality by placing the Moon on an epicycle with the period of the anomalistic month and for the second by placing the epicycle on an eccentric, such that it completes a full revolution on the eccentric in one-half a synodic month. A related inequality, also with a period of one-half a mean synodic month affects the mean anomaly, the motion of the Moon on the epicycle. In Figure 2, the mean sun is at $\bar{S}$, from which the center of the epicycle C moves through the mean elongation $\bar{\eta}$ and the center of the eccentric D moves in the opposite direction through the same $\bar{\eta}$. The result is that C completes one revolution with respect to $\bar{S}$ in a mean synodic month, but two revolutions with respect to the apogee A and the perigee B of the eccentric, the effect being to draw the epicycle closer to the earth at quadrature than at conjunction and opposition, increasing the inequality due to the motion of the Moon on the epicycle. The Moon moves on the epicycle through the mean anomaly $\bar{\alpha}$, completing one revolution in an anomalistic month,

measured from a direction FCE that has an "inclination" to a point E that lies on the apsidal line AB exactly opposite D, such that the distances OD and OE are equal, the effect being to modify $\bar{\alpha}$ to the true anomaly $\bar{\alpha} \pm c_1$ measured from the direction GCO to the earth. The true elongation of the Moon from the mean sun is then $\bar{\eta} \pm c_2$, where c_2 is a function of $\bar{\alpha} \pm c_1$ and the variable distance OC. The parameters of the model are found from observation: the radius of the epicycle r, the mean anomaly $\bar{\alpha}$, and the mean elongation $\bar{\eta}$ from lunar eclipses; the eccentricity e from observations of the Moon at quadrature and octants from the mean sun.

A peculiarity, really a defect, of Ptolemy's lunar model is that it produces a variation of the distance of the Moon from the earth so large that it may be about half as distant at quadrature as at opposition and conjunction. This variation of distance is directly contradicted by the small change in the Moon's apparent diameter and parallax, a flaw noted by Arabic astronomers in the thirteenth century, who proposed alternative models with far smaller variation of distance, and one of these models was later used by Copernicus. Through measurement of parallax, Ptolemy found a confirmation of the close approach of the Moon near quadrature and, as a consequence of his model, a maximum lunar distance of ca. 64 earth-radii, which is a bit too large, and a minimum distance of ca. 33 earth-radii, which is much too small. By a very ingenious method, using the distance of the Moon when the apparent diameters of the Sun and the Moon are equal and the apparent diameter of the earth's shadow where the Moon passes through it—good in principle but not in practice because of its extreme sensitivity to small errors in finding these quantities—he found a solar distance of 1,210 earth-radii. This is too small by a factor of twenty but gives a diurnal parallax of only 3', which is small enough to be neglected for all practical purposes and became canonical until the seventeenth century. For computing eclipses of the Sun and the Moon, Ptolemy's method was to find first the time of mean conjunction or opposition of the two bodies, then the time of true or apparent conjunction or opposition by applying a series of corrections depending upon their true or apparent velocities, and then the magnitude and the duration of the eclipse.

Already Hipparchus had noticed from the comparison of earlier observations with his own that a few bright stars appeared to have shifted their positions with respect to the equinoxes and the solstices. Ptolemy, from a comparison of alignments of stars observed by Hipparchus and himself and from observations of bright stars over a period of about four hundred years, concluded that all of the fixed stars were moving eastward with respect to the solstices and the equinoxes at a rate that he, like Hipparchus, estimated as 1° in a hundred years or 36" per year. The motion is too slow, due to errors of observation, and the motion of the fixed stars had a complex later history, with faster uniform motions than found by Ptolemy but more often with variable motions to account for both Ptolemy's estimate and later observations showing a faster motion. Such a variable motion was still used by Copernicus, but, later in the sixteenth century, Brahe showed that the motion of the fixed stars was, in fact, uniform at ca. 51" per year. After establishing the rate of motion of the stars, Ptolemy finds the longitudes of some number of fundamental stars by measuring their distances from the Moon, then uses the fundamental stars to find the longitudes and latitudes of no less than 1,022 stars that he organizes into forty-eight constellations in his star catalog, which formed the basis of all star catalogs until Tycho Brahe.

The most impressive achievement in Ptolemy's astronomy is the theory of the planets, which provided the foundation of all later planetary theory, including that of Copernicus, and was not improved upon until Kepler. Ptolemy's criterion for ordering the planets, set out in the *Almagest,* is zodiacal period: in descending order, from the fixed stars, Saturn, Jupiter, Mars, the Sun, Venus, Mercury, and the Moon. The Sun, Venus, and Mercury have the same period (one year), and Ptolemy places the Sun between the superior planets (Saturn, Jupiter, and Mars), which reach opposition to the Sun, and the inferior planets (Venus and Mercury), which reach only a limited elongation. The Moon, of course, reaches opposition but is placed lowest since it has the shortest period, may occult all of the higher bodies, and has a large, measurable parallax showing that it is close to the earth. In the *Planetary Hypotheses,* Ptolemy sets out a method of computing the distances of the planets that confirms that the Moon, Mercury, and Venus are below the Sun, since there is adequate space only for them, and the remaining planets above.

The planets have two inequalities: the first a function of longitude, of location in the zodiac; the second, a function of elongation from the Sun. It is the second inequality that produces the most obvious feature of planetary motion, a periodic retrogradation bounded by two stations, which occurs near opposition for the superior planets and near inferior conjunction for the inferior. The second inequality is produced by the motion of the planet on an epicycle; the first inequality, by the motion of the center of the epicycle about the earth. For the superior planets, the motion of the center of the epicycle corresponds to the planet's own motion about the Sun in a heliocentric model, and the motion of the planet on the epicycle to Earth's motion about the Sun; for the inferior planets, the motion of the center of the epicycle corresponds to Earth's motion about the Sun and the motion of the planet on the epicycle to the planet's own motion about the Sun.

Ptolemy's model for both inequalities is shown in Figure 3. The earth is at O and, at an eccentricity e, let M be the center of an eccentric circle of radius R with apogee A and perigee B. Symmetrically to M at the same eccentricity e, let E be the center about which the epicycle moves uniformly, often called the "equant" point, and let the center of the epicycle C move on the circle about M uniformly about E through mean eccentric anomaly $\bar{\kappa}$. The effect of the separation of the center of constant distance M from the center of uniform motion E closely approximates motion according to Kepler's ellipse and area laws, since the circle about M corresponds to the circle constructed on the major axis of the ellipse, with which, for small eccentricity, the ellipse very nearly coincides, and E corresponds to the empty focus of the ellipse, about which the angular motion of the planet is very nearly uniform. In principle, the models of Ptolemy

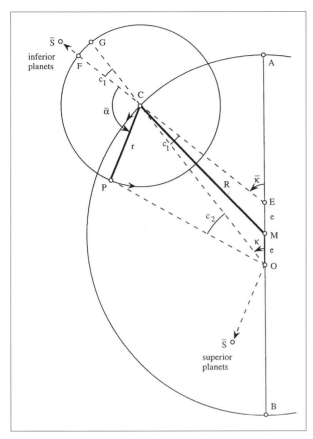

Figure 3.

and Kepler differ by only a few minutes of arc, although inaccuracies in Ptolemy's parameters and other approximations introduce greater errors.

The planet P moves on the epicycle of radius r though the mean anomaly $\bar{\alpha}$ measured from the direction EC extended to the mean apogee of the epicycle F, such that, for a superior planet, CP is always parallel to the direction $O\bar{S}$ from the earth to the mean sun; for an inferior planet, EC always lies in the direction of the mean sun $\bar{S}$. The model produces corrections to two inequalities. The first, c_1, called the "equation of center," corrects $\bar{\kappa}$ to the true eccentric anomaly $\kappa = \bar{\kappa} \pm c_1$ seen from O and $\bar{\alpha}$ to the true anomaly $\alpha = \bar{\alpha} \pm c_1$ measured from the direction OC extended to the true apogee of the epicycle G. The equation of the anomaly c_2, subtended by the radius of the epicycle r, then corrects the direction of the center of the epicycle OC to the direction of the planet OP. Hence, where the longitude of the apogee A is λ_A, the true longitude of the planet is given by $\lambda_A + \bar{\kappa} \pm c_1 \pm c_2$. The parameters of the model are derived rigorously from observation. For the superior planets, e, λ_A, and $\bar{\kappa}$ are found from an iterative computation of considerable

complexity using three oppositions of the planet to the mean Sun, and r and $\bar{\alpha}$ from two observations not at opposition. For the inferior planets, e, λ_A, and r are found through observations of greatest elongations from the mean sun and $\bar{\alpha}$ from an observation not at greatest elongation.

This is but a brief summary of Ptolemy's planetary theory in the *Almagest;* there are additional complications for Mercury and rather complicated models for motion in latitude. The *Planetary Hypotheses* is notable both for the physical, spherical models that Ptolemy developed from the mathematical, circular models of the *Almagest* and for a method of computing the distances and sizes of the planets. The two are related, since the spherical models are contiguous, with no empty spaces, and the distances depend upon this contiguity. Figure 4 shows a cross-section of the spherical model based upon the circles of Figure 3. The epicycle, a complete sphere with the planet just inside it at P, is carried by the eccentric sphere, the inner and outer surfaces of which are concentric to M. Within the eccentric sphere is an inner sphere with its outer surface concentric to M and its inner surface concentric to O. Outside the eccentric sphere is a corresponding outer sphere with its inner surface concentric to M and its outer surface concentric to O. The spheres of a lower planet lie inside the inner sphere, and the spheres of a higher planet lie outside the outer sphere in the same way. The center of the eccentric sphere is M, but the sphere rotates such that the center of the epicycle C moves uniformly about the equant point E, and the epicycle rotates such that the planet moves uniformly with respect to the direction EC extended to the far side of the epicycle. But how can rigid, spherical bodies do this? For the spheres must be rigid to carry the epicycle and the planet (i.e., the bodies are not moving through a fluid medium or empty space). This is the celebrated violation of uniform, circular motion in Ptolemy's models that was noted by Arabic astronomers and Copernicus, and both developed nearly identical alternative models to maintain uniform motion about the equant point strictly through the uniform rotation of spheres.

The parameters of Ptolemy's models give a ratio of the least relative distance $R - e - r$ to the greatest relative distance $R + e + r$ for each planet. Since the spheres are contiguous, the least distance OB of each planet is equal to the greatest distance OA of the planet beneath it. Hence, all that is required is the absolute distance of one planet to compute the absolute distances of all of the

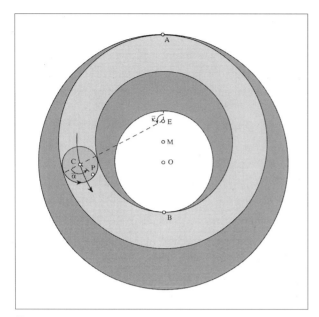

Figure 4.

planets, and in the *Almagest* Ptolemy already found a greatest distance of the Moon of 64 earth-radii and a mean distance of the Sun of 1,210 earth-radii. Hence, beginning with the Moon, he computes the distances of Mercury and Venus, leaving a space between the greatest distance of Venus and the least distance of the Sun, which later Arabic astronomers found ways of closing; beginning with the Sun, he computes the distances of Mars, Jupiter, and Saturn; then, taking the fixed stars to be just beyond Saturn at a distance of 20,000 earth-radii, the limit of the universe. He also reports values for the apparent diameters of the planets at mean distance and of first-magnitude stars, all much too large, as fractions of the apparent diameter of the Sun. Since in the *Almagest* he found the true diameter of the Sun to be 5.5 earth-diameters, he can compute the true diameters of all of the planets, finding that Jupiter, Saturn, and the first-magnitude stars are more than four times the diameter of the earth. Finally, since the volumes of spheres are as the cubes of their diameters, the volumes of the planets in terms of the volume of the earth can be found by cubing the diameters. These distances and sizes, known in Europe through slight variants computed by al-Battānī (fl. ca. 880) and al-Farghānī, (fl. 861), became canonical, and, surprisingly, the adoption of the heliocentric theory initially reduced rather than increased the distances, except to the stars, as long as the distance of the Sun from the earth was taken to be ca. 1,200 earth-radii. The change in these dimensions came only when Galileo

found with the telescope that the apparent diameters of planets and stars were actually far smaller than they appeared to the unaided eye and when a redetermination of the solar parallax in the later part of the seventeenth century greatly increased the distances within the planetary system.

BIBLIOGRAPHY

Crowe, M. J. *Theories of the World from Antiquity to the Copernican Revolution.* New York: Dover, 1990.

Grant, E. "In Defense of the Earth's Centrality and Immobility: Scholastic Reaction to Copernicanism in the Seventeenth Century." *Transactions of the American Philosophical Society* 74 (4) Philadelphia: American Philosophical Society, 1984.

———. *Planets, Stars, and Orbs: The Medieval Cosmos, 1200–1687.* Cambridge: Cambridge University Press, 1994.

Lattis, J. M. *Between Copernicus and Galileo: Christopher Clavius and the Collapse of Ptolemaic Cosmology.* Chicago: University of Chicago Press, 1994.

Neugebauer, O. *A History of Ancient Mathematical Astronomy.* 3 vols. New York: Springer Verlag, 1975.

Pedersen, O. *A Survey of the Almagest.* Odense, Denmark: Odense University Press, 1974.

Taub, L. C. *Ptolemy's Universe: The Natural Philosophical and Ethical Foundations of Ptolemy's Astronomy.* Chicago: Open Court, 1993.

Toomer, G. J. *Ptolemy's Almagest.* New York: Springer Verlag, 1984.

Van Helden, A. *Measuring the Universe: Cosmic Dimensions from Aristarchus to Halley.* Chicago: University of Chicago Press, 1985.

N. M. SWERDLOW

See also Astronomy; Copernicus, Nicolaus; Geoheliocentrism

Public Knowledge

Whether particular kinds of knowledge should be available to everyone or restricted to a select group is a question with a long history. In classical antiquity, Aristotle (384–322 B.C.E.) was reliably reputed to have been the author of two groups of writings: the *esoteric,* meant for initiates only, and the *exoteric,* proper for public circulation. Aristotle's surviving works (except for a few fragments quoted by later writers) all come from the latter group.

These two categories, with their classical pedigree, remained in tension throughout the Western Middle Ages. With few exceptions, the official philosophical learning of the universities (from the thirteenth century onward) should be classified as exoteric, insofar as it formed the subject of open lectures. It was restricted in the sense that these lectures and their texts required knowledge of Latin, but there was no ban on expression of the ideas in the vernacular. Esoteric knowledge occupied a different place, one that, by its very nature, had an ambiguous status. Our evidence for it comes from written texts that, therefore, tended to transcend the secretive, word-of-mouth traditions supposedly characteristic of such knowledge. Thus, writings by Roger Bacon in the thirteenth century, or Books of Secrets from the later Middle Ages, purported to reveal arcane knowledge of a practical kind—the refining of metallic ores, for example, or the construction of mechanical or optical wonders—that had hitherto, they claimed, been the possession of the privileged few. In this way, occult esoteric knowledge and the technical secrets of medieval craft guilds were not much different from each other and stood in stark contrast to exoteric knowledge even (or especially) when "revealed" as "secrets" to the rest of the world.

Thus, when we enter the sixteenth century, we find that a *public* ideal of knowledge was not the basic norm. In contrast to the sensibilities of modern science, ideals of knowledge at the beginning of the Scientific Revolution did not take for granted the general accessibility of natural knowledge. Knowledge, as Francis Bacon (1561–1626) was later to observe, was power, and most people were not prepared to grant that power freely to others. The state had its political secrets, trades had their craft secrets; the schools and universities were unusual in promulgating rather than protecting knowledge. This followed, in part, from their very function as teaching institutions dedicated to the passing on of knowledge, but teaching, this time of an esoteric kind, also went on in the master-apprentice relationships of the craft guilds. What characterized the public knowledge of the universities was the open intelligibility that was held up as the hallmark of true philosophical (including natural-philosophical) knowledge. Aristotle's views on the proper structure of a science dominated university teaching, from mathematics to metaphysics (and even, for many, theology). Aristotle, in his *Posterior Analytics,* stressed a model of demonstrative knowledge that closely resembled the axiomatic-deductive structure of Greek geometry. Starting from sure and universally held starting points, complex and far-from-obvious truths could be deduced through rigorous formal reasoning. Essential to this view of a scientific demonstration, therefore, was the idea that every part of it could be checked and verified. This was, by definition, the reverse of esoteric, and it guided university natural philosophy (as well as mathematical sciences) in the sixteenth century. It is noteworthy, however, that academic natural philosophy usually kept itself aloof from issues of practical use, for which it was seldom clearly relevant.

Elsewhere, and for other purposes, much more controlled ideals of knowledge were upheld. A forum in which this held true was that of aristocratic patronage. In this period, natural philosophers and mathematicians, as well as other kinds of scholars, were beginning to find places for themselves as the clients of wealthy patrons. In the search for such positions and in the endeavor to maintain them, purveyors of knowledge needed to keep their wares—knowledge—as their own possession. A notable example of this appears in the case of the astronomer Tycho Brahe (1546–1601). In the 1590s, Brahe found himself without a patron, having previously relied on the support of a now-deceased king of Denmark. He promptly set about attracting a new one. In 1598 he published a work on his astronomical instruments. He expressed a disinclination to give details of planned new instruments, however, promising instead to reveal them to "distinguished and princely persons" on condition that they not reveal them to others and only when they had shown their "benevolence" toward him. For Brahe, this knowledge was a kind of personal commodity, not a public good.

In 1626 there appeared in England Francis Bacon's utopian work *New Atlantis*. Often hailed as a model for the later Royal Society in the 1660s, Bacon's account in that book of Solomon's House presents an ideal research institution devoted to the creation of new knowledge of nature. The purpose of this knowledge and its pursuit was the common good. But Bacon's was not a vision of a public, an exoteric, science. His research institution was an arm of the state, and only those few people at the top were empowered to decide what discoveries should be made known even to the king himself and what kept secret. Bacon's project for the reform of natural knowledge had been, throughout his career, aimed at strengthening the powers of the centralized state not at disseminating knowledge to everyone.

Ironically, after his death Bacon's emphasis on practical knowledge was taken up by would-be followers in England with the opposite stress. During the Interregnum of the 1650s that followed the English Civil War

(1642–1646), Samuel Hartlib (ca. 1600–1662) and a number of like-minded colleagues set up, with the approval of Parliament, an Office of Address that was intended as a central clearinghouse of information regarding industrial and agriculture techniques. Hartlib's hope, which he regarded as Baconian in spirit, was that the greater availability and circulation of such knowledge would result in increased productivity throughout the country, to the benefit of all. In the 1630s and 1640s, a broadly similar, although topically more wide ranging, scheme had already been instituted in France by Théophraste Renaudot (1583–1653) with the indulgence of the first minister, Cardinal Richelieu. Renaudot intended this Bureau d'adresse to function, among many other things (such as being a free dispensary), as a sort of patent registry, guaranteeing the rights of inventors while making their inventions widely available.

The related problem of persuading those who made their living through their technical knowledge and inventiveness to make their knowledge available to the public troubled the early Royal Society of London for the Improving of Natural Knowledge, founded in the early 1660s. Fellows of the society, attempting to follow Bacon's injunction to learn from artisans, found that such people were very reluctant to give away their secrets to inquisitive gentlemen. Even members of the society sometimes found themselves in dispute over the allocation of credit for inventions, most famously in the priority controversy between Robert Hooke (1635–1703) and the Dutch member of the Académie Royale des Sciences in Paris (who was also a Fellow of the Royal Society) Christiaan Huygens (1629–1695), over the invention of clocks regulated by balance wheels instead of pendulums. Thus, even when money was not involved (and it sometimes was), the concern of natural philosophers with proper credit for their own work could itself work against the rapid publicizing of new discoveries. Huygens, like others, sometimes used the trick of publishing new discoveries in the form of anagrams, to be revealed later, as a means of protecting priority for immature work.

The Académie Royale des Sciences, founded in 1666, was, unlike the Royal Society in England, explicitly designed as an arm of the state. It thus had official duties relating to the issuing of patents, as well as the charge to assist the state in such practical matters as navigation. One of its features during its first three decades of existence, however, was that its publications were often cor-

porate rather than attributed to individual members. The same is true of the sole publication of another scientific society of this period, the Accademia del Cimento in Florence. The Académie routinely published its positive empirical findings (such as work on zoological anatomies) as the collective work of its members, despite the fact that a specifiable two or three were generally primarily responsible. On the other hand, treatises that seemed to be more speculative, such as Huygens's theory of gravity, received notice of their individual authorship. The eventual abandonment in the 1690s of this policy of corporate publication bears witness to the problems of credit and priority that it had created.

Nonetheless, the rhetoric of the Académie, like that of the Royal Society, stressed the Baconian theme of improvement through the medium of the publication of knowledge, in the spirit of Hartlib's Office of Address. Indeed, the perceived importance of priority in discovery worked to promote publication (for example, in the Royal Society's unofficial journal, the *Philosophical Transactions*) rather to suppress it. The common norm that held natural knowledge to be private and esoteric, because valuable, had begun to be supplanted by the norm that such knowledge should be public and exoteric.

BIBLIOGRAPHY

Eamon, William. *Science and the Secrets of Nature: Books of Secrets in Medieval and Early Modern Culture.* Princeton, NJ: Princeton University Press, 1994.

Iliffe, Robert. "'In the Warehouse': Privacy, Property, and Priority in the Early Royal Society." *History of Science* 30 (1992), 29–68.

Long, Pamela O. "The Openness of Knowledge: An Ideal and Its Context in Sixteenth-Century Writings on Mining and Metallurgy." *Technology and Culture* 32 (1991), 313–355.

Stroup, Alice. *A Company of Scientists: Botany, Patronage, and Community at the Seventeenth-Century Parisian Royal Academy of Sciences.* Berkeley and Los Angeles: University of California Press, 1990.

Webster, Charles. *The Great Instauration: Science, Medicine, and Reform, 1626–1660.* London: Duckworth, 1975.

PETER R. DEAR

See also Bureau d'adresse; Hartlib, Samuel; Patronage; Popularization; Books of Secrets

Puritanism and Science

A long-standing dispute exists over whether "puritanism" and, specifically, the period of "Puritan" rule

(1640–1660) were particularly conducive to the growth and institutionalization of science in England. Since the 1930s, affirmative arguments have proffered three interpretations: (1) a direct and consciously desired causal relationship between puritanism and science; (2) a number of parallel intellectual approaches but an inadvertent effect rather than a conscious puritan effort to institutionalize science; and (3) certain social and economic, rather than intellectual, changes pushing forward an interest in natural philosophy at the time the Puritans gained power. The Puritan-science question thus also involves the debate over an internal or external history of science.

The most influential argument, which relied on Max Weber's (1864–1920) ideas of ascetic Protestantism, saw puritanism as a social, rather than a theological or an ecclesiastical, movement. John Calvin's (1509–1564) theological voluntarism emphasized the sovereignty and arbitrariness of God, who laid down laws rather than governed through levels of mediating angels. Nature, like grace, was deterministic, which meant that it was knowable. In exercising his will, God did not contradict reason; man's inherent capacity to know, therefore, was not contradicted by his obligation to believe. A demystified, literal, and historical approach to the Bible and to the Church promoted a new view of nature in which knowledge and control were seen as part of God's benefit to humans. Thus, puritanism paralleled a Baconian approach to natural philosophy. The practicing scientists of the early Royal Society of London were identified as disproportionately Puritan. Nonetheless, the leading protagonist of this argument, Robert K. Merton—whose interest was the reasons for the development and influence of a Puritan ethos and the manner of institutionalization of science in the dominant culture of the seventeenth century—eschewed a conscious causal connection between puritanism and either the development of particular interests and practices or institutionalization itself. In his view, Puritans did not intend (and would not have approved of) the consequences that *inadvertently* resulted from their attitudes and ideas. Such was Merton's influence that the Puritan-science argument is often called the Merton thesis. The two, however, should not be confused. Merton analyzed various other aspects of early-modern natural philosophy, and the Puritan-science debate has developed beyond Merton's original conceptualization.

Later work enlarged upon Merton's arguments and asserted further common characteristics of puritanism and Baconianism: a utilitarian spirit; a concern for the amelioration of material conditions through innovation; a belief in progress; an antiauthoritarian and anti-Scholastic view; a desire to reform the universities; toward the New Philosophy; a belief in the social, economic, and moral value of disciplined labor; an emphasis on the immense powers of human reason; a commitment to the empirical method and to personal experience rather than to tradition; and a desire to regain the original form of things. As well, the theory of accommodation—that God revealed the secrets of nature over time—allowed Protestants to accept without religious demur that the seventeenth-century view of the heavens was different from that apparently stated in Scripture.

Of recent arguments, most noteworthy is Charles Webster's attempt not only to chronicle the development of scientific activity in the mid-seventeenth century, but also to locate historically the cultural conditions essential to its growth. Webster clearly demonstrated the great breadth of approaches and purposes, as well as the widespread involvement of non-university-trained investigators, in comprehending and controlling nature. Crucial to his interpretation was the development of an organized Puritan opposition party from ca. 1626, which used a blend of Foxean Church history and a new millenarianism to produce a "utopian mentality" desirous of overthrowing its "immediate intellectual inheritance." After 1640, Puritans seized upon Baconianism as a way of fulfilling God's providence and of rapidly ameliorating the conditions of existence. Puritan involvement in the London and Oxford natural-philosophical groups helped lead to the formation of the heavily Baconian Royal Society. Webster, however, minimized Merton's argument concerning unintended effects; here knowledge of nature became a self-conscious and highly organized thrust of the "entire puritan movement."

There has also been severe criticism of the Puritan thesis. Proponents were accused of selecting favorable evidence and of ignoring contemporary warnings about the study of nature. As well, values supposedly shared by Puritans and natural philosophers were shown to be dissimilar. So while, for example, both groups favored experimentalism, for Puritans this culminated in the single, unrepeatable, and generally unwitnessed experience of conversion. There was nothing here of the controlled and repeatable experiment increasingly favored by natural philosophers in the Royal Society. Nor was religious experimentalism a rational process.

Much of the criticism has involved a reexamination of the fundamental terms of the debate. For example, Merton's static sense of *puritan* as a generalized *climate of opinion* of social-utilitarian values, and specifically not as a theological and moral reformist point of view, did not accord with seventeenth-century usage and also failed to acknowledge theological or intellectual change. *Puritan* was invented as a term of religious opprobrium, though it grew to have political and even social meanings. Puritans represented a broad spectrum of ideas, but generally they are understood, then and now, as those within the Church of England, until the fragmentation of the 1640s, who wished to reform religious ceremony and organization, who held to a double predestinarian theology, who emphasized sermons and the question of the visible Church, and who pushed for individual and collective improvements in common behavior. *Science,* on the other hand, was not a term used in the seventeenth century for the study of nature. *Natural philosophy,* as this endeavor was usually called, still encompassed a great variety of cultural practices and ways of constructing nature, including even alchemy and astrology. The proper role of rationalism, experimentalism, and mathematics was heavily contested, even among Fellows of the early Royal Society. The degree and pace of change in approaches to, and understanding of, nature are also still matters for wide debate. Broadly construed connections of Puritans and science thus need to be made specific in terms of meaning and effect.

As well, reinvestigation of the narrative of early-modern natural philosophy has shown not only that much of the Continental Scientific Revolution had been completed before 1640, but also that, in England, the degree of activity before then, even in the universities, had been seriously underestimated, so that any supposed Puritan contribution after 1640 had been correspondingly exaggerated. Moreover, it is not clear that there was a surge in scientific literature as a proportion of all publications in the 1640s and 1650s. It was also Protestantism generally, rather than puritanism specifically, which developed greater liberty for the individual investigator of God and the Bible, a trait which may have carried over to the analysis of nature. There has also been methodological criticism concerning the difficulty of demonstrating causation rather than mere compatibility. That some natural philosophers had been or even were Puritans does not establish that their original interest in natural philosophy, or their ongoing motivation, derived from their puritanism. This, of course, also applies to other purported religious connections.

Closer scrutiny of Puritan ideas and policies has reduced the plausibility of a disproportionate connection with natural philosophy. Traits such as asceticism, dedication to a vocational life, desire for the amelioration of conditions, and millenarianism are now understood as conventional in the seventeenth century. Puritans were overwhelmingly concerned with soteriology and with experimentally applying their covenant of grace. Many Puritans expressed fear of natural philosophy because it aggrandized "fallen" human reason and, therefore, might well lead away from experimental religion. In relying heavily on the ideas of Peter Ramus (1515–1572), Puritans contributed to the construction of a new Protestant scholasticism. Puritan emphasis on a priori knowledge and on certainty (of salvation and of assurance) clashed with the increasing emphasis among natural philosophers on probability. Like others, Puritans placed utilitarian value on knowledge of nature, but this knowledge formed no part of puritanism as a distinct set of religious ideas. Pre-1640 school and university statutes written by Puritans insisted on purified religious texts and personnel but placed no greater emphasis on the study of nature. The 1640s and 1650s also reveal only sporadic support in the House of Commons and Council of State for further reforms. While a few of the intruded Masters at Oxford and Cambridge were natural philosophers, so were some of those removed from the universities because of religious unreliability. Nor did contemporaries identify science disproportionately as a Puritan interest. In the 1640s and 1650s, there was great religious diversity, even the continuation of a strong Anglicanism; it is, therefore, simplistic to see the era, and all in it, as "puritan."

Finally, recent research has offered alternative explanations. Increasing recognition of the great variety of methodologies and religious views within the London and Oxford forerunners of the Royal Society has complicated the question of drawing a connection with a single dominant religious catalyst. Earlier figures on Puritans in the Royal Society are now seen as inflated. While frequently also ill defined, Latitudinarian Anglicans, with their greater emphasis on natural religion and reason, and their willingness to accept human fallibility, are seen to have encouraged intellectual cooperation and to have shunned theological dispute and its insistence on certainty, thereby contributing to an intellectual atmosphere in which the new natural philosophy could flourish. Anglicanism was also the dominant religious affiliation among the founders of the Royal Society. However, Anglicans did not share a unified theology or epistemology; as well, Latitudinarians had limited support in the reestablished Church of England after 1660. Since many Latitudinarians did not support or participate in natural philosophy, the earlier methodological difficulty of establishing religious *causation* remains. Notions of culturally coherent ideologies that promoted involvement in, or support for, particular approaches to, and interpretations of, nature have thus proven enormously difficult to establish. They now contend with much more nominalist interpretations that emphasize individual views and personal relationships, while not denying the likelihood of broad ideological benefits from the promotion of natural philosophy.

BIBLIOGRAPHY

Cohen, I. B., ed., *Puritanism and the Rise of Modern Science: The Merton Thesis.* New Brunswick, NJ.: Rutgers University Press, 1990.

Merton, Robert K. "Science, Technology, and Society in Seventeenth-Century England." *Osiris* 4 (1938), 360–632. Repr. New York: Harper and Row, 1970.

Morgan, John. "Puritanism and Science: A Reinterpretation." *Historical Journal* 22 (1979), 535–560.

Webster, Charles. *The Great Instauration: Science, Medicine, and Reform, 1626–1660.* London: Duckworth, 1975.

———. "Puritanism, Separatism, and Science." In *God and Nature: Historical Essays on the Encounter Between Christianity and Science,* ed. D. Lindberg and R. Numbers. Berkeley and Los Angeles: University of California Press, 1986, pp. 192–217.

———, ed. *The Intellectual Revolution of the Seventeenth Century.* London and Boston: Routledge and Kegan Paul, 1974.

JOHN MORGAN

See also Internalist/Externalist Historiography; Reformation, Protestant; Religion and Natural Philosophy

Q

Quadrant

The quadrant is named from its shape, a quarter of a circle. The curved edge is divided from 0° to 90°; at the apex, a cord is attached with a small weight at the other end. On one straight edge is mounted a pair of sights. Holding the quadrant vertically, and aligning the sights on the Sun or a star, the angle of elevation can be read off the degree scale by the position of the cord, which is kept in a vertical line by the weight. This very simple instrument, in its variations, is used for navigation, surveying, and for time telling. Quadrants can be classified as follows:

1. *Altitude.* The plain quadrant, with arc and cord used for taking altitudes. Used by navigators before the invention of the backstaff by John Davis in 1594.
2. *Gunner's.* Used for setting the angle of a gun barrel. Here one straight edge is extended to lodge in the mouth of the gun so that its elevation can be read by the cord.
3. *Horary.* Provided with hour lines, usually curved, designed for a particular latitude of use. The lines can be for unequal (planetary) or equal (mean) hours. A shadow square for trigonometrical surveying was frequently added. A popular version was invented by Edmund Gunter of London in 1623.

The horary quadrant is medieval in origin. The earliest was of brass, with a sliding declination plate that moved in a slot above the arc of degrees. After 1400 it ceased to be universal and had a scale for one fixed latitude. The bulk of the quadrant had a diagram of hour lines. The cord was held over the date on the declination scale, and a small bead on the cord was moved until it cut the noon line. With the cord now set free, the sights were pointed to the Sun, when the position of the bead told the time. This is the mode of action of all horary quadrants.

BIBLIOGRAPHY
Dekker, Elly. "An Unrecorded Medieval Astrolabe Quadrant from c. 1300." *Annals of Science* 52 (1995), 1–47.
Gunther, R. T. *Early Science in Oxford,* vol. 2. Oxford: Oxford Historical Society, 1923.
Turner, Gerard L'E. *Scientific Instruments, 1500–1900: An Introduction.* London and Berkeley and Los Angeles: Philip Wilson Publishers and University of California Press, 1997.
Waters, David W. *The Art of Navigation in England in Elizabethan and Early Stuart Times.* London: Hollis and Carter, 1958.

G. L'E. TURNER

See also Navigation

Qualities

A grasp of the notion of *quality* is essential to an understanding of the Scientific Revolution, for a radically new attitude to such entities constituted the core of the mechanical philosophy. The basic idea had been articulated in the *Categories,* in which Aristotle (384–322 B.C.E.) distinguished qualities from *substances*—things capable of independent existence. Qualities, by contrast—colors, heaviness, the attractive power of a magnet, or the redemptive virtue in holy water, for instance—exist only in association with a substance.

Quality words like *heaviness* are ambiguous, however, for they can refer to two quite different things: the behavior of heavy things, the *fact* that earthy things move downward when unsupported, or to a suspected *cause* of that behavior, something in the element earth that generates and/or guides its motion. The distinction in meaning here is vital. The seventeenth-century disputes about qualities involved both meanings, but the issues were very different according to which sense of the word was involved. Mechanists vigorously denied the Aristotelian presumption that causal qualities existed in abundance (and with it, a Scholastic portrait of God's role in the universe), but they insisted that there were many descriptive qualities that had been prematurely excluded from science by the Scholastics (and others that were frankly illusory, too hastily endorsed by folklore).

Causal qualities had been very important in Scholastic metaphysics, for Aristotelians had not seen a heavy object as falling because it is attracted by the center of the earth, or because it is compelled to move toward the center of the universe by some external agent. Like all "natural" activity, this motion was deemed internally generated: there is some quality (e.g., power, faculty, nature, or virtue) inside a heavy object that guides it toward the part of the universe that is appropriate to it. It would typically possess this quality because of the large amount of the element earth that it contained.

The pursuit of its natural place is not, of course, the only activity of the element earth. Earth also carried the qualities coolness and dryness, so an earthy medicine, for example, would be the appropriate remedy to prescribe for a disease believed caused by an excessively hot, moist condition of the body. Not all activity, however, could be explained in terms of the qualities of the four elements——earth, fire, air, and water—and the exceptions are quite important. A rather obvious example is the activity of building a house. This involves guidance by the architect, as well as the spontaneous inclinations of the building materials. It is, thus, the product of art rather than nature, similar perhaps to the cures associated with pilgrimage to saintly relics. These were probably performed by angel, not qualities.

There was a strong presumption in Scholastic tradition that internal causation was a norm. This notion was effectively built into Aristotelian matter theory via its *hylemorphism* (the doctrine that every corporeal object is a composite substance with two ingredients: matter and form). Matter was conceived of negatively, as dull, inert, passive, and lowly in the scale of Creation, while form was conceived of positively, as a superior principle, responsible for the activity, worthiness—and qualities—of an object. A good analogy for envisaging this resolu-

tion is provided by one particularly important case of it, the standard Aristotelian-Christian conception of a human being. The body represents the matter, while the soul represents the form, and many of the traditional connotations of the soul-body distinction are mirrored by the Aristotelian form-matter dichotomy. This is why the Aristotelian cosmos can plausibly be deemed *animistic* (from *anima,* meaning "soul"), for corporeal objects perform their functions as a result of their containing soul-like qualities, given them by God—and giving them (like humanity) a measure of independence from God. (Yet, since the soul was certainly capable of separate existence, substantial forms created an awkward compromise with authentic Aristotelian doctrine.)

So the Scholastic God ruled the cosmos by a system of decentralized government—established at the Creation, when power was distributed to the objects by implanting forms in their matter. These forms normally acted as his agents in the administration of the universe. A substance like earth had a genuine power to carry things downward and was not dependent on divine grace to do this: God had authorized earth to act on his behalf here. Causal qualities are, thus, a substitute for supernatural action.

The Scholastic God acted via a hierarchy: He appointed angels to turn the celestial spheres, and these passed power on to the stars. These, in turn, focused their beams on the earth and generated the basic qualities of the four elements. The four elements then passed power to any object they constituted. So the actions of a material object were connected back to God only via an extended chain of causal qualities.

At first sight, this appears to be an astrological administration of the world, but, to avowed astrologers, elemental qualities were the mere skeleton of the cosmos, in need of radical supplementation by a whole network of other powers. Being outside the standard hierarchy of causes, such "occult" powers brought God a little closer to his world, yet the contrast with a supernaturalistic worldview remains. So occult powers posed an intellectual threat to religion, and the status of these powers in Christian Aristotelianism was somewhat problematical.

During the the Reformation of the sixteenth century, Scholastic naturalism (and the attached doctrine of qualities) came under severe attack. Indeed, the overt cause of Martin Luther's (1483–1546) break with Rome was his insistence that the keys that Christ had symbolically handed to Peter did not convey a delegated power to absolve sin. In Protestant thought, salvation became a purely supernatural phenomenon. But so was everything else: in an ideal Protestant world, man and matter, pope and king would be stripped of every inherent quality, and all action would be a result of God's direct sustenance.

In the next century and a half, attempts (not necessarily deliberate) were made to extend the reformers' voluntarist interpretation of salvation to the remainder of the universe. To do this, a new physics was needed in which God's involvement in the universe was ensured and causal qualities, the substitutes for divine action, were banished. It thus became necessary to describe the behavior of the material universe in terms of passive matter alone, without involving any activating soul-like forms attached to that matter. This was to become the program of the mechanical philosophy of the mid-seventeenth century.

Although the mechanical philosophers were agreed that the Aristotelian explanation of the action of, say, a knife had to be abandoned, they were not agreed as to what account should be set up in its place. This was partly a function of their skepticism about whether one could describe the causal processes of nature with real accuracy and partly a function of the fact that they individually preferred slightly different explanations. But they would all stress the way the knife and the object cut related to each other, deemphasizing the earlier tendency to locate activity in one object alone. A typical account might run as follows: the knife and the object it cuts are made up of microscopic corpuscles; the cutting edge of the knife is very thin, so the corpuscles of the knife in the immediate vicinity of this edge can insinuate themselves into the gaps between the corpuscles composing the object being cut; hence, when pressure and motion are applied to the knife, the latter corpuscles are forced apart.

This is perfectly straightforward. It is the sort of explanation we could readily imagine someone giving today. Yet, we would not nowadays be inclined to interpret this explanation of the action of a knife as a denial that the knife has a power to cut. The reason that it functioned as such a denial in the seventeenth century was that Aristotelians traditionally viewed the words in which their theories were expressed as precise reflections of the realities of the world. So when they said a knife had a power to cut, they meant that this power had a real existence, that it was lodged in the knife, and that any cutting effected by the knife was caused by this power. Their opponents, however, interpreted the use of human language differently. It expressed our necessarily limited experience of the things that happen in the world about us rather than the reality behind those happenings. To them, the claim that a knife had a power to cut was true only in the nominalistic sense: this was the way we humans had chosen to describe our experience that knifelike objects could be used to perform cuttinglike operations. So the new conception of the operation of a knife does not require the abandonment of the Aristotelian terminology or qualities in the descriptive sense, but the causal conceptions behind them have drastically altered.

In the case of occult qualities, in particular, the New Science was far more accommodating here than the old. Since the deceptions of the senses were now fully accepted, absolute certainty was no longer the hallmark of science, and tentative reasoning from observed effects back to unobservable causes became unexceptionable. So the fact that an agent was insensible did not mean that it was especially unintelligible. Indeed, even the most visible of qualities, such as colors, were now explained via speculative invisible microscopic mechanism. There was, therefore, nothing to stop magnetism or the action of a poison from becoming a routine part of the New Science, and, in this sense, occult descriptive qualities ceased to be excluded—whenever the empirical evidence that they existed seemed good. The alleged ability of a magnet to detect adultery was not acceptable but not because it was occult: for some reason, people lost confidence in the effect.

Since the qualities that were unproblematical to the New Science were purely descriptive, it seemed (superficially) that such qualities could not be explanatory, and contemporaries made much fun of the apparent Aristotelian practice of explaining a (descriptive) quality by automatically positing the causal counterpart, often disguised behind elaborate language. Why does opium help you sleep, asks Molière? Because it contains a dormitive virtue, is his mocking answer. Yet, such jokes depend on oversimplifying the Aristotelian position, and they ignore the fact (alarming to some) that Newtonian gravitation proved remarkably explanatory—even if interpreted peripatetically. The fault with Scholasticism lay in the abuse, not the metaphysics.

To make their claims plausible, that God had not organized the world so that it operated by means of implanted powers, the mechanical philosophers had to demonstrate that a reasonable proportion of the phenomena of the universe were explicable on the assumption that material objects were purely passive in character. The example of the knife indicates how they proceeded here.

Instead of using a "quality of sharpness" to explain the action of a knife, the mechanists based their explanation on the shape of the knife and its motion, combined with the idea that the knife and the object being cut were composed of microscopic particles. This combination—shape, motion, and corpuscularianism—became the characteristic motif of the mechanical philosophy, and the program of applying these ideas to the explanation of the world became enormously popular in the second half of the seventeenth century.

To establish the credentials of their philosophy, mechanists sought to devise plausible explanations for so many phenomena that the reasonableness of supposing matter devoid of active powers became evident. It is important to recognize that they did not, however, seek to use their new ideas about matter to explain all phenomena in the universe. It was important that a few key items were left unexplained by their theory. Some were reluctant, for example, to follow René Descartes (1596–1650) in rigorously applying the theory to animals, for fear that this would suggest that humans, too, were nothing but clockwork. All were agreed that this was not so and that mechanism alone was inadequate to account for human thought. If the mechanist's conception of matter was correct, then it followed, as a rigorous consequence, that a human being was not a totally material object. Its matter had to be activated by a thinking soul. The mechanical philosophy could, thus, function to guarantee the existence of the soul, a conclusion that earlier philosophers had been reluctant to reach. (To them, the existence of the soul had been a spiritual truth to some extent outside the scope of philosophy; hence, heavily dependent on faith rather than reason for its support.)

The new metaphysics similarly appeared to provide proof for the reality of divine participation in the running of the universe. For if no active powers existed, whatever activity there was in the universe could not be of material origin. It had to come from spirits, and, once it was accepted that there were immaterial spirits active in the universe, the step to God himself was very simple. To Descartes, indeed, matter was so inactive that it did not even have the capacity to persist through time. So he was able to draw the radically supernaturalistic conclusion that God had to create the whole universe afresh every instant.

Such conclusions depended heavily on the presumption that matter was totally devoid of causal qualities; yet, this extreme version of the mechanical philosophy proved hard to defend. Descartes claimed that matter was nothing but extension, but we can now see that he implicitly allowed it some causal power—rigidity as well as mere shape, for instance. Similarly, when Robert Boyle (1627–1691) was doing science (as opposed to talking about it), he routinely allowed a few innate powers to his matter, like heaviness or elasticity. Others never sought to strip matter of all of its powers and overtly allowed it a few properties, like Pierre Gassendi's (1592–1655) intrinsic mobility. In practice, then, the mechanical philosophy involved only a drastic reduction in the number of causal powers allowed in the universe, not a complete elimination of them. It avoided the Scholastic abuse without actually denying the doctrine. Indeed, as time wore on, the list of acceptable properties slowly increased. Descartes's elasticity was recognized as such; Newton's gravity came to be interpreted as an innate power; while Gottfried Wilhelm Leibniz (1646–1716) even insisted that activity was the essence of body. By the end of the eighteenth century, matter that was modestly active had become the norm, and a new "dynamical" physics supplanted the mechanical philosophy in the nineteenth century.

BIBLIOGRAPHY

Alexander, Peter. *Ideas, Qualities, and Corpuscles: Locke and Boyle on the External World.* Cambridge: Cambridge University Press, 1985.

Chalmers, Alan. "The Lack of Excellency of Boyle's Mechanical Philosophy." *Studies in History and Philosophy of Science* 24 (1993), 541–564.

Des Chene, Dennis. *Physiologia: Natural Philosophy in Late Aristotelian and Cartesian Thought.* Ithaca, NY: Cornell University Press, 1996.

Dijksterhuis, Eduard. *The Mechanization of the World Picture.* Trans. C. Dikshoorn. Oxford: Clarendon, 1961.

Hutchison, Keith. "Dormitive Virtues, Scholastic Qualities, and the New Philosophy." *History of Science* 29 (1991), 245–278.

———. "Supernaturalism and the Mechanical Philosophy." *History of Science* 21 (1983), 297–333.

———. "What Happened to Occult Qualities in the Scientific Revolution?" *Isis* 73 (1982), 233–253. Repr. in *The Scientific Enterprise in Early Modern Europe: Readings from Isis,* ed. Peter Dear. Chicago: University of Chicago Press, 1997, pp. 86–106.

KEITH HUTCHISON

See also Active Principles; Aristotelianism; Atomism; Matter; Mechanical Philosophy

R

Ramelli, Agostino (1531–1590)

Ramelli was a military engineer by profession, interested in mechanical invention, as were many of his colleagues. He learned his trade in the armies of Emperor Charles V, then moved to France, where he spent the rest of his life and served in the French Wars of Religion. In 1588 he published the largest of the illustrated books of mechanical inventions that came out in the late sixteenth and seventeenth centuries. The book of machines was his masterpiece, printed quite late in his life, after he had been named a king's engineer. A work on surveying, intended to show the potential of his trigonometer, was to have accompanied it but survives only in manuscript.

A Preface on the mathematical arts stresses their utility; machine design is a mathematical art, deriving from mechanics. His machines all work on simple principles but ignore the effects of scale, friction, and the like. Often he seems to delight in presenting many slight variations on a general theme, showing inserts of key details, but without classification or theoretical explanation. Given his military background, many of his machines are understandably applied to the uses of war, even wrenches, jacks, and hoists. Many plates illustrate machinery to raise solid or liquid weights, in the form of cranes and pumps—for drainage, or irrigation, or domestic supply. Some are truly original, among them centrifugal and rotary pumps, whose basic geometry was to appear in later rotary engines. Mills, too, are depicted, among them the first printed illustrations of the interior of windmills. Smaller devices, like cranks, jacks, spanners, and handmills, look drawn from life, but few of the grander designs could ever have gotten off the page. The book's reputation continued through the seventeenth century and even later, despite skepticism about the efficiency of many of Ramelli's designs.

BIBLIOGRAPHY

Keller, A. G. "Renaissance Theaters of Machines." *Technology and Culture* 19 (1978), 495–508.

Ramelli, Agostino. *The Various and Ingenious Machines*. Trans. with a Biography by M. T. Gnudi and Technical Annotations

Agostino Ramelli. From his Le diverse et artificiose machine *(1588).*

and Pictorial Glossary by E. S. Ferguson. Baltimore: Johns Hopkins University Press; London: Scolar, 1976.

ALEX KELLER

See also Automata; Instrument Makers

Ramus, Peter (1515–1572)

Renaissance philosopher, educator, and communicator, Ramus is considered one of the greatest professors of Christian Europe. A forerunner of the encyclopedists of the eighteenth century and the unification movements of the nineteenth, his goals included reforming the teaching of grammar (Greek, French, and Latin), redistributing the functions of logic and rhetoric, adding physics and metaphysics to the liberal arts, increasing the value of mathematics, reconstructing the university curriculum, and arguing with great passion that all knowledge was available to anyone who was willing to use the right method to discover it in his own language. All of these goals were to demonstrate that there was only one true method in learning, that it was based on a new dialectic, and that the dialectic was his own.

Ramus was born at Cuts in the province of Picardy, France. He entered the University of Paris as an impoverished but precocious student in 1527 and completed his M.A. in 1536 with a thesis on the fabrications of Aristotle. Beginning his teaching career at the College of Mans the following year, he reached notoriety by challenging the authority of Aristotle (384–322 B.C.E.), who had been predominant since the first curriculum created at the University of Paris in 1215. His formative years were 1537–1543, when he worked at Mans with a team of colleagues who included his later biographer, Nicolaus Nancel, and his major collaborator, Omer Talon (ca. 1510–1562). Ramus was a workaholic, seldom sleeping more than three hours a night. He was sentenced for his attack on "the art of logic accepted by all nations," as well as for his arrogance, and in 1544 was forbidden by royal edict to teach or write dialectic or philosophy. However, his friend Charles de Guise, cardinal of Lorraine, had him appointed principal of the College of Presles in 1545 and had the ban lifted at the accession of Henry II in 1547.

Ramus, now blessed with royal favor and protection, embarked on a fabled career over the next twenty years. He became Regius Professor in 1551 and Lecturer of the King at the Sorbonne, University of Paris. He converted to the Protestant faith in 1561, the year before the Wars of Religion (1562–1598), and withdrew to Fountainbleu with the king's protection. Ramus became dean of what was later called the College of France in 1565 and left France for Switzerland and Germany in the years 1568–1570. During these war years, he published perhaps his greatest work, *Scholae in liberales artes* (1569) in 1,166 columns. He returned to his college, and, condemned by the Synod of Nimes for advocating secular views of church government in 1572, he was murdered in his rooms on August 26 of that year in the midst of the St. Bartholomew's Day Massacre, allegedly by paid assassins.

Ramus published more than fifty works in Latin and French in his lifetime, and many unpublished works were looted from his study after his death. There were more than two hundred editions of his *Dialectic* (1556) alone in the sixteenth century in numerous languages and versions. Much of his work, however, was inseparable from that of Talon's, and it is often impossible to distinguish who wrote what. In addition, he was always rewriting his own books, changing the phraseology and vocabulary. By 1650 there were more than eleven hundred printings of his works in Europe and hundreds of authors who wrote about him. The works of Ramus and Talon, along with their adversaries and supporters, spread to Germany, Switzerland, Denmark, Poland, the Low Countries, Scotland, and England by the early seventeenth century, and by the mid-seventeenth century to New England, where his logic may have been as influential as the theology of Saint Augustine (354–430) or John Calvin (1509–1564).

Ramus's mission was to establish a Socratic superiority that would invalidate Aristotle and Aristotelianism, and all of medieval Scholasticism, and supplant it with a new and simple method. Ramus argued that logic has the two functions of invention and judgment or disposition, which are applicable to all of the arts, and that a knowledge of how to use them made whatever is known in the world accessible to memory, and rhetoric easy. Thus, once one had abandoned the "stultifying errors" and "wretched confusions" of "the race of Aristotelians," even children could learn to write and speak better, men to interpret art, poetry, music, theology, government, law, and politics, and scholars to discover the boundaries of the social and physical sciences. That Ramus had borrowed most of his ideas from philosophers of the late fifteenth and early sixteenth centuries, and cobbled them together with panache, has contributed to academic debate about his originality from his own time to the present.

BIBLIOGRAPHY

Grafton, Anthony, and Lisa Jardine. *From Humanism to the Humanities: Education and the Liberal Arts in Fifteenth- and Sixteenth-Century Europe.* London: Duckworth, 1986.

Howell, Wilbur S. *Logic and Rhetoric in England, 1500–1700.* Princeton, NJ: Princeton University Press, 1956.

Ong, Walter J. *Ramus, Method, and the Decay of Dialogue: From the Art of Discourse to the Art of Reason.* Cambridge, MA: Harvard University Press, 1958.

Sharratt, Peter. "Recent Work on Peter Ramus (1970–1986)." *Rhetorica* 5 (1987), 7–58.

LOUIS A. KNAFLA

See also Aristotelianism; Educational Reform; Logic

Ray, John (1620–1705)

Born at Black Notley, near Braintree, Essex, England, where his father was a humble village blacksmith and his mother a medical practitioner and herbalist, Ray attended the University of Cambridge, graduating B.A. in 1648 and M.A. in 1651. He was elected Fellow of Trinity College in 1649 and was by then greatly interested in the botany of the County of Cambridge. His catalog of plants, *Catalogus plantarum circa Cantabrigiam nascentium,* was published in 1660, followed by a supplement in 1663. Because his conscience would not allow him to subscribe to the 1662 Act of Uniformity within the Church, he resigned from his university, and, with his wealthy pupil and patron Francis Willughby (1635–1672), pursued his botanical interests further afield.

For many weeks they toured England, Scotland, and Wales in search of plants before undertaking a grand tour of Europe from 1663 to 1666, which was followed by another tour to the west of England in 1667. At this time, Ray had made his home with Willughby at both Wollaton Hall and Middleton Hall, Warwickshire, to catalog all of their discoveries in natural history.

When Willughby died at the early age of thirty-seven, Ray edited Willughby's work on birds and fishes and saw these published before moving back to Essex to work on his own botanical records and collections. In 1690 he published his catalog of British plants, *Synopsis methodica stirpium Britannicarum,* and in 1694 his catalog of European plants, excluding Great Britain, *Stirpium Europeanarum extra Britanniae nascentium syllioge.* He

John Ray. From R. T. Gunther, Early Science in Cambridge *(Oxford: p.p., 1937).*

was the first to attempt the classification of plants, fifty years before the now universally accepted binominal system of the great Swedish botanist Carl Linnaeus (1707–1778).

Ray had turned to insects and spiders by 1700, when he prepared his *Historia insectorum,* which was published posthumously in 1710. Other publications not related to natural history were: *A Collection of English Proverbs* (1671), *A Collection of English Words not Generally Used* (1674), and a trinomial *Dictionary of Latin, Greek and English Names* (1675). Numerous other papers and letters sent to the secretary of the Royal Society, of which he was an early Fellow, were published in its *Philosophical Transactions.*

BIBLIOGRAPHY

Raven, Charles E. *John Ray, Naturalist: His Life and Works.* Cambridge: Cambridge University Press, 1950. 1st ed. 1942.

Stearn, William T. "John Wilkins, John Ray, and Carl Linnaeus." *Notes and Records of the Royal Society of London* 40 (1985–1986), 101–123.

Zeitz, Lisa M. "Natural Theology, Rhetoric, and Revolution: John Ray's *Wisdom of God,* 1691–1705." *Eighteenth Century Life* 18 (1994), 120–133.

                                        JOHN R. PARKER

See also Botany; Lister, Martin; Natural History; Taxonomy; Willughby, Francis

Realism

A position in epistemology, or theory of knowledge, that affirms that humans can grasp the natures of things and know them basically as they are. In the history of thought, *realism* is usually differentiated from both *idealism* and *nominalism*. Idealism, a classical teaching of Plato (428–348 B.C.E.), holds that ideas are what is known and are more real than things, which are only illusions or shadows of the ideas that furnish patterns for them. Nominalism, a medieval teaching deriving from Peter Abelard (1079–1142) and William of Ockham (ca. 1285–1347), maintains—along with realism—that things (*res, realia*) can be known, but not in their natures as universals, only through names (*nomina*) by which they are referenced as singulars. In recent science, realism is also opposed to *antirealism,* or *instrumentalism.* Here the point of contention is not ordinary experience but, rather, theoretical entities, such as quarks and black holes. Realists hold that such entities can be known as existing outside the mind, on a par with ordinary things, whereas antirealists deny this, maintaining that they should be regarded as useful fictions or instruments of calculation, not as having an extramental existence.

In the period before and during the Scientific Revolution, the modern debate was foreshadowed in the Scholastic distinction between a real being (*ens reale*), which, as known, exists in the mind but also outside the mind, and a being of reason (*ens rationis*), which, by its very nature, exists in the mind alone. From the time of Aristotle (384–322 B.C.E.) onward, logical entities were thought of as beings of reason, but, in the mathematical astronomies developed by Ptolemy (ca. 100–ca. 170) and Nicolaus Copernicus (1473–1543), some mathematical entities that were used to explain the motions of the heavens, such as eccentrics and epicycles, were commonly accorded a similar status. Again, in the new sciences of Galileo Galilei (1564–1642) and Isaac Newton (1642–1727), some alleged physical phenomena, such as the earth's motion and universal gravitation, were at first

held by many to be purely suppositional or logical in character and so as lacking extramental existence. Thus, the ontological status of entities and phenomena is a question of long standing in the history of science. One may even wonder about the reality of the Scientific Revolution itself. Does not its real significance depend on whether the earth actually moves around the Sun, and not vice versa? Or is that revolution is itself a fiction, a construct of historians as they attempt to document changing fashions in human thought?

Questions such as these are disturbing, for they can prompt worries about whether, apart from oneself, anything is real, and also about the validity of concepts like science, truth, objectivity, certitude, causality, and demonstration. Yet, doubts of this kind are an integral part of scientific investigation, particularly for researchers who are working at the frontiers of knowledge. Ptolemy, Copernicus, Galileo, and Newton were all at that stage at one time, so it may prove helpful to reassess in our day the doubts each then experienced.

When, ca. 145, Ptolemy wrote his *Almagest,* whose proper title is *Syntaxis mathematica* (Mathematical Compilation), his main task was to systematize the teaching of astronomers to make available a method of computing the positions of the heavenly bodies. By that time, mathematical astronomy had developed independently of the physical astronomy of Aristotle, and it was not expected to give an actual account of the structure of the heavens, which Aristotle's purported to do. As is clear from his *Planetary Hypotheses,* Ptolemy thought of some of his constructions as physically real and others as aids in calculation, but this was not generally known, and it had little influence on the development of physical astronomy. Ptolemy was regarded as essentially a mathematician, and so as a mathematical astronomer. In physical (or philosophical) astronomy, Aristotle remained the competent authority, and, in that discipline, planetary eccentrics and epicycles were only rarely thought of as real.

The case of Copernicus is somewhat different. His *De revolutionibus orbium coelestium* (1543) was written in much the same style as Ptolemy's *Almagest,* but Copernicus was a realist and thought of his work as physical astronomy. Unfortunately, there was little in that treatise that conveyed that impression. To make matters worse, an unsigned Preface was added to it, without Copernicus's knowledge, by Andreas Osiander, a Lutheran theologian who was concerned lest the heliocentric doctrine it contained be seen as contrary to the teachings of Scripture. He therefore stressed that the work he was introducing did not contain a true description of the heavens but furnished only fictive entities that helped simplify the calculations of astronomers. Most readers took the Preface to be written by Copernicus himself and so were not concerned about the reality of the constructions proposed in the *De revolutionibus.* Thus, the question of whether the world system was geocentric or heliocentric never came to a head throughout the sixteenth century.

With Galileo, the situation changed. As a young teacher of mathematics at the University of Pisa from 1589 to 1591, he knew the differences between the world systems of Ptolemy and Copernicus, but he taught the Ptolemaic system as the one most commonly in use in his day. Then, through his discoveries with the telescope announced in 1610, he uncovered new evidence that convinced him of the reality of the Copernican system. This led him to embark on a crusade to convince the Catholic Church that the earth moves around the Sun, even though passages in Scripture clearly state the contrary. Challenged by the Church to demonstrate the earth's motion, Galileo ran into difficulties—not because his basic insight was faulty but because the experimental and observational techniques at his command were too crude to detect such movement, hidden as it is from the senses. Not until the nineteenth century was empirical evidence on hand that would convince the critical observer that the earth actually moves.

With Sir Isaac Newton, the situation was different yet again. Newton had no doubts about the earth's motion, but he was much concerned to uncover the principles that would serve to explain the motion of all bodies on the earth and in the solar system. In his *Mathematical Principles of Natural Philosophy* (1687; 2nd ed. 1713), he laid out his three laws of motion and, with their aid, attempted to demonstrate "that all bodies whatsoever are endowed with a principle of mutual gravitation." He used his methodology of resolution and composition to prove the existence of gravity, but, for a variety of reasons, his demonstration was not grasped by reputable contemporaries such as Christiaan Huygens (1629–1695) and Gottfried Wilhelm Leibniz (1646–1716). Not until the nineteenth century, through the work of philosopher-scientists such as William Whewell (1794–1866) and John Herschel (1792–1871), did gravity come to be accepted as the *vera causa* (universal cause) of falling bodies. Now, of course, there are no longer doubts on the subject, and it is listed among the four basic forces of the universe.

Most practicing scientists are realists. Indeed, many might be called ultrarealists in the sense that they are overconfident in their ability to know not only the world of ordinary experience, but its microstructure and megastructure as well. In such an atmosphere, antirealism may be viewed as a conservative movement that holds in check unlimited faith in the use of theoretical constructions to extend the frontiers of knowledge. Not carried to extremes, it can exert a healthy restraining influence on claims made in the name of science.

BIBLIOGRAPHY

Duhem, Pierre. *To Save the Phenomena.* Trans. Edmund Dolan and Chaninah Maschler. Chicago: University of Chicago Press, 1969.

Harré, Rom. *Varieties of Realism.* Oxford: Blackwell, 1986.

Jardine, Nicholas. *The Birth of History and Philosophy of Science.* Cambridge: Cambridge University Press, 1984.

Koyré, Alexandre. *Newtonian Studies.* Cambridge, MA: Harvard University Press, 1965.

Regis, Louis M. *Epistemology.* Trans. Imelda C. Byrne. New York: Macmillan, 1959.

Wallace, William A. *The Modeling of Nature: Philosophy of Science and Philosophy of Nature in Synthesis.* Washington, D.C.: Catholic University of America Press, 1996.

WILLIAM A. WALLACE

See also Copernicanism; Demonstration; Hypothesis; Theory

Recorde, Robert (1510–1558)

An English physician and a minor civil servant, Robert Recorde is best known for his series of elementary textbooks on mathematics. His first book, *The Ground of Artes* (1542), covered basic arithmetic and its usefulness to merchants and artisans. *The Pathway to Knowledge* (1551) discussed the "first principles of geometrie," namely the definitions, examples, and theorems concerning the geometry of plane figures. He returned to arithmetic in *Whetstone of Witte* (1557), containing what is believed to be the first symbolic algebraic equations.

While his textbooks on arithmetic were popular in their day, his dialogue concerning Ptolemaic astronomy, *Castle of Knowledge* (1556), has received greater attention from modern scholars if only for its brief, favorable mention of Nicolaus Copernicus (1473–1543) and his theories. When he mentions the Copernican controversy, Recorde sets it aside "tyll some other time" with the promise that, at some future point, "you shall not only wonder to hear it, but also peradventure be as earnest then to credite it, as you are now to condemne it." Given Recorde's habit of deferring more difficult sections to later works, this has been generally interpreted by historians as promise of some future pro-Copernican work.

Recorde also wrote *Urinal of Physick* (1547) on the examination of urine for medical diagnosis and a manuscript on the astronomical quadrant that has been lost. Other promised volumes, devoted to the application of mathematics to astronomy, navigation, and timekeeping—including the promised discussion of Copernican astronomy—were never completed.

BIBLIOGRAPHY

Hughes, Barnabas. "Robert Recorde and the First Published Equation." In *Vestigia Mathematica: Studies in Medieval and Early Modern Mathematics in Honour of H. L. L. Busard,* ed. M. Folkerts and J. P. Hogendijk. Amsterdam: Rodopi, 1993, pp. 163–171.

Kaplan, Edward. *"Robert Recorde: Studies in the Life and Works of a Tudor Scientist."* Ph.D. diss. New York University, 1960.

GARY MCINTYRE

See also Copernicanism

Redi, Francesco (1626–1697)

One of the leading naturalists of the seventeenth century, he pushed to make natural history less reliant on such ancient authorities as Aristotle (384–322 B.C.E.) and Pliny the Elder (23/24–79) and more experimental. Born in Arezzo, Redi was educated at the Jesuit College in Florence and received his degree in medicine from the University of Pisa in 1647. His talents came to the attention of the grand duke of Tuscany; by the 1650s, Redi became Court physician to Ferdinando II de' Medici and, subsequently, his son Cosimo III (1642–1723). He participated in the activities of the Accademia del Cimento (Academy of the Experiment) (1657–1667), a scientific academy in Florence advocating a Galilean approach to science fostered by Leopoldo de' Medici (though it is unclear whether Redi was actually a member). By the 1660s, Redi had become one of the leading experimenters at the Tuscan Court. He collaborated with the Danish anatomist Nicolaus Steno (1638–1686), and his work soon became known throughout Europe.

Redi's experimental activities were publicized outside Florence through a series of lively essays, usually written in the form of letters to leading intellectuals and imitating Galileo Galilei's (1574–1642) advocacy of a scientific prose that was accessible (in Italian rather than Latin) and witty. His first essay, *Osservazioni intorno alle vipere* (Observations on Vipers, 1664), described a series of experiments with the snakes in the grand-ducal pharmacy that Redi supervised. Through careful observations of live specimens, Redi identified the fangs as the source of the venom and argued that it was produced by two venom sacs and stored in the cavities of the teeth. Drawing inspiration from William Harvey's (1578–1657) work on the circulation of the blood, Redi further argued that the danger posed by the venom depended on how quickly the poison traveled in the bloodstream (based on countless experiments with animals and occasionally a human subject).

Much of Redi's experimental activities revolved around two practices: the use of the microscope and the development of a control from which he could test the variations in his results. This new instrument and new technique of investigating nature combined most famously in his *Esperienze intorno alla generazione degli insetti* (Experiments on the Generation of Insects, 1668), in which Redi proved that a variety of small animals—from bees to frogs to flies—did not generate spontaneously but emerged from eggs. Again, Harvey was his guide. Placing covered and uncovered animal carcasses and cheeses all over the Medici Court, Redi vividly demonstrated that larvae could form only when flies were allowed to lay their eggs, producing the "spontaneous" worms that had been the proof for Aristotle's idea that all lower organisms generated spontaneously. Not all of his contemporaries agreed with Redi on these points, and the debates about some of his trickier observations—for instance, the evolution of oak galls—were resolved by more skilled anatomists, such as Marcello Malpighi (1628–1694) and Antonio Vallisneri (1661–1730). Yet, in the end, Redi deserves credit for raising important questions about reproduction as a universal principle in nature and for persuading other naturalists, in a manner similar to that of Robert Hooke (1635–1703), to examine more carefully the microscopic world of animals that had previously received little attention.

Many of Redi's questions emerged from his ongoing disagreements with the community of Jesuit naturalists

R

By the 1680s, Redi returned to the more medical subjects with which he had begun his career. He produced his important work in parasitology, *Osservazioni intorno agli animali viventi, che si trovano negli animali viventi* (Observations on Living Animals Found Within Living Animals, 1684), an encyclopedia of hundreds of rather nauseating descriptions of the various parasites, worms, and insects that survived in other animals. During this period, Redi also encouraged a number of disciples to produce essays, following his well-known format (always in an accessible Italian and filled with clear and repeatable results), that furthered his contributions to such fields as comparative anatomy, entomology, and parasitology.

Redi is frequently remembered as a naturalist who set the preconditions to the sort of experimental biology that emerged in the eighteenth and nineteenth centuries, primarily by debunking the idea of spontaneous generation. Yet, like many intellectuals of his time, Redi engaged in a wide variety of cultural pursuits. He was a popular poet at the Tuscan Court, and his *Bacco in Toscana* (Bacchus in Tuscany), an ode to the wines of his region, is still occasionally reproduced. Redi also occupies a place in literary history as the member of the Accademia della Crusca (Academy of the Chaff), Italy's leading literary academy, who supervised the completion of the third Crusca dictionary, a definitive statement on the role of Tuscan in the formation of the modern Italian language. Tending the ailments of the Medici family, debating the origins of words (sometimes inventing them, as Redi did in the case of his mock treatise on the origins of spectacles), and experimenting continuously, Redi led many different lives. He belonged to a community of Italian naturalists and philosophers who refused to see the Catholic Church's condemnation of Galileo in 1633 as the end of Italian science; instead, he devoted his life to applying Galileo's emphasis on sense experience to the less controversial parts of nature, looking at the microscopic world rather than the heavens. In doing so, he created new controversies for scientists to debate and ponder in the ensuing centuries.

Francesco Redi. From Fielding H. Garrison, An Introduction to the History of Medicine, *3rd ed. (Philadelphia and London: Saunders, 1921).*

then working in Italy. His experiments with insects particularly attacked the ideas of the Jesuits Athanasius Kircher (1602–1680) and Filippo Bonanni (1638–1725), two of the most vocal defenders of the Aristotelian view of spontaneous generation. At the same time, Redi published his *Esperienze intorno a diverse cose naturali, e particolarmente quelle che ci sono portate dall'Indie* (Experiments on Diverse Natural Things, Especially Those Brought from the Indies, 1671) in the form of a letter to Kircher. In it, he argued that the snakestones (a calcification found inside the heads of cobras) could not cure disease simply by attaching themselves to the wound and sucking out the poison through their magnetic virtue. By contrast, the Jesuits insisted that this missionary object had unusual medical powers. Neither side was persuaded by the other's arguments, but Redi used this as yet another occasion to demonstrate the simplicity and clarity of his experimental method, describing the repeated failures of his attempts to replicate Jesuit results with the snakestone.

BIBLIOGRAPHY

Baldwin, Martha. "The Snakestone Experiments: An Early Modern Medical Debate." *Isis* 86 (1995), 394–418.

Basile, Bruno. *L'invenzione del vero: La letteratura scientifica da Galileo ad Algarotti.* Rome: Salerno, 1987.

Findlen, Paula. "Controlling the Experiment: Rhetoric, Court Patronage, and the Experimental Method of Francesco Redi (1626–97)." *History of Science* 31 (1993), 35–64.

Tribby, Jay. "Cooking (with) Clio and Cleo: Eloquence and Experiment in Seventeenth-Century Florence." *Journal of the History of Ideas* 52 (1991), 417–439.

Viviani, Ugo. *Vita ed opere inedite di Francesco Redi.* Arezzo: 1924.

PAULA FINDLEN

See also Malpighi, Marcello; Microscopy; Spontaneous Generation; Steno, Nicolaus

Reflection

Refers in optics (and mechanics) to a "bending or turning back" of light (or bodies). Reflection may be considered with respect to its geometry, its causes and, in optics, its relation to the appearance of colors and colored bodies.

The geometrical study of reflected light—*catoptrics,* after the Greek for mirror—and the location of the optical image according to the well-known law of equal angles was a standard topic for mathematicians since antiquity. This law was understood by some as a paradigm of nature acting according to principles of least time, minimum path, or least effort. According to Alan Shapiro (1990), modern geometrical optics began on new foundations with the rapid assimilation of Johannes Kepler's (1571–1630) concept of the pencil of rays (*Paralipomena,* 1604), and, applied to the location of optical images, the method was widely extended in sophistication after midcentury, most notably by Isaac Barrow (1630–1677).

Less certain than geometry were conjectures about the physical causes of reflection. It lends itself readily to mechanical interpretation as a rebound from hard, smooth, dense surfaces. But this simple analogy was incompatible with numerous phenomena. Transparent bodies partly reflect light and, at certain angles of incidence, reflect it totally, whether impinging from, or into, more dense media. Collisions of particles could not account for this or for the smooth regularity of reflection. In his version of the Cartesian pulse, or pression, model, Christiaan Huygens (1629–1695) suggested that reflected light is a pulse in air particles outside bodies, whereas refracted light is a pulse in ether particles inside, but he realized that partial reflection in vacuous spaces could not be accommodated to this model. Isaac Newton

(1642–1727) entertained corpuscular mechanisms and various ethers but also proposed more categorically that "Reflexion" is accomplished "by some Power of the Body . . . evenly diffused all over its Surface."

Finally, the fact that virtually all opaque or transparent corporeal bodies appear colored or—as in the phenomena of thin transparent films—display colors by reflected light posed serious obstacles to a comprehensive understanding of reflection that would also be consistent with other optical phenomena. Newton's heroic attempts foundered on these difficulties. Then, of course, the various chemical aspects of the interaction of light and matter—explored, for example, in the "Queries" to Newton's *Opticks* (1704)—further complicated a picture that at first had seemed, from a geometrical and mechanical point of view, so easy and comprehensible.

BIBLIOGRAPHY

Hall, A. Rupert. *All Was Light: An Introduction to Newton's Opticks.* Oxford: Clarendon, 1993.

Sabra, A. I. *Theories of Light from Descartes to Newton.* London: Oldbourne, 1967.

Shapiro, Alan E. *Fits, Passions, and Paroxysms: Physics, Method, and Chemistry and Newton's Theories of Colored Bodies and Fits of Easy Reflection.* Cambridge: Cambridge University Press, 1993.

———. "The Optical Lectures and the Foundations of the Theory of Optical Imagery." In *Before Newton: The Life and Times of Isaac Barrow,* ed. Mordechai Feingold. Cambridge: Cambridge University Press, 1990, pp. 105–176.

STEPHEN STRAKER

See also Light Transmission; Optics

Reformation, Protestant

The religious movement of the sixteenth century known as the Protestant Reformation had many points of intersection with the Scientific Revolution because many of the leading scientific figures were also people of religious faith or at least very knowledgeable on Christian doctrine. New discoveries in science had a profound effect on religion, and Christian faith helped shape the social acceptance of science. The Reformation began in 1517 when Martin Luther (1483–1546) nailed his ninety-five theses on the church door in Wittenberg, but the movement spread so rapidly that it permanently altered the face of European Christendom within one generation. Calvinism, a second major form of the Reformation, had its center in Geneva under the leadership of John Calvin (1509–1564) and later Theodore Beza (1519–1605). Calvinism was to exercise an enormous influence in Switzerland, Holland, and England. During the same period, fundamental changes occurred in various sciences, culminating in a radical reorientation of natural philosophy by the end of the seventeenth century. When Thomas Sprat (1635–1713) wrote a defense of the Royal Society in the 1660s, he explicitly invoked a parallel between reformation in religion and in natural philosophy, a claim that had become common during the preceding decades of English science.

The Lutheran reformation sought to establish new centers of education in Germany that could teach the authentic Christian faith rediscovered by Luther. The key figure in the educational reforms was Luther's lieutenant, Philip Melanchthon (1497–1560), a professor of Greek at Wittenberg who personally encouraged the dissemination of new scientific knowledge. He gave lectures on physical theory and wrote several prefaces to mathematical works printed in the mid-sixteenth century. Georg Joachim Rheticus (1514–1574), a young mathematician at Wittenberg, visited Nicolaus Copernicus (1473–1543) in Frauenberg and became his only student. Upon his return to Germany, Rheticus sought to publish Copernicus's masterpiece *De revolutionibus,* finally committing the task to the Lutheran pastor of Nuremberg, Andreas Osiander (1498–1552), who added an anonymous Preface to the first edition (1543). The Copernican theory was studied and extended during the 1540s under the guidance of Erasmus Reinhold (1511–1553), the senior mathematician at Wittenberg, who published the first Copernican astronomical tables (*The Prutenic Tables,* 1551). Melanchthon's influence also impacted Lutheranism in Scandinavia, where Tycho Brahe (1546–1601) initiated one of the largest programs of celestial observation in the history of astronomy to date. Brahe adopted Melanchthon's version of Lutheran theology that argued for the religious relevance of astrology, and he sought to combine astronomy, alchemy, and theology into an integrated natural philosophy. Although he failed in this larger task, he proffered a model of the solar system that became enormously influential before being eclipsed by the Copernican system. Brahe's system had the earth as its center, with the Sun encircling it, while the remaining five planets circled the Sun. Under Melanchthon's aegis, the university at Tübingen also became a center of astronomy, with Michael Maestlin (1550–1631) as its

leading faculty member. Maestlin exerted considerable influence on Johannes Kepler (1571–1630), who, in turn, revolutionized astronomy by introducing the notions of elliptical planetary orbits and celestial physics. Kepler's cosmology sought to combine Christian theology with Copernican astronomy and to demonstrate that a heliocentric system was necessary to show the Trinitarian nature of God in the universe. This goal may have grown out of Kepler's Christian belief that the universe was a sacrament, a physical embodiment of God's presence, a belief that would explain why he chose to name his first work by the rather unusual title *Mysterium cosmographicum* (1596).

Calvin never addressed questions of natural philosophy in any direct way, but those influenced by him took cues from his passing comments on biblical texts that mentioned natural phenomena. Calvin's theology emphasized both the radical sovereignty of God and the accommodated nature of biblical revelation. For him, all knowledge of God resulted from God's free disclosure to a humanity incapable of understanding the divine. Consequently, the Bible necessarily had to speak of God by analogy with human things. Calvin specifically invoked accommodation when he interpreted Genesis 1:16, concluding that the knowledge of the precise shape of the heavens could not be learned from exegesis but only from astronomy. The often repeated claim that Calvin condemned Copernicus by an appeal to scriptural texts mentioning an immobile earth has been shown by historians to be false. While Calvin never pronounced on the truth of the Copernican system, his method of exegesis did agree with the Copernican argument that the Bible uses phenomenal language that cannot be properly taken as a theory of nature.

Both streams of the Reformation, Lutheran and Calvinist, found their way into the Church of England and its dissenting parties, where they exercised wide-ranging influence on the transformation of English science in the course of the seventeenth century. Reformation theology stressed understanding nature as a holy task laid on humankind for the glory of God and the advancement of God's kingdom. Francis Bacon (1561–1626), for example, advocated a reconstruction of the sciences based on direct observation of nature that would restore humans to a position of blessedness and benefit. To such figures as Robert Boyle (1627–1691) and John Ray (1620–1705), it was almost axiomatic that knowledge of nature and God would reinforce the piety

R

of believers. The Calvinist doctrine of the radical sovereignty of God implied that the operations of nature resulted from the divine will and that only empirical investigation could discover those divine principles. This voluntaristic conception of God and nature shaped Isaac Newton's (1642–1727) debate with Gottfried Wilhelm Leibniz (1646–1716). Rev. Samuel Clarke (1675-1729), Newton's spokesman, contended that God continually upheld the course of nature and was intimately involved in the daily providence of the world. Although Newton held beliefs similar to Unitarianism, he embraced the traditional Christian notion of God as the supreme Lord of the universe.

BIBLIOGRAPHY

Brooke, John H. *Science and Religion: Some Historical Perspectives.* Cambridge: Cambridge University Press, 1991.

Cohen, H. Floris. *The Scientific Revolution: A Historiographical Inquiry.* Chicago: University of Chicago Press, 1994.

Hooykaas, Reijer. *Religion and the Rise of Modern Science.* Edinburgh: Scottish Academic, 1973.

Merton, Robert K. *Science, Technology, and Society in Seventeenth Century England.* New York: H. Fertig, 1971. 1st ed. *Osiris* 4 (1938), 360–632.

Spitz, Lewis W. *The Renaissance and Reformation Movements,* vol. 2. Chicago: Rand McNally College Publishing, 1971.

Westman Robert S. "The Copernicans and the Churches." In *God and Nature: Historical Essays in the Encounter Between Christianity and Science,* eds. David C. Lindberg and Ronald L. Numbers. Berkeley and Los Angeles: University of California Press, 1986.

KENNETH J. HOWELL

See also Biblical Interpretation; Puritanism and Science; Religion and Natural Philosophy

Refraction

In 1600 an exact law describing the refraction of rays at the boundary of two different media had not yet been found. Fifteen hundred years earlier, Claudius Ptolemy (ca. 100–ca. 170) had searched for it in vain, and medieval optics had not succeeded either. The sixteenth-century contributions of Francesco Maurolico (1494–1575) and Giambattista della Porta (1543–1615) are noteworthy because they were the first scholars who discussed refraction by lenses. Although spectacles had been invented ca. 1300, lenses had never drawn the attention of scholars. Their accounts were, however, based on the qualitative theories of refraction of medi-

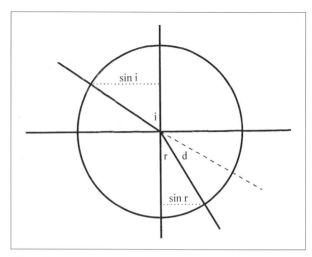

Figure 1.

eval optics. During the first decades of the seventeenth century, Johannes Kepler (1571–1630) developed the modern concept of image formation, and several scholars found an exact law of refraction. Kepler, induced by the invention of the telescope, in 1611 coined the term *dioptrics* for the mathematical study of lenses.

During the very first years of the seventeenth century, Thomas Harriot (ca. 1560–1621) and Kepler tried, independently of each other, to find the law of refraction. Their approaches differed much, as did the results of their efforts. Both started to calculate using a table of angles of refraction by Witelo (ca. 1225–ca. 1280), which contained several errors. When Harriot failed to gain satisfactory results, he started to measure angles of refraction anew. He quickly found that the sines of the angle of incidence and the angle of refraction are in a constant proportion. In modern phrasing: $\sin i = n \sin r$. The constant n is called the *index of refraction* and varies with each refracting medium. Contrary to Harriot, Kepler tried to find a law underlying refraction by means of a rational, mathematical analysis. Each result he checked with Witelo's tables, and each time he rejected it, without starting to distrust those tables. Kepler published his efforts in *Paralipomena ad Witelo* (Supplement to Witelo, 1604). Harriot's results, on the other hand, remained unpublished until the twentieth century.

Galileo Galilei's (1564–1642) astronomical use of the newly invented telescope induced Kepler to write *Dioptrice* (1611), initiating the mathematical study of the properties of lenses and their configurations. Still lacking an exact law of refraction, Kepler used an approximate rule to derive focal distances of some types of lenses and to explain how configurations of lenses can produce magnified images. This rule, which says that the angle of deviation d is one-third of the angle of incidence i, is valid for small angles of incidence and still used today. Kepler not only discussed the ordinary telescope of one convex and one concave lens, but also a configuration of two convex lenses, which had not been used yet to yield a telescopic effect. Kepler never realized his design himself, but, in due course, it would become the type of telescope used for astronomical observation.

Willebrord Snel (1580–1626) discovered the exact law of refraction ca. 1620. It is not clear how he arrived at it, for his manuscripts were lost during the following decades. It is certain that he had conducted experiments on refraction. In the course of the 1620s, his accomplishments became known in scholarly circles throughout Europe. Around that time, René Descartes (1596–1650) also had obtained knowledge of the sine law. Although he was later accused of plagiarism, it is probable that he had found the law of refraction independently. Descartes did not publish the sine law before 1637, and, in fact, lost priority to Pierre Hérigone (d. ca. 1643), who merely mentioned the law in a work of 1637, although his dioptrical theory was based on Kepler's approximation rule.

Descartes not only formulated the sine law, but also applied it to the properties of lenses. He could prove that certain defects of lenses used in telescopes are inherent in their spherical shape. A spherical surface does not generally bring rays from one point into a perfect focus in another point after refraction. This is called *spherical aberration*. Ca. 1626, Descartes derived shapes of perfectly focusing surfaces, which were conic sections. He probably collaborated with Claude Mydorge (1585–1647), who measured indices of refraction to find exact measures for lenses. In *La Dioptrique* (1637), Descartes explained what shape the surfaces of perfectly focusing lenses ought to have and how these can be ground. Subsequent efforts to grind these lenses failed throughout the seventeenth century.

In 1653 Christiaan Huygens (1629–1695) was the first to apply the sine law to spherical lenses, which were used in telescopes and microscopes. He derived a general expression for the focal distance of all types of lenses taking all characteristics of the lens into account. The ultimate goal of Huygens's dioptrical studies was to find a way to correct for spherical aberration. Toward the end of the 1660s, he had developed a highly sophisticated theory of spherical aberration. Moreover, he had designed a configuration of two spherical lenses that emulated the perfect focusing properties of a hyperbolical lens. In 1671 Isaac Newton (1642–1727) showed that refraction of light produces colors, implying that no lens can prevent the colored fringes around telescopic images. With this, Huygens's project stranded, and he never published his dioptrics.

Regarding his theory of focal distances of lenses, Huygens lost priority to Isaac Barrow (1630–1677), who in 1669 published a mathematical theory of image formation that was an extension of Kepler's theory. Barrow discussed images in reflection and refraction, for both plane and spherical surfaces. Barrow's theory was extended further by Newton, whose lectures were not published before 1729. In one of his lectures, Barrow gave, without demonstration, a series of equations for the focal distances of spherical lenses. His condensed and complex presentation made the theory unfit for men of practice. It was obviously too difficult for William Molyneux (1656–1698), for he did not use it in *Dioptrica nova* (1692), a compilation of seventeenth-century dioptrics aimed at explaining the telescope for practical ends. One year later, Edmond Halley (ca. 1656–1743) simplified the core of dioptrics considerably by deriving algebraically a single equation for the focal distance of all varieties of lenses. His paper in the *Philosophical Transactions* for 1693, "An Instance of the Excellence of the Modern Algebra, in the Resolution of the Problem of Finding the Foci of Optick Glasses Universally," was, however, primarily aimed at mathematicians instead of students of practical dioptrics.

BIBLIOGRAPHY

Lohne, Johannes. "Zur Geschichte des Brechungsgesetzes." *Sudhoffs Archiv für Geschichte der Medizin und der Naturwissenschaften* 47 (1963), 152–172.

Pater, C. de. "Experimental physics." In *Leiden University in the Seventeenth Century: An Exchange of Learning,* ed. T. H. Lunsingh Scheurleer and G. H. M. Posthumus Meyjes. Leiden: Universitaire Pers Leiden, 1975, pp. 308–327.

Shapiro, Alan E. "The Optical Lectures and the Foundations of the Theory of Optical Imagery." In *Before Newton: The Life and Times of Isaac Barrow,* ed. Mordechai Feingold. Cambridge: Cambridge University Press, 1990, pp. 105–178.

FOKKO J. DIJKSTERHUIS

See also Light Transmission; Optics; Snel (Snellius or Snel van Royen), Willebrord

Regiomontanus, Johannes (1436–1476)

Born Johannes Müller of Königsberg (Franconia, Germany), this central-European mathematician, astrologer, and printer was the best astronomer of the fifteenth century. By the time he moved as a fourteen-year-old from the University of Leipzig to the University of Vienna, he had already computed a set of astronomical tables. In Vienna, he collaborated with Georg Peurbach (1423–1461), completing the latter's *Epitome of the Almagest,* Ptolemy's (ca. 100–ca. 170) great treatise of mathematical astronomy. Regiomontanus's contribution provided more than a mere summary or finishing touches. In the *Epitome,* he demonstrated (against Ptolemy's own claim) that eccentric alternatives to Ptolemy's models for Mercury and Venus were possible, setting up the geometrical basis for Nicolaus Copernicus's (1473–1543) centering of planetary notion on the mean position of the Sun.

Frontispiece of the Peurbach and Regiomontanus Epitome of the Almagest *(1496).*

Regiomontanus was keenly aware of problems in contemporary astronomy, notably discrepancies between mathematical models and cosmology and between predictions of position and size (e.g., lunar diameter), and he hoped to reform astronomy. Even as he continued to deepen his understanding of Ptolemy, he experimented with models that sought to eliminate the eccentrics and epicycles of Ptolemaic astronomy.

Regiomontanus left Vienna after Peurbach's death in 1461, perfecting his Greek in Italy (1461–ca. 1465) in the entourage of Cardinal Bessarion, a Greek émigré who was a prominent intellectual and patron of learning. Regiomontanus also became involved in the latter's longstanding feud with George of Trebizond, a fellow Greek who had produced a faulty translation of, and commentary on, Ptolemy's *Almagest.* He later (ca. 1467–1471) served as astrologer to the Court of Hungarian King Mathias Corvinus in Buda.

In 1471 he established in Nürnberg an instrument shop and a printing press devoted primarily to works in the mathematical tradition, including his four-hundred-page *Ephemerides* and his popular calendars. Called to Rome in 1475 to consult about the reform of the calendar, he died of plague the following year.

BIBLIOGRAPHY

Gerl, Armin. *Trigonometrisch-astronomisches Rechnen kurz vor Copernicus: Der Briefwechsel Regiomontanus-Bianchini.* Stuttgart: Steiner Verlag, 1989.

Swerdlow, Noel M. "Regiomontanus on the Critical Problems of Astronomy." In *Nature, Experiment, and the Sciences,* ed. T. H. Levere and W. R. Shea. Boston: Kluwer, 1990, pp. 165–195.

———. "Science and Humanism in the Renaissance: Regiomontanus's Oration on the Dignity and Utility of the Mathematical Sciences." In *World Changes: Thomas Kuhn and the Nature of Science,* ed. Paul Horwich. Cambridge, MA: MIT Press, 1993, pp. 131–168.

Zinner, Ernst. *Regiomontanus: His Life and Work.* Trans. Ezra Brown. New York: North Holland, 1990.

MICHAEL H. SHANK

See also Peurbach, Georg; Ptolemaic Astronomy

Reinhold, Erasmus (1511–1553)

The astronomer who established what is today called the Wittenberg interpretation of Nicolaus Copernicus (1473–1543), an approach that adopted Copernicus's mathematical models but not his Sun-centered cosmology.

Reinhold was educated and worked at Wittenberg, the leading Protestant university of Reformation Germany, becoming professor of higher mathematics in 1536 and later dean and rector. His junior colleague Georg Joachim Rheticus (1514–1574) visited Copernicus to learn his theories, wrote the *Narratio prima* (First Account, 1541) describing the new approach to astronomy, and supervised the printing of Copernicus's *De revolutionibus* (1543). There is some evidence that Reinhold had access to Copernicus's manuscript, and his copy of the printed first edition (preserved at Edinburgh) shows extensive technical annotations.

In 1542 Reinhold published a commentary on Georg Puerbach's (1423–1461) *Nova theorica planetarum* (1454), which uses Ptolemaic models, but, on learning Copernicus's method for avoiding the equant, he adopted the models from *De revolutionibus*. He wrote an extensive, but unpublished, commentary on *De revolutionibus* (preserved in Berlin) and set out to enhance the tables of planetary positions supplied by Copernicus. These appeared in 1551 as *The Prutenic Tables* (the adjective "Prutenic," or "Prussian," signaling both the patronage of the duke of Prussia and the homeland of Copernicus). Reinhold's tables were more extensive, and in places more exact, than Copernicus's originals. They were also easier to use and more accurate than the main tables then in use, *The Alphonsine Tables*. *The Prutenic Tables* were quickly adopted by writers of emphemerides and almanacs and consequently spread the name of Copernicus throughout Europe. As the purpose of tables was to calculate the angular position of planets viewed from the earth, it was not required that their users endorse Copernicus's Sun-centered cosmology. Reinhold and many others happily adopted Copernicus's mathematical innovations without changing their allegiance to Aristotle's (384–322 B.C.E.) earth-centered cosmos, although Reinhold may have experimented with a Tychonic planetary system.

Reinhold died of plague at the age of forty-two, leaving many projects unfinished. His student and successor Caspar Peucer (1525–1602) probably completed the *Hypotyposes orbium coelestium,* which appeared at Strasbourg in 1568 and presents a set of models complementing *The Prutenic Tables.*

BIBLIOGRAPHY

Gingerich, Owen. "Erasmus Reinhold and the Dissemination of the Copernican Theory." In *The Eye of Heaven,* ed. Owen Gingerich. New York: American Institute of Physics, 1993, pp. 221–251.

Henderson, Janice A. *On the Distance Between the Sun, Moon, and Earth According to Ptolemy, Copernicus, and Reinhold.* Leiden: Brill, 1991.

Westman, Robert S. "The Melanchthon Circle, Rheticus, and the Wittenberg Interpretation of the Copernican Theory." *Isis* 65 (1974), 165–193.

PETER BARKER

See also Astronomical Tables and Ephemerides; Copernicus, Nicolaus; Copernicanism; Puerbach, Georg; Rheticus, Georg Joachim

Religion and Natural Philosophy

One of the main issues in the debate about the emergence and meaning of modern science is the problem of its relation to the religious traditions of Western culture. According to an interpretation spread during the age of Enlightenment, the Scientific Revolution was the outcome of the struggle for free thought and research, against the authority of the ancient philosophers and the dogmatic spirit of the Christian Churches. Positivist thinkers like Auguste Comte (1798–1857) used this view as the background of the representation of scientific progress as the ultimate destiny of mankind, in the most advanced stages of intellectual and moral development.

In several histories of science written before the beginning of the twentieth century, the concept of a "warfare between science and theology" emerges as a distinctive feature of European culture since the dawn of the modern age. A few decades later, however, the orientation of historiographic work took a radical turn: following the path opened by the pioneer works of Alfred N. Whitehead (1861–1947), Alexander Koyré (1892–1964), Robert K. Merton (1910–), and other scholars, a number of studies have shown the strong connections of scientific ideas, from the late Renaissance until the eighteenth century, with the religious and metaphysical beliefs of natural philosophers.

In the light of these interpretations, the new models of knowledge fostered by the Scientific Revolution of the seventeenth century and the search for the laws of nature often appear not as radical departures from the biblical tradition but as means to confirm and illustrate the Christian view of the world, depending on the decrees of a benevolent and all-wise Creator. Most branches of natural science had reached neither institutional status nor methodological unity at the beginning of the modern age: this simple realization casts doubt on the possibility

Theology and astronomy in harmony. From Petrus de Alliaco,
Cócordátia astronomie cú theologia *(1490).*

of drawing sharp lines of demarcation among the research interests, philosophical commitments, and religious beliefs (or even millenarian hopes) of the protagonists and supporters of the scientific enterprise. The very distinction between the domains of natural philosophy and religion was the result of complex discussions and compromises and was often to be blurred in the efforts to work out a universal standard of truth that might be applied to the whole range of human experience.

On the other hand, it is impossible to neglect the theoretical impact of the discoveries of hitherto unknown phenomena and of the new explanations of the physical world on the traditional doctrines about the creation of the world and man's place in nature. In a historical situation deeply affected by the dramatic experiences of religious struggles within the Christian world and by the skeptical crisis of late-Renaissance culture, the critiques of old beliefs often seemed to shake the foundations of theological and philosophical learning, discrediting the authority of Scholastic teaching and sometimes of Scripture itself. Not only Catholic, but also Protestant, theologians like John Calvin (1509–1564) and Philipp

Melanchthon (1497–1560), in spite of their appreciation of natural knowledge, feared that every deviation from the literal interpretation of Scripture (including the description of the world in the Book of Genesis) meant a challenge to the notion of divine inspiration of the holy text.

The consequences of such worries showed up not only during the long struggles against theological heresies and disbelief undertaken by the Churches, but in the first and best-known instance of the conflict between the traditional view of the world and the New Philosophy: the debate about Copernican astronomy, dating from the second half of the sixteenth century. The work by the Polish astronomer Nicolaus Copernicus (1473–1543), *De revolutionibus orbium coelestium,* was published in the year of the author's death. Its contents questioned some central tenets of the Ptolemaic explanation of the universe, assimilated since the late Middle Ages in the traditional corpus of Christian learning, which was taught in the schools of all Europe. But the view of the system of planets revolving around the Sun (in opposition to the received doctrine of the central position and immobility of the earth) was, according to the first editor of Copernicus's book, Andreas Osiander (1498–1552), only a hypothesis contrived to allow a better calculation of the motions of heavenly bodies, not an explanation of the real frame of the world. This interpretation, together with the acknowledged extravagance of the Copernican doctrines, delayed the reaction of the Catholic Church until the first decades of the seventeenth century. Even after the death at the stake of the Italian philosopher Giordano Bruno (1548–1600) (who, among his theological heresies, had absorbed the Copernican system in his view of an infinite material universe endowed with eternal life and composed of innumerable worlds), the official condemnation of the Copernican doctrine was not pronounced until 1616, when the explosion of Galileo's case compelled the Roman theologians to take a definite stand.

In the first decade of the seventeenth century, Galileo Galilei (1564–1642), a well-known researcher in physics and professor of mathematics at the Universities of Pisa and Padua, had acknowledged his adherence to the Copernican hypothesis, and in 1612 he was denounced as a heretic to the ecclesiastical Court of Sant'Uffizio. In a number of letters written between 1613 and 1615, he tried to disprove this accusation by framing a distinction between the specific roles of the two divine texts, the Bible and the Book of Nature: while the former was intended to expose the moral duties of mankind and the doctrinal bases of faith (to be analyzed and explained by professional theologians), the latter had to be interpreted by skilled inquirers, using sophisticated experimental and mathematical tools. If the conclusions of this reading revealed some truths contrasting with the literal meaning of some scriptural passages, this would depend on the necessity felt by the sacred writer of conforming his speech to the common people's everyday experience.

In the face of this attempt to assert the independence of scientific research from theological restrictions, the Court of Sant'Uffizio declared that the heliocentric hypothesis and the doctrine of the motion of the earth clashed not only with sound philosophy, but also with the express teaching of the Scriptures (especially in Joshua 10:12–13): no Catholic scholar might be allowed to defend or teach Copernican astronomy. The consequences of such a resolution were dramatically played out in the circumstances that led to the second trial and final condemnation of Galileo (1633). The great astronomer was compelled to repudiate his own doctrines and to refrain from teaching and discussing astronomical matters until his death. In the same year, another famous Catholic philosopher, René Descartes (1596–1650), decided to leave unpublished his manuscript *Le monde* to avoid a fate similar to Galileo's. From that moment, the task of reconciling the acceptance of the New Physics with faithfulness to the Church of Rome imposed the adoption of complex and cautious strategies.

The features of this well-known story, however, open a number of historical problems. First of all, it is incorrect to understand it simply as a struggle between faith and disbelief. Most defenders of Copernican astronomy, including Johannes Kepler (1571–1630) and Galileo, meant neither to challenge the idea of an ordered universe directed by God nor to question the authority of Scripture in matters of faith. In the writings of Kepler, the defense of a modified version of Copernicus's theory, conceived as a true description of the solar system, hinged upon the central role of the Sun as the source of the divine energy that enabled the motions of the planets and as a symbol of the unity and harmony of the cosmos. He was convinced not only that the geometrical shapes of the heavenly bodies and of their orbits showed the marks of supreme mathematical wisdom, but also that these numerical relations bore an exact correspondence to the relations of the five perfect regular solids, according to the Pythagorean and Platonic tradi-

tions. This mystical bent was also the source of his view of the universe as a living image of the Trinity.

Galileo also supported the Platonic notion of the Book of Nature written by God in mathematical language. The task of natural philosophers was the interpretation of such language and the explanation of the physical world according to laws acting within both the earthly and the heavenly domains. In spite of his methodological division of labor between science and theology, Galileo took pains to show that a correct interpretation of Scripture supported a number of scientific truths, such as the revolution of the earth around the Sun and the corruptibility of heavenly bodies.

A steady flow of theological and philosophical discussions sprung from the issues raised by the astronomical revolution in the first half of the seventeenth century. The discovery of new planets and satellites, the speculation about the possible infinity of the universe and the existence of other inhabited worlds, and the movement toward the unification of heavenly and earthly physics were alternatively interpreted as signs of a crisis of faith and of the decay of learning or as a confirmation of godly power and of man's high position and dignity in the cosmos.

Even if the leaders of the reformed Churches were often hostile to new ideas and research styles, Protestant countries usually offered a greater freedom for discussions and inquiries. The practice of the personal reading of the Bible conferred a particular responsibility on the believer, looking for the enlightenment of grace, and often entailed the search for deeply symbolic meanings relating to nature and history in the holy text. The great impulse given by religious ideas to natural philosophy in Puritan England during the mid-seventeenth century raised important questions about the possible connection between Protestant ethics and the spirit of scientific inquiry, in the modern sense of the word. Such a thesis, first submitted in a renowned study by Robert K. Merton in 1938, has been the subject of a long debate among social and intellectual historians during the later decades of the twentieth century.

As such discussions have shown, these kinds of questions do not allow for a simple solution. They require a careful assessment of historical and intellectual contexts, whose developments often challenge any effort toward generalization. The fundamental starting point for the evaluation of the religious presuppositions of English science is seen in the tireless work of elaboration

R

and diffusion of a new approach to natural philosophy undertaken by Francis Bacon (1561–1626). One of the most influential characters in the cultural and political climate of his age, Bacon condemned the Aristotelian and Platonic philosophies as barren and unprofitable for the material and moral welfare of mankind and argued that the medieval reliance on authorities must be superseded by direct investigation of nature and by trying to understand the forms and relations of phenomena in order to restore man's original power over the Creation. His *Great Instauration* of learning was not only the condition for economic and technological progress, but especially the way to escape from the evil consequences of original sin and to reinstate the kingdom of charity and peace on earth. The patient and steady work of natural philosophers contrasted both with the contempt of Scholastic doctors for empirical knowledge and mechanical skill and with the efforts of Renaissance magicians to decipher the keys of unlimited power over nature by means of a mystical experience of initiation in alchemical processes. Man's limited faculties after the Fall make researches slow and difficult. Still, they are the only means to improve his condition and to understand the effects of divine power manifested in the Creation. Scientific inquiry, however, must not presume to explain God's ends; the task of the interpretation of nature has to be kept carefully distinguished from the methods and ends of biblical interpretation. The confusion of natural with divine matters is a token of man's overconfidence in his powers and corrupts both secular and sacred knowledge.

In the second half of the seventeenth century, Bacon's ideas assumed prophetic overtones for the Puritans waiting for the end of the Antichrist's dominion. The program of a renovation of learning was often associated with the expectations of the proximate advent of the Millennium and the establishment of the Kingdom of the Saints. During the crucial years of the Puritan revolution (1640–1653), the debates about political and religious themes often included not only the proliferation of speculations about the "new earth" forecast in the Book of Revelation and of scientific utopias—following the Baconian model of the *New Atlantis* (1626)—but also more concrete discussions about the reform of universities and about the creation of institutions intended to promote useful and experimental knowledge. The removal of many royalist professors at Oxford and the modification of traditional curricula also contributed to a different orientation and to the updating of curricula.

The main influences on the institutionalization and promotion of natural philosophy, however, came from the moderate rather than the radical wing of religious reformers. A group of theologians, scholars, and philosophers of different political affiliations—among whom were John Wallis (1616–1703), Robert Boyle (1627–1691), John Wilkins (1614–1672), and Christopher Wren (1632–1723)—had started in the 1640s to hold informal meetings in Oxford and London, with the purpose of describing experiments and discussing scientific problems. These inquirers did not envisage radical transformation in political and social structures or in the organization of the Church; rather, they proposed scientific activity as a model of serious and regular research, inspired by the ideals of tolerance, cooperation, and the free communication of new discoveries. Such a program was incorporated in the statutes of the first public institution expressly intended "for improving Naturall knowledge by Observations and Experiments"—the Royal Society, under the patronage of King Charles II in 1662—shortly after the Restoration of the Stuart monarchy.

Following the historical phases of this process, we can see the alternative interpretations of British science in the seventeenth century as Puritan or Anglican in a different perspective. If the enthusiasm of Puritan reformers often gave a powerful impulse to philosophical debates and to the discussion of research programs, on the other hand the ideological climate of the Restoration was perhaps more favorable to the organization and social acknowledgment of regular scientific work. In the view of the virtuosi (as scientific practitioners called themselves), the concern for the independence of scientific inquiry was balanced by the hope of confirming *The Wisdom of God Manifested in the Works of Creation*—according to the title of a famous work by the naturalist and theologian John Ray (1620–1705). The intention was to strengthen the fundamental principles of natural and revealed religion, rather than stress the theological differences among Churches and sects. The choice of this position was meant both to reject the critiques of science in the name of orthodoxy and to drive back the attacks of deists and freethinkers trying to revive Epicurean or vitalistic doctrines in their original "heathenish" or "atheistic" forms. So neither an abstractly scientific attitude, nor a generic spirit of devotion, but a definite image of Christian science played an important role in shaping a tradition of political and religious moderation, which was to become a typical characteristic of British culture.

The conditions for the development of a scientific frame of mind were very different in the Catholic countries, where the restrictions on free inquiry and discussion were stronger. Descartes's choice of Holland as a safer place than France for his philosophical and mathematical researches is emblematic in this respect. From his point of view, the theological foundation of a mechanical philosophy of nature was the essential condition for confronting the skeptical assaults against both religion and science and to set the basis for a certain and indubitable knowledge. So Descartes tried to persuade the doctors of the Sorbonne and the ecclesiastical authorities to adopt his philosophical system as the surest defense of faith. But many theologians, Catholic and Calvinist as well, saw in the Cartesian view of the human mind and of the world a new challenge both to religious beliefs, such as the doctrine of original sin, and to the authority of Scripture, especially concerning the description of the origin of the world. The methodological barrier built between biblical interpretation and the explanation of nature was obviously inadequate to forbid the overlapping of the two fields and the expansion of the ambitions of scientific explanation.

In spite of such difficulties, the aim of reconciling natural philosophy and sacred science was steadily pursued by many theologians. So Descartes's most sincere follower and friend, the Minim friar Marin Mersenne (1588–1648), made himself conspicuous in the endeavor of showing that the New Philosophy confirmed the view of natural order and God's providence and that it might be used as a powerful weapon against the pantheistic vision of the universe associated with alchemy and the occult sciences, still flourishing in the first half of the seventeenth century.

Some decades later, the brilliant mathematician and experimenter Blaise Pascal (1623–1662) no longer felt the need of reconciling the methods and ends of science with theological concerns; he simply thought that inquiries into natural phenomena, in spite of their practical success, were devoid of metaphysical relevance and unable to satisfy the deepest spiritual needs of human beings.

This evaluation supports the position that the trend toward a sharp separation between the two spheres of human activity could spring from very different motives and interests. Indeed, the two perceived champions of modern infidelity, Thomas Hobbes (1588–1679) and Benedict de Spinoza (1632–1677), claimed the impor-

tance of such a separation. Their purpose, however, was to emphasize the opposition between the criteria for reading the holy texts and the methods of philosophical inquiry rather than to show the complementary role of the two revelations. For Hobbes, every effort to build a theological system was bound to fail through the impossibility of forming a positive idea of God on the basis of the same sensorial data that offered the materials of scientific knowledge. While the experience and reason of every believer made him a competent judge of the meaning of scriptural revelation, the right to define the true doctrines was reserved to the supreme political authority. Spinoza, for his part, resorted to the distinction between the moral and civil purposes of the sacred texts and the aims of theoretical knowledge in order to build a radical interpretation of the Bible, using the same philological and psychological criteria used for deciphering every ancient historical record. The most important meaning resulting from such interpretation was the message of religious tolerance and of reciprocal charity conveyed by the Scripture, which still added nothing to the philosophical understanding of God's nature and of the eternal laws flowing from his unchangeable attributes.

During the last quarter of the seventeenth century, the efforts to accommodate the interpretation of Scripture to philosophical hypotheses about the origin and structure of the physical world tended to ignore the Baconian warnings against the mixture of natural and divine science. A series of tracts, among which were Thomas Burnet's (ca. 1635–1715) *Sacred Theory of the Earth* (1684) and William Whiston's (1667–1752) *New Theory of the Earth* (1696), tried to frame rational explanations for the natural events described in the Scriptures, such as the universal Deluge and the final destruction of the Earth, using the principles of Cartesian or Newtonian physics. The hopes of finding a definite basis for the alliance between reformed Christian theology and natural philosophy, however, found perhaps their most typical expression in the unpublished works of Isaac Newton (1642–1727), the most celebrated scientist of his time.

In the decades preceding the publication of his masterpiece, *Principia mathematica philosophiae naturalis* (1687), Newton had been deeply involved not only in physical, mathematical, and alchemical inquiries, but also in the search of a key for the scientific interpretation of the Bible. His interest was especially focused on the interpretation of the prophecies relating to the end of the world and to the destiny of mankind. This reading of Scripture was founded on the rules of economy and analogy of God's action both in the physical and in the historical world. Such a position implied some important theological consequences, the first of which was a radical simplification of the basic articles of faith and the rejection of the doctrines concerning the Trinity and the divinity of Christ, considered as encroachments of heathen beliefs on the original purity of the monotheistic doctrine. On the other hand, Newton emphasized the need for a method of biblical exegesis showing the marks of certainty and rational evidence, in order to allow the full understanding of God's directions and to show the sure way to salvation for true believers.

Though most of these ideas were not exposed in his published works, Newton did not completely hide the religious inspiration of his system. In the General Scholium of the second edition of the *Principia* (1713), for instance, he referred to the necessity of the voluntary intervention of a personal God, "very well skilled in mechanics and geometry," in order to keep the universe in motion and prevent its dissolution. The emphasis on the direct connection between God and the physical world, resulting from the identification of absolute space with the "place" of divine action, however, exposed even this doctrine to the accusation of pantheism and offered to heterodox authors, such as the freetkinker John Toland (1670–1722), the means of exposing the hidden "atheistical" bent of the Newtonian system.

This kind of criticism was also developed by Newton's main antagonist, the German philosopher Gottfried Wilhelm Leibniz (1646–1716), who stressed at the same time the inadequate conception of a God constantly compelled to mend the work of his Creation. Leibniz chose another way to return modern science once again within a theological frame, by elaborating a metaphysical system centered on the view of the universe as the product of a "pre-established harmony." According to this view, even God's unconditioned will cannot infringe the logical principles constituting the essence of divine intelligence. The act of Creation, therefore, consists in the free choice of calling into existence the most perfect universe compatible with such laws, among the innumerable models of worlds included in his absolute foreknowledge.

Leibniz's work can perhaps be seen as the most ambitious effort to reconcile metaphysical principles and physical laws, necessary truths warranted by the authority of God himself and the vindication of free will, mechanism and finalism in nature. But this remarkable synthesis did not escape the critical examination of Enlightenment thinkers, who often exploited Leibniz's scientific ideas while rejecting their metaphysical presuppositions and criticizing the arguments used for the rational justification of God's providence and the "best of possible worlds."

To sum up, we cannot represent the relation between natural philosophy and religion in the modern world by a comprehensive formula but may, rather, see it as the interaction of various dynamical processes, whose historical results were often very different from the original intentions of the theologians and philosophers involved. Without denying the importance of religious beliefs in shaping the character and aims of the New Philosophy, one must not forget that the search for an ultimate scientific justification of faith, or the use of science as a support for theological knowledge, entailed the risk of dissolving once again the bounds between natural and divine knowledge. The logical plausibility of such a line of evolution finds support in the realization of several historical examples of "theological" approaches to scientific problems that did not succeed so much in shaping the image of a rational religion as in reinforcing a dogmatic view of science. So the holy alliance promoted by the pious inquirers of the seventeenth century would often originate new struggles for the monopoly of certainty, or, at any rate, it would impose on their successors a watchful guard on the boundaries between the two fields, to save their independence without destroying their mutual support, which proved a still more difficult task at the beginning of the eighteenth century.

BIBLIOGRAPHY

Brooke, John H. *Science and Religion: Some Historical Perspectives.* Cambridge: Cambridge University Press, 1991.

Burtt, Edwin A. *The Metaphysical Foundations of Modern Physical Science.* New York: Harcourt and Brace, 1932.

Cohen, I. Bernard, ed. *Puritanism and the Rise of Modern Science: The Merton Thesis.* New Brunswick, NJ: Rutgers University Press, 1990.

Dillenberger, John. *Protestant Thought and Natural Science: A Historical Interpretation.* Garden City, NY: Doubleday, 1960.

Funkenstein, Amos. *Theology and the Scientific Imagination from the Middle Ages to the Seventeenth Century.* Princeton, NJ: Princeton University Press, 1986.

Hooykaas, Reijer. *Religion and the Rise of Modern Science.* Edinburgh: Scottish Academic, 1972.

R

Lindberg, David C., and Ronald L. Numbers, eds. *God and Nature: Historical Essays in the Encounter Between Christianity and Science*. Berkeley and Los Angeles: University of California Press, 1986.

Westfall, Richard S. *Science and Religion in Seventeenth-Century England*. New Haven, CT: Yale University Press, 1958.

White, Andrew D. *A History of the Warfare of Science with Theology in Christendom*. 2 vols. New York: Appleton, 1896.

CHIARA GIUNTINI

See also Arnauld, Antoine; Biblical Chronology; Biblical Interpretation; Book of Nature; Cambridge Platonists; Physico-Theology; Providence, Divine; Reformation, Protestant; Spinoza, Benedict de; Warfare of Science and Theology

Resolution and Composition

The terms *resolutio* and *compositio* were often used as Latin translations for the Greek terms meaning analysis and synthesis and, as such, were used in several different senses. Probably most significant is their use in the discussions of *demonstrative regress* by medieval and Renaissance Aristotelians. Some twentieth-century historians, notably J. H. Randall and A. C. Crombie, have argued that the evolution of this method, which reached its zenith in the writings of Padua School logicians such as Agustino Nifo (ca. 1468–1538) and Jacopo Zabarella (1533–1589), constituted a centuries-long, progressive elaboration of a modern hypothetico-deductive scientific methodology, one whose next small advance was to be found in the methodological writings of Galileo Galilei (1564–1642). Historians and philosophers have since shown that this thesis at least needs significant qualification and that the methodological views of pioneers of the New Science such as Galileo and René Descartes (1596–1650) probably owe more to the notions of analysis and synthesis discussed by ancient geometers.

Discussions of the method of regress usually occur in commentaries on Aristotle's (384–322 B.C.E.) *Posterior Analytics* 1.13, where one finds a distinction between syllogisms that are *demonstrations of fact* (e.g., that which does not twinkle is near, the planets do not twinkle, therefore the planets are near) and those that are *demonstrations of reasoned fact* (e.g., that which is near does not twinkle, the planets are near, therefore the planets do not twinkle). In the first type the *proximate cause* (in our example, *being near*) of the observed effect (*not twinkling*) does not occur as the middle term of the syllogism,

while in the second type it does. This seems to be an attempt to distinguish *explanatory* from *correct but non-explanatory* arguments. Present-day commentators agree that this was not, in fact, supposed to be the key to Aristotle's own account of scientific method, but the regress theorists combined this distinction with some others found in Aristotle (e.g., the distinction between "what is better known to us" and "what is better known in nature") and some ideas probably due to commentaries on Galen's (second century) *Ars medica* to come up with their theory. While they disagreed about its details, the broad outline of the method was clear. Observation yields knowledge of an effect (e.g., that the planets do not twinkle), and, by induction, we establish a general principle (e.g., that what does not twinkle is near). By a demonstration of fact, we come to know the cause. This is called *resolution*, since causes are supposedly simpler than effects. However, at this stage we have only accidental or confused knowledge, since we have started with observation (i.e., with the things that are better known to us). Once we know the cause, we can, by the method of *composition*, construct a demonstration of reasoned fact and so acquire knowledge of the effect. This method is rather obviously circular as so far described—we began with knowledge of the effect, after all—but the regress theorists regarded this new knowledge of the effect as qualitatively different (i.e., as necessary and clear), since it is known through its cause, which is better known in nature. To save the method from its circularity and to account for this qualitative change, the regress theorists posited an intervening contemplative stage (often called *negotiatio* or *consideratio*) between resolution and composition, during which we acquire distinct knowledge of the cause. Unsurprisingly, this stage was the focus of attacks by those skeptical of the regressive method, including Nifo in his later writings.

BIBLIOGRAPHY

Jardine, Nicholas. "Epistemology of the Sciences." In *The Cambridge History of Renaissance Philosophy,* ed. Charles B. Schmitt, Quentin Skinner, and Eckhard Kessler. Cambridge: Cambridge University Press, 1988, pp. 685–711.

Randall, J. H. *The School of Padua and the Emergence of Modern Science*. Padova: Editrice Antenore, 1961.

Wallace, William A. "Circularity and the Paduan *Regressus*: From Pietro d'Abano to Galileo Galilei." *Vivarium* 33 (1995), 76–97.

DAVID DE VIDI

See also Aristotelianism; Demonstration; Logic; Zabarella, Jacopo

Revolutions in Science

The concept of revolution appears in two very different senses in discussions of the development of science. One occurs in the name given to the series of events that mark the birth of science as we know it today, "*the* Scientific Revolution." The time span for this revolution is, roughly, some portion of the era from 1543, the year of publication of both Nicolaus Copernicus's (1473–1543) *De revolutionibus orbium coelestium* (On the Revolutions of the Celestial Orbs) and Andreas Vesalius's (1514–1564) *De humani corporis fabrica* (On the Structure of the Human Body), and 1687, when Isaac Newton (1642–1727) published his *Principia mathematica philosophiae naturalis* (Mathematical Principles of Natural Philosophy). The other sense of revolution occurs in the name used to characterize a set of radical changes and restructuring in a particular branch of science. Unlike "*the* Scientific Revolution," which affected all of science and, indeed, all of human knowledge, this kind of revolution affects primarily a single branch or subject of science. Examples are the Newtonian revolution, the Chemical revolution associated with Antoine Lavoisier (1743–1794), the Darwinian revolution, and the Freudian revolution. Because these two types of revolution are such different occurrences, it is convenient to distinguish one from the other by referring to the first category under the rubric of "scientific revolution" and the second under the rubric of "revolution in science."

Thomas S. Kuhn, whose celebrated *Structure of Scientific Revolutions* (2nd rev. ed. 1970) showed that revolutions are a regular feature of scientific change, later suggested that "*the* Scientific Revolution" was not a unique event, proposing that in the early nineteenth century there occurred a second scientific revolution. Later, I. B. Cohen's *Revolution in Science* (1985) suggested that there have been two other such scientific revolutions, one of which is taking place at the present time.

In the sixteenth and seventeenth centuries, the term *revolution* referred to cycles or periodic returns, often with the image of a wheel or the motions of celestial bodies. It is with the ousting of the English monarch in 1688, referred to as the "Glorious Revolution," and more decisively in the eighteenth century, that the term *revolution* came to be applied to a rapid, sudden, and often violent political overturn, a decisive event. In the nineteenth century, the connotation of the term was broadened to include social and cultural changes embracing successive and lasting consequences. The concept of the Scientific Revolution as employed in the twentieth century, while limited to concepts and practices in the effort to understand natural phenomena, likewise refers to a succession of events and their wider implications.

Several criteria may be used to determine whether a revolution has occurred in a science: (1) the innovator, as well as his contemporaries in his own and other fields, thought of his work as revolutionary; (2) the work had an immediate and profound impact on the field and frequently on related fields, not only overturning traditional concepts and practices, but also opening up new areas for research; (3) historians of science and philosophy now and in the past thought of the work as revolutionary; and (4) a "mythology" of a revolution having been created was established as a tradition among those working in the field.

In the Renaissance and in early-modern Europe, the sense of overturning older knowledge of nature is apparent in the many titles of books containing the words *renovation* or *new*—referring to new experiments, new subjects, and the creation of a new science. In the early seventeenth century, the concept of revolution (in the political and social realm as well as in science) had not yet come into being. Thus, in 1637 in a letter to Galileo Galilei (1564–1642), Raffaello Maggiotti (1597–1658) could indicate that William Harvey (1578–1657) had produced a revolution in biology only by indicating that Harvey had "overturned" all knowledge of the human body, making a discovery comparable in the magnitude of its achievement to the use of the telescope (which "had turned astronomy upside down") or the invention of gunpowder and the magnetic compass.

By the end of the seventeenth century, after the Glorious Revolution and in the wake of Newton's profound achievement, it was recognized that a revolution had occurred. This revolution was seen most clearly in the realm of mathematics—the development of analytic geometry by René Descartes (1596–1650) and Pierre de Fermat (1601–1665) and their successors and of the calculus by Newton and Gottfried Wilhelm Leibniz (1646–1716). Bernard le Bovier de Fontenelle (1657–1757), the permanent secretary of the Paris Académie Royale des Sciences, took note of this great revolution. A sign of it was that a mere beginner in mathematics ("in the first go") could now solve problems that hitherto had challenged the greatest mathematicians, those trained for years on the "thorns of mathematics."

Was there a Copernican revolution, as projected in the famous work by Thomas S. Kuhn (1957)? Kuhn says Copernicus's work produced a revolution in ideas and values, in our conception of the universe and our relation to it. It was not a revolution in astronomy per se, as would be claimed in the eighteenth century, but in its effects on astronomy at a later date and in physics. J. L. E. Dreyer, astronomer and historian of astronomy, said in 1909: "If there was a revolution in astronomy that revolution was Keplerian and Newtonian, and not in any simple or valid sense Copernican." Copernicus's astronomy was a modified Ptolemaic astronomy but not a simpler version. Yet, its realist foundations, in contrast to the instrumentalist character of the Ptolemaic mathematical models, and its systematic nature are what caught the attention of those who studied it, notably Tycho Brahe (1546–1601) and Johannes Kepler (1571–1630).

Kepler, on the other hand, sought an astronomy based on causes, thereby redefining the discipline, and overthrew its classical axioms—uniform circular motion, natural places, and separate laws governing earth and the heavens. Kepler failed, however, to produce a new celestial dynamics and did not alter astronomical practice. That practice was significantly affected when in 1609 Thomas Harriot (ca. 1560–1621) in England and Galileo in Italy began to observe the heavens with the newly invented telescope.

Galileo in mechanics, as had Kepler in astronomy, introduced revolutionary changes, overthrowing time-hallowed concepts concerning "natural" motion, the behavior of falling and projected bodies, and the causes of motion. His work with the telescope, laws of motion, experiment linked to mathematics, and testing by experiment were truly revolutionary, but, large as he looms in the Scientific Revolution, he did not complete the revolution he inaugurated, as he neglected dynamics, both terrestrial and celestial. William Gilbert (1544–1603), as well, may not have created a revolution, but his elaboration of the role of experiment in his *De magnete* (On the Magnet) symbolized and exhibited a revolutionary movement in progress, best seen in the work of Galileo.

Copernicus, Kepler, and Gilbert, therefore, in some measure, inaugurated certain basic features of the Scientific Revolution. We might usefully distinguish between revolutionary discoveries on the one hand and making or constituting a revolution in a science on the other. Newton was unquestionably the creator of a Newtonian revolution in mathematics (together with Leibniz),

mechanics, optics, dynamics, instruments, and methodology. He developed the central concepts in modern (Newtonian) physics of time, space, mass, force, and gravitation. The exalted nature of Newton's *Principia,* often held to have been the high point of the Scientific Revolution, may be seen in a remark by Alexis Clairaut in 1747 that Newton's "famous book of *Mathematical Principles of Natural Philosophy* had been the epoch of a great revolution in the physical sciences."

In the life sciences, Vesalius, while finding contradictions in Galenic anatomy and an innovator in the use of dissection, did not consider himself a revolutionary, nor did his successors. He remained a Galenist in physiology. Paracelsus (ca. 1493–1541) was influential in medicine and chemistry. He challenged the traditional Galenic humoral theory of disease and sought specific substances to cure specific externally caused diseases, which he held were located in specific organs. He also shifted the traditional goals of alchemy to pharmaceutics. He was a revolutionary but not the creator of a revolution.

Harvey, on the other hand, revolutionized physiology by demonstrating the circulation of the blood, a concept absent in traditional Galenic physiology. It led to a profound transformation of physiology not just in his description of the movement of the heart and blood, but also in the transformation of conceptions of the role of the lungs and the nature of digestion. Harvey used dissection in a new way to gain physiological insight— practicing vivisection in his experimentation, utilizing a number of species, and engaging in quantitative and comparative studies. While his work did not revolutionize medical practice, it constituted a biological and physiological revolution.

Was a revolution in method achieved by Francis Bacon (1561–1626) and Descartes? Bacon may have revolutionized the role of method in science (i.e. philosophy), but he did not make a revolution in science. His inductivism was important, as were his emphasis on empiricism, his distinguishing the occult sciences and metaphysics from science, his recognition of knowledge as power and its possibilities for the improvement of life, and his proposal for organized scientific work. Descartes, too, emphasized practical applications as a goal and consequence of proper and effective scientific work. He was truly a revolutionary, thought so, and so did his contemporaries. His clarification of the process of thinking analytically, his emphasis on the mathematical foundations of science, and his important role in the establishment of the mechanical philosophy—the study of nature as essentially the study of matter and motion—were important features of the Scientific Revolution. His version of the principle of inertia is important in the history of mechanics, and his application of the mechanical philosophy to physiology had important consequences in the life sciences. He appears to be truly revolutionary, but his influence on philosophy was not matched by his effect on the sciences.

By the nineteenth century, after the American and French Revolutions, the concept of revolution in science became widespread and general. By the end of that century and in the early twentieth century, a number of scientists and historians (among them Robert A. Millikan, Lord Rutherford, and George Sarton) sought to explain the advance of science by evolution (seen as the cumulative effect of a succession of small increments) rather than revolution. By the turn of the twenty-first century, however, although some sociologists and even historians had challenged the validity of the concept of "*the* Scientific Revolution," the concept of revolution *in* science seemed to be as valid and useful as it has been ever since the advent of modern science in the seventeenth century.

BIBLIOGRAPHY

Cohen, I. Bernard. *The Newtonian Revolution: With Illustrations of the Transformation of Scientific Ideas.* Cambridge: Cambridge University Press, 1980; rev. ed. 1998.

———. *Revolution in Science.* Cambridge: Harvard University Press, 1985.

Hacking, Ian, ed. *Scientific Revolutions.* Oxford: Oxford University Press, 1981.

Kuhn, Thomas S. *The Copernican Revolution: Planetary Astronomy in the Development of Western Thought.* Cambridge: Harvard University Press, 1957; many subsequent printings.

———. *The Essential Tension: Selected Studies in Scientific Tradition and Change.* Chicago: University of Chicago Press, 1977.

———. *The Structure of Scientific Revolutions.* 2nd rev. ed. Chicago: University of Chicago Press, 1970.

I. BERNARD COHEN

See also Scientific Revolution

Rheticus, Georg Joachim (1514–1574)

An astronomer and mathematician and a disciple of Nicolaus Copernicus (1473–1543), Rheticus was born in Feldkirch in Vorarlberg (Austria) to Georg Iserin, the town physician, and Thomasina de Porris. When his father was beheaded for witchcraft in 1528, his patronymic was barred, and Georg Joachim eventually adopted "Rheticus" (after the Roman name for his homeland, Rhaetia). In 1532 he matriculated at the University of Wittenberg, where he became a central element in Philipp Melanchthon's fostering of mathematics and astronomy. He received an M.A. in 1536 and was named to the chair of lower mathematics (i.e., arithmetic and geometry).

He obtained leave in 1538–1539 to visit astronomical centers in Germany. Rumors of Copernicus's revolutionary work compelled Rheticus to obtain additional leave, and he set out for Prussia, arriving in Frauenburg (Frombork, Poland) in May 1539. He immediately became Copernicus's devoted disciple and remained with him for two and a half years. Of astronomers of his generation, Rheticus alone was a fervent advocate of the reality of heliocentrism. In Frauenburg, he composed a précis of Copernican astronomy, the *Narratio prima* (First Account), which was printed in Danzig (Gdansk) in 1540, then again in Basel in 1541. Because of its more elementary and accessible exposition, the *Narratio prima* continued to be valued as an introduction to Copernican astronomy even after the publication of Copernicus's *De revolutionibus* (1543). It was appended to the second edition of *De revolutionibus* (1566) and to Johannes Kepler's (1571–1630) *Mysterium cosmographicum* (1596; 2nd ed., 1621). While in Frauenburg, Rheticus also composed a manuscript on reconciling heliocentrism with Scripture, which was published anonymously in 1651.

Rheticus returned to Wittenberg in September 1541 with permission to publish Copernicus's manuscript, which he took to the printer Johannes Petreius (1497–1559) in Nuremberg the following summer. While seeing *De revolutionibus* through the press, Rheticus accepted a professorship of mathematics at Leipzig and left the job in the hands of Andreas Osiander (1498–1552). Osiander, against Rheticus's wishes, attached an anonymous Preface implying a fictionalist stance toward heliocentrism that was widely adopted.

The remainder of Rheticus's university career was troubled. He taught at Leipzig from 1542 to 1551, including a three-year leave of absence during which he traveled extensively and suffered a mental breakdown. Finally, facing charges of pederasty involving a student, he fled Leipzig in 1551.

He now revived his long-standing interest in Paracelsian medicine (he had memorably met Paracelsus, ca. 1493–1541, in 1532). After studying at the University of Prague, he practiced medicine in Cracow from 1554 until his death in Kassa, Hungary (Košice, Slovakia).

Rheticus's contributions to mathematics were primarily his trigonometric tables. His *Canon doctrinae triangulorum* (Canon of the Doctrine of Triangles, 1551) was the first to give all six trigonometric functions, in this case to seven places at every 10' of arc. During his years in Cracow, he continued working on the monumental tables published posthumously by his disciple Lucius Valentine Otho (ca. 1550–1602) in *Opus Palatinum de triangulis* (1596), a canon of all six trigonometric functions to ten-place accuracy covering every 10" of arc. In addition, Rheticus calculated a sine table for every 10" of arc to fifteen places, which was published by Bartholomaus Pitiscus in 1613 and was not superseded until the twentieth century.

BIBLIOGRAPHY

Burmeister, Karl Heinz. *Georg Joachim Rheticus, 1514–1574: Eine Bio-Bibliographie.* 3 vols. Wiesbaden: Guido Pressler, 1967.

Hooykaas, R. *G. J. Rheticus' Treatise on Holy Scripture and the Motion of the Earth.* (Verhandelingen der Koninklijke Nederlandse Akademie van Wetenschappen, afd. letterkunde, nieuwe reeks, deel 124). Amsterdam: North-Holland, 1984.

Rosen, Edward, ed. and trans. *Three Copernican Treatises: The* Commentariolus *of Copernicus, the* Letter Against Werner, *the* Narratio prima *of Rheticus.* 2nd ed. New York: Dover, 1959.

JAMES R. VOELKEL

See also Copernicus, Nicolaus; Copernicanism; Reinhold, Erasmus

Rhetoric

The term properly denotes persuasive oral and written discourse and an academic discipline. The popular, pejorative connotation of empty bombast, florid language, or crass manipulation has haunted the discipline from the time of the Sophists to the present day. Nevertheless, it was the subject of philosophical study by Plato (428–348 B.C.E.) and Aristotle (384–322 B.C.E.) and became the crowning discipline of Roman education. For both the Greeks and the Romans, the province of rhetoric was the realm of public affairs. As one of the liberal arts, rhetoric, along with grammar and logic, was studied in the *trivium* of the Middle Ages and was a prominent part of the humanities through the nineteenth century in Europe and America. In the mid-twentieth century, the study of rhetoric in the classical sense was revived.

Aristotle defined rhetoric as "the art of finding all the means of persuasion for a particular case." For Cicero (106–43 B.C.E.), it was "the art of persuasion"; for Quintilian (35–96), "the good man speaking well." For some postmodern thinkers, rhetoric includes all communicative discourse, since they believe that all communication is persuasive, cannot escape a subjective bias, and desires to convince others of its point of view. Thus, scientific discourse, in their view, would be rhetorical. Others today see rhetoric more narrowly, as persuasive argumentation in which emotion, authorial character, and wordplay take part. In the period of the Scientific Revolution, rhetoric was generally understood in the narrower sense. The rhetorical works of Aristotle, Isocrates (436–338 B.C.E.), Cicero, and Quintilian were familiar to most scholars of the Renaissance.

Cicero's *De inventione* and the pseudo-Ciceronian text *Rhetorica ad Herennium* provided the usual pattern of study for schools and universities. There the art was divided into five parts: (1) invention, the creation of persuasive arguments; (2) organization, the arrangement of these; (3) style, consideration of appropriate diction, sentences, and figures of speech (tropes and schemes); (4) memory, mnemonic devices; and (5) delivery, voice and gesture for public speaking. During the Renaissance, the last two parts were generally ignored, but invention and style captured the interest of many scholars. Style, treating copious, amplified discourse by means of a great variety of figures of speech, was the subject of many works. Eloquence expressed in classical Latin and, later, in the vernacular was highly esteemed.

In this discussion, rhetoric is treated as it would have been understood in the period of the Scientific Revolution. From the High Middle Ages and well into the Renaissance, rhetoric was treated in conjunction with Aristotle's *Organon,* the tools of reasoning. In that group of texts on logic, induction and deduction and both formal and material aspects of reasoning were imparted. Syllogisms that were perfect in form and matter could yield certain knowledge (*scientia*). This method of proof demanded knowledge of principles or causes in order to arrive at a conclusion that was both formally and materially sound. The proof was termed a *necessary demonstration*. Where certainty could not be attained, probable reasoning came into play. The logic of discovery, directed to finding probable premises, along with probable reasoning itself, was treated in the *Topics*. The title of the work refers to the techniques of invention or lines of argument, termed *topics* (*topoi* in Greek, *loci* in Latin, and commonplaces in English). The work served as a handbook for the practice of debate, formulated in the Middle Ages as disputation. The *Rhetoric* of Aristotle carried the principles of topically based probable reasoning into the realm of public discourse.

Stating that rhetoric is the "counterpart (antistrophos) of dialectic," Aristotle notes in the *Rhetoric* that the two modes of reasoning, induction and deduction, are transformed in rhetoric into the example and the enthymeme. The latter he considered the most powerful instrument of persuasion because it relies on the audience's knowledge of (often hidden) assumptions for its force. In his view, rhetoric shared the topics of discovery, or invention, with dialectic. These techniques he listed in the *Topics* as genus, species or difference, property, and accident. Deciding on genus would determine an entity's general class; species, what makes it different from others in that class; property, its permanent attributes; and accident, what is often but not inextricably associated with it. Under each of these topics, subtopics suggested themselves, for example, comparison, relationship, cause, effect, past and future states. Dialectic, Aristotle thought, could be useful in finding causes or first principles, the first step in arriving at science in the Aristotelian sense. By the time of Cicero, additional topics were added to rhetoric's repertoire, topics usually addressed in considerations of persons and their actions: lineage, education, character, deeds, motives, and occasion.

In an effort to simplify and remove redundancies from the curriculum, Rudolf Agricola (1444–1485) and Peter Ramus (1515–1572) accorded to logic solely the task of invention, leaving to rhetoric only style and delivery. The divorce of invention from rhetoric was to increase the notion that rhetoric was chiefly concerned with style. The influence of these reforms was felt mainly in France and in northern Europe. Desiderius Erasmus (1469–1536) approved Agricola's approach and wrote a very popular work on copious style. Philipp Melanchthon (1497–1560) carried on Agricola's approach in Germany, and, in England and the Puritan Colonies, Ramean concepts of dialectic and rhetoric won many adherents.

In Italy and other areas where the Peripatetic tradition remained strong, rhetoric, as a discipline, was generally compared with dialectic. Both were concerned with investigating opinion on all sides of a question in matters in which certainty or truth was not obvious, either because causes or principles related to the matter in question were unknown or because the matter depended upon contingencies that could not be predicted with certainty. Experts in a field employed dialectic for their own enlightenment, while authors addressed rhetoric to a popular audience. The goals of both differed as well: dialectic's aim was to find what was probably true universally, while rhetoric's was to find "the persuasible" for a particular purpose, as Antonio Riccobono (1541–1599), Paduan professor of rhetoric in Galileo Galilei's (1564–1642) day, expressed it. Dialectical discourse, with its tersely expressed questions and answers, covered disputed topics well, but rhetorical discourse could effect changes in audiences' opinions or move them to action far more readily. But since dialectic's aim was probable truth as opposed to "the persuasible," only dialectic would be appropriate for scientific investigation. Understanding the differences in these three rational processes—demonstration, dialectic, and rhetoric—is critical for understanding what was considered to be proof in scientific discourse during the period of the Scientific Revolution.

Aristotle and Cicero after him described three kinds of rhetorical discourse: judicial, political, and ceremonial. Judicial rhetoric took the form of accusation or defense; political rhetoric considered the beneficial or the harmful; and ceremonial rhetoric offered praise or blame. The tripartite division continued to be taught until the late seventeenth century, when Francis Bacon's (1561–1626) views concerning the arts and sciences began to be taken seriously. Bacon broadened the scope of rhetoric, seeing it as the means by which products of reasoning were referred to the imagination in order to move the will. Rhetoric's office was "to excite the appetite or will." Bacon's views had the effect of associating rhetoric primarily with ornamentation and with its effects on the emotions. In Bacon's view, also, invention in rhetoric was not true invention; that belonged to science. Rhetorical invention was simply the recall of previously stored ideas. The system of the topics in dialectic or rhetoric he thought worthless.

Bacon's views had direct effects upon scientific prose in England. Obviously, ornamentation should have no relevance to science. In the New Science, *verba* (words) should refer to *res* (things) without obfuscation or coloration. Looking to Bacon for its inspiration, the Royal Society, with Thomas Sprat (1635–1713) as its spokesman, eschewed the use of "specious tropes and figures." Sprat called for a reform of scientific discourse that would return its purity and brevity. René Descartes (1596–1650) had also condemned rhetorical artifice and, like Bacon, found dialectical reasoning useless. The art of topical inquiry as a means of discovery in speculative and persuasive reasoning found few advocates by the eighteenth century. Nevertheless, the topics were evidently so familiar to philosophers of the period that they still framed the discussion of subjects in these terms, so much so that one wonders if Aristotle was not right in assuming they are natural mental processes.

Natural philosophers during the beginning of the Scientific Revolution were well trained in the different kinds of argument taught by Aristotle. The topical reasoning of dialectics pervades arguments over the Copernican system, comets, sunspots, mountains on the Moon, and other problems, as various authors explored the genus, properties, accidents, and causes of phenomena. For the most part, they carefully excluded from dialectical and demonstrative arguments the figures of speech and amplification of ideas characteristic of popular prose. For example, Nicolaus Copernicus (1473–1543), familar with the discipline of rhetoric from his studies in Cracow and in Italy, used rhetoric chiefly in the Dedication and Introduction of his *De revolutionibus orbium coelestium* (1543). Since Johannes Kepler (1571–1630) actually taught rhetoric for a time, he was quite aware of its proper use. His writings contain rhetorical passages, but these do not enter into his mathematical demonstrations.

With Galileo, the use of rhetoric in scientific prose reached new heights. He was a consummate master of eloquence who delighted in persuasive as well as scientific argument. Unfortunately, the rhetoric interwoven with the dialectic of the *Dialogue Concerning the Two Chief World Systems* (1638) caused the pope and the examiners ordered to review the work to doubt the sincerity of Galileo's claim that he intended merely a dialectical work and did not desire to persuade readers that Copernicus was right. Soon after Galileo's death, rhetorical artifice in scientific writing fell into disfavor, probably as a result of Baconian and Cartesian notions of rhetoric's proper office.

BIBLIOGRAPHY

Fumaroli, Marc. *L'Age de l'Eloquence*. Geneva: Librairie Droz, 1980.

Jardine, Nicholas. "Demonstration, Dialectic, and Rhetoric in Galileo's Dialogue." In *The Shapes of Knowledge from the Renaissance to the Enlightenment,* ed. D. R. Kelley and R. H. Popkin. Dordrecht: Kluwer, 1991.

Kennedy, George F. *Classical Rhetoric and Its Christian and Secular Tradition from Ancient to Modern Times*. Chapel Hill: University of North Carolina Press, 1980.

Moss, Jean Dietz. *Novelties in the Heavens: Rhetoric and Science in the Copernican Controversy*. Chicago: University of Chicago Press, 1993.

Vickers, Brian. *In Defence of Rhetoric*. Oxford: Clarendon, 1988.

JEAN DIETZ MOSS

See also Demonstration; Dialectic; Discourse, Modes of

Riccioli, Giovanni Battista (Giambattista) (1598–1671)

This prominent Jesuit mathematician and natural philosopher pusued his own interests in such subjects as astronomy and cosmography (roughly, geography) while teaching, during his long academic career at Parma and Bologna, rhetoric, philosophy, and theology. Indeed, his first publication, which went through several editions, was a didactic work on prosody that first appeared in 1640. Riccioli later published extensively on astronomy and on the motion of the earth, his most celebrated work being the *Almagestum novum* (New Almagest, 1651), after Ptolemy's (ca. 100–ca. 170) great work. In geography, his major publication was the *Geographiae et hydrographiae reformatae . . . libri duodecim* (Twelve Books of Reformed Geography and Hydrography, 1661). Both works were speedily followed by second editions, testimony to Riccioli's intellectual stature.

The *Almagestum novum* contains, among many other things, a consideration of the behavior of freely falling bodies, a response to the famous work of Galileo Galilei (1564–1642). A number of other philosophical writers, including several of Riccioli's fellow Jesuits, had already addressed the issue, creating a controversy over Galileo's claim that heavy bodies descend from rest with the speed of fall increasing as the time elapsed. Riccioli presented his own investigations, which had involved dropping weights from the tops of high towers, as confirmation of Galileo's position.

R

The frontispiece of Riccioli's Almagestum novum *(1651) has Urania weighing the Copernican system against Riccioli's geoheliocentric system, with Riccioli's clearly the weightier. Ptolemy looks on approvingly, while his system lies discarded at Urania's feet.*

Riccioli's extensive arguments against the Copernican doctrine of the earth's motion were evidently the product of a determined attempt to provide an intellectually honest foundation for the Catholic Church's official condemnation of Copernicanism following the agitations in its favor by Galileo earlier in the century. As a Catholic priest, Riccioli was bound to oppose belief in the earth's motion, but he did not do so by turning his back on the issue. In the end, he had to conclude that the case for or against the earth's motion was simply not proven—either might be correct, so adherence to the ruling of the Church was at least not in conflict with reason. Apart from such arguments in the *Almagestum novum*, Riccioli also published (1668, in both Italian and Latin versions) what he called a "physico-mathematical argument" against the doctrine of the earth's motion, directed

against the contrary views of the mathematician Stefano degli Angeli (1623–1697) of the University of Padua.

Riccioli's work in the sciences was itself primarily mathematical and focused on the classical mathematical sciences of astronomy and cosmography. These were usually taken to be fundamentally descriptive disciplines (particularly clear in geographical matters), in contrast to natural philosophy, which purported to give causal explanations of phenomena. Riccioli's frequent use of the term *physico-mathematical* betrays his ambitions to be more than merely descriptive, however; he wished to say things about the true physical constitution and workings of the universe. In practice, however, his work concentrated on mathematical issues of measurement, such as the rate of falling bodies, the use of pendulums for timekeeping, the comprehensive cataloging of the positions of the stars, and the exact determination of terrestrial location. He also made qualitative astronomical observations of the appearances of the Moon, the Sun, and the planets and is memorialized in the lunar crater that bears his name.

BIBLIOGRAPHY

Dinis, A. "The Cosmology of G. B. Riccioli (1598–1671)." Ph.D. diss. Cambridge University, 1989.

Grant, Edward. "In Defense of the Earth's Centrality and Immobility: Scholastic Reaction to Copernicanism in the Seventeenth Century." *Transactions of the American Philosophical Society,* n.s., 74 (1984), part 4.

Koyré, Alexandre. "A Documentary History of the Problem of Fall from Kepler to Newton: De motu gravium naturaliter cadentium in hypothesi terrae motae." *Transactions of the American Philosophical Society,* n.s., 45 (1955), part 4.

Sommervogel, Carlos et al., eds. *Bibliothèque de la Compagnie de Jésus.* 11 vols. Brussels: Alphonse Picard, 1890–1932. Repr. *Collège philosophique et théologique,* vol. 6: *Riccioli.* Louvain: Éditions de la Bibliothèque S. J., 1960.

PETER R. DEAR

See also Copernicanism; Galilei, Galileo; Keplerianism

Richer, Jean (1630–1696)

The scientific activities of this French engineer and astronomer essentially date from 1666 to 1673, a period during which he was *élève* (assistant) at the Académie Royale des Sciences in Paris. There are two missions to which he was entrusted—in Acadia (1670) and, above all, at Cayenne (1672–1673)—that gained him celebrity.

R

The first gave him the opportunity to carry out the first astronomical observations on American soil, made with instruments equipped with telescopic sights. His determination of the latitude of the fort at Pentagoûët (today Castine) at Penobscot Bay remained for a long time the most precise observation made in North America (the error was less than a minute).

Besides the discovery of numerous stars in the Southern Hemisphere, the second mission furnished the learned world with two fundamental elements concerning our knowledge of the universe. In the first place, his observations of Mars at perigee (August–November 1672), compared with those made in France by Jean-Dominique Cassini (1625–1712), Jean Picard (1620–1682), and Ole Christensen Römer (1644–1710), carried out at the same time, determined the parallax of that planet to be 25", from which was calculated a figure of 9".5 for the solar parallax (a little larger than its real value of 8".8) and a Sun-earth distance of ca. 25,000 earth-radii. Scientists thereby had available for the first time a valuable estimate of the actual dimensions of the solar system.

In addition, after six months of experiments on a pendulum specially calibrated at Paris before his departure, Richer concluded that the simple pendulum whose arc lasted one second was shorter at Cayenne than at Paris by ca. 2.8 mm and, therefore, that it varied with the latitude. When other observers sent by the Académie to Cape Verde and to the Antilles confirmed the shortening of the pendulum (autumn 1682), thus eliminating doubts concerning the exactitude of Richer's measurements, it had important theoretical consequences: not only did the idea of a universal standard of length founded on the simple pendulum have to be abandoned, but, more important, Christiaan Huygens (1629–1695) and Isaac Newton (1642–1727) demonstrated that terrestrial attraction was stronger at the equator than at the poles and that, therefore, the earth has the shape of an oblate spheroid.

In 1679 at the royal press in Paris, Richer printed the account of his mission under the title *Observations astronomiques et physiques faites en l'isle de Caïenne*. Later, Cassini drew from it the astronomical consequences in his *Élements de l'astronomie vérifiez par Monsieur Cassini par le rapport de ses tables aux observations de M. Richer faite en l'isle de Caïenne . . . ,* printed at the same press in 1684.

BIBLIOGRAPHY

Olmstead, John W. "The Scientific Expedition of John (sic) Richer to Cayenne (1672–1673)." *Isis* 34 (1942–1943), 117–128.

———. "The Voyage of Jean Richer to Acadia in 1670." *Proceedings of the American Philosophical Society* 104 (1960), 612–634.

GUY PICOLET
TRANS. WILBUR APPLEBAUM

See also Académie Royale des Sciences; Cosmic Dimensions; Observatoire de Paris

Roberval, Gilles Personne de (1602–1675)

French mathematician and natural philosopher, most noted for his mathematical work with the theory of indivisibles. Little is known about his early years or his education. He is reported to have undertaken the study of mathematics at the age of fourteen, but he did not take a university degree. Having left home at a relatively early age, he traveled throughout France, evidently earning his living through private lessons. It is also likely that he attended classes at universities in different cities during these journeys.

In 1628 Roberval came to Paris, where he became active in the circle of mathematicians and scientists around Marin Mersenne (1588–1648). He gained a reputation as an able mathematician through these contacts and began an academic career with his appointment as professor of philosophy at the Collège de Maître Gervais in 1632—a position he held until his death. In 1634 he won the triennial competition for the Ramus Chair at the Collège Royal, another position he would hold for the remainder of his life. His connection to the Collège Royal was strengthened in 1655 when he succeeded to the chair of Pierre Gassendi (1592–1655) in mathematics. In 1666 he was a charter member of the Académie Royale des Sciences.

Although he was active in mathematical and scientific research, Roberval published very little. Only his 1636 *Traité de mécanique* and a 1644 edition and commentary on Aristarchus (*Aristarchii Samii de mundi systemate*) appeared in print during his lifetime. A large collection of his writings was issued posthumously in 1693. One likely reason for his reluctance to publish can be found in the fact that the Ramus Chair was awarded on the basis of triennial competition, and his livelihood could be ensured by keeping his methods and discoveries secret.

Roberval's *Traité des indivisibles,* published among the 1693 *Divers ouvrages* by the Académie Royale des Sciences, is his most important single work. In it, he found the areas and arc-lengths of figures and curves by treating continuous geometric quantities as composed of infinite collections of infinitely small parts. Thus, he would consider a curve as an infinite collection of points, or a surface as an infinite collection of lines. Another of his techniques was to consider curves as traced by a "composition of motions" (such as uniform circular motion combined with uniform rectilinear transit). By judicious application of his methods, Roberval investigated a number of important curves (including the cycloid and various forms of the parabola), finding areas, arc-lengths, volumes, tangents, centers of gravity, and other results.

BIBLIOGRAPHY

Auger, Léon. *Un savant méconnu: Gilles Personne de Roberval (1602–1675): Son activité intellectuelle dans les domaines mathématique, physique, mécanique, et philosophique.* Paris: Libraire Scientifique, A. Blanchard, 1962.

Walker, Evelyn. *A Study of the "Traité des Indivisibles" of Gilles Persone de Roberval.* New York: Columbia University Press, 1932.

DOUGLAS M. JESSEPH

See also Académie Royale des Sciences; Collège Royal; Gassendi, Pierre; Infinitesimals; Mersenne, Marin

Rohault, Jacques (1620–1675)

The foremost popularizer and advocate of Cartesian natural philosophy in France during the generation following the death of René Descartes (1596–1650). His *Traité de physique* (1671), a textbook of Cartesian natural philosophy, was widely read and reprinted well into the eighteenth century. He was an active member of the Montmor Academy and other circles of natural-philosophical savants with a reputation as an advocate of experimentally oriented Cartesianism.

In the *Traité de physique,* Rohault tempered any appearance of Cartesian metaphysical dogmatism by posing as an arbiter between the systems of Aristotle (384–322 B.C.E.) and Descartes. He cleverly attached Cartesian corpuscular-mechanical discourse to experimental illustrations and offered Cartesian explanations for various facts and procedures in the practical arts and crafts, about which he displayed impressive exper-

tise. The *Traité* illustrates the shift to experimental legitimation of natural-philosophical claims typical of the mid-seventeenth century.

Rohault held that a corpuscular-mechanical explanatory model is more probable than others, insisting, however, that such hypothetical models be consistent with, and controlled by, unquestioned basic principles of the mechanical philosophy, in its Cartesian form: for example, the doctrines of matter-extension; the three Cartesian elements; the conservation of motion; and the instantaneous, mechanical transmission of light.

The popularity of the *Traité* was due to both the quality of Rohault's text and a remarkable intervention by Samuel Clarke (1675–1729), a protégé of Isaac Newton (1642–1727). In 1697 Clarke published a new Latin translation, adding notes based on Newtonian natural philosophy. In later editions, he expanded the notes, honing their Newtonian edge, so that by 1710 they contained a systematic refutation of Rohault's text. Nevertheless, Rohault's experimental version of Cartesianism, riding above Clarke's notes, remained popular. Rohault's later years were clouded by personal disappointment, through his failure to gain membership in the new Académie Royale des Sciences. He also suffered from the politico-religious backlash against Cartesianism in France in the early 1670s. He tried to mount a counter-attack, in which he argued that only Cartesianism can provide Catholics with a sound interpretation of the Eucharist. It had little impact, and Rohault remained suspect of heresy in some quarters. Nevertheless, Rohault's work significantly shaped the mid-seventeenth-century shift to experimental legitimation of natural philosophy, out of which there ultimately emerged new experimental fields in the course of the next century.

BIBLIOGRAPHY

Clarke, Desmond. *Occult Powers and Hypotheses: Cartesian Natural Philosophy Under Louis XIV.* Oxford: Oxford University Press, 1989.

Hoskin, Michael. "'Mining All Within': Clarke's Notes to Rohault's *Traité de physique.*" *Thomist* 24 (1961), 353–364.

McClaughlin, Trevor. "Was There an Empirical Movement in Mid-Seventeenth Century France? Experiments in Jacques Rohault's *Traité de physique.*" *Revue d'histoire des sciences* 49 (1996), 459–481.

Mouy, Paul. *Le développement de la physique cartésienne, 1646–1712.* Paris: Vrin, 1934. pp. 108–138.

JOHN A. SCHUSTER

See also Cartesianism; Descartes, René; Experience and Experiment

Römer, Ole Christensen (1644–1710)

First demonstrated that light does not cross distances instantaneously and also estimated its speed. Like his countryman Tycho Brahe (1546–1601), Römer was an internationally known astronomer and instrument maker, but he also made other scientific contributions and became a major figure in Danish scientific and governmental circles.

Römer studied mathematics at the University of Copenhagen under Erasmus Bartholin (1625–1698), through whom he came into the task of editing for publication the astronomical observations of Brahe. In 1681 he was named professor of mathematics at the University of Copenhagen. He also became the royal astronomer and director of the observatory, where he devoted many years to observations and the development of new instruments, the establishment of a new Danish observatory, and his studies in thermometry. He also served the realm in a number of advisory roles and became mayor of Copenhagen in 1705.

Römer is best known for his determination of the speed of light. The common opinion of his day, according to both Aristotelian and Cartesian physics, was that light traverses distances instantaneously. However, his work on the motions of the Galilean moons of Jupiter led him to challenge that belief. Establishing accurate tables of the motions of the Jovian moons was a matter of great interest then because, among other reasons, accurate predictions of the eclipses and occultations of the moons could serve as a universal time reference and, therefore, a method for measuring terrestrial longitudes—the foremost navigational problem of the age. Gian Domenico Cassini (1625–1712), who had studied the motions of the Jovian satellites for many years, noted in 1675 a discrepancy between the predicted and the observed motions of the innermost moon (now known as Io). The discrepancy, or inequality, seemed to depend on the distance between Jupiter and Earth. Cassini considered and rejected the hypothesis that the inequality resulted from variations in the time required for light to cover the varying interplanetary distances. Römer, however, took the idea seriously and correctly predicted, in 1676, that Io's eclipse on November 9 of that year would be delayed ten minutes from the calculated time. His correct prediction, along with his explanation that the finite speed of light caused the delay, was published the following year. Römer

Römer making a solar observation. From Peter Horrebow, Basis atronomiae pars mechanica *(1735).*

carried this result further by using then-accepted interplanetary distances to calculate a speed of light—a result that, in order of magnitude, is close to the modern value.

BIBLIOGRAPHY

Balzer, W., and F. R. Wollmerschäuser. "Chains of Measurement in Roemer's Determination of the Velocity of Light." *Erkenntnis* 25 (1986), 323–344.

Cohen, I. Bernard. "Roemer and the First Determination of the Velocity of Light." *Isis* 31 (1940), 327–379.

Meyer, Kirstine. "Ole Römer." In *Prominent Danish Scientists Through the Ages, with Facsimiles from Their Works,* ed. V. Meisen. Copenhagen: Levin and Munksgaard, 1932, pp. 48–52.

Van Helden, Albert. "Roemer's Speed of Light." *Journal for the History of Astronomy* 14 (1983), 137–141.

JAMES M. LATTIS

See also Cosmic Dimensions; Optics; Telescopic Astronomy

Rondelet, Guillaume (1507–1566)

The son of a spice and drug merchant, he studied the liberal arts and Greek in Paris and medicine in his native city, Montpellier. In 1539 he joined the faculty of the Montpellier medical school and—his Protestant sympathies notwithstanding—rose to the position of Regent Professor of Medicine and chancellor.

Rondelet's enthusiasm for the newly revived sciences of botany, zoology, and anatomy marked his entire career. To the detriment of his private medical practice, he performed an autopsy on his dead infant son. On a trip to the Lowlands and Italy in 1549 as personal physician to Cardinal François Tournon, he became particularly interested in whales and fishes and infected the Italian naturalist, Ulisse Aldrovandi (1522–1605), with his passion for ichthyology. Rondelet's major work, *Libri de piscibus marinis in quibus verae piscium effigies expressae sunt* (Books on Marine Fish in Which the True Forms of Fish Are Pictured), was published in Lyon in 1554–1555. Following the model of contemporary illustrated herbals, Rondelet emphasized the identification of marine organisms mentioned in classical texts, but he did not hesitate to challenge the authority of Aristotelian zoology on the basis of his own firsthand observations. Rondelet's correspondents on natural-history matters included Aldrovandi, Conrad Gessner (1516–1565), Luca Ghini (ca. 1490–1556), and Leonhart Fuchs (1501–1566).

Together with Bishop Guillaume Pellicier (himself a Pliny scholar and a frequent companion on Rondelet's botanical expeditions), Rondelet introduced humanist reforms into medical education at Montpellier. His frequent public dissections, botanical demonstrations, and introduction of Dioscorides (fl. 54–68) into the curriculum attracted students from all over Europe to the Montpellier medical school. His lively teaching style was gently satirized by his close friend, François Rabelais, in Book III, Chapter 31, of *Gargantua and Pantagruel*. Rondelet's students included such notable sixteenth-century naturalists as Charles L'Escluse, Matthias de L'Obel, Pierre Pena, Jacques Dalechamps, Jean Bauhin, and Leonhart Rauwolf.

BIBLIOGRAPHY

Joubert, Laurent. "Gulielmi Rondeletii Vita . . . An. Dn. M D. LXVIII." In Joubert, *Operum Latinorum tomus primus. tomus secundus.* Frankfurt: Apud heredes Andreae Wecheli, Claudium Marnium, et Joan. Aubrium, 1599, pp. 186–193.

Reeds, Karen Meier. *Botany in Medieval and Renaissance Universities.* Harvard Dissertations in the History of Science. New York: Garland, 1991.

KAREN MEIER REEDS

Rosicrucianism

The name given to the reformist ideas of a supposed secret society called the Brotherhood of the Rosy Cross, which professed to derive its new philosophy from an itinerant German called Christian Rosencreutz, who was born in 1378 and died at the age of 106 after learning of "Magia and Cabala" from travels in the East and restoring them in accordance with Christianity to make them "agreeable with the harmony of the whole world." It was claimed that Rosencreutz's tomb had been newly discovered in 1604 and provided the occasion for the brotherhood to announce its reformist intentions. First recounted in two manifestos, the *Fama fraternitatis,* published in 1614 but circulating in manuscript from at least 1610, and the *Confessio fraternitatis R. C.* (1615), Rosicrucianism advocated a radical reformation of knowledge. Partly inspired by alchemy and Paracelsian iatrochemistry and partly by the more cryptographic magic of writers like Cornelius Agrippa von Nettesheim (1486–1535) and John Dee (1527–1608), the manifestos hint at a new method of directing and ordering studies according to "sound and sure foundations." The result of applying this new method will be to increase knowledge, to improve the art of medicine, to ease the burden of labor, and to reveal more clearly the "wonderful works of God."

Attracting widespread attention from intellectuals all over Europe, the literature for and against the brotherhood and its aims rapidly proliferated. Among its supporters were the alchemist and utopian writer Johann Valentin Andreae (1586–1654), the mathematician Johann Faulhaber (1580–1635), the leading alchemist Michael Maier (1568–1622), and the mystical philosopher and iatrochemist Robert Fludd (1574–1637). René Descartes (1596–1650) is also known to have been interested in learning more about its proposed intellectual reforms, and it has been suggested that his own turn from mathematical studies to concerns with the correct method for establishing truth was partly inspired by his Rosicrucianism. Similarly, Rosicrucianism has been seen as a significant influence upon the reformist intellectual schemes of Jan Amos Comenius (1592–1670) and Francis Bacon (1561–1626).

Notwithstanding the attention that it attracted from both admirers and some who attacked it, it seems that the Brotherhood of the Rosy Cross never really existed. Certainly, those like Faulhaber and Descartes who hoped to meet with a representative of the brethren never succeeded. The brotherhood seems to have been a fiction developed for allegorical purposes. The most likely author of this fiction is Johann Valentin Andreae, who certainly wrote what has been seen as the third Rosicrucian manifesto, the *Chemical Wedding of Christian Rosencreutz* (1616). In an autobiography written after he had come to reject what Rosicrucianism represented for his contemporaries, Andreae tells us that he wrote a work called *Chemical Wedding* as early as 1604. The published version of his *Chemical Wedding* makes reference to the *Fama* and the *Confessio* and so must be different from the earlier version, but it may well have been closely based upon it. It seems likely, therefore, that the brotherhood supposedly founded by Christian Rosencreutz and described in the *Fama* and the *Confessio* had its beginnings in the youthful writings of Andreae and was developed, if not by Andreae himself, by associates who knew his early work. Within a year of publishing the *Chemical Wedding,* however, Andreae shared the view of opponents of Rosicrucianism that its occultism represented a threat to sound religion.

Strictly speaking, therefore, Rosicrucianism was a very specific and historically rather restricted movement (although it gave its name to other occultist movements from the eighteenth century onward, it has no real continuity with any of them). Frances A. Yates (1972), however, wished to extend the scope of the term, suggesting the use of *Rosicrucian* as "a historical label for a style of thinking." That style of thinking was supposed to combine Hermetic and Kabbalistic perspectives with alchemical interests and enabled Yates to call John Dee a "typically Rosicrucian thinker" and to discern Rosicrucian elements in Francis Bacon and Isaac Newton (1642–1727). It seems fair to say that historians have not accepted this usage.

BIBLIOGRAPHY

Arnold, Paul. *Histoire des Rose-Croix et les origines de la Franc-Maçonnerie.* Paris: Mercure de France, 1955.

Montgomery, John Warwick. *Cross and Crucible: Johann Valentin Andreae (1586–1654), Phoenix of the Theologians.* 2 vols. The Hague: Nijhoff, 1973.

Shea, William R. *The Magic of Numbers and Motion: The Scientific Career of René Descartes.* Canton, MA: Science History Publications, 1991.

Yates, Frances A. *The Rosicrucian Enlightenment.* London and Boston: Routledge and Kegan Paul, 1972.

JOHN HENRY

See also Alchemy; Andreae, Johann Valentin; Fludd, Robert; Hermetism; Iatrochemistry; Kabbalah; Magic; Paracelsus

Rothmann, Christoph (fl. 1555–1597)

R

Counted among the first true adherents of Copernican astronomy, although he came late to the view and recanted in debate with Danish astronomer Tycho Brahe (1546–1601). In 1577 he was appointed *mathematicus* to Wilhelm IV, Landgrave of Hesse (1532–1592), and collaborated with the Landgrave and the noted instrument maker Joost Bürgi (1552–1632) in an ambitious program of astronomical observation at Kassel. Rothmann also prepared several book-length manuscripts. The most important of these are the *Astronomia,* an introduction to astronomy in the Wittenberg manner (accepting some of Copernicus's innovations, but not his Sun-centered system); the *Observationum stellarum fixarum,* which deals in part with the problem of atmospheric refraction; and the *De cometa,* which assigns a celestial position to the comet of 1585. This last provided the impetus for the publication of Brahe's book on comets and the system of the world.

Like his contemporaries Paul Wittich (ca. 1546–1586) and Brahe, Rothmann experimented with different planetary arrangements. Although originally a Wittenberg text, the *Astronomia* contains corrections showing the Sun and the Moon going around a central earth and other planets moving around the Sun. Only Brahe seems to have recognized that any such arrangement with astronomically correct distances required that the orbs for the Sun and Mars intersect, a physical impossibility. When a bright comet appeared in 1585, Rothmann rapidly composed the *De cometa,* containing his observations, and sent a copy to Brahe in May 1586. In Rothmann's book, Brahe found a preliminary endorsement of Copernicanism and, more important, arguments that the substance of the heavens was a continuous fluid through which the planets moved freely. This showed Brahe how to avoid the intersection problem: celestial spheres defined as regions in such a substance would pose no difficulty. In subsequent letters, Rothmann supported Nicolaus Copernicus (1473–1543), while Brahe defended his own system. Against this background, Brahe published the book announcing his new system in 1588 and the correspondence with Rothmann in 1596.

Rothmann finally rejected Copernicanism, although Brahe's story that he persuaded Rothmann to abandon Copernicus while Rothmann was visiting him in the summer of 1589 is doubtful. The modifications to the *Astronomia,* preserved at Kassel, show that Rothmann seriously entertained a Tychonic planetary arrangement even before visiting Brahe. Pleading illness, Rothmann never returned to Kassel but went back to his native Bernburg, although he survived until at least 1597. A successor at Kassel, Willebrord Snel (1580–1626), published Rothmann's stellar observations in 1618 and his book on comets in 1619.

BIBLIOGRAPHY

Goldstein, B. R., and P. Barker. "The Role of Rothmann in the Dissolution of the Celestial Spheres." *British Journal for the History of Science* 28 (1995), 385–403.

Granada, M. A. "Il problema astronomico-cosmologico e le sacre scritture dopo Copernico: Christoph Rothmann e la 'teoria dell'accomodazione.'" *Revista di storia della filosofia* 51 (1966), 789–828.

Moran, B. T. "Christoph Rothmann, the Copernican Theory, and Institutional and Technical Influences on the Criticism of Aristotelian Cosmology." *Sixteenth Century Journal* 13 (1982), 85–103.

PETER BARKER

See also Celestial Spheres; Geoheliocentrism; Reinhold, Erasmus; Wittich, Paul

Royal Academy of Sciences.

See Académie Royale des Sciences

Royal Observatory at Greenwich

Founded to produce aids for navigators in an age of maritime expansion, the Royal Observatory, built in 1676, in its early decades was the only institution in England undertaking a systematic observational program for the improvement of positional astronomy. Its location within the institutional framework of the Ordnance Office created an unprecedented opportunity for continuity in technical and methodological development; the precise course taken depended on the individual aims and characters of its successive directors. The title of Astronomer Royal came to be formally attached to their post in the course of the eighteenth century; the initial use of a variety of descriptions reflects contemporary uncertainty about the nature and scope of their official duties. John Flamsteed (1646–1719), the first of them, retained the post until his death; he was succeeded by a younger rival, Edmond Halley (ca. 1656–1742). Despite continuing controversy, activities at Greenwich provided an influential model for later observatories across Europe, especially with the eventual dominance of meridian-transit techniques.

According to Flamsteed, the building of an observatory in Greenwich Park was first proposed during the reign of Charles I. In that of his son, Charles II, several factors favored the revival of the idea: on the one hand, it was believed that astronomers might soon solve the problem of finding longitude at sea, which appeared increasingly acute as overseas trade grew; on the other, national prestige demanded that the English should keep up with the French, who built their palatial Observatoire de Paris between 1667 and 1671, and even with the Scots, who briefly gained an observatory at St. Andrews in the mid-1670s. The additional impetus that brought the idea to fruition came from Sir Jonas Moore (1617–1679), the surveyor general of the royal ordnance, who had had some experience of astronomy in the course of his career as a mathematical practitioner, teacher, surveyor, and cartographer. In September 1674 he negotiated with the Royal Society for the use of their Chelsea College site, but this proved impractical; in October he announced that he would try "moveing his Majesty for a yearly Annuity" for Flamsteed and set about persuading others to back the scheme.

An opportunity to bring the matter to a conclusion arose in February 1675, when "the Sieur de St. Pierre" (an unidentified associate of Charles II's mistress) proposed an astronomical-longitude method and had it examined by a committee established to review the magnetical theories of Henry Bond (ca. 1600–1678). The committee, through Moore, recruited Flamsteed as a consultant; he succeeded in discomfiting the claimant, arguing that existing star catalogs and lunar tables were inadequate to sustain the proposed method. The committee members and other allies used this incident to persuade Charles II to approve the idea of founding an observatory to remedy these deficiencies.

Flamsteed was appointed "observator" on March 4, 1675, at an annual salary of one hundred pounds, paid by the Ordnance Office. A decision was also made about a site for the intended Royal Observatory, although the warrant for its construction was not signed until the following June; Greenwich is said to have been chosen by Sir Christopher Wren (1632–1723). Wren was also nominally responsible for the design; it is probable, however, that he, Moore, and Robert Hooke (1635–1703) all had a

R

An observing room ca. 1675. From John Flamsteed, Historia caelestis Britannica *(1725).*

hand in the matter. Hooke drew up the plans and helped supervise construction. The Ordnance Office funded the enterprise with an eye to economy, supplying second-hand bricks and lead; the foundations of an earlier building on Greenwich Hill were reused, with the result that none of the new walls was aligned with the meridian. Expenditure was about twenty pounds in excess of the planned five hundred pounds by the time work was completed in the summer of 1676.

It was around this time that views of the observatory's buildings and equipment were engraved by Francis Place after drawings by an Ordnance sketcher, Robert Thacker. These show several large instruments of innovative design, all provided through Moore's generosity: a sextant nearly seven feet in radius, with telescopic sights; two great clocks made by Thomas Tompion (1639–1713); a controversial ten-foot mural quadrant designed by Hooke; and a "well-telescope" with a long-focus lens. The last two of these proved failures, and it was only in the late 1680s that a successful substitute mural arc was

built, at Flamsteed's own expense. On his death, the instruments were removed, as his private property; Halley obtained a government grant to reequip the observatory to an even higher standard.

Flamsteed applied this equipment to the study of a wide variety of celestial phenomena and caused frustration among contemporaries by taking decades to publish a new star catalog. Even in the observatory's earliest years, the Royal Society put pressure on Flamsteed to produce results; he later experienced similar demands from Isaac Newton (1642–1727), who needed Greenwich observations for work on his *Principia mathematica philosophiae naturalis* (1687). In 1710, during Newton's presidency, the Royal Society obtained the right to provide visitors to supervise the observatory, though in practice their attempted interventions proved ineffective. These recurring disputes over the observatory's role and conduct have made its early records (now at Cambridge University Library) of special interest to modern historians of science.

BIBLIOGRAPHY

Chapman, Allan, ed. *The Preface to John Flamsteed's Historia coelestis Britannica, or British Catalogue of the Heavens (1725).* Greenwich: National Maritime Museum, 1982.

Forbes, Eric. *Origins and Early History, 1675–1875.* In *Greenwich Observatory,* 3 vols. London: Taylor and Francis, 1975, vol. 1.

Howse, Derek. *Buildings and Instruments.* In *Greenwich Observatory,* 3 vols. London: Taylor and Francis, 1975, vol. 3.

Willmoth, Frances. *Sir Jonas Moore: Practical Mathematics and Restoration Science.* Woodbridge: Boydell, 1993, ch. 5.

———, ed. *"Flamsteed's Stars": New Perspectives on the Life and Work of the First Astronomer Royal.* Woodbridge: Boydell, 1997.

FRANCES WILLMOTH

See also Flamsteed, John; Halley, Edmond; Telescopic Astronomy

Royal Society of London

Founded informally on November 28, 1660, and formally in 1662, the Royal Society differed from the academies and societies that preceded it in being a democratic but well-run group of men, meeting usually at Gresham College, dedicated to promoting the new experimental natural philosophy (not yet properly science). From Charles II it later received the formal name Royal Society of London for Improving Natural Knowledge, and an official charter drawn up by the members, which granted useful privileges and a ceremonial mace.

The origins of the society, much discussed by historians, go back to ca. 1645, when, as John Wallis (1616–1703) later recalled, a group of "persons inquisitive into natural philosophy . . . and particularly of what hath been called the *New Philosophy* or *Experimental Philosophy*" met at Gresham College to discuss the latest discoveries of the age like the Copernican system, the circulation of the blood, and pneumatics (i.e., the key discoveries of the earlier Scientific Revolution). The members of this group were physicians, clergymen, future academics, instrument makers, civil servants, and gentlemen, all much influenced by Baconianism, including the practical applications of science, but also dedicated to mathematical and theoretical learning. This group continued to meet until 1658, when the death of Oliver Cromwell produced much civil unrest. Meanwhile, several members, including John Wilkins (1614–1672) and John Wallis, moved to Oxford, where they continued to meet, to be joined by Seth Ward (1617–

1689), Thomas Willis (1621–1675), William Petty (1623–1687) and, later, Robert Boyle (1627–1691), Christopher Wren (1632–1723), Robert Hooke (1635–1703), and Richard Lower (1631–1691), among others. Contrary to what has often been said, neither what Boyle would call the "Invisible College" nor the group associated with Samuel Hartlib (ca. 1600–1662) had any direct connection or influence upon the proto-Royal Society. After the restoration of Charles II in 1660, the London and Oxford groups joined together with the addition of Royalists returning from exile. They decided to organize a larger and more formal society, to meet weekly with a presiding officer (Wilkins was the first of several), a treasurer to collect dues of two shillings weekly (William Balle, d. 1690, a landowner and astronomer), and a registrar to record what was done at meetings (William Croone, 1633–1684, physician, Gresham Professor of Rhetoric). The Royal Society really dates from the 1660 meeting, although conventionally either from the Charter of July 11, 1662, or the Second Charter of 1663, that of 1669 being less significant.

The first two charters set out the formal organization, named the first officers and council (the governing body), set out rules for their subsequent election yearly on each November 30 and granted certain privileges. There was to be a president (William Brouncker, 1620–1684, held the post until 1677), a treasurer (Balle was soon replaced by others), and two secretaries (Wilkins, soon replaced, and Henry Oldenburg, ca. 1619–1677, until his death). The twenty members of the council were also named in 1663. All members of the society were now called Fellows (F.R.S.); those named in the Second Charter, Original Fellows. Elections of new Fellows were to be by vote of those present at the meeting where they were proposed. The most important privileges were the right to pass statutes relating to the conduct of the society, its officers, and employees (an amanuensis, or clerk, to copy minutes and letters into bound books as ordered by the secretaries and an operator to assist with experiments, both in their performance and in providing equipment); the right to conduct correspondence with foreigners "on Philosophical, Mathematical or Mechanical subjects"; and the right to appoint printers and to license what they printed. These privileges were to be important in spreading the ideals of the Scientific Revolution, both at home and abroad, an activity increased after Oldenburg initiated the *Philosophical Transactions of the Royal Society.* The treasurer was usually a vice

R

president, of whom several were to be appointed by the president to preside when he was absent; he was also responsible for finances. The secretaries were charged with keeping the minutes, attending all council and ordinary meetings, seeing to entering the minutes into the *Journal Books,* papers read at meetings into the *Register Book,* and letters read into the *Letter Books* with some drafts of replies. Until his death in 1677, Oldenburg saw to all of this, after which the two secretaries shared these duties, until in 1686 they found them so onerous that an assistant secretary (at first called the clerk) was appointed—Edmond Halley (ca. 1656–1742), to be followed by others.

After 1662, as before, the Royal Society served as a showcase for the Scientific Revolution. Now, as in 1645, the members discussed the newest discoveries in natural philosophy and filled the meetings with experiment and discussion. Experiments were "brought in"—either performed or described—supplemented after November 1662 with the work of a curator of experiments (Hooke until 1677), the first salaried officer (no secretary was paid until 1668). The curator was to produce one or more experiments to be shown at each meeting. They might range from the simple, like the repetition of Boyle's air-pump experiments, to new pneumatic experiments, to such complex and difficult experiments as those on blood transfusion. Those present discussed the methods and the results and suggested modifications and extensions. Letters from Fellows and outsiders, usually addressed to the secretary, were read, and these might suggest new experiments. Fellows prepared and read papers on every possible subject. Initially, there were many "histories of trades," as advised by Francis Bacon (1561–1626), accounts of practice in crafts and manufacture. In 1674, when activity languished, Fellows were asked to commit themselves to reading prepared papers at meetings; these usually contained accounts of experiments performed by them rather than involving the showing of experiments, although they might suggest experiments for later performance. So Isaac Newton's (1642–1727) optical papers, written in the form of letters to Oldenburg, provoked Fellows to ask Hooke to repeat key experiments. Similarly, Antoni van Leeuwenhoek's (1632–1723) microscopical experiments were repeated, in accord with the society's motto, *Nullius in verba* (On No One's Word). When Newton was president (1703–1727), he had his curators of experiment, Francis Hauksbee (ca. 1666–1713) and J. T. Desaguliers (1683–1700),

Coat of arms of the Royal Society with its motto Nullius in verba *("On the word of no one"), which expresses the society's insistence on verification by observation or experiment, rather than by the voice of authority or tradition. From Robert Hooke,* Micrographia *(1665).*

repeat his earlier experiments and try new ones for inclusion in his *Opticks* (1704).

This was the serious work of the society and that of a limited number of its Fellows. Many of these were professional men still, all gentlemen, since a university degree conferred that status, although there were also serious practitioners of science with no professional connections, like Johannes Hevelius (1611–1687). There were also courtiers, country clergymen, and landowners who contributed on limited subjects most often on natural history. There were even men of humble birth, such as John Ray (1627–1705), John Flamsteed (1646–1719), and Leeuwenhoek, all welcomed and elected F.R.S. on their merits. Beyond this, there were those who dabbled in science, often knowledgeable in one branch, but often, too, merely interested—like Samuel Pepys (1633–1703) of the Naval Board, who loved seeing or reading about experiments although he could not understand them; he was later to become president. All of these called themselves *virtuosi* (lovers of learning), a term whose meaning degenerated with the years to mean little more than a pretender to knowledge.

From its earliest days, the society was a focus of scientific activity in Britain. Men working the provinces, like Henry Power (1623–1668), a physician who performed original work in microscopy and magnetism and, with Richard Towneley (1629–1707), in pneumatics, sent accounts of their work to the society, were encouraged to publish, and often were made Fellows. Those interested in diffuse natural history of a simple Baconian kind were welcomed but never elected. But promising young men, like Flamsteed, Martin Lister (1639–1712), and Nehemiah Grew (1641–1712), were encouraged to persevere and became notable Fellows. The most important instrument for contact and encouragement was correspondence, undertaken before 1677 by Oldenburg and other Fellows, after that by both secretaries. Correspondence kept established Fellows like Boyle and Wallis aware of what was happening in London when they were absent, and it introduced others, like Newton, to the society and its work. So, too, with foreign scientists: Christiaan Huygens (1629–1695) was already famous when he became a Fellow in 1663 on a visit to London; Hevelius, a persistent correspondent from 1663 onward, sent astronomical data and copies of his books in return for English astronomical observations; René-François de Sluse (1622–1685) sent his mathematical discoveries and was the first foreigner to learn of Newton's; all of the major Parisian scientists, including Adrien Auzout (1622–1691), Jean-Dominique Cassini (1625–1712), Jean Picard (1620–1682), and Ismaël Boulliau (1605–1694), kept in touch through Oldenburg, as did Italian scientists, notably Marcello Malpighi (1628–1694) and, later, Antonio Vallisneri (1661–1730). German medical men sent news; the young Gottfried Wilhelm Leibniz (1646–1716) was encouraged by a patron who knew Oldenburg to send his early work on physics to the society, to which he dedicated it—but the society did not care for it, calling it too little grounded in experiment, although Leibniz was encouraged, and the mathematical work he developed later formed the basis of his interchange, again through Oldenburg, with Newton. This foreign exchange was to continue, increased if anything in the early eighteenth century, when many foreigners were attracted by Newton's eminence after a decade of the society's relative decline. Much of this correspondence (except for the mathematics) was published in the *Philosophical Transactions,* whose existence as published by officials of the society was a decided stimulus to the ideals of the Scientific Revolution. It should be noted that when foreigners attempted to interest the society in work in theology, or pedagogy, or universal learning, they were firmly rebuffed and told that that was not the business of the Royal Society. Nor was the society eager to promote mystical subjects, although the dividing line between chemistry and alchemy was still ambiguous.

The Royal Society was quickly welcomed by the scientific world, and the value of its scientific leadership quickly recognized. Even before Newton's emergence, the reputation of men like Boyle, Wallis, and Brouncker ensured its importance, while its espousal of experimental science gave it preeminence among scientists, even if Cartesians often doubted the conclusions drawn from experiments, as was to occur with those of Boyle and Newton. True, the work done by these individual Fellows in their own workrooms was more important than anything done at meetings; however, the latter provided a forum for presentation and clarification and the discussion stimulated new ideas. Foreigners were impressed by the polite, peaceable, and orderly atmosphere of the meetings, which promoted ease of communication. Individuals working alone added to the reputation of the society as members of it.

Still, the Royal Society was not without its critics. Some feared that the exclusion of religion from its domain must foster atheism, especially since there was no religious qualification for membership. Many feared that the society might infringe upon the privileges and domains of established bodies like the College of Physicians and the universities. The doubts and criticisms were so strong that in 1663 it was decided that the society should publish a work explaining and defending its activities, making it plain that it posed no threat to religion or to any established body, and giving a clear account of its origins, with some specimens of what its Fellows had done. Wilkins was to supervise the author, Thomas Sprat (1635–1713); the work finally appeared only in 1667, delayed by plague, The Great Fire of London, and the Anglo-Dutch War, under the title *History of the Royal Society*. It was not totally effective; in 1669 the society was caustically attacked from the pulpit by the Oxford University orator, while the next year Henry Stubbe (1632–1676), Oxford graduate and country physician, wrote at the request of a member of the College of Physicians the first of a series of works attacking the society on the grounds of religion, ignorance, and the pursuit of trivial knowledge. The society was then defended at all points by Joseph Glanvill (1636–1680), but such attacks continued. In the early 1660s, in *Hudibras,* Samuel Butler (1612–1680) had laughed at astrologers, and now he satirized the virtuosi as pretentious and impractical with their microscopes, telescopes, and air pumps. The most famous attack was the play *The Virtuoso* (1676) by Thomas Shadwell (d. 1692), portraying the leading character as totally impractical and ridiculous. That such satires were popular shows, if oddly, what an impact the Royal Society had on public life.

On the whole, the society was admired and respected by the learned world, which recognized its merits and its aims. Although experiments performed at its meetings, like "only weighing air," might make the king laugh, the work of its Fellows to which the society extended approval was not trivial. Just as it had welcomed Newton's optical papers, so it did Newton's work in mechanics. His *Principia mathematica philosophiae naturalis* (Mathematical Principles of Natural Philosophy), published by Halley in 1687, was licensed by Pepys as president, so appearing, rightly, under the society's aegis. When Newton became president sixteen years later, it was hard to say whether he brought fame to the society or the society conferred honor upon him. Under Newton, the meetings of the Society were once again as lively as they had been in the 1660s.

There has never been any doubt that the Royal Society was then, as it was to remain, an exemplar of the science of the times and one of the leading scientific societies of the world. In the later seventeenth century, as earlier, it consciously and eagerly promoted the ideals of the Scientific Revolution, to which its members contributed, by having experiments performed at its meetings and discussing their significance, by encouraging its members to write papers containing experimental work where appropriate, by recognizing original work wherever it was performed, and by publicizing such work as widely as possible.

BIBLIOGRAPHY

Hall, Marie Boas. *Promoting Experimental Learning.* Cambridge: Cambridge University Press, 1991.

Hunter, Michael. *Establishing the New Science.* Woodbridge: Boydell, 1989.

Lyons, Henry. *The Royal Society, 1660–1942.* Cambridge: Cambridge University Press, 1944.

Moore, Keith, and Mary Sampson. *A Guide to the Archives and Manuscripts of the Royal Society.* London: Royal Society, 1995.

Notes and Records of the Royal Society. 1– (1938–), passim.

MARIE BOAS HALL

See also Académie Royale des Sciences; Correspondence Networks; Gresham College; Oldenburg, Henry; Oxford Philosophical Society; *Philosophical Transactions;* Virtuosi

S

Scaliger, Julius Caesar (1484-1558)

Physician, botanist and, natural philosopher, he changed his original family name—Bordonius—and invented his early biography and his genealogy to present himself as a descendant of the famous Della Scala family, whence the Scaliger. Details of his education are obscure because of the conflicting biographies, but he probably obtained a doctorate of arts at the University of Padua, where he studied under Marc Antonio Zimara, Agustino Nifo, and Pietro Pompanazzi, then later pursued a doctorate in medicine. In 1525 he went to Agen, France, as physician to the bishop there; he vigorously embraced humanism and in 1528 became a French citizen. An expert on Cicero (106–43 B.C.E.), he attacked Erasmus for a satire he wrote on Ciceronian stylists (1531) and wrote a treatise on Latin in which he similarly criticized Lorenzo Valla. He also composed a commentary on Aristotle's (384–322 B.C.E.) *Poetics* (1561) and translated into Latin the pseudo-Aristotelian *De plantis* (1556), Theophrastus's (ca. 371–ca. 287 B.C.E.) six-book *De causis plantarum* (1556), and Aristotle's history of animals (1619), along with several other treatises on botany.

Disputatious by nature, Scaliger is best known for his lengthy critique of the *De subtilitate* of Girolamo Cardano (1501–1576), the more-than-twelve-hundred-page *Exotericarum exercitationum liber XV* (i.e., Book XV of his own *External or Philosophical Exercises,* the first fourteen of which were never published). This is a kind of encyclopedia that treats all types of physical, philosophical, chemical, geographical, technical, and medical problems promiscuously. The work shows Scaliger to be an eclectic Averroist Aristotelian who proposed his thought

as based on observation and experience, not on the systems of the schools. In botany, he was interested in plant classification based on actual specimens, and in medicine he was sought out as a gifted teacher. In dynamics, he offered experimental proof that the medium is not a mover in projectile motion, attributing the motion to impetus. He also saw increasing impetus in a falling body as the cause of its acceleration. Perhaps his most significant contribution was his view of chemical combination as "the motion of [natural] *minima* toward mutual contact so that union is effected," seeing this process to result in a continuous body that itself forms a unit.

BIBLIOGRAPHY

Richards, J. F. C. "The Elysium of Julius Caesar Bordonius (Scaliger)." *Studies in the Renaissance* 9 (1962), 195–217.

Taton, René, ed. *The Beginnings of Modern Science, from 1450 to 1800*. Trans. A. J. Pomerans. New York: Basic Books, 1964.

Van Melsen, Andrew G. *From Atomos to Atom: The History of the Concept of Atom*. Pittsburgh: Duquesne University Press, 1952. Repr. New York: Harper Torchbooks, 1960.

WILLIAM A. WALLACE

See also Aristotelianism; Cardano, Girolamo; Humanism; Impetus

Scheiner, Christoph (1573-1650)

Born in Wald, near Mindelheim in Swabia (southwest Germany), he attended the Jesuit school in Augsburg, continued his studies in the Jesuit college at Landsberg, and entered the Jesuit order in 1595. In 1600 he matriculated at the University of Ingolstadt; in 1610 he joined the faculty of the Jesuit college of the university as professor of mathematics and Hebrew.

Scheiner's talents lay in the mathematical sciences and instruments. Early in his career he became an expert on the mathematics of sundials and also invented a pantograph, a device for copying and enlarging drawings. Upon hearing about Galileo Galilei's (1564–1642) discoveries with the telescope in 1610, Scheiner immediately set out to obtain good telescopes with which to scrutinize the heavens. He first got a glimpse of sunspots in the spring of 1611 and began a study of them in October of that year. His tract *Tres epistolae de maculis solaribus* (Three Letters on Sunspots) appeared in Augsburg early in 1612, under the pseudonym Apelles latens post tabulam. It was the start of a controversy with Galileo over the nature of sunspots.

After reading Galileo's first letter on sunspots, Scheiner published three more pseudonymous letters. His argument in both tracts was that sunspots are caused by dark satellites of the Sun, while Galileo argued that the spots are on the Sun or in its atmosphere and that the Sun is, therefore, subject to change and corruption. Galileo's three letters appeared in 1613 in Rome under the title *Istoria e dimostrazioni intorno alle macchie solari e loro accidenti*. A third of the copies contained reprints of Scheiner's two tracts. Although he was polite to Scheiner, Galileo refuted his arguments, and there was little doubt as to who was the winner of this dispute.

Scheiner went on to publish books on atmospheric refraction and the optics of the eye, and in these works he built on the optical achievements of Johannes Kepler (1571–1630), thus providing important material for later writers on the subject. He also continued his research on sunspots, devising the first equatorially mounted telescope for this research.

In 1624 Scheiner went to Rome, where he stayed for the next eight years. There he published his greatest work, *Rosa ursina* (1630), the standard work on sunspots for more than a century. The attack on Galileo with which Scheiner opens *Rosa ursina* does not take away from its importance. Scheiner agreed with Galileo that sunspots are on the Sun's surface or in its atmosphere, that they are often generated and perish there, and that the Sun is, therefore, not perfect. He further advocated a fluid heavens (against the Aristotelian solid spheres), and he pioneered new ways of representing the motions of spots across the Sun's face.

BIBLIOGRAPHY

Drake, Stillman. "Sunspots, Sizzi, and Scheiner." In *Galileo Studies: Personality, Tradition, and Revolution,* ed. Stillman Drake. Ann Arbor: University of Michigan Press, 1970, pp. 177–199.

McColley, Grant. "Christoph Scheiner and the Decline of Neo-Aristotelianism." *Isis* 32 (1940), 63–69.

Shea, William R.. "Scheiner and the Interpretation of Sunspots." *Isis* 61 (1970), 498–519.

Von Braunmühl, Anton. *Christoph Scheiner als Mathematiker, Physiker, und Astronom.* Bamberg: Buchner, 1891.

ALBERT VAN HELDEN

See also Galilei, Galileo; Telescope; Telescopic Astronomy

Scholasticism. See Aristotelianism

Schooten, Frans van (ca. 1615–1660)

Left a mark in seventeenth-century mathematics through his teaching and his editorial work. He studied at the University of Leiden, in which town his father, Frans van Schooten the Elder, was teaching at the engineering school. He was much impressed by René Descartes (1596–1650), whom he met at Leiden, and by his 1637 *Géométrie*. In the early 1640s, he visited England and Paris, where he was introduced to Marin Mersenne's (1588–1648) circle and read manuscripts of François Viète (1540–1603) and Pierre de Fermat (1601–1665), copies of which he took back to Leiden. He could not find a publisher for Fermat's papers, but in 1646 he issued the first collected edition of Viète's works, the main vehicle through which they were studied in the second half of the century. In 1645 he took up his father's teaching position, but by then he already had been privately tutoring several gifted young pupils, including Jan de Witt (1625–1672) and Christiaan Huygens (1629–1695). Through them he ensured an audience for Cartesian mathematics. In 1649 he published his Latin translation of Descartes's *Géométrie,* which he expanded with lucid commentary. In 1657 he published *Exercitationes mathematicae* and in 1659–1661 a new, enlarged, Latin edition of Descartes's *Géométrie,* which became a key seventeenth-century mathematical book. Van Schooten complemented Descartes's text by his own introductory lectures, a fuller commentary, and substantial contributions by his students. His own mathematical contributions were competent but of limited significance. Among them were the novel geometrical problems that he solved by third-degree equations, including some that led to the case in which Girolamo Cardano's (1501–1576) rules yield no real solution. Mostly inspired by Apollonian propositions, his kinematic constructions of conic sections use instruments similar to the ones that appear in Descartes's *Géométrie*. Van Schoten presented algebra as a powerful tool and the proper language of mathematics—and its power was pointedly illustrated by the work of his pupils, particularly Jan Hudde's (1628–1704) method of *maxima* and *minima* and Hendrik van Heuraet's (1633–ca. 1660) rectification of an algebraic curve.

BIBLIOGRAPHY

Hoffman, J. E. *Frans van Schooten der Jüngere.* Wiesbaden: Steiner Verlag, 1962.

ANTONI MALET

See also Analytic Geometry; Descartes, René; Mathematics

Scientific Revolution

The broad notion that, in course of the sixteenth and seventeenth centuries, thought about nature underwent a more than usually significant change has been with us for almost as long as the change itself. A budding historical conceptualization of the change is to be found in Enlightenment ideas about science and its history and in several currents of nineteenth-century philosophy. A genuinely historical debate over the nature and the causes of the change wrought in, and by, sixteenth-seventeenth-century science, however, started in the first decades of the twentieth century, with the concept of "the Scientific Revolution" itself being coined in 1939. Points of historical debate to come up from the second decade of the twentieth century onward include the scope of the concept in terms of time span and of coverage of scientific disciplines; connections with the notion of "scientific revolutions" in general; continuity and discontinuity; diverse ways to put the past of science in context; how to explain the Scientific Revolution (or portions thereof); how the event fits into European history at large and how it compares with science at other times and in other civilizations; who the protagonists were in terms of individuals, of currents of thought, and of institutions; how mathematics, the mechanical philosophy, unaided observation, experiments, and scientific instruments were connected to one another and what specific role each played in the event; how abstract thought and manual operations were related; how scientists sought to gain credence and legitimacy; in what ways to assign fitting niches for minor contributors and for "losers." There are hosts of other issues, not least of which are growing doubts over whether it might not be better to abandon the notion of "the Scientific Revolution" altogether.

A useful guideline amidst all of this complexity may be gained from looking at the historiography of the Scientific Revolution in terms of successive stages of historization. While it would be misleading to consider present-day states of historical consciousness as the pinnacle toward which all previous eras more or less vainly strove, we may nonetheless maintain that, as in history at large, so in history of science, some growing refinement in modes of understanding of the past has taken place.

Seventeenth-century authors felt the developments in science that went on all around them to be part and parcel of the "quarrel of the ancients and the moderns." Against the idea that ancient Greece and Rome had achieved more than any modern artist or writer or thinker could ever hope to emulate, let alone surpass, recent accomplishments in science were invoked with some frequency to help sustain arguments to the contrary. Whereas this did not lead to significant efforts in historiography, a form of historical consciousness during the Enlightenment did. Authors clustered around the *Encyclopédie* recognized in seventeenth-century science a revolt against previously reigning forces of darkness—a revolt of which they felt themselves to be partisans no less than historians. Besides such rather broadly drawn historical treatments as appeared in the *Encyclopédie* (with René Descartes, 1596–1650, and Francis Bacon, 1561–1626, being pinpointed as the most outstanding heralds of a new way of doing science), several monographs detailing successive events in one or another of the mathematical sciences appeared as well. Here J. É. Montucla's four-volume *Histoire des mathématiques* (1799–1802), in which seventeenth-century mathematical science figured prominently, formed the culmination point for a long time to come.

Starting with some trenchant remarks by Immanuel Kant (1724–1804) in 1787, for 130 years the conceptualization of a drastic, sixteenth-seventeenth-century change in science that did take place was primarily philosophical in nature. William Whewell (1794–1866) recognized the period to have witnessed a particularly dense clustering of those revolutions in science that held his abiding interest as a philosopher of science. Auguste Comte (1798–1857), the founder of positivism, hailed the period as one in which, after the theological and the metaphysical stages human thought unfortunately had to pass through, the third and final stage of positively established science had finally been ushered in. Much more than Whewell's quite refined historical sensibility, the latter conception of the path of science as a triumphal march toward present-day, securely laid knowledge of nature's laws, has fitted in comfortably with how the past of science looks to a modern scientist engaged in looking back. The tendency of history writing in such a mode to yield a much distorted image of the past—as if it were good for nothing but the preparation of our own excellence—comes strikingly to the fore in one of its most influential exemplars, a book by Ernst Mach, *Die Mechanik* (The Science of Mechanics, 1883). Here Galileo Galilei (1564–1642) was portrayed as a Mach-like scientist engaged in the single-handed creation of modern mechanics by replacing Aristotle's (384–322 B.C.E.) rash rationalizations with an unprejudiced recognition of the bare, empirical facts of nature.

It was against such an almost unalleviated conception of the birth of modern mechanics as one sudden, early-seventeenth-century break in the history of science that Pierre Duhem, a French physicist and philosopher of science, in 1913 declared the emergence of modern science to have been a gradual process, the decisive turn toward which he assigned not to Galileo in the early seventeenth century but to a range of Parisian Scholastic thinkers of the fourteenth century. He came to this view upon his discovery of a huge collection of hitherto neglected manuscripts and early printed books by such authors as Jean Buridan (ca. 1295–ca. 1358), Nicole d'Oresme (ca. 1320–1382), and other (in Duhem's original view) precursors of Leonardo da Vinci (1452–1519) (in his slightly later view: of Nicolaus Copernicus, 1473–1543, Galileo, and Descartes). Not that archival materials had previously been ignored by historians of science; rather, in the late nineteenth century, nationalist sentiments had begun to foster the publication of collected works and letters of many pioneers of science, like Johannes Kepler (1571–1630), Galileo, and Christiaan Huygens (1629–1695). But never before had archival findings led to so radical a change in the received picture of the origins of modern science as Duhem inaugurated. Hardly a student of the Scientific Revolution accepts any longer the Duhem thesis in its original, quite radical

guise. Its enduring influence, rather, came from two other resources. In proclaiming continuity to be the predominant feature of scientific advance, Duhem inaugurated a search that has yet to cease for specific ways in which salient components of the birth of modern science followed upon ideas and practices of earlier times. Further, Duhem's drastic and, in many respects, somewhat crudely executed reinterpretation gave rise to a novel level of historization of the past of science. E. A. Burtt and E. J. Dijksterhuis in 1924 and A. Koyré in 1939–1940 published works in which past scientific ideas were not so much ransacked for anticipations and "firsts" but, rather, considered in the context of their own times. What did a given scientist know? What could he know? What made him think the way he did? What underlying problematic and/or metaphysical commitment gave coherence to his thought? Seeking answers to such questions brought with it another, quite radical change in conceptions by historians of the rise of modern science, which now came to be seen as the transition from one particular mode of viewing the world to a drastically altered one. With mutually somewhat different emphases, all three authors characterized the transition as one toward what Koyré labeled the "mathematization of nature." It was in this context that Koyré conceptualized the transition as "the Scientific Revolution of the seventeenth century." (By way of just an expression, "the Scientific 'Revolution'" had occasionally been used from 1913 onward, whereas the obviously related yet general concept of scientific revolutions, plural, goes back to the early eighteenth century.)

Every single book-length study devoted since then to surveying and interpreting the Scientific Revolution finds its origin in the tradition established by Burtt, Dijksterhuis, and Koyré, which from the 1940s and for at least three decades afterward was to dominate ongoing research on aspects of sixteenth-seventeenth-century science. In several respects, it still does. While aimed at establishing historical patterns in which conveniently to cluster successions of scientific ideas and practices of a huge variety and complexity, none of these book-length studies seeks, other than in a set-aside chapter at most, to put the event in its sociocultural context and/or to work a search for causes into the ongoing narrative. Various modes of sociocultural contextualization, as well as efforts to explain the Scientific Revolution, have not been lacking from the 1920s onward. With one partial, and by now quite obsolete, exception (part 4 in volume 2 of J. D. Bernal's *Science in History,* 1954), however, these still await presentation in the format of an ongoing narrative fit for students and/or teachers, which is a remarkable state of affairs for the historiography of what so many historians of science have jointly held to be among the most consequential changes human destiny has ever undergone.

Available books usable as survey interpretations of the Scientific Revolution are, in chronological order:

E. A. Burtt, *The Metaphysical Foundations of Modern Physical Science* (1924, rev. ed. 1932). Here a philosophical thesis, on how, through the advent of modern science, the human spirit has been read out of the cosmos at large, provides a framework for an overview of, in the author's view, drastically novel ideas (mostly those in the mathematical and the corpuscularian mode) from Copernicus to Isaac Newton (1642–1727), with much emphasis on the latter figure.

A. Koyré, *Études Galiléennes* (1939–1940, translated as *Galileo Studies,* 1978). In this most influential of all books to inaugurate the new level of historical consciousness discussed above, Koyré analyzes the Scientific Revolution in the restricted sense he originally assigned to that concept: the deep ramifications of Galileo's and Descartes's radically novel, mathematically idealized treatment of motion. The book does not, therefore, provide an overview as the other books listed here do; yet, if read together with Koyré's *La révolution astronomique* (1961) and his *Newtonian Studies* (1965), one gets an adequate picture of the expanded meaning Koyré in later years gave to the concept.

H. Butterfield, *The Origins of Modern Science* (1949, rev. ed. 1957). Butterfield provides a "general" historian's lecture course that runs from 1300 to 1800, with an inner Scientific Revolution from Copernicus to Newton being effectively distinguished from an outer Scientific Revolution cursorily surveyed in a technically undemanding manner.

E. J. Dijksterhuis, *De mechanisering van het wereldbeeld* (1950, translated as *The Mechanization of the World Picture,* 1961). This is a moderately technical overview of the history of science from ancient Greece to Newton, aimed at showing how the mathematical spirit of the Greeks eventually led to the mathematical treatment of natural phenomena inaugurated by Galileo and Kepler. Focusing much on the mathematical sciences, the book builds on themes previously explored in Dijksterhuis's innovative *Val en worp* (1924, never translated).

A. R. Hall, *The Scientific Revolution* (1954). In this moderately technical survey that runs from 1500 to 1800, Hall treats the creation of modern science at the hands of, above all, Copernicus, Galileo, Descartes, Newton, and Antoine Lavoisier (1743–1794) as the gradually emerging triumph of rationality. The organization of the book is more diffuse than those previously listed, in part because it pays more attention to such nonmathematical disciplines as chemistry and the life sciences.

C. C. Gillispie, *The Edge of Objectivity* (1960). The first five chapters present a concise survey from Galileo to Newton, with the objective nature of the kind of knowledge modern science embodies forming its leading theme.

A. R. Hall, *From Galileo to Newton* (1963). This is a sequel volume to M. Boas-Hall, *The Scientific Renaissance* (1962). Together, these books survey the period 1450–1720 in the same spirit as Hall's previous survey of 1954.

R.S. Westfall, *The Construction of Modern Science* (1971). The author presents a concise survey from Galileo and Kepler through Descartes and Huygens to Newton, overall requiring of the reader moderate scientific proficiency. Westfall seeks to arrive at a balanced treatment of all scientific disciplines at the time by setting off the mathematical and the corpuscularian modes of scientific thought in a dynamic interplay of conflict and harmony that forms the leading theme of the book.

A. R. Hall, *The Revolution in Science* (1983). This is an almost fully rewritten version of Hall's book of 1954, consciously reflecting the ongoing growth in sophistication of specialized studies of facets of the Scientific Revolution. The narrative now runs from 1500 to 1750 and highlights a less marked opposition between rational and irrational modes of thought.

Finally, a multiauthor, themeless overview of the Scientific Revolution arranged according to scientific disciplines, which are treated overall in much more detailed manner, is R. Taton, ed., *La science moderne* (1958, translated as *The Beginnings of Modern Science,* 1964, vol. 2 of *A General History of the Sciences*).

From the late 1960s onward, another level of historical sensibility than the one embodied in the books just listed has gradually come to acquire a shape of its own. Seeking, in most cases, to preserve what gains in responsible historization had been made in the tradition outlined above, proponents of a New Contextualism in the widest sense have become aware of many other respects in which a "view from the times themselves" may serve to heighten our understanding further. Several authors have done this programmatically; others, more by way of an implicit approach than with party colors much in evidence. Historiographical platforms have, in broadly successive order, been provided by Marxism (1930s–1980s), a more or less radical antiscientism (1960s and 1970s, especially), a moderately relativist conception of the scientific endeavor, influenced by T. Kuhn's *Structure of Scientific Revolutions* (from the 1960s onward), and social constructivism (from the 1980s onward).

More or less common threads in numerous efforts to arrive at a New Contextualism are: (1) a heightened awareness of the importance of institutional developments, of patterns of patronage, and of instrumental and experimental practice; (2) a felt need to take "losers" of the Scientific Revolution seriously; (3) an urge not to treat the victory of modern science as a foregone conclusion (let alone as foreordained); and (4) a concern for finding out how the science of the period managed to gain legitimacy in society at large. As a result, near the end of the 1990s the path of science during the period customarily denoted by the term *Scientific Revolution* appeared crooked rather than straightforward, marked by mixed forms rather than by sharp oppositions between old and new or between right and wrong, and, in short, quite as beset by subjective elements as all human enterprises are. In a somewhat polarized climate, the question of how much common ground remains with conceptions of science as embodying at least some degree of objectivity is rarely raised to the level of explicit debate, as it tends to be either affirmed or denied categorically. Meanwhile, so much in earlier, more clear-cut pictures of the Scientific Revolution seems by now to have become blurred that a call for abolishing the concept altogether, as it appears to have become devoid of content, has been raised with increasing frequency since the middle 1980s.

The foregoing characterizes a good part of late-twentieth-century writing on aspects of the Scientific Revolution. Some landmark studies that embody one or more of these approaches include J. L. Heilbron, *Electricity in the Seventeenth and Eighteenth Centuries* (1979); S. Shapin and S. Schaffer, *Leviathan and the Air-Pump* (1985); D. C. Lindberg and R. S. Westman, *Reappraisals of the Scientific Revolution* (1990); M. Biagioli, *Galileo Courtier* (1993). Meanwhile, a first, synthetic, and coherent effort to reap the harvest of the New Contextu-

alism in the format of three interconnected essays on a variety of aspects of seventeenth-century science is provided in S. Shapin, *The Scientific Revolution* (1996). Further, D. Goodman and C. A. Russell, eds., *The Rise of Scientific Europe, 1500–1800* (1991) may be seen as a step in the direction of an integrated narrative of the Scientific Revolution owing to its focus upon the institutional contexts of scientific ideas. J. Henry, *The Scientific Revolution and the Origins of Modern Science* (1997) succinctly fulfills to a considerable extent many of the desiderata for a synthetic study in which the products of the New Contextualism are integrated with the products of the Old Contextualism.

All historiographical tendencies reviewed so far are equally reflected in searches, undertaken from the 1920s onward, to *explain* the rise of modern science. Many authors have sought for causes situated primarily in the realm of ideas. Such explanations have most commonly taken the form of establishing continuities (or rather, in some cases, discontinuities) with currents of thought prior to the Scientific Revolution—medieval Aristotelianism, Renaissance Aristotelianism, such other Renaissance currents as humanism, Neoplatonism, Hermetism, skepticism, and also Copernicanism. Another broad category of explanations has come from causally linking the Scientific Revolution or significant portions thereof to religious currents, whether it be specifically English Puritanism or European Protestantism generally or, still more broadly, Christianity at large. Further, there have been many attempts to explain the Scientific Revolution by reference to elements of budding dynamism in medieval and early-modern European history—to the onset of commercial capitalism, to a rapprochement between abstract thought and manual labor, to a utilitarian concern for making science serve practical ends, to an increasing openness to the vicissitudes of nature coming from the voyages of discovery, to effects of the spread of the mechanical clock, to the acceleration in communications due to the printing press, and to new chances for social legitimation owing to the rise of a specific ideology in which science came to symbolize values and aspirations of rising social groups. Finally, the question of how modern science arose has been considered by way of comparing the fate of science in early-modern Europe with the fate of science in other civilizations—those of ancient Greece, of pre-1600 China, and of medieval Islamic civilization, in particular. As noted, at the end of the twentieth century there existed no study of the Scientific Revolution in which the huge range of purported explanations listed here is worked into a coherent narrative of the event. Rather, a somewhat arbitrary selection among (sometimes from) these causal accounts had achieved "thesis" state. Classic exemplars are the thesis of Boris Hessen on the rise of capitalism, the thesis of Edgar Zilsel on manual labor, the Merton thesis on the Puritan ethic, the thesis of Frances Yates on Hermetic magic, and the thesis of Joseph Needham on China and Europe, all of which have called forth debates of their own. Authors of other significant explanations of the Scientific Revolution include L. Olschki, R. Hooykaas, A. Sayili, J. Ben-David, and E. Eisenstein.

It must be emphasized that the broad lines drawn in the above are drawn not so much from the full literature on the Scientific Revolution, which has reached quite massive proportions, nor from the large amount of source materials that have come to light over the past centuries and upon which so much of that literature has been erected, but chiefly from a much more limited body of literature in which authors have sought to synthesize elements of specialized knowledge into more generalized conceptions. These efforts are marked throughout by a striking divergence in outlook, in intended scope, and in mode of arguing. Since ca. the early 1980s, historians have set out to bring some measure of coherence to studies in this vein, thus, in effect, creating a history of the historiography of the Scientific Revolution. Several works in this metagenre are listed below.

BIBLIOGRAPHY

Cohen, H. Floris. *The Scientific Revolution: A Historiographical Inquiry.* Chicago: University of Chicago Press, 1994.

Cohen, I. Bernard. "The Historians Speak." In I. Bernard Cohen, *Revolution in Science.* Cambridge, MA: Harvard University Press, 1985, ch. 26.

Henry, John. *The Scientific Revolution and the Origins of Modern Science.* London: Macmillan; New York: St. Martins, 1997.

Lindberg, David C. "Conceptions of the Scientific Revolution from Bacon to Butterfield: A Preliminary Sketch." In *Reappraisals of the Scientific Revolution,* ed. David C. Lindberg and Robert S. Westman. Cambridge: Cambridge University Press, 1990, pp. 1–26.

Porter, Roy. "The Scientific Revolution: A Spoke in the Wheel?" In *Revolution in History,* ed. Roy Porter and M. Teich. Cambridge: Cambridge University Press, 1986, pp. 290–316.

H. FLORIS COHEN

See also Craftsman and Scholar Thesis; Internalist/Externalist Historiography; Marxist Historiography; Medieval Science and the Scientific Revolution; Positivist Historiography; Revolutions in Science

Scientific Societies. See Academies

Secrets of Nature

The metaphor of the *secrets of nature* has been one of the most persistent and powerful metaphors in the history of science. To the extent that science attempts to go beyond the obvious and to discover a deeper reality than that revealed to the senses, finding out the secrets of nature may be said to be the goal of all scientific inquiry.

The distinction between common sense versus a deeper understanding of nature is one that goes back to the beginnings of Western thought and has remained a constant feature of natural philosophy ever since. Plutarch (ca. 50–ca. 120) referred to science as the investigation of the "secrets of nature," having in mind such inquiries as where the Sun sets when it sinks into the sea or what becomes of light when its source is extinguished. The astronomer Edmond Halley (ca. 1656–1742) praised Sir Isaac Newton's (1642–1727) prowess in "penetrating . . . into the abstrusest secrets of Nature." Important scientific breakthroughs are still being hailed as discoveries of nature's "secrets." In decoding the mechanism of genetic replication, molecular biologists have proclaimed the discovery of the "secret of life."

The secrets-of-nature metaphor has played upon two different senses of the concept of secrecy, one epistemological and the other sociological. One implies that nature is inherently arcane, the other that natural knowledge is privileged. The most common meaning of secrecy is that of intentional concealment. Thus, to speak of nature's "secrets" is to imply that nature's true character is hidden from view. Cicero (106–43 B.C.E.) wrote that physics was a branch of philosophy that concerned "mysteries veiled in concealment by nature herself." In the Hermetic tradition, nature's secrets were so unfathomable that they could be known only by a divine revelation; they were literally *arcana naturae.*

To the early Christians, nature's secrets were divinely hidden. According to Lactantius, God made humans last in order to hide the mystery of the creation from them, thus setting the stage for the great drama of the Fall. Whether expressed in secular or religious terms (i.e., whether it is God or nature who hides the secret), this conception of nature's secrets makes a fundamental distinction between nature as it appears to the senses and nature as it really is. The sensible world is like a disguise behind which nature's true reality hides.

When coupled with the medieval image of nature as woman, the secrets-of-nature metaphor took on a sexual dimension: nature is modest and unwilling to give up her secrets easily, or she deceives, using various stratagems to fool those who wish to probe her secrets, allowing a glimpse of one aspect of herself but concealing her identity from those who would attempt to know her intimately.

Whereas in the Hermetic and the patristic traditions, nature's secrets were placed in the domain of esoteric or forbidden knowledge, the medieval Scholastics tended to regard the secrets of nature not as permanent mysteries but as phenomena that were merely difficult to comprehend or as events whose causes were unknown. The secrets of nature were thus not intentionally concealed by God or nature but were merely examples of the imperfect state of human knowledge. Since demonstrative arguments could not be adduced to explain them, Scholastic opinion put the secrets of nature outside the boundaries of conventional science.

The early-modern period added a new implication to the secrets-of-nature metaphor: the idea of a secret as a technique or recipe, the sense in which the word was used in the sixteenth-century "books of secrets." The emergence of this connotation of nature's secrets marked a subtle but revolutionary linguistic shift. Underlying this connotation of the metaphor was the view that nature could be understood in mechanical terms as the invisible techniques nature employs for producing various sensible effects. Thus, Francis Bacon (1561–1626) spoke of penetrating "nature's workshop." This sense of the metaphor reflected a new set of research goals for early-modern science. The capacity to artificially reproduce nature's effects was seen as an epistemological guarantee of natural knowledge. As Bacon explained, understanding how works of art are made is akin to taking off nature's veil, "because the method of creating and constructing such miracles of art is in most cases plain, whereas in the miracles of nature it is generally obscure." In the new philosophies, reproducing natural processes became a kind of touchstone against which claims to natural knowledge would be tested. Thus, Robert Boyle (1627–1691) argued that the capacity to produce

mechanically the "forms and qualities" of nature demonstrated the superiority of corpuscularianism over Scholastic doctrine on the nature of matter.

The new philosophers also rejected esotericism and upheld the virtues of open disclosure of scientific knowledge. In the Royal Society, collective witnessing of experimental facts was advanced as the guarantee of objectivity. Yet, experimental knowledge in the Royal Society was never completely open. Although theoretically public, its experimental spaces were, in fact, tightly controlled.

The ideology of science as public knowledge is an integral part of the scientific ethos. Free and open communication of research is regarded as an indispensible component of the scientific method. Yet, the tension between the ideal of openness and the practical need for secrecy has been a constant feature of modern science. Whether used to ensure priorities, to guard against plagiarism, to protect competitive positions in the marketplace, or to keep information from the enemy, secrecy is sometimes a practical necessity in science.

Although the secrets of nature no longer retain the aura of forbidden knowledge, they are no less esoteric and privileged. If anything, scientific knowledge is more the monopoly of an autonomous corporation of specialists than ever before. In the modern setting, the social function of esotericism has been increasingly performed by the construction of disciplinary boundaries. Institutionalization may have replaced esotericism in science, but sociologically its goals are the same: it is a mechanism for protecting the discipline from external criticism and from pollution by outsiders. The paradox is that science, a form of knowledge that is the most open in principle, has become the most closed in practice.

BIBLIOGRAPHY

Bagley, Paul J. "On the Practice of Esotericism." *Journal of the History of Ideas* 53 (1992), 231–247.

Eamon, William. "From the Secrets of Nature to Public Knowledge." In *Reappraisals of the Scientific Revolution,* ed. David C. Lindberg and Robert S. Westman. Cambridge: Cambridge University Press, 1990, pp. 333–366.

———. *Science and the Secrets of Nature: Books of Secrets in Medieval and Early Modern Culture.* Princeton, NJ: Princeton University Press, 1994.

Keller, Evelyn Fox. "From Secrets of Life to Secrets of Death." In *Body/Politics: Women and the Discourse of Science,* ed. Mary Jacobus, Evelyn Fox Keller, and Sally Shuttleworth. London: Routledge, 1989, pp. 175–191.

———. "Secrets of God, Nature, and Life." *History of the Human Sciences* 3 (1990), 229–242.

WILLIAM EAMON

See also Books of Secrets; Hermetism; Porta, Giambattista della

Sennert, Daniel (1572–1637)

Straddled old and new eras of corpuscularian matter theory by promoting an atomist hypothesis based on the protochemical theory of natural *minima*—elementary particles at the limits of divisibility yet with diverse, determinable physical qualities—and on his own evidence from experiment and observation. He understands atoms and *minima* to be identical, because he mistakenly takes Democritean atoms to have chemical properties.

Sennert first proposes that there are such *minima* in his *Summary of Physical Science* (*Epitome scientiae naturalis,* 1618). A year later, in *The Agreement and Disagreement Between the Chemists and the Followers of Aristotle and Galen* (*De chymicorum cum Aristotelicis et Galenicis consensu ac dissensu*), he reaffirms the Aristotelian picture of chemical composition as the interaction of the four elements, all the while suggesting that whatever compounds we form result, in part, from the commingling of *minima.*

In his *Notes on Physics* (*Hypomnemata physicae,* 1636), Sennert stresses that *minima* are imperceptible, yet he suggests observation-based reasons for postulating their existence, interpreting, for example, the vaporization of water as evidence that water is divisible into parts smaller than are perceivable. He further speculates that molecular aggregates of elemental atoms constitute *prima mixta,* which he takes to be the basic structural elements of compound bodies.

Sennert enjoyed a fair audience during his lifetime, but his transitional views and partial Aristotelianism were rejected after his death. By 1671 Robert Boyle (1627–1691), in *An Introduction to the History of Particular Qualities,* emphasized Sennert's role as a defender of substantial forms—albeit in a more sophisticated way than other Peripatetics—given his view that we must explain the variety of natural qualities by appealing to forms and not simply the commingling of elementary particles or their aggregates.

Sennert was also a physician and the author of several medical tracts, including a compendium of disease analyses (such as scurvy and gout) and a guide to the art of surgery.

BIBLIOGRAPHY

Brentini, Pietro. *Die Institutiones medicinae des Daniel Sennert (1572–1637).* Zurich: Juris-Verlag, 1971.

Meinel, Christoph. "Early Seventeenth-Century Atomism: Theory, Epistemology, and the Insufficiency of Experiment." *Isis* 79 (1988), 68–103.

Stolberg, Michael. "Das Staunen von der Schöpfung: "Tota substantia," "calcidum innatum," "generatio spontanea" und atomistische Formenlehre bei Daniel Sennert." *Gesnerus* 50 (1993), 48–65.

An English translation of Sennert's *De chymicorum cum Aristotelicis et Galenicis consensu ac dissensu* is: Culpeper, Nicholas, and Abdiah Cole. *Chymistry Made Easie and Useful; or, The Agreement and Disagreement of the Chymists and Galenists,* appearing in *The Physitians Library.* London, 1622.

SAUL FISHER

See also Atomism; Matter

Series, Mathematical

The key concept in the mathematical theory of series is that an infinite number of terms can be added together and equal a finite value. It is, of course, essential that the terms become smaller and smaller in order to guarantee that the series actually adds up ("converges") to a finite result. Mathematicians of classical Greece paid relatively little attention to infinite series, although some theorems of Archimedes (ca. 287–212 B.C.E.) can be interpreted as involving infinite sums. The first major steps toward the theory of infinite series appear to have been undertaken in the Middle Ages. The fourteenth-century English logician Richard Suiseth (fl. ca. 1350), who was known as Calculator, discovered that

$$\frac{1}{2} + \frac{2}{4} + \frac{3}{8} + \ldots + \frac{n}{2^n} + \ldots = 2$$

Others of this period, notably Nicole Oresme (fl. 1323–1382), investigated other infinite series, although they left no systematic treatment of the topic.

The seventeenth century saw tremendous advancements in the understanding of series. With the development of analytic geometry and the infinitesimal calculus, mathematicians could represent curves and surfaces in terms of equations and use infinite series expansions for functions of all kinds. James Gregory (1638–1675), for example, found a number of important results in the theory of conic sections, and his 1668 result is still known as Gregory's series for the arctangent

$$\arctan\left(x\right) = x - \frac{x^3}{3} + \frac{x^5}{5} + \frac{x^7}{7} + \ldots$$

The decisive step in the development of the theory of series was the discovery of the generalized binomial theorem, which allows the expansion of expressions of the form $(a + b)^n$. In cases in which n is an integer, the theorem delivers the familiar expansion

$$\left(a+b\right)^n = a^n + \binom{n}{1}a^{n-1}b + \binom{n}{2}a^{n-2}b^2 + \ldots + \binom{n}{n-1}ab^{n-1} \cdot$$

where the binomial co-efficient $\binom{n}{k}$ is given by the formula $\dfrac{n(n-1)(n-2)\ldots(n-k-1)}{k!}$. When n takes values other than integers, the resulting equation is an infinite series. The generalized binomial theorem asserts that if x is any number between -1 and 1, and m is any number, then

$$\left(1+x\right)^m = 1 + mx + \frac{m}{2}x^2 + \frac{m}{3}x^2 + \ldots.$$

Isaac Newton (1642–1727) is credited with the first public formulation of the generalized binomial theorem, although he had known the result for a number of years. Others, including Gregory and Nicolaus Mercator (ca. 1619–1687), had used the theorem for some fractional powers of m, but did not have the completely general version of it. Newton employed the theorem to study a wide variety of infinite series, collecting his results into a 1669 treatise, *An Analysis by Equations with an Infinite Number of Terms,* which was eventually published in 1711.

Gottfried Wilhelm Leibniz (1646–1716) undertook researches into the theory of infinite series in the early 1670s, following a somewhat different path than Newton but arriving at many of the same results. In 1674 he obtained the famous series

$$\frac{\pi}{4} - 1 - \frac{1}{3} + \frac{1}{5} - \frac{1}{7} + \ldots.$$

This result, which Leibniz called his arithmetical quadrature of the circle, was based on a transmutation theorem that he used to divide the quadrant of the circle into infi-

nitely many infinitesimal areas and then reassemble them in the form of a series.

The theory of series developed rapidly in the late seventeenth and early eighteenth centuries and emerged as a fundamental part of the infinitesimal calculus, with applications in many different areas of mathematics and physics. This rapid development of the theory of series took place without the benefit of a rigorous and precise formulation of the conditions under which a series converges. As a result, there were frequent disputes about the validity of some uses of infinite series, and, by the second half of the nineteenth century, the whole subject was made more rigorous as part of the reform of the calculus.

BIBLIOGRAPHY

Boyer, Carl B. *A History of Mathematics,* rev. and ed. Uta Merzbach. New York: Wiley, 1989.

Feigenbaum, L. "Infinite Series and Solutions of Ordinary Differential Equations, 1670–1770." In *The Companion Encyclopaedia of the History and Philosophy of the Mathematical Sciences,* ed. Ivor Grattan-Guinness. London and New York: Routledge, 1994, pp. 504–519.

Pensivy, M. "The Binomial Theorem." In *The Companion Encyclopaedia of the History and Philosophy of the Mathematical Sciences,* ed. Ivor Grattan-Guinness. London and New York: Routledge, 1994, pp. 492–498.

DOUGLAS M. JESSEPH

See also Calculus; Infinitesimals; Infinity, Mathematical

Servetus, Michael (1511–1553)

Born in the town of Villanueva de Sigena (Aragón, Spain), during his adolescence and youth he worked as secretary in the Court of Charles I of Spain (also Charles V of Germany). After renouncing the Catholic faith, he published a theological book on the Trinity in 1531, which was condemned by Catholics and Protestants alike. He lived in Paris and Lyons for the following six years. He worked for Trechsel the printers and published editions of the Bible and a Latin translation of Ptolemy's (ca. 100–ca. 170) *Geographia* (1535), which was his first contribution to science. Not only did he improve on the Latin translation, he also contributed to the renovation of geography based on astronomy, and the corrections he made were assimilated by the most prominent geographers, including Sebastian Münster (1489–1552) and Abraham Ortelius (1527–1598).

He became friendly with the physician Symphorien Champier (1472–1538), under whose influence he stud-

The background in this plate from Henricus ab Allwoerden's Historie van Michael Servetus *(1729) shows Servetus being burned at the stake.*

ied medicine at the University of Paris, where he was educated in the humanist trend of Galenism, as opposed to that arising in the later Middle Ages based on Muslim authors. Indeed, he devoted his main medical treatise, *Syruporum universa ratio* (1537), to expounding the therapeutic effect of syrups in keeping with the ideas of classical times as opposed to those of the "barbaric" disciples of medieval Muslims. Subsequently, he practiced medicine in several French cities and finally settled in Vienne, where he lived from 1542 to 1553. Being a practicing physician was no obstacle to Servetus continuing his theological works, the most important of which was *Christianismi restitutio,* which was printed in secret in January 1553. He was tried for heresy three months later but managed to escape and, in his flight from the Catholic Inquisition, tried to make it to Switzerland. In August of that year, he was captured upon orders from John Calvin (1509–1564), who condemned him to be burned at the stake together with a manuscript copy and a printed copy of his last book. The sentence was carried out in Geneva in October 1553.

Despite the outstanding nature of his other contributions, Servetus's place in the history of science is due mainly to his formulation of the pulmonary circulation—the greatest modification made during the sixteenth century to the physiology of Galenism. He expounded his theory in *Christianismi restitutio* because of the prominent role that blood played in his theological doctrine. Servetus made use of anatomical observation to refute the Galenist theory, which held that blood flowed from the right to the left ventricle and deemed that the pulmonary artery served to nourish the lung. He placed particular emphasis on the caliber of the pulmonary artery being too large to be simply a vessel providing nutriment, on the structure of the interventricular septum, and on the position of the lungs in the embryo. It is obvious that he was unaware of the description of pulmonary circulation dating from the thirteenth century by the Egyptian physician Ibn an-Nafis. However, it is difficult to be so categorical about whether other Renaissance authors who expounded the theory and made it known shortly after had heard of Servetus's theory since the fanaticism of Calvin and the Catholic Inquisition succeeded in having virtually all the copies of *Christianismi restitutio* destroyed.

BIBLIOGRAPHY

Bainton, R. H. *Hunted Heretic: Life and Death of Michael Servetus.* Boston: Beacon, 1953.

Fulton. J. F. *Michael Servetus, Humanist and Martyr: With a Bibliography of His Works and Census of Known Copies by M. E. Stanton.* New York: Reichner, 1953.

López-Piñero, J. M. "Serveto, Miguel." In *Diccionario histórico de la ciencia moderna en España,* ed. J. M. López-Piñero et al. Barcelona: Península, 1983, vol. 2, pp. 320–323.

Servetus, Michael. *Michael Servetus: A Translation of His Geographical, Medical, and Astrological Writings with Introduction and Notes.* Trans. Charles D. O'Malley. Philadelphia: American Philosophical Society, 1953.

JOSÉ M. LÓPEZ-PIÑERO

See also Galenism; Harvey, William; Vesalius, Andreas

Severin, Christian (Christen Sørensen; Longomontanus or Langberg) (1562–1647)

Born into a poor family in Denmark, he did not complete his education until 1588. He arrived at Tycho Brahe's (1546–1601) observatory, Uraniborg, in 1590 and remained his primary assistant until Uraniborg's closing in 1597. Longomontanus then toured German universities, taking an M.A. from Rostock. He worked briefly for Brahe in 1598 and 1600. Longomontanus became extraordinary professor at the University of Copenhagen in 1605, sponsored by Chancellor Christian Friis. In 1607 he was appointed professor of mathematics; in 1621, professor of astronomy and higher mathematics. Longomontanus established a tradition of astronomical education at the University of Copenhagen and planned the Round Tower observatory there.

It is difficult to distinguish Longomontanus's contribution to Tycho's work. He apparently supervised the compilation of Tycho's star catalog and was primarily responsible for Tycho's lunar theory.

Upon his death in 1601, Tycho Brahe had failed to reduce his copious observations to finished planetary theories. In Longomontanus's absence, Johannes Kepler (1571–1630) inherited this task with non-Tychonic methods and goals. Longomontanus tried to dissuade Kepler from his physical astronomy and never subsequently accepted his findings.

Longomontanus carried on Tycho's astronomical legacy without the observations, which were in Kepler's possession. He succeeded in composing what was considered Tycho's posthumous testament, the *Astronomica Danica* (1622, repr. 1640, 1663). In it, Longomontanus detailed the geometrical equivalence of the Ptolemaic, Copernican, and Tychonic systems but proclaimed his support for a semi-Tychonic system with a rotating earth. He eschewed Ptolemy's (ca. 100–ca. 170) equant (a point not at the center of the system from which a line to a planet generates equal angles in equal times) in favor of the double-epicycle form of Nicolaus Copernicus's (1473–1543) planetary theory, and he championed uniform circular motion. His solar theory reintroduced a variable precession and had terms inspired by perfect numbers.

BIBLIOGRAPHY

Moesgaard, Kristian Peder. "How Copernicanism Took Root in Denmark and Norway." In *The Reception of Copernicus' Heliocentric Theory,* ed. Jerzy Dobrzycki. (Studia Copernican V: Colloquia Copernicana, I). Dordrecht: Reidel, 1972, pp. 117–151.

———. "Longomontanus (Langberg, Lomberg), Christen Sørensen." In *Dansk biografisk leksikon,* ed. Cedergreen Bech. Copenhagen: Gyldendal, 1979–1984, vol. 9, pp. 109–110.

Thoren, Victor E. *The Lord of Uraniborg: A Biography of Tycho Brahe.* Cambridge: Cambridge University Press, 1990.

JAMES R. VOELKEL

See also Astronomy; Brahe, Tycho; Geoheliocentrism; Precession

Sex and Gender

Historians of science, until the 1970s, minimized women's contributions to the Scientific Revolution and ignored the rhetorical use of gender in scientific discourse. Feminist scholars have since investigated these problems, offering fresh insights into the construction of knowledge and the nature of the scientific enterprise. Sex and gender categorize four different but interlocking topics: (1) the relationship between physiological sexual difference and sociological roles; (2) sexual difference as an object of scientific inquiry; (3) women as scientists; and (4) femininity and masculinity as conceptual metaphors used by scientists. Recent work in these areas overturns three centuries of received wisdom that the Scientific Revolution was entirely objective, untouched by cultural and ideological concerns.

The Relationship Between Sex and Gender

Scholarship defines *sex* as biological sexual difference and *gender* as the social systems, roles, and meanings based on sexual difference. Historian Thomas Laqueur (1990) argues that not only is gender shaped by culture, so also is sex. Before 1700, for example, European thought maintained a "one-sex" model of sexual difference that held that women were inferior, "inside-out" versions of men rather than an incommensurate opposite. This theory shaped anatomical research in striking ways.

Sex and Gender as Objects of Scientific Inquiry

Anatomists investigated the physiology of sexual difference during the Scientific Revolution. Following the logic of "one sex," anatomist Andreas Vesalius (1514–1564) depicted the vagina as an internal penis; when Gabriele Falloppio (1523–1562) discovered the thin tubules between the ovaries and the uterus, he suggested that they were sinews, homologous to male parts. European and Latin nomenclature also reflected this one-sex model, with such words as *testicles* describing both male and female gonads. Other physiological differences, including the unique proportions of the female skeleton, would not be noted until after 1700.

Women as Scientists

For centuries, women managed female ailments, family medicine, and the delivery of children. Some, including Robert Boyle's (1627–1691) sister Mary, published books of herbal remedies and medical advice. Brandenburg midwife Justine Siegemundin (1650–1705) and French midwife Louise Bourgeois (1563–1636) made lasting contributions to obstetrics, including techniques to manage difficult births. The seventeenth-century English Chamberlain family of surgeons developed the obstetric forceps, which they kept a secret from female practitioners. By 1700, "man-midwives" were becoming increasingly popular, contributing to women's medical marginalization in Britain. Female midwives fared better on the Continent, partly because teaching hospitals like Paris's Hôtel Dieu began formally educating women in the seventeenth century.

Many women involved in medicine and science were denigrated for intruding on "masculine philosophy," yet a few made formal contributions to physics, mathematics, astronomy, and biology. Margaret Cavendish (1623–1673), Anne Conway (1631–1679), and others, including Gabrielle du Châtelet (1706–1749), whose translation of Isaac Newton's (1642–1727) *Principia mathematica philosophiae naturalis* (1687) became the standard in French, all participated in natural philosophy through their elite connections to male intellectuals. Other women entered science through the crafts. Wives and daughters like Sofia Brahe (1556–1643) and Maria Clara Eimmart (1676–1707) assisted in astronomy and astrology, scientific illustration, and instrument making. The most exceptional included Maria Winkelmann (1670–1720) and Maria Merian (1647–1717). Assisting her husband, Gottfried Kirch, at the academy in Berlin, Winkelmann made her own discoveries, including a new comet in 1702. When Kirch died in 1710, the academy refused to let Winkelmann take his position although she was the most qualified candidate. She instead assisted several less prominent astronomers, including her son. German entomologist Maria Merian gained more autonomy. The daughter of an artist, Merian illustrated and published works on insects and flowers, developed new printing techniques, and trained other women in scientific illustration. At age fifty-two, she traveled to Surinam, spending two years collecting specimens. Her popular *Metamorphosis insectorum Surinamensium* (1705) provided important evidence against spontaneous generation.

Sex and Gender as Metaphors

Ecological historian Carolyn Merchant, philosophers Evelyn Fox Keller and Naomi Zack, cultural historians Londa Schiebinger and Laqueur examine how the assumptions of societies about gender, sexuality, and the body have shaped science. Merchant (1980, 2nd ed. 1990) argues that the Scientific Revolution led to technological penetration of the earth and women's bodies because nature was no longer seen as feminine and maternal but mechanistic. Fox Keller (1985) analyzes how gender unconsciously shaped epistemological language; Francis Bacon (1561–1626) described the scientific enterprise sexually, with nature as a feminine lover to be captured and controlled by a forceful, male philosopher. Zack (1996) suggests that the scientific ideals of objectivity, distance, and rationality shaped a new, specifically masculine identity for natural philosophers. These expectations were reinforced by René Descartes (1596–1650), Thomas Hobbes (1588–1679), Boyle, John Locke (1632–1704), and Newton, who were all bachelors, freed from the constraints of family life. Schiebinger (1989) and Laqueur (1990) analyze how nature and the body have been used ideologically to validate power relations. Both argue that, starting in the late seventeenth century, Europeans began interpreting anatomical evidence in terms of two incommensurate sexes to scientifically justify women's political exclusion from developing democratic public spheres.

BIBLIOGRAPHY

Keller, Evelyn Fox. *Reflections on Gender and Science.* New Haven, CT: Yale University Press, 1985.

Laqueur, Thomas. *Making Sex: Body and Gender from the Greeks to Freud.* Cambridge, MA: Harvard University Press, 1990.

Merchant, Carolyn. *The Death of Nature: Women, Ecology, and the Scientific Revolution.* San Francisco: Harper, 1980. 2nd ed. 1990.

Schiebinger, Londa. *The Mind Has No Sex? Women in the Origins of Modern Science.* Cambridge, MA: Harvard University Press, 1989.

Zack, Naomi. *Bachelors of Science: Seventeenth-Century Identity, Then and Now.* Philadelphia: Temple University Press, 1996.

LISA FORMAN CODY

See also Cavendish, Margaret; Conway, Anne; Generation; Women and Natural Philosophy

S

Shipbuilding

An old, established, and necessarily conservative occupation. Large vessels, carrying valuable cargoes on dangerous seas, were expensive and complex artifacts whose construction and maintenance required established and wide-ranging skills in finance, design, production, and repairs. The owner-promoter employed a master carpenter to have overall charge of these functions, including supplies and labor. Such Englishmen as Peter Pett and Matthew Baker were the forerunners of both the modern naval architect and the shipyard team.

Design was a matter of set rules, treated as trade secrets; thus, there are few surviving sources from the period, and our knowledge depends on a few papers, contemporary models of larger naval vessels, and recent observation of recovered wrecks, such as the *Mary Rose* and the *Gustavus Vasa*.

The following account is based on an English manuscript of 1608, describing a common merchant vessel of one hundred tons. (Large vessels of one thousand tons or more are known.) It represents a compromise on questions of draft, grounding, stability, and way (or speed), the last only a few knots even in "a bit of a blow."

First, the dimensions of the midship mold, or bend, are determined. These give, within certain proportions, the necessary circular arcs (sometimes elliptical or biquadrate curves were proposed), which were laid out full size for construction. The "crooked" timbers had been marked years earlier on specific standing trees. Next, the plane of length and depth was determined, with the keel between two and three times the breadth at midships. The stem, forming the prow, is a circular arc, and the sternpost raked back somewhat. Set positions fore and aft ("the grype and tuck") determine the so-called rising lines as circular or cubic curves. Next, the narrowings of the plane of length and breadth (not a plane, but a device for calculating offsets) were based on a smoothed mixture of circular, cubic, or even quartic curves, the last at the bow, to give a compromise between a bluff and a sharp vessel. Armed with the preceding dimensions, one can obtain those for the other molds. These molds are rather close together for strength, as given by "timber" and "timber and space." The decks stand on their own supports with suitable camber.

In a similar way, the placing of masts (usually two or three), their heights and widths, and the lengths of spars were determined. After ca. 1620, calculations are often logarithmic, and scaling becomes more sophisticated. Tonnage was calculated by the length at the keel, the breadth, and the depth (all measured in English feet), divided by one hundred. Alternatively, if the bulk of the ship is about one-third of this, the weight of the water equivalent gives a similar figure; thus, ten feet x twenty feet x fifty feet gives a hundred-ton vessel.

Canvas and ropes are subject to similar schemes. The main- and the foremast had two sails each (more on larger ships); the bowsprit, one (and perhaps its own topsail); and the mizzenmast, a triangular lateen sail. Masts were supported by shrouds at the sides and braced by heavy ropes and back-stays. The sails were supported by yards (or spars). Yards were held to masts by parrels, comprising ribs, ropes and trucks (balls). Ropemaking, blockmaking, and so on were specialized trades, requiring many special tools. There were hundreds of technical terms, explained in contemporary guides.

National characteristics varied, depending on local conditions and materials. English ships were immensely strong, but slow compared with the Dutch, because of their proportions and heavy materials (homegrown oak and Scandinavian spars); Spanish ships were sharp and deep; French vessels neat but low-burdened for their appearance, with sharply angled decks. All were intended to go well and steer well, for which ballast and rudder were important, and to bear a good sail, but faults of design and workmanship and unseasoned timbers, owing to considerations of cost, led at best to poorly designed vessels and at worst to loss.

Speed and comfort are not good shipmates, and any design will also be a compromise among cost, strength, seaworthiness, maneuverability, and stowage. Mediterranean fleets included hundreds of different galleys, including, as at the Battle of Lepanto (1571), the descendants of the ancient triremes.

BIBLIOGRAPHY

Baker, William A. "Early Seventeenth-Century Ship Design." *American Neptune* 14 (1954), 262–277.

Goell, Kermit, ed. *A Sea Grammar . . . Written by Captain John Smith*. London: Michael Joseph, 1970.

Mainwaring, Henry. *The Seaman's Dictionary*. London, 1644. Repr. in *The Life and Works of Sir Henry Mainwaring*, ed. G. E. Manwaring [*sic*] and W. G. Perrin. London: Navy Records Society, 1922.

Pepper, J. V. "Harriot's Manuscript on Shipbuilding, c. 1608." In *Five Hundred Years of Nautical Science, 1400–1900*, ed. Derek Howse. Greenwich, England: National Maritime Museum, 1981.

Salisbury, W., and R. C. Anderson, eds. *A Treatise on Ship-building and a Treatise on Rigging Written About 1620–1625*. London: Society for Nautical Research, 1958.

JON V. PEPPER

Signatures. See Correspondences

Skepticism

A philosophical attitude that questions the reliability or even the possibility of acquiring knowledge about the world. Skepticism deeply influenced early-modern discussions about scientific method. Skeptics argue that neither the senses nor a priori reasoning are reliable sources of knowledge about the world.

Skepticism, in the Western tradition, has its roots in Greek philosophy. There were two schools of Greek skepticism. Academic skepticism, which developed within Plato's (428–348 B.C.E.) Academy, maintained that nothing can be known. Pyrrhonian skepticism, formulated by Pyrrho of Elis (ca. 360–275 B.C.E.) and further developed in Alexandria during the first century B.C.E., received its fullest development in the writings of Sextus Empiricus (ca. 200). He criticized the academic skeptics for holding the negative dogmatic view that we can know nothing. He questioned whether we can even know whether we know anything and recommended the suspension of belief. In *The Outlines of Pyrrhonism* and *Against the Mathematicians,* Sextus laid out the Pyrrhonian arguments, known as *tropes,* in a systematic attack on dogmatic claims to knowledge. Each of these modes, or tropes, was designed to show that evidence from the senses is an unreliable source of knowledge about the real natures of things because it leads to contradictory conclusions about the observed object.

Serious consideration of skepticism revived during the Renaissance with the recovery of the writings of the ancient skeptical writers. Coupled with the intellectual crisis of the Reformation, this revival led to a general skeptical crisis in European thought, which prompted many natural philosophers to question the foundations of knowledge about the world and traditional methods for seeking it.

Skepticism played two roles in seventeenth-century natural philosophy: it provided a powerful tool for criticizing traditional Aristotelian methodological prescriptions that had outlined ways of discovering certain truths about the real essences of things, and it led to the formulation of new approaches to knowledge and method. René Descartes (1596–1650) applied the skeptical arguments to all forms of knowledge, arguing that traditional methods did not provide any kind of epistemological warrant for claiming certainty. He used this method of systematic doubt to root out all dubitable claims in his search for a solid foundation upon which to build natural philosophy. In his *Discourse on Method* (1637) and *Meditations* (1641), he showed how claims based on empirical methods and even the results of mathematical demonstration could be doubted in light of skeptical critique.

Descartes believed that his new method could overcome skeptical doubts. He was determined to find some indubitable proposition upon which he could build a natural philosophy that would provide certain knowledge about the real essences of things. Descartes thought that he had found such a proposition in his famous "*Cogito ergo sum*" (I think, therefore I am). Starting from the indubitable *cogito,* he attempted to prove the existence of God, whose necessary veracity provided an epistemological warrant for reasoning from ideas in his mind to the nature of things in the world. On this basis, he claimed that anything we perceive clearly and distinctly exists in the world precisely in the way that we perceive it. Descartes believed that he could proceed to certain conclusions by means of geometrical demonstration. He described his natural philosophy in detail in the *Meditations* and *The Principles of Philosophy* (1644).

Pierre Gassendi (1592–1655) and Marin Mersenne (1588–1648) deployed skepticism to formulate a very different approach to natural philosophy. In his first published work, *Exercitationes paradoxicae adversus Aristoteleos* (Paradoxical Exercises Against the Aristotelians, 1624), Gassendi closely followed the tropes of Sextus Empiricus to disprove the possibility science in the Aristotelian sense. Without the ability to reason from observations to the essential attributes of things, Gassendi considered Aristotle's (384–322 B.C.E.) method to be worthless.

Gassendi thus redefined the epistemic goal of science, replacing certainty with probability. He argued that knowledge consists of probable statements based on our experience of the phenomena. He denied the possibility of acquiring knowledge of the essences of things, thus rejecting the traditional Aristotelian and Scholastic

S

conception of *scientia* as demonstrative knowledge of real essences and replacing it with what he called a "science of appearances," probable knowledge of the appearances of things.

During the second half of the seventeenth century, a group of English natural philosophers associated with the early Royal Society elaborated this epistemology of empirical knowledge cast in terms mitigated skepticism—as Richard Popkin (1979) has called this view—into an account of the degrees of certainty it can achieve. They denied that every kind of knowledge can attain the certainty of mathematical demonstration. Only God possesses knowledge that is absolutely and infallibly certain. Mathematical certainty pertains to mathematics and the parts of metaphysics that can be established by logic and mathematical demonstration that compel assent. Moral certainty, which characterizes knowledge that is based on immediate sense experience or introspection, lies a step below mathematical certainty. A slightly weaker kind of moral certainty characterizes belief and conclusions about ordinary life that are based on observation and the testimony of others. Finally, opinions based on second-hand reports of sense observations can be known only as probable or perhaps as just plausible.

Robert Boyle (1627–1691) elaborated the theory of degrees of certainty into an empiricist epistemology for natural philosophy. He said that theories should be evaluated in terms of their intelligibility, simplicity, explanatory scope, and predictive power and that they are confirmed to the degree that they successfully explain different kinds of observed facts. He noted that intelligibility to a human understanding is not necessary to the truth or existence of a thing. Thus, he believed that the results of natural philosophy could at best attain physical certainty (i.e., a high degree of probability).

John Locke (1632–1704) drew on the tradition of mitigated skepticism and degrees of certainty to articulate a fully developed empiricist epistemology. He claimed that all of our ideas originate from either the senses or reflection on ideas drawn from the senses. He denied that we can attain certainty about things in the world and that we can acquire knowledge of the real essences of things. Acknowledging that this approach represented a major departure from the epistemic goals of both the Aristotelian and Cartesian approaches to natural philosophy, he asserted "that natural philosophy is not capable of being made a science."

BIBLIOGRAPHY

Burnyeat, Myles, ed. *The Skeptical Tradition*. Berkeley and Los Angeles: University of California Press, 1983.

Osler, Margaret J. "John Locke and the Changing Ideal of Scientific Knowledge." *Journal of the History of Ideas* 31 (1970), 1–16. Repr. in *Philosophy, Religion, and Science in the Seventeenth and Eighteenth Centuries,* ed. John W. Yolton. Rochester, NY: University of Rochester Press, 1990, pp. 325–338.

Popkin, Richard H. *The History of Scepticism from Erasmus to Spinoza*. Assen: Van Gorcum, 1960. Rev. ed. Berkeley and Los Angeles: University of California Press, 1979.

Schmitt, Charles B. *Cicero Scepticus: A Study of the Influence of the Academica in the Renaissance*. The Hague: Nijhoff, 1972.

Shapiro, Barbara J. *Probability and Certainty in Seventeenth-Century England: A Study of the Relationships Between Natural Science, Religion, History, Law, and Literature*. Princeton, NJ: Princeton University Press, 1983.

Van Leeuwen, Henry. *The Problem of Certainty in English Thought, 1630–1680*. The Hague: Nijhoff, 1963.

MARGARET J. OSLER

See also Demonstration; Descartes, René; Empiricism; Gassendi, Pierre; Laws of Nature; Locke, John; Mersenne, Marin

Slide Rule

Edmund Gunter (1581–1626) suggested ca. 1620 an instrumental application of logarithms for navigational calculations: a logarithmic scale on the cross-staff permitted computation with a pair of dividers. William Oughtred (1575–1660) tried Gunter's suggestion but found operation cumbersome. Oughtred drew identical logarithmic scales on two rulers ca. 1621, performing calculations by sliding them against each other. Accurate results required excessively long rulers, so Oughtred contracted the instrument, drawing Gunter's logarithmic "scale of proportions" on circles. In successive issues of *Grammelogia* (1631–1634), Richard Delamain (fl. 1630), teacher of mathematics in London, claimed credit for the invention of the circular slide rule. Oughtred then published his account; the physical form described in *Circles of Proportion* (1632) was designed by his instrument maker. There is a single circular scale of logarithms of numbers, with associated trigonometrical functions; the "sliding function" is performed by a pair of stiffly hinged radial arms.

Progression from Gunter's scale of proportion, worked with dividers, to the slide rule in all forms is documented in the priority dispute between Oughtred and

Delamain. The veracity of the latter is questionable; but, early in 1631, Delamain published the first account of a circular logarithmic slide rule. Nevertheless, credit for the invention of linear and circular rules should be Oughtred's and dates to 1622. He published the first description of a linear slide rule in 1633. The conventional slide rule, with one or more runners sliding in grooves cut in a central stock, was described by Seth Partridge in 1662. By 1700 slide rules were not considered general calculating devices, were often ignored in texts on applied mathematics, and were little known outside England. There, particular forms were used, their scales laid out to undertake routine calculations by specific tradesmen, namely glaziers, carpenters, and gaugers. Use was taught by rote and provided no understanding of logarithms or the mathematics of computation. Even a large, well-calibrated slide rule gives approximate answers. Useful in trade, the slide rule was unacceptable in scientific mathematics.

BIBLIOGRAPHY

Bryden, D. J. "A Patchery and Confusion of Disjointed Stuffe: Richard Delamain's *Grammelogia* of 1631/3." *Transactions of the Cambridge Bibliographical Society* 4 (1974), 158–166.

Cajori, Florian. *A History of the Logarithmic Slide Rule and Allied Instruments.* New York: Engineering News, 1909. Repr. Palo Alto: Oughtred Society, 1992.

———. "On the History of Gunter's Scale and the Slide Rule During the Seventeenth Century." *University of California Publications in Mathematics* 1 (1920), 187–209. Repr. Palo Alto: Oughtred Society, 1992.

D. J. BRYDEN

See also Instrument Makers; Logarithms; Oughtred, William; Trigonometry

Sluse, René-François de (1622–1685)

Born in the then politically independent Principality of Liège (now in Belgium), Sluse spent more than ten years in Rome, where his uncle was an influential figure in the Vatican. Appointed canon of St. Lambert, Sluse became, in effect, a member of the Liégeois ruling elite. Although his time was spent mostly in administrative duties, he kept correspondence with many leading intellectual figures, including Blaise Pascal (1623–1662), Christiaan Huygens (1629–1695), Henry Oldenburg (ca. 1619–1677), and John Wallis (1616–1703). He published two historical books and two notes and a book of mathematical content but left hundreds of manuscript pages on many subjects. Besides erudite translations of, and commentaries on, Greek and Latin philosophers, they contain interesting remains of Sluse's work on the laws of percussion, combinatorics, and number theory.

The *Mesolabum* (Of Means, 1659) is a book on the geometrical construction of solutions to problems that mostly correspond in algebraic terms to third-degree equations. Sluse was working in the tradition of François Viète (1540–1603) and René Descartes (1596–1650), using algebra to solve geometrical problems, but he laid open his analytical methods only in the second (1668) edition of the book. Sluse's best-known method of tangents was of use for the kind of curves Descartes called geometrical (i.e., for any conic section, its intersection with a circle can be used to find the roots of third- and fourth-degree equations). Sluse's rule was published, without proof, in the *Royal Society's Philosophical Transactions* in 1672. The next year and in the same journal, Sluse published a few cryptic hints as to how to demonstrate his rule. His unpublished papers show that he drew inspiration from Pierre de Fermat's (1601–1665) method of tangents, which he probably mastered in Rome, and from Jan Hudde's (1628–1704), published by Frans van Schooten (ca. 1615–1660) in 1659–1661. Sluse's rule was found independently by Isaac Newton (1642–1727) as a by-product of his method of fluxions.

BIBLIOGRAPHY

Bernès, A.-C., and P. LeFèbvre. "La correspondance de R.-F. de Sluse: Éssai de répertoire chronologique." *Revue d'histoire des sciences et de leurs applications* 39 (1986), 35–69, 155–175, 325–344.

Le Paige, M. C. "Correspondance de René-François de Sluse." *Bullettino di bibliografia e di storia delle scienze matematiche e fisice* 17 (1884), 427–554, 603–726.

René-François de Sluse (1622–1685): Actes du colloque international. Amay-Liège-Visé, 20–22 mars 1985. *Bulletin de la Société Royale des Sciences de Liège* 55 (1986), 1–269.

ANTONI MALET

See also Algebra; Analytic Geometry; Fermat, Pierre de; Schooten, Frans van; Viète, François

Snel (Snellius or Snel van Royen), Willebrord (1580–1626)

Achieved fame by formulating the law of refraction, which was named after him. He was a professor of mathematics at the University of Leiden. As a student, he had studied law in Leiden and Paris and had visited scholars throughout Europe. He translated and published works of Simon Stevin (1548–1620) and Peter Ramus (1515–1572), among others. In the 1610s, he developed the method of triangulation in his work on the determination of the length of a degree of the meridian, which he published in 1617. He must have arrived at the law of refraction during the last years of his life. It is not known how Snel arrived at the law, for his manuscripts have been lost. At the University of Leiden, Snel taught optics during the winter of 1621–1622, and he might have formulated the law by that time. A note in his copy of *Opticae libri quatuor* (1606) by Friedrich Risner (d. 1580) makes this plausible. He performed experiments on reflection and perhaps on refraction as well. Snel's wording of the law has been preserved in a manuscript containing a summary of his propositions on refraction. As indicated in Figure 1, the eye in O receives a ray of light coming from an object G, which is refracted at R on the surface of the medium. The eye perceives the object in point J on the *cathetus,* GP, the perpendicular on the surface through R. According to Snel's law, the *radius verus* (true ray), RG, and the *radius apparens,* RJ, are in a constant ratio. This can easily be translated into the modern sine law. Snel's accomplishments were known to several scholars. Marin Mersenne (1588–1648) inquired after Snel's optics in 1628. Jacob Golius (1596–1667) looked up Snel's manuscripts in 1632 to verify the law of refraction communicated to him by René Descartes (1596–1650). Descartes published it in *La dioptrique* (1637); although accused of plagiarism, he had probably found the law independently.

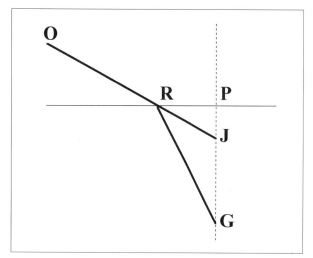

Figure 1.

BIBLIOGRAPHY

Haasbroek, N. D. *Gemma Frisius, Tycho Brahe, and Snellius, and Their Triangulations.* Delft: Rijkscommisie van Geodesie, 1968.

Pater, C. de. "Experimental Physics." In Scheurleer, Th.H. Lunsingh and G. H. M. Posthumus Meyjes. *Leiden University in the Seventeenth Century: An Exchange of Learning.* Leiden: Universitaire Pers Leiden and Brill, 1975.

Vollgraff, J. A. "Snellius' Notes on Reflection and Refraction of Rays." *Osiris* 1 (1936), 718–725.

FOKKO J. DIJKSTERHUIS

See also Light Transmission; Optics; Refraction

Social Class and Science

The Scientific Revolution represents a rise in status of the knowledge and "mechanick artisans." The craftsman-scholar thesis suggests that the revolution was the result of a marriage between the knowledge of the scholar-humanist, on the one hand, and that of artisans, on the other. Many well-known sixteenth- and seventeenth-century authors, such as Georgius Agricola (1494–1555) and Robert Boyle (1627–1691), felt the need to justify their attention to lower-class experience. Based on reports from German-speaking artisans, as well as on his own observations, Agricola wrote a Latin treatise to inform a higher-class audience. Boyle argued for the mutual benefit to be gained from the natural philosopher's discourse with tradespersons but eventually moved the observation, along with the experimental laborers, into the laboratory. Workers, according to Boyle, though honest, could not do natural philosophy, and, according to William Petty (1623–1687), the sons of gentlemen could benefit from trying their hand at practical knowledge and would be eager to prove their superiority to ordinary workmen.

From the 1640s on, science became the province primarily of professionals and businessmen rather than of landed gentlemen or university clerics. Scientific ideas, along with those of Puritanism and parliamentarianism, appealed to merchants, artisans, and yeomen but were developed and dispensed by a new breed of gentlemen in scientific societies. As experimental philosophy developed, artisans built and operated the apparatus, while gentlemen bore witness to the facts. Gentility as an attribute of the credible witness came to be distinguished from noble birth itself but was not a widely distributed quality.

Robert Norman (fl. 1581), a seaman-compass-maker, was one of the few early artisans who actually wrote a treatise (*The Newe Attractive,* 1581) in natural philosophy. William Petty was the son of a clothier. Educated at Caen, Leiden, and Oxford, Petty became wealthy from Irish land holdings, owing to his role in the Cromwellian Settlement (1662), restoring the English monarchy. Robert Hooke (1635–1703) was a highly skilled artisan and an Oxford graduate; he became assistant to Boyle and a natural philosopher in his own right. Although he earned only thirty pounds per year as curator of experiments for the Royal Society, his cash and personal valuables at his death were worth more than eight thousand pounds. Boyle was born into great wealth; his father was the earl of Cork. The family supported his travels on the Continent. He left a very large estate, the personal portion of which alone was valued at ten thousand pounds. Isaac Newton (1642–1727) came from a yeoman family in Lincolnshire; his father, who died three months prior to Isaac's birth, left modest wealth valued at four hundred sixty pounds. His stepfather, the Rev. Barnabas Smith, left him land as part of the marriage settlement, but Newton had to support himself at Cambridge as a sizar (serving at table). He eventually became a freeholder himself.

Not much is known about the early life of Simon Stevin (1548–1620), but some accounts have him involved in commerce. He was, in any case, involved in bookkeeping and became tutor and quartermaster general under Prince Maurice. His countryman Christiaan Huygens (1629–1695) was the son of a diplomat and secretary to the stadholder. Since there was no stadholder between 1650 and 1672, Christiaan was prevented from following in his father's (and grandfather's) footsteps. In Paris, as a member of the Académie des Sciences, he enjoyed ample accommodation in the Royal Library and a generous salary from the king.

Galileo Galilei (1564–1642) came from a family prominent in Florence in the century prior to his birth; it included a magistrate. His father, Vincenzio, was a musician and well-known musical theorist. The family nonetheless experienced financial need, and Vincenzio recommended that his son study medicine. Galileo achieved a regular position as a mathematics instructor in Pisa, with a salary of sixty scudi per year. The professor of medicine, by comparison, received two thousand scudi. When his father died in 1591, Galileo found that the support of his family put greater strains on his financial position. The stresses continued because of the requirements of the dowries of his sisters and his brother's requests for help. By 1609 his salary had risen, but he still needed to take on private students.

René Descartes's (1596–1650) father, Joachim, was a doctor and a member of the Bretagne Parliament at Rennes. His mother had several relatives occupying official positions. The family achieved the status of *chevalerie* in 1668. This process of ennoblement owed much to both his family's official positions and to his own fame. He had been destined for a military career but gave this up for philosophy and science. The sale of land inherited from his mother enabled his travels; a pension from the king of France came only in 1647.

BIBLIOGRAPHY

Hill, Christopher. *Intellectual Origins of the English Revolution.* London: Panther, 1972.

Rossi, Paolo. *Philosophy, Technology, and the Arts in the Early Modern Era.* Trans. Salvatore Attanasio. New York: Harper and Row, 1970.

Shapin, Steven. *A Social History of Truth: Civility and Science in Seventeenth Century England.* Chicago and London: University of Chicago Press, 1994.

RICHARD W. HADDEN

See also Craftsman-and-Scholar Thesis; Ideology, Science as; Marxist Historiography

Society of Jesus

A religious order in the Roman Catholic Church, popularly known as the Jesuits, founded by Saint Ignatius of Loyola (1491–1556) with six companions in Paris on August 15, 1534. The members took the vows of poverty and chastity as well as a special vow of obedience to the pope. The order grew rapidly to 938 members in 1556, 3,500 in 1565, 15,544 in 1626, and 22,589 in 1749. Its growth coincided with the movement known as the Counter-Reformation, in which the Jesuits played a leading role. Heavily engaged in teaching, the order founded colleges and universities, beginning with the college established in Rome by Ignatius himself, the Collegio Romano, and expanding throughout Europe. These followed the course of studies (*ratio studiorum*) laid out by Ignatius and set a pattern for higher education in secular institutions as well. Known as the schoolmasters of Europe, the Jesuits became the major source of scientific contributions within the Catholic world throughout the Scientific Revolution.

Jesuit science during this period has several characteristics that are noteworthy. The Jesuits were intent on the acquisition of knowledge and practiced careful observation and experimentation with optical and newly discovered phenomena such as magnetism and electricity. They had a good sense of the precision required in scientific work and appreciated the value of collaboration, so much so that they could be regarded as a scientific society in miniature. On the debit side, they had a tendency to be eclectic in their enterprises and showed little interest in a coherent philosophy of nature that might tie them together. Related to this was a tension between the scientists (mainly mathematicians) and the philosophers and theologians within the society. Undoubtedly, the scientists were handicapped by the pope's rejection of Copernicanism, which effectively forced them into a prolonged defense of the Tychonian system. Along with this, they inclined to probabilism and fictionalist explanations, encouraging an emblematic view of nature, with its emphasis on signs and metaphors, long after it had been discarded by other scientists.

The earliest work of Jesuit scientists grew out of the teaching of the mathematician Christoph Clavius (1538–1612), "the Euclid of the sixteenth century." Clavius trained many mathematicians at the Collegio Romano and was instrumental in having mathematics made an integral part of the *ratio studiorum*. In astronomy, particularly, Jesuits produced many of the commonly used textbooks and, when the telescope became available, made important discoveries in the heavens. Apart from Clavius himself, whose *Sphaera* (1585) was the classic exposition of Ptolemaic astronomy, the works of Christoph Grienberger (1561–1636), Giuseppe Biancani (1566–1620), Christoph Scheiner (1573–1650), Orazio Grassi (1590–1654), and Giambattista Riccioli (1598–1671) are significant. Biancani propagated Galileo Galilei's (1564–1642) and Johannes Kepler's (1571–1630) discoveries; Scheiner did original work on sunspots; and Grassi, the same on comets. Riccioli, a student of Biancani at Bologna, gave a detailed account in his *Almagestum novum* (1651) of all of the arguments pro and contra the Copernican system, though he himself favored the contra position. He was also an adept experimenter, the first to obtain accurate measurements that verified Galileo's law of uniform acceleration in falling motion.

Optics was a field largely coopted by the Jesuits in the seventeenth century. It started with the *Opticorum*

libri sex (1613) of François d'Aguilon (1546–1617) and reached its culmination in the writings of Francesco Maria Grimaldi (1618–1663), who worked with Riccioli at Bologna and prepared a new Moon map for the latter's text. Grimaldi also discovered the optical phenomenon of diffraction. Others who made notable contributions were Scheiner, Athanasius Kircher (1602–1680), and Honoré Fabri (1607–1688). Kircher's *Ars magna lucis et umbrae* (1646) was a veritable encyclopedia of everything that gives and receives light, from the Sun and the Moon to glowing wood. And it was through Fabri's *Synopsis optica* (1667) that Isaac Newton (1642–1727) learned of Grimaldi's discovery of diffraction.

Magnetism was another area first explored in detail by the Jesuits. Niccolò Cabeo (1586–1650) published his *Philosophia magnetica* in 1629 as a sequel and a rejoinder to William Gilbert's *De magnete* (1600). He adopted Gilbert's experimental method but disagreed with the latter's claim that the earth is a magnet and that this is what causes its rotation. Niccolò Zucchi (1586–1670) used magnetic arguments in 1649 to disprove an annual motion of the earth around the Sun. Kircher wrote two books on magnetism, in one of which, in 1643, he rebutted Kepler's claim that magnetic spokes from the Sun move the planets, whereas in the other, in 1667, he proclaimed magnetic virtue as everywhere in nature and as responsible even for occult phenomena in living things. The three-volume *Cursus seu mundus mathematicus* (1674) of Claude François Milliet Dechales (1621–1678) also included an extensive section on magnetism.

Because of the missionary activity of the society, Jesuits first brought knowledge of astronomical discoveries to China. They then sent materials back to Rome, from which Kircher prepared rich accounts of the marvels of the East in his *China monumentis* (1667). The same occurred with their missions in the New World and in Southeast Asia, which led to new accounts of natural history and atlases that advanced geographical knowledge.

Mention should also be made of the illustrations that adorned Jesuit books throughout this period. The society was convinced of the importance of images for attracting and educating the faithful, and this, along with the interest in emblems, explains the profusion of plates in its publications. D'Aguilon's optics contained engravings based on drawings made by the Flemish artist Rubens. Francesco Lana Terzi (1631–1687) published an unusual work, his *Prodromo* (1670), which contained

S

twenty etchings depicting clocks, air pumps, and other inventions, including a proposed airship to be drawn aloft by four evacuated copper spheres. Gaspar Schott (1608–1666), Kircher's disciple and, like him, an encyclopedist, gave the first account of Otto von Guericke's (1602–1686) air pump and his vacuum experiments and also made Robert Boyle's (1627–1691) work widely known in Germany. He denied, however, that either had produced a true vacuum, since the exhausted space was still filled with ether.

BIBLIOGRAPHY

Ashworth, William B., Jr. "Catholicism and Early Modern Science." In *God and Nature: Historical Essays on the Encounter Between Christianity* and Science, ed. D. C. Lindberg and R. L. Numbers. Berkeley and Los Angeles: University of California Press, 1986, pp. 136–166.

Broderick, J. F. "Jesuits." In *New Catholic Encyclopedia*. New York: McGraw-Hill, 1967, vol. 7, pp. 898–909.

Dear, Peter. "Jesuit Mathematical Science and the Reconstitution of Experience in the Early Seventeenth Century." *Studies in the History and Philosophy of Science* 18 (1987), 133–175.

Jesuit Science in the Age of Galileo. An Exhibition of Rare Books. Kansas City, MO: Linda Hall Library, 1986.

Wallace, William A. *Galileo and His Sources: The Heritage of the Collegio Romano in Galileo's Science*. Princeton, NJ: Princeton University Press, 1984.

———. *Galileo, the Jesuits, and the Medieval Aristotle*. (Collected Studies Series 346). Aldershot, England: Variorum, 1991.

WILLIAM A. WALLACE

See also Clavius, Christoph; Collegio Romano

Soul

Medieval and Renaissance scholars understood *anima* (soul) as the entity whose presence made a thing alive. Following Aristotle (384–322 B.C.E.), they believed that plants and animals as well as humans possessed souls but that only the human soul survived death. United with a properly prepared body, the human soul carried out vegetative and sensitive functions. In the view of most Aristotelians down to the Renaissance, the soul did not require a body for intellectual functions. The mechanical philosophers of the seventeenth century, while not denying the existence of the human soul, argued that organs alone were sufficient for vegetative and sensitive functions. A comparison of the mechanist theories of René Descartes (1596–1650) with the vitalist theories of

William Harvey (1578–1657) in physiology and embryology illustrates how early attempts to banish soul from the science of life foundered upon the variety and complexity of vital functions.

In *De motu cordis* (On the Motion of the Heart, 1628), Harvey showed, contrary to the prevailing Galenic physiology, that blood returned to the heart through the veins and that systole was the active phase of heart motion. Although he likened the heart's motion to that of a pump, Harvey was no mechanical philosopher. He believed that the blood was the seat of the soul and that the heart restored and perfected the blood upon its return from the extremities before pumping it out again. Descartes readily accepted the circulation of the blood but denied that the heart possessed any "unknown or strange faculties" for the restoration of the blood. He claimed that the heat of the heart was sufficient to explain not only the restoration of the blood but cardiac motion as well. Where the vitalist Harvey could readily accept an active systole, the mechanist Descartes found an active diastole easier to accommodate. Descartes dismissed Harvey's assertion of an active systole and claimed, instead, that drops of blood entered the ventricles, were vaporized by cardiac heat, distended the ventricles, and so achieved enough pressure to force open the valves and enter the arteries. Unable to explain active systole in a heart deprived of the soul's vital powers, Descartes returned to the theory of active diastole, which Harvey had already shown was false.

In *De generatione animalium* (1651), Harvey, relying chiefly on the examination of chick eggs at different stages of development, proposed that fetal development took place by epigenesis, by the sequential derivation of parts from a principal particle that, for vertebrates, was the blood. Harvey believed that the blood—the first material to emerge from the homogeneous mass of the egg—became the seat of the soul and, as the source of animal heat and vital spirits, guided all subsequent differentiation. Harvey's willingness to attribute epigenesis to the soul rather than to mechanical processes allowed him to avoid the absurd consequences of preformation.

BIBLIOGRAPHY

Carter, Richard B. *Descartes' Medical Philosophy: The Organic Solution to the Mind-Body Problem*. Baltimore: Johns Hopkins University Press, 1983.

Gorham, Geoffrey. "Mind-Body Dualism and the Harvey-Descartes Controversy." *Journal of the History of Ideas* 55 (1994), 211–234.

Gueroult, Martial. *Descartes' Philosophy Interpreted According to the Order of Reasons,* vol. 1: *The Soul and God.* Trans. Roger Ariew. Minneapolis: University of Minnesota Press, 1984.

McMahon, C. B. "Harvey on the Soul: A Unique Episode in the History of Psychophysiological Thought." *Journal of the History of the Behavioral Sciences* 11 (1975), 276–283.

PETER G. SOBOL

See also Descartes, René; Physiology; Psychology; Spirit; Vitalism

Space

There were at least two main lines of thought about space at the beginning of the seventeenth century: Aristotelians usually conceived of space as an abstraction from body with no reality of its own, and atomists regarded space as something real and independent of body. These divergent lines of thought were clearly linked with debates over the possibility of void space or vacuum. The Aristotelian view culminated in the doctrines of René Descartes (1596–1650) and Gottfried Wilhelm Leibniz (1646–1716). The great champion of the atomist view was Isaac Newton (1642–1727).

To comprehend the debates about space in the early-modern period, one has to understand the context in which these debates were conducted—that is, the Aristotelian theory of place, which was itself developed against the backdrop of Platonic and atomist conceptions of space. Plato (428–348 B.C.E.), in the *Timaeus,* held that space is an everlasting receptacle that provides a situation for all things that come into being. It is not clear whether Plato's talk of space as a receptacle entailed its independent existence; according to Aristotle (384–322 B.C.E.), Plato thought matter and space the same and identified space and place. Aristotle agreed. His primary concept was place, or location in space, as one might say, space being the aggregate of all places. He defined place as the boundary of a containing body in contact with a contained body that can undergo locomotion. But he also asserted that place is the innermost *motionless* boundary of what it contains. Thus, the place of a ship in a river is not defined by the flowing waters but by the whole river, because the river is motionless as a whole. These definitions gave rise to questions about whether place is itself mobile or immobile. They also engendered a problem about the place of the ultimate containing body, the ultimate sphere of a universe consti-

tuted from a finite number of homocentric spheres. If having a place depends on being contained, the ultimate sphere will not have a place since there is no body outside it to contain it. But the ultimate sphere, or heaven, needs to have a place because it rotates, and motion involves change of place. Aristotle recognized these difficulties. In part, his solution was to declare that "heaven is, in a way, in place, for all its parts are; for on the orb, one part contains another."

Aristotle's doctrine and its problems became canonical in the Middle Ages through the commentaries of Averroës (1126–1198), Thomas Aquinas (d. 1274), and others. Aquinas accepted and modified Aristotle's account of the place of the ultimate sphere; the parts of the ultimate sphere are not actually in place, but the ultimate sphere is in a place accidentally because of its parts, which are themselves potentially in place. Aquinas also rejected Averroës's solution to the problem of the place of the ultimate sphere: that it is lodged because of its center, the earth, which is fixed. The technical vocabulary developed to interpret Aquinas's view on the immobility of place was a distinction between material place and formal place. Place is then movable accidentally (as material place) and immovable in itself (as formal place, defined as the place of a body with respect to the universe as a whole). Thus, an anchored ship is formally immobile (with respect to the universe as a whole) even when water flows around it (which thus changes its material place). However, the Thomist views were not universally accepted, in part because they seemed to require the immobility of the universe as a whole. This conflicted with part of the 1277 condemnation by the bishop of Paris of the proposition "that God could not move the heavens in a straight line, the reason being that he would then leave a vacuum." John Duns Scotus (ca. 1266–1308) and his followers rejected the distinction between material and formal place, arguing, instead, that place is a relation of the containing body with respect to the contained body. Since a relation changes with change in either of its relata—here, contained or containing bodies—the place of a body does not remain the same when the matter around it changes, even though the body in question might remain immobile. When a body is in a variable medium, it is in one place at one instant and in another at the next; to capture what is meant by the immobility of place, Scotists said that two successive places are distinct but *equivalent places* from the view of local motion. On the question of the ultimate sphere,

Scotus denied both Averroës's and Aquinas's solutions (requiring the fixity of the universe as a whole, its pole, or its center), claiming that heaven can rotate even though no body contains it and could even if it contained no body; it could rotate even if it were formed out of a single homogeneous sphere.

These debates informed the seventeenth-century Scholastic discussions about place and its two central questions about the immobility of place and the place of the ultimate sphere. For example, the Collegio Romano Jesuit Franciscus Toletus took Aquinas's side against Scotus on both questions. So did Théophraste Bouju, the author of a French-language philosophy textbook, who also kept some Averroist elements in his doctrine. Bouju asserted that place is movable in itself, in what he called situational place, and accidentally, in what he called surrounding place:

> The earth has . . . a surrounding place and can also be said to be in a situational place with respect to the poles of the world. But it cannot change place with respect to its totality; thus it is immobile in that respect and mobile only with respect to some parts that can be separated from the totality and moved into others. The firmament is also in a situational place with respect to the earth, but it cannot change except with respect to its parts and not in its totality, in the fashion of the earth.

There were anti-Thomists as well. Scipion Dupleix, the author of a popular French-language textbook, rejected the Thomist view; he preferred a doctrine he attributed to John Philoponus (fl. first half of sixth century) and Averroës (1126–1198), that when air is blowing around a house, one says that the place of the house changes accidentally. The house is in the same place *by equivalence*. Eustachius a Sancto Paulo, the author of a popular Latin-language philosophy textbook, sided with Scotus: place is a relation between the containing and the contained bodies, and the places of a body in a mobile environment are the same *by equivalence*. He also developed, very briefly, some interesting views about the place of the ultimate sphere: the place of the outermost sphere is both internal place (the space occupied by the body) and external, but imaginary, place—given that the external place is the surface of the concave ambient body. "Imaginary place" thus became the standard answer to

such questions as to where God could move the universe, if he chose to move it, and what there was before the creation of the universe (i.e., before the creation of any corporeal substance. Imaginary places, however, were generally thought of not as real things, independent of body, but on the model of a privation of a measurable thing, like a shadow, given that a privation of a measurable thing can be measured. Similarly, it was held that no time elapsed when time and the world began but that an immense privation of time—an imaginary time—had preceded the Creation.

While late Scholastics agreed in rejecting the independence of space from body, they disagreed about other important issues. Hidden within the debate between Thomists and Scotists on the question of the mobility or immobility of place and the place of the ultimate sphere were issues about the relativity of motion or reference for motion. Some thinkers supported a Thomist doctrine in which the motion of a body is referred to its place, conceived as its relation to the universe as a whole, a universe that is necessarily immobile; others supported a Scotist doctrine in which the motion of an object is referred to its place, conceived as a purely relational property of bodies.

Surprisingly, one can see similar views among various non-Scholastics, such as Descartes and Leibniz. Descartes is well known for his criticisms of Scholastic doctrines in his early works. One can find him asserting, with respect to the Scholastic concept of place: "When they define place as 'the surface of the surrounding body,' they are not really conceiving anything false, but are merely misusing the word 'place.'" He rejected the Scholastic concept of intrinsic place and poked fun at their concept of imaginary space. But, in his mature work, *The Principles of Philosophy* (1644), he developed a doctrine of internal and external place clearly indebted to those he had previously rejected. He asserted that space, or internal place, does not differ from the corporeal substance contained in it, except in the way that we conceive of it; the same extension that constitutes the nature of body also constitutes the nature of space. On the other hand, he defined external place and its relation to space. For Descartes, again, "place or space do not signify a thing different from the body which is said to be in place, but only designate its size, shape and situation among bodies." To determine situation among bodies, however, we must take into account other bodies we consider motionless. So we can define an external place,

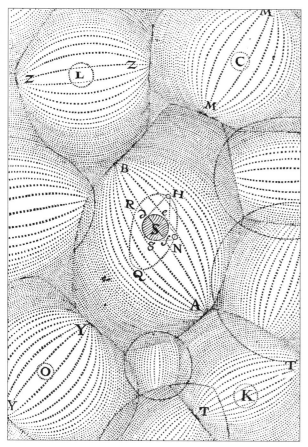

René Descartes, like Aristotle, rejected the idea that a vacuum exists anywhere in the universe. For Descartes, the universe is completely filled with vortices of subtle matter with a role in moving the planets around the Sun. From Descartes's Principles of Philosophy *(1644).*

namely the surface of the surrounding body and ultimately some supposedly motionless points in the heavens, as the fixed and determinate place for the motion of a body. The body then might simultaneously change and not change its place: it might change its external place (its situation) and not change its internal place (its extension or shape). Given that Descartes thought it impossible to discover any truly motionless points in the universe, he also thought that "nothing has any enduring, fixed and determinate place, except insofar as its place is determined in our minds." Thus, for Descartes, place, properly speaking, is internal place, or space, which is to be identified with the nature of body (i.e., its extension), but we can mentally construct a situation, or external place, as the immobile reference for the motion of bodies.

Descartes's choice of a relatively conservative, Aristotelian-inspired theory of space must have been a con-

scious decision. At the time, it was possible to choose from a number of non-Aristotelian concepts of space, originating from attempts to reestablish ancient views, such as Platonism and Epicureanism. Among the new Platonists were Giordano Bruno (1548–1600), Bernardino Telesio (1509–1588), and Tommaso Campanella (1568–1639). All three conceived of space as a container, independent of bodies, but always occupied by bodies. Francesco Patrizi (1529–1597) maintained a more radical line in which three-dimensional space was to be thought of not as substance or accident but as something subsisting in itself, inhering in nothing else. Space is the infinite, immobile container in which God placed bodies, filling some places but leaving others empty. Pierre Gassendi (1592–1655), in his revival of Epicureanism, produced a similar doctrine: God created a single, though finite, world of atoms and placed it in an infinite three-dimensional void space. Thus, Gassendi's world had void spaces inside bodies (i.e., between the atoms) and surrounding the created world.

Isaac Newton continued the penchant for considering space as something real, independent of the bodies existing in it. He stated, in a Scholium in his *Principia mathematica philosophiae naturalis* (1687), that "absolute space, by its nature, without relation to anything external, remains always similar and motionless," and, in the General Scholium to the second edition of *Principia III*, he identified this absolute space with the divine: "He endures always, and is present everywhere, and by existing always and everywhere, he has established duration and space. . . . In him all things are contained and moved."

Newton's views were disputed by Leibniz in his correspondence with Samuel Clarke (1675–1729), who was Newton's stand-in. Leibniz denied that space is an absolute being and that it is an attribute of God (given that it consists of parts). He held, at least in his mature period, that space is an order of simultaneous coexistents: "space denotes, in terms of possibility, an order of things which exist at the same time, considered as existing together, without entering into their particular manners of existing." Hence, for Leibniz, space presupposes the existence of things to be ordered, so space would not exist if there were no bodies and the monads that underlie them. Without bodies, space would be only in God's ideas: "Since space in itself is an ideal thing like time, space out of this world must be imaginary, as the Schoolmen themselves have recognized." Leibniz's space is radically relative, just the actual or possible relations among bodies. Moreover, Leibniz rejected Newton's absolute space by a reduction to absurdity. Leibniz's argument was that there would be no real change if the whole universe were moved without the distances of things with respect to one another being changed or if everything in the universe were placed in a contrary fashion by having east and west flipped. Assuming the principle that nothing is done without a sufficient reason, there would be no reason for God to place bodies in space in one way and not in another, their difference being found only in the "chimerical supposition of the reality of space in itself."

Of course, these propositions were not left unchallenged by the Newtonians, who relied on Newton's citation of a rotating water-filled bucket to argue for the necessity of an absolute frame of reference. The argument over absolute space or space as a body or relational property of bodies continued. Still, one can see, in the great debate between Newton and Leibniz on the relativity and reality of space, the echoes of the previous debates between atomists and Aristotelians and between various Aristotelians, such as Thomists and Scotists.

BIBLIOGRAPHY

Alexander, H. G., ed. *The Leibniz-Clarke Correspondence*. Manchester: Manchester University Press, 1956.

Čapek, Milič. *The Concepts of Space and Time*. Dordrecht: Reidel, 1976.

Descartes, René. *Principles of Philosophy*. Trans. V. R. Miller and R. P. Miller. Dordrecht: Reidel, 1983.

Duhem, Pierre. *Medieval Cosmoslogy: Theories of Infinity, Place, Time, Void, and the Plurality of Worlds*. Ed. and trans. R. Ariew. Chicago: University of Chicago Press, 1985.

Garber, Daniel. *Descartes' Metaphysical Physics*. Chicago: University of Chicago Press, 1992.

Grant, Edward. *Much Ado About Nothing: Theories of Space and Vacuum from the Middle Ages to the Scientific Revolution*. Cambridge: Cambridge University Press, 1981.

Koyré, Alexandre. *From the Closed World to the Infinite Universe*. Baltimore: Johns Hopkins University Press, 1957.

ROGER ARIEW

See also Aristotelianism; Atomism; Descartes, René; Epicureanism; Gassendi, Pierre; Leibniz, Gottfried Wilhelm; Motion; Newton, Isaac

Species

The Scientific Revolution of the sixteenth and seventeenth centuries was a crucial period in the historical development of the species concept. It is impossible to give an accurate account of this concept in its biological use apart from its origin and development in the context of attempts to construct a classification of living things. Classifications of living things prior to this period were largely utilitarian in character. The *De materia medica* of the first-century physician Dioscorides, for example, which was the basis for numerous medieval herbals, classified herbs according to their supposed medicinal value. In his *Historia animalium* (1551), Conrad Gessner (1516–1565) simply arranged animals in alphabetical order according to the common Latin name of each. In neither case was any attempt made to develop a rigorous system of biological classification. A desire to accurately identify the organisms mentioned in the classical writings of antiquity, as well as a desire to bring order to the mass of novel organisms introduced by the voyages of discovery, led Renaissance naturalists to devise new approaches to classification. Critical discussions of the nature of species arose from attempts to construct a "natural" classification of living things.

Foremost among these naturalists was Andrea Cesalpino (1519–1603). In his *De plantis libri XVI* (1583), Cesalpino rejected the medicinal approach to classifying plants by insisting, instead, on a knowledge of their essences (i.e., their similarities and differences of form). Starting from the main genera recognized by Aristotle's student Theophrastus (ca. 371–ca. 287) (trees, shrubs, undershrubs, herbs), Cesalpino divided each group of plants on the basis of certain features (typically, those associated with their reproductive parts) assumed to be essential, terminating in the *infimae species* (lower forms) recognized by herbalists and others. Characters such as color, smell, and taste and those produced by climatic variation were all considered to be accidental properties and, thus, could not be employed in distinguishing species. The same sort of approach, he suggested, could be extended to animals as well. For Cesalpino, as for Aristotle (384–322 B.C.E.), species are eternal and unchanging. In determining species identity by selecting features associated with the reproductive parts, Cesalpino explicitly focused on those structures most directly connected with the propagation of the form of each kind of living thing.

Cesalpino's approach became the conceptual foundation for seminal works in classification by John Ray (1620–1705), Joseph Pitton de Tournefort (1656–1708), and, most famously, Carl Linnaeus (1707–1778). These writers were united in their view that (1) a correct biological classification is representative of the actual order of created nature; (2) the essential characteristics of organisms can be distinguished from accidental ones; and (3) the term *species* refers to the essences of existent particulars. For example, in his *Historia plantarum* (1686), Ray proposed logical criteria for determining species identity by separating accidental from essential variations in plants. For Ray, the true forms of nature (i.e., species) are disclosed by the propagation of "seeds." Whatever characters are constant in such propagation compose the true specific *differentiae* signifying the essence. Ray was quite liberal in his understanding of characters related to propagation, including similarity in parts of the flower, the number and structure of protective leaves surrounding the flower, and the structure of seed cases. All of these characters, however, he considered to be nonaccidental. Tournefort, likewise, in his *Institutiones rei herbariae* (1719), adopted the Cesalpinean distinction between essential and accidental characteristics but simplified botanical classification by focusing exclusively on external variations in flowers. Although simpler and more rigorous than previous systems of classification, it had the disadvantage of providing, at best, a definitional criterion for distinguishing essential from accidental characters, in contrast to the systems devised by Cesalpino and Ray, which included an experimental criterion of species membership based on the propagation of seeds.

Although the work of Cesalpino, Ray, and Tournefort was instrumental in the development of biological classification and in the refinement of the species concept, it was Linnaeus's work that ultimately had the greatest impact. In his *Systema naturae,* originally published in 1735, he undertook a thorough reform of biological classification, including the introduction of the familiar binomial nomenclature (identifying organisms by genus, species designations) used today. For Linnaeus, to know a thing amounts to knowing how to name it correctly, and this requires knowledge of the two terms that define the essence: the proximate genus and the essential difference.

The Cesalpinean tradition of biological classification, culminating in Linnaeus's work, came under fire in the eighteenth century from George-Louis de Clerc, Comte de Buffon (1707–1788), who argued that it is the total morphological resemblance between organisms, rather than just a few "essential" characters, that defines species membership. Prominent French biologists after Buffon, including Antoine-Laurent de Jussieu (1748–1846) and George Cuvier (1769–1832), largely accepted this view of species. It was not until the work of Charles Darwin (1809–1882) that the species concept would be placed on an entirely new foundation.

BIBLIOGRAPHY

Atran, Scott. "Origin of the Species and Genus Concepts: An Anthropological Perspective." *Journal of the History of Biology* 20 (1987), 195–279.

Grieco, Allen J. "The Social Politics of Pre-Linnaean Botanical Classification." *I Tatti Studies* 4 (1991), 131–149.

Mayr, Ernst. *The Growth of Biological Thought.* Cambridge, MA: Harvard University Press, 1982.

Sloan, Philip Reid. "The History of the Concept of the Biological Species in the Seventeenth and Eighteenth Centuries, and the Origin of the Species Problem." Ph.D. diss. University of California, San Diego, 1970.

TIMOTHY SHANAHAN

See also Botany; Taxonomy; Zoology

Spinoza, Benedict de (1632–1677)

Born in Amsterdam, Baruch de Spinoza was one of the most important philosophers of the seventeenth century. Following his excommunication in 1656 from the Amsterdam Jewish community, he changed his name from Baruch to its Latin equivalent, Benedict. He earned his living as a lens grinder and a tutor and died in The Hague.

Spinoza's knowledge of, and interest in, natural science is evident in a number of his works. One of these is *Principles of Philosophy* (1663), an exposition—written in the "geometrical" order of axioms, definitions, propositions, and demonstrations—of Parts I and II (with portions of Part III) of René Descartes's (1596–1650) *Principles of Philosophy* (1644). While he is sometimes critical of both the content and Descartes's presentation of physics in *Principles of Philosophy* Part II, he shows himself to be, on the whole, a sensitive and sympathetic expositor of Cartesian physics. Spinoza's interest in natural science is also manifest in the posthumously published *Correspondence* (1677), which includes, in addition to letters concerning his interests in dioptrics, twenty-eight letters written over a period of fifteen years between Spinoza and Henry Oldenburg (ca. 1619–1677), secretary of the British Royal Society and a close friend of Robert Boyle (1627–1691). This correspon-

Benedict de Spinoza. From A. Wolf, A History of Science, Technology, and Philosophy in the Sixteenth and Seventeenth Centuries *(London: Allen and Unwin, 1935).*

dence includes Spinoza's detailed discussion and criticism of Boyle's interpretations of chemical experiments. Spinoza's best-known work, the posthumously published *Ethics* (1677), contains (in a series of lemmas immediately following Part II, Proposition 13) a brief but important discussion of the foundations of physics, centering on the nature of motion, rest, and individual bodies.

Spinoza's *Theological-Political Treatise* (published anonymously in 1670) explicitly models the interpretation of Scripture on the interpretation of nature and was important in the development of a scientific approach to the history and meaning of the Bible and its constituent books. Both the *Theological-Political Treatise* and the unfinished *Political Treatise* (1677) are intended as contributions to politics conceived as a science, while Part III of the *Ethics* aims to present a scientific account of human psychology, focusing on the passions.

More significant for the Scientific Revolution than Spinoza's contributions to particular sciences, however, is his naturalistic and antisupernaturalistic conception of the universe as a deterministic substantial whole—the

understanding of which constitutes humankind's highest good. He elaborates this conception primarily in the *Ethics*.

Spinoza conceives of nature and God as identical. "God or Nature" (*Deus, sive Natura*) is, he argues, the only genuine substance. This substance is, in many ways, like the God of traditional Western theology: absolutely infinite, eternal, necessarily existent, having an essence identical with its existence, unlimited in power, actively causing all things, and such that the contemplation or understanding of its nature produces intellectual love and eternal blessedness. It is not, however, in any sense personal, and it does not act for any purpose or end. Rather, its activity flows necessarily and in accordance with deterministic natural laws from its own essence. It has infinitely many "attributes" (i.e., "what the intellect perceives as constituting the essence of substance"), of which human beings understand only two: thought and extension. Everything other than God is a "mode" of God and is "in and conceived through" God—that is, everything is a way in which God or nature is qualified or expressed. Because God and nature are identical, in Spinoza's view all science, whether psychological or physical, is knowledge of God, and knowledge of the fundamental nature of thought and extension is knowledge of God's essence. Spinoza's ethical theory identifies "adequate" knowledge with virtue and blessedness; such knowledge, he holds, is grounded in the intellect rather than the mere images of sensory perception.

BIBLIOGRAPHY

Bennett, Jonathan. *A Study of Spinoza's Ethics.* Indianapolis: Hackett, 1984.

Garrett, Don, ed. *The Cambridge Companion to Spinoza.* Cambridge: Cambridge University Press, 1996.

Spinoza, Benedict de. *The Collected Works of Spinoza,* vol. 1. Ed. and trans. Edwin Curley. Princeton, NJ: Princeton University Press, 1985.

DON GARRETT

See also Descartes, René; Religion and Natural Philosophy

Spirit

The fact that the word *spirit* is used today to refer not only to supposedly incorporeal entities but also to material entities of various levels of tenuity or subtlety, from volatile liquids to wispy vapors, is a legacy from past usage. But while today this range of possible meanings

S

causes little confusion and raises no intellectual debate, during the period of the Scientific Revolution things were very different. Certainly there are some Renaissance uses of the word *spirit* that are completely unequivocal, but, more often than not, extreme care is required to correctly interpret what kind of spirits are being invoked, material or immaterial. Spirits were routinely called upon in Renaissance culture to account for various phenomena, and for some thinkers it was clearly important to insist upon the immateriality of spirit, while others were happy to suppose that such spirits could be, and were, material. Difficulties of interpretation most commonly arise at just those points in which spirits are invoked as a kind of bridge between the material and the immaterial realms.

One of the prime sites for discussion of spirits was in the realm of medical theory. Three spirits were said to play an important role in physiology: (1) natural spirit, concocted in the liver from chyle, which nourished the body; (2) vital spirit, compounded in the heart, which heated and vitalized the body; and (3) animal spirit, elaborated in the brain, which gave movement, sensitivity and appetites, and some "lower" mental attributes, such as common sense, imagination, and memory. These were spirits in the material sense: highly subtle fluids that contributed to the functioning of the animal body. In the case of the animal spirits, however, there was some dispute about the nature and the extent of their activity in humans. It seems clear that, for many medical writers, the animal spirits were responsible, at least in part, for higher mental faculties, such as cogitation or understanding. Early theories of brain localization, allegedly supported by observations of brain injuries, suggested that the senses and the imagination were associated with the forepart of the brain; the memory, with the back of the brain; and the higher faculty of the understanding, with the midpart. It was also objected that, if the understanding was held to be one of the higher faculties of the mind and so the province of the immaterial soul rather than the animal spirits, cases of mental derangement could not be understood without assuming the soul to be subject to deterioration. By the same token, madness ought not to be curable by standard humoral therapies, and yet doctors were frequently successful (it seemed) in restoring the insane to their former selves. It was open to the irreligious simply to conclude that all aspects of our mental lives were epiphenomena of the humors and spirits of the body, but even a highly devout physician like

Thomas Willis (1621–1675) found it too easy to explain all mental functions in mechanistic terms, without recourse to the incorporeal rational soul, which he took care to distinguish from his subject.

Behind such technical equivocations about the limits of the animal soul was a firmly held assumption among natural philosophers that matter itself was in some way active. The standard dualism of Christian thought held that matter was dead and inert, animated only by the soul or some other incorporeal spirit. This theologically convenient arrangement was constantly threatened by beliefs about the inherent activity of matter. Willis, for example, in spite of being known as a leading mechanical philosopher and a devout Anglican, rejected the Cartesian view that matter is inert and can be moved only by collision with bodies already in motion, insisting, instead, that atoms are "very active" and even "self-moving." William Harvey (1578–1657), on the other hand, was more obviously indebted to an earlier medical and philosophical tradition. For Harvey, the blood was spirit par excellence. Other medical traditions that blur the distinction between immaterial and material spirits and their functions can be found in Paracelsianism, Helmontianism, and other newly formed, broadly Neoplatonic systems. Although it might seem safe to conclude that medical writers were not concerned with theological niceties, writers on theology have been shown to have been influenced by such medical theorizing, even to the extent of implying that the Holy Spirit and the human soul are material.

Spiritual substances of various kinds figured also in natural philosophy, doing sterling service whenever a source of motion or activity was required in physical systems. For the most part, these notions of spirit seem to derive from Neoplatonic sources. Neoplatonic emanationism supposed that the world was created as a series of emanations ultimately originating from God. The first emanations, directly from God, were light and space, both incorporeal but occupying the three dimensions of length, breadth, and depth. Ether, fire, air, and other increasingly crass forms of matter were formed as light condensed into denser forms. It was, nevertheless, supposed that even the densest forms of matter contained some light within them and that light could activate and move matter. This kind of thinking can be seen in many of the New Philosophers, but it makes its most famous appearance in the thought of Isaac Newton (1642–1727), who repeatedly suggested in the "Queries" with which he finished his *Opticks* (1704, 1705, 1717) that light entered into the composition of bodies, giving them various kinds of activity. In an earlier, unpublished, alchemical work, he had written that the "body of light" was a spirit with a "prodigious active principle," and in his "Hypothesis Explaining the Properties of Light," read before the Royal Society in 1675, he suggested that perhaps "the whole frame of nature may be nothing but various contextures of some certain aethereal spirits, or vapours." Similarly, in unpublished drafts for the "Queries" and in the Scholium added to the second edition of his *Principia mathematica philosophiae naturalis* (1713), he wrote of a "most subtle spirit which pervades and lies hid in all gross bodies" and is responsible for optical, electrical, and physiological phenomena.

The role of active, but nonetheless material, spirits in natural philosophy has only recently begun to be recognized by historians of science, and much remains to be explored. It is already apparent, however, that a consideration of these ideas will help us understand not only interactions between seventeenth-century natural philosophy and theology, but also the nature and development of the mechanical philosophy itself.

BIBLIOGRAPHY

Fattori , M., and M. Bianchi, eds. *Spiritus: IV° Colloquio Internazionale del Lessico Intellettuale.* Rome: Edizioni dell'Ateneo, 1984.

Henry, John. "The Matter of Souls: Medical Theory and Theology in Seventeenth-Century England." In *The Medical Revolution of the Seventeenth Century,* ed. Roger French and Andrew Wear. Cambridge: Cambridge University Press, 1989, pp. 87–113.

Walker, D. P. "Medical Spirits in Philosophy and Theology from Ficino to Newton." In Walker, D. P. *Music, Spirit, and Language in the Renaissance.* London: Variorum, 1985.

———. *Spiritual and Demonic Magic from Ficino to Campanella.* London: Warburg Institute, 1958.

JOHN HENRY

See also Active Principles; Humors; Physiology; Soul; Vitalism

Spontaneous Generation

Beliefs concerning the spontaneous generation of lesser beings in earth, mud, rotting materials, and inside superior plants and animals remained in force in the sixteenth and most of the seventeenth centuries, there being different variants of the two theoretical traditions on this matter dating back to classical times. One was the theory held by Aristotle (384–322 B.C.E.), who defended "self-moved generation" based on the formative force of nature, hylemorphism, and the doctrine of opposed wet-dry, hot-cold qualities. This remained in force in early-modern Europe through Aristotle's own works on biology, the systematization of his ideas by late-medieval Scholasticism, and the reworked version by the Stoics of ancient Rome and Greece, which had been assimilated to a considerable extent by certain of the early Church Fathers. The other theoretical tradition, propounded by Democritus (ca. 460–370 B.C.E.), used the atomist approach to explain the cause of spontaneous generation and survived in the Renaissance mainly in the Epicurean version of Lucretius (ca. 97–54 B.C.E.). In addition to these two traditions, there was also the very broad concept of Paracelsus (ca. 1493–1541) and his followers, based on a vision of the universe as an organism and an *archeus,* a vital principle that directs substances and alchemical forces.

Spontaneous generation was defended in varying degrees by the continuators of traditional doctrines, together with advocates of innovation, including such famous names in different areas during the Scientific Revolution as William Harvey (1578–1657), Johannes Baptista van Helmont (1579–1644), and René Descartes (1596–1650). It was only in the last third of the seventeenth century that criticism denying its existence began to be heard, albeit to a limited extent.

The most influential criticism came from Francesco Redi (1626–1697), head physician at the Medici Court in Florence and a member of its Accademia del Cimento, the institute where he met scientists applying Galilean mechanics to biology. In his treatise *Esperienze intorno alla generazione degli insetti* (Experiments on the Generation of Insects, 1668), Redi used very simple experiments to prove that the larvae on decomposing meat came from eggs laid there by female insects. He placed meat and other organic substances in jars sealed with paper or closely woven fabric and demonstrated that no larvae appeared even after several months, whilst they appeared rapidly on the substances in open jars. However, he declared that the larvae in galls on plants were generated by the same vegetative force that produced fruit. The microscopist Marcello Malpighi (1628–1694) observed that said galls were tumors produced by fertilized insect eggs (1679), a fact confirmed later by his disciple Antonio Vallisneri (1661–1730).

Observations made by classical microscopists from the Netherlands, Jan Swammerdam (1637–1680) and

Antoni van Leeuwenhoek (1632–1723), also contributed to the refutation of spontaneous generation, while the English naturalist John Ray (1620–1705) and the French physician Nicolas Andry (1658–1752) vehemently defended, albeit with little evidence, the sexual generation of intestinal parasitic worms. All of this criticism was related to embryological preformation and other scientific and religious approaches of the period.

BIBLIOGRAPHY

Belloni, L. *Francesco Redi biologo*. Pisa: Domus Galilaeana, 1958.

Farley, J. *The Spontaneous Generation Controversy from Descartes to Oparin*. Baltimore: Johns Hopkins University Press, 1977.

Gasking, E. *Investigations into Generation, 1651–1828*. Baltimore: Johns Hopkins University Press, 1967.

Mendelsohn, E. "Philosophical Biology vs. Experimental Biology: Spontaneous Generation in the Seventeenth Century." *Actes du XIIᵉ Congrès International d'Histoire des Sciences* 1 (1971), 201–229.

Roger, J. *Les sciences de la vie dans la pensée française de XVIIIᵉ siècle: La génération des animaux de Descartes à l'Encyclopédie*. Paris: Armand Colin, 1963.

JOSÉ M. LÓPEZ-PIÑERO

See also Generation; Malpighi, Marcello; Preformation; Redi, Francesco; Vallisneri, Antonio

Stahl, Georg Ernst (1660–1734)

One of the most important contributors to the development of chemistry and medicine in the first half of the eighteenth century. He published extensively, maintained an active medical practice, and held important academic and Court positions. In chemistry, he further developed particulate-matter theories and advanced the phlogiston theory, which provided the most widely accepted theoretical foundation for chemistry before Antoine Lavoisier (1743–1794). In medicine, Stahl defended a strictly vitalist viewpoint, maintaining a firm distinction between living and nonliving matter, and insisted that the two could not be explained by the same principles.

Stahl studied medicine at the University of Jena under Georg Wolfgang Wedel, receiving his degree in January 1684. He then lectured on chemistry there until he was made Court physician at Saxe-Weimar. In 1694 he became professor of medicine at the new University of Halle, where he taught until 1716, when he went to Berlin as physician to Frederick I, king of Prussia.

Stahl's chief contribution to chemistry was the development of the phlogiston theory. His major influence in this regard came from his countryman Johann Joachim Becher (1635–1682), who reorganized the Paracelsian triad of component substances—Mercury, Sulfur, and Salt—into a triad of earths—liquifiable, inflammable, and vitrifiable. The second of these, the inflammable earth (corresponding roughly to alchemical Sulfur) was in a few places referred to as phlogiston by Becher, the term coined from the Greek *phlox,* meaning flame. Stahl developed his chemical system around phlogiston—conceived of as the principle of inflammability—stating, for example, that combustion can be understood as a loss of phlogiston. This system rationalized and systematized many laboratory observations. For example, metals, when heated in a fire, lose their phlogiston and are "burnt" to a friable powder, or calx; this calx, mixed with charcoal, oil, or some other inflammable material, can regain phlogiston from the inflammable material and is, thus, reconverted into its metallic state. Stahlians endeavored to work out difficulties in the system (e.g., the well-known observation that calx weighs more than the metal from which it was produced, in spite of having lost phlogiston). In spite of such difficulties, the Stahlian system was popular among chemists, in large part, because Stahl had emphasized the explanation of the wide range of observable chemical phenomena that was largely glossed over by the more physico-mathematical models of Newtonians. Stahl was suspicious of purely mechanical explanations.

Stahl's system also depended on a vitalist view of matter in which a guiding *anima,* or life force, directed the material changes in living systems. Stahl rejected the notion that a knowledge of chemical phenomena could explain processes such as digestion, growth, or respiration that occur in plant and animal systems; thus, chemistry was not helpful in understanding medicine. Changes in living matter were directed by an *anima* lacking in inanimate materials. When this *anima* ceased to function, death and putrefaction occurred. While Stahl's *anima* bears similarities to the *archeus* of the Paracelsians and the Spirit of Nature of the Neoplatonists, his insistence on vitalism is undoubtedly also tied to his Pietism.

BIBLIOGRAPHY

Duchesneau, François. "G. E. Stahl: Antimécanisme et physiologie." *Archives internationale d'histoire des sciences* 26 (1976), 3–26.

Metzger, Hélène. *Newton, Stahl, et Boerhaave et la doctrine chimique.* Paris: Alcan. 1930.

Oldroyd, David. "An Examination of G. E. Stahl's Philosophical Principles of Universal Chemistry." *Ambix* 20 (1973), 36–52.

Partington, J. R. *History of Chemistry.* 4 vols. London, 1961, vol. 2, pp. 637–690.

LAWRENCE M. PRINCIPE

See also Alchemy; Becher, Johann Joachim; Chemistry; Spirit; Vitalism

Statistics

The mathematical statistics of current scientific practice has two components: the production or collection of quantitative data and the application of a statistical test to confirm or refute a hypothesis. The origins of each of these components lie in the seventeenth century, with the spread of quantification in the sciences and the development of the mathematical theory of probability. Yet, the relationship between them remained unstable until ca. 1900.

John Graunt (1620–1674) became the first practitioner of statistics in 1662 with the publication of his *Observations Upon the Bills of Mortality.* The city of London had been collecting weekly reports on christenings, burials, and deaths by disease (especially the plague) since 1603. In an effort to gain admittance to the Royal Society, Graunt summed and ordered these various London bills into tables and performed minor algebraic manipulations upon them. He also made comments and rough estimations about the population of London, the percentage of people who live to a given age, and related topics. William Petty (1623–1687), who had aided Graunt in his original effort, extended the scope of investigation by including other registers from parish churches, tax reports, and similarly crude sources of data.

Meanwhile, again in 1662, the first systematic treatment of probability appeared as Book IV of the Port Royal *Logique.* Two trends greatly influenced this guide to thinking about probability. The first was the recent mathematical analysis of games of chance, especially by Blaise Pascal (1623–1662), Pierre de Fermat (1601–1665), and Christiaan Huygens (1629–1695). These mathematicians developed the concept of expectation, or the expected payoff of a wager. In part, this concept grew out of the legal context of aleatory contracts, such as insurance policies, annuities, and lotteries. The second trend also came from the legal tradition and concerned the quantification of degrees of belief, as, for example, in the consideration of evidence. The *Logique* instructed jurists to trust the date on notarized documents, since 999 out of a thousand are correctly dated. However, unlike Graunt, the authors of the *Logique* offered nothing but speculation in support of their numbers.

After reading Graunt's work on mortality tables, Jan de Witt (1625–1672) and Jan Hudde (1628–1704) consulted Huygens about applying this data to the pricing of lifetime annuities. At that time, one could buy an annuity that paid one hundred pounds per year for life for seven hundred pounds, and the price did not depend upon the recipient's age. Before the States General of Holland, De Witt argued that he could calculate a fair price for annuities by applying his empirically derived mortality curve, in much the same way that the expected value of a wager could be calculated from the odds of flipping coins.

Two mathematical results further strengthened the perceived link between observed statistical data and the appropriate degree of certainty for a given belief. In 1713 the first proof for the law of large numbers appeared in Jakob Bernoulli's (1654–1705) *Art of Conjecturing.* This limit theorem related the number of samples to the probability that an observation is accurate. Twenty years later, Abraham de Moivre (1667–1754) became the first to derive the equation for the normal curve, in an attempt to deduce rules for the "degree of assent which is to be given to experiments."

BIBLIOGRAPHY

Daston, Lorraine. *Classical Probability in the Enlightenment.* Princeton, NJ: Princeton University Press, 1988.

Hacking, Ian. *The Emergence of Probability: A Philosophical Study of Early Ideas About Probability, Induction, and Statistical Inference.* Cambridge: Cambridge University Press, 1975.

Hald, Anders. *A History of Probability and Statistics and Their Applications Before 1750.* New York: Wiley, 1990.

Stigler, Stephen M. *The History of Statistics: The Measurement of Uncertainty Before 1900.* Cambridge, MA: Harvard University Press, 1986.

Westergaard, Harald. *Contributions to the History of Statistics.* London: King and Son, 1932.

TIMOTHY J. TAYLOR

See also Bernoulli, Jakob I; Petty, William; Probability

Steno, Nicolaus (Niels Stensen) (1638–1686)

Born in Denmark, he initially studied medicine; subsequently, he traveled to Italy and became Court physician to the grand duke of Tuscany. After converting to Catholicism, he moved to Germany to spread the Catholic gospel in the Protestant world. He was buried in Florence.

Steno made several significant anatomical discoveries, including the excretory duct of the parotid gland (Steno's duct) and tear glands in the eye. He investigated the musculature of the heart, brain anatomy, and the action of muscles, which he examined with a microscope. He saw muscle action in terms of the mechanical philosophy, ascribing contraction of a whole muscle to the contraction of its parts, not the influx of hypothetical juices. The arguments were presented mathematically.

Steno also examined sharks and showed that they were viviparous. The dissection of a giant shark in 1666 involved examination of its teeth and recognition that so-called tongue stones found in many strata, especially in Malta, were, in fact, the teeth of sharks. This raised the question as to how such objects could be contained within solid rocks.

To deal with this question, Steno began to make observations of Tuscan strata, looking at exposures at the sides of the Arno River and its tributaries, especially near Volterra. Here many soft sediments may be seen slumping off the cliffs into the valley below. The process is evidently rapid, as many Etruscan graves have been exposed over a few centuries.

Steno proposed a theoretical account of his observations in his *Prodromus* (1669). The book dealt with the general question of how one kind of solid might be contained within another solid. Regarding strata, it seemed that they were formed by the deposition of sediment in water; the seeming organic remains found therein represented organisms that had formerly lived in the water. At the time, this was quite a radical proposal.

Steno went further and hypothesized a sequence of events leading to the dispositions of the strata as he saw them in Tuscany—perhaps near Volterra. The supposed sequence was illustrated by six schematic figures (geological sections), which suggested the deposition of sediment by flooding, the hollowing out of strata by subterranean erosion, and the subsequent collapse of the overlying layers. This sequence was thought to have

Nicolaus Steno. From Fielding H. Garrison, An Introduction to the History of Medicine, *3rd ed. (Philadelphia and London: Saunders, 1921).*

occurred twice. The flooding might have been of the kind described in Genesis.

While Steno's ideas on sedimentation and erosion were crude and were not followed through as he soon gave up his scientific investigations in favor of his missionary work, the *Prodromus* is considered a foundation text in geology. It contained, implicitly if not quite explicitly, the principle of superposition: that, as sediments are deposited, the lower ones are formed first in order of time, so that, when beds are observed in section, the lower ones are the older. Also, Steno understood that the objects found in strata that look like the remains of former living organisms are, indeed, just that. However, his general theory was developed in terms of a biblical time scale, and he was troubled by the theological implications of his geological investigations.

Steno also carried out investigations in crystallography, accounting for the regular structures of crystals in terms of Cartesian matter theory. His theory of the earth, with emphasis on collapse structures, was also probably Cartesian in character.

BIBLIOGRAPHY

Rudwick, Martin J. S. *The Meaning of Fossils: Episodes in the History of Palaeontology*. New York: American Elsevier; London: Macdonald, 1972.

Scherz, Gustav, ed. *Steno and Brain Research in the Seventeenth Century*. Oxford: Pergamon, 1968.

Steno, Nicolaus. *The Prodromus of Nicolaus Steno's Dissertation Concerning a Solid Body Within a Solid*. Trans. J. G. Winter. New York: Macmillan, 1916. Repr. New York and London: Hafner, 1968.

———. *Steno on Muscles. . . .* Trans. M. Emmanuel Collins, Paul Maquet, and Troels Kardel. Philadelphia: American Philosophical Society, 1994.

DAVID OLDROYD

See also Anatomy; Geology/Mineralogy; Theories of the Earth

Stevin, Simon (1548–1620)

As a mathematician, he did important work in statics and hydrostatics, and he is still celebrated as the individual with whom the history of Dutch science really started. But Stevin did not originate in those northern provinces that declared themselves independent of Spain at the end of the sixteenth century. The sudden rise of science in the Dutch Republic in the seventeenth century was much stimulated by immigrants from the southern provinces of Flanders and Brabant, provinces that had been centers of learning for more than a century. Stevin was one of these immigrants: he was born in Brugge but moved to the northern provinces ca. 1580. In Brugge and Antwerp, he had earned his living as a bookkeeper and a cashier, but in Holland he became a mathematician and an engineer.

Stevin settled in Leiden and immediately started to publish works in the fields of mathematics and mechanics. His *Tables of Interest* (*Tafelen van interest*) and *Geometrical Problems* (*Problemata geometrica*) were issued in Antwerp in 1582 and 1583, respectively, but all of his other works were published in the northern Netherlands. In 1585 he published *The Tenth* (*De thiende*), which contains his introduction of what are usually called decimal fractions. Mathematicians were quick to elaborate on this important improvement of their field, but Stevin's proposal for introducing the decimal division in all measures was not adopted for more than two centuries—and then only partly.

More important than his purely mathematical works were the books Stevin published in 1586: *The Elements*

of the Art of Weighing (*Beghinselen der weeghconst*), *The Practice of Weighing* (*De weeghdaet*), and *The Elements of Hydrostatics* (*Beghinselen des waterwichts*). In mechanics, and even more so in hydrostatics, he was the first to resume and continue the work of Archimedes (ca. 287–212 B.C.E.). In hydrostatics, Stevin established the Archimedean principle of the displacement of water by immersed objects in a more elementary and, therefore, more satisfactory manner than Archimedes himself had done. In addition, he was the first to evaluate the forces that a liquid, by its weight, exerts on the bottom and the walls of the enclosed vessel.

It was, however, his demonstration of the law of the inclined plane that appealed most to the scientific and democratic sentiments of Stevin himself. By using the mental experiment of a wreath of spheres hung on an inclined plane, Stevin could demonstrate that the effect of gravity was inversely proportional to the length of the plane, and, as such, it demonstrates an important property of all of his scientific achievements. It appeals only to the intuition and is intelligible to anyone using common sense. According to Stevin, the practice of science should be open to anyone with enough intelligence to follow an argument. He therefore wrote most of his books in Dutch and invented Dutch equivalents for technical terms that were only available in Latin; some of these words are still used in Dutch (like *wiskunde* for mathematics).

Stevin was also active in technical matters. He was granted patents on various inventions by the States General and the States of Holland, the majority of them referring to the subjects of dredging and draining. For the improvement of a mill for pumping water, he went into partnership with a burgomaster of the city of Delft, Johan Cornets de Groot (1554–1640), the father of Hugo Grotius. Together they built watermills all over Holland. His technical expertise was also evident from his book on *The Art of Fortification,* which he published in 1594.

By this time, Stevin had entered into the service of Prince Maurice of Nassau, Stadtholder of Holland and commander in chief of the States Army. The official position he kept until his death in 1620 was rather modest: he was quartermaster and engineer of the States Army. Maurice, however, held Stevin in great esteem. He frequently sat on committees charged with the investigation of matters of defense and navigation; he was entrusted with the organization of a school for engineers that was established in Leiden in 1600; and he was chosen by Maurice as his tutor in mathematics and natural sciences. Being Maurice's tutor, Stevin composed several textbooks, in which he not only condensed what others had written, but also added his own inventions and innovations. All of his textbooks were published in a huge comprehensive edition as his *Mathematical Memoirs* (*Wisconstighe ghedachtenissen,* 1605–1608). Besides mathematics and mechanics, these *Memoirs* contain treatises on the theory of music, bookkeeping, optics, astronomy, and geography. In the book on astronomy, Stevin shows himself to be in favor of the heliocentric model, establishing himself as one of the very first Copernicans in Holland.

BIBLIOGRAPHY

Dijksterhuis, E. J. *Simon Stevin: Science in the Netherlands Around 1600.* The Hague: Nijhoff, 1970.

Stevin, Simon. *The Principal Works of Simon Stevin.* 5 vols., Amsterdam: Swets and Zeitlinger, 1955–1966.

Struik, D. J. *The Land of Stevin and Huygens: A Sketch of Science and Technology in the Dutch Republic During the Golden Century.* Dordrecht: Reidel, 1981.

KLAAS VAN BERKEL

See also Decimals; Fortification; Hydraulics and Hydrostatics; Mechanics

Stoicism

A philosophical system developed in the generation after Aristotle (384–322 B.C.E.) by Zeno of Citium, Cleanthes, and Chrysippus. It was extensively discussed by Cicero and adopted by Seneca. A sharp contrast was recognized with the teachings of Epicureanism. Stoics regarded a correct action as one that fitted with the plan for the evolution of the cosmos and, consequently, studied physics before they studied ethics. They viewed the universe as an organic whole pervaded by an active spirit (the pneuma), a mixture of air and fire that directed the condensation of other elements, and the development of a geocentric, spherical cosmos with a cyclical history. Each cycle ended with a return the original state of pure pneuma.

Stoic physical ideas were revived during the late Renaissance as an alternative to the dominant Aristotelian natural philosophy. Stoicism offered a unified physics of the heavens and the earth and a substance of the heavens that consisted of air or fire rather than a special fifth element. The planets were intelligent creatures capable of moving themselves, and astrology could be understood as a physical interaction between the heavens and the earth. The influence of Stoicism in physics was limited by the revival of Epicureanism in the early seventeenth century, although Stoic ideas continued to be important in alchemy and early chemistry.

The Stoics took their name from the "Painted Porch" decorated with scenes from the Trojan Wars, on the north side of the Athens marketplace, where they first met. The founder of the school, Zeno of Citium (ca. 335–263 B.C.E.), was succeeded, in turn, by Cleanthes (ca. 301–232 B.C.E.) and Chrysippus (280–206 B.C.E.). Only fragments of their works survive. By the Roman period, their doctrines had assumed a stable outline. Cicero (106–43 B.C.E.) reviewed Stoic ideas and contrasted them with those of the Epicureans and the skeptics in his books *On Fate, On Divination,* and *On the Nature of the Gods.* Lucius Annaeus Seneca (ca. 4 B.C.E.–65 C.E.) left an important work on Stoic natural philosophy, the *Natural Questions,* and the opening sections of Pliny's the Elder's (23/24–79) *Natural History* (ca. 77) also presented Stoic ideas. Later contributors ranged from Epictetus (b. ca. 60), who began life as a slave, to Marcus Aurelius (121–180), who spent the last nineteen years of his life as emperor.

In Stoic physics, everything that exists is material and is capable of acting and being acted upon only by contact. Among Aristotle's four causes, material, formal, efficient, and final, therefore, efficient causes receive special emphasis. However, another central idea is that two bodies can occupy the same place at the same time. The pneuma, a material thing, pervades all grosser bodies. Similarly, a cup of wine poured into the sea does not vanish but spreads out to occupy the same boundaries as the sea itself. But the pneuma is not the same everywhere, or the universe would be a featureless expanse.

The pneuma is a mixture of air and fire. This dual nature leads to its identification both with the celestial fire familiar from Plato (428–348 B.C.E.) and Heraclitus (fl. ca. 500 B.C.E.) and with the animating breath or air of Aristotle and later thinkers. At the origin of the cosmic cycle, the pneuma condenses parts of itself to form the heavier elements water and earth. These are driven to the center of the cosmos by currents of pneuma and form the terrestrial globe. Although the radial arrangement of the Stoic elements mirrors Aristotle's terrestrial realm, the four basic elements, earth, water, fire, and air, fill the whole universe, and a single system of physics applies to both the heavens and the earth. The globe of earth and water is surrounded by pneuma contaminated with terrestrial elements that becomes purer and purer toward the periphery of the universe, which is the sphere of fixed stars. Between the earth and the fixed stars there are no concentric spheres, as in Aristotle's system, but a continuous expanse of fluid pneuma. The stars and the planets, including the Sun, are fires that move freely through the fluid heavens. The planets are the natural creatures of the elements that make up the heavens. Being supplied with a superabundance of the fiery pneuma, they are both more intelligent and capable of moving more rapidly than other living things.

The pneuma that directs the evolution of the cosmos performs a cyclical motion inward from the fixed stars to the center of the cosmos and out again to the boundary.

The inward leg of the cycle conveys the influence of the heavens to the inhabitants of the earth, explaining the physical basis for the success of astrology. The outward cycle carries terrestrial material back into the heavens, where it becomes fuel for the celestial fires. But the supply of fuel is limited by the finite size of the terrestrial globe. When all of the fuel is exhausted, the cosmos dissolves back into its primordial state, and the pneuma begins a new cycle that exactly repeats the previous sequence. The cosmos is assumed to be smallest and most dense immediately after the condensation of the heavy elements and to increase in volume as the primordial fire reasserts itself. The Stoics, therefore, admitted the existence of a vacuum outside the sphere of fixed stars to allow for the expansion and contraction of the universe, but they denied vacua inside the cosmos on the ground that they would interrupt the tension of the pneuma.

The transmission of Stoic ideas depended almost entirely upon Latin authors. Although Seneca's *Natural Questions* was known throughout the Middle Ages, it was only during the Renaissance that renewed interest in Cicero placed Stoic ideas before a wide audience. Stoicism became an important influence in literature, especially in moral and political philosophy, during the late fifteenth and early sixteenth centuries. Martin Luther's (1483–1546) objections to Aristotle's natural philosophy created new interest in Pliny, and Stoic ideas began to reappear in scientific contexts.

In a work published in Paris in 1557, Jean Pena (1528–1558) reasoned from the failure to observe atmospheric refraction that there were no boundaries between the terrestrial observer and the fixed stars and that one continuous substance must fill the intervening space. He explicitly connected this substance with the life-giving air that filled the heavens in the account of Stoic cosmology preserved by Cicero. Following Pena, and under the influence of classical authors like Pliny, Christoph Rothmann (fl. 1555–1597) adopted the view that the substance of the heavens was air, with the planets moving freely through this medium. Writers as diverse as Robert Cardinal Bellarmine (1542–1621) and Tycho Brahe (1546–1601) adopted views of the substance of the heavens derived from Stoic doctrines, either to avoid Aristotle's separation of heavens and earth, with its denial of change in the heavens, or as an alternative to Aristotle's celestial spheres. Writers all over Europe revived the Stoic explanation of the causes of planetary motion, signaled by the characteristic phrase that the planets moved themselves "like birds through the air or fish through the waters." Johannes Kepler (1571–1630), in his *Astronomia nova* (1609), criticized this account on the ground that an intelligent planet could not gather enough information as it moved to perform an epicyclic motion, although he retained planetary intelligences capable of sliding a planet up or down the radius vector to the Sun and of making the Sun itself rotate. Kepler also adopted the view that the substance of the heavens was life-giving air and defined the planetary spheres as geometrical constructs in a continuous fluid heaven.

The revival of Stoicism reached its peak in the work of Justus Lipsius (1547–1606), who surveyed all surviving ancient literature in an attempt to recover fragments preserving Stoic ideas. In 1604 he published both the *Handbook to Stoic Philosophy* and a book on Stoic physics that attempted to reconcile it with Christian teaching on providence and free will.

Ironically, although the Roman Stoics largely defeated their rival Epicureans, the revival of Epicurean doctrines in the early seventeenth century caused the eclipse of Stoicism in science. Intermediate figures like Sebastian Basso (fl. 1560–1623) combine Stoic and Epicurean ideas. With Pierre Gassendi (1592–1655) and René Descartes (1596–1650), atomism becomes the dominant physical idea. Stoic vestiges are still apparent in later writers, such as the concept of *conatus* (tendency or endeavor) in Descartes and Newton's views on alchemy and nature of life. Although interest in Stoic physics waned quickly, it made lasting contributions by emphasizing efficient causation and the cosmological role of providence (originally in the guise of the pneuma), and there are indications of substantial Stoic influences in alchemy and early chemistry throughout the seventeenth century (e.g., in the phlogiston theory of combustion). By the end of the twentieth century, a full appraisal of the Stoic contribution to early-modern science had yet to be made.

BIBLIOGRAPHY

Barker, P. "Jean Pena (1528–58) and Stoic Physics in the Sixteenth Century." *Southern Journal of Philosophy* 13 (1985), Supplement: *Recovering the Stoics: Spindel Conference 1984,* ed. R. H. Epp, 93–107.

———. "Stoic Contributions to Early Modern Science." In *Epicurean and Stoic Themes in European Thought,* ed. M. J. Osler. Cambridge: Cambridge University Press, 1991, pp. 135–154.

Colish, Marcia. *The Stoic Tradition from Antiquity to the Early Middle Ages.* 2 vols. New York and Leiden: Brill, 1990.

Hahm, David E. *Origins of Stoic Cosmology.* Columbus: Ohio State University Press, 1977.

Sambursky, S. *Physics of the Stoics.* Westport, CT: Greenwood, 1973.

                                                    PETER BARKER

See also Basso, Sebastian; Celestial Spheres; Descartes, René; Epicureanism; Gassendi, Pierre; Pneuma

Styles of Science: National, Regional, and Local

Many people think of science as necessarily objective and international in character. This view comes nearest to the truth in the twentieth century. This international homogeneity is largely the result of the ease of modern communications. But, if we look at previous centuries, there is a strong argument for the existence of different "national styles" in science. The increasing use of the different European vernaculars from the late sixteenth century helped establish linguistic barriers and reinforce national differences.

In the northern Italian states in the early sixteenth century, the introduction of artillery and the development of fortification provided an incentive for the study of applied mathematics. The emergence of a new profession, the teacher of mathematics, is exemplified by the work of Niccolò Tartaglia (1499–1557). In some Italian universities, the study of medicine and law was particularly strong; Padua is the outstanding example of a faculty of medicine that drew scholars from far afield. The anatomical theater established there in 1594 and in other Italian universities, as well as the creation of a number of botanical gardens, soon inspired similar institutions in other European countries.

It has been argued that the Court system of patronage in Florence was a crucial factor in encouraging Galileo Galilei's (1564–1642) more spectacular astronomical work—hence, his naming of the satellites of Jupiter observed through his telescope the Medicean Planets after his Medici patron. On the other hand, in England after the foundation of the Royal Society (1660), its members did not expect financial support from the king. There was, therefore, no pressure to seek the spectacular. Much of the experimental investigations of members was low-key work intended to do no more than satisfy gentlemanly curiosity. Whereas at the Florentine

Court Galileo fought verbal duels with his enemies, in the England of the 1660s, recently recovered from deep civil strife, sharp controversy was to be avoided. The early Royal Society sought consensus, and there was no room for Galileo's aggressive style.

If England was an intellectual backwater in the sixteenth century, it more than made up for this in the seventeenth century. Here is a reminder that, in emphasizing geographical factors in the analysis of different scientific styles, we should also pay attention to the time factor. Nevertheless, we may risk the generalization that natural philosophy in England was fundamentally empirical in character, a feature that is seen most clearly in the seventeenth century with John Locke (1632–1704). In the eighteenth century, there emerged a British school of pneumatic chemistry culminating in the work of Joseph Priestley (1733–1804), whose empirical approach contrasts with the theoretical analysis of the Frenchman Antoine Lavoisier (1743–1794).

When the Royal Society of London was founded in 1660, its rhetoric was explicitly that of Francis Bacon (1561–1626), who had helped inspire such a sustained collaborative effort, very different from that of the individualistic René Descartes (1596–1650). The Royal Society consistently presented its work as matters of fact. It deliberately avoided associating itself with any particular system. The English were clearly a seafaring nation, and the importance of practical navigation is reflected in institutions such as Gresham College (the meeting place of the early Royal Society) and Greenwich Observatory (1676). Such concerns were obviously absent from landlocked central European countries.

The Dutch, too, were seafarers. In the Low Countries, the development of trade gave prominence to a merchant class, some of the more wealthy of whom acted as patrons for science. At the end of the sixteenth century, land drainage, colonial conquest, and merchant capitalism increased wealth. Some of the science was utilitarian, some was inspired by natural theology, but much arose from curiosity, which extended to many small-scale investigations. In the Dutch universities, the continuing use of Latin as the language of instruction encouraged foreign students and helped break down national barriers. It was only in 1715, after a visit to England, that Willem s'Gravesande (1688–1742) introduced Newtonianism into the Netherlands. His very practical approach helped establish a distinctly Dutch school of Newtonianism, focusing on experimental physics.

The many German nations long remained independent states, with the northern and central states becoming Protestant after the Reformation, while the southern and eastern states remained predominantly Catholic. Both traditions viewed the heliocentric theory with suspicion and were no less hostile to French Cartesianism. Each territory wanted its own university, leading to a dilution of talent, with no national center like Paris. In southern Germany, as in eastern Europe, the Jesuits took over the universities. Paracelsus (ca. 1493–1541) helped turn attention from Aristotelian philosophy toward a more direct experience of the natural world. His alchemical theories may be related to mining in central Europe. The distinguished astronomer Johannes Kepler (1571–1630) thought in terms of divine harmonies. Later, Gottfried Wilhelm Leibniz (1646–1716) built up a grand philosophical system. It was not until the nineteenth century that Germany became a world leader in science.

In France, scientific activity emerged slowly in the seventeenth century. Before ca. 1630, all discussion outside the traditional Aristotelian framework was banned in the universities. However, Jesuit colleges throughout the country made important contributions not only to education, but also to science, notably astronomy. Marin Mersenne (1588–1648), a Minim friar, became the center of a national and international network of correspondence and helped establish a scientific community in France. He kept in touch with his fellow countryman Descartes, who preferred to distance himself from the social life of Paris and live in the Netherlands. There was considerable activity in chemistry and anatomy. The Jardin des Plantes, founded by Louis XIII in 1635, became an important focus for chemistry. Major scientific activity was to move increasingly toward Paris. In the Paris Academy of Sciences, Cartesianism was to become the orthodoxy well into the eighteenth century. A French patriotic preference for Descartes kept (English) Newtonian ideas at bay.

In France, the state apparatus was particularly well developed, and it is not surprising that a government-sponsored Royal Academy of Sciences in Paris became the center of scientific work and authority. Under Louis XIV, we see the functioning of an absolute monarchy. His chief minister, Colbert (1619–1683), drew up plans for an academy to add further glory to *le roi soleil* for his patronage of learning. Also, if science was pursued in a state institution, it could be supervised and controlled. The members of the academy were expected to give advice on practical projects of utility to the state. This implicit control of science in France provides a marked contrast with the laissez-faire attitude of the Royal Society, whose members, unlike the academicians, received no money from the state. Such patronage, however, had the effect of limiting the independence of members. State science in France under the ancien régime may be compared with state industry with government-owned manufactures.

Many European countries remained on the margins of scientific activity. A brief mention must be made of Spain, which had early been influenced by Arabic culture. Jews were prominent in medicine but were often treated harshly by the Spanish Inquisition (1480). Both Spain and Portugal made important contributions to navigation, a natural consequence of their geographical position, but, after the sixteenth century, there was a long period of intellectual stagnation. Some claimed that Catholicism was incompatible with science, but the experience of France demonstrates the contrary. Any analysis of the emergence of modern science in different European countries, therefore, has to look sensitively at the interplay of many local factors, as well as the religious, political, economic, and social context.

BIBLIOGRAPHY

Crosland, Maurice P., ed. *The Emergence of Science in Western Europe.* London: Macmillan, 1975.

Porter, Roy, and Mikuláš Teich, eds. *The Scientific Revolution in National Context.* Cambridge: Cambridge University Press, 1992.

MAURICE CROSLAND

See also Académie Royale des Sciences; Cartesianism; Patronage; Reformation, Protestant; Royal Society of London; Universities

Surgery

Throughout the Middle Ages and into the Renaissance, medicine precisely reflected the prevailing social division between scholarship and craftsmanship. University trained and book learned, physicians worked with their minds, not with their hands. Much of their knowledge was philosophical and theoretical. Surgeons did manual work; they learned their skills by apprenticeship and had the social status of artisans. Their knowledge was practical but limited in scope and application. Not a few surgeons were illiterate; many wrote only in their vernacular

language. In surgery, as in other spheres, the Scientific Revolution was characterized by trained scholars taking an interest in empirical observation and practical investigation and by the craft practitioners developing skills in abstraction and literary expression.

It is noteworthy that, in Italy, medicine and surgery were more closely associated than elsewhere in Europe. A number of Italian physicians were also practicing surgeons, and the Italian medical schools offered lectures on surgery. The remarkable development of anatomical dissection in sixteenth-century Italy may be confidently associated with the fact that, in that country, the manual dexterity and practical reasoning necessary to devise and undertake accurate dissections were not completely dissociated from the intellectual training required to understand and explain the importance of what was revealed. The most famous sixteenth-century surgeon-anatomist was Andreas Vesalius (1514–1564) who, although a graduate physician, lectured on surgery at the University of Padua. In the course of his anatomical demonstrations, Vesalius undertook the dissections himself rather than leave the task to a surgeon to perform, as had been the custom. This was a major intrusion of an academically trained physician into what had previously been a craftsman's domain. The revision of knowledge of human anatomy that resulted was one of the most profound and far-reaching challenges to tradition and classical authority that was to take place in either the sixteenth or the seventeenth centuries.

Vesalius later practiced as a military surgeon, and he endeavored to apply his improved anatomical knowledge to the refinement of surgical technique. For example, he pioneered the surgical drainage of empyema and attempted to refine the practice of venesection. Combating the prevailing prejudice, Vesalius contended that the "use of the hands" was a proper and an integral aspect of medical practice.

All three of Vesalius's immediate successors in the chair of anatomy at Padua—Realdo Colombo (ca. 1510–1559), Gabriele Falloppio (1523–1562), and Girolamo Fabrici (ca. 1533–1619)—made outstanding contributions to anatomical knowledge. All three also had practical experience of surgery. Colombo served an apprenticeship to the leading Venetian surgeon and teacher of anatomy, Giovanni Lonigo, before going on to study medicine at Padua. Colombo's work on the structure of the skeletal musculature expressed his experience of practical surgery. Fabrici enjoyed great fame both as a

S

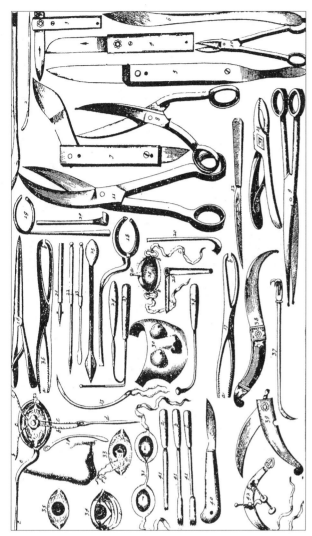

Surgical instruments as depicted in Cornelis Solingen, Alle de medicinale en chirurgicale Werken *(1698).*

Valsalva (1666–1723), who practiced both physic and surgery with distinction in the hospitals of Bologna. Valsalva's investigations of the structure of the otorhinopharyngeal region found many therapeutic applications.

While the Italian surgeon-anatomists represent the embracing of manual investigation by university-trained scholars, the career of the French surgeon Ambroise Paré (ca. 1510–1590) embodies the alternative trajectory of a skilled surgical craftsman invading the scholars' realm by publishing the fruits of his experience. Paré was the son of an artisan and served an apprenticeship to a provincial barber-surgeon. He gained much experience as a military surgeon, radically improving the treatment of gunshot wounds, and rose to be premier surgeon to successive kings of France. Knowing no Latin, Paré wrote in French. He often opposed university authorities, and his works had considerable influence throughout Europe in both the sixteenth and the seventeenth centuries. Drawing upon craft manufacturing and recent improvements in metalworking, Paré advanced the design of several surgical instruments and appliances.

In northern Europe, the artisan tradition in surgery dominated throughout the seventeenth century. An outstanding demonstration of its scientific potential may be seen in the work of Wilhelm Fabry (1560–1634), who, with little formal education, became city surgeon at Berne. He made several important innovations in surgical technique, invented new instruments, and published a major collection of case histories. Important as their contributions were, however, Paré and Fabry were exceptional figures within the social order of the sixteenth and seventeenth centuries. The technical and social progress they achieved was not sustained by their successors. Surgery did not gain the status of a learned and scientific profession until long after the Scientific Revolution.

BIBLIOGRAPHY

Bishop, W. J. *The Early History of Surgery.* London: Scientific Book Guild, 1961.

Conrad, Lawrence I. et al. *The Western Medical Tradition: 800 BC to AD 1800.* Cambridge: Cambridge University Press, 1995.

Lawrence, Ghislaine. "Surgery (Traditional)." In *Companion Encyclopedia of the History of Medicine,* ed. William F. Bynum and Roy Porter. London and New York: Routledge, 1993, pp. 961–983.

MALCOLM NICOLSON

See also Anatomy; Medical Education; Medicine; Paré, Ambroise; Vesalius, Andreas

physician and as a surgeon. He wrote extensively on surgery and made many contributions to the refinement of surgical technique and apparatus. His books on surgery were very successful and went through many editions in several languages. William Harvey (1578–1657) studied anatomy in Padua under Fabrici, and his investigations on the structure and function of the major vessels of the body may be regarded as a culmination of the combination of theoretical reasoning and practical investigation pioneered by the Italian surgeon-anatomists.

The continuation of this tradition of academic surgeon-anatomist into the seventeenth century may also be seen in the work of Marco Aurelio Severino (1580–1656), whose *De recondita abscessuum natura* is often regarded as the first systematic treatment of surgical pathology. Another outstanding example is Anton Maria

Surveying

A discipline whose proper methods were contested between mathematicians and practitioners until a compromise was reached in the mid-seventeenth century. Until the middle of the sixteenth century, the only instruments used by land measurers were rods or lines of variable local lengths, and the duties of surveyors involved tasks we would now associate with land stewards and overseers, as well as the measuring and plotting of land. Indeed, the first text published in English on surveying, printed in 1523, explains the laws relating to manors and the best methods of improving an estate alongside the duties of listing the state and number of buildings, a description of the lands, and the value of all of the properties. The surveying method utilized was mainly linear, except for the use of a pocket compass or a small astrolabe with a compass inset on the backside, to determine "which is East West North and South" on a cloudy day. In the late sixteenth century, however, geometers attempted to obtain control of surveying practice by situating it within the mathematical sciences and declaring their expertise necessary for formulating rules of procedure and necessary tables and designing instruments.

The goal was to incorporate surveying into the expanding practical-mathematics program by promoting geometry as the basis of surveying and angular, rather than linear, measurement as its basic technique. These new methods were to be based upon simplified astronomical instruments, angle measurement, and triangulation. Triangulation was to lure surveyors toward geometry by allowing them to build up an entire map from a single linear measurement rather than roaming about the entire estate measuring distances between significant positions. The instrument used for triangulation, the simple theodolite, was adapted from the astrolabe and had a horizontal circle only, with an alidade (a straight rule with sights mounted at either end) pivoted at its center, and the surveyors seem to have been happy to accept it as a standard instrument. Mathematicians were not content with this development, however, and they proposed even more complex and challenging devices. These instruments, though often described as universal (i.e., appropriate to all surveying problems), were beyond the grasp of the typical surveyor.

The surveyors responded by devising the plane table and the circumferentor, a magnetic compass with two

The first full-scale treatise on the practice of geometrical surveying, showing the surveyer using sighting and measuring instruments.

fixed sights. These two devices were simple to use and circumvented the need for the esoteric skill of angle measurement. They became very popular with surveyors, but the plane table was resisted by geometers because it endangered their entire program for surveying. By the mid-seventeenth century, a compromise was reached in which the needs and abilities of the surveyors were accommodated by a small group of instruments that included the plane table, while surveying nonetheless became a mathematical science, in which some knowledge of angular measurement was essential.

The wider impact of surveying differed according to the local context during the Scientific Revolution. In Italy, although surveyors were firmly embedded within mathematical practice and contributed to land-reclamation and water-management programs, they did not enjoy the rise in status of their military colleagues. In England, on the other hand, William Petty (1623–1687) built his political arithmetic on his experience in the 1650s Down Survey of Ireland. Not only were policy and planning to be based upon the precise data collected in the survey, but he also argued that natural philosophy itself should be made over on the model of political arithmetic and all phenomena dealt with in terms of number, weight, and measure.

BIBLIOGRAPHY

Bennett, J. A. *The Divided Circle: A History of Instruments for Astronomy, Navigation, and Surveying.* Oxford: Phaidon Christie's, 1987.

———. "Geometry and Surveying in Seventeenth-Century England." *Annals of Science* 48 (1991), 345–354.

Richeson, A. W. *English Land Measuring to 1800: Instruments and Practices.* Cambridge, MA: Society for the History of Technology and MIT Press, 1966.

KATHERINE HILL

See also Instrument Makers; Petty, William

Swammerdam, Jan (1637–1680)

A medical man by training and an anatomist, physiologist, and entomologist by vocation, he was able, because of his father's fortune, to live the life of an independent scholar and to devote himself entirely to scientific research. Swammerdam worked along two lines. He started as a human anatomist and an experimental physiologist, studying, for instance, the structure of the spinal cord, the ovary, and animal functions like respiration and muscular action. The majority of these investigations aimed at a critical evaluation of existing knowledge and did not result in new theories and ideas. Swammerdam's most original and innovative contributions to science were in the field of entomology. After 1667 the study of insects was the focus of his scientific work.

The purpose of Swammerdam's entomology was to demonstrate that insects are not the imperfect animals they were commonly held to be. He distanced himself explicitly from traditional views going back to Aristotle (384–322 B.C.E.), according to which insects have hardly any internal structure, come into being by way of spontaneous generation, and reach their adult stage through a series of saltatory changes of form (*metamorphosis*). The principle of uniformity led Swammerdam to the supposition that the anatomy and physiology of insects are no less complicated than those of vertebrate animals. His investigations supplied him with the empirical underpinning of his thesis.

Swammerdam was a confirmed empiricist. His entomological writings contain frequent expositions on the importance of observation and experiment. They were accompanied by sharp criticisms of book learning and rational deductions as primary sources of scientific knowledge. Swammerdam propagated the view that progress in entomology was possible only on the basis of empirical studies. At the same time, he warned his readers that this approach could never lead to the true and ultimate causes of natural phenomena. These would remain forever impenetrable to the scientist. Swammerdam's methodological position also had a religious dimension. As a devout Christian, he considered it an advantage of the empirical approach that it brought

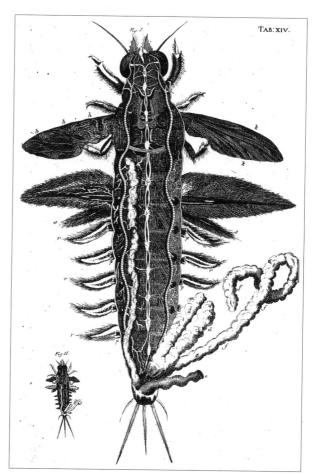

Anatomy of a may-fly, drawn by Swammerdam with the help of a microscope. From John (sic) Swammerdam, The Book of Nature, *trans. Thomas Flloyd (sic), ed. John Hill (1758).*

about a direct confrontation with the wonders of Creation, thus providing the scientist with additional proofs of the existence of God.

Swammerdam's first entomological publication, *Historia insectorum generalis* (1669), contains detailed information on the development of insects. Having studied the process in a considerable number of species, he made it clear that development started, in all cases, with an egg and that there was no trace of spontaneous generation. Moreover, he showed that development from egg to adult stage was a continuous process. Contrary to what was still widely supposed, he did not find any sudden and major changes of form.

Butterflies got Swammerdam's special attention. His manipulative skills allowed him to dissect the chrysalis and to discover structures foreshadowing those of the adult animal. This observation suggested to him that embryogenesis is probably nothing else but the unfolding (*evolutio*) of already existing structures. Swammerdam's rather short and cursory remarks on this topic played an important role in the emergence of the preformation theory that came to dominate the ideas on generation and reproduction until well into the eighteenth century.

Swammerdam's magnum opus was the posthumously published *Biblia naturae* (1737–1738), one of the pioneering works in the history of modern entomology. It dealt mainly with insect anatomy. Swammerdam described a great number of representative species and in much more detail than his predecessors. He did not restrict himself to the shape and position of the organs but also investigated their finer structure; his analysis of the eye and the reproductive organs of the bee are fine examples of his accomplishments as a microanatomist.

BIBLIOGRAPHY

Fournier, Marian. "The Book of Nature: Jan Swammerdam's Microscopical Investigations." *Tractrix* 2 (1990), 1–24.

Lindeboom, G. A. *The Letters of Jan Swammerdam to Melchisedec Thévenot.* Amsterdam: Swets and Zeitlinger, 1975.

Ruestow, Edward G. "Piety and the Defense of Natural Order: Swammerdam on Generation." In *Religion, Science, and Worldview: Essays in Honor of Richard S. Westfall,* ed. M. J. Osler and P. L. Farber. Cambridge: Cambridge University Press, 1985, pp. 217–241.

Schierbeek, A. *Jan Swammerdam (12 February 1637–17 February 1680): His Life and Works.* Amsterdam: Swets and Zeitlinger, 1967.

ROBERT VISSER

See also Generation; Microscopy; Preformation; Spontaneous Generation

Sydenham, Thomas (1624–1689)

A famous London physician, known as the English Hippocrates. At a time when authority and tradition governed medical practice, Sydenham was notably independent. He relied instead on his own observations and so is often described as an empiricist, like his collaborator, the philosopher John Locke (1632–1704). His vivid descriptions of conditions such as gout and hysteria, which he diagnosed in men no less than in women, are classics of medical writing.

His treatments were simpler and more humane than those in general use. Whereas conventional medicines comprised amazing mixtures of ingredients, often secret, Sydenham despised secrecy and introduced simple but effective formulas, including his famous liquid laudanum, made from opium dissolved in sherry. Smallpox he treated by cooling his fevered, dehydrated patients rather than by heating them with drugs and extra bedcoverings.

His dislike of hypothesis did not inhibit him from filling his books with hypotheses of his own. Perhaps the most conspicuous is the *epidemic constitution.* Sydenham believed that each "constitution" superimposed on the prevalent illnesses a characteristic feature, such as abscesses or enteritis, a concept largely ignored by others, both then and since. Its prominence in his writing helped obscure his most important contribution to medical theory, albeit one previously advanced by Johannes Baptista van Helmont (1579–1644), namely that each disease is not a haphazard phenomenon but an orga-

Sydenham's work on therapeutics.

nized entity, a pathological species that exists in its own right no less than a plant or an animal species. Given that each species of disease behaved consistently, it became possible to conceive of specific cures, although Sydenham knew of only one example, the Jesuit bark, or quinine for the treatment of malaria.

BIBLIOGRAPHY

Dewhurst, Kenneth. *Dr. Thomas Sydenham (1624–1689): His Life and Original Writings.* London: Wellcome Historical Medical Library, 1966.

Meynell, G. G. *A Bibliography of Dr. Thomas Sydenham (1624–1689).* Folkestone: Winterdown Books, 1990.

G. G. MEYNELL

See also Empiricism; Helmont, Johannes Baptista van; Locke, John; Medicine

Sylvius, Franciscus (Franz de le Boë) (1614–1672)

Born in the German town of Hanau into a Calvinist family from France, he read medicine at the University of Leiden but graduated from Basel University in 1637. After two years in Hanau, he lived for three years in Leiden, where he met René Descartes (1596–1650), whose thinking had a marked influence on his work. From 1641 to 1658, he lived in Amsterdam—the scientific and cultural center of the Dutch United Provinces at that time. There he struck up a friendship with Nicolas Tulp (1593–1574), the anatomist immortalized in a famous painting by Rembrandt, and with Johann Rudolf Glauber (1604–1668), an adherent of Paracelsian principles and the first to demonstrate the acid and basic constituent parts of salts. In 1658 he moved to Leiden as professor of practical medicine, a position he held until his death and in which he helped make the University of Leiden one of the most prestigious in Europe.

Sylvius made noteworthy contributions to normal anatomy, including those concerning the structures in the brain that bear his name today, and to pathological anatomy, particularly his description of pulmonary tubercles. His considerable prominence in this field stems, however, from his being the main formulator, together with Thomas Willis (1621–1675), of the iatrochemical system which should not be confused with Paracelsianism, or medical chemistry, though it often is. Iatrochemistry was, strictly speaking, the medical system that aimed, during the last quarter of the seventeenth century, to integrate all of the innovations in conflict with Galenism since the Renaissance. Sylvius's iatrochemical system did, indeed, synthesize the breakthroughs made in normal anatomy since the Vesalian movement, the doctrine of blood circulation and subsequent physiological innovations, progress in clinical observation derived from the pathological discoveries made during necroscopies, and Paracelsian conceptions and techniques, but it discarded the metaphysical fundamentals of Paracelsianism and substituted for its panvitalism the marked mechanism found in the thinking of Descartes.

Supported mainly by Glauber's work, Sylvius asserted that the fundamental phenomenon in the workings of an organism was its chemical dissolution (*fermentatio*) and that the mechanism causing disease was its alteration (*acrimonia*) due to either excess acidity or excess alkalinity. The Sylvius iatrochemical system had numerous disciples throughout Europe, and it played, together with Willis's system, a key role in the conflict with Galenism at the heart of academic medicine. Its influence, however, was short lived, for progress in research meant that this system would be superseded in the early eighteenth century.

BIBLIOGRAPHY

Baumann, E. D. *François de le Boë, Sylvius (1614–1672).* Leiden: Brill, 1949.

Beukers, H. "Het laboratorium van Sylvius." *Tijdschrift voor de geschiedenis der geneeskunde, natuurwetenschappen, wiskunde en techniek* 3 (1980), 28–36.

Gubser, A. "The 'Positiones variae medicae' of Franciscus Sylvius." *Bulletin of the History of Medicine* 40 (1966), 72–80.

López-Piñero, J. M. "Silvio y la iatroquímica holandesa y alemana." *Medicina Española* 67 (1962), 164–173.

JOSÉ M. LÓPEZ-PIÑERO

See also Anatomy; Fermentation; Harvey, William; Iatrochemistry

T

Taxonomy

Biological classification, or taxonomic, systems are attempts to organize information about the natural world using observable similarities between organisms. Western cultures long created classification systems with diverse aims and using different methods; not until the eighteenth century was a system proposed that met with near-universal adoption. Prior to the introduction of the Linnaean system, however, most systems were Aristotelian in nature.

Aristotle (384–322 B.C.E.) saw classification as a function of logic and advocated grouping objects on the basis of identification and similarity of immutable essences rather than on accidental characteristics (*History of Animals*). He differentiated between natural and artificial taxonomies; the former revealed fundamental truths about nature and the objects classified, while the latter used selected characteristics to create useful systems. Focusing on essential natures would produce natural, rather than artificial, taxonomic systems. He acknowledged, however, that it was often difficult to determine essential natures and that divisions based on logic would not always accord with intuitively recognized groupings. This dichotomy between systems produced by logic and systems that seemed inherent in the natural world but that could not be justified through similarity of essential natures was to give rise to divergent taxonomic theories and to many different classification systems.

Aristotle did not propose a formal classification of animals, but he declared that organizing them according to their ways of living, their actions, their habits, and their body parts would group together those with similar essential natures. He created two large categories, blooded and bloodless, each of which contained subcategories. Within the blooded were four groups: the viviparous quadrupeds, the oviparous quadrupeds, birds, and fishes. Viviparous quadrupeds, equines, felines, and rodents were then differentiated on the basis of the structure of the skeleton and limbs. Oviparous quadrupeds included lizards, tortoises, and amphibians. Birds were subdivided into eight groups, based on the structure of their feet and preferred food. Fish were subdivided according to whether or not their skeletons were cartilaginous. The bloodless category contained four groups: soft-bodied invertebrates, soft-bodied invertebrates with hard shells, soft-bodied invertebrates with scales, and insects, which were further subdivided into nine groups.

Aristotle's divisions were to form the basis of most natural-philosophical animal classification systems through the seventeenth century. In commentaries on Aristotle's work, Albertus Magnus (ca. 1200–1280) used his methods to organize animals unfamiliar to Aristotle. Many who studied animals, however, were uninterested in complex systems. Bestiaries (illustrated manuscripts dealing with birds, animals, insects, some plants, and natural wonders) from the ancient world often had only a rudimentary classification system that separated birds, mammals, and reptiles from one another, while others did not order their subjects at all. Medieval bestiary authors also usually differentiated between birds, mammals, and reptiles, then created a few subdivisions within those larger groups, such as mammals that ruminate, birds that could be taught to hunt for man, and so forth.

The large number of new animals discovered during the early-modern voyages of discovery gave rise to new attempts to create comprehensive, coherent taxonomic systems capable of accommodating both the familiar and the new life forms being introduced into Europe. Most of these systems were still based on Aristotle. Conrad Gessner (1516–1565) created a classification system that used Aristotle's methods to differentiate animals but ordered the groups alphabetically. Ulisse Aldrovandi (1522–1605), in a ten-volume encyclopedia classifying the known animal kingdom, used Aristotle's schema but added subdivisions that were based on way of life and anatomical criteria and included mythical creatures and deformed specimens. Thomas Willis (1621–1675) adapted Aristotle's system by subdividing blooded and unblooded animals on the basis of differences in the internal structures that seemed most crucial to life, such as the heart or the nervous and respiratory systems. Francis Willughby (1635–1672) and John Ray (1620–1705) collaborated (until Willughby's early death) in attempting to create a rigorous, all-encompassing system to replace all existing systems. Willughby and Ray, focusing on animals and plants, respectively, based their systems on that of Aristotle but created additional subdivisions based on internal anatomy to differentiate among groups. Similarly ambitious attempts were to continue into the eighteenth century, until Carl Linnaeus's (1707–1778) *Systema naturae* divided more than four thousand species of animals into six classes and introduced a standardized biological nomenclature.

Aristotle's student Theophrastus (ca. 372–287 B.C.E.) applied Aristotle's methods to plants. He divided plants into trees, shrubs, undershrubs, and herbs, then grouped the plants by appearance within those categories. This system formed the basis of philosophical taxonomic systems through the seventeenth century; natural philosophers, notably Albertus Magnus and Andrea Cesalpino (1519–1603), used it to structure their taxonomies.

Far more numerous were attempts to classify on the basis of utility. The *De materia medica* of Dioscorides (ca. 40–80) served as the basis of herbal medicine into the eighteenth century but merely divided six hundred plants into three groups: aromatic, culinary, and medicinal. Dioscorides also included a few animals, which he did not attempt to order; over the centuries, the place of animals within herbals shrank until, by the seventeenth century, most included none. Dioscorides discussed only plants of the Mediterranean; his successors added therapeutic plants local to them. Herbals (in ancient and

medieval times written in Latin) expanded, and most (e.g., the anonymous *Ortis sanitatis*) ordered plants alphabetically. Alphabetical ordering was problematic, however, as some plants had many names, while the same name was sometimes used for numerous plants. The rise of printing and the proliferation of herbals printed in the vernacular further exacerbated difficulties with alphabetical classification systems.

Plants introduced into Europe in the early-modern period resulted in a flood of new material to order, much of it sufficiently unusual that attempts to classify either philosophically or artificially seemed impossible. Increasing interest in natural philosophy led many to acknowledge that plant taxonomic systems based on similarity of use resulted in plants being classified together that differed significantly in other respects. Natural taxonomic systems were proposed using a variety of differentiating criteria. Mathius de l'Obel (1539–1616) classified plants by leaf shape; Joseph Pitton de Tournefort (1656–1708), by differences between flowers; Fabius Columna (1567–1650), by both seed and flower characteristics; and Jacques d'Mechamp (1513–1588), by appearance, habitat, and use. Conrad Gessner was the first to clearly differentiate between genus and species, but he applied this concept inconsistently. John Ray, expert botanist and anatomist, used multiple criteria to differentiate among species in his plant taxonomies, as in his animal classifications.

All such attempts failed. By the early eighteenth century, it seemed clear that single-criterion taxonomies produced systems that grouped together plants significantly distinct, while multiple-criteria taxonomies caused arguments about which criteria to include. These problems led to calls for an emphasis on observation and experimentation. With enough information, it would be possible both to classify natural phenomena accurately and to create a new, universal philosophical language whose nouns would make clear an object's place within a taxonomic system.

Attempts in this vein continued but with little success. Finally, the admittedly artificial system proposed in the eighteenth century by Carl Linnaeus found wide acceptance in both the botanical and the zoological worlds. His system solved many classification problems; easy to learn and apply, it could include all animals and plants, and it produced universally accepted names. Increasingly skeptical about the possibility of creating natural taxonomies, scientists and naturalists throughout the Western world rapidly adopted the Linnaean system.

BIBLIOGRAPHY

Cain, A. J. "Linnaeus's Natural and Artificial Arrangements of Plants." *Botanical Journal of the Linnean Society* 117 (1995), 73–133.

———. "Numerus, Figura, Proportio, Situs: Linnaeus's Definitory Attributes." *Archives of Natural History* 21 (1994), 17–36.

George, Wilma, and Brundson Yapp. *The Naming of the Beasts: Natural History in the Medieval Bestiary.* London: Duckworth, 1991.

Knight, David. *Ordering the World: A History of Classifying Man.* London: Burnett Books, 1981.

Mayr, Ernst. *The Growth of Biological Thought: Diversity, Evolution and Inheritance.* Cambridge, MA: Belknap, 1982.

KATHLEEN WHALEN

See also Aldrovandi, Ulisse; Botany; Gessner, Conrad; Natural History; Ray, John; Species; Zoology

Teleology

Nominally, the study of nature in terms of purpose. Frequently, and especially in the Scientific Revolution, researchers also associated purpose with economy; this efficient purpose is summed up by the oft-repeated phrase, "Nature does nothing in vain." Purpose involves the question "why?" and is different from function, which asks "how?"

Before the Scientific Revolution, three main teleological traditions existed. One is Aristotle's (384–322 B.C.E.) final cause, which he considered a purposeful principle, or a goal, wholly immanent within nature: the goal of an acorn is to become an oak tree. Another tradition ascribed the regular sequences observed in nature to the purposes of a limited deity (basically Plato's, 428–348 B.C.E., Demiurge). The third tradition grounded the order of the Creation in the intentions of the unlimited Judeo-Christian God.

The natural philosophers of the Scientific Revolution followed the third teleological tradition. If they sometimes did use Aristotle's term *final cause* or referred to the "wisdom of Nature," they meant it in a Christianized context. Most thought God had designed nature in the most economical manner and utilized purpose accordingly. They took this approach in spite of the objections of Francis Bacon (1561–1626) and René Descartes (1596–1650), who both asserted, without proof, that using purpose in science was unproductive.

William Harvey (1578–1657) used efficient purpose in his discovery and justification of the blood's circulation. He realized that the venous valves opened in one direction only and asked *why* there were so many and *why* they were all oriented toward the heart. Harvey concluded his *On the Motion of the Heart and Blood* (1628) by writing that "it would be very difficult to explain in any other way to what purpose all is constructed and arranged as we have seen it to be."

Harvey's discovery represents the apex of a long medical tradition in which researchers grounded anatomical and physiological studies in purposeful design. This medical use of teleology was by no means an isolated methodology. Researchers utilized the guiding ideas of purpose and efficient purpose in nature throughout the Scientific Revolution.

Researchers employed teleology in the debates over spontaneous generation and the origins of fossils. The microscopist Jan Swammerdam (1637–1680) argued that certain plants did not generate the animals found in them. Rather, God had created these plants for the purpose of nourishing the animals. The naturalist John Ray (1620–1705) asked, if spontaneous generation were true, then why are there sexes and such a "vehement and inexpugnable appetite of copulation?" In the debate over fossils, Robert Hooke (1635–1703) used efficient purpose. He reasoned that, since "nature does nothing in vain," it was contrary for such intricate fossils to have "no higher end than only to exhibit such a form." These and other teleological arguments helped overturn incorrect theories concerning the origins of life and fossils.

Pierre de Fermat (1601–1665) employed efficient purpose to work out the correct proof of the sine law of refraction. Fundamental to his proof was the assumption that nature acts in the most economical manner. Therefore, a light ray follows the path that takes the least time. Christiaan Huygens (1629–1695) used this assumption of least time (now a principle) in developing his wave theory of light. Gottfried Wilhelm Leibniz (1646–1716) also accepted Fermat's principle because of "nature being governed as it is by a sovereign wisdom." In a 1687 letter, Leibniz similarly stated, against Descartes: "Far from excluding final causes and the consideration of a being who acts with wisdom, it is from these that everything must be derived in physics."

Fermat defended efficient purpose by appealing to Galileo Galilei (1564–1642). Galileo had written about the "custom and procedure of nature herself in all her other works, in the performance of which she habitually employs the first, simplest, and easiest means." Galileo was echoing Nicolaus Copernicus (1473–1543), who advised that "we should rather follow the wisdom of Nature, which, just as it has particularly bewared of producing anything superfluous or useless, has, on the other hand, often endowed one thing with many effects." Isaac Newton (1642–1727) repeated this also, stating that nature is pleased with simplicity and does not affect the pomp of superfluous causes.

Finally, thinkers used purpose as a basis for speculation. Tycho Brahe (1546–1601) thought that the purpose of the planets was to be filled with inhabitants. When told about the moons of Jupiter, Johannes Kepler (1571–1630) decided that they had to exist solely for the Jovians. Similar reasoning was exercised for the purpose of the stars. Newton asked: "to what end comets?" He speculated that, generally, comets both nourished and destroyed life, but one in particular may have caused Noah's Flood, "passing the earth to the east."

BIBLIOGRAPHY

Greene, Robert Allan. "Teleology in Seventeenth-Century England." Ph.D. diss. Harvard University, 1961.

McMullen, Emerson T. "Anatomy of a Physiological Discovery." *Journal of the Royal Society of Medicine* 88 (1995), 491–498.

———. "A Barren Virgin? Teleology in the Scientific Revolution." Ph.D. diss. Indiana University, 1989.

Wright, Larry. *Teleological Explanations.* Berkeley and Los Angeles: University of California Press, 1976.

EMERSON T. MCMULLEN

See also Empiricism; Hypothesis; Theory

Telescope

The telescope consists of optical components, mirrors, and/or lenses. Both the refracting telescope, consisting of lenses only, and the reflecting telescope, which uses a mirror as the primary receptor, were products of the seventeenth century. The components, however, had been known centuries earlier. Concave and convex mirrors were known in antiquity and had been treated geometrically by Muslim and Christian authors during the Middle Ages. Convex lenses (*lentium* in Latin, meaning lentil),

first as thick magnifying glasses and then as thin spectacle lenses to correct presbyopia, had been known since the second half of the thirteenth century. Concave glasses—until the end of the seventeenth century, the word *lens* was used for convex lenses only—to correct myopia became known in the middle of the fifteenth century.

Speculation about the miraculous powers of such optical devices are to be found in the works of Roger Bacon (ca. 1215–1292) and are common in the works of sixteenth-century craftsmen and practitioners of magic. The most detailed descriptions were provided by certain English writers of the second half of the sixteenth century, and, on the basis of these, telescopes using a convex lens as the primary receiver and a concave mirror as the eyepiece have recently been constructed. Although these reconstructions do achieve the telescopic effect, such instruments, if indeed they were made, were impractical for several reasons. First, the mirror had to be angled somewhat so that the observer's head did not block the incoming light; second, the observer had to stand with his back to the object; and, third, the combination gives a very small field of view.

A combination using a convex objective and a concave eyepiece was more useful. The first reference to such a device dates from the end of September 1608, when the provincial government of Zeeland in the Dutch Republic wrote a letter to its representatives at the States General in The Hague, recommending an unnamed spectacle maker and his device for "seeing faraway things as though they were nearby." The records of the States General show that this spectacle maker was Hans Lipperhey, who requested a patent on the device. Although he was handsomely rewarded for several binocular instruments he made for the States General, Lipperhey was denied his patent for two reasons. First, several others came forward and claimed the invention as their own. Second, the device was so easy to copy after merely hearing or reading an account of it that the States General judged that it could not be kept a secret.

Indeed, knowledge of these spyglasses spread rapidly, and, by the spring of 1609, three- or four-powered spyglasses were offered for sale by spectacle makers in several major European cities. These devices used as an objective the weakest convex lenses and the strongest concave lenses made by spectacle makers. Making the lenses necessary to make the device more powerful was, however, initially beyond the scope of the craft. Research telescopes, therefore, initially became the province of those rare scientists who had practical skills. Thomas Harriot (ca. 1560–1621) in England and Galileo Galilei (1564–1642) in Italy took the lead. By early August 1609, Harriot was observing the Moon through a six-powered instrument. Later that month, Galileo presented an eight-powered instrument to the Venetian Senate and was rewarded with life tenure and a doubling of his salary as professor of mathematics at the University of Padua.

Galileo's continued efforts to make better and more powerful instruments allowed him to make a series of spectacular discoveries that made him and the instrument famous overnight. By November 1609, he had a twenty-powered instrument with which he studied the Moon. Further improvements allowed him to discover the satellites of Jupiter in January 1610. In March of that year, he published his epoch-making *Sidereus nuncius* (The Sidereal Messenger) in Venice, and later that same year he discovered the strange appearances of Saturn and the phases of Venus. Two complete telescopes and one broken objective lens made by Galileo have survived. Analyses of the lenses shows that, although Galileo could not accurately control the radii of curvature of the lenses and must have worked by trial and error, the objective lenses are nevertheless surprisingly good. The instruments magnified from fifteen to twenty times, and their fields of view were ca. fifteen arc-minutes. Because of the concave eyepieces, these instruments show objects erect and were, therefore, useful for terrestrial as well as celestial purposes. The smallness of the field of view was, however, a limiting factor. At magnifications higher than twenty, the field became so small as to make the instrument impossible to use.

Galileo's lead in telescope making was precarious. By the fall of 1610, other observers, including Harriot, were observing the satellites of Jupiter, and the discovery of sunspots was made by several observers independently in the spring of 1611. But because of the limitations of the instrument, no further important discoveries were made in the heavens until nearly half a century later. Until the 1640s, the Galileo telescope ruled astronomy; by the middle of the century it was replaced by the astronomical telescope.

The new form of the instrument was first described theoretically in Johannes Kepler's (1571–1630) *Dioptrice* (1611). It was first used later in that decade by Christoph Scheiner (1573–1650) for projecting sunspots. In his *Rosa ursina* (1630), Scheiner mentions the advantage of this instrument for direct observing, a much larger and brighter field of view, which negated its apparent disadvantage, the inverted image. During the 1630s, astronomical telescopes made by Francesco Fontana of Naples began to attract attention. In the later 1640s, Fontana was surpassed in skill by Eustachio Divini in Rome.

Astronomical telescopes allowed higher magnifications up to a point. By 1650, magnifications in the best instruments had reached fifty; a decade later, they had reached well over one hundred, and now the shrinking field of view became the limiting factor again. The solution to this problem lay in the addition of a third convex lens, a field lens, a configuration invented by Antonius Maria Schyrlaeus de Rheita (1604–1660) and Johannes Wiesel (ca. 1583–1662) in the 1640s. Henceforth, the most powerful telescopes employed compound eyepieces. Christiaan Huygens (1629–1695), whose telescopes began attracting attention in the 1650s, invented a particular combination of ocular and field lens (the Huygens eyepiece) that resulted in a flatter field and a partial suppression of chromatic aberration.

The astronomical telescope suffered more than the Galilean telescope from optical defects. In 1637 René Descartes (1696–1650) published a quantitative analysis of spherical aberration—in a spherical lens, the focal point varies with the distance of the incident light from the optical axis—and showed that in a spherical-ellipsoidal or plano-hyperbolic lens this aberration was corrected. This announcement led many lens makers to try grinding hyperbolic lens surfaces, efforts that went unrewarded. In the meantime, practice dictated that lens curvature must be kept at a minimum, and this meant that any increase in magnification had to be achieved by an increase in the focal length of the objective. Telescopes thus became longer and longer. Lengths increased from thirty-five feet in 1660 to one hundred forty feet in 1670. Such instruments were virtually impossible to use effectively, and tubes were now increasingly dispensed with. By the end of the century, aerial telescopes of up to two hundred feet were tried. But, except for Jean-Dominique Cassini's (1625–1712) discoveries of the satellites of Saturn and the division in the planet's ring, discoveries made with instruments of comparatively modest lengths, the long refractor had reached its limit.

In the meantime, another theoretical consideration had led Isaac Newton (1642–1727) to abandon the

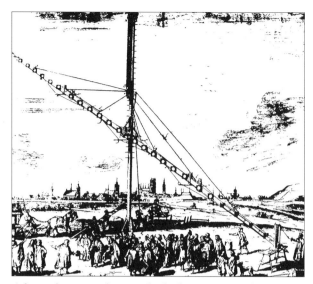

A long telescope without a tube, built to minimize aberration. From Johannes Hevelius, Machina coelestis *(1673–1679).*

refracting telescope. In his celebrated 1672 paper on light and colors, Newton showed that the different colors that make up white light are dispersed by a convex lens and come to a focus at different distances behind the objective. If the primary receptor were a mirror instead of a lens, this dispersion would not occur. Although the possibility of a reflecting telescope had been discussed by several scientists, and James Gregory (1638–1675) had actually ordered one from telescope maker Richard Reeve in the 1660s, Newton was the first (in 1670) to make a reflecting telescope, a small instrument with a primary mirror ca. 1.25 inches in diameter. This instrument was the subject of much discussion, but, except for Newton (who made several), others did not succeed or thought the tarnishing of the mirror made the instrument inferior to the refracting telescope. Not until the 1720s did the reflector become a serious competitor of the refractor.

If the career of the refractor as an instrument of discovery came to a close in the 1680s, its use as a measuring instrument was just then becoming established in observatories. Efforts to turn the telescope into a measuring instrument began with Galileo and his contemporaries. The Galilean form of the instrument does not, however, lend itself to this function because light rays do not come to a focus inside the instrument. In the astronomical telescope, however, the objective focuses light rays in front of the ocular, and, if an object is inserted in this focal plane, it will appear in sharp focus superimposed on the

object. In the early 1640s, William Gascoigne (ca. 1612–ca. 1644) discovered this fact by accident and made a screw micrometer with which to measure distances within the field of the telescope. Because of the English Civil War (1642–1646), however, Gascoigne's instrument remained unknown to the scientific world at large for several decades. In his *Systema Saturnium* (1659), Christiaan Huygens published his method of inserting wedge-shaped metal strips into the focal plane of his telescope for measuring the angular diameters of planets. Building on this method, Adrien Auzout (1622–1691) and Pierre Petit (ca. 1598–1677) in France built a screw micrometer, and its publication resulted in the discovery that Gascoigne had preceded them by more than two decades. At about the same time, Geminiano Montanari (1633–1687) in Italy put crosshairs in a telescope and mounted it on a measuring arc.

Micrometers and telescopic sights quickly became the standard instruments in the Paris and Greenwich observatories for measuring angular distances. As a result, the naked-eye accuracy of one arc-minute, achieved a century earlier by Tycho Brahe (1546–1601) and in the seventeenth century only by Johannes Hevelius (1611–1687), was surpassed. With successive refinements, measuring instruments henceforth gained incrementally in accuracy with each generation.

BIBLIOGRAPHY

Helden, Albert Van. "The 'Astronomical Telescope,' 1611–1650," *Annali dell'Istituto e Museo di Storia della Scienza di Firenze* 1 (1976), 13–36.

———. "The Development of Compound Eyepieces, 1640–1670." *Journal for the History of Astronomy* 8 (1977), 26–37.

———. "The Invention of the Telescope." *Transactions of the American Philosophical Society* 67(4) (1977). (Special Issue).

———. "The Telescope in the Seventeenth Century." *Isis* 65 (1974), 38–58.

King, Henry C. *The History of the Telescope*. London: Charles Griffin, 1955. Repr. New York: Dover, 1979.

ALBERT VAN HELDEN

See also Auzout, Adrien; Galilei, Galileo; Gascoigne, William; Reflection; Refraction; Telescopic Astronomy

Telescopic Astronomy

The telescope came out of the mechanical crafts and was wielded by practitioners of the mathematical sciences, but its impact was on cosmology. In the first century of its existence, the telescope helped shape the new image of the universe.

The discoveries that Galileo Galilei (1564–1642) revealed in his *Sidereus nuncius* (Sidereal Messenger, 1610) bore directly on the debate between the world systems of Nicolaus Copernicus (1473–1543) and Ptolemy (ca. 100–ca. 170). The rough surface of the Moon showed its affinity to the earth and thus bridged the traditional conceptual chasm between the terrestrial and the celestial regions. The satellites of Jupiter answered the objection that, in the Copernican system, the earth would be the only planet to have a moon; now there were four more, and, regardless of what world system one believed in, there were now observed to be several centers of rotation in the universe. The fact that planets were resolved into little disks like moons by the telescope, whereas the fixed stars were not, lent support to the great distance of the fixed stars postulated by Copernicus to explain the absence of an observable annual stellar parallax. Finally, the innumerable hitherto invisible fixed stars revealed by the telescope and the resolution of some nebular patches into individual stars revived the ancient atomist notion that the Milky Way was a congeries of small stars whose light mingled into one streak across the sky.

None of these discoveries fit comfortably into the old Aristotelian cosmology, but they did not prove that it was wrong. Galileo's observation of the phases of Venus, late in 1610, however, proved that, if the traditional cosmology was to be maintained, it would have to be in altered form: Venus and Mercury revolved around the Sun. Further, the discovery of sunspots by several observers simultaneously proved, after some debate, that the Sun and, therefore, the heavens were not perfect and unchangeable. By 1615, then, the telescope had contributed greatly to the undermining of Aristotelian cosmology, as Galileo himself demonstrated in his *Dialogue Concerning the Two Chief World Systems* (1632). Because of the limitations of the Galilean telescope, no major new discoveries were made for the time being, but the impact of the telescopic discoveries was profound in scholarly as well as popular circles.

One immediate problem occasioned by the telescope was the question of the periods of Jupiter's satellites. The idea that the motions of the satellites could be used as a celestial clock that would solve the problem of longitude at sea struck several early observers. The first attempts to calculate tables of these motions was made

by Nicolas-Claude Fabri de Peiresc (1580–1637) (who discovered the nebula in the sword of Orion) and his circle in Provence. Their efforts were discontinued in 1612, when Galileo turned his attention to the problem, on which he worked until he became blind. In 1614 Simon Marius (1570–1624) (who discovered the Andromeda Nebula) published the first tables, in his *Mundus Jovialis*. The pursuit of accurate tables of these satellites occupied astronomers until John Harrison's (1693–1776) chronometers solved the problem of longitude at sea in the eighteenth century.

Making the telescope a regular part of astronomical practice was not easy. In 1610 astronomical practice consisted of making position measurements with naked-eye instruments and calculating orbits. Could the telescope be made into a measuring instrument? Galileo and his immediate successors attempted to do this, but, in the Galilean configuration of lenses, the focal point of the objective lens lies beyond the eyepiece, making this task impossible, and this means that no object introduced into the tube will be in sharp focus. Not until the 1650s, when the Galilean telescope was replaced by the astronomical telescope with its convex eyepiece, was this problem solved. For the first half-century of its existence, telescopy and position measurements remained separate, if complementary, parts of observatory practice.

Some astronomers continued to base their work exclusively (or almost exclusively) on positional measurements and calculations, including Johannes Kepler (1571–1630), Philip van Lansberge (1561–1632), and Ismaël Boulliau (1605–1694). Others, such as Pierre Gassendi (1592–1655) and Johannes Hevelius (1611–

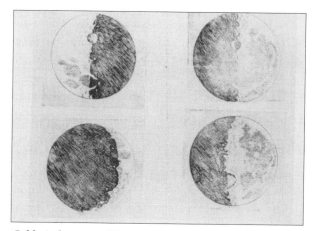

Galileo's drawings of the Moon as seen through his telescope. From his Sidereus nuncius *(1610).*

1687), combined position measurements with qualitative telescopic observations. We must go beyond the narrow astronomical community to find observers who concentrated exclusively on telescopic astronomy, to the virtual exclusion of positional measurements, such as Galileo and Antonius Maria Schyrlaeus de Rheita (1604–1660).

As an instrument of discovery, the Galilean form of the telescope had exhausted its potential by 1612. What remained were several difficult problems: observing the phases of Mercury, solving the riddle of Saturn's appearances, and estimating the angular diameters of all of the heavenly bodies. But the telescope did allow several very important observations. Alerted by Kepler to transits of Mercury and Venus, Gassendi, Johannes Baptist Cysat (1588–1657), and Johannes Remus Quietanus of Rudrauff (fl. 1610–1640) observed the transit of Mercury across the sun in 1631; Jeremiah Horrocks (1618–1641) and William Crabtree (1610–ca. 1644) observed the Venus transit of 1639. These observations gave better figures for the angular diameters of these planets and, more important, gave much improved figures of the locations of the nodes of their orbits, thus making possible more accurate theories of their motions.

The most spectacular result achieved with the telescope after the initial discoveries was the production of moon maps. Although several observers, including Galileo, had published sketches of various phases of the Moon, it was not until the 1630s that serious thought was given to preparing accurate maps of our nearest neighbor. In Provence, Peiresc and Gassendi hired the engraver Claude Mellan (1598–1688), who produced three phases (first quarter, full, and last quarter) in 1637. Peiresc's death that year meant the end of this project. In Brussels in 1645, Michel Florent van Langren (ca. 1600–1675) made the first moon map in which conventions for lunar representation (e.g., illumination from one direction) were used. The most celebrated study of the Moon was done by Johannes Hevelius, whose *Selenographia* (1647) laid the foundation of the science of selenography. But Hevelius's convention for naming lunar features using classical geographical names was gradually replaced by the convention suggested by Giambattista Riccioli (1598–1671) in his *Almagestum novum* (1651), using the names of scientists—the convention still used today.

With the adoption of the astronomical telescope by 1650, telescopic astronomy changed. Because of the larger field of view of this instrument, higher magnifica-

tions now became feasible, and the result was a second wave of discoveries. In 1655 Christiaan Huygens (1629–1695) discovered a satellite of Saturn (now called Titan), and shortly afterward he solved the riddle of Saturn's changing appearances. His *Systema Saturnium* (1659) presented the world with his ring theory, but it also contained the key to making the telescope into a measuring instrument. Huygens also put forward new dimensions of the solar system based on his own measurements of planetary diameters and harmonic speculations. This completely new system of sizes and distances needed only minor adjustments in the following decades.

After Huygens's discoveries, Jean-Dominique Cassini (1625–1712) dominated this aspect of telescopic astronomy for the next three decades. Cassini discovered four more satellites of Saturn (1671, 1672, 1684), as well as Cassini's division in the ring system. He also discovered surface markings on Mars and Jupiter that allowed the determination of their rotation periods.

Huygens's method of measuring apparent diameters quickly led to full-fledged screw micrometers and telescopic sights. It was with these innovations that the telescope became fully integrated in the work of the observatory. Telescopic measurements freed astronomers from the limitation of the discriminating power of the human eye (ca. one arc-minute). By the 1680s, astronomers were routinely making position measurements that were several times more accurate that those of Tycho Brahe (1546–1601). Further, once the limitations of the human eye had been overcome, the accuracy of position measurements continued to increase, so that, by the middle of the eighteenth century, such measurements were approaching one arc-second. Although the refracting telescope as an instrument of discovery had reached its practical limits by then, as a measuring instrument its future was assured.

BIBLIOGRAPHY

Galilei, Galileo. *Sidereus Nuncius; or, The Sidereal Messenger.* Trans. with Introduction, Conclusion, and Notes by Albert Van Helden. Chicago: University of Chicago Press, 1989.

Van Helden, Albert. "'Annulo Cingitur': The Solution to the Problem of Saturn." *Journal for the History of Astronomy* 5 (1974), 155–174.

———. "Christopher Wren's *De corpore Saturni.*" *Notes and Records of the Royal Society of London* 23 (1968), 213–229.

———. "Johannes Hevelius and the Visual Language of Astronomy." In *Renaissance and Revolution: Humanists, Scholars, Craftsmen, and Natural Philosophers in Early Modern Europe,* ed. J. V. Field and Frank A. J. L. James.

Cambridge: Cambridge University Press, 1994, pp. 97–116.

———. *Measuring the Universe: Cosmic Dimensions from Aristarchus to Halley.* Chicago: University of Chicago Press, 1985.

Whitaker, Ewen. "Selenography in the Seventeenth Century." In *The General History of Astronomy*, ed. M. A. Hoskin. 4 vols. Cambridge: Cambridge University Press, 1983–, Vol. 2A, pp. 119–143.

Winkler, Mary G., and Albert Van Helden. "Representing the Heavens: Galileo and Visual Astronomy." *Isis* 83 (1992), 195–217.

ALBERT VAN HELDEN

See also Galilei, Galileo; Hevelius, Johannes; Horrocks, Jeremiah; Langren, Michel Florent van; Observatoire de Paris; Royal Observatory at Greenwich; Telescope

Telesio, Bernardino (1509–1588)

Born of a noble family at Cosenza in Calabria in southern Italy, he also died there. Of his education we know practically nothing. Contrary to a well-established legend, he was never a student or a graduate of the University of Padua. He seems to have been self-taught, and this may explain his freedom with regard to philosophical tradition. Already in the 1540s, he is said to have begun writing "against Aristotle's doctrine," an undertaking that was to occupy him for the rest of his life. In 1563 Telesio met Vincenzo Maggi (1498–1564), a distinguished author of commentaries on the physics of Aristotle (384–322 B.C.E.), to whose critical judgment he submitted his anti-Aristotelian ideas. Telesio apparently emerged with success from this paradoxical challenge, and in 1565 he published in Rome his *De natura iuxta propria principia liber primus et secundus* (On Nature According to Its Own Principles) (i.e., according to nature's principles, not Aristotle's or Telesio's). A revised edition in two books was published in Naples in 1570, and the complete work in nine books appeared in 1586. After Telesio's death, his disciple Antonio Persio (1542–1612) published a collection of Telesian treatises in Venice in 1590.

Criticizing Aristotle's abstract and metaphysical trilogy—matter, form, and privation—Telesio undertook to build a new philosophy of nature on the base of sense perception (*sensus*), defined as the fundamental source of truth in the field of human knowledge. Rethinking in a non-Aristotelian way the notions of space (conceived as an empty capacity to receive bodies and independent of things located) and of time (as independent of motion),

Telesio founded his entire cosmogony and physics on the tangible conflict between two incorporeal natures, *heat* and *cold,* and their associated properties, acting on a corporeal and passive *matter* to control it. He not only sought to explain the birth of a geocentric world in which the fiery heaven encircles an immobile earth, he also placed confidence in the capacity of reason, the exercise of which depends on the activity of man's corporeal and sentient *spiritus* "to obtain rapidly, and without great strain and effort the knowledge of all other things, even of the substance and operation of the soul."

Telesio was one of the most important innovators of the later Renaissance, bringing on the crisis in Aristotelian physics, a determining factor in the Scientific Revolution. For his audacious and isolated undertaking, for which his work was put on the Index of Forbidden Books in 1596, he was recognized by Francis Bacon (1561–1626) as "a lover of truth, a man useful to the sciences, a corrector of certain dictrines and the first of the true philosophers." Galileo Galilei (1564–1642), although far from being a disciple of Telesio or an admirer of his doctrine, did not hesitate to compare him in his *Assayer* (1623) to an eagle soaring over flocks of starlings.

BIBLIOGRAPHY

Atti del Convegno Internazionale di Studi su Bernardino Telesio (Cosenza 12–13 Maggio 1989). Cosenza: Accademia Cosentina, 1990.

De Franco, Luigi. *Introduzione a Bernardino Telesio.* Catanzaro-Messina: Rubbetino Editore, 1995.

Kristeller, Paul Oskar. *Eight Philosophers of the Italian Renaissance.* Stanford, CA: Stanford University Press, 1964, ch. 6.

Sirri, Raffaele, and Maurizio Torrini, eds. *Bernardino Telesio e la cultura Napoletana.* Naples: Guida Editori, 1992.

M. P. LERNER

See also Aristotelianism; Matter; Space; Spirit

Theology. See Religion and Natural Philosophy

Theories of the Earth

There is evidence of close observation of the materials of the earth's crust in Renaissance art (e.g., by Jan van Eyck ca. 1390–1441) and of processes of geological change in the notebooks of Leonardo da Vinci (1452–1519). But, for the earth as a whole, attention was, at that time, chiefly given to astronomical questions. With the

Copernican revolution, incorporating the establishment of Galilean and Newtonian mechanics, a problem began to attract scientific attention, namely the origin of the earth and its history since its first formation. In the long tradition of trying to reconcile faith and reason, it seemed appropriate to propose theories that were compatible with the supposed divinely inspired revelation offered by the Bible and also with the latest knowledge available from natural philosophy. Hence, a genre of writings known as theories of the earth made its appearance in the seventeenth century. These writings exemplified what was called physico-theology.

Among such writings, the most important was probably that of René Descartes (1596–1650). He devised a remarkable "just-so story," which described how three types of corpuscle might have come into being after the first creation of matter (which he regarded as equivalent to space) and the imposition of motion upon the initial matter by divine action. From such a conceptual starting point, Descartes gave a hypothetical account of how the solar system—including, of course, the earth—might have come into being. He also suggested how the various layers of the earth might have been formed, and he sought to account for the occurrence of different mineral substances by suggesting that they were made up of appropriate kinds of invisible particles (e.g., large round ones for quicksilver). Then, finding agreement between his theoretical first principles and the results of everyday observation (along with some venerable ideas about the earth's interior), Descartes triumphantly asserted that his model was satisfactory because it accounted for observations (a notable instance of the fallacy of affirming the consequent).

Descartes's theory of the earth, designed to agree with the principles of physics, is a good example of the application of the mechanical philosophy. Some other theories of the earth were fitted to agree with ideas about earth history arising from biblical lore. The cleric Thomas Burnet (ca. 1635–1715), for example, sought to provide a quasi-Cartesian theory that provided for six stages of earth history that meshed with Old Testament beliefs such as the legends of the Garden of Eden and Noah's Flood and the New Testament belief (actually based on Stoic sources) in a future destruction of the globe in a great conflagration, as well as a rejuvenation of the paradisiacal earth at Christ's second coming.

Other theorists, such as the physician and naturalist John Woodward (1665–1728), propounded theories that supposedly linked biblical history (the Deluge story) with up-to-date Newtonian science, involving the idea that the several layers of the earth's crust settled out after the Flood in order of their specific gravities and that fossils supposedly became entombed in the rocks at the time of the Flood. William Whiston (1667–1752), successor to Isaac Newton's (1642–1727) chair at Cambridge, had the idea that the earth originated from the impact of a comet with the Sun.

Such theories of the earth suffered from the fact that, while they explained certain facts, they failed to provide testable predictions about phenomena that had not themselves been used in the construction of the theories. A notable exception was the theory of Robert Hooke (1635–1703), which sought to explain the occurrence of earthquakes and the existence of different fossil-bearing strata. Hooke's idea was that the earth's poles slowly shift so that the earth moved relative to its ellipsoidal envelope of water; hence, there would be alternating phases of deposition of sediment and erosion at particular points on the planet's surface. Hooke deduced that this movement would slowly alter the direction of the meridian at any given point, and he suggested how such changes might be determined astronomically. The prediction was not actually tested, however; if it had been, it could not have been successful because any such change would have been too slow to detect. This illustrates the point that, in the seventeenth century, ideas about the age of the earth were misconceived, for they were typically based on a biblical time-scale, the earth supposedly being only ca. six thousand years old.

Theories of the earth continued to be proposed into the eighteenth century, but by the nineteenth century they were regarded as speculative and unsatisfactory. In 1797 the Scottish natural philosopher James Hutton published his *Theory of the Earth,* which did make testable predictions; today he is regarded by many as the father of modern geology, but in his own time his representation of his ideas as a theory of the earth did not assist their acceptance.

BIBLIOGRAPHY

Gould, Stephen J. *Time's Arrow, Time's Cycle: Myth and Metaphor in the Discovery of Geological Time.* Cambridge, MA, and London: Harvard University Press, 1987.

Haber, Francis C. *The Age of the World: Moses to Darwin.* Baltimore: Johns Hopkins University Press, 1959.

Laudan, Rachel. *From Mineralogy to Geology: The Foundations of a Science, 1650–1830.* Chicago and London: University of Chicago Press, 1987.

Oldroyd, David R. *Thinking About the Earth: A History of Ideas in Geology.* London: Athlone; Boston: Harvard University Press, 1996.

DAVID OLDROYD

See also Burnet, Thomas; Geology/Mineralogy; Physico-Theology; Whiston, William

Theory

The conceptual structures in terms of which we understand our world are today usually called theories. This notion of theory first took shape in the seventeenth century, though it has roots in earlier natural philosophy. The term *theory* itself was used very broadly, then as now, and was almost never subjected to analysis with a view to more careful definition. We shall not be following this rather casual usage but, rather, the distinctive form of understanding that, by the nineteenth century, the term had come primarily to designate.

Theory, derived from the Greek term *theoria,* became, with Aristotle (384–322 B.C.E.), the activity of contemplation that defined the highest goal of human life. The proper objects of contemplation were things eternal and unchanging and, hence, closest to the divine, to which only *episteme* (knowledge afforded by demonstration from causes) could give access. Primary among these, besides the first cause itself, were the universal features of nature, the essences of physical things. The *theoria* to which all should aspire was contemplation, prompted by wonder rather than by practical ends and directed primarily through the physical world to its unchanging causes.

From the beginning, it was clear that such knowledge was difficult to attain. Even in astronomy, the study of those natural objects closest to the divine, a demonstrative knowledge of the causes of their motions and their changes of brightness could scarcely be claimed. Worse still, Ptolemy's (ca. 100–ca. 170) *Almagest,* the most successful guide to the planetary motions, was at odds with the Aristotelian explanation of those motions in terms of hypothesized spheres that carried the planets. Despite its virtue as a predictor of observed planetary position, the *Almagest* could not lay claim to the sort of causal understanding that *episteme* was held to require.

In the centuries that followed, the models of the astronomer came more and more to be regarded as useful fictions making no claim on truth. When the early-medieval philosopher Hugh of St. Victor divided philosophy into *logica, theorica, practica,* and *mechanica,* the second division, the domain of theoretical knowledge, was taken to include theology, mathematics, physics, and the "mixed" natural sciences that employ mathematical constructions. The label *theorica* came to be associated primarily with the domain of mathematical astronomy, partly perhaps because of the wide influence of the anonymous *Theorica planetarum* (ca. 1270), the most successful technical introduction of its day to the mathematical intricacies of Ptolemaic astronomy. It was clearly a far cry from this to the original usage of *theoria.*

A further shift in the perception of what a theoretical knowledge of nature might achieve came with the nominalist rejection of the central tenets of Aristotelian natural philosophy in the fourteenth century. The nominalists objected, mainly on theological grounds, to the necessitarian emphasis in Aristotle's ideal of demonstration. Instead, they maintained that our knowledge of nature must begin from perceived particulars and restrict itself to generalization, treating universal concepts as no more than names without ontological content. The more radical among them concluded that natural knowledge based on causes could yield only probability at best.

Nicolaus Copernicus (1473–1543) challenged the prevailing skeptical account of what mathematical astronomy could achieve, maintaining that his heliocentric model was to be taken not just as a convenient predictive device but as a true assertion. He could muster an argument of sorts for the realist interpretation he was giving to his astronomy, appealing to the fact that his model could explain some features of the planetary motions that, for Ptolemy, could be no more than odd coincidences. But he could not devise a plausible account of the *causes* of the planetary motions; his epicycles were as difficult to take literally as Ptolemy's had been, and he could not respond to objections to the earth's motion drawn from Aristotelian physics. Worst of all, Tycho Brahe's (1546–1601) computation of the orbit of the comet of 1577 "destroyed the reality of the spheres," as Johannes Kepler (1571–1630) would later put it.

Kepler is, perhaps, the most significant figure in our story. In his youthful *Mysterium cosmographicum* (1596), he amplified Copernicus's claim to give a "reasonable explanation" of what had "aroused astonishment" in the earlier geocentric models. And he attempted a physical explanation of the planetary motions in terms of an *anima motrix* (a moving soul) in the Sun whose force weakens with distance, thus (loosely) accounting for the fact that the more distant planets move more slowly than the ones nearer the Sun. His discovery of the elliptical orbit of Mars, however, allowed a major advance, as the title of his next work indicates: *A New Astronomy Based on Causes; or, A Celestial Physics Drawn from Commentaries on the Motions of the Planet Mars* (1609). His astronomy is no longer going to rest simply on a claim to save the appearances; it is to be based as well on a *physics* of the planetary motions, purporting to explain the causes of those motions. Drawing on analogies with the transmission of light and of magnetic action, he proposes that the Sun rotates and propagates a swirl of immaterial species that alternately attracts and repels and moves the planet onward; its intensity depends on distance and on the mass/bulk of the Sun and the planet. The changing distances between Sun and planet are to be explained by an ingenious suggestion of a magnetic force depending on the orientation of the earth's magnetic poles. The details need not concern us; he continued to modify them in later works. He did not quite reach his goal: a theory that would both predict *and* causally explain the planetary motions in a single quantitative framework. It was left to Isaac Newton (1642–1727) to achieve this, or at least to appear to do so.

But the idea of what such a theory should look like is quite explicit in Kepler's work. It would, initially at least, be hypothetical; its warrant would lie not only in saving the phenomena, but also in providing a testable causal explanation for them. Justification would, thus, proceed backward from effect to cause in an indirect form of inference that Charles S. Peirce (1839–1914) later called retroduction (or abduction). What made it indirect was the possibility that the other causes might explain the effects equally well or better. Kepler hoped, however, that, over the course of time, a single explanatory account could so prove its merits that it could safely be regarded as true.

As the seventeenth century wore on, the term *law* came to be the term of choice for the most basic claims of natural science. "Law" expressed an invariable regularity of action, an invariable correlation of *natures,* or the like. Francis Bacon (1561–1626) and René Descartes (1596–1650) agreed in making the discovery of the laws of nature the primary goal of natural science, though they disagreed fundamentally on how that discovery was to be

achieved. In his *New Organon* (1620), Bacon described a method of induction that would proceed by way of generalizations of gradually widening scope, carried out on observed particulars that could be grouped together under tables of presence, absence, and degree. Descartes, on the other hand, in his *Discourse on Method,* was confident that he could establish the basic laws of mechanics "without basing my arguments on any other principle than the infinite perfections of God." There was no need, he claimed, to test his formulations of these laws against observation. Indeed, when critics of the laws of percussion pointed out that some of the laws ran quite contrary to ordinary experience, Descartes blamed the discrepancies on unspecified impediments, disturbing factors whose influence was, in practice, impossible to predict.

These are the understandings of *law* that have led Bacon and Descartes to be regarded as the paradigm empiricist and rationalist, respectively. But there is another side to each. To illustrate his method of induction, Bacon presents in great detail the set of empirical correlations that lead him to conclude that heat is a species of motion. But since visible motion is absent in most instances of heat, he is forced to postulate the motion of imperceptible particles. There is obviously no way to arrive at such a claim through simple generalization of an observed regularity. And he shows himself to be aware of this: the discovery of latent configurations, latent processes, is a "new thing." Though he has little to say about how such discovery should proceed, he is perceptive in showing how the resultant hypothesis can be tested by the consequences drawn from it. The warrant in this case is no longer the simple empiricist one; the postulated cause of the observed effect lies outside the reach of direct observation. Though Bacon still describes what is discovered as a law, clearly a shift has taken place. What has been discovered or, more exactly, what has been tentatively proposed is a "latent configuration" sufficient to explain a variety of observed effects. What he has, then, is a *theory,* not an inductive law, to draw a distinction based on the type of warrant claimed, a distinction that is still too often glossed over in contemporary scientific writing.

Galileo Galilei (1564–1642) formulated his two laws of motion in kinematic fashion; there was no need, apparently, to invoke either mass or force. He could, then, bracket the *cause* of motion entirely and give his mechanics at least the semblance of demonstration. Isaac

Newton, in turn, claimed to treat the key notions of force and attraction only mathematically, leaving aside the physical issue of the *cause* of gravitational behavior. Though critics like Gottfried Wilhelm Leibniz (1646–1716) and George Berkeley (1685–1753) pointed to the convenient ambiguity of his language, most of his readers were satisfied that he had in some sense *explained* motion. By treating gravity as no more than a simple disposition to move in a certain way, given a particular configuration of masses, motions, and distances, he could claim that he was *deducing* his account of gravitational motion directly from the phenomena. No need, then, for hypothesis, the speculative move from observed effect to unobserved cause that he distrusted and tried to eliminate from science proper. Though most of his contemporaries had accepted the need to include probabilistic inference to unobserved causes within science proper, Newton held out for something closer to the traditional ideal of demonstration. If theoretical explanation could be modeled on mechanics, one could, he implies, extract mathematical principles that would escape the taint of hypothesis. But the sciences of the corpuscular processes underlying the observable world of inductive law would not, as Descartes, Robert Boyle (1627–1691), and John Locke (1632–1604) had clearly seen, yield to this optimistic analogy.

The lure of mechanics as paradigm and the authority of Newton's example led many in the century that followed to regard science as an inquiry into the laws of nature, laws that would rest on some combination of intuition and induction. It was only with the successes of chemistry and optics in the early nineteenth century that causal argument to underlying structure came finally to be regarded as an indispensable part of science proper, and the modern notion of theory as a conceptual construction that rests on the quality of the explanation it gives for the observed regularities of nature came finally to be appreciated.

BIBLIOGRAPHY

Bacon, Francis. *Novum Organum*. Trans. and ed. Peter Urbach and John Gibson. Chicago: Open Court, 1994.

Garber, Daniel. *Descartes's Metaphysical Physics*. Chicago: University of Chicago Press, 1992.

Herschel, John F. W. *A Preliminary Discourse on the Study of Natural Philosophy*. Chicago: University of Chicago Press, 1987. 1st ed. 1830.

Lobkowicz, Nicholas. *Theory and Practice: History of a Concept from Aristotle to Marx*. Notre Dame, IN: University of Notre Dame Press, 1967.

McMullin, Ernan. *The Inference That Makes Science*. Milwaukee: Marquette University Press, 1992.

ERNAN MCMULLIN

See also Demonstration; Empiricism; Experience and Experiment; Hypothesis; Laws of Nature; Realism; Resolution and Composition

Thermoscope/Thermometer

The air thermoscope is a glass flask with a long, thin neck. The flask is warmed, partly expelling air, then inverted with the open end under water. The cooling air contracts, drawing water up the neck. Subsequent alterations in the height of the water indicate temperature changes. Pneumatic experiments recorded in antiquity by Philo and Hero presaged the air thermoscope. Hero's work became widely known in late-sixteenth-century Europe. However, his "fountain that drips in the sun" was a demonstration that water can be raised by heat, and not a thermoscope. The Renaissance also inherited from antiquity a Galenic scale of heat built from the Aristotelian opposites of hot and cold. By the late sixteenth century, the idea of a scale of temperature was familiar, though there was no instrument to quantify it.

The thermometer, which measures, rather than merely indicates, qualitative change, is attributed to the Italian physician Santorio Sanctorius (1561–1636), whose first published account appeared in 1612. By the second quarter of the seventeenth century, such air thermometers had become well known, though there was no common scale. Quite what it measured became problematic as natural philosophers accepted Evangelista Torricelli's (1608–1647) views in 1644 on the variability of air pressure. The sealed liquid-in-glass thermometer dates from 1654 or earlier, the invention of Ferdinand II, grand duke of Tuscany. Through the Accademia del Cimento in Florence, these instruments became well known to the learned world. Subsequent development rested on ensuring comparability, other than through physical similarity. Evaluation of thermometric fluids and attempts to construct rational universal scales of temperature followed, with Robert Hooke (1635–1703) making a notable contribution. The concept of geographically and temporally invariant datum points, such as the temperature of snow, the freezing of water, healthy body temperature, or the melting point of butter, took time to digest. Not until the eighteenth century was the subjectivity of

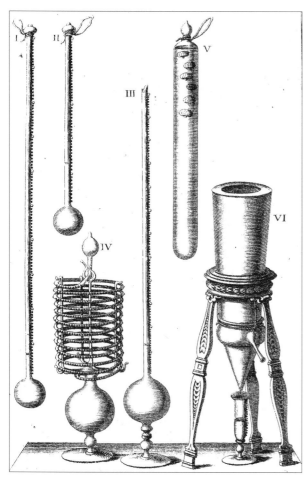

Heat-measuring devices (I–IV). From the Accademia del Cimento's Saggi di naturali esperienze, *2nd ed. (1691).*

the commonsense observation that caves are cooler in summer than in winter generally challenged.

BIBLIOGRAPHY

Chaldecott, J. A. "Bartolomeo Telioux and the Early History of the Thermometer." *Annals of Science* 8 (1952), 195–201.

Middleton, W. E. Knowles. *A History of the Thermometer and Its Use in Meteorology.* Baltimore: Johns Hopkins University Press, 1966.

Taylor, F. S. "The Origin of the Thermometer." *Annals of Science* 5 (1942), 129–156.

D. J. BRYDEN

See also Accademia del Cimento; Heat

Tides

Throughout the seventeenth century, information about tides was reported by scientists and explorers from all around the world. Interest in the subject by natural philosophers was principally promoted by cosmological concerns raised by Copernicanism.

The influence of the Moon on the tides, an idea originating in antiquity, persisted through the Middle Ages and received renewed attention during the Scientific Revolution. Francesco Patrizi (1529–1597) cited observed correlations between the times of tides and lunar positions, in his *Pancosmia* (1591). Johannes Kepler (1571–1630), who was familiar with the work, had postulated attractive forces as causes of celestial motions and concluded that the influence of the Moon's attraction on the oceans creates the tides. The astrological tradition associating the Moon with liquidity and, thus, the tides was rejected by Galileo Galilei (1564–1642).

Galileo noted the periodic diurnal, monthly, and annual variations in the tides and that they were modified by varying depths of waters and by different shorelines. He rejected attraction theories and the role of the Moon, proposing instead a mechanistic explanation that he expounded in his *Dialogues on the Two Chief World Systems* (1632) as a proof of the earth's motion. Because of the earth's daily rotation on its axis, he assumed that the seas on one side of the earth move in the same direction as Earth's annual motion around the Sun, while those on the other side of the earth move in a direction opposite to the annual motion. This, he argued, produces an alternating acceleration and deceleration of these seas. The acceleration causes the water to pile up on one shore, producing a high tide, and, when the sea is on the opposite side of the earth, the deceleration causes the water to slide away from that shore, resulting in low tide.

René Descartes (1596–1650) offered a different mechanistic theory of the tides based on a vortex of matter whirling around the earth and carrying the Moon along with it. Since the Moon is heavier and more sluggish than the matter surrounding it, the matter, moving more rapidly, has to squeeze between the Moon and the earth in order to pass it. This pushes the matter downward onto the surface of the oceans, driving water up onto the shore and producing high tides. When the Moon has passed on, the pressure abates, and the water rises in the oceans and subsides at the shoreline, producing low tides.

Isaac Newton (1642–1727) developed an equilibrium theory of the tides by assuming that the earth was completely covered with water. The attraction of the

Moon draws the water up to form a prolate spheroid, which is elongated on the side facing the Moon, as well as on the opposite side of the earth. A similar prolate spheroid is produced by the attraction of the Sun on the seas. The rotation of the earth beneath these spheroids produces semidiurnal tides, which vary with the cycles of the Moon and the Sun.

BIBLIOGRAPHY

Aiton, E. J. "The Contributions of Newton, Bernoulli, and Euler to the Theory of the Tides." *Annals of Science* 11 (1955), 206–223.

———. "Galileo's Theory of the Tides." *Annals of Science* 10 (1954), 44–57.

Burstyn, Harold L. "Galileo's Attempt to Prove That the Earth Moves." *Isis* 53 (1962), 161–185.

WILLIAM LEWIS HINE

See also Attraction; Galilei, Galileo

Time

As with space, the concept of time involves questions about whether time is dependent or independent of bodies, whether it is mind dependent or not, and whether there is an absolute reference for it or it is radically relative. One can find disagreement over such issues at the start of the seventeenth century. Many Aristotelians thought time dependent on bodies but not mind dependent. Others sided with Augustine (354–430), thinking it independent of the motion of bodies. By the end of the century, the champion of absolute time was Isaac Newton (1642–1727); the great relativist was Gottfried Wilhelm Leibniz (1646–1716).

For Aristotle (384–322 B.C.E.), time is the *number* of motion (i.e., time is the enumeration of motion). There cannot be any time without there being some change; we measure motion by time and time by motion. Consequently, there are as many times as there are motions, and all are able to serve as the definition of time. However, the choice of a motion to measure time is not arbitrary. Although Aristotle thought that time has no reality outside of the motion it measures, he did not think that time has no reality outside of the measurer of the motion: "the before and after are attributes of movement, and time is these *qua* numerable."

The obvious questions raised by the Scholastics of the Middle Ages dealt with the subjectivity of time and its intimate connection to motion. John Duns Scotus (ca.

1266–1308) rejected many elements of Aristotle's doctrine; inspired by Augustine's theory of time as activity of the soul, he argued that, even if all motion were to stop, time would still exist and would measure the universal rest. Questions about the relativity of time also gained theological inspiration through the condemnations of 1277 by the bishop of Paris of certain proposition is derived from Saint Thomas Aquinus, especially the condemnation of the proposition "That if the heaven stood still, fire would not burn flax because God would not exist." The standard late-Scholastic view seems to have been that time began with the motion of the heavens and will end with it also. The Spanish Jesuit Franciscus Toletus (1515–1582) argued an Aristotelian-Thomistic line that, if there were no motion, there would be no generation or time. On the other hand, the textbook writer Eustachius a Sancto Paulo (1573–1640) argued for what may have been the successor to the Scotist line: that time is divisible into real time and imaginary time, the latter being that which we imagine precedes the creation of the world. Another textbook writer, Scipion Dupleix (1569–1661), referred favorably to Augustine's account of time and talked of time measuring both motion and rest.

Similar arguments were also propounded by anti-Aristotelians. Bernardino Telesio (1509–1588) asserted that Aristotle was right about the constant conjunction of time and motion but misundertsood their true relation: "the fact that we always perceive them together is no reason to claim that one of them is the ground of the other, but only, what seems to be the case, that every motion occurs in its own time and that no motion can take place without time."

Questions about the absoluteness or relativity of time were highlighted in the debates between Newton and Leibniz. During the second half of the seventeenth century, it became possible to get a "truer time" using the experimental evidence of the pendulum clock and the eclipses of Jupiter's moons—thus correcting the change in the duration of solar days at different seasons of the year, for example. According to Newton, this truer time was not to be identified with absolute time, which is independent of motion: "all motions can be accelerated and retarded, but the flow of time cannot be changed. . . . Absolute, true, and mathematical time, in itself and by its nature without relation to anything external, flows uniformly." Leibniz denied absolute time, as he had absolute space: as space is the order of simultaneous coexistents, time is the order of successive coexistents. Like space, time is ideal, and absolute time is reducible to absurdity, as was absolute space. Leibniz's argument was that any answer to the question of whether God might have created the world sooner would contradict the principle of sufficient reason: "For God does nothing without reason, and no reason can be given why he did not create the world sooner. . . . If space and time were anything absolute, that is, if they were anything else besides certain orders of things, then indeed my assertion would be a contradiction. But since it is not so, the hypothesis (that space and time are anything absolute) is contradictory, that is, it is an impossible fiction."

BIBLIOGRAPHY

Alexander, H. G., ed. *The Leibniz-Clarke Correspondence.* Manchester: Manchester University Press, 1956.

Čapek, Milič. *The Concepts of Space and Time.* Dordrecht: Reidel, 1976.

Duhem, Pierre. *Medieval Cosmology: Theories of Infinity, Place, Time, Void, and the Plurality of Worlds.* Ed. and trans. Roger Ariew. Chicago: University of Chicago Press, 1985.

Koyré, Alexandre. *From the Closed World to the Infinite Universe.* Baltimore: Johns Hopkins University Press, 1957.

Whitrow, G. J. *Time in History: Views of Time from Prehistory to the Present* Day. Oxford: Oxford University Press, 1989.

ROGER ARIEW

See also Biblical Chronology; Horology; Motion

Torricelli, Evangelista (1608–1647)

Leading Italian mathematician and follower of Galileo Galilei (1564–1642), best known for his invention of the barometer, although his precursory work to infinitesimal calculus and its applications is no less important.

Little is known about Torricelli's early life. He came from Faenza (in Romagna) or from that area. He studied with the Jesuits and later in Rome under Benedetto Castelli (1578–1643), Galileo's former pupil and a pioneer of the science of waters. In 1632, in Castelli's absence, Torricelli answered a letter of Galileo's to Castelli, informing Galileo about the reception of his *Dialogue on the Two Great World Systyems* (1632) in Rome, taking the opportunity of presenting himself as Castelli's secretary and as a mathematician by profession, outlining his studies, and declaring his adherence to Copernicanism.

In 1641, as Torricelli was developing Galileo's theory of motion, Castelli suggested that Torricelli move to Florence to assist Galileo, by then seventy-seven years old and blind. Torricelli left for Florence and assisted Galileo during the last three months of his life. For Torricelli, this was the beginning of a successful career and a period of intense scientific work. He was offered the post of mathematician to the grand duke of Tuscany as Galileo's successor and teaching positions at Florentine academies, primarily at the Florentine Academy (which replaced the largely inactive University of Florence). In the following five years, before his sudden death, Torricelli achieved a series of remarkable scientific results.

It is within the context of the contemporary scientific work of Galileo and his followers, in particular that of Bonaventura Cavalieri (1598–1647), that one should consider Torricelli's work. In 1635 Cavalieri published his *Geometria,* in which he presented his theory of indivisibles, a method for measuring surfaces and volumes, whereby a straight line was moved over a surface and the "trace" it left behind it was used to find the area of the surface (an analogous procedure was used for solid figures). This method facilitated the solution of geometrical problems, although it was criticized for not being satisfactorily rigorous.

Torricelli extended Cavalieri's theory of indivisibles by applying "curved indivisibles"; he showed, among other things, that the area of an infinite hyperbolic solid is finite and proved that the area under a cycloid (the path described by a point on the circumference of a circle rolling on a straight line, above the line) equals three times the area of the circle. He also developed a general principle for finding the center of gravity of plane and solid figures having an axis of symmetry. Torricelli, however, shared the skepticism concerning the rigor of the theory of indivisibles, and, whenever he could, he proved mathematical theorems by the traditional method of exhaustion.

Torricelli gave a broad and detailed geometrical treatment of specific cases of Galileo's theory of motion, including free fall, motion on inclined planes, movement through chords of a circle, and parabolic and projectile motion. He showed, inter alia, that the range of a projectile increases in double proportion to the angle of elevation, composed firing tables for marksmen, and devised an instrument correlating range and angle of elevation. Torricelli's treatment, however, seems to have been purely theoretical; he probably never experimented with

Courtesy Istituto e Museo di Storia della Scienza, Florence, Italy.

projectiles. In the same treatise, Torricelli also extended Castelli's work in hydrodynamics, deducing in particular that the square of the velocity of a jet of water from an opening at the bottom of a container is proportional to the height of the water in the container. These and other results were collected in 1644 in his *Opera geometrica,* the only publication of his to appear during his lifetime.

In the same year (1644), Torricelli invented the Torricellian tube, or barometer, and succeeded in producing an artificial vacuum for the first time. Helped by Galileo's former assistant Vincenzio Viviani (1622–1703), he filled with mercury a glass tube measuring two ells (ca. 120 centimeters) long and sealed at one end, stopped its mouth with a finger, and turned it upside down (sealed end up) in a bowl of mercury. The mercury in the tube descended to a height of ca. one ell (ca. 60 centimeters) above the mercury in the bowl, leaving a space at the top. Torricelli conjectured that this space was empty: to verify this, he added water to the mercury in the bowl and slowly raised the tube. When the mouth of the tube rose to the surface of the water, the mercury in the column flowed down, and the water rushed up into the tube to fill its top, indicating to Torricelli that the space *was*

empty. Moreover, Torricelli believed that the mercury in the tube was in balance with the atmospheric pressure, in contradiction to Galileo's conjecture in his *Two New Sciences* that vacuum exerts a "force." Torricelli repeated the experiment with two tubes, one ending in a large bowl at the top; had the vacuum exerted force, the tube with the large bowl would have had more force since it contained more rarefied matter. The mercury, however, dropped to the same level in both tubes.

The whole topic of the vacuum and the related theory of atomism were delicate subjects, since they contradicted Aristotle and could even be considered heretical. Torricelli did not publish the result of his experiment, but he described it in a letter dated June 11, 1644, to Michelangelo Ricci (1619–1682), a follower of Galileo in Rome, remarking: "We live submerged at the bottom of an ocean of elementary air which is known by incontestable experiments to have weight." Torricelli's experiment was not published until 1663—by his pupil and friend Carlo Dati (1619–1676), under the pseudonym Timauro Antiate.

Many results of Torricelli's work are contained in his correspondence with mathematicians and intellectuals in Italy and France. In 1646, for instance, he produced in a letter to Ricci a universal theorem for determining the center of gravity of geometrical figures by means of a ratio of two values equivalent to two integrals. Though Torricelli at times criticized Galileo, whenever criticism came from outside Galilean circles he assiduously defended and spread Galileo's ideas. He was, with others, involved in a long dispute between Italian and French mathematicians (mainly with Gilles Personne de Roberval, 1602–1675) concerning priority in a number of mathematical discoveries.

Torricelli was active in additional fields of science and knowledge. He performed astronomical observations, though he carefully avoided discussions concerning astronomy or cosmology; he developed a special method of manufacturing lenses, and he gave theoretical advice on drainage. In general, Torricelli's approach to scientific research was theoretical and a priori. He was also known for his polished, brilliant, and witty conversation, and he was active in literary academies, including the Accademia della Crusca. There he gave a series of lectures, *Lezioni accademiche,* on science and general topics, which were published posthumously in 1715.

Torricelli left a series of manuscript works in mathematics that were published in 1919 in his collected works. Despite his clearly important contribution to the Scientific Revolution, by the end of the twentieth century no monograph had been devoted entirely to him.

BIBLIOGRAPHY

Caverni, Raffaello. *Storia del metodo sperimentale in Italia,* vol. 5. Florence, 1897. Repr. Bologna: Forni, 1970.

Galluzzi, Paolo. "Evangelista Torricelli: Concezione della matematica e segreto degli occhiali." *Annali dell'Istituto e Museo di Storia della Scienza di Firenze* 1 (1976), 71–95.

Mancosu, Paolo, and Ezio Vailati. "Torricelli's Infinitely Long Solid and Its Philosophical Reception in the Seventeenth Century," *Isis* 82 (1991), 50–70.

Segre, Michael. *In the Wake of Galileo.* New Brunswick, NJ: Rutgers University Press, 1991.

Torricelli, Evangelista. *Opere.* Ed. Gino Loria and Giuseppe Vassura. 4 vols. Faenza: Montanari, 1919. Faenza: Lega, 1944.

MICHAEL SEGRE

See also Barometer; Hydraulics and Hydrostatics; Infinitesimals; Motion; Mechanics; Pneumatics

Tournefort, Joseph Pitton de (1656–1708)

A prominent French botanist who devised a widely adopted plant-classification system, emphasizing the genus as the primary category of division. As a professional physician, he was concerned with facilitating the identification of plants with pharmaceutical properties, as his *History of Plants Which Grow Around Paris, with Their Medicinal Uses* (*Histoire des plantes,* 1698) attests. Nevertheless, like most other contemporary botanists, such as John Ray (1620–1705), Augustus Bachmann (Rivinus) (1652–1723), and Robert Morison (1620–1683), who proposed competing systems, Tournefort based his classifications strictly upon morphological characters of plants and ignored accidental characters, such as medicinal applications or habitat. Since few of these rival botanists could agree upon which morphological characters were essential to classification, a profusion of incompatible systems arose.

In *Elements of Botany* (*Élémens de botanique,* 1694), Tournefort clearly defined seven hundred genera according to the distinctive features of only two characters, flower and fruit, and provided many detailed illustrations of characteristic species. He also criticized Ray's system for allowing too many characters, although, in practice, Tournefort often included criteria besides flower and fruit in his classifications to achieve more natural genera. The simplicity of Tournefort's system allowed a naturalist to identify quickly a previously classified specimen and to classify confidently many of the newly discovered species being imported in the course of European expansion. Tournefort himself collected many exotic specimens during his royally sponsored travels throughout Europe and the Levant. Although his system was eventually supplanted by Carl Linnaeus's (1707–1778) famous "sexual system," which incorporated many of Tournefort's genera, it remained popular well into the eighteenth century. Tournefort's *Relation of a Voyage to the Levant* (*Relation d'un voyage du Levant,* 1717), published posthumously by colleagues in the Paris Academy of Sciences, combined natural history, systematic botany, and Orientalist scholarship within the genre of the travel narrative.

BIBLIOGRAPHY

Greene, Edward Lee. *Landmarks of Botanical History.* Stanford, CA: Stanford University Press, 1983, pp. 938–964.

Heim, Roger, ed. *Tournefort.* Paris: Muséum National d'Histoire Naturelle, 1957.

Mayr, Ernst. *The Growth of Biological Thought: Diversity, Evolution, and Inheritance.* Cambridge, MA: Harvard University Press, 1982.

ERIC A. URBANC

See also Botany; Ray, John; Taxonomy

Towneley, Richard (1629–1707)

As the head of a wealthy Roman Catholic family with large estates, at a time when English Catholicism was much beleaguered and deprived of all political power, Towneley applied his considerable intellect and energy to the pursuit of natural philosophy. He improved upon the micrometer invented by William Gascoigne (ca. 1612–1644) and used it for accurately determining astronomical positions. He also added an outstanding collection of scientific works to the already splendid family library, and he became the leading member, together with his close collaborator Henry Power (1623–1668), of a group of practicing experimental mechanical philosophers. From 1670 he also collaborated in astronomical observations with John Flamsteed (1646–1719), the future first astronomer royal, to whom he had earlier communicated details of his micrometer. Like Henry Power, Towneley was an early advocate of Cartesianism in England, although he always tempered his theoretical mechanical philosophy with careful experimentalism.

Towneley is usually credited with being the first to realize the relationship between the pressure and the volume of a gas, and what we now know as Boyle's Law was originally referred to as Towneley's hypothesis or Towneley's theory. Robert Boyle (1627–1691) acknowledged Towneley's assistance in arriving at the generalized statement of the relationship between pressure and volume of a gas in the second edition of his *New Experiments Physico-Mechanicall* (1662). Towneley's achievement was the result of his experimental collaboration with Henry Power, beginning in 1653. Inspired by the pneumatic works initiated by the discovery of the Torricellian vacuum, Power and Towneley performed experiments to demonstrate the "elater" or "springiness" of air. Although these initial researches led to no significant conclusion, Power and Towneley were in a strong position to advance pneumatic research after they read the first edition of Boyle's *New Experiments Physico-Mechanicall* in 1660. The experiments they carried out at this time were written up by Power in the early summer of 1661 and were included in Power's *Experimental Philosophy* (1663). Boyle, however, had access to the manuscript describing the experiments after August 1661, and Towneley was in London from the end of 1661. It seems likely that he was able to tell Boyle in person of the full significance of his and Power's work. Boyle was then able to say in the second edition of his *New Experiments* that Richard Towneley had helped him reduce his results to a "precise estimate." Power and Towneley were perhaps able to see in 1661 what Boyle could not in 1660 because their experimental setup enabled them to compare the volume of air, directly measured, with the pressure as calculated, whereas Boyle's setup measured the pressure directly but calculated the volume of air in a way that was, unfortunately, prone to error.

This work subsequently led to efforts by the Royal Society to use the Torricellian apparatus for weather forecasting. Towneley, together with Power, Boyle, John Locke (1632–1704), and others, made systematic barometric observations. This led to the generalization that a fall in the barometric reading indicated a deterioration in the weather. Towneley went on to make detailed measurements of rainfall from 1677 to 1704, which were published in the *Philosophical Transactions of the Royal Society* in 1699, 1702, and 1705. In spite of his talents, Towneley seems to have been reluctant to enter public life. He perhaps judged it safer, as a wealthy Roman Catholic, to avoid drawing attention to himself, with the result that he shunned publication and even avoided becoming a Fellow of the Royal Society.

BIBLIOGRAPHY

Webster, Charles. "The Discovery of Boyle's Law and the Concept of the Elasticity of Air in the Seventeenth Century." *Archive for History of the Exact Sciences* 2 (1962), 441–502.

———. "Henry Power's Experimental Philosophy." *Ambix* 14 (1967), 150–178.

———. Richard Towneley, the Towneley Group, and Seventeenth-Century Science." *Transactions of the Historic Society of Lancashire and Cheshire* 118 (1966), 51–76.

JOHN HENRY

See also Barometer; Gascoigne, William; Pneumatics; Telescope

Translations

The first reception of Aristotle (384–322 B.C.E.) in the Latin West was made possible by a wave of translations in the twelfth and thirteenth centuries, some of which were made directly from the Greek but most from preexisting Arabic translations, often through the intermediary of Hebrew or Spanish. While the quality of the texts thus transmitted was remarkably high, especially given the diverse contexts and languages through which they had passed, one of the great accomplishments of the Italian humanists starting in the late fourteenth century was to begin another wave of translations of classical texts, following new standards of Latin purity and textual criticism. With the help of Byzantine émigrés who taught them Greek and of princes who funded the purchase of manuscripts and their leisure to study, humanist scholars gathered, edited, translated, then published countless ancient works, many of them hitherto unknown. Renaissance *editiones principes,* such as the Greek editions published by Aldus at Venice, especially between 1490 and 1530, set the standards for classical scholarship in many cases down to the nineteenth century; they were followed in the late sixteenth century by editions with facing Latin translations.

Much of Greek mathematics, botany, and geography became available in Latin for the first time thanks to this activity. The rediscovery of Archimedes (ca. 287–212 B.C.E.) through translations by Venatorius in 1544 and Federico Commandino (1509–1579) in 1558 spurred the return to rigorous proof in fields like statics. New translations of Pappus by Commandino in 1588 and of Diophantus by Xylander in 1575 were among the sources of François Viète's (1540–1603) symbolic algebra. Botany was renovated through translations of Theophrastus by Theodore Gaza and by Jacques Daléchamps, who also translated the works of Athenaeus, and of Dioscorides's *Commentaries* (1554) by Mattioli; Mattioli added illustrations and explanations to his translation to aid in identifying the species. The humanist study of ancient natural-historical texts, including Latin works like Pliny the Elder's (23/24–79), generated heated debates over philological emendations (e.g., between Ermolao Barbaro and Niccolo Leoniceno in the 1490s) and brought to the fore the difficulties and risks involved in naming and identifying the species described by the ancients. Ptolemy's (ca. 100–ca. 170) *Geography* was translated into Latin by A. Angeli, with corrections by Johannes Regiomontanus (1436–1476) in 1525, and into Italian by Mattioli in 1548 and served as a model for the development of mathematical methods of cartography.

Even in cases in which the humanists worked on texts that had already been available, their return to the sources (*ad fontes*) was the starting point for reforms with revolutionary consequences. Thus Ptolemy's *Almagest* had been known in the Middle Ages through the *Sphaera* of John of Sacrobosco (d. ca. 1256), which provided only an elementary introduction to the complexity of Ptolemy's astronomical system. In the mid-fifteenth century, Georg Peurbach (1423–1461) began an *Epitome* of the *Almagest,* which was completed in 1463 by Regiomontanus, who knew Greek (while Peurbach did not); when the work was printed in Venice in 1496, its thorough and at times critical reworking of Ptolemy's computations caught the attention of Nicolaus Copernicus (1473–1543), who was studying at Bologna that year. In reading the *Epitome* as a young man, Copernicus acquired both the technical competence required to propose improvements on Ptolemy's system and the admiration that kept him faithful to many of its parameters. Similarly, in transforming the practice of anatomy, Andreas Vesalius (1514–1564) relied in part on the precepts of Galen (second century C.E.), whose *Anatomical Procedures* had been translated in 1531, along with other texts of Greek medicine (including those of Alexander of Tralles and Hippocrates), by Johannes Guinter of Andernach (ca. 1505–1574), his teacher at the University of Paris in 1533. In these cases, a more direct access to the ancient models in different disciplines had rapid and far-reaching consequences.

Humanist translations were not necessarily substantially innovative, however. In the complex transmission of Euclid's (fl. 300 B.C.E.) *Elements* in the Renaissance, the medieval version by Campanus de Novara (ca. 1220–1296) continued to play an influential role. New translations of Aristotle by George of Trebizond, Theodore Gaza, and Johannes Argyropoulos in the fifteenth century did not lead to a radically different presentation of the philosopher, although more attention was paid to Aristotle's natural-historical works than had been in the Middle Ages. Commentaries from late antiquity like those of Simplicius and Philoponus became available for the first time in Greek editions in the late sixteenth century, but the medieval commentaries of Averroës (1126–1198) continued to be standard.

By the second half of the sixteenth century, these translation activities had spread to other languages. Humanist linguistic interests extended to Arabic and Hebrew but did not generate translations of specifically scientific texts. Translations into various vernaculars, on the other hand, became progressively more numerous; they not only made scientific works available to a broader readership, but also prompted interactions between learned and more practical approaches. Euclid rapidly became available in French (1564), German (1558 and 1562), and English (1551 and 1570) as part of a growing interest in practical mathematics. John Dee's (1527–1608) Preface to William Billingsley's English translation of Euclid in 1570 announced the beginning of a few dozen mixed mathematical disciplines: most foundered, but Dee successfully developed the expectation that Euclid's work could be applied to practical concerns. Vernacular translations also appeared early in natural history (Pliny in French in 1562, Dioscorides in Italian in 1544), a field that had broad appeal because of its encyclopedic range and pharmacological usefulness. Texts with a more exclusively specialist audience and those used primarily in schools and universities, notably the works of Aristotle, were in many cases not translated into vernaculars until modern times. Thus, even Nicole Oresme's fourteenth-century French translation of Aristotle's *De caelo* (On the Heavens) was ignored throughout this period and remained only in manuscript.

With the decline of Latin as the language of learning starting roughly from the 1630s, more works of science were composed in the vernacular and were then trans-

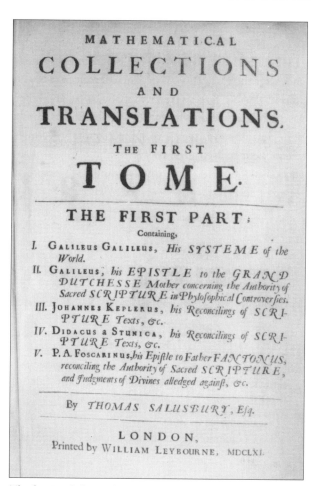

MATHEMATICAL
COLLECTIONS
AND
TRANSLATIONS.

THE FIRST
TOME.

THE FIRST PART,
Containing,

I. GALILEUS GALILEUS, His *SYSTEME* of the
World.

II. GALILEUS, his *EPISTLE* to the *GRAND
DUTCHESSE* Mother concerning the Authority of
Sacred *SCRIPTURE* in Philosophical Controversies.

III. JOHANNES KEPLERUS, his Reconcilings of *SCRI-
PTURE* Texts, &c.

IV. DIDACUS a STUNICA, his Reconcilings of *SCRI-
PTURE* Texts, &c.

V. P. A. FOSCARINUS, his Epistle to Father *FANTONUS*,
reconciling the Authority of Sacred *SCRIPTURE*,
and Judgments of Divines alledged against, &c.

By *THOMAS SALUSBURY*, Esq.

LONDON,
Printed by WILLIAM LEYBOURNE, MDCLXI.

*The first English translations of several significant works of
seventeenth-century physical science and of the relation
between science and theology.*

lated into Latin to ensure their international diffusion.
Thus, Galileo Galilei's (1564–1642) *Dialogue on the Two
Chief World Systems* was translated into Latin three years
after its first publication in 1632 and reedited twice;
René Descartes (1596–1650) himself translated his *Discourse on Method* (1637) into Latin in 1644. These Latin
translations often served as the basis for translations into
other vernaculars. At the same time, Isaac Newton's
(1642–1727) *Principia mathematica philosophiae naturalis,* composed in Latin in 1687, still required vernacular
epitomes, such as the *Elemens de la physique de Newton*
(1738) by Voltaire and Madame du Châtelet.

Throughout the early-modern period, translations
played a crucial role in diffusing and, during the Renaissance especially, inspiring new scientific developments.

BIBLIOGRAPHY

Chartier, Roger, and Pietro Corsi, eds. *Sciences et Langues en
Europe.* Paris: Centre Alexandre Koyré, 1996.

Grafton, Anthony. "The Availability of Ancient Works." In
The Cambridge History of Renaissance Philosophy, ed.
Charles B. Schmitt and Quentin Skinner. Cambridge:
Cambridge University Press, 1988, pp. 767–791.

Lindberg, David. "The Transmission of Greek and Arabic
Learning to the West." In *Science in the Middle Ages,* ed.
David C. Lindberg. Chicago: University of Chicago Press,
1978, pp. 52–90.

ANN BLAIR

See also Dee, John; Guinter of Andernach, Johannes; Humanism; Peurbach, Georg; Regiomontanus, Johannes

Trigonometry

The Greek-sounding name *trigonometry* arose ca. 1595
with Bartholomaus Pitiscus (1561–1613) and referred to
three-angle (triangle) measurement as used in astronomy
and other applications. Previously, phrases like *de triangulis* and *canon triangulorum* had been used; the change
may reflect the influence of sixteenth-century humanism.
Trigonometry already had a long history. The need for
spherical trigonometry arose in the astronomy of Greek
antiquity with Theodosios, Hipparchos, and Menelaos in
the Hellenistic era. Ptolemy's (ca. 100–ca. 170) *Almagest*
gives the most famous example—the rule of six quantities (a sort of sine rule) and the detailed construction of
tables of chords at half-degree intervals to 180 degrees.
These are effectively sine tables at fifteen-minute intervals, and to three sexagesimal places, with tabular differences. Many of Ptolemy's astronomical tables involve
complex interpolations in specific double-entry tables.
This illustrates a common dual theme—the development of the theory of triangles, plane or spherical,
together with the theory and practice of tabulation and
subtabulation.

The subject appealed to both the earlier Christian
and the later Islamic Arab astronomers; they introduced
the idea of tangents and cotangents and took over Indian
work that may have had Greek origins. Abul Wufa (940–
988) added secants and cosecants; such quantities
remained lengths rather than ratios until late in the modern period. Al-Biruni (973–1048) and Al-Ṭūsī (1201–
1274) produced comprehensive works, the latter using
the polar triangle. The tables of Ulugh Beg (1393–1440)
were associated with the work of Al-Kashi (d. 1436),
who solved Ptolemy's interpolation problem as a cubic
equation in sexagesimals. Calculation of the *qibla* (direction of Mecca) was a key motive in some of this work.

In northern Europe, the ablest scholar in this field was the Englishman Richard of Wallingford (ca. 1292–1336). But when work resumed again north of the Alps after the political disruptions of the fourteenth century, not all of the earlier work, in particular that of Al-Ṭūsī, was known there. Georg Peurbach (1423–1461) and Johannes Regiomontanus (1436–1476) were leading figures, the former with his *Epitome* of Ptolemy (which was completed after his death by Regiomontanus in 1463), and the latter with tables of sines and tangents, the *De triangulis omnimodis* (1464), which remained unpublished until 1533. Regiomontanus solved plane and spherical problems by using the *sinus rectus* and *sinus versus* (= 1 – cosine) but not the tangent. The first book of Nicolaus Copernicus's (1473–1543) *De revolutionibus* (1543) contained chapters on trigonometry that were published separately as *De lateribus et angulis triangulorum* (1542).

Copernicus's young associate Georg Joachim Rheticus (1514–1574) published the *Canon doctrinae triangulorum* in 1551, containing all six ratios for every ten seconds of arc and a radius of ten million units, a stupendous achievement. Later, Christopher Clavius (1538–1612) corrected these tables and improved their layout, coining the terms *tangent* and *secant* in 1583. The tables were reprinted in *Thomas Blundeville His Exercises* (1594) to give the English, late in the day, their first complete trigonometrical canon; the work was extended and used for fifty years. François Viète's (1540–1603) *Canon mathematicus* was published in 1579. Later he applied the expression for cos 3x to solve the irreducible case of cubic equations and thereby avoided Girolamo Cardano's (1501–1576) paradox of three real roots arising only via the roots of complex numbers. Many others contributed variations in presentation of methods and results at this time.

The major event at this time, however, was Valentine Otho's publication (1596) of the completion of the tables in Rheticus's great *Opus palatinum* to (in effect) ten places. This was extended by Pitiscus (1561–1613) in 1613 by sine tables to fifteen places. In 1629 Albert Girard (1595–1632) published the means of finding the area of the spherical triangle, discovered by Thomas Harriot (ca. 1560–1621) in 1603, and later seen to link Harriot's logarithmic tangents with hyperbolic non-Euclidean geometry. John Napier's (1550–1617) rules and analogies (1614) are multiplicative formulas involving half angles, suitable for the new logarithmic era.

François Viète, Alexander Anderson (1582–ca. 1619), Henry Briggs (1561–1631), and Isaac Newton (1642–1727) gave various results for angular sections, and, after the early 1660s, Nicolaus Mercator (ca. 1619–1687), Newton, James Gregory (1638–1675), and others gave series whose developments were helpful in tabulation. Harriot and Briggs gave subtabulation procedures, which were rediscovered by Newton and Gregory and generalized by Newton's divided-difference result, as stated in his *Principia mathematica philosophiae naturalis* (1687) for use in comet orbits.

BIBLIOGRAPHY

Debarnot, Marie-Thérèse. "Trigonometry." In *Encyclopedia of the History of Arabic Science,* ed. Roshdi Rashed. London and New York: Routledge, 1996, vol. 2, pp. 495–538.

North, John D. *Richard of Wallingford*. 3 vols. Oxford: Clarendon, 1976.

Pedersen, Olaf. *A Survey of the Almagest*. Odense, Denmark: Odense University Press, 1974.

Zeller, Mary C. *The Development of Trigonometry from Regiomontanus to Pitiscus*. Ann Arbor, MI: Edwards Brothers, 1946.

JON V. PEPPER

See also Logarithms; Regiomontanus, Johannes; Series, Mathematical

Tyson, Edward (1650–1708)

Fellow of the Royal Society, Fellow of the Royal College of Physicians, physician in charge of Bethlehem ("Bedlam") and Bridewell hospitals, natural historian, and comparative anatomist. Tyson received a B.A. and an M.A. from Oxford University and was associated with eminent English natural philosophers such as Robert Hooke (1635–1703) and Robert Plot (1640–1696).

In 1680 Tyson put forth an influential program for the advancement of natural history through the study of specific organisms rather than the compilation of textual references. The first in England to systematically apply the medical tradition of dissection to natural history, he published many careful examinations of particular creatures, both as short contributions to journals, including the *Philosophical Transactions of the Royal Society,* and as independent monographs. Tyson carefully dissected and examined a wide range of creatures, including various monsters, a porpoise, a tapeworm, and a rattlesnake. He was one of the first Europeans to study marsupials, dissecting male and female opossums. His most influential monograph on an individual species was *Orang-Outang* (1699), a report on the dissection of a young chimpanzee with a lengthy essay displaying great classical learning and asserting that the various races of pygmies described by the ancients were really apes and not humans. This claim was important, as Tyson was a strong believer in the Ladder of Nature, viewing apes as the intermediate link between humans and beasts. Finding such links was a principal goal of his science. Tyson was also particularly interested in glands. In human anatomy, his principal contribution was the discovery of the mucilaginous glands of the penis, which are known as Tyson's glands.

BIBLIOGRAPHY

Greene, John C. *The Death of Adam: Evolution and Its Impact on Western Thought*. Ames: Iowa State University Press, 1959. Repr. with a new Preface. Ames: Iowa State University Press, 1996.

Montagu, M. F. Ashley. *Edward Tyson, M.D., F.R.S., and the Rise of Human and Comparative Anatomy in England: A Study in the History of Science*. (Memoirs of the American Philosophical Society 20). Philadelphia: American Philosophical Society, 1943.

WILLIAM E. BURNS

See also Anthropology and Race; Natural History; Species; Taxonomy

T

U

Universal Languages

There are three types of projects involved in the development of universal languages: the creation of (1) real characters; (2) universal languages; and (3) a priori, or philosophical, languages. While they vary in form, most of the projects rest on Aristotelian epistemological assumptions. They assume that nature is an orderly system of essences that can be known and described, that men's mental concepts can be a faithful representation of that system, and that language is or can be a faithful representations of mental notions. In a world of perfect scientific knowledge, ideas would isomorphically represent the things of nature, and words would isomorphically represent ideas.

Proposals and schemes for artificial languages proliferated in the mid-quarters of the seventeenth century. For some, they were an attempt to provide a lingua franca where Latin no longer sufficed. For others with Paracelsian and Rosicrucian tendencies, they were an attempt to restore a prelapsarian language in which names had a natural relation to the hidden natures of things. The schemes were also seen as a means of providing clear and unambiguous communication in a world recently torn by religious and civil strife. The most significant projects, however, came from men with interests in science. Following Francis Bacon (1561–1626), they believed that, in its presently corrupted state, language obscured rather than revealed truth. In order to advance the cause of scientific knowledge, it was necessary to reform language or, better yet, to create an entirely new one. This project claimed the attention of René Descartes (1596–1650), Marin Mersenne (1588–1648), Isaac Newton (1642–1727), and Gottfried Wilhelm

Leibniz (1646–1716), but it was in England in a group associated with the Royal Society that it was most fully developed.

Real characters are marks that depict things or notions rather than written or spoken words. Numbers and signs for chemical elements are a typical example, as (it was mistakenly believed) are Chinese ideograms and Egyptian hieroglyphics. Proposals for real characters shade into schemes for universal languages. These build on Bacon's observation that, to correct the ambiguities and errors of language, there should be only as many words or real characters as there are radical notions. These schemes are based on a lexicon of basic notions. These are root words from Latin and other European languages, usually arranged alphabetically. In addition to the root words, there are affixes for derivations and simplified grammatical endings. The root words, the derivational affixes, and the grammatical particles are each assigned real characters, with the characters for the root words representing the place of the word in the lexicon. With lexicon in hand, one could translate anything written in a real character. Such schemes were developed in England by John Wilkins (1614–1672), the first secretary of the Royal Society, and several others.

Universal languages are based on words from natural languages and do not attempt to give a true or scientific description of things. This was the work of an a priori, or philosophical, language. These were discussed by Mersenne and Descartes and by a group of educational reformers associated with John Amos Comenius (1592–1670), as well as by members of the Royal Society. Full-fledged philosophical-language schemes were developed by George Dalgarno (ca. 1626–1687) in *Ars signorum* (The Art of Signs, 1661) and Wilkins in *An*

Essay Towards a Real Character and Philosophical Language (1668).

Dalgarno and Wilkins based their languages on Aristotelian concepts of taxonomy, which had long been the prevailing method of natural history. In Aristotelian classification, as it was understood in the seventeenth century, substance unfolds itself into essences, or the special forms of being. These are defined by the next-higher genus and the essential, or specific, difference. Thus, a definition of essence is a statement of the genus of the thing and the various properties that distinguish that species from another.

The philosophical-language schemes attempted to arrange all known things and notions on taxonomic tables that divided genera and subgenera according to their differences to produce the lowest species (i.e., the essences, or simple notions, or true divisions of nature). A letter or an ideographic sign was then assigned to each of the genera and differences or to each species or simple notion. The words that are formed from these letters or signs both represent and define the thing. Words are, thus, isomorphic with nature and semantically transparent.

Dalgarno's taxonomic tables, for example, isolate the primitive notions "leguminous plant" (concrete object distinguished by its vascular system) and "medium" (common accident of comparative degree). To signify a "pea," the speaker would combine the linguistic sign for each of these notions. Wilkins's tables more elaborately subdivide all genera and subgenera by their differences until they arrive at the lowest species (e.g., *angelica*, which is classified as an umbelliferous herb, with broad, pale green leaves). Each essential difference is represented by a letter. Thus, the word simultaneously gives a definition of the species.

The overlap between the scientific and the linguistic method can be seen in the collaboration of John Ray (1620–1705), the eminent biologist, who constructed the *Essay*'s taxonomic tables for plants and animals. Just as Wilkins searched for specific differences to define the essences of things, Ray followed Aristotelian principles and looked for the morphological characteristics, such as stems, flowers, and leaves, that distinguish plant species and define the plant's essence.

Wilkins's *Essay* was praised as ingenious, and there were sporadic attempts to revise and develop it, but nothing came of these, and it never received strong support from the more serious scientific figures in the Royal Society, with the exception of Robert Hooke (1635–1703). A substantial factor in the demise of interest in a philosophical language was the fact that taxonomy as a method of scientific inquiry came increasingly into disrepute, and, even in the biological sciences, the Aristotelian foundations of taxonomy were seriously undermined. Robert Boyle (1627–1691) and John Locke (1632–1704) challenged the Aristotelian notion that the real essences or true divisions of nature could be known. While these might exist in nature, men can know only their nominal properties. Taxonomy thus becomes simply a probabilistic account of the order of things. This entirely undermined the epistemological and scientific foundations of a language that would reflect the true nature of nature.

BIBLIOGRAPHY

Eco, Umberto. *The Search for a Perfect Language.* Oxford: Blackwell, 1995.

Knowlson, James. *Universal Language Schemes in England and France, 1600–1800.* Toronto: University of Toronto Press, 1975.

Salmon, Vivian. *The Works of Francis Lodwick: A Study of His Writings in the Intellectual Context of the Seventeenth Century.* London: Longmans, 1972.

Slaughter, M. M. *Universal Languages and Scientific Taxonomy in the Seventeenth Century.* Cambridge: Cambridge University Press. 1982.

M. M. SLAUGHTER

See also Bacon, Francis; Ray, John; Taxonomy; Wilkins, John

Universities

In the frequently polarized intellectual environment of the Scientific Revolution, many contemporaries portrayed the universities as determined opponents of the New Science. As Francis Bacon (1561–1626) wrote in his *New Organon* (the very title of which implied an attack on the Scholastic logic that had long been the basis of university studies): "Again in the customs and institutions of schools, academies, colleges and similar bodies, destined for the abode of learned men and the cultivation of learning, everything is found adverse to the progress of science." For the New Science was based on principles of experiment and mathematics that were in conflict with the Aristotelian-based Scholasticism that continued to be the basic intellectual fare of the universities until the late seventeenth century. Subsequent historians have generally tended to follow this contemporary lead in attributing to the universities a lowly place in the Scientific Revolution, arguing that the latter was a movement that needed to devise a new institutional form—the scientific academy—to replace the uncongenial universities.

Such a view is not without foundation. Naturally, institutions such as universities, which were heir to a long philosophical tradition of Aristotelian-based philosophy deriving from the High Middle Ages, were slow to adopt forms of natural philosophy that contradicted the basic premises on which their integrated philosophical instruction was based. Moreover, the universities, which grew out of the study of the ancient texts recovered in the twelfth and thirteenth centuries, continued to reverence textual authority in a manner that was antagonistic to the Scientific Revolution, with its emphasis on experiment and original inquiry. The choice of the motto of the Royal Society—*nullius in verba* (on the word [or text] of no one)—reflects the strength of such conflict between those defending the traditional bases of intellectual authority and the protagonists of the New Science.

However, as historians have moved beyond such contemporary polemics to investigate the actual record of the universities themselves, a rather more nuanced account of the role of the universities in the Scientific Revolution has begun to emerge. In the first place, there is the indisputable fact that the great bulk of scientists in the period of the Scientific Revolution were educated in the universities—of scientists listed in the *Dictionary of Scientific Biography* (1970–1980) with birthdates between 1450 and 1650, 87 percent were university educated. Moreover, a large percentage were employed in the universities (45 percent of the same sample). In a society in which inherited social position loomed so large, the universities provided a haven for another set of values, in which learning was valued for its own sake and intellectual distinction received recognition—attributes that were to benefit those who wished to devote themselves to new developments in natural philosophy, just as they did those interested in other fields of learning.

Furthermore, the traditional university curriculum did provide some institutional support for aspects of what came to be known as science, even if such support was often partial and inadequate. In the first place, natural philosophy had long been a major part of the undergraduate university curriculum, conferring on it a particular importance. Second, universities had traditionally paid some attention—however limited—to

mathematics. Lastly, the universities, as training grounds for the learned professions, had long supported medical faculties and the sciences, such as chemistry and botany, that were linked with them. In assessing the role that the universities played in the Scientific Revolution, it is useful to turn to each of these three areas.

Since natural philosophy had, for so long, been an integral part of the undergraduate curriculum, changes in natural philosophy were likely to have repercussions for the curriculum as a whole—something that accounts for the often highly charged debates about this subject. By the second half of the seventeenth century, universities throughout Europe were beginning to take account of the developments associated with the Scientific Revolution, with the result that the undergraduate curriculum was becoming more eclectic and less securely anchored in the traditional forms of Scholasticism. Faced by increasing pressure to retreat from Scholastic natural philosophy, many seventeenth-century universities turned to Cartesianism, which, for all of its philosophical novelty, still maintained many points of similarity with Scholasticism. Both were based on a process of philosophical deduction from basic premises, and both integrated natural philosophy into an overarching intellectual system. However, once Cartesian natural philosophy was adopted, it was to have a corrosive effect on the Scholastic curriculum more generally, since the basic philosophical premises of the two systems were fundamentally in conflict. The philosophical materialism to which the dualist Cartesian philosophy could give rise led to it being regarded with suspicion by the religiously orthodox, many of whom turned with relief to the less philosophically explicit system of Isaac Newton (1642–1727).

Part of the incompatibility between the modernized natural-philosophical curriculum and Scholastic philosophy lay in the increasing emphasis accorded to mathematics. Scholastic philosophy, drawing on largely Aristotelian roots, was essentially a system based on qualitative considerations and so did not lend itself to mathematical treatment based on quantitative considerations. Nonetheless, the universities had a long tradition of providing some, albeit often very limited, attention to mathematics, which, in the pattern of education that the Middle Ages inherited from the ancient world, formed the basis of the *quadrivium*—arithmetic, geometry, astronomy, and music. In the early-modern period, the often tenuous tradition of mathematical studies within the universities was strengthened by the humanist program of education, which included, in the manner of the ancients, some provision for the study of mathematics. Partly under the influence of humanism, both the Protestant educators and the Jesuits made mathematics an integral part of their educational program. The increasing need for mathematical practitioners in fields such as surveying and engineering further encouraged the study of mathematics, particularly in countries like the Netherlands, where the recently founded universities were relatively responsive to such social needs. And at some universities, notably Cambridge, mathematics—especially geometry—gradually came to be regarded as a substitute for logic, the traditional foundation for university studies.

Within the universities, however, the study of mathematics had generally been divorced from natural philosophy because quantitative methods did not mesh with the essentially qualitative approach of Scholastic natural philosophy. This situation gradually began to change by the late seventeenth century as the New Science made increasing inroads into the universities, necessitating a change in the structure of the curriculum. It also led to changes in the organization of the professoriate, as the duties of the professors of natural philosophy and mathematics increasingly came to overlap.

For the professors of medicine, the developments associated with the Scientific Revolution presented much less of a challenge than for those teaching natural philosophy or mathematics. Both before and after the Scientific Revolution, Aristotelianism provided a congenial philosophical environment for the biological sciences, with their emphasis on organic form and qualitative, rather than quantitative, explanations. Moreover, the practical needs of medical training had gone some way toward weakening (though by no means eliminating) the emphasis on the study of ancient texts. It is no accident that, in the biological sciences, much of the major work was done in the universities—particularly in the Italian universities, where training for the lay professions of medicine and law had been more deeply entrenched than in the northern European universities, which accorded greater status to the faculty of theology. The medical faculties also provided the institutional setting for the emergence of empirically based sciences, such as botany, zoology, and chemistry, that were relevant to the study of medicine.

Since the medical sciences continued to find the universities relatively congenial hosts, they had less need of the scientific academies that grew up throughout Europe in the seventeenth and eighteenth centuries. The foundation of these new institutions did lead to tension with the universities, but such antagonism generally abated with time, particularly when it became clear that the academies did not seek to compete with the universities in such basic areas as teaching and the awarding of degrees. In practice, too, there was often a good deal of symbiosis between academies and universities, with both institutions drawing on a common clientele and even sharing facilities and equipment. The foundation of the academies was an indication that the universities were not always an appropriate setting for the promotion of scientific research, but this did not challenge what the universities had traditionally regarded as their most basic function: the assimilation and transmission of the store of society's learning.

Though the universities were often slow to assimilate the developments associated with the Scientific Revolution, they were not as impervious as their contemporary critics suggested to adopting the findings of the New Science. By eventually absorbing such new intellectual fare, the universities helped confer on it the sanction of their traditional standing as the custodians of society's learning. Ironically, then, in the long term, the universities played a role in making the New Science respectable and in removing suspicions of it on the part of the guardians of Church and State—many of whom had received their education within the universities.

BIBLIOGRAPHY

Brockliss, Lawrence W. B. *French Higher Education in the Seventeenth and Eighteenth Centuries: A Cultural History.* Oxford: Clarendon, 1987.

Feingold, Mordechai. *The Mathematicians' Apprenticeship: Science, Universities, and Society in England, 1560–1640.* Cambridge: Cambridge University Press, 1984.

Gascoigne, John. "A Reappraisal of the Role of the Universities in the Scientific Revolution." In *Reappraisals of the Scientific Revolution,* ed. David C. Lindberg and Robert S. Westman. Cambridge: Cambridge University Press, 1990, pp. 207–260.

Reif, Patricia. "The Textbook Tradition in Natural Philosophy, 1600–1650." *Journal of the History of Ideas* 30 (1969), 17–32.

Ruestow, Edward G. *Physics at Seventeenth and Eighteenth-Century Leiden: Philosophy and the New Science in the University.* The Hague: Nijhoff, 1973.

Schmitt, Charles B. "Science in the Italian Universities in the Sixteenth and Early Seventeenth Centuries." In *The Emergence of Science in Western Europe,* ed. Maurice Crosland. London: Macmillan, 1975, pp. 57–78

JOHN GASCOIGNE

See also Academies; Aristotelianism; Cartesianism; Educational Reform; Medical Education

Uraniborg

The castle of astronomy; Uraniborg was the name that Danish nobleman Tycho Brahe (1546–1601) gave to the Renaissance manor house he built on the island of Hven. King Frederik II (1534–1588) granted him the lifetime use of the island as part of the feudal exchange of properties, incomes, and services that bound the most important families to the Crown. But this particular gift was also an incentive for Brahe, who had already distinguished himself as a capable astronomer, to remain in Denmark and serve the Crown as consultant in the closely related sciences of astrology and alchemy. Hven was well suited to this assignment: rising above the fog of the sound, it was centrally located in the Danish realm and convenient to Copenhagen, yet isolated from the daily affairs of town and Court.

From its inception, Uraniborg was more than a palatial residence of a great landed aristocrat—it was the embodiment of Tycho Brahe's ideal for a learned household and research center. Construction on the house began in 1576 and continued for the next five years. Tycho sought to replicate on Hven the cultural and scientific life of his uncle's manor at Herrevad Abbey, where Brahe had dabbled in alchemy and observed the nova of 1572. However, unlike the sprawling, medieval Herrevad, Uraniborg was to be a compact Renaissance villa and also a philosophical house, dimensioned according to harmonic ratios. It was a physical expression of the Neoplatonic-Hermetic vision of the universe as a macrocosm that was ordered geometrically and reflected in the human body and spirit—a vision fostered in Renaissance Italy and embraced by Brahe and his circle of friends.

The house was laid out in squares and circles around a central fountain, itself a marvel of hydraulic engineering. On the ground floor there were four rooms, one of which Brahe equipped with several small alchemical furnaces. Across one of the corridors that bisected the

Tycho Brahe, aided by his assistants, before the mural quadrant in his observatory and showing some of the other rooms and instruments at his disposal. From Brahe's Astronomiae instauratae mechanica *(1598).*

house lay the room in which Brahe's famous mural quadrant was affixed to a north-south wall. This arrangement gave the astronomical device stability and permitted meridian measurements to be taken from a protected and heated room. Circular rooms at the north and south ends of the corridor housed the kitchen and the library, respectively, the ceilings of which formed the platforms for the second-story observatories. These were fitted with removable roof sections, which offered shelter from the wind and protected the astronomical instruments when not in use. Two more bedrooms and a long dining hall lay between them. A central stair wound up to a third-floor gallery and led to garret rooms, where student assistants were housed. Underneath it all, in the cellar, lay Brahe's main chemical laboratory, illuminated by skylights radiating from the base of the library. Here Brahe deployed a variety of furnaces and condensers that rivaled those of the most lavish aristocratic laboratories.

The house was centrally located in a square, walled perimeter, inside which was an extensive orchard and botanical garden, with walkways and gazebos. Entryways at the eastern and western corners of the wall were governed by Italianate gate houses; the north corner featured servants quarters, opposite the printing house at the south corner. With its outlying fishing ponds, paper mill, workshop for constructing instruments, and a partly buried observatory called Stjærneborg, Uraniborg was a self-contained manor in the classical tradition, but one designed specifically for the organization of Brahe's scientific enterprise: it was the nerve center for his extended *familia* of dependents, who assisted him with observations, accumulated and reduced data, manned the printing press, and minded the chemical furnaces. With a remarkable array of astronomical quadrants, sextants, and armillaries, each carefully designed and tested for error and precision, Tycho reached the limits of naked-eye astronomy and produced a prodigious amount of accurate data, which enabled Johannes Kepler's (1571–1630) breakthrough in orbital kinematics.

The appearance of Uraniborg was also an important part of its function. Furnished with portraits, Latin epigrams, and the quadrant mural, which was an elaborate painting that depicted the scientific life of the household, the house physically expressed the ideology of its owner and announced that Tycho Brahe's island was a northern center of Renaissance intellectual culture. Uraniborg was, indeed, a jewel in the crown of Denmark and became a regular stop for visiting royalty and dignitaries. But it was an expensive ornament, consuming the income from Brahe's private estates as well as several royal fiefdoms, stipends, and a benefice.

When the winds of politics began to blow against Brahe at the Court of Christian IV (1577–1648), royal grants were recalled, and Brahe closed Uraniborg, moved to Copenhagen, and finally left the country. Uraniborg did not long survive the lord's absence: it was soon cannibalized for building material.

BIBLIOGRAPHY

Beckett, Francis. *Uraniborg og Stjærneborg.* Copenhagen: Selskabet til Udgivelse af Danske Mindesmærker, 1921.

Brahe, Tycho. *Instruments of the Renewed Astronomy.* Trans. Hans Raeder, Elis Strømgren, and Bengt Strømgren; rev. with Commentary by Alena Hadravova, Petr Hadrava, and Jole R. Shackelford. (Clavis Monumentorum Litterarum. Regnum Bohemiae 2, Facsimilia-Translationes 1). Prague: Koniasch Latin Press, 1996.

Christianson, John R. "Cloister and Observatory: Herrevad Abbey and Tycho Brahe's Uraniborg." Ph.D. diss. University of Minnesota, 1964.

Hannaway, Owen. "Laboratory Design and the Aim of Science." *Isis* 77 (1986), 585–610.

Shackelford, Jole. "Tycho Brahe, Laboratory Design, and the Aim of Science: Reading Plans in Context." *Isis* 84 (1993), 211–230.

JOLE R. SHACKELFORD

See also Brahe, Tycho

Ursus (Bär), Nicolaus Raimarus (1551–1600)

Born of peasant stock in Holstein and self-educated, Ursus had a varied career as a surveyor, a tutor in grammar and arithmetic, and a university lecturer in mathematics. From 1591 he was imperial mathematician to Rudolf II in Prague. His published works include a treatise on surveying, *Fundamentum astronomicum* (1588), an account of mathematical methods of use in practical astronomy, and a chronology of the world. *Fundamentum astronomicum* is important for its accounts, derived from Joost Bürgi (1552–1632), watchmaker to Wilhelm IV of Hesse-Kassel, and Paul Wittich (ca. 1546–1586), of the prosthaphaeretic method for solving plain and spherical triangles, a method whereby trigonometrical products and dividends are obtained by addition (*prosthesis*) and subtraction (*aphaeresis*).

The work also outlines a "new" geoheliocentric world system, for which a planetarium had been constructed by Bürgi for Wilhelm IV. Ursus's world system differed from that published by Tycho Brahe (1546–1601) in the same year only in ascribing a daily rotation to the earth and in including the orb of the Sun entirely within the orb of Mars. Brahe reacted by publicly denouncing Ursus as a "dirty rascal" who had stolen the system from him while on a visit to his observatory on the island of Hven in 1584. Modern opinion is divided over Ursus's plagiarism, and it is hard to assess the issue because most of the information about Ursus and his life derives from Brahe and his allies. Ursus struck back in 1597 with *De hypothesibus astronomicis tractatus,* charging Brahe with mathematical incompetence and with dishonesty in claiming for himself a world system in fact invented in antiquity by Apollonius of Perga. In addition, Ursus argued that astronomical hypotheses are mere fictions, designed for purposes of calculation, and he backed this up with a history of astronomy that emphasized the physical absurdity of all of the hypotheses proposed since antiquity. On his arrival in Prague in 1599, Brahe sought to have Ursus and his *Tractatus* condemned and persuaded Johannes Kepler (1571–1630) to write a refutation of the book. The book was duly banned and burned, but the legal action lapsed with Ursus's death and Tycho's appointment in 1600 as imperial mathematician.

BIBLIOGRAPHY

Granada, Miguel A. "Bruno, Brahe, Rothmann, Ursus, Röslin." In *El debate cosmológico en 1588*. Naples: Bibliopolis, 1996.

Jardine, Nicholas. *The Birth of History and Philosophy of Science: Kepler's* A Defence of Tycho Against Ursus *with an Essay on Its Provenance and Significance*. Cambridge: Cambridge University Press, 1984. Rev. ed. 1984.

Rosen, Edward. *Three Imperial Mathematicians: Kepler Trapped Between Tycho and Ursus*. New York: Abaris Books, 1986.

NICHOLAS JARDINE

See also Brahe, Tycho; Bürgi, Joost; Geoheliocentrism; Kepler, Johannes; Wittich, Paul

Utopias

The singular of this term derives from the combination of either the Greek prefix *eu* (good) or *ou* (no) with the noun *topos* (place) and can mean either good place or no place. Often, a utopia is both: an imaginary and an ideal society in which human beings are shown living in peace, harmony, and prosperity. The fact that utopias are fictional does not necessarily mean that they are fanciful flights from the problems of social and political disorder in the actual world. On the contrary, most often the fictional, ideal society is intended to stand in juxtaposition to the disorder of the author's own society and to serve as a paradigm for its improvement or perfection. Achievement of a state of an innerworldly perfection usually entails transformation of existing social and political institutions and reformation of human ethical conduct. The key to these reforms most often lies in advances in knowledge that occur through discovery of new truths or through recovery of ancient wisdom.

A distinctive form of utopias emerged during the seventeenth century, which sought to provide remedies for the social, political, and religious turmoil plaguing the age. What is most intriguing about this specific form is that its utopian solutions derive from a combination of the recovery of esoteric wisdom (magic and alchemy), advances in science and technology, and orthodox (and sometimes unorthodox) religious reforms. The best example of this form of utopia is Francis Bacon's (1561–1626) *New Atlantis* (1626). According to the story, European sailors, who happen on the uncharted island of Bensalem, are immediately struck by the Christian charity of the inhabitants, and they are told that the island was converted to Christianity by a miraculous event shortly after the Resurrection. The Bensalemites received an ark (small chest) containing a letter from one of the apostles, indicating that the island was chosen for special benediction. The Europeans are subsequently told that the island is protected, provided for, and kept healthy through Solomon's House, a laboratory and think tank, the purpose of which is to "found out the true nature of all things (whereby God might have the more glory in the workmanship and men the more fruit in the use of them)." The Europeans are also told that the name Solomon's House was chosen because the Bensalemites possessed King Solomon's *Natural History,* a book that had been lost to the Europeans, and this text guided ongoing efforts to understand nature and to use that knowledge for the "relief of man's estate." While the description of the activities of Solomon's House clearly emphasizes new laboratory research and its technological application, it is equally true that the effort to supplement nature's gifts in order to cure disease, produce well-being, and prolong life closely parallels Paracelsian alchemy and Hermetic magic.

That Bacon is not presenting an escapist fantasy is made clear in the obvious correlations between Bensalem and Bacon's England. The island's geography is remarkably similar to England's, and the references to Solomon are clearly meant to be related to James I, who was hailed as the new Solomon who would bring religious reform, provide political stability, and transform England into the New Zion. Bacon augments this theme of religious instauration by linking utopian social and political conditions to a mastery of nature achieved through a combination of esoteric wisdom and scientific advance.

Tommaso Campanella (1568–1639), an early defender of Galileo Galilei (1564–1642) and heliocentrism, wrote *Città del sole* (City of the Sun), another important contribution to this form of utopianism. Here again, purified (but highly unorthodox) religion, esoteric knowledge, and technological innovation are combined to restore nature to its perfection, to fortify the city, and to make the citizens healthy, prosperous, and virtuous. Campanella actually attempted to usher in a utopian age by staging a political revolt that landed him in prison for twenty years. During his confinement, he wrote *Cittá del sole* and long discourses to the pope and to the Spanish monarch in which he attempted to convince each that he could be the agent for universal religious and political reform. After his release, Campanella and his utopian ideas were entertained, at least for a time, by the pope, the Spanish monarch, and the king of France.

Other influential examples of this particular form of utopianism include Johann Valentin Andreae's (1586–1654) *Christianopolis* (1619), Samuel Hartlib's (ca. 1600–1662) *Macaria* (1641), and James Harrington's *Commonwealth of Oceana* (1656).

This form of utopianism was not the only one to emerge during the Renaissance and the Scientific Revolution. Thomas More's famous *Utopia* (1516) is a case in point. More's utopian program, like those discussed above, is based on a return to religious purity, but, unlike the others, it does not incorporate esoteric wisdom or scientific advances to create idyllic conditions. On the contrary, More is convinced that existing agricultural and manufacturing techniques are more than adequate to meet the needs of the population if ostentation and excessive consumption are eliminated and every citizen shares in the labor effort.

The form of utopianism that combines religious renewal, recovery of ancient esoteric wisdom, and advances in science and technology, while not the only one to appear in the seventeenth century, is a major one, and recognizing its characteristic features helps clarify the intellectual and cultural ambience in which inner-worldly perfection becomes connected to the mastery of nature. In the sixteenth and seventeenth centuries, this mastery of nature was linked to a combination of the recovery of ancient esoteric knowledge and advances in science and technology—Bacon's Solomon's House is the prototypical example. Subsequently, the esoteric traditions of Hermetic magic and Paracelsian alchemy fell into disrepute and were eventually dismissed as pseudoscience. Nevertheless, the distinctive utopian vision, which is rooted in religious yearning for reform and in esoteric dreams of worldly perfection, has remained very much alive in the Western imagination. As religion and esoteric knowledge have fallen to the wayside, science has been given center place as the means of realizing the dream of mastering nature and perfecting society.

BIBLIOGRAPHY

David, J. C. "Utopianism." In *The Cambridge History of Political Thought, 1450–1700,* ed. J. H. Burns. Cambridge: Cambridge University Press, 1991, pp. 329–344.

———. *Utopia and the Ideal Society: A Study of English Utopian Writings, 1516*–1700. Cambridge: Cambridge University Press, 1981.

Emerson, Roger L. "Utopia." *Dictionary of the History of Ideas,* vol. 4. New York: Scribners, 1973, pp. 458–465.

Manuel, Frank E., and Fritzie P. Manuel. *Utopian Thought in the Western World.* Cambridge, MA: Harvard University Press, 1979.

McKnight, Stephen A., ed. *Science, Pseudo-Science, and Utopianism.* Columbia: University of Missouri Press, 1992.

STEPHEN A. MCKNIGHT

See also Academies; Andreae, Johann Valentin; Bacon, Francis; Hartlib, Samuel

V

Vacuum. See Void

Vacuum Pump. See Air Pump

Vallisneri, Antonio (1661–1730)

A student of Marcello Malpighi (1628–1694), Vallisneri advocated the experimental and mechanical philosophies in his writings and in his teaching at the University of Padua, where he occupied a chair of medicine from 1700 until his death. In publications and private letters, he also argued for the Galilean view of the autonomy of science, showing familiarity with those works by Galileo Galilei (1564–1642) officially banned in Italy.

In biology, he focused mainly on issues of generation. Early journal articles (1696, 1700) extended the range of experiments on spontaneous generation, following those of Francesco Redi (1626–1697); these studies, much augmented, were later published as a volume of *Esperienze ed osservazione* (Experiments and Observations, 1713). In *Istoria della generazione dell'uomo e degli animali* (History of the Generation of Man and Animals, 1721), he treated the different roles of eggs and sperm, favoring the mechanist position—dislike of vitalism and occult causes permeates his writings—that ova contain in miniature the fully formed adult organisms. His discussion of parasitic worms found in humans aroused some debate about whether such noxious creatures had infested Adam and Eve; typically, he declined to mingle biblical exegesis with biological analysis.

In geology, too, he rejected as occult those "plastic powers" sometimes used to explain the origin of fossils, and he relegated Noah's Flood to the realm of miracles irrelevant to tracing the earth's history. In his major geological books, *Lezione accademica* (Academic Lecture, 1715) and *De' corpi marini* (On Marine Bodies, 1721), he argued for a long history of fluctuating sea levels, the causes of which he admittedly could not explain.

Vallisneri's writings generally appeared in more than one edition during his lifetime; in each new edition, he would respond to critics in added appendices. His works are best read in the original printings rather than the posthumous *Opere* (Works, 1733), although the latter contains material not published elsewhere. There exists no bibliography of his articles and books.

BIBLIOGRAPHY

Rappaport, Rhoda. "Italy and Europe: The Case of Antonio Vallisneri (1661–1730)." *History of Science* 29 (1991), 73–98.

Roger, Jacques. *Les sciences de la vie dans la pensée française au XVIIIe siècle*. Paris: Armand Colin, 1963. 2nd ed. 1993.

Vallisneri, Antonio. *Opere fisico-mediche*. 3 vols. Venice: Coleti, 1733.

RHODA RAPPAPORT

See also Generation; Malpighi, Marcello; Spontaneous Generation; Theories of the Earth

Valverde, Juan (ca. 1525–ca. 1588)

Born in Amusco, Spain, he read medicine at the University of Padua. His teacher was Realdo Colombo (ca. 1510–1559), a follower of the New Anatomy movement led by Andreas Vesalius (1514–1564) but at loggerheads with him. Valverde was Colombo's assistant during the years when the latter held the chair of anatomy in Pisa (1545–1548) and accompanied him when Colombo was

663

appointed professor in Rome. Valverde lived there until his death, devoted to teaching and anatomical research, almost always in collaboration with Colombo. Like other anatomists working in Italy at that time, Valverde assimilated the renewal of anatomical knowledge that Vesalius had led, but he highlighted the lacunae and errors in his work. This criticism and his loyalty to Colombo explain Vesalius's attack upon Valverde when he had already ceased to work on anatomy (1564).

The first edition of Valverde's anatomy treatise, *Historia de la composición del cuerpo humano,* was published in Spanish in Rome in 1556. It included thirty anatomical discoveries, the most important of which concerned muscles, and also described pulmonary circulation. All of these contributions were derived from his work in conjunction with Colombo or at least had his support. Most of the illustrations are copied from those in Vesalius's treatise of 1543, although there are fifteen originals, some of scientific relevance and one of great beauty depicting a "muscle man." These were the first anatomical illustrations printed using copperplates, those of Vesalius having been printed from woodcuts, and their artistic style is influenced by Michelangelo (1475–1564), almost certainly because of the involvement of the Spanish artist Gaspar Becerra (1520–1570), who had been one of Michelangelo's disciples. The clarity and conciseness of Valverde's work, which was translated into Latin, Italian, and Dutch and reprinted sixteen times, made it the most widely read Renaissance treatise on anatomy in Europe.

BIBLIOGRAPHY

Guerra, F. "Juan de Valverde de Amusco." *Clio medica* 2 (1967), 339–362.

López-Piñero, J. M. "Valverde de Amusco, Juan." In *Diccionario histórico de la ciencia moderna en España,* ed. J. M. López-Piñero et al. Barcelona: Península, 1983, vol. 2, pp. 394–396.

Meyer A. W., and S. K. Wirt. "The Amuscan Illustrations." *Bulletin of the History of Medicine* 14 (1943), 667–687.

JOSÉ M. LÓPEZ-PIÑERO

See also Anatomy; Colombo, Realdo; Vesalius, Andreas

Van Helmont. See Helmont, Johannes Baptista van

Van Leeuwenhoek. See Leeuwenhoek, Antoni van

Van Schooten. See Schooten, Frans van

Varignon, Pierre (1654–1722)

Awarded the degree Master of Arts at the University of Caen in 1682, he was ordained a priest the following year. He gained recognition in the world of science by the publication in Paris in 1687 of his *Projet d'une nouvelle mécanique* (Outline of a New Mechanics). This work, centered on the problems of statics related to the composition of forces and their moments, opened the doors of the Académie Royale des Sciences to him as geometer in 1688. In the same year, he was named professor of mathematics at the Collège Mazarin. Shortly after his admission to the Académie and the publication of his *Nouvelles conjectures sur la pésanteur* (New Conjectures on Weight) in 1690, Varignon became the chief figure in the diffusion of the new Leibnizian calculus. The very great number of treatises he published from

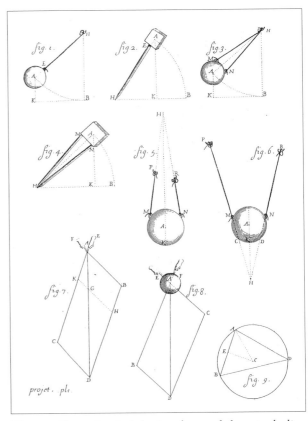

Diagrams illustrating the behavior of suspended moving bodies and of the principle of the composition of forces in parallelograms. From Varignon's Projet d'une nouvelle mécanique *(1687).*

1699 to his death in the annual *Histoire et mémoires* of the Académie are a testimonial to his achievement.

These writings may be divided into two major categories: those bearing on the methods and foundations of differential and integral calculus and those dedicated to the application of the calculus to the science of motion; it is on this point that Varignon's work is important and novel although too often neglected by historians of science. Varignon developed, in particular, the whole of the results expressed in Isaac Newton's (1642–1727) *Principia mathematica philosophiae naturalis* (1687), finding in them specific cases of general rules resting principally on his new concepts, expressed in terms of differentials, of speed at each instant, and of accelerating force at each instant. This work marks, for the construction of the algorithm of kinematics, an essential stage in the analytic elaboration of the science of motion.

Varignon was elected to the Berlin Academy in 1713 and to the Royal Society of London in 1718. Bernard le Bovier de Fontenelle (1657–1757) gave his *éloge* at the Académie Royale des Sciences and aided the posthumous publication in 1725 of three works by his friend: *Éclaircissements sur l'analyse des infiniment petits* (Elucidations of the Analysis of the Infinitely Small), *Traité du mouvement et de la mesure des eaux coulantes et jaillisantes* (A Treatise on the Motion and Measurement of Flowing and Gushing Waters), and *Nouvelle mécanique ou statique* (New Mechanics or Statics).

BIBLIOGRAPHY

Blay, Michel. "L'introduction du calcul différentiel en dynamique: L'exemple des forces centrales dans les Mémoires de Varignon en 1700." *Sciences et techniques en perspective* 10 (1985–1986), 157–190.

———. "Varignon et le statut de la loi de Torricelli." *Archives internationale d'histoire des sciences* 35 (1985), 330–345.

Gowing, Ronald. "Pierre Varignon and the Measurement of Time." *Revue d'histoire des sciences et de leurs applications* 50 (1997), 361–368.

Peiffer, Jeanne. "Pierre Varignon, lecteur de Leibniz et de Newton." In *Leibniz' Auseinandersetzung mit Vorgängern und Zeitgenossen,* ed. Ingrid Marchlewitz and Albert Heinekamp. Stuttgart: Steiner, 1990, pp. 244–266.

MICHEL BLAY

TRANS. WILBUR APPLEBAUM

See also Calculus; Dynamics; Hydraulics and Hydrostatics; Mechanics

Vauban, Sébastien Le Prestre (1633–1707)

The ideal military engineer and administrator of the seventeenth century, Vauban exemplifies the French style of government rationalized through the use of mathematical statistics and methodical techniques. Educated as a simple Burgundian gentleman, he took service in the army, in which he spent the rest of his life, serving on campaign until his last years.

He was chiefly employed in reconstructing the defenses of towns and fortresses, devising new schemes for places acquired by France in his lifetime. Earlier designs show the intelligent use of well-known principles, but later work, such as at Belfort and Neuf-Brisach, was much more innovative, holding the corners of the wall with relatively modest bastions, while the main bastions stand forward, with the ditch or the moat behind them. These were to become the main features of defense, whereas formerly outworks had been subordinate to the main bastions projecting directly from the wall. In attack, too, he was methodical. He would dig a trench parallel to the besieged enceinte, just out of reach of hostile guns; he would then move forward, digging a zigzag trench, then a second parallel, and so on until his forces were quite close to the enemy's outworks, which could be mined before an assault under covering fire. By such means, notably at the siege of Maastricht (1673) and Namur (1692), he captured a number of highly regarded fortresses.

Careful of the lives of his troops in war, of government resources, and of the laboring classes as the nation's principal resource, he sought to rationalize the training of military engineers and to reform recruitment to the army. He also wished to protect the ordinary citizen from exaction and corruption. Being as keen to make the government's revenue more secure and efficient as to help the taxpayer, he proposed to reform the tax system by revising current direct taxes and introducing a 10 percent direct tax.

BIBLIOGRAPHY

Blomfield, Reginald T. *Sébastien Le Prestre de Vauban (1633–1707).* London: Methuen, 1938.

Guerlac, Henry. "The Impact of Science on War." In *Makers of Modern Strategy: Military Thought from Machiavelli to Hitler,* ed. Edward M. Earle. Princeton, NJ: Princeton University Press, 1943. 2nd ed. in Guerlac, Henry. *Essays and Papers in the History of Modern Science.* Baltimore: Johns Hopkins University Press, 1977, pp. 413–439.

Parent, Michel, and Jacques Verroust. *Vauban*. Paris: Jacques Forel, 1971.

ALEX KELLER

See also Fortification

Vesalius, Andreas (1514–1564)

An academic anatomist, as well as a physician and a surgeon, Vesalius is remembered principally for his master work, *De humani corporis fabrica* (On the Stucture of the Human Body) and the principles he propounded in it. Born in Brussels, Vesalius was the son of an apothecary in the service of Charles V, the Holy Roman emperor. He attended the Universities of Louvain and Paris before earning his M.D. at Padua in 1537. The very next day, he was appointed lecturer in surgery at the University of Padua and thus began his academic teaching career.

In 1538, together with his countryman Jan Stephan of Calcar (1499–ca. 1546), an artist who was working in Titian's studio, Vesalius published six large woodcut illustrations of anatomy and physiology designed for use in student instruction. These illustrations and their brief text, the *Tabula anatomicae sex* (Six Anatomical Plates), demonstrate that, at this point in his career, Vesalius still subscribed to many Galenic tenets.

Evidence that his ideas were evolving, however, appears in the notebooks of a German student who attended Vesalius's guest lectures and dissections at Bologna in 1540. The previous year, a newly appointed judge of the criminal court at Padua had become fascinated by Vesalius's work. This interest soon translated into an increased supply of dissection material: the judge provided Vesalius with a constant source of human cadavers, even postponing executions for the the anatomist's convenience. This growth in his opportunities for dissection permitted Vesalius to discover the frequency and extent of Galen's (second century C.E.) anatomical errors and emboldened him to denounce them publicly.

The medium Vesalius chose to present his findings was a comprehensive study of the human body presented in a printed text accompanied by naturalistic illustrations. Designed to challenge many important components of Galenic theory by reporting and graphically displaying his revolutionary discoveries to the scholarly world, this book was a vast illustrated anatomical treatise based primarily on its author's own dissec-

tions. Vesalius was well aware of the enormous importance of his work to the scholarly and scientific world and, therefore, spared no expense in its production.

He devoted more than a year to the creation of its massive text of more than 650 folio pages and its didactic illustrations. Artists from Titian's studio were employed to draw the figures under Vesalius's constant surveillance. These were then carved onto woodblocks in Venice. Insisting that his work be printed by one of the most scholarly contemporary printers, Johannes Operinus, Vesalius personally took the text and woodblocks over the Alps to Operinus's press in Basel. There he completed the final proofreading of the text and of its annotations. The printing of the *Fabrica* was finished, as its colophon states, in June 1543.

Detailed descriptive passages accompany every illustration. Elaborate marginal references from one page to another, to illustrations, and even to details within the illustrations are also included. Such an interrelation of text and illustration had never been achieved before and was not to be equaled until much later.

Examination of the *Fabrica*'s text reveals why it is one of the great classics of medicine. In this single work, Vesalius fully discussed the entire structure of the human body. He described minute details of human structure and carefully integrated its various parts. Relying primarily on his own anatomical investigations in his descriptions of the human body, Vesalius was able to destroy numerous erroneous traditional anatomical beliefs. For example, in the *Fabrica,* Vesalius refuted the Galenic idea that the human jawbone was composed of two bones by explaining that he had examined numerous human jawbones in cemeteries and had never found one divided into two parts.

The Galenic notion that the intracardiac septum was permeable was also attacked by Vesalius, who mocked the idea that any blood could pass from the right to the left ventricle of the heart through seemingly invisible pores. Galen had believed this motion essential to the transformation of natural spirit into vital spirit. Further along in the the course of his human dissections, having consistently failed to find anything like the *rete mirable* (miraculous network) that was traditionally believed present below the human brain and necessary for transformation of vital spirit into animal spirit, Vesalius denied its existence. However, he still believed that the brain moved or pulsated and that the result of this

V

are his principles of investigation on which they were based and which are constantly reiterated throughout their texts. Vesalius believed that, since he had proved, at least to himself, that Galen's anatomical doctrines were based on the investigation of animals, they could not be directly applied to human structure. Moreover, as human structures often varied, an investigator must study the same structure in a number of human bodies before generalizing about it. Vesalius stressed that even his own pronouncements were not to be accepted without empirical verification, and throughout the *Fabrica* he carefully described his own dissection methods for each system. He expected that his readers would be able to make their own investigations and either verify or disprove his findings. By establishing his basic principles of research and setting forth his own antomical discoveries in the *Fabrica,* Vesalius laid the groundwork for the anatomical revolution that provided the foundation for William Harvey's (1578–1657) transformation of physiology.

Unfortunately, Vesalius was not to see this culmination of his work. Shortly after the *Fabrica* was first published, he left academic life and, like his father, entered the service of the Holy Roman emperor. Though he constantly attended and conducted dissections, his primary occupation was as an imperial physician. In 1555 he published the second edition of the *Fabrica,* which contains corrections and revisions of his earlier work on almost every page. Although the second edition is, in many respects, superior to the first, the fact that Vesalius revealed new and important findings in his later effort is frequently overlooked.

Having completed the second edition, Vesalius, who was only forty years old, may well have expected to publish another edition in his lifetime. Unfortunately, when Charles V abdicated in 1556, Vesalius took service with the emperor's son, Philip II of Spain. Vesalius's work did not flourish during his eight years at the Spanish Court, and in 1564 he left Spain ostensibly to make a pilgrimage to the Holy Land. Before embarking on that voyage, he gained a reappointment to the chair of anatomy at Padua. He expected to resume this position after the pilgrimage but, sadly, he never returned to Italy. After he completed his visit to the Holy Land, the ship on which he was returning home was damaged severely in a storm. It made port on the island of Zante, where Vesalius, exhausted from the voyage, died.

Andreas Vesalius. Frontispiece of his De humani corporis fabrica *(1543).*

motion was the production of animal spirits. Investigators had maintained for more than a thousand years that these were the agents of nervous action. Vesalius somewhat reluctantly subscribed to this idea, as did many other investigators even centuries after his death. As the decades passed, however, it was recognized that Vesalius had destroyed the basis for traditional physiology.

The *Fabrica* was considered a classic almost from the first day it was printed. Realizing that few students could afford a copy of his masterpiece, Vesalius created, almost at the same time, a small digest, an *Epitome of the Fabrica.* Intended for beginners, the *Epitome* was initially printed in Latin. Several months later, however, it was translated into German. These student workbooks were very likely the chief means by which students learned of Vesalius's anatomical discoveries. Evidence that they were widely used is that copies of the *Epitome* are rarer today than are those of the *Fabrica.*

More important than any of Vesalius's findings as revealed in either the *Epitome* or the *Fabrica,* however,

BIBLIOGRAPHY

Heseler, Baldasar. *Andreas Vesalius' First Public Anatomy at Bologna: An Eyewitness Report by Baldasar.* Trans. Ruben Eriksson. Uppsala: Almqvist and Wiksells. 1959.

O'Malley, Charles. *Andreas Vesalius of Brussels, 1514–1564.* Berkeley and Los Angeles: University of California Press, 1964.

Singer, Charles. *A Prelude to Modern Science: Being a Discussion of the Historical Sources and Circumstances of the "Tabulae anatomicae sex" of Vesalius.* Cambridge: Wellcome Historical Medical Museum by Cambridge University Press, 1946.

Vesalius, Andreas. *The Epitome of Andreas Vesalius.* Trans. L. R. Lind. Cambridge, MA: MIT Press, 1969.

———. *Illustrations on Work of Andreas Vesalius of Brussels . . . . with a Biographical Sketch by C. M. Saunders and Charles O'Malley.* New York: Dover, 1973.

———. *Vesalius on the Human Brain.* Trans. Charles Singer. New York: Oxford University Press, 1952.

YNEZ V. O'NEILL

See also Anatomy; Dissection; Galenism; Harvey, William; Illustration; Physiology

Viète, François (1540–1603)

The father of modern mathematics, as he has been called, graduated from the University of Poitiers and followed his father's career as a lawyer, spending most of his life in government service in Paris, Rennes, and Tours. By the early 1580s, he was master of requests in Paris and a privy counselor; he was also employed as a code breaker by the government.

However, two periods out of office, 1564–1568, when he was tutor to a Huguenot family, and 1584–1589, when he was forced out of the Royal Court, enabled him to become the most influential mathematician of his time, mainly because of his development of algebraic symbolism, which eventually helped wean mathematics from geometry to algebra. Some of his terminology, such as *coefficient* and *negative,* has survived.

Viète published his *Canon mathematicus* in parts in the 1570s; it comprised trigonometrical tables with explanatory text on plane and spherical triangles, partly following works by Johannes Regiomontanus (1436–1476) (published 1533) and Georg Rheticus (1514–1576) (published 1551) and using the new decimal numbers rather than lengths. He established the tangent formula and may have been aware of the polar triangle. He also produced unpublished astronomical work at this time and later engaged in controversy on calendar reform.

François Viète. From Galerie française *(1821–1823).*

Viète's second mathematical period led to his most important work, including *The Analytic Art,* which appeared mainly between 1591 and 1600. Many of his examples were influenced by Pappus (fl. 300–350) and Diophantus (fl. 250). Analysis was done by considering a problem to be solved; the Greeks contrasted this with synthesis, the building up of results from assumptions. In analysis, proportions were set up (the so-called *zetetics*), and results tested thereby (*poristics*). To this, Viète added *rhetics,* or *exegetics,* the solving of the proportions to make analysis a threefold art, which "claims for itself the greatest problem of all, which is TO SOLVE EVERY PROBLEM" (*In artem analyticem isagoge*).

His symbolism, in which single capital letters represented quantities, vowels represented unknowns, and consonants represented knowns, enabled him to extend the work of Girolamo Cardano (1501–1576) on cubic equations and to improve Ludovico Ferrari's (1522–1567) method for quartics. He related this to the trisection of the angle and duplication of the cube. Viète showed that trisection was equivalent to a cubic of the irreducible case, where all roots are real, and solved it by trigonometry, thus avoiding the puzzling resultant complex numbers that appear in Cardano's method. Viète did not introduce the index notation, using instead Q (*quadratus*) for squared, C for cubed, and so on; he also insisted on homogeneity.

His best-known individual result may be the infinite product for $2/\pi$, obtained from the inscribed polygons to a circle (1593); the method converges rapidly. He was also able to solve a specific equation of the forty-fifth degree given in a challenge by Adriaen van Roomen (1561–1615), who had a low opinion of French mathematics. It was, in effect, to find sin x given sin $45x$, and Viète resolved it into two cubic equations and one quintic. Viète gave all twenty-three positive roots immediately (published 1595). In another problem (1593), he constructed a regular heptagon by *neusis* (Archimedes's, ca. 287–212 B.C.E., solution, also by a *neusis*, survives in an Arab text unknown until the twentieth century) and also reduced the problem to a cubic equation. When the great classical scholar J. J. Scaliger (1540–1609) misguidedly claimed success in circle quadrature and other classical problems, Viète (like Thomas Harriot in England) pointed out the errors; neither received more than abuse for thanks (1594).

In the *De numerosa potestatum ad exegesin resolutione* (1600), Viète gave numerical methods for solving polynomial equations (digit by digit). At the same time, in his *Apollonius gallus* (1600), he attempted to reconstruct Apollonius's lost work on contacts and was able to give a classical construction for a circle touching three given circles; Van Roomen's construction had involved the intersection of hyperbolas. Viète's work on numerical methods and algebra had an immediate effect on Thomas Harriot's (ca. 1560–1621) work in these areas and, subsequently, via René Descartes (1596–1650), Pierre de Fermat (1601–1665), and others, led to the continued algebraicization that is perhaps the main feature of the development of mathematics in the seventeenth century and later.

BIBLIOGRAPHY

Dedron, P., and Jean Itard. *Mathematics and Mathematicians.* Trans. Judith V. Field. London: Transworld, 1973. 1st ed. Paris: Magnard, 1959.

Giusti, Enrico. "Algebra and Geometry in Bombelli and Viète." *Bolletino di storia delle scienze matematiche* 12 (1992), 303–328.

Klein, Jacob. *Greek Mathematical Thought and the Origin of Algebra.* Trans. Eva Brann. New York: Dover, 1992. 1st ed. Berlin, 1934–1936.

Viète, François. *The Analytic Art, Nine Studies in Algebra, Geometry and Trigonometry . . . by François Viète.* Trans. T. Richard Witmer. Kent, OH: Kent State University Press, 1983.

JON V. PEPPER

See also Algebra; Cardano, Girolamo; Harriot, Thomas; Trigonometry

Virtuosi

A term with a variety of meanings, applied to natural philosophers, natural historians, and others during the seventeenth century. Derived from the Italian, the term *virtuoso* was first used in English and French in the mid-seventeenth century to denote someone interested in scientific subjects.

The term was limited by class. Virtuosi were usually of the "gentle" class—including courtiers, landed gentry, and professionals such as physicians and clergymen. Such people had the leisure and the income to practice natural philosophy as an avocation. A person from the lower classes who made his living at natural philosophy, such as Robert Hooke (1635–1703), was often somewhat looked down upon by the virtuoso community. Virtuosi had some education but were seldom university professors, whom they despised as pedantic and behind the times. There was a feminine of the term, *virtuosa,* but the role of women in the virtuoso community varied by nationality, upper-class women playing a much greater role in the salon culture of France than in the more male-dominated intellectual world of England.

Unlike the contemporary usage, which implies expertise in a particular field, the seventeenth-century virtuoso was known for his or her interest in a broad range of subjects. The term could stretch from the most eminent practicing natural philosophers, such as Robert Boyle (1627–1691), to those who merely maintained an interest in science or collected curiosities. A leading virtuoso, such as the English diarist and Fellow of the Royal Society John Evelyn (1620–1706), could be interested in subjects ranging from foreign coins to forests. The virtuoso was characterized by curiosity—*curioso* was a near-synonymous term—and admiration for all things strange and wonderful. However, this admiration did not preclude close observation, analysis, and measurement of curious phenomena. A very common appurtenance of virtuoso culture was the cabinet of curiosities, which included specimens of exotic animals and plants, monstrosities, and antiquities such as ancient medals. Some, but not all, virtuosi emphasized that their studies had no practical use and that wonder and delight were intellectual ends in themselves.

Virtuosi formed a community knit together by common institutions such as academies, webs of correspondence such as that carried on by Henry Oldenburg (ca. 1619–1677), and natural-philosophical journals. Correspondence and journals were particularly important in keeping country virtuosi informed and included in metropolitan intellectual life. Urban virtuosi congregated in certain coffeehouses in England and in salons in France. Virtuosi practiced social rituals such as the exchange of rare and curious objects and visits to one another's homes to view rarities and witness experiments. The community of virtuosi transcended national and confessional boundaries, particularly since many virtuosi were fluent in the common European languages, Latin and French, and wealthy virtuosi made grand tours of Europe, viewing rarities and visiting noted foreign virtuosi. Virtuoso culture became an expression of fashion in some circles, as collecting curiosities, keeping a laboratory, and making chemical experiments became occupations of noblemen and women or even kings, such as Charles II of England. Virtuoso culture proclaimed itself to be apolitical, a retreat from the corruption and self-seeking of Court and politics. The virtuoso movement in England was greatly advanced by the retreat of many nobility and gentry from politics in the Civil War and Interregnum (1642–1660). Similarly, in France during the later reign of Louis XIV, virtuoso culture, centered in Paris, provided one alternative to the Court life of Versailles.

Virtuosi were not universally admired. The term could have a pejorative implication of light-headedness, frivolity, and an obsession with useless trivialities and curiosities. The virtuoso was frequently the target of satirical and anti-intellectual ridicule, as in Thomas Shadwell's play *The Virtuoso* (1676). Shadwell's protagonist, Sir Nicholas Gimcrack, was a gullible fool, promoting such ludicrous projects as producing enough light to read by from a joint of meat. The virtuosa was the target of Molière's *The Learned Ladies* (1672) and the more sympathetic drama by Susanna Centlivre's, *The Basset Table* (1706). Despite the founding of a Society of Virtuosi in England in 1689, the virtuoso movement was in decline by the end of the seventeenth century, as satire

and an increased emphasis on useful learning and humanistic studies made virtuosi unfashionable.

The virtuoso community provided one frequently overlooked necessity for scientific practice—an audience. Virtuosi visited public collections and flocked to lectures and the performance of experiments. If they could afford them, they bought the latest scientific instruments and treatises, as well as natural curiosities. Whether or not a particular virtuoso actively practiced natural philosophy, virtuoso culture spread the ideas of natural philosophers throughout the educated world.

BIBLIOGRAPHY

Findlen, Paula. *Possessing Nature: Museums, Collecting, and Scientific Culture in Early Modern Italy*. Berkeley and Los Angeles: University of California Press, 1994.

Hunter, Michael. *Science and Society in Restoration England*. Cambridge: Cambridge University Press, 1981.

Sutton, Geoffrey V. *Science for a Polite Society: Gender, Culture, and the Demonstration of Enlightenment*. Boulder, CO: Westview, 1995.

Whitaker, Katie. "The Culture of Curiosity." In *Cultures of Natural History,* ed. N. Jardine, J. A. Secord, and E. C. Spary. Cambridge: Cambridge University Press, 1996.

WILLIAM E. BURNS

See also Correspondence Networks; Museums and Collections; Oldenburg, Henry; Popularization

Vision

If the Scientific Revolution represents a historical shift in knowledge about the natural world, how we "see" assumes a central place. Regardless of one's understanding of "science," claims to "visual knowledge" represent a relation (or set of relations) between the world seen and the world we see. Throughout the Scientific Revolution, these relations—among the observer, the medium, and the visible object—were renegotiated. Some things did not change. Old problems persisted (binocular vision; judging size, distance, and shape), and rival theories continued to include conflicting aims and assumptions (mathematical, physical, psychological). But where early theorists tended to emphasize geometrical and formal accounts of *vision,* new efforts focused on the visual effects of material theories of *light*. This shift "from sight to light" was accompanied by a "constant urge," as historians of science have put it, to explain sensation, perception, imagination, memory, and cognition by means of invisible mechanisms.

By tradition, modern theories of vision began with the optical conclusions of Johannes Kepler (1571–1630). Working within the mathematical tradition of medieval perspectivists and benefiting from the ocular anatomy presented by Felix Platter (1536–1614), Kepler displayed his genius by resolving a key question: "How an infinity of rays from each point in the visual field is drawn into a coherent, point-to-point correspondence in the eye." Against tradition, Kepler argued that the crystalline lens refocused intromitted rays on the retina, where vision was made possible. Significantly, Kepler called this image a *pictura*.

Arguably, Kepler's insistence that the *pictura* was a "real optical image" contributed to a different *kind* of confusion. It had long been recognized that, if rays crossed within the eye, the resulting image would be reversed and inverted. But witnesses soon confirmed Kepler's conclusion. Casting light through the dissected eye of a bull, their experiments showed that the retinal image was, indeed, inverted. The dilemma had been recognized since antiquity: If the image in my eye is inverted, why do I see the world right side up?

If Kepler resolved the optical part of vision, the problem was to link his objective *pictura* with the subjective "world we see." Like many before him, Christopher Scheiner (1573–1650) was impressed by the optical analogy of the eye and the camera obscura and, in his *Oculus* (1619) and *Rosa ursina* (1626–1630), was among the first to embrace Kepler's optical findings. But while Scheiner understood how ordinary "errors" in sight could be corrected by lenses, he offered nothing new on the dilemma of vision. Others actively opposed Kepler's claims. In the south of France, Nicolas-Claude Fabri de Peiresc (1580–1637), working with Pierre Gassendi (1592–1655), performed a variety of experiments to refute the concept of retinal inversion, finally postulating a "retinal mirror" to upright the image by reflecting it back toward the center of the eye. Like Marin Mersenne (1588–1648), Gassendi defended a monocular ("Cyclopean") theory of vision, claiming that we see with only one eye (principally the dominant) but in practice that we alternate between the strong eye and the weak eye.

Like Gassendi, Thomas Hobbes (1588–1679) attempted to develop a mechanistic account of vision. During the 1640s, he published three works in which he argued that light itself resulted from mechanical motion propagated instantaneously in a medium by means of a pulse (or wave front). Although he followed Kepler in his geometry of sight, Hobbes argued that vision was made possible as each impinging point (or part) from the visual field made contact in the eye. Here the effect lingered (much like an afterimage), and, if reinforcement by other particles reached a "threshold," a "reactive motion" resulted in the brain. But visual impressions were not simple or passive responses to mechanical contact. For Hobbes, "seeing" was learned. Although he continued to refer to "animal spirits" and *species* (material corpuscles), Hobbes invoked empiricist assumptions to produce one of the first modern mechanistic theories of vision.

Vigorous debate marked the middle decades of the century. Although further research is needed, good evidence suggests that a number of unpublished letters and treatises on optics and vision circulated privately among Peiresc, Gassendi, Mersenne, Fortunio Liceti (1577–1657), and Ismaël Boulliau (1605–1694) during the 1630s and that, afterward, members of this group joined debates among René Descartes (1596–1650), Pierre de Fermat (1601–1665), Hobbes, and Claude Mydorge (1585–1647). The challenge was to combine a coherent geometry of sight with a physical explanation of how light made vision possible.

Here, by tradition, Descartes played a pivotal role. The classic problem of Cartesian dualism was to connect the observer and the observed. If light was transmitted instantaneously and rectilinearly through a continuous medium, the solution was to offer two accounts of the same event, one mechanical (the world, matter in motion), one perceptual (the world we see). The first part of Descartes's solution was to tie the world we see to the body machine by means of "many tiny threads." The second involved innate ideas and a nonpictorial model of visual cognition. Distinguishing between how visual information was conveyed (mechanistically) and how it was represented (signs), Descartes substituted a linguistic theory of vision for earlier pictorial (representational) models. For Descartes, vision was completed by the subject's innate capacity (nativism) to read "natural signs," not to "see pictures."

A turning point in the debate was precipitated by the Molyneux problem. In a letter written to John Locke (1632–1704), William Molyneux (1656–1698) asked a legendary question: If a man, blind since birth, suddenly regained sight, could he distinguish objects (globes from cubes) by sight *alone*? Molyneux's answer in his *Dioptrica nova* (1692) was "no," that seeing is learned; it is not

René Descartes's explanation of how seeing is interpreted physiologically by mechanisms in the brain and can lead to a desire to act.

the eye that sees, "it is the soul." George Berkeley (1685–1753) took the question in a new direction.

Unlike Descartes, whose innate ideas he strenuously opposed, Berkeley argued that vision was learned. Specifically, Berkeley maintained there was not only no necessary connection between words and concepts, there was, indeed, no natural connection between our senses (e.g., vision and touch). Hence, for Berkeley, we do not naturally see distance, as Descartes claimed; rather, we learn to "read" distance in the "universal language of nature." The implications are subtle. If visual signs had no intrinsic meaning, neither were they arbitrary. For Berkeley, meaning was subject to rules of reason and interpretation. The significance of signs was supplied by the subject.

Berkeley broke with tradition. Radical in its empiricism and immaterialism, his theory of vision responded to the two major themes that dominated the Scientific Revolution. Berkeley provided an alternative to the geometry of the "opticians" and the materialism and determinism of the mechanical philosophy. Beginning with the "seeing subject" rather than the material world, he shifted the debate "from light to sight" and solved this riddle of the Scientific Revolution.

BIBLIOGRAPHY

Atherton, Margaret. *Berkeley's Revolution in Vision.* Ithaca, NY: Cornell University Press, 1990.

Lindberg, David C. *Theories of Vision from al-Kindi to Kepler.* Chicago: University of Chicago Press, 1976.

Pastore, Nicholas. *Selective History of Theories of Visual Perception, 1650–1950.* London: Oxford University Press, 1971.

Sabra, A. I. *Theories of Light from Descartes to Newton.* London: Oldbourne, 1967.

Smith, A. Mark. "Knowing Things Inside Out: The Scientific Revolution from a Medieval Perspective." *American Historical Review* 95 (1990), 726–744.

ROBERT A. HATCH

See also Optics

Vitalism

The belief that there exists a life principle independent of mechanical or chemical processes and shared by all living things. It is opposed to materialism, which attempts to explain life, as well as other phenomena, through matter and motion. In a looser sense, vitalism refers to the belief that the universe is permeated with life, that matter is endowed with life, and that many natural processes should be viewed as life processes, a position also known as organicism or hylozoism. For example, the common belief that metals grew in the earth like crops in the field was vitalist in this sense. The term itself was not used during the Scientific Revolution, but a variety of vitalistic hypotheses were put forth. The still great prestige of Aristotle (384–322 B.C.E.) as a philosopher of life influenced early-modern natural philosophers in a vitalist direction. Vitalist interpretations were dominant in the sixteenth century, but, from the early seventeenth century, they were increasingly challenged, and they were eventually defeated by materialist, mechanistic, and chemical theories of life.

The vital principle could be perceived as the soul or as a principle separate from the soul. Soul-based vitalism was particularly strong in the explanation of the nature of human beings, as the belief in a soul as a distinguishing human quality was required by Christian orthodoxy. Thus, René Descartes (1596–1650) held a vitalist theory of man, informed by a soul, along with a mechanist theory of other living things, which did not have souls.

An alternative to defining the the soul as the vital principle was the attempt to locate an intangible principle in specific areas or substances, as William Harvey

(1578–1657) located the heat of life in the blood. This form of vitalism was particularly compatible with alchemical thought, which often ascribed transformation to spirits or seeds inhering within matter. Influenced by alchemical thought, Paracelsus (ca. 1493–1541) and Paracelsian iatrochemists such as Johannes Baptista van Helmont (1579–1644) put forth important vitalistic theories based on spirits as the source of life. Van Helmont claimed that a living body was inhabited by a series of *archei,* or vegetative souls, dwelling in different locations within the body. Vitalism's association with these magical and alchemical beliefs eventually proved to be a liability, and, by the late seventeenth century, chemists increasingly defined spirits as material substances extracted by distilling rather than as incorporeal substances.

Vitalism in the sense of organicism persisted during the Scientific Revolution as a legacy of ancient Stoicism with its belief in a universal soul, or pneuma, permeating the universe and of alchemical thinking. The reaction to the extreme materialist position of Thomas Hobbes (1588–1679) often took pneumatist form as natural philosophers such as Henry More (1614–1687) and Anne Conway (1631–1679) extended the idea of the soul as vital principle to all living things. More ascribed power over nature to a "plastic spirit," invested with power by God and blamable for those phenomena that were difficult to reconcile with God's benevolence and perfection, such as monsters. Other natural philosophers, such as Robert Boyle (1627–1691), attacked this form of vitalism as tending to pantheism and the denial of God's ultimate power. This was the argument of Boyle's influential *A Free Enquiry into the Vulgarly Receiv'd Notion of Nature* (1686).

Less spiritual forms of organicism, such as that held by Isaac Newton (1642–1727), ascribed "vegetative" qualities to matter itself, refusing to draw a sharp distinction between living and nonliving matter. The common belief in spontaneous generation tended in the same direction. However, the general tendency of the Scientific Revolution was toward a mechanistic interpretation of matter as dead. Some feminist scholars have argued that the marginalization of organicist ideas in the course of the Scientific Revolution was part of a project of reenvisioning nature as dead and machinelike and, therefore, as exploitable for economic gain without moral compunction, and that this was related to the alleged intellectual marginalization of women during the period. Other historians assert that the belief that matter was endowed

with life tended to support radical ideas of the political importance of the common people, whereas mechanistic ideas that held that matter was dead and acted only as directed by divine providence tended to support monarchical and aristocratic politics.

During the late seventeenth and early eighteenth centuries, vitalism as a theory explaining the living world persisted particularly among physicians and on the European Continent, where a vitalist medical theory based exclusively on the human soul received its classical formulation from the German physician Georg Ernst Stahl (1660–1734). Vitalist theories of life would experience a strong recrudescence during the late eighteenth century and the Romantic period.

BIBLIOGRAPHY

Clericuzio, Antonio. "The Internal Laboratory: The Chemical Reinterpretation of Medical Spirits in England (1650-1680)." In *Alchemy and Chemistry in the Sixteenth and Seventeenth Centuries,* ed. Piyo Rattansi and Antonio Clericuzio. Dordrecht: Kluwer Academic, 1994.

Dobbs, B. J. T. *The Janus Faces of Genius: Alchemy in the Thought of Isaac Newton.* Cambridge: Cambridge University Press, 1991.

Merchant, Caroline. *The Death of Nature: Women, Ecology, and the Scientific Revolution.* San Francisco: Harper and Row, 1980.

Smith, C. U. M. *The Problem of Life: An Essay in the Origins of Biological Thought.* London: Macmillan, 1976.

WILLIAM E. BURNS

See also Active Principles; Alchemy; Helmont, Johannes Baptista van; Mechanical Philosophy; Soul; Spirit; Stahl, Georg Ernst

Vives, Juan Luis (1492–1540)

Born in Valencia, Spain, he studied at the Universities of Valencia and Paris. From 1512 onward, he lived in the Netherlands, where he was a professor at the University of Louvain and became one of the main thinkers of Renaissance humanism, together with his close friends Desiderius Erasmus of Rotterdam (ca. 1466–1536) and Thomas More (1478–1525). Between 1522 and 1528, he was the private tutor of Mary Tudor and a professor at Oxford. He returned to the Netherlands after Henry VIII's first divorce and died in Bruges.

The relationship between Vives's work and science must be considered in the context of his ideas on education, which include the need for direct and practical learning on "natural things" beginning with primary education. Consequently, he was a fervent defender of the new positive appraisal of technology, as opposed to the Platonic and Aristotelian tradition, which scorned the "mechanical arts" as being tasks fit merely for slaves and serfs. In *De tradendis disciplinis* (On the Disciplines, 1531), his main epistemological treatise, he recommended that one should learn from craftsmen and pay special attention to techniques not only because of their practical utility, but also because they provided more direct knowledge of nature than that obtained from speculation.

The general aim of Vives's epistemology was to reject the dialectics of the Scholastics as a means of evaluating the truth or falsity of scientific knowledge. He believed that the different disciplines should be separate from metaphysics and be structured on the basis of the phenomena gained from experience. Hence, in his treatise *De anima et vita* (1538), he dismissed the debate on the essence of life and the soul as of no interest and concentrated instead on analyzing their manifestations. Believing medicine to be the model of *ars* (practical learning), he subjected it to an extensive, in-depth analysis.

His commentaries on natural philosophy and pure mathematics, on the other hand, were more superficial, since he did not understand the modifications of Aristotelian physics in the later Middle Ages. Vives used the word *experimentum* but only in reference to experience, recommending careful observation as a general alternative to Scholastic speculation. His thought had great influence—directly or indirectly—on the scientific renewal.

BIBLIOGRAPHY

Gilbert, N. W. *Renaissance Concepts of Method.* 2nd ed. New York: Columbia University Press, 1963.

Noreña, C. G. *Juan Luis Vives.* The Hague: Nijhoff, 1970.

Rossi, P. *Il filosofi e le machine.* Milan: Feltrinelli, 1962; *Philosophy, Technology, and the Arts in the Early Modern Era.* Ed. Benjamin Nelson, trans. Salvator Attanasio. New York: Harper and Row, 1970.

JOSÉ M. LÓPEZ-PIÑERO

See also Aristotelianism; Craftsman-and-Scholar Thesis; Educational Reform; Experience and Experiment

Viviani, Vincenzio (1622–1703)

The life and work of this Florentine mathematician have been relatively little studied, considering the large number of manuscripts he left. He apparently owes his fame more to having been a pupil of Galileo Galilei (1564–1642) and having served the Tuscan Court than to his contribution to mathematics.

Viviani's mathematical talent as a sixteen-year-old student was brought to the attention of Grand Duke of Tuscany Ferdinand II de' Medici (1610–1670), who introduced him to Galileo, then blind and under house arrest. Viviani moved to live with Galileo and assist him as amanuensis, and the relation between the two mathematicians took the form of that of father and son. After Galileo's death, Viviani gradually became a central figure in Tuscan science: among other things, he helped Evangelista Torricelli (1608–1647), also an assistant of Galileo, perform the barometric experiment in 1644, was a leading member of the Accademia del Cimento in Florence between 1657 and 1667, and fulfilled a series of engineering and advisory tasks for the Court. Viviani's published works, however, are mainly restorations of classical works, in the tradition of Renaissance mathematics, contributing little to the contemporary progress of mathematics. Viviani never received a university posi-

Courtesy Istituto e Museo di Storia della Scienze, Florence, Italy.

tion; he was granted pensions by King Louis XIV and by the grand duke of Tuscany and received high honors, such as foreign membership in the Royal Society of London and the Académie Royale des Sciences in Paris.

Viviani, a fragile, hesitant man and a perfectionist, was all of his life under the burden of Galileo's memory. He called himself "Galileo's last pupil" and amassed material related to Galileo and his work, to the benefit of historians. He planned to collect and publish Galileo's works but did not manage to carry out the project; yet, one of his most important written contributions is the earliest biography of Galileo, drafted in 1654 and published posthumously in 1717. Viviani presents Galileo as a Renaissance genius and as a practical man and relates, among other things, the famous doubtful story of Galileo refuting Aristotle (384–322 B.C.E.) by experiments performed from the top of the Leaning Tower. The biography became the cornerstone of the tradition in historiography of science presenting Galileo as the founder of modern experimental sciences.

BIBLIOGRAPHY

Favaro, Antonio. "Vincenzio Viviani." *Amici e corrispondenti di Galileo*. Florence: Salimbeni, 1983, vol. 2, pp. 1009–1155.

Procissi, Angelo. *La collezione galileiana della Biblioteca Nazionale di Firenze*. 3 vols. Rome: Istituto Poligrafico dello Stato, 1959–1994.

Segre, Michael. *In the Wake of Galileo*. New Brunswick, NJ: Rutgers University Press, 1991.

MICHAEL SEGRE

See also Accademia del Cimento; Barometer; Galilei, Galileo; Torricelli, Evangelista

Void

Doctrines about the void and vacuum were fairly stable at the start of the seventeenth century. The majority view was held by Aristotelians, who denied that there is any vacuum in nature (i.e., any void inside bodies or outside the universe). But atomists required the void as the emptiness that surrounds atoms and as the area beyond the region occupied by bodies. These positions became more contested during the seventeenth century, with atomists and vacuists seeming to derive empirical support for their position with the invention of the barometer and the air pump.

Early-modern theories about the possibility of the void were developed in the context of Aristotelian doc-trines and their successive interpretations. Aristotle (384–322 B.C.E.) denied the existence of the void. He argued that the void is impossible, if it is thought to be a place with nothing in it (i.e., a location actually existing apart from any occupying body). Further, he concluded, against the atomists, that motion is impossible in the void, using an argument deriving from his principles of motion. A body moving by impact moves in proportion to the force exerted on it and in inverse proportion to the resistance of the medium in which it is situated. Since a void would provide no resistance, the body would move with a speed beyond any ratio—but such instantaneous motion is impossible.

Most Scholastics attempted to soften these arguments, not so as to accept the existence of the void, but to accept its possibility (i.e., to argue that God could create a void). Although attacks on Aristotle's views about the void preceded the condemnations by the bishop of Paris of various propositions in 1277, they gained theological inspiration from them. Among the relevant condemned propositions was "That God could not move the heavens in a straight line, the reason being that he would then leave a vacuum." As a consequence, there were numerous discussions of Aristotle's argument about the impossibility of motion in the void, many of them prompted by an internal criticism of Aristotle's position; in particular, it was noted that, in his system, the heavens have a determined speed of rotation but are not slowed down by the resistance of any medium. If one applied Aristotle's reasoning about the impossibility of motion in the void to the heavens, then the heavens would have to rotate with a speed beyond any ratio. Rejecting Aristotle's reasoning might lead one to conceive of an internal resistance to motion, thus invalidating the conclusion that a body would move with a speed beyond any ratio (i.e., instantaneously) in the void. The doctrine that became standard was that motion in the void would not be instantaneous and that, although they did not naturally occur, vacuums were not impossible supernaturally. The Jesuit Franciscus Toletus agreed with Thomas Aquinas (d. 1274), against Aristotle, that motion in the void would not be instantaneous. The Paris textbook writer Eustachius a Sancto Paulo (1573–1640) called motion in the void extremely probable and distinguished imaginary space above the heavens from vacuum, properly speaking. Others, such as Scipion Dupleix (1569–1661), also denied Aristotle's argument against the impossibility of motion in the void, asserting that the speed of the motion would not be due just to the resistance of the medium, but also to the weight and shape of the moving body.

René Descartes (1596–1650) actually hardened the position, looking more like Aristotle than the Aristotelians. He argued for the impossibility of empty space, both in and out of the world. Thinking of a vessel, its concave shape, and the extension that must be contained in this concavity, he asserted: "it would be as contradictory of us to conceive of a mountain without a valley, as to conceive of this concavity without the extension contained in it, or of this extension without an extended substance." In fact, he decided that, if God were to remove the body contained in that vessel and did not allow anything else to take its place, the sides of the vessel would thereby become contiguous. Others, such as Thomas Hobbes (1588–1679), denied the vacuum almost as strongly as Descartes did. For Hobbes, "every part of the universe is a body and that which is not a body is not part of the universe; and because the universe is all, that which is not part of it is nothing, and consequently nowhere." Thus, there can be no vacuum; imaginary space or extramundane void is "nothing but a fiction and a non-being." Gottfried Wilhelm Leibniz (1646–1716) followed Descartes and Hobbes in rejecting empty place. For Leibniz, voids are imaginary: "Since space in itself is an ideal thing like time, space out of this world must be imaginary, as the Schoolmen themselves have recognized. The case is the same with empty space within the world, which I also take to be imaginary." Moreover, voids are contrary to Leibniz's principle of plenitude, to his principle of the identity of indiscernibles, and, ultimately, to his fundamental principle of sufficient reason: "it is impossible that there should be any principle to determine what proportion of matter there ought to be, out of all the possible degrees from plenum to a void, or from a void to a plenum." Given that there is any degree of matter, there cannot be a void.

Samuel Clarke (1675–1729), as Isaac Newton's (1642–1727) representative, disagreed with Leibniz. For Clarke, empty space outside the world would not be imaginary but real. It would not be a space void of everything but void only of body, and God would be present in that space. Thus, separate, absolute, infinite void space is God's immensity, though it is not equivalent to God, only a property of God.

In these respects, Clarke was following the general tenets of atomism—for example, those advanced by

Pierre Gassendi (1592–1655) in his revival of Epicureanism. However, not all atomists required voids in which their atoms could move. Sebastian Basso (fl. 1560–1620), in particular, denied the void, preferring to fill the interstices between his atoms with an elastic ether.

The debates between vacuists and plenists intensified by the middle of the seventeenth century with the invention of the barometer by Evangelista Torricelli (1608–1647). The barometer was a tube four feet in length, sealed at one end, filled with mercury and inverted in a bowl of mercury. Interestingly, not all of the mercury flowed out of the tube—there was an apparently empty space at the top of the tube. Blaise Pascal (1623–1662), convinced that the empty space was a genuine vacuum, experimented with the barometer. Among other things, he had the apparatus taken to the top of a mountain to confirm his suspicion that the height of the column would be shorter at the top than at the bottom. According to Pascal, the weight of the air, not nature's abhorrence of vacuum, held up the column of mercury. Others—Descartes, in particular, who seems to have suggested Pascal's experiment—agreed that the changing height of the column of air was telling against some Scholastic accounts of vacuum, but they disagreed that the empty space was a genuine vacuum: after all, light passed through the supposedly empty space. Questions of this kind were bracketed by experimenters such as Robert Boyle (1627–1691), who deemed them too metaphysical and not amenable to experimentation. Subsequent work on barometers and air pumps was conducted within an experimental program in which the vacuum was a space almost totally devoid of air, not a space in which there are no bodies at all.

BIBLIOGRAPHY

Duhem, Pierre. *Medieval Cosmology: Theories of Infinity, Place, Time, Void, and the Plurality of Worlds*. Ed. and trans. Roger Ariew. Chicago: University of Chicago Press, 1985.

Garber, Daniel. *Descartes' Metaphysical Physics*. Chicago: University of Chicago Press, 1992.

Grant, Edward. *Much Ado About Nothing: Theories of Space and Vacuum from the Middle Ages to the Scientific Revolution*. Cambridge: Cambridge University Press, 1981.

Koyré, Alexandre. *From the Closed World to the Infinite Universe*. Baltimore: Johns Hopkins University Press, 1957.

Shapin, Steve, and Simon Schaffer. *Leviathan and the Air-Pump: Hobbes, Boyle, and the Experimental Life*. Princeton, NJ: Princeton University Press, 1985.

ROGER ARIEW

See also Aristotelianism; Atomism; Barometer; Epicureanism; Pneumatics; Space

Wallis, John (1616–1703)

English mathematician and influential figure in seventeenth-century science. He received a thorough grounding in classical languages and in 1632 entered Emmanuel College, Cambridge, where he pursued the traditional undergraduate course of study and took the degree of Bachelor of Arts in 1637. He followed this with additional studies in theology, anatomy, astronomy, and other branches of natural philosophy; he reports (evidently with some exaggeration) that mathematics was "scarce looked upon, with us, as Academical Studies then in fashion." In any event, his mathematical education seems to have been largely self-directed.

Wallis took the degree of Master of Arts in 1640 and was ordained in the same year. He served as a private chaplain for several years after his ordination and made a name for himself among the Parliamentary forces in the English Civil War (1642–1646) when he was shown a letter written in cipher and managed to crack the cipher in a matter of hours. This episode led to his subsequent employment as a cryptanalyst for the Parliamentarians, who rewarded him well for his efforts. In 1649 Wallis was appointed (by Parliamentary order) Savilian Professor of Geometry at Oxford, despite the fact that there was little in his public record to recommend him for the position. Nevertheless, within a few years he established himself as one of the most prominent mathematicians of the era.

Wallis's mathematical publications are many and varied; they include treatises on infinitesimal methods, encyclopedic surveys, polemical tracts, and editions of classical authors. His most influential work, *Arithmetica infinitorum,* appeared in 1656 as part of a two-volume mathematical collection entitled *Operum mathematicorum.* The *arithmetic of infinities* is Wallis's term for his method of finding areas and volumes of geometric objects. The basic idea derives from the method of indivisibles introduced by Bonaventura Cavalieri (1598–1647). Wallis took surfaces to be infinite collections of infinitely narrow parallelograms and then used an inductive technique for evaluating infinite sums. For example, in studying properties of the series of cube numbers, he observed that

$$\frac{0+1}{1+1} = \frac{1}{2} = \frac{1}{4} + \frac{1}{4}$$

$$\frac{0+1+8}{8+8+8} = \frac{9}{24} = \frac{3}{8} = \frac{1}{4} + \frac{1}{8}$$

$$\frac{0+1+8+27}{27+27+27+27} = \frac{36}{108} = \frac{4}{12} = \frac{1}{4} + \frac{1}{16}$$

$$\frac{0+1+8+27+64}{64+64+64+64+64} = \frac{100}{320} = \frac{5}{16} = \frac{1}{4} + \frac{1}{16}$$

Because the remainder term grows smaller as more terms are included, Wallis concluded that, in the infinite case, the ratio 1:4 holds. He then applied this arithmetical result to the geometric problem of finding the area under the curve $y = x^3$, treating the area as an infinite sum of infinitesimal "cubic elements" and obtaining a version of the integral $\int x^3 dx = \frac{1}{4}$. In the *Arithmetica infinitorum,* Wallis extended his methods and applied them to the problem of finding the area of the circle. The work culminated with the famous infinite product $\frac{4}{\pi} = \frac{3 \cdot 3 \cdot 5 \cdot 5 \cdot 7 \cdot 7 \ldots}{2 \cdot 4 \cdot 4 \cdot 6 \cdot 6 \cdot 8 \ldots}$.

Wallis's *Mechanica* (1671) and his *Treatise of Algebra* (1685) are two other important mathematical publications.

John Wallis. From Wallis's A Treatise of Algebra *(1685).*

The former uses the method of indivisibles to examine the nature and the principles of motion and includes investigations into the balance, centers of gravity, percussion, and related topics. The latter attempts a full exposition of the principles, history, and applications of algebra; an expanded Latin version published as the second volume of his three-volume *Opera mathematica* included significant letters and papers from Isaac Newton (1642–1727) and other British mathematicians.

Wallis was also a significant figure in the religious life of his day. He served as secretary to the Westminster Assembly of Divines, which met from 1644 to 1647. He took the degree of Doctor of Divinity at Oxford in 1654 and held forth in sermons and pamphlets on controversial theological issues. His evident fondness for controversy led him to pursue a bitter and long-running quarrel with Thomas Hobbes (1588–1679) that ranged over issues in mathematics, philosophy, theology, and politics, among other areas.

Wallis was also influential in the development of the Royal Society. He was a member of the so-called "Invisible College" in London in the 1640s, which met regularly to discuss scientific matters, then of the Oxford group that succeeded it. He was instrumental in the organization of the Royal Society: he was a charter member at its founding in 1660 and its president in 1680. He published dozens of letters and articles in the *Philosophical Transactions* on topics ranging from astronomy to linguistics to medicine.

BIBLIOGRAPHY

Prag, Adolf. "John Wallis (1616–1703): Zur Ideengeschichte der Mathematik im 17. Jahrhundert." *Quellen und Studien zur Geschichte der Mathematik, Astronomie und Physik* 1 (1931), 381–411.

Scott, J. F. *The Mathematical Work of John Wallis, D.D., F.R.S. (1616–1703)*. London: Taylor and Francis, 1938.

Scriba, Christoph J. "The Autobiography of John Wallis, F.R.S." *Notes and Records of the Royal Society* 25 (1970), 17–46.

———. *Studien zur Mathematik des John Wallis (1616–1703): Winkelteilungen, Kombinationslehre und Zahlentheoretische Probleme*. Wiesbaden: Steiner Verlag, 1966.

DOUGLAS M. JESSEPH

See also Cavalieri, Bonaventura; Infinitesimals; Royal Society of London; Series, Mathematical

Ward, Seth (1617–1689)

A founding Fellow of the Royal Society, Ward was known for his work in mathematics before becoming bishop of Exeter (1662) and Salisbury (1667). Born in Aspenden, Hertfordshire, England, Ward took degrees at Cambridge (B.A. 1637, M.A. 1640) and was later appointed Savilian Professor of Astronomy at Oxford (1649–1661). During these years, he became involved in a debate with John Webster (1610–1882) concerning reform of the university curriculum. In his *Vindiciae academiarum* (1654), Ward opposed claims by Webster, Thomas Hobbes (1588–1679), and William Dell (d. 1664), arguing that reform was unnecessary, that recent works in the sciences were not neglected, and that the New Science—particularly the mathematical sciences—flourished in English universities. Ward's most focused work appeared as an attack against the planetary theory of Ismaël Boulliau (1605–1694). In his influential *Astronomia Philolaica* (1645), Boulliau had proposed a new cosmology that opposed Johannes Kepler's (1571–1630) "ageometrical methods" and "magnetic fibers." At the suggestion of Sir Paul Neile (ca. 1613–1686), Ward published *In Ismaelis Bullialdi astronomiae philolaicae fundamenta inquisitio brevis* (1653), followed by *Astronomia geometrica* (1656). In the latter work Ward claimed to produce a more accurate theory. Responding in 1657, Boulliau acknowledged an error but argued that Ward had mistakenly identified his planetary theory with the "simple elliptical" hypothesis: movement of the planets in an orbital ellipse in which the empty (nonsolar) focus served effectively as an equant point (i.e., a point not at the center of an ellipse about which a planet generated equal angles in equal times). Applied to Mars, Ward's hypothesis would yield a maximum error of almost 8' in heliocentric longitude rather than the 2.5' calculated from Boulliau's theory. Although the Boulliau-Ward debate was not resumed, interest in the "elliptical way" spread rapidly as a number of works by English followers of Boulliau guided post-Keplerian astronomy to its pre-Newtonian conclusion. By the time of Isaac Newton's (1642–1727) *Principia mathematica philosophiae naturalis* (1687), Ward had left a large legacy of sermons but had published little science. Most of his manuscripts and letters are lost.

BIBLIOGRAPHY

Debus, Allen G. *Science and Education in the Seventeenth Century: The Webster-Ward Debate.* London: MacDonald; New York: American Elsevier, 1970.

Pope, Walter. *The Life of Seth: Lord Bishop of Salisbury.* Ed. J. B. Bamborough. Repr. Oxford: Oxford University Press, 1961, first ed. 1697.

Wilson, Curtis. "Predictive Astronomy in the Century after Kepler." In *Planetary Astronomy from the Renaissance to the Rise of Astrophysics,* ed. C. Wilson and R. Taton, Part A: *Tycho Brahe to Newton.* Cambridge: Cambridge University Press, 1989, pp. 161–206.

ROBERT A. HATCH

See also Boulliau, Ismaël; Educational Reform; Keplerianism

Warfare of Science and Theology

Although some early-modern churchmen were suspicious of developments in science, the concept of an innate structural conflict between science and religious dogma began not during the Scientific Revolution itself, but in the eighteenth-century Enlightenment, and reached its fullest development in the late nineteenth century. Anticlerical French Enlightenment philosophers such as Voltaire (1694–1778) and the Marquis de Condorcet (1743–1794), author of the posthumously published *Esquisse d'un tableau historique des progres de l'esprit humain* (Sketch of the Progress of the Human Mind, 1795), were among the first to integrate the history of science with general history. Although most of the Enlightenment philosophers were not atheists, they were passionate enemies of established religion, particularly Catholicism, and appealed to science as a liberating alternative and a better path to God. They interpreted particular episodes of the Scientific Revolution, especially the trial of Galileo Galilei (1564–1642), as expressing a fundamental conflict between a vilified dogmatic religion based on authority and an idealized empirical science based on observation. Although the idea of innate conflict between religion and science was weaker in England than in France, due to the greater strength of natural theology in England, the warfare thesis was also compatible with a tradition in Protestant thought that depicted "priestcraft," and particularly the Catholic Church, as obscurantist. The Scientific Revolution, like the Renaissance and the Reformation, could be portrayed as a stage in the liberation of Western thought from the Church-dominated Middle Ages.

The interpretation of the Scientific Revolution as a revolt against dogmatic religion was strengthened in the nineteenth century by factors including the decline of natural theology and intellectual conflicts over Darwinian evolution and the philological study of the Bible, known as the *higher criticism.* On an institutional level, there were bitter struggles against members of the clergy and Christian religious bodies who opposed the establishment of nonsectarian or secular educational institutions. The period was also marked by the rise of evolutionary and dialectical concepts of the development of human society in which religion was seen not, as some Enlightenment philosophers had seen it, as an evil enemy of human progress but as a necessary stage in humanity's history that had been transcended in an age of science. The positivist philosophy of Auguste Comte (1798–1857), which identified human history as passing from a theological, to a metaphysical, and, finally, to a "positive," or scientific, stage, was particularly influential in placing science and religion at odds. Comte, a pioneer in the history of science, identified the late sixteenth and the early seventeenth centuries—the time of Francis Bacon (1561–1626), Galileo, and René Descartes (1596–1650)—as the period when science liberated itself from theology and metaphysics and identified these early-modern scientific thinkers as founders of positivism.

The warfare thesis received its classic formulation in the English-speaking world in several influential late-nineteenth-century works of intellectual history and history of science. The Irish intellectual historian W. H. Lecky (1838–1903), in his *History of the Rise and Influence of the Spirit of Rationalism in Europe* (2 vols., 1865), argued that the seventeenth century was marked by the triumph of reason over religious dogma and superstition, a process in which science played a central role. He and others argued that the rise of rationalism and skepticism and the decline of supernatural approaches could be seen in developments such as the decline in the belief in witchcraft and in the portentous nature of comets and monsters.

Focusing more strongly on science, the English-born American teacher of chemistry and medicine J. W. Draper (1811–1882), in his *History of the Intellectual Development of Europe* (2 vols., 1861) and *History of the Conflict Between Religion and Science* (1875), and the American Andrew Dickson White (1831–1914), in *A History of the Warfare of Science with Theology in Christendom* (2 vols., 1896), revived the anticlericalism of the Enlightenment but in a much more documented and systematic form and with a characteristically nineteenth-century belief in progress. Draper, in particular, was deeply affected by the struggles over Darwinism in England and America and was a bitter enemy of the Catholic Church. His *History of the Conflict Between Religion and Science* was written in the period immediately following the *Papal Syllabus of Errors* (1864), which condemned rationalism and liberalism, and the promulgation of the doctrine of papal infallibility by the First Vatican Council in 1870. In this atmosphere of conflict between intellectual freedom and the Catholic Church's claims to dogmatic authority, Draper portrayed the Church as the great enemy of science and liberty, pointedly contrasting the many economic and social benefits resulting from science in the nineteenth century with the poverty and backwardness of the Church-dominated Middle Ages and using high-toned rhetoric concerning the blood on the hands of the Catholic Church. Draper portrayed science, which he claimed (erroneously) had never allied itself with civil power, as pure and spotless, presenting Galileo and Giordano Bruno (1548–1600) as heroic martyrs of science and victims of the persecuting Catholic Church. Draper was not an atheist, and he concentrated his antireligious fire on Catholicism. Antiscience statements and actions by Protestants received comparatively little attention, and Draper claimed that the Reformation, by breaking the intellectual monopoly of the Church, had been an important contributor to the rise of early-modern science. Draper also greatly admired medieval Islamic science, which he believed had played an important role in the rise of European science by stimulating resistance to Church domination of European thought. Draper believed that this struggle between science and Catholicism, reason and faith, would soon be fought to a finish. Science would inevitably triumph, relegating Catholicism to the dustbin of history, although Protestantism might possibly adapt to the dominance of science if Protestant theologians were willing to accept a sharply restricted intellectual role. Draper's works were widely reprinted and translated into all the major European languages as well as Polish, Portugese, and Serbian, exerting much influence in America and Europe.

Whereas Draper was a scientist who became a historian, Andrew Dickson White was a humanist who served as first president of the American Historical Association, as well as a diplomat. His opinions were shaped by fierce struggles against Protestant religious bodies to establish America's first nondenominational private university at Cornell, of which he became the first president. His *History of the Warfare of Science with Theology in Christendom* appeared in bits and pieces for several years, in lectures and in short books and periodical articles, before being gathered into a book. Like Draper's, White's work was reprinted and translated many times. White also conceived the history of science as a struggle between natural and supernatural explanations in which heroic scientists always eventually triumphed over obscurantist clerics, represented in his work by the extreme antiscience statements of a vociferous minority, frequently quoted out of context. Again like Draper, White argued that more moderate religious figures and positions played a relatively unimportant role in the struggle. Some of White's quotations are inaccurate, such as one he prominently featured in which the Protestant leader John Calvin (1509–1564) allegedly rejected Copernicanism as antibiblical. In fact, not only is the quotation spurious and inconsistent with Calvin's theological method, but Calvin's writings contain no mention of Nicolaus Copernicus (1473–1543). White treated statements by scientists themselves of religious motivations for their work as remnants of theological backwardness, irrelevant to scientific achievements or actually hindering them.

Although their overall interpretations were similar, White was less obsessed than Draper or the French Enlightenment thinkers had been with the Catholic Church, much less of a factor in the American than the European political context, and largely avoided Draper's anti-Catholic rhetorical flourishes, carefully pointing out instances in which Protestants had also been enemies of science. Rather than the Church or Catholicism, White tended to identify the enemy as the persistence of medieval thinking. He also tried to distinguish himself from Draper by claiming not to be antireligious but antitheological, although Draper had also claimed not to be antireligious, and by picturing the conflict between religion and science not as a fight to the finish. Instead, White claimed that the establishment of an autonomous science would purify religion, making it wholly spiritual.

Neither Draper nor White, who included social sciences such as anthropology and political economy as well as physical and biological sciences in his narrative, focused specifically on the period of the Scientific Revolution, a concept neither employed. Their interpretations did, however, place events that would become associated with the Scientific Revolution as central in the ongoing struggle to emancipate science from religion. Draper saw an Age of Reason beginning in Europe in the sixteenth century with the rise of heliocentric astronomy playing a key role, and White's history prominently featured the trial of Galileo. The conflict thesis was carried into twentieth century scholarship on the period of the Scientific Revolution. The French intellectual historian Paul Hazard (1878–1944), in his influential three-volume *La crise de la conscience européene* (The European Mind, 1934), put forward an interpretation of the late seventeenth century similar to Lecky's, although more detailed in argument. He also saw science as part of an overall cultural change from faith to reason. The American philosopher of religion E. A. Burtt (1892–1989), in *The Metaphysical Foundations of Modern Physical Science* (1925), restated the conflict thesis but at a deeper level. Burtt was less concerned with tracing the debates over specific issues such as Copernicanism and more concerned with asserting the ultimate incompatibility of the impersonal rule-governed universe of the physical sciences rooted in Newtonianism and the personal God of Christianity. Burtt was also much more sympathetic to religion and more ambivalent about science than White and Draper had been. He admired the intellectual achievements of science but found the mathematized

and abstract world picture of science deeply dehumanizing and spiritually impoverishing in comparison to the medieval one, which he believed put human beings at the center. Although less nostalgic, the Russian-born historian of the Scientific Revolution Alexander Koyré (1892–1964) took a similar position in *From the Closed World to the Infinite Universe* (1957) and other works.

Despite the persistence of the conflict model, twentieth-century history of science was marked by a more complex awareness of the relation of science and religion. The most significant development eroding the conflict thesis was the growing realization of the compatibility of science and religion, and even the positive contributions of religion to scientific advance. This growing awareness marked both internalist and externalist approaches to the history of science. The revival of interest in the intellectual history of medieval science and its influence on the Scientific Revolution led by Pierre Duhem (1861–1916), a devout French Catholic physicist and historian, fostered a more ambiguous notion of the relation of science and religion. The English philosopher Alfred North Whitehead (1861–1947), in *Science and the Modern World* (1925), argued on a more general level that Western science was rooted in the ideas of medieval theologians about a rational God and an ordered universe. Internalist historians also connected scientific ideas with religious ideas about Creation. This interpretation has been extended by some scholars, the most extreme example being Stanley Jaki, who considers the Scientific Revolution and scientific thinking itself to be an offshoot of Christian theology. Among externalists, the influential thesis put forward in the American sociologist Robert K. Merton's (1910–) *Science, Technology, and Society in Seventeenth-Century England* (1938) identified a particular religious movement, Puritanism, as one of the sources of scientific advance during the seventeenth century, rejecting the notion of a structural conflict of science and religion. Other externalists rediscovered the functions of science in Catholic and Protestant religious apologetic or the religious or millenarian motivations of important scientists, such as Isaac Newton (1642–1727). At the end of the twentieth century, even the trial of Galileo was being interpreted as a struggle in which religious and scientific motivations were to be found among both Galileo's supporters and his defenders. The decline in the heroic image of the scientist and science also contributed to the abandonment of the warfare thesis by historians of science, although it still occupies a prominent place in popular culture. Historians of the Scientific Revolution identified complex interactions between various religious and scientific positions rather than as representations of an all-encompassing conflict.

BIBLIOGRAPHY

Brooke, John Hedley. *Science and Religion: Some Historical Perspectives.* Cambridge: Cambridge University Press, 1991.

Cohen, H. Floris. *The Scientific Revolution: A Historiographical Enquiry.* Chicago: University of Chicago Press, 1994.

Daston, Lorraine. "History of Science in an Elegaic Mode: E. A. Burtt's *Metaphysical Foundations of Modern Physical Science* Revisited." *Isis* 82 (1991), 522–531.

Hooykaas, R. *Religon and the Rise of Modern Science.* Edinburgh and London: Scottish Academic Press, 1972.

Welch, Claude. "Dispelling Some Myths About the Split Between Theology and Science in the Nineteenth Century." In *Religion and Science: History, Method, Dialogue,* ed. W. Mark Richards and Wesley J. Wildman. New York and London: Routledge, 1996.

White, Edward A. *Science and Religion in American Thought: The Impact of Naturalism.* Stanford, CA: Stanford University Press, 1952.

WILLIAM E. BURNS

See also Biblical Interpretation; Galileo and the Church; Internalist/Externalist Historiography; Puritanism and Science; Religion and Natural Philosophy

Wendelin, Gottfried (Vendelinus) (1580–1667)

His astronomical discoveries and learning were admired by René Descartes (1596–1650), who sought his opinion on his *Geometry,* and by a number of other leading contemporary natural philosophers, whom he met and with whom he corresponded.

He was born in Herck, in the province of Liège, and studied at the Latin schools at Herck and Tournai, at the University of Louvain, and at the University of Orange, where he obtained a doctorate. In the course of his career as priest, teacher, and Church official, he worked and lived in Belgium, the Netherlands, France, Italy, and Germany. He returned to his native land in 1612 and remained there for the rest of his life. He was head of the Latin school in Herck until 1620, and then parish priest in Geet-Bets and Herck until 1648. From 1648 to 1658, he was an official of the Cathedral of Tournai, and the last nine years of his life he lived quietly in Ghent with a nephew.

Wendelin's studies ranged over several fields. He published books on the Church Fathers, the Salic laws, and Latin poetry. He was the first to note that, as the amplitude of a pendulum increases, so does the time it continues to oscillate; moreover, the number of oscillations increases with a lowering of the ambient temperature.

In his astronomical works, *Loxias seu de obliquitate solis diatriba* (Loxias; or, A Learned Discourse on the Obliquity of the Sun, 1626), *Lampas* (1644, 1658), *Eclipses lunares ab anno 1573 ad 1643 observatae* (Lunar Eclipses Observed from 1573 to 1643, 1644), and *Teratologia cometica* (A Study of Monstrous Comets, 1662), as well as in his correspondence with fellow astronomers such as Giambattista Riccioli (1598–1671) and Pierre Gassendi (1592–1655), he showed himself to be a staunch Copernican, familiar with the ideas of Johannes Kepler (1571–1630), and an important contributor to astronomical theory. He was the first to argue that the obliquity of the ecliptic varied over time, oscillating 30' about a mean of 24°. He applied Kepler's third law of planetary motion—that the squares of the periods of the planets are proportional to the cubes of their distances from the Sun—to the Galilean satellites of Jupiter. He also reduced the horizontal parallax of the Sun to less than 15 arc-seconds, constituting a substantial increase in the generally accepted size of the solar system. These contributions were based partly on assiduous observation and calculation and partly on harmonic speculation similar to that employed by Kepler.

BIBLIOGRAPHY

Godeaux, Lucien. "Godefroid Wendelin." *Biographie nationale publiée par l'Académie royale de Belgique* 27 (1938), cols. 180–184.

Silveryser, Florent. "Godefridus Wendelinus et les 'causes secondes.'" *Ciel et terre* 49 (1933), 54–62, 83–88, 111–116.

———. "Godefroid Wendelin: Sa vie, son ambience et ses travaux (1580–1667)." *Bulletin de l'Institut Archéologique Liégeois* 58 (1934).

ALBERT VAN HELDEN

See also Copernicanism; Kepler, Johannes; Keplerianism; Parallax

Whiston, William (1667–1752)

The third of the nine children of Josiah Whiston and Katharine Rosse, he was born in the rectory of Norton Juxta Twycross in Leicestershire. He attended the grammar school at Tamworth and was admitted to Clare College, Cambridge, in 1686.

Whiston defended Thomas Burnet's (1635–1715) *Sacred Theory of the Earth* for his bachelor's degree and, through his own *New Theory of the Earth* (1696), earned a place with Burnet, John Ray (1620–1705), and John Woodward (1665–1728) as one of the "earthmakers" of the seventeenth century. Whiston's special contribution centered on his theory that it was the near passage of a comet at the time of the biblical Deluge that gave rise to the Great Flood. Whiston believed he had shown "the mathematical demonstration of the cause of the flood from astronomy." He discussed his theory with Richard Bentley and Isaac Newton (1642–1727) and built on Newton's idea that the condensed vapors of comets could supplement rainwater. Whiston's 1696 work appears to have been received favorably by Newton, who chose Whiston as his deputy in 1701. The following year, Whiston succeeded Newton as Lucasian Professor of mathematics at Cambridge.

Whiston delivered the Boyle Lectures in 1707 under the title *The Accomplishments of Scripture Prophecies,* in which he continued to use chronological studies to show the exact time of the fulfillment of certain prophecies. His mathematical lectures in Cambridge were published in Latin and English; the texts were in use for more than fifty years and were important in popularizing Newton's work.

Whiston was expelled from Cambridge in 1710 following his publication of *Sermons and Essays on Various Subjects* (1709), in which he expressed heretical views on the doctrine of the Trinity. Newton, though himself not orthodox in theological doctrine, dissociated himself from Whiston, whose fanatical pursuit of primitive Christianity made him an object of contemporary derision. After 1710 Whiston generated an income by giving lectures on astronomical topics and publishing charts of eclipses. He made several attempts to win prize money by schemes for finding longitude. Whiston translated Flavius Josephus from the Greek; his text has gone through many editions to the present day.

BIBLIOGRAPHY

Farrell, Maureen. *William Whiston.* New York: Arno, 1981.

Force, James E. *William Whiston.* Cambridge: Cambridge University Press, 1985.

Whiston, William. *Memoirs of the Life and Writings of Mr. William Whiston by Himself.* London, 1749.

MAUREEN FARRELL

See also Physico-Theology; Theories of the Earth

White, Thomas (1593–1676)

Philosopher, priest, and leader of a faction of English Catholics known after his pseudonym as "Blackloists," Thomas White has long been a forgotten figure. However, his significance for the Scientific Revolution, well recognized by his contemporaries, is now apparent: with wide-ranging contacts over Continental Europe, he was particularly important as a synthesizer of old and new ideas. White was traditionally schooled in the works of Aristotle (384–322 B.C.E.) and Thomas Aquinas (d. 1274); his contact with the new thought came particularly through his association with the Mersenne circle in Paris in the 1640s. His cosmological treatises, *De mundo* (1642) and *Peripatetical Institutions* (1646), are remarkable for incorporating many elements of the New Science within an essentially Scholastic framework.

Despite insisting on the need to retain Aristotelian first principles and procedures, White contrived to present versions of both Copernicanism and atomic theory. Some ambiguity was inevitable. For example, he claimed the possibility of a central Sun within a nominally earth-centered universe by redefining the universe's center point as the circumference of the earth's whole orbit. He then explained the orbital motion of Earth, as required by Nicolaus Copernicus (1473–1543), by postulating a continuing force as demanded by Aristotelian physics: prevailing winds activated the sea, which, in turn, pushed the earth. Similarly, while still in the old manner insisting on the uniqueness of the earth within a finite universe, White foresaw the possibility of empirically verifying the new model with modern methods, after a sufficiently powerful telescope had been developed to enable observation of stellar parallax. White effected a similar synthesis in physics, in which he again reconciled two apparently incompatible theories: that of *minima naturalia* (smallest parts of matter) associated with Aristotelianism and that of discrete particles of matter, which derived from the alternative and newly revived atomic tradition.

White's reputation became obscured by his notoriety in theology and politics, but he importantly exemplifies an intermediary position in the transition from Scholasticism to the New Science.

BIBLIOGRAPHY

Henry, John. "Atomism and Eschatology: Catholicism and Natural Philosophy in the Interregnum." *British Journal for the History of Science* 15 (1982), 211–239.

Jones H. W., ed. *Thomas Hobbes: Thomas White's De Mundo Examined*. London: Bradford University Press with Crosby Lockwood Staples, 1976.

Southgate, Beverley Charles. *"Covetous of Truth": The Life and Work of Thomas White, 1593–1676*. Dordrecht: Kluwer Academic, 1993.

BEVERLEY SOUTHGATE

See also Aristotelianism; Atomism; Copernicanism; Religion and Natural Philosophy

Wilkins, John (1614–1672)

Played an important role in the popularization of the New Science in seventeenth-century England. In his *Discovery of a World in the Moone* (1638) and *Discourse Concerning a New Planet* (1640), he attempted to bring Copernican astronomy, the implications of Galileo Galilei's (1564–1642) telescopic observations, the idea of a plurality of worlds, and the possibility of flight to the Moon to the general reader. He also addressed the problem of authority and argued for a Galilean approach to Scripture that would leave science independent from religion. In *Mercury; or, The Secret Messenger* (1641), he dealt with codes and symbolic representation; in *Mathematical Magick* (1648), he explained the basic principles of mechanics and suggested how these principles might be used to construct a variety of practical and fanciful devices. His mission in these early works was to introduce the uninitiated to the study of nature. His imaginative treatment of lunar inhabitants and flying chariots inspired considerable literary adaptation.

Wilkins played a key role in the organization of scientific activity during the Interregnum and Restoration periods. While warden of Wadham College, he attracted a considerable portion of the English scientific community to Oxford. The Wadham group of the 1650s was an immediate predecessor of the Royal Society. While at Wadham, Wilkins began his efforts to bring natural philosophers of different religious persuasions together to cooperatively pursue scientific experimentation and to encourage younger natural philosophers. Together with Seth Ward (1617–1689), in *Vindiciae academiarum* (1653), he defended the universities, humane learning, and the current state of university science against the attacks of radical sectaries.

Wilkins played a leading role in the founding of the Royal Society and served as one of its secretaries. He was heavily involved in both its administrative affairs and its

John Wilkins. From A. Wolf, A History of Science, Technology, and Philosophy in the Sixteenth and Seventeenth Centuries *(London: Allen and Unwin, 1935).*

experimental program until his death. He played a major role in supervising the composition of Thomas Sprat's (1635–1713) *History of the Royal Society* (1667), a combined history and apologia for the society.

Wilkins's lifelong interest in a simplified, more precise language and the development of a universal character and language culminated in *An Essay Toward a Real Character and a Philosophical Language* (1668), a work he hoped would facilitate scientific communication, international commerce, and religious understanding. Wilkins was one of the founders of linguistics.

Wilkins, who had become bishop of Chester in 1668, played an important role in seventeenth-century and modern discussion concerning the relationships between religion and science and the development of a rational theology. His emphasis on the importance of moderation and tentativeness in both scientific and religious discourse and on the compatibility of religion and science led him to a Latitudinarianism that would make the established Anglican Church more inclusive and to an epistemology that emphasized the probable nature of human knowledge. If at Oxford he was criticized for his protection of Anglicans, during the Restoration (1660) he was criticized for his protection of Dissenters. Wilkins has been a central figure in scholarly discussions concerned with the relationship between Latitudinarianism and science, Puritanism and science, and the role of the universities in fostering or hindering the teaching of the natural sciences.

BIBLIOGRAPHY

Moss, Jean Dietz. *Novelties in the Heavens: Rhetoric and Science in the Copernican Controversy*. Chicago: University of Chicago Press, 1993.

Shapiro, Barbara, *John Wilkins, 1614–72: An Intellectual Biography*. Berkeley and Los Angeles: University of California Press, 1968.

Slaughter, Mary M. *Universal Languages and Scientific Taxonomy in the Seventeenth Century*. Cambridge: Cambridge University Press, 1982

Subbiondo, Joseph L., ed. *John Wilkins and Seventeenth-Century British Linguistics*. Amsterdam and Philadelphia: John Benjamins,1992.

BARBARA SHAPIRO

See also Oxford Philosophical Society; Popularization; Royal Society of London; Universal Languages

Thomas Willis. From Fielding H. Garrison, An Introduction to the History of Medicine, *3rd ed. (Philadelphia and London: Saunders, 1921).*

Willis, Thomas (1621–1675)

Born in Great Bedwyn, England, and educated at Oxford University, he graduated with a B. Med. in 1646 a few months before Oxford was conquered by the Puritans. Despite having been a volunteer in the Royalist forces, he became a committed member of the innovative group, including William Petty (1623–1687), Robert Boyle (1627–1691), and John Wilkins (1614–1672), among others, that transformed Oxford into the center of the New Science until the end of the Commonwealth (1660). Robert Hooke (1635–1703) and Richard Lower (1631–1691) worked with him as assistants while they were young students, and Lower remained associated with his research for the rest of his life. Willis graduated D. Med. following the Restoration of the monarchy in 1660 and was appointed professor of natural philosophy at Oxford in recognition of his loyalty to the Royalist cause. The return of teaching to Scholastic methods, however, proved to be incompatible with his modern ideas, perhaps the reason for his move in 1665 to London, where he remained until his death, having won great renown as a physician while continuing to participate in the group mentioned earlier, which also founded the Royal Society.

Willis's work may be divided into three stages. In the first, he focused on iatrochemical doctrine—parallel to, but separate from, that formulated by Franciscus Sylvius (1614–1672)—which he expounded in *De fermentatione* (1656) and applied to fever at a later date (1659); it synthesized Paracelsian principles with the scientific innovations of that time. In the second stage, he concentrated on the nervous system and related diseases. His numerous contributions in his treatise *Cerebri anatome* (1664), a milestone in the history of neuroanatomy, included many details of the vegetative nervous system, a new classification of cranial nerves that was generally accepted for more than a century, and an iatrochemical interpretation of nerve functions. Following his "pathology of the brain and nerves," *Specimen* (1667), on scurvy and convulsive disorders, he published a book on hysterical and hypochondriac complaints (1670) in which he upheld their nervous character—the basis of neurosis as formulated in the late eighteenth century. His *De anima brutorum* (1672) covered not only the dynamic principle of animal life, but also comparative neuroanatomy and provided outstanding descriptions of mental and nervous illnesses.

Willis devoted his final years to attempting to provide an experimental basis for pharmacology, expounded in his treatise *Pharmaceutice rationalis* (1674–1675), in which he also provided clinical descriptions, including the first in Europe of diabetes mellitus.

BIBLIOGRAPHY

Isler, H. *Thomas Willis, 1621–1675: Doctor and Scientist.* New York: Hafner, 1968.

López-Piñero, J. M. *Historical Origins of the Concept of Neurosis.* Cambridge: Cambridge University Press, 1983.

———. "Willis y la iatroquímica inglesa y de los países latinos." *Medicina española* 67 (1972) 228–237.

Meyer, A., and R. Hierons. "On Thomas Willis' Concepts of Neurophysiology." *Medical History* 9 (1965), 1–15, 142–155.

JOSÉ M. LÓPEZ-PIÑERO

See also Lower, Richard; Oxford Philosophical Society; Paracelsus; Pharmacology; Physiology

Willughby, Francis (1635–1672)

The eldest son of Sir Francis Willughby, who, between 1580 and 1588, built the magnificent Wollaton Hall at Nottingham, England, which is now Nottingham Natural History Museum. Great attention was given to the education of young Francis, who was diligent in his studies of the classics and mathematics. His admission to Trinity College, Cambridge, enabled him to take a B.A. in 1656 followed by an M.A. in 1659, during which period he was a pupil of John Ray (1620–1705). Both men, being of like minds, took great interest in the advancement of natural science, which they pursued during journeys throughout Britain both before and after their grand tour in Europe, with the object of collecting specimens and gaining all possible information about natural history. They returned with many treasures to Wollaton Hall, and Willughby immediately started to work toward publishing his findings on the animal kingdom. But nothing was published because he thought his work imperfect. Urged on by Ray, he continued and gave permission for publication before he became ill and died. Ray took on the editorial work and the first of Willughby's works, *Ornithologiae libri tres,* on birds, was published in Latin in 1676 and in English in 1678. It contained a vast amount of original observation. In 1686 Ray edited and published Willughby's second work, *Historiae piscium libri quatuor.* This history of fishes contained carefully described specific observations, and several subscribers paid for the production of the engraved illustrations, including the diarist Samuel Pepys, who paid

for no less than fifty. Both works were highly praised at the time. Willughby, like Ray, was one of the early Fellows of the Royal Society, founded in 1660. Both were in frequent correspondence with Martin Lister, F.R.S. (1639–1712), on the subjects of spiders and entomology, and papers by all three friends were published in the *Philosophical Transactions of the Royal Society.*

BIBLIOGRAPHY

Welch, Mary A. "Francis Willughby, F.R.S. (1635–1672)." *Journal of the Society for the Bibliography of Natural History* 6 (1971), 71–85.

Willughby, Francis. *Historiae piscium libri quatuor.* Ed. John Ray. London, 1686.

———. *Ornithologiae libri tres.* Ed. John Ray. London, 1676.

JOHN R. PARKER

See also Lister, Martin; Natural History; *Philosophical Transactions;* Ray, John; Zoology

Witchcraft

In the Christian cosmology of Europe before the late eighteenth century, the Devil was believed capable of tempting human beings to pay him homage normally paid only to God, to enter agreements with humans according to the terms of which humans received powers over nature and humanity not attainable by any other means (i.e., to perform acts that were not physically caused and were not miracles), and to perform acts that harmed or illicitly influenced other humans by these occult means. Both a pact with the Devil (which presumed the sin and crime of idolatry) and harm to others by occult means (whose Latin designation was *maleficium*) constituted the crime of witchcraft. In addition to these two primary features, witches were also thought to bear the mark of the Devil on their bodies, to have demonic companions (familiars), and to be capable of flight and shape-shifting, and they were accused of gathering collectively to pay homage to the Devil (the Sabbath), sacrifice infants, and engage in sexual promiscuity. Until the fifteenth century, witchcraft was not clearly distinguished from general sorcery (as it still is not in French; the German *Hexerei* was distinguished from *Zauberei* in the early fifteenth century, and the English witchcraft was distinguished from magic or sorcery somewhat earlier), which was consistently condemned in Scripture, by the Church Fathers, and in later theology and canon law. From the fifteenth century on, however, sorcery divided into learned magic (either natural or diabolical) and witchcraft proper, an Old English word originally meaning diviner.

The division reflects both a social and an intellectual change. The sixteenth and seventeenth centuries saw a vigorous debate concerning the validity of learned magic, one that raised some of the most important questions about scientific explanations that the period knew, but witchcraft bore the brunt of most trials and condemnations during the most intense persecutions, ca. 1560–1660. The general ideas concerning the nature of witchcraft and the necessity for punishing it were first laid out in detail in a work by two Inquisitors, Heinrich Krämer and Joseph Sprenger, entitled *Malleus maleficarum* (Hammer of Witches), published in 1486. A very large literature was produced in England and on the Continent into the early eighteenth century.

Before the mid-sixteenth century, trials for witchcraft usually took place in ecclesiastical courts. After that date, however, they generally took place in secular courts, partly as a result of the new powers acquired by secular courts as a consequence of the Reformation. A second consequence of the Reformation was the prevalence of trials for witchcraft in areas that were religiously divided and a considerably smaller number of trials in areas that were religiously homogeneous. Although gender differences among those accused and tried varied from place to place, approximately four women were tried for witchcraft to every man who was charged. Of the women, unmarried or widowed older women whose neighbors suspected them of causing harm to humans or property were most frequently accused, tried, and convicted.

The distribution of accusations and prosecutions for witchcraft was not uniform throughout Europe. Prosecutions in Continental Europe were carried out according to the Romano-canonical Inquisitorial legal procedure, which usually required a confession for conviction and used torture to obtain a conviction when other evidence pointed to the likely guilt of a suspect. Continental witch trials usually focused on the offence of idolatry (i.e., pact with the Devil). English common law prohibited the use of torture, but, since 1542, witchcraft had been a statutory crime in England and there were several large-scale prosecutions for witchcraft as well. In England, the prosecutions usually focused on the harm (*maleficium*) allegedly caused by the witch. In Scotland, witchcraft became a statutory crime in 1563. The best

recent estimates suggest that ca. 110,000 people were tried for witchcraft in the sixteenth and seventeenth centuries and that ca. 60,000 were executed.

Popular beliefs about—and fears of—witchcraft suvived longer than the mass persecutions and the tolerance of courts even to admit individual accusations. Generally, the withdrawal of elites, including magistrates and judges, from accepting charges of witchcraft was one of the most prominent features of the decline of prosecutions and, eventually, beliefs. Philosophical skepticism contributed to that reluctance, as did a growing transformation of theories of physical causation and the limitations on the use of evidence derived from supernatural sources. In addition, elites began to withdraw from a cultural world that they had long shared with the general population, and the condemnation of popular beliefs as erroneous increased during the later seventeenth century.

BIBLIOGRAPHY

Briggs, Robin. *Witches and Neighbours: The Social and Cultural Context of European Witchcraft.* London: HarperCollins, 1996.

Cohn, Norman. *Europe's Inner Demons.* New York: Basic Books, 1975.

Kors, Ian C., and Edward Peters. *Witchcraft in Europe, 1100–1700: A Documentary History.* Philadelphia: University of Pennsylvania Press, 1972.

Levack, Brian. *The Witch-Hunt in Early Modern Europe.* London and New York: Longman, 1987. 2nd ed. 1993.

EDWARD PETERS

See also Glanvill, Joseph; Magic

Witt, Jan de (1625–1672)

The son of a prominent family in the Netherlands, in the early 1640s de Witt belonged to the circle of young mathematicians whom Frans van Schooten (ca. 1615–1660) introduced to Cartesian geometry. From his years as a Schooten student came his *Elementa curvarum linearum* (published in the 1659–1561 edition of René Descartes's, 1596–1650, *Geometry*), one of the first textbooks in analytic geometry. It shows that straight lines are represented by first-degree equations involving two unknowns. As for quadratic equations, among other things, de Witt identifies ellipses, parabolas, and hyperbolas by studying their equations and reduces the equations to canonical form.

From 1653 to his assassination in 1672, de Witt was grand pensionary of Holland with responsibilities equivalent to those of a prime minister of the Netherlands. Out of his concern for improving public finances came his 1671 *Waerdye van Lyf-renten naer proportie van los-renten* (Treatise on Life Annuities), one of the first attempts to use probabilistic notions in an economic context. It deals with annuity prices, a standard seventeenth-century means for public institutions to raise money. The individual buying a life annuity on someone (usually a healthy child) paid a lump sum in exchange for the beneficiary receiving an annual income for life. Drawing inspiration from the mathematical elucidation of the notion of expectation in games of chance in Christiaan Huygens's (1629–1695) book (1657) on the subject, de Witt assumed that, when a person has a chance of winning A and an equal chance of winning B, then he has an expectation of winning (A + B)/2. De Witt combined this notion with two hypotheses: that uniform rates of mortality for the age intervals 4–53, 54–63, 64–73, and 74–80 obtain (i.e., the chances of dying are the same for all of the years in a given interval) and that the chances of dying in these intervals keep the ratios 1:3/2:2:3 (i.e., someone 74 or older is three times as likely to die as someone between 4 and 53). On these hypotheses, De Witt demonstrated that Holland could sell annuities at sixteen years' purchase (a life annuity of one florin would cost sixteen florins) rather than at fourteen years' purchase, as was customary, and they would still be profitable to buyers (i.e., investors could mathematically expect the annuity beneficiary to receive by the end of his or her life at least as much as she or he would if the money were lent at 4 percent, which was then the usual lending rate).

BIBLIOGRAPHY

Barnwell, R. G. *A Sketch of the Life and Times of John de Witt, Grandpensionary of Holland, to Which Is Added His Treatise on Life Annuities.* New York: Pudney and Russell, 1856.

Coolidge. J. L. *The Mathematics of Great Amateurs.* Oxford: Clarendon, 1949. 2nd ed. 1990, pp. 119–131.

Hacking, I. *The Emergence of Probability.* Cambridge: Cambridge University Press, 1975, pp. 111–121.

Rowen, H. H. *John de Witt, Grand Pensionary of Holland, 1625–1672.* Princeton, NJ: Princeton University Press, 1978.

ANTONI MALET

See also Analytic Geometry; Probability; Schooten, Frans van; Statistics

Wittich, Paul (ca. 1546–1586)

Recognized by his contemporaries as an ingenious mathematical astronomer, he never published any of his work, and his reputation nearly vanished. In the 1980s, several copies of Nicolaus Copernicus's (1473–1543) *De revolutionibus* (1543) have been identified as heavily annotated in Wittich's hand, and these marginalia give a greater appreciation of his influence as an itinerant teacher of technical details of the New Astronomy. In particular, diagrams in a copy of Copernicus's book show that Wittich had proposed a partial geoheliocentric system, an embryonic form of the Tychonic system. Marginalia in another copy of *De revolutionibus* show Wittich at work on the prosthaphaeresis method, whereby multiplication and division could be reduced to addition and subtraction through the use of trigonometric identities.

Wittich matriculated at Leipzig in 1563, which places his birth ca. 1546. Three years later, he enrolled at Wittenberg, and in 1576 at Frankfurt an der Oder, where he tutored the Scot John Craig in astronomy; Craig took the prosthaphaeresis method back to Edinburgh, and there informed John Napier (1550–1617) about it.

By 1579 Wittich was back home in Wratislavia (Wrocław), serving as tutor to the Hungarian humanist Andreas Dudith. In 1580 he traveled to Hven to visit Tycho Brahe (1646–1601). Brahe reported that Wittich "was a man very skilled in mathematics." Later, Wittich turned up at the Court of Wilhelm of Hesse in Kassel, where he spoke freely of his own mathematical methods and of Uraniborg, Brahe's observatory and workshop. Brahe was outraged to learn that Wittich was giving away what he considered to be his own technological secrets. Wittich went next to Vienna, where he died at about age forty.

While at Hven, Wittich had shown Brahe his annotated copies of *De revolutionibus,* and, after Wittich's death, Brahe made a decade-long effort before he was able to buy these volumes. Although Wittich had stopped short of a full geoheliocentric system, his diagrams must have played a seminal role in Brahe's own cosmological thought.

BIBLIOGRAPHY

Gingerich, Owen, and Robert S. Westman. "The Wittich Connection: Conflict and Priority in Late Sixteenth-Century Cosmology." *Transactions of the American Philosophical Society* 78 (1988), Part 7.

Thoren, Victor E. "Prosthaphaeresis Revisited." *Historia mathematica* 15 (1988), 32–39.

OWEN GINGERICH

See also Brahe, Tycho; Geoheliocentrism; Logarithms

Women and Natural Philosophy

The subject may be understood as concerned with: (1) ideas or images of women, or of a supposed female principle, in theories or traditions of natural philosophy; (2) relations between large numbers of women, or women generally, and science or natural philosophy; and (3) particular activities of noteworthy individual women in relation to systems or projects of natural philosophy, their own or those of others.

Virtually all intellectual, creative, or scientific activity before 1700 was carried out by elite, privileged sectors of the population—usually, by persons with inherited incomes, or who worked under the auspices of royal, aristocratic, or ecclesiastical patrons; or persons with positions at universities. The overwhelming majority of these individuals were male.

Sixteenth- and seventeenth-century conceptions of women and of "the female" (the earth regarded as a mother and nature as a female, for example) are multiply problematic. These conceptions come mostly from men. Further, they partly reflect features of language (feminine inflections, for example), which long precede the Renaissance. Christian and Greco-Roman conventions also play an important, but opaque, role in the formation of images of women and nature in the period.

The foregoing noted, western European expansion into the rest of the world from the early 1400s onward reflects (and perhaps partly creates) energies and ideologies that dominate the sixteenth and seventeenth centuries. The creative intelligence, theoretical and practical, of the period is clearly correlated with this expansion; this is transparently evident in Francis Bacon's (1561–1626) writings (and those of others) on natural philosophy and technology. Both impulses, and the mechanist naturalism of the New Philosophy, were identified in the language of the time as markedly "masculine." The worldview underlying these patterns was fashioned by talented, highly self-confident, dominant males, acting usually without even indirect involvement by women, and the language in which their achievements

is repeatedly expressed is redolent of conquest and control, with nature, whose secrets will be wrung from her and who will yield to their forcefully applied suit, characteristically conceived as a female. Metaphor and connotation for the New Science were definitely "masculinist," whatever the empirical and theoretical warrant was.

Some recent scholars have reconstructively assembled a "world that was lost" in an ideal of a comprehensive natural philosophy that preceded seventeenth-century mathematicized mechanist naturalism and that was holistic, vitalist, and organicist and prefigured contemporary trends or positions in ecology and feminism. What substance such reconstruction may have would point importantly to a female role in natural philosophy prior to 1600 and, perhaps, in rearguard contestation of the new developments after that year.

In fact, no women philosophical writers are identifiable before 1600. There were women healers and midwives in peasant society, and women found a role in religious movements as prophetic writers and charismatic public figures. These correspond strikingly to the positions as licensed physicians and ordained priests from which women were everywhere barred, by firm convention when not by explicit legal statute. Women were also denied entrance to the universities.

On the plane of popular culture, the position and role of women in respect of ideology or worldview, particularly in relation to nature, are unclear. The sixteenth and seventeenth centuries were the period of the most developed and intense prosecutions for witchcraft in European history. Many thousands of people were executed for witchcraft throughout Europe in this period, and ca. 80 percent of them (in some areas, more) are estimated to have been women. Although some scholars have sought to make a case for witchcraft as part of a premechanist worldview or a "gynoculture," there is no serious evidence for this.

In the later seventeenth century, there developed a view that women were well suited to natural philosophy and ought to receive some education in it. These ideas stem partly from notions of women's practical domestic duties and the technical skills they involve, but more fully from the egalitarian educational theories of John Komensky (Jan Comenius, 1592–1670) and his Dutch disciple Anna Maria van Schurman (1607–1678), and find explicit developed enunciation in the remarkable feminist tract *An Essay to Revive the Ancient Education of Gentlewomen* (1673) written by Bethsua Makin (ca. 1612–ca. 1674). Sister of John Pell, a Fellow of the Royal Society, Makin had serious interests in the New Science and urged female education in this direction. Hers was not a solitary voice. Wide numbers of upper- and middle-class women were taught or interested themselves in basic knowledge, and some experimental work, in botany, chemistry, and physics.

It has already been intimated that women in general played only a minor role in the Scientific Revolution. Even the great majority of the servants and laboratory assistants of scientists were male. On the other hand, a number of individual women were prominent in developments, especially in the seventeenth century. Principally, though not without exception, members of royal and aristocratic families, these women were involved in the New Science through written correspondence and conversation with leading philosophers and scientists. In a few cases, original philosophical theorizing appeared in published form. Marie de Gournay (1565–1645) edited the essays of Montaigne. Princess Elisabeth of Bohemia (1618–1680) was one of the sharpest and most important of the many correspondents, and critics, of René Descartes (1596–1650). Margaret Cavendish, duchess of Newcastle (1623–1673), was an undisciplined but original formulator of her own natural philosophy in a series of published volumes. Two of Robert Boyle's (1627–1691) sisters were his philosophical and theological intimates: Mary, countess of Warwick (d. 1678), and, especially, Katherine, Viscountess Ranelagh (d. 1691). Boyle lived the last twenty-three years of his life in Lady Ranelagh's house, where he had a laboratory. Christina, queen of Sweden (1626–1689), was keenly, and intelligently, interested in natural philosophy and invited Descartes to her Court, where he died. The letters of Marie, marquise de Sévigné (1626–1696), display her great enthusiasm for Cartesian natural philosophy. Her daughter, Françoise-Marguerite, marquise de Grignan (1646–1705), carried on these Cartesian commitments, declining the proposed gift of a pet dog to her own daughter Pauline in 1690 on the declared Cartesian ground that such an irrational, but incontinent, natural machine would be unwelcome. Marie Du Pré (b. ca. 1640) wrote a number of poems on Descartes's work. Anne, Viscountess Conway (1631–1679), was an original Neoplatonist metaphysician, whose posthumously published treatise engages, among other topics, the limits of mutation of natural objects. Sophia, electress of Hanover

Johannes Hevelius and his wife Elizabetha, who frequently assisted him in observation, measuring the angular separation between two stars. From Hevelius's Machinae coelestis *(1673).*

(1630–1714), interested herself in natural philosophy, which she discussed with Gottfried Wilhelm Leibniz (1646–1716), as did her daughter, Sophia Charlotte, queen of Prussia (1668–1705). Damaris, Lady Masham (1659–1708), was both custodian of the philosophical heritage of her father, the Cambridge Platonist Ralph Cudworth (1617–1688), and friend and public advocate (in correspondence with Leibniz) of the philosophy of John Locke (1632–1704). Also a published advocate of Locke's views was the extremely able Catherine Cockburn (1679–1749), whose spirited defense of Locke appeared when she was only twenty. One striking—and remarkable—feature of the ideas of some of these thinkers, among them Princess Elisabeth, Newcastle, Conway, Masham, and Cockburn, is their degree of comfort with materialism. They view human beings as unitary embodied individuals; none finds it perplexing, or shocking, to think that God could endow (and perhaps has endowed) chunks of matter with thought (i.e., without need of a special separate spiritual substance).

Another important dimension of women's role in the course of the Scientific Revolution is as contributors primarily in astronomy and entomology, especially in Germany. Particularly notable were Maria Sibylla Merian (1647–1717), who published and illustrated books on caterpillars and flowers, and a series of astronomers, the earliest of them Maria Cunitz (1610–1664), who published simplified versions of Johannes Kepler's (1571–1631) astronomical tables. As in other areas, by the end of the seventeenth century or in the early eighteenth, the increasing professionalization of all scientific activity came to exclude women, even in areas in which they had practiced with acknowledged success.

BIBLIOGRAPHY

Atherton, Margaret, ed. *Women Philosophers of the Early Modern Period*. Indianapolis: Hackett, 1994.

Merchant, Carolyn. *The Death of Nature: Women, Ecology, and the Scientific Revolution*. New York: Harper and Row, 1980.

Meyer, G. D. *The Scientific Lady in England, 1650–1760*. Berkeley and Los Angeles: University of California Press, 1955.

Phillips, Patricia. *The Scientific Lady: A Social History of Women's Scientific Interests, 1520–1918*. London: Weidenfeld and Nicolson, 1990.

Schiebinger, Londa. *The Mind Has No Sex?* Cambridge, MA: Harvard University Press, 1989.

PETER LOPTSON

See also Cavendish, Margaret, Duchess of Newcastle; Conway, Anne, Viscountess Conway; Sex and Gender

Wren, Christopher (1632–1723)

Architect, mathematician, and astronomer, he is most widely remembered for his prolific work as an architect. However, his contributions to science deserve to be regarded as equally significant and spanned most fields of scientific knowledge. Furthermore, he was a central figure in the Oxford circle of scholars whose activities in the 1650s led to the founding of the Royal Society in 1660.

The son of a prosperous cleric, Wren joined Wadham College, Oxford, in 1649. Already a precociously talented youth, at Oxford Wren came into contact with anatomist and mathematician, Charles Scarburgh (1616–1694), John Wilkins (1614–1672), John Wallis (1616–1703), and Robert Boyle (1627–1691), among others. He also met there Robert Hooke (1635–1703), with whom he later worked closely on the rebuilding of the City of London churches. Taking his degree in 1651, he continued his studies as a Fellow of All Souls College until appointed professor of astronomy at Gresham College, London, in 1657. In 1661 he was appointed Savilian Professor of Mathematics at Oxford, a post he retained until 1673. By that time, he was already surveyor of the king's works (1668) and had built the Sheldonian Theatre in Oxford (1664–1669), produced a plan for rebuilding London after the Great Fire of 1666, designed a number of City churches, and constructed a model for the proposed rebuilding of St. Paul's Cathedral. Although almost exclusively engaged in architectural matters, Wren continued to remain involved with the Royal Society. He was an active president (1680–1682) but ceased to contribute original scientific work. He retained royal favor throughout his career, and his buildings include a number for scientific purposes, notably the Royal Observatory at Greenwich (1675–1676).

Wren's scientific work in the 1650s and 1660s spanned an astonishing range, but the key disciplines were mathematics and astronomy. He wrote a treatise on spherical trigonometry and worked out the rectification of the cycloid. He made improved astronomical instruments, constructed a model of Saturn, proposed a method for representing the course of a comet, and made a survey of the Moon. His work also included anatomy, physiology, physics, meteorology, and microscopy. He assisted Scarburgh in dissection and, always a skilful draftsman, produced drawings and models of the muscles and the human eye. He devised an important experiment to transfuse the blood of one animal into another. He studied insects under the microscope and made drawings of what he saw. He advocated the measurement of weather and wrote an important treatise on the laws of impact (1668). These studies influenced or anticipated the work of others.

It should be emphasized that these sciences were not regarded as separate fields at that time, and it was not considered unusual in the early Royal Society for scholars to contribute to a broad spectrum of studies. The Oxford circle was characterized by intellectual excitement, curiosity, and an emphasis on mathematics. In

Christopher Wren. From Lawrence Weaver, Sir Christopher Wren: Scientist, Scholar, and Architect *(London: Country Life, 1923).*

addition, Wren had extraordinary practical talents and was exceptionally clever at devising instruments to provide practical demonstrations of his theories. His instruments included a weather clock, surveying instruments, mechanical devices, and an improved telescope with an adjustable aperture. He certainly built on Galileo Galilei's (1564–1642) theoretical and experimental approaches to investigating the mechanistic universe and on René Descartes's (1596–1650) highly theoretical work in mechanics, especially with regard to the laws of impact. But Wren's approach was Baconian in spirit. Instruments and the development of quantitative techniques enabled him to observe, test, and then draw empirical conclusions. He discarded an idea if a better solution or hypothesis was put forward. For example, he agreed that Christiaan Huygens's (1629–1695) view that Saturn's appearance was due to the presence of a uniform and symmetrical ring was a stronger, neater, and more elegant solution than his own view that Saturn was surrounded by a corona or elliptical ring. Also Baconian in temper was his emphasis on large-scale information gathering (e.g., in meteorology).

The diarist John Evelyn called Wren a "prodigious youth," and Isaac Newton (1642–1727) regarded him as one of the best geometers of the day. Wren's immense architectural output and his position as arbiter of English architectural taste for forty years have tended to obscure the impressive scientific output of his earlier years. Although he has been the subject of many biographies, with few exceptions relatively little has been written about his scientific work. However, it is now argued that his career was not so much one that abandoned science for architecture but one in which architecture had long been part of the traditional domain of science, grounded in mathematics. The shift was professional rather than intellectual. Wren's range of work; his concern with neatness, symmetry, and elegance so characteristic of mathematics; his genius for practical construction and instrumentation; and his key role in the formation of the Royal Society combine to ensure that he should be regarded as a central figure in the English Scientific Revolution.

BIBLIOGRAPHY

Bennett, J. A. *The Mathematical Science of Sir Christopher Wren.* Cambridge: Cambridge University Press, 1982.

Colvin, Howard. "Wren, Sir Chrisopher (1632–1723)." In *A Biographical Dictionary of British Architects, 1600–1840.* 3rd ed. New Haven, CT, and London: Yale University Press, 1995.

Hunter, Michael. "The Making of Christopher Wren." *London Journal* 16 (1991), 101–116.

Wren, Christopher, Jr. *Parentalia; or, Memoirs of the Family of the Wrens,* 1750. Repr. London: Gregg, 1965.

SOPHIE FORGAN

See also Architecture; Gresham College; Mixed Sciences; Oxford Philosophical Society; Royal Society of London

Wright, Edward (1558–1615)

He left teaching at Cambridge University to move to the practical world of navigation and cartography, where he produced his best work. Entering Cambridge in 1574, he graduated B.A. (1581) and M.A. (1584) and held a college Fellowship (1587–1596). The turning point of his career was his attachment to the earl of Cumberland's ill-fated voyage to the Azores (1589), which convinced Wright that improvements in navigational science were necessary, and he produced these in the early 1590s, including a solution by the addition of secants of the construction of the Mercator chart, presumably independently of earlier solutions by John Dee (1527–1608) ca. 1559 and Thomas Harriot (ca. 1560–1621) in 1584.

The Spaniards and the Portuguese had led the field in such work earlier, but Wright's work, published in 1599, maintained its influence in England throughout much of the seventeenth century. It was a compendium of the main problems in mathematical navigation of the time, excluding the longitude problem, which was not solved, except by dead reckoning, until the mid-eighteenth century. Wright also provided assistance for William Gilbert's (1544–1603) *De magnete* (1600).

After Cambridge, Wright supported himself by various mathematical lectureships in London, including the East India Company's, and worked as a surveyor in the New River project for supplying London with fresh water. His work was well known in England and Holland. His English translation and editing of John Napier's (1550–1617) logarithm tables of 1614 was published in 1616 with a Preface by Henry Briggs (1561–1631) and reissued two years later. His translation of Simon Stevin's (1548–1620) *Hafenvinding* was published in 1599, and he wrote on instruments (1614).

BIBLIOGRAPHY

Dawson, Georgina. "Edward Wright, Mathematician and Hydrographer." *American Neptune* 37 (1977), 174–178.

Waters, David W. *The Art of Navigation in England in Elizabethan and Early Stuart Times*. London: Hollis and Carter, 1958. Repr. London: HMSO, 1978, 3 vols.

JON V. PEPPER

See also Cartography; Gilbert, William; Navigation

Z

Zabarella, Jacopo (1533–1589)

The foremost representative of secular Aristotelianism in the generation before Galileo Galilei (1564–1642), Zabarella taught logic and natural philosophy at the University of Padua (1564–1589). Besides commentaries on Aristotle's (384–322 B.C.E.) *Posterior Analytics, Physics, Meteorology,* and *On the Soul,* his major works were two compendia, the *Logical Works* (1578) and *On Natural Things* (1590). Best known now for his contributions to logic and scientific methodology, he perfected the theory of the demonstrative regress, according to which scientific knowledge is acquired by a twofold process of first ascending from particular effects and experiences to universal causes and then demonstrating, in turn, those effects from their causes. For John Herman Randall, Jr. (1961), this was the source of Galileo's scientific method, though subsequent scholars have largely discounted any direct influence.

Zabarella also developed a theory of the middle, or mixed, sciences that, contrary to the prevailing view, afforded sciences such as astronomy and optics full demonstrative status despite their borrowing principles from pure mathematics. Nevertheless, Zabarella's approach to the study of nature remained causal and qualitative in the traditional Aristotelian vein, rather than mathematical.

Zabarella's use of Aristotle and other authorities was both eclectic and critical: his sources included newly recovered Greek commentators such as Philoponos and Simplicius, as well as medieval commentators such as Thomas Aquinas (d. 1274), Walter Burley (ca. 1275–ca. 1345), and Averroës (1126–1198). Expert in Greek, he could consult the Greek text of Aristotle and the commentators and could suggest where the text might be emended, but he resisted the tendency of the humanists to expunge all medieval barbarisms from his work, preferring philosophical precision to classical elegance. His works were widely influential in Italy, Germany, and England until the mid-seventeenth century, and modern scholars of Aristotle still consult his commentaries with profit.

BIBLIOGRAPHY

Mikkeli, Heikki. *An Aristotelian Response to Renaissance Humanism: Jacopo Zabarella on the Nature of Arts and Sciences.* Helsinki: Societas Historica Finlandiae, 1992.

Randall, John Herman, Jr. *The School of Padua and the Emergence of Modern Science.* (Saggi e testi 1). Padua: Antenore, 1961.

Schmitt, Charles B. "Experience and Experiment: A Comparison of Zabarella's View with Galileo's in De Motu." *Studies in the Renaissance* 16 (1969), 80–138.

W. R. LAIRD

See also Aristotelianism; Logic; Mixed Sciences; Resolution and Composition

Zoology

The branch of today's biology that studies the animal world, or what is now called the animal kingdom. The earliest extant zoological studies are by Aristotle (384–322 B.C.E.), whose descriptive and analytical work, often directly from animal specimens (*History of Animals, On the Parts of Animals, On Generation, On the Movement of Animals*), was once termed the most accurate before the nineteenth century. Pliny (23/24–79) is the next most frequently cited author for zoological natural history, followed by Aelian (ca. 170–ca. 230), Isidore (ca. 560–636), and the thirteenth-century encyclopedists: Thomas of Cantimpré (fl. 1200–1270), cited anonymously as *De natura rerum* (On the Nature of Things) until the eighteenth century, Vincent of Beauvais (ca. 1190–ca. 1264), Bartholomaeus Anglicus (fl. ca. 1250), and Albertus Magnus (ca. 1200–1280), all of whom compiled standard learning more than they studied animals from live or dead specimens. Albertus includes some personal observation, and Frederick II Hohenstaufen (1194–1250), in the practical hunting treatise *De arte venandi cum avibus* (On the Art of Hunting with Birds), even more. However, in the study of the world per se, the dramatic return to the direct methods of Aristotle receives impetus from the humanism of fourteenth- and fifteenth-century Italy, the movement that sought to retrieve the texts of the classical authors in a form as close to that in which they were written as possible, through the direct, critical study of the manuscript tradition. This approach to texts is analogous to the approach of sixteenth- and seventeenth-century anatomists and naturalists as they returned to the study of the natural world for its own sake (i.e., as God's Creation) but not solely in relation to man's use of it either in daily life or as religious and spiritual metaphor (as in the medieval bestiary tradition).

The revolutionary approach of the fourteenth- and fifteenth-century humanists became the model for the naturalists and other observers of natural phenomena in the sixteenth century. In the attempt to understand the wealth of creatures observable locally and, increasingly, from exotic lands outside of Europe, naturalists corresponded and exchanged specimens and observations. Conrad Gessner (1516–1565) was the clearinghouse and critical intellectual filter for much of this activity in what we call zoology. Naturalists who fed their direct observations of animal morphology and behavior into his *Historiae animalium* (Histories of Animals, 1551–1587) included Pierre Gilles (1490–1555): *Elephanti nova descriptio* (New Description of the Elephant); William Turner (1510–1568): *Avium praecipuarum . . . historia* (History of the Principal Birds, 1544) and "Letter to Gessner on Fish" (1557); Pierre Belon (1517–1564); *L'histoire naturelle des estranges poissons marins* (Natural History of Exotic Marine Fish, 1551) and *L'histoire de la nature des oyseaux* (History of the Nature of Birds, 1555); Guillaume Rondelet (1507–1556): *Liber de piscibus* (Book on Fish, 1554); Ippolito Salviani (1514–1572): *Aquatilium animalium historiae* (Histories of Aquatic Animals, 1554); John Caius (1510–1573): *De*

canibus Britannicis (On British Dogs) and *De rariorum animalium . . . historia* (History of Rare Animals, 1570); and Thomas Penney (d. 1589), to whom Gessner bequeathed his insect notes and drawings, later cut up and incorporated, without full understanding, in Thomas Mouffet's (1553–1604) *Insectorum theatrum* (Theater of Insects, 1634). Their high level of descriptive analysis created the new standard. Ulisse Aldrovandi (1522–1605) of Bologna, relying on direct experience and on correspondence with, and published works by, among others, Gessner (some of which Aldrovandi owned on suffrance from the Inquisition), produced a multivolume animal natural history (1599–1606 and posthumous to 1639), attempting to revise categories. There followed later John Johnston's (1603–1675) derivative *Historia naturalis* (Natural History, 1650–1661).

Belon includes a comparison of the dolphin brain with that of man and an illustrated comparison of the skeletons of bird and man (1555), the beginnings of comparative anatomy. Aldrovandi's pupil Volcher Coiter (1534–1576) published his work on comparative anatomy (1572) before Aldrovandi's works began to appear. Some questions of classification (e.g., cetae vs. pisces) were confronted as early as Edward Wotton's (1492–1555) *De differentiis animalium* (On the Differences Among Animals, 1552), using classical sources and some observation, though criteria would remain elusive until Carl Linnaeus (1707–1778). Zoological paleontology began with Leonardo da Vinci's (1452–1519) recognition of shell fossils as marine-animal remains, a viewpoint taken by Girolamo Fracastoro (ca. 1478–1553), though Gessner's *De omni rerum fossilium genere* (On Every Kind of Fossil, 1565) did not theorize; that would wait for Nicolaus Steno's (1638–1686) *De solido intra solidum naturaliter contento dissertationis prodromus* (Precursor to a Dissertation on a Naturally Contained Solid Within a Solid, 1669), contesting the biblical "Delugist" explanation of fossils.

Francis Bacon (1561–1626), in his search for a valid method to "dissect nature" with the tool of human understanding, using both empirical and theoretical reasoning (as Paolo Rossi has pointed out), paved the way for increasingly sophisticated analyses of natural phenomena by experiment, which he undertook for portions of his *Instauratio magna* (Great Renewal, 1603–1626). His influence went beyond his published works to the founding of the Royal Society in 1662. Under the further influence of René Descartes's (1596–1650) emphasis on mechanics and measurability in his *Discourse on Method,* (1637), in which he cites William Harvey's (1578–1657) work on the circulation of the blood and on embryology, experiment (including physiological experiment) was to become the norm in natural science. John Ray (1620–1705), also a Fellow of the Royal Society, made strides with Francis Willughby (1635–1672) in systematizing birds (1676) and fish (1686) in more natural and practical (for identification) categories than had been found before.

An important tool of biological description is illustration, our exacting tradition of which, while evident in the model books of medieval decorators (of margins, capitals, and the like), begins with Giovanni de' Grassi's (d. 1398) and Jacopo Bellini's (d. 1471) animal drawings and includes those of Leonardo da Vinci and Albrecht Dürer (1471–1528), as well as the artists employed by Gessner and Gessner himself. The Vatican manuscript of Pier Candido Decembrio's (1399–1477) *De animantium naturis* (On the Nature of Animals) illustrates the transition from a dominant reliance on received authority (in Thomas de Cantimpré [fl. 1200–1270], Decembrio's source) to analytical description in the illustrations in the 1590s by Teodoro Ghisi (1536–1601). Once the ground was laid by the humanistically inspired naturalists, illustrators such as Jacopo Ligozzi (1547–1626) in the employ of the Medici, Ghisi for the Gonzaga, and John White (fl. 1585–1593) on his visits to America were increasingly able, applying the refined techniques of perspective, to portray animals in nature convincingly and with descriptive accuracy. Refined illustration was crucial to the conveyance of anatomical understanding in the work of Carlo Ruini (ca. 1530–1598) on the horse (1598) and Girolamo Fabrizio de Acquapendente (ca. 1533–1619) on embryology and comparative anatomy (1600–1621), as it had been in Andreas Vesalius's (1514–1564) human anatomy (1543). The role of artists in the development of answering what Ernst Mayr (1982) has called the *what* phase of biological investigation was crucial, for, as Leonardo da Vinci noted, words are not enough to describe the visible world. The seventeenth century would begin to ask and to answer the *how* questions, although scientifically satisfactory answers to the *why* questions (nonteleological, within systems) would be left to the post-Darwinian ages.

The microscope opened new fields of observation and experiment. In 1625 Francesco Stelluti (1577–1653) published the minutely observed anatomy of the honey-

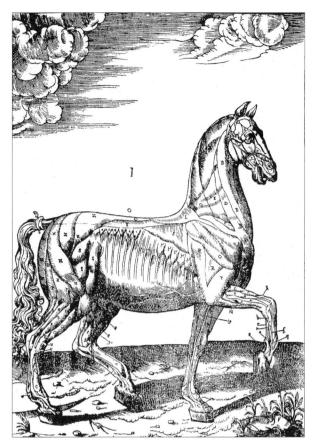

Carlo Ruini's Anatomia del cavallo, infermita, et suoi rimedii *(1599) was the first book devoted exclusively to the anatomy, physiology, and therapeutics of an animal.*

bee on a broadsheet for Pope Urban VIII (whose Barberini insignia was the bee). He was followed by Robert Hooke (1635–1703), curator of experiments for the Royal Society, collaborator with Robert Boyle (1627–1691), and a trained artist, whose further revolutionary *Micrographia* (1665) disclosed the cell in plants and the microstructure of insects, fish, and skin, thereby founding microanatomy and histology, and by Marcello Malpighi's (1628–1694) *De pulmonibus* (On the Lungs), discovering Harvey's hypothesized capillaries (1661), *De bombyce* (On the Silkworm, 1669), and *De formatione pulli in ovo* (On the Formation of the Chick in the Egg, 1673). Antoni van Leeuwenhoek's (1632–1723) epistolary studies (1680–1714) launched comparative microanatomy, microembryology, and bacteriology. Jan Swammerdam (1637–1680) preceded Giovanni Alfonso Borelli (1608–1679) in understanding the role of air in respiration (1667) and exhibited subtle observation, dissecting techniques, and classification in *Biblia naturae* (Bible of Nature, written in 1675; published 1737–1738).

BIBLIOGRAPHY

Cole, F. J. *A History of Comparative Anatomy from Aristotle to the Eighteenth Century*. New York: Dover, 1975.

Hoeniger, F. D., and J. F. M. Hoeniger. *The Development of Natural History in Tudor England, and The Growth of Natural History in Stuart England from Gerard to the Royal Society*. (Folger Booklets on Tudor and Stuart Civilization). n.p.: University Press of Virginia, 1969.

Mayr, Ernst. *The Growth of Biological Thought: Diversity, Evolution, and Inheritance*. Cambridge, MA: Harvard University Press, 1982.

Nissen, Claus. *Die zoologische Buchillustration: Ihre Bibliographie und Geschichte*. 2 vols. in 3. Stuttgart: Hiersemann, 1969.

Pyle, C. M. "The Art and Science of Renaissance Natural History: Thomas of Cantimpré, Pier Candido Decembrio, Conrad Gessner and Teodoro Ghisi in Vatican Library MS Urb. lat. 276." *Viator* 27 (1996), 265–321.

CYNTHIA M. PYLE

See also Aldrovandi, Ulisse; Gessner, Conrad; Illustration; Microscopy; Natural History; Taxonomy

INDEX

B